campaign 72

campaign 72

Press Opinion from New Hampshire to November

Editors: *Edward W. Knappman*
Evan Drossman
Robert Newman

MODERN MEDIA INSTITUTE
556 Central Avenue
St. Petersburg, FL 33701
(813) 821-9494

FACTS ON FILE ▪ 119 WEST 57TH STREET ▪ NEW YORK, NEW YORK

CAMPAIGN '72:

Press Opinions from New Hampshire to November

Copyright, 1973, by Facts on File, Inc.

All rights reserved. No part of this book may be reproduced in any form without the permission of the publisher except for reasonably brief extracts used in reviews or scholarly works. Editorials reprinted with permission of cooperating newspapers, which retain their copyrights. Published by Facts on File, Inc., 119 West 57th Street, New York, N.Y. 10019.

ISBN 0-87196-351-5

Library of Congress Catalog Card Number: 72-94169

PRINTED IN THE UNITED STATES OF AMERICA

Preface

To fully understand either the present or the past, we must know more than merely what happened; we must try to discover why it happened. Rarely is the answer more sought after or more elusive than during and after an American presidential election. The purpose of this book is to present a composite answer to the question: Why did Americans re-elect President Richard Nixon in 1972?

Nearly 700 opinions on the issues, personalities and results of the 1972 presidential campaign have been reprinted in this survey of editorials from 117 U.S. newspapers covering every significant development from the first primary in New Hampshire to the final balloting in November. Viewed from an immediate perspective, these editorials try to explain what happened. Looking back at them from the future, these editorials will serve as documentary evidence of contemporary attitudes and opinions during the 1972 campaign.

Each chapter is introduced by a brief, objective summary giving the factual background necessary for a full understanding of the editorials. The editorials reprinted are selected to present a balanced cross-section of the arguments, ideas and analyses on every side and facet of the issues, reflecting not only the major national political viewpoints, but also the views of regional, local and special interests. All editorials are reprinted in full-text exactly as they appeared in the cooperating newspapers.

The material in Campaign '72 *originally appeared in the regular twice-monthly issues of* Editorials On File. *The bracketed numbers in the introductory factual summaries—e.g. [See pp. 267-278]—refer the reader to material previously published in the regular issues of* Editorials On File.

Edward W. Knappman

Contents

Preface * v

I. THE PRIMARIES

Muskie Wins in New Hampshire * 11

Wallace Favored by Florida Voters * 21

Illinois Democrats Back Muskie,
   Reject Mayor Daley's Candidates * 31

McGovern Wins Easily in Wisconsin * 38

Nixon, Jackson Challenged on Funding * 48

Humphrey Wins in Pennsylvania;
   McGovern Sweeps Massachusetts * 52

Muskie Withdraws from Primaries * 59

Contenders Split Vote in Eight Primaries * 64

Wallace Shot at Campaign Rally * 71

Wallace Wins in Maryland, Michigan;
   McGovern Captures Rhode Island, Oregon * 78

McGovern Defeats Humphrey in California * 84

New York Voters Support McGovern Delegates * 95

Five Men Caught in Democratic Offices * 100

II. THE CONVENTIONS

Democrats Debate the Credentials
   of California and Illinois Delegates   *   104

McGovern Wins First Ballot Nomination   *   112

Eagleton Chosen as Vice Presidential Candidate   *   120

Democrats Adopt Broadly-Worded Platform   *   124

Eagleton Quits Following Mental Disclosures   *   129

Daley Supports McGovern; Meany Remains Neutral   *   140

Nixon Backs Agnew's Renomination   *   145

Newspaper Guild Endorses Democratic Ticket   *   148

Shriver Replaces Eagleton on Ticket   *   150

Wallace Declines Third Party Bid;
   Schmitz Nominated by American Party   *   157

Nixon, Agnew Win Renomination Easily   *   161

Pro-Agnew Group Wins Reform Fight   *   170

Delegates Back Nixon's Platform   *   174

Protestors Fail to Disrupt Convention   *   179

III. THE CAMPAIGN AND THE ELECTION

GOP Finances, Watergate Raid Investigated   *   182

McGovern Revises Welfare, Tax Reform Plans   *   188

Shriver Cites Lost Chance for Peace;
   McGovern Aide Visits Hanoi's Negotiators   *   193

Former White House Aides Indicted
   for Roles in Watergate Bugging Raid   *   197

Opinion Polls Show Wide Nixon Lead   *   202

Newsday Drops Endorsements;
   Most Papers Back Nixon's Re-election   *   206

McGovern Outlines Vietnam Plans   *   211

House Bars Watergate Investigation;
   GOP Sabotage Efforts Reported   *   215

Newspapers Endorse Nixon by Wide Margin   *   219

Imminent Vietnam Peace Announced
   Two Weeks before Presidential Vote   *   252

Nixon Wins Landslide Victory;
   Democrats Retain Edge in Congress   *   257

Index   *   285

Cooperating Newspapers

Akron (Ohio) Beacon Journal (174,000)
Albany (N.Y.) Knickerbocker News (71,000)
Albuquerque (N.M.) Journal (66,000)
Anchorage (Alaska) Daily Times (13,000)
Ann Arbor (Mich.) News (37,000)
Atlanta Constitution (209,000)
Baltimore Afro-American (29,000)
Baltimore News American (201,000)
Baltimore Sun (165,000)
Biloxi (Miss.) Daily Herald (37,000)
Birmingham (Ala.) News (76,000)
Boston Globe (261,000)
Boston Herald Traveler Record American (211,000)
Buffalo Evening News (284,000)
Burlington (Vt.) Free Press (45,000)
Charleston (S.C.) News & Courier (66,000)
Charleston (W.Va.) Gazette (60,000)
Charlotte (N.C.) Observer (170,000)
Chattanooga (Tenn.) Times (64,000)
Chicago Daily Defender (21,000)
Chicago Daily News (435,000)
Chicago Sun-Times (536,000)
Chicago Today (429,000)
Chicago Tribune (768,000)
Christian Science Monitor (Mass.) (216,000)
Cincinnati Enquirer (195,000)
Cincinnati Post & Times-Star (234,000)
Cleveland Plain Dealer (403,000)
Cleveland Press (374,000)
Columbia (S.C.) State (107,000)
Columbus (Ohio) Dispatch (222,000)
Dallas Morning News (243,000)
Dallas Times Herald (232,000)
Dayton (Ohio) Daily News (113,000)
Denver Post (255,000)
Denver Rocky Mountain News (205,000)
Des Moines (Iowa) Register (246,000)
Des Moines (Iowa) Tribune (109,000)
Detroit Free Press (593,000)
Detroit News (640,000)
Emporia (Kans.) Gazette (10,000)
Fall River (Mass.) Herald-News (42,000)
Fort Worth (Tex.) Star-Telegram (98,000)
Gary (Ind.) Post-Tribune (72,000)

Greenville (S.C.) News (91,000)
Hartford (Conn.) Courant (160,000)
Honolulu (Hawaii) Advertiser (74,000)
Honolulu (Hawaii) Star-Bulletin (124,000)
Houston Chronicle (303,000)
Indianapolis News (183,000)
Indianapolis Star (225,000)
Kansas City (Mo.) Star (310,000)
Kansas City (Mo.) Times (324,000)
Lincoln (Neb.) Star (27,000)
Little Rock Arkansas Democrat (74,000)
Little Rock Arkansas Gazette (108,000)
Long Island (N.Y.) Press (418,000)
Los Angeles Herald Examiner (513,000)
Los Angeles Times (966,000)
Louisville Courier-Journal (233,000)
Louisville Times (172,000)
Madison Wisconsin State Journal (71,000)
Memphis Commercial Appeal (214,000)
Miami Herald (383,000)
Miami News (86,000)
Milwaukee Journal (347,000)
Minneapolis Tribune (238,000)
Nashville Tennessean (139,000)
Newark (N.J.) Star-Ledger (246,000)
New Bedford (Mass.) Standard-Times (73,000)
New Orleans States-Item (128,000)
New Orleans Times-Picayune (199,000)
Newsday (L.I., N.Y.) (459,000)
New York Daily News (2,130,000)
New York Post (623,000)
New York Times (846,000)
Norfolk (Va.) Ledger-Star (105,000)
Norfolk (Va.) Virginian-Pilot (129,000)
Oakland (Calif.) Tribune (208,000)
Oklahoma City Times (103,000)
Oklahoma City Daily Oklahoman (181,000)
Omaha (Neb.) World-Herald (129,000)
Orlando (Fla.) Sentinel (129,000)
Philadelphia Evening Bulletin (634,000)
Philadelphia Inquirer (464,000)
Phoenix Arizona Republic (170,000)
Pittsburgh Post-Gazette (236,000)

Portland (Me.) Evening Express (30,000)
Portland (Me.) Press Herald (56,000)
Portland (Me.) Sunday Telegram (112,000)
Portland (Ore.) Journal (135,000)
Portland Oregonian (244,000)
Providence (R.I.) Journal (67,000)
Rapid City (S.D.) Journal (31,000)
Richmond (Va.) News-Leader (121,000)
Richmond (Va.) Times-Dispatch (144,000)
Roanoke (Va.) Times (63,000)
Rochester (N.Y.) Democrat & Chronicle (143,000)
Rockford (Ill.) Morning Star (62,000)
Rockford (Ill.) Register-Republic (35,000)
Rock Hill (S.C.) Evening Herald (16,000)
Sacramento (Calif.) Bee (167,000)
Saginaw (Mich.) News (61,000)
St. Louis Globe-Democrat (293,000)
St. Louis Post-Dispatch (326,000)
St. Louis Review (unreported)
St. Petersburg (Fla.) Times (163,000)
Salt Lake City (Utah) Deseret News (84,000)
Salt Lake City (Utah) Tribune (108,000)
San Diego Union (152,000)
San Francisco Chronicle (479,000)
San Francisco Sun Reporter (9,000)
San Jose (Calif.) Mercury (128,000)
San Juan (P.R.) Star (48,000)
Seattle Times (245,000)
Sioux Falls (S.D.) Argus-Leader (50,000)
Springfield (Mass.) Union (79,000)
Syracuse (N.Y.) Herald-Journal (126,000)
Toledo (Ohio) Blade (175,000)
Topeka (Kans.) Daily Capital (63,000)
Tulsa (Okla.) Daily World (110,000)
Wall Street Journal (497,000)
Washington Post (500,000)
Washington Star-News (302,000)
Wichita (Kans.) Eagle (60,000)
Winston-Salem (N.C.) Journal (78,000)
Winston-Salem (N.C.) Twin City Sentinel (46,000)
Worcester (Mass.) Telegram (63,000)

Campaign '72:
MUSKIE WINS NEW HAMPSHIRE VOTE, McGOVERN SECOND WITH 37 PER CENT

The New Hampshire presidential primary, the first of 23 contests leading up to the Democratic and Republican nominating conventions, took place March 8. Public attention focused on the Democratic race in which Maine's Sen. Edmund S. Muskie captured 46.4% of the vote. South Dakota's Sen. George S. McGovern finished second and received a surprising 37% of the ballots cast. Los Angeles Mayor Sam Yorty, Rep. Wilbur Mills (Ark.) and Sen. Vance Hartke (Ind.) were far behind in the voting. Muskie won 15 and McGovern five of the state's 20 delegates to the national convention.

While Muskie remained the Democratic frontrunner, McGovern's strong showing in Muskie's neighboring state convinced many observers that the Maine senator had not lived up to expectations. Muskie's victory came despite the vehement opposition of New Hampshire's largest newspaper, the *Manchester Union Leader*, and its publisher, William Loeb, who supported Yorty's effort. McGovern, who campaigned extensively in the state, received support from what had always been considered to be one of his weakest constituencies—the blue collar workers. His strong showing was generally viewed as having given him the status of a serious contender for the Democratic nomination.

In the Republican primary, President Nixon, who did not campaign in the state, received 68% of the vote—10% less than he received in the 1968 New Hampshire primary. Nixon won all the state's 14 delegate votes. His two rivals, California's liberal Rep. Paul N. McCloskey and Ohio's conservative Rep. John M. Ashbrook, polled 20% and 11% of the vote, respectively.

PORTLAND EVENING EXPRESS
Portland, Me., March 8, 1972

The New Hampshire presidential preferential primary is over, and one of the things it proved is that a bevy of presidential candidates can spend a million dollars or so, between them, in one of the smallest states in the union to obtain an inconclusive result.

Sen. Muskie, the central figure, did not win big in the "beauty contest" part of the primary, but he did not lose it, either. And he may do even better in the delegate count, which is still incomplete.

Sen. McGovern is acting like a winner, but he only captured about a third of the Democratic votes cast, and this is the third time this year he has lost to Sen. Muskie in a popularity contest. If Sen. Muskie wins most of the 20 delegates, then McGovern will have lost three times in the delegate selection fight.

President Richard Nixon won, on the GOP side of the ballot, but his left-wing and right-wing foes took 30 per cent of the votes, and this may be a little disturbing, since Mr. Nixon was given 77 per cent of the total four years ago.

The more notable of the also-rans were found on the Democratic ticket. Rep. Wilbur Mills spent as much as $250,000 as a write-in and only received 5 per cent of the vote, while Mayor Yorty, backed by the state's biggest newspaper, took only 7 per cent.

What should be remembered, in the Muskie-McGovern struggle, is that while the Maine man has a chance to win the nomination, his rival is given almost no chance at all. Nevertheless, the word will be carried to Florida, which votes next week, that Muskie should have outdone all of his opponents combined, since New Hampshire lies adjacent to his home state. That however, does not necessarily follow. Sen. Muskie made mistakes, he was spread too thin, and now he must face George Wallace in Florida, and try to finish second in the race there.

Portland Press Herald
Portland, Me., March 9, 1972

Senator George McGovern may have won more in losing the New Hampshire primary than Sen. Edmund S. Muskie gained in winning it.

That, at least, is the construction by some of the analysts. But when the pundits and prophets and other experts are through explaining how Senator Muskie didn't win it would be well to remember that he polled more votes than any other Democrat and that he finished with a comfortable margin over Senator McGovern, the closest competitor.

A luxurious margin would have been preferred, of course. Everyone likes to "win big." It would have served Senator Muskie to greater advantage had he captured 58 per cent of the vote in New Hampshire rather than 48 per cent. Lyndon B. Johnson took 49 per cent of the vote in 1968 and it was a numbing defeat. But Lyndon B. Johnson was an incumbent President.

The implications of a political beauty contest, which is about what the New Hampshire primary really amounts to, are to a large degree what the press decides they are. If Senator Muskie had won by an overwhelming margin, there could have been only one interpretation. Even then, some would have derided it as merely a demonstration for a neighbor just as some now contend that he should have fared better as a neighbor.

Senator McGovern's feat was impressive but not astounding. He has been campaigning in New Hampshire for some 13 months. In these recent critical weeks he virtually moved into the state while Senator Muskie had to be giving attention to Florida and several other states.

We suspect that Senator Muskie was hurt less by publisher William Loeb's attacks than he was by his own response to that barrage. We doubt that Loeb's hostility had much more effect in New Hampshire than Kevin Phillips' words had in Maine. Readers of Loeb's Manchester Union Leader must be accustomed to his diatribes and manipulation of the news and consider it in context. Some may have been disappointed that Senator Muskie would permit himself to be drawn into conflict at that level. Certainly the Loeb support did little for Mayor Sam Yorty.

In recent weeks, too, there has been a concerted "Stop Muskie" effort. That's a penalty front runners sometimes must pay when everyone else in the field admits he is behind. It is Ed Muskie, not Richard Nixon, that some of the Democrats are running against.

President Nixon had no difficulty in sweeping the Republican vote although he, too, might have been happier with a larger percentage.

Senator Muskie's showing in New Hampshire may make the primary trail a bit bumpier for him. But he did win and with a thoroughly respectable margin.

BOSTON HERALD TRAVELER
Boston, Mass., March 9, 1972

The last place to look for informed and unimpeachable punditry about the results of New Hampshire first-in-the-nation presidential primary would be in the camps of the candidates. Presidential primaries in the Granite State may be the only electoral contests in which more than one candidate claims victory.

There are, it seems, numerical victories, delegate victories, psychological victories and moral victories, depending on one's preconceptions and predeterminations. The chief interest, of course, was focused on the Democratic primary, which every reliable poll and politician predicted would be won by Maine's Sen. Edmund Muskie, the "front-runner" who only lately began to look back over his shoulder.

Conflicting claims, widely divergent analyses and prognostications aside, Sen. Muskie did in fact win the Democratic sweepstakes with about 48 per cent of the Democratic votes. Since he was expected (almost required, according to some observers) to win at least 50 per cent of the total vote, Sen. George McGovern, whose long active political troops blitzed the state, also claims some sort of victory by collecting nearly 37 per cent of the vote. Why Sen. McGovern's 37 per cent of the vote is equally important or more important than Sen. Muskie's 48 per cent of the vote will be tirelessly (and fruitlessly) argued.

Every quadrennium the public seems to forget that the presidential primaries amount to a sort of process of elimination, at least for those candidates who must prove their mettle in them. So although Sen. Muskie failed to eliminate Sen. McGovern in New Hampshire by a landslide that would shake the White Mountains, neither man has accomplished more than what the election returns record.

Round One is over and the only two major contenders survived the contest. Mayor Sam Yorty of Los Angeles and Sen. Vance Hartke of Indiana should simply go home. Rep. Wilbur Mills, who waged a write-in campaign, should go back to the Ways and Means Committee, but will probably go South to test his political muscle in the selection of other delegate slates.

The results of the Republican primary, on the other hand, were indisputably clear. President Nixon was endorsed by nearly 80,000 voters—or by about 70 per cent of the ballot-markers in the GOP column. With a challenger to the left of him and a challenger to the right of him, President Nixon passed up campaigning for global statesmanship and won handsomely. As a matter of fact, President Nixon received more votes than both Sen. Muskie and Sen. McGovern combined.

Rep. Paul McCloskey, the liberal Republican from California, and Rep. John Ashbrook, the conservative Republican from Ohio, did their best to discredit President Nixon and his administration, but their best was worse than mediocre. The effect of the cross-fire was to make President Nixon the centrist candidate which, all things considered, is a fairly accurate description. Rep. McCloskey and Rep. Ashbrook were "protest" candidates—with antithetical beefs—as distinct from the competitive candidates in the Democratic column.

Perhaps the strongest—yet most overlooked—showing in the entire balloting was made by Vice President Spiro Agnew. If the "Agnew may be dumped" claque finds the time to read the numbers, they may be dismayed (if not deterred) to learn that approximately 43,000 voters in the Republican primary took the time to write-in the Vice President's name on the ballot. (And so did nearly 2000 Democrats.)

If one wants to play further with the numbers, more New Hampshiremen wrote-in their preference for Spiro Agnew for Vice President than voted for Sen. Muskie or for Sen. McGovern. That fact scarcely indicates, as the Democratic contenders claim, that their victories reflect widespread anti-administration sentiment. In short, the office-holders did much better than the office-seekers.

The Boston Globe
Boston, Mass., March 9, 1972

The big political show is over up to the north of us, and now the nation's pundits and oracles are busy telling the voters the meaning of what the latter have just done. It is perhaps a harmless occupation and occasionally even an instructive one, and so we add our own voice to the babel.

The New Hampshire primary results surely gave Sen. Edmund S. Muskie of Maine a victory in the year's first presidential balloting, but his 48 percent just as surely was not as much of a victory as he had hoped for. What some had thought would be a steamroller this year may be having trouble in its boiler. Only time will tell.

Perhaps the real victor on the Democratic side was Sen. George McGovern of South Dakota. His 37 percent of the vote surpassed all expectations, and may increase his chances significantly as the candidates go on to the other primaries. Yet it was not quite the stunning upset that former Sen. Eugene McCarthy scored against ex-President Lyndon Johnson four years ago. That vote, in its effect, took Mr. Johnson out of the White House. But there are two ways of viewing this.

Oone is to say that President Richard M. Nixon, unlike Mr. Johnson, won a heartening victory in the Republican primary with 69 percent of the vote, unlike Mr. Johnson who had not even been on the ballot. Still, in gathering 20 percent support, against the President, antiwar Rep. Paul N. McCloskey of California scored no mean accomplishment.

And the other way of viewing the Granite State results is to say that 89 percent of the Democratic voters and 20 percent of the Republicans cast their ballots for candidates who want to stop the war in Southeast Asia. This may have significance in a state that had been strongly Republican and pro-Nixon. Perhaps New Hampshire once again was telling us something.

Lastly — and this is for sure — the results up north show the utter futility of a newspaper's trying to tell the people how to vote. Once again the candidates backed by William Loeb, publisher of the Manchester (N.H.) Union-Leader, went down to defeat.

Rep. John Ashbrook of Ohio, the Republican right-winger, received only 10 percent, and Mayor Sam Yorty of Los Angeles polled only six percent on the Democratic side. This preserves intact the New Hampshire publisher's record of never having backed a presidential winner.

And for that matter, it ought to offer a lesson to all the media, including ourselves, not to get too smarty-pants. End of punditry.

The New York Times
New York, N.Y., March 9, 1972

Whether the Democratic voter was for Muskie or McGovern, the Republican for Nixon or McCloskey, the results of the New Hampshire primary are encouraging, in at least one respect, to everyone in both parties who likes fair play and does not want to see gross abuse of the power of the press.

The voters overwhelmingly rejected the advice of The Manchester Union Leader, the state's largest newspaper, which as usual shrieked its vilifications against the leading candidates. President Nixon was denounced as "stupid" and "a doublecrosser"; Senator Muskie was described as "Moscow Muskie." Both won their respective primaries. The Union Leader's preferred candidates—Republican Representative John Ashbrook and Democrat Sam Yorty—each finished a poor third. Mr. William Loeb's brand of journalism met a richly deserved rebuff.

On the Democratic side, Senator Muskie won an adequate if unspectacular victory. Having finished first in the Arizona and Iowa caucuses and having won the nation's first primary, he has thus far managed to cling to the position he has staked out for himself as the Democrat with broad appeal who has a better chance than anyone else to unite the party against Mr. Nixon.

Senator George McGovern, however, has shown that intensive campaigning and an aggressive, sharply defined stance on the issues can evoke considerable support even in Mr. Muskie's home region. Mr. McGovern benefited from his record of early and well-known opposition to the Vietnam war. More surprisingly, he ran Senator Muskie a close race in the working-class wards of Manchester, the state's largest industrial city. His radical positions on tax reform and economic policy apparently appealed to low-income Democrats. On the basis of this McGovern showing, Mr. Muskie and the other rivals for the Democratic nomination can be expected to bear down more heavily on "bread-and-butter" issues.

President Nixon won the Republican primary easily as expected. Representative Paul McCloskey nevertheless achieved a highly creditable performance in obtaining one-fifth of the vote while opposing an incumbent President. Much of the independent vote and the volunteer effort on which he depended were undoubtedly diverted to the McGovern campaign, a more exciting contest.

Mr. McCloskey has demonstrated courage and political leadership in raising some of the issues—continued heavy bombing in Vietnam, the mania for secrecy, the favoritism toward big corporations—on which the Administration is particularly vulnerable.

When many better-known members of his party have taken refuge in silence or accommodated themselves to much that they disapprove, this combative young Congressman has kept flying the proud banner of progressive Republicanism. It is an old and honorable political tradition which publisher William Loeb's father—an aide to Theodore Roosevelt—understood even if his son has forgotten it.

©1972 by The New York Times Company. Reprinted by permission.

THE WALL STREET JOURNAL.
New York, N.Y., March 9, 1972

Senator Muskie won the New Hampshire primary, but came out second best in his struggle with the "phantom candidate" he said the press had him running against. Senator McGovern came in second, but established himself as a candidate a few cuts above Mayor Sam Yorty, Senator Vance Hartke and the guy with the rat. And there are 22 more presidential primaries to go.

We've been scribbling on the back of an envelope, trying to put it all in perspective. One per cent of the New Hampshire Democratic turnout was some 850 votes. So if Senator Muskie could have added 8,500 votes to the 48% he actually received, he would have come up with 58%, clearly enough to put him ahead of the phantom. Conversely, if Senator McGovern's handshaking had converted 8,500 fewer souls, he would have wound up not with 37% but with 27%, respectable perhaps, but still falling quite a ways back toward the sideshow category.

At the time of the last presidential election some 116,535,000 persons were of voting age. About 78,964,000 actually cast ballots. In New Hampshire itself, the 1968 turnout was 297,000. The Democratic nominee then received 131,000 votes, compared with 85,000 for all the Democrats together in Tuesday's voting. Incidentally, this turnout is good as primaries go.

So all in all, it's somewhat sobering to contemplate the impact 8,500 New Hampshire voters can have on a candidate's future; who knows what stroke of pure chance might change that few minds? Not that this is anything new; there once was a Texan who picked up the nickname "landslide" Johnson by squeaking through a senatorial primary by 87 votes, but who parlayed it all into a presidential career. The element of chance and luck is a great part of the glamor and mystery of politics.

Still, there is warning here about attaching too much significance to primary results, and especially about confusing them with some sovereign "voice of the people." True, New Hampshire is a bit of a special case because of its small size and strategic timing. Still, it is not that much an exception; with 11 Democratic candidates on the Florida ballot next week, what great moral or ethical lesson is there if one of them finishes 5% ahead of the pack?

Now, clearly presidential primaries are a historic part of the American political tradition, one of our treasured institutions. They obviously test the mettle of the candidates in a number of different and important ways. But it is not clear, at least to us, that this test requires 23 of them.

This number is up from 15 in 1968 due largely to the efforts to "reform" the Democratic Party. Now the cutting edge of the reformers is pointing to the effort and expense involved in the proliferation of primaries reform has wrought, and wants to reform *that* by a single nation-wide primary.

Well, there are also other ways to test a candidate's mettle—in the organizational effort at party caucuses, in appealing to the party faithful at conventions, yes, even in bargaining in smoke-filled rooms—that we find far from irrelevant to his ability to govern a nation. By cut and fit over the years, our institutions have managed to incorporate all of this.

So an important thing to remember in this season is that while primaries are a treasured part of "the democratic process," they are by no means all of it—at least if by that phrase we mean not some civics-book maxim but the real process by which real democracies have won their success in the real world.

Pittsburgh Post-Gazette
Pittsburgh, Pa., March 9, 1972

THE OUTCOME of the New Hampshire primary indicates that even though Sen. Edmund Muskie got the most votes in the Democratic Presidential contest, he now faces a steeper uphill road. In a switch on that advertising slogan, No. 1 must try harder than ever.

For the Muskie strategy had been for the Maine senator to come out with a huge majority in neighboring New Hampshire. Such a bandwagon shove thus would overcome tighter races or even setbacks in primaries farther from home. But it didn't work out that way as Mr. Muskie got only 48 per cent of the New Hampshire Democratic vote.

The reason was what the Muskie camp calls the "spoiler strategy" of other Democratic candidates. Others one at a time can select their primaries to cut down Muskie.

That is why Sen. George McGovern's impressive-looking 37 per cent of the vote could be deceptive for him. For if it helps zap Muskie eventually, it likely will be Sen. Hubert Humphrey or even Sen. Ted Kennedy who would be the beneficiary, rather than Mr. McGovern.

At least the primary should have washed out for good such hopefuls as Los Angeles Mayor Sam Yorty (6 per cent of the vote), Congressman Wilbur Mills (4 per cent), and Sen. Vance Hartke (3 per cent).

On the Republican side President Nixon came through with a smashing 69 per cent. Still, it was significant that Congressman Pete McCloskey got 20 per cent, as the liberal Californian has attacked Mr. Nixon headon about such issues as the Vietnam War. Moreover, Mr. McCloskey got twice as many votes as conservative challenger Congressman John M. Ashbrook of Ohio, who avowedly was running to push Mr. Nixon more to the right.

Does this mean Mr. Nixon will need to pay more attention to his liberal flank even within the GOP? Or does this primary result weigh little against the fact that Republican conservatives work harder in elections and therefore count more? (Note: The same consideration skews results on the Democratic side, where liberals traditionally campaign more vigorously for their men.)

So despite the results in New Hampshire the money still has to be on both President Nixon and Sen. Muskie as the eventual candidates. If this proves true, Americans may raise more questions than ever about the multiplicity of primaries and the wear and tear on candidates and campaign finances which they represent.

* * *

But this year a reservation must be made about any such analysis. The Democratic reform of convention delegate selection procedures does make a difference from previous years. That is, each presidential primary means that there are that many delegates sewed up for each of the candidates (from New Hampshire 15 for Muskie, 5 for McGovern, for instance).

This will make for a more splintered convention and keep any candidate from being swept into the nomination by either a group of kingmakers or by some bandwagon effect. So the primaries will mean a lot more this year than in the past.

That is why Mr. Muskie cannot be discounted unless he takes a real nosedive somewhere further along the long primary trail. For, after all, Mr. Muskie is going to have a lot of committed delegates at the Miami Beach convention, too, "spoiler" strategy notwithstanding.

LEDGER-STAR
Norfolk, Va., March 8, 1972

The results from yesterday's New Hampshire primary make risky criteria on which to base ultimate conclusions. But some tentative observations perhaps are in order.

Senator Muskie's so-so showing had to be disappointing to the Maine Democrat. Despite his efforts to shrug off the facts that he failed to surpass 50 per cent of the vote and that Senator McGovern was surprisingly close behind with about 37 per cent, the outcome was a mild setback. Mr. Muskie is still the party's frontrunner, to be sure, but he obviously is running more slowly and not as far in front.

No doubt Mr. McGovern will take heart at his showing, but probably the greater gainers were a couple of Democrats named Humphrey and Jackson who weren't really in this race. They're concentrating on next Tuesday in Florida. Meanwhile, Mr. McGovern remains a long-shot candidate for the nominatioin.

Although the Republican party presidential primary drew less attention, tentative judgments can be made here, too. Mr. Nixon did not do any better really than it was expected he would do, but significantly he didn't do any worse either. The conservative challenge of Congressman Ashbrook faltered; the anti-war crusade of Congressman McCloskey, which invited comparison with the solid McCarthy showing against President Johnson four years ago, wasn't a great deal stronger. Mr. Nixon captured about 70 per cent of the vote, leaving a mere 30 per cent for the other challengers.

With respect to the McCloskey challenge, it will be remembered that it was principally a public disenchantment with the war that contributed to Mr. McCarthy's big 1968 vote and the subsequent decision by Mr. Johnson not to run again. The people are still disenchanted with the war, more so, we would guess, and the prisoner issue continues to sadden and frustrate the nation. But the failure by Mr. McCloskey to draw a larger vote suggests that the American people are not unaware of the steady and effective job Mr. Nixon has done in disengaging the U.S. from the Indochina fighting. And indeed the turnaround over the past three years has been so dramatic that even much of Mr. McCloskey's anti-war vote might be interpreted in a sense as an endorsement at least of the Nixon direction on the war. It may merely be that some of the voters are dissatisfied with his pace and his method.

But a presidential primary remains a preliminary match-up of candidates leading to the election in November. And, overall, political conclusions to be drawn from the New Hampshire voting yesterday are themselves preliminary. But, alas, there is more to come—a great deal more perhaps than the people wish to see and, before it is all over, doubtless more than most candidates will wish to see.

New York Post
New York, N.Y., March 8, 1972

Perhaps the clearest thing that can be said about the New Hampshire primary is that it increased the suspense and multiplied the imponderables of campaign '72.

In arithmetical terms President Nixon scored a decisive victory over his two Republican challengers, Congressmen Pete McCloskey and John Ashbrook. But what appears to be about a 7-3 margin will be cause for less rejoicing in the private Nixon councils than is reflected in the inevitable victory proclamation. As the incumbent Chief Executive recently returned from a trip to China that blanketed the nation's media for many days, Mr. Nixon's triumph fell some ten per cent below his 1968 showing as a candidate for the nomination in the same state's primary. About two thirds of the opposition votes were rolled up by McCloskey, running on a platform largely comparable to those of the leading liberal Democratic aspirants.

Without seeking to read excessive meaning into a single primary involving a small state and a limited number of voters (with independents free to roam into either primary), it is fair to suggest that the returns dispute the image of Mr. Nixon's invincibility in November. Moreover, despite the wide disparity between McCloskey's views and those of Ashbrook, a voice of the GOP's extreme right wing, one thrust was common to both men's campaign—the charge that the Nixon Administration has been repeatedly guilty of disingenuousness in its dealings with the people. Credibility—or lack of it—was the issue that dominated the GOP primary, and in those terms Mr. Nixon was scarcely a landslide winner.

* * *

Sen. Muskie's victory in the Democratic primary was also less significant in many respects than the vote amassed by Sen. McGovern, his leading opponent in this contest. He did not obtain a clear majority, and McGovern ran notably stronger than early surveys had predicted. Muskie, however, was the target of an infamous, insistent campaign of defamation by William Loeb's notorious Manchester Union Leader—an exercise which led to what may have been a costly emotional episode. Nevertheless McGovern's adherents can cite his totals as compelling evidence that he has ceased to be the invisible man so often projected in the polls.

Other aspects of the primary will feed political speculation for many days—the remarkable Agnew write-in and the failure of Loeb-supported rightist Sam Yorty to make any inroads in the Democratic race. The returns invite the hope that the crowded Democratic field may be reduced by the departure of Yorty, Vance Hartke and possibly Wilbur Mills, none of whom proved serious factors.

As the full returns are analyzed, many obscure and conflicting meanings will be read into them. But next week the scene will shift to Florida and there will be other faces in the cast. At this stage it may be wisest to remember that the date is now March 8, and the form charts may be subject to many changes before the summer conventions and November's day of national decision.

The Washington Post
Washington, D.C., March 9, 1972

"Victory" and "defeat," even "setback" and "surge," are highly relative terms when you employ them in the context of the quadrennial New Hampshire primary. Mr. Nixon, for instance, overwhelmed his two Republican opponents, Representatives Ashbrook and McCloskey. Yet three out of every 10 Republicans who voted in Tuesday's contest voted for one of Mr. Nixon's two opponents, and the President attracted a smaller percentage of the Republican vote than he had in either 1960 or 1968—campaign years in which he had no effective opposition, but in which he also did not have the power and prestige that accrue to the incumbent President. Thus his showing can be (and has been) interpreted as a triumph by some and as a dark omen by others. Just so, Senator Muskie failed to meet previously set standards and expectations, so that his 48 per cent of the vote was at once enough—and not enough—to "win."

The point is that these things are traditionally measured in quicksilver where the New Hampshire primary is concerned, weighed against a set of constantly shifting assumptions and values. In consequence there are two quite separate kinds of result to tally. One is the delegate count. The other is the psychological warfare effect. And at this early stage in the national political proceedings the second can be at least as influential as the first in determining the convention result. On this count, Senator McGovern, confounding the expectations of many with his 37 per cent of the Democratic vote, clearly was the "winner" of the New Hampshire primary. He has demonstrated a capacity to produce a very respectable percentage of the vote in a fragmented primary and gone a long way to undermine the notion that his candidacy was somehow, endemically, a lost cause.

We mean to take nothing from his particular achievement in noting that the two fairly constant elements of New Hampshire primary history, however, are first, surprise, and second, evanescence. Estes Kefauver in 1952 and 1956, Henry Cabot Lodge in 1964, Eugene McCarthy in 1968—it is almost as if the voters of New Hampshire had a contract with the rest of us to produce the desired "upset," inviting us first to make our predictions and then to sit back and watch them be disproved. The question, as David Broder put it in The Post a few days back, was who would the voters of New Hampshire "victimize" this year? Well, they pretty much spoiled the ambitions of Senator Hartke and Mayor Yorty, but an awful lot wasn't expected there. If they "victimized" anyone, it was Senator Muskie. We have, all along, had a feeling that Senator Muskie was in some sense letting his frontrunner role victimize him and his campaign as well, that both were sorely in need of liberation from its particular tyranny. Florida will tell us more. For now it is enough to wonder whether the voters of New Hampshire might not have liberated Senator Muskie in the very act of victimizing him.

The Louisville Times
Louisville, Ky., March 9, 1972

Before New Hampshire's primary this week we suggested that it couldn't be expected to prove much. The state is both too small and too untypical of the country as a whole to provide much insight into how the nation feels about the men who want to be President.

Only if the results of the primary could be used to build a bandwagon for the winner, we thought, could the voting have real national significance.

Well, the voting is over, and we see little reason to revise our opinion.

On the Democratic side, Senator Muskie got the most votes but considerably fewer than some of the polls and pundits had expected him to get. Certainly he did not sweep everything before him among voters he consistently referred to as neighbors, and his bandwwagon, if he has one, revealed certain squeaks. Senator McGovern, on the other hand, definitely trailed Muskie but he did quite a bit better than many had expected. It may well be that his showing will inspire both his workers and his financial contributors in the primaries ahead.

And, if the New Hampshire primary achieved nothing else, it apparently put an end, for this year anyway, to the pretensions of Senator Hartke and Mayor Sam Yorty of Los Angeles. They did so badly it is hard to see how or why they would continue to clutter up the list of candidates.

On the Republican side, President Nixon won handily enough though he didn't campaign in person. His challenger from the right, Representative Ashbrook, received only about 10 per cent of the vote. If this is the best he could do in a state regarded as basically conservative, it indicates that President Nixon doesn't have too much to fear from the right—except to the extent that it gets angry and refuses to give him campaign money. The President's challenger from the left, Representative McCloskey, did much better than Ashbrook but even so received only 20 per cent of the vote, and it is not now clear whether he will continue to contest for the Republican nomination.

If there is any kind of straw in the wind to be detected in the New Hampshire primary, it seems to us that it might be in the showings of McGovern and McCloskey. Both men did somewhat better than many had foreseen. Both men, one Republican and the other Democratic, had made their long opposition to the Vietnamese war the principal basis of their appeal to the people not of just New Hampshire but the country.

It is conceivable, though we would not want to press the point, that the McGovern and McCloskey showings indicate that the Vietnamese war remains a very real and effective issue, and that President Nixon's hope that it would be muted will not be realized.

THE DALLAS TIMES HERALD
Dallas, Tex., March 9, 1972

IF, FROM THE New Hampshire primary, anyone emerged smelling like a rose, it was Richard M. Nixon.

Without campaigning, the President coasted to a 70 per cent victory margin in the Republican contest. Reps. Paul McCloskey and John Ashbrook, his liberal and conservative challengers respectively, collected the remaining 30 per cent and expressed satisfaction therewith.

In truth, though, the Great Revolt against Nixon simply failed to make much headway in New Hampshire. Had the dovish McCloskey not been campaigning around the country for well over a year, he likely would not have garnered the 20 per cent share of votes he got. As for Ashbrook, his was a spirited and utterly earnest campaign—high-toned and wholly attentive to gritty issues of deep concern to his fellow conservatives, such as the President's Red China trip and Nixonian deficit-spending. Mr. Ashbrook got 10 per cent of the votes.

Four years ago, the New Hampshire primary may have been pivotal in Lyndon Johnson's decision not to seek re-election. Johnson had received 49.4 per cent of the Democratic votes; challenger Eugene McCarthy, 42.2 per cent. An authentic revolt was brewing in Democratic ranks, and the incumbent President simply sidestepped it by opting for retirement.

But no such intra-party revolt is in prospect for Mr. Nixon. He is presently serene in the enjoyment of public favor. The voters seem little exercised about his policies—on the war, deficit spending, or Red China.

No doubt this should be a warning signal to the President's Democratic rivals. In New Hampshire, neither Edmund Muskie (48 per cent) nor George McGovern (37 per cent) commanded overwhelming support.

True, McGovern did far better than expected. But he was the only credible alternative to Muskie, and as the campaign wore on, Muskie's image sagged. Overexposure in the media probably didn't help; neither did his tearful attack on newspaper publisher William Loeb; nor, more fundamentally yet, his seeming lack of commitment to anything in particular. "Trust Muskie," he begged. "Why?" the majority of New Hampshire's voters replied.

Well, at any rate, the nomination is by no means sewn up. Twenty-two more presidential primaries lie ahead, and in these, both Muskie and McGovern will face such feisty competition as George Wallace, Hubert Humphrey, John Lindsay, and Henry Jackson, all of whom stayed out of the New Hampshire race.

Right now, on to next week's primary in Florida—and then we'll all have another look-see at who's ahead.

THE RICHMOND NEWS LEADER
Richmond, Va., March 8, 1972

South Dakota's Democratic Senator George McGovern likes to be called the "David of the Plains." He went to New Hampshire and lobbed some stones, and undertook to impose himself on the granitic voters there. He did marginally well. At this writing, he has garnered 37 per cent of the Democratic vote, which is not so good when you consider that he has been wandering around in New Hampshire for more than a year, but not so bad when you consider that he is, well, George McGovern.

With equal presumption, Maine's Democratic Senator Edmund Muskie likes to be regarded not so much as Senator McGovern's Goliath, but as a contemporary Abraham Lincoln. When the first New Hampshire voter surveys were taken a year ago, Senator Muskie was said to have the support of 65 per cent of the Democrats. He has wound up with about 48 per cent. One wonders whether Lincoln would have understood. Attribute that dramatic drop less to the effectiveness of 'David' McGovern's stones than to the voters' displeasure over Mr. Muskie's determination to be on every side of almost every issue, and to be on the wrong side of all the rest. Senator Muskie has sought to occupy the middle ground in the national Democratic party. But he evidently has made the mistake of equating a centrist or moderate stance with far-left positions that are alienating the ultimate muscle of the national Democratic party that is an amalgam of blue-collar labor and white-collar middle class.

Senator Muskie is perhaps best known for the statement he made last summer in a room above Ralph's Supermarket in Watts: The Senator said that no black could hack it as a vice-presidential candidate. He also is well-known for his advocacy of compulsory busing; for his waffling on the matter of Vietnam; for his statement that the FBI is "a dangerous threat to fundamental constitutional rights"; for his Florida statement condemning the space shuttle; for his comment that the Attica prison uprising shows that "we have reached the point where men would rather die than live another day in America"; and for his support of the militant leftists who undertook to shut down Washington D.C. two years ago.

Every candidate is subject to the elements of accident and caprice. But Senator Muskie seems to have a penchant for the self-inflicted political wound. Perhaps the only Democratic candidate in New Hampshire who was consistently sillier was Indiana's Senator Vance Hartke: He went to New Hampshire and said that everyone should be guaranteed a set of new false teeth.

A comment about the Republican vote is to the point. President Nixon was opposed by two candidates—California Congressman Paul McCloskey from the left and Ohio Congressman John Ashbrook from the right. Mr. Ashbrook endeavored to teach Mr. Nixon a conservative lesson. The President received 69 per cent of the Republican vote, in contrast to his 77 per cent showing as a non-incumbent four years ago. Nevertheless it was clear from the beginning that the Ashbrook candidacy was a mistake. Yesterday's vote proved that: Mr. Ashbrook walked away with a grand total of 10 per cent of the vote. This can be viewed only as a distinct blow to conservative aspiration.

Yet the essential story out of New Hampshire is the story of 'David' and 'Abe.' In spite of his relatively strong performance, it would be wrong to take Senator McGovern seriously. And perhaps New Hampshire's fundamental damage to Senator Muskie was this: Prior to New Hampshire, it was believed that nobody was really mad at him; New Hampshire disclosed that—on the contrary—quite a few Democrats are. It is likely that this will be borne out next week in Florida, where the issue of compulsory busing probably will show the depth of voter antipathy to dubious 'David' and ambivalent 'Abe.'

Arkansas Gazette.
Little Rock, Ark., March 9, 1972

TURNING POINTS in presidential politics have been found sometimes in the earlybird New Hampshire primary but certainly there was nothing resembling a turning point in New Hampshire this time around.

There were just two Democratic candidates in New Hampshire to be taken seriously as aspirants for the nomination. One of them, Senator Ed Muskie of Maine, went in in New Hampshire as the frontrunner for the nomination, and he came out as the frontrunner, with about 48 per cent of the New Hampshire vote. The other, Senator George McGovern, ran a strong second with about 37 per cent of the New Hampshire popular vote, and he remains in serious contention for the nomination in spite of the small percentages of support he gets in the national opinion polls.

Certainly George McGovern has every reason for encouragement. He continues to show strength as a vote-getter in spite of the fact that he is not nearly as well known as the two leading (in the polls) Democrats, Muskie and Hubert Humphrey.

On the other hand it is difficult to sustain suggestions that Senator Muskie has suffered a setback. No matter if New England is his home territory, the fact remains that Muskie won. He got nearly half the total vote and would have gotten more than half, certainly, if Wilbur Mills and Mayor Sam Yorty of Los Angeles had not been siphoning off small "conservative" percentages of the vote that Muskie could have expected to receive in a two-way contest with McGovern. Muskie is somewhat more of a centrist than McGovern, or at least he is so identified in the public mind.

Wilbur Mills got about 4 per cent of the vote, on an expensive write-in campaign organized by the Memphis PR man, DeLoss Walker. Mr. Walker has had better days in his time. What Mills is up to remains as much a mystery as ever. In New Hampshire the effect was to help McGovern, who is hardly Mills's hero. In a broader context, the Mills campaign in New Hampshire did help Hubert Humphrey, somewhat, indirectly, in the latter's contest with Muskie, and possibly this is what Mr. Mills has in mind. Unless it is to keep George Wallace out of Arkansas. Or to win the vice presidential nomination. Who knows?

In any event "New Hampshire" has come and gone and nothing decisive has happened.

Florida is next, and we are prepared to predict that nothing decisive will happen there, either. Nearly everybody is in the race in Florida and, accordingly, George Wallace will probably win the plurality with 30 per cent of the vote, say, and a sweep of the redneck counties across the Northern tier. The lineup of the other candidates will be important and significant but we rather doubt that anybody will be made or broken in Florida with the exceptions of Senator Henry M. (Scoop) Jackson and Mayor John Lindsay, who have to make respectable showings in Florida or give up the whole idea of becoming president.

On to Wisconsin and California!

THE ARIZONA REPUBLIC
Phoenix, Ariz., March 12, 1972

Despite all the analysis, the two victors in New Hampshire's presidential primary were plainly President Nixon and Sen. Hubert Humphrey.

President Nixon easily walked away from his two Republican primary opponents, capturing almost 70 per cent of the popular vote and all 20 Republican delegates to the party convention in San Diego.

And Senator Humphrey, who will vie with 10 opponents in his first primary contest for Florida Democratic delegates next week, obviously gained when Sen. Edmund Muskie, up until New Hampshire the party's leading presidential contender, was doused by his close race with Sen. George McGovern. McGovern has about as much chance as Pat Paulsen of getting the Democratic presidential nomination in Miami.

Senator Muskie seriously damaged his New Hampshire bid and his presidential image nationwide when he publicly excoriated Manchester Union Leader publisher William Loeb for opposition to his candidacy. Muskie's emotional outburst toward the end of the campaign sent liberal Democrats scurrying into the McGovern camp.

McGovern, who conducted a low-keyed campaign that soft-pedaled his extreme positions on the national guaranteed income and complete U. S. surrender in Vietnam, emerged as the angel of moderation to those alienated from the Muskie camp.

However, New Hampshire is hardly a representative state. And entirely too much false significance has been attributed to the primary game. The late Sen. Estes Kefauver not only won all 12 Democratic delegates in New Hampshire's 1952 primary campaign, forcing President Harry Truman to step out of the race. He also scored primary victories in Nebraska, Illinois, New Jersey, Massachusetts, Oregon, South Dakota, and California.

But the 1952 Democratic convention, deadlocked until the third ballot, turned to Illinois Gov. Adlai Stevenson, who was not previously a primary candidate in any state. And Stevenson passed over Kefauver for the vice presidential spot, selecting instead Alabama Sen. John J. Sparkman.

It is too early to say anything with certainty about the outcome of this year's summer conventions. Primaries rarely do little more than confuse things. But barring the completely unexpected, President Nixon and Vice President Agnew will almost surely be renominated by the Republicans at San Diego.

The atomization of the Democratic Party, with more than a dozen presidential candidates in 24 primaries, will almost inevitably result in a hopelessly deadlocked convention that will probably turn in desperation to Senator Humphrey. His selection of a running-mate would then alone determine if this year's race is to be a repeat of 1968.

THE INDIANAPOLIS NEWS
Indianapolis, Ind., March 10, 1972

This week's vote in New Hampshire demonstrated, among other things, the perils of political front-running.

It had been widely assumed that Sen. Edmund Muskie of Maine would walk away with the Democratic balloting. The early polls showed Muskie with a comfortable lead, while his principal rival, George McGovern, trailed rather badly. As it worked out, Muskie netted 48 per cent of the Democratic ballots, McGovern 37. What produced this outcome is uncertain, although many feel that Muskie's emotional response to criticism played an important role.

Whatever the reason, McGovern received a boost in his effort to overtake Muskie, although the latter remains the favorite. Most political observers believe McGovern's chances at the nomination remain rather slim, so the effect of his showing could be to throw the nomination race to some other Democratic contender. Sen. Hubert Humphrey of Minnesota, party standard-bearer in 1968, c o u l d prove to be the major beneficiary.

In the Republican column, President Nixon easily outdistanced his two Republican rivals—Rep. Paul McCloskey of California on the left and Rep. John Ashbrook of Ohio on the right. Nixon garnered about 69 per cent of the vote, McCloskey 20, and Ashbrook 10. That deployment of votes hardly implies an anti-Nixon prairie fire, but the figures do suggest some sparks of party discontent. When 30 per cent of the voters cast their ballots against an incumbent chief executive of their own persuasion, there is no particular cause for presidential rejoicing.

This point is especially notable when we reflect that neither of Nixon's opponents is nationally well-known. McCloskey has been campaigning in the state for a long time, of course, and person-to-person communication is supposed to be the way to get across to New Hampshire voters. Ashbrook's campaign was late-starting, and has received comparatively little publicity. In view of this and the added fact that Nixon is undoubtedly perceived as "conservative" by many voters in contrast to McCloskey, Ashbrook's showing could be a premonition of further troubles down the line.

The New Hampshire vote is small and may not be typical of feeling nationwide. Florida and other primaries will tell us more about the situation in each party. In the meantime, the Granite state results have given both political front-runners cause to re-examine their positions.

RAPID CITY JOURNAL
Rapid City, S.D., March 9, 1972

If any one event has sent hopes soaring in the camp of Senator George McGovern's followers in South Dakota, it has to be the outcome of the New Hampshire primary election.

Instead of finding himself near the bottom as results came in Tuesday, South Dakota's presidential hopeful captured a solid 37 per cent of the vote and, in the process, shook the leading Democratic contender, Sen. Edmund Muskie of Maine. But that is just one spin-off result of his strong showing. Claiming a victory because he did so much better than he had dared hope, McGovern has been catapulted into the foreground as a viable vote getter and someone to be reckoned with in the Democratic presidential nomination race.

South Dakotans committed to McGovern's cause have never wavered in their enthusiasm, but, until Tuesday, they probably operated mostly on loyalty and faith in their candidate. If they listened to McGovern's own words that his low standing in national polls was unimportant, they could only be haunted by the fear that the polls were substantially correct. New Hampshire may change all of that.

National Pollster George Gallup has something to say about polls in primary elections. They are, he says, little better than pilot studies — mere straws in the wind — and no one should regard them as anything else. The reason polling in primary elections is less reliable than in general elections is that primaries often draw small turnouts. Combined with the ability of political parties to turn out the faithful, this makes primaries very difficult to predict.

So far as we know, Gallup did not have a poll taken in New Hampshire for Tuesday's election. His sampling of opinion nationwide, however, has never given McGovern more than 6 per cent. New regard for McGovern among voters across the country should be reflected in upcoming Gallup Polls because of what happened in New Hampshire Tuesday.

But already proved by McGovern is the fact that outstanding organization, persistent hard work and fearless campaigning by a man from South Dakota cannot be ignored.

The Detroit News
Detroit, Mich., March 9, 1972

Senator Edmund Muskie, touted as front-runner in the crowded field of D e m o c r a t i c candidates, has thrown a shoe coming out of the starting gate. It doesn't eliminate him from the sweepstakes but obviously it slows him down.

Muskie needed at least 50 percent of the Democratic vote in tne New H a m p s h i r e primary to avoid embarrassment and maintain the momentum of his campaign. He got only 48 percent against a field of weak opponents, some of whom are unknown outside their own home towns.

Putting on a brave face for the press, Muskie referred to New Hampshire as his third solid victory in a row. This reference was evidence in itself that he did not consider his showing in New Hampshire strong enough to stand alone. The previous two "victories" were party caucuses in Iowa and Arizona where he took 34 percent and 38 percent of the votes respectively.

If it's any consolation to the Muskie camp, New Hampshire provided none of the candidates with brilliant victories.

Senator George McGovern did enjoy a "moral victory" by winning 37 percent of the Democratic total, thus losing by less than expected. As election day approached, he seemed to get stronger and Muskie weaker.

Muskie went into the New Hampshire campaign with the endorsement of UAW President Leonard Woodcock but the pattern of voting indicates a strong measure of labor support for McGovern. In the final days of the campaign, McGovern apparently managed to overcome the label of "one-issue candidate" and broaden his appeal. This may spell more trouble for Muskie in the future.

The remainder of the Democratic c a n d i d a t e s — Senator Vance Hartke, Los Angeles Mayor Sam Yorty, Edward Coll and the write-in candidate, Rep. Wilbur Mills — divided approximately 15 percent of the vote among them. Their showing was not quite but almost on a par with that of comic Pat Paulsen, who won about 1 percent of the total on the Republican ballot.

President Richard Nixon was unsurprisingly the big vote-getter of the New Hampshire primary. He got 69 percent of the GOP vote, thus repudiating the attacks upon him f r o m the left by Rep. Paul McCloskey and the right by Rep. John Ashbrook. Still, he fell short of his 79 percent in New Hampshire in 1968.

In the wake of this week's primary, New Hampshire maintains its reputation as the place where a strong victory doesn't necessarily mean anything but a weak victory may mean near-disaster.

Now, it's on to Florida, which could prove another near-disaster for Senator Muskie. There he faces an even larger and a more potent field of candidates, i n c l u d i n g Senator Hubert Humphrey, New York Mayor John Lindsay, Senator Henry Jackson and, of course, Alabama Gov. George Wallace.

The Florida polls show Wallace well ahead with Humphrey and Muskie far behind and battling for second place. McGovern, flush with moral victory in New Hampshire, will return to reality.

New Hampshire indicated that the Democrats have no strong favorite. Florida will only confirm that indication. The first two primaries of 1972 will have proven mainly the disarray of the Democratic Party.

ST. LOUIS POST-DISPATCH
St. Louis, Mo., March 9, 1972

If there is anything heartening about the political circus just brought to a merciful end in New Hampshire it is the strong showing of Senator George McGovern of South Dakota who obtained 37 per cent of the vote in the crowded Democratic presidential preference primary. Senator Muskie, the current Democratic front-runner from the neighboring state of Maine, won 48 per cent, but his victory was not big enough to give his campaign a substantial lift.

Senator McGovern, on the other hand, scored what he called "both a moral victory and a political victory." While as a New Englander Mr. Muskie had a head start, Mr. McGovern had nothing going for him except integrity, industry and a program that more than a third of the Democratic voters found compelling. The outcome should be a national boost to his presidential aspirations. This is additionally so because Mr. McGovern apparently won five of the 20 Democratic national convention delegates, leaving Mr. Muskie with 15, short of an expected sweep.

As *Post-Dispatch* correspondent Thomas Ottenad reported from the scene, "Mr. McGovern now becomes a serious and credible challenger, something he was not before Tuesday's vote." Throughout the months of dreary politicking in the state, Mr. McGovern kept his cool, which is something Mr. Muskie, who also worked to the point of physical exhaustion, apparently did not.

There is substantial opinion that Mr. Muskie's emotional outburst in Manchester at the end of February tarnished the image of calmness and deliberation he has presented to the public. What the Senator did was to challenge a newspaper attack on himself and his wife. During a public denunciation of the *Union-Leader*, published by William Loeb, Mr. Muskie wept. The candidate's tears can easily be explained by campaign exhaustion, but Mr. Muskie's lack of judgment in the way he attempted his counter-attack is not reassuring. He could have laughed off the newspaper attack, or ignored it.

As became obvious Tuesday, the influence of the *Union-Leader*, New Hampshire's largest daily, is not very great despite the blustering of Mr. Loeb, an arch-conservative. Mr. Loeb went all out to support the least likely Democratic candidate in the race, Mayor Sam Yorty of Los Angeles. Mr. Yorty got 6 per cent of the vote, which was 6 per cent more than he deserved but in any event an inconsequential total. Even Representative Wilbur Mills of Arkansas, chairman of the House Ways and Means Committee, got 4 per cent in a write-in vote.

On the Republican side, President Nixon won 69 per cent of the vote, easily fending off the challenge from the left (Representative Paul McCloskey of California, 20 per cent) and from the right (Representative John Ashbrook of Ohio, 10 per cent). The major GOP significance is the further weakening of Mr. McCloskey's chances.

Although Mr. McGovern came off unexpectedly and encouragingly well in New Hampshire, he still has a long way to go if he is to put together a national constituency large enough to win him the Democratic presidential nomination. If he does not make it, at least he will have conducted a forthright campaign addressed to the important issues before the country. Like Adlai Stevenson, his major service may be talking sense to the American people. It is good to find that so many New Hampshire voters appreciate the Senator from South Dakota.

Minneapolis Tribune
Minneapolis, Minn., March 9, 1972

We leave to pollsters and pundits the task of interpreting the percentage distribution of votes in the New Hampshire presidential primary election. Our own view of this first preference primary of the election year is that it shows preferences for president in only the most general, predictable way; that the results form little basis for predicting the outcome next November; that, instead, the New Hampshire exercise says more about the candidates than the voters.

For example, it seems evident that candidates on the left of both parties meant themselves to be taken more seriously than did those on the right. Conservative Republican Ashbrook was seldom in the state. His Democratic counterpart, Los Angeles Mayor Yorty, proclaimed pristine conservatism by insisting that he, unlike the majority of the nation, had never questioned the rightness of American policy in Vietnam.

In contrast, the showing by left-of-center candidates was impressive. No one gives Republican Paul McCloskey a chance of taking the nomination from Mr. Nixon. But McCloskey campaigned hard, criticizing on a number of issues an increasingly popular President who has proved more liberal than most expected four years ago. And in New Hampshire, a substantial minority of Republican voters responded by supporting McCloskey.

Similarly, the main question about liberal Sen. George McGovern has been how far behind the pack of Democratic centrists he would remain. McGovern, like McCloskey, was undeterred by the odds against him. He ran a carefully organized campaign in New Hampshire, capitalizing on lessons learned by supporters of Eugene McCarthy in 1968 and, later, those of Robert Kennedy. And he stood by positions less popular than some taken by the most prominent Democrats — Sen. Muskie, who was on the New Hampshire ballot, and Sen. Humphrey, who was not. Like McCloskey, he predictably received less support than his party's front-runner. But McGovern clearly achieved his objective of adding greatly to his stature as a candidate.

The net effect, in our view, is encouraging. The American process of nominating presidential candidates and electing one of them is long, grueling and complex, a strange mixture of salesmanship and issues. Primary campaigns therefore should be more than contests for votes alone or demonstrations of physical endurance. They should also be tests of leadership in which the results indicate the degree to which candidates have successfully explained their stands. A number of them seem to have done so in New Hampshire.

Los Angeles Times
Los Angeles, Calif., March 9, 1972

In 1968 the incumbent President was the loser in the New Hampshire primary. Lyndon B. Johnson got a majority of the Democratic votes, but Sen. Eugene J. McCarthy's surprising showing, coming on the heels of the Tet offensive, in Vietnam, helped push Mr. Johnson out of the race altogether. And meanwhile Richard M. Nixon swept the New Hampshire Republican vote.

This year the incumbent President was the winner in New Hampshire. In his own party's primary Mr. Nixon easily held back the challenges from the right—Rep. John Ashbrook (R-Ohio) got only 10%—and from the left—Rep. Paul N. McCloskey (R-Calif.) took only 19%.

And the results in the Democratic presidential preference primary must have been satisfying to the President.

For the Democrats have no Richard M. Nixon this year. New Hampshire, unrepresentative though it is of both the nationwide Democratic Party and its full choice of candidates, has tarnished Sen. Edmund S. Muskie (D-Me.) a little bit, and set up Sen. George McGovern (D-S.D.) a little bit, and all in all has underscored the Democrats' quandary. They have no obvious candidate to put up against Mr. Nixon, and he is looking formidable.

How much McGovern's strong showing—36% to Muskie's 48%—reflected positive support for him and how much reflected disenchantment with Muskie is an intriguing question. Muskie's emotional attack on the publisher of the Manchester Union-Leader may have damaged him. People are put off by presidential candidates who can cry in public. Muskie's weepy response to the publisher's nasty attacks on his wife may be one of those signs that mark a crucial turn in a candidate's fortunes.

Another factor was that McGovern campaigned harder than Muskie, who was diverted by commitments in other states, especially to next week's Florida primary.

But the Florida primary, it looks now, will also be a good deal less than decisive, even though every potential Democratic candidate except Sen. Edward M. Kennedy (D-Mass.) is entered. The presence of George Wallace, the referendum on the busing issue and the President's mischievously adroit manipulation of it muddy the waters so much that the Democratic candidates are reduced to fighting for second place behind Wallace, the presumed winner. Again, a cause of satisfaction for the President.

As for Mayor Yorty, the kindest thing you can say is that he is no more serious a candidate for President now than he was when he declared. He is talking about campaigning in California, and maybe Nebraska, but he's had his fling. Let him sell his Yortymobile and stay home. His ridiculous campaign is making a national joke of a great city. And, after all, he was elected to be mayor of Los Angeles, wasn't he?

The Salt Lake Tribune
Salt Lake City, Utah, March 9, 1972

Does the New Hampshire primary election prove anything? The answer usually depends on subsequent developments. As the nation's earliest presidential primary, New Hampshire's March voting is eagerly looked to for portents. But the signs are not always totally reliable.

For example, in 1964, pundits watched New Hampshire's Republican primary to see who had the initial edge, Sen. Barry Goldwater or New York Gov. Nelson Rockefeller. When the ballots were counted, Henry Cabot Lodge, then U.S. ambassador to South Vietnam, not even a declared candidate as a write-in.

In 1960, it wasn't the New Hampshire results that put the late John F. Kennedy over the top, but preferential tallies in Wisconsin and West Virginia. However, four years ago, Sen. Eugene J. McCarthy's strong showing on the Democratic ballot, 42 percent of the total, against 49 percent for President Johnson's stand-in, is credited with pushing LBJ into reluctant retirement.

Tuesday's New Hampshire returns should at least discourage such candidates as Sen. Vance Hartke and Los Angeles Mayor Sam Yorty on the Democratic side as well as cause Republican Rep. Paul McCloskey and Rep. John Ashbrook to wonder if the race is worth pursuing.

The man with every right to feel heartened by Tuesday's vote is Sen. George McGovern, who showed with his 36 percent of the Democratic total that he can run a campaign that attracts more than token votes. While Maine Sen. Edmund S. Muskie won the Democratic primary with almost 50 percent of the vote, he did not overwhelm McGovern, and that's going to be noticed no matter how much the New Englander scoffs at "phantom" figures.

Sen. Muskie still leads in the convention delegate column, and that's where the nomination will be determined. But there is still time for mass defections before the convention actually gathers. Had the senator from Maine captured a heftier majority, over 55 percent, his bandwagon would have been off to a galloping start. It's still in heavy traffic.

Sen. McGovern can be especially encouraged as a truly credible nominee. The other Democratic hopefuls, Sen. Hubert H. Humphrey, Sen. Henry Jackson, New York Mayor John Lindsay, to a certain degree Rep. Shirley Chisholm, can also consider the contest as undecided as it was in February. The Republicans, with their candidate, President Nixon, facing no serious inner-party challenge yet, can relish the prospect of Democrates tearing each other up.

What did New Hampshire's primary divulge? Above all, that President Nixon is holding a wide strip of middle ground among Republican voters in New Hampshire; that Sen. Muskie was not as popular as he should be in his native territory; that remaining primaries are more important to Democrats searching for a worthy opponent to Mr. Nixon than was the New Hampshire vote. In politics as in weather forecasting, the first week in March can be too early to decide the outlook for summer, much less fall.

Campaign '72:
WALLACE WINS FLORIDA PRIMARY; HUMPHREY TOPS JACKSON, MUSKIE

Alabama Gov. George C. Wallace won the Florida Democratic presidential primary March 14, winning 42% of the vote in a field of 11 candidates. He picked up 75 of the state's 81 delegates to the Democratic National Convention. Second place went to Sen. Hubert H. Humphrey (Minn.), the party's 1968 presidential candidate, who won 18% of the vote and the remaining six delegates. Sen. Henry M. Jackson (Wash.) finished in third place with 13%, while Sen. Edmund S. Muskie (Me.) was in fourth place with only 9% of the Florida vote. Following his relatively unimpressive victory in New Hampshire [See pp. 267-278], Muskie's Florida showing severely damaged his reputation as the front-runner for the nomination. The remaining seven candidates, including New York Mayor John V. Lindsay, Sen. George S. McGovern (S.D.) and Rep. Shirley Chisholm (N.Y.), together received 18% of the vote.

Wallace's Florida victory was expected as he had dominated the contest from the beginning by making his total opposition to school busing for racial integration the central issue in the campaign. The other candidates had wavered between qualified opposition and full endorsement of the concept. On primary day Floridians also cast votes on the busing issue directly through two non-binding questions on the ballot. The results: 74% of the voters supported a constitutional amendment to prohibit busing and guarantee the right of a student to attend the public school nearest his home; 79% favored an equal opportunity for quality education for all children and opposed the return to a dual system of public schools. (The second question had been put on the ballot by Gov. Reubin Askew, who actively opposed the anti-busing effort.)

In the Republican primary President Nixon received 87% of the vote and captured all of the state's 40 delegates to the GOP convention. Nixon's nominal challengers, Rep. Paul McCloskey Jr. (Calif.), who had announced his withdrawal from the presidential race March 10, and Rep. John Ashbrook (Ohio), polled 4% and 9% of the votes.

The Dallas Times Herald
Dallas, Tex., March 16, 1972

EDMUND MUSKIE blew it—not just the Florida presidential primary, but his candidatorial cool, for good measure.

It wasn't just that Muskie, long regarded as the front-running Democratic presidential candidate, gathered in a measly nine per cent of the vote, barely ahead of John Lindsay's seven per cent and way behind George Wallace's 42 per cent.

No, Muskie then had to commit another of his increasingly frequent faux pas: He had to uncork a pettish attack on Wallace.

Now when a given opponent has won a landslide victory (as did Wallace) in a state sometimes regarded as the U.S. in microcosm, it would seemingly behoove the runners-up to behave graciously about it. Muskie didn't. Instead, he called Wallace "a demagogue of the worst kind" and "a threat to the unity of this nation." Whereby he gave Wallace a marvelous chance to respond with charitable forgiveness. Being a canny fellow, Wallace did just that—and assuredly made himself additional votes.

All of which casts increasing doubt on Muskie's potential as a candidate. Even more than the New Hampshire primary—where he won only a plurality in what was basically a two-man race with George McGovern—last Tuesday's contest in Florida shows Muskie to be an inadequate vote-getter. Somehow his image as the cool, collected man of reason doesn't come across. Well, certainly it doesn't come across when he indulges in personal vituperation, such as he hurled in New Hampshire at publisher William Loeb ("a gutless coward," said Muskie) and in Florida at George Wallace.

Worse, Muskie misreads the temper of the electorate. What bothers him most about Wallace, one gathers, is Wallace's opposition to racial-balance busing. Yet in a straw vote referendum Florida voters by 3 to 1 endorsed a constitutional amendment to outlaw busing. Muskie favors busing. And he thinks anyone who doesn't is a redneck bigot.

Not so. For in the same referendum, the voters endorsed by an even wider margin the principle of equalized education for all children. What's bigoted about that, senator?

At all events, the Florida primary shows that the voters in this microcosmic state don't care for leftish candidates. Muskie, McGovern, Lindsay, Chisholm—among them they garnered only 26 per cent of the vote. To George Wallace, to the anti-busing, law-and-order-minded Scoop Jackson, and to Hubert Humphrey, with his now-moderate rhetoric went all the rest of the votes.

There's a very definite lesson here. And it's one Muskie ought to heed—if it isn't already too late. The farther left a candidate leans, the worse his prospects appear. If a Democrat's to have any chance at all against Richard Nixon, he's got to straddle the center. Muskie and McGovern can talk all they wish to "the poor, the black, and the young."

But George Wallace, Scoop Jackson, and Hubert Humphrey are talking to a lot of other folks, too. And so far, they're the ones who are getting the votes.

Tulsa Daily World

Tulsa, Okla., March 16, 1972

THE FLORIDA primary has shaken up the PRESIDENTIAL pot; no doubt about that. It has scrambled the Democratic candidates and their roles as winners, losers, good guys and bad guys; spilled the cards all over the floor until no one knows exactly what the deck will look like when it is put back together.

It is easy enough to see some of the messages from the Florida voters. They have made Gov. GEORGE WALLACE of Alabama a force that cannot be laughed off. They have destroyed the myth that Sen. EDMUND MUSKIE would be a runaway nominee. They have given a lift to Sens. HUBERT HUMPHREY and HENRY JACKSON and made the race tougher for New York Mayor JOHN LINDSAY and Sen. GEORGE MCGOVERN.

Most of all, these voters have demonstrated that the great mass of people, mostly in the middle-class economic group once labeled the silent majority, are not going to respond to the appeals to disaffected minorities or sophisticated eggheads.

If the Florida vote is a true indication of the temper of the land, the school busing issue has been badly underrated. That means candidates like LINDSAY and MCGOVERN are out of touch with the main body of Democrats and even HUMPHREY and MUSKIE are going to look at their hole cards and perhaps shift their emphasis in a more "conservative" direction.

This can be only a tentative judgment, because it is not yet established that Florida's thinking is typical of the nation. We know there is a wide disparity among the States; certainly the results in the first two State primaries dramatize it.

But Florida has so many elements of population that the voting there cannot be dismissed as simply a Southern phenomenon. Even though GOVERNOR WALLACE is still a most unlikely nominee for the Democratic Party, he obviously is going to the National Convention with a good handful of delegates and will play more than a bit part in the nominating process.

The 9 per cent vote given MUSKIE weakens his position and makes the next few weeks critical for him. He must bounce back quickly or he will be just another candidate struggling to survive at the convention.

If there is one big winner in the Florida vote, it is probably RICHARD NIXON. Not because he swept the State's 40 GOP convention delegates, but because the voting left the Democrats with so many question-marks that it almost looks as though their lineup is loaded with losers.

It's still early in the game, of course, but the combination of GEORGE WALLACE, busing and middle-class reaction has left the field of Democratic hopefuls staggering, confused and in some cases suffering from shell-shock.

Richmond Times-Dispatch

Richmond, Va., March 16, 1972

To all of the nation's presidential aspirants, sunny Florida has telegraphed a message that they will ignore at their peril: Far from being the "minor flap" that South Dakota's myopic Sen. George McGovern has called it, compulsory busing is a major concern of middle America.

The results of Tuesday's Democratic presidential primary in that state constituted a thundering condemnation of the bizarre practice of massively transporting children in circles to promote racial balance in public schools. Busing was the dominant issue, and Floridians gave a majority of their votes to the two candidates who had vehemently denounced it — Gov. George C. Wallace of Alabama and Sen. Henry M. Jackson of Washington. For emphasis, the voters decisively rejected the concept of compulsory busing in a referendum.

Consider the disastrous performance of those allegedly strong contenders who had piously endorsed massive busing outright or who had implied their approval of it. McGovern, who is in favor of busing everyone's child except his own, and New York Mayor John Lindsay, who seems to favor busing in every community except Fun City, each received only 6 per cent of the vote. Maine Sen. Edmund S. Muskie, supposedly the leading candidate for the Democratic nomination, tried to pretend throughout the campaign that he had never heard of busing. He received only 9 per cent of the vote.

By contrast, Minnesota Sen. Hubert Humphrey, a master vacillator, began his campaign by pooh-poohing the busing issue, finally grasped its significance, and ended up saying he favored one-way busing only, from poor schools to good schools. Thus, unlike McGovern and Lindsay, Humphrey could not be labelled an ardent pro-buser, a fact that may have been partly responsible for his finishing second in the primary, with 19 per cent of the vote.

Florida's primary results cannot be dismissed as a manifestation of Deep South racism. Florida is not a typical Southern state, for it is now home for thousands of Americans who have immigrated from other regions, and especially from the North. The racial views of these people were shaped in New York, in New Jersey, in Maine, in Minnesota and in scores of other Northern and Midwestern environments. Moreover, Floridians not only rejected busing, they overwhelmingly endorsed, in approving another proposal on the ballot, the concept of equal educational opportunities for all children, black and white. Clearly, the people of Florida are willing to accept school integration achieved by reasonable means.

Any candidate who cannot comprehend the results of the Florida primary, who cannot accept them as a measure of the public's antipathy to busing, or who cannot understand that it is possible simultaneously to oppose busing and to favor equal educational opportunity for all children is duncical indeed. Accordingly, Muskie should turn in his Lincolnesque stovepipe hat for a cone-shaped cap, for his post-primary remarks suggest that he missed the whole message.

The primary results, he whined, revealed "some of the worst instincts human beings are capable of." With that churlish observation, Muskie insulted not only the voters of Florida but concerned parents everywhere. Is parental anxiety about busing's adverse impact upon the physical and educational welfare of children one of "the worst instincts human beings are capable of"? In making such an asinine charge, Muskie displayed appallingly insensitivity to the anguish of millions of honorable Americans who oppose busing not because they are racists but because they consider it tragically wrong to use America's children as the major tools to dismantle the racial dualism that characterizes American society.

Muskie's remark also revealed that he has no more grace than stamina. Campaign pressures turned him into a sniveler in New Hampshire, and defeat has made him a carping boor in Florida. The American people are not likely to admire such temperamental characteristics in a potential president, and it is possible that when Muskie mouthed the Florida insult he preached his own political funeral.

It would be a mistake to assume that the message of the Florida primary was beamed exclusively to Democratic presidential hopefuls. Over the noise of the primary's post-mortem can be heard an SOS meant for President Nixon. Floridians want busing halted, and they rallied to Wallace because he was the candidate who most vigorously championed their cause. If no other leader emerges, he may go on to play a decisive role in the presidential campaign, possibly to Mr. Nixon's detriment. For many foes of busing who now look to Wallace would turn to the President if he used the power and prestige of his office to provide relief from this iniquitous practice. Mr. Nixon reportedly is drafting a new announcement on busing. He would do well to consider the SOS from Florida, and consider it carefully, before he sends his statement to the printers.

The Miami Herald
Miami, Fla., March 16, 1972

GEORGE WALLACE won Florida by a landslide. He also won it by surprise — including his own. He carried every county. He carried every congressional district save one. He even carried Dade County, but only with 27 per cent of the vote compared to his statewide plurality of 42 per cent.

The analysts are busy at their charts and even at their microscopes. What happened in Florida?

For one thing, there were 11 Democratic candidates and the so-called "liberal" vote was splintered. Yet if we look at the spectrum, the "conservative" candidacies of Gov. Wallace And Sen. Henry Jackson piled up 682,000 votes to the "liberals'" 539,000.

What, however, is the true spectrum? Jackson is a populist domestically with a hard line abroad. Wallace is a populist and a racist with no known comprehension of foreign policy.

Then there was busing. The anti-busing amendment straw vote drew nearly as many votes as all those of the 11 Democratic candidates. The straw vote in favor of a continued program of integration drew even more. An anomaly.

Is Florida a microcosm of the national electorate? Politically, it certainly is variegated. In the Sunshine State there are many Floridas. In Presidential matters, however, most often Florida is conservative.

Many conservative Democrats and some re-registered Republicans voted openly for Wallace with no intention of voting for anyone but Richard Nixon in November. This switcherooing has happened more than once in Florida, most recently in the High-Burns contest for the Democratic gubernatorial nomination in 1966.

If Florida is a miniature model of the United States, does the Wallace sweep mean a hard rudder to the right? We'd like to see more returns, say from more politically oriented Wisconsin, before making a judgment.

So, what happened?

We think that George Wallace skillfully put together everything that rubs peoples' nerves raw, the frustrations, the things that make living painful, the issues in government no voter can get at directly. The Wallace campaign was a mobilization of discontent, orchestrated by a superb demagogue in simplistic phrases.

Whatever happened, George Wallace is right. He is now a national, not a regional, figure. The Democratic Party, which he shattered in Florida, must reckon with him.

So must sober Americans who know that discontent must have answers lest it become total disunity; that these answers are not simple or emotional, and that the kind of leadership contrived by Wallace in Florida is not along a path to glory but to the destruction of the human values which the power-hungry in every age and in every place seek first to corrupt.

Miami, Fla., March 15, 1972

"They" done sent "them" a message.

Florida's outsized vote for Alabama Gov. George Wallace, though it varied from district to district in intensity, reads about as clearly as Gov. Wallace's speeches:

Governments are run by big shots who forget the source of their power lies in people. Governments and other fatcats live it up, give money away to no-accounts for no decent reason and do not respond to the needs of the folks who carry crushing tax burdens.

Governments try to readjust people's natural social arrangements by carting kids unnecessarily on buses instead of just leaving people to work things out for themselves.

"Send them a message," read George Wallace's ads. The message has to be one of protest.

Sens. Henry Jackson and Hubert Humphrey subdued their New Dealism under attacks on busing. They pulled the second and third highest vote. They received the message clearly. Both are alive politically to test their slightly new image in some other state.

Sen. Ed Muskie, embittered by what he feels were erroneous press estimates of his status, plans to maintain his campaign. But more than any other candidate his chances have been seriously damaged in Florida.

Serious harm, also, was rendered to New York Mayor John Lindsay. He fought hard in Florida, spent much and barely edged out Sen. McGovern, who made an effort but hedged it enough so that he now appears neither helped nor hurt, just still in the fight.

President Nixon, of course, won the Republican primary solidly. He was not pitted against George Wallace and, besides, he proved his ability to defeat the Alabaman back in 1968.

With an almost solid Wallace delegation, except for six Dade Countians, headed for Miami Beach in July, Florida certainly seems in a mood now to lay a sort of vengeance on Democratic liberals, perhaps through a return to Mr. Nixon in November. We still do not believe the national party will nominate a five-state winner in 1968 to do battle with the incumbent.

Everyone expected George Wallace to win Florida. His victory exceeded the general assumption. It is an embarrassment to party leadership which now will have no opportunity to influence national party platform policy nor even play the participating host. Those duties will fall to Wallace delegates and none of the in-Democrats even know who they are.

Gov. Wallace deserves recognition of his victory. His outrage at the unresponsiveness and contrariness of government is no more than ours, but his method of stating it has prevailed this time.

We hope there is not an overreaction to his win. Smoldering outrage can carry elections but it doesn't really generate solutions of the problems that started it in the first place.

24—Florida Primary

The Birmingham News

Birmingham, Ala., March 15, 1972

Whether or not his impressive victory in Florida's primary transforms Gov. George Wallace into a serious contender for the national Democratic Party's presidential nomination, it can't help but serve as the two-by-four to get the donkey's attention.

Florida is far from a typical Southern state. That, in fact, is one of the reasons the candidates put such emphasis on the state's primary—that is, put emphasis on it before it became obvious that George Wallace was going to win it big. Then they began to play it down.

The point is that Florida is a composite of the U. S., and its voters may be considered to represent cross-section thinking in this country.

And Florida's Democratic voters said resoundingly, unmistakably, that they don't like much of what they've been seeing and hearing.

Most attention was given the bussing issue in Florida, and some analysts no doubt will try to explain away Gov. Wallace's showing as some sort of racist aberration. But the very same voters who favored Wallace and who voted three to one against busing for racial balance in schools voted four to one in favor of equal, nondiscriminatory educational opportunity for all children.

That's not racism; it's a call for a return to realism in educational policies.

But more than busing was involved in the Florida vote. Essentially, Gov. Wallace succeeded in articulating the deep sense of frustration and resentment many voters feel in this country. They feel that the government goes along its way doing as it pleases, ignoring them except at election and tax time, and that there hasn't been a great deal they could do about it.

George Wallace convinced them that they *can* "do something about it," and their response was a shout of approval.

We believe that the results are convincing proof that the majority of rank-and-file Democrats don't support the ultra-leftist policies just about every one of their leading candidates espouse.

We believe that it indicated, too, that the voters are tired of the constant criticism and harassment of the incumbent President and government. This is not just a comment on their effort to undermine a responsible Vietnam withdrawal policy by the current President; it goes back to President Johnson as well, who was hounded unmercifully by the arrogant know-betters.

The way politics is being played in this country nowadays, it may be impossible for *any* candidate to govern effectively once elected President. The voters in Florida said they're tired of that.

The Wallace and Henry Jackson votes combined totaled 55 per cent on the Democratic side, and this is a clear vote against the course the Muskies and McGoverns have been urging the party to take, particularly on defense and foreign policy issues.

Even the fact that the second man in the vote was Hubert Humphrey was significant, for Humphrey is seen much more by most voters as a moderate, center-road candidate than the others.

Humphrey and Jackson probably gained most among the Democratic also-rans. Sen. Muskie's nine per cent showing will seriously affect his nomination drive. So, in our opinion, will his post-election comments devoted almost exclusively to a denunciation of Gov. Wallace and all he represents. Voters aren't much drawn to the sour-grapes loser.

McGovern's and Lindsay's six per cent each—well . . .

The combined vote of the leading Democratic liberals — Humphrey, Muskie, McGovern, Lindsay, Chisholm —was about 44 per cent of the total Democratic vote. But when the 400,000-plus Republican voters who gave President Nixon an overwhelming vote of confidence in their own primary are considered, the Democratic liberals all together got the support of fewer than a third of the Floridians voting.

As we said, that ought to get the donkey's attention.

ST. LOUIS POST-DISPATCH

St. Louis, Mo., March 16, 1972

The Florida presidential primary results did not so much prove that George Wallace is a national candidate, as he claimed, as that bussing could easily be exploited into a national issue.

Despite Gov. Wallace's heady Democratic victory, with 42 per cent of the votes, he is not yet in any position to be more than a regional candidate, if that. He missed the filing deadline in such big industrial states as Illinois and Ohio, and can expect only a handful of convention delegates from Pennsylvania and some other states above the Mason-Dixon line. Even in Georgia, which Wallaceites considered a challenge, the Alabama governor failed to pick up a single delegate in 10 district conventions over the weekend.

Nor, from a national standpoint, can Florida's Democratic voting be considered anywhere near conclusive. Senator Humphrey showed new strength, Senator Jackson rode Mr. Wallace's anti-bussing stand into third place, and Senator Muskie won only 9 per cent of the votes. But Florida, with its Dixie North and heavy influx of prosperous and semi-prosperous retirees in the south, can hardly be regarded as a cross section of anything but Florida.

Neither did Florida provide a clear picture of the bussing issue. It is true that 74 per cent of the voters favored amending the Constitution to prohibit "forced" bussing, but 79 per cent supported a straw ballot question in behalf of equal educational opportunities for all children regardless of race or residence and against a return to dual school systems. The anti-bussing proposition drew more votes, however.

What to make of that? Do Floridians both oppose bussing to integrate schools and support school integration? Or is it simply that more of them were against bussing than were against racial segregation? Certainly the bussing straw vote helped the Wallace vote, offering new evidence that this emotionally-charged issue invites political manipulation by those who stoop to that.

Bussing is in many ways a synthetic issue. The Florida question about "forced" bussing was loaded, for children have long been "forced" to ride busses for various purposes, including segregation. Nationally, President Nixon has elevated the issue beyond the realm of reason by talking of bussing to achieve "racial balance," which no court has ordered and no one has even defined. Mr. Nixon is working on a congressional message on the subject, while the House is insisting on a host of anti-bussing amendments to the aid-to-education bill.

What the bussing issue requires is not exploitation but perspective. For it is, as Senator Muskie observed, the most potentially divisive issue presently confronting the country. Stopping the school bus has become a euphemism for applying the brakes to civil rights progress. And the Florida results should not intimidate those candidates—Muskie, McGovern, Humphrey—who refuse to pander to racist sentiment or politically-inspired fears, and who will talk sense.

That role requires political honesty and courage. A premium should be set on those values in the elections to come.

The Chattanooga Times
Chattanooga, Tenn., March 17, 1972

From the welter of conclusions drawn from the results of Florida's preferential primary Tuesday, only two seem sound enough to stand on bases for predictions of pre-convention trends in the Democratic party. And even they have to be subjected to the stresses suggested by a vote taken under unusual circumstances in an atypical state.

The first is obvious. George Wallace of Alabama is a stronger candidate within the ranks of the party he manipulates at home and has disavowed nationally than many thought. He had been expected to ride the school busing issue to a big lead. For him to take 42 per cent of the total, more than double runner-up Hubert Humphrey's 18 per cent, was surprising.

Nor does all his strength stem from the emotion-laden busing controversy. A special poll taken of 400 persons as they left the voting booth revealed that they were about equally divided in considering busing and economic issues as of first importance. Those who said they had voted for Mr. Wallace were not so strongly influenced by economic questions of taxes and prices, but the governor had stressed this issue and is certain to have captured some votes on its appeal. The presumption follows that he could rely on his populist demands for more services to the poor and higher taxes for the rich in states where busing was not as hot an issue as in Florida.

The second conclusion is that Mr. Humphrey's somewhat tarnished image as a "has-been" has been significantly brightened. Freed from the burdens he carried four years ago as the vice president of a discredited Administration, Sen. Humphrey revealed much of his earlier ebullience and political savvy in picking the issues and appealing to the visceral responses of the voters without approaching the demagogic overtones of the Wallace race. Mr. Humphrey has re-established himself as a candidate in the running for the nomination.

We do not believe Sen. Edmund Muskie, who has been the unenviable target of concentrated attacks as the front-runner, was hurt as badly as some would claim. His was a lost cause in Florida—and perhaps much of the South—from the start, because he is honest enough to say he does not think school busing is an issue of paramount importance in today's world. Sen. Muskie has had lapses in which he showed bitter anger or distress; they hurt him. These are not the things the voters long remember, however, and he is a man who tends to gain rather than lose from the way he answers questions. The road to Miami is still a long one, on which strengths can be developed or weaknesses can destroy.

The non-binding referendum on busing both showed the predictable opposition, three-to-one, and brought out the voters to swell the Wallace total. Those who make the most of this result say little or nothing of the still higher percentage, four-to-one, which favored quality education for all and no return to segregated schools.

George Wallace can be given no reasonable chance to win the Democratic nomination for president. There is no doubt, however, that he is the oil in the Democratic tank. As long as he is present, cohesiveness will be close to impossible.

The Virginian-Pilot
Norfolk, Va., March 16, 1972

Alabama's Governor George C. Wallace received more votes in the Florida primary Tuesday than Hubert Humphrey, "Scoop" Jackson, and Edmund Muskie put together.

Had Mr. Humphrey or Mr. Jackson or Mr. Muskie pulled Mr. Wallace's vote, or had any one of the leading "respectables" made a respectable race against Mr. Wallace, the candidate's camp-followers and the experts would be finding national significance in the showing.

But under the curious ground rules that apply to Governor Wallace, his votes don't really seem to count in the Democratic primary.

Even among the red, white, and true-blue believers in Mr. Wallace, there aren't many who seriously think he is ever going to be President of the United States. Their hero himself talks of influencing the Democratic Party platform and having a say in the choice of the nominee at the convention next summer.

Obviously Mr. Wallace is going to have some say about who'll be the Democratic nominee, and a greater say about who won't be the nominee. He is the apparent winner of 75 of Florida's 81 convention delegates and he probably will win additional delegates in other primaries. But Mr. Wallace is only going to do well in states where he is on the ballot and can exploit popular resentments. (See Joseph Alsop's column on the opposite page today.) He cannot hope to overcome the opposition of almost all the established leaders and the power brokers within the Democratic Party. He might destroy the party, but he cannot capture it.

If Mr. Wallace isn't going to be nominated, then why did a half-million people vote for him?

Because a vote for Mr. Wallace is a "free" vote, and a protest vote. It is most obviously a vote against busing, reinforcing the nearly 3-1 rejection of busing in the Florida straw vote. It is also a protest against all the targets of Mr. Wallace's wrath, and against conventional politics and politicians. By voting for Wallace, the man in the street says that he doesn't like the way the country is going. That is always tempting.

Some statistics should be useful. In 1964 Governor Wallace ran very well against a series of stand-ins for President Johnson in Democratic primaries. In April he got 33.8 per cent of the Wisconsin vote, and in May he polled 29.8 per cent in Indiana and 42.8 per cent in Maryland. (That was when "white backlash" was coined to explain the Wallace vote as an expression of resentment against the civil rights movement.) After the early primaries Mr. Wallace withdrew from Presidential politicking, and Barry Goldwater pursued a "Southern strategy" to the GOP nomination and disaster in November. There was little evidence of the "white backlash" in the November returns.

In 1968 Mr. Wallace stayed out of the Democratic primaries and campaigned as an independent for President. He carried five Deep South states and received 13.6 per cent of the total vote. (He got 28.9 per cent of Florida's votes in '68, running third.) Significantly, the Wallace vote, as measured by the polls, fell off sharply in the campaign's closing weeks.

But if the Wallace vote is a protest again against busing, taxes, and whatnot, it is also an evidence that the Democrats' "respectables" aren't exciting the people.

The big loser on Tuesday was Edmund Muskie, who finished fourth with just 9 per cent of the vote. The Democratic "front-runner" is now in serious trouble. His campaign was premised upon snowballing through the early primaries, stampeding the waverers, and cinching the nomination before the convention met. After Florida, Mr. Muskie is holding a melted snowball; if he can't produce a solid victory in a big state soon there will be a stampede away from him to the likeliest-looking winner.

That very well could be Hubert Humphrey, who ran second to Mr. Wallace with 18 per cent of the Florida votes. Mr. Humphrey, the erstwhile joyful warrior, is rejuvenated and restyled this year. He is anxious for a rematch with Mr. Nixon, whom he came close to defeating in '68 against all odds. The Democrats were bitter, bloodied, and broke in '68. They aren't in '72, at least not yet, and Lyndon Johnson is off in Texas. The ever-eager Mr. Humphrey looks like the Democrats' fail-safe selection, the man the party can always turn to.

Of the others, Mr. Jackson (3rd, 13 per cent) and Mayor John Lindsay (5th, 7 per cent) stayed alive on Tuesday. Both campaigned extensively in Florida, escaped humiliation in the numbers game, and can't claim much of a positive showing. In the liberal sweepstakes, Senator George McGovern (6th, 6 per cent) and Representative Shirley Chisholm (7th, 4 per cent) had little to lose, and did.

President Nixon won 87 per cent of the Republican votes, and conservative challenger John Ashbrook did poorly (9 per cent) in a state where he had hoped for right-wing support. But while the GOP house is in order, Mr. Nixon may have to reckon, too, with Mr. Wallace. The Democrats are in disarray, as Florida shows, and that is tailor-made for Mr. Wallace. If he tastes another triumph or two, will he again run for President on his own ticket? And if so, will he help or hurt Mr. Nixon? It is too soon to say.

Portland Press Herald
Portland, Me., March 16, 1972

Ed Muskie's dismal showing in the Florida primary, following hard on the heels of his less-than-spectacular win in New Hampshire, takes much of the forward motion out of a campaign that has depended on momentum from the beginning.

Still, it would be foolish to count Sen. Muskie out at this point on the basis of these first two primary results. He remains the frontrunner, although Sens. McGovern and Humphrey are breathing hotly down his neck right now, and Sen. Jackson is getting up some momentum of his own.

A poll taken in the closing days of the Florida primary showed that the two dominant impressions voters there held of Muskie were that he was "too emotional" and that he waffled on the issues.

The first impression obviously sprang from his tearful outburst in the snows of New Hampshire. As for the second, in a state where everyone has very strong opinions on the subject of "forced busing," Muskie's temperate views may have sounded indecisive.

The busing issue, which dominated the Florida race, is one reason the primary results there may be misleading.

There are stronger, more important tests ahead for Muskie. If he wins the Illinois primary next week, as expected, it will go a long way toward getting him back on the momentum track heading into such crucial primaries as Wisconsin, Massachusetts and Pennsylvania.

Those are primaries in which Sen. Muskie must make a good showing. Any further stumbling could prove fatal to the Maine senator's presidential ambitions.

Arkansas Gazette
Little Rock, Ark., March 24, 1972

Much too much has been made of the Florida primary, for reasons that we have previously set forth in some detail. But if the fratricidal warfare among the Democratic candidates continues on the present scale, with continuing fragmentation of the popular vote and the delegate votes, the outlook for a deadlocked convention will grow stronger and stronger.

If the convention did deadlock, there wouldn't be much question in our mind about what would happen or who would be the nominee even if he did not lift a hand to gain the nomination.

Let us imagine this situation and scene at the Democratic Convention in Miami Beach in July—

It is Wednesday night and the seventh ballot is under way. Governor Dale Bumpers has just had the floor to announce that "Arkansas, the land of Opportunity, casts its votes for Wilbur Mills." Senator Ed Muskie is still leading, barely, with Senator Hubert Humphrey a few votes behind, and neither is anywhere near a majority. Senator McGovern has a sizeable package of votes and nearly a third of the delegates are divided among Senator Henry M. Jackson, Governor George Wallace, Mayor John Lindsay, Congresswoman Chisholm and, Congressman Mills. The McGovern forces have refused to join Muskie; the Wallace and Jackson forces have refused to join Humphrey. The hour is late, the delegates are tired and apprehensive. At this juncture California yields to South Dakota and a delegate takes the microphone to announce: "South Dakota, with the full approval of Senator George McGovern, places in nomination the name of Senator Edward M. Kennedy..."

One can imagine the response, at such an hour, to the magic name. The situation would be perfectly made for a stampede like the one in which Wendell Willkie won the Republican nomination in 1940. The memory of Chappaquiddick would very likely be lost in the wild surge of sentiment, of yearning for "Camelot," of instinctive reaching for the standard under which the Democrats marched to victory in 1960.

The developing possibility of Senator Kennedy's nomination is one that many of us in the Democratic Party will regard with mixed feelings, if only in the knowledge of the physical danger that any Kennedy faces now if he becomes a candidate for president, and in the knowledge that the Nixon Republicans would wage undoubtedly the dirtiest campaign of which they are capable, which is about as dirty as campaign politics can get. Nevertheless, it is entirely possible that the youngest of the Kennedy brothers shares the potential for greatness that his martyred brothers had. In any case the Kennedy possibility will become more tangible with each fragmented primary.

The Washington Post
Washington, D.C., March 16, 1972

Last week—and somewhat prematurely, as it turns out—we observed that Senator Muskie's fair-to-middling performance in the New Hampshire primary could conceivably have the effect of liberating him from the tyranny of frontrunnership and all its self-imposed restraints and obligations. Well, if he was liberated last week, the vocabulary of freedom hardly has a word to describe his condition after Florida. The senator's meager 9 per cent of the Democratic vote in the primary there Tuesday surely removed his last shackle; and in the Illinois and Wisconsin contests that lie immediately ahead, he faces a challenge that could be critical to his candidacy: namely, whether he can stage a decisive comeback. Second perhaps only to the spectacle of a public figure's confessing a sin on live television, the American public seems most sympathetic to the spectacle of a politician's stoutly fighting his way back from apparent defeat. Senator Muskie may not have a lot of chances left. But he has this one enormous chance.

Other candidacies and reputations will be put to different tests. We surmise that Mayor Lindsay will have to prove rather more cost-effective as a vote-getter, a turner on of the liberal-left constituency to survive many more primary contests. Senator Humphrey, who did best of the orthodox candidates running in putting together the classic elements of the Democratic coalition, will be obliged to demonstrate a consistent capacity to do so, just as Senator Jackson will be obliged to demonstrate that he can acquire a larger slice of the electorate than that part which doesn't *quite* have the courage of George Wallace's convictions. Those who are hoping that the next big multi-candidate primary (Wisconsin) will settle or at least somewhat clarify all these confusions and party choices, may be in for another disappointment. Some of the wiser heads in politics are predicting that not until the Massachusetts and Pennsylvania primaries anyway—both on April 25—will the choices begin to narrow significantly.

We have saved the worst for last—George Wallace's splendid showing. It can be (and already has been) argued of course that Governor Wallace took only about the same percentage of the total vote cast in both parties (around 30 per cent) that he took in the state of Florida in the 1968 election. And from this and other data it is possible to adduce relatively reassuring evidence that the Wallace vote may be a kind of given, a hardcore constant that does not necessarily presuppose a growing momentum for his candidacy. If such perspective should have the effect of discouraging some of the other Democratic candidates from any inclinations they might have to appropriate some of the governor's outrageous appeals, it could be useful. But we think it is equally important just now for those Democrats who are not George Wallace to face up to the importance of his candidacy and of the principal issue on which he will be playing.

That there remains at this time within the electorate a profoundly split collective personality on matters of race and school, was demonstrated by the Florida votes on two separate referenda—one to restrict school desegregation in practice, the other to endorse it in principle. For just as members of Congress have lately been winning votes to provide support for desegregating schools with votes to prevent those schools from desegregating, so the Florida voters supported both moves. The strange combination of passion and ambiguity that marks the public response to this issue, taken together with Governor Wallace's effort to heighten the passion and eliminate the ambiguity, represents a principal and growing challenge to all of the Democratic candidates, to the party as a whole and especially to whomever the party nominates.

The New York Times
New York, N.Y., March 16, 1972

No election could have followed the expected pattern of voting more clearly than did the results of the Democratic primary in Florida. It could hardly have surprised anyone that Mr. Wallace polled a substantial fraction of the vote. Most of Florida is culturally and racially part of the old rural South. Many of its city-dwellers are recent arrivals from the farms and small towns of neighboring Georgia and Alabama. Under these circumstances, Mr. Wallace's minority victory is unimpressive, despite much post-election comment to the contrary.

It is, in fact, encouraging that a majority of Florida's Democrats voted against Mr. Wallace's demagogic fakery. But with that opposition split among ten candidates, it was naturally almost impossible for any single rival to best him.

The second and third place showings of Senators Hubert Humphrey and Henry Jackson in contrast to the poor showing of Senator Edmund S. Muskie are also subject to misleading interpretation. When several candidates are running who have similar views, the pressure, as we have previously observed, "is to concentrate on particular ethnic blocs and interest groups and not to develop the broader consensus which can unite many different kinds of Democrats. The candidate who can get the maximum response from one or two narrow segments of the party may thus do best in the primary —next to Mr. Wallace—and yet prove nothing about his ability to make the broad appeal which alone can defeat Mr. Nixon."

That is what occurred in Florida on Tuesday. Senator Humphrey relied upon his leadership in civil rights dating back to 1948 to rally black voters and his assiduous courtship of the Jewish community for the past quarter-century to pile up a respectable vote, especially in Miami and its environs. Senator Jackson also made much of his championship of Israel's cause. Both Mr. Humphrey and Mr. Jackson supported the space shuttle, which is popular with Florida workers. Both moved strikingly close to the Wallace position on school busing. This mish-mash of ethnic and special interest appeals on which Senators Humphrey and Jackson concentrated proves nothing.

The New Hampshire primary showed that Senator George McGovern is well-qualified to defend the most liberal viewpoints within the Democratic party; the Florida primary proved that when he has to share that role with Mayor Lindsay and Representative Chisholm, all three are weakened. If their respective votes had been combined, they would have outpolled Senator Jackson and given Senator Humphrey a stiff battle for second place. As it is, the three were also-rans.

Senator Muskie was originally established in the minds of party leaders and the press as front runner because it was believed that in a race against President Nixon—not against other Democrats—he could get the normally Democratic ethnic and liberal votes plus the crucial one or two per cent additional votes among independents that could make the difference between victory and defeat in November. What happened in New Hampshire and Florida does not necessarily undercut that reasoning. Senator Muskie waged a campaign which appealed to Floridians to vote on national rather than special interest issues. In the many primaries and state conventions still to be held, the Democratic candidates can best serve their party by avoiding personal rancor and concentrating on the broad national issues on which a potential President has to be judged.

©1972 by The New York Times Company. Reprinted by permission.

The Burlington Free Press
Burlington, Vt., March 16, 1972

THE RESULTS OF the Florida Presidential preference primary have really separated the men from the boys. Especially significant are the following:

(1) In a field of 11 Democratic candidates, George Wallace won a massive victory with 42 per cent of the vote. He also captured 75 of the 81 convention votes, giving him by far the largest number of votes accorded any Democratic candidate in this election year. Is it really so certain that Wallace won't be nominated by the Democrats?

(2) Hubert Humphrey came in second with a respectable showing of 18 per cent and the other six convention votes. A rerun of the 1968 Nixon-Humphrey battle seems a distinct possibility.

(3) Henry Jackson demonstrated unexpected strength with 13 per cent of the vote, but most observers doubt he has any chance for the nomination. He's a prime Vice Presidential possibility, however.

(4) Edmund Muskie suffered a drubbing, receiving only 9 per cent of the vote. He is probably finished as a candidate to be taken seriously.

(5) John Lindsay spent huge amounts of money, much of it on a lavish television saturation campaign, and he spent more time in the state than most other candidates, yet he suffered a crushing rejection — only 7 per cent of the vote. This was a fitting response to the shallow opportunist from New York.

(6) It was said that Lindsay and George McGovern would split the "liberal" vote. What "liberal" vote? Together the two of them received fewer votes than Henry Jackson!

(7) Some observers were suggesting yesterday that the Democrats may have to turn to Teddy Kennedy. If the Democrats do they will be committing political suicide. Kennedy's recent far-out statements (Northern Ireland, amnesty, etc.) and peculiar conduct (cheap allegations in the ITT flap) have angered large segments of the American public.

(8) On the Republican side, President Nixon won another smashing victory with an incredible 87 per cent of the vote and all 40 convention votes. John Ashbrook, the conservative challenger, won 9 per cent of the vote and Paul McCloskey, the liberal challenger who can't decide whether to stay in the race or not, received a dismal 4 per cent of the vote.

(9) On the important three straw vote questions, 74 per cent of Floridians want to prohibit forced busing of school children, 79 per cent want to provide equal opportunity for quality education for all children, and 79 per cent want to allow prayer in the public schools. The results only confirm the overwhelming public opposition, throughout the nation and among both blacks and whites, to forced busing.

(10) As of this writing, it appears there are only three "live" candidates for the Democratic nomination: Wallace, Humphrey and Kennedy. And Humphrey is obviously the only one of the three who would have a ghost of a chance of defeating President Nixon. — F.B.S.

28—Florida Primary

DAILY NEWS
New York, N.Y., March 16, 1972

We refer to political earthquakes in the Sunshine State's Democratic presidential primary on Tuesday.

Gov. George C. Wallace of Alabama was (let's face it) the big winner, with 42% of the vote, as against the 30-32% forecast by most polls and many experts.

Hubert H. Humphrey, with 18%, greatly increased his chance to get the presidential nomination. Sen. Henry M. Jackson (Wash.) also did well.

But Mayor John Vliet Lindsay of New York City, after spending gobs of money in Florida and shamelessly waving his charisma around right out in public down there for weeks and weeks, crawled across the finish line with a pathetic 7%.

Gov. Wallace

Why should Lindsay and his comrade political oddball, Sen. George McGovern of South Dakota (6%), not just quit right now?

Sen. Edmund Muskie of Maine, long considered the front runner, flopped on his Lincolnesque face in Florida, and may not be able to rise again.

The Wallace triumph interests us the most.

Gov. Wallace long has cozied up to the many voters who detest professional "liberals" and what he calls "pointy-headed intellectuals" (terrific phrase).

Nowadays, he also aims political appeals at middle-income Americans with their tax and other troubles, and doesn't overlook his numerous fellow-haters of forced school busing for integration's sake.

So-o-o, the Alabaman (not Alabamian, please, Mr. Printer) won, not only in conservative northern and central Florida, but also 'way down south, where "liberals" and Yankee immigrants abound.

All this, as Wallace says lip-smackingly and chop-lickingly, is giving national Democratic leaders St. Vitus's dance. And we think that's just fine—though we also think a President Wallace would be hard to take.

The Wallace showing in Florida should, it seems to us, impel both parties' leaders to discount very heavily the "liberal" noise-makers around the nation, listen carefully to the current beefs and bawls of the so-called common people (who aren't common at all, friends), and tailor the 1972 presidential platforms accordingly.

Should that come to pass, we believe Gov. Wallace would rate some sort of top-grade medal for public service—though, to repeat, we hope the little fighting cock never will become President.

WORCESTER TELEGRAM.
Worcester, Mass., March 16, 1972

Two down, 22 to go.

With the Florida presidential primary behind us, the Democratic race seems more complicated than ever. On the Republican side, President Nixon appears stronger with each passing contest, not only because of his own showing but also because of the stalemate among Democrats.

But reaching sweeping conclusions based on Florida or any other primary state would be a mistake.

Gov. George Wallace's strong showing was the surprise of the day. He was generally expected to be the top vote-getter; but he got more votes than Senators Hubert Humphrey, Henry Jackson and Edmund Muskie put together. He won more than 40 per cent of the vote, compared to 29 per cent in the final presidential race in Florida in 1968 with only two others on the ballot.

Wallace obviously attracted far more than just hardcore segregationist and protest votes to win that big.

While there is no question that the Wallace style has a basic appeal to racists and anti-intellectuals, he also is getting a wider audience from people who are tired of conventional politics and who have a general unease they can't articulate about their lack of ability to gain access to the bureaucracy of big government.

What will Wallace do with his political power, provided it lasts through the primaries? He may be able to exercise some leverage at the Democratic convention, though it does seem highly unlikely he could overturn the party machinery at Miami and win nomination. He may be warming up for another effort to test the strength of his American Party which siphoned off 10 million votes in 1968.

One thing seems certain: the Wallace phenomenon represents a challenge to the political establishment, and other candidates may have to work harder to make the political process more responsive to the aspirations and desires of many disenchanted voters.

The real loser in Florida was Senator Muskie; his status as a frontrunner is now questionable. New Hampshire provided some hint that the Maine senator's voter appeal is less than overwhelming, and his Florida showing may have been affected by that performance. He must gain much ground quickly if he is to keep the reverse snowball process from building up further. A win in Illinois next week will not be enough. But he has time to recover.

Humphrey worked hard, capitalized on his name and did twice as well as Muskie. That tends to refute Muskie's argument that Wallace's appeal to the voters' "worst instincts" was the main cause of his setback; he and Humphrey basically represent the same political philosophy. Still, Humphrey's performance should give him little cause for over-confidence.

Jackson tested his conservative views on the Floridians, but he just could not compete with Wallace. While his third-place finish was creditable, it was hardly enough to give him real momentum. And Florida should be one of his best states.

The Sunshine State provided a High Noon in the battle of the liberals, Sen. McGovern and Mayor Lindsay. Both finished as expected: in a virtual tie and well out of it. McGovern lost some of his New Hampshire luster.

It's Illinois next week, to be followed by the Wisconsin primary — an important contest — two weeks later. Massachusetts and Pennsylvania are next to voice their preferences. By then, some of the questions of Florida — "Is Wallace for real?" and "Just how strong is Muskie?" — may be answered. In the meantime, with two primaries behind us, the chances anyone is going to need a moving van around 500 Pennsylvania Ave. next January look slimmer and slimmer.

The Standard-Times
New Bedford, Mass., March 17, 1972

The Florida presidential primary proved that, to nobody's surprise, the self-styled friend of the "little people," George ("Sock it to 'em") Wallace still possesses considerable ability as an actor and salesman.

Although there is little substance to the man or to anything he says, his simplistic solutions to complex problems are ever appealing. A classic example of this in the Florida election concerned the busing controversy.

It is estimated that the Democratic candidates who campaigned in Florida spent well over $2 million. But their expensive campaigns, and all other issues, were overshadowed and blurred by the busing matter. Wallace, exploiting the deep feeling in Florida against compulsory busing to desegregate public schools, made this his major issue. He opposed it.

By contrast, McGovern and Lindsay took firm stands for busing and Muskie and Humphrey straddled the issue. Jackson lined up with Wallace against forced busing.

Wallace's victory, based on 42 per cent of the votes, was no more than a reflection of the fact that the voters also approved overwhelmingly a proposed amendment to the U.S. Constitution prohibiting forced busing to achieve racial balance in the public schools.

In other words, what happened in Florida on Tuesday has no national meaning — the referendum vote on busing has no legal effect, and the Wallace victory is insignificant because he has no chance of winning the Democratic nomination.

Actually, his triumphs at the polls in 1968 were reasonably regarded more seriously because he mounted the most serious third-party threat in years. But running within the system, as a Democrat, he stands no chance and, as in Florida, his role is no more than to spoil and confuse.

And confuse it certainly did, as far as the other Democratic contenders are concerned. Muskie's defeat in Florida, following his unimpressive victory in New Hampshire, turns the race for the party's nomination into a wide-open scramble, with no candidate holding a clear lead.

Even though we agree with the Maine senator's views on the subject, it is not clear that he gained anything by assailing Wallace in his post-Florida vote public comments. Wallace is, after all, a non-issue, and anybody who wants to vote for him has a right to do so.

Assuredly, Mr. Muskie must do very well in the primaries in Illinois and Wisconsin if his flagging campaign is to gain new momentum. These prospects are inhibited by the fact that Mr. Humphrey got what he wanted in the Florida vote—second place; it was a long way back of the Wallace figure, but still twice that of the Muskie total. Humphrey appears to be Muskie's principal rival in Wisconsin.

Lindsay wanted enough votes in Florida (his first run as a Democrat) to make him a credible candidate; McGovern obviously hoped to buttress the strong showing against Muskie that he made in New Hampshire — but because the issue was busing, and they were both for it, Florida was no place for either to prove anything decisive.

Jackson, principally because he also received more votes than Muskie, is encouraged to stay in the race, but here again, his stand against busing was the only real factor involved.

In other words, for all it really proved, Floridians could have saved a lot of time (and the candidates a lot of money and energy) if the Sunshine State's presidential primary never had been held.

Obviously, those whose cash registers rang cheerily because of it wouldn't agree.

The Boston Globe
Boston, Mass., March 16, 1972

Give George Wallace his due: the governor of Alabama won the Florida Democratic primary and won it bigger than just about anybody had expected he would. The aftershocks of Florida are still reverberating in the foundation of the American political system.

Wallace got more than twice as many votes as Hubert Humphrey, his nearest competitor; and the Wallace total was greater than the combined support of Humphrey, "Scoop" Jackson and Ed Muskie.

Another way of looking at the results is to observe that more than twice as many Floridians voted for other Democratic or Republican candidates as voted for Wallace.

Was the Wallace vote "racist"? To pose the question is to raise semantic difficulties which are subject to interminable controversy, but a candid answer must include a conditional yes.

The Alabama governor, a demagogic Dixie politician in a tradition considerably older than Huey Long, did undoubtedly benefit from racial anger and fear. But the "racist" interpretation is inadequate to the arithmetic of the results. Not all Wallace voters are racists, conscious or otherwise. Nor are all adversaries of busing for purposes of school integration racists, nor are advocates of busing and integration free from "racism." America is learning these things, too slowly.

No, George Wallace has been talking to people in terms they understand about things that concern them deeply. Because he is a skilled talker, he has been persuasive. That his political bandwagon depends for its momentum on some of the meanest and most vicious impulses of mankind is tragic and obnoxious.

George McGovern took a charitable and sensible view of the Wallace vote when he refused to accept the idea that it represented unadulterated racism.

McGovern said, and one tends to agree, that many Wallace voters were just registering a protest against things as they are—an attitude presently shared by citizens of every political persuasion.

The danger, and it is a real danger, is that this feeling of disillusioned anger at an unsatisfactory society may find expression in support for Wallace around the nation. As a virtual unknown quantity, the man received almost 10 million votes four years ago. He is correct in saying he no longer is a regional candidate.

Florida is an odd state. In the last 25 years, it has almost tripled its population. It is tropical, Southern, urban, rural and conservative. Seventy percent of its electorate chose either Richard Nixon, who won its 15 electoral votes, or Wallace in 1968. It has elected Claude Kirk governor, rejected G. Harrold Carswell for US Senate and chosen the distinguished Reubin Askew as its governor and "Walkin' Lawton" Chiles as US senator.

It is, in short, a state from which political inferences should be drawn carefully, if at all.

Floridians voted 74-26 against busing and 79-21 in favor of quality education for everyone and against return to a dual (segregated) school system. These superficially inconsistent figures make generalizations about this strange election extremely risky.

Any "stop-Wallace" movement on the part of the Alabama governor's liberal opponents would be a panic reaction and one simply not justified by Wallace's unquestionably stunning performance in a single, unique state. It would tend to build his strength.

But the fragmentation of the Democratic center and left is clearly working in his favor. If all of the other Democratic candidates insist upon fighting him, they will in fact be playing his game. For some of the also-rans in Florida, this is a fact worth pondering.

The Detroit News
Detroit, Mich., March 16, 1972

George Wallace's startling victory in the Florida primary illustrates above all the failure of the Democratic Party to develop strong moderate leadership as an effective alternative to Wallace demagoguery.

Senator Edmund Muskie, who had to settle for fourth place and 9 percent of the Democratic vote, warned in a bitter post-election speech that Wallace constitutes a threat to national unity. Very true.

But that threat exists in part because neither Muskie nor any of the other candidates has managed to capture the imagination of Democratic voters and unify the party's moderate sentiments. While Wallace was holding his bloc of voters together in Florida, his 10 weak opponents were dividing the remainder among them.

Some Democratic leaders shrug off Wallace's backing as "the bigot vote." Wallace certainly is a bigot and no doubt many people support him because they recognize in him a fellow bigot who expresses their point of view exactly.

But we suspect that many who vote for Wallace do so because he seems to be concerned about their legitimate complaints. With the finesse of a consummate demagog, Wallace has for the wrong reasons put himself on the right side of a host of issues not the least of which are taxes and bussing and big government.

If Wallace's foes start addressing themselves positively to the mundane frustrations which Wallace has been exploiting, they will stand a chance of blunting his disruptive influence. It is no mystery why Senator Jackson shot up from virtual obscurity to beat out Muskie for third place in Florida. Jackson conducted a strong anti-bussing campaign.

The thinking of Florida's voters on that issue was decisively expressed in a straw vote. They balloted 3-1 against the forced bussing of school children away from their neighborhood schools. They also voted overwhelmingly in favor of equal opportunity for quality education for all children.

In short, they favor integration but not at the heavy cost and inconvenience of illogical bussing programs. That is exactly the view of many moderates and liberals, so these straw votes cannot be dismissed as the hypocrisy of essential bigotry, as some bussing advocates suggest.

The big loser of the Florida primary was Senator Edmund Muskie. Stumbling out of New Hampshire where he got slightly more than 46 percent of the vote — not the 48 first reported — he hit the skids for the second time in a week. When you come in fourth, it's hard to maintain the claim that you are the "front-runner."

Meanwhile, aside from Wallace, Hubert Humphrey has become the man to watch. In his first outing against Muskie, he beat the senator from Maine and took second place in the field of 11 candidates. If Muskie continues to fall apart, Humphrey is poised to replace him as the most likely to succeed at the Democratic Convention next summer.

This assumes, of course, that anybody other than Ted Kennedy will be able to win the nomination after Wallace gets through splintering the party into a dozen pieces.

THE CINCINNATI ENQUIRER
Cincinnati, Ohio, March 16, 1972

WHEN THE FIELD of presidential aspirants is as large and diversified as it is this year for the Democrats, it is too much to expect any single primary to be decisive. Instead, each primary generates a few faint rays, a few clues that, taken together, tell us the direction in which the party is moving.

The significance of Tuesday's balloting in Florida, accordingly, lies less in who won than in who lost—and by how much. And certainly the most prominent of the losers was Sen. Edmund S. Muskie (D-Maine). Only a week earlier, Senator Muskie, though he ran first in the New Hampshire primary, garnered far fewer votes than his supporters anticipated. Now, in Florida, he has encountered an electoral disaster. He polled no more than 9% of the Democratic votes; he lost in every one of the state's 12 congressional districts; he won not a single convention delegate, and—most important of all—he appears to have done poorly among every category of Florida voters and particularly poorly among Florida's Negroes.

Senator Muskie remains the personal choice of strategically placed Democratic leaders across the country—a circumstance that is likely to give him more convention votes than a half dozen of the primary elections. But he appears to have lost the momentum his candidacy enjoyed early in the year following his formal announcement. Just as each state-level victory makes the next state an easier target, so each setback makes the next state more difficult. Senator Muskie's political fortunes in Florida undoubtedly suffered from his poor showing in New Hampshire. And his prospects in Illinois and Wisconsin are likely to be dimmed by what happened in Florida.

Florida had the best news for Sen. Hubert H. Humphrey (D-Minn.), whose popular vote was roughly twice Senator Muskie's. As we suggested a week ago, any faltering of the Muskie campaign serves principally to enhance Senator Humphrey's outlook—a diagnosis with which the ebullient Senator Humphrey obviously agrees.

To a lesser extent, the Florida returns brought encouragement to Washington's energetic Sen. Henry M. Jackson. Although he entered the race with a serious name-recognition problem, Senator Jackson outdistanced Senator Muskie by 50% and collected as many votes as New York Mayor John V. Lindsay and Sen. George S. McGovern (D-S.D.) combined.

Senator McGovern spent little time or money in Florida, but Mayor Lindsay made a major race of it. Neither has anything about which to rejoice.

The happiest of the Democratic candidates Tuesday night, of course, was Alabama's Gov. George C. Wallace who polled 42% of the popular votes, carried 11 of the 12 congressional districts and won 75 of the 81 convention votes. Governor Wallace claims that his Florida victory makes him a national—rather than simply regional—candidate, a reference, no doubt, to the extent to which Florida's inward migration has made it something of a microcosm of the nation. Yet Governor Wallace has made strong showings in primary races before—in Maryland, Wisconsin and Indiana in 1964, for example—without accomplishing anything more than reminding other Democratic candidates that the party still has a large constituency for which Governor Wallace is the authentic spokesman.

In Tuesday's Republican race, the Florida returns ended, for all practical purposes, any serious threat to President Nixon's renomination. The President collected 87% of his party's primary returns.

Now the focus shifts to next week's Illinois primary, which promises to provide still more clues to what lies ahead.

MUSKIE VICTORIOUS IN ILLINOIS AS DALEY MACHINE IS REBUFFED

Sen. Edmund S. Muskie (Me.) won the Illinois presidential preference primary March 21 with 63% of the vote against his only rival on the ballot, former Sen. Eugene J. McCarthy (Minn.), who received 37% of the vote. In the contest for convention delegates, Muskie won 59 committed delegates while his major opponent in this separate ballot, Sen. George McGovern (S.D.), who did not engage in the preference contest, won 14 delegates, about half his goal. Chicago Mayor Richard J. Daley, leader of the state's Democratic organization, won control of a large block of 80 to 87 uncommitted delegates. On the Republican side, there was no presidential preference vote but 46 of 48 delegates elected to the national convention were committed to President Nixon. Two were uncommitted.

Interest in the Illinois primary results focused on the local races for governor and state's attorney where the powerful machine of Mayor Daley suffered surprising setbacks. Independent Daniel Walker, a Daley critic, won the Democratic gubernatorial nomination with 52% of the vote against Lt. Gov. Paul G. Simon, the organization candidate. State's Attorney Edward V. Hanrahan, cast adrift by the Daley organization, won renomination by a 100,000-vote margin over Raymond K. Berg, the organization choice, and independent Democrat Donald Page Moore. Hanrahan, a staunch "law and order" campaigner, had been dropped by the organization following his indictment last August on charges of obstructing justice in connection with the investigation of the December 1969 police raid on a Chicago apartment in which two Black Panthers were slain. [See Vol. 2, pp. 1116–1120] Daley said afterwards he would support both Hanrahan and Walker in the general election.

Chicago Daily Defender
Chicago, Ill., March 27, 1972

Though muffled, the overriding issue in the Hanrahan stunning victory in last Tuesday's primary was not the controversial State's Attorney's defiance of the Democratic party organization, it was not his stand on law and order, nor was it his promise to make the streets safe for decent citizens. The silent issue which brought him an unprecedented triumph was his conduct in the Black Panther killing case and his indictment for obstructing justice.

The vote was in effect an approval of the murder of the two Black Panther leaders. It was a psychological white backlash with an intensity seldom reflected in American politics.

That the Democratic party organization had a hand in the Hanrahan victory is not at all an improbable assumption. For many of the wards which gave Hanrahan healthy percentage votes, were under strict party control. The victory was no accident, nor was it brought about solely by Republican voters who ignored their party label.

It was a well planned conspiracy to keep in power a racist, a man who, as State's Attorney, has demonstrated his antipathy to black people throughout his administration of justice. The most sinister aspect of the whole drama is the support Hanrahan is getting for his anti-racial policy and attitude. It is a kind of demonstration that will sustain and give currency to the advocacy of black separatism and strengthen the pillars of black power.

The Register-Republic
Rockford, Ill., March 23, 1972

Illinois politicians are still rubbing their eyes with disbelief over the surprising results of Tuesday's primary election.

It had been generally expected that many Republican voters would take advantage of the recent federal court ruling and cross over to the Democratic primary, where there were more contests.

But the extent to which voters crossed over astounded everyone — and produced some major upsets.

Illinois Democrats had hoped to turn out one million voters, but when the final count was made some 1.4 million persons had voted the Democratic ballot.

The big loser was the Illinois Democratic machine, controlled by Chicago Mayor Richard J. Daley. Maverick Daniel Walker, who walked 1,200 miles through the state in a unique campaign, upset the organization candidate, Lt. Gov. Paul Simon, in gaining the nomination for governor.

In Cook County, State's Atty. Edward V. Hanrahan, who had been dumped by Mayor Daley, swept to a stunning victory over the machine candidate, Raymond Berg, and independent Donald Page Moore.

The extent of the crossover was especially noticeable in Winnebago County, where four years ago 24,000 voters went to the polls and Republicans outnumbered Democrats by a 3-1 margin.

This week, more than 38,000 votes were cast, and the Democratic turnout topped that of the Republican party by 5,000 votes in the city and some 2,000 in the county. In the 34th District Democratic state Senate race between Betty Ann Keegan and Gerald Wernick, for example, 15,515 Democratic votes were cast, as against 8,476 Republican ballots.

Now the big unanswered question is whether Republicans who crossed over in the primary will remain in the Democratic column in the November general election. That applies to the entire state as well as to Winnebago County.

By being able to select either party ballot, Illinois voters had the opportunity of making their decisions on the basis of the candidates, rather than party labels. The fact that so many voters took advantage of that opportunity is a healthy development on the Illinois political scene.

There was a message in this week's primary election. Each political party must offer top-drawer candidates, and the endorsement of a political machine is by no means a guarantee of victory.

It could well mean the dawn of a new political era in Illinois.

THE INDIANAPOLIS NEWS
Indianapolis, Ind., March 24, 1972

To serious students of the taxpayers' revolt which has broken out in state after state, the upset victory of a challenger to Mayor Richard Daley's machine in this week's Illinois primary should come as no great shock.

The issue was not one of general ideology since both Democratic hopefuls were certified liberals. The race centered principally on the question of taxes. Dan Walker, the maverick, decisively beat Lt. Gov. Paul Simon, Mayor Daley's choice to represent the Democratic party in next fall's gubernatorial race, primarily because Simon proposed an increase in the state income tax. Perhaps taking a cue from Hoosier tax boosters, Simon suggested the tax hike as a way of reducing property taxes.

Walker zeroed in on Simon's proposed tax boost, promising to hold the line on taxes and to bring economies into government spending. It seems reasonable to suppose Walker will pursue the same strategy in his race against Gov. Richard Oglivie, who is in trouble because he earlier led the way to an increase in state taxes. Sensing voter distaste with this stand, Oglivie now opposes future boosts in Illinois taxes.

Illinois, of course, is no political aberration. Voters in Connecticut, for example, were so irate at the initiation of a state income tax last year they forced the legislators and governor to negate the tax before it was ever collected. There is a loud and clear message in all this for political contenders in Indiana. We hope they are listening.

Chicago Tribune
Chicago, Ill., March 23, 1972

A Political Earthquake...

How do you analyze an earthquake? Tuesday's primary results have left the Illinois political scene littered with rubble, and it's hard, amid the devastation, to figure out who was upset and who was the victor.

Certainly the Daley machine suffered an upset—and the farther one goes from Chicago, the greater will be the tendency to play up this defeat. The liberal Eastern press is already singing joyous requiem masses over what it regards as the remains of the Cook County Democratic organization.

It is true that there were defections from the Daley ranks, especially among whites who stuck with Mr. Hanrahan, despite his having been dumped by the organization. They looked on him as a law-and-order state's attorney who would protect their neighborhoods from crime [which a good many of them equate with keeping blacks out]. But in fact, Mr. Hanrahan's credentials as a Daley man are much more valid than those of the machine candidate, Raymond Berg. Mr. Berg, like Paul Simon, the organization's unsuccessful candidate for governor, was a sort of foster child, adopted under the exigencies of circumstances. Neither of them aroused much enthusiasm among the party faithful, even in the machine wards where there is only one God and he is the Democratic precinct captain. These wards went obediently for Mr. Berg, but with less than the usual unanimity, and they were the only ones he carried.

The Daley organization has a remarkable capacity for recovery. Every effort will now be made to suggest that Mr. Hanrahan was the favorite all along. It will be interesting indeed to see how conscientiously Mr. Hanrahan can carry out his duty to prosecute the election officials who have been arrested for helping the machine harvest fraudulent votes for his recent opponent.

The Daley machine's upset really came about less because of defection from within than because of the carpetbagging Republicans who took advantage of their new freedom to cross party lines in the primary, and who did so in vast numbers, conservatives to vote for Mr. Hanrahan and others, for varying reasons, to vote for the liberal Messrs. Walker or Moore.

And crossing over in such large numbers, Republican conservatives contributed to the defeat of some of their own organization's most important candidates.

If any general conclusion can be drawn from the primary, it is that voters tend increasingly to vote according to what they think and how they feel rather than how they are told. As this tendency spreads, it will ultimately spell trouble for all political organizations, including organized labor, which went all out for Mr. Simon, but in vain.

The independence of voters is encouraged by recent court and legislative actions. The Illinois restrictions on crossing over in primaries were scrapped by a recent federal court decision. On the same day as the primary, the United States Supreme Court handed down a more far-reaching decision ruling out all state residency requirements, for state and local elections, of more than 30 days. This will affect 49 states, including Illinois, and will erode further the discipline of the traditional local party organization. Finally, there are the new teen-age voters, especially on campuses, who have no ties to and little respect for the old-time political organizations.

The growing influence of young and independent voters may not contribute to the traditional politician's peace of mind and can have unfortunate side-effects. But the trend seems inescapable and in general it should be a healthy one.

...And Some Aftershocks

In pondering the possibilities of next November, the Republicans should take no comfort in the thrashing Dan Walker gave to Paul Simon and the Chicago Democratic machine. The defeat exposed the weaknesses of Mr. Simon and his regular organization colleagues, but it also laid bare the pitfalls of practicing orthodox politics in a state filled with angry and increasingly independent voters.

Mr. Walker proved himself a formidable candidate. He was well-financed, well organized, and even glamorous. His 1,000 mile walk across the state proved to be a public relations coup.

Unlike Gov. Oglivie, who is straightforward and always himself, Mr. Walker demonstrated an uncanny ability to straddle issues and jump all over the ideological spectrum and get away with it. Not since Sen. Robert Kennedy took both the black vote and the George Wallace vote in Indiana in 1968 has any candidate proved so agile.

In Chicago, he posed as the champion of the lake shore liberals in their crusade against the machine. Downstate, he portrayed himself as a country boy fighting the city slickers. Beyond the hearing of his liberal financial backers, Mr. Walker talked right wing to suburban conservatives, coming out against busing and amnesty for draft dodgers.

He scored his biggest points, tho, by touching upon that issue which runs thru Illinois politics like an inflamed nerve—high taxes. As George Wallace did with busing in Florida, Mr. Walker played the issue for all it was worth, and it gave him an enormous plurality downstate and a tremendous Republican crossover vote. He took conservative Du Page County by a ratio of 3 to 1. As Du Page County Clerk Ray MacDonald put it: "Our tax assessments just came out. The taxpayers are wild." When Mr. Simon came out for a tax reform program with income tax increases, he was doomed.

Gov. Oglivie has nothing to be ashamed of on the tax issue, and Mr. Walker knows little about state finances—but this won't keep him from making an issue of taxes.

One factor which may be of help to Mr. Walker's opponents in both parties is that his election as governor could well throw the state into legislative chaos. The legislature is now fairly evenly divided between both party organizations and is able to function only under a sort of armed truce.

Put a governor opposed to both sides in the Statehouse and open warfare could result. As one observer put it on election night: "You could end up with the state being run by the Illinois Supreme Court."

How Mayor Daley will handle this situation remains to be seen. His followers are not adept at the intricacies of split-ticket voting, and it would be difficult for him to oppose Mr. Walker and support the rest of the Democratic state ticket.

The Republicans will have to make an unprecedented effort to hold on to the Statehouse and all their legislative seats. They will unfortunately be crippled in this effort by one of the side-effects of Tuesday's primary. Because of the huge Republican crossovers and the plethora of G. O. P. primary candidates, some of the party's strongest men in the legislature failed to win renomination. Among them was House Majority Leader Henry J. Hyde, whose unnecessary defeat was a loss not only to his district but to the state.

ST. LOUIS POST-DISPATCH
St. Louis, Mo., March 24, 1972

The surprising results of the races at the statewide level overshadowed the importance of the Illinois primary in the presidential sweepstakes. While the debate over whether Edward Hanrahan's victory and Paul Simon's defeat tarnished the Daley image continues, a more subtle development should not be ignored. The mayor may be able to recoup after the setback suffered by the two regular party candidates, if indeed he considered it a setback in the first place. But will he be able to recoup at the Democratic convention?

It has been a long time since Mayor Daley went to a convention without controlling the Illinois delegation. Not so in 1972, unless of course he decides to support Senator Muskie before departing for Miami Beach. Thanks to the reforms by the party's Fraser-McGovern Commission, Illinois Democrats elected most of their delegates. At last count 59 of the elected were committed to Senator Muskie, 14 to Senator McGovern and 87 won on a non-platform as uncommitted.

Most of the uncommitted, although not all, were slated by the party and it is only in this slate that Mayor Daley will enjoy unrestricted control. This could diminish his brokerage power at the convention, at least to a more proportionate and reasonable level.

There is also the matter of the preferential primary. Although Senator Eugene McCarthy lost, as expected, he did attract 438,802 votes and in Illinois this is not insignificant. Added to Senator Muskie's 747,674 votes, the total may be big enough to discourage an inclination by the mayor to switch at the convention to Senator Jackson or Senator Humphrey.

Consequently, it is in the contest over delegates and in the preferential race where the results of the party's reform efforts in Illinois may be more penetrating.

Chicago Sun-Times
Chicago, Ill., March 23, 1972

The populist sentiment that has been growing in the United States, the revolt against political figures and entrenched and arrogant political organizations, spread over Illinois Tuesday and seeped deep down into wards and precincts. Mayor Daley's Democratic organization took a beating in some respects worse than the last time it lost a primary fight for the nomination for governor, 36 years ago. And its vaunted ability to deliver the vote in Chicago crumpled in the neighborhood revolt to rally around State's Atty. Edward V. Hanrahan.

There was a new mood abroad Tuesday that changed trandtional voting patterns and produced strange crosscurrents. For example, while maverick Daniel Walker won the Democratic nomination for governor after a campaign of vilification against the Daley organization, the winning candidate for lieutenant governor was Neil F. Hartigan, one of Mayor Daley's closest political associates. And while Hanrahan was cleaning up in Chicago, opposed by liberals and nominally by the party organization alike, liberals and independents succeeded in nominating five anti-organization candidates for the Illinois Legislature.

Walker's unprecedented victory told much of the 1972 temper of the voters who are fed up with old scandals, who resent the closed-circle aspect of so much of the political system and who are worried about high taxes. Walker's walk across the state brought him widespread recognition and galvanized support among individual voters. He built a Downstate organization in two years that in some areas outmanned the regulars. At the 11th hour he capitalized greatly on a candidate statement by his rival, Lt. Gov. Paul Simon, which was widely but mistakenly taken to mean Simon favored an increase in the state income tax.

Walker benefited greatly also by a switchover of Republicans who this year took Democratic ballots. So did Hanrahan, producing an unlikely combination — the liberal corporation lawyer who wrote the Walker report critical of Chicago police in the 1968 convention violence and the man under indictment for allegedly obstructing justice in protecting policemen after the Black Panther shooting.

The attitude of many Republicans was summed up by Martha Mitchell, wife of the former U.S. attorney general, who telephoned Hanrahan and said, "Ed, I'm a Republican but you're my kind of Democrat."

Hanrahan demonstrated that an energetic and eye-catching campaign can win votes. His showing in Chicago wards also demonstrated that many loyal party workers were content with Mayor Daley's first judgment about Hanrahan — despite the unresolved indictment. Mayor Daley supported Hanrahan for re-election last December until objections from some other candidates persuaded the slatemakers to abandon Hanrahan and go to Judge Raymond K. Berg.

Berg relied almost exclusively on the "organization" to give him the nomination at the polls; his appeal to independent voters was minimal. The organization delivered him hardly many more votes than independents turned out for Donald Page Moore.

Hanrahan demonstrated that a tough prosecutor's attitude, a willingness to fight for political survival and an appeal to the individual voter fearful of crime and changing social conditions can pay off. He won desite a finding by two bar associations that he was unqualified and the opinion of all the major media including The Sun-Times that Hanrahan has an abysmal record of performance in his office.

The big question now is how Mayor Daley's people can recover from this worst defeat since Gov. Henry Horner successfully broke an attempt to dump him for renomination in 1936. Like Walker, he rolled up heavy Downstate, anti-Chicago City Hall support to beat the then Chicago mayor, Edward J. Kelly, Daley's mentor. But unlike Walker, Horner had political ties and communications inside the organization and could easily rejoin it. With Chicago help he was re-elected.

Walker is a different case. His antagonism to what he calls boss politics goes deep. He has said he would accept Daley's support but makes no commitments. It will be interesting to see how the relationship between the mayor and the maverick nominee for governor will work out.

Characteristically, Daley rolled with the punch and said he'd support Walker — the people had spoken. It was obviously much easier to him to accept the Hanrahan nomination.

There is no doubt now that Hanrahan emerges as a great local political power, having demonstrated his own personal vote-getting ability. He can demand a seat alongside Daley in the party's councils. He is a tempestuous, impulsive person and there is no question that great changes are due in the local picture. A new role also is due for Hartigan who took 66 percent of the vote in his contest. The independent movement within the Chicago organization should and can have greater influence. The victory of Mrs. Dawn Clark Netsch over an incumbent organization state senator, the successful defiance of an attempted purge by State Rep. Robert E. Mann and the nomination of three other independent legislative candidates are symptomatic of changing conditions at the ward level in Chicago. These are good signs for a more politically healthy city.

We hope that Simon and Moore, whom we supported continue in positions of influence within the Democratic Party. Our respect for them remains high. They both are of the caliber needed in public offices.

CHICAGO DAILY NEWS

Chicago, Ill., March 22, 1972

The Illinois primary election revealed a Democratic Party in violent turmoil, and an electorate torn by emotional riptides. The Cook County organization and its boss, Mayor Daley, were jolted when their man was decisively beaten in the state's attorney race and again when the candidate carrying their colors was beaten for the nomination for governor.

But the question of whither the Daley organization — important and intriguing as it may be — is of less moment than the question of what the election says about the temper of the voters. For two issues dominated the picture, or at least the Democratic part of it. One was taxation — a stubborn, angry, indiscriminate resistance to any whisper of a higher tax bill. The other was security. Any hope that time had begun to drain off the passion enveloping the interlocked issues of race and law-and-order was dashed, for the moment at least. Those issues, as illuminated by the primary vote, must now be measured and dealt with as the successful candidates of both parties head for the final reckoning in November.

The Hanrahan victory

Edward V. Hanrahan surmounted incredible obstacles to win the Democratic nomination to succeed himself as state's attorney of Cook County.

He is under criminal indictment for conspiracy to obstruct justice in the Black Panther murder investigation. Both the Chicago Bar Assn. and the Chicago Council of Lawyers proclaimed him unqualified. The Daley organization that had nurtured him cast him out. The major media condemned him.

Everybody rejected him, one might say, but the people. The Democratic voters — with a substantial boost from Republicans who switched allegiance — gave him a resounding vote of confidence. In so doing, they rejected two stout adversaries, the independent Donald Page Moore and the highly praised former supervising judge of the Chicago Traffic Court, Raymond K. Berg, whom the regular organization endorsed after dumping Hanrahan.

Never within memory has the Daley organization taken a beating like this. And considering that the Daley forces also saw their gubernatorial favorite, Paul Simon, whipped by a man they viewed as an upstart (of which more below) it was a defeat to shake the organization to its roots, and from which it may never fully recover. No one may yet count the Daley machine out, but it will be bleeding internally for a long, long time

How could Hanrahan win against such odds? One reason is doubtless that a lot of voters, including switchovers, are fed up with the Daley machine and took pleasure in humbling it.

But the main reason, we fear, is that Hanrahan offered himself purely and simply as the tough guy who could and would deal harshly with the hoodlums and the dissidents, and by inference keep the fractious racial elements in their place. This was the banner that rallied the backlash elements of city and suburbs, of all political persuasions. There probably wouldn't have been enough of them to swing it if there hadn't been two other candidates to fractionize the majority. And the question of how the electorate will split when Hanrahan goes against the powerful Republican, Bernard Carey, remains to be seen. But for the moment it's Hanrahan's day in the sun — and a gloomy day for the cause of social concord in Cook County.

Walker over Simon

No less griping to the Daley forces than Hanrahan's triumph was Dan Walker's toppling of the organization's candidate for governor, Paul Simon.

Simon was and is a wholly different kind of man from Hanrahan — liberal, attractive, with a statesmanlike record in government and a spectacular record as a vote-getter.

Walker came to the race with excellent credentials as a business executive and a public man, and he made political history by plodding hundreds of miles through the Illinois countryside and urban areas, wringing tens of thousands of hands and learning the people's views.

But two factors figured most importantly in Walker's victory: antipathy toward the Daley organization (even though Simon was demonstrably no Daley minion) and — once more — the tax phobia. Simon said frankly and, we believe, correctly, that the state should get rid of the personal property tax and take the tax off food, even if this meant increasing the income tax. Walker accused Simon of plugging for a higher income tax, and Simon couldn't scrape off the opprobrium. So it will be Walker vs. Richard Ogilvie in the finals.

Lieutenant governor

Ironically enough, the man the Democratic voters chose as Walker's running mate was Neil F. Hartigan, the attractive young Chicagoan whom Daley had persuaded Simon to take as his running mate. Hartigan beyond doubt has appeal of his own, but it could well be in this instance that a quirk in ballot positioning and a similarity in names had as much to do with his victory as his political prowess. As the ballot lined up it was easy for the uninitiated to conclude that Hartigan was in fact Walker's running mate rather than Neal E. Eckert, the equally young and attractive mayor of Carbondale who had Walker's blessing for the post. But it should be said in fairness that Hartigan had campaigned the state vigorously on his own and it was not until recent weeks that his name had blossomed alongside Simon's in political posters and fliers.

Congressional races

As expected, Congressman Roman C. Pucinski, with only token opposition to his bid for the Democratic senatorial nomination, won overwhelmingly. But the fact that his largely unknown challenger, W. Dakin Williams, got as many votes as he did should remind Pucinski that he faces a formidable contest when he takes on Sen. Charles H. Percy in November.

The outcome of the key contests for congressional nominations in the North Shore's new 10th District reflected the same spirit of independence the voters had shown higher up on the ticket.

Able Independent Democrat Abner J. Mikva easily won his contest for the party's nomination against Nicholas B. Blase, who had mustered more organization support and sought to raise the carpet-bagging issue against Mikva, recently remapped out of his South Side Chicago district. Mikva's long record of opposition to the machine and his accomplishments in Congress were factors in his victory.

On the Republican side Samuel H. Young, a moderate, beat Floyd T. Fulle, the county commissioner endorsed by Gov. Ogilvie and most of the district's township Republican leaders. Fulle's involvement in the County Board's maze of waste, extravagance and patronage doubtless figured in his defeat, but Young's seemingly lone fight against formidable odds appealed to voters tired of entrenched GOP power.

The Morning Star
Rockford, Ill., March 23, 1972

Not even the most astute politician could have predicted the extent of the effect of a federal panel's ruling which opened the gates to party switching in Illinois in time for this week's primary election.

And nowhere in the state was the effect of the decision felt more acutely than in Winnebago County.

In the last presidential election year primary four years ago, 24,000 voters went to the polls in Winnebago County, with Republicans outnumbering the Democrats by three to one.

Tuesday, despite inclement weather, more than 38,000 votes were cast and in both the city and county the Democratic vote exceeded Republican ballots — by almost 5,000 in the city and more than 2,000 in the county.

It is documentary evidence that former Republican voters switched parties in droves to the Democratic column. Years of Republican domination in Winnebago County have been brought to a sudden end.

Democrats are chortling with glee. Republicans are stunned.

But the big question mark is whether the voters will love the Democrats in November as they did in April.

THAT SIMILAR question is subject to debate the length and breadth of Illinois in the aftermath of rebel Democrat Daniel Walker's stunning upset victory over Lt. Gov. Paul Simon for the Democratic nomination for governor.

Chicago Democratic Slatemaker Mayor Daley's powerful organization suffered a crushing twin setback — the defeat of Simon and the victory of incumbent State's Atty. Edward V. Hanrahan, who had been dumped by Daley and replaced by Raymond Berg.

The Daley organization simply could not deliver enough regular Democratic votes to overcome the surge of Republican crossovers in the normally Republican Chicago suburbs and elsewhere in the state which put Walker over the top.

It is premature to forecast the dissolution of the Daley dynasty. Daley and Hanrahan will have no trouble smoking the peace pipe, but the Daley-Walker relationship is another matter.

Walker has traversed the state condemning the Daley Democratic machine and fence-mending will be no simple chore. Walker has challenged Daley and he has won. It is Daley who must compromise. And eventually he will.

WHAT HAPPENED in Winnebago County may have shocked Republicans and elated Democrats, but it is a lesson from which both parties should profit.

It has its roots not in either the Republican or Democratic parties, but rather in the hearts and the minds of the voters who are seeking more able and more responsive government and are taking searching looks at the candidates rather than the party labels.

In Winnebago County, in Chicago and throughout the rest of the state that is the message that should come through loud and clear to the master politicians of both parties.

If the two parties will not offer the best possible candidates, if they continue the long trend of business as usual politics, the voters will go elsewhere in their search for candidates to represent them.

The voters are demanding solutions to the problems that are plaguing them these days, not warmed-over promises.

The people of Illinois have spoken through the ballot box. The political parties — both of them — should realize, ponder and act on their message.

St. Louis Globe-Democrat
St. Louis, Mo., March 23, 1972

The clearest implication of the results in the Illinois primary election is that voters of every political stripe turned out in droves Tuesday to overturn the long-powerful political machine of Chicago Mayor Richard Daley.

In that, they were markedly successful. Lt. Gov. Paul Simon, of Troy, who carried Daley's endorsement for the Democratic nomination for governor and was expected to win with comparative ease, was beaten narrowly — but convincingly — by Chicago lawyer Daniel Walker, a political newcomer who conducted a vigorous statewide campaign independent of Democratic leaders.

☆ ☆ ☆

Walker's victory over the favored Simon was one of two major political upsets in the Illinois primary. In the race for Cook County state's attorney, Daley-backed candidate Raymond Berg was beaten soundly by incumbent Edward Hanrahan.

In this race the deciding factor appears not so much an anti-Daley movement as it does a law-and-order issue. Hanrahan's victory seems clearly a sign of voter determination to put a man in office who stands for strict enforcement of the law.

The public has refused to buy the indictment of Hanrahan and several other Chicago law enforcement officials on charges of conspiracy in connection with the raid on a Black Panther party apartment two years ago in which two Panther chiefs were killed.

A great majority of voters in Cook County have demonstrated as voters throughout the country are doing that they are fed up with ultraliberal permissiveness toward criminal elements. The law-abiding citizenry want a man like Hanrahan who believes in getting tough when necessary to protect the public.

☆ ☆ ☆

In the gubernatorial race the win by "Walking" Dan Walker — a nickname he earned by his 1,200-mile foot-stumping campaign of Illinois — has to be viewed in the main as a refutation of the party's machine. Walker carried downstate Illinois — which should have been Simon's heaviest vote-getting area — by some 50,000 votes.

There were other factors in Walker's victory, such as the political capital he made over the confusion about Simon's tax stand, but he could never have captured Simon's stronghold if the Lieutenant Governor's image hadn't been blurred by the Daley association.

In the other primary contests there were few surprises. Democratic presidential hopeful Sen. Edmund Muskie won handily on two fronts, beating back a challenge by Sen. George McGovern for Illinois delegate support and easily outdistancing former Sen. Eugene McCarthy in the Illinois presidential preference primary.

The showing raises Muskie's stock, which has been sagging, as a contender for the Democratic nomination for President.

One of the ironies of Tuesday's election is that voters who wanted to get away from the Chicago influence on state politics will find two Chicagoans in the two top spots on the state Democratic ticket in November. Walker's running mate will be Neil Hartigan of Chicago, hand-picked by the Daley organization to run for nomination as the Lieutenant Governor candidate.

THE POST-TRIBUNE

Gary, Ind., March 23, 1972

How do the Illinois primary surprises shade the national political picture?

The answers aren't as clear as these two simple facts:

Fact one, Chicago Mayor Richard Daley's machine was badly embarrassed by Edward Hanrahan's sizable victory over machine-endorsed Raymond K. Berg for the Democratic Cook County state's attorney nomination, and by Daniel Walker's apparent narrow triumph over organization-backed Paul Simon as the party's choice for governor.

Fact two, Sen. Edmund Muskie, who was regarded as slipping in the race for the Democratic presidential nomination, easily won the popularity contest where former Sen. Eugene McCarthy was his only opponent while delegate candidates pledged to Muskie in a separate contest fared much better than those backing Sen. George McGovern.

But the underlying answers to the original question are keyed more to two other questions: (1) How much of the Daley organization loss is attributable to the youth vote with 18-year-olds eligible to vote for the first time? and, (2) How well can the Daley machine regroup for the national convention and the fall vote?

The first of these questions is the more important because it applies to every state.

The Daley giant killers (well, giant wounders, anyway) are vastly different. Still, they shared two qualities calculated to appeal to youth. Both proved themselves fighters. Both, in the current instance, were fighting "the establishment" insofar as that is represented by the Daley organization, last of the really potent big city machines. If youth was a major factor then those attributes — willingness to fight and opposition to entrenched power — will have meaning elsewhere.

It seems certain Hanrahan will be welcomed back into the machine of which he was once a major cog. In fact the very size of his victory was proof that many generally loyal to the organization would not go along with the dumping of one they regarded as a veteran fellow-marcher. The fact that Hanrahan had been dumped primarily to appease the black vote angered by a Hanrahan-directed bloody Black Panther raid is vital but will take careful weighing. Will the machine failure to win under those circumstances mean it may pay less attention to black demands? Will the failure of the organization to beat a man whom blacks so heavily opposed further weaken black ties to the machine?

Those are among the imponderables in regrouping the Chicago machine. That in itself raises two vital national questions:

Will Daley come back strongly enough to have his usual control of the Illinois convention delegation which makes him so powerful a convention lever, or will there be more independence on the part particularly of downstate delegates, none of whom are legally committed even to those under whose names they were listed on the ballot?

Will the Chicago organization be weakened enough to prevent its returning the Illinois presidential and gubernatorial votes back to the Democrats?

Daley's machine is hurt, but until it is determined how badly and by whom, the meaning of the Illinois surprises remains clouded.

THE LOUISVILLE TIMES

Louisville, Ky., March 24, 1972

The breakdown of Mayor Daley's automatic voting machine this week cannot be regarded as a sign that it is soon to be junked. The Cook County Democratic organization has, although not often, survived defeat before. Richard J. Daley is a politician noted for his ability to roll with the punch.

Undoubtedly the victories of Daniel Walker in Illinois' Democratic gubernatorial primary and Edward J. Hanrahan in the Cook County state's attorney's race will precipitate changes. Mr. Daley is 70 and the potential successors to the "boss" long ago began jockeying for position. This week's results will make that infighting even more pronounced.

Victors Weren't Allies

If Mr. Walker and Mr. Hanrahan had been allies, or even compatible political types, the blow to the organization might have been severe. But they emerged from contrasting schools of politics—and while much of the sentiment that lay behind their victories came from the same sources —they drew votes for different reasons.

Both were liked by newly enfranchised 18-to-20-year-olds. Both benefited from a switchover of Republicans who took Democratic ballots as the result of a federal court decision striking down Illinois' restrictive registration laws.

But Walker is a maverick who dramatized his lone-wolf campaign with a 1,200-mile walk through Illinois. Hanrahan, on the other hand, is the archetypal machine politician—a real chip off the Daley block—who blundered in handling the 1969 Black Panther shootout, was indicted and abandoned by the organization that nurtured him.

That gave him an appeal to the Right and he was lionized by no less a person than Mrs. John Mitchell who got on her telephone to call him "my kind of Democrat." The result was heavy strength in Republican suburbs where Walker was also attracting support, not for his ideology, but for his "populist" image as a man in revolt against the entrenched political establishment.

Mayor Daley recognized that appeal by accepting as his gubernatorial candidate Illinois' popular lieutenant governor, Paul Simon, long a "Mr. Clean" in the state's dirty politics. The endorsement cost Mr. Simon his independent status, and his frankness in advocating a higher income tax to offset "less equitable" levies was a final blow.

What About Adlai?

Mayor Daley has indicated that since "the people have spoken" he will support Mr. Walker and Mr. Hanrahan. More of a question mark is the attitude of Sen. Adlai Stevenson II who is lukewarm toward Mr. Walker. An even larger question is whether the Republican crossovers will return home in November or stick with the Democrats who brought them out of the fold.

Politics is a game of alliances and Chicago has been described as a city of alliances, with Mr. Daley as its most skilled alliance-maker. The fascination ahead lies in watching new ones form as the old ones crumble in the wake of Tuesday's performance.

The Star-Ledger
Newark, N.J., March 23, 1972

After the New Hampshire and Florida primaries, the Illinois Democratic contest took on a grim connotation for front-running Sen. Edmund Muskie. If the Maine senator had fared badly in yesterday's primary, his candidacy would have been in deep trouble.

But it appears that Senator Muskie has managed to stage a comeback with his impressive showing in Illinois. He beat Eugene J. McCarthy in the presidential popularity contest and ran well ahead of Sen. George McGovern in a separate primary contest for delegates to the Democratic National Convention.

For a concerned Senator Muskie, this was a welcome — and urgently needed — reversal of the also-ran form he displayed in Florida. He ran up a strong vote in defeating former Senator McCarthy, but this was expected, since the latter no longer is seriously regarded as a major rival for the nomination.

In a pragmatic political perspective, his pickup of delegates was more important, although the wily Mayor Daley of Chicago, the Democratic boss in Illinois, arranged to have half of the delegation remain uncommitted for tactical purposes — i.e. Daley's tactical purposes — at the convention.

The Illinois primary should provide a needed psychological lift for the badly sagging Muskie candidacy. He not only has been having problems with the surprising Senator McGovern, but there were signs in the Florida primary that Sen. Hubert Humphrey has begun to pick up momemtum.

However, the Muskie candidacy is still considerably short of being trouble-free. The first two primaries revealed that he is highly vulnerable, and there isn't any firm assurance at this stage that he has a lock on the Democratic nomination.

It is apparent that Senator Muskie has had problems establishing himself as a strong, assured candidate, the one that Democrats have believed right along has the best chances of the available aspirants to defeat President Nixon in November.

What happened in New Hampshire and Florida has stirred doubts and misgivings about the Muskie candidacy among Democratic leaders. But while the Illinois primary has given Mr. Muskie a respite, it is clear that he must prove himself again as a potent vote-getter in the crucial Wisconsin primary in April, where all the major candidates will be in contention.

The Wisconsin fight, in a fuller context, could be a determining element in the political future of Senator Muskie as a candidate of national, impressive stature. It could answer many questions for the senator — and the Democratic party.

The New York Times
New York, N.Y., March 23, 1972

Senator Edmund S. Muskie claims a "solid victory" in the Illinois Democratic primary and former Senator Eugene McCarthy "a significant achievement." The statements are as predictable as the results, but Mr. McCarthy's adjective is clearly more in need of modification than Mr. Muskie's.

A winning margin of 63 per cent is "solid" by any political standard outside the Iron Curtain, especially since Mr. McCarthy spent an estimated $250,000 on a media campaign in Illinois while his financially strained opponent reportedly spent only about one-fifth of that.

More important, while the Muskie vote *was* a vote for Muskie, the McCarthy vote was also a vote for Senator McGovern. Since the contender from South Dakota chose to stay out of this preferential primary, his followers were pressed to indicate their preference for Mr. McCarthy—if for no other reason than to further slow down the front-runner from Maine.

Where Senators Muskie and McGovern confronted each other head-on—in the separate voting for convention delegates—the Democrats of Illinois gave the former all the best of it. Mr. Muskie comes away with 59 more seats at the convention to 14 for Mr. McGovern. The lion's share of 87 are uncommitted, which means almost all are at the disposal of Mayor Daley of Chicago. As of now, that too could be a plus for Mr. Muskie, toward whose candidacy the Mayor has been distinctly friendly.

Yet it is not far-fetched to suggest that the day's results for Mayor Daley can in the long run do the candidate who eventually emerges as this year's Democratic standard-bearer as much harm as good. The Mayor's two top candidates for state office went down to defeat, though it is true the loss of his hand-picked choice for State's Attorney to the incumbent—Edward V. Hanrahan—may not be much of a blow. The Mayor had originally favored Mr. Hanrahan and dropped him only when he was indicted for obstructing justice in the case of a fatal police raid on the Black Panthers three years ago. Had Daley done otherwise he would have forfeited the black vote.

There is thus no reason to doubt the Mayor's pledge to back Mr. Hanrahan in the fall, but there is real doubt that he will go all out for Daniel Walker, who upset Lieut. Gov. Paul Simon, the Daley candidate, in the primary race for Governor. The maverick Mr. Walker wrote the "Walker Report," which found Mr. Daley's policemen guilty of a "police riot" at the time of the Democratic convention four years ago. Ever since, Mr. Walker has attacked the Chicago boss in unsparing language.

In the circumstances it is conceivable that the Daley machine will roll with less than its customary efficiency in November. Running for the Presidency four years ago, Senator Humphrey lost Illinois by 3 per cent, though the Mayor led an all-out campaign for the ticket. A reduced effort in November could hurt Mr. Muskie as a nominee more than the primary helped him as a candidate.

© 1972 by The New York Times Company. Reprinted by permission.

PORTLAND EVENING EXPRESS
Portland, Me., March 23, 1972

With the vote count practically complete in Illinois, Sen. Edmund S. Muskie has scored a respectable if not a staggering victory over "Clean Gene" McCarthy in the "beauty contest" part of the state primary, at the same time he has done very well in the fight for delegates to the national convention. Unless there is a slight change in the totals, the senator will have 59 delegates, Sen. McGovern will capture only 19, and the other 87 are "uncommitted," which means they will take their orders from Mayor Daley of Chicago.

Despite the nit-picking that some national columnists will indulge in, we think it is fair to say that Sen. Muskie's campaign train is back on the track, with the next big test coming in Wisconsin in less than two weeks. His margin in the "beauty contest," and in the delegate chase, too, might have been larger but for the fact that 200,000 below-21 voters registered and enrolled in the state, most of them in Cook county where they also may have voted en masse against Daley's candidates. The majority no doubt preferred McCarthy and Sen. McGovern, and this preference may also be a factor in Wisconsin.

Muskie's victory is likely to help his fund-raising efforts, and it will immeasurably boost the morale of his workers, who were becoming discouraged over the setbacks in New Hampshire and Florida.

One would think that Mayor Daley would also be discouraged over the setbacks he suffered on Tuesday, with his candidates for governor and attorney general both defeated, though one contest is close. He will probably try to make peace with his foes, since a cardinal precept in politics is that if you can't lick 'em, join 'em. Yet Daley's star may be setting, in an era where the historic political disciplines no longer exist.

McGOVERN WINS WISCONSIN PRIMARY; WALLACE FINISHES 2ND, MUSKIE 4TH

Sen. George S. McGovern (S.D.) won the Wisconsin Democratic presidential primary April 4, polling 30% of the popular vote and capturing 54 of the state's 67 delegates to the national convention. Alabama Gov. George C. Wallace finished second in the field of 12 candidates, receiving 22% of the vote, and Sen. Hubert H. Humphrey of Minnesota came in third with 21%, winning the remaining 13 delegates. Maine's Sen. Edmund S. Muskie, once considered the front-runner in the race for the nomination, finished fourth, receiving only 10% of the votes. New York Mayor John V. Lindsay, who finished sixth behind Sen. Henry M. Jackson (Wash.), announced his withdrawal from the contest for president late April 4.

Analysis of the results was complicated by the cross-over system which permitted Republicans to vote in the Democratic primary. Nevertheless, it was generally acknowledged that McGovern's win rebutted the charge that he was a one-issue candidate standing on his opposition to the war. McGovern, whose efforts in Wisconsin had been better organized than those of the other candidates, had hit hard on economic issues. Gov. Wallace, who campaigned very little in the state, also had stressed economic matters and tax reform in his bid for the "protest-vote."

After the Wisconsin Democratic primary, the race for delegates to the national convention stood as follows: Muskie, 96.2; McGovern, 92.5; Wallace, 75; and Humphrey, 19. (1,509 votes are needed to win the nomination.)

In the Republican primary, President Nixon won 97% of the Republican vote against token opponents who had not campaigned in Wisconsin.

THE MILWAUKEE JOURNAL
Milwaukee, Wis., April 5, 1972

Discontent struck in several directions in the Wisconsin presidential primary.

For Sen. McGovern it meant a great lift. Well organized, hitting hard, promising a "new day in America," the once lonesome campaigner from South Dakota won an impressive victory in a crowded Democratic field. Running well in virtually all areas, he took nearly a third of the vote, snatched most of the convention delegates and proved that he is much more than an antiwar candidate with a narrow constituency. If not now the leading contender for the nomination, he is very close to it.

Disenchantment produced another winner of sorts in Gov. Wallace, who took second place away from Sen. Humphrey, the ebullient Minnesotan who many thought would win the state. It is disturbing, for Wallace has slickly offered answers to everything and solutions to almost nothing. True, he apparently profited greatly from Republican crossover voters, free to wander because of token opposition to President Nixon, who easily won the Republican primary. Nonetheless, it is a sad comment on Wisconsin and the condition of American political leadership that so many saw some value in a vote for the Alabama demagog.

Humphrey, of course, is still very much alive. Whether the same can be said of Sen. Muskie of Maine is another matter. While Humphrey was hurt, Muskie was gravely damaged. He has plunged from front runner to also-ran in only a few weeks. His ability to garner major endorsements has not been matched by an ability to galvanize ordinary voters. Even in Polish-American areas of Milwaukee, where he was supposed to be strongest, he lagged badly.

For the two other main Democratic candidates — Sen. Jackson of Washington and Mayor Lindsay of New York — Wisconsin also proved a rugged survival test. Jackson hangs on, hoping for a better showing elsewhere. Lindsay, probably wisely, has quit.

Wisconsin thus helps thin the pack and clarify the issues. With 20 primaries remaining, the ultimate result is still purely speculative. It seems increasingly clear, however, that this is the year of the alienated voter. The candidates, understanding this, will be talking more and more about tax reform, restoring a sense of trust in government and a score of related questions. Channeled along constructive lines, it can strengthen the nation.

Wisconsin State Journal
Madison, Wis., April 6, 1972

Wisconsin voters, displaying their historical independence, gave resounding victories Tuesday to the two most diverse candidates in the whole Democratic pack, liberal Sen. George McGovern from South Dakota, and conservative Gov. George Wallace of Alabama.

Since his announcement as a presidential candidate away back on Jan. 18, 1971, McGovern has been campaigning in this state. He worked the political field the longest and the hardest and he won favor over the crowd of fringe candidates and the tired old pros who considered themselves "front runners."

While all the professional Democrats would like to disown Wallace, the election proved beyond doubt that he hit a responsive chord with voters generally. Democratic, Republican, and Independent.

The feisty little southerner told the people what they wanted to hear about high property taxes, low farm prices, and "$20,000-a-year bureaucrats running around Washington with peanut butter sandwiches in their brief cases."

While his Democratic opponents were looking down their noses at the Alabama governor and the issues he raised, his strong showing in this state will help make him a voice to be heard at the Democratic National Convention, though we do not consider him presidential timber.

Wisconsin has long been noted as the political graveyard for presidential hopes, and the latest casualty is New York's mayor, John Lindsay. Other fringe candidates, such as the Democratic poet laureate, Eugene McCarthy, should follow Lindsay into political oblivion.

The blatant political brawling in the Democratic primary in recent weeks with the cheap appeals to religious and ethnic groups in the bitter vote struggle was proof positive that a better way should be found to give the people a voice in selecting party candidates.

Senate Democratic Leader Mike Mansfield and Sen. George Aiken (R-Vt.) wisely protested the wasteful March-through-June primaries in 24 states, and suggested the wide array of primary contests should be eliminated. Some better format for a national referendum should be studied.

Polling 98 per cent of the Republican vote in the primary, President Nixon remained above the Democratic political brawling of the Wisconsin campaign. While the Democrats demeaned themselves in the bitter internecine struggle, the President gained in presidential stature.

The President, however, would be wise to give pause to the clear voice of Wisconsin voters who expressed their anguish over the horrible war in Vietnam by their votes for McGovern and their concern over property taxes, low farm income, and high prices as evidenced by their ballots for Wallace.

This is the real lesson of the Wisconsin primary.

ARGUS-LEADER
Sioux Falls, S.D., April 6, 1972

South Dakota friends and supporters of U.S. Sen. George McGovern for president have real cause for jubilation in the senator's victory in Wisconsin.

Senator McGovern, in leading the field decisively and gaining support among all voting segments in Wisconsin, has given his chances of winning the nomination at the Miami convention a real boost. Those chances may still seem remote but make no mistake: the Democratic race for the presidential nomination has taken a decided turn. Primaries in Massachusetts, the home state of Sen. Ted Kennedy, and in Pennsylvania, will be very important to McGovern.

In voting for McGovern and placing Gov. George Wallace of Alabama second, the Wisconsin voters in the Democratic primary seem to indicate that they feel their government is not listening to them, and is not responsive. Wallace has been saying this a long time; so has McGovern, who says his solutions to the problem are more constructive than those of Wallace.

It is interesting to note that McGovern, Wallace and Sen. Hubert Humphrey were careful not to knock each other personally or knock the candidates who trailed in Wisconsin. This was in sharp contrast to Sen. Edward Muskie's performance in Florida, where he rapped Wallace as a demagogue.

Wisconsin's primary is an open one, which means that Republicans may vote in the Democratic primary and vice versa. McGovern, from all reports, did well in Republican areas, a feat which he has demonstrated in his own state, of South Dakota. President Nixon, as anticipated, won overwhelmingly on the Republican ballot. How McGovern and Nixon might do against each other in Wisconsin in November is something else again.

Wisconsin must be marked down as a disappointment for Humphrey, who has been called the Badger state's third senator in the past when Wisconsin had two Republican senators and Humphrey, as a Minnesota neighbor, provided a contact for Democrats. Nevertheless, Humphrey came out of Wisconsin with some delegates. He has tasted early defeat before . . . and to rule him out of the running now would be premature.

At any rate, Wisconsin demonstrates that McGovern must be rated a foremost contender for the Democratic nomination, along with Wallace and Humphrey.

For South Dakotans, it means that there are two chances of placing a citizen or native of this state at the top of the Democratic ticket: McGovern or Humphrey, who was born at Wallace, S.D., and still has an interest in the family drug store at Huron.

The Detroit News
Detroit, Mich., April 10, 1972

The failure of any single Democrat to speak the mind and win the confidence of his party's moderate rank and file was illustrated again in the Wisconsin presidential primary.

Between them, Senator George McGovern and Alabama Gov. George Wallace, representing the opposite extremes of the Democratic Party, captured 52 percent of the vote.

Some voters of course supported these men because of a close political affinity with them, because of — not despite—the candidates' extremism.

But many, we believe, turned to McGovern and Wallace not because they support those men's basic philosophies, but because McGovern and Wallace articulated some crucial issues—taxes, inflation, big government — in a forceful and persistent manner. Had a more moderate candidate with charisma and good leadership qualities done the same, he would have won much of this support.

True, the good showing by McGovern and Wallace resulted in part from the fact that Republicans, having nothing more exciting to do, crossed over to vote in the Democratic primary and create mischief. Yet, the fact that they managed to create mischief shows again the absence of a strong — candidate to represent the moderate sentiment of the party.

Such a man could have mustered sufficient strength to withstand such dabbling by Republicans he; could have marshalled the votes that were otherwise fragmented; he could have attracted some of those Republican votes to himself.

Senator Muskie was supposed to be the man who could do this. But he has proven a weak campaigner who fails to project an image of confidence. Senator Humphrey made a run at it, but to many voters he was used political goods.

In short, the demogogues won because the moderates had weak representation.

But hark! Moderation may yet win. McGovern is apparently giving some thought to two facts — one, that he will not be able to depend on cross-overs as regular fare; two, that if he remains too far from the middle of his party, he has small chance of getting the support of the national convention. So now one of his spokesmen tells us that McGovern intends to show "that he's not a radical, not a left-wing kook that the newspapers imply. The blue-collar voter will see a very conservative man who talks sense to him."

McGovern a conservative? It is a peculiar campaign, indeed.

Actually, McGovern is one cat unlikely to change his spots, though his managers may try to give him protective coloration in certain primaries. Basically, he represents and will continue to represent the party's left wing. With Lindsay gone from the field, McGovern represents the remaining hope of that wing.

If he gets nominated, a possibility we regard as remote, he will do so because the ultraliberal segment of the party holds solidly together while the rest of the party remains divided. Even with Lindsay's vote added to his own, McGovern would have gotten only 37 percent of the vote in Wisconsin; but with no powerful moderate to challenge him, he didn't even need that much to score a "victory."

The Wall Street Journal observes that the reform of the delegate-selection process for the Democratic National Convention may benefit "the ideologically oriented sectors of the party at the expense of the victory-oriented ones, resulting in a huge overrepresentation of the left." In that case, the party would indeed be in trouble.

Under those circumstances, McGovern conceivably could get the nomination. If that happened, the Democratic Party would find itself in the same position the Republican Party found itself in back in 1964, when Barry Goldwater was able to rule the convention but hadn't a chance in the world of getting elected president.

Chicago Sun-Times
Chicago, Ill., April 6, 1972

The Wisconsin presidential primary, in which 1.12 million citizens voted in the hot Democratic contest, offered the first real look at how competing candidates performed in a cosmopolitan Northern state whose demographic makeup comes close to making it a microcosm of America. When its voters speak, as they did Tuesday, they speak, to a great degree, for the nation as a whole.

They have spoken now for Sen. George McGovern and by a solid plurality. In a field of six major candidates, each one of whom could have done well, the South Dakotan won 30 per cent of the vote. He won these votes across the entire spectrum of the electorate, capturing blue-collar workers, farmers, students, white-collar suburbanites, Polish voters on Milwaukee's South Side, Menominee Indians and upper-middle-class citizens in the professional and managerial groups.

It was the kind of coalition that Franklin D. Roosevelt forged just 40 years ago, when the country was also in deep economic trouble, and the kind of coalition that Robert F. Kennedy was beginning to forge before he was assassinated four years ago.

If there is a message, it is that Wisconsin voters spoke in a loud, clear voice for candidates who discussed the issues close to the heart of the average man and woman.

As they did in Illinois March 21, Republicans in wholesale numbers switched to vote in the Democratic primary. Only 282,000 voted the GOP ticket, with President Nixon taking virtually all of these. The Republican switchovers appeared to be divided mostly between McGovern and Gov. George C. Wallace of Alabama, who ran second with 22 per cent of the vote.

It should be noted that Wallace, who narrowly beat out the earlier odds-on favorite, Hubert H. Humphrey of neighboring Minnesota, addressed himself in Wisconsin to the same problems as did McGovern. These are runaway inflation, catastrophic property taxes, waste in government spending, leaders who are unable to extricate the nation from the Vietnam War. Wallace's campaign in Wisconsin was only marginally racist, in contrast to Florida where the fake issue of busing was the code word for everything else that is wrong in America today. But Wallace's appeal to Wisconsin voters, in contrast to McGovern's, was emotional, negative and superficial and gave no solutions as McGovern did. McGovern won 54 convention delegates, Humphrey 13 and Wallace none.

A word should also be said about New York Mayor John V. Lindsay, who bowed out of the presidential race when he received only 7 per cent of the Wisconsin vote. He is to be commended for withdrawing with grace and style, before bitterness between his own followers and those of other candidates could set in.

The primary election system, as Winston Churchill once remarked about democracy, is more inefficient, wasteful and clumsy than anything yet contrived by the minds of men — except for all the other systems. Wisconsin demonstrated who has the ability to hold a coalition of voters together and who has not. Other primaries will offer further proof, but the Democratic Party seems well on the way toward paring down the field to a few good, voter-tested candidates.

THE CINCINNATI ENQUIRER
Cincinnati, Ohio, April 6, 1972

THIS YEAR'S assortment of candidates for the Democratic presidential nomination is too large and too diversified for anyone to expect a single state primary—or even a combination of two or three primaries—to produce one, undisputed favorite, as the preferential primaries frequently have done in the past.

It now seems far likelier that the primaries, as they continue to unfold across the country, will serve the nearly as significant purpose of narrowing the field.

The New Hampshire primary, for example, persuaded Sen. R. Vance Hartke (Ind.) that his presidential campaign was going nowhere. It should have been similarly instructive for Mayor Sam Yorty of Los Angeles.

The Florida primary, topped by this week's balloting in Wisconsin, produced substantially the same handwriting on the wall for Mayor John V. Lindsay of New York. Despite an ambitious, well-financed campaign (which featured in its closing days an open bid to Wisconsin Republicans), the mayor has become another of the season's dropouts.

No one can survey the Wisconsin returns without wondering whether the onetime front-runner, Sen. Edmund S. Muskie (Maine), is similarly near the end of his rope. Senator Muskie has yet to offer a startling performance at the polls this year; indeed, his Florida showing (8.8%) and his Wisconsin showing (10%) suggest that his status as a front-runner has hung principally on the early endorsement of a few would-be kingmakers around the country. Now there is evidence that even that support has begun to erode. New Jersey's top Democrats are in the process of switching from the Muskie column to the uncommitted column, and a survey by Newsweek — even before the Wisconsin primary—indicated that nearly a dozen states that looked like Muskie territory in January are now fair targets for the other candidates. Senator Muskie is likely to find the trend difficult to reverse.

It is similarly difficult to see how Sen. Henry M. Jackson (Wash.) can remain actively in the field.

Also in desperate need of good news is Sen. Hubert H. Humphrey (Minn.), who, in three bids for the presidential nomination, has yet to win a state primary. He retains powerful support in the party; but sooner or later, he must begin demonstrating appeal at the polls as well.

Perhaps the most curious aspect of the Wisconsin campaign was that the first- and second-place winners presented, with several notable exceptions, the same basic campaign message. Sen. George S. McGovern (S.D.) and Gov. George C. Wallace of Alabama differ on Vietnam, amnesty for draft evaders and civil rights. But their efforts to exploit deep-rooted discontents about the state of American society, the frustrations of the "little man," vague feelings about the inequity of the tax structure sounded as though they had been cut from the same cloth. Senator McGovern confirmed the similarities in their appeals in an interview yesterday morning, although he noted that their solutions differed.

Despite Senator McGovern's good showing in New Hampshire and his significant victory in Wisconsin, the Gallup Poll continues to show him as the choice of precisely 6% of the Democrats polled. What he achieved in Wisconsin was the result of a prodigious, expertly organized, year-long campaign. Whether he can put his assets to work elsewhere —particularly among party professionals and among the nation's labor leaders— will be the ultimate test of his viability.

Chicago Tribune
Chicago, Ill., April 6, 1972

In making winners of Sen. George McGovern and Gov. George Wallace, the voters of Wisconsin have thrown the Democratic Presidential race wide open and confounded pundits and professional politicians alike.

Nothing went as the preprimary "conventional wisdom" had supposed. Sen. Edmund Muskie, who had been crowned front-runner in the forecasts just a few weeks ago, was sent reeling.

Sen. Hubert Humphrey, Wisconsin's "third senator," held enough of his labor support to remain in contention, but the loyalties he was supposed to have commanded as a "good neighbor" evaporated with the opening of the first polling place.

"Glamorous" John Lindsay, who was going to sweep to a Kennedyesque victory with a grand coalition of blacks, the young, feminists, old people, Chicanos, etc., etc., was instead swept aside and out of the race.

To many it all seemed incredible in its lack of logic. Mr. McGovern seemed an antiwar liberal with "far out" economic ideas, with no one but the students to cheer him on. Yet he took black votes, labor votes, the votes of conservative Republican cross-overs from the Fox River Valley, and those of farmers and tradesmen who lived across the Mississippi River from Mr. Humphrey's Minnesota.

Mr. Wallace had been dismissed as a racist redneck with little Northern appeal, yet he pulled Republican and Democratic votes from all over the political spectrum, including those of people who said Mr. McGovern, the liberal, was their second choice.

By the old rules, this was illogical, but according to the patterns which are emerging in election year 1972 it makes a great deal of sense. These patterns were apparent in the antibusing vote in the Florida primary and in the antitax, antiestablishment vote in last month's Illinois contest.

The electorate is in a mood to protest. It is not interested in grand visions for the future, ideological philosophizing, personal glamor, or ethnic appeal. It is angry over its latest tax bill, uneasy about its pension plan, worried about the price of meat, and tired of politics as usual.

In Wisconsin, it ignored the Viet Nam crisis, the redundant rhetoric, and the endless slogans and television commercial promises. It seized upon the two men who, aside from the obvious also-rans, were given the least chance of receiving the Democratic nomination. There was no better way to protest.

The Wisconsin primary was not conclusive. Sen. Henry Jackson, who finished fifth, is remaining in the race and looking to the Ohio primary as a means of rekindling his hopes. Mr. Humphrey is planning a comeback try in Pennsylvania. Mr. McGovern faces another test in Massachusetts and Mr. Wallace has a rough fight on his hands in Michigan and Indiana.

It is too early to tell what effect the mood of the electorate will have on President Nixon's reelection chances. Whatever the outcome of the Democratic scramble, the voters have made it clear they want some changes made. They have made the election a new ball game, and they have rewritten the rules.

PORTLAND EVENING EXPRESS
Portland, Me., April 7, 1972

The results of the Wisconsin primary must be as big a disappointment to Sen. Edmund S. Muskie as his defeat in Florida, where a number of candidates cut up the vote.

Yet he insists he is still a viable candidate, and is the only Democrat who, firmly planted at the center of the political spectrum, can unite the various factions of the Democratic party.

There is a good deal to that, and it is likely that if Sen. Hubert Humphrey were the winner, representing the party's conservative wing, there would surely be a third party on the liberal side led by Sen. McGovern or Eugene McCarthy.

By the same token, a victory for McGovern no doubt would bring about a third party on the right, led by George Wallace. But Muskie is a centrist, though lately he has been leaning a bit toward the left in an effort to capture the voters nominally attracted to Mayor Lindsay and McCarthy, and it would be much more difficult to put together a third-party movement aimed at the Maine senator.

It will probably help the senator, as he gets ready to tackle Hubert Humphrey in Pennsylvania and Sen. McGovern in Massachusetts on the 25th of this month, if someone will come up with a fairly accurate estimate of the extent of the Republican crossover vote, and where it went.

No doubt thousands of Republicans, with no contest on their own ticket, voted for Wallace, and he took away votes from Muskie in the Polish wards in Milwaukee. It might be that other thousands voted for McGovern, in their conviction he could not be nominated anyway, to injure the chances of Humphrey and Muskie. So the primary result is not an accurate reflection of just how the front runners fared at the hands of Democrats alone. In other words, take away the GOP vote and the gap between Muskie and Wallace and McGovern would have been much narrower.

Now we go on to Pennsylvania and the Bay State, in less than three weeks, and it is here that Sen. Muskie must do well.

The Burlington Free Press
Burlington, Vt., April 6, 1972

THE RESULTS OF the Wisconsin Presidential primary election couldn't be more encouraging for the Republicans!

George McGovern received the most votes by far, with George Wallace coming in second, and together these "protest votes" totaled more than half of all those cast on the Democratic side of the ballot.

Hubert Humphrey's showing was especially poor when it is remembered that he was known for years as "the third Senator from Wisconsin." As for Edmund Muskie, it was another total disaster — he received only a third as many votes as McGovern!

The remaining candidates cannot be taken seriously. John Lindsay, with a measly 7 per cent of the vote, dropped out of the Presidential race Tuesday night. Henry Jackson, with only 8 per cent, probably will do likewise in due course.

On the Republican side of the ballot, Richard Nixon received an incredible 97 per cent of the ballots cast. Paul McCloskey on the left and John Ashbrook on the right each received only 1 per cent of the votes.

The post-election surveys are likely to prove anew, however, that Nixon won a far bigger victory than the vote totals show. Unquestionably he was the only big winner on either side of the ballot in Wisconsin on Tuesday. Post-election surveys in New Hampshire, Florida and Illinois revealed that a remarkably high percentage of voters casting Democratic ballots in the primaries plan to vote for Nixon in November, and there is every reason to expect the same was true in Wisconsin.

McGovern, of course, hasn't a ghost of a chance of being elected President. He is simply not Presidential material. The Republican glee would be unrestrained if either McGovern or Wallace were nominated by the Democrats.

The Communist offensive in Vietnam comes at just the wrong time for McGovern. The idea of McGovern coping with Vietnam war policy in the White House is simply too ludicrous to even contemplate.

42—Wisconsin Primary

BOSTON HERALD TRAVELER
Boston, Mass., April 6, 1972

Let's see if we have everything straight now.

Sen. Edmund Muskie received 47 per cent of the vote in New Hampshire, and that was supposed to be a "terrible setback"; but Sen. George McGovern got only 30 per cent of the vote in Wisconsin, and that's supposed to be a "smashing triumph."

Sen. Hubert Humphrey made a "surprisingly strong" finish in Florida with 19 per cent; but he suffered a "great disappointment" by polling a mere 21 per cent in Wisconsin.

The fact that Gov. George Wallace received more votes than all of his rivals in Florida didn't surprise too many people because that, after all, is a Southern state; yet he polled more votes than all but one of his rivals in Wisconsin, which is about as far North of the Mason-Dixon Line as you can get.

McGovern's win in Wisconsin is supposed to represent a big "victory" for the liberal hard-core and the New Left; but Wallace, Humphrey and Sen. Henry Jackson (the "conservatives" or "old fogies" in the Democratic contest) received 51 per cent of the vote there.

If all the statistical mumbo jumbo leaves us a bit confused, we'll have to confess that for pure amusement the primaries remain the best show in town. And we can rest assured that unlike ball players in the major leagues, the runners in the White House Derby will never go on strike.

It's true that a few of them have abandoned the field. The latest drop-out, Mayor Lindsay, quit after he "peaked" in Wisconsin with 7 per cent; but there are several candidates left in the arena who haven't even done that well to date. There's Sen. Eugene McCarthy, for example, who's consistently been polling about one per cent of the vote. (Yes, he got 37 per cent in Illinois, but that wasn't really a contest; his only rival was the erstwhile Democratic "front-runner," Sen. Muskie.)

Though the Democratic field has been narrowing a bit, for some odd reason the primary winners have been getting a steadily smaller share of the vote; Muskie won New Hampshire with 47 per cent, Wallace took Florida with 42 per cent and McGovern grabbed the prize in Wisconsin with 30 per cent. On the Republican side, however, President Nixon's winning majorities have been getting progressively larger (70 per cent in New Hampshire, 87 per cent in Florida, 97 per cent in Wisconsin). The way things are going, by the time the primaries are over, Mr. Nixon ought to be getting well over 100 per cent, and the Democratic "winner" may be lucky to run up a score as high as the discouraging figures that have already driven Lindsay, Hartke, Yorty and McCloskey out of the race.

There are still roughly 20 primaries left to go this season, so there will be plenty of time for more serious—and whimsical—comment. But we can't resist adding a few last political notes and postscripts here.

Yesterday (with tongue in cheek, we hope), Sen. Mike Mansfield remarked that Hubert Horatio Humphrey—who has made three tries for the White House, but has never won a contested primary in any of the 50 states—is "the freshest face among the present lot."

When asked the other day what his Democratic "dream team" would be, Vice President Agnew replied: "Humphrey-Muskie—why break up a losing combination?"

And last but not least, the following item appeared in the New York Daily News on the morning after John Lindsay counted the votes and threw in the towel: "Milwaukee, April 4—Winding up his Wisconsin campaign, Mayor Lindsay wrote off his rivals for the Democratic Presidential nomination as 'losers' today . . ."

It will be pretty difficult for anyone else to top that statement for honors in the "famous last words" department.

BUFFALO EVENING NEWS
Buffalo, N.Y., April 5, 1972

Perhaps the most promising way to sort out the results in yesterday's crowded Democratic presidential primary in Wisconsin is to look first not at the winner, clearly Sen. George McGovern, but at the losers.

John Lindsay, whose late-blooming liberal candidacy never clicked, has now prudently withdrawn, thus saving himself a lot of futile effort and his backers a lot of money. Another irrevocable loss was suffered by Sen. Henry Jackson. Whether he formally withdraws, Wisconsin voters gave his sputtering conservative candidacy a decisive shove toward oblivion. While both of these retain some ticket-balancing credentials for vice president, neither now has any realistic chance at the top nomination.

Also in Wisconsin, as in New Hampshire and Florida, Sen. Edmund Muskie, with only a puny 10 per cent of the vote, did poorly. He isn't eliminated yet, but he leaves Wisconsin weaker than he entered and, from one-time front-runner, he has been reduced to hanging on by his finger tips.

Add to this the fact that Sen. Hubert Humphrey finished only third in a state he had hoped to win, and the fact that Alabama's scrappy Gov. Wallace may have benefited substantially from Republican cross-over votes which would go to President Nixon in the fall, and the victory of Sen. McGovern looks most impressive. He has gone much farther in these spring primaries than many, ourselves included, thought he would. He has picked his states carefully, husbanded his limited resources (something Sen. Muskie has failed to do) and gradually built a momentum which clearly transforms him into a major contender in the race.

With the liberal Lindsay out, Sen. McGovern has effectively consolidated his hold on the Democratic left. Now he can concentrate on picking up votes in the moderate-to-liberal range and is a serious threat to Sen. Muskie, whom he faces in the Massachusetts primary on April 25.

Indeed, April 25 may well be Sen. Muskie's last chance in these primaries.

That same day, while facing Sen. McGovern in Massachusetts, he is also locked in a tough three-way battle in Pennsylvania, with Sen. Humphrey and Gov. Wallace. There lingers the feeling that the Maine senator may be everyone's second choice. But if he doesn't soon trounce some opponent of real stature — McGovern on his left or Humphrey on his right — he simply cannot remain a viable contender with any hopes of beating President Nixon.

After Wisconsin, then, it looks as though Gov. Wallace dominates the right, Sen. McGovern the left, and nobody yet holds the decisive center of the Democratic constituency. Both McGovern and Wallace emerge in stronger positions to appeal to this centrist constituency. Besides Humphrey and Muskie, McGovern now has a real chance to win enough of the center to claim the nomination. But if none of those three shows a consistent gain from here on out, the more likely development at the Democratic convention will, it seems to us, be an effort to draft Sen. Edward Kennedy.

Pittsburgh Post-Gazette
Pittsburgh, Pa., April 6, 1972

WISCONSIN'S presidential primary Tuesday showed that the sentiment for major change within the Democratic party is so great that an "anti-establishment" candidate conceivably could win the Presidential nomination at Miami Beach.

With the two "outsider" Georges, McGovern and Wallace, finishing one-two in Wisconsin, that possibility cannot be discounted. Of course, there have been primary-sweeping rebels in the past, Estes Kefauver in 1952 and 1956, and Eugene McCarthy in 1968, who eventually were smothered by the traditional Democratic organization when convention time came.

* * *

But there are a couple of differences this time. One is the revamping of the delegate selection process (proposed by a committee headed by Senator McGovern, incidentally). Unlike previous conventions, mayors and governors will not come to the convention with huge blocs of delegates they can switch this way and that. The traditional party leaders may not have the leverage they had in the past to stop the mavericks.

The other factor is that the primaries to date have shown an amazing "aginner" spirit on the part of Democratic voters. And it has been the candidates who could rub this raw edge of unhappiness who have been the most successful — the showing of the two Georges in Wisconsin being the latest example.

Now Mr. McGovern and Mr. Wallace have quite different ideas of which direction they want the party to go (although both have strong strains of populism in their approaches). But the sum of their efforts has been to hammer the middle to pieces.

Senator Muskie or Senator Humphrey might be the kind of centrist leader who could pull the country together for a good presidency. But the Democratic voters seem to be shunning this approach.

Maybe this is just contrariness in the primaries, a thumbing of the nose at the establishment, a gulping response to the simple approach (McGovern: "Get out of Vietnam NOW." Wallace: "Stop busing NOW.")

Or maybe it shows that rank and file Democrats are not only upset about affairs in the country but also in the Democratic party itself. Maybe they really want a new direction, and, if so, it could make Miami Beach a new ball game indeed.

At first glance, Wisconsin would seem to be happy news for the Republicans with this splintering of the Democratic party. But if the "raw edge of unhappiness" the voters are demonstrating concerns matters in general, then the Nixon administration with the problems of the Vietnam war, inflation, and the rest might be in great danger of the "throw 'em out" feeling, too, come November.

Wisconsin did thin the ranks of candidates, with Republican-turned-Democrat John Lindsay dropping his presidential bid. Indeed, it was Mr. McGovern's ability not only to organize a grass-roots effort on the left but also to hold it intact against the attractiveness of Mr. Lindsay which doomed the latter's hopes.

* * *

Now the action moves to our state of Pennsylvania and to Massachusetts, both of which hold primaries April 25. Here may be the final head-to-head struggle between Mr. Muskie and Mr. Humphrey, and a reading on what the party's center can do to hold off the "outsiders."

Wisconsin shows that even if 1972 isn't the year of the re-making of the Democratic party, it will see posed the sternest challenge yet to the "way it's always been done" in the oldest continuous organized political party in the world.

The Star-Ledger
Newark, N.J., April 6, 1972

The Democratic primary in Wisconsin was really a matter of survival for presidential aspirants, but it appears to have given significant impetus to the candidacy of Sen. George McGovern, who ran a professional, well-planned and organized campaign.

And it showed in the results, with Senator McGovern rolling up an impressive vote to head the large field of Democratic candidates, some of whom did not even campaign.

Alabama Gov. George Wallace, who ran ahead of Sen. Hubert Humphrey, continues to be a hairshirt for the Democrats. But the governor's strong electoral showing must be realistically evaluated on the basis of a heavy crossover of Republican voters and a revolt by Wisconsin voters against some of the heaviest property taxes in the country.

But it is apparent that the governor cannot be written off by other Democratic contenders: The strong race he made in the Northern primary gives him an imposing showcase when it is coupled with the expected hefty vote he pulled in the Florida contest. Mr. Wallace is going to be a thorny problem for other Democrats if he continues to attract large electoral support.

The fourth place finish for Sen. Edmund Muskie is another disquieting portent for a candidate who was regarded as a front runner. The senator's indifferent showings in the primaries thus far could have troubling implications for his candidacy, possibly leading to a reassessment by party leaders on whether he is still the man the Democrats will bank on to defeat President Nixon next November.

At the moment, Senator Muskie has shown little to indicate that he can carry this difficult assignment. There will have to be a dramatic reversal of form in future primaries if the Maine senator is to be regarded as a serious choice for the Democratic nomination.

The Wisconsin primary put an end to the national ambitions of New York Mayor John Lindsay, who pulled out as a candidate after a mediocre showing, with only seven per cent of the vote. After looking at the returns, it was apparent that the mayor, who left the Republican Party last year, got the message.

The Wisconsin results reveal that the Democrats have some frustrating problems to resolve. While Senator McGovern has emerged as a major contender, it is apparent that Governor Wallace could be a source of inordinate embarrassment for the party. Thus far he has overshadowed both Muskie and Humphrey, two candidates formerly regarded as top choices for the Democratic nomination.

There is a disquieting mood of disarray among Democratic candidates who appear to be confused and uncertain over how to deal with the "Wallace problem." Senator McGovern frankly concedes that Governor Wallace has seized on two issues—controversial school busing and high taxes—that have broad, potent voter appeal. And other Democratic candidates will have to address themselves to these issues.

But this raises philosophic and moral problems, too. Mr. Wallace has not been above demagogic appeals, exploiting fears and misconceptions of voters. It is doubtful that Democratic contenders would let themselves take this road, even if it assured one of them the party's nomination.

ST. LOUIS POST-DISPATCH

St. Louis, Mo., April 5, 1972

Senator McGovern's smashing victory in the Wisconsin presidential preference primary is a manifestation of diligence, an intelligent and well-organized campaign, a platform that said the right things and, most of all, a candidate with character. The primary constituted an upheaval among Democratic presidential contenders, and if it caused some to fall by the wayside perhaps Wisconsin voters have provided explanations.

Mr. McGovern staked a great deal on Wisconsin; his fine organization there was not an accident. It has now propelled him into the front ranks of the Democratic contenders if it has not made him the current front-runner. The Senator from South Dakota has not only received a great psychological boost; having won a test of political skill and public drawing power, he should find it easier to obtain campaign funds and followers for the remaining primaries.

Senator Muskie of Maine, the leading Democrat earlier in the year, may not have been knocked out of the race but he has been hurt badly. He came home fourth in a field of 12, with about 10 per cent of the vote. Mr. Muskie says he will not quit, and it is true that each primary must be evaluated individually, but it is pretty obvious by now that his campaign has not caught on.

Senator Humphrey also suffered a blow to his prospects. With 21 per cent of the vote he was nosed out for second place by George Wallace, who probably benefited from Republican crossovers but whose strong showing, nonetheless may be a portent. By many political standards Mr. Humphrey should have won in Wisconsin, and had he done so he might have finished Mr. Muskie. As a veteran and popular Minnesota politician Mr. Humphrey has many friends in neighboring Wisconsin, but obviously there were not enough.

How did Mr. McGovern manage to get some 30 per cent of the vote? Look at the field. Mr. Humphrey is mostly sound on domestic issues, but he has a war-hawk record and he humiliated himself with his waffling on the busing issue. Mr. Muskie's views have been hard to define. Mr. Wallace got the hard-hats (there are more of them than we like to think). Mayor Lindsay of New York, suffering from the handicap of leaving the GOP and joining the Democrats, garnered only 7 per cent, and bowed out of the race.

And then look at the state. Wisconsin may be the most anti-war state in the nation. Mr. McGovern's record of opposition to the Vietnam war is impeccable. He said not long ago: "If we can't do well in Wisconsin, I don't know any state where we are going to do well." Mr. McGovern unquestionably attracted a large number of new young voters, a welcome indicator. The voter registration in Madison, which has a student population of more than 30,000, has risen by 60 per cent since 1968. Many of the new votes were expected to go to Mr. McGovern.

While Mr. McGovern's victory is extremely heartening, it would be a mistake to regard it at the moment as the kindling of a prairie fire. Mr. McGovern has a somewhat specialized constituency, and it has yet to be demonstrated that he can put together the combination of elements that will win the Democratic nomination for him this summer, and take his party to victory in November. But as of today, when Mr. McGovern is viewed against the field that turned out in Wisconsin, the Senator from South Dakota may well be the man behind whom the Democrats had better unite.

The Washington Post

Washington, D.C., April 6, 1972

Forgetting, perhaps, the built-in eccentricity that marks this country's political institutions as a whole—the electoral college, the madcap convention, the loosely defined political party—people at about this point every four years start trying to make the primary results yield up a sense of order and direction which they cannot provide. For the criss-cross, accident-prone, part local and part national primary contest is as weird and improbable in its own right as every other part of the system by which this nation chooses its leaders. And the Wisconsin primary, both because it comes when it does and because it occurs in one of those states in which voters may cross over party lines, has a way of producing a result that brings on confusion bordering on panic in those of us who want to know what's going on. Accordingly, so far as we have been able to judge, the question on most peoples' minds in the immediate aftermath of Tuesday's primary may be stated as follows: what do we know now and when are we really going to know something, and how are we even going to know when we know it?

At the very least, it should be possible to identify what has been learned from Wisconsin. George McGovern, by virtue of his organizational skill and diligence and his apparent ability to relate abstract issues to the immediate concerns of the voter, has demonstrated that he is a good candidate—a far more effective one than most people had supposed and one who has thus far outdistanced Senator Muskie not in delegate votes but in political skill. Senator Muskie has as yet shown very little in the way of being a good politician—and we use the word "politician" in its best sense. Perhaps the greatest surprise of the campaign has been his apparent inability so far either to organize his tremendous campaign assets or to make his views seem relevant to the lives the voters he is wooing. We would submit that what is available to be learned from the primaries to date lies more in what can be thus observed about candidate performance than it does in unearthing voter trends. And we suspect that Senator Muskie's early failure to produce votes in the expected numbers says more about his particular qualities as a campaigner than it does about voter views on the big issues or about the death of "centrism" and the rest.

Is the drive for the Democratic nomination going to take the form of a series of inconclusive slugging matches from now until convention time in Miami? Will Miami see the delegates presented with a collection of half-dazed contenders staggering around the ring, each of whom has been seriously disabled by the others? In fact, there are contests ahead that should begin to produce some conclusive results and to eliminate some of the contenders. Vice President Humphrey, who did fairly well—but not awfully well—in Wisconsin, could go a long way toward extinguishing Senator Muskie's reduced prospects by beating him in Pennsylvania; should the former Vice President also do well in Ohio and beat Governor Wallace in West Virginia he would have shown a likelihood of surviving the pre-convention course. Senator McGovern's next trick, if he is to accomplish one, will be beating Senator Muskie in Massachusetts. It is not impossible that whoever survives these contests will be in a position to acquire crucial numbers of delegate votes in the California and New York primaries. And because, despite the reforms of Democratic party rules, delegates are still free to vote finally as they wish, it is also not impossible that a "brokered" result will occur, some decision representing an accommodation between candidates with hefty and decisive blocs of votes.

We do not sketch out this possible scenario by way of expressing nostalgia for what is known as the "old politics" or even by way of firmly predicting that any one of the candidates now in the running will end up with the Democratic nomination. The point is that the post-Wisconsin snapshot does not necessarily represent what things will be looking like several weeks hence. We do think, however, that Wisconsin has confirmed a few things people already suspected—that George Wallace is a large and very troublesome element in the Democratic picture this year; that the other candidates and the party itself will be obliged to acknowledge the discontents that are the source of his strength and to deal with them not by contempt or (worse) imitation, but head-on and in an honorable, authentic way; that there is no substitute for a skillful campaigner—and no earthly help for one who's not so good.

The Birmingham News
Birmingham, Ala., April 6, 1972

Looking back at Wisconsin:

Sen. George McGovern has every right to feel elated at his victory in Wisconsin, which was the first real showing of any return on his investment of more than a year of campaigning and more than a million dollars in quest of the presidency.

Realistically, however, his victory in Wisconsin no more makes him the front-runner for the Democratic nomination than George Wallace's victory in Florida made him the front-runner.

McGovern in victory still managed to get only 30 per cent of the vote. The next two finishers, Wallace and Sen. Hubert Humphrey, got 43 per cent between them, and they are the most prominent candidates appealing to the center-to-right viewpoint within the Democratic Party.

Add Sen. Henry Jackson's eight per cent and more than half of the Democratic voters of Wisconsin—a pretty liberal state, traditionally—rejected the politics of the far left represented by McGovern and Sen. Edmund Muskie.

If McGovern is elated, Muskie must be utterly dejected after Wisconsin. It would be difficult to recall a more complete political collapse in so brief a time as that suffered by the Maine senator.

Since 1968, when he impressed observers as the party's vice presidential candidate, and especially since 1970, when his election eve pitch for Democratic congressional conidates won smash political reviews, Muskie had been conceded to be the leader among Democratic hopefuls.

Now, after only four primaries, he has sunk virtually out of sight, politically. His nine per cent and ten per cent showings in Florida and Wisconsin, respectively, the only states where he has been thrown against all of the other candidates, have not only shattered his image as a winner, and perhaps his confidence, but almost certainly have dried up some sources of financing for his campaign.

The "why" of Muskie's decline is not easy to pinpoint. It may be that his high standing was artificial from the start—that his lead in the polls only reflected the absence of any other really strong candidate and the fact that most rank and file Democrats had only vague impressions of him as a strong, silent, middle-of-the-party type who could help put the pieces back together.

Once the campaigning started in earnest and "the real Muskie" began to emerge—not a centrist, but a man who had positioned himself solidly on the left wing; not a strong, dependable sort, but a testy, short-tempered one—the voters began thinking seriously about alternatives.

Sen. Muskie may yet make a comeback. He apparently intends to try, judging from his comment Tuesday night that he doesn't "know the meaning of the word quit" (despite the efforts of the voters of Florida and Wisconsin to explain it to him). But that would take a reversal almost as dramatic as his sudden fall.

So, who then?

McGovern? George McGovern is not going to be the Democratic nominee, unless the Democratic convention succumbs to a mass political death wish.

George Wallace? Wallace isn't going to be the nominee, either.

What both of them *are* going to do is force the party to look for a candidate who isn't as closely identified with either ideological extreme as McGovern or Wallace, one who—theoretically, at least—could get the support of all but the diehards on either side.

And who has been positioning himself most neatly in that vicinity?

That's what Hubert Humphrey was smiling about Tuesday night, despite his third-place finish in Wisconsin.

The Dallas Times Herald
Dallas, Tex., April 6, 1972

APART FROM their Christian names, George S. McGovern and George C. Wallace have little in common.

Yet as they battle for the Democratic presidential nomination, both have the very same thing going for them—popular discontent.

It was discontent — with busing, with welfare, with crime and taxes—that fueled Wallace's remarkable victory in the Florida presidential primary.

It was discontent—with high taxes and old faces—that put McGovern over in last Tuesday's Wisconsin primary, with 30 per cent of the vote. And it was discontent, one scarcely need add, which put Wallace close on his heels with 22 per cent, against Hubert Humphrey's 21 per cent, Edmund Muskie's 10 per cent, and Scoop Jackson's eight per cent.

Wisconsin was 1972's fourth presidential primary. It permits more specific conclusions than could previously be drawn. And foremost among those conclusions is that of all the Democratic contenders, Wallace and McGovern are talking most directly to the voting American.

Muskie? Well, what is Muskie really in favor of, anyway? Or, for the matter of that, what is he against?

As for Humphrey, he appears to coast on the affection in which even many conservatives hold him.

Of the two leaders in Wisconsin, George Wallace may well prove the more formidable. For the discontent that he channels so ably appears to proceed from deeper, more far-flung wellsprings than in McGovern's case.

High taxes-McGovern, too, is against. But Wallace was talking about high taxes while McGovern was still hung up on the war issue. And how theatrically Wallace talks about them! With pursed lips, insolent eyebrows and pugnacious fist, he heaps more scorn upon the "foundations" and the "big money" men than McGovern can conceive. Given one more week to campaign in Wisconsin, Wallace would surely have cut even deeper into the victory margin that McGovern's extensive campaigning and student backing afforded him.

Assuredly, much of the discontent on which McGovern feasted in Wisconsin won't be spread before him in other states. His attacks on defense spending, for example, would go down poorly in Texas. He's aggressively in favor of busing. While he wants to take from the Pentagon, he wants to give generously to welfare clients.

Not so with Wallace, who's already staked out a huge anti-busing constituency, and who, thanks to Wisconsin, has proved himself more than just a regional, one-issue candidate. McGovern has yet to prove as much.

But what this year's key primaries — Florida and Wisconsin — have already proved is that there's a vast protest vote out there. He who asks shall receive, and he who seeks shall find.

The Arizona Republic
Phoenix, Ariz., April 6, 1972

The first reading of the Wisconsin election results made George McGovern's supporters jump with joy. It's true that Senator McGovern's solid victory gives him at least a temporary lead in the ebb and flow of Democratic presidential nomination prospects.

But we think the most significant result of the Wisconsin primary was the establishment of George Wallace as a serious candidate for the Democratic nomination. It's quite likely, of course, that part of the conservative Southerner's ability to grab second place in a Northern liberal state was due to the crossover of Republican voters who were able to vote in the Democratic primary.

But it's even more true that Wallace's ability to win in Florida and in Wisconsin gives him a stature in the Democratic Party that was completely lacking back in the days when he didn't know whether he would run as a Democrat or an Independent.

Whether the Wallace vote came from Democrats or Republicans, the Wisconsin voters were obviously sending out a clear warning to both parties not to take the protest vote lightly.

Mayor John Lindsay has withdrawn from the race, in the face of the poor showing (7 per cent of the vote) he made in Wisconsin. That should move the Democrats a little closer to the unity and stability they need if they are going to successfully challenge President Nixon.

Lindsay's withdrawal, however, will make Arizona Democrats question the soundness of this state's fancy new way of electing convention delegates. As you may recall, six of Arizona's 25 votes are pledged to Lindsay on the first ballot at the Democratic national convention. At the time the sweepstakes were being held, we said no one in his right mind would think that the New York mayor reflected the thinking of anything like 20 per cent of Arizona Democrats. Now that he's out of the race, the pledging of delegates so early in the year seems even less wise than it did back in February.

There are some important primaries—Pennsylvania, Indiana, California—in the offing, and each Democratic candidate is pledged to take part in some or all of them. But the folly of allowing each state to choose a different primary date is becoming more evident with each election.

THE RICHMOND NEWS LEADER
Richmond, Va., April 6, 1972

Primary votes often are protest votes, and the results of yesterday's Wisconsin primary indicate that the voters there are not altogether enthusiastic about the way things are going with the national Democratic Party. Wisconsin is a vastly peculiar State—from the roadside bars in the cow counties to the beerhalls of Milwaukee and Racine, from the lumbermen of the north woods to the football fanatics of Green Bay. It is a State with a profoundly demagogic political heritage of LaFollette, McCarthy, and Proxmire. It is a State that has interred many national politicians: John Kennedy crushed Hubert Humphrey in the 1960 primary, and in 1968 Eugene McCarthy swept the primary to complete the destruction of Lyndon Johnson. Now George McGovern and George Wallace have combined to put Edmund Muskie in the ground.

Big Ed ought to step down. In none of the four primaries held thus far has he done particularly well. He has finished fourth in Florida and Wisconsin—averaging 9.5 per cent of the vote in those States. In both States, he ran only two percentage points better than that would-be Democratic golden boy, John Lindsay, who now has retired from the field. The Senator from Maine has come across as self-righteous, querulous, peevish. The quondam front-runner, he initially sought to be gingerly centrist. There turned out to be no vigor in him but the distemper of his adjectives. In a vain attempt to gain support, he progressively has moved to the far side of the Democratic left. Surely the ghost of Abraham Lincoln is telling him: "Get out. Get out." But Muskie plods on.

George McGovern stands today as a beaming example of where plodding can get you. The Senator from South Dakota declared himself available for the Democratic nomination in Sioux Falls on January 18, 1971. (The only successful presidential candidate to announce farther in advance of the election was Andrew Jackson.) Senator McGovern has been trudging along ever since, yet something persistent says that he simply does not have the goods to become the Democratic nominee. One pictures him toeing the ground and saying, "Aw shucks." But with the burial of Big Ed in the Wisconsin graveyard, George McGovern today is the essential Democratic advocate of the new politics—aside from Edward Kennedy.

Of course, the other major story out of Wisconsin is the performance of George Wallace. In the 1968 general election, the suzerain of Alabama carried just 8 per cent of the vote; yesterday he walked away with 22 per cent, enough for second place. Once again this black-browed outlander has exploded out of the South to bedevil the nation's political establishment. Once again, a large segment of the electorate has rallied around his flag of neo-populism, anti-elitism, and revival-tent corn. Yet far be it for any politician—for anyone at all—henceforward to label Mr. Wallace as merely a red-neck rabble-rouser. He has gone into the North and, once again, muddled the mandate. He is going to make things lively for the national Democrats in Miami Beach.

And in the results of the Wisconsin primary, it is possible to see what the story of Miami Beach will be. On one side will be Hubert Humphrey and his warmed-over New Deal rhetoric, representing the party regulars and traditionalists. On the other side will be George McGovern and Edward Kennedy with their virulent leftism, representing the Democratic insurgents and self-styled moralists. The result of the consequent encounter probably will determine the course of Democratic politics for the next generation. The possible outcome at the convention? A Humphrey-Kennedy ticket, which would go down to defeat in November. Then Edward Kennedy, the leader of the Democratic radicals, would emerge as the titular head of the Democratic party—as Edmund Muskie did four years ago. But there would be a difference: Senator Kennedy would go forward, unhindered by other Democrats, to 1976.

The Virginian-Pilot
Norfolk, Va., April 6, 1972

Senator Edmund S. Muskie's clobbering in Wisconsin is all the more brusing because he had more to gain than any other candidate in the Presidential primary there. Once conceded to be the Democratic front-runner, Mr. Muskie is turning into a fourth-runner: his finishing place in Florida and now Wisconsin. His New Hampshire and Illinois laurels are turning brown.

Suddenly Senator George McGovern has credentials. Although he announced for the '72 nomination before any other Democrat, he was taken seriously by few until he took Wisconsin. How much credibility he can add between now and the July convention is uncertain. His progressive approach seems to be better fitted to Wisconsin's political history than to the national mood. Maybe, though, Mr. McGovern is communicating broadly.

George C. Wallace ran just behind him. In a way, that figures. Governor Wallace's showing hardly was more spectacular than his 1964 Wisconsin stunt, which was to collar a third of the Democratic ballots in a race with President Johnson's stand-in. Hubert Humphrey was so concerned about a Republican cross-over vote for Mr. Wallace on Tuesday that he urged Republicans to stay in their fold and support President Nixon. And while Mr. McGovern usually is classified as a liberal and Mr. Wallace as a conservative, in populism they tend to overlap. Each benefited from voter disgust with the drift of national government; indeed, the size of the protest vote may be the most significant lesson of the Wisconsin story.

Poor Mr. Humphrey! The Senator from Minnesota expected to receive better than a yellow ribbon from his Wisconsin neighbors. If he finds some satisfaction in Mr. Muskie's further fall, and remains convinced that the two candidates who outran him cannot be nominated, he nevertheless must be pained by his failure to move ahead.

As predicted, Wisconsin served to trim the Democratic field. Mayor John Lindsay surveyed his 7 per cent vote and went home to New York. Senator Henry M. Jackson was all but knocked out, too, having been out-Wallaced, as he was in Florida, by the genuine article from Alabama.

Well, the last always have a problem. But what is binding the first to the Biblical prophecy? The image that Senator Muskie offered of himself—the common-sense man from Maine, the Lincolnesque figure, the keeper of the old virtues, the magnet of agreement—has not been convincing in the candidate who shows strain, louses up his schedule, and repeats cliches. Perhaps it all goes back to Manchester; maybe that day he stood in a truck and wept he should, in the immortal words of Joe Jacobs, have stood in bed.

THE WALL STREET JOURNAL.

New York, N.Y., April 6, 1972

Richard Nixon continued his string of startling victories in the Democratic presidential primaries, as Wisconsin deepened rather than dispelled the confusion in Democratic ranks. Indeed, Senator George McGovern's plurality there probably means we should start to take seriously a possibility that sets Republican lips smacking.

The Wisconsin results brought only discouragement to the Democrats trying to establish themselves as a cut above the pack. Senator Hubert Humphrey finished third, behind Senator McGovern and Governor George Wallace. Senator Edmund Muskie was a distant fourth. After finishing sixth, Mayor John Lindsay sensibly withdrew from further contention. So Senator McGovern has established himself not only as a serious possibility but as the clear candidate of the left.

Given the erratic nature of the primary outcomes so far, it's obviously a mistake to read too much into any one of them. But Senator McGovern will now have the left of the Democratic Party to himself while other candidates carve up the center and right. This means the Senator could win in states where he could not beat any one of the other candidates in a two-man race.

It also remains to be seen who benefits from the "reform" of the delegate-selection process. One thesis is that the more open process will benefit the candidates with the best grass-roots organizations, probably meaning those with hefty financing and labor-union support. The alternate thesis is that the "more democratic" process will benefit the ideologically oriented sectors of the party at the expense of the victory-oriented ones, resulting in a huge over-representation of the left.

Thus the actual nomination of Senator McGovern, though we would hardly regard it as likely at this point, can no longer be dismissed as inconceivable. It's worth a moment to contemplate what this will mean in the general election.

In the wake of Wisconsin there will be talk about Senator McGovern running as an "anti-establishment" candidate, appealing to the "alienated" voters who picked either the Senator or Governor Wallace. This is not a wild description of what can happen in primaries; in retrospect, support from Wallace voters was the key to Eugene McCarthy's mysterious early success in 1968. But no such coalition of opposites is likely to hold together very long.

What a McGovern nomination would mean, rather, is something much closer to Richard Nixon versus the left-most third of the Democratic Party. The Republicans know something about the result of this type of politics from their experience with Barry Goldwater, and nothing could delight them more than for the Democrats to go marching off to the beat of an ideological drum.

We hasten to add that it would be an over-interpretation of the Wisconsin results to regard this as more than an outside possibility at this point. We think it more likely that the centrist candidates will start to recoup in the large-state primaries that now impend.

Even so, Wisconsin was nothing if not a victory for Senator McGovern. And what the Senator personifies is the chance that the Democrats will do in 1972 what the Republicans did in 1964.

EVENING HERALD

Rock Hill, S.C., April 8, 1972

Because of Sen. George McGovern's impressive showing in the Wisconsin presidential primary, the possibility of his capturing the Democratic nomination is being discussed seriously in some quarters for the first time.

The Wall Street Journal, which is not favorably disposed toward McGovern, noted in a recent editorial that McGovern's nomination is "a possibility that sets Republican lips smacking."

The newspaper figured that if McGovern should get the nomination it might be a rerun of the 1964 election — only in reverse.

According to this line of reasoning, McGovern would be the Barry Goldwater of the Democrats, "marching off to the beat of an ideological drum." The only support McGovern could count on in a race against Nixon, said the Journal, would be from the "left-most third of the Democratic Party."

Perhaps the financial publication is correct. But we see another possibility.

For one thing, voters this year might be less likely to believe charges of "extremism" that were so successfully used against Goldwater in 1964, and certainly would be employed against McGovern. Many people will remember that Lyndon Johnson, to the dismay of liberals, disappointed as a "peace president" and actually followed some of the Vietnam policies advocated by Goldwater.

Moreover, times have changed. There is widespead discontent in the country today, and it's not limited to students and left-wing intellectuals. People are deeply unhappy about the war, about unemployment, about rising prices, and about a host of other things that affect their daily lives.

It's the kind of political and social climate which causes voters to stray from the center, and makes them susceptible to answers offered by the left and right. Therefore McGovern's simple solution to the American involvement in Indochina — "let's get out now" — has great potential appeal to the mass of people.

Furthermore, McGovern is a more sophisticated campaigner than Goldwater was. Also, unlike the Arizona senator, he possesses intellectual depth. Goldwater, despite his admirable honesty and candor, frequently seemed fairly naive, both in the way he conducted his presidential campaign and through the solutions he suggested to the nation's problems.

Considering these factors, McGovern might appeal to a broader segment of the population than Goldwater did eight years ago.

Whether our theory is better than the Wall Street Journal's theory remains to be seen. We agree with the Journal, though, that McGovern's nomination is no more than an outside possibility at this point.

Nevertheless, it's fun to speculate.

NIXON AND JACKSON CRITICIZED FOR NOT LISTING CONTRIBUTORS

Before the Federal Election Campaign Act of 1971 came into effect on April 7 [See pp. 168–173], the willingness of the presidential candidates to comply with the spirit of the provision in the law requiring disclosure of all campaign contributions over $100 became a matter of controversy when John W. Gardner, chairman of Common Cause, a citizens' lobby, urged President Nixon March 30 to disclose the sources of his campaign funds received before April 7.

A letter, published in part by the *New York Times*, allegedly from one of Nixon's campaign aides to businessmen requesting contributions had stated: "We have a deadline of April 7th to meet for this important gift phase of the drive, because that is the effective date of the new Federal campaign law which will require reporting and public disclosure of all subsequent campaign contributions in excess of $100, which we all naturally want to avoid...." The *Times* also reported that Maurice H. Stans, a principal Nixon fund raiser and former secretary of commerce, had privately urged wealthy businessmen to make contributions before the disclosure law took effect.

Among the Democratic candidates, Sen. George McGovern, Sen. Edmund Muskie, Sen. Hubert Humphrey, and Gov. George Wallace had made public lists of campaign contributions received before April 7.

The *Times* reported April 2 that a Boeing Co. official had worked for Sen. Henry Jackson, the only major Democratic candidate who had not disclosed the sources of his campaign funds, in the Wisconsin primary using company funds to pay for his expenses and newspaper advertising space for Jackson. Boeing said the official was on a mixed business-political trip and had used company expense funds only as a "matter of convenience" on a temporary basis. Jackson said the effort was unauthorized and "an indiscretion" but not illegal as long as the official reimbursed the company.

THE ATLANTA CONSTITUTION
Atlanta, Ga., April 3, 1972

Ever so slowly the nation is getting a better picture of political campaign contributions. Even Gov. George Wallace has weighed in with a list of 30,000 campaign donors. He joins Sens. George McGovern, Hubert Humphrey and Edmund Muskie in listing the sources of their funds.

But President Richard Nixon remains a holdout. His fund-raisers have been pointing out that beginning April 7 it will be necessary under a new federal law to disclose the lists. Some of the letter-writers have said "we will want to avoid" giving out the lists, and suggests contributions before that date.

Sham. That's the only word for it. Nixon owes it to the United States and to the voters to disclose how much campaign money was raised prior to the effective date of the new law. He needs to make clear where the money has come from, and the country needs to know what contractors (if any) have made big contributions.

Another man who needs to deal with campaign issues is Sen. Henry Jackson of Washington. He is the last remaining serious Democratic candidate who has not disclosed how he affords the jet airplanes and huge staffs which are the essential accoutrements of presidential campaigns.

The country is not very tolerant in 1972 of candidates who won't level about the sources of their funds. It feels it has a right to know who is putting big money into a political campaign. And it is absolutely right in insisting that the political process can be skewed by an abnormally large contribution.

Nixon and Jackson should tell us quite simply where they are getting campaign funds. That would end the controversy. Or do they fear that some of the names on the list would start an even bigger controversy?

The Philadelphia Inquirer
Philadelphia, Pa., April 2, 1972

For those who believe, as we do, that economic influences lie at the very foundations of the democratic process, 1972 so far has been a year for restrained jubilation. The main reason for exuberance has been, of course, passage of the federal campaign spending law, which goes into effect April 7 — the end of this week.

It is thus with disappointment that we survey the recent frantic efforts to circumvent both the letter and the intent of election financing reform — nationally and in Pennsylvania.

The quest for big contributors to President Nixon's re-election campaign is capitalizing on the deadline pressure.

Most of the arguments used by Maurice H. Stans, the chief Nixon fund-raiser, are unbreachably private. But a recent letter to businessmen from Thomas P. Pike, a faithful helper, may be symptomatic. The letter, published in part by the New York Times, said:

"We have a deadline of April 7th to meet for this important gift phase of the drive, because that is the effective date of the new Federal campaign law which will require reporting and public disclosure of all subsequent campaign contributions in excess of $100, which we all naturally want to avoid . . . You may rest assured that he (Mr. Nixon) will be personally apprised of your support."

And in Pennsylvania, funds are being raised across the state by something called "Campaign '72 Committee," an effort led by Gov. Shapp. We don't like the way it is being done either, though the new law will have little to say about it.

The fund, so far, is not designated as supporting any specific candidate for national office. Thus even after April 7 it is not required under federal law to report or reveal the source of its money. If and when any of the funds are spent on a national candidate's behalf, presumably, only the expenditures will be recorded publicly.

This is typical of the still-gaping loopholes in the campaign spending reform machinery. No prudent observer expected all national candidates to refrain from rushing to get in under the deadline, although most of the Democratic Presidential candidates have — commendably — volunteered disclosure. Such voluntary candor is a more honorable response to the loopholes, we believe, than imaginative evasion. But clearly Congress should tighten the new law next year.

And Gov. Shapp, who professes utter independence from vested economic interests, would do well to make state campaign spending reform — on the federal lines, but even tighter — a major legislative effort of his administration.

The Courier-Journal

Louisville, Ky., April 4, 1972

With the help—not wholly voluntary—of the mass media, President Nixon has created a curious, and unprecedented one-way communication with the American people. He can reach us but we can't reach him. We can see him but he can't hear us. He is always with us but there is no dialogue. 'Always visible but never reachable' has become his trademark and his strategy.

—Common Cause chairman John Gardner

THERE ARE so many subjects to which Mr. Gardner's words could apply that it may be a slight shock to realize that his argument referred to the campaign spending act that goes into effect this Friday. Partly because of pressure constantly exerted by his public-interest lobbying group, Common Cause, and partly because of the leadership of Senator McGovern, the precedent of *voluntary* disclosure of the sources of political finances has been well advanced in 1972, but with no help from the President.

Before the effective date of the new Federal Election Campaign Act, the public received voluntary disclosures of political gifts from Senator McGovern, Representative McCloskey (now out of the race), Mayor Lindsay, and Senators Humphrey and Muskie—all within a single month. Governor Wallace also has committed himself to disclosure.

Case of beating the deadline

Yet there are silent candidates. When the President signed the new elections act, he forecast: "The legislation will guard against campaign abuses and will work to build confidence in the integrity of the electoral process." Rather than build that sort of confidence, Mr. Nixon has been stubbornly silent up to now about his presidential re-election war chest.

Others in the Silent Service have been Senator Jackson and Representative Mills on the Democratic side, and Representative Ashbrook, on the Republican. But wait! Senator Jackson has, indirectly and defensively, made one disclosure—$299 in Boeing Company traveler's checks that a young employe of the defense contractor has laid out for ads in Wisconsin newspapers. And, perhaps as a prize for his singular status as the Senator's only recognized donor, the Boeing aide will get his company's money back.

Can anyone survive?

The Senator from Washington — often dubbed the Senator from Boeing—seems not to realize the conclusion people will draw from this episode: If one disclosure has revealed a seeming conflict of interest, what would full disclosure uncover?

Moreover, announcements made later, under the provisions of the new law, just may not help any of these reluctant dragons. Most people will just assume, and rightfully, that vast amounts of money had been collected and disbursed before the deadline.

It seems, and this is one of the surprising political developments of 1972, that candidates who won't come clean are not likely to survive the competition this year—except the President, that is. And, in a year in which disclosure is a genuine issue for the first time, how can he be sure *he* will survive?

PORTLAND EVENING EXPRESS
Portland, Me., April 4, 1972

Americans sometimes like to think of themselves as landlords owning the residence at 1600 Pennsylvania Ave., Washington, D.C.

They rent it to certain very select families on a four-year lease, renewable once.

But our politics has become such that a disenchanted public often suspects that it no longer owns the property at all, that it has been taken over by a few "fat cats" who can afford to operate it and decide for themselves who will occupy it.

Life magazine has charged that the present occupant of The House has done a considerable favor for affluent backers. The ITT mess involves more of the same sort of alleged "buying and trading."

But it is no longer a matter only of what may actually happen in the meeting of obligations by politicians indebted to big money supporters. The sense of moral decline lingers because the implication of obligation is unmistakable.

People who contribute $100,000 to Richard Nixon's campaign, $50,000 to Senator Muskie's bid, $75,000 to Hubert Humphrey or John Lindsay, may never ask anything at all in return. But the country knows that they're in a position to ask favors and that the recipient of campaign gifts cannot close his ears to such pleas.

The new law on reporting donations, which becomes effective this week, may be a step in the right direction. But it would seem that if the people want to retain their title to the White House they will have to finance the campaigns of all those who strive to occupy it.

THE NASHVILLE TENNESSEAN
Nashville, Tenn., April 2, 1972

WHEN HE signed the new campaign financing law last month, President Nixon praised the law and said that providing the facts about campaign financing would "guard against campaign abuses and work to build public confidence in the integrity of the electoral process." Unhappily, Mr. Nixon's words and his deeds do not square.

* * *

According to reports in the New York Times, Mr. Maurice H. Stans, the former Secretary of Commerce and now Mr. Nixon's chief political fund raiser, has been privately calling on big businessmen to make anonymous donations to the Nixon campaign before April 7, when the campaign law goes into effect. After that time, every political committee will be required to make public each donor of more than $100, along with his occupation and address.

Mr. Stans has been a very busy man, hopping around the country for secret meetings with wealthy Republicans, all of whom are being told the same story: that they should make big donations now and that nobody will ever know except the Nixon administration. Then, for the public record, they can make small donations later to the GOP.

Out on the West Coast, one of Mr. Nixon's fund raisers sent out a rather amazing letter calling for the same thing and warning of public disclosure later "which we all naturally want to avoid."

Mr. Nixon can, of course, sit back and pretend that he knows nothing of these things and, if pressed, explain it all away by saying that his supporters may have gotten overzealous. But that is hardly going to be credible, not when the man closest to him is Mr. John Mitchell, his campaign chairman, and one of the closest is Mr. Stans, who is the money raiser and the man who is on intimate terms with the biggest fat cats of the Republican party.

Campaign funding is a necessary business. It takes lots of money to run even in primary campaigns and a great deal more to run an election campaign. The present methods of funding campaigns in this country are not the most rational or best that could be devised, but at least the focusing of public attention on the source of campaign funds is a major step forward.

As of this writing, all but one of the major Democratic contenders have made public their lists of contributors, even before the April 7 deadline. Sen. Henry Jackson is the lone holdout so far.

The Democrats who have divulged their sources of funds might have taken the cynical course that Mr. Nixon has taken and waited until after the deadline to put their contributors on record. Elsewhere in this section, Reporter Jim Squires has dealt with the subject of campaign financing and some of the big contributors.

* * *

For all of the rationalizations and excuses from the Nixon administration on why it has decided not to make public its full list of contributors up until now, the fact remains that Mr. Nixon is not only the leader of his party but the President of this country, and as such should set the example of probity and make public his own sources of funds received before April 7. That would help more than most to bolster public confidence in the integrity of the electoral process.

50—Campaign Contributions

The Providence Journal
Providence, R.I., April 11, 1972

A new law that went into effect April 7 requires political candidates to disclose every political contribution of $100 or more made in their behalf.

When he signed the new law last February, President Nixon declared: "By giving the American public full access to the facts of political financing, this legislation will guard against campaign abuses and will work to build public confidence in the integrity of the electoral process."

The new law stands as a long-needed reform, and Mr. Nixon's words aptly summarize its intent and promise.

But a fly remains in the ointment. With the April 7 deadline approaching, some politicians started beating the bushes in a furious burst of activity to collect as much as they could on the quiet *before* the full disclosure rule went into effect. Among these busy collectors was Maurice Stans, former commerce secretary in the Nixon Cabinet and now the chief fund-raiser for the Nixon campaign. It is understood that quite a few wealthy patrons were persuaded to make generous contributions before April 7 when it was explained to them that these gifts could be kept secret, but that if they waited until after the deadline, similar gifts would become part of the public record.

Most of the major Democratic presidential candidates have observed the spirit as well as the wording of the new law. They have ignored the April 7 deadline and voluntarily disclosed all contributions received before that date.

But President Nixon has not chosen this course. The White House has studiously refrained from disclosing whatever contributions may have been made to the Nixon campaign prior to April 7.

In an address the other day, John W. Gardner, chairman of Common Cause, called attention to this matter. He thought it odd that Mr. Nixon was keeping his contribution list secret, while so many Democratic contenders were disclosing theirs.

"When will we hear from the President of the United States?" Mr. Gardner asked. "Should not he, above all others, provide moral leadership in this matter? Isn't this, above all else, one thing he should make perfectly clear?"

Those are pertinent questions. They are especially pertinent when directed to a President who, as recently as February, was applauding full disclosure as a means to give the American public "full access to the facts" and as a step toward building "public confidence in the integrity of the electoral process."

Buffalo Evening News
Buffalo, N.Y., April 7, 1972

The new law governing the financing of campaigns for national elective office, which takes effect today, should throw refreshing public light on this twilight zone of U. S. politics and help restrain the soaring cost of seeking office.

The reforms aren't as comprehensive as we would have liked, especially the omission of an independent national election commission to oversee the reporting of campaign contributions. But they're a lot stronger than what has existed. They're stronger, too, apparently, than many congressmen who voted for them a few months ago would now prefer.

The law limits how much a candidate and his family can contribute to his own campaign, a provision aimed at the very rich. It limits to 10-cents-per-voter how much a candidate may spend on political advertising, a major source of steeply rising costs. But probably most important, it requires periodic public disclosure of how campaign money is spent and where it comes from, even down to names and addresses of contributors of $10 or more.

It is this latter provision that has prompted some congressmen, such as Rep. George Danielson (D., Calif.) who voted for the bill in January, to complain now that it "is a clear case of over-legislating."

"These people don't want their names published—they don't want their employer to know. Sometimes they don't want their wives to know," he says. "I'm afraid if I make available the names and addresses of my contributors, my opponents and every mail-order house will start asking them for money. I don't want to dry up these small contributions—they're what I depend on."

Such second-thought reservations, not to mention the way administration fund-raisers and perhaps some Democrats, too, have scurried around trying to bring in big contributions before the tightened reporting provisions take effect, suggest that this reform may have real bite to it. They also suggest that the essential strength of this law from the public's point of view lies less in its ceilings on spending, which in some respects are circumscribed and porous, than in its public disclosure requirements and their threat of embarrassment.

What the public really should insist on, as this new law becomes effective, is that those running for Congress and the presidency conform in good faith to its enlightened spirit as well as its stricter letter. And before Congress agrees to any changes, as some House members particularly are already proposing, this law deserves a fair trial in its present form in the 1972 campaign.

Albuquerque Journal
Albuquerque, N.M., April 7, 1972

A new national law designed to close loopholes in present statutory restrictions on campaign spending will go into effect today — bearing some loopholes of its own.

The largest of these may be its effective date — meaning Congress should have enacted the law much sooner than it did.

The act doesn't cover campaign contributions made prior to April 7. The obvious result: A huge flow of money already has gone to candidates and their committees enabling donors to preserve their anonymity. Such contributions can be made to any presidential candidate through dozens of dummy Washington committees which — through a loophole in the expiring Corrupt Practices Act — do not have to file public accountings.

John Gardner, chairman of Common Cause which plans to monitor compliance with the new law, said there was evidence that before the law became effective "the President . . . collected the biggest war chest of political contributions in the history of the country."

Aides have said President Nixon plans to comply fully with the law but would make no disclosures of pre-April 7 contributions.

Gardner cited another loophole. The law requires candidates for the U.S. Senate to file reports with the secretary of the Senate; congressmen with the clerk of the House, and presidential candidates with the General Accounting Ofice, an arm of Congress. These three offices are charged with investigating complaints and then referring cases they believe to be valid to the Justice Dept.

Gardner aptly comments: "The built-in conflict of interest in having Congress monitor its own activities is clear. So is the fundamental inconsistency of assigning an employe to investigate and supervise his employers."

We can take some solace in the fact campaign spending this year may help boost the economy. But Congress manifestly will have to go back to the drawing board.

The Sun
Baltimore, Md., April 4, 1972

"Dear Fellow American: Now that President Nixon has announced that he will be a candidate for re-election, we need your help. . . ." So begins a letter mass mailed not long ago from the Finance Committee for the Re-Election of the President. It is signed "Maurice Stans, Chairman." It asks for money, and at one point says in parentheses "If you can give $25.00, $50.00, $100.00 or more, this is the time to do it!" You bet it is! If you give now, before the new campaign reporting law goes into effect next month, no one need ever know.

Mr. Stans isn't leaving that point up for misinterpretation for the really big givers. He and his agents have been traveling around the country telling the kind of people who give by the thousands of dollars that they'd better give before the new law takes effect April 7. The point is, that then, later, if the government does something beneficial for the giver or his corporation, union or what have you, no one can link that favoritism to reciprocity. Yet that is exactly what the law—hailed by the President and others in his party—is supposed to do, to bathe the campaign contributor and recipient in sunlight, "the best disinfectant," as publicity in this area has often been called.

It used to be possible for candidates to say they couldn't disclose contributions because their opponents wouldn't. No more, after the new law goes into effect. And no more before then for President Nixon and Democratic Senator Henry Jackson. Every other bona-fide candidate for the Presidency, including Gov. George Wallace, has already disclosed funds received for the 1972 campaign—every phase of it—for the period before the new law required it. The President and the senator will have a lot of explaining to do if they do not join the others.

THE BLADE
Toledo, Ohio, April 6, 1972

EVEN before it becomes effective tomorrow, there are signs of efforts to weaken the new Federal Election Campaign Act which was designed to bring light into the hidden world of campaign financing. As a lobbyist for Common Cause, one of the act's supporters, expressed it: "Members have finally read the law and realized what they have gotten themselves into."

One provision requires that every contributor of more than $10 be listed by a candidate. Rep. George Danielson (D., Calif.) has promised to introduce an amendment to raise that to $100. "I can't see how a contribution of less than $100 is going to corrupt anybody," Mr. Danielson said. He described the frustration of many members over detailed reports required of small donors: "These people don't want their names published—they don't want their employers to know. Sometimes they don't want their wives to know. I'm afraid if I make public the list of my contributors, my opponents and every mail order house will start asking them for money. I don't want to dry up these small contributions—they're what I depend on."

Rep. Wayne Hays (D., Ohio) has a different approach. He would take responsibility for watch-dogging the reports away from the House clerk and give it to a House administration subcommittee, which could be a little like leaving the bull in charge of the china shop. "Self-protection lies in the protection of one's colleagues," is the way an objector to the Hays move phrased it.

On other fronts, the Conservative Party of New York has filed suit, contending that the law limits freedom of political activity, and there has been great activity by lawyers searching for loopholes. They have found some, chief of which is a provision that reports are not required from committees that take in less than $1,000. This has resulted in a ploy described as the "$999 Committees," limited only by the number of fancy names which their creators can think up for them.

What is most surprising is that the act passed both houses of Congress by wide margins to become effective in an election year. But since it is on the books, it should be given an opportunity to work. Everyone is aware of the abuses of past spending practices, and the need to somehow cut back on the astronomical costs of winning public office. If the act has a chance to correct these wrongs, it deserves a try.

ST. LOUIS POST-DISPATCH
St. Louis, Mo., April 10, 1972

The federal Election Campaign Act, now in effect, "will guard against campaign abuses and will work to build public confidence in the integrity of the electoral process," said President Nixon when he signed the bill on Feb. 7.

In the last two months, the chief Republican fund raiser, Maurice Stans, has been rushing from one city to another, including St. Louis, to urge well-heeled donors to give before the April 7 deadline. The Republican war chest now reportedly amounts to more than $10,000,000 and it is doubtful that much of it will be reported.

This gives the new law an inauspicious start. A law is as good as its enforcers want it to be. The enforcers in this case are the comptroller general for presidential candidates, and the clerk of the House and secretary of the Senate for congressional elections. These are the same functionaries, as a spokesman for Common Cause notes, who have done nothing but rubber-stamp the inadequate campaign reports filed under the old Corrupt Practices Act.

As a practical matter, the new law will probably not be effective this year, thanks to Mr. Stans and former Attorney General John Mitchell who have raised much of the money Richard Nixon needs for November. Although Democrats have also solicited funds, all but one of the presidential candidates have followed George McGovern's lead and disclosed the sources of their contributions. The exception is Senator Henry Jackson.

By contrast, Mr. Mitchell adamantly refused to release publicly the names of contributors to his candidate. "We will comply with the law when it becomes effective," he said. This sounds as though the game plan here is to adhere to minimum standards when public interest actually requires maximum levelling with the people who are tired of double talk, secret fund raising and shredding machines.

Detroit Free Press
Detroit, Mich., April 7, 1972

THE SENATOR from Boeing, Henry M. Jackson, wasted no time returning fire after he, or rather Boeing, was caught red-handed. The New York Times disclosed this week that a Boeing official had used travelers' checks issued to the company to purchase campaign advertising for Sen. Jackson.

The Federal Corrupt Practices Act prohibits corporations and their officials from making campaign contributions. In his defense, the senator said it would be a violation only if the official failed to reimburse the company. That defense, it seems to us, is pretty weak.

Last month, after Sen. George McGovern and others began revealing the names and amounts of campaign contributors, Sen. Jackson labeled the actions "gimmicks." And we suggested here that until Jackson came forward with his own list, "we would have to assume his backing comes from the aerospace industry."

We haven't seen anything since to change that assumption.

The Oregonian
Portland, Ore., April 4, 1972

Sen. Henry Jackson's duel in the frosty Wisconsin air with the New York Times over campaign efforts of a Boeing Co. official is the only spark that has jumped out of that state's presidential primary campaign that goes to the voters today.

That such a mini-controversy involving, according to Jackson, only $299.62 paid for political advertising with Boeing-issued traveler's checks, is a testimony to the boredom the primary has generated. But is is also evidence of a growing concern over who is paying the political bills in this country.

The Boeing Co. is a giant corporation with huge government contracts in the aero-space programs, but it also is a corporation with a reputation in its home state of being politically naive and of having an old-fashion idea that if it builds a good product it can ignore politics. The company has often ignored its own friends.

Rodney W. Scheyer, the 31-year-old accountant for Boeing and a former football player, tried to combine company business with a campaign effort to help Jackson. The senator said he was unaware of Scheyer's efforts but will cover the small expenditures out of his own campaign chest.

Payment of the Boeing expenditure, Jackson said, would prevent the company from being in violation of the federal Corrupt Practices Act that prohibits corporations and their officials from making campaign contributions. In the past, the laws have not kept candidates of both parties from getting major contributions from both corporations and labor unions. What has been harmful has been the inability of the voters to find out who is supporting whom.

Oregon's new election laws require a preliminary report not later than seven days before an election, but the loophole here is that a candidate does not have to report all of his contributions and the names of his donors until 30 days after the election. By that time the issue is usually moot.

Large corporations are prone to give employes with expertise in political campaigning leaves of absence, which is what young Scheyer should have obtained. Labor unions usually don't bother with such niceties. They have set up parallel organizations to do the political jobs.

Sen. Jackson raised the issue of "honorariums," a term lifted from the academic world that describes payments to politicians, often for speeches before an organization that has an interest in legislation or of a candidate's election. The senator suggested the New York Times, which worked so diligently to expose the Boeing employe, ought to look at the honorariums paid some of the other candidates by groups interested in legislation.

In Florida, there is good political mileage in running against the New York Times. But in Wisconsin, the heartland of progressive politics and government, the voters will not pay that much attention to such an issue. In the closing hours of a campaign, new controversies seldom have much impact on the voters. In well-publicized races they have already become strong leaners.

Campaign '72:
HUMPHREY TOPS PENNSYLVANIA VOTE; MASSACHUSETTS GOES TO McGOVERN

Sen. Hubert H. Humphrey (Minn.) won his first presidential primary with 35% of the vote in Pennsylvania April 25. Gov. George C. Wallace (Ala.) was second with 21% and Sen. George S. McGovern (S.D.) third with 20% of the votes. Sen. Edmund S. Muskie (Me.), who was the only active campaigner in the state besides Humphrey, finished in fourth place with 20% of the vote even though most of the state's Democratic leadership had supported him. In the separate balloting for delegates to the national convention, Humphrey won 57, McGovern 37, Muskie 29, and Wallace 2 committed delegates. No Republican presidential primary was held in Pennsylvania.

In the Massachusetts preference primary held the same day, Sen. McGovern, who had campaigned extensively in the state, won 52% of the vote in a field of seven candidates. By sweeping the state's 102 delegates to the national convention, McGovern took the lead in the national delegate count. Sen. Muskie, who had the endorsement of the state's Democratic leaders but who had run a limited campaign in the state, received 22% of the vote. Muskie's disappointing showing here and in Pennsylvania, combined with McGovern's triumph, led the former frontrunner to withdraw from further participation in the primaries April 27. [See pp. 532–536] Sen. Humphrey, who did not campaign in the state, finished third with 8% of the vote. Gov. Wallace was fourth with 7% of the vote.

In the Massachusetts Republican primary, President Nixon received 82% of the preferential vote against token opposition from Rep. Paul McCloskey (Calif.) and Rep. John Ashbrook (Ohio).

Pittsburgh Post-Gazette
Pittsburgh, Pa., April 27, 1972

TUESDAY'S PRIMARIES in Pennsylvania and Massachusetts boosted Hubert Humphrey's stock, pushed George McGovern ahead in the convention delegate race, showed awesome protest strength for George Wallace, winged the already crippled Edmund Muskie, and effectively snuffed out Henry Jackson's bid for the Democratic nomination for the Presidency.

News reports yesterday said Muskie was ready to drop out of the race.

Yet the eerie result was that these vital big-state primaries really settled so little. We must slog through more primaries before the trend is decisive, and the possibility grows that there will be a deadlock at the Miami Beach convention in July out of which a compromise candidate could emerge.

The reason even the Pennsylvania and Massachusetts primaries left so many issues up in the air was that the winners carry so many liabilities with them. (For an analysis of why see Tom Wicker's column on this page today.) Indeed, the only reason experts didn't cross off Mr. Muskie completely after so many disastrous primaries is because he is the only candidate more or less acceptable to the various segments of the party. But his succession of primary losses will make it harder and harder for him to get workers and money for the primaries ahead.

* * *

Pennsylvania Governor Shapp jumped in early for Mr. Muskie and got egg on his face Tuesday. Ohio's Governor Gilligan is in the same uncomfortable fix with the primary in his state next week. It's doubtful Mr. Muskie will pick up important new converts to join these abashed men.

The Humphrey showing was a clear demonstration of strength by organized labor, and a converse shellacking for the political organizations of Governor Shapp and of Peter Camiel in Philadelphia. Mr. Humphrey clearly still has voter appeal as shown by the crowds surging to shake his hand during his campaign walks on the sidewalks of Pittsburgh. The contrast with similar efforts by Mr. Muskie was painful.

To date Mr. Muskie's standing has been maintained by his lead in committed delegates to the national convention. But Tuesday's primaries cost him even that distinction as Mr. McGovern's big delegation win in Massachusetts (108) plus 37 in Pennsylvania puts the South Dakotan ahead 234½ delegates to Mr. Muskie's 128½.

Despite the Humphrey and McGovern gains in Pennsylvania, the big story was the whopping Wallace vote. True, the Alabama governor really was in a virtual three-way second place with Senators McGovern and Muskie, all badly trailing Senator Humphrey. But he got a much bigger vote than anticipated.

Why?

Clearly it was a protest vote, based to a great extent on race and on the "busing" issue which has poked the sore boil recently, especially in Allegheny County. But undoubtedly it went beyond that to a protest in general.

In Allegheny County, for instance, 65 of the 129 cities, boroughs and townships gave him the lead, and five more (including Pittsburgh) put him in second spot. Mr. Wallace led not only in the mill towns of Etna, McKeesport, Duquesne and Clairton, but also in such suburban areas as Penn Hills, Plum Borough, and O'Hara, and McCandless Townships. Mr. Humphrey took most of the rest, with Mr. McGovern winning in affluent suburbs where Republicans are in the majority and the relatively few Democrats are liberals. (Mr. Muskie won in just one area, Harrison Township.)

The protest vote is particularly interesting because the voter turnout Tuesday in Pennsylvania was normal. If people were so upset, why didn't more turn out? Was there uncertainty, or disgust with all the candidates? Is the bitter protest confined to blue-collar workers squeezed in the economy and worried about the gains of blacks; and to anti-Vietnam War groups? Or is this the tip of the iceberg of a deeper running protest?

* * *

Curiously, Mr. Muskie got a long start in the Democratic race because of his calm presentation on Election Eve 1970 in response to efforts by President Nixon and Vice President Agnew to whip up support through the "law and order" issue. Does the decline of Mr. Muskie mean that the public in 1972 doesn't want calm, but angry protest instead?

Here, indeed, is something for the Democrats to reckon with; and the Republicans, too, as the "ins" customarily get the blame for conditions which bug people. The 1972 election campaign could turn quite bitter and ugly.

WORCESTER TELEGRAM.
Worcester, Mass., April 19, 1972

The patterns shaped by the tea leaves Tuesday in Massachusetts and Pennsylvania look more and more like a High Noon confrontation in the midsummer heat of Miami.

The impressive primary victory here in the Bay State of Sen. George S. McGovern, which saw him take about half of the total popular vote in a crowded field, and all but a handful of delegates, coupled with the clear win in Pennsylvania by Sen. Hubert Humphrey, may be read as the strongest signal yet that the Democratic convention less than a dozen weeks hence is headed for deadlock.

The campaigns of the Massachusetts and Pennsylvania winners spell out the likelihood for stalemate.

McGovern's big support — and much of the energy for his carefully calculated campaign here — came from the younger, dissident, most liberal wing of his party. If any state primary were to be fertile territory for this kind of "new politics," McGovern's camp shrewdly perceived, it would be Massachusetts.

Humphrey's drive in Pennsylvania was "old politics" all the way. The former vice president surrounded himself with top labor figures and directed his campaign at President Nixon in an old-fashioned Democratic appeal to traditional party loyalties. As a result, he won only his first state primary in 12 years of campaigning for the presidency. Both Humphrey and McGovern seem to have a deep-down zest for campaigning.

That kind of fervor seems lacking in Sen. Edmund S. Muskie, who, if not undone by this week's voting, obviously has suffered a serious double setback. The Maine senator's only hope now seems to lie in staying close enough to keep afloat financially until the convention, then being the deadlock choice to heal the wounds from a McGovern-Humphrey brawl.

The ground lost by Muskie in the few weeks since the first primary in New Hampshire is readily apparent. He topped McGovern by nine percentage points in the Granite State and lost to him here by about 30.

The showdown between the two senators from the midwest appears certain to go right into the convention hall itself, assuming both continue to do well in the primaries ahead. Bitter floor fights over delegate seating and platform issues were in the cards between the new and old wing Democrats from the start. The McGovern and Humphrey wins Tuesday will only intensify that polarization between reform and regularist factions.

Many observers were predicting last year that the Democrats would need to latch on to a single candidate early in the year and ride with him hard to have any hope of winning back the White House. Muskie looked like the man to fill that role. Ironically, had he avoided the primary-by-primary route, he might have strengthened his chances of emerging in July as the compromise choice. But defenders of the primary system have long pointed out that the process has value in measuring a candidate's potentialities for the highest office by putting him to the test in the full glare of national attention.

Alabama Gov. George Wallace's fight with Humphrey for third place in Massachusetts and for a share of second place in Pennsylvania with McGovern and Muskie continues to point up an unarticulated restiveness in the electorate that first surfaced in Florida but seems to have roots outside the South.

What has not changed since the start of the series of primaries that began in the snows of New Hampshire is the obvious support enjoyed by President Nixon within his own party. He was the choice of eight out of ten Republican voters in Massachusetts, despite the opposition of a conservative congressman on one side and a liberal on the other. The latter, Rep. Paul McCloskey of California, had dropped out of the race after New Hampshire but appealed for votes in the Bay State as a protest against renewed air strikes in Vietnam.

And another thing that has not changed — has grown, in fact with each passing primary — is the lingering likelihood that most Democratic voters will have wound up putting crosses in the circle that translates "None of the above."

The Standard-Times
New Bedford, Mass., April 27, 1972

The Massachusetts presidential primary was an expression of popular wishful thinking and continuing distrust of the power factions of government, state or federal, known as "the establishment."

There was little to choose, as regards issues and personal charisma, between the two Democratic presidential candidates most concerned, Sen. George McGovern and Sen. Edmund Muskie.

But in a remarkable turnaround of preference since last February, the voters gave McGovern a triumph, and all the state's 102 delegate votes for the first ballot at the national convention, and rejected so thoroughly the candidacy of Muskie that he is now on the sidelines.

On the Republican side, President Nixon captured a comfortable 80 per cent of the vote. However, when an unknown like Congressman McCloskey, who already had withdrawn officially, gets 15 per cent or more, as he did, Mr. Nixon has had a rebuff.

Probably few, very few, of the voters involved in this drastic shift of sentiment — Muskie was favored 46 per cent to McGovern's 11 per cent in February polls, but lost the primary 22 per cent to 52 per cent — could separate the two men on matters of public concern, on their qualifications, on their persuasiveness or on personal integrity.

But McGovern had the smell of the sod, and Muskie, who should have, with his Polish farmer background, did not. McGovern put together an organization of new voters and independent mavericks like Congressman Drinan and economist John K. Galbraith. Muskie signed up the establishment, like Boston's Mayor White and Attorney General Quinn.

And McGovern campaigned for votes in the traditional door-to-door way, while Muskie, by his own declaration, looked for a showing in the delegate column, which is to say, that Mayor White et al were running, not Muskie.

This was not sound strategy in a state that demands even its Kennedys canvass the hustings at election time. That did not appear to escape McGovern's notice; at the windup he was touring the state with a new generation of the Kennedy family.

If a particular event signaled the upcoming downfall of Sen. Muskie, it would be his dismally inept maneuver in tearfully responding to a harsh presentation of Muskie and wife by New Hampshire publisher William Loeb. Massachusetts is tough, liberal and weathered in political warfare; this exhibition of oversensitivity left its mark.

The Pennsylvania primary also was an unhappy show for our Maine neighbor. He campaigned hard there, and McGovern did not. Yet the latter finished ahead of him. Second to Sen. Hubert Humphrey — front-runner all the way — George Wallace who hardly campaigned, remains an important factor.

A disturbing element in both primaries was evidence that the Democratic candidates are seeking support with oratory of the pie-in-the-sky tradition. Sens. Muskie and McGovern hammered at the renewed bombing in Vietnam, a legitimate issue, indeed. But both deplored high taxes and unemployment and lack of credibility in government.

Do they, or the electorate, actually believe anyone promising lower taxes can deliver same in these times; that employment can be increased while cutting back on space and military expenditures, huge providers of jobs; or that candor is possible in government when Muskie himself found that publicly expressed doubts about a black vice presidential nominee nearly ended his public life?

Primaries, they have been saying, don't mean much. That in Massachusetts rebutted this theory, we would say. It put McGovern out front in the race. It left the state's best-known Democrats, who jumped too soon, out of the convention delegate picture. It confirmed Massachusetts' reputation for being deeply antiwar. And it should remind the electorate that wishful thinking is all right at this stage; but something more practical must be demanded of actual nominees for the White House.

The Boston Globe

Boston, Mass., April 27, 1972

After George Wallace captured the Florida primary March 14, George McGovern was the one rival with the perceptivity, candor and courage to interpret the results as a protest against things as they are.

On Tuesday, Sen. McGovern proved that for those with the passion and dedication to get out and vote about it in this state, he was the candidate who most clearly expresses their dissatisfaction.

This is not to say that the Wallace vote in the tropics in mid-March and the McGovern vote in the north in a chill late-April of this perplexing primary year are the same thing. They are not, any more than Cape Ann is Cape Kennedy.

Indeed, citizens of this state might well scan and ponder the Pennsylvania results of Tuesday before basing any conclusions about the national temper on the Massachusetts results.

Pennsylvania said Hubert Humphrey and George Wallace just as loud as Massachusetts said McGovern.

It is no disservice to George McGovern and his stunning, pollster-confounding victory here to suggest that the Commonwealth of Pennsylvania is about twice as big as the Commonwealth of Massachusetts and is considerably more centrally located, geographically and otherwise.

Despite the remarkable McGovern showing in New Hampshire, many analysts and other political professionals refused to take the South Dakotan seriously. Newsweek magazine observed that McGovern was "cursed by a lingering suspicion that his votes are all concentrated on the campus."

Massachusetts is an odd place to prove the fallacy of that argument, and, yet, it would seem that in Boston and places like Andover, Stoneham and Winthrop, his landslide margins are inexplicable on such flimsy grounds.

Instead, let it be said that he was talking to people about things that they cared about in terms that they understood, and people believed he meant it. Simple. Fundamental. Thorough. Respectable.

"Charisma" is a word that has worn awfully thin recently. It refers more to a candidate's style than to the response that style evokes. Fred Harris, John Lindsay and Birch Bayh all probably had more "charisma" than good, grey George McGovern.

But perhaps people aren't looking this year for glamour, defined as an artificial attractiveness. It is more probably that Democrats and Independents who want a change in administration and policy are seeking instead the real thing. And good, grey George McGovern, in giving it to them, may have more "charisma" than any of his more glamorous competitors.

"They" say he may win Massachusetts but that he cannot be nominated and that he cannot, if nominated, be elected. "They" did not believe sixty days ago that he could win anything. "They" believed that Ed Muskie had it wrapped up.

All you can really be sure of at this point in this unpredictable presidential year is that "they" seldom know what they are talking about, even when they mean what they say.

George McGovern clearly convinced most of the Massachusetts voters that he does, indeed, mean what he says.

He also worked at politics so professionally that the "pros" were left at the post.

On the night of March 17, in the Garibaldi Club in North Plymouth, a mostly Italian neighborhood some 35 miles south of Boston, the "Democratic Valley Boys" picked a banjo concert in the interest of George McGovern. About 125 people showed and had a marvelous time.

According to Jody Deetz, an anthropologist's wife who ran the affair, the committee sent $250 to McGovern headquarters in Boston, which sent back enough to pay the headquarters' telephone bills. There were about 60 volunteers, none of whom expected to get a thing out of the effort except the satisfaction of victory and, optimistically, the election of their candidate.

They won.

At the time, the so-called "Establishment," the elected Democratic officeholders of the commonwealth, were virtually invisible, relying apparently on what they thought were organizations to deliver for Muskie. It was not to be.

The "Establishment" must be perceived to be a "paper tiger." The Emperor is displayed in his birthday suit. Jody Deetz is the new Establishment, and what she does works. Even if you loathe McGovern, you have to concede that the system is supposed to work that way.

More than two million Democrats and unenrolled voters were eligible to cast ballots on Tuesday. About one of four of them did so.

Whether an 80 percent sampling would have produced different results cannot be known. What can be known is that the political process was open as it has never been before. Given that openness, the people who cared about their candidate were able to win for him.

But Massachusetts, superficially dismissed by television commentators as the most "dovish" state, is a poor place to look for a national trend. What Sen. McGovern did here was to catapult himself from the category of a long-shot possibility to that of a major contender, a force to be reckoned with.

And that should mean a lot to his people in Indiana and Ohio next week and in the major primaries still to be decided.

The Philadelphia Inquirer

Philadelphia, Pa., April 27, 1972

Inevitably, of course, the Democrats will nominate a candidate for President when they meet in Miami Beach in July. But the difficulty of that undertaking — to say nothing of predicting its outcome — becomes increasingly apparent as the primary season progresses.

Back in the days before they started counting the votes, a favorite scenario was that Sen. Edmund Muskie would have the nomination all locked up by the time everybody got to the convention and the delegates would need to interrupt their good times there just long enough to make it formal and pick a running mate.

But now the Pennsylvania and Massachusetts primaries have added such new dimensions of disaster to the Muskie candidacy that his only hope seems to be that the new frontrunners would deadlock and the convention might turn to him as everybody's second choice. While anything is possible in politics, Sen. Muskie's spectacular failure thus far to attract votes hardly establishes him as a man the Democrats could enthusiastically send forth to challenge President Nixon.

As for the new frontrunners, Sen. Humphrey demonstrated here in Pennsylvania (in his first major primary victory in three Presidential bids, incidentally) that there is still life in this happy warrior and the labor organizations on which he depends so heavily.

But the bitter memories of 1968 linger on, and the residual disenchantment of the party's more liberal wing becomes more apparent as Mr. Humphrey's prospects brighten.

Meanwhile, the new darling of that element — Sen. George McGovern — continues to confound the pundits as voters respond to his outspoken views and his impressively effective volunteer organization. But the problem of his candidacy was illustrated in a bitter attack by Sen. Henry Jackson on the day Sen. McGovern moved into a substantial lead in the race for delegates.

Mr. McGovern, his Senate colleague charged, has become "the spokesman for some of the dangerous and destructive currents in American politics" and is giving "extremism of the left ... a respectability it ought not to have" in the Democratic Party. Can the party nominate a man who inspires that kind of division in the ranks?

And George Wallace? We agree with Mr. McGovern that the vote the Alabama governor received here in Pennsylvania, coming on top of impressive showings elsewhere, means that he has to be taken seriously as a significant factor and a candidate who is "touching the sources of anger and frustration in the country."

But we cannot take seriously the possibility that the Democratic Party would nominate George Wallace for President of the United States.

So that brings us once more to Sen. Edward Kennedy, who said again only Tuesday that he would not run even if drafted.

One consolation in all this is that at least the Democrats know where they will be meeting to choose their candidate. At the moment, that's one thing the Republicans can't say.

The Greenville News

Greenville, S.C., April 28, 1972

This week's primaries in Massachusetts and Pennsylvania failed to produce a clear-cut leader in the crowded race for the Democratic presidential nomination. They did, however, offer support, in varying degrees, to the candidacies of the major contenders — with the exception of Sen. Edmund S. Muskie who now has been virtually pushed completely out of the race.

The two primaries, added to Muskie's poor showing in earlier contests, were not so much resounding victories for the other candidates, as they were unquestionable defeats for the Maine senator. Sen. Muskie now has been beaten by Hubert Humphrey, George McGovern and George Wallace.

Sen. Muskie has failed to capture the imagination of Democratic voters anywhere on the political spectrum. His decision to pull out of the remaining primaries is an admission of this failure. His campaign which began with a loud bang has now fizzled into merely a position of availability in the event of a draw at the national convention.

Sen. Humphrey, on the other hand, gained a new boost by his win in Pennsylvania. This demonstration of his continued appeal to blacks and labor can be expected to add funds to his campaign chest, as well as to draw strong support from many segments of the party's leadership who recall that he came close to beating Richard Nixon in 1968.

The most surprising candidate to emerge from the primary competition is Sen. George McGovern, an avowed anti-war liberal. He has steadily gained momentum, climaxing in his big victory in Massachusetts. Along the way he has, to date, picked up more committed delegate votes to the Democratic National Convention than any other candidate.

McGovern's success reflects a number of factors, including general dissatisfaction with United States participation in Vietnam. His win in Massachusetts, where he received more than 50 per cent of the vote, can be attributed largely to the fact that he was running in Kennedy country with members of the Kennedy family and its organization taking active part in the campaign.

The machine he is building could, in fact, be shifted intact to Sen. Edward Kennedy if McGovern should switch his support to Kennedy to break a convention deadlock. The possibility of such a deadlock and a Kennedy candidacy grows with each state primary, despite Sen. Kennedy's firm statement that he will not accept a draft.

And, then, there is Alabama Gov. George Wallace doing what he loves to do best — upsetting the political apple cart. With only token appearances in Massachusetts and Pennsylvania, he made extremely strong showings. He ran a little better than Muskie and McGovern in Pennsylvania and about broke even with Humphrey in Massachusetts for third place.

This should make it clear to the Democrats — if they haven't gotten the message before — that Wallace is a force which must be reckoned with. If he continues to garner a respectable percentage of the votes in future primaries, he will go to Miami in July in a very strong bargaining position.

So, the primaries plod on, and the Democratic party seems further away than ever from selecting a presidential standard bearer. There is still a way to go, and time for one candidate to steamroll over the others. But, as of now, the race appears headed for an exciting photo finish at the national convention.

ST. LOUIS POST-DISPATCH

St. Louis, Mo., April 27, 1972

As he viewed the results of the Pennsylvania primary on Tuesday, Senator Hubert Humphrey remarked that the vote had confirmed him as the choice of the "vital, progressive center of the Democratic Party," by which he meant that he had displaced the erstwhile front-runner, Senator Muskie of Maine, who has now withdrawn from further participation in the primaries, in the minds of Democrats and independents aiming at a consensus powerful enough to capture the White House in November.

If this so, it represents an odd turn in the road Mr. Humphrey has traveled since he came to national attention as the ultra-liberal young upstart from Minnesota. He gave up his liberal credentials when, as Vice President, he became an enthusiastic advocate of President Johnson's misguided Vietnam War policies. In the current primary campaigns he has temporized on both foreign and domestic issues. If he has indeed become the choice of the center it is because Mr. Muskie faltered.

In 1968 and again in 1970 Mr. Muskie appeared to the nation as a decent, competent and solid man, deserving of confidence and respect. He is the same man today, but somewhere along the line he was apparently persuaded by manipulative advisers that he should present an image that did not always ring true. The voters became aware of confusion and misjudgments in his camp, and the 1968-1970 personality faded.

Senator Humphrey thinks he has moved into Senator Muskie's vacated slot in the national consciousness, leaving the far right to Gov. George Wallace of Alabama and the far left to Senator George McGovern of South Dakota. This is a bit too simplistic, we think. For example,

Mr. Humphrey has major support among old-line politicians and labor unions; organized labor put him over in Pennsylvania. But Mr. Wallace has backing among the hard-hats, and Senator McGovern has shown drawing power among workingmen.

An interesting element in the Democratic race just will not go away. On the very day that labor money and organizational muscle were carrying Mr. Humphrey to victory in the Keystone State Senator Kennedy of Massachusetts, a non-candidate, was addressing the Atlantic City convention of the United Auto Workers, whose leadership had endorsed Mr. Muskie. Mr. Kennedy was mobbed by enthusiastic delegates, who voted informally but nearly unanimously to support him if he should decide to run.

The possibility of a Kennedy draft is going to be hanging over the July convention unless some candidate sweeps into Miami Beach with enough obvious clout to be a potential winner. Had all gone as planned, that could have been Mr. Muskie, but it is doubtful now. It is hard to see Mr. Humphrey, a too-familiar face, in such a role, which leaves (if George Wallace is eliminated) Senator McGovern, whose triumph in Massachusetts and strong showing in Pennsylvania Tuesday added to his political stature.

It is beginning to appear that George McGovern may be the only Democratic candidate whose campaign has the chance of rolling to the convention with enough power to win quickly and shut off any incipient draft-Kennedy movement. If that occurs Mr. McGovern will have proved that his consistent moderate liberalism is the real Democratic center, and what most people want.

The New York Times
New York, N.Y., April 27, 1972

Although the Democratic party is a house of many mansions, it contains only two centers of power. The first consists of the trade unions who can furnish money and invaluable manpower in getting out the vote. The other comprises intellectuals and students on the nation's campuses and their middle-class liberal allies who have the personal commitment and the leisure time to devote to political canvassing.

Senator Edmund Muskie's basic problem as a Presidential candidate has been that he is not the candidate of either of these power centers. The unions are determined to achieve the renomination of Senator Hubert Humphrey. Their efforts finally paid off in the Pennsylvania primary.

The students, intellectuals and many—though not all—liberals have been equally committed to the candidacy of Senator George McGovern. For these activists, the Vietnam war is the overriding issue. Mr. McGovern since 1963 has been in the forefront of the fight against the war. As long as he had any chance of winning the nomination, they were deaf to the appeals of any latter-day convert to the antiwar opposition such as Mr. Muskie.

Caught between the pro-Humphrey unionists and the pro-McGovern liberals, Senator Muskie has seen these contending forces grind down his gallant effort to reunite the party and oppose President Nixon with a politics of hope and national reconciliation.

His political peers within the party recognized the logic of his candidacy. He gained endorsements from Senators, governors and other party leaders across almost the entire spectrum of the party. It was their perception of him as the candidate most likely to unite the party that made him appear to be the frontrunner. These endorsements lured Senator Muskie into a high-risk strategy of trying to create an unstoppable bandwagon. With the wisdom of hindsight, it is possible to see that a wiser course for Mr. Muskie would have been to enter only a few primaries and wait for his mutually antagonistic rivals to fight it out. He remains "everybody's second choice," but in primaries it is the partisans and not the peacemakers who prevail.

In adversity, Senator Muskie remains the sober, decent thoughtful public man he has always been. The odd dynamics of this year's primaries have brutally punished his political plans but—whether or not he announces his withdrawal from further primaries today—they have not destroyed his credibility as a potential President.

Senator George McGovern's victory in the Massachusetts primary and his relatively strong showing in Pennsylvania have moved him from an underdog to a viable national candidate. Tuesday's results were more convincing than his previous victory in Wisconsin, where he won with only 30 per cent of the vote and where heavy Republican participation in the Democratic primary cast doubt on the validity of the result.

Republicans could not vote in the Massachusetts primary although independents could. Mr. McGovern demonstrated that, given time to campaign and intensive organizing efforts by his volunteer supporters, he could draw votes in working-class neighborhoods as well as in the liberal suburbs.

Despite the powerful psychological boost which it gives the McGovern forces, the Massachusetts results are far from conclusive. Two qualifying factors are immediately apparent. Senator McGovern had no active opposition, yet he polled a bare 52 per cent majority of the total popular vote. Moreover, that total vote—although sizable by the standards of Massachusetts where a low turnout in primaries is traditional—was still well under half the vote cast for Hubert Humphrey in November, 1968. In Massachusetts as elsewhere, the McGovern supporters are committed activists and they got their voters to the polls. No comparable effort was made in behalf of Senator Muskie once he decided three weeks ago not to invest time or money in Massachusetts.

In Pennsylvania, Senator Humphrey gained a critical victory in his comeback attempt. He won with only 35 per cent of the vote while his three active rivals—Senators McGovern and Muskie and Governor Wallace—ran almost exactly neck-and-neck in dividing the rest of the vote. But since Mr. Humphrey had previously not won in any state, he urgently needed this show of strength, limited though it was.

©1972 by The New York Times Company. Reprinted by permission.

St. Petersburg Times
St. Petersburg, Fla., April 27, 1972

A bore has been defined as a person who talks when you want him to listen; as a man who, when you ask him how he feels, tells you.

For too many Americans, those definitions are beginning to fit the Democratic presidential candidates. That's a way of recognizing a new and inevitable factor on the political scene after only six of the 23 Democratic primaries — the boredom factor.

THE SPARKLE of New Hampshire and Florida have worn off. The public's sagging interest is reflected in media coverage (the three Bay area TV stations didn't even broadcast special programs on the Pennsylvania and Masschusetts results).

It's a shame. Difficult as is this bone-wearying primary course, it's the only way we've got to sort out the strong from the weak. And the important primaries in Ohio, West Virginia, Oregon and California still are ahead.

The boredom factor works to the advantage of President Nixon, who can campaign best merely by doing his job. It also boosts the secret wish of some convention delegates for a fresh candidate to revive the public's appetite for politics.

In any case, the campaign mill is grinding its way methodically toward the convention. After Tuesday's primaries in Pennsylvania and Massachusetts, the Democrats are closer to a two-way contest between Sens. Hubert H. Humphrey and George S. McGovern. George Wallace got 21 per cent of the Pennsylvania vote to place second, but he still is more a spoiler outside the party's mainstream than a serious threat for the nomination. Sen. Edmund S. Muskie ran poorly in both primaries. There was speculation that he would announce the end of his campaign at a news conference this morning.

IT STILL appears that no candidate will enter the convention with the 1,509 delegate votes necessary for the nomination. At this time, Humphrey and McGovern have that essential momentum. Unless the convention is deadlocked and looks outside the primary field, the choice now seems between those two.

Humphrey's strength still is his deep experience, his stamina and his strong support by labor. His weakness is the limp attitude with which some Democrats face a re-run of 1968.

McGovern's strong points are his new face, his record on the war and his surprising victories with modest funds in Wisconsin and Massachusetts (52 per cent). But he is bitterly opposed by some labor leaders and his support in some states — such as Pennsylvania and Florida — has been narrowly based in suburbs and near college campuses.

THE NEXT big tests are Ohio and Indiana May 2 and Michigan May 16. The boredom factor no doubt will rise, but the primaries are doing their job of telling the candidates the voters' mood, and testing the strengths and skills of those who might become president. They are tough, but worth it.

THE STATES-ITEM
New Orleans, La., April 30, 1972

Sen. Edmund S. Muskie's withdrawal from the Democratic presidential primaries sharpens the contest for the remaining candidates.

From here on out, it looks like a two-man struggle in the primaries. Sen. Hubert H. Humphrey has laid claim to a "progressive vital center" in the Democratic Party. And Sen. George S. McGovern has the liberal-reformist field all to himself.

Then, of course, there remains Gov. George Wallace to dog the steps of both senators.

Sen. McGovern already has indicated he plans to nibble away at Sen. Humphrey's so-called progressive center, and that means appealing to blacks, labor and the old party regulars. The South Dakota senator has going for him a snowballing image as the Cinderella candidate of 1972. Should he upset Sen. Humphrey in Ohio, Sen. McGovern's bandwagon could gain the momentum to carry him through the California primary to the nomination.

California appears to be the showdown state. Sen. Humphrey must win in Ohio and again in California to have a solid chance at the nomination. Sen. McGovern must at least run strong in Ohio, where Sen. Humphrey is favored, and win in California to arrive aboard a bandwagon and draw the "progressive center" behind him at the convention. Should either fail to gain the clear profile of a winner, the convention could turn into a free-for-all. And under such circumstances even Sen. Muskie might have a final chance.

The Virginian-Pilot
Norfolk, Va., April 27, 1972

Confounding the experts, contradicting the polls and surveys, and scrambling the theories, the American voter is engagingly unpredictable.

He has stood the conventional political wisdom on its ear in the first months of this election year.

Consider what has happened in recent weeks. Before the Presidential primaries started, the conventional wisdom was that Edmund Muskie of Maine was practically a sure-thing to become the Democratic nominee. In the event Mr. Muskie stumbled, those who were prone to conspiracy and/or romance suggested that the Democrats would look to Teddy Kennedy. John Lindsay, the handsome Mayor of New York, was considered an interesting long-shot who might woo the voters with superslick television techniques. Hubert Humphrey was dismissed as a retread, but a dependable enough fail-safe selection. George Wallace was a nuisance. And George McGovern, who had been the first to announce for the Presidency, simply wasn't taken seriously. Henry (Scoop) Jackson was more likely to be nominated than George McGovern, the experts would have told you.

Almost all of the "expert" judgments have been reversed in the first few primaries. Mr. Muskie is beginning to look like a Democratic George Romney, a terrible thing to happen to any politician, and the bandwagon upon which a lot of the "old pros" were leaping just a few weeks ago has collapsed like the famous one-hoss shay. Mr. Lindsay is out of the race; he didn't sell in Florida or Wisconsin. Mr. Jackson ought to get out of the race—his popularity is zilch, or thereabouts. Meanwhile, Hubert Humphrey seems to be getting younger with every speech. And George McGovern and George Wallace are about the only candidates exciting interest among the voters.

The results Tuesday in the Massachusetts and Pennsylvania primaries reinforced the trends that were evident earlier in New Hampshire and Florida and Wisconsin. Mr. Muskie was dealt a double setback that just about finished him, or so it seems, and the contest narrows now to Mr. Humphrey v. Mr. McGovern. (Mr. Wallace is a nuisance still, but a nuisance who gets an embarrassingly large vote. And the conspirators and romantics still see Teddy Kennedy in the wings.)

Mr. Humphrey proved in Pennsylvania that he can, too, win a Presidential primary, but his triumph was upstaged by Mr. McGovern's Massachusetts runaway. The Senator from South Dakota won a clear majority of the Bay State's votes and all 102 delegates from Massachusetts. With the delegates that he got in Pennsylvania, where he barely campaigned, Mr. McGovern now leads in pledged votes. While the captains and kingmakers prefer Mr. Humphrey for the most part, it is beginning to look as though the Democratic troops want Mr. McGovern, the candidate who promises the biggest change from the Humphreys and Nixons.

At least, that is how Mr. McGovern is being perceived. He himself is more professorial than radical, and indeed he and Mr. Humphrey are both liberal Midwesterners with many more similarities than differences in outlook and record over the years. But one is coming to symbolize the center and the status quo, and the other is becoming the champion of change and the liberal wing. There are the seeds of the strife that destroyed the party in '68 in such a showdown, symbolically. But fratricide isn't inevitable if the party senses victory. And, in any event, the convention is scheduled for July 10-13, leaving several weeks in which to bind up wounds before the campaign in the fall.

If George McGovern weren't a credible nominee for President before Tuesday, he certainly is now. Furthermore, it looks as though he may get the lion's share of Virginia's votes at the convention in July. That alone indicates this is an unpredictable year.

Detroit Free Press
Detroit, Mich., April 27, 1972

AND THEN there were three, but not the three any forecaster might have expected six weeks ago.

Ohio and Indiana, West Virginia and Michigan, California, New York and a dozen other primaries are still ahead before the Democrats convene in July. But as of today, it seems to us, the three names most likely to be heard most are George McGovern, Hubert Humphrey and — no, not George Wallace — Edward M. Kennedy.

If Edmund Muskie does not admit now that his miserable showings in Massachusetts and Pennsylvania have destroyed his candidacy, it could only be because blood as cold as the Atlantic at Kennebunkport flows in his veins. Muskie's supporters are agonizing over the fact that in only one primary yet has he done as well as he was supposed to have done, and in Tuesday's important tests he simply ran miserably. He got 22 percent of the vote in Massachusetts and nary a delegate. In Pennsylvania he ran back in the pack and picked up 31 delegates of 137.

Easily the biggest winner was McGovern, who got all 102 Massachusetts delegates and 32 of Pennsylvania's, even though his campaigning in Pennsylvania was minimal at most. McGovern, two months ago the serious Democratic contender given the least chance to win, is now quite clearly the front-runner.

And he won his races in unexpected places. Called anathema to the working man, he carried working class districts. A Protestant, he carried Catholic wards in Boston. And, as expected, he carried the votes which went four years ago to Gene McCarthy.

Hubert Humphrey's victory, while not so outstanding on its face, was nonetheless vital to his candidacy. As he had admitted, a bad showing would have finished him. Now he has not only won his first state primary in 12 years of trying, but he can expect to pick up some of the Muskie followers.

Humphrey also has some strong union states, particularly Ohio next week and Michigan on May 16, ahead of him.

It was somewhat pathetic, though, to see the pillar of the Democratic establishment trying to wrap himself in the anti-establishment flag just because many of Pennsylvania's leaders had endorsed Muskie. No wonder George Wallace was complaining that Humphrey had stolen his best stances. Humphrey, who discovered "the politics of joy" in a joyless 1968, has now discovered that most Democratic voters are disenchanted with where their party's at.

Which, as we have noted before, is why McGovern and Wallace are doing so well.

The greatest impact of Tuesday's primaries, though, might be on the party's most eminent non-candidate, Ted Kennedy. In spite of the love fest he wallowed in at the UAW convention, we remain convinced that Kennedy does not really want the nomination this year. At 40 he can afford to wait, to get Chappaquiddick farther behind and to win the nomination by acclaim.

But the party pros might see it differently. No matter how slim their chances they are always looking for a winner. It is not difficult to see Humphrey and McGovern going to Miami with heavy first ballot strength, and Wallace playing the role of spoiler.

Many Democrats would be reluctant to let Humphrey have the nomination again, either because they don't like him, because he is a tired warhorse or because he has already lost once to President Nixon. At the same time, George McGovern may still have a hard time convincing some of the pros that he is for real or that he could beat Mr. Nixon. Some, too, think of him—mistakenly, we believe—as a visionary.

Given a stalemate or a bloodbath at Miami, it is not hard to envision the Democrats demanding that Kennedy run, and it would be difficult for him to refuse a genuine draft, no matter how much he might not want it.

Much could happen to upset that forecast, and at this moment the odds are against it. The odds, in fact, are that George McGovern, whose campaign strategy and organization have been flawless, may finally convince the doubters.

In such a disorganized organization as the Democratic Party, this by no means makes him an odds-on favorite. But from the way he's been going it does make him for the first time, the man for the others to try to beat.

THE DENVER POST

Denver, Colo., April 27, 1972

STATE PRIMARIES such as those in Massachusetts and Pennsylvania don't necessarily tell us — at least this year — who's going to be the Demcratic presidential candidate. That question apparently is going to be decided finally only at the convention in Miami.

But these primaries are telling us where and where not to look for a winner. They do tell us which candidates have the best organizations and the most personal appeal to voters.

On the basis of the Massachusetts and Pennsylvania primary results, the contenders who look most like winners now are Sen. George McGovern and Hubert Humphrey.

As for Sen. Edmund Muskie, the former frontrunner in these sweepstakes, one major cause of his failure in Massachusetts is depicted in Mary McGrory's column elsewhere on this page: an incompetent, lackadaisical personal organization.

But in Pennsylvania, another factor had to have hurt him. There he had the backing of both the state and Philadelphia Democratic organizations. And he spent 17 or 18 days in the state campaigning. Yet he was beaten not only by Humphrey, who spent an equal amount of time stumping the state, but by Alabama's Gov. George Wallace — who campaigned only one day in the state.

That kind of defeat really has to sting. It says the unkindest sort of thing about the candidate's personal appeal.

Muskie insisted Tuesday night that he would hang in there and fight, but he undoubtedly was aware that decision depended less on his personal willingness than on the willingness of others to put up the money for his campaign.

Thursday morning, Muskie announced that he was pulling out of remaining primaries—a sure sign that his financial backers had cut off the flow of cash.

So the Massachusetts and Pennsylvania primaries have shown us one more place not to look for a winner.

And those primaries have established McGovern as undoubtedly the new front runner in this race, with Humphrey coming up on the outside. But now the spotlight switches to the next major primaries May 2 in Indiana and Ohio.

With Muskie out, McGovern should have relatively clear sailing in Ohio, and a chance to cement his gains with the relatively conservative Democrats whom he wooed in Massachusetts.

FOR HUMPHREY, the road ahead is harder. He has established himself as a major candidate with his win in Pennsylvania, but must take on Wallace head-to-head in Indiana. And he must do well there to retain his standing.

Until May 2, in any case, the meaning of Massachusetts and Pennsylvania clearly is that those looking for a winner in the Democratic presidential race must look mainly to McGovern and Humphrey.

St. Louis Globe-Democrat

St. Louis, Mo., April 27, 1972

In the here-today, gone-tomorrow Democratic presidential race, Senator Hubert H. Humphrey has forged ahead with his solid victory in Pennsylvania.

But Governor George C. Wallace continues to be the political surprise of 1972. In winning second place in Pennsylvania, he even surprised himself.

Senator George C. McGovern also is continuing to confound the experts. By crushing Senator Edmund S. Muskie in Massachusetts, he has come close to knocking out the former front-runner.

Muskie, like a punch-drunk fighter, is dead on his feet. It is reported he may quit the race today.

☆ ☆ ☆

Humphrey's win in Pennsylvania is far more significant than McGovern's victory in Massachusetts because the former is more than twice as large as the latter and has a greater cross-section of voters.

McGovern, by contrast, was given an extra lift by the political machine headed by Senator Edward M. (Ted) Kennedy and the whole Kennedy clan. This has always been a Kennedy stronghold and any candidate who wins the Kennedy nod in this state is almost a shoo-in winner.

The South Dakotan also has become the Pied Piper of the anti-war movement, which obviously is stronger in Massachusetts than Pennsylvania.

Governor Wallace's showing in Pennsylvania again was the big surprise. No one believed he would win second place in this pivotal state.

If Wallace's strength in the South is added to his increasing strength in the North, it is obvious that his anti-Establishment campaign is being taken seriously by voters and that his strength is continuing to grow. He is a force the Democratic Party regulars will have to reckon with whether they like him or not.

When Senator Muskie went into his tailspin, he left a vacuum. The big question was who would fill it.

Pennsylvania gives us the answer. Democratic voters have chosen Hubert Humphrey because he represents the progressive center of the party.

George McGovern, who represents the Democratic left, is winning most the party's left-wing. But it is extremely doubtful he can seriously challenge Humphrey nationally. He is too radical. The history of both major parties is that they don't nominate extremist candidates. McGovern probably will prove no exception to this rule.

☆ ☆ ☆

Humphrey's win in Pennsylvania does not insure him the nomination. Nothing is certain in the volatile, changing Democratic race. This is a dog-eat-dog scramble to the wire. If Senator Muskie can be almost eclipsed in the span of several months after overshadowing the field for so long, anything can happen.

Even though Humphrey does appear to have the momentum that could carry him to victories in crucial tests in Ohio and Indiana (May 2), Michigan (May 16), California (June 6) and New York (June 20), he will have to continue running at top speed to fight off his challengers.

As Senator Muskie discovered, the political wind shifts in a hurry. One trip, one blunder, and the huge pack of pursuers can catch the front-runner and devour him.

OREGON JOURNAL

Portland, Ore., April 27, 1972

The field of Democratic presidential candidates was bound to trim itself down to a manageable size before the arduous primary course had been completed.

A few months ago, when a dozen or more prominent names were tossed about as likely prospects, few would have foreseen that the contest would shake down to a head-on clash between Sens. George M. McGovern and Hubert Humphrey.

It may not be at that point yet, but it is close to it after the votes were counted in Massachusetts and Pennsylvania. It's possible that one or the other won't win the rest of the primaries. There's George Wallace, whose particular brand of demagoguery continues to show disturbing appeal. The names of the others also remain on the ballots and some of them will campaign actively.

One who has abandoned the campaign trail is Sen. Edmund Muskie, whose fading aspirations were shattered when Humphrey beat him badly in Pennsylvania where the two had campaigned hard and head-to-head for what they regard as the center position of the party, and when McGovern outpolled him by more than 2-1 in his neighboring New England state.

Muskie's only hope is that no one else will have the nomination nailed down by convention time. That would give him a chance to test the theory that he is everybody's second choice. Second choices don't show up in votes, but they may surface in deadlocked conventions.

Of course, the primaries do not necessarily assure nomination, but a candidate would rather have those victories than not have them going into the convention.

Right now the rest of the trip through the primaries concentrates on the new front-runner, McGovern, who is proving to have much wider appeal than his detractors thought he would have, and Humphrey, whose contention that he is not a has-been gained support in Pennsylvania.

It is ironic, and perhaps a sign that the old political rules are changing, that there should be a McGovern-Humphrey showdown. Neither is from a big state with a big bloc of votes—that was one of the old rules.

McGovern's South Dakota indeed is one of the smaller states and it also happens to be the native state of Humphrey, although he represents its eastern neighbor, Minnesota.

When McGovern was building a Democratic party in South Dakota he received the active help of Humphrey, who continued to have an interest in his home state. The two have had a long personal relationship, although their brands of liberalism have carried them to certain differences, as the old and the new inevitably do.

So it has come, somewhat surprisingly, that friends and neighbors from the northern plains—with different personalities and styles—are riding hard against each other in the hope of becoming president of the United States. Politically, their similarities are greater than their differences. Humphrey would seem to represent the old and McGovern the new and that more than anything else may set the tone of their campaign.

After a few more contests in the East, Oregon's May 23 primary looms more and more as a critical test to determine who carries the brightest image of victor into the convention.

THE RICHMOND NEWS LEADER
Richmond, Va., April 26, 1972

Following the 1970 Congressional elections, President Nixon described Edmund Muskie as "the George Romney of the Democratic Party." Yesterday's returns from the Pennsylvania and Massachusetts primaries confirm that appraisal: Senator Muskie ran a poor second in Massachusetts (22 per cent of the vote) and at this writing, with 98 per cent of the precincts reporting, he is running third in Pennsylvania (21 per cent of the vote). The Senator is entitled to the wishful verbal indulgences of a failing candidate: "We did rather well in winning delegates. We've turned the corner. We're on the way up again." But in Massachusetts he won only 7 of 102 available delegates; in Pennsylvania, 29 of 137. Rationalizations aside, the Senator is a candidate in defeat.

The romneyization of Senator Muskie has been as swift and as total as that of any candidate in the nation's political history. Created the front-runner in 1968 by a press filled with apoplectic disenchantment for Hubert Humphrey, Richard Nixon, and Spiro Agnew, the Senator from Maine now is being destroyed by his creators. One need only quote Senator Muskie to understand that this is a man experiencing his last hurrah. These days he exudes an aura of desperation—a fuzzy radical brimming with the isolationism of the new left, a candidate who clearly has failed to define a constituency. In the four primaries in which he has taken on the Democratic field, he has averaged 15 per cent of the vote. In Massachusetts, where there were but two candidates, he ran second; in Florida and Wisconsin he ran fourth; in Pennsylvania he barely held on to third.

The candidate with whom much of the press currently is enamored is George McGovern. As far as winning the Democratic presidential nomination is concerned, the South Dakota Senator's chances are about equal to the chances of Elmer Fudd. But the Senator has been uncharacteristically shrewd in selecting his primaries, and he has the former Kennedy organization doing most of his electoral thinking for him. So he has won the Wisconsin and Massachusetts primaries, and has done rather well in Pennsylvania. Yet he is much too much of a philosophical hayseed for most of the ideological elitists in the Democratic Party. The likelihood that he ever will run against Richard Nixon remains just about zilch.

Pennsylvania was critical for Hubert Humphrey. He won the primary there—his first State primary victory in 12 years of coveting the presidency. Happy Hubert (his doctor, Edgar Berman, jokes that the Humphrey energy in a man just a month short of 61 is "a serious genetic defect") has taken to hair tint, dark face powder, wide ties, bootlike shoes, and Oscar de la Renta suits ("Yes, I'm a modern man. I love the good life. I don't want to go around looking like a sad sack...."), and won the Pennsylvania primary with 35 per cent of the vote. He cashed in on a lot of accrued political debt. But practically everywhere he went in Pennsylvania—practically everywhere McGovern and Muskie went as well—there was the visage of the cheshire cat from Alabama. In his continuing campaign to bedevil the nation's political establishment, George Wallace ran second in Pennsylvania, after campaigning there for three days. You can't blame the other Democrats for wishing that he would go away.

The results of the Democratic primaries thus far indicate nothing so much as that the Democratic Party is in shambles. Muskie is out of it. Humphrey is a has-been. McGovern comes across like Moon Mullins at the Playboy Club. Yet the question persists: Why doesn't Teddy Kennedy, the essential popular force in the Democratic Party, come forward and endorse George McGovern. The South Dakota Senator stands for everything that Kennedy stands for; many of the most effective staffers in the several Kennedy campaigns now are strategizing for South Dakota George, although their hearts most likely are not in it. If there ever was a candidate who deserved the Kennedy blessing, it is George McGovern. But Kennedy declines. And the question persists: Why?

MUSKIE WITHDRAWS

Announcing his withdrawal from "active participation" in the presidential primaries, Sen. Muskie called his campaign strategy to date "a mistake," because it required "a major effort and a major expenditure of resources in every primary with a maximum impact in none." As a result, Muskie said, "I do not have the money to continue." Muskie pledged to continue "to speak out on the issues." His only apparent hope for the nomination now rested with the possibility of a draft at a deadlocked Democratic Convention in July.

EVENING HERALD
Rock Hill, S.C., April 29, 1972

Sen. Ed Muskie has attributed his demise in the presidential race to a basic error in campaign strategy — trying to enter as many primaries as time, money and energy allowed him to. It wasn't until after the Wisconsin fiasco that he changed plans and decided to concentrate on a few large states.

It's our observation, however, that this strategy was not necessarily a mistake, at least not until it became evident that Muskie was not as strong a vote getter as his supporters had anticipated and his funds and other support started drying up.

What did Muskie in, we believe, was that he lacked both the warm, outgoing, exuberant personality of a Hubert Humphrey, and the determination of a George McGovern to offer voters clearcut alternatives on the main issues of the times.

There was nothing exciting about the man, at least not on the surface, and both the voters and the press sensed it. Although he was capable of deep emotions — his occasional outbursts of temper proved that — he essentially came across as too solid, too aloof, too dull, and too wishy-washy.

Apparently Muskie had hoped to duplicate what John F. Kennedy accomplished in 1960 when JFK swept primary after primary. What the Maine senator lacked, however, was Kennedy's appealing personality.

So Muskie's basic flaw was that he failed to compensate for his lackluster image by giving voters a choice on the issues. He finally tried that approach in Pennsylvania, but by then it was too late.

Maine Sunday Telegram
Portland, Me., April 30, 1972

To feel compassion for a punctured politician is wholly out of style.

Yet compassion for Ed Muskie is what we feel.

We felt that compassion as the pundits and commentators gloated over Muskie's defeats in the primaries.

For a year and a half previously Ed Muskie had been the darling of TV commentators and newspaper columnists. They fawned over him as the Lincolnesque man from Maine whose honesty, whose sincerity, whose open earnestness marked him, in their eyes, as the ascending new star in a new, refreshing kind of American politics.

Yet today those same commentators twist the knife into the same Ed Muskie they once adored.

Why?

We ask: Did these political pundits admire Muskie the man: or did they merely jump on his bandwagon because for so long and so early the public opinion polls indicated Muskie was the magic name, the favored front-runner, the only Democrat who might unseat Richard Nixon, whom so many pundits dislike?

Were these fickle fellows out there, swimming with the tide of what they thought would be a tidal wave for Muskie?

Then came the early primaries, just one-third of the primaries, and the tide changed. It ran against Muskie. And the commentators whose darling he had been, turned against Muskie.

Now, broke, battered and despondent, Muskie has withdrawn in effect from the race for the Democratic nomination. The one time glamorous front runner is a lonely drop-out, one third down the track. And we feel compassion.

More importantly, we ask: Can the tide change again? Can Muskie again become a magic name?

Yes, we think it may, just possibly, despite Muskie's inept race and more inept withdrawal.

In running, Muskie assumed he was in the lead too confidently. In getting out of the race, Muskie assumed he was beaten too humbly.

We never leapt on the Muskie bandwagon with wild eyed enthusiasm early in the game, when it was popular to opine that Muskie was the appointed saviour of the Democratic cause.

And today we are not leaping off the bandwagon posthaste because turning one's back on Muskie seems to be the fad of the moment.

At the start we gave our opinion that Muskie had about a 50 per cent chance to win the Democratic nomination.

Today we still feel he has a fifty per cent chance to win.

And we are far from giving up the Muskie ship. We still feel that if we had to choose between Humphrey, McGovern and Muskie for the next President of the United States, we would select Muskie without any hesitation at all.

Since this opinion goes against the tide of fashion, we will give a few reasons why we are still in Muskie's corner among the Democratic candidates. Our reasons are not rooted simply in local Maine affection for a Maine man.

Here they are. . . .

1. In Democratic primaries, the extremes attract. We think McGovern is an extremist. We think Wallace is an extremist. And dear old Hubert Humphrey we think is simply an extremely durable campaigner for a losing cause, namely HHH.

2. But we do not think the Democratic party is an extremist party. There are, after all, millions more registered Democrats in the United States than there are registered voters in any party. And we are fairly sure that the majority of voting Americans are not extremists. So come the final votes at the Democratic nominating convention, we doubt the delegates will nominate either an extremist or a has-been, unless they seek defeat for their party.

3. Muskie, as the closest thing to a centralist running in the Democratic herd of candidates, is a dull performer in the primaries. We never expected otherwise. As a political figure, Muskie is dull rather than vibrant, moderate rather than magnetic. (Not wholly bad qualities in anybody who could sit in the White House). One result is that Muskie has failed to attract enough exuberant enthusiasts in his primary campaigns. His organization has been too stuffy, too "establishment" to produce many such workers. Muskie relied overmuch on high-sounding endorsements, collecting testimonials like Ponds Cold Cream, rather than on door-bell ringing salesmen who have successfully hawked McGovern.

4. By the time Humphrey, McGovern and Uncle Tom Cobbely and all get to the Democratic convention in Miami our guess is they will be battered, bloody and bitter from fighting each other. The Democratic party is likely to be in shreds of divisiveness. As the shifting roll calls go on, that modest nugget of delegates believing in the man Muskie may be the only segment to hold fast. Slowly it may grow, as desertions erode other ranks.

Then on the umpteenth roll call the Muskie tide could suddenly swell. He will be in the hall, with no tin-cans tied to his tail, no political blood feuds on his hands. The popular opinion polls which months ago showed Muskie the most popular of Democrats among voters may then spring to delegates' minds and make their forgotten weight felt.

Hence, our conviction stays: There is a fifty-fifty chance that Ed Muskie of Maine will emerge as the Democratic candidate.

We are still on the Muskie bandwagon and will stay there. Partly because we think still that Muskie has a fifty per cent chance of winning; but mostly because we are 100 per cent convinced that if any Democratic candidate were to win the next election, the nation would be better and safer under Muskie than Humphrey, McGovern or Wallace, or Kennedy.

Pittsburgh Post-Gazette
Pittsburgh, Pa., April 28, 1972

SENATOR Muskie was wise to withdraw from active contention in the presidential preference primaries. The favorite at the start, he somehow didn't ignite the voters in the primaries, and more of the same would have have been unnecessary torture all around.

Now it can be seen that a Muskie problem was that he didn't have a power base, in contrast to Senator Humphrey's support by organized labor and Senator McGovern's backing by the anti-war forces, the young, the academic community, and a good slice of the liberal wing of the Democratic party. He did get a convincing number of endorsements by party leaders, but increasingly it is evident this doesn't mean much any more with the decline of the political machines and the rise of the independent voter.

But also to many voters Mr. Muskie had seemed like a pipe-smoker who at first appears wise and reserved until one wonders whether the pipe covers the fact that he has little to offer. Regardless of how he came across to voters, by every objective standard Mr. Muskie has plenty to offer, and that is why it is good that he is not withdrawing from the race itself.

Senators Humphrey and McGovern are the major contenders now, but if they cut each other up so much in the remaining primaries that the convention in Miami Beach becomes deadlocked, Mr. Muskie might look good again after all as the best bet to unite the party to defeat President Nixon. That, at least, is what he is betting on as the final spark of hope in a campaign launched so brightly only 114 days earlier.

The New York Times
New York, N.Y., April 28, 1972

President Kennedy used to say: "Victory has a hundred fathers but defeat is an orphan."

In the aftermath of his decision to withdraw from an active campaign in the primaries for the Democratic Presidential nomination, Senator Edmund S. Muskie has occasion to ponder that melancholy proverb. Although he received more than one man's share of bad advice and was the recipient of an inordinate amount of backstabbing from erstwhile political allies, he knows that he alone will have to carry the burden of defeat. No one else will claim the orphan.

Fundamentally, Senator Muskie misjudged the effect which a succession of primaries would have upon his kind of candidacy. It was not simply that he was whipsawed by rival candidates concentrating on one primary at a time while he entered them all. It was also that in primaries, the voters who go to the polls are somewhat atypical of the party as a whole and of the entire electorate. Most are either deeply committed to a particular cause such as ending the war in Vietnam or they are angry and want to cast a protest vote.

A candidate like Mr. Muskie who has broad appeal but no clearly defined constituency finds himself at a severe disadvantage. Personal qualities which made him a strong candidate when matched against Mr. Nixon in the public opinion polls proved to be handicaps when Senator Muskie was matched against rival Democrats in the primaries.

As adversity developed, Senator Muskie and his managers tried to gain for him a sharper image in people's minds. But though he keyed his rhetoric a little higher, he continued to come across to voters as basically what he is—a thoughtful New England liberal with a cautious, realistic approach to what is possible in legislation and policies. His talents are for building a consensus, working out compromises, reconciling diverse views. Senator Muskie has moral commitment and his own style of idealism, but no amount of image retouching could make this quiet man sound like an angry populist or a fiery radical.

Senator Muskie's true qualities are now his one surviving political asset. Having released his delegates and quit the primaries, he can be nominated only in the highly unlikely event that a divided and distracted convention turns to him because it finds his qualities essential in its nominee. Politically, it is a slender hope but emotionally, it is consoling for any man to know that his character is his fate.

© 1972 by The New York Times Company. Reprinted by permission.

The Detroit News
Detroit, Mich., April 30, 1972

Having tried a wide assortment of o t h e r strategies without success, Senator Edmund Muskie has now decided to try the Ted Kennedy strategy. That strategy is simply to avoid the hassle of the primaries, work behind the scenes and hope that lightning will strike at the national convention.

This is a long-shot strategy, but the chances of success can hardly be rated less than the chances that Muskie could win the nomination after a series of humiliating defeats in primaries from one end of the country to the other.

Unfortunately — for him — he already carries the loser's taint, which will be the big difference between himself and Senator Kennedy at Miami Beach. If a compromise candidate should be needed at a deadlocked convention, Kennedy and not Muskie will be sitting in the catbird seat.

In theory, Muskie had a great idea. He would get into the race for the Democratic nomination at an early hour, establish himself as the front-runner and sweep to success on an inexorable tide of popular support.

In reality, his assumption of the role of front-runner made him the major target of the strategies of all the other candidates. They whittled him, squeezed him and whipsawed him until there was nothing left.

Muskie's worst single miscalculation probably was his belief that big-name endorsements and the backing of state political machines would magically be translated into votes at the polls. His faith was r e f l e c t e d in a column which appeared several days before the Massachusetts primary:

"During all this time the Muskie campaign has been barely sputtering, but now all the politicians will see their own names on the line. They will call their friends who will call their friends and presto, victory ought to come to Muskie. It sounds suspiciously easy, but politics often works that way in Massachusetts."

It did not, obviously, work that way this time.

With Muskie no longer active in the primaries, the forthcoming contests will provide a clearer picture of the relative strength of Senator McGovern and Senator Humphrey, though the presence of Alabama's Gov. George Wallace will in many cases still prevent a head-to-head contest between those two.

Wallace shares the blame — or the credit, as you will — for fragmenting the Democratic votes and preventing Muskie from maintaining front-runner status. He probably will continue to take enough votes to prevent either McGovern or Humphrey from going to the convention with a clear mandate.

Thus, Wallace could be more responsible than anybody for the selection of Senator Ted Kennedy as a compromise Democratic nominee.

By the way, few realistic political observers any longer doubt that Kennedy is a candidate. He delivers his daily disavowals in what can only be described as campaign speeches. This week, for example, he went to Atlantic City ostensibly to advocate a national health insurance program in a speech to the UAW convention and t h e n stayed to deliver a political blast at President Nixon.

Asked about future plans, Kennedy said as usual that he won't be a candidate. UAW delegates smiled knowingly back and waved a banner proclaiming: "Kennedy for President." Let the r e c o r d show that the banner did not throw the senator into a fit of dismay and anger.

WINSTON-SALEM JOURNAL
Winston-Salem, N.C., April 28, 1972

THERE are many theories to explain Sen. Edmund Muskie's breathtaking slide from "frontrunner" to "also-ran" in the race for the Democratic presidential nomination.

Some say that Muskie tried to occupy the "vital center" in a year when most of the voters are angrily perched in the left or right wing of the party. A less sophisticated version of the same theory is that the American people want to hear candidates who have something to say, even if what they say is disagreeable — and Sen. Muskie went out of his way to avoid controversial positions. Still another explanation is that Muskie spent too much time collecting endorsements from political brokers and not enough time building grass-roots organizations in a year when power-brokers are not in style.

There is probably some truth in each of these theories. But what do they add up to?

They add up the fact that only the toughest, shrewdest, most resilient of men can survive the meatgrinder which we sportingly call an American presidential campaign.

If a candidate cannot raise a considerable amount of money early in the campaign, he drops out even before the primaries begin — as Sen. Harris did. If his record is so bad that even a lot of money and a handsome phiz can't hide it, he falls by the wayside — as Mayor Lindsay did. If he naively steps into a pitfall, as George Romney did in 1968 with his "brainwashing" comment, he is snickered out of the running. If he is capable but almost completely colorless to most voters, as Sen. Jackson seems to be, the odds are against him.

These were not the weaknesses which pushed the Man from Maine back into the crowd of long-shots who hope for a miracle at Miami Beach. But he displayed other weaknesses, and he displayed too many of them. His personal staff was mediocre, and his organization, spread too thin, was weak. He committed the cardinal sin of misreading the mood of the voters when he blasted the Florida electorate for preferring George Wallace.

But the awesome demands of our system are not limited to organizing skills and cerebral judgment. The physical demands are enormous, too, and more than one candidate has committed errors when he was bone-tired from shaking hands, making speeches, flying, driving and walking from place to place in the hectic search for votes. If he had not been exhausted, Edmund Muskie probably would not have wept on the doorstep of a New Hampshire newspaper that had insulted his wife. But wept he did, and the murmur that went around the nation — do we want an unstable man in that office? — was audible.

It is a brutal, costly, almost irrational system which often seems to make little sense. But those who survive it are not ordinary men, and there is something to be said for that.

The Charlotte Observer
Charlotte, N.C., April 29, 1972

What happened to Sen. Edmund Muskie in recent weeks may go down in history as a classic example of how the American presidential primaries tend to produce losers, not winners.

For nearly two years, Muskie was counted the man most likely to win the Democratic nomination and to beat President Nixon. But his front-runner position put him at a decided disadvantage. It made for over-confidence on the part of his staff and advisors.

While other candidates were organizing support at the grassroots and seeking alternative positions on the issues, Muskie was playing it safe. He remained too long in the middle instead of building a base of voter enthusiasm.

Basically, Muskie is a decent man who won many friends and admirers over the past three years. His presence in the 1968 presidential campaign was like a ray of sunlight. Among the candidates on the three major tickets, he alone stood out as a national unifier. He was probably the best thing the Democrats had going for them in the uphill fight to keep the White House.

Sen. Muskie's televised speech on the eve of the 1970 congressional elections, which thrust him into the front-runner position, showed him to be a man of calm, firm common sense. In contrast to the divisive campaign tactics of both President Nixon and Vice President Agnew, Muskie that night gave the nation a glimpse at a kind of leadership it had not witnessed for many months.

Yet in the end, this calm and centrist approach did not prove effective in rallying the voters. Is it because, perhaps, there is something different in the nature of primaries themselves? Do voters behave differently there, perhaps thinking of the primary mainly as a place to express grievances? The showings of George McGovern and George Wallace suggest that.

So we have sympathy for Sen. Muskie. He set out with a popular appeal that seemed to be based upon his position as centrist and peacemaker, but in the primaries the voters were not looking for that. Will they be looking for it, though, in November? Perhaps.

His departure from the primary campaign will narrow the choice facing voters. It will focus attention on the alternates posed by Sen. Hubert Humphrey and Sen. George McGovern. And unless the party can rally around one of these two in Miami next summer, Muskie could still emerge as the man the Democrats turn to in compromise. He is, after all, an acceptable "second choice" for many voters.

BUFFALO EVENING NEWS
Buffalo, N.Y., April 28, 1972

We do not rejoice in the sad destruction of the presidential candidacy of Sen. Edmund Muskie, who remains a man of intelligence, integrity and generally impressive stature. Announcing his withdrawal from "active participation" in the remaining presidential primaries, the Maine senator observed that he had "no choice. I do not have the money to continue."

But of course that isn't the basic reason behind the swift collapse of a candidacy formally announced only 16 weeks ago. More fundamental is why the senator now lacks the money that once flowed so generously to him and now still flows to other candidates with less optimistic prospects a couple of months ago. The answer is that Sen. Muskie's unity image has somehow consistently failed to attract enthusiastic support among Democratic voters.

Almost beginning with his formal announcement in January, Sen. Muskie looked slightly fuzzy on the issues. He seemed eager not to displease anyone on highly divisive policy questions from Vietnam to bussing to tax reform. His tearful response to a harsh newspaper attack in New Hampshire turned off some voters. He spread his resources too thin, as he acknowledged yesterday, in promising to enter all of the first eight primaries. But he also relied too heavily on a bandwagon pulled by proxy power — through prestigious but non-negotiable endorsements from state figures like Govs. Shapp of Pennsylvania or Gilligan of Ohio.

In a phrase, Sen. Muskie, who cultivated a Lincolnesque image, increasingly emerged as a hesitant candidate playing it disappointingly safe.

His hopes for the Democratic nomination now rest on the possibility that at a deadlocked national convention in July he would provide a compromise choice more acceptable to the supporters of Sen. Hubert Humphrey or Sen. George McGovern than either is to the other.

That could happen, of course, but it looks somewhat improbable at the moment. His withdrawal gives both Sens. McGovern and Humphrey clearer shots at the nomination. And even in deadlock some fresher face, unblemished by Muskie's poor showings in the spring primaries, might seem more attractive to convention delegates.

The Muskie withdrawal suddenly intensifies interest in next Tuesday's Ohio primary. It sharpens the rivalry between Sen. Humphrey, a centrist candidate backed by organized labor, and Sen. McGovern, representing the more anti-establishment left. And it also poses speculative questions about which rival will benefit most, or how this turn of events may affect the fortunes of others like Sen. Edward Kennedy. For now, though, it is enough to ponder the tantalizing parallels between the self-destructing Muskie candidacy and classic Greek tragedy, a kind of American political nobility humbled by unforeseen events mercilessly flowing from the flawed conception of the central figure in the drama.

The Washington Post
Washington, D.C., April 27, 1972

Judging from the mortifying fate of just about every assumption with which we began this political year, we can only assume now that any pronouncement of the death of Senator Muskie's candidacy — even his own — would be bound to guarantee its revival. Nevertheless, it seems to us that the Senator's dismal showing in the Pennsylvania and Massachusetts primaries on Tuesday, taken together with his earlier buffetings, invites a little comment on the condition of his campaign and a little speculation as to how it came about. The Senator, one hears, has been victimized by an "anti-establishment" mood among the voters —a hypothesis that certainly seems to have a measure of truth to it and one that is expressed not just by a number of those known as "political observers," but also by numerous of the observed.

We would enter a caveat or two, however, and a couple of qualifications concerning this line of thought. It seems to us that something other than a particular body of views identifiable as "establishment" (or "centrist" or even "old hat") is what is being rejected by voters who are rejecting the Muskie candidacy. Many of the Senator's positions and appeals have been virtually indistinguishable from those of the candidates who have trounced him. He is certainly no more "old hat" than Hubert Humphrey who won the Pennsylvania primary. And from the war to the environment—with appropriate stops in between for economic and tax questions—Senator Muskie has taken stands and issued position papers very much in keeping with what is said to be the current public mood. We would argue, therefore, that it is less a substantive set of "centrist" views than an establishmentarian style which has offended or at least failed to attract the voters—and by style we mean something more than mannerism, something of a special spirit that has seemed to infuse his whole campaign.

That spirit—part innocent, part arrogant—in our view accounts for much of the lassitude and unprofessionalism and inattentiveness and indifference that have marked the campaign effort itself at the technical level. And we think it can be approximately rendered as follows: "It *has been decided by those who know best* that Senator Muskie is to be the Democratic nominee. Please stand by for further instructions." In consequence, something artificial has characterized much of that flow of high-level endorsements he has received. And something abstract and overformulated has characterized much of the rationale for his candidacy, much of the argument for supporting him. We have been put in mind—in some respects, anyway—of that moment eight years ago when the Republican "establishment" made a very similar kind of decision that Governor Scranton, not Senator Goldwater, ought to be the next President and one could all but hear the collective sigh: Well, thank God that's settled—now what shall we talk about?

If any one thing seems to be demonstrably on the voters' minds in these primaries, it is that *they* are going to speak up and register a few ideas and 'settle' this thing, that they are **not** going to be taken for granted or buy what is thought to be best for them by someone else. This view of things, while coming only to the edge of what is being hailed (a little loosely, we think) as the "new populism," does have the advantage of making room for the rather surprising strength shown by Hubert Humphrey in some of the primaries that have taken place. We are wary of the "populism" formulation because that movement has had such a mixed and largely unfortunate history, because fed-upism (whether with crime, corruption, politicians as a class, taxes, Korea or student riots) is not so novel a political motivation among voters as is now being supposed, and because we think the simple single term blurs more than it explains. It hardly does justice, in our view, to the exceedingly impressive and successful campaign Senator McGovern has been waging.

Here again, as in the case of Senator Muskie's style as distinct from his opinions, we suspect that it is less a matter of left or right viewpoint than of perceived authenticity that is moving voters. It seems indisputable to us that there are new and different currents moving within the electorate at the moment and that they have much to do with discontent, a sense of grievance and thoroughgoing impatience with official deceptiveness and incompetence. What Senator McGovern (and Governor Wallace in a less surprising way) has managed to do is relate his own larger and firmly held and occasionally rather "way out" political views to these sentiments, translating everything from his unequivocal position on the war to his well-known views on defense spending into a currency that is relevant to the voters' concerns, that evidently relates to what is on their minds. Surveys show, to be sure, that many of those supporting the Senator are quite oblivious to the actual implications of some of his positions and that they are admiring him for a capacity to speak out and to defy the ordinary wisdom, as they think of it, passed on by politicians. Doubtless, as the campaign goes forward, much of the confusion will be dispelled and conceivably the response will be quite different. For now, it may be enough to say that the difference so far in the curves of the Muskie and McGovern campaigns reflects a difference between telling the voters to vote for a candidate because he should win and telling them *why* he should win and asking for their votes.

THE CINCINNATI ENQUIRER
Cincinnati, Ohio, April 30, 1972

UNLIKE THE OTHER candidates for the Democratic presidential nomination who have fallen by the wayside in the state primaries, Sen. Edmund S. Muskie (D-Maine) has not renounced his candidacy. He has merely suspended it.

Given the dismal fortune Senator Muskie has encountered so far in the primary marathon, his decision not to campaign further was realistic. His attempt to keep his name in consideration as a viable nominee rests on two prospects.

The first is that neither Sen. George S. McGovern (D-S.D.) nor Sen. Hubert H. Humphrey (D-Minn.) can attract 1509 delegates votes at the Democratic National Convention and, therefore, be nominated.

The second is that, if such a deadlock occurs, Senator Muskie will be turned to as a compromise candidate. On the strength of Senator Muskie's primary showings, this does not appear credible at first blush.

One would guess that the convention would turn rather to Sen. Edward M. Kennedy (D-Mass.), who, whatever his reasons (a genuine disinterest in the nomination this year or extraordinary shrewdness), has chosen not to be bruised and bloodied by the primary wars.

If, however, Senator Kennedy truly is not available or if delegates do not rush to him, then Mr. Muskie would become a prospect simply because some of those associated with the Kennedy family would prefer him to Senator Humphrey. The antipathy for Senator Humphrey has been apparent and, therefore, one could expect an effort to steer any McGovern delegates abandoning ship to Senator Muskie.

One can suspect that there even may have been some understanding along this line as part of the Muskie removal of himself from an active role in the primaries. At least the McGovern people were saying privately that Mr. Muskie would bow out even before the votes in Pennsylvania and Massachusetts were counted. And Mr. Muskie was being seen as preferred by McGovern supporters over Mr. Humphrey if there should be a deadlock.

Whatever the preference of some of the party kingmakers, however, there are other considerations. Mr. Muskie, in starting out as the consensus front runner and then floundering as an also-ran, has left a poor image of himself as a vote getter. His campaign strategy and organization were so poorly managed as to draw criticism even from visible supporters, such as Ohio's Governor Gilligan. Mr. Muskie spread himself too thinly geographically in seeking to blitz the primaries and he was spread as well in terms of issues. Mr. McGovern is identified with the Vietnam War, Mr. Humphrey with the economy and Gov. George C. Wallace of Alabama with busing, but Mr. Muskie is hardly identifiable at all. This may have occurred because the polls identified him as the front runner and his strategy was simply to try to keep that identity.

In terms of delegates so far, Senator McGovern is well in front, with Senator Muskie second and Senator Humphrey and Governor Wallace in a virtual tie for third. Therefore, it becomes important whether (1) Muskie delegates slip away toward the center to Senator Humphrey or to the left to Senator McGovern before the convention and (2) whether voters who would have voted for Mr. Muskie in the forthcoming primaries shift further left or toward the center.

The situation that has emerged, with Mr. Muskie going to the bench for possible recall, is of a candidate of the left, a candidate of the center and a candidate of the right, with those to left and right harvesting the votes of protest and dissent while the center counts on party and country not to wander to either extreme. Labor support is perhaps Senator Humphrey's strongest card in the battles ahead.

DEMOCRATIC PRESIDENTIAL CANDIDATES SHARE VICTORIES IN EIGHT PRIMARIES

Eight primaries in the race for the Democratic presidential nomination were held in seven states and the District of Columbia during the first half of May.

In contests held May 2, Sen. Hubert Humphrey (Minn.) scored victories in Indiana and Ohio. In Indiana, Humphrey won 47% of the vote and 55 delegates to the national convention defeating Gov. George Wallace (Ala.) who, registering his strongest showing outside the South to date, won 42% of the vote and the remaining 21 delegates. Maine's Sen. Edmund Muskie received the remaining 11% of the vote. In Ohio, Humphrey won 41.5% of the vote with Sen. George McGovern (S.D.) finishing a close second with 39.3%. Humphrey captured 77 delegates to McGovern's 63. The Ohio balloting was marred by a massive voting-machine tie-up in Cuyahoga County (Cleveland) which led to widespread disenfranchisement and calls for a new election. Sen. Henry Jackson (Wash.), after finishing fourth behind Muskie in Ohio and having failed to win a single convention delegate in the primaries thus far, withdrew from all future contests.

Gov. Wallace was victorious in the Alabama primary May 2, winning control of his home state's 37-member delegation to the convention. Favorite son Rev. Walter H. Fauntroy headed the delegate slate that won in the District of Columbia primary held the same day.

In the Tennessee presidential preference primary held May 4, Wallace won 68% of the popular vote and gained the state's 59-member delegation to the national convention, which was bound by state law to support for two ballots the winner of the preferential vote. Tennessee voters also balloted on a non-binding referendum on busing similar to the one held in the Florida primary. [See pp. 312–324] The proposed law on busing won by a large majority.

In the North Carolina Democratic primary held May 6, Gov. Wallace won 50% of the vote to defeat former Gov. Terry Sanford who received 37%. Wallace won 37 convention delegates. Busing was an important issue in the North Carolina campaign.

In primaries held May 9, Sen. McGovern won in Nebraska polling 41% of the popular vote to Sen. Humphrey's 35% and capturing 15 convention delegates to Humphrey's 7 in a separate ballot. In the West Virginia preference contest, Humphrey won by a 2-1 margin over Wallace.

On the Republican side, President Nixon captured all convention delegates in primary contests held during the period.

The Dispatch
Columbus, Ohio, May 7, 1972

NO MATTER how they divided up Ohio's presidential election delegates, this state taught the candidates a precious lesson — philosophical extremism is an illigitimacy in American politics.

Ohio, called by historians the "mother of presidents," always has been considered not only vital to election to the U.S. presidency, but as a bellwether regarding citizen concerns.

OUR STATE'S electorate is a composite of all the political factions to be found in the nation and candidates do well to tailor their approach to the thinking of the average Ohio voter.

Last Tuesday's Democratic presidential primary election demonstrated this point in the campaign conducted by Sen. George McGovern in his efforts to overcome the pre-election edge held by his chief rival, Sen. Hubert Humphrey.

AS RECENTLY as last month, in primary elections in Wisconsin and Massachusetts, Mr. McGovern deserved to be called the "messiah of the new morality," an epitaph which has been attached to him ever since 1948 when he basked worshipfully at the feet of Henry Wallace, the most liberal of the original New Deal era liberals.

Until Ohio, Mr. McGovern, who once studied for the Methodist ministry, keyed his "new moralism" pronouncements to soft and tender views about amnesty, marijuana and Gay Liberation while heaping scorn at what he called America's wicked war crimes, needless tensions about Communist Russia and the dictator tactics of the late J. Edgar Hoover.

IN OHIO, however, Mr. McGovern learned what his rival candidate, Senator Humphrey, knew all along—that the book "The Real Majority" was correct in contending the vast bulk of voters is in fact "unyoung, unpoor and unblack."

That is why he started complaining about high taxes and hinting he and his fellow liberals may have indeed allowed the law-and-order issue to be slighted. Too, he went so far (for a liberal, that is) as to raise a question about the busing of school children.

OHIO FORCED Candidate McGovern to seek the center of the political spectrum and with a vengeance.

The question about a candidate like George McGovern is whether he learned a permanent lesson. The nation may be told in this week's primaries in Nebraska and West Virginia, in Michigan on May 16, and in Oregon on May 23.

Even if he continues to collect pledged delegates, it will be to no avail in November if he forgets his Ohio lesson—the great mainstream of the American body politic does not cotton to extremism.

THE PLAIN DEALER
Cleveland, Ohio, May 5, 1972

Ohio was a good laboratory in which to test Democratic candidates for the presidency. It is a swing state. It tilts as the nation tilts, and almost invariably lands on the winner's side in presidential contests.

In its trouble-plagued primary Tuesday Ohio gave Sen. Hubert H. Humphrey 41.5% of his party's statewide preference votes. It gave Sen. George McGovern 39.3%. The fallen front-runner, Sen. Edmund S. Muskie, got 8.9%; the newest dropout, Sen. Henry Jackson, got 8.1%, and former Sen. Eugene McCarthy got 2.2%.

This means to us that the Democratic party is gravitating into two nearly equal major factions: the central, traditional-liberal group which Humphrey represents—and the new-liberal, antiestablishment group represented by McGovern.

There is also a maverick bloc led by Gov. George C. Wallace of Alabama. It is compounded of northerners who are just plain against everything; Dixiecrats, warriors on the racial fronts and Democrats who are going to vote for Nixon anyhow.

But the two major factions led by Humphrey and McGovern are sure to fight out the main battles from here on to the nominating convention floor in July at Miami Beach.

Humphrey is striving to hold onto the coalition which was the Democrats' mainstay since Franklin D. Roosevelt. He has got organized labor and a good deal of rank-and-file labor; a good part of the urban minorities, some of the party establishment and a share of farm vote.

McGovern has captured the peace vote, the youth vote, the antiestablishmentarians. He has taken the lead in demanding tax reform, and is the chief critic of the military-industrial complex, pledging he will cut back the Pentagon, reduce U.S. armed forces and stop racing in the nuclear arms area.

Ohio did not prove to be "the West Virginia of this campaign," as McGovern's campaign coordinator, Pierre Salinger, thought possible. It did not mark McGovern as the emerging meteoric winner, as West Virginia did in 1960 for John F. Kennedy.

McGovern stood off Humphrey almost 50-50 in the state. He won over Humphrey in three out of four congressional districts in Greater Cleveland. And he is now reaching for more centrist blocs of voters.

That is how we read the vote facts in the Ohio test tube. It is a battle within the bosom of the Democratic party, not to be decided until the ultimate vote at the national convention.

AKRON BEACON JOURNAL
Akron, Ohio, May 3, 1972

The Ohio primary was the most fouled-up election in memory and the race for the Democratic presidential nomination may have been the closest anywhere so far in 1972. With the final count still hours away, Sen. Hubert Humphrey of Minnesota appeared to have won the 38 at large delegates to the national convention, but Sen. George McGovern of South Dakota was leading in the contest for district delegates.

McGovern said he was delighted with his showing in Ohio, and he had reason to be.

Little known here until about 10 days ago, he had no support from organization Democrats and very little from labor leaders, yet he showed strong appeal to rank and file voters, holding Humphrey almost even statewide and running ahead in many areas.

If the Democratic presidential race was a standoff between Humphrey and McGovern before, that's what it was after Ohio voted. The only thing that was changed by the Ohio primary was the status of Sen. Henry M. Jackson of Washington. After running fourth here, behind Humphrey, McGovern and the recently withdrawn candidate, Sen. Edmund Muskie of Maine, Jackson announced that he would not campaign in any more primaries.

That the vote count in Ohio would be slow was known in advance. Never before had the voters of either party been confronted with such a formidable set of ballots — five slates of at-large delegates and alternates plus varying numbers of slates of district delegates and alternates.

But as it turned out, it wasn't the ballot, with its multiplicity of choices, that caused the big trouble. It was the incredible bungling of election officials, particularly in Cuyahoga County, where voting in some precincts didn't even begin until after the normal closing time.

It goes without saying that the mishandling of the election in Cuyahoga County and elsewhere must be investigated and that the bunglers must be removed.

The results might not have been any different, if the election had been conducted properly, but this is beside the point. Depriving any citizen of his right to vote is intolerable.

THE INDIANAPOLIS NEWS
Indianapolis, Ind., May 3, 1972

The checkerboard pattern of Indiana's primary, with many key races still in doubt, yields one conclusion: Hoosier voters have declared their independence.

This was most obvious, perhaps, in Marion County, where unslated candidates made a spectacular showing against the regular Republican organization. In the spotlighted races, State Sen. Joan Gubbins and State Rep. Robert L. Jones beat the slate to win renomination, in clear-cut victories for the conservative wing of the party. Former State Sen. Dan Burton, running unslated for the 11th District congressional nomination, fought slated candidate William Hudnut to a standstill.

In related upsets, Republican voters also dumped the liberal Rev. Lawrence Voelker from his legislative post and nominated conservative candidate Paul Burkley in the 42nd legislative district. These and other results suggest that conservative feeling has resurfaced in the Marion County GOP, and that organization slates no longer have the magic they seemed to possess in previous primaries. That reassertion of spirit could prove beneficial to the GOP as it looks to the fall election.

Hoosier Democrats were not without a conservative rebellion of their own. Again the organization was leaning one way, while a hefty portion of rank and filers moved off in another. Minnesota Sen. Hubert Humphrey won the presidential primary with considerable backing from party leaders and the chieftains or organized labor. That win, combined with his recent showing in Pennsylvania and Ohio, could well spur him on toward victory at the Democrats' convention in Miami Beach. But even here a conservative flare-up was visible.

In obtaining a sizable hunk of Democratic votes, Alabama Gov. George C. Wallace racked up his best Northern showing to date. He apparently did well among union members, despite the fact that labor leadership is strong for Humphrey. As in Wisconsin and Pennsylvania, he tapped a vein of rightward sentiment in the Democratic Party. Forty-plus per cent of Hoosier Democratic votes for Wallace is a portent that both political parties will have to weigh as they map their November strategies.

Taken together, the ballotings suggest a concerted movement to the right by Hoosier voters. Whether that movement will break through to effective political representation depends on what the major parties and their candidates decide to do about it.

The Detroit News
Detroit, Mich., May 4, 1972

When Alice went through the looking glass, she found a land where you had to run as fast as you could just to keep in the same place. Therein, the presidential primaries of 1972 continue to resemble something out of Wonderland.

Senator Hubert Humphrey won last Tuesday's Democratic primary in Indiana but not by sufficient margin to justify saying he forged ahead.

The count is so slow and the votes so close in the Ohio primary that the winner remains unknown. But enough votes have been counted to show McGovern can neither win a spectacular victory nor suffer a devastating defeat.

Wallace, meanwhile, lost to Humphrey in Indiana but got more votes than he ever got before in a Northern primary, thereby remaining a significant factor in the race for the Democratic nomination.

Thus, the major contenders hold approximately the positions they held previously. The primaries continue to serve as a process for winnowing out slow runners rather than creating a durable and obvious front-runner.

Following the example of Senator Edmund Muskie, who withdrew from active participation in the primaries, Senator Henry Jackson has now announced he will not campaign further in the primaries although he remains a candidate for the nomination. Mayor John Lindsay of New York has long since bit the dust along with a host of other marginal candidates who couldn't make the grade.

Senator Humphrey got a sample last Tuesday of the whipsawing which ripped Muskie to bits. Wallace cut into him in Indiana while McGovern was doing the same in Ohio. It was close enough to show Humphrey the perils of running in too many places simultaneously.

For the moment, McGovern finds himself on an uncomfortable plateau. By doing surprisingly well in several races, he had given a sense of momentum to his campaign, gotten his picture on the covers of the newsmagazines and created great expectations. Ohio has done little or nothing to accelerate the momentum or fulfill the expectations. He turned out to be not a miracle worker but another candidate grinding and slogging it out.

The pressure has never been on Wallace, of course, to prove he can win. He regards any inroads he makes upon the votes of party regulars as so much gravy. But he has now won enough votes so no one in the Democratic Party any longer regards him as a political joke. In Michigan, for example, labor is so concerned it has now formed a coalition to try to stop him.

So that's the kind of race the contest for the Democratic nomination has become and promises to be — a contest in which candidates fight off threats with the hope of simply staying in the race. As the Queen said to Alice: "If you want to get somewhere else, you must run at least twice as fast." Nobody's running twice as fast yet.

St. Louis Globe-Democrat
St. Louis, Mo., May 4, 1972

If Hubert Humphrey ever stops talking, it probably will be because he's speechless over what happened to him in Ohio.

Ohio was supposed to be another Pennsylvania for Humphrey, giving him the chance to prove Democrats in a heavily industrialized state prefer him over George McGovern.

Instead, Ohio was bad news for Humphrey from the moment he got up Tuesday until he left Cleveland at a late hour, with the results still not complete.

Because of incredibly inept election arrangements, many polling places were not open until others were closed. This brought charges and counter-charges from McGovern and Humphrey. The eloquent Hubert corrected a reporter to say he not only denied the McGovern camp's accusations — he denounced them.

Meanwhile, next door in Indiana, George Wallace was uncomfortably close to Humphrey, getting 42 per cent of the vote to 47 per cent for the former vice president. This was Wallace's best showing to date in a Northern state.

When the smoke cleared in Ohio, it appeared Humphrey and McGovern were at a stand-off, with the dreaded possibility McGovern could be the real winner.

So it's on to West Virginia, Nebraska, Michigan, Oregon, New York and California with the choice narrowed. Sen. Henry Jackson, perhaps the ablest Democrat of them all, withdrew as an active candidate after a poor showing in Ohio.

From here on out it appears to be a head-on race between Humphrey and McGovern, with Wallace very much in a position to hold the reins for some real horse trading before the Democratic convention opens July 10.

The New York Times
New York, N.Y., May 4, 1972

For many months, it was the hope of some starry-eyed Democrats that their party would settle early upon one strong contender for the Presidency, thereby avoiding the bitterness of a protracted struggle for the nomination and saving money and energy for the main battle against Mr. Nixon. But the smooth logical resolution of its problems is not the Democratic party way, and could hardly be expected from such a complex heterogeneous coalition.

The voting in the first ten primaries has indeed served to narrow drastically the choice of candidates and at the same time to polarize the party—as usual. Senator Edmund S. Muskie has been driven to the sidelines, where he has now been joined by Senator Henry Jackson, the long-shot favorite of some party conservatives. Defeat in Wisconsin had earlier caused the withdrawal of Mayor John Lindsay, the long-shot favorite of some liberals.

If the nomination can be decided in the primaries—and that is a considerable if—the choice now lies between Senators George McGovern and Hubert Humphrey, with Gov. George C. Wallace having no chance of nomination but very much of an unpredictable disruptive force.

Their neck-and-neck finish in the balloting for the at-large delegates in Ohio suggests that Senators McGovern and Humphrey may be closely matched in strength—which represents a truly striking advance on Senator McGovern's part from his original starting position. Ohio is more typical of the nation in social composition than some of the early primary states such as New Hampshire and Florida, and particularly is it typical of that part of the nation where the Democrats have their greatest support. The virtual standoff in the Ohio voting and the pattern of voting in that state are therefore significant indicators of the balance of power within the national Democratic party. Senator McGovern is most popular with young voters and middle-class liberals. He is making unexpected headway among industrial workers but Senator Humphrey still has an edge with those voters and heavy support from blacks and older people.

A critical but imponderable issue is the extent to which the McGovern and Humphrey supporters are mutually antagonistic. The McGovern side could well argue that the Humphrey voters are "brass-collar Democrats" who will vote for any nominee the party selects, while in contrast a Humphrey nomination would evoke furious disaffection among the younger and more radical McGovern Democrats. The Humphrey side naturally discounts this disaffection, believing that in the end most McGovern voters would accept Mr. Humphrey.

Governor Wallace's volatile performance in the primaries adds to the uncertainty. His strong showing in Indiana is not in itself significant. A Democratic Presidential candidate has carried Indiana only once in the last 32 years. Moreover, that conservative state permits Republicans to vote in the Democratic primary. But it is clear that a sizable fraction of Democrats in Indiana and elsewhere are prepared to vote for Mr. Wallace if he is an independent candidate in November. As the candidates fight their way through to the possibly decisive primaries in California and New York, practically nothing else is clear except that the party is deeply divided and that composing its differences at Miami Beach may prove even more difficult than usual.

©1972 by The New York Times Company. Reprinted by permission.

The Standard-Times
New Bedford, Mass., May 6, 1972

Now, four more presidential primaries later, where do we stand in terms of being able to determine who is likely to do what?

Sen. Hubert H. Humphrey of Minnesota won the most delegates, but Sen. George McGovern of South Dakota did so well that it not only cheered his supporters but stimulated a substantial flood of large contributions to his campaign. There is an indication that, for the first time, Mr. McGovern has penetrated the Eugene J. McCarthy "inner circle," and that some of Mr. McCarthy's backers now have swung to the South Dakotan.

Gov. George C. Wallace of Alabama, still given no chance of winning the nomination by professionals, nevertheless picked up respectable momentum, polling 42 per cent of the popular vote in Indiana. In view of the fact that a Democratic presidential candidate has carried Indiana only once in the last 32 years, presumably Mr. Wallace must still be described as an outsider, but potentially disruptive.

Finally, Sen. Henry Jackson, until now the hope of some Democratic conservative elements, has joined Mayor John Lindsay, and Sen. Edmund S. Muskie on the sidelines.

Thus, with ten primaries behind us, the picture presented suggests some kind of new balance between McGovern and Humphrey, which is, first of all, a large gain for the former.

In Ohio, for example, McGovern managed to hold Humphrey about even, which was impressive because the Minnesota senator had been considered the heavy favorite during most of the campaigning.

With the exception of Mr. Wallace's strong showing, probably Mr. Humphrey's description of the Ohio voting as a "standoff" between him and Mr. McGovern might well be applied to all of the Tuesday voting. Perhaps we are now then on the threshold of a campaign period in which the two leading Democratic contenders will emphasize the differences of view between them, as well as those between them and President Nixon.

If it is conceded that Ohio represents a fairer cross-section of American voters than any state in which a primary election has been held thus far—and this may well be the case—the suggestion is that the two leading contenders are reasonably well-matched, although, assuredly, their strength lies in different areas.

It is assumed that Humphrey has greater appeal to conservatives and labor, based on past performances, and that McGovern is more favored by youth and liberals, but the Ohio results remain so clouded that it is impossible to know whether this picture was altered.

In any event, the difficult task remaining for these two is to give to the voters a clear picture of the alternatives they offer, at the same time hoping that they will not so divide the party over these alternatives as to make mending at convention time an impossibility.

Humphrey supporters have suggested most of McGovern's following could accept a Humphrey nomination; whether the reverse is true is unknown, nor is it known to what degree Mr. McGovern's more liberal approach to problems of world and nation will appeal to younger blacks and union members, whose older counterparts have inclined to the Minnesotan.

The Democrats remained divided, the primaries have not yet established a clear front-runner, the confusion remains—but the field of contenders is much reduced, and it is time for the hopefuls to define themselves specifically.

The Greenville News
Greenville, S.C., May 6, 1972

The primaries this week in Ohio and Indiana produced another casualty in the ranks of the Democratic presidential hopefuls and turned the race for the party's nomination into a three-way draw. The results point to a heated national convention battle this summer in Miami.

Sen. Henry M. Jackson's withdrawal after an extremely poor showing in Ohio was not unexpected. The most conservative of the Democratic candidates, with the exception of Alabama Gov. George Wallace, Sen. Jackson was never able to stir the enthusiasm of the voters.

The low percentage of votes he received in Ohio, after a long and vigorous campaign, finally forced him to the sidelines. He now joins Sen. Edmund S. Muskie in the wings as an "available" compromise candidate in the event of a deadlocked convention.

The race in Ohio was one of the more important contests of the primary series. It is a large industrial state, fairly representative of the county at large.

The virtual tie in the Buckeye State between Sen. Hubert H. Humphrey and Sen. George McGovern kept Sen. Humphrey's candidacy alive, but it was a victory for Sen. McGovern as well. Running to the left of the former vice president, Sen. McGovern proved without a doubt that he has appeal for a large segment of Democratic voters.

It is interesting that in Indiana Sen. Humphrey met the same type of stiff opposition from the right of the party in the person of Gov. Wallace who racked up a percentage of votes impressive enough to convince anybody that he no longer can be considered purely a regional candidate. Sen. Humphrey must find it a bit strange to suddenly have become the center-of-the-party candidate.

The position is bound to be a bit uncomfortable for the long-time liberal senator, especially in light of the rising candidacies of Sen. McGovern and Gov. Wallace. As the situation now stands, the trio could go to Miami in fairly equal positions of strength.

The clear-cut division of voter support among Humphrey, McGovern and Wallace indicates that while all three may have an important say about who the party's candidate will be, none of them so far has shown enough strength to grab the top prize for himself. The possibility grows with each primary that Sen. Jackson, Sen. Muskie, Sen. Edward Kennedy or some dark horse may yet be called to center stage to try and unite the party for the November elections.

Los Angeles Times
Los Angeles, Calif., May 5, 1972

Apparently there was a Democratic presidential primary election in Ohio Tuesday. But the voting went forward in some areas with considerable difficulty, especially in Cuyahoga County, which produces about 25% of the Democratic vote in the state and includes Cleveland. Thousands of Cuyahoga Democrats were frustrated by polling places that never opened, lack of voting machines and machines that did not work.

The voting machine supervisor for Cuyahoga County saw the situation more clearly than anyone else. "The only way to have prevented this fiasco was not to have held the election," he observed philosophically.

But two days later, as Ohio officials got accustomed to the idea that an election had been held and the returns began to pile up, some tentative judgments are possible. Sen. Hubert H. Humphrey appears to have won, but of possibly more significance is the fact that Sen. George S. McGovern managed to hold Humphrey just about even. This, in a state where Humphrey had been considered the easy favorite until a few days before the primary.

Humphrey demonstrated again that he retains a constituency among organized labor and blacks and older liberals. But McGovern apparently was successful in making inroads among ethnic groups and blue-collar workers, and he may get as many as 55 Ohio delegates, five more than the number he said he had to have to make a respectable showing. While the primaries are attracting the most attention, McGovern has been quietly working, with considerable success, to round up delegates in the non-primary states. This reflects his talent for tight political organization, which may be the most significant, if often overlooked, aspect of his success so far.

Overshadowed by the fiasco in voting procedures in Ohio were the results in Indiana; Humphrey won, but only by 5 percentage points over Gov. George C. Wallace, who ran stronger than he ever had before in a Northern state. Wallace also decisively knocked down a challenge in his home state the same day. The bad news candidate of 1972 may turn up in Miami with a larger wrecking crew than was thought likely only a few weeks ago.

A week ago Sen. Edmund Muskie fell by the wayside. Sen. Henry Jackson quietly ducked out of active competition this week. Who can tell what will happen in succeeding primaries, including the big one June 6 in California with its 271 delegates?

No one can be certain. But after all that is why we have elections—to find out. It seems to be the best way.

THE COMMERCIAL APPEAL

Memphis, Tenn., May 7, 1972

MORE THAN two-thirds of the registered voters of Tennessee thought the state's first presidential preferential primary election so unimportant they didn't bother to vote.

As for the results of the half-million votes which were cast, you needn't have tuned in on radio or television on election night to find out. As predicted, Alabama Gov. George Wallace swept up about 68 per cent of the ballots in the Democratic primary, leaving the other 10 in the field to chop the remaining votes into small segments. With the outcome so predestined, no wonder Tennessee saw little of the candidates, and that so few Tennesseans thought it worth a trip to the polls.

What probably got out those who did vote was the issue of public school busing. The statewide referendum on a constitutional amendment to prevent busing for the purpose of school desegregation undoubtedly brought in a goodly bundle of votes for Wallace, an outspoken foe of busing.

Wallace and the busing opponents would like to think that this election gives them momentum. Time will tell, but at the moment it is difficult to see the Tennessee primary as much more than an emotional escape valve for the anti-busing people.

On paper, George Wallace has won the 49 Democratic delegates Tennessee will send to the July convention at Miami Beach. Presumably they would be committed to him on the first two ballots. But these delegates, to be chosen under the party's new rules demanding representation for all kinds of minorities and factions, have yet to be selected. Some of them will be blacks, who are unlikely to feel any loyalty for Wallace.

By the latest count, George McGovern leads in Democratic delegates with 285½. Hubert Humphrey has 181. And Wallace is third with 169 — if you count all 49 from Tennessee, which would be pretty risky.

Governor Wallace may not know until the Tennessee delegation is polled on the first convention ballot just where he stands with the state he won so easily.

THE REFERENDUM on busing was no more meaningful than a Gallup Poll. The people who bothered to vote had a chance to express their feelings. Now they've done it. They've let their congressmen know they want a law to prevent federal judges from issuing school desegregation orders which require busing. The 4-1 outcome is now a matter of record, in case anyone ever wants to look it up.

And that's about all the great, first Tennessee presidential primary meant, except that it allowed the electorate to express some current frustrations — and it gave Knoxville a chance to vote in liquor by the drink.

THE NASHVILLE TENNESSEAN

Nashville, Tenn., May 6, 1972

FOR SUPPORTERS of Governor George C. Wallace the Tennessee preferential primary was an overwhelming success, but for the state it was little more than an expensive way to confirm facts that were already well known.

The primary, which cost at least $300,000 and did not bring money into the state as anticipated, proved that the people in this state do not like busing for racial balance in public schools. But, then, everybody knew that. As the proponent of that view Mr. Wallace's election was a foregone conclusion. Even though three-fourths of the eligible voters did not choose to participate, it is unlikely that the outcome would have been any different had the turnout been large.

In retrospect it seems clear that mistakes and events reduced the primary to virtual insignificance in terms of having a bearing on the national political picture. The timing was disastrous, for the primary was sandwiched in between other contests in which other candidates had better reason to spend their time and money. Also the primary was held so late that candidates who may have given Mr. Wallace competition had already been forced out of contention by other state tallies.

Mr. Wallace benefited from a heavy Republican cross-over vote, as evidence by the large number of traditional GOP precincts which voted in the Democratic column. Of course it is impossible to tell if GOP partisans were trying to spoil the Democratic contest, if Mr. Wallace's appeal drew support across party lines or if — as in Davidson County — Republicans were induced to cross over so that they could have a voice in local elections. In any case, Mr. Wallace did not need the Republican votes to win in Tennessee.

But Mr. Wallace will gain from his victory in Tennessee, even if he does not get the convention support of all the 49 delegates bound to him by state law — a real possibility because of national Democratic party rules. By rolling up a clear majority of 68% Mr. Wallace's momentum has been pushed along — perhaps enough to help him win in North Carolina today where he faces his only serious challenge in a Southern primary. A North Carolina win would give Mr. Wallace a clean sweep of all Southern primaries.

With each passing primary Governor Wallace presents more of a problem to the national Democratic party. There is no clear indication from Mr. Wallace that he will be in the party come November.

Despite the fact that Mr. Wallace is now talking to other issues — big government, tax loopholes, the plight of "the little man" in dealing with the political system, his followers in this state seem satisfied to have his victory in Tennessee a win against busing.

Nobody knows for sure where the Wallace candidacy is going. To Miami Beach and the Democratic convention, it seems certain. But he confirms that he will take only about 300 delegates with him — and that is some 1200 delegates shy of victory. Mr. Wallace has sent his message to Washington on busing. Now the Democratic party waits to hear his message on what his future political party plans will be. Will he stay in, or will he bolt? Until that is clear he will continue to serve as Democratic spoiler, a role he played to perfection in Tennessee Thursday.

The Des Moines Register

Des Moines, Iowa, May 11, 1972

Senator George McGovern survived the pains and perils of being a presidential primary front-runner in the Nebraska preference polling. With most of the vote counted, he had a solid six percentage points lead over Senator Hubert Humphrey.

Although most state Democratic leaders and organized labor backed Humphrey, McGovern had been rated a slight favorite until a few days before the Nebraska election.

In the Alice-in-Wonderland way of primaries, Humphrey's loss is not considered a serious setback. This is particularly true since he won two to one over George Wallace in West Virginia the same day. But, although the McGovern victory is not being treated as a great boost, the pundits had already concluded that a McGovern loss would be a "serious blow" — evidence that McGovern couldn't withstand concentrated political attack. So it goes.

It isn't clear yet how many delegates McGovern will gain in Nebraska (the presidential preference vote is not binding on delegates). The steady accumulation of delegates in other states has given the South Dakotan an early lead in assured convention votes.

Over the weekend, youthful supporters swamped precinct caucuses and the state organization in conservative Oklahoma, assuring McGovern at least 15, possibly 29, of the state's 39 delegates.

And although McGovern did not enter the West Virginia primary, his volunteer organization made a strong bid for some of that state's 35 convention delegates.

St. Petersburg Times

St. Petersburg, Fla., May 11, 1972

West Virginians often say that if all their mountains were flattened out, the state would reach from coast to coast. That's a way of describing rough terrain, and it's also a way of saying that West Virginia — non-Southern, non-Eastern and non-Midwestern — is a politically significant state.

THAT IS why Sen. Hubert H. Humphrey's decisive primary victory there Tuesday in a head-to-head contest against Gov. George Wallace was so important to his campaign.

It gave Humphrey momentum. That makes two Democrats who have it. Sen. George McGovern added to his momentum with his victory over Humphrey and Wallace in Nebraska, even though Humphrey led in delegates.

But to Democratic convention delegates at Miami Beach, Humphrey's West Virginia is more important than McGovern's Nebraska. If Humphrey wins the nomination, he is a solid bet to carry West Virginia in November against President Nixon. Humphrey won the state in 1968, and Johnson and Kennedy carried it in the two previous elections. Kennedy's primary victory in West Virginia over Humphrey in 1960 was the turning point of his campaign.

Nebraska, in contrast, went to Mr. Nixon in both 1968 and 1960.

After these primaries, the Democratic contest looks more than ever like a two-man race between Humphrey and McGovern, with both still building support. The grueling test of the primaries is doing its job. By convention time, it will reveal which of the two is stronger.

The Birmingham News

Birmingham, Ala., May 11, 1972

There was considerable significance in the results of day before yesterday's Democratic primaries that no amount of post election confidence can hide.

Senator Hubert Humphrey's West Virginia total of 68 per cent of the vote, with slightly less than 80 per cent of the boxes reported, was an especially encouraging result for the Minnesotan who saw his nomination fortunes crumble there beneath the Kennedy machine in 1960.

And, although George Wallace virtually wrote off West Virginia late last week, his 32 per cent of the total, which might go a little higher as the scattered rural boxes where he showed most of his strength trickle in, he did passably well considering the effort expended.

Humphrey has displayed the ability to bounce back from his earlier problems in getting his campaign under way. His durability, despite a tendency shown early this year to swap sides on certain issues, may prove to be his greatest advantage between now and the voting roll call at Miami Beach.

Nebraska, despite the exhuberance displayed by Senator George McGovern and his suporters, was not the thumping victory they tried to make it appear to be.

McGovern's 41 per cent of the Cornhusker vote to Humphrey's 35 per cent makes him something considerably less than a solid Democratic asset in that state.

This was the day after President Nixon's strongly-worded announcement of far more stringent military tactics in Vietnam. The North Dakota senator, one of the Senate's more outspoken doves, did not carry a majority of his own party in a state next door to his home base. And, certainly, this gives rise to reasonable speculation about McGovern's bedrock voting pull on the major issues that Americans will hear much about before next November.

There'll be several more tests, extravagant claims and much jockeying for the backing of the polls by July. As the total of all the primaries held by that time may prove—and probably will prove — they cost lots of money and fill the air with challenges and newspaper columns with much froth and less substance, but not too often do they decide who will grab the brass ring at nomination time.

The Charlotte Observer
Charlotte, N.C., May 8, 1972

George Wallace's vote in North Carolina's Democratic presidential primary effectively eliminated Terry Sanford from contention as even a long-shot possibility for the nomination. It also offered more evidence of the strong discontent that is running through the country.

North Carolinians simply did not take Mr. Sanford seriously as a presidential contender. Polls indicated that he was regarded as a "favorite son," and many people seemed to wonder whether he was merely a stalking horse for some major candidate.

Thus we had a primary, the only one of its kind this year, in which voters could not feel that any of the contenders was apt to become president. What, then, did they use the primary for? It is clear that it was used largely as a protest mechanism. And that could only reverberate against Mr. Sanford, who has never been primarily a man of protest, as Mr. Wallace has been.

Mr. Sanford has served this state exceedingly well in the past, and he should not view the results as any kind of personal repudiation. We never regarded him as anything like a major contender for the Democratic nomination, though we felt that if North Carolinians would take him seriously as a contender, he might become a viable alternative in a convention deadlock. The North Carolina primary results rule that out. There are too many other compromise candidate possibilities, and Mr. Sanford's loss of a Southern state — his own — will hardly recommend him to convention brokers as a good bet.

Mr. Sanford already has been of significant service to the state during his brief tenure as president of Duke University, and we hope he will resume that role with renewed vigor.

Gov. Wallace's candidacy would have been substantially set back if he had lost in North Carolina. But it is not substantially enhanced by the victory, since outside the South most people probably assumed he would carry any Southern state in a primary.

Mr. Wallace is still not a serious possibility for the presidential or vice presidential nomination, if for no other reason than that such a nomination would shatter the party and drive away many of those who are necessary for any Democratic victory. But he continues to enhance his role as a spoiler for the convention.

Pittsburgh Post-Gazette
Pittsburgh, Pa., May 11, 1972

THE MOST significant outcome of the latest round of presidential preference primaries was the shellacking Governor Wallace took in West Virginia.

There Senator Humphrey won two-to-one in the only head-to-head confrontation between these two particular candidates in the 1972 campaign. Whether one considers West Virginia a border state or northern, it was an important indicator. Certainly, had the conclusion gone the other way, Mr. Wallace would have a great deal to crow about.

The outcome is particularly interesting in view of the inroads Mr. Wallace made in the April 25 Pennsylvania primary in southwestern Pennsylvania, which has some characteristics similar to West Virginia.

Probably labor influence was stronger there in holding the rank-and-file to Humphrey. Maybe the seriousness of the idea of a Wallace presidency has begun to sink in so that even persons upset about present conditions in our country have become cautious about balloting for him.

We'll have a clearer picture on that next week in the Michigan primary where Mr. Wallace is expected to do quite well.

But the importance of the West Virginia primary is that it can be used to counter any notion that Mr. Wallace and what he stands for are inevitably sweeping the nation.

* * *

The other primary Tuesday was in Nebraska where Senator McGovern continued to show his appeal and vote-getting strength by edging Mr. Humphrey.

Oddly enough, though, Mr. McGovern now is experiencing the perils of being a front-runner. He is being tut-tutted for not having won bigger in Nebraska, when a month ago his present winning streak would have seemed highly improbable.

It's much like New Hampshire where Senator Muskie got "only" 48 per cent and was virtually declared a loser by the commentators for not outstripping the opposition (including Mr. McGovern) by a far greater margin.

THE LINCOLN STAR
Lincoln, Neb., May 10, 1972

Regardless of how the presidential primary election turned out, the campaign leading up to the voting Tuesday was different in several respects than the Kennedy-McCarthy confrontation in Nebraska in 1968.

Sens. Hubert Humphrey and George McGovern played to smaller crowds, for one thing. Certainly, there were ready-made crowds that Humphrey and McGovern could work — such as the McGovern benefit concert in Lincoln, the Cornhusker spring football game and the Ak-Sar-Ben races — but the candidates didn't draw them.

The McGovern whistle-stop tour, a strategy acquired from the late Robert Kennedy's organization, failed to generate the turnouts that thronged the Platte valley depots when RFK stumped the state in 1968. Those that came were enthusiastic, but one got the feeling that the undecided, the just plain curious, were not there. Those that stood on the sidings would have been there blizzard or earthquake, and McGovern had their votes — or a large share of them — anyway. Sen. Humphrey similarly failed to turn out the people in any appreciable numbers.

The rotten weather last weekend had something to do with it. But more than the weather, the lack of large crowds can best be attributed to organization and scheduling. Robert Kennedy's advance men herded people to the depots and courthouse lawns. Schedules were set days in advance, not, as in 1972, a few short hours before Humphrey or McGovern came to town. The camps of the two front runners might have done great canvassing work, but the organizational work was not reflected in crowd size.

A record voter turnout might take the edge off this argument. Perhaps there was great underlying interest, but on the hustings, the Democratic presidential primary was not a pulse-quickening affair.

Another difference — it seemed different, at least — was that this year the candidates spent an unnecessary amount of time explaining their positions on petty issues. Maybe, in the case of McGovern especially, they were forced to. But at a time when war, inflation, farm income and other major issues are — or should be — of major concern to Nebraskans, it is too bad that Humphrey and McGovern had to spend so much time on abortion and marijuna. Their answers to the real problems facing this country didn't get a decent hearing.

Toward the end, the Nebraska primary was written off by many observers and the major networks as inconsequential. It might have seemed that way because of the lack of enthusiasm generated and the necessity to debate picayune issues, as well as the fact that Nebraska packs a meager punch when it comes to delegate-counting. But it was important to the candidates. For McGovern, to demonstrate he could win close to home and blunt Humphrey's momentum. And for Humphrey, too, despite his statement that a loss here wouldn't hurt him. He could have spent much of the last week in California.

Campaign '72:
GOV. WALLACE SHOT IN MARYLAND; MURDER ATTEMPT SPARKS GUN DEBATE

Alabama Gov. George C. Wallace, campaigning in Maryland May 15 on the eve of Democratic presidential primaries being held there and in Michigan [See pp. 691–696], was seriously wounded in the chest and stomach by pistol shots as he addressed a rally at a shopping center in the Washington suburb of Laurel. Three other persons were struck by bullets before security personnel could subdue the alleged assailant, identified soon afterwards as Herman Bremer, a 21-year-old white man from Milwaukee. Wallace, who underwent five hours of emergency surgery following the shooting, was taken off the critical list the next day, but a bullet remained lodged dangerously close to his spinal cord resulting in paralysis from the hips down.

While Gov. Wallace recuperated from his wounds, federal and state officials began prosecutions against Bremer and investigations into his background. Preliminary inquiries revealed that Bremer had been arrested in 1971 and charged with possession of a concealed gun. He was released after pleading guilty to a lesser charge and paying a fine. The attempted assassination revived the debate on gun control and the protection of political celebrities. During the controversy, the Senate Judiciary Committee's subcommittee on juvenile delinquency voted May 17 to limit the sale of handguns to law enforcement agencies and the military unless such weapons were found suitable for "lawful sporting purposes."

THE WALL STREET JOURNAL.
New York, N.Y., May 16, 1972

Immediately after the assassinations of President John Kennedy, Martin Luther King and Sen. Robert Kennedy, Americans were subjected to the most sustained self-flagellation in history. One after another, commentators and columnists, theologians and teachers, psychologists and sociologists insisted that "we are all guilty," and proceeded to bludgeon 200 million Americans with the crime of collective guilt.

The attempted assassination of Gov. George Wallace rekindled some of that same effort to indict an entire society, the very thing Edmund Burke said he did not know how to do. But for the most part there was commendable restraint all around. We don't know if it will continue that way, but for now the TV and radio networks have not once again subjected viewers and listeners to swarms of accusers trying to saddle them with the guilt of specific violent acts.

The United States has suffered more than its share of violence throughout its turbulent history, as Alan Otten details alongside. It seems to us likely that certain historical and social factors, such as a heterogeneous society, instant communications and impassioned politics, may influence at least the way violence is expressed. But that is a far cry from the accusation that violence proves Americans somehow a cut below the rest of humanity. For while violence can be found in the American tradition, a larger part of that tradition is willingness to work within the bounds of tolerance and fair play to resolve differences.

Accusations of collective guilt are really moral cop-outs because they destroy moral judgment altogether. By denying that men have even the most fundamental control over their behavior, the notion of collective guilt rejects the very essence of our Judeo-Christian tradition. By viewing society as an organic whole instead of as an aggregate of individuals, it rejects the unique individuality in each person.

Further, open-ended accusations against "society" may well breed rather than diminish violence by spreading guilt feelings among those who are clearly not guilty, and by failing to place responsibility on those who clearly are. Logically, if everybody is guilty, then it follows that no one is really guilty.

It is important to deplore every aggressive act. It is important to try to understand and eliminate the frustrations that feed aggression. But it is likewise important to repudiate the dangerously fashionable notion that all of us pulled the triggers of the guns in Dallas, Memphis, Los Angeles, and Laurel, Md.

TWIN CITY SENTINEL
Winston-Salem, N.C., May 17, 1972

Here on the eve of our national bicentennial as "mankind's last and best hope," we still can't seem to curb an impulse to violence that focuses almost relentlessly on our political campaigns.

Once again, as before, we are keeping solemn vigil over the bed of yet another victim of this madness; once again, as before, we are demonstrating to the rest of the world how dangerous we can be when our blood is up.

But the world knows who and what we are. It doesn't forget it. It is here in this country, that our violent past is casually ignored. We pretend to be the best-behaved of all nations, and in the main we probably are. But when a political leader like Gov. Wallace can't even speak his piece without being shouted down and struck with oranges and rocks and now bullets, then we have lost something crucial to our very survival: That measurable quantum of civility that allows any man to speak what he believes loud and clear, and to speak it to those who share his beliefs, without being cut down like an animal.

That is what civility is. We no longer have it in our land.

And this is the most savage irony of all — the fact that *we* must learn once again how essential a quantum of tolerance is to our system. After the madness and conflicts of our past, after all we have suffered at the hands of murderous zealots and mad men, a sense of political tolerance ought to be second nature to us.

But it isn't; and so another victim has fallen, another political "decision" made by a bullet instead of the ballot.

Gov. Wallace, like his Democratic opponents, like the President himself, has every right to aspire to any office in the land. It is as much his land as anybody else's. He has the right not only to seek higher office but to speak what he believes to be the truth and to encourage others to join with him. When he was deprived of that right Monday afternoon by a man with a pistol, then something was pulled loose inside all of us.

The candidate and his family have lost far more than the rest of us, even if he survives and returns to his vigorous campaigning. But we have lost something too, all of us. We have lost one more fight and given up one more foot of this country to mad men and anarchy.

And there is only so much we can surrender before we surrender all of it. If this impulse to violence succeeds in driving our political office-seekers into secure studios, if we are forced into an era of the canned, snipped, edited, tailor-made political candidate simply because the streets aren't safe for such men and women, we may find that we have pushed this delicate, tempermental, precariously perched democracy of ours beyond its limits.

ST. LOUIS POST-DISPATCH
St. Louis, Mo., May 16, 1972

The shocking attack on Gov. George Wallace of Alabama as he campaigned in Maryland for the Democratic presidential nomination should give every American pause. What kind of country is it, what kind of climate are we living in, that impels people to seek political decisions by bullets? Can our society survive the hatred that seems all too ready to spring to the surface and vent its frustrations in mindless violence?

When such things can happen it lends credibility to the belief that one obstacle in the way of a decision by Senator Kennedy of Massachusetts to become a candidate for the presidency this year is the fear of assassination. This is understandable in a man whose two brothers, one a President and the other an aspirant for that high office, were murdered. But what a commentary!

The attack on Gov. Wallace shows that violence has no political ideology. John Kennedy and Robert Kennedy stood to the political left, George Wallace to the right—and Martin Luther King stood simply for human rights. But fanatics who disagreed with them brought them down. The whole idea of America is that political differences shall be settled at the ballot box, not through the barrel of a gun. The violent repudiate this principle.

This newspaper is in almost total political disagreement with George Wallace, and it must be said that in his manner and his actions he himself courted violence. Yet the place for the nation to express itself on what George Wallace stands for is the polling booth. Every American must feel a sense of shame and trepidation at what occurred in Maryland. Must every candidate walk in fear?

The answer is Yes, unless somehow the root causes of America's malaise can be singled out and dealt with by leaders dedicated to bringing back harmony and rationality. There is no doubt that the official violence and brutality of the Vietnam War has contributed to a climate in which distrust, frustration and desperation indicate courses of antisocial action. Violence in Indochina has its counterpart in crime in the streets and the urge to settle scores by brute force, not argument.

George Wallace is not a leader who can bring men together; quite the contrary. But he has the right to test his political philosophy in the marketplace, so that the people may decide. Injuring him will not injure what he stands for; only votes will do that. So we hope that Mr. Wallace recovers rapidly and completely from his wounds, and that the shooting will somehow generate more tolerance for the expression of thoughts that may be abhorrent.

The San Diego Union
San Diego, Calif., May 19, 1972

American citizens, heartened by the news that presidential candidate George Wallace is out of danger from the bullet wounds inflicted by an assassin, are praying for his full recovery.

Concurrent with their prayers it is apparent that Americans also are doing a great deal of soul-searching in an effort to discover the root causes of the social illness that leads to such attacks upon public figures.

As study goes forward, comments are heard that the United States of America is a sick society, that it is sliding backward into a primeval barbarism, and that a bent for violence that has been endemic for years has become the rule rather than the exception.

This is nonsense. If Americans will but look about them they will see the strength and resilience of their society. Our moral standards, despite aberrations, are high, our laws are just, our institutions are outstanding, our Constitution still is an example to the world and most of the 200 million American citizens are respectable, hard working, loyal and responsible.

Indeed if the majority of Americans have erred in respect to the increase in violence it is because of the healthy aspects of their society, not its sickness. It appears that Americans simply have not yet settled on the permissible boundaries of right and wrong, nor have they defined adequately the permissible boundaries of dissent.

All responsible citizens will agree that the vitality and progress of the United States depends upon the freedom of its people to challenge the decisions of their government and institutions through legitimate channels. They also agree that such dissent should be given great latitude.

However, in their desire to provide the greatest possible range of opportunities for disagreement, Americans may have let their innate sense of tolerance gain the edge over their reason.

Through permissive court decisions, benign law enforcement and overly liberal laws, Americans have given tools to many persons who are far more than responsible dissenters. In doing so they also have shifted the focus of national interest from the accomplishments of the good citizens to the actions of the violent few.

While persons committed to violence and assassination may have many motives for their behavior, or even none at all, it also is true that they live in a larger society and are encouraged by its attitudes.

Thus, as we look at the events that led to the shooting of a presidential candidate, we must by all means look to our national weaknesses and correct those that can be corrected. Equally important, it will benefit all Americans to review the sources of national strength and to rededicate themselves to nourishing the qualities that made the United States the envy of the world for almost two centuries.

The New York Times
New York, N.Y., May 21, 1972

The scenario has become terrifyingly familiar. After the assassin's bullets—the numbing shock, the fear of a wider plot or spreading chaos, then the shame and finally the explanation—accurate but inadequate—that, really, in so large a country there can never be safety from the demented deeds of a minute fringe of the insanely and unpredictably violent. And so it was again when sudden shots felled Governor Wallace last week.

It is true that individual psychopaths have been primarily responsible for these assassinations and murderous assaults. Specific changes in policies and practices including stricter gun control, better police protection for candidates and an end to reckless campaign activities are essential to defeat these irrational attempts.

But the violent fantasies acted out by psychopaths reflect like a distorting mirror the stresses and failings of the larger society. Political assassination is rare in some countries and is becoming common to this one. Why is this so? If the secondary contributing causes can be discerned and corrected, the fantasies of these would-be killers may change their shape and the deterrent restraints which government erects against them may prove more effective.

The deeper disease is a widening gap between the American self-image of a country that values human life and the reality of a growing preoccupation with the competitive drive for power, the need to get to the top, no matter how many others must be trampled in the climb to prominence or notoriety.

The corrupting element is growing resort to violence in word and deed, the effort to gain recognition through individual or group force. Most violent crimes are committed by society's failures.

The right to bear arms, intended to signify merely the nation's right to self-defense, has been distorted to make many Americans consider it the sign of manhood to speak through the barrel of a gun. National honor abroad and personal success at home have become fatally entangled in the delusion that might makes right. When the laws or facts are inconvenient, they are circumvented, shredded and ignored.

The rush for power in business and in politics turns irrational as well as unsatisfying because the goals have become blurred. Mutual suspicions in a divided society make it easy to rationalize the ruthless threat of force. In the process, old bonds are broken and the fabric of family, friendship, community and country becomes frayed. The violent act is the reckless bid for recognition of those who slump from alienation to despair. It is the insane imitation of the way power is seen abused in the total environment—in military operations abroad and business tactics at home.

Such a pollution of the political environment is as deadly as the fouling of the air and water, but like the latter it can be halted. The country has the heritage and the institutions to free itself from the tyranny of violence and fear. What is needed are leaders and policies —at all levels of representative government—courageous enough to heal the divisions which too many now exploit as an avenue to power. Americans must seek guidance from those who shun self-righteous bombast —in politics, government, business and military affairs —and find strength instead in rational debate and reasoned action.

©1972 by The New York Times Company. Reprinted by permission.

St. Louis Globe-Democrat
St. Louis, Mo., May 16, 1972

The shooting of Gov. George C. Wallace as he campaigned in a shopping center in Laurel, Md., is another national tragedy and an indictment of our way of life.

Governor Wallace, a courageous man who has attracted widespread support across the nation for his vigorous campaign against school busing, big government, wasteful federal spending and high taxes, has now been struck down by a man who fired a gun at close range, hitting the Governor four times — three times in the right arm and once in the right side.

Suddenly the presidential race has been turned into a nightmare. An ugly cloud now hangs over the Democratic presidential contest. It is hoped that it will not trigger reactions and counter-reactions that could further polarize and divide the nation.

We pray that Governor Wallace will recover from his wounds and be able to resume his campaign that has stirred so many Americans to his side that he is the favorite in today's preferential primaries in Michigan and Maryland.

This senseless shooting of Governor Wallace, coming as it does so soon after the assassination of President John F. Kennedy, the slaying of his brother Robert F. Kennedy and the killing of civil rights leader Martin Luther King, could again inflame and divide the nation at a time when there is a need for unity.

It is getting to be so dangerous for anyone to run for high public office in the United States that it is a wonder that any man or woman still risks his or her life in this climate of hate and violence.

This chain of violence, if not stopped, can undermine our whole society.

In our opinion the single, most identifiable cause of this rash of assassinations and shootings of the nation's highest public figures is due to the permissiveness in our society that has allowed violence to become an accepted way of protesting and seeking change.

The George McGoverns, the Eugene McCarthys and others who spur on the violent and the violence-prone mobs and scream hate and invective at the President almost daily have done much to foster this climate of violence.

When unreasoning men running for the highest office in the land look the other way when their supporters rampage and destroy, and even encourage these hoodlum tactics, how can reason and order survive?

When violence is exalted on television and in films until it makes the viewer almost sick to his stomach, isn't it time that the nation re-examined its motives and goals?

An anything-goes society that turns its back on moral values and respect for the law is a society that hasn't the backbone or the courage to administer the stern but fair justice required to deal with the man with a knife or gun.

The wounding of Governor Wallace is another warning that a sickness is engulfing our society — a sickness that must be cured if our nation is to survive.

The Standard-Times
New Bedford, Mass., May 20, 1972

Among the early comments on the shooting of Governor Wallace, written when it was not known whether he would survive—were these:

"Little as this newspaper shares Governor Wallace's opinions, we earnestly hope for his quick and complete recovery . . ."

"Never mind what George Wallace stands for. The attempt to assassinate him was a foul and terrible act."

"Never mind the political consequences of this senseless deed. The only thing men of reason and decency can hope for is that Mr. Wallace recovers, as speedily as possible."

One word described these begrudging, qualified reactions to the felling of an American presidential candidate by a gunman. Shocking.

The first comment states, in effect, that even though one disagrees with Mr. Wallace, one should not hope for his death.

The second admonishes Americans not to place first in their thinking the political image of the governor, but to try and remember that he never deserved to be the target of an assassin.

The third — the most brutal — declares that the limited category of "decent and reasonable" men should not despair about what the shooting may have done to their political strategies and goals, but should give priority to hoping that the victim recovers.

Taken in concert, the theme of these comments could be taken to mean that this presidential candidate is one whose outlook and influence is so despicable that many Americans might be expected to countenance, if not wish for, violence against him.

This is, in our opinion, an insulting appraisal of the American people. There may be some who wished Mr. Wallace physical harm but they are deranged, we would say, or else they have been misled by exactly the kind of thinking (he's bad, but don't kill him) reflected in the comments quoted above.

It's going to require a national effort to disentangle violence from dissent in this nation. We regret that an oracle of opinion and influence like the New York Times and its associate editor, Tom Wicker, should have been the authors of these qualified appraisals on the shooting of a prominent American public servant.

THE DAILY OKLAHOMAN
Oklahoma City, Okla., May 17, 1972

EXPRESSIONS of shock and dismay in the aftermath of the pistol attack on Gov. George Wallace are strikingly similar to the reaction evoked by earlier acts of political violence in the nation.

The frequency with which violence is intruding on the political process is taken as a symptom of some deep-seated malignancy which afflicts the entire nation. Concern is expressed for the future of representative government if affairs have reached such a pass that public figures no longer can express their views freely without placing their lives in jeopardy.

Similar expressions were heard after the shootings of President John F. Kennedy, Sen. Robert F. Kennedy and Dr. Martin Luther King. In all those prior instances, the assessment of some sort of collective national guilt was widely accepted. Although a single triggerman was responsible for each attack, the plural pronoun "they" was commonly used initially in assigning blame.

The present instance is no exception. In a singular display of emotional disarray, a Wallace supporter at Montgomery, Ala., deplores the violence as "awful," and then goes on to say that "we wish we could blow the whole state of Maryland up." The fallen Wallace is quoted by a campaign worker as having asked after the shooting where "they" got him.

The fact is that much of the political violence that has occurred in this country over the years has been the senseless work of unstable notoriety seekers lacking in any rational motivation. Politicians of enough national stature to attract the attention of such individuals have recognized the near impossibility of preventing assassination attempts.

To Abraham Lincoln is attributed this comment: "What does anybody want to assassinate me for? If anyone wants to do so, he can do it any day or night if he is ready to give his life for mine."

The price of assassination has been marked down since the brooding John Wilkes Booth gave his life for Lincoln's. Unless the U. S. Supreme Court rules otherwise, Sirhan Bishara Sirhan, the Jordanian convicted of assassinating Sen. Kennedy, will escape the gas chamber under a state supreme court finding that the death penalty is "cruel or unusual punishment" and therefore is in conflict with the California constitution.

Sen. Kennedy was aware of the risks he was taking as a presidential aspirant. "I play Russian roulette every time I get up in the morning," he told friends. "But I just don't care. There's nothing I could do about it anyway." His brother, the late president, had expressed a similar fatalistic attitude, as had Martin Luther King.

After observing that the nation had suffered more than enough from the intrusion of violence into its political processes, President Nixon said of the Wallace shooting: "We must all stand together to eliminate this vicious threat to our public life. We must not permit the shadow of violence to fall over our country again."

But there's little actually that the people can do to prevent the random acts of erratic individuals. The candidates themselves are in a position best to take the precautions that could discourage attempts on their lives.

A first imperative would be to overcome the urge to mix in close quarters with crowds in order to engage in what President Lyndon Johnson used to characterize as "pressing the flesh."

Chicago Daily Defender
Chicago, Ill., May 17, 1972

The bullets that fell Alabama Governor George C. Wallace are symptomatic of the emotional hysteria that accompanies the struggle for power in American politics. The morbid scene at Laurel, Md., was in retrospect a vivid re-enactment of previous tragedies that in the past have punctured the air with their hair-raising inerruption of a flaming campaign.

Wallace's unflagging rhetoric on school busing has cut a deep emotional swath in the consciousness of the people on both sides of this burning issue. To those who hold contrary conviction to busing, George Wallace was a knight in shining armor going forth to do battle with the citizens who believe that court injunctions should be obeyed and that busing is the best available mechanism for hastening the end of the racial imbalance which has plagued the American schools and impeded public education far too long.

Wallace has poured all his forensic skills into the debate on integration. Viewed in historical perspective, he has moved up a wrung in the ladder of moral compunction. He moved from "Segregation today, segregation to-morrow and segregation forever," the central theme of his inaugural address when he was first elected Governor of Alabama—to the acceptance of integration as a badge of progress in the leveling process of education. However, he stands four-square against court-ordered school busing to achieve racial balance.

Yet, he uses torrents of oratorical phrases in his indefatigable advocacy of "law and order." It is a contridiction for which the Governor of Alabama has been at pain to find supporting logic. He has set in motion the fury of which he is now the victim. We hope from his recovery will emerge a man with a greater sense of his moral responsibility to his countrymen and to his nation.

The Des Moines Register
Des Moines, Iowa., May 17, 1972

Admirers and critics of George Corley Wallace join in indignation and sorrow at the shooting which left him in grave condition, with both legs paralyzed, perhaps for life.

Americans are right to reproach themselves for the large amount of violence in their culture, illustrated anew by the shooting. But they need not panic.

This assassination attempt, plus the successful assassinations of President John Kennedy, Senator Robert Kennedy, Dr. Martin Luther King, jr., Lee Oswald and Malcolm X do not add up to a trend to assassinate political figures, still less political leaders of any one persuasion. All but one of these victims were killed by a loner, not by members of any organized group with a political goal. Malcolm X was a possible exception.

The fact that the victims were conspicuous political figures is coincidence, not a sinister new trend. Lonely, hating men may emulate a type of behavior which attracts a large amount of popular and media attention. But five killings of political figures by such a job lot of lone assassins do not add up to any sort of trend.

Quite different were the political killings which marked the Algerian-French struggle of some years ago, with Arab killing Arab and Frenchmen killing Frenchmen as well as each other, to enforce extremist views.

Quite different also was the campaign of Japanese militarists in the 1930s to kill or cow the leaders of more moderate views. Still different was the international campaign of the violent wing of the Anarchist movement in the period from the 1860s to 1914 to kill government leaders as "propaganda of the deed."

The shooting of Wallace does point up a need for greater precautions by presidential candidates and for them. (Do the candidates need to walk through crowds shaking hands?)

But it would be foolish for the country to try to prevent such random follies as the Wallace shooting by wholesale cracking down on dissenters.

If stricter gun-control laws are needed (and we think they are), it is because the United States has one of the highest rates in the civilized world for deaths due to firearms, in all three categories: accidents, suicides and homicides. Thousands of Americans die each year in each of these three ways by gunfire.

A gun control law making it more difficult for unstable people to get handguns probably could reduce the number of killings. But it couldn't prevent the occasional fanatic assassin from trying his deed.

The Boston Globe
Boston, Mass., May 21, 1972

Behind the attempted assassination of Governor George Wallace lies the larger question of rage in our society. The person who leans on his car horn in a traffic jam, the parent who tells his child, "I'll kill you if you do that again," are presumed to have the built-in controls to stop there. But an occurrence like the one last Monday raises the question of how far the threshold of violence can be raised on such levels before it pushes the deranged person over the top.

Psychiatrist Robert Coles says, "The everyday difficulties that people are having that cause them to be annoyed with each other, in my opinion, are not to be confused psychologically with the acts of an assassin. Nor should the difficulties that a society is having be quickly brought up as explanations for such acts."

Agreed. And this is not intended to be a "mea culpa." Rage is a legitimate emotion and some expression of it may be more useful in reducing acts of violence than the super-polite atmosphere that has produced lynchings in the South or the tidy-mindedness of places like Japan and Sweden where rage is expressed in the form of suicide.

In a society that puts incredible pressures on its members, that compels people to conform against their natural instincts, instincts, that fosters isolation and loneliness, most people respond with extraordinary patience and generosity toward each other. And, as Dr. Coles indicates, it would be an outrage to escalate the everyday rhubarb into a potential assassination.

But there are points, unrecognized and unremarked in our daily lives, at which the natural outburst gets close to the firing point and, because they are so largely unremarked, it may be worth giving them a thought.

The Archie Bunker malapropism when he tells wife Edith to "stifle yourself" may turn out not to be a joke. The words "I'll kill you" could be taken literally. After the shooting at Laurel, Maryland, the manager of a local store said, "It's awful and we wish we could blow up the whole state of Maryland." Someone in the crowd had shouted, "Kill him,'" and the reaction of a few on that night's talk shows was that Governor Wallace should be dead.

None of these remarks was intended to be taken seriously. But police statistics show all too clearly that bombings, knifings and shootings are taking place with increasing frequency. And, when a 10-year-old child has a gun and uses it to shoot a friend with whom he has had an argument, as happened here last Tuesday, it becomes obvious that the gap between the message and the act is narrowing.

The current television advertisement for a headache remedy that shows a middle-class housewife wavering as in a heat storm and promising herself "I will not shout at my children" strikes an all too familiar chord. And it echoes the pathetic fantasy of the man charged with shooting Governor Wallace who once wrote "I like to think that I was living with a TV family and there was no one yelling at home and no one hit me."

The constant pressure of crowding, the unending assault of noise, time saving devices that indicate the need for yet more time, competition at home and in the office and a too-remote bureaucracy everywhere are all part of the pileup of pressures that drive the desperate to acts of violence.

And, in the background, we have a country divided over the war in Vietnam, broken apart on issues like school busing, wracked by unemployment, and in the throes of a political campaign in which bombast too often outweighs reason.

If it seems impossible to do anything about the big issues, if the councilor is always out, if the insurance company and the car salesman won't come through, at least we can think twice about adding to the aggravation by shouting at each other. In the end, it is on this level that push really comes to shove and it is here that we can start de-escalating the climate of violence in America.

THE ROANOKE TIMES
Roanoke, Va., May 17, 1972

In the first startled reaction to the shooting of Alabama Gov. George Wallace, The Associated Press gathered, among others, these three statements:

From presidential candidate George McGovern: "If we've gotten to the point in this country where a public figure can't speak out on the issues of the day and seek the presidency without being shot, then I tremble for the future of our nation."

From Joe C. Phillips, a Wallace campaign worker in Oklahoma: "Mister, if they want a fight, they've got one . . . If they kill Wallace, I'll spend the rest of my life running them down. I'm not afraid of them."

From Los Angeles Mayor Sam Yorty: "Governor Wallace . . . was quite critical of many of the militant anti-law enforcement activists and, without knowing any more facts, I would assume that's probably part of the background of the attack. . ."

Those are gut reactions, and probably they are quite close to what many Americans assumed when the news first came out. The natural tendency was to think that Mr. Wallace, a controversial public figure, was shot by someone who disagreed with his political views. It is the kind of initial reaction people probably had when they heard of the shootings of John F. Kennedy, of his brother Robert, of Martin Luther King Jr.

The easy assumption has, in most cases, been proved entirely wrong. In virtually every assassination in this country in the 20th century, the killer has been shown to have no ideological motive—none, at least, that would make sense to the average person.

Demonstrably, there was no political conspiracy behind the slayings of the Kennedys; and who are "they" that the Oklahoman Mr. Phillips is ready to fight? No group, it appears; just a lone, 21-year-old Midwestern white youth whom not even his immediate family could fathom.

This is one frightening feature of the violence visited on political figures in our time: It is most often random. The victim is chosen not for his views but because, in the muddled mind of the attacker, he is prominent and he represents some kind of force, authority or whatever that must be struck down.

There may be no particular lesson to draw from this, which is what makes such sorrowful incidents the more frustrating. At least we need not, just yet, tremble for our nation's future because political factions are prepared to gun each other down. They are not. What we must tremble for is the vulnerability of human beings like George Wallace who can get in the way of crackpots in any city or hamlet across the nation.

Des Moines Tribune
Des Moines, Iowa, May 19, 1972

Several columnists have expressed relief that George Wallace's assailant wasn't black. One feared that if the shooting had been done by a black person, it might have triggered a race war. (See article by William Raspberry on this page.)

Concern about the color of the would-be assassin was shared by many. One of the first questions asked when word was flashed of the attack on Wallace was about the attacker's race. Reporters recognized the public's interest in this by pointedly describing Arthur Bremer as a white man.

The interest is understandable. Wallace came into the public eye as a segregationist. The assailant's race could provide a clue to the motive for the shooting at a time when little was known except that Wallace was shot.

But the anxiety expressed lest this be the deed of a black person is disturbing. Is America so racist that the guilt of one person would be imputed to a whole class of persons solely on the basis of that one person's race?

Guilt is individual, not collective. It is depressing that people were concerned about the color of the assailant's skin and relieved that it was white.

WINSTON-SALEM JOURNAL
Winston-Salem, N.C., May 31, 1972

TWO little girls, step-sisters, ages 3 and 6, lay clinging to each other against the curb of a shopping center street. Both were crying. Both had been shot. One was trying to wipe the blood from the other's hair and clothing.

Their father lay dead in the middle of the street.

It was just another day in America, in North Carolina. Another "loner," as they always seem to be described, had very calmly shot down a dozen people, including himself, at a Raleigh shopping center. A young man, perhaps insane, perhaps physically ill, had spread his own secret tragedy into the lives of a crowd that never knew he existed.

In Concord, the National Guard was still on duty, maintaining an uneasy peace after the civil disorder there. It all began when a black man was shot in a grocery store.

In Hollywood, Clint Eastwood, the world's number one box office attraction, still hasn't made up his mind whether he will make a sequel to "Dirty Harry," the cop who defies his superiors' orders and stalks criminals so he can shoot them in the head with his .44 magnum.

It all falls into place. Murder is a national option. It's so much a part of our entertainment, our news, our lives, that some of us accept it as a natural response.

So when we get angry, when we get drunk, when we go insane, and the time has come for us to react, the murder which was planted there long ago by hundreds of movies becomes one of a long list of responses we have to choose from.

Murder, assassination, war, rage have always been with us. But in our state of civilization, which we would like to believe is advanced, our textbook learning tells us that these things are basically repulsive. Yet murder rates continue to climb. Rage simmers more than ever beneath even the calmest personality.

And murder seems increasingly to be the option of the enraged.

So what do we do about it? Take away everybody's guns? Make the enraged turn more to bombs or knives? Certainly the tools of murder should come under some form of regulation, but no one believes that strict gun laws will eradicate the problem altogether.

Perhaps we should start combing our society for the "loners" and misfits. But does that mean we lock up all the Albert Einsteins who shun people simply so they can have some peace and quiet within their own minds? Does it mean that we must strive for a uniform national personality?

Perhaps we should mount a new campaign against mental illness, much like the war on poverty, mobilizing every social worker in the nation to peer into every home for the demented and almost demented.

All these things are likely to be mentioned at some time or other as reaction to the ever mounting number of senseless killings on our streets. But the fact is that there is no formal program we can start to deal with murder as a national aberration.

Instead, we must have a national commitment from those people who build our tastes and styles. It will cost nothing, injure nobody. Simply, it is to remove murder from its current prominence in entertainment.

This doesn't mean that high school kids will never learn that Caesar was stabbed. Rather, it means that murder as a casual, look - him - in - the - eye - then - shoot - him pastime, must be rejected.

Gunsmoke, Bonanza and Mannix can stay with us. They can even have a shooting or two. But explicit, cold-blooded, slow motion, blood-spraying killing, must end.

Such a demand seems like a small thing in the face of what is a national crisis with violence. But small things like entertainment seem to be shaping our personalities while we're unaware of it. And we suspect that this subliminal erosion of our character, this wearing away of values by repeated exposure to non-values, is at the heart of our new-found violence.

The Chattanooga Times

Chattanooga, Tenn., May 17, 1972

Physicians are laboring helpfully and with hopefulness to start George Walace on the road to recovery from wounds inflicted by a would-be assassin. The American people, as completely stunned as a diverse—and sometimes perverse—society can be over a single savage act, are deeply introspective as they probe for the cause, and a cure, for recurring political bloodshed.

The litter of a rented room and acquaintances' recollections of an outwardly quiet and inwardly turned young man offer only faint clues as to the motivation of the Alabama governor's assailant, 21-year-old Arthur Herman Bremer. It was a jigsaw puzzle with many pieces blank.

Concerned citizens obviously will wonder why Bremer, a Milwaukee white never known for any depth of philosophical or political leanings, could come to the point of an attack on Gov. Wallace, the archetypical Southern segregationist who has only recently and selectively softened his outspoken expression of racial bias.

Much more are Americans worried about the underlying causes of the outburst of violence, the latest in a sickeningly long series of attacks on public figures in the past decade.

Crime in the streets, many are saying, spawns the acts of assassins; the truth is that those so accused have been remarkably free of criminal records (an exception is James Earl Ray, serving 99 years for the slaying of Dr. Martin Luther King).

A permissive society, others will argue, encourages youth to pay no heed to laws or moral codes. But whom do we indict? The parents, the adults of today, where permissiveness begins? Or the young people who have never known the restraints of compassionate care or loving guidance?

The nation is wracked by the demands of minorities, bitter in their demands and violent in their reaction to the "establishment," still others assert. But how do we weigh this without reckoning the rankling weight of generations of lynchings of body and mind by color-determined rulers who went largely unpunished?

No one should dare attempt a definitive answer to the dread question, "Why?", with a simplistic conclusion. It doesn't exist, in its entirety, either in a blanket condemnation of the people, or the theory of a wholesale conspiracy. It is made up of bits and pieces of national policies and individual attitudes, of the unforgettable past and of the sometimes unendurable present, of societal trends and of personal acts. It is made up of all of us, and each of us.

The cure will not come all at once nor from a single source. It will come when the leaders in all fields set the direction and the pace of the march toward realization of our objectives, when political demagogues are quieted and pulpiteering humbugs lose their listeners.

It will come when every responsible American begins to think how to apply influence and expend energy on easing the tension involved in public issues, on solving problems rather than creating them, on spreading the rights of equality of opportunity rather than regarding them as personal privileges.

The Dallas Morning News

Dallas, Tex., May 17, 1972

IN RECENT years, it has been fashionable in some quarters to idealize and romanticize violence as a means for political self-expression. This fashion has been condoned, excused and praised by prominent opinion leaders in the media, in the church, in the academies and even in the government.

In the beginning, the accent was on the breaking of laws of a relatively minor nature. But fashions demand an avant-garde, those who are eager to go farther and farther in following "the dictates of conscience."

In our sickening atmosphere of permissiveness, violence against laws was escalated into violence against property. Then it became the fashion to commit violent acts against the rights of others. Finally, as we have seen in recent years, the fashion of violence has grown to include political murder.

When mobs of hoodlums smash a college or a city block, this destruction is excused as merely a form of "propaganda of the deed." The hoodlums are portrayed to the public, not as bullies but as activists, dissenters.

If boors shout down a speaker with whom they disagree or prevent him from speaking at all, their boorishness and violence are hailed as evidence of their passionate concern, their involvement in the problems of society.

INEVITABLY THIS trend has produced "activists" who have abandoned all traditional forms of political disagreement, who no longer attempt to debate or discuss or present alternatives to the ideas of those with whom they disagree—they just kill those who do not share their own beliefs.

And when they commit such outrages, all of the fashionmongers who have prattled of the "dictates of conscience" as an excuse for violence are greatly shocked. All of those who have gushed over vicious crimes and praised them as "demonstrations of solidarity" point to society and pronounce it sick.

George Wallace is a man who speaks for millions of Americans who regard him as the spokesman for their convictions.

Whether or not you agree with those convictions, he has the right granted him by God and the Constitution to speak out for them. And his audiences have the right to hear what he has to say.

YET THROUGHOUT this campaign, his right and theirs have been violated again and again by "dissenters" who have tried to shout him down, "activists" who have hurled rotten eggs, rocks and bottles. And on Monday afternoon a man tried to silence Wallace forever.

We have now reached the point at which candidacy for the office of President of the United States carries a risk almost as great as military combat.

The 12-month span preceding a presidential election has become a time in which the men who seek the office are in grave peril. And in each of the past three election years, Americans have seen one of their leaders shot down. The situation now threatens not only the personal safety of candidates but the survival of democracy itself.

It is time to act against the forces and the intellectual fashions that have produced this situation. It is time to crack down on those thugs whose favored form of political action is to beat up or shout down or murder those they oppose. We must demand swift, sure and strict justice for those who violate the political right to speak up and be heard.

These creatures and the political violence they practice are poisonous. If our democratic society does not deal with them now, the days of democracy in this country are numbered.

THE EMPORIA GAZETTE
Emporia, Kans., May 17, 1972

Another prominent American has been shot. The list continues to grow: John Kennedy, Robert Kennedy, Martin Luther King, Malcolm X, John Connally, Medgar Evers; now Gov. George Wallace of Alabama, the number three man in the race for the Democratic nomination for President.

It is a disgusting state of affairs that men cannot run for high public office or become national figures in the United States without fear of being murdered.

Some of the killings have been called political assassinations. Only the murder of Robert Kennedy can clearly be classed as political. Sirhan Sirhan assassinated Mr. Kennedy on behalf of a national political cause.

Mainly the killers have been more like madmen than political assassins. Lee Harvey Oswald, James Earl Ray, Jack Ruby, etc., apparently were not supported by political forces.

↑ ↑ ↑

The insanity of the shootings makes them all the more frightening. When there is no reason to the attacks, defense is nearly impossible.

No public figure is safe. Men like Ronald Reagan, Edward Kennedy, Robert Dole, Eugene McCarthy, Jesse Jackson, George McGovern — especially President Nixon—are in danger. There is no way to provide absolute protection for them.

What is to be done?

All reasonable precautions must be taken.

Politicians must abandon the common practice of mingling with crowds of people during their campaigns; Presidents must not allow themselves to be clear targets for high-powered rifles equipped with telescopic sights; national figures should stay out of open cars on public streets.

How sad it is that America has come to this.

↑ ↑ ↑

Meanwhile, Americans join in the hope that Governor Wallace will recover fully from his wounds. The Alabama Governor has many political enemies and his beliefs may not be in the best interest of the good of the nation.

But the proper place to defeat political opponents is at the polls. Governor Wallace knew he was a likely target for violence, yet he carried on bravely. May his recovery be quick and complete.—R. C.

The Birmingham News
Birmingham, Ala., May 19, 1972

Each time some violent incident involves a public figure speculative news stories come tumbling one upon the other saying that we must halt all flesh-to-flesh contact in the public forum.

These commentators counsel what amounts to an arrangement whereby public people, including political campaigners, must be kept safe in a vacuum, away from all contact with the masses, as sterile as the incubator that nestles the premature infant.

Any such arrangement through which the office holder must always remain removed from those who placed him there or the campaigner who represents the admonition: Listen, but do not touch, would place a barrier that the average citizen, even though he held malice for none, could not penetrate.

The total impersonality of an arrangement whereby there must be no contact between the people and a public figure, as tragic as this has proved to be otherwise within the past 10 years, simply should not be permitted to come about.

People respond in various ways to other people who are offering an idea or themselves for public approbation, but mostly the response becomes more spontaneous when the petitioners stand where they can be seen "live," or even touched, as they push their way through the throng.

There simply is no substitute for the passing handclasp, the friendly wave or the pause to speak for a moment with an elderly person or child. If some of this is political "smaltz," there's no substitute for it. Warmth doesn't come through a layer of grease paint or a camera.

Take away the free-and-easy campaigning style of today? Never. You might as well banish the George Wallaces and Hubert Humphreys and George McGoverns of today's public world as to deprive them of the right to mingle with the people.

There are some for whom close public adulation is as necessary as the air they breathe, and the roar of the crowds as needed as food and water.

Some way should be devised to protect our public people better. But to remove them from the outstretched hand of people would be to deny both the very element that gives their real or imagined relationship meaning.

The Cincinnati Post
TIMES ★ STAR
Cincinnati, Ohio, May 16, 1972

The dreadful shooting of Gov. George C. Wallace of Alabama as he stumped for votes in Maryland proves that this violence-prone country needs a safer kind of presidential campaigning.

To put it plainly, the United States has too many psychopaths with guns to let candidates for our highest office go about freely shaking hands with the public.

This may be a harsh judgment, but how many Presidents, presidential candidates and national leaders does America have to lose before it realizes that it cannot afford campaigns as usual?

The United States has been plagued for a century by political assassination, but recently that ugly crime has become frighteningly more frequent: John F. Kennedy in 1963, the Rev. Dr. Martin Luther King Jr. and Robert F. Kennedy in 1968; now the attempt on Wallace in 1972.

Even the new practice of assigning Secret Service agents to leading candidates did not protect Wallace. In truth, these days no candidate for the presidency can walk into a crowd and know for sure that he will emerge alive.

President Nixon and the Democratic hopefuls should learn from the Wallace shooting that they should campaign from the safety of the TV screen, by issuing public statements and by making speeches only before carefully screened audiences.

The factory-gate appearance, the shopping-center speech, the mass rally are obsolete in this television era and too dangerous in this age of assassins. All the candidates ought to agree not to campaign in such risky ways.

We know that every time such limits on campaigning are suggested, objections are raised that it is "not democratic to isolate the candidates from the people."

Well, democracy consists of letting the people choose among all the candidates, not just the ones that our armed maniacs let survive.

The public should insist that all the candidates take the same precautions.

This country is passing through troubled times and to come out of them we need all the leadership we can get. That does not mean turning our national candidates into clay pigeons and settling for the only one who is left.

WALLACE WINS MICHIGAN & MARYLAND; R.I. & OREGON VOTE FOR McGOVERN

On May 16, the day after he was seriously wounded in an attempted assassination while campaigning in Maryland, Gov. George Wallace of Alabama scored impressive victories in the Michigan and Maryland Democratic presidential primaries. By capturing 51% of the Michigan vote, Wallace won his first clear majority in a primary in a northern state. Sen. George S. McGovern (S.D.) finished second in Michigan with 27% of the vote; Sen. Hubert H. Humphrey (Minn.) finished third with 16%. In the Maryland primary Wallace won with 39% of the vote to Humphrey's 27% and McGovern's 22%.

To reflect his share of the popular vote in Michigan, Wallace would have to receive 69 delegate votes. But, since the actual delegates would be named by a state convention controlled by anti-Wallace forces, it was expected that he would get less. Several explanations were offered for Wallace's sweeping victory in Michigan. With no party affiliation required to vote in the primary, large numbers of Republicans and independents may have crossed over to vote for Wallace. His adamant opposition to school busing to promote integration was believed to have won him many votes; Michigan had witnessed several major judicial and legislative battles on the busing issue during the previous year. It was also thought that Wallace's tally may have been pushed up by a sympathy vote following the shooting.

Based on his proportion of the popular vote in Maryland, Wallace won 41 delegates committed to him for at least two ballots at the convention. However, since all the Maryland delegates selected were known to be favorable to McGovern or Humphrey or genuinely uncommitted, there was some question as to the firmness of the Wallace committment.

Sen. McGovern won the Oregon and Rhode Island Democratic presidential primaries held May 23. In Oregon, McGovern won 50% of the vote and 34 delegates in an almost uncontested campaign. Wallace finished second, Humphrey third. In Rhode Island, McGovern received 41% of the popular vote and all of the state's 22 convention delegates, although he had made no personal appearances in the state. Sen. Edmund S. Muskie of Maine finished second with 21% of the vote, Humphrey was third with 20%, and Wallace fourth with 15%.

The delegate count following the May 23 Democratic primaries was: McGovern, 505; Wallace, 323; Humphrey, 294; and Muskie, 160.

In the Republican presidential primaries, President Nixon scored overwhelming victories in all four contests.

Detroit Free Press
Detroit, Mich., May 18, 1972

READING MICHIGAN'S primary election returns can be something like reading the Bible: Look long enough and evidence can be found to support almost any conclusion.

But a few stand out without any searching:

- Michigan voters of both parties are dissatisfied with the way things are going, whether in Vietnam, in Washington or in federal courts.

- Democrats expressed their disapproval by voting for George Wallace and George McGovern, and Republicans did the same.

- George Wallace, healthy or invalided, is going to be hard for either party to ignore, especially the Democratic Party. His whopping victory in Michigan and his healthy plurality in Maryland gave him six primary victories, more than any other Democratic candidate. More important, he has taken himself and his candidacy to three separate sections of the country and has either won or done surprisingly well in all.

- The biggest loser was, without any doubt, Hubert Humphrey. Perhaps we were hearing things that weren't being said, but we could not help sense, in listening to his own post-primary analysis, an air of defeat and resignation. The party faithful, the union members and the blacks who had long been his base of support in Michigan all but vanished. Though Sen. Humphrey did not do badly in Maryland, he did miserably in Michigan.

- *Two issues stood out above all others —forced school busing and the Vietnam war—and the people of Michigan want no part of either. One issue was captured by Gov. Wallace, the other by Sen. McGovern, and Sen. Humphrey was left waffling on both.*

It does nothing to diminish the impact of the results to point out that Gov. Wallace would not have scored so impressive a win without a heavy Republican crossover, or that a great many people who voted for him Tuesday expect to vote for President Nixon in November. To our mind, Gov. Wallace himself was not really the issue. We did not believe before and we do not believe now that he has any more chance of winning the Democratic nomination than a Michigan salmon could survive an Alabama August.

What was important was that he was the lightning rod for massive voter discontent, an issue both parties are going to have to cope with. If busing is to become a useful tool of desegregation and quality education—a question over which Nixon or any other President has no control—reasonable account is going to have to be taken of parental fear. Parents are afraid, and they showed it, of racial turmoil and even lower quality than the education their children get now. The fears may be exaggerated, as Pontiac's experience seems to be showing, but the existence of that fear as a fact of life cannot be ignored.

The Michigan results, it seems to us, give little comfort to either party. However they are sliced, the size of the turnout and the distribution of the votes show that most people voted against, not for. They are against the Vietnam war and against Mr. Nixon's Supreme Court. They are against the Democratic center, against deficit spending and against things as they have been.

The Democrats are going to have to grapple with the issues Gov. Wallace has raised or see a defection by some of their former staunchest supporters. Mr. Nixon is going to have to end the war and concentrate on domestic problems or lose a number of traditionally Republican votes.

If there was a bright side, it was only visible to Republicans. The Democratic Party, after Tuesday, is now in disarray. With Mr. Humphrey went the old center coalition. We have trouble seeing how the Wallace and McGovern wings can compromise their differences, even until November. And after the assassination attempt on Gov. Wallace Monday, we are hard put to imagine Ted Kennedy or his family letting his name be put in nomination.

THE SAGINAW NEWS
Saginaw, Mich., May 18, 1972

The grim irony of it is apparent enough. As expected, Alabama Gov. George C. Wallace has won the Michigan and Maryland presidential primaries—and won them by margins bigger than even he or the political analysts had forecast. But the irony is now wrapped in a dilemma—perhaps the greatest in modern day politics.

Obviously from a political standpoint this is Mr. Wallace's finest hour and perhaps the last big one he'll enjoy before the Democratic National Convention in July.

But the cause for rejoicing in the Wallace camp is of necessity tempered—overshadowed and shattered by a would-be assassin's bullets. As a nation, even those among us who do not favor Mr. Wallace for President, mourn the fact that we have managed to spill yet more blood over another election campaign supposedly carried out in the best democratic traditions of a free society.

Today Mr. Wallace lies seriously wounded in a Maryland hospital. Thankfully, all indications are that he will survive the treacherous attack upon his life even though the medical prognosis leaves some doubt that he may ever walk again.

Therefore, the dilemma. At this point the political career of Gov. Wallace must be marked uncertain—the confident and determined predictions from his side that he will carry on even if he has to do so in a wheelchair notwithstanding. We are not prophetic enough to read what this portends for the remainder of the campaign year.

What is certain is that a Wallace recovery in time to make an appearance in Miami Beach would have a tremendous emotional impact on all people. As we are all well aware, we are an emotional people. But what happens from here on or after such an appearance is too much to guess at. It boggles our imagination.

As far as the vote for Mr. Wallace in Michigan and Maryland, it may take weeks to analyze. He figured to do exceedingly well in both states and he certainly has. But just how much of his vote was pure Wallace vote, how much of it (in Michigan) was cross-over and how much of it was last-minute protest in sympathy and anger over what happened in Laurel, Md., only careful post-primary election survey will determine.

All that safely can be said is that the shooting of Mr. Wallace on the eve of the two primaries cast both in a new light. It did give Mr. Wallace additional voter help which he didn't need anyway.

The fact is that Mr. Wallace worked Michigan hard. He was out after the protest vote and it was early conceded that he would get it and carry the state. So there is no way to demean or dismiss his victory in Michigan. That would be foolish. Earliest surveys of precinct results do clearly indicate, however, that he was helped by the cross-over and the sympathy vote.

The defection in Michigan, however, seems to have hurt Sen. Humphrey worse than it hurt Sen. McGovern. McGovern fell only reasonably below what he had hoped for, Sen. Humphrey well below. There is in this the suggestion that a good deal of labor vote went to Mr. Wallace. Very little if any of it was safely counted in the McGovern corner.

Beyond this it is difficult, next to impossible to venture, save for transient observations. Michigan, in a troubled election year, has survived a traumatic primary experience and behaved itself well. All candidates have been treated cordially and with respect—for the most part. For this we can be proud.

Aside from this, the abhorrent event in Laurel, Md. has added to the list of imponderables. The future is even more difficult to read as it applies to Mr. Wallace and the Democratic party. All we can say is thank heavens the dreadful thing that happened Monday didn't happen here.

The Virginian-Pilot
Norfolk, Va., May 18, 1972

Governor Wallace's tragic wounding occurred just as his state-primaries campaign was cresting. Maryland and Michigan—a Border and an industrial state—were the last of his key targets. Mr. Wallace's next big job was to work on uncommitted delegates already chosen in such nonprimary Southern states as Georgia and South Carolina. Also, he faced the chore of bucking up delegates only theoretically pledged to him in such primary states as North Carolina and Tennessee.

The Wallace victories on Tuesday, the day after the Alabama insurgent was gunned down, were overwhelming. In both Maryland and Michigan Mr. Wallace received nearly half the votes, with Senators McGovern and Humphrey sharing the leavings. Never before had he carried states of such strategic location.

Mr. Wallace's shocking misfortune did not materially influence Tuesday's results. If some voters were swayed by sympathy and outrage, others were guided by what they perceived to be a new realism. That Mr. Wallace would win had been foreseen.

But the would-be assassin's work is certain to affect Mr. Wallace's race for the Democratic Presidential nomination over the rest of the course. The Wallace staff has discussed wheelchair appearances and an enlarged role for Mrs. Wallace, who already has proved to be a powerful asset to her husband's politicking.

But as the extent to which Mr. Wallace may recover is uncertain, so is the full impact of his remarkable performance upon the Democratic National Convention in Miami Beach. All along there has been doubt that Mr. Wallace could be nominated. The bullets fired into him in a Maryland parking lot complicate the prospects.

Mr. Wallace never has been broadly representative. Despite his adoption of Populist-like causes, his basic reputation is for his race protest. School-busing more than economics made him a winner in Florida, Tennessee, North Carolina, Maryland, and Michigan, and earned him red ribbons in Wisconsin, Indiana, and Pennsylvania. (Ironically, a third Wallace issue, law and order, was mocked by the easy availability of the pistol so horribly employed against him.)

This much can be said with certainty: The power of the Wallace campaign already has been felt in the Nation's political affairs, as in President Nixon's call for a moratorium on court orders for busing just two days after Mr. Wallace won in Florida; in Senator Humphrey's switch from a no-compromise civil rightist to a busing opponent; and in Senator McGovern's discovery that maybe the Federal judges are overly concerned with racial imbalance after all.

And this much may be said with some assurance: The force of the Wallace campaign is far from over.

The Detroit News
Detroit, Mich., May 18, 1972

Backers of George Wallace "sent them a message" in this week's primaries in Michigan and Maryland. If the message was not entirely clear, it was certainly loud enough to make all politicians sit up and take notice.

The Alabama governor's victories this week reflected in part public sympathy for a man shot down on the campaign trail. Still, Wallace was clearly the favorite in Michigan before the attempt on his life. Voters, in short, were already riled up about something.

Mainly, we think, they were riled up about the prospect of cross-district bussing of school children. They recognized Wallace as the leading, unequivocal foe of bussing and through him registered their own opposition at the polls.

Since Wallace benefited from Republican cross-over votes, his victory in Michigan must be regarded as a bipartisan one. Many Republicans crossed over simply to cloud the Democratic results, fully expecting to vote for President Nixon next fall.

However, many crossed over because they genuinely like Wallace's brand of politics. Some probably wanted to strengthen his hand at the Democratic National Convention on cross-bussing and other issues which deeply concern them. Although they will vote Republican in the fall, they see Wallace as a means of influencing the Democratic platform and the selection of the Democratic candidate.

While the shooting in Maryland and the Wallace election victories are the big story of the moment, this week may have produced a more significant story for the long run. That story lies in the weak showing of Senator Hubert Humphrey, as compared with Senator George McGovern, in this key Northern state where Humphrey got more votes than Mr. Nixon in 1968.

Just ahead lies the crucial primary test in California, where the Democratic winner will take all 271 delegate votes. Wallace has not entered his name on the ballot there, and his ability to conduct an effective write-in campaign has been further reduced by the bullet which immobilized him this week.

Having finished third behind Senator George McGovern in Michigan, Senator Humphrey goes into the California campaign on the down beat. McGovern's chances appear improved. For the first time, it really looks as if McGovern, written off as a face in the crowd of Democratic candidates in the beginning, could win the Democratic nomination.

Michigan may thus have played a very important role in the outcome of the presidential race of 1972. By giving McGovern a springboard for his plunge into the remaining races, it may have assured his nomination — and the reelection of President Richard Nixon.

This speculation does not take into account the possibility that George Wallace might resume his efforts following the Democratic convention as a third-party candidate. Should he do so, the election might end up in the House of Representatives.

The bullet lodged near his spine raises a question mark over all this. Was that bullet the beginning or the end of George Wallace's career in presidential politics?

THE ANN ARBOR NEWS
Ann Arbor, Mich, May 18, 1972

AIDED by Republican crossovers, an undetermined sympathy vote and his own growing popularity among large voting blocs, Gov. George Wallace of Alabama won Michigan in a big way Tuesday.

A 50 per cent triumph in a fairly crowded primary in a liberal northern industrial state is positively Rooseveltian in scope. Among the crestfallen today are Sen. Humphrey, who did badly here, and Sen. McGovern, who was merely swamped.

Wallace's win was dramatic, surprising, complete. And rounding out the picture was the sad fact that the governor had to take this high point in his career literally lying down.

* * *

BUT NOW the imponderables begin. The predictions were that Wallace had peaked after Maryland and Michigan. That from here on it was all a flat plane. That the governor's influence would hold steady rather than rise until the opening gavel at Miami Beach.

Now who can be sure? In politics one can take nothing for granted. Gov. Wallace's usefulness to the Democratic party, or at least to its centrist and conservative factions, has been magnified. The whole question of his electability on a national scale is being re-examined.

In that sense, "they" are getting the message. Translate "they" to the power brokers. It has been widely assumed that Wallace isn't really after the presidency at all, that all he really wants is to reshape the Democratic party and alter its direction.

But just as sure as Penn Central makes little green cabooses, Gov. Wallace would accept second spot on the national Democratic ticket. And given this kind of potential access to the White House, Wallace could be prevailed upon to have his rough edges smoothed out to make him more acceptable to all voters.

* * *

THIS IS not far out stuff. LBJ in 1960 and Spiro Agnew in 1968 were tapped for the number two spot to the consternation (and dismay) of many. If the governor sufficiently recovers from his wounds, he could provide the biggest surprise of Miami Beach.

At this point, a write-in for Gov. Wallace in California is a possibility. He may appear on the Oregon ballot. Maryland and Michigan were supposed to be the end of the trail, but all bets are off now.

The extent to which "they" have received the message George Wallace has sent out will be seen shortly. As the sportswriters dearly love to say, it's another ballgame now.

The New York Times
New York, N.Y., May 18, 1972

Much more than a floodtide of sympathy over the despicable attempt on his life went into the victories scored by George C. Wallace in this week's two key Democratic primaries.

That fully half the primary voters in Michigan, stronghold of the United Automobile Workers, recorded their preference for the wounded Alabama Governor is startling testimony to the persuasiveness of his appeals to fear and frustration. His share of the Democratic vote was more than triple the 16 per cent that went to labor's oldtime favorite, Senator Humphrey.

In Maryland, where Mr. Wallace was struck down by bullets on the eve of the primary, four Democrats out of every ten cast their primary ballots for him. Though this result was more in line with forecasts, it also underscored the depths of the discontent that finds inchoate expression in the Wallace column.

What all this will mean at the Democratic Presidential convention or at the polls if Governor Wallace emerges as a third-party candidate, no one can tell while he lies with a pistol slug still lodged at the edge of his spine and no definitive word on how permanent his paralysis will prove.

If he does regain his health, even though confined to a wheelchair, the Governor will remain a formidable campaigner. The four successful Presidential campaigns of Franklin D. Roosevelt made it plain, even in a pretelevision era, that losing the use of one's legs need not be a deterrent to political activity.

Mr. Wallace could wage the electronic equivalent of the "front porch campaign" of the McKinley-Harding era when delegations of voters were brought to the candidate rather than the other way round. Via television, he could also reach large numbers of voters without making a physically exhausting canvass.

* * *

In the short term, the Alabama Governor's misfortune may work to the political advantage of Senator McGovern. Although public opinion research in the Democratic primaries suggests that Mr. Wallace and Mr. McGovern in the main attract significantly different voters, there unquestionably are some disenchanted voters who are prepared indiscriminately to vote for any anti-establishment candidate. The absence of Mr. Wallace as an active candidate in the period of his hospitalization may lead such voters to concentrate behind Senator McGovern.

For the longer term, a Wallace third party vote, particularly if it is swelled by a sizable sympathy vote, would harm both Democrats and Republicans in November. The strong probability is that the same five states in the Deep South that went to Mr. Wallace in 1968 would rally to his banner again, thereby depriving President Nixon of those electoral votes.

But the much cloudier question is who would be hurt most in the North, Mr. Nixon or his Democratic rival. Prior to the Michigan balloting, most observers had taken it as certain that a Wallace independent candidacy might well block Democrats from victory in such pivotal states as New Jersey, Ohio, Illinois and Michigan itself, all with big electoral votes. Now doubt is cast on that theory by the post-primary findings of The Times/Yankelovich survey in Michigan that the Alabaman cut much more heavily into the potential Nixon vote than he did into the support that any Democratic nominee might expect. By contrast, Louis Bean, the wisest of political statisticians, estimates that outside the South 70 per cent of the 1968 vote for Wallace came from Democrats.

Having survived an attempted deadly decision by bullets, Mr. Wallace may yet have his opportunity to influence the nation's decision by ballots.

©1972 by The New York Times Company. Reprinted by permission.

Wisconsin State Journal
Madison, Wis., May 23, 1972

As far as the professional politicians are concerned, the Maryland and Michigan primaries — which Gov. George Wallace won last week — aren't really over yet.

Although the delegates are nominally pledged to the Alabama governor, election loopholes permit non-Wallace Democrats to fill numerous seats on the delegations, ready to jump to one of the other candidates after the second ballot.

A majority of the Michigan voters — 51 per cent — in the Democratic column voted for Wallace, and a plurality of 39 per cent endorsed his candidacy in Maryland.

But his actual delegate support at the convention will not reflect those victories.

The will of the people will not prevail in full for those states.

Regardless of one's views about Wallace, the technicalities of these state primaries are unjust to his candidacy.

Agents for both Sen. George McGovern and Sen. Hubert Humphrey are working on the Maryland and Michigan delegates who have only a nominal pledge to Wallace.

The political pros know that Wallace, who lies wounded in a hospital bed, stands little chance of holding many delegates beyond the bare minimum required by law, two ballots.

It is also believed that the Democratic convention will require many ballots before a presidential candidate is nominated, underscoring the significance of the loopholes in the primary system.

Clearly, the visibility of some uniform, national primary would expose such mechanisms designed to serve the party organizations and not the will of the people.

The inequity of the primary regulations in those states, moreover, underscore how the Democratic party's well-publicized reform efforts are less than effective. It was McGovern who co-chaired the commission.

We have no reason to believe that Wallace, if he had the upper hand in the delegate scramble, would institute any better system.

But we haven't heard the liberal voices loudly protesting the injustices being visited upon a vote winner in two states.

Chicago Tribune
Chicago, Ill., May 18, 1972

One significant and gratifying aspect of Gov. George Wallace's primary victories in Michigan and Maryland is that Monday's assassination attempt was not much of a factor in them.

The measurable "sympathy vote" was very small. In Maryland, he did about as had been predicted before the shooting, and his total was actually below what he received in the 1964 primary. In Michigan, according to reporter Bill Jones, the shooting prompted a large turnout of Wallace supporters who might otherwise have neglected to vote, but changed no minds.

It would have been a sorry reflection on the intelligence of the American electorate if very many people had decided to vote for George Wallace for President simply because he had been shot.

Michigan and Maryland were triumphs for Mr. Wallace, nevertheless. As even network television commentators noted, he must be viewed as a national figure of some stature and his political movement as one of consequence. The pundits can no longer dismiss him as a backwoods demogog with little following.

Will Mr. Wallace, confined to a wheelchair or not, go on to win the nomination? We doubt it. He capitalized on his areas of strength and surprised everyone, but he may now have exhausted his potential. The only remaining primaries of note are Oregon [May 23], California [June 6], New Jersey [June 6], and New York [June 20], and he isn't likely to win any of them. Our guess is he will take his 312 delegates to Miami and function more as a kingmaker than candidate.

What Mr. Wallace's victories do underscore is the apparent impossibility of the candidacies of his two major opponents, Sen. George McGovern and Sen. Hubert Humphrey. Mr. McGovern has made skillful use of this year's changes in the Democratic Party's delegate selection system and has amassed a sizable delegate total, but, with relentless hammering by Mr. Wallace and others from the right, his "Populist" veneer is wearing thin and exposing the leftist ideology beneath. His strong position in favor of busing, for example, demolished him in Michigan. Mr. McGovern may still swing the nomination, but, as the polls are showing, he would be a weak entry against President Nixon.

Mr. Humphrey still occupies the center, but has been squeezed so by Mr. McGovern on the left and Mr. Wallace on the right that there's not much maneuvering space left. Sen. Edmund Muskie and Sen. Henry Jackson amply displayed their inadequacies on the primary circuit.

Who then, Teddy Kennedy? Monday's assassination attempt has undoubtedly reinforced his doubts about running and has already dampened the fires of the draft Kennedy movement. We also wonder if he would have permitted his wife to make public remarks about her emotional fears if he had definite plans to run.

John Connally? A possibility, as our political editor, George Tagge, noted several months ago. But if they chose Mr. Connally, the Democrats would be depriving themselves of their major issue—the economy. How could they blame Mr. Nixon for what Mr. Connally did or did not do as secretary of the treasury?

One of the functions of the primary system is to pare down a large field of candidates to a viable few. In the Democrats' case this year, it would seem to have pared down the field to nothing.

THE SUN
Baltimore, Md., May 22, 1972

Casting a vote for George Wallace for presidential nominee at the Democratic National Convention may be unpleasant for such party leaders as Governor Mandel, but he says he will do that if he is a voting member of the Maryland delegation. His position is correct. All at-large delegates, as well as all members of the delegation whose districts were carried by Governor Wallace, should follow the Governor's example, however strongly they may object to what Mr. Wallace represents.

Senator McGovern has publicly urged two wavering Maryland delegates loyal to him to obey the law and vote for Wallace. Any delegates who choose to break the Maryland law at the convention would not be prosecuted, it is being assumed, since state law can't apply in Florida—but it might be possible to prosecute them under conspiracy statutes, since their decision to break the law would have taken place in Maryland.

As to that point, even if prosecution were not possible, delegates should follow the spirit and letter of the law. That is true for all delegates, no matter in what direction their loyalties lie, but it is perhaps particularly true for McGovern supporters. We say that because many supporters of both the Georges are particularly distressed that the public will is not always heeded in high places. For McGovern supporters who are out to demonstrate that the system can work and that basic changes and reform can be brought about by the people—for these supporters to rebuke the people and ignore the law just because they disagree with it would be criminally ironic. And it can only increase the anger and frustration of the Wallace supporters. It may even increase their number.

The Washington Post
Washington, D.C., May 19, 1972

We have this terrible confession to make: we do not know who is going to win the Democratic nomination. Indeed, having pondered the voting results in seventeen different primaries now, having added, subtracted and otherwise fiddled with various combinations of the votes already cast, and having listened to candidates and voters alike attempting to explain what it all means, we are growing increasingly less confident in predicting what any of it portends for tomorrow—let alone for next July or November. Only a very few things do seem self-evident to us in relation to the primaries so far. And we shall concentrate on these.

The first has to do with Governor Wallace's showing, and from it our other conclusions flow. It is not necessary to overstate the meaning of his victory at the polls this past Tuesday to observe that Michigan and Maryland have reconfirmed that his success has become a central fact of the 1972 campaign. Whether or not Governor Wallace has—as many were predicting he would well before Michigan and Maryland—pretty well reached the upper limit of his delegate strength with these two primaries, whether or not the savage attack on him in Laurel will prevent further campaign exertions, and whether or not his forces will have mustered sufficient strength to "broker" the Miami convention, the solid showing of Governor Wallace in primaries, North and South, will remain a matter of great consequences within the Party. It has already influenced the responses of the other candidates to the issues at hand, and neither the Michigan nor Maryland result seems likely to diminish that influence. So the candidates' response—and that of Party officialdom—to Governor Wallace's success becomes increasingly important. And it has been thus far, in our opinion, wholly inadequate.

It is appalling that the trend we noted in this space last week to deny the Governor his duly elected delegate strength proceeds apace. In Maryland, we learn, as in Tennessee, efforts are under way to figure out how to deprive the Wallace forces of the first ballot representation to which they are entitled. From Michigan comes identical news: it is already being pointed out that although Michigan state law requires that the Governor's preference vote strength be reflected in first ballot delegate support, state law does not impose penalties on those delegates who choose to defy it. Read McGovern or Humphrey for Wallace in the news accounts describing these intentions, and you will have no trouble imagining the uproar and charges of rigging and bossism that would be filling the air. More to the point is the fact that anyone who is counseling such an ethnically dismal course is also demonstrating an invincible insensitivity to the kind of grievance on which the Wallace campaign has been able to capitalize, to the issues that underlie his appeal. Never mind for the moment that to pursue these tactics would be to undermine the validity of the Democratic reforms as a whole, it would also be to confirm the belief of so many of his supporters that they have, one way and the other, been tricked and sweet-talked and cheated out of what is politically their rightful due.

The way to combat Governor Wallace's appeal is on the issues—not with backroom treachery. And this brings us to the candidates' own responses, to their way of defining themselves and one another. Governor Wallace's brutal victimization by a gunman no doubt will have its effect on the tone and tenor of the remainder of the campaign. But we see no reason why it should prevent the other candidates from challenging, in a straight-forward and tough-minded way, the kinds of solutions he has been proposing to our national ills. In fact, we fear that his being invalid is more likely to be invoked as an excuse for ducking a real confrontation on the issues with Mr. Wallace—although what has been needed all along is clarification and definition, as distinct from vagueness and obfuscation. If there was any notion hanging around that a flight from clarity and sense into enigma would be helpful on the busing issue, Michigan should have demonstrated that this is a no-win game. There is, for example, a way of defining clearly and rationally and persuasively what the meaning, limitations, advantages and disadvantages of busing may be—in fact, Chief Justice Burger, in a far from radical decision, spelled out such a position last year. We cannot help thinking that a little bravery and forthrightness in pursuing such a view on the stump would pay off far better than a run for cover.

This defining of view and stand, this sharpening of distinctions on the issues is also required of Senators Humphrey and McGovern in relation to one another. We do not have in mind the aimless and mischievous attack on Senator McGovern for holding a "radical" view on abortion, a charge that bids fair to become the Quemoy-and-Matsu of this election. There are far more central things to talk about, more central to either man's potential for conducting the office of the presidency. No doubt the pressures of the crucial California primary will draw them toward sharpened attacks on one another. Our only hope is that they will avoid the ad hominem game, and attempt to dispute each other on issues that really matter. We have a feeling that that is what their prospective electorate is waiting for. We have a profound conviction that this kind of serious and straight talking is also the only answer to Governor Wallace.

The Evening Star
Washington, D.C., May 17, 1972

Monday in Maryland wasn't a day many residents will like to remember. There was pervasive shock and sadness at the shooting of Governor Wallace within the borders of the Free State, which prizes its long history of toleration and responsible politics. But though this ugly drama was closest to them, Marylanders yesterday did not, from all indications, allow it to affect their political judgments in any remarkable degree.

Certainly some "sympathy votes" were cast for Wallace, but apparently on nothing comparable to the scale of such voting in Michigan. Indeed it's difficult to tell if the violent episode had any measurable effect on the Maryland returns. For though the turnout was relatively heavy for a primary, it wasn't sensational. And Wallace, taking 39 percent of the votes, did no better than many observers had predicted two weeks earlier, and not as well as he did in the state's 1964 primary. It may be, however, that the shooting arrested the boomlets that were seen rising in the final week for Senators Humphrey and McGovern, shaving their vote totals.

Marylanders generally, it appears, voted yesterday just as they had planned to vote before the shocking news of Monday afternoon.

As expected, Wallace led the 11-candidate field by a margin that should give him considerable satisfaction. It was no small victory. But the fact remains that most people voted for someone other than him—again in contrast to Michigan—and we submit that Maryland can take some pride in that result.

There is yet another unknown factor in the Maryland balloting: Undoubtedly a great many people voted for him altogether as a protest gesture, with no desire ever to see him become president. Still, the votes themselves are unequivocal, and they give Wallace 41 of Maryland's 53 delegates to the Democratic national conventon. Nor must there be any quibbling about his entitlement to all the convention support he has won. A state law binds delegates to support on the convention floor the candidate who wins in their congressional district. They must stay with him for two ballots, or until he receives less than 35 percent of the votes needed to nominate. But recently Maryland's attorney general, Francis B. Burch, expressed doubt that the law is enforceable. The national convention will be held outside his state and its rules differ from Maryland law. But all the state's delegates should feel bound by that law, morally as well as legally, and Maryland officials should emphasize that they will make every effort to enforce it.

Humphrey failed to show the strength that many of his supporters, who included some of the state's leading political figures, had expected. But he and McGovern, with 27 and 22 percent of the votes, respectively, and six delegates apiece, both acquitted themselves well, in view of ther late-starting campaigns, Wallace's residual support in the state and the imponderable effects of the assassination attempt. And the voters did likewise, in their refusal to let Monday afternoon's awful incident get in the way of their political reasoning.

The Providence Journal
Providence, R.I., May 25, 1972

The lesson in the state's Democratic presidential primary is clear: behind an attractive candidate, dissidents in a party can muster the skills, dedication, and hard work to defeat an entrenched organization, its prestigious leaders, and its trained professional cadres of party workers.

Months ago, when Sen. Edmund Muskie of Maine was the front-runner in the presidential race, Gov. Frank Licht, Mayor Joseph A. Doorley Jr. of Providence and just about every major figure in Rhode Island's Democratic organization enrolled in his cause. Then Mr. Muskie withdrew from active campaigning.

There is little doubt that it is difficult to heat up a campaign for a man who has taken himself out of active campaigning. But the state's Democratic leaders kept up the fight, hoping, no doubt, that a combination of prestige and machine would make Mr. Muskie a surprise winner Tuesday.

But meanwhile, supporters of Sen. George S. McGovern of South Dakota went to work. It would be easy to characterize their victory here as a victory of amateurs over professionals. But what really happened is that the amateurs — amateurs only in that day-to-day politicking is not their daily bread — outplayed the organization at its own game.

Workers were mobilized across the state; voting lists were translated into door-to-door canvassing lists. Sheer hard work in the streets developed the voting strength that Mr. McGovern showed so plainly. It was the kind of campaigning that swept Sen. Eugene McCarthy to national prominence in 1968.

To make this point is not to underrate Mr. McGovern as a candidate. With the withdrawal of Senator Muskie, Mr. McGovern inherited not only the place of front-runner; his own appeal has grown within the Democratic Party — among the young, among blue collar workers, among the affluent and intellectuals.

In combination, the senator and his workers swept the board; the Providence city organization could not even deliver to Muskie what had been rated as a machine stronghold. Any party leaders who get to Miami for the national convention will be traveling as visitors — strictly on their own.

THE BLADE
Toledo, Ohio, May 29, 1972

So George McGovern won the Oregon and Rhode Island presidential primary. So what else is new?

Yet the fact that this item of news can be accepted in such ho-hum fashion tells a lot about the flabbergasting way in which the 1972 presidential campaign has gone. Five months ago, even three months ago, if anyone had said Senator McGovern would be the frontrunner in the Democratic race to the extent that an Oregon or Rhode Island victory would be kissed off as unsurprising, he would have been hooted from the room.

Everybody knew (everybody but Mr. McGovern and his most starry-eyed followers) that Senator Muskie all but had it wrapped up, and that only the pesky intervention of Senator Humphrey threatened that. To be sure, there was Mayor Lindsay competing with colorless Senator McGovern for the vote of the left, and Senator Jackson and Governor Wallace edging in from the right. But so what?

Then came Florida and Wisconsin and Pennsylvania and Massachusetts, and the picture was irrevocably scrambled. The distressing assassination attempt on Mr. Wallace made it even more so.

Instead of the "obvious" scenario of last January, Mr. Muskie wasn't even in the contention for the Oregon primary which was to have been his penultimate victory, and Mr. Humphrey decided to duck it to concentrate on California. Contrary to every winter expectation, it is Mr. McGovern who goes to the great showdown in California with the big Oregon victory under his belt.

Mr. McGovern might lose in California. He might be denied the presidential nomination in any event, and if he got it, he might not be able to defeat President Nixon. But the fact that his victories in Oregon and Rhode Island evoke little else but yawns shows not only how far he has come, but how risky it is to underestimate the candidate from South Dakota.

The Miami News
Miami, Fla., May 25, 1972

Sen. George McGovern is headed for the California primary campaign today exuding the sort of leadership that few thought he possessed when the presidential contest began.

His comfortable victories Tuesday in the Oregon and Rhode Island elections indicated that his bandwagon is gaining momentum as it heads for the most important state on the primary circuit. He picked up all 22 delegates in Rhode Island, all 34 in Oregon, he is leading in the polls to take all 271 in California.

Although the New York contest looms large on June 20, California is considered more important because the New York delegates can be divided among the leaders whereas the whole California delegation goes to the winner.

Gov. George Wallace isn't on the California ballot, which means that the chief contenders will be Sen. McGovern and Sen. Hubert Humphrey. And while McGovern's campaign has been gaining momentum, Humphrey's seems to be losing steam. The former vice president suffered a serious setback when he finished behind Wallace in Oregon and Muskie in Rhode Island, taking third place in both elections.

If Humphrey doesn't repair his prestige with a victory or extremely close second place finish in California, McGovern will arrive in Miami Beach in July in excellent shape to take the nomination.

The Oregonian
Portland, Ore., May 28, 1972

Where will all the "anti" voters go in the November election in Oregon? That's the problem to be solved by victorious nominees and their strategists as they study the statistics of Tuesday's primaries. For examples:

The Democratic presidential preference and all of Oregon's delegates to the national convention in July were conceded to Sen. George McGovern long in advance, as Humphrey, Muskie, Jackson, Wallace, et al, left him a clear field.

But almost 50 per cent of Oregon majority party voted for the 10 names on the ballot other than McGovern's. If McGovern is nominated at Miami Beach, as now appears much more than likely, will a majority of the non-McGovern voters swing to him, or to the certain Republican nominee, President Richard M. Nixon?

It will be noted that Gov. George Wallace ran second, far ahead of Sen. Hubert Humphrey, and Sen. Henry M. Jackson ran fourth, well ahead of Sen. Edmund Muskie and non-candidate Sen. Edward Kennedy. With the Democratic Party's dominance in voters' registration, a switch of anti-McGovern voters to the Republican nominee might assure another Nixon victory in this state.

Ex-Sen. Wayne L. Morse, nominated by the Democrats to challenge the Republican he endorsed in 1966, Sen. Mark Hatfield, won on a plurality. The combined vote for ex-Rep. Bob Duncan, State Sen. Don Willner and Ralph Wiser was greater than 50 per cent of the Democrats Tuesday. Sen. Hatfield also ran into an "anti" vote in the GOP primary, but won by a comfortable majority over Lynn Engdahl, Kenneth Brown and Ralph Wiser.

Hatfield's unbroken record of election victories — for the Legislature, secretary of state, governor and senator — have all been achieved with strong help from defecting Democrats.

McGOVERN'S WIN IN CALIFORNIA PUTS HIM CLOSE TO NOMINATION

Sen. George S. McGovern (S.D.) won the California Democratic presidential primary June 6, capturing 47.1% of the popular vote and 271 delegates to the Democratic National Convention. Sen. Hubert H. Humphrey (Minn.) won 41.7% of the vote, but did not pick up any delegates in the winner-take-all primary. By winning an additional 99 delegates in primaries held the same day in New Jersey, South Dakota and New Mexico, McGovern gained such a wide lead over his rivals in the delegate count that he seemed very likely to win a first-ballot nomination in the July convention.

With such a large block of delegates at stake, the California campaign was the hardest-fought primary of the year. Sen. Humphrey directly attacked McGovern for the first time, hitting hard at the South Dakotan's positions on defense spending, tax reform and welfare benefits. With polls showing him trailing McGovern by a wide margin, Humphrey challenged McGovern to a series of television debates, which were nationally broadcast May 28, 30 and June 4. After the returns came in, McGovern conceded that Humphrey's criticisms had cut into his victory margin. McGovern hinted that the details of some of his programs might have to be revised to take account of these criticisms.

A "stop-McGovern" movement, reportedly led by Gov. Jimmy Carter of Georgia, apparently failed to attract significant support at a meeting of the National Governors' Conference in Houston June 5-7. Both McGovern and Humphrey took time out from their campaigning to appear at the conference. It was reported that McGovern had indicated a willingness to modify some of his programs. Many Southern governors were fearful that a McGovern candidacy might lead to Democratic defeats in state and local contests.

Maine Sunday Telegram
Portland, Me., June 4, 1972

It is June, time for editorial writers to eat words they wrote in January. In January, we did not give McGovern a chance. Today he looks like a winner.

What makes McGovern magic, when Muskie turned out to be mush?

In January who in Maine would have guessed that Ed Muskie might get to the Democratic convention with a threadbare 159½ delegate votes? And that McGovern might go trumpeting to Miami with 1200 delegates, all but a shoo-in on the first ballot?

Yet if McGovern wins all 271 votes in California on Tuesday and picks up the majority of New York's 278 votes on June 20, then the unknown man from insignificant South Dakota, will probably become the Democrat nominee for President.

Already, he has 502 delegates, trailed by Wallace with 323, while the erstwhile standard bearers and early front-runners Humphrey and Muskie have 294½ and 158½ each.

McGovern is outspending Humphrey in California 5-1. Humphrey money has dried up. A couple of revealing details are that in San Francisco, McGovern had outbought Humphrey on three out of four major TV outlets there. In San Diego, McGovern has booked $5,600 of TV time, and HHH is down for a total of $332. McGovern has 50,000 young volunteers working in 82 regional offices, staging what politicos call "the most intensive campaign ever mounted in a California primary."

Somewhere out there, Muskie's name is still on the ballot.

But if HHH closes the gap, it is rumored that Sen. Ted Kennedy will publicly declare what others long have said; Kennedy will, if necessary, campaign for McGovern at the last moment.

Many insiders have long whispered that it is Kennedy money, Kennedy friends, Kennedy organization, Kennedy volunteers that have pushed George McGovern into the lead.

While McGovern is the favorite to win California, it is possible that Humphrey's appeal to the minorities — the blacks, the Mexican-Americans, the Jewish vote, the elderly, and the Democratic "regulars," could stop McGovern in California; and blunt the expected McGovern victory in New York.

If this happens, then HHH will go to the convention with 900 delegates, close on the heels of McGovern with 950. And the convention will be deadlocked.

Enter the power-broker, George Wallace, the man with perhaps 400 delegate votes in his pocket.

Wallace has campaigned on the threat to "send them a message." In a deadlocked convention, Wallace may be in the catbird's seat, able to deliver a message in the strongest language known to politicians. If Wallace wants to, Wallace may be able to stop McGovern in the stretch. Wallace might be able to throw his 400 votes or so to Humphrey or Muskie on a crucial ballot and change the tide.

Here is the reason for the parade of phony visits to the bedside of the wounded Wallace by his erstwhile political enemies . . . Humphrey, Nixon, Muskie, Kennedy, and Democratic National Chairman O'Brien.

At Miami, watch them fawn upon Wallace. Each recognizes Wallace for the power broker he has become.

Further each recognizes that if Wallace bolts the Democratic convention, he could spearhead a "Democrats for Nixon" campaign. And such a move could cost any Democratic nominee about three million votes in November.

The one man most unlikely to concede enough to Wallace is McGovern.

Our hunch is that the Democratic regulars will do their utmost to play Wallace and McGovern against each other, in order to deadlock the convention and prevent the nomination of McGovern.

If they do this, then McGovern supporters could make the riots at the Democratic convention in Chicago four years ago look like a curtain raiser.

But the Democratic "regulars" may be tempted to. For they know that with rank and file Democrats, McGovern is too far leftist; too permissive; too pacifist; too much in favor of "acid, abortion and amnesty," as Senate Republican leader Hugh Scott labelled him.

Ten Democratic governors, secretly polled, say McGovern would run worse than any Democratic nominee in their states, and hurt the entire Democratic ticket.

Gallup polls across the nation, show that Humphrey is still the choice among rank and file Democrats over McGovern, 35 to 19 per cent.

If McGovern is thrust upon these Democrats by the convention, they may vote for Nixon, by the millions.

But at this writing, the McGovern camp is so confident of victories in California and New York that they have already booked Constitution Hall in Washington D.C. for two days and nights of victory celebrations, June 22 and 23. They have also booked Madison Square Garden in New York City for June 14. Some tickets for these events have price tags as high as $5,000. And the same old glamor names will be in attendance: Simon and Garfunkel, Peter, Paul and Mary; Mike Nichols; Elaine May; Bette Davis; Dustin Hoffman; Goldie Hawn; Paul Newman; Ben Gazzara; Shirley MacLaine. And Mrs. Robert F. Kennedy will give a picnic at Hickory Hill for upper crust McGovernites.

Sounds fun, for the Manhattan — and Hollywood crowd. And precisely the kind of antics that will turn millions of Democrats away from candidate McGovern, one time farm boy from South Dakota.

Out of the ashes of Chicago, the Democrats revised their way of choosing convention delegates, to make their convention more representative.

Their dilemma now is that, they may end up with a candidate who does not represent rank and file Democrats. And they could lose this election by a landslide.

The Sun Reporter
San Francisco, Calif., June 3, 1972

The most significant fact of the 1972 presidential election is that 25 million young voters between 18 and 20 years of age will exercise their franchise for the first time. These young voters are registering Democratic 3 to 1. Forty years ago under the leadership of Franklin Delano Roosevelt the Democratic Party developed a philosophical thrust that has been amended but not changed over the last four decades. The dreary circumstance of 18 years of U.S. involvement in Vietnam, which has led to the slow, progressive erosion of America's stability at home as well as its standing in the world community lead us to conclude that a Democratic victory in the 1972 presidential election demands the development of two new types of leadership in the Democratic Party:

First, the nomination of a Democratic standard-bearer intelligent enough, creative enough and courageous enough to develop out of the morass of Vietnam new techniques for governing the nation which will provide for the utilization of our national resources to feed the hungry, care for the sick, give work to the jobless, provide decent housing for the homeless, clean up our air and waters and educate all of our children properly;

Second, such a man needs a party committed to using its resources for the rebuilding of a new coalition which will revitalize the Democratic Party in the same image as accomplished by Franklin Delano Roosevelt forty years ago. Such a new coalition of forces for dynamic change will being together peace advocates, women demanding equality of the sexes, small farmers fighting to survive against giant agri-businesses, idealistic young people, racial minorities, blue collar workers, conservationists, consumer advocates, civil libertarians, educators, and finally, enlightened business and professional people--all of these diverse elements of the population dedicated to building within the Democratic Party a broad new coalition which will redirect the nation away from the destructive path of the military-industrial-political complex which makes war be in Indochina, propagates neo-colonialism against the colored peoples of Asia, Africa and Latin America, and by slow, erosive procedures attempts through fear and intimidation to create constitutional fascism in the United States.

California Democrats on June 6, 1972 in the presidential preference primary have an opportunity to give their 271 delegates to a man whose public service record in the U.S. Senate since 1968 and during the preceding '72 presidential primary campaigns qualifies him to lead the broad new Democratic coalition in America. Because of his record of consistent opposition to the war in Southeast Asia involving his profound articulation of the economics of the Vietnam war, the politics of the Vietnam war and the destructive domestic and international role of the Vietnam war, the Sun-Reporter endorses Senator George McGovern and urges your vote for McGovern in the June 6 Democratic presidential primary election.

Of the seven other candidates vying for delegates to the National Democratic Convention, none of them can serve the cause of the new democratic political coalition demands as well as Senator George S. McGovern. Moreover, the millions of newly enfranchised young Democratic voters will not vote for the old nor be inspired by a retread; they will only support the inspiring leadership of the new politics offered by George McGovern.

THE SACRAMENTO BEE
Sacramento, Calif., May 26, 1972

The decision the Democratic voters will make in the June 6 California presidential primary is of far-reaching importance. It even may dictate who will be the Democratic candidate and well could determine who will serve in the White House the next four years.

The Bee is endorsing the candidacy of US Sen. George McGovern of South Dakota because he is offering a program of fresh, innovative ideas to solve the problems now debilitating both the spirit and economy of this nation.

The old political formulas seem unable to break the pattern of crushing and inequitable taxes, scandalously high unemployment in the midst of great national plenty and a war policy which is poisoning the nation's spirit and threatens the economy.

More than any candidate in recent history, Sen. McGovern has been refreshingly candid in detailing how he proposes to solve these problems. Some of his ideas have been tagged as radical or unworkable but close analysis proves these labels to be false. He is offering constructive proposals to get this country moving forward again. He is challenging old ideas which have failed, and for this he deserves great credit.

The Democratic voters are fortunate that both of the leading candidates in the California primary are distinguished and responsible national leaders. This newspaper proudly supported Sen. Hubert Humphrey of Minnesota when he was the Democratic nominee for the presidency in 1968. Nothing has happened to dampen The Bee's respect and admiration for the former vice president.

The problems that must be faced now, however, have become aggravated and in many cases have taken radically different form. The division between young and old has become acute. The understandable disenchantment over high taxes and pockets of privilege has increased. The more militant attitude of racial minorities demands new insights and greater sensitivity. Old programs, worthy as they may be, will not meet the challenge of today.

George McGovern has demonstrated he has the confidence both of the young and the elderly. The farmer in the Midwest trusts him and he understands the problems of the worker. He believes in the free enterprise system and knows the businessman must be free of unfair controls to make it work.

Sen. McGovern wants to build an economically strong America and to achieve full employment by filling the unmet needs of the nation. As a World War II combat pilot, awarded the Distinguished Flying Cross for valor, he understands the need to keep the nation militarily strong but he is opposed to the waste of billions of dollars in military boondoggles.

McGovern has demonstrated his personal courage and honesty. He has the program to get the country moving and he has the instincts to move in the right direction. He has the qualities today's leadership demands. He would make an admirable president at a time of great need.

Oakland Tribune
Oakland, Calif., June 8, 1972

Of all the ingredients that meshed so harmoniously to give Sen. George McGovern his convincing victory in the California Democratic primary, particular attention must be given to the evident "populist" thrust of his campaign.

Whether it's the "wave of the future" or a throw-back to an ancient political age (depending on one's historical perspective), populism is a force to be reckoned with in this presidential campaign.

For in winning the support of nearly half of California's Democrats, or roughly one-fourth of the state's voters, the South Dakota senator certainly made an appeal that evoked a strong and positive response from a sizable segment of the electorate. The words that he consistently used, and the campaign promises that he consistently made, can only find definition in the populist context.

Populism emerged near the end of the 19th century as an agrarian-blue collar political reform movement seeking to break the power of the railroads, middlemen, corporations and, as one collective phrase put it, "all entrenched money."

Urging wholesale changes in political, economic and government conditions without particular concern for the effect of such changes, the Populist party built its appeal on simplistic solutions and assorted panaceas to remedy the problems of the day with one-shot cure-alls.

In the voting, it never really gained much public support, and the Populist presidential candidate in 1892 won but eight per cent of the vote.

In appealing more to the heart than to the head of the electorate with a whole new bag of similar simplistic solutions to virtually all of the nation's ills, George McGovern has precipitated a true rebirth of populism's emotional exuberance.

His California victory seems to reflect a public disenchantment with the status quo — whether that condition is defined as the war in Vietnam, inflation, high taxes, poverty or the continuing international arms race.

It appears that many of the California Democrats who marked their ballots for McGovern did so more to register unhappiness with the so-called "old style" Democrats, as represented by Sen. Hubert Humphrey, than to endorse, for example, McGovern's $32 billion defense cut proposal or his scheme to give every American $1,000.

The "anti-establishment" or populist sentiment was particularly reflected in the New Mexico primary, where McGovern split the vote about evenly with another Democrat who fits the populist mold, Gov. George Wallace of Alabama.

If McGovern proves to be his party's choice in Miami Beach next month, at least the issues in the November general election will be easy to define.

Americans have always supported genuine progress in a well-ordered, pragmatic manner. Despite populism's current successes, there is not yet sufficient evidence to suggest most citizens truly believe a faith shot through with emotion and pie-in-the-sky panaceas should be the basis for national policy.

Herald Examiner
Los Angeles, Calif., June 13, 1972

According to a survey by the New York Times, a striking 40 per cent of California voters who supported Sen. Hubert H. Humphrey in that state's primary say they will abandon their party and vote for President Nixon in November if Sen. George McGovern wins the Democratic nomination.

Exaggerated or not, nationally representative or not, the finding dramatically underscores the potentially disastrous problem now confronting the Democrats and their leading contender for the White House. To have even a remote chance of victory in November, party unity must be restored. And the prospect is far from encouraging.

The situation shapes up as a close mirror of the Goldwater-Johnson showdown in 1964. Barry Goldwater, a hawk of the right wing, had an enthusiastic base constituency which propelled him into the Republican nomination. GOP moderates subsequently joined Democrats to give a resounding victory to his nonextremist rival, Lyndon Johnson.

McGovern, a sell-out dove on Vietnam whose basic constituency is the radical left, faces the same looming disaster in reverse. Unless he can broaden his appeal, a majority of voters are all but certain to support President Nixon's generally middle of the road position.

Goldwater never really tried to moderate his original platform. Sen. McGovern, more astute politician, for some time has been trying to soften and broaden his own — and the attempt in the end may be as disastrous as not to try.

Much of his popular appeal is based on the sincerity he has projected. From now on every retreat from his original stands will diminish that image. In trying to clear his biggest hurdle, George McGovern could wind up as just another fence straddler whose sincerity is doubted by friend and foe alike.

Los Angeles Times
Los Angeles, Calif., June 8, 1972

A few short months ago, it appeared almost impossible that Sen. George S. McGovern might win the Democratic presidential nomination, but Tuesday the Democratic voters of California placed the nomination almost within his grasp.

McGovern's victory over Sen. Hubert H. Humphrey fell far short of the margin that a poll had found a week before the election. Nevertheless, he captured the state's 271 convention delegates, and the importance of his victory cannot be discounted. In defeating Humphrey, McGovern beat a man who has been riveted into the political consciousness of the country for 25 years and who came close to winning the Presidency four years ago.

On the day he won in California, McGovern picked up 68 to 70 of New Jersey's 109 convention delegates, 10 of New Mexico's 18 and all 17 of the delegates in his home state, South Dakota. McGovern will go the convention with at least 1,100 of the 1,509 delegates needed for nomination, and he very likely will have accumulated considerably more by convention time.

The California primary demonstrated McGovern's strength, but it also revealed his vulnerability. He was forced on the defensive by Humphrey's attacks on his tax reform measures, his proposals to cut the defense budget by billions, and his income supplement proposals.

But as McGovern campaigned across the country, it became apparent that he had attracted to his banner a large and resourceful crew of bright, vigorous young men and women. The "new politics," if there is a "new politics," concerns basic issues, but the young men and women for McGovern have applied the old politics of careful organization and have used these methods with more skill than the party professionals. The new breed, whether or not they can put McGovern in the White House, may influence the Democratic Party and the country for years to come.

It also may be said that the absence of Gov. George C. Wallace's name on the California ballot distorted the results. If Wallace had entered the primary and had been able to campaign, he undoubtedly would have drawn more votes than he received in a last-minute write-in drive.

And if there was any doubt before that President Nixon would lead a cohesive, unified Republican Party into the November election, there was none after Tuesday's California primary. Rep. John Ashbrook, a conservative opponent of the President, made only a nominal showing. As if to underscore the point, the Republican voters of the 35th Congressional District defeated Rep. John G. Schmitz, an extreme right-wing Republican critic of Mr. Nixon.

But McGovern obviously has caught the mood of a large element in the Democratic Party. If this mood extends within and beyond the party and persists through the summer and fall, he could be a formidable candidate against President Nixon.

The Oregonian
Portland, Ore., June 8, 1972

Sen. Hubert Humphrey did a little better than expected against George McGovern in California, which means he was not crushed. If McGovern did not get all of the political bandwagon he was looking for in California, he did get all of the political parade of 271 delegates, a victory unthinkable only 90 days ago.

Sen. Humphrey is left with the mathematical hope that McGovern will be several hundred delegates short on the first ballot and that after that the fortunes of the Prairie Populist will recede. This is the politics of optimism.

McGovern's victory in New Jersey over Humphrey is as significant in assessing his appeal as was the California test. In New Jersey McGovern swept over the forces of the old politics, digging for the first time into the northern working and ethnic votes that have long been Humphrey's trump. Further, New Jersey will make New York (June 20), with its complicated delegate election system, easier and more certain for McGovern.

McGovern rolled over rural New Jersey, as expected, but also collected strong support in the wealthy suburbs and among those most knowledgeable about the issues. As in California, Humphrey continued to have strong appeal among Jewish voters.

What McGovern seems to be proving is that political ideology, given a near-death blow in the Goldwater defeat, is even less important in 1972 than the kind of man the voter perceives the candidate to be. Voters are not always stupid. They know all about the campaign promises and they also know that presidents are prisoners of the Congress and other forces that thwart their best intentions.

Leadership in both parties will be making a mistake if they believe McGovern is another Goldwater and will lead Democrats to a crushing defeat. This may well happen if President Nixon's popularity can continue to grow, but it won't be for the same reason that President Johnson crushed Sen. Goldwater. The voters liked Goldwater the man, but he scared to death far too many of them.

Successful presidential candidates since Franklin Roosevelt in modern times have run against something. Eisenhower was the exception, winning on integrity, the father image and the nation's general admiration for his role in World War II. He had the trust of the voters, and if McGovern can build on the trust reflected in his grandslam of four primary victories in one day, it may not matter too much with the voters what he's saying about busing, defense expenditures, withdrawal in Vietnam and $1,000 in every pot for each citizen — or that there's no money in sight to pay for all these things without more taxes.

And it won't matter that McGovern is a ponderous speaker, who when forced to smile almost seems a caricature of a man delivering the treasurer's report at a PTA meeting. It all reflects "non-politics," and with the voter, the "non-politician" is always in season.

The San Diego Union
San Diego, Calif., June 8, 1972

For many months the citizens of California have been hearing from political experts that the Golden State was in a state of incipient revolt against all government, that this irritation would be expressed at the polls on June 6.

The primary election has come and gone, and if there is any feeling of outrage at government it is certainly of less than landslide proportions.

For example, President Nixon, the highest symbol of authority in the United States of America, who did not campaign personally, won nine votes for each one that went to his opponent, Rep. John Ashbrook.

Moreover, the people of California gave solid approval to nine of the 10 state propositions on the ballot last Tuesday — including two bond issues, totalling $600 million, that will assist veterans and school children.

Even the single negative vote was, in fact, positive. It defeated resoundingly Proposition 9, which sought, in the name of good environment, restrictions that would have brought California's citizens to their knees economically. Hopefully, this obvious faith of the people in more regular approaches to good ecology will spur the Legislature promptly to enact and enforce stronger restrictions against pollution.

Finally, while the public was assaulted with political hyperbole before and after the election about "winning it all" and "bandwagons," the pragmatic Democrat officials who will gather in Miami next month have to worry over some significant statistics.

Principal among them will be the fact that California, like the other 20-odd primary elections to date, exhibits that neither Senator Humphrey nor Senator McGovern, who are currently the two leading contenders for their party's nomination, have an across-the-spectrum appeal to Democrats.

Senator Humphrey clearly has not been appealing to youth. By the same token, it is doubtful that Senator McGovern appealed in California to labor, the Jewish vote, Negroes and many Americans of Mexican extraction. Senator McGovern did not carry the state's largest county — Los Angeles — or populous Ventura, San Bernardino or Orange counties. His relatively slight 5 per cent plurality over Senator Humphrey could have been offset if six other Democrats were not also in the primary race.

All of this will be of little comfort to the Democrat delegates in Miami. They must deal with an internal fight for party leadership. They are worried about the carry-over indebtedness from 1968 of several million dollars. They cannot ignore the immense popular vote for Governor Wallace in the primaries, and, even before the convention begins, they face a bruising fight over who shall be seated as delegates.

The Des Moines Register
Des Moines, Iowa, June 8, 1972

"I can't believe we won the whole thing," George McGovern told ecstatic supporters in Hollywood Tuesday night after early returns indicated he would add a crucial California primary victory (271 delegates) to earlier wins in New Jersey, New Mexico and his home state of South Dakota where he was unopposed.

His parody of the disbelieving, but distressed, Ralph of the commercial delighted his audience, but it scarcely fitted the situation. There was no disbelief, let alone distress. McGovern and the polls had predicted wins, and win he did. The wins brought his assured first-ballot convention delegate strength to more than 900. And he has been all but conceded at least 200 New York delegates in that state's June 26 primary. He is getting close to the 1,509 needed for nomination.

In contrast to the McGovern camp, there is genuine disbelief and acute distress among traditional Democratic party wheelhorses who still can't believe the South Dakotan has almost won the whole nomination. Those suffering from political indigestion at this prospect include labor leaders, state and county chairmen and a number of moderate as well as conservative Democratic governors.

They fear McGovern is "too radical" for the majority of American people. It isn't merely that they disagree with McGovern's minimum income and tax reform plans or his proposals to slash defense spending. They fear Nixon would swamp both him and the rest of the ticket, including themselves in some cases.

Their fears are understandable. But McGovern in the last five months has been overcoming even more substantially grounded omens of doom with stunning regularity.

In its first presidential opinion sampling of 1972, the Gallup Poll showed McGovern the choice of only 3 per cent of Democrats polled. But in Iowa precinct caucuses that month, the nation's first, McGovern won a fourth of the state's national convention delegates. He has been building ever since.

When his campaign star began to rise dramatically in April, there were confident predictions it would set in California. Would a state suffering extreme unemployment in defense industries vote for a candidate who wants further defense cutbacks? Would a state which elected a governor who denounced "welfare loafers" vote for a candidate who proposes a minimum income payment for everyone?

It would and did. The McGovern "star" is almost out of reach of those so desperately trying to haul it in.

RAPID CITY JOURNAL

Rapid City, S.D., June 8, 1972

Pulses in both political parties are pounding harder, thanks to the ever-growing number of Democratic National Convention delegates claimed by presidential hopeful George McGovern.

The South Dakota senator has virtually mesmerized the news services and political analysts who are now preoccupied with the "McGovern Phenomenon." But it has to be the pros in both parties who are excited.

Turning over in the minds of Democrats is the question of whether McGovern could defeat President Nixon, should McGovern be the Democratic presidential candidate. Conversely, it is understood that Nixon's political advisors are almost yearning for a McGovern candidacy. They are said to believe he can be shown to be so far to the left side of the political spectrum that Nixon can defeat him handily and perhaps bring about a fundamental political realignment in the process.

What was good Republican strategy before McGovern's sweep of four primary elections Tuesday may still be good. Some of the ammunition the GOP has stored for use against McGovern was incorporated in Hubert Humphrey's losing campaign in the high-stakes California race. Humphrey hoped aerospace industry workers would see McGovern's military spending cutback proposal as a threat to their jobs. The pros now are probably trying to decide whether that gambit helped Humphrey to do better than pre-election polls indicated he would do. If so, it could also help Nixon.

The Democratic pros (only a few of McGovern's advisors are recognized as being traditional pros) seem not to know which way to turn. McGovern's campaign has taken on the dimensions of a juggernaut, and no politician wants to get run over. Yet, as columnists Rowland Evans and Robert Novak note, many Democratic governors feel threatened by McGovern. And there are other signs of resistance causing McGovern to give attention to disarming hostile party leaders and calming the nervous ones.

Stress inside the Democratic party comes from visible infighting and the supreme air of confidence emanating from the McGovern camp. This stress is exacerbated by Nixon's successful trips to Peking and Moscow and improved reports from the Vietnam war.

Perhaps the most difficult task now is to determine whether McGovern's primary victories represent rank-and-file party support or superb McGovern organizational work geared to winning delegates. Obviously, his opponents failed to develop strategy to win delegates under Democratic Convention Reform Commission rules that McGovern himself helped write. Yet before California, Gov. George Wallace had more total votes than Humphrey, who, in turn, led McGovern.

With the now seemingly rapid swing toward McGovern, 1972 could be one of the strangest chapters in political history if the scenario ends up with Republicans hoping for a McGovern candidacy for reasons that suit the GOP cause.

THE ANN ARBOR NEWS

Ann Arbor, Mich., June 11, 1972

NOW THAT Sen. George McGovern has successfully run the gauntlet of state primaries, his critics are singing a different tune. Now they are saying the South Dakota senator will have to be de-radicalized.

Others are saying that the Democrats are about to pull off a feat similar to the Republicans in 1964, i.e., nominating a man so far out of the mainstream of political thinking as to be unelectable.

McGovern admittedly has a selling job ahead of him. If he gets the nomination next month as now seems likely, he must win over labor and a host of governors and senators who have staked out anti-McGovern positions.

* * *

THE FEAR is that McGovern on the national ticket will drag down Democrats all along the line, similar to the disastrous GOP defeat in 1964. In many respects, however, the situations are not analogous, and neither is McGovern the kind of politician who would go into Tennessee and advocate selling off TVA.

The truth of the matter is, McGovern is not as far left as his critics believe. The keystone of his program to the people has been the trinity of fundamental tax reform; a swift conclusion to Vietnam; and cuts in defense spending. These are not radical proposals and the only pity is that these issues were not raised much earlier.

On other matters, McGovern is less precise and his arithmetic open to suspicion. He will have to develop his welfare reform and redistribution of income proposals in language the people can understand.

No question about it, he is going to have to learn the politics of accommodation and learn it in a hurry. There is too much disunity in the party and too much antipathy to his candidacy. If McGovern cannot provide leadership in this respect and practice the politics of accommodation, his nomination may be a gesture of little value.

* * *

THE DEFEATISM that seems to pervade the Democratic party at this point is not McGovern's fault. The Democrats are afraid, mortally it seems, of a man who comes on television wearing the American flag in his coat lapel. But that's just the image of the man, and the Democrats need to unite to defeat Nixon where he is vulnerable — on the issues.

The question now is whether McGovern can unite his party without compromising his own strong principles. His problem is that he has to be true to his own populist - protest politics while showing that he can work with the other factions of his party.

He can start by playing up his South Dakota origins. Any state that can elect Karl Mundt to the Senate at the same time as McGovern is no hotbed of radicalism.

McGovern's choice of a running mate is crucial. The Wallace delegation at Miami will be large and not easily bought off. Obviously he won't accept Wallace on the ticket, so that leaves a southern running mate as a wide open possibility. This might appease the Wallace backers.

In that event, Gov. Reuben Askew of Florida would be a fine candidate for vice president. So would former North Carolina Gov. Terry Sanford, now president of Duke University. Picking either of these two men would also moderate McGovern's positions in the public eye.

Realistically, the Democrats have little choice but to unite under McGovern. The alternatives (Muskie, Humphrey, Wallace) are less and less acceptable as the convention nears. Can McGovern beat Nixon? Could Truman beat Dewey? Would Lyndon Johnson decline re-election? Rhetorical questions, of course. Nixon's party is a minority party, and there is plenty that can go wrong for the Administration between now and November. Protest politics could put Sen. McGovern in the White House.

AKRON BEACON JOURNAL
Akron, Ohio, June 8, 1972

Sen. George McGovern didn't win in California by as big a margin as the polls had projected, but that he won at all is remarkable, considering his advocacy of a $30 billion cut in defense spending, which is so important to the state's economy.

Sen. Hubert Humphrey took pains to let Californians know about his opponents stand on arms spending — and about his radical tax program as well — but it didn't seem to hurt McGovern. At least, not enough.

The 271 delegates McGovern picked up in California, plus those he won in New Jersey, New Mexico and South Dakota the same day, put him over the 900-mark — three-fifths of the way home to the Democratic presidential nomination. His delegate strength at this point exceeds by over 100 the combined totals of Gov. George Wallace, Sen. Humphrey and Sen. Edmund Muskie.

California didn't prove that McGovern can win in November, nor even that he would do better against President Nixon than some more conservative Democrat.

What was proved, we think, on Tuesday — in California and elsewhere — is that Humphrey has had it. California was a must for him. He needed those 271 delegates to stay alive.

Even if McGovern is stopped at Miami Beach — an unlikely prospect now — Humphrey is an improbable compromise choice. Too many McGovern delegates would refuse to switch to Humphrey even if McGovern asked them to do so; in their eyes Humphrey still is a symbol of Lyndon Johnson's Vietnam policy.

Chicago Sun-Times
Chicago, Ill., June 11, 1972

Like Lord Byron's Assyrian, Sen. George McGovern of South Dakota has come down like the wolf on the Democratic fold. The most reliable (and conservative) count indicates that he will go to Miami Beach one month from now with—at most—only a relative handful of delegates required to give him the nomination on the first ballot.

In the meantime, his chief rivals—if that is the word — Senators Hubert Humphrey of Minnesota and Edmund Muskie of Maine — are acting as if there is still a good chance that McGovern can be headed off at the pass. Quite frankly, we can't see it. Projecting beyond the remaining states in which delegates have yet to be chosen, McGovern is likely to have about 1,380 delegates out of 1,509 needed to nominate. He can probably pick up the rest before the convention in dribs and drabs. Former Democratic National Committee Chairman John Bailey, for example, is sitting on 25 uncommitted Connecticut delegates.

And the pattern is repeated across the country. There are another 25 uncommitted New Jersey delegates, to say nothing of Mayor Daley's 92 uncommitted. But the mayor is unlikely to announce his support for any candidate until after the Illinois delegation caucus on July 9, the day before the convention, by which time the issue will probably have been decided.

In the meantime, what have Humphrey and Muskie done? Well, Humphrey has backtracked on a statement he made only two weeks ago to the effect that he "could not" accept Alabama Gov. George C. Wallace as a running mate; later he said that "under certain conditions" Wallace would be acceptable although such a pairing would be unlikely.

Never mind that Humphrey demands agreement by Wallace to a liberal Democratic platform; the fact remains that Humphrey, who at this point is looking and acting like a tattered coat upon a stick, is apparently doing everything he can to muster the forces of conservatism within the party to stop McGovern—no matter what alliances that requires. This is not the Hubert Humphrey one used to know; this is not the fighter for liberal causes who helped the black, the deprived, the elderly. This is an aging Faust who forgets that Mephistopheles must sometime be paid.

Muskie, for his part, says that he cannot support McGovern at this point because this would mean that delegates would go to the convention "with nothing to decide." One wonders what his position would be if the rigors of the primary trail had turned out differently and that the predictions of the political soothsayers a year ago had proved to be true and that the Maine senator had himself locked up the nomination by now. Indeed, his references to McGovern proposals which are "very unacceptable to a very large portion of the people" sit ill with the memory of Muskie in Wisconsin scrambling to keep up with McGovern's suggested innovations.

We think McGovern has earned the right to run against President Nixon. We will decide, as the issues are developed, whether we will support Mr. Nixon or his Democratic opponent in the fall. But McGovern should take care lest a willingness to listen to voters and modify his programs turns into a facile ability merely to bend with the wind.

The Detroit News
Detroit, Mich., June 8, 1972

Senator George McGovern's primary victories this week in four states, including California, bring the Democratic presidential nomination virtually into the senator's grasp. The question no longer is whether he can get it, but, as in the case of the pup that caught the car, what he will be able to do with it.

Despite the nimbus of optimism that surrounds his campaign, McGovern must know that his real problems are just beginning.

At his victory party in Hollywood, he asserted: "We have started well in pulling the Democratic Party together and, in a larger sense, pulling the entire country together." He was whistling as he passed the graveyard.

Only the day before, he had visited Democratic governors at the National Governors' Conference in Houston in a fruitless effort to erase their fears about what his candidacy might do to the party. After McGovern's visit, most of the Democratic governors said they still don't think he can be elected.

Expressing a sentiment obviously not restricted to Southern Democratic leaders, Gov. William L. Waller, of Mississippi, declared: "If McGovern is nominated, Democrats might as well forget the 1972 election."

McGovern's achievements in the primaries obviously cannot be dismissed as trivial, but there is a certain illusory quality about them that also cannot be dismissed.

True, he has won the most delegates. But, putting it another way, he has collected the largest number of splinters in a badly splintered party. The popular votes cast in these primaries have been widely distributed among a field of several candidates.

At this point, there is no more reason to believe that McGovern can unify his own party and win the fall election than there was reason to believe in 1964 that Barry Goldwater could do those things as the Republican presidential candidate.

Paradoxically, McGovern's vulnerability was illustrated in California, even as he made a clean sweep of that state's 271 delegate votes. Several days before the election, polls had shown him winning by as much as 20 percentage points. Actually, he failed to get a majority of even the Democratic vote and edged out Senator Hubert Humphrey by only 8 percentage points.

The ability of Humphrey to close such a gap suggests the vulnerability of McGovern when another candidate takes off the kid gloves and punches at his weak points. No candidate had done that until Humphrey went into action belatedly in the last days of the California campaign.

Humphrey made some headway even though much of the impact of his attack got lost in the famous Humphrey verbiage. What will happen to McGovern in the final election when an expert like Richard Nixon gets to work on him?

McGovern stands far left of the great middle of the American electorate. When people find out what he really thinks, they shun him in droves. He could, in fact, lose the election on a single issue — his unremitting effort to emasculate the armed defenses of this country.

So McGovern may have climbed a pile of delegate votes almost to the summit but in doing so he has put the Democratic Party in a real spot. It is getting a candidate who will have to be de-radicalized before he can be offered for public consumption.

Chicago Tribune
Chicago, Ill., June 11, 1972

To Sen. McGovern's supporters, his four-state primary sweep Tuesday night was the grand finale in his triumphant march to the Democratic nomination. They see him now as an irresistible force who has swept aside all comers and who will unite all factions of the party behind his liberal standard and lead them on to glory.

This is a splendid example of wishful thinking. Mr. McGovern won his victories, all right, but the results are not all that rosy.

The California primary was on a winner-take-all basis [in violation of the party's McGovern Commission recommendations, we might note] and so the state's 271 delegates went to McGovern. But he cannot claim, as several liberal commentators have already tried, that his California win is a reflection of widespread national popularity. With nearly all precincts reporting, he defeated Sen. Humphrey by only 5 percentage points, not the 20 points predicted by the polls. Statewide, he drew only 45 per cent of the vote.

In New Mexico, he barely outpolled Gov. George Wallace, who didn't even campaign. In New Jersey, a supposed cinch for McGovern, he came away with only 71 of 109 delegates.

This has been pretty much the story of the entire McGovern campaign: pluralities rather than majorities; dazzling victory celebrations that mask gaping weaknesses. He was a disaster in the South. He was badly defeated in several northern industrial states, Illinois among them. He has won nine primaries and now controls more than 900 delegates, but a large hunk of this delegate strength came not from primaries, but from his skillful exploitation of the caucus system of delegate selection. This was the same method Sen. Barry Goldwater's forces used to win the 1964 Republican nomination for him.

Mr. McGovern has proved he can beat Mr. Humphrey, but Gov. Wallace has dogged him every step of the way. Mr. Wallace has won six primaries, controls 326 delegates, and, until California, led the entire Democratic field in the popular vote. Contrary to what is known as "the conventional wisdom," Mr. Wallace's supporters are not sympatico with Mr. McGovern. In contests matching both candidates, Wallace supporters rejected Mr. McGovern on ideological grounds and may well bolt the party if he is nominated, especially the rural southerners and northern backlash elements.

On the basis of numbers alone, Mr. McGovern has failed to appeal to what Republicans have called the party mainstream. More importantly, he has failed to prove he can beat Richard Nixon. At the National Governors Conference in Houston, 28 Democratic governors were asked to raise their hands if they thought McGovern could carry their states. Only three did.

Sen. Humphrey, Sen. Edmund Muskie, and others are hoping this will give rise to a stop-McGovern movement at the convention. As things stand now, we don't expect such a movement to succeed, not because Mr. McGovern will go to Miami with 1,250 of the 1,509 delegates needed for the nomination, but because the anti-McGovern forces can produce no viable alternative to him. They are in the same shape as were Scranton & Co. at the 1964 Republican convention—divided, disorganized, and with a proven record as losers.

So Mr. McGovern may very well win his nomination. But instead of a triumphant march to glory, we see dissension developing along ideological lines, and the party coming apart at the seams.

The Evening News
Newark, N.J., June 8, 1972

We have it on no more popular authority than Sen. George McGovern that "nothing is certain in politics." For cases in point, take California and New Jersey—which Sen. McGovern did, but not in ways that sages and polls predicted.

The Prairie Populist was given a chance in Eastern Establishment New Jersey, but barely. After all, arrayed against him in the ranks supporting Hubert H. Humphrey were just about all the stalwarts of Democracy's Old Order. To envision a Democratic convention without chairs for Sal Bontempo, Harry Lerner, Bill Kelly and Charlie Marciante would be like having a ball without a band.

Yet, when the counting in New Jersey's precincts was done, it was Sen. McGovern leading the state's long line of Democratic delegates; Hubert Humphrey's boys from the back rooms were nowhere in the delegate listings.

A strange happening that, especially in a state with close to the highest per capita income in the country—and in behalf of a presidential candidate who would take chunks of taxes from those earning over $12,000 a year, confiscate inheritances over $500,000 and dole out $1,000 annually to all, whether they worked or not.

California, where funny money pops up periodically, told a different story. There, Sen. McGovern was held to be so far out front that all that would remain for Hubert Humphrey would be the choice of a gracious way to throw in the towel. But the magical 20 per cent margin did not materialize for Sen. McGovern and, at last sounding, Sen. Humphrey was battered but still beating a trail to Miami.

Disparate as its components may seem, there's no denying the substance of the McGovern phenomenon. What is there about this latter day Robin Hood that makes the well-to-do seem so anxious to give to the poor, the needy and even the lazy? Perhaps it's a mixture of belief and disbelief.

Belief in Sen. McGovern's possession of virtues like honesty, directness, the best of what once was great and good in America. A repudiation, too, of the kind of duplicity, greed and chicanery that unbalanced our wealth and our values and got us involved abroad against the popular will. These beliefs represent Sen. McGovern's pluses, as supported in primaries from wintry New Hampshire to late spring's Wisconsin, California and New Jersey.

But there's also disbelief. Oddly, that seems to produce pluses, too. For many who have been voting for Sen. McGovern obviously choose to ignore his radical pronouncements about wealth and national defense, or don't take them seriously enough to believe they might prevail if he's elected President.

Just what the Eastern Establishment stalwarts can do about the McGovern phenomenon between now and Miami in July becomes less clear with each passing primary victory. It's true that conventions rarely heed primaries. No more recent reminder is needed than Chicago in 1968.

But, as Sen. McGovern happily concedes: "Nothing is certain in politics." And one can be sure he's counting on that also being in his favor.

DAILY NEWS
New York, N.Y., June 8, 1972

Sen. George McGovern (D-S.D.) didn't win the California presidential primary Tuesday as overwhelmingly as some polls predicted.

California's winner-take-all-delegates rule is grotesque.

President Richard M. Nixon outpolled McGovern in California.

All that is true. Nevertheless, it seems clear to us that McGovern has become, as politicians say, the man to beat.

He is the man for Democrats worried about their party's future to beat, if they can, at their July 10 Miami Beach national convention.

And he is the man for the Republicans to start fighting right now in dead earnest. Never mind the talk that he would be duck-soup for President Nixon—or the yarn (fostered, we're convinced, by wily Democrats) about how McGovern can't carry a single Southern state if nominated for President. He wasn't going to get anywhere in the primaries, either; and look at him now.

Sen. McGovern

All real Republicans, we believe, and all patriotic Democrats, should begin working now to defeat McGovern.

If McGovern becomes President, he can be counted on to do his utmost to wreck the Vietnam war effort and betray Southeast Asia to the Communists.

Also, you can look for him to strive to weaken the U.S.A. militarily throughout the world . . . to bankrupt the government via outlandish handouts and giveaways . . . to cripple initiative and destroy work incentives with idiotic tax "reforms" . . . and in other ways to make America over into a ruinous hulk of a once great nation.

Such goings-on of a President (God forbid) McGovern have been foreshadowed by his every utterance and political act up to, say, three months ago.

His current efforts to appease Southern Democrats, Northern conservatives, and admirers of Gov. George C. Wallace are transparent political maneuvers which McGovern could be expected to forget within minutes after being inaugurated, God forbid, President of the United States.

Hence, we think it is the duty of true Americans to unite and stay united against this person so long as he has a ghost of a chance of becoming, God forbid, President. In this fight, we have nothing to lose except our country as we know and love it.

THE WALL STREET JOURNAL.
New York, N.Y., June 8, 1972

The California primary campaign made it clear we have misjudged George McGovern in two important respects.

It is already fashionable in punditdom to tot up where we all went wrong about his political prospects. For our part, we had allowed for the importance of devoted partisans in primary campaigns, but had not expected the vacuum that was created by the collapse of Senator Muskie and the rest of the Democratic field. We also underestimated the appeal of Senator McGovern's cool television personality. He has the knack (warning to Republicans) of winning elections by getting himself attacked.

The second misjudgment is even more interesting. To wit, we wrote that his nomination might produce a 1964 in reverse. We still think he could quite possibly lead his party down to dire defeat, but not quite for the reasons Barry Goldwater did. Senator McGovern has by now made it quite clear he is not about to go into Tennessee to talk of selling TVA, or do anything else to rub his ideology into anyone's face.

We do not feel particularly contrite over this particular misjudgment. After all, the Senator's stock speeches ring with phrases like, "I think the overwhelming majority of the American people are dissatisfied with the leadership of both parties. . . . It's a leadership that has consistently told us one thing in public while advocating a different course in private. . . . I think they're tired of politics as usual. . . . I think there's a tide running in this country that provides the motive force of the McGovern campaign, and it's a tide that above all else would restore some measure of truthfulness and openness in the councils of government."

When a politician talks like that, we feel we really are entitled to conclude that his ideology is something less than a model of flexibility. All the more so if he comes up with a slogan—"Right. From the Start"—that promises nothing if it does not promise consistency. These are promises of blunt talk, but Mr. McGovern's blunt talk has proved devilishly hard to understand.

In The New York Review of Books, for example, he said, "I propose that the actual corporation income tax be returned to its 1960 level by the elimination of the special loopholes that have been opened since then." Those of us who knew the corporation income tax level in 1960 was 52% somehow got the idea he was advocating an increase from the current 48%.

It seems we missed the fine print. Or anyway, the Senator took out an ad in this paper to assure everyone he only wanted to change depreciation rules and the like. (Eileen Shanahan of The New York Times remains puzzled, since an increase to 52% from 48% happens to make the arithmetic come out right for the $17 billion the Senator says his proposals would raise.)

In an Iowa speech last January, Senator McGovern talked of inheritance taxes and said, "we must set a ceiling on the amount that might be received and then place a 100% tax on all gifts and inheritances above that amount. . . . Even if the ceiling were set as high as $500,000 . . ." Richard Reeves of New York magazine somehow got the idea the Senator wanted to tax inheritances of over $500,000 at 100%. But the ad in this paper explained he had suggested no ceiling "on inheritances at $500,000 or any other level."

We're not quite sure what the Senator said about excess profits taxes last August, but somehow Tom Wicker of the Times got the idea that "Senator McGovern is proposing that an excess profits tax (on the Korean war model) be levied." In that ad the fine print comes again, "I have not suggested the imposition of excess profits taxation on general corporate income of a cyclical nature, nor that which is derived from sound growth or from innovation and invention. I have suggested that during the present period of inflationary stress, profits derived solely from wage limitations and price increases should, in equity, be subject to taxation when excessive."

Senator McGovern, we now learn, is not in favor of repealing laws restricting abortion, it's only that he wants such decisions left solely to the woman and her doctor. He would cut military manpower by 30% but not close any bases important to local economies, or anyhow none that voters have asked about. And so on.

Now, it is our habit when these matters come up to express considerable sympathy for the poor politician; Americans always expect him to stick to his principles but do what the voters want. In Senator McGovern's case, in particular, the problem seems to be no sort of deviousness but a tendency to believe any staff paper where the figures somehow add up right on the bottom line.

Still, if Senator McGovern is not going to pull a Barry Goldwater but a politics as usual, it really would be nice if we could be spared all that talk so dear to those devoted partisans—all the stuff about how other politicians are slippery but Senator McGovern is consistent, about how all the rest are deceivers and only he is truthful.

The New York Times
New York, N.Y., June 8, 1972

The most astonishing climb out of obscurity in recent American political history has carried Senator McGovern almost within grasp of the Democratic Presidential nomination. His sweep of all four primaries Tuesday, plus the virtual certainty of another big victory in New York June 20, makes it probable that he will enter the convention next month only 200 delegates short of clinching the nomination on the first ballot.

Unquestionably the strength of the tide in Mr. McGovern's favor will bring feverish last-ditch efforts at fused resistance by those who never have had much enthusiasm for his candidacy—Chicago's Mayor Daley and a handful of other still-powerful big-city bosses, the leadership of organized labor, Southern Governors and other party potentates with deep reservations about his program or his electability.

But the stop-McGovern forces will have to reckon with two compelling deterrents to overaggressiveness in attempting to muscle the South Dakota Senator aside. One is the absence of any potential rival with demonstrated mass appeal; the other—and even more forceful—is party awareness that a recourse to old-fashioned wheeling and dealing to block Mr. McGovern at Miami Beach would so outrage all the reform elements active in his ascent that the Democrats might be irretrievably fragmented.

At best the party must face the possibility that Governor Wallace, the other prime beneficiary of the politics of disaffection in this strange primary campaign, will seek to rally his followers behind a third-party bid. Whether such a bid would, on balance, take more electoral votes away from the Democratic nominee or from President Nixon is an open question. But whatever chances a Democrat might have to triumph in the face of a Wallace defection would plummet to near-zero if a convention gang-up on McGovern sparked a fourth-party challenge led by the army of young activists so prominent in his dramatic spurt to the top.

* * *

That combination of realities makes it important to both Senator McGovern and his party that he devote the bulk of his energies in the month remaining before the convention to demonstrating his capacity to unify the discordant Democrats and to clarifying the now hazy details of his controversial positions on everything from taxes to Vietnam.

It is hard to believe that the impressive delegate total amassed by Mr. McGovern necessarily reflects considered voter backing for all the elements in his program, especially since he has himself had great difficulty in indicating just what his program entails, what it would cost or how it would answer specific national needs. The primary spur for McGovern votes, it would appear, is a widespread questioning among the electorate of vested centers of authority, political and economic, and a consequent eagerness to identify with a candidate who gives an impression of earnestness in challenging established approaches to solving the country's problems.

But, even on that basis, the McGovern constituency has been more effective in marshalling delegate strength than in piling up a huge numerical majority of votes. Despite the sweep in California and New Jersey and the victories that went before, an Associated Press tabulation of the popular vote in the eighteen primaries held thus far shows Senator Humphrey actually ahead of Senator McGovern by a thin margin, with Governor Wallace not far behind.

A quality of desperation nevertheless seems to have come into the Humphrey candidacy as the former Vice President strives to keep the twilight from closing around his long career. Only panic could explain his extraordinary suggestion in Houston yesterday that he might, if Governor Wallace subscribed to the Democratic platform, accept him as a Vice-Presidential running mate. If these are the tactics to be used to frustrate the McGovern rush toward nomination, they had better be forgotten before they bring lasting disgrace to the Democratic party.

©1972 by The New York Times Company. Reprinted by permission.

TULSA DAILY WORLD
Tulsa, Okla., June 8, 1972

TO READ and hear about the California Democratic PRESIDENTIAL primary is almost like watching someone commit suicide.

Does the Democratic Party have a strange death-wish in these peculiar times, that it would nominate a GEORGE MCGOVERN to be its No. 1 national leader? Or is it merely a commentary on the entire roster of Democratic candidates that SENATOR MCGOVERN is considered the most likely of the lot?

We give full credit to the organizing genius of the Senator, to his ability to attract zealous campaign workers from the ranks of the young in particular, and to his unfathomable capacity for winning the support of people who apparently do not care what he believes or would do as PRESIDENT.

He is the candidate of the "aginners," and today that may be all a man must offer to be accepted as a Messiah by the dissatisfied and disgruntled.

But nominated for PRESIDENT?

That is the clear prospect now, incredible as it may seem. The Democrats are actually about to nominate for the nation's highest office a man who was a joke as a candidate in 1968 and who only a few weeks ago was straining for 5 per cent recognition in the national polls.

If we appear appalled at this prospect, it is not that we expect McGOVERN to be PRESIDENT. Perhaps he would be the easiest man for RICHARD NIXON to beat. But in our view the greatest hope of the country is for the two major parties to put up the best possible candidates, so that even if a stunning upset occurs the United States will still be in good hands.

We do not have that confidence in GEORGE MCGOVERN.

Perhaps our dismay may be suspect, since we are not likely to support PRESIDENT NIXON'S opponent no matter whom the Democrats nominate. In that case, let's look at it from a strictly Democratic viewpoint. Within the last week, here is what Gov. JIMMY CARTER of Georgia, a moderate Democrat, has written about his party's outlook. Following are some of his comments:

"What we find in the Democratic Party today is the same potential for disaster that the Republicans demonstrated in the 1964 PRESIDENTIAL election.

"Because of the new delegate-selection mechanisms, Republican crossover voting in Democratic primaries and a frightening lack of public awareness of his stands on basic issues, Sen. GEORGE MCGOVERN has become our party's frontrunner.

"It is almost inconceivable to see that Democratic convention delegates could nominate a candidate who cannot possibly win, because he favors forced busing of students, amnesty for draft evaders, $1,000 Government handouts to every American and a social spending program which would mount up Federal deficits of more than $100 billion while undermining U.S. defense capability by $32 billion."

Many, many other Americans should share GOVERNOR CARTER'S fear of a MCGOVERN nomination—not because he probably couldn't win but because there is no way to rule out the possibility—no matter how remote—that he *might*.

ST. LOUIS POST-DISPATCH
St. Louis, Mo., June 9, 1972

It is somewhat amusing to witness the tortured arguments of Republican pundits who are advising the Democrats not to nominate George McGovern because he cannot win. This process began two or three months ago when it appeared Mr. McGovern might be a formidable contender for the Democratic presidential nomination, and it has continued to the present (even after Mr. McGovern has demonstrated pretty conclusively that he is a winner).

No doubt the Republicans would like to encourage the opposition to nominate a pushover for President Nixon, and they just might get their wish. But political realists will understand that Mr. McGovern has qualities that make him perhaps the most dangerous opponent for the President that the Democrats could select—a man who engenders confidence (no credibility gap), a man with a progressive program, a splendid organizer, a fresh personality.

If Senator McGovern has correctly sensed the national mood the question may not be whether he can win but whether he can lose. In 1952 the national mood demanded Gen. Eisenhower; no Democrat could have defeated him that year. If today, 20 years later, there is another surge of the popular will in the direction taken by Mr. McGovern, no Republican, least of all one suffering from Mr. Nixon's handicaps, has a very good chance of winning.

St. Louis Globe-Democrat
St. Louis, Mo., June 8, 1972

Sen. George McGovern's supporters are claiming the victories in four primaries Tuesday have virtually assured McGovern the Democratic nomination on the first ballot.

This is not true.

McGovern probably will go to the Democratic Convention July 10 with more delegates pledged to him than any other candidate, but he is far from being a shoo-in nominee. In fact, the odds are against him for very good reasons.

The principal reason he can't be regarded as the inevitable choice is the fact that the Democratic party will want to nominate a candidate it believes can win in November.

George McGovern just does not qualify on this score.

A Gallup Poll of a representative sampling of Democratic voters in the nation (carried in the current U.S. News & World Report) shows that Sen. Hubert Humphrey outdistances McGovern in every region of the country.

☆ ☆ ☆

In the East, Democratic voters prefer Humphrey over McGovern 28 per cent to 24 per cent; in the West it is again Humphrey over McGovern 28 per cent to 24 per cent; in the Midwest Humphrey's margin is 40 per cent to 21 per cent, and in the South it is Humphrey 33 per cent to 10 per cent.

Why then does McGovern now have about 900 delegates and the prospect of going into the convention with about 1200?

Because he has been the beneficiary of three factors that have worked for him and against Humphrey. They are:

(1) The Kennedy organization and all of its resources have given him the kind of aggressive, professional campaign team that has not been seen since the late President John F. Kennedy was running for the presidency.

(2) His young and aggressive backers have by far the best knowledge of the new Democratic delegate rules and procedures and are using this advantage to take over party caucuses and capture delegates even in areas where McGovern does not appear strong.

(3) He has benefitted from the big Communist offensive in Vietnam which revived the war issue and crystallized anti-war votes behind him.

Despite all the extravagant claims by his backers, McGovern did not live up to expectations in California.

His final victory margin there was only about 5 per cent—a far cry from the 20 per cent margin they were forecasting.

He just narrowly defeated Gov. George Wallace in New Mexico even though the hospitalized Alabama Governor had no chance to campaign.

In New Jersey, where Humphrey put on only a limited campaign, McGovern's margin was only slightly more than 10 per cent even though his supporters put on an elaborate, expensive campaign.

☆ ☆ ☆

All in all it was not a signally impressive performance and certainly did not indicate any kind of Democratic mandate for McGovern. When the amount of campaigning and money spent by McGovern forces is considered, it becomes less impressive.

The leaders of the Democratic party know from long experience that a man as far left as McGovern can't be sold to the American electorate.

The great majority of people are just not going to buy McGovern's radical income redistribution plans—his proposal to guarantee every person a $1,000 income; his dangerous plan for cutting $32 billion willy-nilly from the annual national defense budget; his virulently hostile attitude toward business, reflected in his proposals for much higher taxes, and removal of expansionary tax incentives.

For these reasons Hubert Humphrey is still very much in contention for the nomination although his image as a one-time loser doesn't inspire many in the Democratic party.

A more formidable candidate than Humphrey may still be Sen. Edward M. (Ted) Kennedy who will be in the wings in the event the convention turns from McGovern to a candidate it regards as more viable.

☆ ☆ ☆

Kennedy has said he doesn't want the nomination. But he hasn't said he would turn it down if it was offered to him.

When the convention starts, keep a close eye on his backers. They can be counted upon to make a strong drive for a Kennedy draft.

In which case, McGovern could look around and find the powerful Kennedy team that is now behind him has disappeared.

THE RICHMOND NEWS LEADER
Richmond, Va., June 8, 1972

We now have the tallied opinions of California's Democratic voters, and—45 per cent to 40 per cent—they evidently prefer George McGovern to Hubert Humphrey. Given the incredibilities of California, it is difficult to know whether to be more amazed at the stampede to McGovern or at the casting of Humphrey as the conservative in the campaign. But if one is looking for nuggets of good news in the California returns, he ought to seize on the disparity of McGovern's California performance in contrast to how the pollsters predicted he would fare: They said he would defeat Humphrey by 20 per cent; McGovern actually defeated him by 5.

The reason for this comparatively poor showing may be directly attributable to the effects of Hubert Humphrey's one-week attack on George McGovern's extremism. What Humphrey did to McGovern suggests the vulnerability of McGovern's positions on practically everything—and they are extreme indeed. For instance:

Levy confiscatory taxes on every individual earning more than $12,000 annually. Increase the taxes on corporations by $17 billion and abolish their investment tax credits—thereby wiping out the major sources of jobs for the poor. Close the "loopholes" that allow municipalities to sell tax-free bonds and that permit oil and mineral prospecting companies to use depletion allowances to develop new sources of extractive wealth. Confiscate 77 per cent of any estate larger than $500,000 at death. Compel children to ride school buses for reasons of race. Provide amnesty for draft dodgers and AWOLs. Legalize marijuana. Legalize abortion for unwanting mothers. Cut the defense budget by more than $30 billion. Junk the space program. Withdraw every American soldier from Vietnam within 90 days.

It would be nice to believe that Senator McGovern has been consistent on every issue. Surely that is what he wants the public to believe. But on the matter of Vietnam, to take one example, he has been all over the field. In an interview with the New York Times in 1965 he said: "I support the strafing (of North Vietnamese targets) ordered by President Johnson because I agree (that) when our forces are attacked and our interests are under fire, we have to respond with appropriate retaliation." In recent years he has run from that position all the way to the opposite end zone. Now on Vietnam, as on so many other issues, he is beginning to edge toward mid-field. In the words of James Reston, who looks kindly on the McGovern candidacy, the Senator is a man with "radical programs and (an) army of radical organizers." He should not be allowed to succeed.

The prospect of a McGovern candidacy may be relished by conservatives who support Richard Nixon. Yet the Senator is a deft demagogue, and the American people have been suckered before. His nomination would mean that the radical left of the Democratic Party, fueled by Henry Wallace but shoved into a third-party ghetto by Harry Truman in 1948, had taken control at last. George McGovern is a compeller, a leveler, an isolationist who would destroy the nation's defenses and invite national suicide. Like all true demagogues, he presumes to offer something for everyone: "A lot of people will write it all off as just more rhetoric, a something-for-everyone budget. It is a something-for-everyone budget. And I think it's about time that we have a budget like that." From the nomination, he could go on the presidency. With something-for-everyone McGovern in the White House, the American people soon would discover that he could provide nothing for anyone. Let them not find out too late.

The Birmingham News
Birmingham, Ala., June 8, 1972

Southern Democratic governors, led by Georgia's Gov. Jimmy Carter, are understandably concerned about the disastrous political effects on their states' politics that would surely come, if Sen. George McGovern were to receive the Democratic nomination.

And if that wasn't enough, along with McGovern commencing to trim his sails on such things as taxes, a not uncommon tactic when the time of great decision nears, Hubert Humphrey stands up and says a Humphrey-Wallace ticket is conceivable.

The time to seek a way to put a stop to the McGovern steamroller narrows. When the bandwagon fever mounts the crush to get a good seat can be stifling. After Tuesday's victories in four states McGovern may be virtually unstoppable.

McGovern has been compared more than once with Barry Goldwater, whose well-organized party enthusiasts corralled the nomination for him at the expense of a rout at the polls in November, 1964.

Who can blame Carter and other governors, particularly in the South, for wanting to head off a candidate whose image would likely goad overwhelming numbers of voters to pull the big lever for the other party? McGovern may have great popular appeal in some parts of the country, but not in the South. His nomination would virtually ensure a sweep for President Nixon in November—or perhaps a Nixon-Wallace split of the vote, in the event the governor again makes a third party campaign after the convention.

In an anti-McGovern sweep, state and local Democratic contestants would be left in the same position many Democratic nominees found themselves when the South went for Goldwater in '64.

McGovern, aware of the concern among Southern Democratic governors, dropped in at the National Governors' Conference in an effort to reassure the uneasy Southern chief executives.

After McGovern's visit, Carter said, "I really can't say that my attitude toward him has changed."

McGovern was conciliatory: He said he wouldn't rule out selecting a Southerner as a running mate; he suggested possible shifts on the issues, if the convention platform committee were to differ with his key proposals on tax reform, welfare reform, etc.

But there is a limit to McGovern's flexibility. Just as Goldwater had to keep extremists among his enthusiasts happy, McGovern also has to please his far-out crowd. He can't make the radical chic and the ultra-liberals happy and please most Southern voters at the same time. The Southern Democratic governors undoubtedly are aware of this.

Carter and his colleagues may lack the clout to stop McGovern, but the Southern Democratic governors have every reason to be apprehensive about the havoc McGovern as a nominee would cause their state Democratic Parties in the fall.

THE STATES-ITEM
New Orleans, La., June 10, 1972

A first ballot nomination is now within Sen. George McGovern's reach. At the very worst, he will go to the National Democratic Convention in July only 200 to 300 delegate votes short of the 1,509 required for nomination.

And so in the coming weeks, the South Dakota senator will be intensifying his efforts to win over uncommitted delegates, attempting to mend his fences with organized labor and, in general, trying to allay the fears of those in the party especially in the South, who feel he is an uncompromising radical.

It will be a delicate tightrope walk.

For example, uncommitted black delegates, whose support Sen. McGovern needs, have served notice that they will demand concessions in the party platform which may prove unacceptable to some conservative southern and border state delegates, whose support the senator also needs.

It is clear that Sen. McGovern will have to move toward the center by modifying some of his original policy statements and recommendations. He will have to do so not only to win the nomination, but the support of a majority of Americans.

The job should not be too difficult.

If there is one thing Sen. McGovern has shown himself not to be it is an ideologue. He is nothing if not a pragmatist. His astuteness as a politician consistently has been underestimated by political observers.

Sen. McGovern has been talking lately about the possibility of a McGovern-Muskie ticket. This, of course, is a device to soften up delegates committed to the Maine senator as a prelude to their possible release. Sen. Muskie, for his part, has stated repeatedly that he is not interested in running for vice president again. Indeed, there is some question about whether Sen. McGovern would need additional support, should he win the nomination, where Sen. Muskie can offer it. There are those, for example, who think that Sen. McGovern might be better off with someone like Gov. Reubin Askew of Florida as a running mate.

In any event, the task before Sen. McGovern is clear. He must broaden his base of support, not only to win the nomination, but to assure a unified Democratic party in November.

The Washington Post
Washington, D.C., June 7, 1972

We count ourselves among that not-so-silent majority of political observers whose expectations have been confounded over the past several months by Senator McGovern's success at the polls. From New Hampshire on—except for the anomalous Florida primary—he has consistently demonstrated not just the worth of a diligent and well-run campaign organization, but, more important, a capacity to engage the minds and emotions of an increasing number of voters, a capacity to make his own distinctive view of things seem relevant to their concerns.

The senator's victory in California and his successes elsewhere Tuesday, taken together with earlier primary and convention results, now make him a good deal more than what you would call the "front-runner"—especially when you consider how easily and loosely that term has been handed from candidate to candidate in the past few months. To be sure, Senator McGovern does not have the Democratic nomination locked up. But he is not all that far from possessing what might be called the critical mass of delegates, a number so near the number needed for nomination as to ensure that the necessary remainder will come over. That is one important element in his chance of success. The other is that it is very difficult to sketch out a course or a series of moves by which someone else might get the nomination now.

Mindful of the way in which our own assumptions have been disproved by the primary results, we would still risk the observation that this last point is particularly true of Senator Humphrey. The former Vice President has done much better in the primary contests than people supposed he would when he got into the race last winter and it was widely judged that he would be one of the early casualties of the Muskie "juggernaut." Still, it seems to us that Hubert Humphrey's prospects for nomination rested largely on success in the primaries—required it, in fact—and that the only way in which he could get the nomination at this point would be via a course of action ultimately self-defeating to his candidacy. Theoretically and even practically, we suppose, Mr. Humphrey could still mobilize sufficient strength from among uncommitted delegates and party leaders to turn back the McGovern tide or at least to stop it short of victory. Conceivably he could do so and redirect the nomination either to himself or to some third candidate who broke a deadlock. But apart from the seemingly small possibility of things working out that way, there is a separate problem for Mr. Humphrey, namely, that to acquire the nomination in this fashion and against the current of the primary results is the one thing he cannot afford, the one thing bound to diminish the value of the nomination for him in particular, and also the one thing most likely to bring about holocaust in Miami.

For Senator McGovern, we would say, the imperatives work almost exactly the other way around. As primary champion and a man who is not just unencumbered by any connection with the Chicago strongarming of 1968 but also by much connection at all with the regular organization of his party, he is under an entirely different set of restraints and obligations. Senator McGovern, in short, should (and presumably will) spend much of the next few weeks wheeling and dealing. He will, that is, if his candidacy for the presidency is to be waged with the same degree of seriousness that it has been so far in the primaries. This is the moment when George McGovern will doubtless be reaching out to party leaders and officials around the country, seeking to enlarge his constituency and calm genuine fears about his positions on a number of issues and make possible a winning of the nomination in such a way as to give him a good crack at winning the fall elections.

There has been a certain amount of grotesque chit-chat about possible "accommodations" with Governor Wallace on Senator McGovern's part. While there is no doubt that the Wallace contingent at Miami deserves to be treated fairly and accorded its due, the availability of other delegations with which to treat and the irresponsibility of elevating Governor Wallace and all the tawdry things he stands for to co-equal status with the nominee, make these suggestions seem wholly cynical to us. The moves toward accommodation that we foresee have more to do with the taming of some of Senator McGovern's position paper views. Both his income redistribution/tax reform plan and his proposed reductions in defense expenditures stand in need of some reconsideration and rearrangement. The dollar figures in both appear to be gravely flawed, and one must suppose that efforts to rework the income redistribution plan would be matched —at the very least—by efforts to revise the defense spending plan in a way that takes account of the ramifications of the recent Moscow accords. It is likely that these two intricate subjects which have been dealt with only by labels and generalities in the give-and-take of electioneering, could stand some rethinking on the part of the senator and that he would be the first to concede that he should not be wedded to programs that do not squarely address the conditions they purport to. At the same time, it is also likely that any such moves on his part would be greeted with cries of "sell-out" on the part of some supporters and gloating wiseacre remarks about trimming and expediency on the part of political commentators. Still, it is our view that Senator McGovern will risk these things because he is so plainly a serious candidate for both the nomination and the presidency. Tuesday's primary results and all that went before leave no doubt about that.

Campaign '72:
McGOVERN SWEEPS NEW YORK PRIMARY, WITHIN 200 DELEGATES OF NOMINATION

Sen. George S. McGovern of South Dakota, the leading contender for the Democratic presidential nomination, swept 230 of the 248 elected delegates in New York's primary June 20. McGovern's victory in New York, the last major contest in the series of 23 primaries held since the New Hampshire balloting March 7, increased his total committed delegate strength to within 170 of the 1,509 needed for nomination at the party's convention in July. McGovern had fielded delegate slates in 37 of the 39 New York congressional districts. His principal rivals ran only minimal campaigns in the state.

In other New York Democratic primary battles the same day, the dean of the House of Representatives, Judiciary Committee Chairman Rep. Emanuel Celler, 84, who had served in Congress for fifty years, was narrowly defeated by Elizabeth Holtzman, 30. Rep. William F. Ryan won by a 2–1 margin over Rep. Bella S. Abzug, whose former district had been eliminated by reapportionment. Rep. John J. Rooney defeated Allard K. Lowenstein and Rep. Jonathan Bingham defeated Rep. James H. Scheuer in other New York congressional primaries.

New York Post
New York, N.Y., June 21, 1972

There were poignant individual victories and defeats in the New York Democratic primary, but it shed no great clarifying light on the national or state political future.

As expected, George McGovern's delegates—running with only a few uncommitted slates as opposition—scored impressively. This brings him closer to the Presidential nomination at Miami, and narrows considerably the number of delegates he still needs for his goal of a first-ballot victory. McGovern's speech at his New York headquarters was understandably a plea for party trust in him as the head of a "new coalition." He reassured those who fear his programs that there is "nothing they need be alarmed about," and that he plans to make America "a whole, happy, and confident people again."

But for political realists who look beyond rhetoric there was nothing in the New York results that could be considered a trend, far less a tide. Despite the anti-Establishment mood of the recent succession of state primaries, the incumbents in New York largely kept their hold on the nominations. In the two dramatic Congressional contests where incumbent Democrats ran against each other because of Republican gerrymandering of their districts, there was little choice between the contenders on the score of their Congressional records. The victories of William Ryan over Bella Abzug and of Jonathon Bingham over James Scheuer were personal rather than ideological victories, although both victors had solid liberal accomplishments as a base for their triumph.

Here, as in other instances, personality and style counted for more than political ideology.

In one Congressional race there was a sharp liberal-conservative confrontation—that of Allard Lowenstein's bold challenge to John Rooney. Here we feel that the better candidate came out at the short end of the vote. Lowenstein's refusal to concede defeat, and his decision to go to court on the charge of voting irregularities, are a mark of the determined, principled stance he has all along shown. But in another instance where a liberal-conservative issue was at stake—the Queens contest for Emanuel Gold's seat in the State Senate—Gold's victory over Jerry Birbach was a good omen for the further pursuit of the Forest Hills housing project in a spirit of reasoned liberalism.

The vivid cliffhanger contest was in the Brooklyn Congressional district where a young district leader, Elizabeth Holtzman, won narrowly over the dean of the House Democrats, Emanuel Celler. It shows that long Congressional service, along with the prerequisites of power and seniority, can be effectively challenged by an attractive and articulate candidate. Our own feeling was that Celler's experience as chairman of the House Judiciary Committee should not be lost to his New York constituents. Nevertheless the results show that no Congressional "big name" can take victory for granted.

We add a note about the fortunes of two other women who got considerable notice as candidates. Bella Abzug, who made much of her role as a champion of women's rights, was defeated by a considerable margin. Judge Nanette Dembitz, who ran for the State Court of Appeals as an insurgent without organization support, but who ran primarily as a judge not as a woman, scored the second highest vote of the four candidates vying for three nominations. There is a moral here, but we think it is again one of personality rather than of ideology.

DAILY NEWS
New York N.Y., June 22, 1972

SEN. GEORGE McGOVERN

—was the big winner in the New York State presidential primary, scooping up some 225 of the 278 delegates to the July 10 Democratic National Convention in Miami Beach.

McGovern thus demonstrated anew the power of tightly, shrewdly organized minority voting blocs to defeat loosely organized opponents.

Some of our Republican friends are chortling that, if this economic illiterate wins the Democratic presidential nomination, the Republicans will carry all 50 states for President Richard M. Nixon, plus both houses of Congress.

For the nation's sake, let us hope so. But the Republicans would be historic fools to take any such thing for granted. The time to begin working in earnest to defeat this prairie Populist is now—not tomorrow—but now.

We thought there was—

GOOD NEWS, AND BAD NEWS

—from other aspects of Tuesday's primary.

It seems a shame that Rep. Emanuel Celler (though we by no means have always agreed with him), after 50 years in Congress, was defeated for renomination by a no doubt nice little gal (but how experienced is she?) named Elizabeth Holtzman. Don't count Mr. Celler out yet, though—there is still the Liberal Party.

Under the head of good news, we feel, came Rep. John J. Rooney's win for renomination over Allard Lowenstein, head of Americans for Democratic Action, and need we say more?

And we cannot grieve over the defeat of Mrs. Bella Abzug for the Democratic nomination for Representative from the 20th CD by Rep. William Fitts Ryan.

Ryan, we believe, is at least as economically illiterate as McGovern. But Mrs. Abzug tried to muscle him aside after she had been gerrymandered out of her seat in Congress, when she should have sportingly recognized that this is how the ball bounces in politics.

Suggestion: The Abzug, we think, could make a name for herself in television as a female Archie Bunker, just as Mayor J.V. Lindsay, another primary loser, should do well as the glamorpuss hero of some TV soap opera.

Detroit Free Press
Detroit, Mich., June 22, 1972

THE HARD PART is ahead of him.

Considering that George McGovern came out of nowhere 15 weeks ago and now has the Democratic nomination all but assured, it would seem that he has done at least all that could be expected of a presidential candidate. He won 10 of the 23 primaries he entered, showed an ability to organize and to lead that no one expected, and demonstrated a vote-getting ability unseen outside South Dakota.

The result is that with Miami Beach 18 days away, he is less than 200 delegate-votes short of the 1,509 he needs. He has more votes than all other candidates combined.

It is conceivable, of course, that he can be stopped. Hubert Humphrey, hungering pathetically for one last hurrah, is stooping to almost any outrage. Edmund Muskie is once more standing in the rain, hoping that the lightning will strike. And George Wallace still remains a potent force.

These and others might just possibly combine to stop him, but it is only a possibility—unless McGovern himself commits some error or takes some stand catastrophic to his cause.

That is the hard part ahead, and clearly George McGovern is already working on it.

Even in the full flush of his one-sided victory in New York, Sen. McGovern was talking about unity.

"Because we do represent a new coalition of political forces in this country," he told his supporters, "there are some who have expressed fears about us. They have nothing to be alarmed about. We want harmony and justice, not bitterness and special privilege."

George McGovern is not about to repeat the mistakes of the Republican Party in 1964, when Barry Goldwater all but read out of the party any of those who did not buy his brand of extremism.

"Anyone who joins us in all sincerity, we welcome," Goldwater said in his acceptance speech. "Those who do not care for our cause we don't expect to enter our ranks."

Having overwhelmed those Democrats who did not originally care for his cause, McGovern is now trying to enlist them in his ranks.

He has decided not to appear before the Platform Committee Saturday, so that he will not seem to be trying to force his programs on the party. In Colorado he gave away three delegates, in the cause of harmony, he legitimately could have claimed.

At the same time, McGovern cannot afford to alienate his advocates. Many of his delegates will not go to Miami Beach to select a candidate, but to nominate George McGovern. Many were outside in Grant Park four years ago, and they were ignored. Now they are demanding to be heard.

Even if everything works right, McGovern still faces a steep uphill fight. His party will be more behind him than with him. He faces an incumbent President who has made relatively few mistakes and scored two spectacular foreign policy coups. By November, we'd bet, all Americans will be out of Vietnam.

Mr. Nixon should and probably will be the heavy favorite. But these past 15 weeks must have taught him one thing: Don't underestimate George McGovern. Unless Mr. Nixon listens to John Mitchell again, he won't.

THE CINCINNATI ENQUIRER
Cincinnati, Ohio, June 21, 1972

SEN. GEORGE S. McGOVERN has based much of his campaign on a reputation of forthright candor on the issues. Indeed, many voters have found great appeal in Senator McGovern (as in Gov. George C. Wallace) because "you know where he stands."

Thus, it would be politically disastrous for Senator McGovern to don too often the two-faced Janus mask affected by practitioners of the "old politics" (as, for example, he did in May, when he told the radical New York Review of Books that he would soak the rich and then told the establishmentarian Wall Street Journal that he wouldn't).

But this, in turn, presents Mr. McGovern with a new dilemma—how to assuage the fears of moderates that he is "too radical." It would appear that Senator McGovern and his supporters (including many commentators in the news media) have developed an ingenious ploy to deradicalize his image without presenting Senator McGovern as a trimmer and a waffler.

An example of this ploy came during his recent visit to the Governors' Conference in Houston. When braced by a number of governors about his rather startling proposals on income distribution and welfare, Senator McGovern made no real effort to defend them on mathematical, economic, social or legal grounds. Instead, he said, "Look, Congress will always provide the balance against any programs that I recommend."

One governor had the perfect comeback, which he recounted later: "He seemed to be saying, 'Don't worry. If you think I'm a wild-eyed nut, Congress will keep me in line.'"

What's more, upon reflection, the cop-out to the control of Congress seems to be just an updated version of the political chicanery Mr. McGovern so deplores in others. Instead of changing his tune to fit his audience, he tells critics of his program that, in effect, his program will never come to pass.

The gambit may well make Mr. McGovern the first presidential candidate in history to appeal for support on the grounds that his program would never be implemented. But his tactics reassure no one. Those who oppose his proposals can more easily fight them by electing Senator McGovern's opponent, if Senator McGovern should be the Democratic nominee, thus precluding the need to rely on the whims of Congress. Those who support Senator McGovern's ideas, on the other hand, could have good reason to feel betrayed, or at least to question how sincerely he believes in them himself.

The Oregonian
Portland, Ore. June 22, 1972

George McGovern's default victory in New York brings to an end his long, expensive campaign in 23 Democratic primaries, of which he has won 10, and virtually guarantees his nomination to oppose President Richard M. Nixon in November.

It is no longer credible that Hubert Humphrey, Edmund Muskie, George Wallace, et al, can muster a coalition to stop Sen. McGovern's nomination. It would be a losing game. If successful, the Democratic Party would be so divided it would have no chance of defeating President Nixon — a questionable chance even with the increasingly popular McGovern as the nominee.

Nothing pays off like success. McGovern's is attributable in part to his bold and even radical foreign and domestic promises, in part to his talent for grassroots organization, and in part to the millions of dollars ($2 million in California's primary alone) he has raised and spent.

The Gallup Poll released for today discloses that McGovern finally has overtaken Humphrey as the first choice of Democrats polled for the nomination. The poll probably still lags behind Democratic voters' sentiment. But the June 11 Gallup Poll showed President Nixon leading McGovern among all voters, 53 per cent to 34, in a two-man race, and winning a three-way race, should Gov. George Wallace defect from the Democrats because of McGovern's nomination, by these margins: Nixon 43 per cent, McGovern 30 per cent, Wallace 19 per cent.

The June 11 poll should not fan overoptimism at Nixon headquarters, however, given McGovern's demonstrated capacity to overcome Democratic Party resistance and make converts in that party, among liberal Republicans and among left-leaning independents.

President Nixon has not done badly, himself, in making converts. His dramatic initiatives toward military and economic detente with the Communist powers, China and Russia, and his startling reversal of domestic and overseas economic policies, including wage and price controls to fight inflation, have generated strong support.

McGovern has yet to win the support of the chieftains of organized labor and he has aroused widespread apprehension among middle-class and upper-class business and employe groups with his share-the-wealth, tax-and-spend programs which Senators Humphrey and Muskie say would bring defeat of the Democrats in November. But he has also struck responsive chords among a segment of the citizens by his promises to pull all U. S. forces out of Indochina, without a political settlement, and his radical proposals to cut defense spending.

Sen. Edward M. Kennedy of Massachusetts has dimmed speculation that he would help McGovern win organized labor's support by accepting second place on the ticket. His least equivocal of many statements now is that "there are no circumstances under which I would accept a nomination for any national office this year." Still, he has not endorsed McGovern. But the odds are that he will be working for McGovern's nomination at Miami Beach in the national convention starting July 10.

With Sen. McGovern within 200 delegates of nomination, it is hardly credible that the convention would choose party suicide by nominating anyone else. That, in fact, was decided in the winner-take-all California primary, in which Humphrey was the victim. The New York victory, with other presidential hopefuls staying out, merely added delegates without a contest, as did the Oregon primary in May. But McGovern's best chance against Nixon might be to insult Wallace and get him to run as an independent again.

The New York Times
New York, N.Y., June 22, 1972

Any lingering doubts over the probability of Senator McGovern's success in capturing the Democratic Presidential nomination have been all but dissipated by the size and strength of his victory in the New York primary. Winning 230 of the state's 248 elected delegates, the South Dakota Senator now appears to be within easy striking distance of a first-ballot nomination.

Now more than ever, Mr. McGovern needs to clarify his position. He has come this far by addressing himself to the country's desire for basic change—in foreign policy, tax structure, welfare system and ways of improving the economy. Yet his primary victories, impressive as they are, hardly indicate a sweeping popular endorsement of the way he intends to carry out his program. In spite of his prolonged campaign, the details of that program are still vague and have already been subject to casual modification.

In making further modifications, Mr. McGovern could soften his program to the point of innocuousness or he could produce a specific and believable blueprint for reform. In the former case he would recapture an undetermined number of voters on the right wing of his party who, moved to panic by some of his unorthodox talk, might bolt to President Nixon. But in salvaging these, he could run the danger of losing many of the five million or so new young voters toward whom he has largely been pitching his campaign and on whom he is counting to wipe out the narrow lead that Mr. Nixon enjoyed over his Democratic opponent four years ago. The same problem presents itself in Senator McGovern's eventual choice of a running mate. Ideological balance suggests a conservative; ideological compatibility suggests a liberal.

In trying to respond to these opposite pulls—to some extent a problem for all major party Presidential candidates—Mr. McGovern will have to move with more than mere caution. He will have to move with plausibility. It is true that compromise is the essence of democratic politics; but let compromise once take on the flavor of expediency, the candidate—especially as idealistic a candidate as George McGovern—would suffer a loss of credibility that could quickly translate itself into loss of support.

© 1972 by The New York Times Company. Reprinted by permission.

Buffalo Evening News
Buffalo, N.Y., June 26, 1972

The defeat of Brooklyn's veteran Rep. Emanuel Celler in last week's primary comes as a rather painful reminder of just how regionally distorted the seniority-ridden hierarchy of Congress is—especially when the Democrats are in the majority. For Mr. Celler is not only the dean of the House. He is the only non-southerner among the ten most senior House members and also the only non-southern chairman of any of the half-dozen most important committees. His big-city-oriented liberalism as head of the Judiciary Committee has been a lonely island in a sea of Dixie conservatism or rural-focused southern populism in most other key committee and House leadership posts.

When Mr. Celler finishes this term, he will have rounded out 50 years of continuous membership. The next in line, Rep. Wright Patman of Texas, is six years behind him and the only other member of either house whose service predates the Roosevelt New Deal. In the Senate, the man with most seniority (Ellender of Louisiana) goes back only to the start of the second Roosevelt term.

But there, too, the monopoly of the South in the top seniority posts is no less pronounced than in the House.

The Republicans have no such regional distortion, although on their side, too, it is the more conservative and rural states and districts that tend to keep the same members in Congress long enough to build high seniority. What makes the seniority structure so peculiarly a Democratic problem, however, is that the very region which bestrides every Democratic Congress like a Colossus is the one that gets brushed off in every national Democratic convention and platform.

It is this paradox of a party that thunders its civil-rights liberalism from every national soap-box and then lets the conservative South dominate its leadership structure in Congress that has caused so shrewd a Republican critic as this area's Rep. Barber B. Conable to refer to the congressional seniority system as "the Democrats' Southern Strategy." And now the retirement of Rep. Celler will just further underscore the point by letting Congress whistle Dixie all the louder.

THE DAILY OKLAHOMAN
Oklahoma City, Okla., June 25, 1972

NEW YORK's primary elections provided at least one hopeful omen. Bella Abzug, the flamboyant, abusively profane representative in Congress, lost her bid for re-election. As a result, women who are striving for true equality with men can breathe a bit more easily.

Ms. Abzug, a militant leftist, was running against William Fitts Ryan, a male liberal with a congressional record fully as wild as her own in terms of conventional politics. But she expected, even demanded, an automatic endorsement from all women, and that she did not get.

Many feminists agreed with the assessment of a fellow worker who had quit Bella Abzug's Washington office.

"She is vulgar, profane, and abusive to her staff and people who don't go along with her ... She is, in a word, unbearable."

Jean Faust, of the New York chapter of the National Organization for Women (NOW), announced that her group was supporting Ryan on the grounds that women have a responsibility to oppose female chauvinism as well as male chauvinism. A district poll had showed women leaning toward Ryan two to one, a trend apparently verified by the election. Such discerning females should help quiet fears of the Women's Lib movement.

THE BLADE
Toledo, Ohio, June 24, 1972

SOMETHING OLD and something new both took a beating in the New York election. As if to underscore the unpredictability of voters' tempers, Democrats in New York City rejected Emanuel Celler, the voice of experience, and Bella Abzug, the voice of impassioned change.

But voter unpredictability left a pattern hard to discern. Mr. Celler was beaten by a woman, Mrs. Abzug by another liberal. Elizabeth Holtzman, who was born two decades after Mr. Celler first took his seat in Congress, probably came close to the mark when she said: "I think the people of the district here are tired of the old politics."

Mr. Celler did indeed represent the old. He is 84, and has served since 1923, under Warren G. Harding and eight other presidents. In all that time, he had primary opposition only once. Over the years he established a pioneering record as a civil rights leader. But he annoyed many of his constituents in Brooklyn by his support of the Vietnam war, the anti-ballistic missile, and the Lockheed loan, and by keeping up his private law practice even though he long had been chairman of the powerful House Judiciary Committee. Miss Holtzman, 30 years old, capitalized on Mr. Celler's support of the war and accused him of dragging his feet on consumer legislation and of "high-handed opposition" to the women's rights amendment.

Across the East River in Manhattan, Mrs. Abzug had a different problem. A freshman representative, she had made her mark by her flamboyancy and by being outspoken on any given subject but particularly in support of women's liberation and the new politics. Her difficulty was that a Republican legislature had reapportioned her district out of existence. Here she made a fatal error. She had a choice of three districts in which she could run, and she chose one represented by five-term William Fitts Ryan, who has a voting record as acceptable to liberals as Mrs. Abzug's but lacks the same stridency of voice and manner, and who had a much better organization to help him. He won by a margin of 2 to 1.

It is unlikely that this will be the end of Mrs. Abzug's career. She has a way of making herself heard above the crowd. And it may not even be the end for Mr. Celler. He is afflicted with a fairly virulent case of a disease called office-holding, and besides calling for a recount of Tuesday's vote he is considering running in November as the candidate of the Liberal party, a powerful segment of New York City politics. After all, that's the banner under which John Lindsay was elected mayor the last time around.

98—McGovern Wins N.Y. Primary

THE MIAMI NEWS
Miami, Fla., June 29, 1972

WAY down yonder in the land of cotton, old times are not forgotten. The Prairie Populist, George McGovern, has invaded the South's red hills and turnip greens territory with an ancient theme.

The South is being exploited by divisionists, the senator says, stealing a 100-year-old headline from Atlanta Constitution editor Henry Grady.

It was Mr. Grady, a man of vision, who determined in his day that a New South was aborning in the region. His foresight was keener than he ever suspected, however, for gestation even yet has not been completed.

"You are kept apart so you can be separately-fleeced," Sen. McGovern tells Southern audiences. His Southern Strategy, therefore, emerges as the old Henry Grady theme that racial animosities so divide the South that her growth is retarded.

The senator poetically stood under a statue of the old Georgia populist and racist, Tom Watson, to make his pitch in the give-'em-hell style dear to the Southern heart.

"What is right has always been called radical by those with a stake in things that are wrong," he said. He charges the Republicans with the radicalism of the Old South.

Thus in an odd twist the South finds itself exposed to a Presidential campaign whose theme goes back to the Reconstruction days.

Sen. McGovern would cast himself in the role of Henry Grady and would be glad to hand over the Tom Watson coattails to President Nixon. If this does not seem entirely consistent, that too is traditional with the South.

Populism to the South has been a theory of conspiracy by the Yankees or other foreign interests to somehow do Southerners in. It has been elastic enough to include almost anyone who can come up with an appropriate foreign devil.

But the senator, at least, has not backed off the basic liberalism on which his own populism is based. Despite the primaries which showed in the votes for George Wallace how much of the South still clings to the past, he has chosen to buck the trend with an opposite page from Southern history.

The South, then, will hear opposing claims to populism and different versions of which is the high road. But it won't be the first time and we expect few surprises.

In the land where the black-eyed pea reigns supreme, such a mixture becomes palatable as a kind of political hoppin' john.

The Times-Picayune
New Orleans, La., June 26, 1972

> You shall see a bold fellow many times do Mahomet's miracle. Mahomet made the people believe that he would call a hill to him, and from the top of it offer up his prayers, for the observers of the law. The people assembled; Mahomet called the hill to come to him, again and again; and when the hill stood still, he was never a whit abashed, but said: If the hill will not come to Mahomet, Mahomet will go to the hill.
> —Francis Bacon, Essays: of Boldness

Will a bold fellow like Sen. George McGovern "many times do Mahomet's miracle"? By analogy, the "people assembled" might be the South Dakotan's zealous disciples; the "hill," the "center" of the American electorate — whose circle stretches far beyond the Democrat party's.

"I was advised every day by pundits and some of my advisers to move toward the center," said the senator from the Black Hills to some Bronx apartment dwellers shortly before his New York primary victory.

But, with the boundless faith of Mahomet, he added, "the center is moving to us."

So the great debate proceeds among columnists and others as to whether it is McGovern the Immutable who has an outside chance of becoming the next great stone face on his homestate's Mount Rushmore, or whether his distinctive feature will earn him the title of McGovern the Great Compromiser once, as seems likely, he becomes the Democrat nominee for president next month.

Peter Lisagor of Chicago Daily News, for example, seems impressed with the insistence of McGovern's chief political strategist Frank Mankiewicz that a "move to the center" to placate party regulars and old-time professionals, including many Southern governors, is out.

Such talk, says ex-Kennedy camp follower Mankiewicz, only reflects the "desire" of those speculating. Conversely, the ex-columnist-turned-promoter might be projecting a currently orthodox McGovern image and party line — the same "Selling of the Candidate" his forces attempted in primary races as they filmed, developed and edited select McGovern quotes and bestside angles for distribution to TV stations willing to use the politically canned "news."

For his part, Joseph Kraft of Publishers-Hall Syndicate sees the McGovern problem not as refusing to compromise but as showing himself "too casual about the issues to impress the Democratic heavyweights," who themselves command a good number of voter-troops.

Placing the primaries in perspective, columnist Kraft concluded: "To gain the support of thoughtful people, he (McGovern) needs a better reason than that he happened to win a small number of primary elections in which only a tiny fraction of the Democratic electorate voted for him."

McGovernites, of course, like to represent the primary results as a popular mandate, whereas examination of the vote statistics proves the opposite is true. Chicago Daily News black columnist Carl T. Rowan, though partial to McGovern, illustrated that fact with statistics.

Prior to the June 20 New York primary but after the California contest in which Alabama Gov. George Wallace was only a write-in candidate, Mr. Rowan observed that the South Dakotan claimed neither a majority nor a plurality but "less than a third of the votes cast in all the primaries" up to then. Sen. Hubert Humphrey had 4.01 million, Sen. McGovern 3.93 million and Gov. Wallace 3.60 million.

By weekend no popular vote tally was available from New York. But even if the liberal Democrats of the Empire State were to raise the McGovern count to a majority, the combined primary results would hardly represent a nationwide plebiscite. Hence, the talk of a single national primary.

Shortly the McGovern camp anticipates announcing the acquisition of the magic 1,509 delegate votes to make the July 10 Democratic nominating event as suspenseless as the Republican one for President Nixon.

Much of that dedicated McGovern coterie would come from the juggernaut which, as Public Broadcasting System's Sander Vanocur observed, capitalized on the McGovern-engineered party reforms and "packed the caucuses" with tactics similar to the Old Politics but with new and younger faces. Only an estimated 20 per cent of the Democratic delegates will have attended a previous party convention.

Reluctance to scandalize his volatile troops may be a reason why Sen. McGovern says he will not go to the center, contending instead the center must move to him.

Witness, for example, the Congressional Quarterly's quote of Howard T. Robinson, executive director of the Congressional Black Caucus: "The better part of these new delegates are for McGovern, and how they'll act is anyone's guess. If things seem to be going their way, they'll probably try to be orderly. But if McGovern fails to win the nomination, they'll tear the convention hall down."

Ah, such pure dedication to democracy in action!

Finally, there's the professed aversion to smoke-filled rooms as part of the honest-to-pete New Politics. The South Dakotan should safeguard his credibility ratings by setting straight former California Assembly speaker Jess Unruh, who opined on PBS the night of the California primary: "Oh, he'll (Sen. McGovern) get by on a lot of backroom deals that aren't visible."

If the hill will not come to Mahomet, will Mahomet have to go to the hill?

St. Louis Globe-Democrat
St. Louis, Mo., June 22, 1972

George S. McGovern's lopsided victory in the New York state primary is being hailed by the South Dakota senator and his faithful followers as the clincher in his bid for the Democratic party's nomination to oppose President Richard M. Nixon in the November election.

In chalking up his 10th primary win out of 23 contests over the last three and a half months, the supremely confident McGovern predicted he would be named his party's presidential candidate on the first ballot at the Democrats' national convention next month in Miami Beach.

McGovern even went so far as to assure Democratic leaders across the country he's already mapping a campaign against President Nixon.

There is no question that the New York results boost the South Dakota senator's candidacy stock considerably. He captured an overwhelming majority of the state's 278 delegates. Unofficial returns give McGovern a minimum of 225 New York delegates. This puts him within about 200 votes of the 1,509 needed for his party's presidential nomination.

☆ ☆ ☆

But the Democratic convention is still more than two weeks away. McGovern's shoo-in optimism could be premature. Despite the impressive record the senator has compiled along the primary trail, he has never caught fire within the party establishment.

The old-line Democrats, who don't like McGovern's brand of far-out politics, will without doubt try all the gambits they know in a "block McGovern" movement.

There is, for example, no sign at this stage of the political game that either Senators Hubert H. Humphrey or Edmund S. Muskie — who could put McGovern over the top now by endorsing his candidacy and releasing their delegates in a bid for party unity — have any intentions of joining the McGovern camp.

Very much to the contrary, both appear still to consider themselves as contenders for the No. 1 spot on their party's ticket in November. Humphrey and Muskie quite likely are holding out for the possibility of a deadlocked convention, on the theory that if McGovern doesn't win on the first ballot his support will immediately start to slip.

If McGovern's power base erodes, it will be a wide open convention. There could be unprecedented turmoil. No candidate would have the nomination in his pocket.

The factor of McGovern himself also must be considered in the Democratic race. The senator's support has come largely from party liberals who go along with his radical proposals for welfare and tax revisions and massive cuts in defense spending. This far-left stance has made the party establishment wary of McGovern.

Of late, there has been pressure from party leaders for McGovern to modify his policies, to make him more acceptable to the vast number of Americans who do not lean noticably to the left or right but cleave to the center.

There are indications that McGovern may be trying to soften his statements. In a recent appearance before a congressional panel, in which he discussed his proposal for redistributing the nation's wealth through wild tax changes, he hedged by saying that his original plan was subject to modification.

The Democratic front-runner very easily could stub his toe by trying to adjust his stride to please party leaders and other groups who have until now reserved their support for Humphrey or Muskie or Alabama Gov. George Wallace.

But whatever happens between now and convention time, it's almost a sure bet that the old-line Democrats will do everything they can in Miami Beach to stop McGovern.

Their reason is very basic: The party leaders want a winner and they don't think McGovern is the man. They don't believe McGovern stands a chance of beating President Nixon. They want a candidate who will be more acceptable to vast middle-road America with more moderate views than McGovern has expressed.

Another thing which seems dead certain is that the Democratic convention will be the wildest in political history. The Democrats' new reform rules, designed to send more minority groups to the convention, likely will cause unparalled challenges of delegates.

The most logical prediction at this time is that this convention process will be chaotic. It's impossible so far to see anyone as a clearcut winner in the early balloting.

The Washington Post
Washington, D.C., June 23, 1972

By most estimates, Senator George McGovern has almost all the delegates he needs, either in hand or in prospect, for a first-ballot nomination, and while no candidate ever thinks he has enough money, he probably is in a position to attract a sufficiency of that. But where his cup runneth over, where he is rich beyond measure, is in a super-abundance of unsolicited advice. Having confounded the predictions and expectations of all the experts—including, one would surmise, some of his own most zealous supporters—he is now being freely counseled to abandon the fresh and often radical doctrines that have carried him through an almost impossibly testing obstacle course from New Hampshire to New York and to make himself more conventionally acceptable. He is being told that his voice is flat and his style colorless, that he doesn't exhilarate or electrify. It is being said that he must "clarify" the positions he has taken up to now, which is another way of saying that he must modify them to the taste of one or another of the challengers that he has disposed of along the way. In brief, he is being hassled and chivvied to become precisely the antithesis of what he has presented himself to be, which is something new and apart from the old political establishment, and to seek security in some hypothetical Center where the decisive votes of the American electorate have always been supposed to be.

Well, there may be great political wisdom in a lot of this, but frankly, having been among the pundits who grossly misjudged the McGovern candidacy from the beginning, we are sufficiently shell-shocked by his stunning successes to be chary —at least for now, mind you—with advice. Just for one thing, we're not quite as certain as we thought we were about just where that Center is to which Senator McGovern is now being asked to move. True, his total popular vote, in all the primaries he contested against a proliferation of candidates, is not the truest register of voting sentiment across a representative sample of the electorate. But it says something about a degree of popular disenchantment with things as they are that does not encourage conventional reliance on the old politics.

For another thing, it is important to consider who is doing most of the hassling. Who is it that's saying that McGovern would be a "disaster" for the Democrats? Who is heaping scorn upon his boisterous, hot-eyed, tireless army of party irregulars who have outfought and outorganized and outworked the organization regulars? Who is telling the senator that what was good enough in January and June, and presumably will be good enough in July, will not wash in November because it's too woolly or too wild? The answer is that today's chorus of advisors-without-portfolio to George McGovern is made up in considerable measure of (1) columnists and commentators who still can't believe, or admit, that he's all but won the whole thing and that they were horribly and consistently wrong about his prospects; (2) governors and other party leaders who backed losers in the race and are likewise unwilling to concede to their own supporters that they made a mistake; (3) the losers themselves who would like to find some vindication of their own performance by forcing Senator McGovern to repudiate his; and (4) old hands from earlier Democratic administrations and/or campaigns whose current put-downs of Senator McGovern reflect at least in part their concern about how they can still scramble aboard the bandwagon, after having missed it, and where—or even if— they can find a suitable seat.

None of this is to suggest that a campaign fitted to the zany rough-and-tumble of the primaries does not need some overhauling and refitting before it's ready for the big struggle in the fall. Large parts of the McGovern program on taxes, welfare, defense, and foreign policy, as it has been unfolded on the dead run these past months, have struck us as hastily assembled, in some cases misconceived, and in others incomprehensible, and therefore susceptible to what could be fatal misunderstanding. Mr. McGovern would not be the first candidate to be victimized in the fall by false impressions and distorted images allowed to form in the spring under the particular pressures of primaries involving disparate electorates in widely differing states. So there is obviously a need for re-thinking and re-statement and we gather that process is under way. There is also an urgent need for reconciliation with substantial elements of the party who find the senator's philosophy, to say the least, unsettling, and that need also seems to be recognized by the more responsible and realistic members of the McGovern camp including, we would judge, the candidate himself; he did not get where he is by being entirely insensitive to his political imperatives.

Whether he will, or can, adjust enough to bring some greater cohesion to his sorely divided party is something else; there are enormous differences to be reconciled. How much he *ought* to change is also something else which nobody should be too quick to be categorical about; it might just be that a low-key, plain-spoken gentle revolutionary is what a large number of voters really want.

No self-respecting pundit, ourselves included, could consider letting George do it all by himself without at least a little critical counseling from time to time. But as of right now, we do not count ourselves among those who feel sufficiently in tune with whatever it is that is roiling the American electorate to be offering him advice with any confidence. In short, when you look at his record, you have to ask yourself just who it is—the senator or the rest of us—who is most in need of going back to the drawing-board.

Campaign '72:
FORMER CIA MEN CAUGHT IN RAID ON DEMOCRATIC NATIONAL OFFICES

Five men were arrested at 2 a.m. June 17 while engaged in an apparent espionage raid on the headquarters of the Democratic National Committee in the Watergate Hotel in Washington, D.C. The raiders, who were in possession of electronic eavesdropping devices and photographic equipment when captured, included James W. McCord Jr., a former Central Intelligence Agency employee currently working as a security agent for the Republican National Committee and the Committee for the Re-Election of the President. Also arrested were Bernard L. Barker, the group's alleged leader, Frank Angelo Fiorini, Eugenio L. Martinez and Virgilio R. Gonzales. All reportedly had CIA links in the past and had been involved in anti-Castro activities in Florida.

John N. Mitchell, President Nixon's campaign manager, denied June 18 that any of those involved in the raid were "operating either on our behalf or with our consent." Republican National Committee Chairman Sen. Robert J. Dole (Kans.) echoed Mitchell's position. Democratic National Chairman Lawrence F. O'Brien called for a full-scale FBI investigation into the incident and termed the raid a "blatant act of political espionage." O'Brien announced that the Democrats were filing a $1 million civil suit against the Committee to Re-Elect the President for its alleged involvement in the raid. The Justice Department disclosed June 19 that the FBI had begun an investigation of the affair.

ST. LOUIS POST-DISPATCH
St. Louis, Mo., June 20, 1972

The abortive raid on the headquarters of the Democratic National Committee by five men with burglary tools and sophisticated eavesdropping devices and photographic equipment has profoundly disturbing implications for the integrity of the country's political processes. Even if we accept at face value the expressions of dismay and disapproval by John N. Mitchell, chairman of the Committee for the Re-election of the President, and Senator Robert J. Dole, chairman of the Republican National Committee, the fact that the raid occurred indicates that there is a market for political data gathered by the grossest kind of invasion of privacy. The natural inference that someone is prepared to pay for and use campaign material garnered at the highest level by such despicable methods suggests how unrestricted political surveillance has become a fact of life in the nation.

While the housebreaking at Democratic headquarters would be unsettling enough as an independent unauthorized entrepreneurial venture, the unrefuted circumstantial evidence leads to the suspicion that it was more than that. Since James W. McCord, one of the raiders, is employed as a security agent by the Republican National Committee and the Committee for the Re-election of the President, the suspicion arises that he was working for his employers in this enterprise. Both Messrs. Mitchell and Dole must have known of and valued Mr. McCord's eavesdropping specialty when they hired him. It may be surmised too that the former employment by the CIA of Mr. McCord and of Bernard L. Barker, the reputed leader of the group, did not go unappreciated. Mr. Barker also is reported to have important Republican Party links in Florida.

In the light of this background and in view of the Nixon Administration's support for wiretapping and eavesdropping, even without court orders in alleged domestic security cases, the whole episode has a distasteful aura which cannot be dispelled by bland and unelaborated disclaimers from top Republican strategists.

A thorough FBI investigation, which has been promised, is fully warranted. But since that agency has itself engaged in illegal wiretapping and since it had been politicized by the late director J. Edgar Hoover and is now headed by a Nixon appointee, even its report on the raid cannot be anticipated with complete confidence. Yet considering the possibly damning ramifications of this case and the difficulties of getting to the bottom of them, it must be recognized that no matter how nonpartisan the FBI's investigation may be, the agency's report may be incomplete. Time will show whether a further inquiry seems to be called for in order establish confidence that this form of contemptible political activity will not be tolerated.

ARKANSAS DEMOCRAT
Little Rock, Ark., June 22, 1972

We won't dwell on the comic-opera aspects of the weird case in which several bumbling would-be wire-tappers — one with high-level Republican connections — apparently plotted to bug the offices of the National Democratic Committee. Suffice it to say that poor Larry O'Brien, who has longsuffered in silence as the Nixon Administration gilded its record, seems to have gone giddy over the thing. Having finally found something (anything!) to gibe the GOP with, he's thrown dignity and restraint to the wind. Ergo, the million-dollar lawsuit against the Committee for the Re-election of the President, in whose hire one of said bumblers seems to have been. The suit seems an improbable solution, if the only feasible one that's yet appeared, to the ponderable question of how the Democrats can ever get the party out of hock. The unanswered question, in that rationale, remains: Why a mere million, which would hardly pay the interest on the party's staggering debts?

Our concern, rather, is that the serious aspects in this case not be obscured by the absurdities. A minor question is why the subdued, almost apathetic response by the administration. We can't believe it actually had anything to do with the bizarre scheme — sitting as it is in the political catbird seat, with nothing to gain in such an escapade (What could it possibly hope to overhear?) and everything to lose. But rather than firmly and unequivocally dissociating the administration from the thing, Ron Ziegler, the President's mouthpiece, persists in trying to trivialize it. It's understandable that he would want to play it down, lest it blow up into an issue the Democrats can get their teeth into; but the fact remains that the incident is anything but trivial. And ignoring it won't make it go away.

By the sheerest coincidence, it was a Nixon appointee to the Supreme Court — Justice Lewis F. Powell — who pointed up the seriousness of this case. In a court opinion on an unrelated case — delivered ironically on the same day that the alleged wiretap plotters were arrested — Mr. Justice Powell wrote:

"The price of lawful public dissent must not be a dread of subjection to the unchecked surveillance power. Nor must the fear of unauthorized official eavesdropping deter vigorous citizen dissent and discussion of government action in private conversation. For private dissent, no less than open public discourse, is essential to our free society."

No evidence has yet appeared that the attempted eavesdropping in this case was either authorized or official. But the implications — and the gleeful insinuations by O'Brien & Co. — of official involvement, official sanction, or at the least official indulgence, not only reflect badly on the administration. They also raise serious questions in the public mind that merit more than the "routine" investigation the FBI has promised and more concern than the pooh-poohing the government has given the matter so far.

Democratic Office Raided—101

THE DENVER POST
Denver, Colo., June 20, 1972

SURVEYING WHAT IS KNOWN so far about the bizarre attempted burglary and bugging of the Democratic National Committee headquarters in Washington, our impression is that it is the Republicans who need a better security system.

One of the five men arrested during the break-in at Democratic headquarters was employed at the Committee for the Re-election of the President, Nixon's main campaign committee, as a security expert. He was hired, according to Committee Chairman John N. Mitchell, Nixon's former attorney general, "to assist with the installation of our security system."

But this guy may not be around much longer. Anyway, he probably was hired to assure the President's campaign committee of security against opponents such as Democrats and nosy newspapermen. And that, obviously, is not the Republicans' real problem.

What they need is a security system to protect them against some of their friends and supporters.

For instance, another of the men caught in the Democrats' headquarters is a Miamian who is reputedly an important Republican party wheel in Florida. He is also reported to have been one of the top CIA planners of the spectacularly bungled Bay of Pigs invasion of Cuba in 1961.

With helpers of that caliber, the GOP clearly needs all the security protection it can get.

What puzzles us right now, though, is why Larry O'Brien, the Democratic national chairman, is demanding a full investigation of this whole idiotic caper.

Admittedly, it is only human for O'Brien to be curious as to who gave the five burglary suspects the $6,500 in crisp new bills found on them and in their hotel rooms. He might be smarter, though, to smooth the whole thing over, if that would keep the Republicans from finding out who was responsible for this odd affair.

FOR WHOEVER FINANCED this caper either has far more money than brains—in which case he can be expected to foul the Republicans up again in some way—or else he is secretly the Democrats' best friend.

After all, no admitted Democrat could have dreamed up a more attention-getting way to impugn the intelligence and integrity of the main GOP campaign organization. So why would O'Brien want to cramp this character's imaginative style?

THE RICHMOND NEWS LEADER
Richmond, Va., June 22, 1972

As they demonstrate daily, the Democrats are becoming increasingly desperate for ammunition—any ammunition—with which to assault President Nixon. So when an employee of the President's re-election organization reportedly was discovered, hand thrust deep into a cookie jar and body wrapped in bugging equipment at the Democratic National Headquarters in the Watergate complex, candidates and other party leaders could barely restrain their well-orchestrated cries of horror and outrage.

Larry O'Brien, the Johnson hangover and Democratic National Chairman, set the tone by exclaiming that the "bugging incident . . . raised the ugliest questions about the integrity of the political process that I have encountered in a quarter century. No mere statement of innocence by Mr. Nixon's campaign (staff) will dispel these questions." Senators Humphrey, Muskie, and McGovern chimed in with suitably ominous pronouncements, all intended to imply that if the police had arrived sooner on the scene, they might have found Richard Nixon at the wheel of the getaway car.

It is predictable election-year Mickey Mouse, of course, but surely the Democrats are pushing our sense of humor too far. When George Wallace was gunned down, we watched—in slow motion, no less—as a man stepped up to the Governor, pulled the trigger five times, then was beaten to the ground and carted off. Yet despite the TV coverage, Arthur Bremer still rates an "alleged" before every reference to his being a "would-be assassin." President Nixon, who was not filmed at the Watergate nor sneaking over the White House fence, finds himself tried and convicted in absentia, while hordes of hopeful Democrats scout around for an appropriate length of rope.

What makes the Democrats' performance even more shameful is the easy availability of an alternative explanation for the incident. Mike Mansfield, hardly a Nixon-lover, read beyond the headlines and discounted the possibility of Republican double-dealing: Mansfield apparently noted that the Nixon employee arrested in the alleged raid, as well as four other men from Miami captured with him, all have long histories of involvement with the CIA and the Cuban liberation movement. Whatever they hoped to gain—perhaps proof that the Democratic platform will support recognition of Red Cuba—probably had more to do with personal politics and politics within the Cuban exile community in Miami, than with national politics and the re-election of President Nixon.

Presumably we will know the right answers before long, as scoop-happy reporters from the Washington Post and the New York Times try to tie everything to the White House. Whether we will accept the answers remains a separate matter—particularly if the Democrats insist on parading more puffed-up outrage. After all, the ITT "affair" proved absolutely nothing, showed absolutely no wrongdoing, and resulted in not one indictment, let alone one conviction. Yet the average American continues to conceive of the ITT sideshow as a replay of Teapot Dome. The raid on the Democratic National Committee Headquarters will share the same fate, unless we all—including Democratic leaders—bone up on our civics books and remember the injunction about "innocent until proven guilty."

Chicago Tribune
Chicago, Ill., June 22, 1972

You'd think Santa Claus had come six months early, the way Chairman Larry O'Brien of the Democratic National Committee is carrying on—and in a sense, this is just what has happened. Only this Santa came in the form of several men; they didn't come down the chimney of Democratic headquarters, they sneaked in a door; and when they were caught at 2:30 a.m. they weren't carrying gifts, they were carrying eavesdropping equipment. Best of all, from Mr. O'Brien's point of view, some of them were linked indirectly to the White House.

There is nothing the Democrats need more, at the moment, than a good, lively issue. The war and the economy are rapidly losing their appeal as issues, and it looks as if the Democratic Party is going to find itself with an unplanned candidate, in the form of Sen. McGovern, whom many of the party regulars look upon with something less than enthusiasm. The bugging attempt came at the perfect moment, and Mr. O'Brien deliberated for a full 15 seconds [as Republican Chairman Bob Dole put it] before leaping upon it as proof of Republican "gutter politics." He has even filed a $1 million damage suit against the Committee for the Reelection of the President, a Republican campaign group with which one of the alleged eavesdroppers was linked.

The bugging scheme is a deplorable example of stupidity and contempt for the law, especially at a time when the Supreme Court has just ruled that the government itself cannot resort to eavesdropping, even in cases affecting the domestic security, without court approval. It is hard to believe that it had the participation, approval, or knowledge of any official Republican organization, let alone the White House. More likely it was the brainchild of a few individuals who may have hoped to make points for themselves by picking up Democratic secrets and passing them along.

Whatever the facts, they should be determined as soon as possible so as to prove—or disprove—Mr. O'Brien's pointed insinuations. He can feel safe filing the suit because he knows it probably won't come to trial before the election and can then be conveniently forgotten. If his charge that the Republican Party is officially involved proves true, then so will his charge of gutter politics. But in this country [except in the Democratic National Committee] people are generally considered innocent until proved guilty; and lacking further evidence, it is Mr. O'Brien who is guilty of gutter politics and of charging guilt by association.

The Des Moines Register
Des Moines, Iowa, June 28, 1972

Democratic National Chairman Lawrence O'Brien has asked the President to have the attorney general name a special prosecutor "of unimpeachable integrity and national reputation" to investigate the attempted bugging of Democratic national headquarters.

Democrats are trying to make political capital out of the arrest of five men caught apparently in the act of planting electronic bugs in the party's national offices. One of the five was in charge of security for the committee to re-elect Nixon. Two of the men carried address books with the name of a former White House consultant. Democrats filed a $1 million civil suit against the five men and the Commitee to Re-elect the President.

The attempt of the Democrats to get political mileage out of the incident paradoxically makes the suggestion that a special prosecutor be named a good one. If for any reason the men are not successfully prosecuted, or their motives are not revealed, there is certain to be widespread suspicion of a political cover-up. One would not have to be a partisan Democrat to share in that suspicion when the heads of the FBI, the Justice Department and the committee being sued by the Democrats are all political associates.

The one thing worse than attempted illegal political espionage would be a whitewash of the attempt. Even the appearance of less-than-vigorous prosecution and full disclosure would be severely damaging.

If the White House has nothing embarrassing to hide, it ought to welcome the suggestion for the appointment of a special prosecutor. The public, as well as the Democratic Party, is entitled to assurance that this politically explosive case will be dealt with in a non-partisan manner.

The Tennessean
Nashville, Tenn., June 21, 1972

AS A PLOT for the television series "Mission Impossible," it would have been entertaining but as an actual mission into the offices of the Democratic National Committee, the five-man breakin raises ugly questions about the political process and about the administration in power.

* * *

One of the five men who staged the breakin was, when arrested, the security coordinator for the Committee to Re-Elect the President, the chief campaign agency for Mr. Nixon which is headed by Mr. John Mitchell, the former attorney general.

The man, Mr. James W. McCord Jr., also did work for the Republican National Committee, according to Chairman Robert Dole, who has severed relations with him.

Mr. Mitchell, who was technically Mr. McCord's boss, said the man had other clients which his committee didn't know about. He threw in an ambiguous statement about security problems of his own committee and finally said "we will not permit or condone" such activities.

For a man charged with the re-election of Mr. Nixon, Mr. Mitchell seems singularly uninformed about a great many things. He knew nothing about the problems of selecting San Diego as the first GOP convention site and had no idea that ITT was offering a financial commitment—so his testimony in the ITT case indicated.

Who would hire a security coordinator without knowing something of his other clients and relationships? That would be the first breach of internal security. Admittedly, Mr. Mitchell may not have hired him, but somebody did. And therein lies deep suspicions which are buttressed by the fact that this has been a government hag-ridden by its own fears and uncertainties.

Nothing else can explain its love for wire-tapping, the Army's surveillance of peace groups, the Agnew attacks on the media, the subpoenaing of reporters' notes, the raucous cries against a "treasonable" opposition, the desperate wrigglings in the face of the "Anderson papers," the sly, but persistent urging that "fat cat" contributors to the campaign fund give massively before the law making such contributions public went into effect, and the chortling plans of the Committee to Re-Elect the President to us all and any weapons to meet its goal.

Whether the breakin at the Democratic headquarters was part of that philosophy isn't known. But Democratic National Chairman Lawrence O'Brien has announced a one million dollar damage suit against the Committee to Re-elect the President and the five men accused of breaking and entering.

He has cited civil rights laws protecting voting rights, charges invasion of privacy and violations of the 1968 Safe Streets Acts forbidding wiretapping by private parties.

* * *

"As far as I am personally concerned," said Mr. O'Brien, "there is certainly in every sense a clear line (in this incident) to the Committee to Re-elect the President . . ." How plainly that clear line will be revealed depends, ironically, on the FBI and the Justice Department, whose old boss is now chairman of the Committee to Re-elect the President.

The Louisville Times
Louisville, Ky., June 21, 1972

As opera bouffe, the bungled burglary of the Democratic party's national offices would be a bust. Its music is atonal; its story is pure Art Buchwald and its cast is even more inept than the Marx Brothers ever pretended to be in their zaniest moment.

Its revelations about the state of American political morality are even more fascinating than the inevitable speculation as to the culprits' motives. For it is hard to believe that any skilled political operative would be stupid enough to hire so rank a band of amateurs.

According to one report from Washington, wiretapping equipment of the type seized went out "with high-button shoes." Among the bugging devices were transmitters powered by flashlight batteries and microphones the size of half-dollars. One wiretap expert was incredulous when the equipment was described; another found it shocking that five men were involved.

"If they follow the usual route, they hire only one man . . .," was his comment. Another belittled the idea of bringing in outsiders rather than hiring "local, top talent. . . . They know the field, they have the contacts."

But had the plot succeeded, what would have happened to the information? Would a politician turn it down? It is doubtful. All he would demand is that he never know how it was obtained. It is the same dodge that is used in collecting campaign funds. Political morality has it that the candidate is not tainted by illegally collected money if he is unaware of the source. That, of course, is pure hokum.

So, the issue is not who hired the burglars because—at least to our way of thinking—no one could be quite that stupid. The relevant question is who would have used the illegally obtained information. And, we think, no politician could truthfully say he would have turned his back on it if he thought he could benefit through its use.

The upshot is another blow at the credibility of our political system and all the FBI probes will not erase that, the FBI's own credibility being what it is today. Most of the damage naturally falls to the Republicans because it was their employe who got caught.

The general public probably won't hold that against the GOP, though. Some of the party's big contributors might, however. They probably are Scotch enough to think that the party has better things to do with their money than to pay a loser like J. W. McCord Jr. $14,000 a year for services as "security coordinator."

The Charlotte Observer
Charlotte, N.C., June 24, 1972

The mere thought of a Republican National Committee employe's being nabbed inside Democratic National Committee headquarters wearing rubber surgical gloves and armed to the teeth with photographic equipment and electronic listening devices was enough to move one to laughter. But now the laughter is being replaced by grim speculation.

Democratic Chairman Lawrence O'Brien has filed a $1 million suit against the Committee for the Reelection of the President, naming this influential group as co-conspirators in a plot to "bug" Democratic headquarters. Mr. O'Brien's action will probably be dismissed by some as no more than a political maneuver. To some extent it is that. The Democrats have a decided interest in prolonging this embarrassment to the GOP and the President's committee.

But seeking answers is also very much in the public interest — if only to dispel the ugly questions raised by the intrigue that placed five men inside Democratic headquarters early last Saturday morning.

One of those arrested — James W. McCord — is a former CIA agent who has worked recently as a "security specialist" for the Republican National Committee and the Committee for the Reelection of the President. Mr. McCord was hired several months ago by former Atty. Gen. John Mitchell (who is the President's campaign chairman) and occupied an office in Republican headquarters.

The man who apparently led the midnight raid was Bernard Barker, who also worked closely with the CIA and who apparently helped plan the 1961 Bay of Pigs operation. The other men also have been active in anti-Cuban activities.

Some of the questions raised in this case are obvious. Who engaged these five men and for what reason? Or did they act on their own? Police found about $6,500 in new, consecutively numbered bills (mostly $100 bills) on their persons and in their hotel room. Where did this money come from? And what did they hope to find in the Democrats' files and confidential reports? What information did they expect to get from "bugging" Democratic communications? And what of the indications of ties to the President's reelection committee?

Police investigations turned up a notebook with some intriguing entries. It contained the name and home telephone number of E. Howard Hunt Jr., a former CIA agent who has been working as a consultant to White House special counsel Charles W. Colson. It also contained the notations "W. H." and "W. House." Among the possessions of one of the arrested men was a personal check from Mr. Hunt in the amount of $6.

The common bonds between the suspects and Mr. Hunt may well be their backgrounds in the CIA rather than their current employment. (Mr. Hunt was a CIA agent for 21 years, until resigning in 1970.) But that raises still more questions, perhaps more ominous ones than those related to Republican-Democratic politics.

Now four more men are being sought in connection with this and possibly other "buggings" and burglaries. And an obscure 800-member organization of right-wing, anti-Castro Cubans is coming into the picture. Was it involved? Did it seek only to discredit the Democrats and thus help assure a Republican victory? Or did it have even more dangerous objectives?

There are other questions. Where has the FBI been? Perhaps in some way it led police to make the arrests. Yet it appears possible that a large band of rightwing extremists, ambitious enough to attempt to turn national events through use of a private spy system, has been operating dangerously close to some of its objectives. And does the CIA still have contact with these people? The spectre of a secret rightwing group with close ties to the government's own giant spying apparatuses should be disturbing to anyone concerned about freedom.

We hope this episode will not now be dismissed as mere election-year maneuvering, embarrassing, perhaps, but of no great consequence. Every aspect of the case should be seriously pursued. Much more than political partisanship is involved.

THE ARIZONA REPUBLIC
Phoenix, Ariz., June 24, 1972

Sen. Barry Goldwater is understandably amused by the inflated rhetoric and $1 million suit against Republican officials by high-ranking Democrats because some people connected with the campaign to re-elect President Nixon were caught either installing or removing wiretap equipment designed to eavesdrop on business conducted at Democratic National Committee headquarters in Washington.

Senator Goldwater would be the last person to condone such political espionage. But his amusement obtains from his own experience as a presidential candidate eight years ago, when Moira O'Conner, a pretty 23-year-old Democratic spy, boarded his campaign train as a "reporter," and used her good looks and cover as a journalist to collect juicy tid-bits for the Democrats.

Miss O'Conner, who openly admitted connections with the Democratic National Committee, was paid by California Democratic strategist Richard Tuck to spy on the Goldwater campaign operation and publish an anti-Goldwater newspaper based on information she collected before she was discovered by the senator's associates.

The Democrats also tried in 1964 to fake an espionage attempt and blame the Republicans by informing the press that Louis Flax, night teletype operator in Washington for the Democrats' nationwide communications network, was being paid large sums of money by the GOP to furnish them with copies of Democratic teletype transmissions.

A trap was arranged by the Democrats, and reporters and photographers were on hand to witness a supposed clandestine meeting between Flax and his Republican contact, at which he was to be paid for his regular delivery.

When Flax arrived with the material, pre-screened by the Democrats, it was openly accepted by Republican National Committee executive director John Grenier in his office — hardly unusual under the circumstances. But there was no pay-off — indeed Grenier refused to pay for the information — and no proof that any prior arrangement existed between Flax and the Republicans to steal Democratic secrets.

Senator Goldwater knows as well as any political strategist, however, that intelligence gathering is a standard part of professional political operations. Undoubtedly, there are times when such surreptitious activities are conducted unlawfully. And they are often done without the knowledge or sanction of party leaders or those running campaign operations.

There is still much that we do not know about the alleged wiretapping of Democratic National Committee headquarters by James McCord, security chief for the Committee to Re-elect the President, and others. Former Atty. Gen. John Mitchell, head of the President's re-election campaign, has firmly denied that McCord was acting in the committee's behalf, and there is no reason to believe otherwise.

There is, however, a considerable difference in the way Democrats and the press have reacted to this latest political spy story. When Senator Goldwater and the Republicans were victims of beautiful spies and James Bond tactics of the Democrats, the stories were featured as light asides in an otherwise heated, issue-oriented campaign year.

But now that the Democratic campaign sanctuary has supposedly been breached by GOP functionaries — one of them a former CIA agent — a hue and cry against treachery and reprehensible political tactics has been echoed and re-echoed by the Democrats at the expense of President Nixon and his supporters.

For the Democrats, it is an obvious attempt to get some publicity and sympathy when their political fortunes are at an all-time low. And so far as press critics are concerned, Senator Goldwater probably put things into perspective when he said that the Republicans are likely being blamed only because their spies are not "well-stacked."

Democratic Convention:

CALIFORNIA, ILLINOIS DELEGATIONS DISPUTED IN PRE-CONVENTION STORM

The composition of the large California and Illinois delegations was the subject of a legal and political battle during the weeks preceding the Democratic National Convention. Both supporters and opponents of Sen. George S. McGovern, the front-running candidate, recognized that the results of these disputes would have a crucial effect on McGovern's chances for a first-ballot nomination. These were the major developments:

■ D. C. District Court Judge George Hart Jr. ruled June 19 against a suit seeking to bar a slate of Illinois delegates led by Chicago Mayor Richard Daley from the convention on the ground that the slate had been selected in defiance of the party's new reform rules requiring proportional representation of blacks, women and young people. [See pp. 325–333] The next day the D. C. Court of Appeals ruled that the challengers had the right to seek a ruling on the question by the party's Credentials Committee.

■ On June 26 a coalition of uncommitted delegates and supporters of rival presidential candidates on the Credentials Committee voted 72–66 to take away 151 of the 271 delegates McGovern won in California's winner-take-all primary. [See pp. 726–737] Other candidates would be awarded these delegates in proportion to their percentage of the vote in the primary. The majority based its ruling on the opposition of the party's reform commission—which had been chaired by McGovern—to winner-take-all primaries. Although he later recanted, McGovern at first angrily threatened to bolt the party if he lost the nomination because of the decision, which he termed "an incredible, cynical, rotten political steal."

■ The Credentials Committee June 30 voted 71–61 to oust the Daley delegates and seat the challengers, which included 40–50 McGovern delegates.

■ Judge Hart upheld the rulings of the Credentials Committee on both cases July 3.

■ The Court of Appeals July 5 upheld the ruling on the Illinois case but ruled 2–1 against the Credential Committee decision on California, declaring it "arbitrary and unconstitutional."

■ Meeting in emergency session at the request of Democratic Party officials, the U.S. Supreme Court ruled July 7 by a 6-3 vote to void all previous court decisions and to deliver both cases to the full convention for settlement. The majority declared that the judicial intervention in the political process that had occurred was unprecedented and against the public interest.

(As the opening of the convention neared, officials in Miami, recalling the disturbances at the 1968 Chicago convention, laid plans for controlling expected crowds of demonstrators. Reluctantly, city officials voted to allow demonstrators to camp in local parks.)

Oakland Tribune
Oakland, Calif., June 30, 1972

The Democratic Credentials Committee is guilty of both a legal and ethical outrage in voting to strip Sen. George McGovern of more than half of his California convention delegates.

Sen. McGovern won California's entire bloc of 271 delegates to the Democratic National Convention in our state's traditional "winner-take-all" primary election earlier this month.

The primary was open from the onset to any interested candidate. There was, in fact, a crowded field of nine candidates. The rules were known, and accepted, by all in advance. After a vigorous campaign, McGovern was the undisputed winner.

Now, the Democratic Credentials Committee in Washington says it wants to go back and change California's rules. It has voted to deprive McGovern of 151 of his 271 delegates, allocating them instead to other candidates on the California ballot in proportion to the total vote count.

If the full Democratic National Convention sustains the committee ruling, it will be committing a grave injustice.

We do not quarrel with any contention that a process of proportional delegate selection may have merit. Equally convincing arguments can be made for either winner-take-all or proportional primaries.

The point is that the California legislature and, through it, the people of California, long ago selected the winner-take-all method. The place to make any changes is in the legislative halls in Sacramento, not in a committee meeting in Washington, D.C.—and most certainly not retroactively to the advantage of one or another candidate.

Ethically, the action of the Democratic Credentials Committee at this late date is a particularly sorry breach of American concepts of fair play.

Neither of the two candidates most prominent in the effort to deprive McGovern of his full slate of California delegates, Sens. Hubert Humphrey or Edmund Muskie, opposed the winner-take-all system before the election. In days when their political prospects seemed brighter they did, in fact, enthusiastically pursue the California winner-take-all plum.

What is particularly unfortunate about this attempt to plunder the California Democratic delegation is that it occurs at a time when the fairness of the nominating process is, as it were, on trial in the minds of many skeptics.

The Democratic party this year, both nationally and in Sacramento, went to unusual lengths to institute reforms in the selection process guaranteeing grass roots participation.

To have such efforts, not to mention the will of the California legislature and the vote of its citizens, overturned in a highhanded "political deal" in Washington would be tragic and would have far reaching consequences.

The Courier-Journal
Louisville, Ky., July 30, 1972

THE STEAL of California delegates from Senator McGovern that was accomplished at the behest of Senator Humphrey this week is very likely to be overturned when the Democratic convention meets in Miami Beach. The question that is haunting thoughtful Democrats, however, is what price the party, and ultimately the nation, will have to pay for one leader's ambition.

The success of the California challenge offends history and principle, but it may not yet have "blown the convention and the party sky-high," to cite the words of political reporter David Broder. In view of the Democrats' tradition of feuding, but coming together for a campaign, it's perhaps too early to say that the nomination now would be worthless to Senator McGovern. What must annoy party "regulars" is the paradox that it must now be admitted that Senator Humphrey couldn't win the nomination, or the election, without a miracle of reconciliation.

There is irony in the party reform effort that provided the basis for the California challenge. When Democratic leaders met in March, 1969, four months after the Humphrey defeat, to organize the Commission in Party Structure and Delegate Selection, their chairman fired them up with a pledge to save the party from ever having "another convention like the one we had in 1968." That chairman was, of course, Senator McGovern.

It's often supposed that the reformers outlawed "winner take all" primaries like California's. Yet that isn't true. A compromise reached in 1970 allowed exceptions to the general rule that state delegations would give proportional representation to all candidates, whether entered in convention or on a ballot. The California exception was an overtly political compromise, and was acknowledged as such by Senator McGovern. He yielded on the point only after a former John Kennedy aide, Fred Dutton of California, convinced him that the reform rules would have to permit the Golden State one more round of winner-take-all politics in 1972, or the party guidelines wouldn't have been adopted by the national committee.

It was the broad understanding of this by party leaders that made this week's Credentials Committee vote so shocking. The committee examiner, another former Kennedy aide, Burke Marshall, had ruled on Tuesday that Senator Humphrey's challenge was "without merit" in law or in party rules. Yet the victim of 1968's disunity, Senator Humphrey, has come back to haunt his party by getting the rules of the game changed after it was played.

Before California Democrats voted June 6, the major candidates, including Senator Humphrey, had agreed they would abide by the rules, whether to their taste or not.

It must be counted one of the tragic effects of presidential ambition that Senator Humphrey, an intrinsically decent man, could be driven now to such a reversal. While his decision to lead the stop-McGovern effort was understandable, his use of the California tactic was not.

Admittedly, the work of pulling the party back together will be all the harder after the bitter words of the past few days, but history says it can be done. One can remember the slanders exchanged by supporters of John Kennedy, Lyndon Johnson and Adlai Stevenson in 1960, the walkouts that left Harry Truman with the "loneliest campaign" of 1948, and the traumatic Al Smith-Franklin Roosevelt clash of 1932 for examples of elections won after bitter conventions.

The Democrats must remember that four more years of war, Nixonomics and "strict construction" on the Supreme Court is the alternative to their potential collapse. It's time for a bystander to talk some sense to the party, and one who could do it is Senator Kennedy. If it is true that he is on call to the McGovern campaign for the best use of his influence at the proper time, this may be the moment to issue that call in the name of party unity.

Arkansas Gazette.
Little Rock, Ark., July 1, 1972

WHAT governs in the test of the California primary dispute is the simple rule of equity: All the Democratic presidential candidates entering the California primary knew what the state law was in reference to the apportionment of delegates, and none of the candidates challenged the law at the time. It was only after the election was over that Senator Hubert Humphrey disputed California's "winner-take-all" system.

What is appalling now is the Credentials Committee's astonishing decision to sustain, narrowly, Humphrey's contest and thus to change the rules of the game after it has already been played.

It does not matter what had been George McGovern's position on "winner-take-all" in the general application, nor what Humphrey's position had been. Both of them went into California knowing and accepting the rules which applied there, and, indeed, Humphrey said then that anyone challenging the outcome would be a "spoilsport" — which, unquestionably, he has proven himself to be, repeatedly, in the course of this year's campaign for the presidential nomination.

The most pitiable spectacle in this year's campaign has been the decline of Hubert Humphrey. In this last desperate bid to become president, Humphrey has compromised himself again and again, brazenly, twice in the context of the California primary alone. In addition to his flip-flop on the "winner-take-all" issue, Humphrey reversed himself twice on whether George Wallace is vice presidential material. In a few short weeks since the climactic stage in California Humphrey has found Wallace (1.) unsuitable as a vice presidential nominee, (2.) suitable, and (3.) unsuitable again. A third reversal on Wallace may be anticipated now, for Humphrey's last chance for the Democratic nomination must depend upon some kind of desperate deal with George Wallace's bloc of delegates at the Convention.

If somehow Senator Humphrey does manage to euchre Senator McGovern out of the prize that McGovern has earned at the polls, then the nomination itself will not be worth to Humphrey the "pitcher of warm spit" which John Nance Garner once assessed as more valuable than the vice presidency.

So much for Hubert Humphrey.

It is, actually, the Credentials Committee majority that bears the final responsibility for what might become a disaster even worse then "Chicago, 1968." The Credentials Committee's decision was cynical, grossly partisan, certainly; but it was also a political blunder of incomprehensible dimension. If the California primary had been allowed to stand on its own merits, on the rule of equity, the accepted delegate counts would not have changed and the outcome would have been accepted generally, if sometimes grudgingly. Now the contest has been reopened, McGovern's hold on the nomination has been shaken, and the McGovern forces outrageously wronged. The McGovern people around the country would not accept defeat, if it were to come, in such shocking circumstances.

If the Democratic Convention or the federal courts right the wrong done in the Credentials Committee, there will still be an awful rancorous controversy dividing the party as it moves toward the election. The damage may or may not prove irreparable but it was all so unnecessary. The only real winner in the California primary dispute is Richard M. Nixon.

The Standard-Times
New Bedford, Mass., June 24, 1972

"Reforms" for the selection of delegates to the Democratic national convention, worked out by a committee headed by Senator George McGovern, the party's leading presidential candidate, could well become the bitterest issue at the convention.

When the McGovern committee finished its work last year, the party national chairman, Lawrence F. O'Brien, said, "Never has a political party so totally changed its way of doing business in such a short period of time... and there will be no turning back... by the new party."

McGovern's partner in leading the reform commission, Rep. Donald M. Fraser, from Hubert Humphrey's Minnesota, also hailed the changes. Among other things they provided that a state's delegation should have "reasonable relationship" to the state's population in sex, race and age.

But Chicago Mayor Richard J. Daley, among others, had a contrary idea about delegate selection. He and his advisers selected a slate that was successful at the polls but which does not adhere to the guidelines. The national committee took a challenge to the courts, and a federal judge has declared the party cannot enforce its "reforms."

No individual delegates or groups of delegates "shall be barred" from the convention "because of (their) race, age or sex," said the judge. This endorsed the claim by the Daley group that to deny them their seats was to disenfranchise the voters who chose them—however they might have gotten on the ballot—a logical argument.

The judge in turn, has been overruled by an appeals court, on the narrow ground that since the Credentials Committee has not yet taken action the Daley group's "constitutional rights" had not yet suffered.

We would say the chances of survival of the guidelines are dim. The "reforms" are in reality an intrusion by the party into basic voting rights. It is naive, as well as unconstitutional, to attempt to tell the electorate what it must vote for.

If there's a difference in decreeing that a legislature should include "a reasonable relationship" of women, blacks and youths and ordering the same for a state-elected delegation, it is not readily apparent. Indeed, there is no way of assuring a "proper" balance without handpicking an entire state's delegate candidates, thus ruling out the possibility of an "unofficial" candidacy. If the McGovern reformers seek an openly and freely-elected delegate body, the questioned reforms do not assure it. Mayor Daley may be dictating locally; the reforms dictate nationally.

The national committee has its problems, with more than 1,000 of the 2,600 delegates so far chosen already challenged. Whither now? It may well be that the only change between the raucous 1968 convention and the upcoming one will be in the absence of "planned demonstrations," no more hired bands and conscripted marchers. This is one McGovern reform that should be adhered to.

THE INDIANAPOLIS NEWS
Indianapolis, Ind., July 3, 1972

There is a line in Shakespeare which says: "For 'tis the sport to have the enginer hoist with his own petard."

A rough translation in modern English would say there is poetic justice in seeing somebody blasted by a bomb (that's what a "petard" is) he has set for others. In either version, the saying is relevant to Sen. George McGovern in the wake of a ruling that California delegates to the Democratic convention must be divided up among the various candidates who ran there.

McGovern and his followers are crying "foul" because this decision reduces his California delegate total from 271 to 120, bestowing the remainder on Sen. Hubert Humphrey and other entries in the California sweepstakes. Yet the proportional division required by the credentials committee (and reversible by the convention) is the very formula McGovern's own reform commission had recommended. And it is a formula other primary states have followed, to McGovern's benefit.

Primary winners in Michigan, Indiana, Florida, Maryland, etc., have had to divide up delegates with candidates who trailed them in the voting, preventing any of those winners from making a decisive breakaway in delegate strength. Only California among the crucial primary states went against this asserted "reform," and that arrangement, too, redounded to McGovern's advantage. He was thus the beneficiary of his own "reforms," and of their violation as well.

Indeed, this pattern has run throughout the Democratic contest in non-primary states. The complicated formulae and techniques proposed by the McGovern commission were best understood by McGovern and his helpers, and have provided the senator with the bulk of his delegates. We have been treated to the interesting spectacle of a purely one-way reform—advancing the political interests of its sponsor and damaging the interests of his competitors.

Add the fact that McGovernites danced with glee last Friday when the credentials committee unseated Illinois delegates led by Chicago Mayor Richard Daley, and replaced them with a group committed chiefly to McGovern. This despite the facts (a) the ousted delegates had been duly elected by the voters, and (b) McGovern hadn't even been entered in the Illinois primary. No matter; the important thing was to drive home the "reforms" — and assist McGovern.

But, in the committee's California ruling, one such reform has been turned against McGovern, and his followers are distraught. While proportional breakdown of delegates in Michigan suits them fine, they don't want a breakdown in California. There they want it winner-take-all, and never mind that this arrangement violates reformist principles.

The Charlotte Observer
Charlotte, N.C., July 1, 1972

After months of sailing along smoothly, upsetting all expectations of his performance, Sen. George McGovern is experiencing some bumps. The Democratic nomination for president, within easy reach only a few days ago, has suddenly receded from him. Can he repair the damage and go on to win, or will his delegate total begin to melt away?

The vote of the convention credentials committee, apportioning the big California delegation among several candidates and denying Sen. McGovern 151 first-ballot votes that had been his, was the biggest in a series of recent reversals. Others included his premature claim on the nomination (a claim based on a staff miscount of delegates), and some overreaching claims of support among blacks, as in South Carolina.

All of these things, while angering Sen. McGovern and prompting some public remarks that he already regrets, give aid and comfort to his rivals. They suggest that the McGovern bandwagon has slowed and that at last the plain-speaking senator is making some costly mistakes.

In fairness to Sen. McGovern, the vote of the credentials committee on the California question did look like dirty pool. Before the California primary, the senator sought to arrange an apportionment of the state's 271 convention delegates according to the results of the primary. But Sen. Humphrey and others insisted that the winner-take-all requirement of California law be adhered to. Once the voting was done, however, and Sen. McGovern was the winner, roles were reversed.

Yet, the maneuvering among credentials committeemen for their votes on the question was not the "political steal" that Sen. McGovern immediately claimed. It was an open and fair fight. Like the quest for the nomination itself, it was a test of resourcefulness and strengths. In that instance, the Humphrey, Muskie, Wallace, Chisholm, Jackson and labor forces united to win. Sen. McGovern has a chance to overturn the decision at Miami Beach.

What hurt the senator more, perhaps, was his intemperate reaction to news of the credentials vote. His threats to disavow the convention and its nominee could come back to haunt him. The remarks rivaled Edmund Muskie's outburst and tears in front of the Manchester, N.H. newspaper offices.

Sen. McGovern's later remarks suggest that he himself realized the outburst was a mistake. "I don't want to dwell any more on anything that sounds like a threat," he said. That sounded more like the man who rolled implacably through the primaries, gaining strength in every new contest, impressing voters with his decency.

The senator stands to be hurt, too, by the threats of some of his supporters who claim the Democratic Party will be torn apart if Sen. McGovern is denied the nomination. That amounts to wild talk. If Sen. McGovern is denied the nomination, it will not be because of the California decision alone. Other factors will have to come into play. Other candidates have gone to conventions with nearly the strength of Sen. McGovern and been denied, and the party survived.

A race for president is a long, gruelling, chancy enterprise. Right has little to do with winning it; might has a great deal. The McGovern forces have been handed a setback. If they keep their heads, employ the imagination and resourcefulness they have displayed before, they can recoup. If they lash out self-righteously they may lose. The setbacks amount to a test of their will.

THE SAGINAW NEWS

Saginaw, Mich., July 3, 1972

Few would argue that the presidential preferential primary system in this country is in need of an overhaul. But the way to go about it is not the way the Democratic party's National Convention Credentials Committee has chosen to go about it.

The path it has taken puts the party on a straight course to chaos as it heads to Miami Beach. It may well be, in fact, as Oliphant pictures it in the accompanying cartoon, on the way to its own funeral in its own fashion in this election year 1972.

Be this as it may, only one word sums up the national credentials committee's 73-65 decision to take away from Sen. George McGovern more than half (151) of the delegate votes he won in California's winner-take-all primary. The word is incredible.

"It's the principle of the thing," argues the credentials committee in defense of its action reapportioning California's 271 delegates among all contenders on that state's ballot according to percentage of votes received. Well, perhaps there certainly is principle involved here—but the very action of the committee flies in the face of all principle.

In essence, what the committee has done is to flout California state primary election law and ignore a judicial finding that Mr. McGovern was indeed entitled to all of California's delegates. The judge who ruled wasn't weighing the merit of state election law. He was simply recognizing that the law existed and that it was there to be followed until the state changed it; that it was not subject to redefinition at the whim of losers who had found no quarrel with it before the election was held.

That kind of logic has been stampeded by the National Democratic Convention Credentials Committee—stampeded no doubt to halt the stampede of the McGovern presidential nomination campaign. What the esteemed committee has done—which still remains subject to full convention ratification—is to rewrite a state's election rules to alter the score after the game has been played. The fact that it was played with a clear understanding of the rules before the fact obviously makes no difference.

There is in all this a transparent cynicism, if not a death wish on the part of the party's power brokers. As one unnamed AFL-CIO official disgusted with the committee's ruling put it, "they're willing to destroy the party in order to stop McGovern."

That may be closer to the truth than any who are making this decision would be willing to admit. It won't be covered by the specious reasoning that XcGoVern got less than half of all of the votes cast in California in a field of ei ht candidates. Less than half of the popular Vote made Richard M. Nixon President four years ago.

What sticks out is that the Democratic party bosses are having a hard time accepting George McGovern. George McGovern has taken them on at their own game state by state accepting the rules as they were written. He has won in California where it was winner take all and in New York where it was take what you earn.

In face of this, the credential committee's decision is indeed incredible. George McGovern has used a few other choice words. What his followers are calling it is unprintable.

At a time when the Democratic party desperately needs all of the unity it can get in November, it stands on the brink of a nervous breakdown. How unity can emerge from the current dissension we do not know. But then we've never pretended to understand how the Democrats do it.

As they so often remind everybody, they love a good fight They're headed for humdinger in Miami Beach all over again.

All we know is that two days before the California primary Hubert H. Humphrey said only a "spoilsport" would challenge that state's winner-take-all system after running and losing. Mark Mr. Humphrey as a "spoilsport.

The primary system needs a revamping to be sure. Perhaps in California. Certainly in Michigan where the cross-over vote should be prohibited. Whatis needed most of all is fewer primaries. What we need least of all is the kind of thing thatasresulted post-California. After all of those delegate reforms, it's bad for the faith, ruinous to loyalty and participation.

But as Mayor Daley recently put it, "Do you want to follow the rules—or do you want to win?"

OREGON JOURNAL

Portland, Ore., July 6, 1972

The potential implications of the Democratic Credentials Committee's attack on the winner-take-all primaries are worth pondering.

That the taking of California delegates from Sen. George McGovern was a political power play, rather than a semi-judicial determination of the merits of a dispute, is beyond question.

But the party, and its rules, are very much a part of the political process that produces American government. If those rules are subject to change on the basis of political force after the fact, the process of governing is corrupted.

In overruling a federal district judge, a U.S. Court of Appeals panel recognized as much when it ruled that the California delegation was constitutionally selected, thereby restoring to McGovern the delegates that the credentials committee sought to take from him. That decision, if it survives other challenges, helps to restore the fairness of lawful rules to the nominating procedure.

It is worth noting, too, that nearly the entire election process is governed by the winner-take-all concept. President Nixon got less than a majority of the popular vote in 1968, but he won all of the presidency. And how else could it be? He did have a majority in the electoral college, but the electors came out of winner-take-all elections in every state.

Whether for federal, state or local office, the eventual winner, of course, takes all. In the nominating process, some states require a run-off between the top two vote getters if no candidate receives a majority in the primary. But in Oregon and many other states the top vote getter in the primary wins his party's nomination— not just part of the nomination, but all of it—even though his total falls far short of a majority.

Presumably all would agree that at some point winner has to take all, unless someone wishes to divide a governor's office, let's say, with 52 per cent of the responsibilities assigned to the winner and 48 per cent to the loser.

Gets ridiculous, doesn't it?

The Appeals Court came down on the side of reason. There are different ways to do it, but state laws must be allowed to provide methods for voters to make a binding decision. At that point, winners win and losers lose. The important thing is that the decision is based on a vote of the people, not backroom tests of strength. Hopefully, the court ruling will stand.

The Topeka Daily Capital
Topeka, Kans., July 7, 1972

Without saying why, the U.S. Circuit Court in Washington Wednesday leaped headlong into the thorny thicket of politics by reversing a lower federal court's decision not to question actions by a political party.

The Democratic national convention's credentials committee, meeting in advance of the July 10 convention in Miami, decided the "winner-take-all" California rule was invalid and divided the delegates among contenders. Sen. George McGovern, D-S.D., lost 151 of the 271 California delegates.

In another action, the credentials committee dumped a 59-man delegation headed by Mayor Richard J. Daley of Chicago, from Illinois and substituted for it a challenging delegation with leanings toward McGovern's presidential candidacy.

The issues were taken immediately to federal district court by the losers. Judge George L. Hart had held that even though the party actions might not be cricket and might be dirty pool, he found no constitutional question involved.

In truth, there is no constitutional question involved and the final decision of the Democratic convention will be the factor in seating or barring convention delegates.

The entire protest before the courts is whether the courts have any business at all trying to require members of a political party to obey the rules that party has established for its operation.

The Circuit Court in Washington clearly has overstepped the constitutional separation of governmental powers and even clouded this misstep by interposing its opinions on political questions.

These political questions, which the court considered in a special Fourth of July session, may or may not influence the nomination of McGovern, either by making it simpler for him to assemble a first-ballot victory, or by upsetting the convention to the point resentment of the court's interference in political differences within a political party could actually damage McGovern's position.

It was one thing for the U.S. Supreme Court to step into the apportionment field. That was a legal field. So many inequities existed in apportionment of voters in congressional and legislative districts that some action not only was necessary, but change has been workable and healthy.

But for a court to step into the political processes of a national party as it proceeds toward choice of its presidential nominee goes beyond judicial propriety.

It is, whether by accident, circumstance or design, affecting the people's choice of a nominee who, if fate decrees, might be the president of the United States, the man who holds all federal judicial appointive powers.

The U.S. Circuit Court in Washington is obviously out of bounds.

The Dallas Morning News
Dallas, Tex., July 8, 1972

IN THE MATTER of the courts overruling the Democratic Credentials Committee, the Democratic National Committee has charged that such action "has thrown the country into a constitutional crisis."

Seeking relief from a lower court ruling, the Democratic National Committee's lawyer declared:

"The courts have never intruded in this way into the quarrels of political candidates. Now that the Court of Appeal in the District of Columbia has done so, we have no recourse but to ask the Supreme Court to restore the judiciary to its proper place in the constitutional scheme of things."

Regardless of the action of the Supreme Court, the "proper place" of the judiciary in these political squabbles is highly debatable, as recent headlines make clear.

The Democratic lawyer's contention that the Constitution "intends that political parties settle political disputes" may be hard to document, for there were no parties when the Constitution was written. The party system evolved outside the framework of the constitutional specifics.

There is ample evidence, however, that the architects of the Constitution meant to insulate the judiciary from "political disputes." And there is good reason to keep it that way.

For one thing the parties' main purpose, so far as the American people are concerned, is to name candidates—the most important being the presidential candidates.

But naming candidates is not the same thing as naming government officials. The parties are not official government agencies; they serve primarily to provide the people with alternatives to vote for. That being the case, as private rather than governmental organizations, they have had wide leeway in setting their own internal rules and settling their own internal disputes.

If one of the parties does poorly in choosing its candidates or commits injustices that raise questions as to its fairness, the voters are not automatically compelled to live with the erring party's failure or unjust result, they can merely vote for the other party's candidates. If both major parties fall down on the job, third parties arise and show them the error of their ways.

For that reason, it has been the custom to regard the voters, not the courts, as the final arbiters of the parties' methods and results in the candidate selection process.

In brief, it makes sense to let the party settle its own squabbles and get on with the chore of naming candidates. In November, the voters will rule, far more decisively than the courts can rule, on how well or how badly they carried out that task.

ST. LOUIS POST-DISPATCH
St. Louis, Mo., July 9, 1972

While the Supreme Court's strong desire to keep out of the Democratic Party's delegate fight is understandable enough, the court has not really done that in its 6 to 3 vote staying actions of an appeals court.

The lower court had concluded that the party's credentials committee was wrong in unseating 151 delegates pledged to Senator McGovern of 271 elected in California's winner-take-all California primary. The same court upheld the party committee's action unseating 59 of Mayor Daley's slated Illinois delegates.

By staying both orders of the appeals court, the high court has let the party committee overrule California election law, without any prospect for McGovern supporters to seek legal remedies. At the same time the court has freed Mayor Daley's Chicago organization to pursue its case against the party's own rules in state courts. It is hard to escape Justice Douglas's dissenting opinion that the court majority, though contending it had no time or precedent for deciding the merits of the case, found an oblique way of deciding the merits.

Moreover, the decision is suspect on its assertion of lack of precedent. To be sure, as the majority says, there is no precise case where the court in the past intervened with work of a party on the eve of its convention. But the court has intervened in party conduct of primaries, most particularly in overruling the old Democratic lily-white primaries in the South.

As Justice Marshall contends, in his strong dissent, both constitutional issues and governmental action were similarly involved here. California's primary was conducted under state law. It was the first step in a process designed to select a candidate for president. California's voters had a right to expect that the results would be counted as provided by law and previously accepted by the Democratic Party.

That is roughly what the appeals court said—that the process of electing a president could not "be placed outside the law" and that the courts had a duty to avoid "grave injury to the fairness and legitimacy of the process." As between the Supreme Court and the appeals court in Washington, it seems to us that the appeals court had the better of the argument.

Yet that makes no difference. The practical result of the high court ruling is to deprive Senator McGovern of delegates won fairly according to law and accepted party rules, and to drop the issue on the Democratic National Convention floor tomorrow. Naturally every other prospective candidate is applauding the court's decision; together they have formed a coalition to try to stop the man who roundly defeated all of them in primary after primary.

It is a sorry spectacle of obstructionism by men the primary voters said they did not want against a man a majority of voters favored, and it is a particularly dangerous spectacle for the Democratic Party and the ambitious men who claim to be its loyal leaders. For if they deny Senator McGovern on the floor the delegates he won in primary elections, they will be affronting not only the Senator and his supporters but millions of primary voters and the party's own self-respect. What a way to head into an election campaign against a rival party united behind an incumbent president!

The San Diego Union

San Diego, Calif., July 8, 1972

If the Democrats worry at all about the attitude of the average American toward their party or his puzzlement over their public agonies, they might try to see themselves as others see them.

At a time when there is a great body of opinion already extant that political activity is a charade, the Democrats are staging tonight a telethon to raise money to pay off four-year-old debts. The telethon, in addition to calling attention to the unfairness of the debt delinquency, thrusts our politics even deeper into the circus atmosphere.

Or Democrats might consider the more serious image question raised by the unseemly but deadly serious party flap over the allocations of 271 California delegates and 59 Illinois delegates to the Democratic National Convention.

A U.S. Court of Appeals ruling restoring all of California's delegates to Senator McGovern, who won a plurality of the vote, may have been correct in its equities, but it did little to quiet national concern over the direction that politics is taking in the United States of America.

It was a strange day in our land when the Democratic Credentials Committee undertook to establish itself as the final authority on both Illinois and California election laws.

The decision of the U.S. Supreme Court yesterday to stay the opinion of the lower tribunal regarding California delegates, and to take no action on the Illinois stalemate, temporarily threw the issue back into the political arena, but it only added to the uncertainty and turmoil because no final resolution of the problem is assured. As Justice Thurgood Marshal, who dissented, noted, now the possibility is raised that the Supreme Court may have to declare the Democratic convention itself void if the party cannot settle its own disputes in Miami.

Moreover, intrusion of the courts into what has been, historically and traditionally, a matter for state political decisions holds a potential for damage far beyond a single party. It is part of an accelerating national trend of taking all issues to court and of appealing them to the ultimate.

Thus, we have seen the Supreme Court rule that secret government documents may be purloined and published. We have seen the court withhold the right to publication for the first time in history. We have seen the court strip immunity from newsmen, and even members of Congress under certain circumstances. We have seen the courts assume the power to divide states into political districts, and we have seen their power grow in many ways over the legislative and executive branches of governments, as well as over political party structures.

Solomon perhaps could suggest a solution to the deteriorating balance of powers but the average citizen is hard put to suggest an alternative so long as the political institutions exhibit an inability to solve their own problems, as is true with the Democrats in 1972.

The Register-Republic

Rockford, Ill., July 9, 1972

As the Democrats head for Miami Beach to make their presidential choice, they're fussing and feuding in true party tradition. There's nothing unusual about that.

But this business of opposing factions hauling each other into court and demanding judicial adjudication of their differences is both unprecedented and dangerous — and could make a donnybrook a debacle.

Fortunately, the Supreme Court has most prudently told the Democrats to settle their own squabbles.

We believe it is a tragic mistake to inject the judicial process into what heretofore have been strictly political party matters.

There is no constitutional issue involved. The U. S. Constitution makes no provision for presidential nomination. The process has evolved through individual party rules and disagreements should be resolved by the parties, not the courts.

In roundabout fashion, it could be alleged with some justification that President Nixon played a major role in the determination of the Democratic presidential candidate if the challengers had been adjudicated by the Supreme Court. Four of the nine Supreme Court justices are Nixon appointees.

What's worse, a court ruling would have the effect of taking away the rights of the voters to be heard in the selection of party presidential candidates.

It is too late for that now, but the original courts of jurisdiction should have refused to have anything to do with the squabbles.

The California unit rule challenge, the Illinois challenge over a duly-elected 59 delegates headed by Mayor Daley of Chicago, and other lesser credentials disputes are the outgrowth of the most serious effort any party ever has made to further open its nominating procedures to party members from all walks of life.

It would be tragic to the American political process if this effort were to boomerang to the extent that it served to exclude the rank-and-file party voter from a decision-making role.

The zealous reformers appear to have a temporary majority in the Democratic party this year, power that many traditional party voting blocs find extremely hard to swallow.

They should be permitted to resolve their differences within the party structure, to seek their own accommodations. To have their disputes resolved by the courts could only widen the breach and accentuate the bitterness.

Over the years, the Democrats have had more than their share of political quarrels. But always before they have settled them in the political arena and patched up their differences.

A donnybrook? That's to be expected.

But a debacle? For the good of the American political system we hope not.

THE WALL STREET JOURNAL.
New York, N.Y., July 10, 1972

So the Democratic National Convention will convene with Hubert Humphrey, the stalwart of the old guard, arguing that the key California delegation must be split up in the spirit of reform; with George McGovern, the standard-bearer of reform, arguing that the winner-take-all system has always been good enough for California and ought to be good enough one more time. And with the Democratic presidential nomination hinged on the outcome of the argument.

The reform commission Sen. McGovern once headed felt in principle that convention votes ought to be divided up in proportion to the votes for each candidate, and Sen. Humphrey's forces succeeded in selling this principle to the Credentials Committee in the case of California, where the primary was won by Sen. McGovern. In voting to split the delegation the committee deprived the Senator of 151 votes that would give him a first-ballot victory. The convention will vote tonight on whether to accept or reject the committee report.

For all the irony, we find it difficult indeed to quarrel with Sen. McGovern's position on the immediate question. His commission took the moderate course of not flatly outlawing winner-take-all primaries this year. All of the candidates in California understood that, and there was no challenge to the arrangements until the outcome was known. By what right does the Credentials Committee change the rules at this stage of the game?

If you don't look too hard it's even possible to square Sen. McGovern's position on California with his position on Illinois, the other major credentials challenge. In this case the Credentials Committee has thrown out Mayor Richard Daley's delegation on the grounds that its slate-making procedures did not produce the proper proportion of women, blacks, youths and other minority groups. Here Sen. McGovern sees the room for compromise he does not see in California. The Illinois argument, he points out, is not whether to change the rules but whether pre-established rules were violated.

Yet more profoundly, we think, the question in the Illinois case is one and the same with the question in the California case. By what right does the Credentials Committee, or the convention itself, second-guess the voters?

The question, of course, is gravely subversive to the reform movement that has been sweeping the Democratic Party. If the citizens of California want to establish a winner-take-all primary, as though their laws they have, what reform commission can rightly overrule them? Even more centrally, if the voters of Illinois want to elect a delegation with a disproportionate number of old men, who is to say they cannot?

The proferred answer is that the reforms are made to make the party more representative of "the people." This answer lasts about as long as it takes to ask why, if the reforms look at the proportion of women and youths, they do not look at the proportion that has not graduated from college. The 1970 census found that 89% of the population over 25 had not completed four years of college. How about an 89%, or maybe 85%, quota to make the party representative of these voters?

The answer is perfectly simple. More women, blacks, and youths, especially the women, blacks and youths the reform movement has motivated to fight the traditional power-holders, would take the party in the issue direction the reformers want to go. Non-college-graduates would take it in exactly the opposite direction on a host of issues: busing, patriotism, amnesty, abortion, marijuana, homosexuality, welfare reform, gun control and on and on. These are the issues on which a highly educated elite wants to impose its views on the body politic; a Washington Post survey finds that 45% of the McGovern delegates have taken post-graduate work, compared with 4% of the American population.

It is, of course, clear that the reformers do not see themselves in any such way. They entirely lack the self-awareness and refreshing candor that allows Sen. Humphrey to say that if he had won in California his posture on proportional representation would be one of "fighting for every delegate I could get." Rather the reformers *know* the only reason they do not get their way is that the party does not represent "the people"; why, everyone they know thinks the same way on all those issues.

This division between a self-segregated educated elite and the mass of the people is in fact one of the gravest dangers to the body politic today. Since the mass lacks the money, leisure or symbol-manipulating skill that win places in the convention process, its only chance to make itself heard is through the polls. We are headed for trouble if the results of the polls can be overturned to fit the tastes of elites, whether the old elite embodied in Sen. Humphrey or the new elite embodied in Sen. McGovern.

That, it seems to us, is the greatest principle at stake in the credentials fight tonight. Of course we will hear symbols about reform and representation being manipulated by both sides. That is how elites compete, and their competition makes the democratic process work by giving the mass a choice.

But it pays to remember that, whether in the case of the Humphrey forces on California or the McGovern forces on "reform" generally, when the symbols are used to overturn elections they are used in the pursuit not of justice but of power.

The New York Times
New York, N.Y., July 9, 1972

There is no such thing as a painless revolution. As the Democrats go through the ordeal of drastically reordering the balance of power within their party, they are once again learning that old human truth.

Four years ago, the delegates at the Democratic National Convention voted to change the ways in which delegates are chosen in the non-primary states, to impose standards on the representative character of state delegations as far as women, youth and minorities are concerned and to establish new rules of party procedure. Many of the delegates four years ago probably did not foresee the far-reaching effects of the changes which they set in motion. But all of these changes were duly approved by the Democratic National Committee and are now being put into effect.

The reforms augmented by the candidacy of Senator George McGovern with its basic anti-establishment theme have achieved a kind of peaceful political revolution. Peaceful but not painless. Such old-line politicians as Mayor Richard Daley of Chicago do not like to be told that they cannot put their delegations together at private meetings with loyal henchmen but instead have to run well-publicized caucuses with the widest possible participation.

Old-timers do not like to be told that they have to give up their seats to unknown 19-year-olds because their delegation is short of the requisite number of young people. Men accustomed to viewing politics as a masculine game rather like professional football do not like to be told they have to allot half of the delegation to women. Dominant factions do not like to share their power with blacks or Chicanos.

It is no surprise that the majority of delegates going to Miami Beach are attending their first national political convention. Similarly, it is no surprise that wrangling over credentials has produced an unprecedented number of challenged delegations, two of which—California and Illinois—have carried their disputes to the nation's highest court. The Court has now bucked the challenges back to the convention through a stay of a lower-court decision, leaving unresolved what the majority conceded are "important constitutional questions." The Court's failure to rule at once on the merits could compel it later to resort to "drastic" remedies, as Justice Marshall warned, possibly even to the point of ordering a convention rerun. The crisis this would create can only be certainly averted if rival factions sort out their differences amicably at Miami Beach, forestalling the need for further Court action.

In theory, reforms could have been introduced gradually over a period of two or three conventions, thus giving the party more time to adapt. But historically, radical change seems to follow a rhythm of its own. Denied for a long period, it suddenly gathers force with startling haste.

The turmoil through which Democrats are now passing may seem wasteful and disorderly, and in some respects it is. But this turmoil also marks the release of new energies and the arrival of new strength. If this upheaval means that over the long term the Democrats have in fact captured the loyalty and enthusiasm of millions of young voters as well as many others previously disenfranchised or apathetic, the turmoil of these days will have been a small price to pay for those enormous gains. Tightly run political parties can be decorous and orderly. But so are cemeteries.

© 1972 by The New York Times Company. Reprinted by permission.

The Birmingham News
Birmingham, Ala., July 1, 1972

Of all the bizarre happenings of this last half of the 20th Century—and they have been plenteous—the upcoming Democratic Convention in Miami promises to be the very most, dad.

Already, because of its wildly assorted mixture of both the cussed, the kooky and the curious, the event is being hailed as Woodstock South.

Miami Beach Mayor Chuck Hall, Police Chief Rocky Pomerance and six city councilmen are nervously proclaiming, "Peace, brother," while 60,000 Miami Beach residents, less concerned with the resort's image, are pleading for more power and guns for police against the anticipated invasion by thousands of Hippie, Yippie-type protesters.

Among the weird assortment of non-delegates who'll be piling into the beach party are:

—The Yippies (Youth International Party), who estimate a total of 50,000 demonstrators will show up;

—The National Welfare Rights Organization, which will march to demand a $6,500 guaranteed annual income for a family of four;

—The Vietnam Veterans Against the War, which will have an anti-war march and provide drug information sessions;

—The Southern Christian Leadership Conference) refused permission to build another Resurrection City similar to the tents and wooden huts erected in Washington in 1968) will march for remedies for unemployment, welfare reform and adequate health care for the poor;

—Peoples' Party, which will conduct sessions on "alternative politics;"

—And women's lib groups, The Women's National Political Caucus and the National Organization for Women (NOW), which will attempt to inform women delegates of key votes in the convention's committees.

While police and city fathers are making every effort to develop techniques and methods designed to placate demonstrators and avoid violence, a group of private citizens are threatening to force city officials to carry out their sworn duty to prosecute infractions such as inciting to riot, obscenity, smoking pot or using drugs, parading nude and open profanity.

To preserve order, Chief Powerance has a 250-member police force, 100 men from the county public safety department, about a 100 from the Miami police force, about 400 from the state and an unspecified number from the Florida marine patrol.

The estimated cost of extra peace keeping measures brought about by the influx of demonstrators is conservatively placed at $500,000 plus, with Uncle Sam footing the heaviest part of the bill. Portable toilets alone will cost about $115,000 to install and maintain.

Any attempt to put the Miami Beach affair in some historical context in advance of its happening would be futile. However, we expect that deep within the complex forces moving these assorted groups to the convention site is the mystique of instant remedy for national problems and the nursery philosophy that if we cry loud and long enough, kick and scream, mother will give in and let us have our way, regardless of the reasonableness of our demands.

Despite the fact that the Democratic leadership must be shuddering inwardly at the prospects for chaos at Miami Beach, it has been strangely silent, apparently fearful of antagonizing potential demonstrators. Faced with a convention delegation which will be composed of about 80 per cent neophytes, perhaps the leadership feels to preserve order in the convention hall itself will exhaust whatever resources it has, and Miami Beach will just have to look after itself.

To say that chances for a productive convention where reason prevails is threatened is to state the obvious. We do not believe the vital political process of nominating persons to fill the two highest offices of the land should be subjected to the intolerable psychological pressures of the threat of violence. We do not believe the Democratic Party, the electoral process or the nation is served by such tactics.

And we believe a large part of the responsibility lies squarely in the laps of Sen. George McGovern, Sen. Hubert Humphrey, Sen. Edward Muskie, Democratic Chairman Lawrence O'Brien and other Democratic leaders. Their silence must be interpreted as giving tacit approval.

The Miami News
Miami, Fla., July 5, 1972

The Miami Beach City Council will consider another batch of ordinances today designed to hamstring the non-delegates in town for the Democratic convention. Even though the visitors have taken the initiative in expressing their peaceful intentions, some of the city officials are still trying to keep the young people out of the parks and off the streets.

To their credit, Mayor Chuck Hall and Councilman Leonard Haber have shown they know what the First Amendment is all about and have voiced no objections to free assembly. We wish other members of the council were equally enlightened.

We would urge Councilmen Jerome Green and Robert Goodman, who have political ambitions beyond Miami Beach, to apply the first rule of long political life: Vote for what is right, not what is expedient for the short term.

In their longterm wisdom the voters prefer a leader who votes his convictions even when they disagree, when the issues are critical. Furthermore, though we have no instant poll we expect the Beach constituency is rapidly changing its collective mind on the matter of approved, rather than impromptu, campsites as well as on punitive ordinances.

Nationally known newspapermen and television commentators, on hand in advance of the Democratic delegates themselves, are telling the rest of the U.S. every bit of trivia that's happening at Miami Beach. The Council ought to broadcast to the nation there is, indeed, a degree of maturity among the members by disposing of the proposed ordinances forthwith and freeing their own police to act logically on campsites.

The Dallas Times Herald
Dallas, Tex., July 7, 1972

THE APPROVAL by the Miami Beach City Council for the use of a public park as a campground for protest groups has been hailed by both police and demonstrators as a boon to a peaceful Democratic convention — on the outside, at least.

The council reversed an earlier vote at the insistence of Miami Beach Mayor Chuck Hall, who said the welfare and safety of Miami Beach's 87,000 residents and convention visitors could depend on a favorable vote on the campground request.

Police Chief Rocky Pomerance, who has gone several extra miles in seeking to deal gently with the protest groups, said he believed a controlled site will make it easier to maintan law and order, in contrast to the turmoil which marred the 1968 Democratic convention in Chicago.

It must be noted in both sorrow and disgust that the capitulation of the Miami Beach council to the threats and blackmail of the protest groups is a sign of the times. The business of the convention does not rquire the presence of hundreds of far-out protesters and if they want to stage their act in front of the TV cameras they should be prepared to provide their own housing and other necessities.

For the moment, the Hippies, the Zippies, the Vietnam Veterans Against the War, the gay activists, the Southern Christian Leadership Conference, the National Welfare Rights Organization and the National Tenants Association are happy about their campground victory. One Zippie leader said they were going to "unite for social change."

If the convention outsiders are united and peaceful, they are different from the elected delegates who will toil inside their fortified headquarters behind barbed wire and heavy security precaustions. Bitter battles are in prospect on every front — from the platform to credientials, from the supporters of George NcGovern on the left through the middle bloc of Hubert Humphrey and Ed Muskie, on to the right contingent of George Wallace.

Regardless of the outcome, this Democratic convention will be a historic event. Operating under new rules and with most of its delegates attending their first convention, the session may result in the death of the old Democratic party. Whether a new party emerges with any strength and cohesiveness remains to be seen.

Blackmail worked for the protest groups on the outside of the convention hall. We hope that other forms of blackmail don't stampede those on the inside of the convention into adopting extremist positions or nominating those who will divide rather than unite the Democratic party and the nation.

Democratic Convention:

McGOVERN NOMINATED ON FIRST BALLOT AFTER WINNING CREDENTIAL FIGHTS

The Democratic National Convention that met in Miami Beach, Fla. July 10-13 marked a major shift in the balance of power within the party. Ninety per cent of the more than 3,000 delegates had never before attended a national convention; only 60 delegates were members of Congress. The power and representation of big city machines and organized labor were considerably reduced; most of the party regulars who were in attendance had opposed the convention's ultimate choice, Sen. George McGovern. Forty per cent of the delegates were women, 25% were under 30 years of age and nearly 14% were black.

McGovern's strength was tested as soon as the convention's opening ceremonies were completed when the critical credential disputes came to the floor. The California and, to a lesser degree, the Illinois disputes focused the power of most of McGovern's rivals in a coalition to block his nomination on the first ballot. An early showdown on the floor became inevitable after McGovern rejected a compromise on the California dispute proposed by Maine's Sen. Edmund Muskie, a member of the "stop-McGovern" coalition. Late July 10 the delegates voted 1618.28 to 1238.22 to restore the 151 challenged California delegates to McGovern, demonstrating that the South Dakota senator had the necessary strength for a first ballot nomination. The Illinois question was taken up next. The McGovern forces had sought to compromise the issue, suggesting the seating of both delegations with half votes, but the Daley group had refused. The delegates voted 1,371 to 1,486 to reject Daley's appeal from the decision of the Credentials Committee. Acknowledging the futility of their efforts to stop McGovern in light of the votes on credentials, Sens. Hubert Humphrey (Minn.) and Muskie withdrew July 11 from the presidential race.

On July 12 the delegates gave the party's nomination to Sen. McGovern on the first ballot. McGovern received 1715.35 votes (1509 were needed for nomination). Sen. Henry Jackson (Wash.), backed by labor after Humphrey's withdrawal, finished second in the balloting with 525 votes. Gov. George Wallace (Ala.) was third with 381.7 votes, Rep. Shirley Chisholm (N.Y.) fourth with 152 votes and Duke University President Terry Sanford fifth with 77.5 votes.

St. Louis Globe-Democrat
St. Louis, Mo., July 12, 1972

It is supremely ironic and revelatory that Sen. George S. McGovern's crushing California delegate victory that knocked Sen. Hubert H. Humphrey and Sen. Edmund S. Muskie out of the race and virtually assured McGovern the Democratic presidential nomination was achieved at the expense of disenfranchising 1.9 million California voters.

In drawing up the new McGovern rules, the Democratic Party envisioned the creation of another Camelot in which the highest order of political chivalry and pureness of heart would prevail. According to the script, Senator McGovern, that valiant knight armed with the sword Excalibur, would go forth and slay any challenger to the integrity of Camelot.

But a funny thing happened on the way to the Democratic National Convention. Camelot became somewhat flawed. Those noble principles of equality gave way to the imperative of winning—at any cost.

☆ ☆ ☆

With all of their new politics colors flying, the McGovern delegates ramrodded the insidious, undemocratic winner-take-all concept through the convention Monday night to reverse the ruling of the credentials committee.

If one wants to engage in mental gymnastics, there are all kinds of arguments that can be used to support this disenfranchisement.

The defense used most often Monday night in Miami was that the new McGovern rules still permit and recognize winner-take-all primaries. In taking 151 California delegates from McGovern and giving them to other candidates in proportion to their vote totals, the credentials committee had changed the rules of the game after the rules had been made, the McGovernites charged.

And so, mounting their white chargers, the McGovern legions rode roughshod through the Democratic convention to impose this victor-take-all rule on the assembled delegates. And, in so doing, George McGovern and his Round Table of Sir Lancelots and Sir Galahads fell off their white horses.

Stripped of its euphemism (winner-take-all), the rule that the McGovern delegates so vehemently defended is simply a device that gives the winner of the most votes in a state presidential primary all of that state's convention delegates, even when a candidate receives less than a majority of the votes, as was the case of McGovern in California.

☆ ☆ ☆

What makes this action by the McGovern delegates and the Democratic convention so incredibly ironic is that it directly contradicts the whole import of the new McGovern rules. These rules, painstakingly drafted after long and tedious hearings, were designed to make certain that every segment of our population is fairly represented at the Democratic National Convention, and to end the old inequities that prevented minorities from gaining a voice in the quadrennial assembly of the party.

And so what happens?

The Democratic Party, as one of its first orders of business at its national convention, ratifies and gives its stamp of approval to this odious, disenfranchising, all-or-nothing rule. The logic apparently being that a rule, no matter how unjust, is a rule. Principles be damned! It must be followed—and so it was.

And so this, ladies and gentleman, is how it was that the Democrats ushered in the golden age of McGovernism and alleged equal representation for all—unless you happen to have some delegates that the smiling senator from South Dakota wants.

And this is how it was that Hubert Humphrey came to utter his tearful last hurrah as his visions of the White House faded forevermore. In view of what happened Monday night at the convention he certainly had a great deal to cry about. Camelot may never be the same again.

St. Louis, Mo., July 12, 1972

Ousting Chicago Mayor Richard J. Daley's delegation in Miami Beach could have serious repercussions on George McGovern's probable candidacy.

Not the least of these is the hypocrisy of the delegates.

Chiding Daley's delegation for being short of women and black delegates, the convention replaced him with the Rev. Jesse Jackson's challengers—which includes few whites or older voters.

The convention action also threw out a delegation selected by thousands of Chicagoans and replaced it with a group handpicked behind closed doors.

The convention apparently believes this is democracy in action. It seems to us to be closer to the processes of government under military junta.

On a practical political basis, the Democratic candidate is also going to find the key, pivotal state of Illinois may end up in the Republican column. Without the full weight of Daley's supporters, Chicago doesn't build up those dubious majorities for Democratic candidates.

And voters won't forget that the so-called reform candidates, met in Miami Beach, don't practice what they preach.

BUFFALO EVENING NEWS
Buffalo, N.Y., July 11, 1972

The Democratic national convention has had its climax in the very first act, and now it is apparently downhill all the way for Sen. George McGovern. All the way, at least, until the start of his fall campaign against President Nixon.

The smoothness of the McGovern forces' take-charge performance during the opening-night festivities at Miami Beach is one more warning, if another were needed, of just how foolish the Republicans would be to underrate him.

They could summon his Democratic rivals as expert witnesses to testify on that subject — especially on the way in which they all allowed themselves to get put on the moral defensive in the convention's first crucial make-or-break roll-call. Perhaps the out-maneuvered stop-McGovern forces were already beaten and had no other choice. But if the only way they could hope to prevent the front-runner from buttoning up a first-ballot nomination was to change the rules of the California primary after it was over, and strip McGovern of 151 delegates he had won there, then you have to wonder: Why didn't some of them let him have it and keep their own dignity?

Sen. Humphrey in particular, it seems to us, demeaned himself by leading this insupportable effort to win with convention muscle what he couldn't win from the California voters. And Sen. Muskie looked little better by staying aloof on the California challenge until yesterday and then making a futile call for a talk-it-over compromise before coming down lamely on the side of stripping McGovern of his California votes.

Besides getting caught on the weak side of the California argument, the stop-McGovern forces showed their ineptness further by not even making the most of the case they did have. For the best argument against the convention's acceptance of a winner-take-all delegation from one state only is that this outcome leaves the Democratic Party with an indigestible precedent for the future. But that argument was hardly heard during this morning's debate.

If one large state can follow the winner-take-all principle while others do not, after all, then that one state's convention influence is bound to be magnified in comparison with the others. So if the California precedent stands, then we must assume that many other large states may try to maximize their own influence by doing likewise. This, indeed, was precisely how the winner-take-all system of voting in the Electoral College came about. The Founding Fathers assumed the electors would divide their votes within each state, but once a few states cast their votes as a bloc, all soon did likewise in self-defense.

So even while voting to accept the California primary results this time, the Democratic convention still has to decide whether to let that or any other state defy its proportional representation "reform" principles again.

For Sen. McGovern, with the momentum all running his way and a first-ballot nomination now all but assured, his next big challenge is the unification of his party in preparation for the hard, uphill campaign still ahead. How well disciplined his legions of delegates will prove to be for that phase of the operation remains to be seen. Their triumphant ouster of Mayor Daley's Chicago delegation does not seem much of a harbinger of party unity, but that is another story that isn't played out yet.

Pittsburgh Post-Gazette
Pittsburgh, Pa., July 12, 1972

ASIDE FROM the undetermined impact it will have on the presidential election, the ouster of Mayor Daley from the convention in the wee—and, for him, weeping—hours of yesterday morning is a signal event.

The man who ran everything inside and outside the convention hall in his own city four years ago, the man who bossed the podium from his seat on the convention floor, the man who bossed Chicago up to now without effective challenge, the last of the great, big-city bosses, the boss of bosses, may be finished as king-maker in the Democratic Party.

Mayor Daley

With a man like Daley, of course, there is always the chance of a phoenix rise from the ashes of November, if there are ashes. (It's certain that he's burned up over what happened yesterday but not certain that he'll burn down McGovernism in retaliation.)

Neither a Hitler nor a Jefferson, he was nonetheless tough and proud, right up to the end. He forced the McGovern generals and even the Chicago delegates challenging his delegates to offer a compromise, to fall, in effect, to one knee and, with bowed heads, admit that they needed Richard Daley in November. And then he told them to go to hell. He would take all or nothing.

Then, it was their turn. They gave him nothing.

Whether or not he was in the Miami vicinity—only God and Daley's top henchmen presumably knew at that point—he certainly was not in the convention hall and is not likely to be there the rest of the week.

Mayor Daley hand-picked his delegates, the way he always had, regardless of the new party guidelines. He thought he could get away with it, because he was (1) The Boss and (2) the Democrats needed him more than they needed their new, anti-boss guidelines.

Apparently, the din of the disorders of four years ago still rang in his ears, and he missed hearing the steady, low beat of the quiet revolution going on in his own party.

The Des Moines Register
Des Moines, Iowa, July 12, 1972

Everybody is commenting on the differences between this national convention of the Democratic Party and all other conventions of that party or of the Republican Party. The differences are many — more women, young, blacks, Chicanos, amateur politicians, etc. Overriding these differences is the atmosphere of newness, change, replacing the old guard.

What seems to us most striking in this change is the loss of influence of organized labor.

For at least 40 years labor unions have been identified with the liberal political philosophy of the United States. They were part of the New Deal coalition of Franklin Roosevelt. Now we find, dramatically in this Democratic convention, the labor bosses on the side of conservatism, resistance to change.

It may be an exaggeration to say, as Walter E. Fauntroy, nonvoting delegate of the District of Columbia, did, that "if Senator McGovern wins, he will be the first Democratic nominee in 40 years who will not have been selected by big labor." But there is no doubt that labor has had a powerful voice in such choices.

The AFL-CIO leaders are almost all opposed to McGovern and were among the prominent backers of the attempt to deny McGovern the full California delegation. They lost on each maneuver. The mention by the McGovern camp that Leonard Woodcock, president of the United Auto Workers Union, might be a choice for the vice-presidential nomination on a McGovern ticket did not weaken the labor opposition to the South Dakota senator.

The change in the Democratic party rules, the wave of new delegates and the skillful organization of the McGovern campaign all have played a part in the decline of labor influence. But the change in labor union political philosophy is also a major factor.

Organized labor represents the status quo or status quo ante these days — much more than big business does. George Meany, head of AFL-CIO, remains a hardline anti-Communist. He is opposed to President Nixon's overtures to China and Russia — let alone George McGovern's policy of ending U.S. participation in the Indochina war. He opposes the McGovern cuts in the defense budget.

Leading labor executives are against strong civil rights activism, including busing for school desegregation. Many labor unions still are the chief barriers to fair employment. They are opposed to foreign economic aid; they want protective quotas on imports and curbing of foreign investment by business.

So it should be no surprise that the labor unions oppose McGovern and are especially unhappy with the reforms in the Democratic party. They prefer the old-time bosses of the party and their dependable deference to labor union power.

What is surprising is that the McGovern crowd was able to dislodge the labor leaders, who now face a terrible dilemma. They don't like President Nixon and are traditionally allied with the Democrats, but they can't stand a McGovern nomination. We can expect that McGovern will try to mend his fences with labor leaders, but he is in a strong position not to make many compromises with them.

The Evening Star
Washington, D.C., July 12, 1972

For Hubert Horatio Humphrey, defeat in the California and Illinois credentials battles yesterday was the last presidential hurrah. Not just for 1972 but — at age 61 — almost certainly forever. And it was a measure of the man that, when the handwriting on the convention wall was clear for all to see, he stepped down without rancor and released his delegates rather than prolong the fratricidal bloodletting at Miami Beach.

For Edmund Muskie, at 58 (who also withdrew yesterday), tonight's nomination of George McGovern of South Dakota can hardly be less conclusive. It is conceivable that, should President Nixon massively defeat McGovern in November, Muskie might get a second shot at the Democratic nomination in 1976. But if that scenario should be played out, there are others — such as Senator Kennedy — better placed to make a bicentennial bid.

No man yearned for the presidency more than Hubert Humphrey. And that thirst for high office was not entirely selfish. The senator from Minnesota, from that day in 1945 when he launched his political career by winning the mayorship of Minneapolis, has been consumed by the desire to give of himself to the people of his city, his state, his country.

To a certain extent, Humphrey's 1972 campaign foundered on a set of unrelated circumstances. He probably entered the race too late and entered too many primaries. Muskie's early entry deprived him of the support of many party regulars and kept organized labor on the sidelines. Senator Jackson's unsuccessful candidacy deprived Humphrey of campaign contributions from the Jewish community which could have tipped the scales in his underfinanced California primary battle.

Finally, it was the unrelenting and to a certain extent mindless hostility of younger voters which doomed Humphrey's candidacy. For the young, the world began in 1965 when President Johnson, with the support (naturally) of Vice President Humphrey, committed the United States to massive intervention in Vietnam. That "betrayal," coupled with the events at the Democratic National Convention at Chicago in 1968, made Humphrey anathema to voters who were not yet born when he was in the forefront of liberalism. In the end, even blacks for whom Humphrey had done so much deserted his banner in droves for that of McGovern.

But if 1972 was too overheated a year for Humphrey to be given his due, it is certain that history will recognize him as an honorable man who acted as a force not just for change but for progress. As Humphrey put it in his withdrawal statement yesterday, his is "no withdrawal of spirit, or of determination to continue the battle I have waged all my public life on behalf of those who had no voice." He will continue that battle in the Senate.

While Chicago's Mayor Daley is unlikely (having been ousted from the convention) to turn the other jowl and work vigorously for McGovern in Illinois, the politics of retribution has never been Humphrey's style: He can be counted on to do what he can to restore party unity in anticipation of McGovern's campaign against Mr. Nixon.

So the way is clear now for McGovern's nomination this evening on the first ballot, despite token opposition from the supporters of Governor Wallace, Jackson and perhaps others. For Humphrey, the Happy Warrior of yesteryear suffering from withdrawal pains, there remains only the satisfaction of knowing, as always, that he did his best.

DAILY NEWS
New York, N.Y., July 12, 1972

TO WIN A BATTLE

Sen. George McGovern's super-heated steamroller rampaged through the opening session of the Democratic National Convention, flattening everything in its path.

The display of raw, old-style political power by the practitioners of the "new politics" piled the casualties in dazed heaps.

A humble Hubert Humphrey (D-Minn.), apostle of "the politics of joy," tossed in the towel yesterday, as did Sen. Edmund Muskie (D-Maine), the party's Hamlet.

Humphrey and Muskie exited more or less smiling. Not so Chicago Mayor Richard Daley, who radiated no resigned sweetness or gentlemanly light after the McGovern juggernaut rolled over him.

The mayor has reason to be bitter. McGovern's fanatics ground him into the dust not because they had to win the Illinois delegate challenge—as was the case in California—but for the sheer joy of humiliating the man they have detested since 1968.

It was a political blood feud, and not even McGovern—who occasionally shows a sober awareness of political realities his ultraist followers lack—could leash the Frankenstein's monster he created. It was not a happy portent for the South Dakotan, his party or the country.

McGovern may be the starry-eyed idealist his flacks make him out to be. But he has been around politics long enough to know that one way—

TO LOSE A WAR

—in politics is to exact petty revenge on party foes or trample them when they are down.

McGovern is assured—if anything is certain in this world—of carrying the Democratic banner against President Richard M. Nixon this fall. But his victory cup may be laced with poison.

Moderates, regulars and labor chieftains within the party had little love for McGovern to start with. The battering they received from his runaway machine may drive many of them to the sidelines, there to sulk and lick their wounds, during the campaign.

The senator's legions have shown their power. But they may quickly learn there is more to politics than flexing muscles and throwing weight around.

Chicago Tribune
Chicago, Ill., July 12, 1972

He is still mayor of the nation's second largest city. He remains the great chief of the Cook County Democratic Central Committee. He may well save his local ticket in the fall, and conceivably could assist the party to great victory in 1974.

But as a national political figure, as the man to whom Presidents paid homage and before whom Congressmen groveled, as "the whole ball game" in the Democratic Party, Richard J. Daley has lost his clout.

His decline has been swift and spectacular. Perhaps the first symptom was Mr. Daley's "slash across the throat" gesture so well remembered from the 1968 convention. The last moment came Monday night as the likes of Ald. William Singer and the Rev. Jesse Jackson pushed rudely past the mayor's floor leaders to shout "victory!" and to seize the mayor's seats as permanent members of the Illinois delegation.

It may be argued that the anti-Daley forces gained little. This is Sen. McGovern's convention, it might be said, not the Democratic Party's. Tho they control the convention, the McGovern forces may have cause to regret their harsh treatment of the party regulars in November. Mr. Daley can cost McGovern the election. He still controls at least 1 million Cook County votes and the easiest way to split a ballot is to start at the top.

Because of his propensity for scene-stealing and mulishness, Mr. Jackson has apparently riled the Chicago liberal camp so much that many now want nothing more to do with him. Mr. Singer has become a national hero to the liberals, but back in Chicago the regular precinct captains are so angry that we may see many of the independent victories in the March primary evaporate in November.

But Mr. Daley gained nothing. The "political genius" whose motto was "We want everything" has lost one of the biggest. The apparent Democratic nominee-to-be for the Presidency of the United States has decided he can win without him.

This comes on the heels of a police controversy in which such one-time stalwarts as Rep. Ralph Metcalfe have turned against him. It follows a Democratic primary in which a political unknown beat his candidate for governor, in which he tricked himself into turning against his protege, State's Attorney Edward V. Hanrahan, only to have Mr. Hanrahan turn against him and win.

Mistake after mistake after mistake. Mr. Daley is now 70 years old. Younger men in the party have tired of waiting in the wings and Mr. Hanrahan is among them.

A detailed diagnosis of Mr. Daley's malady requires more space than this page provides, but basically it seems a failure [perhaps unwillingness] to perceive. He failed to perceive that Mr. McGovern's young shock troops had grasped the science of his power politics and could use it against him. He failed to see the discontent in the black wards until more than 40 per cent of the black vote in the March primary went against him. He dismissed the Singer group as a band of crazies, and then turned around and gave them the public support and credibility they needed by invading their caucuses with mobs of patronage storm troopers.

He failed to see that the times had changed, that what went before no longer works. He is still boss of the 11th ward, but the 11th ward is no longer the world.

McGovern Nominated on First Ballot—115

Chicago today American
Chicago, Ill., July 12, 1972

SEN. HUBERT HUMPHREY is out, Sen. George McGovern has the Democratic Presidential nomination all but formally locked up, and Miami Beach is looking like the climactic event in one of the great reversals in history; an upset that couldn't happen. It made us think briefly of Gen. Cornwallis' surrender at Yorktown, the defeated redcoats marching out with fifes shrilling "The World Turned Upside Down." Here is another upside-down victory, with the regular troops, the well-drilled, seasoned professionals, routed by an army of untrained malcontents who seemed to have nothing going for them but a cause they believed in.

The parallel won't stretch very far. There was no Cornwallis and no Gen. Washington in sight Monday night; no formal surrender, no ceremonies, few expressions of good sportsmanship [Humphrey's game announcement of his withdrawal was one of the few]. McGovern's steamrolling victories made his opposition, not him, look like the underdog. And for half his party, McGovern's triumph right now feels very much like defeat.

McGovern's forces—and how fitting the word sounds now—rolled over the opposition to give the senator what he needed: 151 challenged delegates from California, 59 challenging delegates from Chicago.

The result in Chicago was to deal a splintering blow to the Democratic machine under Mayor Daley, and at the same time to make thousands of Democratic voters furious at McGovern and his supporters. It is hard to see how things could have worked out any worse for Democratic chances in Illinois next November.

In California there is less reason for bitterness. Democrats there did vote, presumably, with the knowledge that the winner of the primary would get everything and the loser nothing. But in Chicago it was the winning voters who got nothing; the delegates they elected were pushed out in favor of delegates nobody elected. And no amount of explaining party rules about slating can make that fact any more acceptable.

Some of the angry voters are discussing legal actions. We don't readily see that recourse is possible, short of demanding that the convention be held over again. But their resentment is unlikely to die down before the general election.

In his position of defending the sacredness of the vote, Mr. Daley may have won a moral victory in his state. But that's a sorry anticlimax for an organization that made such a specialty of real victories. Outside of Cook County at least, Daley has been drastically weakened as a political power. And in our view, the person chiefly to blame is Richard J. Daley.

Thruout the delegate battle, his forces used tactics of maximum stupidity. The regular delegates had a good case, but instead of arguing it, they made themselves look like arrogant elitists demanding power as their due. A political computer, if there were such a thing, might have judged Daley in the right; flesh-and-blood decision makers trying to give their party a new image could hardly help opposing him.

Mr. Daley may recover from his disaster at Miami Beach. In politics, tho, no comeback is possible from inflexible self-righteousness. He and the organization will either adjust to changing times and tempers, or they'll find that Miami Beach was just the first installment.

As for the heir-presumptive to the Democratic Party, we'll have to get used to seeing . . .

CHICAGO DAILY NEWS
Chicago, Ill., July 12, 1972

The long, high political ride of Richard J. Daley turned the sharp corner that leads to the pasture at about 3 a.m. Tuesday morning.

When he got the word the mayor must have felt a stabbing pain in the heart. For a political godfather of Daley's vanishing breed is a realist. And as a realist he can read the fateful message better than any of his subordinates. A godfather can sometimes be gracious, but he can never be humble. He must prevail, and he must protect the image of his omnipotence and his dignity. Daley was not only whipped and humbled by a pack of political upstarts, they did it in head-on combat; they did it before the assembly of national Democratic leaders; they did it in front of the whole nation.

It was this kind of power deterioration in the face of bold new demands that helped make it possible for 59 motley dissidents with no special clout or even much claim to leadership to raise a challenge to Daley's divine right to represent Chicago in the Democratic Party's national councils. Even so, their challenge could hardly have got off the ground except for that fatal rigidity of the feudal machine. Through arrogance or blindness or helplessness to bend the system, Daley ground the new party rules for delegate selection under his heel and handpicked his own slate. A national convention bent on rallying the masses to a philosophy of "new politics" could not condone this final hurrah of bossism, and threw out the Daley crew.

Daley was not the only one to draw a sharp and painful breath when the word came. George McGovern knows there is still life in the Daley machine. He knows there may be enough life in it to take Illinois away from him in November and destroy what fighting chance he might have for the Presidency. Had Daley been willing to take half a loaf, McGovern would gladly have given it to him. But Daley could not bend; no feudal ruler can.

So Daley has been humiliated and deposed as a power in the national party and the impact of that defeat will work its harsh and cumulative damage on the Cook County machine.

The machine is far from defunct, as McGovern, if he is the candidate, will see. But the forces of change have dealt the mayor a punishing blow from which the aging boss will never fully recover. We are bound to say, with due respect for a man who has always loved and served Chicago by his lights, that it was bound to come.

And nothing will ever be quite the same again.

Because this was a moment of high importance in the political history of Chicago, it may serve a purpose to consider how it happened, and what it means for the future.

What brought Daley down at Miami Beach was not so much the 59 challengers who provided the immediate weapon, but an inexorable shift in the character of the times and of the community comprising his realm — and his inability to cope with that change. For a long time it was enough to provide the people with tall buildings and street lights and expressways and a bustling economy. For a long time it served to rule these docile folk with a disciplined political organization that bestowed rewards for services rendered — and swift and sure punishment for ingratitude or faithlessness.

But in these past two decades the revolution of rising hopes and needs sweeping the world and the nation has been surging through Daley's domain. It has been manifesting itself in many ways but at its core is the quest of the individual to have something and be somebody in his own right. This changed the emphasis from bricks and mortar and the arbitrary bestowal of political favors and handouts to job opportunities and educational opportunities and the chance of everyone to better himself and to play a dignified role in bringing these things about.

The "revolution" hasn't yet realized its full potential in Daleyland. But it has acquired formidable power all the same, and the mayor simply hasn't been able to stem it or tame it or adjust to it. There is no give in a feudal power pyramid. Its strength is rigid discipline, and when the discipline begins to go, the base of the pyramid begins to crumble. When all the old devices — five bucks for a vote, a city job for Uncle Pete, a building code crackdown for a political ingrate — no longer serve, there is nowhere to turn. The political machine begins to cough.

THE RICHMOND NEWS LEADER

Richmond, Va., July 13, 1972

This world tends to reward the stubborn, and shortly before midnight perhaps the most stubborn member of the United States Senate won the most coveted prize that a major political party can bestow. George McGovern declared for the presidency 18 months ago—farther in advance of the convention than any other major-party nominee except Andrew Jackson. He benefited extensively from brilliant exploitation of new Democratic Party rules that he is largely responsible for writing; yet this exponent of the "new politics" has risen from political impotence to the plateau on which he stands surrealistically today primarily through masterful machining of the "old politics" of sheer power. But sitting on the convention floor amid the euphoric tumult last night, one sensed that he was witnessing something out of Tennyson: By nominating George McGovern, has the Democratic Party not initiated a headlong charge into the valley of death?

On May 17, 1971, Time magazine wrote of George McGovern: "His singular intensity seems sometimes to sweep him beyond the fine limits of good judgment. He ends up beyond any serious constituency, too strident on the war, too quick to embrace any dissenter, suspected finally of being an opportunist." Truly, there can be no doubt that the Democrats have given us a ruggedly colorless radical who heretofore has not minded being labeled as such. He is a compeller, a leveler, a redistributionist, an isolationist, an anti-militarist who would invite national suicide. He is a man full of radical programs championed by radical organizations. He nourishes preposterous views on everything from amnesty to economic paternalism—views that contain little wisdom or restraint, yet views that endeared him early to the self-styled Eastern intellectual establishment and the hawkeyes in Harvard's department of sociology.

The anointment of this disciple of Henry Wallace is an event of singular significance in American political history. It means that the Henry Wallace left, relegated to a third-party ghetto by Harry Truman in 1948, has taken control of the Democratic Party. And this raises once again the matter of the extent to which the "new" in George McGovern's new politics is based on chimera. The views he champions have been hanging around the Democratic playground for a long time. In most of his proposed programs, there is a near absence of imagination. Yet he is full of the self-fulfilling prophecy so dear to leftist exhortation, and his supporters love him. There is a good deal of evidence that the American people and the unhappy stalwarts of the Democratic Party view him with creeping dislike.

An interesting and potentially crippling contradiction was suggested in the results of surveys released by pollsters Louis Harris and George Gallup early this week. They indicated that the more the people come to comprehend what George McGovern is all about, the more they regard him as an extremist. This gives us the essential reason behind the bitter dissatisfaction of the Democratic regulars. It also shows us the way to one of Senator McGovern's major tasks if he is to have any prospect of electoral success: He has opened a seismic fault in the Democratic Party, and in order to breach it he will have to reconcile the blue-collar Democratic rank and file whom he has spent so much of his time alienating. The remarks of United Steelworkers president I.W. Abel in his seconding speech for Senator Henry Jackson suggest that the task will not be particularly easy for South Dakota George.

It will not be easy because the nominee may be trapped by the fanaticism of his own supporters. These participants in the McGovern children's crusade are intransigent, as they proved in a 25-minute confrontation with him in the Doral Hotel last night. They constitute the energetic, over-educated minority that is largely responsible for the McGovern nomination, but they have no concept of what a small minority they comprise. These are the detesters of the system, the abhorers of materialism, come to this concrete clutter of materialistic capitalism to nominate their man. They are driven by diehard hostility, by unalterable images of their own self-purity. And they will not be denied. George McGovern discovered that in the Doral Hotel last night. Even though he has said many times that "the youth are closer to the truth," last night he found himself in the tightening bind fashioned by the youth; he discovered, as philosopher Irving Kristol has told us, that "the disasters of life begin when you get what you want."

But to reconcile the electoral majority, this nominee who is so wildly far from the national center must mute his extremist views, and he already has begun to do so. He has moved to the front; now he must move to the center. Retreating behind a veil of vagueness, he has started the long process of trying to unsay all his radical statements. Through rhetorical evasions, he has started to cover his tracks back to the middle, but the question remains whether he can do so without his armies noticing. George McGovern surely knows, as electoral analysts Richard Scammon and Ben Wattenberg have written, that the majority of American voters are "unyoung, unpoor, unblack; they are middle-aged, middle-class, middleminded." Without those people, without capturing the loyalties so crucial to Democratic prospects, George McGovern cannot win. And the Democratic Party will remain nothing more than the functional equivalent of a third party; there will be no worth to the Democratic prize.

"Men go crazy suddenly and in herds," columnist Smith Hempstone has written. "They regain their sanity slowly and one by one." There is no limit to the extent of human self-delusion, as we saw in the Miami Beach Convention Center last night. Yet the question at hand is whether Democratic politics have ideologized so much that the national Democrats can regain their sanity at all. Can the Democrats survive their own democracy? One suspects that the delegates here have accurately expressed the sense of the convention, but through their nomination of George McGovern they have expressed the sense of neither their party nor the American people. Surely the peacenik-populist from the prairie did not come to this convention carrying an overwhelming mandate from the primaries. In the primaries, George McGovern ran second to Hubert Humphrey in terms of total popular votes received, and George Wallace ran a close third.

Last night, Senator Abraham Ribicoff described Senator McGovern as "the man for America's future." Maybe so. One hopes not. But if the party of Mr. Jefferson has gone on an ideological trip, the rational among the American public must start taking George McGovern seriously; we have scoffed this guerrilla politician too long. Richard Nixon may be a GS-100 President. George McGovern is the general of the armies of "commitment" and ideological chic—armies that enjoy sympathy in vast segments of the media. It is time to do battle with those armies. Georgia's Governor Jimmy Carter said the other day that the nomination of George McGovern would "decimate our (Democratic) ranks in the national Congress and Statehouses throughout the nation." For its own good, the electorate must see to it that Governor Carter is right—that riding Senator McGovern's coattails turns out to mean riding the whirlwind.

George McGovern is a living leftist cliche. He has written off the South. He has declared war on the American family that earns more than $12,000 per year. He is a philosophical radical the likes of which this nation never has seen. He has emerged victorious from a vituperative, soul-sundering party fight. In the immediate future he will attempt to ride out the convulsions that are the result of that fight: He will seek conciliation; he will try to control the centrifugal forces within the party. Finally, during the presidential campaign, this stubborn man will do all he can to neutralize the desire of the voters to stampede to the Republicans. The American people—and only the American people—have the power to instruct him in the verities of what Tennyson had to say.

THE LOUISVILLE TIMES

Louisville, Ky., July 12, 1972

Barring the intervention of extraterrestrial forces, Sen. George McGovern will be the presidential nominee of the Democratic Party. The vote on the California delegation brought his prize within reach. The withdrawal of Sens. Edmund Muskie and Hubert Humphrey has made his victory a foregone conclusion.

But it will be a costly victory, some say a worthless one. Mayor Richard Daley of Chicago, who was active in Democratic politics before some of the delegates who voted to deny him a seat at the convention were born, has been insulted. AFL-CIO President George Meany is hostile, for reasons that are clear only to himself. The South feels alienated again. Gov. George Wallace yet may sit out the campaign. Other governors, including our own Wendell Ford, mayors and congressmen are fearful of a McGovern candidacy. The party is in debt and divided. According to the conventional wisdom, this all adds up to catastrophic defeat.

The Democrats would not be in such deplorable condition if Humphrey and Muskie had begun the sensitive task of reconciliation several weeks ago when it was obvious their own candidacies were finished. The credentials fights could have been settled amicably, keeping Mayor Daley in the fold. Party officials could have been reassured that the talk about McGovern's "radicalism" was only campaign rhetoric. Even Meany might have come around once it became evident that he was alone in left field.

Instead we were treated to the sorry spectacle of such stalwart liberals as Humphrey, Muskie and Rep. Shirley Chisholm, actively encouraged by the AFL-CIO, ganging up with the likes of Wallace in an "anybody but McGovern" coalition. When the convention started, virtually no one was for the South Dakota senator except a near majority of the delegates. Finally, the hopelessly indecisive Muskie proposed, and then flubbed, a peacemaking attempt. By then, it was too late. Everybody was playing for keeps and the damage had been done.

It was inevitable, perhaps, that the party would go through a convulsion at a time when the old establishment is being replaced by a new one. Such far-reaching change is almost always accompanied by resistance, conflict, and predictions of disaster. The old pros in Miami are openly distrustful of the women, young people and blacks who have taken over an important role in the decision-making process. The first-time delegates are scornful, in their idealistic way, of the closed meetings, arm-twisting and boss rule which determined the selection of nominees in the past.

Some of the traditional elements in the party fear McGovern will lead them in a Goldwater-type plunge back to minority party status. Ford apparently thinks so, although Lt. Gov. Julian Carroll believes otherwise. Actually, there are few parallels to the Goldwater fiasco. McGovern is a different sort of man who rose to the leadership of his party in a different way under different circumstances.

★

Other observers foresee the formation of a new Democratic coalition to replace the one that kept the party in power, with one break, from 1932 to 1968. Daley, Meany and Wallace may simply be anachronisms in this new alignment of political forces. If a new coalition is being born, it will have an extremely difficult time winning this year. But one suspects that the energies unleashed in Miami Beach this week will have a profound affect on the political landscape in the years to come.

AKRON BEACON JOURNAL

Akron, Ohio, July 13, 1972

There's a lot of mourning in print these days for the passing of the old labor-poor people-big city machine coalition that worked pretty well for the Democrats through the decades since Franklin Roosevelt got it cranked up in 1932. As if somehow George McGovern and the party reforms did it in, and they ought to be ashamed.

It has made reams of plausible, readable and more or less nostalgic reading matter in newspapers and magazines, and on it have been based dire pronouncements that the party, by deliberately smashing its own house, is committing suicide.

But it doesn't scan—at least the blame-placing what-caused-what part. And a glance back at history, with its succession of coalitions that have flourished and perished while parties survived, inclines us to think the report of the party's death has been grossly exaggerated.

★

The 1932-on coalition was already showing signs of rigor mortis in 1968. The years since have only made its demise more apparent; the party reforms and "the McGovern phenomenon" are reactions to it, not its cause.

In 1932 organized labor was struggling to achieve power. Its leadership was lean and hungry, and had every reason to want change. The poor also wanted change. The Democrats offered it.

Big-city Democratic machines were riding high—drawing their power from patronage and poverty. The bosses could deal out jobs as they saw fit, and deliver emergency help to the poor family in trouble, without red tape; in return they had legions of loyal followers who would vote as they were told.

But it's different now.

★

Big Labor has achieved power. Much of its top leadership is now as "establishment" as the "entrenched interests" it thunders against—and is equally uninterested in any alterations more fundamental than a fatter slice of "more-of-the-same." George Meany's hawkishness on the war and the push of many leaders for import barriers are among the symptoms of the urge to protect the manor house.

The spread of civil service and the growth of public programs to deal with problems of poverty eroding boss-power, have sent the big-city machines the way of the dinosaur. Richard Daley's in Chicago is the only large one still showing vital signs—and even this last one's pulse seems to be flagging. There's nothing left here to "coalesce" with.

Still with us are the poor— a term that needs to be read loosely, to include many not literally "poor" by any accepted statistical standard, yet who view themselves as getting pushed around. They still tend to back the Democratic Party, for reasons different in detail but essentially the same as before.

There is no longer the concurrence of interest among those three live power groups. And it isn't party reforms that did it, or George. It's the march of history, changing things as it always has and inevitably will.

★

Whether the party's hotly debated broaden-the-base reforms can cement together for 1972 a new sort of coalition—one Americans may later look back on as "traditional" and somehow sacrosanct—we don't pretend to know. The party has done it before, every 30 or 40 years, as history made necessary.

Nor do we know whether the McGovern strategy and tactics that served him well in the primaries and the convention can do for him and the party the much more steeply uphill job necessary for success in November.

But both seem intelligent reactions to evident reality, whether they succeed or not. It was useless to try staying with "the old politics"; something different had to be tried.

We don't think it's mad temple-smashing, or the end of the world, or the death of the Democratic Party.

ARGUS-LEADER
Sioux Falls, S.D., July 13, 1972

South Dakota's Senator George McGovern has won the top prize of his party—the Democratic nomination for president of the United States.

His achievement at Miami Beach ranks as one of the great success stories in politics. He was the first candidate to announce for president for the 1972 campaign. He made his announcement in Sioux Falls on Jan. 18, 1971. The announcement drew a ho-hum reaction from most of the national politicians and press. How could a senator from a small farm state be taken seriously?

Since then, McGovern and his close friends have waged a determined, professional campaign to get him the nomination and to try to elect him as president of the United States. He also happened to be the architect of party reform. The new Democratic party, from rules to platform, which will come out of Miami Beach to do battle in the fall campaign, bears his stamp.

His dream of getting the nomination was called an impossible one. But it wasn't. He has won—and won big. The larger test—the battle against President Richard Nixon for the White House—lies ahead.

McGovern's ideas about which direction this country should take with respect to defense, welfare, taxes and redistribution of income, busing and a host of other questions are liberal and leftist. They do not reflect the mainstream America that we have known. They do reflect the new politics of change, of dissatisfaction with the way things are and a desire to effect radical changes in the system.

George McGovern — one-time college teacher, decorated World War II bomber pilot, grassroots politician from a small state—embarks on the biggest battle of his lifetime: a quest that comes only to two chosen individuals every four years.

We congratulate him for his personal victory and attaining the nomination of his party for president. This is an historic first for a South Dakota citizen and the state. No other South Dakota citizen has had the nomination of either major political party, although U.S. Sen. Hubert Humphrey, a native son, has served as vice president.

In our opinion, the American voter is not likely to turn the government, the economy and the system in the direction which McGovern has in mind. His new politics, based on hard grassroots work and skills he developed in South Dakota and in Washington service, will provide a tough challenge for President Nixon and the Republican party. His political foes will underestimate George McGovern at their peril. His is a new face on the political scene, which is likely to be a plus factor for him.

The forthcoming campaign, between Nixon and McGovern, will give the voters a clear choice. The electorate's decision on Nov. 7, 1972 will be a landmark in determining which direction this country will take as it nears the start of its third century.

The Washington Post
Washington, D.C., July 14, 1972

If the past year should have taught us anything about the political condition of this country, it is that the old definitions will not do—and especially will they not do to analyze or describe the successful candidacy of Sen. George McGovern, who won his party's nomination for President Wednesday night. Orthodoxy would require, for example, that Senator McGovern now be urged to "move to the center." Yet it seems to us that one thing Senator McGovern's preconvention campaign has amply demonstrated is that the American voter has rendered obsolete the familiar conception of where the center lies, that too many issues and attitudes now defy the old left-right schematic distinctions to make possible some ready location of a "center" midpoint between them. Similarly, we would suggest that nothing is more likely to lead to an intellectual dead-end than the current effort to measure Senator McGovern in terms of the degree of his "radicalism." Senator McGovern, after all, has scarcely proposed anything more "radical" than some of Richard Nixon's larger policy departures in office—from the overturning of 30 years of China policy to the espousal of a guaranteed annual income. So we would argue that the relevant question about Senator McGovern's views is not whether they are "centrist" or "radical" but whether they are foolish or wise.

That Senator McGovern's emphasis in the preconvention campaign reflected a preoccupation with legitimate new issues that are properly coming to the center of national concern seems indisputable to us: the inequities of the way in which we as a nation tax and redistribute our income; the skewed priorities and outworn assumptions that have led us into so costly and disastrous a war as Vietnam and which are reflected in our outsized and nigh uncontrollable military expenditures; the fundamental crisis in confidence the American people are experiencing in relation to the institutions that so profoundly affect their lives. Where Senator McGovern has set forth specific programs to counter these ills or permitted himself to talk freely about less specific plans, we believe that he has endorsed or at least identified himself with a number of questionable propositions. There are elements of both his defense spending plan and his earlier tax and income redistribution scheme which sorely require revision. These, together with certain aspects of his prospective program for ending U.S. involvement in the war while assuring the return of our prisoners, are among the major subjects on which we expect there will be not just debate but also response from the candidate as the campaign wears on. But our own preliminary judgment is that it would be another miscalculation of the man and the meaning of his nomination to attribute those more controversial or even offensive parts of his program to his presumed leadership of some well-organized and extreme (or "radical" or "left wing") faction within the Democratic Party. For one thing that does seem certain at this point is that Senator McGovern in fact reflects and represents a very powerful current of thought and bent of mind within the party on his approach to the major issues and his definition of them.

The fact helps account, we think, for the extraordinary atmosphere of the Miami Beach convention, a potentially explosive gathering that turned out to be marked instead by a strange quality of easy patience and even bonhommie. This, of course, was due in large part to the actions of others—the good sense of Lawrence F. O'Brien, who conducted the convention brilliantly, the good fellowship of Hubert Humphrey, who got out when his candidacy could only be continued at the expense of the party and its nominee. But there was something larger at work, we believe, in Miami Beach among the Democrats, something closely connected with the McGovern candidacy and something that strongly affected the tone of the proceedings. It was an elusive but real sense among the participants of reunion and even liberation—liberation from the nightmare of Chicago and from the closed door, stale-air evasion and dissembling that led to it. It was a sense that the party might just be on the verge of re-establishing its identity and continuity and making peace with itself.

That observation will seem to many wise heads preposterous at the very least, coming as it does on the heels of unprecedented labor leadership disaffection, a drastic reduction in the prospect that the Southern element of the old coalition can be retrieved and the dramatic refusal of the convention to seat the delegation of the last of the party's great city machine politicians, Richard Daley. Nor would we argue that the absence of physical violence or disturbance should be confused with an absence of profound disagreement on the part of many important party members with the ideology and the constituency that prevailed. What we would observe is that Senator McGovern both in his manner of winning this nomination and his thematic emphasis may have helped make the party able once again to live with itself. For the theme we have in mind, that which animates the platform as it did Chairman O'Brien's opening remarks and as it has Senator McGovern's campaign, is one which accepts responsibility for what has gone wrong, which makes that the basis not just of new policy but also of a party continuity of a very peculiar but genuine sort. *Let us come out in the open and see who is strongest and let everyone play by the rules,* the convention seemed to say. *Let us concede that much of what has gone so wrong has been our own work. That is the only way in which we can even affirm the rather basic fact of who we are—not to mention the only way in which we can pick up the pieces and figure out where to go.*

The Democratic convention and its nominees—Senator McGovern and Senator Eagleton—may well turn out to represent a ticket that is wrong on substantial points of program or that is politically and/or ideologically unequal to the elective test. It could prove inadequate to the challenge of mobilizing a majority Democratic vote by failing either to reconcile disaffected elements of the party or to compensate for their loss. But the extraordinary process of procedural reform and identification of the issues that appear to be moving the electorate somehow contrived in the convention to create a situation in which one felt the Democrats were beginning their 1972 campaign in the only way they could—if they were to have a fighting chance. For that they owe much to their candidate.

The Salt Lake Tribune
Salt Lake City, Utah, July 15, 1972

Techniques that won Sen. George S. McGovern the Democratic presidential nomination and left the party split and embittered, won't work in the election campaign against President Nixon. That is what everyone says and they may be correct. But there are indications that Sen. McGovern doesn't agree.

It has been widely noted that the party reforms which lessened or eliminated the influence of some party stalwarts; the bruising convention delegate seating fights; the alienation of big labor, left the Democratic nominee a major party rebuilding job before he can hope to win in November. The disaffection is real. It is the price the so-called "new politics" paid to establish its preeminence in the Democratic Party.

Sen. McGovern is aware of the party split and even before he secured the nomination made overtures to heal it. Selection of Sen. Thomas F. Eagleton of Missouri as his running mate is further indication that Sen. McGovern is moving to mend fences. Sen. Eagleton is a loyal supporter of labor and a former backer of Sen. Edmund S. Muskie's presidential aspirations.

These overtures to party harmony notwithstanding, Sen. McGovern can go only so far toward making amends without risking losing what his major advisers see as the more important support of the "new Party" which nominated him. Thus it appears that the main thrust of the McGovern effort toward party rebuilding and victory will be directed at perfecting and expanding techniques which produced his overwhelming convention support.

If that strategy is followed it means huge registration drives among newly enfranchised youths, reform rhetoric and national grassroots organizing. "There are all kinds of people out there just waiting to get back into politics," says Gary Hart, the young Denver lawyer who managed Sen. McGovern's nomination victory. By marshaling huge armies of new voters McGovern strategists apparently hope to win back labor leaders and regular Democrats who fought his nomination by demonstrating that the regulars' self interest lies with supporting the new party. If the gambit works, Sen. McGovern will be able to restore a measure of party unity without having to give in on the issues which caused the splits.

It is much the same with the electorate as a whole. No doubt the candidate will be more careful what he says between now and November. But he cannot back down too far without destroying his shining knight image. By bringing in millions of young voters and capitalizing on what the McGovern camp sees as a legion "of voters lying in the weeds for Richard Nixon to go by," the nominee hopes to build strength without watering down the basic positions which led to his nomination.

By the standards of establishment politics the smart thing for Sen. McGovern to do is go to great lengths to compromise and reunite the party he took the lead in splitting. But the country will be the better if he keeps compromise to a minimum and goes after those "all kinds of people out there" instead.

At this stage a McGovern-Nixon contest could give the nation a rare choice of alternatives. But if Sen. McGovern decides to bend too far in order to win back the disaffected, the gap between choices will narrow. By November there may no longer be a choice at all. Sen. McGovern's highest duty as the Democratic candidate is to provide American voters with a genuine alternative.

The State
Columbia, S.C., July 14, 1972

THE EMERGENCE of Sen. George S. McGovern as the Democratic presidential nominee is, at one and the same time, a tribute to the man and a threat to the nation.

But out of Senator McGovern's extraordinary achievement at Miami Beach there emerges something else — the demonstrable fact that organization and determination can turn a political institution upside down and inside out. Therein lies an object lesson for Democrats and Republicans alike.

Reduced to its essentials, the McGovern strategy was simple enough: Change the party rules (through the guise of "reform") so as to permit maximum participation of those voter groups most susceptible to Senator McGovern's radical ideas. Generate enough enthusiasm at the local level to insure the loyalty of those groups throughout a long and often bitter campaign. Meanwhile, continue promising discontented Americans prompt and positive relief from their burdens they feel to be most oppressive.

The pay-off came at Miami Beach, where McGovernites outnumbered and outmaneuvered the old-line Democrats who were still trying to play by pre-McGovern rules. The opposition was overridden, with the result that control of the Democratic party (at least on the national level) rests in the hands of a strange and motley assemblage of ultra-liberal professionals and ultra-zealous neophytes drawn from the ranks of youth, women, and minority groups.

What Senator McGovern has done is to put together a coalition of enough minorities (by catering to their special interests) to constitute a working majority within the Democratic party. Whether he can do the same with the electorate at large remains to be seen — and therein lies both the threat and the challenge to middle America.

It is becoming increasingly evident that Senator McGovern now is seeking to broaden the base of his support by attracting voters who have shied away from his earlier pronouncements. True, he still clings to his "bug-out" Vietnam policy, which lies somewhere in between surrender and appeasement. But some of his positions on social and economic problems are being steadily modified so as not to scare away any more of the middle Americans whose support he will need in November.

His task, and a difficult one it is, is to retain his image as the shining knight of "new politics" while building a supplemental constituency from the ranks of citizens who are not willing to throw the entire "establishment" overboard.

We don't think he can turn the trick. For one thing, he is too well established as a radical on the basis of statements already recorded. For another, if he achieves credibility as a reasonable man of moderation, he will lose credibility with the very forces which brought him to his present eminence. And, finally, his restructuring of the Democratic party so badly erodes the position of established party leaders that many of them will write off the presidential election in hopes of being able to rebuild the party out of what looms as its 1972 wreckage.

But the McGovern performance (stretching over four years and culminating this week at Miami Beach) should warn Americans of all parties and all persuasions that new political forces are at work. Unless equally effective forces are set in motion — and soon — the McGovern effort to remold the United States into his own image may come uncomfortably close to success.

God help America if he succeeds.

Democratic Convention:
SEN. EAGLETON NOMINATED FOR V.P. AFTER KENNEDY TURNS DOWN OFFER

Sen. Thomas F. Eagleton of Missouri was named as Sen. McGovern's choice as a running mate July 13 and was nominated for the vice presidency on the first ballot by the convention early July 14. Eagleton, a 42-year-old Catholic with a liberal voting record and close ties to organized labor, reportedly was asked to join the ticket after similar offers had been made to Sen. Edward Kennedy (Mass.) and Sen. Abraham Ribicoff (Conn.) and turned down. Florida Gov. Reubin Askew and United Auto Workers President Leonard Woodcock were also alleged to have been high on McGovern's list of possible vice presidential candidates.

ST. LOUIS POST-DISPATCH
St. Louis, Mo., July 14, 1972

The average Missourian will be pleased, we think, at the selection of Senator Thomas F. Eagleton of our state to be the running mate of Senator George McGovern. He is an attractive political figure, 42 years old, who has shown himself repeatedly as a strong campaigner. Although the choice was a complete surprise to the public, Mr. Eagleton has assets that commend him highly.

He can be, in a way, a bridge between the old and the new politics; he speaks the language of the crusty professionals and he is endowed with the progressive ideas of the newcomers. He should be in a good position to act as a conciliator, and his first task may be to help Mr. McGovern repair the breaks in party harmony. It is significant, we think, that among Mr. Eagleton's first comments on learning of his selection was an expression of regard for Mayor Daley of Chicago, the archetype of the Old Guard boss who was ousted from the convention by McGovern supporters.

Mr. Eagleton said that Mr. Daley was a pro who would support the Democratic ticket, and this will be an important factor in whether the Democrats carry the key state of Illinois in the fall. Mr. Eagleton also observed he has friendly ties with labor, some segments of which have been turned off by Mr. McGovern. He is a Roman Catholic, which presumably will give the ticket added strength in areas in which Mr. McGovern has been weak, although we tend to discount the importance of this factor.

Mr. Eagleton, as a native of St. Louis, brings to the ticket an understanding of big-city problems which Mr. McGovern, a representative of a plains state, may be held to lack. He has a liberal voting record in the Senate, where he has been an outspoken opponent of militarism abroad and wasteful defense spending. His thinking generally is compatible with that of Mr. McGovern.

In addition, he will go before the American public as a rather nice contrast to the ineffable Spiro Agnew, assuming Mr. Nixon retains the current Vice President as his running mate. Indeed, the contrast is so profound that it might well cause the President to dump Mr. Agnew for a more presentable candidate.

We do not know all the considerations that went into the selection of Mr. Eagleton, but we think that the only liability he affords the ticket is his lack of national recognition. And that can be overcome before November.

The Kansas City Times
Kansas City, Mo., July 15, 1972

Tom Eagleton of Missouri is certainly not, as some said when the moon was setting over Miami, one of politics' "perfect nobodies."

He is neither perfect nor a nobody. Indeed, because he is an extremely able, attractive young senator, an articulate speaker and an energetic campaigner, we would guess that his presence will to a degree strengthen the Democratic ticket. Obviously he swims in what Senator McGovern regards as the new mainstream of American life.

Whether McGovern is correct in his assessment of an America that he has invited to "come home" will be determined in November. Meantime, Eagleton should be of assistance in merchandising the point of view set forth by the presidential nominee in his acceptance speech.

This is not to say that the Missourian's presence on the ticket will tilt the scales in McGovern's favor. Only rarely in history has the choice of a vice-presidential nominee made that much difference, the most conspicuous exception being Lyndon B. Johnson who did so much for John F. Kennedy in 1960. (And, ironically, former President Johnson's name was only rarely invoked at Miami Beach, which says something about the ability of the new Democratic Party to create its instant nonpersons.)

The Eagleton selection did, however, come as a surprise of considerable proportions but then, if you recall the political scene of several months ago, so did the McGovern nomination. If McGovern seemed to be reaching deep into the barrel, remember that Eagleton has earned considerable respect in the party in his brief tenure as a freshman senator.

He has, according to all reports, worked conscientiously at his job, and although we have certainly disagreed with some of his positions, he has won admiration as a comer in public life. Some of the party powerhouses recognized that fact last winter when they used him as political anchor man in a congressional TV response to President Nixon's State-of-the Union address.

Denied what appeared to be just about everyone's first choice, Senator Kennedy of Massachusetts, McGovern did have a problem. Some of his constituents were offended because the selection was to be dictated, not freely made. Others felt that the ticket should have greater balance in the hope of widening its November appeal. Some sulked because they or their constituencies were ignored in the selection process.

Such things happen, even at a reformed convention, and at Miami Beach they led to the extreme of charades that saw first-ballot votes cast for the likes of Martha Mitchell, Mayor Daley and Archie Bunker. For the first time the discipline of a carefully orchestrated (although more rock 'n' roll than symphonic) convention appeared to break down. And everybody must now regret the ultimate timing of a candidate's acceptance speech at 2:35 a.m., hardly prime TV time for the initial national exposure.

As to the balance that Senator Eagleton does bring to the ticket, its value may be debated. He is a Roman Catholic, but frankly we doubt that a more sophisticated electorate is going to be swayed by religion in politics. He has some close ties to labor and has carefully tended to that alliance in his Senate votes. He is of a border state or of the lower Midwest, but a man of the city, whereas his leader is of agrarian America.

Philosophically, he is something of a McGovern soul mate and clearly is a man in whom the South Dakotan has confidence. Perhaps above all, he is young, even younger than George McGovern. The factor of youth is not to be underestimated in the new Democratic scheme of things. Indeed, Richard Nixon may just meditate on that fact should he decide to seek a new running mate of his own.

At any rate, the decision is made and with some ringing, middle-of-the night, neo-Populist oratory, the McGovern-Eagleton ticket is on its way. It has a tough road to travel, and a great deal of political pacification to perform.

Missouri's contribution to the new wave just may be considerably more helpful than some of the tired and weary masses of Miami expect.

Eagleton Completes Ticket—121

LEDGER-STAR
Norfolk, Va., July 14, 1972

Senator McGovern, either by choice or because he really had none, has reached into the more obscure ranks of the Democratic party to find a running mate. Senator Thomas Francis Eagleton of Missouri was not entirely a surprise selection, to be sure; his name had been a part of the speculation for several days. But he is, in terms of the national electorate, among the least known of the possibilities. This obviously bothered some delegations, including Virginia's. As Chairman Fitzpatrick said: "It's going to be hard enough (in Virginia) with McGovern, and Eagleton adds nothing."

Senator McGovern obviously encountered some difficulty in filling out the ticket. His first choice, Senator Kennedy, turned him down, and several other likely candidates, including two Southern governors, withdrew themselves from consideration.

Apparently Mr. McGovern feels, though, that Mr. Eagleton will complement the ticket and strengthen it in specific ways.

★ ★ ★

No doubt Mr. Eagleton can add some breadth. For example, he backed Senator Muskie for the nomination and hence could contribute somewhat to a healing of the party's wounds. Mr. Eagleton also has friendly ties with organized labor, something Mr. McGovern seems not to possess. The point of Mr. Eagleton's religion—Roman Catholic—has been made, but that is of scant significance in 1972, as evidenced by the fact Mr. Muskie's religion, also Roman Catholic, was hardly mentioned during all of his campaigning in the primaries. Mr. Eagleton has an urban background, and this might prove helpful in that the crisis of the cities is such a big domestic issue. Mr. Eagleton also is young —only 42—but apparently, judging from the way the convention went, Mr. McGovern already has a large slice of that vote.

★ ★ ★

Perhaps the point of Mr. Eagleton's selection is that he is not likely to hurt the ticket in any appreciable way and he may help to broaden its appeal in some quarters where Mr. McGovern is considered weak.

But the contest on which the people will be making their decision lies between Senator McGovern and President Nixon. And our guess would be that Senator Eagleton will not alter that simple reality very much.

The Boston Globe
Boston, Mass., July 14, 1972

Perhaps the remarkable thing about Sen. George McGovern's choice of Sen. Thomas F. Eagleton (D-Mo.) to be his runningmate is the absence of a factor which has influenced the naming of a Vice-Presidential candidate in both parties in years gone by.

Dumped overboard along with other excess baggage was the notion of geographical distribution, the notion that the runningmate had to come from the South (or West) if the top standard-bearer was from the North (or East). Both of the Democratic nominees are mid-Westerners, though Missouri may be said to tilt somewhat southward. Sen. McGovern is going for the heartland.

The geographical factor has been a demeaning one and it was time that it should go. It has resulted in some poor choices, without naming any names, and in a decade scarred by assassinations the risk of such a choice becoming President is simply too great.

The same consideration ought to hold for ethnic and religious factors, in a country where all men are created equal. But cynics, who call themselves realists, would say we are not ready for this yet. If they are right, it may help the Democratic ticket in that Sen. Eagleton is partially Irish and a Catholic.

But what many voters want to know about most today is the capability of a Vice-Presidential nominee to assume the Presidency should that high office be thrust upon him. It is an awesome burden, and another Missourian, Harry S Truman, spoke for all such when he told reporters in 1945 that "I felt like the moon, the stars and all the planets had fallen on me."

A graduate of Amherst and Harvard Law School, Sen. Eagleton brings to the nomination a good record of four years as attorney general of his state, another four years as its lieutenant-governor and three and a half years in the Senate. On the war he is a dove, and on our social ills, a conciliator.

In a notable speech at Suffolk University two years ago he was optimistic that "the current crisis of fear and violence can be reversed," urged youth to work within the system for political change, and said the country will "make the gravest mistake of a lifetime if it indicts this generation of youth, because we will be losing our entire future."

In urging youth then to "find your causes in the common human needs and common hopes that unite us, not in the fears and hatreds that divide us," he struck the same note that had such effect later that year in the election eve telecast by Sen. Edmund S. Muskie of Maine.

Now the Democrats have met, chosen and are going home. Next month it will be the Republicans' turn. And speaking of going home...

OKLAHOMA CITY TIMES
Oklahoma City, Okla., July 15, 1972

ALL THOSE cries of "Thomas who?" which followed the announcement that McGovern's running mate would be the junior senator from Missouri were evidence that a lot of delegates and reporters had gone to Miami Beach without doing much homework.

Sen. Thomas F. Eagleton was not Sen. McGovern's first choice, and there was no secrecy about that fact. The list of those who were either offered the post or asked if they might be available was long. Some were rejected by McGovern supporters. Some turned him down cold. And some suggested politely that there must be someone who would be of greater value to the ticket.

BUT EAGLETON was a logical choice, in every sense. From the time he first dipped a toe in political waters, Tom Eagleton has been labor's man. In the Senate, he managed to compile a 100 per cent score with COPE, the AFL-CIO political arm, and a 94 per cent rating from the ADA, the left wing of the Democratic party.

Big Labor's money is vital, if the Democrats are to have a chance this year. But George Meany had led the Stop McGovern forces, and during the convention steelworker I. W. Abel had said labor will never forget that McGovern has failed them in the Congress. So what more logical than to complete the ticket with a young, handsome labor lawyer from the Senate? His Ivy League law degree, his close links to the AFL-CIO, and his work on the District Committee (which D. C. blacks regard as their own) can bring some wandering elements back into the fold before election day — if traditional patterns mean anything.

The Standard-Times
New Bedford, Mass., July 15, 1972

Measured by today's outlook, the chances of victory in November for the Democratic presidential ticket were not strengthened by the selection of Sen. Thomas Eagleton of Missouri to be vice-presidential running mate for Senator George McGovern.

Ideologically, McGovern and Eagleton are two peas in the same pod, far to the left of its center. The liberal Americans for Democratic Action rates McGovern as 96 per cent faithful to its views and Eagleton at 90 per cent. Only 11 of the 100 senators had higher "marks".

Such similitude hardly widens the appeal of a ticket that needs the support of disenchanted middle-ground and organization Democrats. The balance of Democratic slates like Humphrey-Muskie, Johnson-Humphrey, Kennedy-Johnson, Roosevelt-Garner, Roosevelt-Truman — winners or near-winners — is missing.

Indeed, the 1972 Democratic pairing recalls the disastrous Republican one of 1964, Barry Goldwater and an unknown congressman, William E. Miller, look-alikes all the way.

However, as has been made only too apparent, it is risky to rate a tactic by Sen. McGovern at face value. Many hours of consultation — seemingly with party leaders a conspicuously absent item at the convention — preceded the selection. And, as far as is known at this time, only Sen. Kennedy had prior consideration over Eagleton.

The presidential nominee, then, must be counting on other factors — the "winning ways" of Eagleton, who has never lost an election in rising from country attorney to attorney general of his state, lieutenant-governor and senator. He is young, 42, a big-city politician and a Roman Catholic.

Nevertheless, the McGovern power base is represented by the convention that nominated him. And even for that diverse group, the nomination of Eagleton appeared to hold little appeal. Instead of clearing the agenda with an overwhelming endorsement of their leader's personal preference, the convention drew out the night hours — missing valuable prime exposure time for the ticket — by horsing around with other nominations and displays of egotism by opportunists like Sen. Mike Gravel of Alaska and former Massachusetts Governor Endicott Peabody.

Meanwhile the endorsements given by Senators Humphrey and Muskie, the unsuccessful challengers to McGovern, to the choice of Eagleton were perfunctory, an example being Humphrey's "he's a fine man." And Rep. Wilbur Mills, powerful member of Congress, who had vigorously sought the vice-presidential place and the only candidate thoroughly approved by labor union leaders, was not even consulted by McGovern.

The composition of the Democratic ticket may arouse electorate excitement as the campaign develops. It is unlikely. The slate may, however, move Vice President Agnew off the Nixon ticket. What the Democrats have come up with is a presidential team of such liberal image that President Nixon can afford to risk alienating his right-wing Agnew backers. They have nowhere to turn, and are not likely to sit out an election in which the McGovern-Eagleton combine seeks to take the reins of government.

St. Petersburg Times
St. Petersburg, Fla., July 14, 1972

In the American political system, the ideal candidate for vice president should be well qualified to assume the presidency, he should support the party's platform, he should come from a key state and he should help the ticket, preferably with political strengths aimed at the weaknesses of the presidential candidate.

Sen. Thomas F. Eagleton, George McGovern's choice for vice president, meets two of those standards. The former prosecutor, state attorney general, lieutenant governor and since 1968 U.S. senator is qualified to be president. He has an exceptionally strong and progressive Senate record and has impressed Senate observers with his legislative ability and political skill. But he is not well know and does not now have strong appeal to any of McGovern's weaknesses — labor, the South, the Jewish vote or the big cities.

From a political viewpoint, Eagleton seems to have two, perhaps three, clear assets:

—As a Catholic, he brings religious balance to the ticket.

—His selection should repair a party split in a swing state where Gov. Warren Hearnes has been bitterly anti-McGovern. But Missouri, which narrowly went for President Nixon in 1968 by 811,932 to 791,444, has only 12 electoral votes.

—We suspect that Eagleton will be an effective national campaigner and an attractive TV personality. He defeated an incumbent senator (Edward V. Long) and a veteran congressman (Thomas B. Curtis) in his 1968 race. But in national recognition, Eagleton starts from where Spiro T. Agnew was in 1968.'

Gov. Reubin Askew decided wisely in not allowing his name to be in the final consideration for the spot. Askew, still in the first half of a first term, is needed too badly in Florida to seek the vice presidency.

THE INDIANAPOLIS STAR
Indianapolis, Ind., July 15, 1972

It's kind of interesting to think a b o u t Senator Edward M. Kennedy's refusal of the vice-presidential spot on the Democratic ticket reportedly offered h i m by Democratic presidential nominee Senator George S. McGovern.

If personal ambition is a factor with Kennedy, as it seems to be with most politicians, McGovern's offer could have had all the attraction of a p a i d vacation at the South Pole.

Had Kennedy accepted and the ticket won this fall, what would have been the position of the then vice-president in 1976?

At age 46 Kennedy could have been a locked-out glamor candidate of glamor candidates for the presidency in the nation's 200th year. Squarely in his way, assuming no cataclysms in the interim, would have stood the incumbent President, George McGovern.

Would a political party refuse to nominate for a second term a sitting president of its own political faith? Could a serving vice-president challenge his own "boss" resident at the White House? Hardly, unless something had gone badly amiss.

And in that case Kennedy would presumably have found himself sitting out another four years as vice-president — if the ticket had again been elected.

Then—at long last—Kennedy could h a v e expected his party's nomination to the top spot.

He would still have been under 50, true. Likely he'd have become a seasoned vice-president. But a wee bit shopworn? Quite possibly.

In any case his watchword over eight long years would have had to have been patience, patience—patience!

Suppose, though, that he had accepted the McGovern bid, but the ticket had lost this fall.

Then, four years from now, instead of being in a position to offer himself as a newly minted candidate for nomination as his party's front runner, he could have found himself—a Muskie.

The least-scarred partner in a ticket that had failed to commend itself to a majority of the voters, he could have been the titular head of his party only to find that voters in primaries and convention delegates alike had fallen quite out of love with him.

Win or lose, McGovern's proposition that Kennedy join him on the 1972 Democratic ticket was hardly one to make Kennedy jump for joy—if he has presidential aspirations of his own.

Kennedy's refusal of the offer may be the first swallow of summer, 1976.

Minneapolis Tribune
Minneapolis, Minn., July 14, 1972

By selecting a little-known but vigorous young senator as his running mate, Sen. McGovern lived up to one of the two specifications he listed in advance for his selection.

The specifications were for a candidate "well qualified to take over the White House on a moment's notice" and whose views are "in the same ballpark as mine."

Sen. Thomas Eagleton, 42, is a liberal, antiwar Missouri Democrat whose views on many issues are similar to those of McGovern. But whether he is qualified by experience to take over the White House "on a moment's notice" seems doubtful. His experience in the Senate is less than four years, while his previous principal experience in government was as attorney general and later lieutenant governor of Missouri.

Eagleton is a Catholic, so his selection broadens the religious appeal of the ticket—just as Sen. Muskie added a similar appeal to the Humphrey ticket in 1968. As a border-state man and Muskie supporter, Eagleton also brings other conventional political advantages to the ticket.

By selecting a liberal like himself rather than a Southern conservative like Wilbur Mills, McGovern has given the public additional evidence that he intends to offer the public a clear alternative to the ticket President Nixon will head.

THE ROANOKE TIMES
Roanoke, Va., July 15, 1972

Like many another vice presidential nominee before him, Sen. Thomas F. Eagleton of Missouri starts out poorly known to the national electorate. But by almost any political standard he should prove an asset to his Democratic running mate, Sen. George S. McGovern.

Granted, the Missourian will not much strengthen the Democrats' appeal in the South. Dixie looks unredeemable anyway for McGovern and his reconstituted party. Eagleton brings other benefits which may help more: his good relations with labor, his border-industrial state-big city origins, his Roman Catholic religion, his youth.

This is ticket-balancing in the old style, one indicator that Sen. McGovern earnestly desires to unify Democrats. Another sign that the new politics is like the old. Sen Eagleton is good-looking himself and has a photogenic family, which is a help to any candidate for public office right down to the ward level. As a freshman in the Senate, he has worked quietly but effectively, often impressively.

In his acceptance speech early Friday, the vice presidential nominee won friends easily. He is no stump speaker or classical stylist, but his appearance of candor and sincerity blends in well with that of his running mate. His talk was positive, upbeat, lightly spiced with humor—and he, as well as other platform speakers, contrasted his muted approach with the abrasive belligerence that has become the hallmark of Vice President Agnew.

Sen. McGovern may have reason to be thankful that Sen. Edward Kennedy declined to run with him. With all his political assets, the youngest Kennedy still is haunted by Chappaquiddick, a specter that could mock the tone of moral crusade that the South Dakotan set in his own acceptance speech.

At the same time, in the campaign McGovern might have found himself overshadowed by Kennedy, who was the sentimental hero of the convention and delivered its only passionate, stem-winding oration. Sen. McGovern will be more comfortable with Sen. Eagleton. They could make a formidable team to confront Nixon-Agnew or Nixon-Connally this fall.

DESERET NEWS
Salt Lake City, Utah, July 14, 1972

Four years ago when Richard M. Nixon announced the name of his running mate, Americans scratched their heads and asked:

Spiro who?

Now the question going the rounds if: Who is Thomas F Eagleton?

Until George McGovern called on him Thursday to be his running mate on the Democratic ticket this year, few Americans ever heard of Senator Eagleton. Fewer still were acquainted with his views.

There's room for wondering about the wisdom of Senator McGovern, himself still a largely unknown quantity in the hinterlands of America, in selecting such an obscure figure as a running mate. At least Richard Nixon had himself long been well known when he called on Spiro Agnew to share the Republican ticket with him in 1968.

But in this era of rapid communications, as Mr. Agnew himself has demonstrated, Americans need not remain in the dark very long about the record and qualifications of any public figure once he gains a national platform.

Consequently, it shouldn't be long before the public becomes well aware of the liberal voting record the 42-year-old Eagleton, a Roman Catholic from St. Louis, has compiled in his first term as Senator from Missouri.

Since Eagleton is considered an ally of organized labor, his selection for the vice presidential nomination looks like a key part of Senator McGovern's efforts to reunify his party following the divisive Miami convention.

Moreover, just as Maryland's Agnew reflected a GOP effort to make inroads in the South, McGovern's selection of a running mate from Missouri looks like part of an effort to win back a section of the country that was once solidly Democrat.

The office for which Senator Eagleton has been nominated can no longer be accurately described in the words of John Adams, the first American to serve in that post, as "the most insignificant office that ever the invention of man contrived."

Most voters have come to realize that the Vice President must not only be personally and politically compatible with the President, but also should be qualified to hold the top office if called upon to do so. Nine times in this nation's history the Vice President has become President.

In addition to presiding over the Senate, the Vice President serves on the National Security Council and may often represent the White House on important foreign assignments. Some political scientists think the Vice President should be assigned other duties of real substance with the aim of making him, in effect, an "assistant president" and relieving some of the burden on the President.

Americans will be keeping some high standards in mind as they assess the record and potential of the nominee from Missouri, one Thomas F. Eagleton.

St. Louis Review
St. Louis, Mo., July 28, 1972

The selection of Senator Thomas F. Eagleton as a candidate for the vice-presidency brings to our attention once again the issue of Catholics in politics. The significant difference this time is that there was great sentiment in favor of Mr. Eagleton because he was a Catholic. In 1960 there was much sentiment against John F. Kennedy for the same reason. This is perhaps a growth of some sort in what is considered to be the American political attitude.

Other differences exist, too. In 1960 Mr. Kennedy felt constrained to take a stand against government aid to parochial schools at least partly to neutralize anti-Catholic sentiment. Senator Eagleton successfully led a fight to keep abortion out of a family aid program and this "pro-Catholic" position doesn't seem to have hurt his attraction as a candidate.

While some may be happy with this apparent turn about in affairs, it does not strike us as completely satisfactory. It is all based on the assumption that there is a significant Catholic vote and that there was at least in 1960 an anti-Catholic vote. Both assertions are dubious.

We don't think there should be either. Voting should be concerned with issues. The personality of candidates will naturally enter into the consideration in so far as the candidates do or do not generate trust and confidence, but their religious affiliation should receive no consideration whatsoever.

It is difficult to conceive of a real Catholic issue in American politics even though the Catholic Church may have taken a stand on a particular problem. Abortion for instance is not primarily a Catholic issue. It is a moral issue which confronts our whole society. Government aid to education is an issue which is also much broader than its sectarian aspect. Justice is involved as is the interpretation of the First Amendment.

We hope the candidates this year will not exploit the so-called Catholic issues to gain the alleged Catholic vote. Both Mr. Nixon and Mr. McGovern should be judged on their stand on the real issues. The real issues sometimes have a moral aspect but it is not sectarian. Politics should not be divorced from morality but it should be divorced from sectarian labels. A real sign of political maturity in our country would be a lack of concern about Catholic candidates, Catholic issues or the Catholic vote. We could focus attention however on moral issues, morally concerned candidates and the conscientous electorate.

Chicago Tribune
Chicago, Ill., July 15, 1972

After studying his choice of running-mate, one can only presume that Sen. George McGovern must be supremely confident of his election chances. The name of Sen. Thomas F. Eagleton isn't going to add much to them.

The function of the running-mate, while ostensibly to be a potential President, traditionally has been to compensate for the weaknesses of the man on top of the ticket. Hence Lyndon B. [Texas] Johnson was enlisted by Ivy League John F. Kennedy in 1960.

Mr. McGovern's weaknesses are many.

He is an apparent dissenter in the anti-busing South. Big Labor despises him. Wall Street [for reasons mentioned above] is terrified by him. Mayor Daley's Illinois regulars are out for his head. According to what they call "the conventional wisdom," Mr. McGovern's Vice Presidential selection should have reflected a concern for these things.

To placate the South, he might have picked Terry Sanford of North Carolina or Gov. Reubin Askew of Florida. To mollify labor, he might have opted for one of their own, as he suggested he might do by dropping hints about Leonard Woodcock of the United Auto Workers. To make both the South and Wall Street happy, he might have taken Rep. Wilbur Mills of Arkansas. For the salvation of the Illinois vote, there was Adlai Stevenson, begging for the job.

Instead he went for Mr. Eagleton, a 42 year old liberal from Missouri, an industrial border state that manages to be midwestern, southern, and western at the same time. Tho a liberal [McGovern says their views coincide], Mr. Eagleton has strong pro-labor and pro-farm views and so is considered merely a moderate by many. He is a Roman Catholic, a family man, a World War II veteran, a Harvard grad, and, as Shirley MacLaine noted, he is "pretty." But what Mr. Eagleton chiefly is, in terms of this election campaign, is unknown.

We can't pretend to know what goes on in that whirring and buzzing political mind of Mr. Govern's, but it seems that Mr. Eagleton's only real advantage is that he does not offend. The radicals will accept him because he is anti-war, the labor skates have no complaints with his voting record, and the middle Americans have to agree that he is middle American. But inoffensiveness is not a quality to stir up campaign fervor. Mr. Eagleton is no Teddy Kennedy.

Maybe it doesn't make much difference anyway. As I. W. Abel, president of the United Steel Workers, put it: "It doesn't matter if it's Kennedy or Woodcock on the ticket. McGovern is still on the top."

Democratic Convention:
BROADLY-WORDED PLATFORM ADOPTED; CONVENTION ENDS WITHOUT DISORDERS

The delegates to the Democratic National Convention July 11–12 adopted with only minor changes the broadly-worded platform drawn up by the party's Platform Committee two weeks earlier. Generally, the platform called for increased federal spending for a variety of domestic needs and reduced foreign military commitments. Specifically, it called for "an immediate and complete withdrawal of all U.S. forces in Indochina" and advocated a "long-term public commitment" to Israel's military preparedness. The platform was acceptable to Sens. McGovern, Humphrey and Muskie.

The delegates rejected a number of minority proposals calling for more radical stands on tax reform, welfare, abortion and homosexual rights. They also rejected a number of conservative planks, including one flatly opposing school busing. Gov. George Wallace made a dramatic wheelchair appearance at the convention in an appeal for support of the conservative minority planks.

On July 13 the convention delegates endorsed revised party reforms designed to moderate the fears of party regulars. Democratic congressmen had voted 105–50 June 28 to condemn the Rules Committee's proposals for more drastic reforms as "not in the best interest of the party."

With Sen. McGovern's acceptance speech, the convention drew to a close. Only minor incidents involving the demonstrators camped outside the convention were reported. More than 5,500 troops had been on station in case of trouble.

The Dispatch
Columbus, Ohio, July 12, 1972

WRITERS of the 1972 Democratic party platform presented their proposals in Miami Beach Tuesday night and delegates found planks laden with splinters.

Before a motion to adopt the manifesto could be entertained, a long list of minority reports was debated and the bulk of them were shouted down by voice vote.

AS IS THE case with most platforms, this one contains promises both idealistic and lavish. Even so, the document either omits or dilutes many of the original planks which had been preached along the pre-convention trail by Sen. George McGovern.

The document skates close to fantasy and follows the tradition of previous Democratic thinking such as that found in the New Deal, the Fair Deal and the New Frontier.

PLATITUDES are foundation blocks for the platform. It calls for life styles for all persons so they can feel life is worth living, a social environment whose institutions promote the good of all and a physical environment whose resources are used for the good of all.

Democrats call for guaranteed jobs for all, a redistribution of wealth and assurances the federal government will pick up the slack for employes and local political subdivisions when an industrial plant moves or closes.

But financing is not detailed.

THEY WANT Congress to abolish the seniority system although many chairmanships are held by elder statesmen of the Democratic party.

The Democrats, anticipating a full national health insurance program, want to expand Medicare in the interim.

The party asks "forthwith" withdrawal of American military forces from Indochina, cautioning it believes there is nothing to be gained by debating who got the United States into that sorry affair.

WHAT THE platform writers obviously found was that it was difficult to remain rational and at the same time outmaneuver President Nixon on issue after issue which he had pre-empted.

Richmond Times-Dispatch
Richmond, Va., July 5, 1972

The proposed Democratic party platform is shoddy and shaky, and no wonder. It contains hardly a scrap of solid lumber. Obviously, the carpenters simply nailed together bits of soggy driftwood they found bobbing on the surface of radical liberalism and slapped on a little shellac. The result is a rickety structure that leans, sags and quivers in the breeze.

Only a brief examination of some of the platform's salient features will show what an irresponsible piece of work it is.

The platform unfairly scathes President Nixon's economic policies and promises that a "first priority of a Democratic administration must be eliminating the unfair, bureaucratic Nixon wage and price controls." A Democratic administration, the platform declares, would substitute better wage and price controls. What kind of controls would they be? Well, the platform hedges. A Democratic program to curb inflation would be strong and fair, swift and tough. The platform speaks vaguely of controls on "profits, investment earnings, executive salaries and prices, as well as wages," as if wages alone have been affected by Mr. Nixon's program. But nowhere is the platform specific about the kind of wage-price control program it favors.

And while it insists that inflation must be conquered, the platform also advocates programs and policies that would aggravate inflation: Cost-of-living escalators to cause the value of savings bonds and Social Security payments to rise automatically as prices go up, income supplements for the working poor, public service projects to guarantee a job for all" and so forth. Meanwhile, a Democratic administration, tuided by the proposed platform would discourage economic growth — which could create jobs — by imposing taxes and pursuing policies designed to redistribute the wealth.

The platform's pronouncements on foreign affairs and defense would be laughable were they not so serious. A Democratic administration would defend "America's real interests and maintain our alliances, neither playing world policeman nor abandoning old and good friends." It would, however, abandon old friends in Southeast Asia by ceasing "all U.S. military action in Southeast Asia" and by terminating "military aid to the Saigon government, and elsewhere in Indochina...." It would reduce "overseas bases and forces," but it would maintain in the Mideast a military force "amply sufficient to deter the Soviet Union from using military force" on behalf of the Arabs in their aggression against Israel. How a blanket promise to reduce "overseas bases and forces" might dilute this firm commitment to Israel is ignored.

America's government, the platform states at one point, should be the "servant, not the master, of the people..." Elsewhere, however, the platform advances proposals that would make the people even more subservient to the government than they are now. Under a Democratic administration, the federal government would assume awesome power over elementary and secondary education. And the pernicious practice of coercive busing to promote racial balance, the policy of a "master" if ever there was one, would continue.

One more contradiction deserves to be noted. At the outset, the platform builders denounced "opportunistic politicians," but at least one feature of the platform is a manifestation of opportunism in its crudest form. The platform promises the "appointment of women to positions of top responsibility in all branches of the federal government to achieve an equitable ratio of women and men. Such positions include Cabinet members, agency and division heads and Supreme Court justices." Further, a Democratic administration would include "women advisers in equitable ratios on all government studies, commissions and hearings."

Even The New York Times, which could be expected to view the platform sympathetically, denounced this silly pledge of allegiance to the quota concept as "sheer vote-trapping." Ability, not sex, should be the primary consideration in filling such governmental posts. Besides, asks the Times, if the platform promises quotas for women "what happens to all the other elements of the population seeking quota representation?"

Numerous other flaws can be found in the platform and some responsible Democrats surely will seek to patch it up at the party's Miami Beach convention. But don't expect any major changes. The same radicals who put it together probably will succeed in defending it, and it is likely to emerge from the convention as shoddy and as shaky —as it went in.

FORT WORTH STAR-TELEGRAM
Fort Worth, Tex., June 29, 1972

Bearing the stamp of the populist mood which prevailed during its five-day gestation period, the Democrats' platform draft was delivered Tuesday amidst a flood of tears for the American consumer.

The document, distinctly anti-business in its thrust, was endorsed by all major Democratic candidates except George Wallace, whose campaign manager described it as "a suicide note for November." The Wallace forces promised to carry their fight to the floor of the Miami convention beginning July 10.

George McGovern, the nominee-apparent, campaigning in the South, said he was pleased with the proposed platform, and well he might be. It seems tailor-made to fit the broad outlines of his campaign posture: Level out the wealth, pull back the military, run the school buses as "another tool" to accomplish desegregation.

All of this transpired pretty well according to script, but it is astonishing to us that so little blood was left on the floor. For example, not an opposition shot was fired, apparently, by delelates from the oil-producing states when the platform writers agreed to "abolish the oil industry's cherished import quota system."

In this plank we see a prime example of how the business-baiting "new politicians" permit their emotions to outrun their powers of rational thought.

The oil import control program, in effect since 1959, was adopted for several excellent reasons, and the wisdom of President Eisenhower's action has been demonstrated over and over again. It is increasingly clear that foreign oil is neither cheap nor dependably available. To become overly dependent upon it would be folly.

But it is the general tone and direction of the proposed Democratic platform—not any individual plank—which gives us pause. It is the old "break up the Yankees" cry, applied now to a vague congeries of "large conglomerates" and big business in general. It is the demagogic impulse to level everything down—and never mind the fact (and it is a fact) that in recent years the employes of this country's corporations have been getting more than seven-eighths of the corporate income available for division, and the shareowners less than one-eighth.

The platform as it stands is a fraud and a swindle upon the American working man.

That working man is interested, and rightly so, in more jobs and money. But this proposed platform addresses itself not to more jobs and money but to querulous bickering over the present supply—which, all things considered, is not too bad at that.

Making General Motors smaller and the government bigger isn't doing the "little man" any favors. Has no one yet learned that there's no way to "redistribute" something that hasn't been produced? Has no one yet learned that wealth and income cannot be created with alluring slogans and utopian dreams?

The Washington Post
Washington, D.C., July 11, 1972

At this writing, the outcome of the Democratic Convention's credentials fight is yet unknown, and the convention's platform deliberations—which will doubtless be influenced by the way the credentials fight is resolved, if it is—have yet to take place. They have been scheduled for this evening, to be sure, but everything is subject to change in a political convention, especially when the Democrats are involved. Even so, it seems to us that a few observations can be made at this moment on what is likely to be a principal element of conflict over the prospective party platform—namely, its so-called "busing plank." Should the convention be in shape to go forward with the platform this evening, then the odds are that this will be Governor Wallace's night—the first moment thus far at Miami Beach in which the Alabama governor and his supporters will have become a principal focus of attention.

Traditionally (and this convention is no exception), the specific language of party platforms is less important as a guide to future policies of an elected administration than it is as a guide to the political complexion of the party at a given moment. Its language and its compromises and fuzzinesses and inconsistencies in particular reflect something of both the prevailing public mood and the relative clout of the various elements within the party coalition. Thus, there are three variations on the "busing" plank in the Platform Committee's draft: a committee-backed, McGovern-favored plank, a Wallace plank and a plank that Senators Muskie and Humphrey had a hand in and which represents a kind of middle position between the other two planks.

Contemplating this focal point in the party's platform, conflict is necessarily to be struck by the strange context in which it occurs, a context which is worth noting because it says something not just of the meaning of the busing argument but also of the manner in which the party as a whole has changed. The plain fact is that black delegates are present at the Miami Beach convention in unprecedented numbers; and yet mention of the party's obligation to bring about racial justice specifically for black Americans is notably scant in the proposed platform. It is also a fact that the black delegates at Miami Beach, functioning as a caucus with sharply divided groups within, have concentrated their energies thus far on the more conventional assertions of power politics that go with a nominating convention, even as "busing"—a more or less conventional civil rights or desegregation issue for Democratic gatherings has been dominated by white delegates arguing with each other.

To some extent this unfamiliar condition represents a wholesome development within the party itself. For the presence of large numbers of black delegates, their comfort in conducting a classical political drive to gain and exert influence, and the fact that they have (along with various black lobbyists and protestors) bent their attention to issues other than the establishment of constitutional rights (jobs, income maintenance programs)—all this suggests that a certain number of the critical battles of the past have in fact been won, that the party like the country can at least begin to move on to issues other than the time and pace of granting what should have been granted long ago and what never should have been in question in the first place.

At the same time, there are disturbing aspects of the convention which also go a certain way to explain the framework in which the "busing" dispute takes place. Only four years ago and even in the wake of the turmoil in the cities and the dispute over the conclusions of the Kerner Commission, the Democratic platform made a point of recording the party in favor of strong execution of the provisions of the Civil Rights Act of 1964—possibly the last occasion on which the party would witness a fairly clearcut North-South argument over implementation of civil rights for blacks.

What is distinctive in this year's platform is the dwelling upon the rights of practically every other group imaginable within the society, the downplaying of the issue as it has traditionally been applied to blacks and the fact that the single issue—"busing"—on which the orthodox struggle has come to turn now crosses regional lines: George Wallace is not representing a Southern resistance movement; rather he is exploiting the genuine confusions and legitimate controversies that surround the issue nationwide and he has plenty of Northern support in his cause. It is worth remembering that the Wallace minority plank on busing, calling for "immediate relief from busing" and for an exercise of congressional power to limit the courts contains very little that is at odds with the position taken by Michigan's liberal Democrats who have been fighting the Detroit and Pontiac decisions in Washington.

All this surely has something to do with the eerie silence of the platform as a whole on certain aspects of the fulfillment of black people's rights, and it does not bode particularly well for the convention's disposal of the issue. As it happens, the draft plank of the committee itself is far from radical or militant or even overly precise. The key sentence, embedded in a couple of paragraphs of unexceptional generalities merely accepts "transportation" as one of several "tools" to achieve desegregation and asserts that it should remain "available" as such in accord with certain "Supreme Court decisions." Perhaps because the black political community is itself divided on this question and certainly because the white political community is so frightened of it, there is a fairly strong chance that one of the alternative planks will have a good run on the convention floor. The party, however, should stick with the language as drafted by the committee. That language is hardly extreme or inflammatory. In a minimal way it acknowledges the authority of the federal judiciary to remedy violations of black people's constitutional rights. That strikes us as being the minimum that the reconstructed Democratic Party should do.

Detroit Free Press

Detroit, Mich., July 13, 1972

MIAMI BEACH — When they needed it most, the McGovern supporters came up with the secret ingredient no one suspected they had — discipline.

They were known for being smart, dedicated and energetic. But the old pros are also smart, dedicated and energetic, and here this week the old pros had the extra incentive of fighting for their lives. So the smart money said that when it came to the push and shove of convention politics, the balloting, the maneuvering, the willingness to suppress causism for concert, the amateurs wouldn't have it.

The smart money was wrong. From the meetings of the rules, credentials and platform committees in Washington last month until the last shout of approval of the platform itself Wednesday morning, the McGovernites kept it all together.

The greatest danger to their success — as it will be from now on — came not from the anti-McGovern coalition but from their own enthusiasm. As hundreds of experts have written in millions of words, they represent an amalgam of separate causes which coalesced behind McGovern because his campaign embraced more of them than did anyone else's. But they were neither pros nor dedicated Democrats.

They made mistakes. The most grievous, of course, was their failure to dominate the Credentials Committee as they dominated the other committees. It was this failure which could have cost them the vital 151 extra votes in California.

They almost overkilled George Wallace and the Platform Committee. After the Alabama governor, then in a suburban Washington hospital, rejected a moderate plank which referred to school busing as only one tool which might be used to promote quality education, the McGovernites threatened to push through a plank practically demanding busing. In the end, moderation prevailed and the final version said, "Transportation of students is another tool to accomplish desegregation. It must continue to be available according to Supreme Court decisions."

They threatened to shatter over such issues as women's lib, abortion reform, legalization of marijuana and the ending of criminal penalties for consensual homosexuality. Each of these had its advocates, and if anyone of them had stirred too much friction within their mutual camp, it could have provided the wedge the opposition needed.

But the dangers, though real, were also reckoned with. McGovern strategists had seen every possibility and had planned accordingly.

The tip-off, as everyone now recognizes, came on the first crucial vote Monday night on the South Carolina credentials challenge. The details are too complicated to repeat here but essentially it was a noble battle but on a disastrous battlefield. To win the battle would have been to lose the war.

Responding to more discipline than anyone knew they possessed, they deliberately lost the battle. They lived to fight another day — on the far more important California challenge.

From then on it was easy. Some of them must have been torn at times Tuesday night and Wednesday morning, as individual minority reports on the platform came before them. But the price of fervor was too high, and suddenly these amateurs, these causists, became pros.

This is not to say that the platform they adopted or the campaign that will be waged this fall will be just another campaign run on just another platform. It is not a radical document, but it is reformist. Much of it isn't going to be popular with large elements of the citizenry, whether they are beneficiaries of oil depletion allowances or scared householders who like to keep a .38 in the dresser drawer for self-protection. No accommodation was made to the real issues raised by George Wallace, which could be fatal in the finals.

But the fact is that an overwhelming proportion of the delegates here put it together, are willing to stand on it and are willing to defend it. And the man who put them all together, into one cohesive mold, is their candidate. He is, without any question, his own best strategist. What he did in one year of planning and four months of campaigning was to build a powerful structure on organization and education.

It may easily come apart in the strains of the campaign. Too much divisiveness remains, too much bitterness, too many dashed hopes. Too many power brokers may have been offended for a winning coalition to emerge.

But Republicans who tend to underrate McGovern's chances four months from now might do well to remember where and who he was four months ago.

The Virginian-Pilot

Norfolk, Va., July 13, 1972

With the voluminous Democratic Party platform to draw upon, Senator McGovern need not ever be at a loss for words in his quest of the Presidency. For that matter, President Nixon will find the document a help in attacking the Democrats at some points.

It differs from platforms of other years in being assembled not by a few closeted politicians, but by a 150-member committee that held 30 public hearings throughout the country. Political scientist Richard Neustadt was the committee's guide. If nothing else, the Democratic platform is a fascinating compendium of everything that all shades of the American people want, or think they want, in 1972.

Ironically, the delegates now pressing their demands on Congress excluded, for the most part, Congressmen from their midst. In fact, elected officials of any sort form the great minority of this convention. It is an enthusiastic assemblage of political newcomers.

But the old folks will have their day. One plank provides that the aged, like the young and other minorities, be represented hereafter at conventions in proportion to their numbers in the population.

What with birth-control programs and lengthening life spans, the nation's senior citizens soon will be in a position to inherit the Democratic Party, or what's left of it. They should live so long.

(The Arrangements Committee brought back former House Speaker John McCormack to introduce a platform section, and the faded old eagle, ticking off a few achievements of the Roosevelt-Truman era—Social Security and what-not —reminded the delegates gently that the old politics had not been entirely bereft of progress.)

Among the platform's less forthright planks is the one on busing. It is an embarrassment, shrinking from any mention of the dreaded word, saying only that "transportation" is another tool to accomplish desegregation. It reminds one of how the Democrats in the 1950s used to tiptoe through the tulips on fair employment practices. Governor Wallace appeared with stronger stuff, a resolution condemning busing, and he served as a sort of tar baby against which the liberals punched. They got their kicks in roaring down the Wallace antibusing proposals, along with other far-right sentiments from preservation of capital punishment to prayer in the public schools.

The rich get short shrift in the platform. Verily, it is easier for a camel to get through a needle's eye than for anyone with a sizeable income to get a favorable place in the Democratic platform. The convention's oratory has been marked by vows to abolish "tax-welfare aid for the wealthy, the privileged, and the corporations."

The platform is unusual in facing, here and there, the Democrats' own defaults. It notes, for instance, that the Democratic Party must share responsibility for Vietnam, but says the task now is to end the war, not decide who is to blame for it. It pledges "as the first order of business, an immediate and complete withdrawal of all U.S. forces from Indochina. All U.S. military action in Southeast Asia will cease."

Thanks to the public hearings' input (a much-used word here), the Democratic platform is strikingly different from the party's 1968 model. They could be separated by a decade instead of a mere four years. The current version shows a much greater sense of social justice. It seeks legal counsel for juveniles in trouble, better education for mentally retarded children, protection of the rights of prisoners.

It also would replace the sacrosanct Highway Trust Fund with a single Transportation Trust Fund to aid local transit systems as well as roads. Recognizing the core cities' burdens, it would encourage urban-suburban cooperation in education of children.

Many of the dozens of proposals are meritorious; all are worth pondering as reflecting the hopes and fears in these United States.

San Jose Mercury
San Jose, Calif., July 13, 1972

There were no surprises in the Democratic party platform, adopted by the delegates to the national convention early Wednesday morning. Sen. George McGovern should be comfortable in its company.

It is a commonplace among political observers to downgrade party platforms, insisting they are little more than exercise yards for party ideologues. That may be too harsh a judgment.

The Democrats, to nobody's great surprise, adopted a platform calling for immediate withdrawal from Vietnam, the closing of tax loopholes, replacing welfare with a system of income grants and the continued utilization of busing to achieve school integration. These are McGovern positions from top to bottom, and the Senator will have the opportunity to take them — and his own political future — to the people this fall.

To the extent that the platform reflects the sentiments of a majority of Democrats, it suggests that the party may, in fact, unify behind the McGovern candidacy. The real question, of course, is whether the convention, controlled effectively by McGovern delegates and McGovern ideology, accurately mirrors the Democratic party as it exists in cities, towns and rural areas across the country.

This is one of the things the November election will determine. Unlike President Nixon, George McGovern will not be defending the record of an administration. He will be asking the people to trust his view of what the future should be, not what he has done in the past to shape the present. Consequently, the McGovern candidacy and the Democratic party platform — which is a McGovern platform down the line — will be linked inseparably in the minds of the voters.

It is probably not stretching the point to suggest that George McGovern will be elected or defeated largely on the appeal — or lack of it — of the Democratic platform.

This is one aspect of the party platform — any party's platform — that is all too often overlooked. It can give the challenger a useful tool and a handy identity, should he lack a sufficiently forceful one of his own. Consequently, it is a mistake to view the party platform merely as a list of campaign promises, and it is the tendency to view all platforms in just this light that thrusts them into undeserved disrepute after the election.

No party, no President, no Congress — indeed, no nation — operates in a vacuum. Circumstances always alter cases, and what may be not only feasible but desirable as a platform plank in July may prove to be unwise or unattainable, or both, the following March or April. This should hardly be held against political parties or individual politicians; to the contrary, the ability to adapt to changing circumstances is a quality to be desired in public men. President Nixon, for example, has demonstrated great flexibility in the past three and a half years, much to the benefit of the nation and to the improved prospects for world peace.

The Indianapolis Star
Indianapolis, Ind., July 13, 1972

Radical delegates listened more or less politely to Governor George Wallace, but their response, like much else at the Democratic National Convention, was rigged.

On orders from the McGovern radical command, the delegates listened with closed minds. Wallace's attempt to influence the platform was — before he made it—doomed.

The delegates shouted down, one by one, Wallace's proposals to curb "senseless, asinine busing of school children," maintain a strong national defense, cut welfare spending and foreign aid, strengthen law enforcement, demand release of prisoners of war, allow prayers in schools, authorize states to impose capital punishment and affirm the right to bear arms.

Wallace had won the Democratic primaries in states with a total population of more than 32 million and placed second in primaries in states with a total population of over 26 million. That is some evidence of the extent to which his views on key issues are shared by other Americans.

The rejection of the Wallace proposal at the convention is one significant measure of how far the radical Democrats are out of touch with millions of Americans.

It is another instance of the dominant idea behind leftist thoughts and actions — that the leftists know better what is good for the people than the people do.

The radicals in control of the Democratic convention have shown they know how to cast a hex.

As spells sometimes do, this one may return to hex the sorcerers who cast it—in November.

The Evening News
Newark, N.J., July 13, 1972

Because the platforms of political parties frequently bear little relevance to the campaign program a party's presidential nominee ultimately puts together, or to what he can reasonably be expected to accomplish, they tend to be catch-all documents, distinguished mostly by the multiplicity of the issues, frequently minor, that they cover and the vagueness of the language in which they are couched.

The platform adopted by the Democratic convention in Miami Beach fits into the accepted mold. In addition to obvious issues of major import that offer no surprises (get out of Vietnam posthaste, massive federal programs for the cities, mass transit, the environment, etc.) we are exhorted to choose our own "life styles" without fear of discrimination or prosecution, to refuse to ingest nonunion lettuce and to break up large conglomerates.

Enhancing the occasional aura of unreality one finds in the document is the lack of specificity. We are spared the vulgarity of price tags on an idealistic program of guaranteeing jobs for everyone, and on replacing the existing welfare system; we are not told how an "equitable" distribution of wealth would be accomplished or what constitutes an "appropriate" occasion for the taxing of environmental polluters.

The platform finally adopted unmistakably matches the liberal convictions of the day. That it was not even more liberal can be attributed to the new moderation being practiced by the McGovern organization as it faces up to the reality of appealing to the American political center in the campaign that lies ahead.

To insure that the platform as fashioned in committee did not undergo any radical re-structuring on the floor of the convention, McGovern aides were on hand to head off minority-sponsored plans on abortion and guaranteed incomes ($6,500 for a family of four).

Similarly, the McGovern forces made sure that Gov. Wallace enjoyed no success in trying to turn the convention rightward. Down to defeat went the Wallace anti-busing proposal in favor of one that identified busing as only "one tool" in the desegregation of schools. Other Wallace proposals on national defense, welfare, tax relief, foreign aid, and cutting back on the federal bureaucracy never got anywhere.

In short, the platform projects a generalized, occasionally profound, sometime silly, program that the liberal Sen. McGovern can live with and run on, with considerable room for maneuvering, as he seeks to tone down the radical image some of his public statements have fostered.

Adoption of the platform without any significant amendment also demonstrates that the Democratic party in this era of New Politics is now firmly in Mr. McGovern's control and ready to do his bidding.

THE TENNESSEAN
Nashville, Tenn., July 13, 1972

THE DEMOCRATIC party has a new presidential nominee and a new platform, and the latter is pretty much what the former wanted, even if everybody isn't happy with it.

In a marathon session Tuesday night, Gov. George Wallace and others who wanted substantial changes failed to make very many in the platform hammered out before the convention began. Governor Wallace's dramatic appearance at the convention and his speech in behalf of the minority reports which embodied his political philosophy didn't sway the convention.

* * *

Tossed out in the voice voting, in addition to a strong anti-busing proposal were a reaffirmation of the right to bear arms, support for capital punishment, a proposed constitutional amendment to permit prayer in the schools and stringent curbs on foreign aid. Also rejected on roll call were proposals to establish a $6,500 guaranteed income for a family of four and a plank on abortion.

The delegates did vote to strengthen a provision supporting a U.S. military commitment in Europe and the Mediterranean to deter Soviet pressure. The platform had already stressed the continuing need for a robust Atlantic Alliance and a "partnership of equals" with West Europe. It pledges to work in greater cooperation with the European Economic Community and upholds the liberal trade policies set forth by President Franklin D. Roosevelt.

The platform pledges "an immediate and complete withdrawal of all U.S. forces in Indochina" and the "cessation of all military action in Southeast Asia. Vietnam will, of course, remain a crucial issue of the campaign unless President Nixon makes good on his promise to end it by November.

The Democratic platform sets forth some positive and humane economic goals: Jobs for those who want to work and can, an "adequate income" for those unable to work; protection against inflation; programs to improve the nation's urban and rural blight and a major reform of the tax system to make taxes more equitable up and down the line.

* * *

It was in the area of taxation that the McGovern forces' handiwork is most clear. This represents a shift in thinking on economic policy away from preoccupation with growth to that of redistribution of wealth. It recognizes an increasing frustration among the middle income taxpayers who bear the lion's share of the cost of government in this nation and an incipient tax rebellion on the part of many who want that load to be shared equitably by all.

Both Senator McGovern and Governor Wallace have found response to this theme has been fervent across the land and while big business is apprehensive, it has become clearer in recent years that middle Americans — caught between relentless inflation and high taxes—are going to have change, one way or another.

The social planks commit the Democratic party to reverse the present drift away from basic concepts of individual rights and liberties and to move to restore confidence in constitutional guarantees—a confidence that has been seriously eroded by the government practices of surveillance and other infringements on the privacy of Americans.

The platform pledges an end to an injustice against the aged who are on Social Security by permitting them to earn more without sacrificing their benefits. It calls for a national health insurance program that would include preventive medicine and protection against catastrophic illness wiping out the savings and the means of Americans.

The platform contains a section on women's rights and a proposal to grant Indians first priority in allocation of federal surplus lands.

* * *

The Democratic platform obviously doesn't completely satisfy everybody, not even Senator McGovern. It particularly doesn't satisfy Governor Wallace and those who think a number of its provisions ought to be stronger. Still others think some planks ought to be weaker. It would be difficult, if not impossible to write a party platform that would satisfy every faction and segment of the party.

It is a political cliche that platforms are "made to stand on, but not to run on." It may well be that the presidential nominee tends to dress the platform in the clothes of his own policy. Nevertheless, as a statement of ideals and goals, the Democratic party document is one that the nominee can both stand on and run on in good conscience.

WORCESTER TELEGRAM.
Worcester, Mass., July 13, 1972

Reflecting in general the views of the man whose nomination was assured even before yesterday's balloting, the 1972 Democratic Party platform provides Sen. George McGovern with the stage from which he hopes to make his way to the White House. It is a curious structure.

The platform, as adopted, indicates McGovern's eagerness to avoid major embarrassments during the campaign and to bring about some sort of party unity. The delegates respectfully listened to Gov. George Wallace tell them that "75 to 80 per cent of the American people are against senseless, asinine busing of school children" — but then went on to shout down his entire eight-part package of dissenting planks. And an even clearer demonstration of McGovern power came when the convention defeated a number of amendments favoring liberal abortion policies, nondiscrimination against homosexuals and all the major goals of the National Welfare Rights Organization, including a $6,500 income guarantee for a family of four. Similarly torpedoed was the populist call for repealing the income tax code and substituting a system of lower tax rates and personal credits, but no deduction.

Still, the platform is enough to make every conservative or moderate hair stand on end: Immediate withdrawal from Vietnam — although McGovern has softened his own attitude, hinting that he would leave residual U.S. forces in Thailand until the American war prisoners are returned — replacing the welfare system with income grants, closing all tax "loopholes" and accepting busing as a means of achieving racial balance in schools.

The document is wholly doctrinaire with a strong populist flavor. It pays lip service to the free enterprise system, but the praise seems merely ornamental. It sees American industry in terms of "the power of corporate giants". It appears preoccupied with class distinctions — the "rich", as contrasted with the "working people" and the "poor". In places it sounds like a declaration of socialist principles: "We must restructure the social, political and economic relationships throughout the entire society in order to insure the equitable distribution of wealth and power." And in the best egalitarian fashion, the platform also calls for "an equitable ratio of women and men" in federal appointments and proportional representation of the "poor" at all levels of the Democratic party

There are serious contradictions. The platform demands "an end to inflation". But then it endorses a long shopping list that would feed the fires of inflation, more federally subsidized housing, a $2.50 minimum wage, free maternity benefits, expensive health care and heavier tax burdens on industry.

The platform stresses the social, political and economic ills of the nation, concluding that the Republicans in general, and the Nixon administration in particular, are largely to blame. It neglects to mention that, except for four years, the Democrats have controlled both houses of Congress for 40 years.

It has been said that party platforms are important only during convention time, to be tucked out of sight soon after the confetti is swept up. It may be that the new Democratic document, too, will wind up on a dusty shelf.

It may also be that the McGovern platform does not truly represent the philosophy of most Democrats. If it does, the party has pulled up stakes and moved to new and shakier ground.

Campaign '72:
EAGLETON REVEALS MENTAL CARE; FORCED TO RESIGN FROM TICKET

Democratic vice presidential candidate Sen. Thomas F. Eagleton (Mo.) disclosed July 25 that he had been hospitalized on three separate occasions during the 1960s for nervous exhaustion. His treatment had included electro-shock therapy. Eagleton's revelation caused a serious crisis for his already divided party and for his presidential running-mate, Sen. George S. McGovern (S.D.) As concern among party leaders and political observers grew over Eagleton's mental fitness and his lack of candor in not disclosing his past illness earlier, McGovern muted his initial support for Eagleton and finally asked for his withdrawal. Eagleton resigned from the Democratic ticket August 1.

Eagleton's initial disclosure of his psychiatric past came only hours before the Knight newspaper chain reportedly was going to break the story. Declaring he was fully cured of his past afflictions, Eagleton said, "I've learned how to pace myself and . . . measure my own energies and know the limits of my endurance." McGovern called Eagleton "fully qualified . . . to be the vice president . . . and, if necessary, to take on the Presidency." While admitting he had been unaware of Eagleton's mental history when he offered the nomination, McGovern said he would not have hesitated to select Eagleton even if he had known of it. McGovern said July 26 his decision to keep Eagleton on the ticket remained "absolutely" irrevocable.

McGovern's campaign manager Gary Hart admitted July 27 that no staff member had seriously checked into the backgrounds of potential running mates. However, another senior McGovern aide reported that Eagleton had been asked if "there are any skeletons in your closet." Eagleton had replied "no." (Eagleton later indicated that he did not regard his hospitalization as a "skeleton.")

Columnist Jack Anderson charged July 27 that Eagleton had been arrested several times for reckless and drunken driving in Missouri. Anderson said he had received the information from a source "whose reliability is beyond question." Eagleton called the charges a "damnable lie" and an "attempt to drive me off the ticket."

Although Eagleton reported July 28 that McGovern "was for me 1,000 per cent" and emphasized his own determination to "stay in the race," it was apparent that McGovern's support for him was weakening. "I'm with Sen. Eagleton all the way until he and I have had a chance to talk," McGovern said. Democratic Party Chairman Mrs. Jean Westwood appearing on NBC's "Meet the Press" July 30 said, "It would be the noble thing for Tom Eagleton to step down." Her sentiments were echoed by Vice Chairman Basil Paterson.

Eagleton's withdrawal was announced by McGovern July 31. He said Eagleton's health "was not a factor" in the decision, but public reaction "continues to divert attention from the national issues that need to be discussed" and serves only to "further divide the party and the nation." Eagleton acknowledged that "growing pressures" necessitated his withdrawal and indicated he would continue to campaign for McGovern.

On August 1, the day Eagleton submitted his formal resignation, Anderson publicly retracted his charges, saying he now knew them to be untrue and that they were "an outgrowth of a political smear campaign in 1968" as Eagleton had maintained.

THE MILWAUKEE JOURNAL
Milwaukee, Wis., July 27, 1972

A confusing political year has been further clouded by Sen. Eagleton's disclosure that, earlier in his fast moving career, he was briefly hospitalized three times for nervous exhaustion — with two of the visits involving electric shock treatment for depression.

As a man of 42, Eagleton today seems sound of mind and body. He cites a recent medical checkup as proof. He is highly regarded in the Senate. Colleagues call him "solid" and "hard working." They say he is quick witted and slow to anger.

Yet as a vice presidential candidate in a nation that sets almost superhuman standards for men in high office, Eagleton's medical history could add significantly to the political difficulties already facing his partner Sen. McGovern. Surely Eagleton, as he acknowledges, was wrong in not telling McGovern about the nervous disorders before the ticket was formed. Although McGovern loyally declares that it would have made no difference, he deserved to know and now must be anxiously wondering: Will voters, upon reflection, generally accept Eagleton as a restored man and a useful political leader? Or will he be widely and unfairly stigmatized as unworthy?

In this regard, it should be remembered that in varying degree we've all had feelings of depression, sleepless nights, bouts with "nerves." We are people with emotions, not machines. Eagleton's problems were perhaps out of the ordinary. Yet instead of trying to treat himself with pills and alcohol as so many do, he sensibly sought professional help, underwent treatment and since 1966 has apparently made adjustments indicative of an intelligent, evolving human being learning to cope successfully with life stresses. Numerous persons now thriving in prominent positions have done likewise, many undergoing shock therapy.

Eagleton's medical history, therefore, basically suggests strength, not weakness. Whether citizens see it that way in the coming days will be a major test of America's maturity.

The Virginian-Pilot

Norfolk, Va., July 27, 1972

The disclosure that Senator Thomas Eagleton, the Democratic nominee for Vice President, was hospitalized for nervous trouble in 1960, 1964, and 1966 is a hot potato politically.

It is not the sort of thing that can be exploited openly by the Republicans. But it isn't going to help George McGovern and the Democratic ticket.

The issue, if that's the word, is bound to cause a quantity of bad jokes. Beyond that, it is difficult to say whether or how much it will hurt the Democratic ticket. But the best that can be expected is that the matter will be kept in perspective, that Mr. Eagleton will not be misjudged by the voters, and that the election will be decided upon the issues—in short, that Mr. Eagleton's medical record won't change things. Which would mean that Mr. McGovern has plenty of problems still, even if Mr. Eagleton isn't to be a new one.

Certainly, the facts ought to be kept in perspective. Mr. Eagleton hospitalized himself during December 1960 as the result of exhaustion and fatigue from the campaign in the fall, when he was elected Attorney General of Missouri. "I pushed myself terribly hard, long hours day and night," he explained at his news conference with Mr. McGovern Tuesday.

He was hospitalized for the second time in 1964, when he spent four days at the Mayo Clinic for a check-up during the Christmas holidays. He had "a kind of a nervous stomach situation," again as a consequence of overwork. "I am like the fellow in the Alka-Seltzer ad who says I can't believe I ate the whole thing," he quipped.

The third time he was hospitalized was in September 1966, "once again for exhaustion and fatigue," for a period of three weeks. Mr. Eagleton was counseled by a psychiatrist and received shock treatments, which are used in cases of depression. He is just 42 now and in good physical shape, he says. "I still am an intense person, I still push very hard. But I pace myself a great deal better than I did in earlier years."

Mr. Eagleton is the sort of super-achiever who drives himself relentlessly toward the top. For such to drive themselves too hard occasionally isn't uncommon. But "psychiatrist" remains a dirty word in American politics, suggesting not the help of a specialist (such as Ann Landers is always recommending) but a scandal of some sort. In an age of big-city tensions, we still seem to insist upon the old small-town virtues in our politicians.

The fact that Mr. Eagleton had been hospitalized for nerves was no particular secret in Missouri politics, and had never been used against him in campaigns in the state. That ought to be the pattern in the Presidential race, too. For the question really isn't whether Mr. Eagleton is fit and stable to be Vice President—he is, on the record—but whether the American people prefer to have him or Spiro Agnew a heartbeat from the Presidency.

THE LOUISVILLE TIMES

Louisville, Ky., July 27, 1972

President Nixon diplomatically has told the people around him not to comment on Sen. Thomas Eagleton's revelations concerning his mental problems of several years ago. And Clark MacGregor, head of the Republican presidential campaign, has indicated that the senator's medical history should not be a campaign issue.

But that does not necessarily mean that in fact it will not be an issue. Nor does it mean, in our view, that it should not be decently but candidly discussed.

For most people, mental problems are and should be a private affair. But Eagleton is a public man. He is seeking a high public office, the vice presidency of the United States. If he achieves it, he will be only one mortal man away from the presidency and the most pressure-crowded office in the world.

The people have every right to all the available information on Eagleton's past troubles so they might make a reasonably informed judgment on how he might react to such pressure; if fate called upon him.

For that reason, we hope Eagleton will reverse the position he reportedly took Tuesday when he said he would not release the written reports of the two doctors who treated him. He said the medical histories were written in professional language, not for public consumption.

This is not, in our opinion, an acceptable argument. No doubt the medical reports are written in medical language incomprehensible to most of us. But there is no shortage of qualified physicians capable of taking the reports, once they are published, and interpreting them in terms the layman can understand.

In no other way, as far as we can see, can the public have final assurance that Eagleton's problems of the past were no more than he says they were: the simple result of overfatigue. In no other way can he put to rest the inevitable rumors, the existence of which he acknowledged, of possibly more sinister causes, including alcoholism.

Eagleton's candor now is particularly important for he was apparently less then completely candid with Sen. George McGovern. McGovern recalls having asked him before presenting him to the Democratic convention whether there were "any problems in his past that were significant or worth discussing at that time."

In saying "No" and thereby withholding information on mental breakdowns that required hospitalization and psychiatric treatment, Eagleton was not being candid.

We assume—certainly we have no information to the contrary—that whatever problems Eagleton had are far behind him and that he has, as he says, learned to pace himself to prevent the buildup of intolerable pressure. Moreover, he is not the first man in politics to have difficulties of that sort.

In the May, 1964, issue of *Good Housekeeping* Mrs. Barry Goldwater revealed that her husband suffered a couple of nervous breakdowns many years before after intensive work in connection with the family department store. Goldwater apparently was not hospitalized. The only therapy mentioned was rest — at Honolulu after the second incident.

And George Wallace, according to one biographer, was discharged from the Air Force after World War II with "10 per cent nervous disability." This presumably was service-connected, Wallace having flown as flight engineer in several bombing raids over Japan.

Besides, how many men in any field are totally, solidly stable at all times?

But it is Eagleton's case that is at issue now, and we believe he must make all the facts public. To do less would be to do a disservice to Senator McGovern, to his party, and, most important, to his country.

New York Post
New York, N.Y., July 26, 1972

No matter how much sympathy he deserves for fighting back against the private torments that led to his voluntary hospitalization on three occasions, the fact that stands out starkly in Sen. Eagleton's story is his avowed failure to tell Democratic nominee George McGovern the whole truth before he was designated for the Vice Presidency.

Whether McGovern would have been willing to choose him in the light of these disclosures can never be retroactively evaluated. Nor do we pass any medical judgment on Eagleton's contention that he has vanquished the personal problems that beset him. We must assume he is convinced that he has.

But the tragic reality is that his lack of candor in the period preceding his selection has cast fatal doubt on the credibility of his candidacy. His continuance on the ticket can only produce cruel, diversionary conflicts in a year when real issues should be sharply defined and debated.

At 42, Sen. Eagleton retains many chances to prove his capacity for high office. In this year of a great national decision, however, he has disqualified himself by his apparent act of concealment. In fairness to McGovern and to the many dedicated people who have enlisted under his banner, we believe that Eagleton should withdraw.

The San Juan Star
San Juan, P.R., July 27, 1972

Only the most rabid political partisan would relish the Gethsemane Sen. Thomas F. Eagleton, the Democratic vice presidential nominee, is going through.

We have the deepest sympathies.

But while recognizing the motes in all our eyes, this is not a case that can be viewed with the equanimity one might greet such revelations concerning the assemblyman, the garbage man or the school principal.

This is a health-background case involving a man who could become president of the United States.

Sen. Eagleton is supposed to be a bright fellow and is a cum laude graduate of Amherst and Harvard Law. He served as attorney general, lieutenant governor and United States senator from Missouri.

He supposedly knew what the score was and what game he was playing in.

Yet he consciously chose not to tell Sen. George S. McGovern before McGovern chose him as his running mate that in the past, while fatigued and under strain, Eagleton had to place himself in the hospital three times and twice underwent psychiatric care and shock treatment.

The "candor" of the health-background revelations, praised so highly by Sen. McGovern, came only after newspaper reporters were zeroing in on Eagleton health history, spurred on by many rumors. So, not much credit there.

Our psychiatrist friends tell us it is very possible for a man of Eagleton's makeup to function A-ok if he does learn to pace himself, as the Senator says he has learned to do, and has been doing, since 1966.

"If by fate or tragedy, I should succeed to the Presidency," he says, "I would pace myself."

Question: How does a President "pace himself" during something like the Cuban missile crisis?

As McGovern's right-hand man, Frank Mankiewicz, frankly put it: "It (the Eagleton affair) is not a plus."

And as Tom Eagleton himself must know now, there is no way his remaining on the Democratic ticket can help to elect George McGovern.

Arkansas Democrat
Little Rock, Ark., July 26, 1972

The sad revelation yesterday of Sen. Thomas Eagleton's emotional problems (hospitalized three different times for a total of two months) is more damaging to George McGovern than Eagleton.

The young senator from Missouri couldn't help being sick. But the Democratic Party's presidential nominee certainly didn't have to choose him as his running mate. And his face-saving comment that he didn't know about Eagleton's problems before he selected him and that it wouldn't have mattered if he had makes him appear even more ridiculous. Don't the Democrats have the right to expect their standard-bearer to be a little more careful? It's troubling to note that of the two men McGovern asked to be vice president, Ted Kennedy and Tom Eagleton, one has a history of panic and the other, instability.

As he says, Senator Eagleton may be completely cured, and we hope he is. But in such a complicated world as this, a man with his medical record shouldn't be only one heartbeat away from the presidency.

It's not as if McGovern didn't have time to check. Two weeks before the convention, Eagleton's name was being bandied about by McGovern's aides to the extent that the Washington Post's chief political writer interviewed him about his views on the vice presidency. Also, it's not as if McGovern didn't have other choices. Twenty-four names were on his list (including Wilbur Mills) when his aides started the selection process at breakfast in Miami Beach. They cut it to seven by 10:30 a.m., and the final choice was between Eagleton and Mayor Kevin White of Boston. At 3 p.m.—one hour before the deadline—McGovern decided to go with Eagleton.

His decision and the careless way he made it do not say much for McGovern's ability to lead this country.

BOSTON HERALD TRAVELER
Record American
Boston, Mass., July 28, 1972

With all due sympathy for Sen. Thomas F. Eagleton — and a lot of it has been earned by the distinguished public service of this talented and self-driven man — it seems all but incredible that he should continue to be the Democratic candidate for Vice President of the United States.

The crucial issue is not his dramatic admission that the stress of politics, on three occasions, caused him to seek psychiatric help. Many other talented and useful members of society have resorted to such mental aid, including electric shock treatment, just as routinely and beneficially as most of us resort to family doctors for physical assistance.

The really crucial issue is that Sen. Eagleton, in his bombshell press conference, blandly admitted that he failed to inform the Democratic nominee for President of his past when George McGovern asked him if it contained anything potentially damaging.

He said there was not and Sen. McGovern took him at his word. The fact is that both are certainly experienced enough to know that any shadow of mental illness — however temporary or subsequently cured — is or should be automatic grounds for disbarment to the second most important position in the nation.

Sen. McGovern says he accepts the claim of Sen. Eagleton that the latter's mental problems have been overcome and were not important enough to have been brought to his attention in the first place.

We do not buy that. We do not believe Sen. Eagleton would have got the designation if Sen. McGovern had known the whole story. And we do not believe that Sen. Eagleton has any moral justification whatever for having withheld the damaging truth from his leader.

In doing so he displayed a most serious lack of sound judgment and responsibility, hardly in keeping with his driving ambition. Sen. McGovern can continue to try to fudge this point, but it is the one absolutely inexcusable fact which no words can really obscure.

What also cannot be obscured, incidentally, is that Sen. McGovern failed to make the kind of detailed check on an all important appointment which should have been routine. He is at least partially responsible for the unexpected cross he now bears — and he will bear it so long as Sen. Eagleton fails to realize how totally he has disqualified himself.

Omaha World-Herald
Omaha, Neb., July 28, 1972

Let's assume that Tom Eagleton's mental health is sound and will remain sound.

There is another aspect of this astonishing episode which as we see it overrides the question of health. It is the record of deceit over 12 years which grows more damning as the story unfolds.

In 1960, 1962 and 1966 Eagleton did not tell the truth about the reason for his hospitalizations. The files of the St. Louis Post-Dispatch show that in each of these instances a physical ailment was given as the reason.

It is true that other politicians have misled the public about their health, but the fact that Eagleton's deception is not unique does not excuse deception.

* * *

The record shows that Eagleton has lived with his deception since 1960, and that he failed to tell Sen. McGovern of his psychiatric treatment when asked if there were anything of significance in his background that the presidential nominee should know.

The deception continued until this week when he told the story to Sen. McGovern and then to the press.

Some commentators have seen fit to praise Eagleton and McGovern for their alleged courage in making a public disclosure.

The fact is that the Knight Newspapers, Time magazine and other news gathering agencies were closing in on the Eagleton story and were about to publish it. The McGovern-Eagleton camp knew the story was going to break and tried to salvage as much face as possible by speaking out a few hours before the newspapers and magazines did.

* * *

Such action requires no courage nor does it deserve praise. It is an act of self-preservation.

We have some sympathy for Sen. McGovern in this episode despite the fact that he and his staff should have explored Eagleton's background before McGovern named him as running mate. It is a heavy burden for McGovern and a blow not wholly deserved.

We have no such sympathy for Sen. Eagleton. He practiced calculated deceit and is paying the consequences.

The Des Moines Register
Des Moines, Iowa, July 28, 1972

The disclosure that Senator Thomas Eagleton was hospitalized three times for mental upsets underscores the haphazard way vice-presidential candidates are chosen.

Eagleton became a serious contender for the nomination on the last day of the Democratic convention, apparently after others declined the post. A top aide to George McGovern said, "There wasn't time to run an FBI check." When Eagleton's name came up at a meeting of McGovern's staff, rumors were reported about drinking and medical problems. A few phone calls satisfied the staff man assigned to check them out that they were groundless.

McGovern's nomination did not come as a bolt from the blue. He emerged as a leading contender months before the convention. McGovern came to Miami Beach with far more delegates than any other candidate and was a clear favorite for the nomination, but the selection of running-mate was left to the last minute.

This is typical of the way both parties choose vice-presidential candidates. Richard Nixon's selection of Spiro Agnew as his 1968 running-mate a few hours before the convention ratified the choice stunned even Agnew. Presidential candidates who run for years for their party's nomination invariably delay the selection of a vice-presidential nominee and make the choice almost as an afterthought.

It's hard to view this as anything but a reflection of low regard for the office: When delegates to party conventions abdicate their responsibility and meekly rubber-stamp the choice of the presidential nominee, they declare in effect that the job isn't important, so why fuss? This attitude persists in the face of the historical fact that eight of the country's 37 presidents assumed the nation's highest office from the vice-presidency.

A convention that deliberated over the choice of vice-president would not necessarily pick a man without flaws, but negative features in a candidate's background are more likely to be revealed in a contest than when the candidate is hand-picked. If nothing else, democratic nomination by an open convention would give the vice-presidential candidate stature in his own right and make him the party's, rather than one man's, choice.

Both parties are talking extensively about reforming the political convention process. The talk and action to date have been directed almost exclusively to improving the selection of presidential candidates. The Eagleton incident is a reminder of the need to extend reform measures to include the way vice-presidents are chosen.

The Washington Post
Washington, D.C., July 27, 1972

It is a measure of this country's persistent myopia where the office of the vice presidency is concerned that, amid all the rejoicing over the manner in which our presidential nominating process is being reformed, most of us have managed to ignore the fact that vice presidential candidates are still chosen pretty much as usual: they spring full bloom from the brow of the presidential nominee—often as the result of frantic last-minute political calculations and often in the form of men little known to the nominee himself, let alone to the delegates who ratify his choice. In other words, while we tend to scrutinize our presidential candidates overtime, we tend to take our vice presidential candidates on faith. And subsequently, even as we tend to demand everything of a President, we tend to forgive everything in a vice president. This habit—which the nation has been indulging over the past four years—seems to rest on a durable capacity to put out of mind the single critical qualification for the vice presidential office, namely, fitness to take over the presidency. Three out of our last five Presidents, it is worth recalling, have come to power via the vice presidency, either upon the death of the incumbent or as a consequence of position and influence gained in the lesser office. One-third of all American Presidents served previously as vice president.

We record these thoughts by way of saying, first, that both President Nixon and Senator McGovern have engaged in the worst aspects of this process in the not dissimilar manner in which they have made their choices. That it is scarcely fair to the electorate goes without saying. That it is scarcely fair to the presidential candidate himself, or to the party or to the prospective vice presidential nominee became quite plain in the revelations made by Senator Eagleton in South Dakota Tuesday. We will get around, in time, to the implications of Mr. Nixon's choice of Mr. Agnew to run again—our views on the subject of his fitness for office are not the greatest secret in the land. But for now it seems more urgent and more apt to try to make sense of the meaning of Senator Eagleton's disclosures. That they are, in some respects, an almost natural consequence of the chaotic and thoughtless way in which vice presidential candidates are chosen, says nothing one way or the other about their gravity or their implications for the voters who must make a choice.

Senator Eagleton's disclosure in a post-nomination press conference that he had on three occasions since 1960 been voluntarily confined to hospital for treatment of disorders triggered by "nervous exhaustion" and involving shock treatment raises first a medical-psychiatric question which neither we nor other laymen can readily answer. It is the question of whether this particular history implies a condition that could or would recur in some fashion sufficient to inhibit him from acting well under the prospective pressures of high executive office—including the office of the presidency. One can easily overdo the "Fail Safe," dramatic aspects of the office, to be sure. And compassion as well as humility and sophistication in these matters further argue against taking the harsh and mindless view that a man who has experienced what he evidently has is automatically proven unequal to the strain. The point is that *we do not know* and that there is apparently no more information to be forthcoming, so that, at the very least, the valid question of his fitness has been raised—one for which there is no available answer.

The second question raised by the disclosures has an answer and an unhappy one at that. Did the senator, for whatever seemingly plausible reason, behave with remarkably bad judgment in failing to make these facts known to Senator McGovern before his selection was announced? We believe the only answer is, yes. Evidently, Senator Eagleton was sufficiently troubled by the potential impact of this information on the electorate to have—by his own account—lived for many years in fear of its revelation. And evidently too he and his wife discussed its relevance to his prospective choice as Senator McGovern's running mate before the choice was actually made. Yet, by the candidates' joint account, Senator Eagleton did not make any of this known when Senator McGovern asked whether there was anything in the record that could be dredged up to embarrass his candidacy. We do not think it speaks particularly highly of Senator McGovern's own judgment in this matter that he should so easily have said that had he known what he now knows it would not have altered his decision. But one must at least allow that the presidential candidate was responding to an accomplished fact and that he was very possibly operating in what he regarded as a no-choice situation. The choice he *should* have had, the decision he *should* have been free to make and to weigh with those in the party whom he consulted, was never available to him. It was made for him in Senator Eagleton's silence and in the apparent lassitude and indifference of some of Senator McGovern's staff aides who should have been doing a lot more checking of their own.

It seems to us beyond question that, taken together, the unanswerable question concerning Senator Eagleton's condition and the answerable question concerning his performance in this matter have created—and will continue to create—an enormous, probably crippling, burden for Senator McGovern's candidacy. By direct extension, it has created an equal burden for the party that nominated him. Except as that party acquiesced in the pell mell designation process that resulted in Senator Eagleton's nomination, it does not bear real responsibility for what has occurred. If there is to be a remedy, however, it must ultimately proceed from within the Democratic Party—and, in the last analysis, from Senator Eagleton. For it is our judgment that the burden imposed by the presence of Senator Eagleton on the ticket can only be removed by his withdrawal as a candidate.

The Burlington Free Press
Burlington, Vt., July 28, 1972

THE PUBLIC SHOULD keep in perspective the disclosure by Senator Thomas Eagleton that he was hospitalized three times between 1960 and 1966 for "nervous exhaustion and fatigue."

Eagleton, the Democratic Vice Presidential nominee, also disclosed that he had undergone psychiatric treatment, including electric shock therapy, on two of the three occasions.

The general response to these disclosures has been calm, a tribute to the good sense and understanding of most Americans. Unfortunately, there have been exceptions: One newspaper bannered a headline that Eagleton is a "mental case," which he clearly is not. And an unthinking campaign manager attempted to exploit the matter by reviving "rumors" about the health of other national candidates.

Eagleton demonstrated a great amount of courage by making the disclosures in the manner he did. He has gained our admiration.

We are somewhat surprised that the disclosures have raised such a commotion. The fact is that a lot of Americans — some estimates say 20 million or more — have sought psychiatric care, and there is nothing even remotely shameful about that. Experts tell us that almost all human beings, at some times in their lives, suffer periods of depression — some longer and more severe than others, of course.

Those of us who have not suffered from nervous exhaustion have no reason or excuse for pointing the finger at someone less fortunate: "There but for the grace of God go I."

Perhaps Eagleton should have informed Senator George McGovern, the Democratic Presidential nominee, of the medical history prior to the selection of a runningmate at Miami Beach. And perhaps some Republicans will seek to make political hay out of the Eagleton case by reminding voters, not so subtly, of the "extreme tensions and pressures" of high national office. But regardless of the mistakes made or contemplated, we strongly suggest that the Senator from Missouri is deserving of more compassion than is generally accorded political leaders in an election year.

If the public will keep this matter in perspective, it is possible that national attitudes toward Eagleton's type of illness will be changed, and the nation's mentality would be far healthier than it appears to be at the moment.

Whatever happens politically to Thomas Eagleton, he already has made a singular contribution to the betterment of our national life by his demonstration of courage this week. — F.B.S.

The Sun Reporter

San Francisco, Calif., July 29, 1972

Democratic Vice Presidential Nominee, Thomas F. Eagleton's failure to disclose to Democratic Presidential Nominee, Senator George McGovern, that he was hospitalized three times for "nervous exhaustion and fatigue", requiring electric shock therapy for depression (on two of those occasions), grievously destroys one of the great strengths of the McGovern-Eagleton ticket: its credibility. Three major issues will aid the Democrats in their struggle for the White House: the war in Vietnam, the current national economic crisis, and credibility, with honesty, in the executive branch of government.

We understand and sympathize with Eagleton on his reluctance to make his private medical affairs a part of the public domain, but the office of Vice President of the United States, one-third of whose occupants have succeeded to the presidency, is too important for personal considerations and the possibility of personal honor being given any degree of primacy consideration over the physical and mental well-being of candidates who aspire to such important high office. We do not propose here to discuss the medical pros-and-cons of a person, previously treated by electric shock therapy for some form of depression (the type and degree yet unknown), being chosen by the electorate for the office of vice president. The burdens of both the presidency and the vice presidency are awesome, and a considerate people on the basis of simple charity would not want to endanger the health of any vice president who had previously succumbed to the rigors of nervous exhaustion, fatigue, and depression. Moreover, the nation and McGovern have the right to assume that a person so afflicted would not permit the nation unknowingly to call him to such high office.

With President Nixon, Agnew, and spokesmen for the National Committee to Re-elect the President issuing statements to the effect that they will not make the health of Vice Presidential Nominee Thomas Eagleton a campaign issue, the stage is set for covert and sublingual waging of this campaign by merely mentioning such a denial once every day between now and Nov. 7.

The Democratic candidate for president, George McGovern, bears many awesome responsibilities in his endeavor to create a new constituency and to develop new priorities for the American electorate for the remaining third of the twentieth century. He does not need the added burden of a presidential running mate with a precarious health problem in the area of mental illness. The electorate should be expected to choose its president and vice president on the basis of the issues of war or peace, a government serving the many or the selected few, and the question of integrity and honor in the highest level of government; and the nation should vote for men found to be not only dedicated to these principles but possessed of both mental and physical health so as not to compromise their respective leadership roles in the difficult, challenging days ahead.

We urge Senator Thomas F. Eagleton to relinquish the vice presidential spot on the national Democratic ticket, to continue his service to the nation as the junior Senator from the State of Missouri to which he apparently has been able health-wise to successfully adjust, and to more adequately provide for his pursuit of the role of husband and father as well as a patriotic and honorable member of the Democratic Party.

ST. LOUIS POST-DISPATCH

St. Louis, Mo., July 31, 1972

To his credit, Senator McGovern has refrained from a hasty decision on whether Senator Eagleton should continue as his vice-presidential running mate. But just where Mr. McGovern stands is not so clear. As the public understands it, he has been telling Mr. Eagleton he wants him on the ticket and at the same time hinting to news reporters that he hopes he will quit.

This may be shrewd political maneuvering, if the public understanding is correct, but it is somewhat demeaning to Mr. McGovern and unfair to Mr. Eagleton. The Missouri Senator has responded to the attacks on him with skill and aplomb, and these attacks have included some of the most vicious (and contemptible) questioning by a few members of the news media in our experience. Mr. Eagleton has not lost his composure, nor even his sense of humor; we can think of no more severe test of his ability to withstand pressure.

Mr. Eagleton's public appearances in the last week have met with warm response. He has reason to believe he will be an asset to the ticket; indeed, he is probably the best campaigner of the top candidates of either party. There is evidently a widespread sympathy for the fact that prior to six years ago he received psychiatric treatment for nervous exhaustion; his record since that time has been one of good health.

There is justified criticism of the fact that Mr. Eagleton did not find a way to inform Senator McGovern of his past illnesses before he was selected as the vice-presidential candidate. But is that sufficient to bar him from the ticket? And if so, what does it say about Mr. McGovern? It would seem to say that he failed to make a thorough check into the background of the man he was asking to be his Vice President (and possible successor).

Actually, Mr. McGovern had no reason, from anything on the record, not to select Mr. Eagleton, and if Mr. Eagleton was nationally unknown at the time, his name is now a household word. That is an asset. But irrespective of Mr. Eagleton's assets, we think one can argue from the negative in favor of Mr. McGovern's keeping him on the ticket. That involves the choice of a replacement.

There are plenty of able Democrats available to step in should Mr. Eagleton be dropped, but the choice would be made, on Mr. McGovern's recommendation, by the Democratic National Committee. It would be an atmosphere of deals and smoke-filled rooms. Replacing Mr. Eagleton might be a blow to the ticket from which Mr. McGovern and his new running mate would have difficulty recovering. And would it not reflect on Mr. McGovern, as to his ability to make decisions and stick to them? Would it not risk a defection by intellectuals and young people, who lack medieval notions about nervous ailments and who regard Mr. McGovern as a man of compassion and high moral caliber?

It is not just a simple matter of "dumping" Mr. Eagleton and choosing a replacement. The decision makes demands on Mr. McGovern's integrity as well as his judgment. He is under the greatest pressure and he must analyze carefully his own prospects and those of his party. In the end he may feel that he must ask Mr. Eagleton to step down.

If it comes to that, we suppose there would be no practical alternative for Mr. Eagleton but to accept the decision. He cannot be ousted without his consent, but it would hardly be possible for him to continue if he and Mr. McGovern were in disagreement. The two men are to meet tonight, and we hope that if Mr. McGovern should be leaning toward dropping Mr. Eagleton he will delay his decision.

To our mind Mr. Eagleton's record of public service, his ability as a campaigner, the public response to him, and his fine performance in recent days commend him for the post to which he now aspires. If that is not clear to Mr. McGovern today, it should be before this week is up.

The Oregonian

Portland, Ore., August 1, 1972

Sen. Thomas F. Eagleton walked the last mile to his confrontation with Sen. George McGovern breathing determination to stay in the race for the vice presidency. He left the meeting a beaten man, cashiered by the presidential nominee he said he will continue to support in the name of Democratic Party unity.

It should not have happened. And nothing hereafter will restore the patina of courage and integrity which Sen. McGovern has sought to overlay his campaign. The nominee stands convicted by his own words of sacrificing his hastily chosen running mate on the altar of political expediency.

The only issue before the American people was whether or not Sen. Eagleton's history of psychiatric treatment in the 1960s raised an unacceptable risk to the national welfare and security should he be elected vice president.

Distinguished psychiatrists have said it would not. And Sen. McGovern himself said he was "fully satisfied" that Eagleton's "health is excellent." In the "joint" decision (a word hardly applicable), Sen. McGovern said, "health was not a factor."

Both men made it clear that the motivating factor was the damage to the McGovern campaign caused by the public interest in Sen. Eagleton's belated admission that he had entered the hospital on three occasions and had been given electric shock treatments on two of those occasions.

Sen. McGovern decided that his chance of being elected president would be improved by unloading the man he had chosen without adequate investigation to be his running mate, thus making Tom Eagleton of Missouri the first vice presidential nominee in history to be dumped.

Rather than improving his chance to be president, the decision may have destroyed his opportunity. If health was not a factor, then political expediency was the factor. Sen. McGovern's image is tarnished. He did not have the courage to carry on with a companion whose name became a "household word" overnight because of the disclosure of an old illness.

"Integrity," "credibility," "courage," and such self-glorifying words have been the hallmarks of Sen. McGovern's publicity campaign. What are the young voters and the not-so-young idealists to think now? There is nothing shameful about illness. Sen. McGovern could have made his stand on that. It was less than honorable not to do so.

ARGUS-LEADER
Sioux Falls, S.D., July 28, 1972

At the Miami Beach Democratic convention, George McGovern, the presidential nominee of his party, asked Thomas Eagleton if there were anything he should know about the latter's past that would have a bearing on his running for vice president.

Eagleton, a United States senator, told McGovern "no." In doing so, he misled McGovern and did him a grave disservice. McGovern made a grave error in not double-checking, despite Eagleton's assurance.

And at Miami Beach, the McGovern staff knew of some recurring rumors about Eagleton's health, but there was no time on that last frantic day of the convention to check them out. McGovern didn't learn of Eagleton's health problem until after the presidential nominee arrived in South Dakota.

This situation doesn't say much for McGovern's staff, which turned up problems with other potential candidates. And it leads to the question of whether No. 2 men on tickets should be decided upon and chosen in the kind of frenzied and limited time available such as was the case at Miami Beach.

In disclosing Eagleton's record of psychiatric care, both McGovern and Eagleton said they thought this was the best way to do it: to let the public know, because this is the day of open politics.

Yet, Eagleton has refused to release the medical records of his three hospital treatments for nervous exhaustion. So the openness of the disclosure of the senator from Missouri is open to considerable question. When he entered the hospitals at various times, his illnesses were described as something else in statements to the press.

McGovern, despite a present inclination to keep Eagleton on the ticket, could very well find himself asking for Eagleton's resignation. If he does not, the doubts created by Eagleton's illnesses could greatly reduce McGovern's chance of attaining the prize of the presidency.

In standing by Eagleton at Sylvan Lake this week, McGovern was considerate and kind. But he has a tough gut decision to make on Eagleton that goes to the heart of the matter: Could Eagleton, if he became president, stand the heat in the kitchen?

The answer is probably no, for a vice presidential candidate who says he's going to campaign six days and take Sundays off between now and November. Matters involving government have a way of happening overnight or on Sundays, as well as weekdays.

Under the circumstances, it will be more surprising if Eagleton stays on the ticket, than if he leaves. The problem for George McGovern is one that he shouldn't have had, and didn't deserve, in his achievement of winning his party's nomination.

The New York Times
New York, N.Y., July 28, 1972

The issues that should concern American voters in the Presidential election are now obscured by the belated revelation of Senator Eagleton, the Democratic nominee for Vice President, that he was three times hospitalized for nervous exhaustion and depression.

We believe that the only way the campaign can be turned back into a true test of the programs and leadership qualifications of President Nixon and his Democratic rival, Senator McGovern, is through the voluntary withdrawal of Senator Eagleton from the McGovern ticket.

Unquestionably, Mr. Eagleton has shown no incapacity for performing in public office—and performing well. But the pressures he has experienced as Attorney General of Missouri, as Lieutenant Governor of that state and as a United States Senator are in no way comparable to the fearful pressures of the Presidency. And it is as a potential President that Mr. Eagleton must now be regarded.

It is possible, as Senator McGovern has said, that "there is no one sounder in body, mind and spirit" than his running mate. But the regrettable fact is that the state of scientific knowledge in the field of mental illness is not such that anyone can speak with certainty on such matters. That would be true even if Senator Eagleton were willing to permit release of his full medical history.

None of this raises any question about Mr. Eagleton's ability to continue his successful career in the Senate, where he is highly regarded, or in any other endeavor that would allow him to "pace" himself, as he says he has learned to do. But unfortunately no President since Calvin Coolidge has enjoyed the luxury of a world geared to so personal a need. Every President seeks relaxation, on a beach or a boat or a golf course, when opportunity presents itself; but there can be no flight from the demands of the office when decisions of fateful importance need making—and the severity and duration of these periods of maximum tension are not subject to control.

It is painfully evident that, in a manner all too familiar in the designation of Vice-Presidential candidates by both major parties, little attention was given by Senator McGovern to learning all he should have known about his running-mate's strengths and weaknesses in the only terms that are of genuine importance to the country—his readiness to take on the duties of President. It is no less evident that Senator Eagleton was himself grievously at fault in not revealing his medical history to Mr. McGovern when the nomination was first offered.

There is clear merit to the suggestion that all nominees for President and Vice President be required to make detailed disclosure about their health well before Election Day. But, whatever happens on that proposal, it would be a helpful contribution not only to the McGovern candidacy but to the health of the American political process for Senator Eagleton to retire from the field and permit the Presidential contest to be decided wholly on the issues.

© 1972 by The New York Times Company. Reprinted by permission.

THE ATLANTA CONSTITUTION
Atlanta, Ga., July 29, 1972

Sen. Thomas Eagleton should resign promptly from the Democratic ticket.

The Democratic National Committee should choose another candidate who is compatible with the views of Presidential nominee George McGovern

Then this Presidential campaign should proceed on the issues, not on the alleged frailties of one candidate.

McGovern has stood up like a man in defending Eagleton. He has won respect by not bowing to the pressures to dump the Missouri senator.

Eagleton has taken a hard knock. He thought he had lived down his mental problems. He considered himself recovered. It is clear the public does not agree.

This nation has tried to teach itself about mental illness. It has tried to understand that treatment for mental illness is as possible as for physical ailments. Sometimes it reaches that level.

A psychiatrist has put this in focus for us: "A history of recurrent depression does not preclude brilliant accomplishment or success. I would not hesitate to engage the services of an individual of demonstrated capacity despite such a history. I would read his books, listen to his music, enlist him to teach me or my children, or accept him as my physician or attorney... However, to positions in which reliability is a major factor, he brings a significant degree of risk."

Which is another way of saying that Eagleton possesses all the possibilities of being an excellent senator or Cabinet officer. He also has talents in those areas which brought him to the attention of McGovern and the nation.

This nation is not, however, so poor in administrative talent that it must take a risk of this magnitude.

Compassion compels the nation to wish Eagleton well.

Necessity requires him to withdraw from the vice presidential candidacy.

St. Louis Globe-Democrat
St. Louis, Mo., August 1, 1972

Many individuals interested in the political scene have been suspicious, or convinced, as far back as Senator George S. McGovern's announcement that he was seeking the Democratic presidential nomination that the senator is less than candid and verges on hypocrisy.

These early conclusions were based on McGovern's vacillation respecting his campaign pledges.

Since the days immediately preceding the Democratic Convention in Miami Beach, followed by the convention proceedings and culminating now in Senator McGovern's callous, devious and autocratic firing of Sen. Thomas F. Eagleton as the vice presidential candidate, even a casual political observer must conclude that McGovern is a grievous threat to the nation and the Democratic Party.

There is considerable doubt that McGovern has the authority to circumvent the will of the convention and capriciously, arbitrarily dismiss Senator Eagleton.

☆ ☆ ☆

Except for mindless Democratic Party lackeys and a few representatives of the left-wing urban press in America there has been no evidence of a widespread demand for Senator Eagleton's removal, either by the public or responsible Democratic party leadership.

On the contrary, polls among citizens throughout the country produced a heavy majority in favor of Senator Eagleton's retention as the vice presidential candidate, even though a significant number of those questioned believed Senator Eagleton had erred in not making his medical history known to McGovern when he was notified of his selection.

☆ ☆ ☆

Senator McGovern's sinister, cowardly and lying tactics in maneuvering to bring about Eagleton's removal from the ticket prove beyond question McGovern cannot be trusted to be the President of the United States.

When the news of Senator Eagleton's medical history broke, Senator McGovern announced his "1000 per cent support" for Senator Eagleton. Subsequently, the presidential nominee advised Senator Eagleton repeatedly, in private, that he supported Senator Eagleton.

At the same time, at his vacation retreat in Custer, South Dakota, when Senator McGovern was assuring Senator Eagleton of his support, Senator McGovern visited the dining room occupied by the media. There he talked at length with several representatives of television news staffs and the urban press, letting them know in unmistakable language that he was preparing to remove the Missouri Senator from the vice presidential spot.

Such treacherous and sneaky tactics are not the mark of a man who can be trusted to be the President of the United States.

How can the voters of America rely on the moral judgment of an individual of this caliber when he is confronted with decisions affecting the welfare of the nation?

It is evident that Senator Eagleton has recovered from his illness, but there is serious doubt that Senator McGovern has recovered from his.

The McGovern credibility, which he embroidered with his gaudy "new politics" to lure young dedicates to his banner of pseudo idealism, has been smashed to smithereens.

His conduct in the Eagleton issue not only laid bare a lack of public honesty and political guts, it showed him as a blatant opportunist, who would dump his own choice for running mate in the interests of bald expediency.

It seems clear one reason, perhaps the chief reason, McGovern spited Eagleton was because he had been advised, or believed, he could not get money for his campaign chest from what party angels are left — unless he made Senator Eagleton quit.

☆ ☆ ☆

The low moral values which motivate the presidential nominee have been sharply pointed up by St. Louis' Collector of Revenue John K. Travers, who commented that if McGovern could tolerate the "unpleasant events" surrounding Senator Edward Kennedy — his first choice as a running mate — then his actions toward Eagleton "are totally unjustified."

Most citizens recognize the despicably irrational resolution concerning the Missourian's health.

Most Americans believe that individuals who prove by subsequent conduct that they have recovered from such health difficulties as Senator Eagleton experienced in the past should be admired for their courage and strength and accepted as productive citizens.

McGovern's actions in fact rule that any citizen who has a misfortune in health should be forever barred from productive life in high office.

This is absurd and a reflection on every American who has had the fortitude to redeem himself from whatever previous misfortune he might have experienced. Such a conclusion is an affront to a high percentage of Americans who have had similar experiences.

Senator McGovern's phony facade should become apparent now even to the disenchanted youth and left-wing militants in the Democratic party who were beguiled into believing that Senator McGovern conducted an open convention.

☆ ☆ ☆

Nothing could be further from the truth. Senator McGovern's tactics in controlling the convention were successful only because of the naivete of the inexperienced delegates who were so determined to change the party structure.

We agree that Senator Eagleton displayed great loyalty to the Democratic party in succumbing to the presidential nominee's dictates, but we do not accept the conclusion that McGovern's actions were in the best interest of the Democratic party or the two-party system or in the interest of the nation.

We are certain that we join with millions of Americans in praying that the distress brought so viciously on Senator Eagleton will not impair his health or his future.

Perhaps it may be all for the best, since Senator Eagleton will not be part of a crushing defeat looming for the national Democratic ticket in November.

Chicago Tribune
Chicago, Ill., August 2, 1972

In the name of political expediency, Sen. Thomas F. Eagleton has been thrown to the wolves. Sen. George McGovern's "1,000 per cent" support of his choice for the Vice Presidency has dwindled to zero. Thus ends an episode unprecedented in American Presidential politics, an episode marked by amateurish bumbling, cynicism, bad judgment, and deceit — in all respects a tragedy of errors.

If anyone is entitled to sympathy in all this, it is Mr. Eagleton himself. It remains an open question whether his medical past was cause to disqualify him for high office, but he felt it was not. He claimed a substantial support for his position from an enlightened American public and pleaded for the chance to vindicate himself at the polls.

This was denied him. He has been thru a grueling political wringer and his career is in something of a shambles, but he has emerged as a good sport about it.

While one feels sympathy for him, he is not to be absolved from blame. He was so driven by political ambition that, rather than dealing openly with his medical problems [as Sen. Harold Hughes of Iowa dealt with his alcoholism], he took pains to hide them for more than a decade. He hid them when it became clear he had a chance for the Vice Presidential nomination and after he had been selected. When they were forced out into the open, he attempted to dismiss them as nothing more than a broken leg [which one does not normally try to conceal].

There can be no sympathy for the man who is most responsible for the Eagleton affair — George McGovern. He selected Mr. Eagleton with only a cursory, last-minute check of his background after Sen. Kennedy and others refused to join the ticket. When he learned of Mr. Eagleton's psychiatric treatment, he kept quiet about it until confronted by newspaper correspondents responsibly seeking confirmation of their story. Instead of granting that confirmation, Mr. McGovern tried to get the whole thing over with in a quick news conference.

He promised Mr. Eagleton his unqualified support, but then backed down in the face of pressure from campaign fund raisers and his mentors in the Eastern liberal press. Rather than openly demanding Mr. Eagleton's resignation then, he surreptitiously dropped hints to reporters of his displeasure and let such operatives as Mrs. Jean Westwood, national Democratic chairman, do his dirty work for him.

The guilt is to be shared by his staff: by Frank Mankiewicz, who said: "This word 'shock.' Boy, that's a tough word for the public," and then did nothing; by Gary Hart, who gave his overwhelming approval to Mr. Eagleton; and by Gordon Weil, whose job it was to check out the rumors concerning Mr. Eagleton's past. There is discredit also for the editorialists who might be expected to have a modern, enlightened attitude toward mental illness but instead called on Mr. McGovern to drop Mr. Eagleton in a ruthless display of political pragmatism.

But Mr. McGovern was the man in charge, the man who made the final decision. He is the man who would be President.

Mr. McGovern, his staff, and the liberal press have rationalized their actions as necessary to return the campaign to "a discussion of issues," not personalities. Their obvious hope is that everything will be forgotten. It won't. The Eagleton affair is a blot on the record and an issue which will dog them into November, not because of Mr. Eagleton's health but because of their own failure to deal with the problem responsibly.

The Charleston Gazette
Charleston, W. Va., July 29, 1972

It is difficult to imagine anyone not being thoroughly sympathetic to Sen. George McGovern and his Democratic vice presidential running mate, Sen. Thomas F. Eagleton of Missouri, in the dilemma in which they now find themselves.

In mid-July, when Eagleton was nominated, he appeared as a bright new personality on the national political scene — a young (42) man who had risen swiftly to a position of respect in the U.S. Senate, an attractive man who knew the issues and who demonstrated a remarkable ability to articulate them.

Then, on last Tuesday, Eagleton himself made the disclosure that could bring his political world tumbling around him: On three different occasions, in 1960, 1964 and 1966, he voluntarily submitted to hospitalization for nervous exhaustion; he was treated by a psychiatrist and underwent electric shock treatments on two of the occasions, but "for the past six years since 1966 I have experienced good, sound, solid health."

Sen. McGovern said promptly that "I wouldn't have hesitated one minute" in choosing Eagleton anyway, "if I had known everything Sen. Eagleton has said here today."

Other political leaders of both parties rallied to Eagleton's defense. Sen. Barry Goldwater, the 1964 Republican presidential nominee, summed up the sentiment in these words: "Eagleton, by his courageous performance, has indicated the truth of his claim that his health is now 'solid and sound,' both for the fall campaign and for the possibility of serving as vice president."

The American Psychiatric Assn., without direct reference to Eagleton, said the judgment of a person who suffered mental depression would be completely restored following recovery from the illness. The APA added that countless thousands have resumed normal activities after successful treatment for mental depression by various methods, including electroshock.

The Gazette contacted three prominent psychiatrists, and their evaluation is the same: Eagleton should be a stronger person as a result of his therapeutic experience; it is common for people suffering from nervous exhaustion and depression, including those treated by electroshock, to return to a fully normal and productive life in their professions or occupations, with no recurrence of the illness; on the basis of what they know of Eagleton's health history from the news media, this would give them no hesitancy about voting for him.

The decision for McGovern and Eagleton, therefore, is strictly a political one. They have to decide whether this could cost them the election.

Voters who think the Eagleton revelation is going to cost McGovern the election should ask themselves if it has changed their vote. And if it hasn't, why do they assume it has or will change any American's vote?

DAYTON DAILY NEWS
Dayton, Ohio, July 29, 1972

As they have been agonizing days for Sen. Thomas Eagleton, these last few have been agonizing for the nation, too. It has had to begin deciding what it feels and thinks, what it really feels and thinks, about a sinuous issue. One of the sternest disciplines of a democracy is that, at such moments, it won't let its people off the hook. Voters can weigh competing advice and scout opposing directions, but finally even the plainest voter must turn to himself for the answer.

Partisan calculations aside, there is no compelling reason for Sen. Eagleton to resign from the ticket.

He is not the most impressive of candidates. Sen. George McGovern had better men and women available to him even after he had received the polite regrets of the obvious choices. And Sen. Eagleton must be severely faulted for failing to tell the presidential nominee of his medical history. He was asked, and Sen. Eagleton's explanation that the matter didn't occur to him is not convincing. He has conceded that rumors about it have harried his career, something that doesn't slip a politician's mind. Like rivals at a bargain counter, Sen. Eagleton's ambition apparently elbowed his good judgment aside.

But that said, what remains to make a case against the vice presidential nominee?

Even his political opponents are quick to grant that Sen. Eagleton has been an able, conscientious and decent-minded legislator. He wagered his ambition on doing a careful, thoughtful job, rather than on handy expediencies. A comparison is u n a v o i d a b l e: Vice President Agnew takes his pleasures from playing the political game usually to demean and often to hurt people, like a thug tackle on a slightly disreputable football team.

Sen. Eagleton's medical history is a legitimate public concern. His lapses into depression do not seem to have been acute, however, although neither were they merely post-campaign blues. That the senator sought psychiatric treatment is an indication of strength. Persons with shallower self-knowledge and less real confidence would try to brazen the matter through, forcing up a good front without actually solving the problem.

Sen. Eagleton says he has solved the problem, and there is no reason to dispute that. He has been a vigorous public official for the last six years. Some informal statute of limitations should apply. A man is well who steadily acts well; there is really no other criterion.

Whether psychiatry is an evil totem to the electorate is a matter of political calculation rather than of justice. The decision will be a difficult one, and probably a close one, for Sen. McGovern. It will be less to his benefit but more to his credit if Sen. McGovern chooses justice.

The Kansas City Times
Kansas City, Mo., August 8, 1972

Thomas F. Eagleton has emerged from his week of trauma as a man to be admired, a man who held up calmly and confidently under extreme personal and political pressure, and then bowed gracefully to the harsh decision of his running mate. We cannot say the same for George McGovern.

That, too, is a harsh judgment, yet one that from our point of view is entirely justified. Senator McGovern quite obviously had been traveling an uphill road to the White House; now he is climbing a mountain. Whether he can make it remains to be seen. His performance in handling the Eagleton case gives little reassurance to Democrats that he can.

McGovern is a political man and, perhaps inevitably, he made a purely political decision. He was the one, or so it seems, who bowed to the pressures of the moment. In seven days he moved from a position of "1,000 per cent support" for Tom Eagleton to the decision that he must go, a fact that hardly speaks for McGovern's candor and decisiveness. This in spite of the way in which the Missouri senator had performed during that period. And in spite of the fact that, by McGovern's own admission, he had talked to three of Eagleton's doctors, and that they felt he had made a full recovery from what had been diagnosed as depression.

But health, McGovern said, was not a factor. He pinned his case for dumping his own vice-presidential choice on the assumption that Eagleton's past medical history would continue to divert attention from the national issues that needed to be discussed. That is the excuse given for moving from total support to abandonment and it is an excuse that seems to insult the intelligence of the American voters. McGovern appeared to be saying that as a people we lack the sophistication and the maturity to make rational judgments on both personalities and issues, that we have failed to reach the point where a medical history such as Tom Eagleton's is not an indelible mark on a person's record. And he further seemed to be saying—although he would reject the contention—that a medical record of this type, involving psychiatric treatment, precludes the possibility of a man seeking such high office. At least the implication was there.

At any rate, the decision has been made, and our sympathy and understanding go out to Senator Eagleton. We see no possible reason why this unfortunate week should foreclose a future public career. His past service, his performance the last several days and his obvious ability as a public man hold high hopes for such a continuing career. His error in this whole matter was in failing to inform Senator McGovern, in advance of the nomination, of his medical history, although Eagleton had assumed as, we imagine, do many Americans, that curing such a mental condition is very much like healing a broken arm.

But that, McGovern has told us, was not the focal point for decision. The presidential candidate will now proceed to put a new show on the road and, under the circumstances, it will be no easy task.

George McGovern, it seems to us, has fallen in the estimation of many Americans who had been willing to hear him out as an alternative to Richard Nixon.

THE WALL STREET JOURNAL.

New York, N.Y., August 2, 1972

Senator McGovern has in effect admitted that he came up with an astonishing blunder in the most important single decision he has faced in public life. Having set things right by securing his running-mate's withdrawal, he now asks to be President of the United States.

Coming as it does atop the air of otherworldliness that has attended the McGovern candidacy, the blunder raises questions not only about the man but more profoundly about the impulses that have made him a paramount figure on the American scene. The McGovern supporters got the kind of candidate they asked for, all heart and good intentions. By now they are learning that in the real world much more is demanded. Perhaps they are even starting to suspect that in picking a President there may be other qualifications that are even more important.

All of us make mistakes, of course, and Senator McGovern can offer excuses that would be perfectly adequate in most contexts. He was the victim of a mammoth lapse by Senator Eagleton, who assured a McGovern aide he had no skeletons in his closet though he had been hospitalized and received shock treatment for nervous illness. Senator McGovern was also the victim of the haste and pressure that typically surround vice-presidential decisions.

But not all of us ask to be President, and these excuses are precisely the type a President cannot offer. He must bear the ultimate responsibility for his decisions and his staff work; and the details of the case—with Senator McGovern talking to Senator Eagleton for 45 seconds and aides asking about skeletons only after the decision was made —do not exactly leave the presidential candidate fully exonerated. And whatever the deficiencies of the way Vice Presidents are chosen, it has served other candidates since the advent of the convention system in 1832 without anyone else having to withdraw his choice.

A breakdown in staff work, even on so important a decision, would not seem nearly so significant if it were a more-or-less isolated incident; after all, President Nixon had his Carswell case. But Mr. McGovern has become something of an expert in withdrawals. Prior to withdrawing his running-mate, he withdrew his income maintenance plan, which we are told is being reworked, and his tax reform proposals, which have given way to Wilbur Mills' now-you-see-it-now-you-don't approach.

The typical pattern seems to be one of the Senator discovering the world is a more complicated place than he thought it was. On previous matters we have been told that the "direction" is right and the trouble is merely with "details." Of course the income-maintenance plan can be made to add up; a new vice-presidential nominee can be found, and so on. But what plausible reason is there to believe the directions themselves have been treated with any greater realism? If we abjectly withdraw from Vietnam, for example, how realistic is it to expect to maintain a credible commitment to Israel, even by assuring the Israelis we are 1,000% behind them?

This is a question that should be put not only to the Senator, but to his erstwhile supporters. Many former supporters, at least to judge by the columnists in the press, have been turned against him by the Eagleton episode, and particularly by Mr. McGovern's indecisiveness in dealing with it. But in a real sense, these supporters have created a candidate in their own image.

If enough people in the nation want a candidate who is above all "candid" or "honest" or "trustworthy" as these people define those terms, the political system will obligingly supply a candidate who purports to fulfill their desires. But if the desires are defined in a way that can be met only by monkish isolation from the complexities of the real world, there is going to be trouble when their candidate encounters those complexities.

For in fact, public issues are seldom black-and-white, seldom matters of "honesty" or even "candor." Those who suggest issues can be resolved in those terms simply do not understand reality. This is not always bad; there is a place in the world for Saints who push aside reality and set unblemished moral examples. But a President needs above all the ability to deal with complexity and ambiguity. Those who demand that a President be a Saint as well are simply asking too much.

HOUSTON CHRONICLE

Houston, Tex., August 2, 1972

The Tom Eagleton affair adds up to a severe loss to the Democratic Party.

The loss was compounded by the indecisiveness exhibited by Sen. George McGovern before he finally asked Sen. Eagleton to step down as his vice-presidential running mate.

When the Democratic National Convention ended, McGovern faced the task of pulling a divided party together behind his leadership as the presidential nominee. McGovern and his staff knew they had little time to accomplish this task. Working in their favor was some degree of momentum generated at the convention by the massive news coverage and the enthusiasm of McGovern's supporters.

The issue of Sen. Eagleton's health brought to a halt McGovern's unity efforts and even caused divisiveness among some of his stalwart supporters. And any momemtum gained from the convention has vanished. What good now are pictures of McGovern and Eagleton waving from that high, blue rostrum?

Instead of working on campaign issues, McGovern and his staff have been entangled with the health issue since July 25 when Eagleton revealed he had been hospitalized three times for psychiatric treatment.

Instead of Vietnam, the economy, employment and defense spending being discussed, the vice-presidential candidate has occupied center stage. McGovern was right when he said rather plaintively that the medical issue clouded all others.

McGovern's own indecision magnified his problem. Eagleton, when he first disclosed his history of mental illness to McGovern, offered to withdraw. This was the course urged by McGovern's advisers. Instead, McGovern chose to announce his 1000 percent support for Eagleton, then over a week's time progressively withdraw that support until he had to make a different decision and tell Eagleton that he wanted another name on the ticket. If made a week earlier, that decision would have eased the pressures on Eagleton, who handled himself well considering the circumstances, and would have put the party back on the campaign trail sooner.

Now, McGovern and his staff must come up with another name. McGovern said he will be "very cautious and very careful." But serious damage to the party's chances have already been done. Error compounded by error.

The Saginaw News

Saginaw, Mich., August 3, 1972

To what extent the Thomas Eagleton affair has further eroded public confidence in the democratic (small "d") process in this country, there is no way to measure. That is something for future historians to brood over.

Turning to the realities of the present, however, this much is certain: Sen. George McGovern is going to have his hands full trying to unseat Richard M. Nixon as President. Given the current political climate in this country, it is doubtful that he could have come close with Sen. Eagleton staying on the Democratic national ticket as his vice presidential running mate.

That problem, of course, no longer exists. Sen. Eagleton has resigned from the ticket in the aftermath of revelations that he had three times been treated for nervous exhaustion and periods of mental depression—twice receiving shock therapy. That is fact. Allegations that the young Missouri senator also had a drinking-driving problem are unfounded and deserve to be discounted. Faith is partially restored that Washington columnist Jack Anderson, who added this bit of agony to an agonizing week for Sen. Eagleton, has retracted his statements and apologized for jumping the gun without conclusive evidence in hand.

Thus, for the moment at least, an unprecedented and by all odds one of the saddest and most traumatic episodes in American political history has ended. It has ended the only way that it could. A correct course of action has been followed.

This may sound heartless and there will be those who disagree. There is already disagreement among various factions of the Democratic party, Anderson's error of judgment aside, over the dumping of Eagleton. They are those who believe Eagleton has been pilloried on the altar of political expediency.

They can go beyond that, too, by arguing persuasively that Sen. Eagleton's past ailments pale by comparison when measured against any number of social misfits and assorted poor characters who have been sent to high public office.

It is not quite that simple. In light of today's realities it is incumbent that major political parties present top of the ticket candidates with impeccable personal credentials. As we have seen in this lamentable case, the public has become far more discerning through a more discerning press.

It is no disgrace to be a highly-motivated individual with high-energy, high-devotion attitudes toward the job—be it in public service or private employment. Many individuals are. It is no disgrace to come apart at the seams as the price for that drive.

Where Sen. Eagleton made his mistake was in not revealing this health background information to Sen. McGovern when the Democratic presidential nominee had chosen him and asked if there was anything in his past which might prove troublesome later.

In Failing to do this, Sen. Eagleton made a serious error as subsequent revelations have demonstrated. As a candidate for office only a heartbeat away from the presidency, he became a liability to the ticket—not a help as he insisted.

In this Sen. McGovern himself does not escape blameless or without additional harm to his cause. In the eyes of many he now looks much like John Mitchell as a selector of candidates. Not too thorough. Correctly, however, he just as Sen. Eagleton, had to come to the pragmatic moment of truth. For Eagleton to have stayed on the ticket would have diverted public attention from the campaign issues—and likely would have diluted it as well.

As it is, the McGovern campaign now has additional yardage to make up. Any man without a sense of compassion toward Sen. Eagleton is without compassion. But we don't recall when we've seen the party both men represent with a greater stockpile of problems with the voters out there just ahead in November.

Still, it is one thing to make an error in judgment and blunder forward in stubborn refusal to yield to the reasoned judgment of others. Painful though it has been for both men, Sens. McGovern and Eagleton have done the far better thing regardless of the eventual outcome.

St. Louis Post-Dispatch

St. Louis, Mo., August 2, 1972

Senator McGovern and his staff have met the first crisis of their campaign, the disclosure of Senator Eagleton's past illness, and their performance indicates that at the moment there are some serious problems confronting the Democratic ticket, whoever the new running mate may be. These troubles have nothing to do with the decision to drop Mr. Eagleton, which we believe to be a serious and perhaps disastrous mistake. Rather, they pertain to those transcendent issues on which the voters are likely to make up their minds one way or the other on the Senator from South Dakota.

Foremost in significance, in our opinion, in the way Mr. McGovern handled, or mishandled, the Eagleton affair was what it appeared to say about his quality of leadership. And we include here the control which Mr. McGovern apparently either was unable or unwilling to exercise over his staff, which went about assiduously undermining Mr. Eagleton's position at the very moment that Mr. McGovern was publicly proclaiming support for the Missourian.

One clear measure of leadership is the willingness of the commander if not to protect his subordinates then at least to share their rigors. In this respect, Mr. McGovern did little for his image by cooling it in the hills of South Dakota while the wolves were relentlessly snapping at his partner. A leader who does not offer loyalty is unlikely to receive it in his time of need.

Then there is the matter of conduct under pressure. Mr. Eagleton performed with grace; Mr. McGovern came off as an intimidated man. As one whose political ambitions were so thoroughly discounted by the media less than a year ago, Mr. McGovern more than any person in public life ought to realize that the press can be wrong in its assessment of political "realities." Yet when several eastern newspapers said Mr. Eagleton's candidacy was untenable and demanded his withdrawal, Mr. McGovern hastily sacrificed his man. The action may have left open the possibility of certain editorial endorsements later on, but the country may well wonder at what point expediency becomes incompatible with principle.

Other questions come to mind. Mr. McGovern has consistently stressed candor and honesty as a theme in his campaign. What will he answer when critics say, "Yes, but when the chips were down see how he rewarded these qualities"? How can the grassroots populist, who proclaims "complete faith in the fairness of the American people," explain himself when by every indication there was overwhelming public support for Mr. Eagleton?

The last issue, too, may reveal a fundamental although not necessarily irreparable weakness in the McGovern campaign. The McGovern organization was superb in capturing the nomination, but the skills which achieved that end—building local organizations, mastering party procedures, packing countless caucuses where delegates were selected—may not be totally sufficient unto themselves when it comes to winning a national election. Mr. McGovern's delegates were committed to him by law, but the voters who selected the delegates are not. The Eagleton experience suggests that the McGovern organization may be underrating the need to keep current with the public's mood.

It is possible that Mr. McGovern, a modest and decent man, has been overwhelmed with the fact of his nomination. If so, he had better recover his poise in a hurry and his staff had better begin looking at realities. Perhaps he can salvage something constructive from the wreckage caused by his callous dumping of Mr. Eagleton. There is not too much time.

Campaign '72:
DALEY AGREES TO SUPPORT McGOVERN; MEANY'S AFL-CIO VOTES NEUTRALITY

Chicago Mayor Richard J. Daley said at a news conference July 17 that he "will support every candidate on the Democratic ticket, federal, state and county" as he had always done in the past. Daley's statement, viewed as an endorsement of the presidential candidacy of Sen. George McGovern (S.D.), did not specify that his organization would take an active role in working for the party's national ticket. Daley's relations with McGovern had been strained since he and 58 other Chicago delegates were unseated by pro-McGovern forces at the Democratic National Convention [See pp. 854–863].

Sen. McGovern was unsuccessful in his attempt to gain the support of organized labor's top leadership. On July 19 the Executive Council of the AFL-CIO voted for the first time in its 17-year history not to endorse the Democratic presidential ticket. The 27–3 vote to remain neutral reflected the wishes of President George Meany, who said afterward that the vote represented a "showdown with the new politics" made necessary when "a small elite of suburban types and students took over the apparatus of the Democratic Party."

The effect of the council's vote was to deny the 13.5-million-member federation's campaign contributions, estimated in 1968 at $10 million, to either presidential candidate and to deprive both parties of the vote-getting services of its Committee On Political Education (COPE). The council's vote of neutrality did not apply to "the election of our friends" in congressional races, or prevent individual unions within the AFL-CIO from endorsing a presidential candidate. (There were already strong indications that at least four large affiliated unions would announce their support for McGovern. Meanwhile, one of the largest unions not affiliated with the federation, the International Brotherhood of Teamsters, had voted July 17 to endorse President Nixon's candidacy [See also pp. 955–959].)

THE KANSAS CITY STAR
Kansas City, Mo., July 19, 1972

Mayor Richard J. Daley, still simmering over his role as a nonperson at the recent Democratic festivities in Florida, has broken his silence to announce his support for "every candidate on the Democratic ticket—federal, state and local." In his unrestrained enthusiasm, the mayor forgot to mention the name of the man who heads that ticket. Indeed, about all the Chicago political chief said, after reading a 102-word statement, was that the statement spoke for itself.

The performance was typically Daley, totally predictable and possibly exaggerated in its importance. For while Senator McGovern obviously wanted the support of the mayor's organization, it is by no means clear what that support will mean in November. And less clear what Daley himself wants it to mean. Certainly the mayor, publicly embarrassed at Miami Beach and previously a loser in the two most important state races in the March primary, cannot offer the 1972 ticket what he once could offer—say, a John F. Kennedy. His backing in Cook County gave the 1960 Democratic ticket the state of Illinois and the keys to the White House.

But 1960 is not 1972, and there is little chance that Daley can deliver in Chicago as he delivered then. Or that, deep down inside, he really wants to. The question is not the lip-service support expressed in a statement (that spoke for itself), but the precinct energy and dollars that the mayor will invest. The question is not whether Daley has made his final peace with McGovern (which is improbable considering, for example, their different viewpoints on the war, on law and order and other issues), but whether Daley and his people will embrace the McGovern Democrats of Cook County and Illinois. That seems even more improbable.

All of which seems to leave the national ticket with something less than high hopes in Illinois. If Senator McGovern is counting on Daley to flex his muscles vigorously in the manner of the old Daley, he had better count again. The senator can read statements, too, and as Mayor Daley said, the statement spoke for itself.

It didn't speak. It whispered.

Chicago Tribune
Chicago, Ill., July 18, 1972

Ending his long, self-imposed exile, Mayor Daley has stepped back into the public eye and said the obvious: "I am a Democrat. I will support every candidate on the Democratic ticket, federal, state, or local."

If the backers of Sen. George McGovern think this means they have it made, that Mr. Daley will now march off arm in arm with Ald. William Singer, they're dreaming.

We're back in the real world now. This is not Miami Beach, where the McGovernites ran everything. This is Cook County, where the mayor is still boss and where Mr. Singer [tho he has proclaimed himself number one liberal in the world] is still only alderman of the 43d Ward. In Miami, CBS' Mike Wallace went to the Rev. Jesse Jackson for the inside dope on Illinois. In Chicago, no one does.

Of course Mr. Daley said he will support the ticket. In 1964, Gov. Nelson Rockefeller and Sen. Robert Taft said they'd support Barry Goldwater's ticket. To have done otherwise would have required their leaving the party. But saying is not the same as doing. If the McGovernites are expecting another 1960, in which Mr. Daley gave John F. Kennedy Illinois and the Presidency, they're crazy.

First of all, Mr. Daley has nothing to gain from the election of Mr. McGovern, any more than he does from the election of gubernatorial candidate Daniel Walker or Mr. Singer's liberal allies in the lake shore wards. In terms of control of the Democratic Party, these people are his enemies. Mr. McGovern will not stump for the election of such conservatives as Rep. Roman Pucinski and Rep. Daniel Rostenkowski. Mr. Walker will not work for State Sen. Robert Cherry and other machine legislators. Mr. Singer's great goal in life is not the reelection of State's Atty. Edward V. Hanrahan.

So, will Mr. Daley waste one campaign dollar, one illegally posted campaign sign, or one minute of a precinct captain's time on extolling the virtues of McGovern-Walker-Singer liberalism? Heavens no. He will devote his money and effort where he needs them most—helping his state ticket, his legislative candidates, and Mr. Hanrahan.

Secondly, Mr. Daley's biggest post-convention problem locally is not the Singer forces but his own lieutenants. They want revenge on McGovern and Singer. Is Mr. Daley in a position to deny them this?

The liberals contend that the regulars can't afford such revenge; that a machine vote [like a stolen vote] is always a straight ticket vote. That is true of about 300,000 voters in Chicago, most of them residents of the black ghetto. It is not true of the rest of the Democratic constituency, of the Poles who regularly split their tickets to vote for Polish names on the Republican ballot, of old-line Democratic Jews who helped give Sen. Adlai Stevenson a 400,000 vote county plurality in 1970 and then turned around and nearly defeated Sheriff Richard Elrod. Ticket splitting is no mystery to them.

These people are angry. Their votes for delegates in the March primary were taken away from them by the McGovern-Singer cabal. The ousted Daley delegates included the first four Spanish-speaking representatives ever elected to anything in Chicago. Also ousted was the publisher of a community newspaper chain which circulates in Mr. Singer's lake shore wards. The city's Poles, Irish, Germans, and Italians were disenfranchised. Mr. Daley could publicly embrace Mr. McGovern and it wouldn't make one bit of difference.

THE LINCOLN STAR
Lincoln, Neb., July 18, 1972

An Illinois state senator told the Chicago Daily News in a story published over the weekend that Chicago Mayor Richard J. Daley has agreed not to campaign aggressively against the top of the Republican ticket. In exchange for Daley's "cooperation," according to Rep. Eugene Schlickman, Arlington Heights, Ill., the Nixon administration would free millions of dollars of federal aid withheld from the Chicago area.

Mayor Daley's statement Monday shook much of the credibility from that report. At the same time, Sen. McGovern should not feel too secure in the belief that Daley belongs to him, heart and soul.

The Chicago mayor said Monday that "I am a Democrat. I am chairman of the Democratic Party of Cook County and have always supported the nominee of the Democratic Party. I will support every nominee on the Democratic ticket, federal, state and county."

This promise of support, sent in a telegram to McGovern, was conditioned on the support of Daley's slate of local candidates by the group of challengers who replaced the Daley delegation at last week's convention. One can imagine McGovern insisting on that support-in-return being offered.

Daley did not promise to beat the bushes for McGovern; he didn't even mention him by name. But he did promise to support the ticket, which is going a lot farther than many McGovern backers were prepared to give him credit for. His statement might be an answer to the Daily News story in which the mayor indicates he will not sell out to a Nixon promise to release withheld federal aid funds. Or, more likely, it is merely an expression of a political virtue not held in high esteem by the new politicians. And that is loyalty to party.

St. Louis Globe-Democrat
St. Louis, Mo., July 19, 1972

Chicago Mayor Richard J. Daley's obviously reluctant support of George McGovern portends the difficulties the Democratic presidential nominee will repeatedly encounter in his quest for backing from the professional politicians.

Daley, while supporting "every candidate on the Democratic ticket," didn't mention McGovern by name. It's obvious that while the mayor will work to elect his local candidates, little door-to-door campaigning will be done for McGovern.

Without heavy Democratic majorities in Cook County to overcome downstate Republican votes, the McGovern-Eagleton ticket would be in real trouble in Illinois.

Other Democratic mayors, governors and congressmen—also trying to win re-election while avoiding being identified with McGovern—may come up with similarly cold-shouldered endorsements.

CHICAGO DAILY NEWS
Chicago, Ill., July 19, 1972

It was nice of Mayor Daley to promise to support the whole Democratic ticket, and we can understand how elated Sen. McGovern must have been when he called the mayor to thank him and was invited to visit our town. But if we were McGovern we would not start counting Illinois chickens just yet. The mayor did not get where he is in Cook County politics by wearing his heart on his sleeve, or by giving away his game in advance. He may not be angry with McGovern personally, but he was humiliated by a McGovern convention that unseated his whole delegation and, by Daley's interpretation, negated the sincere and valid votes of a host of Daley Democrats. Compounding this, a lot of the young conventioneers looked suspiciously like the rabble that gave the mayor all that grief in 1968. If Daley were merely to forgive and forget, he would be surrendering the field to a gaggle of wrongheaded upstarts.

So Daley smiled through his chagrin, reasserted his unswerving loyalty to the party, and carefully unveiled a piece of a proposition that may very well give the McGovernites fits on election day.

He said he would support the whole ticket, but naturally he would expect the McGovernites to do no less. And that would involve their giving full and unstinting support to State's Atty. Edward V. Hanrahan in his bid for re-election.

But Hanrahan is notoriously a chicken bone in the throats of the Rev. Jesse Jackson, Ald. William S. Singer, and the great bulk of their liberal-minded, McGovern-worshipping supporters. And "regular" Democrats Rep. Roman Pucinski and Rep. Daniel Rostenkowski, in the eyes of the "new politics" crowd, aren't much better. Will the McGovernites go all out for these Democrats? If not, we would be astonished if Daley would order any doorbells rung for their man.

To veteran Daley-watchers, there were two other significant aspects of the mayor's press conference. One was that he did not once mention the name McGovern. The other was that he smiled mysteriously when asked whether, having proclaimed himself in favor of the whole Democratic ticket, he thought he could hold his fellow "regulars" in line. "You know," he said gravely, "I never hold anyone in line. This is a decision they will have to make on their own. After all, this is a day when everyone has their own independent thoughts."

Ho, ho, and ho. The day when the mayor's organization henchmen have their own independent thoughts will be the day the Chicago River runs pure and limpid.

Mayor Daley quite clearly considers that it is Singer, Jackson, and McGovern—not he—who have defected from the party he has known and loved and led. The mayor isn't especially worried about November, so far as his own bailiwick is concerned. Now they can come to him. On skinned knees.

ST. LOUIS POST-DISPATCH
St. Louis, Mo., July 21, 1972

Mayor Richard J. Daley's endorsement of "every candidate on the Democratic ticket, federal, state and local," was not exactly a ringing pledge to go to battle for the McGovern-Eagleton ticket. Realistically, however, such an austere endorsement is about all that could be expected at this time. The mayor has an image to worry about and an instant reconciliation chock-full of platitudes would have sounded pretentious and contrived.

Whether the endorsement is a prelude to support of a more substantial nature remains to be seen. Mr. Daley could have remained silent or, as Sam Yorty of Los Angeles did in the 1960s, supported the standard bearer of the other party. But Mr. Daley realizes that if Senator McGovern loses badly in Illinois, the Daley ticket in Cook County may also be swept under. And if Senator McGovern wins without the active support of the mayor, an eventuality quite conceivable, the pipeline of influence and prestige from city hall to White House would be clogged, if not completely broken.

Omaha World-Herald
Omaha, Neb., July 19, 1972

"I am a Democrat... I will support every candidate on the Democratic ticket, federal, state and local."

That was Mayor Daley talking and setting to rest the rumors that he would either remain silent about his intentions or declare himself for President Nixon.

Neither of the latter courses was plausible, not for a man who has built his political life around the Democratic party.

But the cryptic statement, in which he did not mention the presidential nominee, probably gives little joy to the McGovern camp. There are varying degrees of support the Chicago mayor might choose to give.

If he spends Cook County Democratic dollars and Cook County political energies on behalf of candidates for state and local office—with barely a nod in the direction of the national ticket—Sen. McGovern would not be getting the kind of help he needs in a key state that went to Nixon by an eyelash in 1968.

In brief, Daley could give the national candidates support, but not the all-out support of which his machine is capable. By so doing, Daley could keep himself in good standing within the party and in a position to enjoy victory or ride out the defeat of the national ticket.

Meanwhile, it is worth noting that Daley has kept on good terms with the Nixon administration. If he should give minimal support to McGovern and Illinois happens to play a key part in a Nixon victory, that combination of circumstances would seem to be a bearable one for Mayor Daley.

The Standard-Times
New Bedford, Mass., July 21, 1972

The AFL-CIO Executive Council decision to remain neutral in the presidential election appears to stem from many more considerations than disavowal of the candidacy of Senator George McGovern.

The council chairman and AFL-CIO president, George Meany, singled out McGovern as the reason for the first occasion that the nominee of the Democratic party has not received AFL-CIO endorsement. McGovern has, indeed, voted against "big labor," notably in opposing outlawing state right-to-work laws.

But it would be naive to think that an old hand like Meany does not understand that McGovern has represented a normally conservative state—which, incidentally, has a right-to-work law—and that such electorate influence on his voting could be shucked once McGovern were in the White House.

Already the before-and-after McGovern is apparent in the nominee's hurried trip to Washington to vote for a liberal minimum wage bill of little appeal to South Dakotans. The senator's message is clearly, "Don't judge me by what I have been on labor matters, but what I can be if elected."

Rather than a repudiation of McGovern, the AFL-CIO vote represents "our showdown with the new politics," a political adviser to Meany told the New York Times.

"A small elite of suburban types and students took over the apparatus of the Democratic party," he said, and "arrogantly excluded" traditional leaders, including those of organized labor.

This strikes us as a more believable basic reason for "big labor" disenchantment. Additionally, there are developments in the ranks of labor itself that urge a course of official neutrality on the hierarchy.

The union leader most outspokenly in McGovern's corner is Jerry Wurf, head of the AFL-CIO American Federation of State, County and Municipal Employees, an activist of the "public be damned" school. Wurf told his union's convention in May that "the big crap game is now in the nation's capital . . . all the laws being passed in all the states are lousy . . . "

His attitude is reflected in the mounting criticism of labor leaders by the general public and union members. About six union members in 10 feel the leadership is not responsive to the public interest, and 55 per cent of the public, including 41 per cent of union members, believe unions have grown too powerful and should be curbed. Meany and the majority of his council cohorts may well be apprehensive about the Wurf tangent.

There is the further consideration of the endorsement of President Nixon made by the powerful Teamsters Union. If Nixon is re-elected, with the AFL-CIO tied to McGovern, Teamsters President Frank Fitzsimmons would have high-priority claim on the White House ear.

As to practical effects, the AFL-CIO neutrality will hit Senator McGovern hardest in the campaign coffer. The funds of COPE, AFL-CIO political arm, will be diverted to congressional candidates; AFL-CIO member unions that endorse McGovern will have to organize political arms for the "voluntary" giving that the law requires in political contributions.

The neutrality should add more votes for Nixon than it takes away from McGovern. We say this because unions, just as with the National Association of Manufacturers, are not able to "deliver" votes of the membership. But a departure from a traditional course of endorsement may prompt many union members to support the status quo.

An interesting development of the impartiality decision may come with the Republican convention in August. Will the council vote be interpreted by President Nixon as a kind of negative backing that calls for some reciprocity in the labor planks in the Platform? Or will the GOP continue to call for "vigorous" enforcement of Taft-Hartley, which provides for right-to-work laws?

Despite Meany's ringing repudiation of both McGovern and Nixon, one would hope that the neutrality in which he was so influential is based on a concern for the long-run best interests of unions and the public.

The Charlotte Observer
Charlotte, N.C., July 20, 1972

The labor movement is headed straight toward the rocky shoals of disunity and discord, with the ship's captain clinging to his own delusions and pride as stubbornly as a Capt. Queeg. That may be more important in the long run than what the AFL-CIO does in the presidential election.

George Meany forged much of the relative unity that has prevailed in the AFL-CIO in recent years. In the process, his forces won out over the more flexible and socially responsible elements once led by Walter Reuther. But now Mr. Meany's single-mindedness, once an asset in creating unity, is proving to be big labor's greatest liability. Because of it, we expect to see a major breakup within the AFL-CIO in the years immediately ahead.

So far Mr. Meany is simply refusing to face the reality of George McGovern's victory in the Democratic party. Although Sen. McGovern has a record of friendliness to labor, he has never been simply a "Cross it with Meany" senator and Mr. Meany is not forgiving him for that independence.

The principal Meany delusion is that he can hurt McGovern and emerge intact. The reality, as we see it, is that if he keeps on this course the AFL-CIO will suffer a loss of unity that will not end with the November election.

The decision by the AFL-CIO on Wednesday to take no position in the presidential election probably will be seen by the McGovern forces as something of a victory. They expect to receive the support of some major unions in the AFL-CIO, most notably Leonard Woodcock's auto workers and Jerry Wurf's government workers. At the same time, President Nixon probably will have the support of the maritime, operating engineers and building trades unions. Already he has won the Teamsters' endorsement.

All of this will put the AFL-CIO's unity in peril, and Mr. Meany is likely to increase the peril because even though he recommended formal neutrality by the AFL-CIO his feelings of animosity toward Sen. McGovern have made him move in no neutral way at all. For instance, while still in Miami Beach he ordered the AFL-CIO News to give front-page space to the anti-McGovern speech made at the Democratic convention by the Steelworkers' I. W. Abel.

Mr. Meany, in fact, can hardly be neutral. He maintains very tight control of COPE, the AFL-CIO's political arm. COPE will be hip-deep in campaigns throughout the country, and it cannot avoid actions that will help or hurt the Democrats' national ticket. Since COPE is ostensibly an instrument of all of the unions of the AFL-CIO and Mr. Meany's obstinacy has encouraged those unions' different stances on the McGovern candidacy, there will be new discords related to COPE's use of union money.

We believe Mr. Meany is leading the AFL-CIO into a disaster. It may well lead to a complete restructuring of the labor movement, one that he more than anyone else will have reason to regret.

Daley Backs Ticket; AFL-CIO Neutral—143

The TENNESSEAN
Nashville, Tenn., July 2-, 1972

WHAT MR. GEORGE Meany wants, Mr. George Meany gets within the AFL-CIO executive council. As a result the Democrats are facing the first general election in 40 years without the endorsement of Big Labor.

★ ★ ★

The vote by the council was 27-3 in favor of Mr. Meany's wish that neither Mr. Nixon nor Senator McGovern would share in the considerable financial and manpower reserves of organized labor. The lopsided vote was achieved although as many as half of the council members are believed to favor the Democratic nominee.

The 117 individual unions were left free to endorse either candidate and some already have. Senator McGovern said he believes that most eventually will come around to the Democrats. Many locals of the United Auto Workers, now an independent union, are expected to provide strong support for Senator McGovern while the Teamsters have already pledged to defeat him.

But there is little indication that the executive council decision marks an end to the Roosevelt coalition that brought labor into the Democratic camp. The vote does represent a personal triumph for Mr. Meany.

However, Mr. Meany's impressive victory and his iron grip on federated unions may be short-lived. There are reports that many leaders of AFL-CIO unions are in a rebellious mood and may see the presidential election as an opportunity to dethrone the 77-year-old potentate. If Senator McGovern manages to appeal to labor's rank-and-file or if he proves a formidable challenger to the President, Mr. Meany may be left looking something like an old eccentric bucking modern trends.

On the other hand, if Mr. McGovern loses badly in November, Mr. Meany could find himself being held personally responsible for four more years of President Nixon's economic policies — policies which have been repugnant to most labor organizations—and to him. In his present frame of mind Mr. Meany would probably take Mr. McGovern's loss as a compliment.

★ ★ ★

There is no doubt that the loss of AFL-CIO backing will prove a serious blow to Senator McGovern's chances. Big Labor has been a decisive factor in Democratic victories in 1948 and 1960. Even when the Democrats have lost, Big Labor has been given credit for turning debacles into horse races. In 1952 and 1956, candidate Adlai Stevenson received only luke warm support, but union solidarity did help the candidate in many regions and carried over to enable congressional candidates to win.

In 1968, the last minute surge for Vice President Hubert Humphrey almost proved to be enough to defeat Mr. Nixon. Labor provided the money and the work that made that surge possible.

In this incredible year it appears that a powerful man, out-of-step with both political parties, has succeeded in pushing his will on 13.6 million union members. Those who oppose Senator McGovern as a radical of the left may be shocked to learn he does not have an impressive pro-labor record, but such a record could hardly be expected of a representative of South Dakota, where labor unions are not a strong force or concern and the vote usually is two to one Republican.

★ ★ ★

Mr. Meany said the nominee, not the party, should be held responsible for the council decision. This may be true, but it is also true that Mr. Meany's own personality was of paramount importance. It probably will be remembered when this year's political history is recorded that Mr. Meany's personality, not Mr. McGovern's politics, cost Senator McGovern labor's votes.

THE ROANOKE TIMES
Roanoke, Va., July 23, 1972

This being a democracy, everybody has the right to be an amateur psychoanalyst and try to figure out why George Meany, president of the AFL-CIO, doesn't support the Democratic nominee for President, George McGovern. The Wall Street Journal tried its hand recently and came up with the idea that Mr. Meany sorta feels it in his bones that he is not for Mr. McGovern.

This newspaper, which has just as much right to play psychoanalyst as anybody else without certified credentials, sticks to its first conclusion: Mr. Meany just can't stand the idea of a Democratic president he doesn't have hooks into. After four Democratic Presidents who jumped when he said to, and lay down when he said to, the old fellow just can't stand the idea of a Democratic candidate not hog-tied, bound and delivered to Mr. Meany.

The remarkable thing is that other people don't see the enormous benefits that come from Mr. Meany guessing wrong and backing the wrong Democrat before the convention. Rank and file union men can now vote as they dern well please without the feeling that they are disgracing Big Brother. Rank capitalists could—but probably won't—wonder how that old radical (quickly stereotyped) could be opposed by the AFL-CIO and still be such a radical. Have Big Finance and Big Labor become brothers under the skin?

Even George McGovern, the peerless and fearless Senator from South Dakota, can't see what he has lucked into. Now that AFL-CIO unions have been set free to vote as they please, he and Senator Eagleton, vice presidential candidate, are out trying to do for themselves what Mr. Meany won't do for them.

After consultation with the chief Indian in the Black Hills, Mr. McGovern any day now may send up smoke signals: I AM SO SORRY I VOTED FOR SEC. 14 (B) of the TAFT-HARTLEY ACT. Fact is, that is one of the best votes he ever cast. It enables states to pass laws guaranteeing the right to join a union and the right not to join a union.

After hours of psychoanalysis, it appears here that Mr. Meany has guessed wrong; the right-wingers have guessed wrong in thinking Mr. McGovern is some kind of a nut; and Mr. McGovern is guessing wrong in not recognizing the benefit of his remarkable position, one rarely held before by a Democratic candidate for President: the position of being a friend of organized labor but not a possession of organized labor. In brief: Everybody is crazy but us; and that is a typical position of amateur editorial psychoanalysis in a free country.

The News and Courier
Charleston, S.C., July 21, 1972

The decision by George Meany, president of the AFL-CIO, to sit out the 1972 election without supporting either candidate did not do much good for Sen. George McGovern. It might do him considerable harm.

While Mr. McGovern expects the rank and file of union men to disregard Mr. Meany — and many no doubt will do so — the removal of the blessing of the top leadership surely will slow down some of those who have been voting Democratic by habit. Furthermore, money and squads of doorbell ringers which would have been working for McGovern now will transfer to congressional campaigns.

Without professing admiration for Mr. Meany, The News and Courier believes he took a courageous stand in breaking the Democratic allegiance of organized labor. In times past, some union bloc votes went Republican. We believe that every citizen, regardless of his walk of life, should make up his own mind in deciding whom to support — and whether, in fact, he wants to vote at all. Mr. Meany put a pox on both houses.

The Cincinnati Post
TIMES ★ STAR
Cincinnati, Ohio, July 20, 1972

Sen. George S. McGovern, the Democratic presidential nominee, says he is "disappointed" at the refusal of the AFL-CIO executive council to endorse his candidacy.

Such is understandable, especially considering that he is the first Democratic nominee to be so shunned by the labor moguls since the AFL-CIO combination was put together in 1955. And the bulk of big labor's traditional support of the Democratic nominee goes back much further, being unbroken through the Roosevelt years.

BUT, NICE as all endorsements are, the South Dakota senator and his aides well know that failure to receive the blessing of George C. Meany & Co. is no reason to jump off one of the Black Hills.

Endorsements are becoming more and more meaningless, as voters of all classes become more and more independent.

No one in recent years started off with more important endorsements, ranging from governors and senators to the head of the United Auto Workers, than did Sen. Edmund S. Muskie of Maine, who fared so badly in his presidential bid.

And to go way back in disproving their impact there was the classic endorsement of Wendell Willkie by CIO President John L. Lewis which was supposed to have such an effect on the 1940 election. Union members overwhelmingly ignored the instructions of the Big Boss and helped sweep FDR back into office by 449 electoral votes to 82.

Leonard Woodcock, head of the United Auto Workers, couldn't do any better, when his union members this year went overwhelmingly for George Wallace in the Democratic primary in Michigan.

SO PRESIDENT NIXON, who had no chance for an AFL-CIO endorsement, has no particular reason to cheer at big labor's rejection of Senator McGovern.

And he might well reflect that the labor endorsement he has received, from the Teamsters, also was given him in 1960 when he was defeated by John F. Kennedy.

As recent history has proved, the only endorsement that really counts, after all, is the vote cast on election day. And we'll have to wait until the first Tuesday in November for an accurate reading on that.

THE WALL STREET JOURNAL.
New York, N.Y., July 19, 1972

We detect a certain amount of sympathy in the business community for George Meany's reservations about the Democratic ticket this year. Not that business shares the AFL-CIO's concern about Mr. McGovern's several "anti-labor" votes during his 10-year Senate career. The South Dakotan has not been one of the heroes at the U.S. Chamber of Commerce or National Association of Manufacturers, and these groups would probably feel more generous than Mr. Meany in viewing those McGovern votes as merely anomalous lapses.

Indeed, we suspect Mr. Meany is less upset than he lets on about Mr. McGovern's past positions on Taft-Hartley, right-to-work, and the minimum wage. It's easily explained that prior to 1968 a Senator representing rural South Dakota would feel few compelling pressures to keep organized labor happy. Mr. Meany surely appreciates that as soon as Mr. McGovern cast his eye on the White House his votes on issues of interest to labor matched those of Senators Muskie and Humphrey, who were said to be acceptable to Mr. Meany.

Nor can Mr. McGovern's views on Vietnam explain Mr. Meany's hostility to the Democratic nominee. The AFL-CIO chief is opposed to outright "surrender" in Southeast Asia, a position he finds incompatible with Sen. McGovern's pledge to pull out lock, stock, and barrel in 90 days, no matter what Hanoi does. But Sen. Edward M. Kennedy would do no less than Mr. McGovern, yet Mr. Meany would have found Sen. Kennedy acceptable. Mr. McGovern said he would "beg" Hanoi, if necessary, for the return of American POWs. Senator Kennedy more than a year ago said he would "crawl on my hands and knees" to Hanoi if that's what it took to get the POWs. No difference there.

It's clear neither Mr. Meany nor his blue-collar constituency are as anxious to abandon traditional social values as Mr. McGovern's most ardent followers seem to be. Yet this is hardly the bread-and-butter issue that usually has been paramount with labor.

On the bread-and-butter side, perhaps the AFL-CIO chief is as apprehensive as his counterparts in management are about the economic impact of a McGovern presidency. As our Lindley H. Clark Jr. reported last week, Michael K. Evans, president of Chase Econometric Associates, fed into a computer those McGovern proposals that could conceivably get through Congress. The result, said Mr. Evans, would be a recession in 1974 and an unemployment rate of 7%. Maybe Mr. Meany came to the same conclusion without a computer, merely by passing his hand over the McGovern proposals.

It's always difficult to read Mr. Meany's mind. Maybe he himself doesn't know why one man should be less acceptable than are others who are for the most part cut from the same cloth. If so, we would be inclined to sympathize with Mr. McGovern as he tries to figure out what it might take to woo Mr. Meany. Then too, the campaign is young. Like Bobby Fischer, Mr. Meany may be playing hard to get.

The remaining possibility is that there is simply no specific basis for Mr. Meany's behavior, that it doesn't result from this vote or that statement but from an accumulation of passing impressions. When successful men get to be 77-years-old, they often grow impatient with data, arguments and wooing. They have seen it all, have developed their instincts and "feel of things," and simply know.

OREGON JOURNAL
Portland, Ore., July 21, 1972

The official neutrality of the AFL-CIO on the presidential race seems more an act of humoring an aging boss than an expression of political preference.

Decisions of the member unions in the weeks ahead will tell. But the early evidence is that most of them will endorse Democrat George McGovern, a few Republican Richard Nixon, and a minority will indeed remain neutral.

If that is the way it works out, the official position taken by the AFL-CIO executive board will not represent the sentiment of the AFL-CIO at all, but only that of its president, George Meany.

At any rate, unless there is a change of mind between now and November, the AFL-CIO will break tradition by not officially supporting the Democratic presidential nominee.

Meany has yet to provide a rational explanation for his opposition to McGovern. True, he has nitpicked the McGovern voting record and has come up with enough differences that he could build a one-sided case against the candidate.

But that doesn't make sense as the real reason, for such an unbalanced assessment could be made against anyone. As United Auto Workers President Leonard Woodcock said, McGovern's labor record is around 95 per cent which places him near the top.

Meany has objected to McGovern's position on Vietnam and defense spending. Yet, Sen. Edward Kennedy's position is nearly identical and the AFL-CIO president indicated that he'd be happy with Kennedy as the candidate.

What this suggests, unless the aging labor warrior comes up with a better explanation, is that it is a matter of personal pique. McGovern first was not to be taken seriously, then was not the preferred candidate, and finally could not be stopped.

Meany, like the late J. Edgar Hoover and many congressional committee chairmen, may suffer from the malady that afflicts many men who acquire power and influence. They can't let go of it, even when their causes might be better served by younger leadership. When their power fails them, as Meany's did at the Democratic convention, defeat is hard to accept.

Regardless, George Meany got his way, and his way does not appear to be representative of the mighty organization over which he presides. Perhaps, indeed, it was a last hurrah. In the country's changing political scene, there is a lot of that going around these days.

Campaign '72:
NIXON DECISION TO RUN WITH AGNEW FOLLOWS DEMOCRATIC CONVENTION

White House Press Secretary Ronald Ziegler announced July 22 that President Nixon had chosen Vice President Spiro Agnew to be his running-mate in the November election. Ziegler said the decision had been reached "a short time after the Democratic convention." The announcement put an end to speculation that the controversial Agnew might be replaced by John Connally Jr., who had resigned as treasury secretary in May [See pp. 717-719]. Several liberal Republicans, including Sens. Jacob Javits (N.Y.) and William Saxbe (Ohio) had urged President Nixon to replace Agnew.

The Virginian-Pilot
Norfolk, Va., July 24, 1972

It isn't surprising that President Nixon wants to keep Vice President Agnew on the Republican ticket this year. Any attempt to dump the outspoken Vice President would have gotten Mr. Nixon into trouble with his own troops. Nevertheless, the announcement that Agnew's the one removes the last, lingering suspense that might have spiced the Republican convention next month.

There was never any question that Mr. Nixon will be renominated, and really there wasn't much question that Mr. Agnew would be retained in the No. 2 spot. But as long as the likes of Senator Javits, who is close to the last liberal in the Republican Party, were saying that Mr. Agnew ought to be replaced, and as long as the hypothetical possibility remained, there was something that the experts could chew over and speculate upon. Now the Republican convention threatens to be the dullest ever, outdoing the Democrats in '64. Everybody knows who'll be on the ticket, nobody cares what's in the platform, and who wants to listen to the speeches?

Certainly Mr. Nixon would have been willing to dump Mr. Agnew if he had judged that to be expedient politically. He has treated the Vice President as distantly (and properly) as he himself was treated by President Eisenhower. And even a lot of Republicans would be willing to concede that Richard Nixon would dump his mother from the ticket to win. (Agnew associates have maintained, meanwhile, that the Vice President would bow out voluntarily if he thought that his presence on the ticket would be bad for the Republicans.) But the speculation that Mr. Agnew would be replaced by former Secretary of the Treasury John Connally or Governor Nelson Rockefeller or somebody was unrealistic.

For the fact is Spiro Agnew is first in the hearts of the rank-and-file Republicans. "I haven't met one Republican yet who doesn't think that the Vice President is more popular than the President," Barry Goldwater says. As the alliterative critic of Democrats, kids, kooks, liberals, and the press, Mr. Agnew has been feeding the faithful just the rhetorical red meat they want. That is one of the main reasons why he is fabulously successful as a fund-raiser, particularly with moneyed right-wingers.

But his partisan popularity is something of a liability at the same time. "He has been programmed to massage right-wing psyches, and given an almost completely negative function as a critic of the left," conservative columnist Kevin P. Phillips wrote. "As a corollary of this, he has been denied the chance to spell out some of his own ideas and programs which would make the sum total of what he says more appealing to the general public." Mr. Agnew is "controversial," and the idea that he might become President frightens a lot of people. The polls show that the public tends to equate Mr. Agnew with George Wallace. Each has a reputation for saying what many want to hear, but neither is regarded as the kind of man people want in the White House.

That is the political paradox which attaches to Mr. Agnew's career, and his future role. He became a household word by doing the dirty work for Mr. Nixon, and lost a lot of political respectability by being the GOP's hatchet man. If he and Mr. Nixon are reelected, the Vice President will be an obvious prospect to run for the No. 1 spot in '76, as did Mr. Nixon in '60, Lyndon Johnson in '64, and Hubert Humphrey in '68. But to be credible as a future President, and a leader of the Western world, Mr. Agnew will have to be less loud-mouthed, less partisan, less the Spiro the Hero we've come to love and/or hate. His image (if you will pardon the term) will have to be transformed. Can he lay down his big stick and start to speak softly?

The Louisville Times
Louisville, Ky., July 26, 1972

Although the Republican Party's private polls have undoubtedly shown that Vice President Spiro Agnew will strengthen the ticket this year, President Nixon did take some risks in deciding to keep the winning combination of 1968 intact.

Agnew, it is true, is an effective orator at GOP fund-raising events. His savage attacks on the alleged "radicalism" of the opposition are comforting to old guard Republicans. Judging from his remarks about Sen. George McGovern, he will probably be assigned similar chores this autumn while the President plays the role of an above-the-battle statesman.

But as fondly as he may be regarded by the party's Neanderthals, Agnew has not yet demonstrated that he is an asset in an election year. In 1968, it is worth remembering, Mr. Nixon started out way ahead. During the months that Spiro Agnew became a household word, the President's lead was cut to almost nothing. And then in 1970, Agnew sallied forth to rally the silent majority in behalf of Republican congressional and gubernatorial candidates. When it was all over the party's gains were slight and its losses quite serious. Many moderate Republicans were offended by the vice president's irresponsible rhetoric and his hatchet job on former Sen. Charles Goodell of New York.

Agnew could even turn out to be a liability this year. His attempts to portray the Democrats as apologists for a whole catalog of evils may fire up some Southerners and Wallaceites, but it will choke off whatever support the GOP might have hoped to get from young people, blacks and fair-minded moderates of both parties. Mr. Nixon doesn't expect much help from the campuses and ghettos anyway, but it is not in his interest to alienate them completely. He might have been wise to select a running mate more attuned to their needs and problems.

A potentially more serious problem for the Republicans is the possibility that voters will ask themselves whether Agnew is really the sort of man they would like to have as president. He has not shown the dignity or intellect most people expect in their chief executive. He shoots from the hip and seldom speaks knowledgeably about a complicated issue. Like Gov. George Wallace, he attracts supporters who appreciate his phrase-making and fighting style, but who wouldn't trust him in the White House. Yet his re-election would not only put him within a heartbeat of the presidency for another four years, but would make him the probable Republican nominee in 1976.

The Nixon strategists have evidently taken all this into consideration and concluded that Agnew would be more helpful than one of the party's bright young men, like Mayor Richard Lugar of Indianapolis. The White House apparently feels the team that nearly blew the 1968 and 1970 elections will be unbeatable this time. Perhaps there are plans to merchandise a new, more diplomatic Agnew. Perhaps, as is widely assumed, the President is so far ahead he could win with Black Beauty on his ticket. But let's not forget that Mr. Nixon has a habit of losing ground as he heads toward the finish line. By the end of October, Agnew may begin to hang like lead around his ankles.

The New York Times
New York, N.Y., July 24, 1972

When Richard M. Nixon picked Spiro T. Agnew as his Vice-Presidential running mate four years ago, it seemed incredible that a man would be chosen to stand next in line for the Presidency who had experience neither in national government nor in foreign affairs.

His nearly four years as Vice President have done nothing to dissipate the public's anxieties about Mr. Agnew. He has shown himself to be a man without comprehension of the American tradition of civil liberties or the meaning of the First Amendment. As an emissary abroad, he has been a jet-propelled embarrassment. To the dismay of all citizens who covet the good name of this democracy, Mr. Agnew has publicly and effusively endorsed dictators in Europe, Asia and Africa.

If he has learned anything about the nation's serious domestic problems, Mr. Agnew has kept that knowledge to himself. He remains the man who said in 1968, "If you've seen one slum, you've seen them all." Periodically, his press agents and political allies suggest that he has serious ideas about Federal-state relations and other real concerns, but those ideas—if they exist—remain buried under a slag heap of partisan claptrap.

Mr. Nixon's political rationale for keeping Mr. Agnew on the ticket is clear enough. Confronted with the prospect of conservative Democratic defections from the McGovern-Eagleton ticket, the President feels confident enough of carrying Texas not to need his chief Democratic recruit, former Treasury Secretary John B. Connally, as his running mate. Mr. Agnew's alliterative nonsense is soothing to those conservative Republicans who are distressed by Mr. Nixon's journeys to Peking and Moscow.

Vice President Agnew is a campaigner able and willing to take the partisan low road while Mr. Nixon remains not only above the battle but also beyond accountability. The decision was not unexpected but it is still a dismal augury for the fall campaign.

© 1972 by The New York Times Company. Reprinted by permission.

The San Diego Union
San Diego, Calif., July 26, 1972

President Nixon had remarked so often about the folly of breaking up a "winning team" that it was only a long-shot proposition that he might choose a new running mate for 1972. All along, the idea of replacing Vice President Spiro Agnew on the Republican ticket seemed to fascinate critics of Mr. Agnew more than it did members of the official White House family.

Mr. Agnew was relatively unknown in national politics when he became the Republican candidate for vice president in 1968. His name now approaches the familiarity of the "household word" which, four years ago, he jokingly conceded it was not. The controversy he provoked at times has served mainly to reveal his character — that of a clear-headed man with the courage of his convictions.

The vice president's determination to "tell it like it is" has had a healthy effect on some of the targets of his criticism. While at first accused of attempting to intimidate segments of the mass media, he actually has instigated a round of soul-searching in the communications industry which in the long run can improve its credibility with the public.

Mr. Agnew has shown himself to be a serious student of major issues confronting our government, as his position next to the President demands. The stature which Mr. Nixon discerned in him in 1968 has been made all the more evident by his performance as vice president. The Republican Party has good reason to view a Nixon-Agnew ticket as a "winning team" for 1972.

EVENING HERALD
Rock Hill, S.C., July 26, 1972

President Nixon's fairly predictable decision to keep Spiro Agnew as his running mate might be wise from a political standpoint, but one wonders whether it is best for the Republican Party or the country in the long run.

Looking at it from a short-range perspective and going no further than the November election, Agnew will be more of an asset to Nixon than a liability.

While his presence on the ticket provides the McGovern forces with a handy target, the Vice President has become pretty adept at dishing out fairly strong politicial medicine himself.

Moreover, Agnew's candidacy most likely assures Nixon the dedicated backing of arch conservatives, who are peeved at the President for his "liberal" foreign policy moves.

Had Agnew been replaced, many of these people might have denied the ticket financial and manpower support, and "gone fishing" on election day.

In addition, Agnew's seeming candor and his colorful verbal lashings of the liberal Eastern establishment press, war protesters, and intellectuals have endeared him to many Americans.

As far as we can tell, he will be good for the Republicans this fall.

But looking further ahead, Agnew's presence on the ticket could present a real problem for Republicans in 1976.

If Nixon and Agnew are reelected, the Vice President would be in line for the GOP's presidential nomination in four years.

This possibility could easily lead to a bitter split within the party, since GOP liberals and moderates are not likely to be overly enthusiastic about an Agnew candidacy. It could make for a dismal situation for the GOP and a delightful one for the Democrats.

Carrying this speculation one step further, the possibility that Agnew may be elected President (or will get the post should something happen to Nixon) is of considerable concern to many Americans.

The country likely could survive an Agnew administration without falling apart. But the Vice President's position on social issues, his apparent lack of sensitivity, and his repeated attempts at polarizing the American public make him questionable presidential material in the eyes of many thoughtful citizens.

Roscoe Drummond, in a column we didn't publish because it became outdated with Nixon's announcement to stick with Agnew, made a worthwhile recommendation regarding a vice-presidential nominee for the GOP.

He suggested that Nixon should leave it up to the convention to choose a running mate, perhaps from a list of candidates submitted by the President himself.

This would have accomplished two purposes: It would have gotten Nixon off the hook regarding Agnew, and it would have made the Republicans appear as reform-minded as the Democrats. Even George McGovern, with all the talk of reform, still insisted on picking the vice presidential nominee himself.

THE INDIANAPOLIS STAR

Indianapolis, Ind., July 28, 1972

Speculation that Mr. Nixon might not choose Vice-President Spiro Agnew to be his running mate again ended when the President announced he wants Agnew to stand for re-election.

It is noteworthy that much of the conjecture that Mr. Nixon might prefer to run with former Treasury Secretary John Connally—on the premise that he would make a stronger candidate than Agnew—originated with newspaper columnists who are committed anti-Nixonites. Such pundits argued that Agnew had become an embarrassment to the administration and would hurt the Republican ticket were he to be renominated at Miami next month.

A look at some cold facts tends to refute that view.

Fact one is that in the nation's first presidential primary this year, in New Hampshire, Agnew received more votes by write-in than Senator Edmund Muskie won with his name on the Democratic ticket —and Muskie won his party's primary in the Granite State. What makes Agnew's accomplishment even more impressive is the fact that Muskie, as a Maine resident, is a fellow New Englander to New Hampshirites.

Fact two, a Gallup Poll taken two months after the New Hampshire primary showed that Republican voters heavily favored Agnew for renomination. Other polls, sampling Democratic, Republican and independent voters, placed Agnew as high as third in the "most-admired American" category.

Perhaps the most formidable fact in relation to Agnew's strength lies in New York, which now has the nation's second largest number of electoral votes—41. In 1968, New York was entitled to 43 electoral votes. At that time Mr. Nixon lost them to Democratic candidate Hubert H. Humphrey, who defeated Mr. Nixon by 370,542 popular votes.

Now consider this point: Four days before Mr. Nixon announced that Agnew would be his running mate again, Kieran O'Doherty, founder and vice-chairman of the Conservative Party of New York, said that if Vice-President Agnew were denied re-nomination it would "foreclose" any chance in New York of a Conservative indorsement of the Republican national ticket. Were the Conservative Party to withhold indorsement, an expected strong effort on the part of Governor Nelson A. Rockefeller to win New York's electoral votes for Mr. Nixon would be in jeopardy. That the Conservatives have ballot-box clout was demonstrated in 1968 when James L. Buckley, running on that ticket, defeated Democrat Richard L. Ottinger and Republican Charles E. Goodell to become New York's junior senator.

There have been various analyses of why Mr. Nixon decided to go again with Agnew. One, based on a sort of armchair psychology, agonizes that Mr. Nixon still remembers and remains bothered by the fact that President Dwight Eisenhower did not indorse him for re-election as vice-president at an early stage in 1956. Another is that the McGovern-Eagleton slate has positioned itself so clearly to the left that there is no real reason to replace Agnew with someone who might have provided a fresh attraction to moderates of both parties.

We think the main reason concerns simple arithmetic—a question of adding up the various indications of vote-getting strength the vice-president has clearly displayed.

Chicago today American

Chicago, Ill., July 24, 1972

IN AN ordinary election year, President Nixon's decision to keep Vice President Agnew as his running mate would seem a tactical mistake, or at least an unnecessary risk.

Conventional wisdom would be this: Mr. Nixon is running against Sen. George McGovern, a thorogoing liberal whose sweeping ideas for economic reforms and military cutbacks scare the pants off most conservatives. Agnew is a strong vote-getter among conservatives, but Mr. Nixon is sure of their support anyway and needs no extra insurance. Where he does need strengthening is in the center; to offset the 18-to-20-year-old new voters who undoubtedly will lean toward McGovern, he should try to attract as many as possible of the middle-of-the-road or undecided voters. So he should pick a candidate with broader appeal than Agnew, one whose specialty is attracting new votes rather than entertaining voters who have already been convinced.

That, as we said, would be the conventional wisdom, and ordinarily would make perfect sense. But this is not an ordinary election year.

In 1972, for reasons that a sociologist might be able to explain more readily than a politician, the trend is to pull apart instead of seeking the center; to emphasize rather than soften differences. It seems as tho the parties, the candidates and the voters all feel an impulse to sort themselves out, to resolve some kind of identity crisis. This year the idea is not just to pick a President but to define more clearly what kind of nation this should be.

Mr. Nixon could hardly have picked a better way to express this trend than his choice of Agnew. With him on the ticket an already clearcut choice becomes practically polarized. Agnew is perhaps the best available symbol for everything that divides the two ideological camps. For conservatives, he is a two-fisted slugger standing up against namby-pamby idealists, do-gooders and the welfare state; for liberals, he is an educated oaf who perfectly represents an insensitive, big business-oriented administration. This time that haunting X quantity, the undecided voter, is likely to be a small minority, hardly more than a splinter group.

Mr. Nixon's selection of Agnew is more than a choice, it is a challenge. And whatever the campaign textbook says, this is the right year for it.

The Evening Star and The Washington Daily News

Washington, D.C., July 24, 1972

It probably occurred to President Nixon that he could add some suspense and theatricality to an otherwise predictable Republican convention by holding off to the last minute his announcement that he wants Spiro Agnew on the ticket with him again this year. But it would have been transparent. And considering the choice he made, it is just as well it came when it did.

The 1972 campaign now comes into sharper focus. The President and the vice president are for the most part political duplicates, with Agnew somewhat to the right of his boss. Senators McGovern and Eagleton reflect carbon-copy liberalism. For reasons that have yet to be made wholly clear, neither of the presidential candidates saw fit to choose as running mate someone who might appeal to those millions of centrist voters who do indeed exist and who may well be torn between Mr. Nixon and McGovern. For what it is worth, the Republican and Democratic tickets are in no way Tweedledum and Tweedledee. The voters must make a clear-cut choice.

For Agnew, the President's decision must be highly gratifying. If he has given the press and some segments of the public a good many lumps over the years, they have given him the same, speculating almost from the 1969 Inauguration that come 1972 he would be dumped from high office to return to his modest political base in Baltimore County. And the decision will no doubt delight the Republican right wing — the Buckleys and Ashbrooks and others whose announced disaffection earlier this year settled down to a keep-Agnew tactic.

This newspaper several times has suggested that Mr. Nixon could do better. In no way do we subscribe to the fashionable liberal view that the vice president is in the category of arch-villain, nor were we questioning his honor, honesty and capability of doing a good job. But any time a man runs for or becomes vice president, the question arises as to whether he would make a good president. Up to now, we have concluded that despite his many admirable qualities, Agnew has not measured up to presidential timber.

Then comes the question of what is smart politics. The President has shored up his conservative base and he has strengthened his appeal to Wallaceite Democrats and other voters who might ordinarily vote Democratic but who have come to believe that Agnew speaks their language. Yet it is difficult to believe that more than a handful of these people, had Mr. Nixon chosen another running mate, would have given up a chance to vote against the McGovern-Eagleton ticket. Meanwhile, what of all those independents and moderate Democrats, listening to McGovern but troubled by him, who might well have responded to the choice of a younger, more progressive person in the Republicans' No. 2 spot? We believe their numbers are many. They very well could make the difference.

Perhaps, like Spassky or Fischer, the President is such a professional that he can look four or five moves down the board and know everything will turn out all right. Perhaps. Mr. Nixon said he does not want to break up "a winning team." Actually, the team did not win by all that much in 1968. It will be quite a battle this year, too, in a political climate that has changed and keeps changing. In short, what the Republicans and the country need is a new Agnew, a vice president and a campaigner who will spurn the heavy-club approach, who will seek not only to rouse the already converted but appeal to those in the middle who are searching for the positive and the rational in what some call the old politics.

Campaign '72:
NEWSPAPER GUILD BACKS McGOVERN; ACTION RAISES OBJECTIVITY ISSUE

The 14-member executive board of the American Newspaper Guild broke the union's 40-year tradition of neutrality in presidential elections when it voted July 13 to endorse the candidacy of Sen. George McGovern. Charles Perlick Jr., national president of the 33,000 member Guild, said the decision had been taken because "compelling human pressures pushed the Guild off the thin illusory edge of neutrality and into the arena where the battle will be fought."

Announcement of the decision brought an immediate reaction from Guild members who saw the action as potentially discrediting the objectivity of all journalists. A number of influential national editors and reporters signed petitions disavowing the board's action. Sen. Barry Goldwater (R, Ariz.) charged the media with downplaying the story in an attempt to sweep the issue under the rug. He said the Guild's action raised "suspicions [of] what I believe to be a built-in bias in favor of radical Democrats."

The Washington Post
Washington, D.C., July 24, 1972

The endorsement of Senator McGovern for President by the Newspaper Guild, which was announced at the Democratic Convention by Guild President Charles A. Perlik, has predictably stirred a lot of outcry among partisan Republicans (as well as among newspaper people in and out of the Guild). Senator Goldwater, for example, called it "one of the most interesting and least written about stories" of the Democratic Convention. Apparently sensing something furtive or clandestine, he went on to declare that "the public has a right to know a lot more about it."

Well, we would agree with that — although the story was in fact fully covered by this newspaper and many others. Still, newspaper readers have a rightful interest in any open display of political partisanship by an organization composed in part of working reporters and editors and other newsroom employees who are supposed to be objective, fair, unprejudiced and non-partisan in their work. So we would like to talk about this issue today, strictly For Your Information, and also commend to you an article on the subject elsewhere on this page today in which Mr. Ben Bagdikian describes in some detail the process by which the Guild arrived at its decision to endorse a presidential candidate for the first time. You can judge for yourself whether that process was democracy in its purest form. The protest already mounted by scores of Guild members raises at least some doubt about that. But leaving that question aside as an internal problem for the Guild, the question remains whether it was a sensible, useful and — perhaps most important — *professional* thing to do, even assuming that it accurately reflected the sentiment of the Guild membership. The short answer, in our view, is that it was not.

We would not question the Guild's right, in theory, to endorse political candidates in the same way that other trade unions do. The issue is whether this particular union, representing this particular group of workers, is not obliged, almost by definition, to foreswear any participation in partisan political processes. We would think it is, and not for the reason that the Guild's endorsement of Mr. McGovern might somehow induce its members to slant their news reporting or editing in favor of the Democratic candidate. The flash flood of petitions signed by Guild reporters in protest of the action taken by their union leadership is eloquent testimony to the integrity of the great body of serious, professional reporters and editors — and especially of those dealing with national politics. As Mr. Bagdikian points out, it is no more reasonable to suspect that these Guild members will be influenced in their work by their union's endorsement of Senator McGovern than it is to suspect that they will be tilted towards President Nixon by the fact that the overwhelming majority of their publishers — the people they work for and who have quite a lot to say about the course of their careers — are generally conservative and, thus, more sympathetic to Republican candidates for President.

In short, it is not the professional news reporters and editors themselves who will be influenced adversely by the Guild's action, and neither is it their product — which can be regularly tested for tilt, in any case, because it is out there, all of it, on display every day. On the contrary, the problem is in the fact that for a newspaper to be effective, it must not merely be fair and non-partisan in its handling of news; it must also *appear* to be fair. The problem is in the eye of the beholder and that is why anything which offers strong reason to suspect the objectivity of those who handle the news — anything which shakes the reader's trust and confidence — is that much more extra, un-needed freight for any working reporter or editor. It not only robs their work of believability but arouses the suspicion of news sources as well. That is why the Guild's endorsement of Senator McGovern, as a practical matter, is so troublesome, not to say reprehensible. For them the Guild's endorsement is an encumbrance they neither need nor want and it is greatly to their credit that so many of them are moving—by petition or paid ads or local voting in repudiation of their leadership—to shake it off.

THE WALL STREET JOURNAL.
New York, N.Y., July 28, 1972

Senator Barry Goldwater is not alone in feeling that it was improper for the Newspaper Guild to endorse Senator George McGovern's presidential candidacy. At least one Guild unit voted to disavow the union's endorsement, a chapter of the Sigma Delta Chi journalism fraternity also criticized it, and much of the national press—including The Washington Post, Time, and The New York Times—editorialized against the endorsement.

We share the concern that the move, the first such endorsement in Guild history, was symbolically unwise. But we don't think that it was all that important substantively. It reflects certain aspects of the press, but is unlikely to change them.

After all, it is pretty well acknowledged that journalists, particularly on the larger newspapers, tend to be rather liberal. Therefore it isn't too surprising that many of them would be more sympathetic to Mr. McGovern's liberal activism than to Mr. Nixon's more cautious and less ambitious view of government's proper role. The important question is to what extent journalists can put aside such personal preferences when they write news.

Those who have difficulty being objective are unlikely to be affected by the Guild's position. After all, the Guild was formally neutral in the 1964 presidential campaign, yet that did not prevent reporters from a prominent newspaper and a prominent radio-TV network from smearing candidate Goldwater by reporting that he was planning to meet with German neo-Nazis soon after the election.

Even more certainly, none of the many conscientious, disinterested newsmen who exist throughout all levels of the media are likely to abandon their journalistic integrity because of the Guild decision.

Still, it was disconcerting to hear the Guild's national president explain that the executive board endorsed Mr. McGovern because "compelling human pressures pushed the Guild off the thin illusory edge of neutralism. . . ." It is just such an "illusory edge" that the media's critics frequently deplore. Furthermore, such admissions reinforce the trenchant criticisms of Daniel Moynihan, who last year charged that journalists have become advocates of the "adversary culture," that they disparage and set a tone of pervasive dissatisfaction with society's values and premises.

But aside from giving aid and comfort to journalism's critics, the Guild endorsement and rationale are regrettable in that they seem to abandon even the goals of impartiality and objectivity. Any journalist knows that strict impartiality and objectivity are difficult to come by, but professional newsmen understand that if journalism is to maintain its integrity news writers must pursue an objective intent; there is plenty of room for comment and opinion once a reasonably impartial base has been laid.

Pure neutrality may indeed be illusory, just as illusory as, say, adherence to the Ten Commandments. Fortunately, the reaction to the endorsement suggests that a good many journalists understand the point: merely because a standard can never be completely fulfilled is no reason whatever to abandon the standard itself.

The New York Times
New York, N.Y., July 22, 1972

During its three and a half years in office, the Nixon Administration has evinced undisguised hostility toward working reporters and has attempted by threats and by legal and economic reprisals to intimidate television networks, influential metropolitan newspapers, and magazines.

This war on the press goes well beyond that which always exists between any administration and the journalists who write about it. It also goes well beyond the merely verbal threats and admonishments of Vice President Agnew although even those, it should be noted, are not isolated forays. It forms part of a coordinated Administration campaign which includes speeches and comments by White House aides and other middle- and upper-level Government officials, and which is consciously intended to disparage the press and to undermine public confidence in its fairness and integrity.

This verbal onslaught is not a mere matter of harassed public officials "letting off steam" by answering back their critics, which of course they have every right to do. It has the political objective of discrediting the national press and television, centered in Washington, New York and the big cities generally, where President Nixon has always been weakest.

The Administration's animus and its aggressive attempts to rein in the press are visible on many different fronts. In the Pentagon Papers case, the Administration tried to impose prior restraint on the publication of news, a policy wholly alien to American tradition and expressly forbidden by the First Amendment. The Justice Department has used subpoena power to coerce reporters to turn over their notes, and to testify before grand juries on matters which they learned in a confidential professional capacity—a most sinister line of action which now unfortunately has the approval of the Supreme Court.

Under cover of legitimate criticism, implicit threats are made to block the renewal of television station licenses or to take legislative action against networks. President Nixon has vetoed funds for public broadcasting. He has also virtually destroyed the White House news conference, an important forum in which reporters used to be able to force a Chief Executive to provide at least a partial accounting to the public of his policies and the motives behind those policies.

The relationship of the Nixon Administration with the press, a critically important relationship in a self-governing society and one which receives special protection in the Constitution, can thus only be described as dismal. It is exactly the opposite of the "open Presidency" which Mr. Nixon promised four years ago.

Because of the Nixon Administration's record, it could be argued that the Fourth Estate has the responsibility to oppose Mr. Nixon's re-election. The repeated disparagement, intimidation and coercion of the press are not only a broad public issue but also a specific concern of reporters and editors.

Yet the decision of the American Newspaper Guild's executive board to endorse the candidacy of Senator George McGovern is wrong in principle and mistaken in tactics. The Guild clearly includes members of diverse political viewpoints. The union leadership cannot and should not try to speak for them as if they were a political bloc. Moreover, impartiality and fairness in reporting and editing the news are the central ideals of the news profession, never perfectly attained but striven for every day. While it is true that a large part of the Guild's membership has nothing to do with preparing, reporting or editing the news, the union contains enough strictly professional journalists to warrant its avoidance of taking positions on public issues or political personalities. To do otherwise is to cast a shadow of doubt upon the profession's commitment to its own ideals.

Needless to add, the endorsement is a tactical blunder inasmuch as it gives such Administration spokesmen as Senator Goldwater another excuse to attack the credibility of the press. Because members of the press have special rights under the First Amendment, they have a special responsibility to exercise their other rights as citizens with circumspection. Political endorsements are a right which those who are directly concerned with reporting the news would do well to forgo.

© 1972 by The New York Times Company. Reprinted by permission.

The Charleston Gazette
Charleston, W.Va., July 28, 1972

To paraphrase Joseph Fouche's often repeated comment, the Newspaper Guild's endorsement of Democratic presidential nominee George McGovern is more than a mistake; it's a blunder.

The right of the union to endorse Mr. McGovern over Mr. Nixon isn't at issue. Whether the union should have exercised its right is.

By breaking precedent the Guild has placed its reportorial members, especially those who will be covering the autumn election campaign, in an impossible position.

At best, reporting is an imprecise science. Reporters, no less than chiefs of state, aren't immaculately conceived. The most conscientious reporters err even when they write about unimportant matters, and presidential campaigns are anything but uncomplicated.

All reporting is subjective in part. Straight news stories can't include every last detail of what happened. Reporters must select some information and throw away other information.

Guild members accompanying either nominee along the campaign trail, in addition to the normal pressures encountered on such assignments, will have dangling above their typewriters their union's official certification of the McGovern candidacy.

The least mistake, if it benefits the senator, will subject a reporter to accusations of bias from the President's supporters, and his union's embracing of Mr. McGovern will lend credibility to these charges.

Describing the character, quality, subtleties and daily particulars of a presidential race presents a tough challenge to the most qualified reporter. All he can hope to accomplish — all his readers should expect him to accomplish — is to furnish honest, balanced accounts of what is going on.

Obviously occasional errors of judgment, taste and fact will blemish the copy of the best reporters. But these errors, 99 times out of 100, are attributable to human frailty not malice. Neither are they, as Vice President Spiro Agnew is so fond of intimating, a component of some giant East Coast liberal establishment conspiracy.

Guild reporters in this year's campaign, however, are going to be hard pressed to justify mistakes solely on grounds of human fragility.

Their union has done them and Mr. McGovern a great injustice.

THE INDIANAPOLIS NEWS
Indianapolis, Ind., July 17, 1972

The Newspaper Guild has compromised principles of honest journalism by endorsing a presidential candidate.

The Guild last week endorsed the candidacy of Sen. George McGovern, breaking a 40-year tradition of remaining free from direct political participation. The union has thus played right into the hands of the news media's critics, notably Vice-President Agnew. When he talks about liberal bias in the future, his remarks will carry substantially more weight.

The fact is that political participation makes the press' performance suspect, even when it is honest and above-board. The most impartial reporter suffers in the public eye from the kind of action the Guild has taken in the name of the profession.

What is sad, too, is that the Guild endorsement is symptomatic of a so-called "new journalism" that makes no pretense about objectivity but is overtly activist and ideologically motivated. Too many reporters come out of journalism school believing they are specially anointed to mold opinion, not just report the facts.

Guild leaders have done the press a disservice. And, curiously, they have forfeited the right to get upset about Mr. Agnew's broadsides.

Rocky Mountain News
Denver, Colo., July 26, 1972

SINCE IT WAS FOUNDED in Cleveland 39 years ago, the American Newspaper Guild, which as a labor union represents 33,000 reporters, photographers and clerical workers, most of them in large cities, never has endorsed a candidate for President.

That tradition was broken last week when the Guild's 14-member executive board voted to endorse Sen. George S. McGovern during the Democratic convention in Miami Beach.

Guild President Charles A. Perlik Jr. explained that "compelling human pressures pushed the Guild off the thin, illusory edge of neutralism and into the arena where the battle will be fought."

The line between neutralism and partisanship may be thin, all right, but it is by no means as "illusory" as Perlik would have us believe.

Most newsmen, whatever their political persuasions, lean over backwards to be fair in their reporting, and the endorsement of Sen. McGovern by an organization that speaks for newsmen is bound to raise doubts in the minds of the readers.

Sen. Barry M. Goldwater, R-Ariz., says the Guild action confirms his belief that newsmen favor "radical Democrats" over conservative Republicans like himself.

The truth is that reporters are as skeptical of politicians, left and right, as they are of editors and editorial writers, which might be a good thing for all concerned.

Fortunately, hundreds of reporters from New York to Minneapolis have signed petitions opposing the Guild action and disavowing the endorsement of Sen. McGovern or any other candidate.

Delegates from the Denver local who attended the national convention in Puerto Rico voted 5-to-3 to oppose Perlik's move, based largely on the conviction that the Guild, representing people covering politics in an active way, should not take any kind of partisan stance to compromise their reportorial credibility.

We insist a newspaper reporter should detach himself, as far as possible, from the events and personalities he is covering so as to present the most objective possible view to the public.

For the Guild to take sides in a presidential election campaign, or any other political contest, is a handicap most reporters can cheerfully do without.

Campaign '72:
McGOVERN NAMES SARGENT SHRIVER TO REPLACE EAGLETON ON TICKET

Democratic presidential nominee Sen. George McGovern (S.D.) Aug. 5 chose R. Sargent Shriver to succeed Sen. Thomas Eagleton as his vice presidential running-mate. [See pp. 912-925] Before settling on Shriver, McGovern offered the nomination to several of the same men he had originally considered for the post during the Democratic Convention as well as to Sen. Edmund Muskie (Me.), who weighed McGovern's offer for 24 hours before rejecting it because of "family duties."

The Democratic National Committee nominated Shriver Aug. 8 with the only significant opposition coming from the Missouri delegation which cast its 73 votes for Sen. Eagleton.

Shriver, 56, a Catholic and an in-law of the Kennedy family, was the first director of the Peace Corps under President Kennedy and served as first director of the Office of Economic Opportunity under President Johnson. He also served as ambassador to France under the Johnson and Nixon administrations. Shriver has never held an elective office.

St. Louis Globe-Democrat
St. Louis, Mo., August 8, 1972

Democratic presidential candidate George S. McGovern is having a tough, deflating time to find a vice presidential candidate to run on his ticket. He has asked one prospect after another and they have turned him down one after another. Does no one want to be running-mate with McGovern?

He again sounded out this week Sen. Edward (Ted) Kennedy, Sen. Hubert Humphrey and Sen. Abraham Ribicoff. Each said No. Others mentioned, who professed no interest, included Florida Gov. Reubin Askew, Sen. Frank Church and Sen. Gaylord Nelson.

The latest from the McGovern hat-in-hand front seems to be Edmund Muskie, ex-candidate for the presidency.

What a wry commentary if the presidential nominee were to hoist Muskie to the second spot.

McGovern dumped Sen. Thomas F. Eagleton because of past mental treatments for depression which seem to have completely cured the Missouri senator. Now presumably the nominee is entreating Muskie, who went on an emotional weeping jag when campaign ardors got depressive.

Candidate McGovern is making a travesty of his vice presidency problem by publicly conducting a safari for a No. 2 man, and no takers so far willing to join him on the ticket.

Not that we blame any of them.

The Hartford Courant
Hartford, Conn., August 6, 1972

After what is being aptly described as one of the most bizarre weeks in American political history, Senator McGovern has finally tapped someone else to be his running mate on the Democratic national ticket.

The party's Presidential nominee announced last night that he wants Sargent Shriver to take a shot at the Vice Presidency.

In addition to his more tangible assets as a diplomat and former ambassador to France, a pioneer in American Peace Corps and antipoverty programs, a longtime big-city experience in Chicago, and the fact he is Catholic, Mr Shriver basks in the charisma of the Kennedy family to which he is related by marriage.

Senator McGovern and probably many Democratic leaders had clung from beginning to end to the hope that Senator Kennedy himself would accept the Number 2 spot on the ticket.

And when it finally became plain Senator Kennedy meant "No" when he said it, wracking events were set en train that the Democrats will long remember.

Senator McGovern reached into the hat and came up with the name of Senator Eagleton. The melancholy story of what followed does not have to be gone over again here.

That shabby episode was followed all last week by an incredible game of hide-and-seek, "try, try again," or what you will. At least a half dozen prominent Democrats were approached by Senator McGovern—several for a second time around—and all had reasons why they did not want to stand for the vice Presidential nomination. Senator Kennedy (again), Senators Muskie (almost), Humphrey, Ribicoff, Governor Askew of Florida, Senator Nelson of Wisconsin, all had other fish to fry. They were content as they are, they had obligations elsewhere, they had personal family reasons for pushing aside the proferred coronet. How much pique, how much pessimism over Democratic prospects figured in the turndowns we shall never know. And perhaps it isn't just that Vice Presidential candidates are picked in the wrong way, as the growing debate claims. Perhaps few people want the job, say nothing of the task of striving for it.

In any event, the scramble last week, and all that led up to it, can hardly have been a help to getting the Democratic campaign off the ground. For all the vaunted organization Senator McGovern has been credited with putting together in the last four years, it apparently stood him in little stead in finding a running mate. It can hardly help a Democratic Party already rent and wracked by internal controversies. It was a week of confusions, bafflement and disappointments for the party's Presidential nominee himself.

There are indeed three months left in which to try to recoup the disadvantages the Democrats have put upon themselves in the last three weeks alone. It will be fascinating to see how they go about it.

The Dispatch
Columbus, Ohio, August 7, 1972

SARGENT SHRIVER, George McGovern's latest choice to be the Democratic party's vice presidential candidate in the November election, is at once a most presentable and a most provocative figure.

This 56-year-old Washington attorney is attractive and has a fine personal record. There probably are no skeletons in his closet. He has impeccable taste, for he is not just a socialite, he is of the rare social elite.

MR. SHRIVER is listed among the nation's wealthy and upperclass people. And it is especially significant he is aligned with the Establishment which orbits along the Atlantic seaboard.

As the wealthy are wont to do, Mr. Shriver married wealth. His wife is the former Eunice Kennedy, sister of the late President John Kennedy.

She is a daughter of the environs of "good old Boston, home of the bean and the cod, where the Lowells talk only to the Cabots and the Cabots talk only to God."

WHEN THE Kennedy family needed someone who personally was identified with Establishment ways of big business ventures, such as the giant Merchandise Mart in Chicago, Mr. Shriver was its choice.

When President Kennedy needed Establishment expertise to direct the Peace Corps, he turned to his brother-in-law.

And when President Lyndon Johnson needed a man to run the Office of Economic Opportunity and later one of wealth and social aplomb as his ambassador to Paris, Mr. Shriver was the obvious choice.

THUS, SARGENT Shriver is the antithesis of everything the forces supporting George McGovern stood for as they battled to gain the presidential nomination for their man last month in Miami Beach.

Labored rejections by a half-dozen other prospects for the selection as running mate may have been part of a grand strategy, that what Mr. McGovern wanted after all was a touch of the so-called Kennedy charisma. And Mr. Shriver was as close as he could get.

BUT IN THAT effort, Mr. McGovern is co-opting the very concerns which fashioned his nomination. For it definitely was not the wealthy, the social elite, the Establishment which pleaded the McGovern case from New Hampshire to California to Miami Beach.

But there he stands holding his impeccable Establishment credentials — Sargent Shriver, George McGovern's candidate for vice president.

The Washington Post
Washington, August 6, 1972

Sargent Shriver is a man of considerable accomplishment and of considerable talent and ambition. He is Senator McGovern's designated choice to replace Senator Eagleton as the Democratic Party's vice presidential nominee. In ordinary times—can anyone remember when they last were?—these two facts would have been sufficient to ensure Mr. Shriver's nomination by the party and they would also have been sufficient to make both timely and apt a discussion of Mr. Shriver's qualifications—his weaknesses and his strengths as a candidate. But in light of the gathering confusion concerning the kind of show the newly convened Democratic National Committee intends to put on at its nominating meeting this week, it seems to us the better part of valor to wait until Mr. Shriver is nominated before assessing the meaning of his nomination.

More than simple discretion argues for getting around to Mr. Shriver's record later. For we believe there is a related subject which takes precedence over the subject of the man himself, and that is the circumstances under which he has been chosen. We refer to what might be called "the second week that was"—the week in which you were nobody if you couldn't let it be known that you too had turned down an offer of the vice presidential nomination, the week, that is, which followed the joint announcement of Senators McGovern and Eagleton that Mr. Eagleton was getting off the ticket. The evident disarray and lack of discipline of the Democrats during those days seem to us far more likely to be on people's minds just now than the identity or biography of the new candidate. They must certainly be on the collective mind of the Republican Party and its presumptive candidates who have had the treat of watching the Democratic fun preoccupy both participants and observing public—even as such potentially explosive issues as the Watergate scandal go by almost unremarked.

Listening to Senators McGovern and Eagleton on their broadcast news conference the other night, one could have supposed that Mr. McGovern had the question of succession well in hand, that he was aware of the damage that had been done his candidacy by the incredible events of the week preceding Senator Eagleton's removal, and that his fellow Democrats—mindful of all this and also of the shrieking need to restore some semblance of dignity to the process of the vice presidential choice—would have determined to help Mr. McGovern recoup the party's losses. On the contrary, there followed a week of recrimination as to whose fault the Eagleton mess had been and something in the way of a vice presidential auction—with a sequence of announcements concerning those who had refused to bid. As pure political theater, Senator Muskie's performance must surely rate as the most extraordinary of all—the ostentatious turndown preceded by the period of musing and capped by the lengthy statement of his reasons for refusal, a statement including an offer to help Senator McGovern if the Senator so desired but a solid pledge to campaign for congressional and gubernatorial candidates across the country. When you consider not just the manner in which this second highest office in the land has been treated this past week, but also the nature of its present occupant, you have to wonder what more can be done to the poor office of the vice presidency.

In his address last night Senator McGovern attempted to retrieve some of the damage by reminding listeners of the crucial issues of the campaign as he saw them. He also pushed his earlier public explanation of the reasons for asking Senator Eagleton to get off the ticket a good deal farther than his remarks of last Monday evening. Mr. McGovern lent unfortunate credence to the belief that Senator Eagleton's removal from the ticket was solely owing to some national prejudice against persons who had received psychiatric treatment and that in the face of this overwhelming public response he had — against his own wishes — determined that Mr. Eagleton's presence on the ticket would displace, as an issue, the more important issues between the two parties. As a political tack, it seems to us that there are two things wrong at least with this position. One is that it does not comport with the word coming out elsewhere from the McGovern camp as to the nature of the Senator's decision. The other is that Mr. McGovern can hardly be doing his candidacy much good in portraying himself, by indirection, as a man helpless to express and enforce his will on such a major decision owing to the resistance of others. So while we found much in Mr. McGovern's speech on the issues to agree with and while we think Mr. Shriver is a very considerable man, we would observe that if this is in fact to be the ticket, it—and the Democrats—have much to overcome. Openness is not chaos, and credibility rests on more than mere assertions. The observing public is waiting to see something about the Democratic ticket—and it is waiting to see something more than who the candidates are.

THE SUN
Baltimore, Md., August 7, 1972

Sargent Shriver, first of all, deserves a good mark from the Democratic party for cheerfully taking on a vice presidential assignment which, by the time it reached him, had lost nearly all of whatever luster it ever had. Second, Mr. Shriver's designation by Senator McGovern as his choice for the vice presidential nomination—a matter subject to the action of the Democratic National Committee this week—is of special interest to Maryland. This state is in the unusual position of seeing two native Marylanders, Mr. Shriver and Mr. Agnew, selected for the vice presidency by the presidential candidates of the two major parties. An Agnew vs. Shriver contest for Maryland votes in November would give a localized touch to the campaign.

Mr. Shriver, of course, cannot be expected to win the election for Mr. McGovern, but it is just possible that he can help to rescue the Democratic campaign from the disaster that has been threatening it since the end of the convention—to help pull it out of the swamp of indecision and poor decision in which it has been caught. The responsibility for this state of affairs rests primarily on Mr. McGovern, who managed by inadvertence to focus public attention on the haphazard way in which vice presidential candidates are chosen. The Senator undertook to use his television time Saturday evening to put his campaign against President Nixon in motion, but he still has a good distance to go toward setting out specific proposals. Moreover, his rationalization of the Senator Eagleton episode did him little credit and his designation of Mr. Shriver for the second place on the ticket was made to seem a secondary part of his broadcast.

Mr. Shriver has been listed informally as a vice presidential prospect all along; his political assets seemed to put him on an equal footing with others on the lists, and he might well have been chosen at the start if the subject had been given the careful attention it should have had. Mr. Shriver is a known quantity. His record as director of the Peace Corps was outstanding. He probably did as well as any one person could have done with the formless Office of Economic Opportunity, the agency set up by President Johnson for a war on poverty. As ambassador to France for Mr. Johnson and briefly for Mr. Nixon, Mr. Shriver performed capably and stylishly. He worked diligently for Democratic congressional candidates two years ago, after putting aside thoughts of running for the governorship of Maryland. He has the Kennedy connection, he has a direct knowledge of American business, he is personable and he is a hard worker.

As we said, by the time the offer of the vice presidential nomination reached him its luster was worn away. Democrats who have been dismayed at the events of the past two weeks can hope, however, that Mr. Shriver will give a measure of breadth and stability to the campaign and thus contribute to a reasoned discussion of the public issues at stake this year. Mr. Shriver shows a becoming willingness to take on a tough job in trying circumstances.

PORTLAND EVENING EXPRESS
Portland, Me., August 7, 1972

Ever since Sen. George McGovern and the Democratic National Committee gave the heave-ho to Sen. Thomas Eagleton, a week or so ago, McGovern has been combing the political woods for someone else to run as the vice-presidential candidate.

Last Friday he got around to asking Sen. Edmund S. Muskie if he would join the ticket, after being rebuffed by Sen. Hubert Humphrey, Sen. Abraham Ribicoff, Sen. Edward Kennedy, Sen. Frank Church, Gov. Askew of Florida, and perhaps a few others.

Characteristically, Sen. Muskie flew home to talk with his family before making up his mind. On Saturday morning he politely declined the honor. We think he did the right thing, and we applaud him for it.

The senator told reporters it was a family and not a political decision — "my family was the central question in the decision."

But Sen. McGovern had a fall-back candidate, and only a short time later he announced that Sargent Shriver, Sen. Kennedy's brother-in-law, had agreed to run as the vice-presidential candidate. It is not likely that the national committee, when it meets tomorrow, will reject him.

There are several reasons why Muskie should have accepted McGovern's invitation, and several others why he should have reacted negatively, as he did.

Sen. Muskie has been through the presidential rat-race, and he acknowledged on Saturday that it has been a physical as well as an "emotional drain." It would have been almost impossible for the senator to add luster to his fine record, since this election holds very little promise of a Democratic victory. Who wants to be a two-time loser?

Then there is the question of compatability. Politicians are like chameleons in what they say and do, but Mr. Muskie led the fight against McGovern on the California credentials issue, and he had some bad things to say about him during the primary campaigns. It's likely that had Muskie joined the ticket the Republicans would have dredged up these tidbits in an effort to embarrass the Democrats. Furthermore, McGovern is a Populist, while Muskie is not, and it might have been difficult for the Maine man to swallow some of the proposals his colleague has made in the areas of taxes and defense and welfare.

Taking the other view, Sen. Muskie no doubt could have helped Sen. McGovern, as we pointed out only the other day. He is a Catholic, he represents the ethnic groups, labor likes him, and the South can tolerate him, and he would have added geographical balance to the ticket.

Still, the Muskie of 1972 is not the Muskie of 1968, when he was a fresh, able, Lincolnesque figure who inspired confidence in millions of voters. When he decided to run for the top spot in 1970, he ran ahead of the pack for many months, but then Humphrey entered some of the critical primaries, to cut into the vote Muskie otherwise would have enjoyed, McGovern turned out to have the better organization, and between the two of them they drove Big Ed far down in the rankings.

So, weighing the pros and cons, the senator has opted out, and he will achieve far more in the Senate as one of its leaders than had he made the race and lost again. Of course if the South Dakota senator wins, then Muskie may have second thoughts. But with McGovern's credibility beginning to dim, this does not look like a Democratic year, and tomorrow we will examine the reasons why Sargent Shriver accepted the somewhat dubious honor that Sen. Muskie rejected.

Newsday
Long Island, N.Y., August 7, 1972

What qualities should the country demand in a vice president? Although neither political party has bothered to prepare a checklist, it's not all that complicated. The candidate should know how big government functions, both the bureaucracy and the Congress. He needs a grasp of foreign policy, particularly big-power realities. He should (today, especially) have a feel for the problems of the cities and counties. In addition to all this, he should be a leader: a man possessed of energy, charm, robust health and the ability to sell his ideas.

We suspect Sargent Shriver would score high if the vice presidency were awarded on the basis of a Civil Service exam. As organizer of the Peace Corps under President Kennedy, he proved his skill in stirring the government to action and in handling relations with Congress. As ambassador to Paris he conducted diplomacy so well that President Nixon kept him on. And it should not be forgotten that Shriver was president of the Chicago Board of Education for five years. That ought to make anyone an expert on the local government crisis which besets us all today.

If Shriver has handicaps, they probably lie in his lack of electoral experience and in his longtime membership in the Kennedy clan. Two things can be said on the latter point. There were no Kennedys pulling strings in the background when Shriver, his family impoverished in the depression, won a scholarship to Yale, was elected chairman of the Yale Daily News (a big honor on campus) and graduated cum laude. And he showed personal independence by staying on with President Johnson (as first head of the Office of Economic Opportunity—the war on poverty) when his in-laws were breaking all ties.

On his record so far, Shriver is a handsome addition to the Democratic ticket. The fact that he was third choice (or fourth or fifth or whatever) is more a commentary on the system than the man.

It is much too early to render a judgment on the Presidential candidates and their programs, but we do welcome Senator McGovern's selection of Shriver as a positive step in upgrading the office of vice president.

THE DAILY OKLAHOMAN
Oklahoma City, Okla., August 7, 1972

JUST when it appears that nothing possibly could happen to make bad matters worse for George McGovern's ill-starred presidential quest, he receives another setback.

His latest reverse is the refusal of Maine Sen. Edmund S. Muskie to join him on the Democratic ticket. Muskie had been the fourth prospect within a week to withdraw from contention as McGovern's running mate.

He previously had been rebuffed for a second time by three men who had declined during the Democratic convention to run with him. Refusals had come from Sens. Edward M. Kennedy of Massachusetts, Abraham Ribicoff of Connecticut, and Hubert Humphrey of Minnesota.

Other possible contenders who have said they weren't interested include Florida Gov. Reubin Askew and Sens. Frank Church of Idaho, Birch Bayh of Indiana and Gaylord Nelson of Wisconsin.

In a fiasco of bad judgment and indecision which didn't reflect credit on either man, Sen. McGovern earlier had dumped Sen. Tom Eagleton of Missouri after the latter's belated disclosure of a medical history embracing electric shock therapy for mental depression.

In addition to the appalling staff work which was reflected in Eagleton's choice, McGovern's credibility suffered enormously when he forced the Missourian off the ticket after having expressed complete confidence in him and having said he would have chosen him even if he had known of his medical record.

Close associates of Sen. Muskie had indicated earlier that he entertained strong misgivings about the prospects for the Democratic ticket. One of the senator's associates was quoted to the effect that he thought things were "in such bad shape that it's virtually a lost cause."

Democratic politicians of national stature aren't eager to become associated with what increasingly has the appearance of a lost cause. Those who harbor even low-key presidential aspirations are reluctant to join McGovern on the ticket.

McGovern had been expected to announce his choice well in advance of the scheduled meeting Tuesday of the Democratic National Committee which must confirm the nomination. The delay suggested the difficulty McGovern was having in finding a willing running mate.

The New York Times
New York, N.Y., August 8, 1972

With the designation of Sargent Shriver as the Democratic Vice-Presidential nominee all but official, American voters can begin to give full attention to what both President Nixon and his Democratic challenger, Senator McGovern, have rightly called "the clearest political choice of the century."

The fundamental issues of economic and military policy, of approaches to human dignity and the quality of life that divide the two parties have now been sketched by Mr. McGovern in Saturday's televised announcement of his new running mate. He indicts the Nixon Administration for dividing the country and failing to fulfill its pledges of peace and prosperity. His own goal is to help turn America's course into a journey "inward toward the most powerful aspirations of the human heart." A totally different estimate of both the record and the potentialities will emerge when the Republicans gather two weeks hence to renominate Mr. Nixon and Vice President Agnew. Indisputably, the gulf is wide; the campaign task for both parties will be to persuade the country that not only are their objectives valid but that they have the programs, will and capacity to translate them into reality.

* * *

For the Democrats this task has been made substantially harder by the agony that has gone into filling the second spot on their ticket. The circumstances surrounding the original choice of Senator Eagleton and the week-long indecision over whether he would stay or go raised troublesome questions about Mr. McGovern's own judgment and even the trustworthiness of his commitments. These questions will provide abundant campaign fodder for his enemies, even though the damage to the ticket would have been vastly greater had Mr. Eagleton remained.

One solid effect of the whole tragic affair was that it awakened the country—we hope permanently—to the distortions in the yardsticks traditionally applied by both parties in selecting their Vice-Presidential candidates. How many extra votes the running mate might attract has obscured to the point of total exclusion any concern for his adequacy to fill the Presidency if fate decrees.

In exercising his second opportunity to round out the Democratic slate, Mr. McGovern was decidedly conscious of the need for putting first things first. Unfortunately, none of the six highest on his preference list would accept the nomination. The most disappointing rejection of all came from Senator Muskie, who only a few months ago was an odds-on favorite to head the ticket and who remains, in the judgment of many, the Democrat best qualified to occupy the White House. Although a variety of personal and political considerations influenced the half-dozen turndowns, their sum will be widely read as a vote of no confidence in Mr. McGovern's chances of victory and an index of the depth of the splits in the party.

* * *

The man who will now be his running mate, Mr. Shriver, brings many attractive qualities. In contrast to Senator McGovern's shy, almost diffident, manner, Mr. Shriver is an ebullient salesman, as he proved by his brilliant success in launching the Peace Corps at the start of the Kennedy Administration and again by the fact that the coldness of official relations between the United States and Gaullist France interfered little with the warm personal relations he built up as Ambassador to Paris in both the Johnson and Nixon Administrations. He was less impressive, however, as first field marshal of President Johnson's oversold "War on Poverty."

Mr. Shriver's chief assets are dynamism, charm, an engaging blend of practicality and idealism and, probably most persuasive to politicians though most dubious in any legitimate value scale, a link by marriage to the "magic" of the Kennedy family name. Whatever else, as measured against his opposite number on the Republican ticket, Mr. Shriver more than holds his own.

Both parties are now squared away for a fateful contest on the issues.

© 1972 by The New York Times Company. Reprinted by permission.

ARKANSAS DEMOCRAT
Little Rock, Ark., August 8, 1972

The problem of course is, that there has to be a vice presidential candidate. The law requires it. But it's certainly been nothing but a pain in the neck to George McGovern. Without it, he would have been off and running three weeks ago, whereas until now the best he's been able to do is to pose in front of Mount Rushmore and to make a dramatic trip back to Washington to vote for a raise in Social Security that was sure to pass anyway.

But now it's settled. R. Sargent Shriver, a brother-in-law of the Kennedys and the first director of the Peace Corps, accepted the job. The fact that he was the fifth or sixth choice didn't seem to bother him. Why should it? He's been looking for something to do for a long time.

Back in 1964, he wanted to run as Lyndon Johnson's vice president and Lyndon wanted him, too, but this allegedly got scotched by Shriver's in-laws, according to Kenneth O'Donnell, a Kennedy aide who wrote about it in Life Magazine. Hubert Humphrey was the choice of the Kennedys, and they made Pres. Johnson take him. Bobby Kennedy was at that time planning ahead, and he figured that only one member of the family ought to be in presidential politics at one time. So Shriver led Johnson's War on Poverty, resigning in 1968 to become ambassador to France. He stayed there at President Nixon's request and helped set up the Paris peace talks.

Early in 1970, there were rumors that he would become the chairman of the Democratic Party, but nothing ever came of that. In May, he decided to run as governor of Maryland, so he resigned his post in Paris and came home, where he began checking his chances. In deciding not to run, he established his credentials as a wind-tester. Marvin Mandel got 83 per cent of the vote against four opponents in the Democratic primary and picked up 65 per cent of the vote in the general election. But Shriver was hungry for politics, so he created something he called "Congressional Leadership for the Future" and went around the country campaigning for Democrats in 1970. That's why his selection is being greeted with cheers by Democrats in the Congress.

And actually, Shriver is as good a choice as McGovern could have made under the circumstances. To fill a job no one wants, you have to first find a man looking for a job who has time on his hands. Shriver is a sincere, well-organized individual, who has had enough real-life experiences (everything from operating his own business to seeing a 16-year-old son through a marijuana-possession charge) to bring some practicality to the ticket. Also, he presents no threat to Teddy Kennedy's ambitions in 1976, because few persons really think the Democratic ticket has a chance of winning this year. (We like the way that Sen. Ernest Hollings, D-S.C., put it: "McGovern couldn't carry the South, with Robert E. Lee on the ticket.")

Shriver is expendable, but at the same time he makes a classy runningmate. Of course, he has some problems in rationalizing his views with those of McGovern's. For instance, he gave at least tacit approval to President Nixon's Vietnamization program, which McGovern disparages. And his opinion of abortion — especially the views of his wife, who heads a nationwide movement against it — are not similar to McGovern's. But these things shouldn't present much of a problem. In fact, McGovern may be so happy to have an acceptable vice presidential nominee that he might change his views to fit Shriver's. Why not? McGovern already has done a lot of changing since he stepped off the primary stump.

THE CHRISTIAN SCIENCE MONITOR
Boston, Mass., August 7, 1972

Senator McGovern has tried to cut the string of losses both to his own candidacy and the future prospects of the Democratic Party with his naming of Sargent Shriver as running mate.

Those losses grew acute with a questioning of his own judgment and the quality of the men around him when Senator Eagleton's medical history surfaced. But they did not begin there. They began with a series of decisions in the McGovern camp which made the candidate appear too unbending toward the traditional elements in the Democratic Party. Senator McGovern had come by the nomination as a candidate decidedly to the left of his competition. And while his guess of the *direction* of change in his party may well have proved correct, he may have guessed wrong on the *pace* of change. Most voters wanting change want it to come about by evolution, keeping hold on what is useful until something clearly better comes along. But the Senator's camp had showed signs of the revolutionary's one-trackness, and this is distrusted.

The Senator, by the Eagleton affair, has been forced back to a more pragmatic position within the Democratic constituency. This may prove to have its rewards, if not in November, then at least in mending party affections for the future.

This is not to reflect on the personal qualifications of Senator Eagleton for office. He may have been done an injustice by the fact that the public discussion of his case would not end, preventing a confrontation between Senator McGovern and President Nixon.

Nor is this to ignore the damage done to the campaign as one major Democrat after another — from Senator Humphrey to Senator Ribicoff to Senator Muskie — rejected the second spot on the ticket. These refusals, which actually began with Senator Kennedy during the convention, will be read by the public as a vote of no-confidence in the ticket, regardless of the reasons given. Each refusal had the effect, if not the intention, of a rebuke to the judgment of the McGovern forces which controlled the convention.

There is no question, then, that in terms of the November race Mr. McGovern is more in the hole than he was three weeks ago. Then he had run up a string of successes that had made him and his men appear to be political wizards. The impression that he had some kind of infallible "winning formula" proved a myth. He has had to put a whole new campaign together.

Any objective observer would have to say this badly hurts his chances against Mr. Nixon.

But there is also a positive side to the recent McGovern misfortunes. First, each appeal to a Senator Humphrey or a Senator Muskie, though spurned, will not be lost on those who thought Mr. McGovern had grown too "new politics" arrogant for their vote.

Second, though Mr. Shriver will not by himself be able to deliver labor or other estranged party elements, he will generally be confirmed by party pros, voters, and the press as a reasoned choice. Mr. Shriver is an energetic and engaging man. He has marital though politically more tenuous ties with the Kennedy family. He is associated with a decade of national Democratic politics, and is thus a link with the traditional and progressive Democratic past. His record in launching and selling the Peace Corps under John Kennedy, in running the Office of Economic Opportunity under President Johnson, should make him a credible candidate with youth, minorities, and the city vote. He is not new to big-time politics. He will likely campaign with flair and zeal, a counterpoint to Senator McGovern's more sober campaign style.

Third, the latest Gallup Poll shows voters still give the Democrats the edge over the Republicans, by 53 to 47 percent, as the party they consider best able to meet the problems of the country. This is the same margin as in 1968 and 1960, perilously close elections. Mr. Nixon no doubt is running ahead of his party, just as he is running personally ahead of Senator McGovern. But at least the poll shows that Mr. McGovern, if he can only catch up with his own party, is in a race worth running.

One final advantage Mr. McGovern may gain out of his recent adversity lies in the nature of the Democratic constituency itself. Democrats, though they are the party of the numerical plurality, still consider themselves the party of adversity, the under-represented, the underclass. The recent ordeal of Senator McGovern may make him appear more one of their kind.

In any event, the Senator has endured the Eagleton affair with a display of intense seriousness but not of distress. This too could help him, as surely as he needs all the help he can get.

The Charlotte Observer
Charlotte, N.C., August 8, 1972

Sargent Shriver will bring to the Democratic ticket some distinct political advantages, but he has yet to prove he has the qualities that should be possessed by a man in a position to succeed to the presidency. To that evaluation anyone may logically retort: But look at the alternative who will be on the Republican ticket, Spiro Agnew. Even so, we are less than overwhelmed.

Only a few hours before the Shriver selection was announced, it appeared that Sen. Edmund Muskie would accept the nomination. That would have created no great enthusiasm, but Sen. Muskie has a very good public record and he would have been a most respectable running mate and, we think, vice president. He is a man of substance, though the indecisiveness which he showed throughout his presidential campaign raised some legitimate doubts about how he would perform as president.

After Sen. Muskie declined, some of the principal figures on Sen. George McGovern's staff won their arguments on Mr. Shriver's behalf. Frank Mankiewicz, Gary Hart, Henry Kimmelman and other leading campaign aides had looked favorably upon him all along. Sen. McGovern agreed to take their advice only after seeking other candidates.

The advantages which the party gains with the selection of Mr. Shriver are clear enough. He brings "freshness" to the ticket, as a number of congressional Democrats immediately noted with satisfaction. He also brings with him some of the Kennedy aura, as well as the confidence of many of the Kennedy people. His Maryland and Illinois connections will help the ticket; and so, perhaps, will his Catholic faith, a factor of decreasing importance in national politics but significant still in many urban areas.

Mr. Shriver had a good record in directing the Peace Corps. He engendered enthusiasm for it in its early days, and he was a successful salesman of it in dealing with Congress. He brought imagination, too, to the poverty program, though its ultimate bureaucratic failures may stand against him. As ambassador to France at a time when Gen. DeGaulle had sent Franco-American relations into a very awkward phase, his personality and zest helped repair some of the damage.

But we have doubts about Mr. Shriver's substance. In a way he reminds us of John Connally, though certainly Mr. Connally's poor record as governor of Texas is many notches below Mr. Shriver's administrative performances. The two share an ability to win attention, convey enthusiasm, dazzle people with their energy and, in general, make waves as super-salesmen. Given George McGovern's low-key manner and undazzling personality, Mr. Shriver will add fervor to the ticket. But is that the main ingredient it needed, and should that be a leading qualification for the vice presidency?

To Mr. Shriver's credit, his interests in public life have been directed toward solution of some of our basic problems — problems which others have been less effective in drawing attention to. He has flair as a leader, and he sometimes has been superb at bringing out the best efforts of subordinates.

And certainly it is an advantage to the ticket to have a man who does not accept the vice presidential nomination reluctantly. Mr. Shriver is, and has been, rarin' to go. He wants to prove things, and he desperately wants to make good — at the top. Those are not unimportant considerations.

We will watch with interest for indications that we are wrong in doubting his depth and constancy. Many men who have been called dilettantes midway in their political careers — Franklin Roosevelt springs to mind as one of those — have proved to be much better than that. We hope Mr. Shriver will.

ST. LOUIS POST-DISPATCH
St. Louis, Mo., August 8, 1972

Considering the catastrophic blow suffered by the national Democratic ticket in the dropping of Senator Eagleton as the vice-presidential nominee, Senator McGovern is fortunate in being able to enlist Sargent Shriver, an able and attractive executive and a member of the Kennedy clan. Mr. Shriver lacks experience in seeking public office, but he has an excellent background and he should add a bit of dash and glamor to the ticket.

Senator McGovern's difficulties in finding a replacement for Mr. Eagleton suggest that the leading Democratic politicians are gloomy about the South Dakota Senator's chances of defeating President Nixon in November; no one wants to ride the coattails of a loser. But it would be a mistake, we think, to dismiss too lightly the possibility of a McGovern victory. About three months of campaigning remain, and if Mr. McGovern and his advisers, including Mr. Shriver, can put their house in order quickly and begin to move, the lost time of the last three weeks may be made up.

After all, the issues remain, and they are pretty much what they were when George McGovern announced in January 1971 that he would seek the presidency—the Vietnam War, overspending on defense, the need for radical change in domestic priorities. Mr. Nixon, as reported the other day by James Deakin of our Washington Bureau, intends to concentrate this year on the issues rather than personalities, and has so informed Vice President Agnew. This is a constructive approach and we hope that both Democratic and Republican campaigners will follow-through.

But no one knows what will happen in the heat of a campaign. In view of the Democrats' travail, Mr. Nixon might suppose that he and Mr. Agnew have so much going for them that they need only to speak in platitudes and avoid mistakes in order to win. That is what Gov. Dewey thought in 1948 and scrappy Harry Truman, the underdog, carried the attack and won. Mr. McGovern is the underdog, and as he has pointed out, it is a familiar role. He can be expected to make the most of it.

Mr. Shriver's selection, assuming it is confirmed at the current meeting of the Democritic National Committee, should assure the active participation in the campaign of Senator Kennedy of Massachusetts, if that were not already assured. For Mr. Kennedy himself there is a unique opportunity, through his brother-in-law Mr. Shriver, to influence the course of the campaign. The circumstances could be significant with respect to Mr. Kennedy's future.

Mr. Kennedy, with his own trauma at Chappaquiddick in the background, has now seen how avidly some elements of the press and television pounced on Mr. Eagleton's health problems; he has a good idea what he can expect should he run for President later on. Since his ideas are quite the same as those of Mr. McGovern, he can observe without political risk how those ideas fare in the market place. Should Mr. McGovern and Mr. Shriver lose, Mr. Kennedy would be in a position to evaluate his political future, on the basis of a sort of test run, with greater accuracy. Should they win, well, Mr. Kennedy is only 40 years old.

It is to be hoped that Mr. McGovern is working on the reorganization of his staff with the intention of plunging into his national campaign the moment his choice of Mr. Shriver is confirmed by the national committee. He abruptly lost the winning momentum generated in the primaries and at the convention; perhaps Mr. Shriver can help him make a new start without more fumbling.

The News and Courier
Charleston, S.C., August 8, 1972

Sargent Shriver, even as fifth or sixth choice, adds something positive to the Democratic presidential ticket, namely the Kennedy clan's power and money.

Still vigorous at 56, Mr. Shriver was the first head of the U. S. Peace Corps, an agency formed by his late brother-in-law, President John F. Kennedy. To his credit, Shriver made the agency work despite an abundance of doubters. He later became director of President Johnson's Office of Economic Opportunity and more recently served as President Nixon's ambassador to France.

Mr. Shriver says the Kennedy family, particularly matriarch Rose Kennedy, is excited over his nomination. George McGovern probably is excited that the Kennedys are excited. Shriver, a wealthy man in his own right, has access to the Kennedy political exchequer, a virtue McGovern counted as his list of available running mates dwindled.

With an in-law on the ticket, the Kennedy family can be expected to go an extra mile with McGovern. Shriver's presence gives additional credence to the popular conjecture that McGovern is a front for Sen. Edward Kennedy and his presidential hopes for 1976. The Republicans won't have an incumbent in the White House in 1976 and, barring a McGovern victory, the Democrats will still be licking their wounds.

With approval of Shriver by the Democratic National Committee virtually assured, it is understandable that McGovern looks forward to smoother traveling. The Eagleton affair was a dilemma produced by McGovern himself with the able assistance of his zealous and idealistic legions. If times do settle, Mr. McGovern shouldn't be surprised to find that his credibility has become a prime issue.

After Sen. Eagleton told the world about his past health problems, Sen. McGovern said: "If I had known every detail of what he has discussed this morning, he would still have been my choice for vice president . . . I'm behind him 100 per cent." Within a few days he dropped Eagleton.

Newsweek magazine quotes McGovern's comment on Shriver as a possible successor to Eagleton: "Shriver! Who wants him? All that Shriver talk is coming from Shriver himself." Within days McGovern was down to Mr. Shriver on the availability list.

Perhaps this lack of credibility is one reason why McGovern had a hard time lining up a successor to Eagleton. The savvy prospects no doubt considered that Mr. McGovern in recent weeks has displayed a knack for letting his mouth trap him in politically embarrassing corners. The voters will wonder, too.

Time will tell how much McGovern has been hurt. Many will argue the old pros wouldn't have let it happen this way. As the controversy wanes, however, the exposed character and temperament of George McGovern are left in plain view of American voters.

The News American
Baltimore, Md., August 10, 1972

DRUNKS and little children, according to the old saying, get destiny's special protection from their own weaknesses. The same may well be true of George McGovern, at least in the selection of Sargent Shriver as his last-choice running mate for the White House.

In finally enlisting Shriver to be his first mate, the Democratic presidential nominee has given the impression of a man who somehow has done the right thing in spite of himself—almost miraculously.

His appallingly inept handling of the Eagleton fiasco was bad enough. Yet he managed to damage his leadership image still further by having his vice presidential offer subsequently spurned—in public—by potential substitutes ranging from Senators Humphrey to Ribicoff to Muskie.

The next effect was that of experienced officers refusing to sign on for a voyage they regard as doomed as the Titanic. Inviting Shriver aboard, as a result, clearly was the last major option open to the captain.

All things considered, Shriver might properly have been McGovern's first choice. Next to Sen. Edward Kennedy, his brother-in-law, Shriver stands to bring more strength and badly-needed cohesion to the party ticket than any of the men McGovern wanted before him.

Just consider. With Kennedy definitely refusing to run, Shriver was and is the one man who can give the McGovern ticket a touch of the Kennedy mystique it so desperately has needed.

He not only is married to the Kennedy family, he embodies its image. Energetic, articulate, handsome, ambitious and a Roman Catholic, he is best known to millions as the man who was picked to oversee the successful take-off of President John Kennedy's idealistic Peace Corps.

And that's not the half of it. His successful business background appeals to moderate Democrats. His work as head of the party's poverty programs under President Johnson earned him the confidence of the blacks, the young and many labor leaders. His long and distinguished service to his party has the appreciation of virtually all its traditional leaders.

Why McGovern was unable to see all this, and act accordingly from the first, is something only he could explain. The fact remains that he finally did so, however belatedly, and perhaps unwittingly has thus done himself and the Democratic Party a real favor.

Or maybe it was that special destiny that looks after bumblers, helping them when they need it most and deserve it least.

The State
Columbia, S.C., August 8, 1972

THE CHOICE of R. Sargent Shriver Jr. as the vice presidential running mate for Sen. George McGovern is bound to strengthen the Democratic ticket—except within those segments of the electorate which have no taste for Kennedy politics.

Mr. Shriver is more than just an in-law of the Kennedys (he married the sister of the late President John F. Kennedy). He is a credible representation of what the Kennedy brothers have stood for in their individual and collective biddings for minority bloc votes, Roman Catholic support, and liberal government.

As the first head of the Peace Corps and later as the initial director of the Office of Economic Opportunity, he established a reputation as a hustling public servant, capable of opening avenues of communication with new segments of society without alienating the old. Subsequently, as ambassador to France, he gained diplomatic experience which should shore up Senator McGovern's manifest weakness in that field.

Indeed, the combination of charisma and connections which Shriver brings as a vice presidential candidate may tend not just to shore up but to show up Senator McGovern. And if, as Number Two, he tries harder, he may wind up running faster than his principal.

But irrespective of his personal performance and campaign persuasiveness, Mr. Shriver is saddled with a presidential program and a political platform which goes far to the left of anything proposed by President Kennedy. And in one particular area of discussion, he may encounter some difficulty in reconciling McGovern's cut-and-run Vietnam policy with that of President Kennedy.

Nevertheless, it is probable that a McGovern-Shriver ticket will attract more support than would have a McGovern-Eagleton slate, even if Senator Eagleton's psychiatric problems had never come to light.

The manner in which that episode was handled ultimately proved a greater embarrassment to Senator McGovern and the Democratic party than to Senator Eagleton.

We anticipate that the immediate impact of the Shriver selection, which undoubtedly will be ratified by the Democratic National Committee today, will be twofold: it will get the Democrats back on track after their derailment in Missouri, and it will—or it should—shake the Republicans out of some of the complacency which had begun to set in after the Miami Beach Democratic convention and the Eagleton debacle.

Sargent Shriver will add a touch of pizazz to the Democratic ticket. In all probability, he will be able to tap some sources of campaign funds which were closed to Senator McGovern. He may be able to re-establish working relationships with some of the Democratic power brokers who had their noses put out of joint by McGovern's new breed—or should we say brood—of supporters.

Whatever the outcome, the presidential race from now on out promises to be more lively than would have been expected a week ago—and more threatening to those who fear the catastrophe of a McGovern victory.

San Jose Mercury
San Jose, Calif., August 8, 1972

Sen. George McGovern, the Democratic presidential nominee, is rapidly becoming his own worst enemy. The harder he tries to retrieve a lost advantage, the more inept he winds up appearing.

The latest case in point is Sargent Shriver, the latest McGovern choice for a vice-presidential running mate.

After failing to interest at least a half-handful of party regulars in the job — in the wake of the Tom Eagleton fiasco — McGovern was able to persuade Shriver to join the ticket. Shriver, a Kennedy in-law and a highly capable man in his own right, is a former ambassador to France and former director of the Peace Corps. His loyalty to the Democratic party and to the Kennedy family, which has supported Sen. McGovern from the beginning, is as obvious as his credentials are impressive.

Consequently, when George McGovern told reporters Sunday night that "I think we now have the best possible man," the Senator was hoping doubtless that the nation would take his words at face value and ignore their context. That is neither possible nor desirable, especially when it is realized that the American people will be passing judgment in November not only on a set of political and ideological differences but upon the individual men who will attempt to give form to those programs.

The nagging question persists: If George McGovern thought Sargent Shriver was "the best possible man" for Vice President, why didn't he submit his name to the Democratic national convention last month in Miami Beach?

McGovern's opinion regarding the relative desirability of Sargent Shriver for Vice President carries about as much conviction as the earlier McGovern pledge of "1,000 per cent support" for Sen. Thomas Eagleton, when that vice-presidential nominee was under fire for failing to disclose a history of treatment for emotional exhaustion.

The point in all this is that George McGovern, even before the presidential campaign can fairly be said to be under way, has shown himself to be as expedient a politician as any he ever scored for the same sin.

Apart from that, the entire vice-presidential mess to date has cast grave doubts upon McGovern's judgment, on the thoroughness of his staff work and, perhaps most important of all, on his standing as a genuine leader within his own party.

The frantic scrambling to find a vice-presidential nominee after Eagleton's resignation suggests that few of Sen. McGovern's colleagues are either drawn to him personally or feel they are in his political debt. Certainly there was no rush to support the candidate-in-distress, no closing ranks to meet the common enemy head-on. The fact that George McGovern is not a team player was never more clearly, nor for him more bitterly, illustrated.

For the American people, the implications of this cannot be overstressed. How can a President who commands no great allegiance or affection within his own party hope to push his programs through even a friendly Congress? The stalemate would be complete, of course, should the American people elect George McGovern President and give him a Republican Congress or a Congress narrowly divided between Democrats and Republicans.

In such a case, only a President with great personal authority among the people, a man of proven judgment and political deftness, could hope to accomplish anything. On the basis of his performance so far, George McGovern is not that man.

Campaign '72:
WALLACE RULES OUT 3rd-PARTY BID; AMERICAN PARTY NOMINATES SCHMITZ

Alabama Gov. George Wallace (D) announced July 29 that, on advice of his doctors, he "was not a candidate for the presidential nomination of the American party." Wallace had been the party's 1968 nominee when he achieved one of the best third-party showings in U.S. history. Wallace continued to undergo medical treatment for the paralysis suffered since he was shot by Arthur Bremer in Maryland May 15 [See pp. 681–690]. Bremer, convicted Aug. 4 on nine counts including attempted murder, was sentenced to 63 years in prison. The jury of six men and six women took only 90 minutes to determine Bremer's responsibility and sanity.

The American party convened in Louisville, Ky. Aug. 3 with many delegates still intent on nominating Wallace. Only a personal telephone call by the governor to the convention blocked a draft. The next day, the delegates proceeded to nominate Rep. John Schmitz (R, Calif.) for president and Tennessee publisher Tom Anderson for vice president. Both nominees are members of the John Birch Society. The party platform adopted the same day stressed local rule, law and order, strong drug laws, a ban against busing for integration, a generally isolationist foreign policy, and a call for military victory in Vietnam.

(A July 24 Harris Poll predicted a Wallace withdrawal would mean a net gain of five precentage points for the candidacy of President Nixon over Sen. McGovern.)

The New York Times
New York, N.Y., August 1, 1972

Governor Wallace's announcement that he will not run for President on a third-party ticket makes official a campaign advantage that President Nixon must have been anticipating with relish. So distinct are the potential benefits for Mr. Nixon—in every section of the country—that some political observers hint at an understanding between the President and Mr. Wallace, with a formal link to be established and, presumably, some political reward for the Alabama Governor in the offing.

Neither evidence nor logic back up this supposition, however. The Governor had no realistic alternative to recognizing that the heavy damage inflicted on his health by the despicable attempt on his life made any active independent campaign virtually impossible. That was especially true for a man whose basic appeal is to the passions of the electorate.

It seems plain that Mr. Wallace's immediate ambition is to capitalize on the prestige he has gained within the Democratic party by virtue of his impressive showing in the primaries and the sympathy and concern understandably accorded him by party celebrities of every stripe after the atrocious assassination attempt. With that purpose in mind, an arrangement with the Republicans would be counter-productive.

Given the Governor's view, he has only to sit back during the campaign and watch the grass grow. If the party wants him to speak out for the ticket, it will have to make concessions to him on policy. If not, he apparently sees a McGovern defeat in November, with himself prominent among the influential party chiefs who will in time pick up the pieces.

The strategy is shrewd but, if it gives the Democrats pause, there are compelling reasons why that pause should not be long. Any concession of principle on the scale Mr. Wallace would require would be not only morally unthinkable but politically even more disastrous than resistance to the Wallace philosophy—especially for a candidacy like Senator McGovern's.

© 1972 by The New York Times Company. Reprinted by permission.

Richmond Times-Dispatch
Richmond, Va., August 1, 1972

It would be naive to assume that Gov. George C. Wallace's withdrawal from the presidential race will eliminate the Wallace factor from the campaign. During the Democratic primaries, this man received more than three million votes. The people who supported him remain a part of the electorate and, presumably, remain troubled by the concerns that Wallace so forcefully articulated. Three million voters cannot be ignored simply because their leader has retired from the contest.

Polls indicate, and reason suggests, that most Wallace voters will now transfer their allegiance to Republican Richard M. Nixon, whose general philosophy they should find far more palatable than the views of Democrat George S. McGovern. Mr. Nixon's opposition to compulsory busing, which McGovern has endorsed as an acceptable tool for desegregating public schools, should be enough to lead most Wallace supporters into the Republican camp. And it is reasonable to assume that most of them are offended by some of McGovern's camp followers—the abortionists, the pot-smokers and the Gay Liberationists, for example—who would use the Democratic party to promote radical changes in American society.

Still, it would be foolish for the Republicans to believe that they can take all of Wallace's supporters for granted. Not all of them were attracted to the Alabama governor by his fierce denunciation of busing. Many were motivated by a vague dissatisfaction with things as they are and found solace in his criticisms of big government and big business and in his appeal for a better life for "the average man." McGovern's promises to impose higher taxes upon "the rich" and to return government "to the people" might appeal to many of the voters who supported George Wallace.

To win the enthusiastic backing of Wallace's followers, then, the Republicans must do more than condemn compulsory busing. They must make a vigorous and positive effort to demonstrate that the responsible moderation of Richard Nixon would do more to strengthen American society, do more to improve the lot of "the average man," than the irresponsible radicalism of George McGovern. This will not be an easy task, and the Republicans will commit a grave error if they approach it as such.

WORCESTER TELEGRAM
Worcester, Mass., August 8, 1972

The American Party has made its nominations for the coming presidential campaign. Party officials hope to have their slate on the ballot in all 50 states.

But no matter how strenuously John G. Schmitz and Thomas J. Anderson campaign, the American Party will be only a shadow of what it was in 1968, when it got almost 10 million votes and carried five states.

Four years ago, the American Party's candidate was George C. Wallace, the hero of millions of Americans who deemed themselves ignored by the major parties. They responded to Wallace's populist rhetoric with enthusiasm.

But without Wallace, the American Party is like the Battle of Austerlitz without Napoleon. Schmitz and Anderson are able exponents of the conservative viewpoint, but they have never "stood in the schoolhouse door," they have never taken on the "pointy-headed bureaucrats" with Wallace's breezy pungency, and they do not have his special identification with the race issue.

It may be that they will be able to coalesce conservative discontent with the Nixon performance to some extent, but it seems unlikely that they will be enough of a factor to cut into his electoral vote total. Most conservatives will take one look at McGovern and vote for Nixon anyway, despite his alleged flaws.

One key factor in the American Party's success or lack of it may lie in George Wallace himself. If he remains silent, most of his supporters will vote for Nixon. But if he should go on television and endorse the Schmitz-Anderson ticket, it might make a difference in some of the border states. It seems unlikely, however, that Wallace will do anything that might help McGovern.

Like the Bull Moose Republicans in 1912, the American Party of 1968 was a one-man vehicle. Wallace's mantle cannot be transferred to others, even if he should want to do so.

THE COMMERCIAL APPEAL
Memphis, Tenn., August 3, 1972

THE AMERICAN Party will convene in Louisville, Ky., today, but its hopes of giving a voice to many discontented Americans have pretty well disintegrated.

Gov. George Wallace of Alabama says the doctors won't allow him to run for president, and without Wallace the American Party won't have much to sell.

The history of third parties in presidential politics shows that they almost always are built around the charisma of an individual. Wallace, as the American Party's 1968 nominee, polled more than twice as many popular votes as any other third-party candidate in history. His third-man electoral vote had been topped in only one other presidential election in this century — by Theodore Roosevelt as the Progressive Party's man in 1912.

But the bullets which shot George Wallace down at a mid-May rally have left him too weak to campaign. The momentum he had going in the primaries has slowed to a halt. Running as a Democrat he was uncovering a popular vote which identified with the feisty Wallace, especially in his attacks on the integration of schools by busing. But when the Democrats brought Wallace to their convention platform to speak, it was evident that the party was in Senator McGovern's hands and headed in the opposite direction from most of the things Wallace stands for.

THE MEN and women who have supported Wallace have not cared so much about his party label as about his philosophies. Where, then, do they have to go when he is at odds with the Democratic leadership and also says his health will not permit him to run again under the American Party banner? The most likely beneficiary is President Nixon. Wallace's name on the ballot as a third-party nominee could have hurt Nixon more than McGovern. Now, even if the Wallace following "goes fishing" on Nov. 7, it means the President scores a net gain, for there will be less to siphon off his support in several key states.

As for the American Party, it can spend the campaign fighting things out with the People's Party, which has just chosen as its presidential candidate Dr. Benjamin Spock, who is more dovish on Vietnam than Senator McGovern.

The Courier-Journal
Louisville, Ky., August 6, 1972

WHAT CAN ONE SAY about the American Party's convention last week in Louisville, with its valiant but hopeless attempt to reconcile the political realities of 1972 with a Stone Age view that the best government is no government?

An acquaintance of ours says it was like a meeting of the Flat Earth Society, especially since George Wallace wasn't available to pump the juice of populism into the limp veins of right-wing conservatism.

Maybe so. Our dire prediction of tumult in the streets if Louisville hosted this convention has come back to us in the form of a heaping plate of crow (as we chew we are consoled only by the well-said maxim that if one must eat crow, the time to do it is while it's still warm). But could anyone have anticipated that without the Alabama governor to blend passion into the prejudice, the convention would spin off into such a giddy state of unreality? What outsider, no matter how unkempt his hair or wild his views, could muster up enough outrage at this silly business to want to march on the convention?

What did drift into Freedom Hall was an ideological flotsam from the distant, Birchite right; a sprinkling of passionate advocates of obscure causes; and a noisy array of those "love it or leave it" people who blame almost everything that ever happened on "the Communist conspiracy." It was a fearful political carnival, a flag-draped hall of mirrors in which the issues were the bright illusions. The point of it all seemed to be a chance for the delegates to reassure themselves, and each other, that they are right in insisting on an America that never was.

In the end, Governor Wallace wouldn't sacrifice what's left of his health to bring order out of this chaos. So the convention draped the mantle on California's Representative Schmitz, a man even more reactionary than his principal roll-call rival, Georgia's Governor Maddox. But Mr. Schmitz does seem to have at least one useful asset: a sense of humor. After this convention, he'll need it.

Admittedly, some of the week's speeches had a certain zip, although criticism always can be counted on to sound more lively than the dull business (which the American Party and Governor Wallace resist) of problem-solving. And at least one plank in the party's new platform—a pledge to end secrecy in government—is as up to date as the SST. But it's hard to find another.

Health care, for example. The platform committee had a hard time with this one, because the populists share the widespread view that everyone is entitled to decent medical attention, whatever has to be done to achieve it; while the conservatives cower in dread that this could mean forcing doctors into a more efficient system. The compromise, therefore, is a pallid assertion that the advantages of medical achievements should be available to every citizen through the free enterprise system. Whoopee. But how?

Welfare and Social Security? The conservatives have made some mental adjustments since the 1930s, when these concepts of governmental help for the poor and the aged struck them as the final triumph of Karl Marx. Now the most they can find to say is that these are good things if not abused. Wham. Opposition to abortion, sex education, busing "for purposes of social experimentation or racial balance," scatter-site public housing except when the neighbors (ha, ha) approve? President Nixon, who also keeps a close eye on public opinion polls, couldn't agree more. So much for moral leadership.

And, finally, the nitty gritty stuff of conservatism: The age-old opposition to deficit spending (even Mr. Nixon finally saw that Lord Keynes knew more economics than Harry Byrd), the yearning for impenetrable barriers to trade or other competition from the world outside, the xenophobia about the United Nations and almost everything else —except Chiang Kai-shek—in foreign affairs, the stress not on individual freedom but on property rights, not on corporate responsibility but on "the private capital investment system," not on how to solve problems but on how to blame them on everybody else.

Don't get us wrong. No party's platform will stand up to close scrutiny. All are a schizoid blend of diverse viewpoints; and if the American Party's is more unfocused than most it's just an indication of how big a tent it takes to hold both right-wingers who wish Washington would blow away and populists who want the benefits that only big government can bring.

The best thing to do in such a dilemma is change the subject, which is what national chairman T. Coleman Andrews Jr. did so poetically in his kickoff address: "This country was built on blood, sweat and tears, but today it's being replaced by sex, dope and queers." In a world full of problems, that's the way it is. Oh, alas for those simpler days of blood, sweat, Ma's apple pie, the robber barons, the 60-hour week, minorities who "knew their place," and—oh, yes—a flat earth.

The Star-Ledger
Newark, N.J., August 2, 1972

Governor Wallace has bowed to the physical realities of his incapacitation inflicted by the demented attempt on his life. He has removed himself as a candidate for President on a third party ticket, a decision generally regarded as enhancing the candidacy of President Nixon.

It is reasonable to assume that the surprising large number of voters who cast ballots for the Alabama governor will more likely fall to Mr. Nixon than the Democratic Presidential candidate, Sen. George McGovern. Ironically, the primary successes of Sen. McGovern were due in substantial degree to a populist appeal that paralleled the line taken by Gov. Wallace, including such broad-based issues as tax reform and the frustrations of the constituency with the establishment.

There is little doubt, even now with Mr. Wallace out of the campaign, that a third party vote, swelled by a sizable sympathy outpouring, would have cut more deeply into the Republican vote than the Democratic. The strong possibility is that the same five states in the Deep South that were carried by Mr. Wallace in 1968 will now swing over to President Nixon.

The issue is not that clear cut, however, in the North, where there are heavier concentrations of electoral votes. In such pivotal states as New Jersey, Ohio, Michigan and Illinois, there is no certainty that the Democratic votes pulled by Gov. Wallace will automatically go to Mr. Nixon.

But the impressive primary victories, coupled with the sympathy and concern evoked by the despicable attempt on his life, have made Gov. Wallace his own man, in political terms. He is in a position where he could wield broad influence in the Democratic Party, rather than seek an accommodation with the Republicans that would in the end be self-defeating.

Gov. Wallace could seek policy concessions, but any compromises along these lines would be deeply hurtful to the McGovern candidacy, on moral as well as political terms. It is extremely doubtful that the Democratic Presidential candidate would accept any arrangement that would profoundly compromise basic principles he has espoused.

The Miami Herald
Miami, Fla., August 8, 1972

ACCORDING to the Presidential candidate, there is a vast conspiracy between the Republicans and the Democrats. The candidacy of George McGovern was really "set up" by Richard Nixon, so that the Republican candidate can point to the Democrat and say to people: "You don't want that, do you?"

So much for the Presidential candidate. The Vice Presidential candidate thinks that Mr. Nixon is after "one-world government" and would "mongrelize the race." He likened women as public speakers to a dog standing on its hind legs—"When it does it at all, you're surprised." ("Sir, a woman preaching is like a dog's walking on its hind legs. It is not done well; but you are surprised to find it done at all." — Samuel Johnson, Boswell's Life, July 31, 1763.)

So much, indeed, for the American Independent Party and its candidates, lame-duck GOP Rep. John G. Schmitz of California and Tom Anderson, Nashville, Tenn. farm magazine publisher, both prominent members of the John Birch Society. In politics, it takes all kinds, we say conspiratorially.

The Virginian-Pilot
Norfolk, Va., August 7, 1972

Here is the line-up for the Presidential race this year. The Democrats wanted Teddy Kennedy and got George McGovern. The American Party wanted George Wallace and got John Schmitz. The Republicans are going to get Richard Nixon, and seemingly that's what they want.

The American Party (it used to be the American Independent Party) is the creation of Alabama Governor George Wallace, who won 10 million votes as its candidate for President in 1968. Mr. Wallace was a candidate for the Democratic nomination this year and said that he would not run as an independent or accept a draft by the American Party. But the delegates to the convention in Louisville last weekend wanted to draft him nevertheless, and it was necessary for Mr. Wallace to address the convention by telephone to head off the draft movement. He told the delegates, some in tears, that "the doctors have told me it would not be in the interests of my health. . . . I want to get well." Mr. Wallace, who remains hospitalized and partially paralyzed, will be months recovering from Arthur Bremer's bullets.

While the American Party without Mr. Wallace is a body without a head, the electorate may be surprised when they come to know more about former Representative John Schmitz, the man who was nominated for President on the first ballot by the delegates Friday, outpolling Georgia's Lieutenant Governor, the ineffable Lester Maddox.

Mr. Schmitz is a long-time member of the John Birch Society with far-right views. But contrary to the stereotype of the Bircher as a humorless kook, he has a sense of humor that is constantly catching others unawares. (Once at a gathering of right-wingers he approached a gentleman wearing a brown suit and a tan shirt and remarked, "I didn't know we were supposed to come in uniform.") He first attracted attention in 1964 when he was elected to the California legislature as an avowed Bircher, the first to hold major office, and he graduated to the House of Representatives in 1970, representing the Orange County (California) district where San Clemente is located — which made him President Nixon's Congressman. He was beaten by a more orthodox Republican in the June 6 primary, and some think that he was tripped by a wisecrack. He had said that he didn't mind Mr. Nixon's going to China and Russia, "but he might come back," and many Republicans resented the remark.

As its candidate for Vice President, the American Party ratified the selection by Mr. Schmitz of Tom Anderson, another John Bircher with a sense of humor. Mr. Anderson is the president of Southern Farm Publications and has won a conservative following through his column in *Farm and Ranch* magazine, in which he characterized Dwight D. Eisenhower on one occasion as "the most overrated man since Santa Claus." He has been characterized himself as "the barefoot wit" of the John Birch Society. The Schmitz-Anderson ticket won't win anything like Mr. Wallace's vote, but the pair promises to be good for a few laughs. Considering the earnest righteousness of George McGovern and the one-two of the Republicans, Spiro Agnew's banality and Richard Nixon's unctuousness, a few laughs will be more than welcome.

The Greenville News
Greenville, S.C., August 9, 1972

There is not much chance that John G. Schmitz, nominee of the American party, can win the 1972 presidential sweepstakes — even in this confused election year. He could, however, influence the outcome of the election by drawing votes away from President Nixon, just as Dr. Benjamin Spock, running on the other extreme of the political spectrum under the people's party label, is expected to nibble at Sen. George McGovern's ballot total.

The nominees of both splinter parties are avowed extremists. Mr. Schmitz, a lame-duck GOP congressman from California, and his running mate, Tom Anderson, a Tennessee weekly newspaper editor, are members of the radical right-wing John Birch Society. Dr. Spock's participation in various leftist causes is well known.

The American party was born in 1968 as Alabama Gov. George Wallace's personal vehicle in his campaign for the presidency. Delegates to the party's Louisville convention realized well the dependency of the party on Governor Wallace, and it was only after the governor, citing his physical condition as the reason, firmly refused to be nominated, that the convention turned to the Schmitz-Anderson ticket.

The ticket is not likely to have the voter appeal of a Wallace candidacy. The nominees actually stand to the right of Gov. Wallace's position on some issues. It would be a political miracle if Mr. Schmitz could revive the badly-splintered American party to even a portion of its 1968 strength. Only George Wallace had the potential to make the American party a major third-party movement this year.

This is not to say that the Schmitz-Anderson team will not get votes, even without the support of a strong party organization. And the votes they do get are likely to be President Nixon's losses.

The Schmitz appeal will be to ultra-conservatives who feel that both the President and Senator McGovern are too liberal, but who would have voted for Mr. Nixon as the lesser of two evils. Mr. Schmitz will get the "Red under every bed" voters, those who feel strongly that the President's relations with the Communist approach treason.

The base and width of Mr. Schmitz' support will be more narrow and confined than Governor Wallace's would have been on the same ticket. Even a small measure of support, however, could make the difference in the election in some states where a tight Nixon-McGovern race is expected, such as California.

A possible ray of hope for the Republicans is that Dr. Spock and his People's party will help even the score by draining a sufficient number of far-left votes from Senator McGovern. Dr. Spock's platform embraces just about all the liberal concepts that George McGovern felt were too radical to be included in the Democratic party platform.

The baby doctor, thus, will have a similar appeal to the left that Mr. Schmitz will have to the right. The country will be fortunate if they simply cancel each other out.

The American party, however, may do more damage to President Nixon's campaign than the People's party will do to Senator McGovern's drive for the White House. This is because the American party does have some organization left over from 1968. The machinery is still there to get Mr. Schmitz and Mr. Anderson on the ballot in a number of states. This is an important legacy Governor Wallace has given his party.

The People's party, on the other hand, has little organization and even less formal structure. These are facts, no doubt, which make Senator McGovern very happy.

Both splinter parties represent, as splinter parties usually do, the extremes in American political philosophy. But given the right circumstances in this uncertain election year, they could have a lasting impact on the future direction of the country.

The Birmingham News
Birmingham, Ala., August 11, 1972

All through the years when national Democrats were pushing civil rights and Gov. George Wallace was pushing back, the governor liked to refer to himself as an Alabama Democrat. Not to be confused with the Democrats of the Kennedys, Hubert Humphrey and so on.

But this election year Wallace went all the way with the Democrats. He entered primaries, amassed a goodly sum of delegates and went to the convention with confidence that, if he could not be nominated, at least he would make his influence and issues part of the party platform.

But the delegates, overwhelmingly for Sen. George McGovern, listened politely for the most part and decisively voted the Wallace platform proposals down.

Now Wallace finds himself in a party further to the left even than it was when he would have no part of it in the '60s.

What are his prospects, assuming as always that Wallace has not relinquished ambition for higher office, as a Democrat in a party in which McGovern, who wrote the convention rules, will be titular head, however the election goes, until 1976?

We have no answer. But Wallace must seethe with frustration at having proved that a sizeable constituency relishes his message, only to have the Democratic Party pay no heed.

The only possibility of Wallace again becoming a serious force in the restructured Democratic Party's nominating process would be for voters to inflict a Goldwaterish wipeout on McGovern in November.

Unless the present drift of "new politics" is—and Wallace and others will certainly work toward that end —repudiated, he will be as effectively shut out of the party as he was in 1964 despite his convincing growth as a force in national politics.

The question has been asked, will Wallace support McGovern in November? Of course not, though he may give aid to selected Democratic nominees in House and Senate races.

A McGovern victory would put Wallace back 10 years in the political spectrum, about where he stood while protesting school integration when buses were politically neutral modes of transporting school children.

In that case Wallace could after November resume the third party route, switch to the Republican Party, work with other conservatives to wrest control from McGovern, or content hmself as the dominant force in Alabama politics.

Portland Press Herald
Portland, Me., August 15, 1972

When Arthur H. Bremer pumped a bullet into the spine of George Wallace, he did something more than simply cripple the Alabama governor. Bremer's bullets also effectively shot down Wallace's American Independent Party.

Aside from Ted Kennedy, George Wallace is about the only major American political figure around who could be said to possess an abundance of charisma. It was largely this ill-defined, extremely personal quality upon which Wallace's third party movement was built.

When the American Party — which is what it now calls itself — held its convention in Louisville, Kentucky, recently, the extent of the party's dependence upon the Wallace personality was fully realized. Delegates refused to believe that Wallace would not be their presidential nominee until the governor personally telephoned the convention to explain again his physical inability to perform as a candidate.

Without Wallace, the American Party has collapsed as a viable political force. Without Wallace, hundreds of thousands of votes that went to the party in 1968 are expected to drift into the Nixon column this year.

The Louisville convention eventually constructed a presidential ticket with a couple of John Birch Society activists. What remains of the party, thus, has fallen to the control of a crankish, discredited organization at the farthest fringes of the political right.

The Wallace Party is dead, proving that personal charisma is not the firmest foundation on which to build a political movement.

Republican Convention:
NIXON AND AGNEW WIN RENOMINATION; PRESIDENT CALLS FOR 'NEW MAJORITY'

The 1972 Republican National Convention, with little of the drama of the Democratic nominating session in July, renominated President Richard M. Nixon and Vice President Spiro T. Agnew Aug. 21–23 in Miami Beach. Nixon's name was placed in nomination by Gov. Nelson A. Rockefeller (N.Y.), the President's chief rival at the Republican convention in 1968. In the balloting Aug. 22, Nixon won 1,347 votes, the only dissenting vote being cast for Rep. Paul N. McCloskey Jr. (Calif.). Agnew was renominated Aug. 23 by a vote of 1,345–1 with two abstentions. The dissenting vote was cast for David Brinkley, a National Broadcasting Co. commentator.

From the moment when party chairman Sen. Robert Dole (Kan.) welcomed delegates to the convention Aug. 21, the main theme of the convention emerged as a call for Democrats who were dissatisfied with the policies of their party's nominee, Sen. George S. McGovern, to work for the re-election of President Nixon. Another point made many times was Nixon's refusal to concede the youth vote to his rival. The President's only public appearance before making his acceptance speech was before a cheering rally of Young Voters for the President Aug. 22.

In his acceptance speech Aug. 23, Nixon appealed to the nation to give him a "new majority" to continue "the progress we have made in building a new structure of peace in the world." He directed special appeals for support to the young, the elderly and disaffected Democrats. Referring to the Democratic convention, he insisted that "many of the great principles of the Democratic party" had been abandoned. The choice in the election, he asserted, was "not between radical change and no change" but "between change that works and change that won't work." In an apparent reference to the delegate quotas used for the Democratic convention, Nixon declared Americans should not be divided into quotas. "The way to end discrimination against some is not to begin discrimination against others."

Echoing many of Nixon's points, Agnew warned in his acceptance speech Aug. 23 against pushing the nation back to an era when "people were judged not by their ability and energy but by their skin pigmentation and their ancestry and the church or synagogue they attended." In an apparent response to criticisms of his aggressive tone in previous campaigns, Agnew said he was "the President's man and not a competing political entity." Agnew met with reporters Aug. 24 to say he welcomed "the chance to be able to campaign totally on the issues" in contrast to his role in 1968 as "the cutting edge" for the party.

WINSTON-SALEM JOURNAL
Winston-Salem, N.C., August 23, 1972

SAY what you will about Richard Nixon, he is some politician!

Ten years ago, after his defeat for the governorship of California, he looked like a goner. As he lay there on the canvas, he even told reporters, "You won't have Nixon to kick around any more."

As recently as February of last year, he was running behind Sen. Edmund Muskie of Maine in the Harris poll — 49 to 46 per cent.

And still more recently, a year ago this month, only 27 per cent of the voters polled by the Sindlinger organization said they would vote for him.

But today in Miami he stands at the top of the political heap, a clear shoo-in for re-election in November.

Within his own party all is harmony. On the liberal side, Gov. Nelson Rockefeller of New York, who fought him bitterly for the nomination in 1960, now hails him as a statesman of finest feather. On the conservative side, Gov. Ronald Reagan of California, who sought to beat him for the nomination in 1968, now guarantees the purity of his conservatism.

And all across the land the great, invincible Democratic coalition put together by Franklin D. Roosevelt lies in smithereens.

Where are the Catholic voters? They know that Nixon is against abortion and for a $200 tax credit to parents with children in parochial schools.

What about the Jews? Nixon has given Israel even more than McGovern can promise.

What about the Solid South? Nixon is against busing (and even though the buses are rolling again this week, that doesn't seem to hurt him).

What about labor? With the kind cooperation of Sen. McGovern, Nixon has won over some of the leaders and neutralized others. And the platform, which is his creation, even is silent on one of the most sacred canons of Republican theology, the right-to-work laws.

How about the farmers? Nixon is selling $1 billion of wheat to the Soviet Union.

And the young people? Nixon has wound down the draft and has taken the foot soldiers out of Vietnam.

All this leaves mighty slim pickings for the Democrats.

Even the man's failures seem to add up to his advantage.

In 1970 he promised to balance the budget. Actually, the deficits for the first four Nixon years will come to something like $100 billion. If a Democrat had done it, this same convention would be calling for his impeachment. But not one whisper about "fiscal irresponsibility" has been heard at Miami.

Four years ago he promised to end the war in Vietnam, and he said again and again that the war would no longer be an issue in this campaign year. Actually, he extended American involvement to Cambodia and Laos and resumed the bombing of the North that President Johnson had halted. But most of the country only knows that he took out the foot soldiers, and it doesn't care about the rest.

He promised again that he would keep the United States supreme in decisive strategic weapons. But in Moscow he conceded to the Russians superiority in numbers of missile launchers and weight of nuclear warheads. Again, if a Democrat had done it, the Republicans would be calling for impeachment. But the Nixon magic made the Moscow visit an unalloyed political triumph.

☆   ☆   ☆

How has Mr. Nixon done it? How did he climb to this peak from the low point of a year ago?

It was done by a combination of action and motion. The wage-price controls of August, 1971, were action, and the public liked that. The Peking and Moscow trips were motion, and people liked that too. The mining of Haiphong harbor and the resumed bombing of the North were action again, and again the public responded.

Add to all this the fumbling of Sen. McGovern and his helpers, and you find Mr. Nixon now leading in the polls with an advantage of almost two to one.

So Richard Nixon, the down-and-outer of 1962, is very much the Champ in 1972. And barring miracle or catastrophe, he will still be the Champ on the morning of Nov. 8.

THE COMMERCIAL APPEAL
Memphis, Tenn., August 25, 1972

IT WAS A CONFIDENT, self-assured President Nixon who came forward Wednesday night at Miami Beach to accept the Republican nomination for his re-election.

Acceptance speeches at these events are generally rousing calls to the party to get out and work for the candidate, with as many peppy catch phrases as the writers can think up. But Mr. Nixon used another tack. He wasted little time imploring Republicans to come to the aid of the party. Their unity in support of his return for another four-year term was assumed.

THE TONE which Nixon set for his campaign is upbeat and positive. He addressed himself to all Americans, issuing a big, fat, happy invitation to disgruntled Democrats and independents to try his middle-of-the-road politics. Nixon sought to leave the impression that those who ride with him down the middle of the road will soon find it widening into a superhighway with beautiful and unobstructed scenery on both sides.

In his exuberance, the President did tend to exaggerate. Despite his war on crime and drug abuse, the view today is not as rosy as he pictured it. The rate of inflation has been curbed, but it is still unacceptable. The economy is good but erratic. The war in Vietnam has been wound down, but is not ended. But then these are the criticisms being made by Senator George McGovern as the Democrats' presidential nominee.

Mr. Nixon chose to tell it his way with words which would make Americans feel good about themselves. He proved, indeed, that he can outdo Hubert Humphrey, his 1968 opponent, in the so-called politics of joy.

For example, he pointed out the Republican young people in the convention hall as typical of cleancut American youth, leaving it to the television viewer to visualize the contrast with the street ruffians outside the hall who were doing their utmost to make a bad impression on the public. He noted that senior citizens on Social Security are not welfare people but have worked for what they receive and have a right to respect. Americans as a whole are better off than people anywhere else in the world, he said, and even if taxes are too high they're not as bad as in other countries. In short, the system of capitalism and free competition, Mr. Nixon assured the nation, is far superior to anything else devised by man.

In himself the President saw fulfillment of "the American dream," and he held his door open to those who "believe in the American system."

Hewing to the positive line, the President made no apology for not having brought the Vietnam War to an end as yet. He could have dumped South Vietnam when he took office and blamed everything on Lyndon Johnson, he said, but that was not how American presidents, since the time of FDR, have dealt with foreign obligations. So while struggling to terminate the war he has been busily building a peace for the future in talks with Peking and Moscow. And who can top that?

The other Nixon theme, which will be exploited from now until Nov. 7, was that Senator McGovern's economic plans are unworkable and that in foreign affairs the Democratic candidate goes against everything America stands for. Until McGovern, he suggested, dedication to a strong United States defense has brought nothing but bipartisan agreement.

THUS, PRESIDENT Nixon sees himself as the latest in a solid and unbroken line of right-thinking chief executives, starting with Franklin Roosevelt and proceeding through Truman, Eisenhower, Kennedy and LBJ. All American voters who see anything good in any of them, Nixon implies, are now eligible to join the "new majority" which he expects to renew his lease on the White House.

Nixon didn't exactly say that Americans never had it so good, but he tried in the Miami Beach spotlight to convince the people that if they want to keep what they've got they had better not let George McGovern get a handhold on the government.

TULSA DAILY WORLD
Tulsa, Okla., August 17, 1972

PERHAPS the Republicans should be grateful to Rep. PAUL McCLOSKEY of California for trying to put some life into their National Convention, which threatens to be about as exciting as a three-hour wait in a bus station.

But on the other hand, they know him pretty well by now.

Yesterday the GOP Rules Committee barred McCLOSKEY from having himself nominated for PRESIDENT at the Miami Beach convention next week. They ruled that any candidate to be placed in nomination must have at least a majority of the delegates in three States.

Some will complain that the Republicans are being arbitrary and choking off all opposition to PRESIDENT NIXON. That argument might stand up if McCLOSKEY had any real support in a genuine opposition move against MR. NIXON. But the fact is that he will have exactly one vote in the convention, because he got a few votes in the New Mexico PRESIDENTIAL primary.

McCLOSKEY has made a determined effort to advance his own name by running as a liberal Republican against the PRESIDENT. He didn't get enough support in the primaries to make it worth while to continue. Why should the convention clutter up its proceedings by letting anyone who has one vote be nominated as a gesture of vanity?

One of the things wrong with political conventions is the great amount of time wasted with futile, often quixotic, empty motions. They have a certain amount of ritual to go through, but here is a case where everyone knows RICHARD NIXON is going to be renominated unanimously. Why fool around just to let somebody named McCLOSKEY make a hokey pitch for the tv cameras?

If there were a genuine opposition candidate with substantial support, of course he should have his day at the convention. But the GOP proceedings will not lose an iota in any way by keeping McCLOSKEY off the rostrum.

The Seattle Times
Seattle, Wash., August 25, 1972

THOSE political pundits who had been advising the nation that President Nixon intended to remain largely above the campaign battle, allowing lesser administration figures to bear the brunt of the attack on Senator McGovern, widely misjudged Mr. Nixon's zest for political combat.

It did not take the President long, after mounting the podium at Miami Beach for his acceptance speech, to take off the gloves.

The way to reach the goal of adequate employment levels without war or inflation, Mr. Nixon said, is "not to take a sharp detour to the left which would lead to a dead end for the hopes of the American people...

"Our opponents," he observed, clearly warming to the battle, practice "the politics of paternalism... Their proposal to pay $1,000 to every person in America insulted the intelligence of the American voters."

McGovern lately has been trying to back away from his $1,000-to-everybody proposal (why not $10,000 or $50,000 or $1 million?), but he has not backed away fast enough to keep an old political master like Mr. Nixon from recognizing a fat target when he sees one.

BUT to move from the ridiculous to the single issue that is of greatest importance to all of the world's peoples—war or peace—the President, in his Miami Beach address, added a significant phrase to his 1968 call for "an era of negotiation rather than confrontation" with the Communist powers.

"*Within the short space of four years in our relations with the Soviet Union,*" he said, "*we have moved from confrontation to negotiation to COOPERATION in the interests of peace.*"

In other words, the two nuclear superpowers have reached a third stage—beyond simply the absence of confrontation (remember the American and Russian tanks gun-barrel-to-gun-barrel at the Berlin wall) and beyond simply a continuance of negotiations—to active cooperation in preventing major war.

Evidence of that cooperation abounds in recent weeks: The arms-limitation treaty, for instance; the Russian refusal to provide Egypt with long-range offensive weapons (leading to the ouster of Soviet military advisers from that country), and the steps taken by both superpowers to prevent Vietnam from distorting their relations on larger issues.

THIS progress in rolling back the threat of nuclear war will be the centerpiece of the record Mr. Nixon will set before the country in his bid for re-election.

But for all of that, he's not above trading punches with a challenger who must place his hopes in a free-swinging attack. It should make for a lively campaign.

The New York Times
New York, N.Y., August 25, 1972

President Nixon's acceptance speech to the Republican National Convention was an extraordinary address for an incumbent to deliver. Instead of expounding the accomplishments of his own Administration and explaining how he plans to extend and improve upon them in the next four years, Mr. Nixon devoted most of his energies to calling upon the electorate to fear Senator McGovern and the Democrats.

"In asking for your support, I shall not dwell on the record of our Administration which has been praised, perhaps too generously, by others at this convention," he said. Coming early in the speech this sentence sounded like a bit of engaging modesty, until it became evident that it was, in fact, a line concocted to enable him to pivot away from his own record and make a savage, partisan attack on the opposition.

Except for a concluding "upsweep" section on the hope for peace, the thrust of the speech was overwhelmingly negative. It was as if Mr. Nixon has not been President at all but is still the office-seeker and partisan sharpshooter, ever on the attack. It was also an intellectually tired and empty speech—one that fell back on old material and barely reworked "cheer lines" from previous campaigns.

Thus, the quote from Lincoln about America being on God's side was lifted from the last paragraph of the first Nixon acceptance speech in 1960. The passage about Tanya, the Russian girl, was the same one that he used in his address to the Russian people earlier this year. "Peace is too important for partisanship," is a slight variation of the line Mr. Nixon used in the last campaign to avoid any discussion of how he intended to "end the war and win the peace" in Vietnam.

Indeed, Wednesday night's speech had the same purpose as the carefully crafted "basic speech" which he repeated over and over again in 1968 and—with some different phrases—in 1960. That purpose is not to engage in the democratic process of debate, of argument and counter-argument, of explaining problems to the people and trying to guide them in the direction a leader thinks they should move. Mr. Nixon seeks the opposite. He seeks to obscure the hard choices, to package issues in ways that sound pleasing to listeners but actually commit him to nothing, and thereby to evade a leader's responsibility rather than to exercise it.

* * *

There can be little doubt that Mr. Nixon's performance was effective in partisan terms. With the skills he has relied upon in a quarter-century of campaigning, he set up straw men and bravely struck them down. He placed the well-calculated innuendo; he deployed the usual dubious or unprovable statistics; he made complex issues pivot like dancing bears and leap through rhetorical hoops; he stirred fear and then came down firmly on behalf of convictions shared by everybody.

"I believe in the American system." And who in this campaign does not?

"We have launched an all-out offensive against . . . permissiveness in our country." What does it actually mean, if anything, to launch an attack on permissiveness?

Dusting off an applause line from his 1968 standard speech, Mr. Nixon said, "I want the peace officers across America to know that they have the total backing of their President in their fight against crime." Does that mean they did not have the backing of President Kennedy or President Johnson? Or that Senator McGovern is pro-crime?

"Let us be generous to those who can't work without increasing the tax burden of those who do work," Mr. Nixon said. No one can be generous and thrifty at the same time; the President's own welfare reform plan would involve substantial additional Federal expenditures. In like vein, the President denounced the local property tax but said nothing about the broad-based tax that would have to be imposed to take its place.

The taint of demagoguery sadly infected even the President's discussion of the Vietnam tragedy and also of his initiative toward China and Russia, where his critics would readily concede his constructive efforts. Mr. Nixon laid down three unexamined but applause-provoking criteria for a Vietnam peace. He promised never to abandon American prisoners of war, but did not say how endless bombing would get them back. He promised never to impose a Communist government on South Vietnam, but did not explain how he would end a war in which the political future of South Vietnam is the central issue. He promised never to "stain the honor of the United States of America," but did not say why it is honorable to rain bombs on the Vietnamese people because they are Communists at the same time that he is making friendly overtures to far more powerful Communist nations.

If he keeps to the pattern of his past campaigns, President Nixon will reiterate endlessly between now and November what he said on Wednesday evening. Sections of the speech may be omitted or their order of delivery shuffled on other occasions, but this is probably "the speech" for the Nixon campaign. If so, it is no happy augury for a reasoned and responsible discussion of the nation's serious problems.

© 1972 by The New York Times Company. Reprinted by permission.

Minneapolis Tribune
Minneapolis, Minn., August 24, 1972

President Nixon, in accepting his party's nomination last night, made world peace his No. 1 campaign theme. "More than on any other single issue, I ask you, my fellow Americans, to give us the opportunity to continue these great initiatives (with China and Russia) which can contribute so much to the peace of the world."

This means that Americans will choose between two peace candidates in the November election—candidates with clearly different approaches to peace. The President emphasizes his vision of a lasting peace brought about by improved relations between the United States and the two big Communist nations. Development of that kind of peace requires, the President argues, a continued high level of military spending and a continuation of basic U.S. policies in Vietnam. Sen. George McGovern, in his acceptance speech and in a subsequent speech when Sargent Shriver was selected as his running-mate, has emphasized his proposals to end the war immediately and to reduce military spending greatly.

We think military spending can and should be reduced, though not as drastically as McGovern suggests, and we favor a more rapid end of American participation in the war. But we also strongly applaud the President's efforts to improve relations with China and the Soviet Union.

In 1968, in an earlier acceptance speech, Mr. Nixon spoke of the need to replace "an era of confrontations" with "an era of negotiations." That change is taking place, and the American people have responded to the President's initiatives. According to a Gallup Survey published this week by Newsweek, Americans consider the President's trips to China and Russia his most important accomplishments.

The irony of the President's emphasis on peace initiatives with China and Russia is, in our opinion, that America is dropping record tonnages of explosives on a small country that we went to war against as part of the Cold War against China and Russia. While he seeks better relations with them, what began as France's colonial war against Vietnamese goes on. And so does the rhetoric about staining America's honor and, somewhat disguised, the domino theory.

The domestic portion of the President's speech seemed to lack compassion for America's poor and for those who suffer the effects of discrimination. "People on welfare in the United States," the President said, "would be rich in most of the nations of the world today." While this statement may be true in terms of dollar income, it hardly reflects the misery and degradation experienced by many poor Americans.

The President said America's elderly want "retirement in dignity and self respect," but did not mention that his administration is withholding funds for housing programs that help the elderly. He criticized McGovern's income-redistribution plan as "a scheme where government gives money with one hand and takes it away with the other." But he also mentioned his own goal of reducing local property taxes by providing more federal revenues to local communities. Whether this is good or bad, it involves a process of giving and taking—and presumably would even mean taking some money, directly or indirectly, from people who are too poor to own property.

In his presentation last night, the President seemed relaxed and confident. The reception given him by his own party, as well as the broader public receptivity indicated by the polls, gives the President every reason to be confident. George McGovern told his fellow Democrats: "Never underestimate the power of Richard Nixon to bring harmony to Democratic ranks." It is a long time until election, but at the moment the opposite seems to be taking place.

THE BLADE
Toledo, Ohio, August 23, 1972

THIS ALMOST certainly is Richard Nixon's moment of greatest triumph. It is greater than his previous nominations at Republican national conventions — twice as presidential standard-bearer and twice earlier as vice presidential candidate—because now, as an incumbent he enjoys a breadth of unified support and genuine admiration within his party that goes beyond the political pragmatism and opportunism which accounted for his past candidacies. And the experience of this hour of acclamation at Miami Beach is probably greater than Mr. Nixon can expect even if he does indeed achieve the hoped-for victory of landslide proportions in November.

As the giant kickoff rally that the 1972 GOP national convention represents proceeds through its carefully orchestrated preview of the campaign ahead, the oft-cited comparison between the Nixon-McGovern race this year and the Johnson-Goldwater one in 1964 unavoidably comes to mind. But what is more intriguing — and probably more accurate — than the similarities is the contrast between the two situations. As ought to have been more apparent than it was at the time, the 1964 campaign did not really offer the highly touted choice between conservative and liberal candidates; in definition of conservatism, Lyndon Johnson if anything fit the category more appropriately than Barry Goldwater did. And as subsequent history starkly demonstrated, the winner's conduct of the Vietnam war turned out to be far more hawkish than the pledges of the loser, who bore the militant label during the campaign.

This time, the advantage that the incumbent appears to have gained is the opportunity to emphasize a choice for the electorate, and one which is based, paradoxically, on his neutralization of the opponent's principal points against him. In effect, the President is taking over Senator McGovern's issues and making them his own.

THAT is most dramatically evident in the case of the war. It was the foundation of the McGovern cause, and Mr. Nixon should by all political logic—if there is such a thing—be indefensibly vulnerable to the charge that he has not ended the conflict as he promised in 1968 to do. Yet, the President seems so far to be succeeding in actually turning that failure to his favor by withdrawing U.S. combat troops, reducing American casualties to a tiny fraction of what they were when he took office, and contending that he can do no more in the absence of conciliation from Hanoi without grave risk to prisoners of war and remaining U.S. air and support forces.

Moreover, through his bold moves toward new relationships with Soviet Russia and especially Communist China, Mr. Nixon has focused attention anew on internationalism in American policy as the route to peace, while scorning the McGovern calls for a lower American presence abroad and reduced spending for defense as "neoisolationism."

That is part and parcel as well of the Nixon response to Senator McGovern's demand for higher priorities in the domestic realm. The President reiterates that the "new era" of global detente negotiated from a position of continued American strength is the prerequisite for solution of pressing problems at home. The implication is that he will devote more effort to domestic affairs as foreign problems are eased — or that he would if the Democratic-controlled Congress only would act on the programs he advances. Meanwhile, the more Mr. McGovern discusses his own ideas for dealing with these problems, obviously the more he is subject to criticism on the substance of his proposals. The President could hardly be in a better tactical position to trap his opponent coming or going.

For all of that, nothing can be taken for granted as to the outcome of the campaign itself. In politics, such certainty is always hazardous. But what is clearly certain is that George McGovern has a great deal of work cut out for him, not only to put his own divided forces into better condition for a difficult fight but, more important, to confront the overwhelming advantage the incumbent holds.

And the very fact that the President has managed to put himself at this moment in such a commanding position of superiority — barely a year after things could scarcely have looked worse for him — goes a long way to explain why he and his party's delegates in Miami Beach are riding a crest of such confidence.

OREGON JOURNAL
Portland, Ore., August 24, 1972

The Nixon-Agnew ticket comes charging out of the Republican National Convention, riding high in the polls and backed solidly by a united party.

The quadrennial gathering was less a convention than a dramatization of a party's enthusiastic support for the incumbent team seeking a second term.

What dissension existed, and it was there, was carefully played down and the picture given to the public was meticulously staged to give the impression that everybody, including the young, are on the Nixon bandwagon.

The GOP convention contrasted sharply with the previous Democratic assembly, where debate ruled and party differences were fought out for all the world to see. There was jubilation and disappointment, victory and defeat and only in the closing hours was there an attempt to give the appearance of unity.

But a question has bugged some delegates to the GOP convention: Was it too well staged, too harmonious to be believable, too obvious?

People have differences, and fight them out, and then get together again, and then disagree some more even while working for a common cause. Will they identify more readily with the Democratic convention, which was real if tumultuous, than the tidy, placid reunion of the Republicans?

At best, the GOP had little chance of drumming up much excitement. The party holding the White House just doesn't have the opportunity when it is gathering for the formality of renominating the incumbent. But the Republicans may have overdone the solid-front theme.

An issue of this campaign already is the matter of openness, candor, letting the public in on the decision-making even if it hurts.

As President Nixon goes into the campaign with all the odds in his favor, the question of trust could be his Achilles heel.

There is the Watergate bugging incident, and the undisclosed campaign fund of $10 million, deliberately collected before the law requiring full disclosure went into effect. These are incidents that strike at the heart of the issue of trust.

If the convention came through to the public as a bit too neatly packaged, that could offer further ammunition to the Democrats for an issue they will seek to develop.

THE DENVER POST
Denver, Colo., August 25, 1972

WE WERE IMPRESSED this week by the joyous, brisk efficiency with which the Republicans went about the renomination of President Nixon and Vice President Agnew.

Much of the joy, of course, resulted from the fact that the President's lead over Senator McGovern in the opinion polls is so substantial.

And the briskness derived from the convention's wasting precious little time on deliberation. In fact, there was not much to deliberate; almost everything had been worked out in advance.

AS INDICATED BY his speech, the President plans to take the high road, to run on his record and to invite a "new majority" of Americans to create a fresh consensus. He cast himself, "not as a partisan of party, which would automatically divide us, but as a partisan of principles which can unite us."

His toughest line of the night was: "Let us reject the policies of those who whine and whimper about our frustrations and call on us to turn inward."

It was a subdued Vice President Agnew who accepted renomination, also. He challenged the "piecemeal, inconsistent and illusory policies of George McGovern" and let it go at that.

NOT THAT THIS campaign strategy won't change should the polls suddenly show the Democrats closing the gap appreciably. In that case, the President very likely will come out jabbing.

But as of now, the form of battle, if not all the substance, has emerged.

Mr. Nixon casts himself as the seasoned solver of problems; McGovern is the innovator, a man impatient with the pragmatic approach. If these roles can be preserved, the President can concentrate on his Vietnam accomplishments — which are considerable, his highly-successful efforts to establish and maintain communication with China and Russia, and with his rapidly-succeeding domestic economic programs.

IT WOULD BE wrong, we sense, simply to make note of this Republican convention as a well-oiled performance that went off right on schedule and let it go at that.

It seems to us that if there had been any fundamental, deep-set gripes with Mr. Nixon or the way he has done his job, they would have surfaced — all the floor managers in the hall notwithstanding.

Los Angeles Times
Los Angeles, Calif., August 25, 1972

If the delegates to the Republican National Convention fail to see that the future of the Republican Party lies in broadening its base, as we were arguing yesterday, President Nixon clearly understands that his election in November depends upon his widening his appeal.

The President's acceptance speech was an open bid for the votes of uneasy Democrats. Sensing that George McGovern is vulnerable, the President went on the attack, striking for McGovern's weak points, notably his ideas about defense and the national economy—and making his own pitch for those groups of traditional Democrats, including workingmen, Catholics, ethnics, Jews and white Southerners, whom he hopes to bring into his "new coalition."

The speech was, as nearly all acceptance speeches are, and as George McGovern's last month certainly was, undistinguished in expression and unimpressive in delivery.

In substance nothing in it was new; it was a collection of issues reduced to slogans. Its interest lies in what it forecasts about the rhetorical content of the President's campaign. It is reasonable to suppose that, as in 1968, Mr. Nixon's acceptance address pretty well foreshadows what he is going to be saying on the stump.

In that respect, we confess to some disappointment. Mr. Nixon has been a better President than his presentation of himself at the Miami Beach convention hall. He has a stronger and more subtle grasp of issues than he revealed in his speech.

Any politician, and Mr. Nixon is a superb practitioner of the craft, could reply that after all a political speech is a political speech, and where is a political speech more appropriate than to the party convention that just nominated you. True enough, and in evidence any politician could introduce the fact that Mr. Nixon got much less applause for mentioning the U.S.-Soviet arms agreement, which is probably the most notable achievement of his Administration, than for declaring that "we will never abandon our prisoners of war," which as a sentiment is unexceptionable, but as a statement of policy is as vapid as McGovern's applause-getting litany of last month, "Come Home, America." So perhaps to ask for a statesman's speech at a political convention is a bit much.

But it does seem to us that the President, riding as he is a wave of popularity, had the opportunity Wednesday night, and still has it, to rise above using the vote-luring, applause-getting rhetorical chords he played in his acceptance speech. He had the opportunity, and still has it, to talk soberly and substantively about the central issues of this campaign: how to adjust to the changing world, how to manage the economy, how to work toward social justice.

There is a choice in this campaign; is it too much to ask the two candidates to talk to us with some recognition that we can go beyond slogans to make the decision on the basis of mature discussion?

Naturally enough, Mr. Nixon is currently making the most of his good fortune in having George McGovern as his opponent. But in the longer run the independents and the Democrats whose support the President seeks are probably more interested in what Mr. Nixon will do for the country than in what Mr. Nixon thinks McGovern will do to it.

The Burlington Free Press
Burlington, Vt., August 25, 1972

A MAJOR TURNING POINT in the history of American politics and government is occurring this year. This is the most significant change since the election of Franklin D. Roosevelt four decades ago, and the subsequent construction of the Democratic-labor coalition.

The old Rooseveltian coalition was shattered finally this year, and the new ruling coalition — which could last as long as the old — has emerged in unmistakable fashion.

The architect, the spokesman, the inspiration of the new majority is Richard M. Nixon, widely regarded already as one of the truly great Presidents of American history.

He has built the coalition with many of the vital and diverse elements of the Rooseveltian one — the workers, the young people, the various minorities. But there are really no distinct minorities in the new majority, as the President noted in his acceptance speech at the Republican National Convention Wednesday night. They are all Americans who believe in America, who will help to build America, who will defend America, who know there is far more right with our nation than wrong with it.

Nixon's new majority consists of millions of Democrats as well as Republicans. And the numbers will grow following the President's invitation of Wednesday night: "Six weeks ago our opponents in their convention rejected many of the great principles of the Democratic party. To those millions who have been driven out of your home in the Democratic party we say come home, not to another party but to the great principles we Americans believe in together."

The construction of this new majority was accomplished totally through the forceful leadership of Richard Nixon, and even some of his severest critics express admiration. It is all doubly remarkable because the President has achieved this during a period of divided government — his own party in charge of the executive branch and the opposition party in charge of the legislative branch.

* * *

CAN THE NEW MAJORITY, whose construction so much reflects the personality of one man, survive after the Nixon years? The Rooseveltian coalition, of course, survived Roosevelt by a quarter of a century.

The new Nixonian coalition appears destined to survive its architect, although a clearer forecast will have to await the cumulative results of the Nov. 7 election, the further achievements of President Nixon during the next four years, and the selection of his successor in the nation's bicentennial year of 1976.

Richard Nixon's new majority is built upon the sturdiest of foundations: Faith in America's future. That is the prevailing national political faith which has sustained our nation through every crisis for 196 years, and that is the faith which must sustain our nation through the years of adventure and greatness ahead. — F.B.S.

DAYTON DAILY NEWS
Dayton, Ohio, August 25, 1972

The Republican party has completed its pre-election victory celebration and gone off to campaign behind a leader who, in accepting his renomination, typically misrepresented his opponent's proposals and offered fake alternatives. The Old Nixon is with us again, as he has been in almost every national election since 1952.

The difference four years has made is that Mr. Nixon now poses more statesmanly, with some justification. He seems almost to have accepted the fact that he really is the President. At his best, there is a kind of amazed dignity about him these days.

The convention that verified that for him did not, however, show Mr. Nixon or the Republican party at their best. So anxious were its controllers to force general agreement into unamity that they even denied poor Rep. Paul McCloskey Jr. his lone delegate and only grudgingly allowed him the one vote his disaster won for him.

Some after-images:

The convention made an effort to avoid the thinly covered race-baiting that the administration sometimes has encouraged, and it worked to display its sprinkling of Negro delegates. But the message that came through was an old one up-dated: that Negroes are all right in their place. It is progress of a sort that the place is now judged to be the middle class.

As a result, welfare recipients could be denounced anew and presumably without racist taint. The current thrust of the GOP seems to be from racial chauvinism to class chauvinism. Since the well-off, well-educated are doing okay, it must be the fault of the welfare recipients themselves that there are few jobs for them. The truth would be uncomfortable, so the myths are embraced.

The Democratic convention was a-boil with new ideas, some good and some not so good but ideas in any case. You can search the GOP platform in vain for one. It is compound of certitudes and of assumptions, many of which have been left unchallenged too long. As the Nixon administration does, it reflects the most recent soundings of the pollsters. Mr. Nixon's deviations from the current mean of mass opinion never has exceeded the negligible. He is the nation's foremost follower.

Free of decisions about who its nominees would be, this convention had a rare chance to risk introspection, to glance around the country and to measure itself against the important changes of recent years, to rethink such habits as its uncritical, even passionate embrace of technology and "development" for their own sake.

The GOP did none of that, however. Its delegates merely lived it up. Given the current polls, you can hardly blame them, but the result was neither memorable nor important.

The Evening Bulletin
Philadelphia, Pa., August 24, 1972

If the 1972 Republican convention seemed to some to be dull in the certainty of its outcome and the lack of controversy in its proceedings, President Nixon's speech last night accepting renomination capped a grand design that is anything but dull.

It is nothing new for Republicans, as the minority party, to appeal across party lines for the support of Democrats and political independents. That, in recent decades, has been a necessity.

But what was different this time, what was brought to a climax in Mr. Nixon's speech, was the clear conviction that there is the opportunity for the Republicans to become the majority party in 1972 and for a good many years to come.

The prospect of such a historic shift makes the contrast in Republican and Democratic conventions profoundly interesting and important beyond the superficial judgment that the former was a contrived extravaganza and the latter a lively donnybrook.

But if the Republicans put on a show of unity that was remarkable even for Republicans, and if the Democrats engaged in a struggle that was bitterly fratricidal even by Democratic standards, it is what lies behind their respective unity and chaos that could bring a long-term alteration in the national political balance.

Mr. Nixon clearly feels that the forces which won the Democratic nomination for Senator George McGovern, and the process by which they won, and the policy directions in which they trend are too radical a break from centrist politics either for the Democratic Party to knit its wounds or for the country to accept its candidate.

President Nixon believes, and sounded the note as did other Republican speakers at the convention, that the McGovernites can be branded and isolated from the mainstream as irresponsible, and indeed alien and hostile to the American system and to American traditions.

So Mr. Nixon's appeal to Democrats to "join us as members of a new American majority bound together by our common ideals" — to "come home," not to another party, but to "the great principles we Americans believe in together" — was a formulation designed to drive a deep and perhaps permanent wedge in Democratic ranks.

And his appeal is not simply to dissidents among the regulars. In the new majority that he would shape this year he challenges the McGovern forces vigorously in that very area where their greatest hopes seem to lie — among the millions of new voters. If Mr. Nixon is right in his expectations of youth support, the implications will be far-reaching indeed.

The question is, will the American electorate see the Republican Party in the great centrist role in which is has been cast by Mr. Nixon? Will it find convincing the broad and moderate program adopted, the conciliatory tone of this remarkable convention under Mr. Nixon's firm control?

Will it be convinced by the record of administration achievement Mr. Nixon and his party so proudly cite? And will it be frightened by the specter of extremism he raises against the opposition?

There are flaws. The eloquent appeal for unity among Americans will recall the theme of bringing America together that the President struck in his campaign of 1968. The Nixon Administration's performance in the field of human relations will certainly be one area of bitter controversy in the campaign.

And while the President points with deep and understandable pride to the initiatives he has made in dealings with Russia and China, and emphasizes peace and bipartisan cooperation in achieving it, the continuing American involvement in the Vietnam war is not seen by many Americans as precisely the commitment to national honor that he presents it. Dissent on this score is not confined to the violent hoodlums who "demonstrated" outside the Republican convention.

But if the President is politically vulnerable on these and other counts — including an unemployment rate that remains too high despite general economic advance — the strength of the Republican position under Mr. Nixon amply justified the confidence that the convention exuded and his acceptance speech heightened.

Thus far his Democratic opposition has done little to impair that confidence. It is still far too early to suggest that Senator McGovern cannot overcome the advantage held by the incumbent President.

But the series of missteps by Mr. McGovern and his managers have done nothing to diminish the President's hopes for transforming what has been a natural Democratic majority into a natural Republican one.

The Standard-Times
New Bedford, Mass., August 26, 1972

For many persons, we would say, the Republican convention that reaffirmed confidence in the team of Richard Nixon and Spiro Agnew illustrated what may be a crucial issue between the two major parties at this stage in the campaign.

Inside the Miami auditorium, in an atmosphere of unity, confidence and direction, the incumbent President was inviting "everyone listening to me tonight . . . to join our new majority—not on the basis of the party label you wear on your lapel, but what you believe in your hearts."

Outside in the glare of anti-riot lights from a helicopter, a disheveled rioter, rejecting a plea from another dissenter to abstain from violence, muttered, "Hell, man, this is a night this country is going to remember."

And he rejoined the tire-slashing, passerby-roughing, rock-throwing, obscenity-calling activity of a minority.

The muscular street melee—protesting, no less, the use of U.S. muscle in Vietnam—could only have been deplored by the McGovern campaign. But that will not dispel the impression that this was a contrast between violence and order with political overtones.

Here is an issue tailor-made for the umbrella that Mr. Nixon was extending, because violence in behalf of any cause has become a tiresome, grotesque spectacle, an issue of the heart. Deliberately, it must have been, neither the President nor the Vice President mentioned the goings-on outside.

But the GOP team touched upon several other issues dividing it from the Democratic nominees, issues not of war or peace, solvency or bankruptcy, but the kind, like rioting on which people want to be counted. These were amnesty for draft-dodgers and busing.

On amnesty, the President did not vow vengeance on those who refused to serve; instead, he implied that sympathy for them was an affront to the 2.5 million who did serve, and the 55,000 who have died—an understated but nevertheless solar plexus disavowal of the McGovern position. A foursquare stand against busing was woven into the text, several times repeated, that all aspire to be Americans, not items in a quotaized nation.

However, it was on foreign policy, not domestic matters, that the President pitched his appeal for support in November. He stated it flat out: "More than on any other single issue, I ask you . . . to give us the opportunity to continue these great initiatives which can contribute so much to the peace of the world."

Foreign policy is, indeed, Mr. Nixon's strongest asset, the least pregnable to a McGovern assault and, in fact, the Democratic nominee's weakest claim on the presidency. Whether it ranks as the No. 1 issue with the voters is problematical, although a settlement of the Vietnam war would enhance its priority.

Vice President Agnew, whose manner and speech were subdued in the best understudy tradition, summed up the "basic issue in '72" as a choice between the piecemeal, inconsistent and illusory policies of George McGovern and the "sound, tested leadership of Richard Nixon."

But he also emphasized the foreign policy aspect, noting that in his travels he had found the President recognized as "the pre-eminent international statesman in the world."

Mr. Nixon ticked off other differences between himself and his opponent — the $1,000 welfare bonus, an "insult" to the intelligence of voters; a renewed pledge to appoint judges "who share my philosophy that we must strengthen the peace forces against the criminal forces." But he was careful not to portray any of this as a man-against-man contest, a posture the administration apparently is going to avoid in the campaign.

Instead he pictured the choice as between individual initiative vs. governmental paternalism, confidence in the American system vs. distrust of it, of effort to improve on the goals of American presidents vs. frantic tinkering in search for a new millennium —tearing down the edifices to fix the windows.

The labels that Mr. Nixon pinned, by implication, on Senator McGovern may not be accurate, but the Democratic nominee has been placed in the position of proving they are not.

Senator McGovern was even then engaged in proving he is not what he has seemed to be, seeking a rapprochment with two "old politics" leaders of the party, former President Johnson and Chicago's Mayor Daley, and explaining to the American Legion convention that his proposed slashing of military spending does not mean he is settling for inferior national defense.

While the future looks promising for the Republican ticket, there were no signs of taking anything for granted in the convention proceedings. The Nixon womenfolk were outstanding. Most factions were heard. Youth got an unprecedented share of the limelight.

We got the distinct impression that the task of Senator McGovern and the Democratic party in showing cause for a change in leadership has been made the more difficult by what went on in Miami.

The Louisville Times
Louisville, Ky., August 25, 1972

The preliminaries are over. The conventions at long last—at very long last—have been finished. The two political parties have concluded their quadrennial prime-time orgies of self-congratulation and viewing with alarm. Now they can get on with the serious business of trying to knock each other down and, if possible, out.

There is a temptation to infer that the differences of demeanor of the two 1972 conventions say something illuminating about the basic, permanent differences between the two parties. That is, the chaotic, exhuberant, and vital Democratic convention shows that the Democrats are chaotic, exhuberant, and vital while the orderly, cosmetic, and bland Republican convention shows that the Republicans are orderly, cosmetic, and bland.

Unhappily for that theory, in 1964 it was the Republicans who were chaotic (remember the Goldwaterites booing Rockefeller?), exhuberant, and vital. It was the Democrats then who were orderly, cosmetic, and bland (does anyone remember anything about the 1964 Democratic convention?).

There also may be a temptation to infer that the very orderliness, the obvious split-second timing and control of the uneventful and, let us face it, boring Republican convention turned people off politically. We are not at all sure this is true. Whether the people were more repelled by the Republicans' orderliness than by the Democrats' lack of it is, as far as we are concerned, an open question. A clue to the answer will be found in the voting in November.

About the only excitement at the Republican convention was provided by the Republicans' most physical opponents, the street demonstrators. Again, we cannot read people's minds, but on this point we would guess that the demonstrators accomplished exactly what they did not want to accomplish—that is, they created sympathy for those they attacked, the Republican delegates and the Republican President. In fact, as some observers have suggested, the demonstrators may have been the best thing the Republicans had going for them at Miami Beach.

There is an additional temptation in commenting on the two conventions: that the differences between the two platforms indicate the great divide between the two parties. To an extent this is, we believe, true. On certain issues, the war, for example, and busing, the platforms pretty much spell out genuine differences. But on the whole platforms historically have been merely massive platitudes. They are the most talked about and least acted upon element in politics. Can anyone tell by reading the platforms specifically what either party plans to do about the problems they both deplore—inflation, unemployment, environmental pollution, welfare?

If we have given the impression here that we view the end of the two conventions with some sense of relief, the impression is quite accurate. We look forward with a kind of hopeful trepidation to the campaign proper. Hopeful, because we believe it possible that the two nominees, intentionally or not, will from time to time illuminate the issues and tell specifically what proposals they have in mind for our problems. With trepidation, because while this is possible, history indicates that it isn't probable.

The San Diego Union
San Diego, Calif., August 24, 1972

While quadrennial presidential political campaigns in the United States of America really have no formal beginning, acceptance speeches by the presidential candidates are as definite a starting point as any.

In this respect, it is noteworthy that in the presidential squareoff of 1972 both President Nixon and Sen. George McGovern have used the same basic theme in accepting the support of their respective parties for the highest office in the nation: "Come Home America." Sen. McGovern employed the catch phrase frequently a month ago. Last night President Nixon used the theme directly on two occasions, and frequently in the undertones.

It was equally clear after the President's eloquent message last night that the candidates are poles apart in their interpretations of the words. The Democrat challenger believes that home is a sharp detour to the left, as the President noted last night. On the other hand, Mr. Nixon believes that America is on course — apart from a few aberrations. Moreover, he is convinced that the course is illuminated by principles that have guided at least the last five presidents of the United States, both Republicans and Democrats.

The principles are familiar to all of us. President Nixon believes that Americans should be generous with the unfortunate, but that they should work for what they earn if they are able. He holds that endeavor and achievement should dictate the rewards not artificial mathematical or ethnic quotas. He opposes federal paternalism, permissiveness and laws that offer criminals more protections than they do the law abiding.

However, from the response at the convention last night it also is evident that President Nixon struck the most responsive chords when he spoke about the immutable honor, leadership, strength and responsibilities of the United States.

He received the greatest response when he urged Americans not to abandon the system that made us the greatest nation on earth, not to abandon our allies, not to retreat to isolationism and to keep our strengths so that we may speak with conviction in the councils of the world.

The spontaneous response when he declared that he would never abandon American prisoners of war was heart warming. Surely the prolonged applause when the President said that it is time that the United States gave the long overdue honor and respect to the 2.5 million Americans who served with distinction in Vietnam echoed in hearts across the land.

All told the President drew the distinction between his opponent and himself with eloquence, clarity and conviction. Americans will have a definite choice of homes in November.

The Christian Science Monitor
Boston, Mass., August 24, 1972

Richard Nixon is now the Republican candidate for re-election to the presidency of the United States and barring some unlikely and unforeseeable event the probable winner, and that prospect need not dismay any American regardless of personal and partisan feelings.

We do not like everything he did during his first term. His tax cutting pleased his own constituency at the expense of the economy. It was one reason the inflation broke loose after he became President. We think he should have moved sooner and faster to wind down the war. He has been a partisan on race relations, a sectarian on federal aid to private schools, and a politician rather than a statesman on backing Israel against Arabs.

But, overall, his first term has witnessed a quieting down of discontent in the United States. The amount of credit due to him is arguable. But conditions are easier, more comfortable, less dangerous than they were when he took office. The prospect of a change in Washington has become unsettling in the minds of many who live outside the Republican faith. The alternate prospect of a second Nixon term is reassuring to many who would normally vote for Democrats.

This is, of course, precisely why he was renominated almost unanimously by the Republicans and why he seems to be the likely winner in November. The American people sense in Richard Nixon something of the same capacity they sensed in Dwight D. Eisenhower to smooth over the internal rivalries, frictions, and discontents which from time to time set Americans against Americans. And undoubtedly they like the calming and reassuring effect of his foreign policies. The danger of more war has receded. The Americans are more nearly at peace with the outside world now than they have been at any time since Joseph Stalin and Adolf Hitler filled that outside world with danger. He gave them the two things they most wanted: less war and, however belatedly, a prospect of economic stability. So he is in line for a second term.

And this prospect need not overly dismay even those who for personal or partisan reasons will vote against him. He has been running for re-election ever since he walked into the White House. Many of the political things done to gain his re-election are unattractive. The list seems likely to be longer by the time the "Watergate caper" is sorted out. But he will never be running again for re-election. In a second term he could and certainly would be less a partisan, more a president of all the people.

THE ARIZONA REPUBLIC
Phoenix, Ariz., August 24, 1972

President Nixon's acceptance speech at the Republican convention will be remembered as one of the greatest of this century. His appeal for a "new American majority bound together by our common ideals" had the sweep and majesty of "One nation, under God, with liberty and justice for all."

"This nation proudly calls itself the United States of America," Mr. Nixon said. "Let us reject any philosophy that would make us the divided people of America."

In a way, the President was reacting again to the sign carried by a child at one of the 1968 Nixon rallies in Ohio. "Bring Us Together" said the sign.

"I address you, my fellow Americans, not as a partisan of party, which would automatically divide us, but as a partisan of principles, which can unite us," the President told the nation in his speech at Miami Beach Wednesday evening.

Inviting Democrats to join him, the President said, "Come home — not to another party, but to the great principles we Americans believe in together."

Then, to the millions in the television audience, he said:

"I ask everyone listening to me tonight — Democrats, Republicans and Independents, to join our new majority — not on the basis of the party label you wear in you lapel, but what you believe in your hearts." Proving he was willing to go beyond narrow political partisanship, Mr. Nixon aligned himself — in one respect at least — with all of the "five Presidents in my voting lifetime," namely Franklin D. Roosevelt, Harry Truman, Dwight Eisenhower, John F. Kennedy and Lyndon Johnson. Four of them were Democrats.

"They had differences on some issues," he said, but they were united in "their total opposition to isolation." They all insisted that this country "assume the responsibilities of leadership in the world community."

Because it is a changing world, President Nixon has directed American world leadership into new channels that, for the first time in decades, hold forth a real hope for his goal of "a generation of peace."

His trips to Peking and Moscow have changed the shape of international relationships. His negotiation of the Strategic Arms Limitation accords with Russia is the first long step toward ending the frightfully expensive nuclear missile race without making the U.S. a second-rate military power.

In penetrating the Bamboo Curtain and reducing the Iron Curtain, President Nixon has opened the way for trade activity which will not be tremendous at first, but which already has provided an outlet for surplus American wheat. Our trade deficit is becoming more manageable, thanks to newly negotiated dollar exchange rates, but the President is opposed to economic isolationism just as strongly as to political isolationism.

Unlike Democratic Candidate George McGovern, President Nixon is unwilling to crawl on his knees to Hanoi or to impose a Communist government on our South Vietnam ally. Such a course, says Mr. Nixon, might be good politics, but it would be "disastrous to the cause of peace in the world." Without surrendering to the enemy, he has kept his peaceful pledge of four years ago by ending the American ground combat role in Vietnam and bringing home more than half a million American troops.

In his final appeal for the new majority, President Nixon voiced "the dream of mankind since the beginning of civilization.

"Let us build a peace which our children and all the children of the world can enjoy for generations to come," he said. While Sen. George McGovern has displayed complete lack of understanding of world affairs, President Nixon has accomplished major goals and is on the road to future achievements. This speech alone, with its clarion call for a new majority, assures him an enduring place in American history.

THE SUN
Baltimore, Md.
August 24, 1972

Both the renomination of Vice President Agnew last night and the reaffirmation of the party's faith in small-state predominance on Tuesday afternoon remind anyone who needed reminding that the Republican party today and into the foreseeable future is going to be run by its conservative wing. This week's events only strengthen the conservatives' hold, first displayed eight years ago with the nomination of Senator Barry Goldwater, if not 12 years ago, with the nomination of Richard Nixon. For a long time prior to Mr. Nixon's first nomination, the party's presidential nomination was thought of as a gift of the liberal, internationalist, Eastern, urban leaders of the party. These were the men who so regularly defeated Senator Taft, the last time with General Eisenhower. In that year, 1952, the liberals made their usual gesture of respect to the conservatives in the hinterlands and Congress by giving the number two spot on the ticket to Mr. Nixon.

If 1952 and 1960 are ancient history, 1968 certainly is not. In the Republican convention that year, Mr. Nixon was nominated despite the opposition of the very states that this year have been urging the party to change its delegation selection process: New York (which went for Nelson Rockefeller then), Massachusetts (also Rockefeller), Pennsylvania (ditto). Ohio and California were for their own governors. Of the 10 largest states, only three were for Nixon at the 1968 convention, and two of those were Southern: Florida and Texas.

The smaller states of the West, Middle West and South not only nominated President Nixon in 1968, they elected him. And these are precisely the states in which Vice President Agnew is most popular, the states that are maintained in power in the party by the delegate-apportioned rules adopted Tuesday at Miami Beach. Four years is a long time, but it would appear that in 1976 the small, conservative states will be the dominant Republican states and Mr. Agnew will be the dominant Republican personality.

Like most Vice Presidents Mr. Agnew performed primarily political chores in the past four years. The cliche became that he was "Nixon's Nixon," fighting adversaries with the same rhetorical ferocity that Mr. Nixon displayed in the 1950's on behalf of President Eisenhower. There are some indications that the Vice President would like to abandon this role for that of political healer, if the Republican ticket wins re-election. That would be a constructive step.

The Detroit News
Detroit, Mich., August 27, 1972

As one of the original critics of the Spiro Agnew style of political rhetoric, we applaud the vice-president's announcement that from now on he will try to tone it down.

His truculence and his preoccupation with phrase-making have reduced the effectiveness of his refreshing and often cogent views of the political scene. People tend to forget the substance of his remarks and remember the controversial language in which he delivers them.

At times, not only his language but also his taste has been bad. Nobody laughed when he made reference to "fat Japs." He was sent to the woodshed by members of his own party in 1968 when he asserted that Hubert Humphrey was "soft on communism."

When he plays it straight, as he did last week in his acceptance speech at Maimi Beach, the vice-president makes a favorable and lasting impression on his listeners. His carefully-reasoned remarks, delivered in a calm but forceful style, contrasted favorably with the acceptance speech of his opposite number, Sargent Shriver, whose bounciness, bordering on flippancy, may become very tiresome to political audiences during the next 10 weeks.

One does not need clairvoyant powers to understand why Agnew has decided to change his own style. He has his eye on the future. He is correct in believing that a more conciliatory approach will improve his chances of getting the presidential nomination and winning the presidency in 1976.

The prospect of the presidency does have the effect of making some men more responsible. If the prospect can break Spiro Agnew of the habit of reckless language, who knows?—it might even break George McGovern of the habit of reckless promises. Well, we can dream, can't we?

BUFFALO EVENING NEWS
Buffalo, N.Y., August 24, 1972

In accepting renomination last night, Vice President Agnew gave what must surely be scored as the best speech of his political career. Whether this was a "new Agnew," looking for the first time a little beyond the vice presidency toward something bigger in 1976, or whether it was the same Agnew under a new set of campaign marching orders from his chief, his whole performance was a delight to see and hear.

From his opening look at the vice presidential office itself to his incisively developed theme that this must be "one America" and not a quota-computed collection of "splinter groups," here was campaign oratory at its graceful best. We were particularly intrigued by his perceptive reading of the vice presidency as an office dedicated to two primary functions — "to serve the President and to learn from the President." Much controversy about it, he said, would be quieted if the fact were better accepted that "the vice president is the President's man and not a competing political entity."

Whether he was thereby subtly reminding his critics that the controversial "old Agnew" had only been working under orders, or telling his fans that the blander "new Agnew" was being kept under presidential wraps, he left both elements to decide for themselves. But on the fundamental point, that the vice president is necessarily and even constitutionally the President's man, he was being both correct and candid — and candid in a way that Hubert Humphrey, for instance, must often wish he had emulated during all the years he served a Johnson war policy he later tried unsuccessfully to disavow.

For all its thoughtful qualities, there was nothing soft in Mr. Agnew's acceptance speech. In posing the issues cleanly and clearly, he minced no words but shunned the rhetoric of overstatement and abrasive satire. There was not an "effete snob," a "radiclib," a "nattering nabob of negativism" or any other old-style "Agnewism" in the whole speech. Unifying, anti-divisive, solidly pro-Nixon, it was an appeal to the best in America. It was pitched throughout to an issue-oriented level which we hope both he and the President, whose man he says he is, will sustain throughout the campaign.

HOUSTON CHRONICLE
Houston, Tex., August 28, 1972

Since the Republican Party convention, much is being said about the "new Spiro Agnew." We find both political and personal reasons for this development.

The opening remarks of Agnew as he accepted the nomination as the party's candidate for reelection as vice-president set the stage:

"Surely much of the controversy about the vice-presidency could be quieted if we would accept the fact that the vice-president is the president's man and not a competing entity.

"A president lives in the spotlight, but a vice-president lives in the flickering strobe lights that alternately illuminate or shadow his unwritten duties. It is sometimes uncomfortable. It is sometimes ego-diminishing. But it is also quietly rewarding."

Agnew was saying he has been a good soldier, carrying out the task assigned to him. In the 1968 presidential campaign, and subsequently, he lashed out at "radicals" and chopped away at the press, welfare loafers and dissenters in general. A man who was considered quiet and reserved by his colleagues, a man little known outside his home state of Maryland, became a controversial figure, much sought after as a speaker and much cheered for his angry rhetoric. Politically, it was a successful tactic.

Now politics dictate different tactics and we will therefore see a change in Agnew's approach. The Republicans, with leadership in the polls and dissension among the Democrats, want to avoid excesses, point to the record and campaign on the issues. They want to ride the tide, not muddy the waters. Thus, the party can afford for Agnew to tone down his message.

The vice-president's convention address gave the impression that he, personally, welcomes the change. He seemed more relaxed in his milder approach. He deplored labels, and in later press conferences deplored the labels attached to him.

Agnew is strong in his own right. Changing his image doesn't mean changing his conservative beliefs. He worked hard to succeed as a lawyer and in politics and has done his homework as vice-president.

Though he is still "the president's man," Agnew has now given notice that he will be undertaking a little more freedom of action.

The Virginian-Pilot
Norfolk, Va., August 25, 1972

Trustworthy, loyal, obedient, and reverent, if not so thrifty, the delegates did their duty at Miami Beach and renominated President Nixon and Vice President Agnew for a second term.

The Republican convention followed the script—and there really was a script, a copy of which fell into the hands of the press. But if the convention was dull and phony, it left no wounds. Not one Republican went away mad, at least not visibly.

Ever since he was nominated by the Democrats in July, Senator George McGovern has been trying to make peace with his party's soreheads. The effort has been only partly successful. While Mr. McGovern has been photographed, smiling, with Mayor Daley and Lyndon Johnson just this week, and while he has been courting recalcitrant Southerners, enthusiasm for the ticket is the exception, and not the rule, in state after state. Many Democrats, running scared like Senator Spong, are keeping a discreet distance from Mr. McGovern; others, such as the AFL-CIO's George Meany, remain totally unreconstructed. By contrast, everything was sugar substitute and light for the Republicans this week. One by one, the barons of the GOP—Barry Goldwater, Ronald Reagan, even Nelson Rockefeller—swore fealty to the GOP's liege lord, outdoing each other in praise of Richard Nixon. *Is it not passing brave to be a king, and ride in triumph through Persepolis?*

All samplings suggest that the Republican ticket is so far in front that Messrs. Nixon and Agnew could not snatch defeat from the jaws of victory, a la 1948. The enemy now is not George McGovern, but overconfidence. Friends of Mr. Nixon, such as columnist Kevin P. Phillips, already are speculating upon the content and direction of his second term. The only genuine issue among the Republicans was the delegate-selection system for 1976, stirring talk of an Agnew vs. Chuck Percy race then.

It is obviously premature for Republicans to worry about '76. But the moment Mr. Nixon is re-elected on November 7—assuming he is not Thomas E. Dewey reincarnated—he will become a lame-duck President. Inevitably, Mr. Nixon's second term will be marked by wars of the Republican succession. The focal point will be the Vice President, who is the man to beat in '76, political precedent (Nixon in '60, Johnson in '64, Hubert Humphrey in '68) suggests.

Spiro Agnew—Spiro Who?—was unknown when he was chosen by Mr. Nixon in '68. But he became a household word in a short time, and a dirty word to a lot of people. Mr. Agnew was assigned the hatchetman's role by the White House and did the job vigorously. He earned an identity in the process that is a liability to him now, politically. To be the blunt instrument of the Republicans is fine for fund-raising, but bad for a candidate for President.

The role assigned by Mr. Nixon to the Vice President is one that he himself performed as Eisenhower's Vice President, prompting the talk that Mr. Agnew was "Nixon's Nixon." There is also talk that insiders at the White House are cool toward the Vice President, as said of Mr. Nixon in the Eisenhower years. But when Mr. Nixon became President in his own right, he was full of surprises. What will be Mr. Agnew's role in the second term? What will Mr. Agnew's Agnew be like?

Republican Convention:
RESULTS OF DELEGATE REFORM FIGHT SEEN AS VICTORY FOR AGNEW FORCES

A delegate reform proposal to increase representation for the populous states at the 1976 convention was defeated Aug. 22 by a 910–434 vote of the convention. The result was generally interpreted as a victory for those Republicans working for the nomination of Vice President Agnew as the 1976 presidential candidate.

The complex formula approved by the convention was to award each state six delegates at large and three for each Congressional district. In addition, states that carried the vote for the Republican presidential nominee would receive an extra four and one-half bonus delegates plus additional bonus delegates equal to 60% of their electoral vote. Another bonus delegate would be awarded each state for each senator or governor elected between conventions and another for a Republican majority Congressional delegation. Under the rejected reform plan, the populous states would have received 400 bonus delegates based on their Republican voting strength.

The convention's decision went against a U.S. District Court ruling by Judge William B. Jones in the District of Columbia April 28. He had held that the bonus system was unconstitutional because it unfairly discriminated against the largest, most populous states.

The convention approved Aug. 22 an amendment to the Rules Committee's report, calling upon the party chairman to appoint a representative of "a black Republican organization" to the party's executive committee. The report, adopted by voice vote, called upon the Republican National Committee and state committees to take "positive action to achieve broadest possible participation by everyone in party affairs, including such participation by women, young people, minority and heritage groups and senior citizens in the delegate selection process." There was strong and vocal opposition among the Republican delegates to the adoption of any quota system similar to that used by the Democrats to increase representation for women, young people and minority groups.

BUFFALO EVENING NEWS
Buffalo, N.Y., August 18, 1972

With so-called conservatives firmly in control, the Republican National Committee has adopted a formula of allocating delegates for future conventions which continues to favor small states and discriminates rather blatantly against the large states where most of the voters live. Since this seems to have the tacit blessing of the administration, no one expects a successful challenge on the convention floor.

The arithmetic is complicated, but the new rule has the effect of greatly magnifying the small-state favoritism that is implicit in any allocation of votes based on electoral rather than popular votes. It will do this with such gimmicks as giving the same number of "bonus" delegates to every state that goes Republican, regardless of the state's size. That principle has already been ruled unconstitutional by one federal court, and how it will fare on appeal we have no idea.

What does puzzle us, though, is why the Republicans, who overwhelmingly supported a constitutional amendment in Congress in 1969 to abolish the Electoral College and go over to direct popular voting to elect future Presidents, should now face in the opposite direction when it comes to nominating them.

Another thing that puzzles us is the fact that the winning formula, adopted over the strenuous objections of New York and nearly all other large-state spokesmen, was co-sponsored by none other than Texas' John Tower, a senator from the nation's fourth largest state, and Buffalo's Jack Kemp, a congressman from the second largest state. If there is some persuasive explanation as to how the best interests of New York and Texas could be served by giving the smallest state as big a prize for going Republican as the largest state would get, we'd like to hear it.

FORT WORTH STAR-TELEGRAM
Fort Worth, Tex., August 16, 1972

Sen. Charles H. Percy, the Republican senior senator from Illinois, pleaded in a speech the other day for reforms in the process of selecting delegates to Republican national conventions, to expand representation for minority groups and women. Senator Percy later commented that it was not the first time that he has raised this question with his GOP colleagues.

But whereas his earlier proposal did not attract a lot of attention, this time there was a flurry of reaction, with charges that Senator Percy is trying to "McGovernize" the Republican party, with an eye to seeking the GOP presidential nomination in 1976.

And, indeed, there are obvious parallels in both timing and content betwen Mr. Percy's plan and the one launched just after the 1968 Chicago Democratic convention to reform the party's convention machinery and its delegate selection process. Senator McGovern was one of the chief architects of the Democratic remodeling job, and his long-held presidential aspirations have been served by its results in admirable fashion thus far.

Another Illinois lawmaker, Rep. Philip M. Crane, who is several shades more conservative in his politics than Mr. Percy, has been quick to blow a whistle on the senator's budding GOP reform movement. He views it as "elitist and totalitarian" and as a move that would wreck the GOP.

Representative Crane is joined by other Republican congressmen who see the proposed delegate-selection changes as a simple power grab by Senators Percy, Javits of New York, and a few other GOP liberals.

For the benefit and guidance of his fellow Republicans, Mr. Crane cites the example of the fate of the Chicago delegation at the recent Democratic convention in Miami Beach, when the legally elected delegation was supplanted on a partisan basis by a delegation that "did not reflect the ethnic makeup of Chicago" and one of whose leaders had not voted in the Democratic primary.

Congressman Crane, who is expected by many to be a challenger to Sen. Adlai Stevenson III, in 1976, thus has thrown down a gauntlet which may signal a new political brawl under the banner of reform, this time in the ranks of the Republican Party with the possibility of having considerable effect on the presidential race four years hence.

DAYTON DAILY NEWS
Dayton, Ohio, August 20, 1972

If the Republican party is not embarrassed by its pre-convention efforts at reform, it ought to be. Already years behind the Democrats in involving women, blacks and young voters, the GOP is fighting not to catch up but to stay behind. Its elders and power figures are busy with a remarkable attempt to fasten their political party, whose object presumably is to win elections, to a foundation of elitism and exclusion.

Not that the issue will matter greatly this year. President Nixon currently is the front-runner by several lengths in the presidential campaign. He has the advantage of being the incumbent and is working the advantage fully.

His party, however, continues to lag behind the Democrats in registration and in general voter preference. As if to insist on that long-run handicap, Mr. Nixon's aides have been undermining even modest proposals for broadening the base.

It appears now that the convention will offer little more than paternal pieties and good but unsupported intentions to women, minorities and the young. The delegate selection formula is being gimmicked to hamper moderate Republicans in the populous East and disproportionately favor conservatives in the South and in the small towns and suburbs of the Midwest.

In its seeming determination to avoid serious reform, the GOP is like an inventor-entrepreneur laboring long and fixedly into the night to perfect the lesser mousetrap.

The New York Times
New York, N.Y., August 23, 1972

The search for a fair formula for allocating delegates to the next Republican National Convention has ended in failure. Instead of facing the issue on its merits, the delegates in Miami Beach unfortunately became entangled in the ideological and personal power rivalries within the party. Contending conservative and progressive factions fought—to the first frontier, but scarcely the last—in the struggle to determine the G.O.P.'s post-Nixon leadership in 1976.

The issue is whether the delegates are to represent people or whether they are to represent states. A population formula squares with the one-man, one-vote principle. A state formula tends—as do the Electoral College and the United States Senate—to overrepresent the small states. At this convention, eight states with 49 per cent of the nation's population, which four years ago actually cast 52 per cent of Mr. Nixon's popular vote, have only 37 per cent of the delegates. Some of the discrepancies are enormous. Thus, Alaska has twelve delegates and New York 88, although this state has sixty times as many people. Arizona has eighteen delegates while California has 96, a ratio of approximately one to five, as against a real ratio of one to eleven in population.

Before the convention opened, a rules subcommittee last week approved a plan to bring representation into line with population. But the full committee overturned it and substituted the so-called "Miami Beach compromise," which was not a compromise at all but a clear victory for the small states and the old way of doing things.

The cosponsorship of this plan by Senator John Tower of Texas and Representative Jack Kemp of Buffalo, N. Y., strongly suggested White House backing. Senator Tower is a long-time ally of Mr. Nixon. Representative Kemp, a former California resident, is a Trojan horse who will have difficulty explaining to New Yorkers why he cosponsored a plan so manifestly unfair to his adopted state and so strongly opposed by Governor Rockefeller and other state party leaders.

Ideology helps account for Mr. Kemp's action. Conservatives believe that bolstering the strength of the smaller states of the South and West will make it easier to nominate a conservative in 1976. For that reason, Gov. Ronald Reagan of California backed the Tower-Kemp plan, even though his state would suffer under it.

Since the Republican politicians have failed to meet the challenge of reform, the courts once again may have to do their work for them. For a decade, the Supreme Court has held that such disproportionate arrangements are unconstitutional in electing members of Congress, state legislatures and many local government bodies. The application of this principle within political parties is less well defined, but a Federal district court has already ruled that this year's allocation of delegates in the Republican National Convention could not be used again. Since the delegates have not gone far enough in devising a new formula to meet the one-man, one-vote criterion, the courts may once again have to make a determination more consistent with constitutional democracy.

© 1972 by The New York Times Company. Reprinted by permission.

PORTLAND EVENING EXPRESS
Portland, Me., August 22, 1972

The only genuine interest generated at the Republican national convention arose when liberals and conservatives split over the issue of apportionment of delegates at the next convention in 1976.

The rules committee has debated the question for days, and late last night appended a "California compromise" to the earlier "Miami compromise", actually a victory for party conservatives who have reportedly decided that Spiro Agnew should be next in the line of presidential succession.

So an earlier victory by the big states where the liberals are strong was wiped out, and today they may make a fight on the floor for the plan that, until it was scuttled, would have given a bonus of 500 delegates added to the regular 1,346, on the basis of the 1972 vote. Nearly all of the bonus would have gone to the heavily-populated states.

The conservatives want to keep control of the convention four years from now in the hands of leaders and delegates from the smaller, right-wing states and thus shut off any opposition to the ticket they decide to support.

So we may be watching a replay of 1964, when the right-wingers captured the convention and nominated Barry Goldwater. Only time will tell if the new apportionment formula, provided it is accepted by the convention this afternoon, turns out to be a hollow victory.

THE SUN
Baltimore, Md., August 18, 1972

If genuine political debate unexpectedly breaks out at the Republican National Convention, it likely will develop over the liberal-to-moderate wing's attempt to broaden participation in the party nominating procedure. That seems the lone question open to the floor, the one element that holds any promise for the huge and potentially drowsy audience that is expected to tune in. The nominations this year are clearly cast. And nobody is going to argue over a platform that carries a White House imprimatur.

But what of 1976 and future conventions? As matters now stand the Republican party is in the hands of a collection of small border and Southern states. Reformers, though set back in earlier pre-convention attempts, want it changed. They argue that, to represent more people, a new formula must be devised to strengthen the larger states by increasing the size of the convention. It seems a reasonable endeavor, given the frequent and legitimate appeals from women, blacks and youth for greater representation in the political process. The Democrats went through it, and they seemed at last month's convention to have escaped unharmed. In fact, they have begun implementing further refinements as a result.

One doesn't have to look far to make out a needy case for the Republican party. The Maryland delegation to Miami Beach is composed of 26 members, 16 of them chosen by direct election, the remainder selected in a caucus dominated by party professionals. Only 5 of the 26 are women, 3 are black and just 1 is under 30 years of age. In fact, the average age for a Maryland Republican delegate is 48, and nearly half of the 26 are over 50. Other border and Southern states are said to be similarly restricted in scope, and many are over-represented at party conventions because of the methods used to reward delegations with extra members in states that voted Republican in previous presidential elections.

If the liberal reformists bring their fight to the floor, it will provide not only entertainment but a healthy turn in party politics. Even if it doesn't work, the courts have already shown a willingness to consider the question, and in fact have ruled favorably in a similar case. Many Republican conservatives who wish to maintain the status quo charge that the reform movement is nothing more than an attempt to deny Vice President Agnew the 1976 presidential nomination. Indeed, this may be a motivating consideration. Still, if Republicans hold back the trend toward reform it will soon dawn on voters that the GOP is a small and exclusive group. And how much can a nomination be worth under those conditions?

Long Island Press
Long Island, N.Y., August 20, 1972

The Republican National Convention, which opens tomorrow, may lack excitement and suspense. But it could be the party's most significant convention in years and probably will shape the future of the Grand Old Party.

To the public, the nominees and the platform are most important. As far as the 1972 election is concerned, they are.

But to the party, the key question is convention rules, a question which could determine which GOP faction dominates the 1976 convention, and probably the party for many years ahead.

The rules involve proposed reforms to open the party to more representation by women, young people and minorities. They also include a bitter battle between large and small states, with Mr. Agnew's possible candidacy in 1976 at stake.

This year's convention will see many new faces — more women, more blacks, more young people — though not as much so as at the Democratic convention last month. The Democrats reformed their rules after the 1968 convention, mandating representation by all groups in relation to their proportion of the state population.

A Republican reform panel had recommended quotas for the GOP, but this was anathema to the conservatives and was discarded. In its place, Republican liberals led by Sen. Jacob Javits and John Gardner, chairman of Common Cause, suggested a rule requiring state parties to assure participation in GOP affairs by ethnic minorities and youths.

That was changed to require only that state parties assure all segments of the voting population an equal opportunity to participate in party affairs.

There are plausible arguments against a quota system. But the fact remains that, until this year, the young have hardly been represented in any party, and women and minorities have been greatly under-represented.

The Democratic party reforms changed that—at their convention. The Republican convention, too, will see greater representation by women, youths and minorities.

But lip service alone will not democratize the party. Quotas worked for the Democrats. If the Republicans don't want quotas, they will have to demonstrate that they can achieve similar results without them. Otherwise, the party that the hard-liners think they are protecting will in the long run, suffer.

* * *

The question of state representation is even thornier, and the debate over it could be the high spot of the convention.

The plan the national committee approved favors small, safely Republican states over larger, more populous ones. It was adopted despite the warnings of New York GOP Chairman Charles Lanigan that "sectional politics will tear us apart."

The formula would add 600 delegates to the 1976 convention, to be distributed among states that vote Republican this year. Thus, a small midwestern or southern state which supports Mr. Nixon might have proportionately more influence in 1976 than a New York or Illinois — if the President were to lose there — even if the larger states had Republican governors or senators.

Mr. Agnew's interest clearly lies with the smaller, more conservative states. The "eastern establishment" has never been enamored of the vice president and it would be to his advantage next time around if its power were diminished.

But the Republicans must remember that they are the minority party by national registration, and that they have not won an election in the last half century with an ultra-conservative candidate. It has only been with moderates such as Presidents Eisenhower and Nixon that the GOP has been successful in wooing enough independent voters for victory.

The question the party must decide this week is whether to widen its base, and its popular appeal, or to return to the limited appeal of a Goldwater or a Taft.

While the situation may look rosy for the GOP in 1972, it, too — like the Democrats — faces some basic decisions which could affect the future of American politics.

THE INDIANAPOLIS NEWS
Indianapolis, Ind., August 19, 1972

The Rules Committee of the national Republican party made a wise move this week when it adopted the so-called "Miami compromise" in the dispute over apportionment of delegates.

Adoption of this formula is now up to the rules committee of the convention and the delegates themselves, and it is to be hoped as a matter of common justice and common sense that the plan is ratified. It has the merit of meeting legitimate objections to the current system of distributing delegate votes in the national GOP, while forestalling the effort of certain elements in the party to "McGovernize" the national convention of 1976.

The system envisioned by the compromise would enlarge the total delegate allotment and give weight to population factors, which answers complaints that the present method of sorting delegates is injurious to large states and overly generous to small ones. But it would keep the "bonus" feature which rewards Republican performance, assigning extra delegates to states which vote for the GOP in presidential elections.

This bonus, moreover, would incorporate population factors. Five votes will be awarded simply for going Republican in the presidential balloting; but other bonus votes will be determined as a percentage of the state's electoral vote, so that the larger and more populous the state the greater its extra delegate total. The result seems eminently fair to all concerned.

Republican national chairman Robert Dole observes that "the Miami compromise essentially preserves all that was valuable from our old system—a victory incentive bonus, and then goes beyond that. It appears to me constitutionally acceptable, and it provides a true incentive for state parties to go all out for victory for the President this November. Smaller, traditionally Republican states will be rewarded if they carry for the President—and that is as it should be. Large states where the President wins will receive proportional bonuses, but not so large that a few states could dominate a convention—and that is as it should be."

From most reports it appears the GOP has turned its back on the idea of quotas, which is to the good. Now if the party repels the liberal attempt to stack the next convention for the Eastern states and adopts instead the plan endorsed by Dole it will have done a good job of work in fashioning its rules for '76.

THE SPRINGFIELD UNION
Springfield, Mass., August 22, 1972

While Gov. Sargent pushes a plan for making GOP delegations to future national conventions more reflective of the states' ethnic, age and sex character, Gov. Meskill of Connecticut supports another change in the delegate structure.

Meskill backs a plan that would award "bonus" delegates to states on the basis of GOP victories in governorship, senatorial and House elections, as well as the presidential election.

The plan clashes head-on with that favored by the convention Rules Committee, which would give a "bonus" to any state that merely supported the party's presidential nominee in the election.

The Rules Committee version is regarded as conservative — perhaps geared to help Vice-President Agnew win the GOP nomination in 1976, if he seeks it. It would do this presumably by building the convention strength of the Southern and Western "Old Guard" at the expense of the big Eastern industrial states.

But the conservative tag may be misplaced. It is, for instance, a liberal aim (that of Gov. Sargent, among others) to broaden the base of party membership across the country. Yet, the larger the role of voting patterns in apportioning delegates, the more exclusive the party becomes. This is not the way to make the GOP a party "of the people."

The GOP Rules Committee hits closer to the target, but even more pertinent to the goal would be to base delegate strength, state by state, strictly on population.

THE PLAIN DEALER
Cleveland, Ohio, August 16, 1972

Liberals in the Republican party are strenuously urging GOP leaders: "Broaden our appeal. Bring in more of the young, the black, the ethnic, the women, the issue-oriented voters. Otherwise the party will perish."

But the GOP leaders move warily and slowly. Compared with the Democrats' pace, the pace of the Republican party, historically, is elephantine. The GOP examines today's type of reforms very gingerly.

For example, William C. Cramer, GOP convention rules chairman, rules out quotas for women, for those under 25, for blacks or other minorities.

That could be called foot-dragging on reform. Quotas have been officially proposed by the GOP's Delegates and Organizations Committee, as well as by party liberals.

But Cramer and others may have reason to drag their feet on such techniques as sex or race or age-group quotas. Quotas can be unjust. They can screen out merit and screen in tokenism.

Cramer could argue that drastic reforms and a quota plan badly damaged the Democratic party this year. It abruptly changed delegate selection, the makeup of the party's national convention and thus the method by which the Democrats picked nominees for president and vice president.

It can easily be shown that quotas, seeking to be just to the groups formerly unrepresented, yielded a mix of Democratic delegates heavy with idealistic amateurs, light on delegates with practical experience. Fully 85% had never been at a national convention, and most of those had never done front-line party duty before.

Yet the liberals are right. It is imperative for the Republican party to make genuine effort to bring in more young, black, nationality-group, female, activist and lower-income voters. To preserve a healthy two-party system, either party must be flexible enough to represent the whole nation.

The liberal Ripon Society's national political director, Daniel J. Swillinger, warns: "The 1972 national convention will provide Republicans with their best—and perhaps last—opportunity to open up the party before it is overwhelmed by the pro-Democratic votes of under-35, issue-oriented voters."

He says the GOP should allocate more delegates to large swing states (California, New York, Pennsylvania, Ohio, Texas, Illinois). Those states contain more of the minorities and the young proportionally.

But that is an indirect way to broaden participation among the left-out groups. Much more direct appeals and more than lip-service reform are needed. Surveys show there are more self-professed Democrats and independents than Republicans in this country. The GOP is a minority party, and minorities have to try harder.

Chicago Daily Defender
Chicago, Ill., August 22, 1972

Bowing, with a bit of reluctance, to the massive resistance mounted against its plans, the Republican reform group dropped all efforts to require quotas for youths and racial minorities in the GOP convention delegations. The proposal, patterned after similar reforms adopted by the Democratic Party, has come under heavy attack from conservative Republicans who regard it as a move to block the possible nomination of Spiro T. Agnew for President in 1976.

The reform group endorsed 13 proposed rules changes designed to broaden participation in party affairs, one of which would encourage states to have men and women equally represented on their delegations.

But instead of requiring the representation of youths in proportion to their voting strength as urged by a special panel of the Republican National Committee, the group settled for strengthening an existing rule banning any discrimination in delegate selection.

Besides urging greater participation by women, youths and racial minorities, the proposals endorsed by the group are aimed at opening up the delegate selection process by requiring open meetings, prohibiting poxy voting, abolishing fees and assessments of delegates and eliminating the automatic selection of party officials as delegates.

With the precedent already established by the Democrats, the Republican Party can ill afford creating the impression that it does not want the broadest possible participation of all segments of the voting population. The reform group proposals are in line with the march of events.

The Detroit News
Detroit, Mich., August 21, 1972

Whether newsmen are overpublicizing the Republican controversy over proposed convention reforms or not, the GOP really owes the news media a debt of gratitude for the stories. They provide the most interesting developments to come out of Miami Beach before the opening of the GOP convention today.

The proposed reforms reflect the intentions of the more progressive Republicans to change the apportionment of delegates to ensure more representation for blacks, women and young people in 1976 and to give the larger states a bigger share of the delegates. The aim is to open up the Republican Party and the convention to groups which have been underrepresented in both.

Critics of the proposals, chiefly from the conservative wing of the party, see the moves aimed chiefly at the future of the party. They contend the reformers merely want to make certain that neither Vice-President Agnew nor any other conservative is the 1976 presidential nominee. Agnew's supporters are chiefly white, middle-aged, Southern and rural and his backing obviously would be diluted by any move that would increase representation of blacks, young people and big city voters.

On the surface at least, the President is staying out of the power struggle and so presumably is the vice-president. Yet in the long run the decision probably will have to be made by Mr. Nixon even though he cannot be a candidate for reelection in 1976. For the party recognizes that the 1972 election comes first and that its plans for the future must not jeopardize its chances this year.

Even the Republican reformers seem to be opposed to the kind of "quota democracy" the Democrats imposed on themselves through their new rules. Yet with the addition of millions of 18 to 21-year-olds to the voting rolls the GOP would be shortsighted if it did not make new efforts to enlist them under its banner. With blacks and other minorities now more aware than ever of their growing political power, the GOP cannot afford to overlook their strength either. Yet if the party makes too many overtures in these directions, it faces the prospect of a loss of support — or even a third party movement — from its conservative backers.

Whatever the outcome, the GOP concern about 1976 is unlikely to become so serious as to interfere with its efforts in 1972. Yet any reform at the 1972 convention that broadens the party's appeal in the future ought to bring some dividends in November, 1972, let alone November, 1976.

Chicago Tribune
Chicago, Ill., August 23, 1972

It's ironic that the most troublesome issue the Republicans have had to face in their 1972 convention is how to divide up the seats and power for their 1976 convention.

Th rules changes approved yesterday after heated hearings and a good deal of convention hall maneuvering are interpreted as a victory for the small states over the big states; the rural states over the urban states; the conservatives over the liberals; and, more specifically, the conservative potential candidates for 1976 such as Vice President Agnew and Gov. Reagan over the more liberal contenders such as Sen. Percy.

It was all of these, in varying degrees, but when the dust settles the squabble is likely to end up more important as a matter of principle than in practice. The difference between the extreme positions looked deceptively big in numbers because the total number of delegates is to be raised from 1,348 to about 2,100. But in relative percentages—and thus influence—the differences are probably too small to be decisive for or against any candidate.

The nine largest states, including Illinois, now have 40.1 per cent of the total delegate vote, admittedly less than warranted either by their population or the number of Republican voters in the state. Liberals sought to raise this percentage to about 47 per cent; the approved changes would give them about 43 per cent, assuming their present political complexion.

The 15 smallest states, conversely, now have 13.8 per cent of the delegates. Liberals would like to have cut this to 10.1 per cent; the approved changes give them about 12.5 per cent.

Even if the big states all vote Democratic and the small ones all Republican, the variation would not be overwhelming.

The same goes for the wording of the provision designed to bring in more women and minority members [which at present tends to mean liberal] as delegates. It really doesn't make all that much difference whether state committees are told to take "positive steps" toward this end or to try "in good faith" to do so. After all, a remarkable advance in this direction has been made in 1972, without any formal instructions at all.

In short, the Republicans might have spent their time better than on maneuvering for position in the uncertain conditions that will exist four years hence. The conservative forces were well organized and their cause a good one, namely to keep the party from drifting into the hands of big city Republicans who might turn it into a carbon copy of the Democratic Party. There is merit to their contention that small states are entitled to somewhat greater influence per capita than larger states; that is part of the system. But they needn't be afraid of allocating seats more nearly according to the number of Republican voters in each state than either the present formula or the new one does.

San Jose Mercury
San Jose, Calif., August 19, 1972

The Republican party has been grappling with a number of proposed "reforms." For the time being, the Republican Rules Committee has said no to a proposed duplication of the quota system employed by the Democratic party in selecting its delegates to the national convention.

The GOP rules-makers instead have opted for a ban on discrimination because of sex and age, and for statements of commitment to an "open party" system.

The proposal for adoption of a "proportional representation" system requiring so many men, so many women, so many youth and so many members of minorities as delegates was unceremoniously scuttled.

We'll have no "McGovernization" of the Republican convention, was the reaction of GOP pros.

Nevertheless, the GOP rules-makers will urge that the Republican convention support a "good faith" proposal that each state "endeavor to have equal representation of men and women in its delegation" at future conventions.

Now the fear among some liberal Republicans is that failure to copy the Democratic quota system will invite charges that the GOP is anti-progressive.

Such charges undoubtedly will come. But the much-hailed quota system for delegation selection already is being subjected to some second-guessing. Indeed, it has been observed that the Democratic quotas gave short shrift to the poor, the elderly, several ethnic minorities, the working class and lawn bowling devotees, to name only a few.

A breakdown of the Democratic convention's "reform delegation," in fact, gives substance to complaints that the so-called reforms supplanted one elite with another. Thirty-nine per cent of a cross-section of the Democratic delegates were found to have post-graduate degrees, contrasted with less than four per cent in the total population. One in four had some college, compared to one in eight in the nation. Almost one-third of delegates had family incomes over $25,000; the national average: one in 20. Only six per cent had incomes under $5,000; the national average: 19 per cent. An analysis of the black delegates showed a similar disparity between them and the nation's blacks.

This is not to discount the broader participation in the political process which was evident at the Democratic convention. It is rather to question if quota systems really perform the wonders their advocates proclaim. The record to date suggests that they do not.

The Republican party, however, embarks on an alternative route at great risk. Despite brave talk of massive realignments of party loyalties, the GOP yearly sees new registrations running heavily in the opposition's favor. More persons now call themselves independents than Republicans. This means the GOP must give more than lip service to its invitations for broader participation.

Republican Convention:
PLATFORM REFLECTS NIXON POSITIONS; DOCUMENT ADOPTED WITH ONE CHANGE

The convention approved the Republican party platform by voice vote Aug. 22. The delegates adopted the platform, written largely under the guidance of the White House, virtually intact, adding only a plank calling for preferential hiring and promotion of Indians within federal agencies dealing with Indian affairs to the 140-page document. A proposal to prohibit President Nixon from submitting deficit budgets was rejected by a voice vote.

Plank by plank, the platform reflected the President's views on Vietnam, labor, disarmament, school busing, welfare reform and other subjects. It also charged that the Democratic party "has been seized by a radical clique which scorns our nation's past and would blight our future." The omission of the traditional GOP stand against compulsory unionism and in favor of "right to work" laws was seen as part of the White House's effort to woo the votes of disaffected Democrats from the ranks of organized labor. Among the major policy positions detailed in the platform:

- A declaration that the U.S. should not perform an "act of betrayal" by overthrowing the Saigon government. "We most emphatically say the President of the U.S. should not go begging to Hanoi."

- A categorical rejection of "all proposals to grant amnesty to those who have broken the law by evading military service."

- A demand that the nation's welfare system "simply must be reformed."

- A statement that the party "irrevocably" opposed school busing for the purpose of racial integration.

- Praise for organized labor for "advancing the well-being" of the American free enterprise system and backing for collective bargaining as the "cornerstone of the nation's labor relations policy."

The Oregonian
Portland, Ore., August 22, 1972

There is marked contrast between the Vietnam war planks in the platforms of the two major parties:

The Democrats "pledge, as the first order of business, an immediate and complete withdrawal of all U. S. forces in Indochina. All U. S. military action in Southeast Asia will cease . . . any resolution of the war (must) include the return of all prisoners . . ."

The Republicans "will continue to seek a settlement . . . which will permit the people of Southeast Asia to live in peace under political arrangements of their own choosing . . . the President's proposal to withdraw remaining American forces from Vietnam four months after an internationally supervised ceasefire . . . and all prisoners have been returned is as generous an offer as can be made by anyone . . ."

But it is more productive to examine the record of President Nixon's accomplishment in extricating America from the war with honor, not just the promises.

As the Republican National Convention convened Monday in Miami Beach, it was announced in Saigon that U. S. troop strength in Vietnam had fallen below 39,000, more than a week in advance of the Sept. 1 deadline the President had set for that mark.

The measure of that achievement is reflected in comparison of 39,000 with 543,000, which was the peak U. S. strength in April, 1969. There are about 100,000 U. S. forces still involved in the war from air bases in Thailand and Guam and aboard ships of the Seventh Fleet. But these, as well as the remaining U. S. ground troops in Vietnam, would surely be withdrawn on resolution of the war.

Presidential action, not just pledges, has proved the intent of the Nixon Administration to achieve peace at the soonest time possible — peace, not surrender. No amount of eloquence in platform planks or in convention oratory can match that performance in the scales of public opinion on the war issue.

Mr. Nixon is scheduled to make yet another troop withdrawal statement next Monday, with the probability that the Vietnam contingent will be cut to 25,000 or lower, or less than 5 per cent of the 1969 figure. But even more significant information on the war in Vietnam, present and future, could come in the President's address accepting nomination for a second term.

The Courier-Journal
Louisville, Ky., August 28, 1972

THE REPUBLICAN platform makes it perfectly clear that the party intends to play a cruel game with one of the most serious and most emotional issues bothering the people during this presidential campaign.

First, the party declares a noble goal for itself: "We are committed to guaranteeing equality of education opportunity and to completing the process of ending de jure school segregation."

But how does it propose to achieve that goal? By opposing "busing for racial balance," on the ground that it creates "division within communities and hostility between classes and races" (the reason that Dixie's governors used to cite for opposing the very idea of desegregation and every civil rights bill passed during the 1960s). By favoring the "neighborhood school concept" (a "concept" devised to justify the continued segregation of black schoolchildren in ghetto neighborhoods). By proposing "$2.5 billion of federal aid to school districts to improve educational opportunities and build facilities for disadvantaged children. . . ."

It's a strange map the party has drawn, for it points the way to neither equality of opportunity nor the end of segregation. Busing —which everyone concedes is one of the least desirable ways of ending segregation—is opposed, yea, even unto a constitutional amendment prohibiting it. But the platform mentions not a single means by which the Republicans intend to redeem their pledge to end de jure segregation. Nor does it even say that President Nixon will come up with one later.

Of course, there *are* other ways. If President Nixon doesn't know them, he may find them listed in the Democratic Party platform: "School attendance lines may be redrawn; schools may be paired; larger physical facilities may be built to serve larger, more diverse enrollment; magnet schools or educational parks may be used." These methods have been used more widely than busing to bring about desegregation.

But, as the Supreme Court has noted, these methods aren't always viable, and when they aren't viable, busing may be called for. "Transportation of students is another tool to accomplish desegregation," the Democratic platform states. "It must continue to be available according to Supreme Court decisions to eliminate legally imposed segregation and improve the quality of education for all children."

That "quality of education for all children" is what both parties say is the real school issue in this campaign. The Democrats, paraphrasing the Supreme Court's 1954 decision in *Brown v. Board of Education*, contend that "equal access to quality education for all our children" is the very purpose of school desegregation. But President Nixon and the Republicans pretend that quality education and desegregation aren't related.

After the courts' efforts to achieve desegregation have been squelched, the Republican platform implies, the federal government will spend $2.5 billion to buy "high-quality education" for those kids who have been stranded in the ghettos.

Even if this were a good-faith promise, $2.5 billion in "new" federal money wouldn't begin to bridge the educational-opportunity gap between the ghettos and the suburbs of this country. But the $2.5 billion that President Nixon has proposed isn't even "new" money. It's money that has already been authorized by Congress—but not spent by the President—for other educational needs.

The criticism that several House Democrats leveled against President Nixon's compensatory education bill when it was introduced last March still holds: If Mr. Nixon *really* wants to improve education for needy youngsters, he doesn't need a new law to do it. Title I of the 1965 Elementary and Secondary Education Act authorizes full funding of more than $6 billion for this purpose. Yet current outlays under Title I total about $1.5 billion, and President Nixon hasn't asked that they be increased.

The Democrats, by calling for full funding of Title I, plus additional help for educationally deprived children, seem to have a more realistic idea of the magnitude and seriousness of the "quality education" problem. Their proposals, Mr. Nixon will point out, will cost more money. And so they may be more unpopular. But if the cry for "quality education" is anything more than a dodge around the segregation issue, surely the voters see that more money is the first essential step toward solution.

Mr. Nixon won't fight the battle along those lines. He'll continue to call only for no busing and more funds for the ghettos, which, being translated, means "separate but equal." And we all know how well that idea worked.

CHICAGO DAILY NEWS
Chicago, Ill., August 22, 1972

Hope springs eternal that one or the the other party will write a campaign platform rooted in principle. It didn't happen last month in Miami Beach; it didn't happen this week. Perhaps it's too much to ask on the eve of the quadrennial contest for the Presidency. Perhaps platforms should be written midway between campaigns.

The Republican platform is at least more amenable to labor than it would be if President Nixon didn't see a chance to move profitably into a breach in organized labor's ranks. That's why a right-to-work plank, handiwork of the party's conservative wing, got squeezed out. By the same token, there doubtless wouldn't have been a plank calling for federally assisted day care for children if women's rights hadn't become quite an issue this year. Mr. Nixon had vetoed daycare legislation passed by the Democratic Congress. The platform took backhanded note of that fact by opposing "proposals which are ill-considered, incapable of being administered effectively," etc.

But in reaching out for women and working people the platform did not ignore the sources of its conservative strength in such matters as its anti-school busing plank, its flat opposition to amnesty, and its jibes at the Democratic Party, which it says has been captured by a "radical clique" that, among other things, would perpetrate "an act of betrayal" in Vietnam. Businessmen are soothed by a promise to drop wage and price controls "at the earliest possible moment."

Predictably, a great deal of space is devoted to Congress' derelictions with regard to Mr. Nixon's legislative programs. Still languishing "in the opposition Congress," the platform points out, are sweeping proposals covering land use, park lands, air and water quality, noise, ocean dumping, and other environmental matters. And while opposing "the principle of a government-guaranteed income" and deploring welfare loafers, it powerfully endorses Mr. Nixon's own welfare reform program, which has been bottled up by the Senate all year.

All of this is, of course, peripheral to the main platform themes, which will also serve as the twin campaign themes: the withdraw-with-dignity policy in Vietnam and the you-never-had-it-better economic theme.

Altogether it is a platform reflecting confidence in a political strategy that the polls testify has the support of an overwhelming majority of Americans. It reaches out cautiously toward groups that have not traditionally been friendly to the party, but it is meticulously careful not to prod any present supporters to desert to the enemy.

And since the name of the game is to win, and since platforms are, after all, utensils designed to enhance the chances of success, it must be adjudged a shrewdly wrought springboard.

The Dallas Morning News
Dallas, Tex., August 22, 1972

Although basically a sound document, the Republican platform unfortunately contains no strong stand against compulsory unionism.

Writers ignored pleas by Reed Larson, executive vice-president of the National Right to Work Committee, and others to include a reestablishment of the principle of right to work as a basic civil and human right.

Larson bolstered his argument with results of a national opinion poll, which indicated that a majority of the nation's union members in each voting category—Republican, Democratic and independent—favor party platforms pledging to eliminate forced unionism. Of the Republicans surveyed, 73 per cent favored a strong stand for right to work.

States now can outlaw compulsory unionism as a requisite for holding a job.

Republicans, of course, are looking forward to getting many labor votes this fall, and omission of the plank is seen as a concession to labor leaders, who are cool to Democrat George McGovern's candidacy.

Nevertheless, a strong stand for right to work and individual liberty would have strengthened the platform in the minds of conservatives.

The Providence Journal
Providence, R.I., August 23, 1972

By its tone as well as its content, the 1972 Republican platform symbolizes not only the confidence of a party in power, but also the widespread GOP belief that it will fall heir in November to a new constituency, a constituency of the generally satisfied center. It is a proud document, laden with the expected encomiums for President Nixon, yet one with harsh rhetorical overtones that indicate a bruising campaign ahead.

* * *

On Vietnam, the Republican platform draws a clear contrast with the Democratic posture, which calls for "immediate and complete withdrawal of all U.S. forces." The GOP, naturally, praises the President for having withdrawn all U.S. ground combat forces, and registers firm support for his conditions of settlement, including continued backing for the Thieu government in Saigon. It is something else again, however, to describe the Vietnamization program, as the platform does, as "successful." Such a view takes no notice of the continuing dependence of the Saigon government on U.S. bombing to fight off the North Vietnamese.

On defense spending, the Republicans deliver a sharp, if indirect, rebuke to Sen. George McGovern, the Democratic nominee, by decrying "meat-ax" cuts in Pentagon outlays. The platform specifically advocates retention of several major—and costly—weapons programs; in this area, Mr. McGovern has declared they are not needed. The Democratic plank, in contrast, declared that "the military budget can be substantially reduced with no weakening of national security."

On the domestic economy, the GOP platform also indirectly assails Mr. McGovern, saying the party opposes "deceitful" tax reforms that would raise taxes for middle-income families. This is an unmistakable thrust at the McGovern income maintenance proposal. But the platform, while declaring that the Republicans "flatly oppose programs or policies which embrace the principle of a government-guaranteed income," oddly ignores the fact that the President's welfare plan does precisely that.

Sharply drawn differences between the two parties also appear in their treatment of amnesty for draft evaders (conditionally favored by the Democrats, flatly opposed by the Republicans) and busing (the Democrats regard it as "another tool to accomplish desegregation" while the Republicans are categorically opposed).

* * *

What may be most significant from a comparison of the two party platforms is not so much the positions on specific issues, important as these are, but the political outlook that each platform represents. These documents, both thoroughly political in nature, point up the fact that both Mr. Nixon and Mr. McGovern feel ready to benefit from newly forming coalitions of voter support. Mr. Nixon is paying special attention to the South, to Catholics and to working men and women, while the Democratic nominee professes to see a new coalition of the disaffected, especially the young, the poor, the blacks, the farmers and the intellectuals.

The contrast between the two parties' view of the nation is as marked as that between them on any single issue. The Democratic platform declares that "skepticism and cynicism are widespread in America," while the GOP document seeks to present the nation as embarked on a "calmer sea with a sure, steady hand at the helm" and undergoing a "saga of exhilarating progress."

The tone of the two platforms also highlights the extent to which the politics of 1972 have polarized the two parties along ideological lines. The Democrats have swung to the left (although hardly to the extent of a "convulsive leftward lurch" as the GOP platform asserts), while the Republicans are moving briskly to stake out a newly broadened claim to the moderate conservative center.

With so much going for the Republicans, especially the built-in advantages inhering to an incumbent President, the harsh tone of some of their platform rhetoric appears excessive. For example, by declaring that the Democratic Party has been "seized by a radical clique," and implying that the Democrats are "bemused with surrender" in Indochina, the language of the Republican platform does scant honor to the party's responsible traditions.

* * *

One might expect that an incumbent President (Mr. Nixon closely supervised the platform drafting) would be more restrained. But the calculated aggressiveness of its language, some of it tougher in tone than Mr. Nixon originally sought, indicates that those shaping GOP policy now feel assured of the wisdom of sharply partisan attacks on the Democrats. The Republicans now sense that they are dealing from strength, and if there is a measure of fierce contentiousness in their platform document, it reflects a political reading of the nation's temperament. The November results will tell whether this reading has been accurate and will indicate to a significant degree whether the Republicans are on their way to becoming the nation's new majority party.

Detroit Free Press
Detroit, Mich., August 23, 1972

THE DEMOCRATIC platform was the result of a pitched battle among the assorted forces in the Democratic Party, a battle waged in the open by political amateurs. As a result, it included the program the majority of the delegates wanted, but some pretty silly trivia as well.

The Republican platform, on the other hand, was crafted in secret by presidential handmaidens, polished in the White House, and delivered to the delegates in Miami like the Ten Commandments. And, like the children of Moses, the delegates accepted it.

It's a good thing some 70 percent of them are first-timers. It's not a platform which the Republicans would have accepted four years ago, and certainly not one on which Mr. Nixon would have run.

Which tells us more about the futility of these quadrennial exercises than about what we can expect for the four years to come.

The platform, for instance, promises that the GOP "will press for expansion of contacts with the peoples of Eastern Europe and the People's Republic of China." Four years ago Richard Nixon was the most energetic exponent of the cold war, and for anyone to have suggested rapprochement with communist nations would have invited screams of "treason."

The GOP platform promises "to continue to pursue sound economic policies that will eliminate inflation, further cut unemployment, raise real incomes and strengthen our international economic position."

The facts, of course, are that unemployment is higher than it was four years ago and that the cost of living went up faster in Mr. Nixon's first 30 months than it did even in Lyndon Johnson's full term. As Sylvia Porter pointed out yesterday, the pace of inflation did not begin to abate until Mr. Nixon adopted the Democratic policies he and the Republican Party had earlier denounced and sworn to avoid. Wage and price controls were anathema, and Mr. Nixon repeatedly said he would never devalue the dollar.

On foreign policy, the platform gets carried away with itself to say that "historians may well regard these years as a golden age of American diplomacy." Given the President's penchant for "the greatest day," "the greatest event," "the greatest week" and other first and greatests, one suspects that particular line came straight from the Oval Office.

We do not suggest that Mr. Nixon should be faulted for his innovations, or that the GOP platform should ignore them. Quite the contrary, Mr. Nixon has indeed changed the nature of post-World War II foreign policy and deserves full credit. He has expanded trade with Russia and opened the door to China.

Through skill, luck or both he has kept the lid on in the Middle East, and if he gets the blame when things go wrong he must be given the credit.

But it's hardly a golden age when the war in Vietnam goes on because of his obsession with saving face, or relations have soured with India because of his "tilt" to Pakistan while professing neutrality, or Japan feels less secure and Latin America more neglected.

He has, in the past year, cut unemployment slightly and reduced the rate of inflation, but it's going overboard a bit to hail all this as due solely to Republican genius, achieved over the opposition of Democratic trouble-makers.

We would not expect a political platform to confess the party's sins and ask the people to balance the good against the bad. In politics the failures are never mentioned except by the opposition.

But Mr. Nixon has a record on which he can and will have to run, a record which will be remembered far longer than the sycophantic simperings offered in the platform.

Now that he is safely renominated, minus one dissenting vote from New Mexico, we hope Mr. Nixon has the dignity to ignore his lackey's excesses and offer the people some of the moderation the platform promised but never delivered.

The San Juan Star
San Juan, P.R., August 23, 1972

In general, the Republican platform, like always, is a windy pitch for votes, something for everybody—small business, cities, states, environmentalists, nature lovers, artists, scientists, children, young people, old people, ladies, blacks, the Spanish-speaking, Indians, Alaskan and Hawaiian natives, consumers, veterans.

In short, as a subtitle says, the Republican Party pledges "a better future for all." The Democrats, of course, claim they will deliver on the same bill of goods.

Anyone who has followed closely the record of the Nixon administration the last three and one-half years would just about know what the platform says, without reading the Platform Committee's product. The platform is, without deviation, strictly a Nixon platform—not unusual for a party which has its man in the White House and wants to keep him there another term. Indeed, Nixon's nomination came right on schedule Tuesday night.

The Democratic platform, written by all the divergent elements at that earlier convention, is not wholly McGovern, not unusual when the party is out of power. The GOP platform is entirely Nixon. It is his own case for re-election.

Voters who care to read both documents, and can screen out the purely partisan color, will find real differences from which to choose.

THE WALL STREET JOURNAL
New York, N.Y., August 22, 1972

Possessed as it is of a commanding lead in the early stages of the presidential sweepstakes, the Republican Party might reasonably have been expected to exercise some restraint in bidding for support from the myriad pressure groups that have become so much a part of our politics and society.

Such restraint would have shown an awareness of and response to the popular discontent with the rising cost and pervasiveness of government which has made itself evident in a number of ways in this year's primary election campaigns.

There is not much restraint to be found, however, in the draft Republican Party platform that will come before the party's convention today. Not only does it point with pride to a proliferation of federal programs and activities under three and a half years of Republican administration, it promises a great deal more of the same if President Nixon is reelected in November.

Even though it was written with strong guidance from the White House, the platform in at least one instance partly relents on a form of spending that the President rejected when it was brought forth by the present Congress. The President vetoed as too costly a bill authorizing federal child day care centers for working mothers. But after renewed insistence from women's rights groups, a plan supporting federal assistance for centers that would be set up privately or by state and local agencies was included in the 1972 platform.

Other spending promises tumble out of the new platform like apples tumbled from a well-stocked barrel. New tax incentives and more loans are to be available for "Small Business." Commodity programs and other efforts to expand farm income are to be pursued. Greater federal involvement in education is promised. There is no mention of the massive federal borrowing that already has been used to finance Nixon administration programs. While this expansion is already straining the nation's credit resources, further debt would no doubt be needed to keep the platform promises.

We, of course, are aware that party platforms have traditionally been designed to offer something for everyone and traditionally have been regarded with some skepticism as to how accurately they reflect the intentions of a party seeking votes. We also are aware that if the President wins a strong mandate and a friendlier Congress in November, he may very well adopt a more conservative stance than he has displayed so far.

But there can be no certainty of that, and at any rate we suspect that there may be more significance to be found in this platform document than in many of those of the past. The especially wide net the platform casts in its bid for votes makes it clear, if there had been any lingering doubts, that the Republican Party, in its view of the federal role in our governance, our economy and our society, has moved leftward in an effort to occupy the vital center of American politics. The platform preamble, in fact, claims control of that center by saying that the party's "moderate" goals are those historically sought by *both* major parties. The Democratic Party, it argues with little cause for challenge, is not the party of old but has been seized this year "by a radical clique which scorns our nation's past and would blight her future."

The bid to occupy the center—and thus become the nation's dominant party, would seem to have a strong chance of success. Just as surely as a successful occupation of the center squares on a chessboard by Bobby Fischer leaves his opponent with reduced options, the Democrats seemingly have been forced into a far-out and uncomfortable corner. But in order to play the center properly and for the general good of all, it is necessary for a party to have a reasonably clear concept of where the center actually is.

The danger that confronts the Republican Party is the danger of overreaching in an excess of zeal to co-opt the social programs that have been more traditionally the offerings of Democrats. It may well get the government and nation into more serious fiscal and economic difficulties than it already confronts.

A great deal has been said about the real choice the November election will offer, and beyond doubt that is true in many important respects. But we suspect that a good many voters see less choice than many analysts imagine. Given the radical position of the Democrats, for many it will be the Republicans or nothing. If that proves to be the case, we hope the Republican Party will not misread the mandate. It should keep in mind that a good many of the votes it will receive may well be from voters who would have preferred less, not more, than the Republicans are offering.

THE KANSAS CITY STAR
Kansas City, Mo., August 22, 1972

Wondrous are the ways of political parties when it comes to writing a platform. Consider, for example, what happened at Miami Beach as the Republicans suddenly realized (having received the word from the White House) that this was Be-Kind-to-Labor Year. Mr. Nixon wanted a platform that would be attractive to labor. On the whole, Mr. Nixon has been getting what he wants.

Traditionally, the G.O.P. has included in its platform a provision which vowed to preserve the federal act that permits states to enact right-to-work laws. Mr. Nixon ran quite comfortably on such a platform four years ago. Traditionally, too, the Democrats in their official party declaration have called for repeal of that law.

This year the Democrats stayed with tradition. Even so, Senator McGovern (for other reasons, including one of his votes opposing repeal of the law in question) failed to gain the imprimatur of George Meany and the top hierarchy of the AFL-CIO.

Mr. Nixon obviously has no hope of gaining that endorsement. Even so, at his urging, the platform writers decided to omit any reference whatsoever to right to work. The theory, we suppose, is that sometimes silence wins voters, or at least may forestall any further endorsements of the Democratic ticket by various unions acting independently.

Now it may be concluded that since the Democratic right-to-work plank favorable to labor did not influence George Meany and his executive board, a Republican plank silent on the issue would have no more effect. Of course it won't. But both parties, we note, have gone further. Each, using different language, has also written into its platform (on which the G.O.P. is to take final action today) language which seems to cater to the growing protectionist sentiment of organized labor.

Mr. Nixon, by instinct and philosophy, is an advocate of free trade. The Democratic party was the home of Cordell Hull, who espoused the cause of this nation's first reciprocal trade law. Yet here we have both parties paying only lip service to liberal trade, and speaking, if we hear them correctly, in the language of the protectionists.

What either party says about right-to-work laws is, in all probability, not too important except in the campaign context. It is not the kind of promise that is likely to affect any administration or any Congress. But what the parties say about trade—as vital as it is to the American economy—can be of considerable importance.

In this area, a platform can set the mood for an administration that must (as the next one will) seek new trade negotiating authority from Congress. And there is no way to avoid the impression that in the writing of both platforms, protectionists have scored a victory. Such victories are not, as we see it, in the interest of the nation as a whole.

Oakland Tribune
Oakland, Calif., August 23, 1972

The party platform agreed to by the Democratic National Convention last month was, by and large, a product of the thinking and a reflection of the philosophies of the man delegates later selected as their candidate for the presidency.

In turn, the Platform Committee of the Republican National Convention listened attentively to White House suggestions in preparing the document made public Sunday and adopted last night.

Which is as it should be. Platforms should honestly and clearly reflect the consensus opinion of each party's membership and leadership.

So now, with the official adoption of the Republican platform, the differences between the two party's policies, which this year appear considerable, can be illuminated by and for the public.

Under the welfare heading, for instance, the Democrats emphasize the need for "income security" and flatly promise federal assistance for those who claim they need it.

The GOP welfare plank declares the "nation's welfare system is a mess" and offers a "decent level of payment to the genuine needy." But the big differences come in the Republican insistence that all adult welfare applicants register for work or job training and to accept such offers when made.

In net, the Democrats offer a government guaranteed income. The Republicans specifically reject that principle.

Another big difference is in defense policy, where the GOP platform warns against meat-ax slashes in spending that would substantially weaken this nation's deterrent capability.

The Democrats' defense plank calls for major reductions in virtually all defense spending categories and particularly in overseas forces.

On Vietnam, the Democrats would, if McGovern is elected, immediately withdraw all U.S. forces from Indochina and presumably abandon our allies in South Vietnam and other countries to whatever fates the Communists would have in store for them.

The GOP position endorses the continuing Administration effort to negotiate a settlement with Hanoi that would permit the people of Southeast Asia to "live in peace under political arrangements of their own choosing."

Perhaps the most glaring platform difference is on the touchy school busing question. Here, the Democratic policy statement describes busing as "another tool to accomplish desegregation." The Republican position rejects "busing for racial balance" and favors consideration of an "appropriate constitutional amendment to that effect."

On amnesty, tax reform and health care there are equally evident differences between the two party positions, with the Democrats consistently taking a more liberal position.

Thus, for all the voters a comparison of the two party platforms now offers a singular opportunity. Without particular regard to candidate personalities, it is now possible to confirm the thrust of one's political philosophy, or indeed, to find out a new, more comfortable political "home."

St. Louis Post-Dispatch
St. Louis, Mo., August 24, 1972

In adopting an uncompromising plank against amnesty for young men who have fled the country to avoid military service, the Republicans have badly confused leniency or forgiveness with a total repudiation of the Administration's Indochina war policies. Any hint of the latter, of course, would be repugnant to the political beatification of Richard Nixon that is taking place in Miami Beach. Accordingly, the platform states: "We reject the claim that those who fled are more deserving, or obeyed a higher morality, than those next in line who served in their places."

But as the Democrats correctly perceived last month, amnesty can be proposed without any mention of "higher morality" or, conversely, the immorality of the war. *Their* platform simply says that when the fighting has ended and the troops and prisoners of war are back home an amnesty shall be declared "on an appropriate basis," a phrase hinting at some sort of conditional appropriate service. Thousands of young Americans are in exile because of their convictions or their fear of the draft. The object for both political parties ought to be to devise some way of making them useful citizens again. Neither banishment nor prison, which are the only possibilities under the Republican platform, is satisfactory.

Omaha World-Herald
Omaha, Neb., August 22, 1972

President Nixon's open wooing of political support from organized labor seems to have resulted in the watering down of his party's strong position on the right to hold a job without being compelled to join a union.

The GOP platform indicates displeasure with forced unionism, but makes no mention of the "right to work." This is something more than a semantic difference; "right to work" has been one of the strong points of Republican labor policy and is the name usually applied to state laws forbidding the closed shop.

Mrs. Lorraine Orr, a Nebraska delegate, said she and others waged a hard fight to strengthen the "right to work" plank, but there was "no way" it would be inserted in the platform.

We suppose that in terms of campaign strategy, the platform writers — and the White House — see some advantage to be gained in softening of position on one of organized labor's key issues.

It sounds to us, however, like a retreat from principle, an approach to the sacrifice of the already precarious rights of millions of nonunion working people.

Chicago Tribune
Chicago, Ill., August 24, 1972

If the purpose of a political party platform is to mean all things to all people, then 1972 is sure to be a vintage year. Rep. Roman Pucinski, Democratic candidate for the Senate, said of the Democratic platform that Calvin Coolidge could have run comfortably on it. The platform approved by the Republicans this week might have been equally agreeable to the late Socialist candidate, Norman Thomas.

Of course party platforms have never been gems of precision or consistency. Their phrases are like bubbles—glittering, appealing to the eye but dissolving at a touch of analysis. This year's platforms seem more ambivalent than ever — the Democrats' because they couldn't agree on what to say, and the Republicans' because of a calculated effort to appeal to a variety of voting blocs including labor and other erstwhile Democrats who dislike Mr. McGovern and might be lured into the Republican fold.

True, there are some controversial areas where the parties are willing to take strong and distinctive stands: For example the war, busing, amnesty for draft evaders, and the taxation of business. But in general, what differences remain are in tone or semantics rather than in substance. The Democratic drift is toward more and more government intervention in our lives [except with respect to wage and price controls, which they first demanded and now promise to end]. The Republicans, tho drifting in the same direction, are fortunately far behind.

The two parties use almost identical words in calling for such things as the equitable distribution of taxes, the rights of women, better education, faster justice, the security and Israel, and a cleaner environment.

In their passionate courtship of labor, the Republicans have sacrificed their traditional support of right-to-work laws guaranteeing a worker the right to hold his job without having to join a union. Nor can one any longer find the commitment to strengthen laws protecting us from crippling strikes, especially in transportation, or to restore the equilibrium between management and labor without which collective bargaining becomes a farce and the public often become the victims.

The voter is left to his own devises in trying to determine what each party means by its honeyed phrases. And here the Nixon administration has the advantage of being able to point to its achievements, which are substantial while the Democrats can only carp and promise to do better, without saying precisely how.

If party platforms are to continue to move toward one another, we may soon find that they can be abandoned and not be missed.

Both documents are feeble as expressions of political philosophy and blueprints for action. They can be summarized in two words — forgettable manifestoes. And we predict they will soon be forgotten.

Republican Convention:
SITDOWN FAILS TO DELAY SPEECHES; POLICE ARREST 1,100 PROTESTERS

More than 1,100 protesters were arrested after attempting to block traffic in the streets around the convention area Aug. 23. Although the stated aim of the demonstrators was to delay the acceptance speeches of President Nixon and Vice President Agnew, the convention session began only seven minutes behind schedule. Protesters were prevented from gathering in large groups by the use of CS or "pepper" gas, which also affected some delegates as they entered the hall. Only 38 minor injuries were reported as police adopted the highly mobile, but low profile tactics devised by Miami Beach Police Chief Rocky Pomerance.

Ignoring the advice of most of their leaders, some demonstrators slashed tires, overturned garbage cans and assaulted delegates. Most of those arrested were freed on nominal $10 bail fees within 24 hours. Smaller demonstrations had been held Aug. 20-22.

The Detroit News
Detroit, Mich., August 28, 1972

Since reaching its tumultuous peak at the 1968 Democratic Convention in Chicago, militant protest has been slowly expiring as a technique of political propaganda in this country. The noise made by protesters at the Republican National Convention in Miami Beach last week was another death rattle.

In saying this, we don't dismiss as trivial the pain and discomfort suffered by convention delegates and residents of Miami Beach at the hands of the protesters. There's nothing trivial about having your car or bus disabled or about being mauled, kicked and spat on by marauding hippies, zippies and revolutionaries.

However, there was small inclination of the part of anybody — including TV newsmen who once acted as apologists for protesters — to preserve the fiction that such protests are spontaneous exercises in democracy by youthful idealists concerned about the morals of their country.

Certainly, many of the young people protesting at Miami Beach were sincere young idealists. But their actions were neither spontaneous nor compatible with the democratic process. Their harrassment of delegates at a political convention violated basic democratic principles; moreover, that harassment was carefully orchestrated by some of the oldest professional malcontents in the business.

The country has grown thoroughly disenchanted with militant protest; the public now sees the strings that manipulate the puppets. Fewer and fewer young people allow themselves to be used. Some who once considered militant protest a worthwhile tool have abandoned it as unproductive. All this has diminished the ranks of flatulent outfits such as the "People's Coalition for Peace and Justice."

The organizers of the Miami Beach disturbances had announced that "tens of thousands" of protesters would flock to Miami beach to disrupt the GOP convention. Between 3,000 and 4,000 — enough to cause plenty of trouble, to be sure — actually showed up.

Although they s u c c e e d e d in making life miserable for some of the residents and delegates, the protesters lacked the force of numbers they n e e d e d to achieve their announced goal, which was to bring the convention to a grinding halt. Time and again in the past year, street protest in America has met with similar failure.

For some, of course, protest has become a lifetime occupation which apparently will never lose its lure, w h a t e v e r the discouragements. Among familiar faces in the roving gangs on the streets of Miami Beach were those of Rennie Davis and David Dellinger, two of the infamous Chicago 7.

Does justice never complete its mission? These men participated in the riots at the Democratic National Convention in 1968. After a long and stormy trial, they were convicted in 1970 and sentenced to five years in prison. They were set free, and they remain free, pending appeal.

Since his conviction of inciting riot in Chicago, Davis has appeared in the vanguard of "Stop the Government" demonstrations on two different occasions in Washington, D.C. He helped organize the Miami Beach demonstrations and, along with Dellinger, took part in those demonstrations.

Four years from now, Democrats and Republicans will hold their national political conventions again. There should be many new faces of politicians at those conventions. But if you like a sense of the familiar, don't worry. You probably can depend on seeing Dellinger and Davis — without followers, perhaps, but with their bullhorns roaring and their everlasting appeals still pending.

THE MILWAUKEE JOURNAL
Milwaukee, Wis., August 26, 1972

The antiwar demonstrators failed in their attempt to disrupt the Republican convention Wednesday night. From almost all sides it is agreed that the police acted in a level headed manner. Miami Beach was not a repetition of the 1968 Democratic convention in Chicago. But the key point was made, that the Vietnam War is still a major divisive factor in the country today. Its continuation rips at the fabric of American society and domestic peace. No mere calls for unity and bipartisan understanding, such as the president made in the convention hall, can mend that rupture. Only a true end to the bombing and the war will succeed in doing that.

The Miami Herald
Miami, Fla., August 25, 1972

NON-VIOLENCE, like beauty, is in the eye of the beholder. Ah, well, the Republican Convention is over, and with it a chapter in the streets of Miami Beach which ranged from hoodlumism to heroism.

The purpose of granting the so-called non-delegates a sort of asylum in Flamingo Park was to contain and control them rather than to accommodate them. Thus the community escaped the major outrages of Chicago in 1968, when fewer dissenters were arrested but many more persons were injured under an inept security plan.

For this, all thanks to an intelligent, smooth-working plan which involved law enforcement officers, the swift-dealing courts of justice, volunteer pacifiers and civil officials who respected the right of dissent but had no patience with the assumed right of violent protest.

While many of the non-delegates honored their non-violence pledge, those who did not brought dishonor on the whole anti-war movement and should be punished for their acts.

There is nothing as frightening as a mob.

The hoodlums who slashed tires, immobilized cars and buses and personally assaulted delegates need to be identified. The vandals who "trashed" store fronts (a relative few) must be held to an accounting for their acts.

But let us say a word for the whole community. That word is pride.

We are proud that Miami Beach and Greater Miami made it possible for two great political parties to preserve the electoral process.

This was a patriotic contribution to the American way. Made with some sacrifice, psychologically and physically, it will stand as a brighter chapter in history than two ugly nights in the streets. If the truth be known, the Republicans came within an ace of not being able to hold a conventional convention at all.

180—Convention Protest Fails

THE DALLAS TIMES HERALD
Dallas, Tex., August 25, 1972

BACK IN the late '60s, when street protest reached its zenith, goodly numbers of the broadminded took pains to note how the protesters were only exercising their good old American right of free speech. That was relatively easy to say during a time of ferment on all intellectual fronts.

The times are quieter now. And wrenched from their late-'60's context, the demonstrations in Miami Beach this week reveal the real nature of all such efforts to change "the system" by main force.

It is not merely that the protests at the Republican convention were ugly and sordid. It is, above all, that they were so silly, so puerile, so — yes, even so pathetic.

The demonstrations, according to a manual the protesters circulated among themselves, were designed "to signal America's refusal to accept a war criminal as a presidential candidate . . . to isolate and defeat Richard Milhous Nixon, 37th President of the United States."

To which end, the assorted protesters — nearly all of them White Anglo-Saxon Protestants in their 20s — puffed pot, paraded about in the near-buff (girls, too), yelled obscenities at delegates, whipped up on a few bystanders, slashed tires, and as the paddy wagons hauled them away, chanted, "All we are saying is give peace a chance."

One protester, seizing a 7-year-old girl, shrieked, "Your mother is a murderer! President Nixon is a murderer! He kills little girls like you!"

Cruel? Of course. Absurd. Yes; that, too. And how very illustrative of the egocentricity and juvenility of the protesters. They are reminiscent of three-year-olds bawling for attention. One longs to whack their bottoms soundly.

Do they really, honestly, truly think such tactics to be of benefit to their cause? Evidently they do. Whereby they are rendered all the more pathetic. They simply know nothing of the world their bodies inhabit. So far from "isolating" Richard Nixon at Miami Beach, one suspects they have merely won him new votes, and themselves new antagonists.

Omaha World-Herald
Omaha, Neb., August 25, 1972

As we understand it, one of Miami Beach's advantages as a political convention site is its isolation. It is an island city, surrounded, in effect, by a moat. It can be sealed off from onslaughts by the violent.

Obviously, this inherent defensive advantage was not exploited properly during the two conventions, and particularly not in the case of the Republican gathering.

There were numerous incidents of violence against people and property. Delegates and uninvolved citizens were set upon and about 1,200 "demonstrators" were arrested.

In retrospect, it appears that the local authorities erred in cooperating so thoroughly with the various "protest" groups that converged on Miami Beach, and in allowing them to camp out in Flamingo Park.

A more prudent alternative would have been to make the city secure by barring the disrupters from Miami Beach, and blocking their various marches and offensive formations at the causeways.

By now it should be fully recognized by the authorities that any gathering of the volatile New Left groups is more likely than not to produce lawbreaking and violence, often on a large and threatening scale.

Giving them the benefit of the doubt in advance or — as some of the TV commentators did — trying to play down the viciousness of their activities, is dangerous folly.

THE LOUISVILLE TIMES
Louisville, Ky., August 23, 1972

No one paid much attention the other day when a few nude zippies marched in front of Miami's convention hall and a group of anti-war veterans flew the American flag upside down. The police kept their distance.

Yesterday's sporadic demonstrations and "mass arrests" conveyed no sense of crisis.

How different it was from the heady days of 1967 and 1968 when the youth of America intimidated the educational bureaucracy, helped unseat the President of the United States, and demanded nothing less than a complete transformation of our society. In a period of three or four years, a generation by modern standards, the marching young forced a major political party to reform itself, persuaded us to widen our neckties and the bottoms of our trousers, exposed us as slaves to hypocrisy and inhibition, and shocked us with their addiction to skinny dipping in public.

Nowadays, they can't even raise an eyebrow among the pensioners in Flamingo Park. The demonstration as we have come to know it is clearly dead.

Is the Miami escapade, then, the last pathetic gasp of the once formidable youth movement? Has all progress on the road to Consciousness III come to a halt? What has become of the humorless, sometimes violent, but unquestionably sincere youngsters of the 1960s who promised to lead us into an era of peace and love? Are we on the threshold of another silent generation?

It's too soon to make any assumptions of course, but there is considerable evidence of a return to squaredom. Students are reported to be taking their studies seriously again and worrying less about the relevance of their courses. College fraternities, reviled by the revolutionaries of 1968, are enjoying a revival. Beer is said to be competing with pot at parties and marriage is back in fashion. Girls are trying out for cheerleading teams in record numbers. It's hardly surprising that the mining of Haiphong harbor caused little more than a ripple of anger.

Even clothes are coming back into use. According to the *Times* movie critic, nudity is no longer considered a necessary ingredient of every motion picture. Most surprising of all, President Nixon, the symbol of the straight society, is enjoying unexpected popularity among voters under 25.

At the same time, members of the establishment have adopted many of the outward trappings of the protestors. Bankers and lawyers wear long hair and bell bottoms, listen to rock music and talk about doing their thing. Being hip is fashionable. It is becoming increasingly difficult to distinguish between revolutionaries and the managers of the corporate state. We suspect that overexposure had as much to do with the decline of protest marches as anything else. Back in the good old days, any teen-ager who showed up in public with a sign made the evening news and the front pages. Magazines clogged our homes with instant analysis of the revolution. Sociologists assured us we were indeed hypocrites, just as the kids said. Long before war, injustice, poverty and hate were overcome, everybody young and old alike, became bored with the whole business.

It's too soon to proclaim an end to the Age of Aquarius, however. The really serious dissidents of the 1960s and early 1970s have decided that working for George McGovern or Ralph Nader or women's liberation is a more productive way to remake society than marching mindlessly into a fussilade of tear gas bombs. And they are obviously right. Demonstrations like the one in Miami may arouse some nostalgia for the glorious past when kids ruled the streets, but they won't bring us any closer to universal peace and love.

Herald News
Fall River, Mass., August 28, 1972

The demonstrators outside the Republican Convention did not affect the proceedings there. Nevertheless, it is disturbing to the American people to realize that anti-riot gas had to be used to disperse the demonstrators. Moreover, the security precautions to protect not only the President but the delegates to the convention were on a far larger and more intense scale than usual.

The precautions were justified, not perhaps so much because of the demonstrators as because of the possibility of an attack such as the one that crippled Governor Wallace last spring. No one has forgotten that Arthur Bremer's diary revealed his primary target was President Nixon, and it is a safe bet that the danger from an isolated psychotic was more vividly in the minds of the security agents than any serious danger from the anti-war demonstrators.

The fact is, however, that something has changed in the temper of the nation, and both the demonstrations and the security precautions reflect it. Even though there was nothing at Miami that even approched the disturbances in Chicago four years ago, enough did happen to prove that the free and easy atmosphere of political conventions in the past is no longer possible.

All Americans will regret its passing and will hope that, sooner or later, it will return. Meantime, there is no avoiding the evident fact that as long as the present climate persists, security precautions and special police are needed to safeguard our political processes and the lives of our elected officials.

The State
Columbia, S.C., August 29, 1972

IF CRITICS of the National Republican Convention think it was "orchestrated," what have they to say about the rabble-rousing in the streets aimed solely at anarchy?

The "orchestration" of the street demonstrations at the GOP convention began during the Democratic convention when the organizers, who had cooled it for Sen. George McGovern's nominating event, urged the hoard to return in protest to President Nixon.

The hooligans of the Left kept the date. They did their thing. Tuesday they roamed the streets, smashing windows, cursing pedestrians, beating on passing automobiles, and looting a beer truck and liquor store. There were 210 arrested near convention hall.

Wednesday night was worse. The South Carolina delegates' bus was one of the prime targets for terrorism, the men and women jostled, spat upon, taunted with obscenities.

The rabble weren't children at play. They knew what they were doing. It was planned and led by revolutionaries. Their mission was to disrupt a legitimate political activity. More than 800 were arrested.

The provocation was disgraceful. Equally so is the silence by the political leaders whom these hoodlums have chosen to support. The anarchists should be repudiated.

HOUSTON CHRONICLE
Houston, Tex., August 25, 1972

For an exercise in self-defeating futility, we don't think we have ever seen a better example than the rampage of the "crazies" element of the antiwar demonstrators in Miami Beach the final night of the Republican National Convention.

Youthful demonstrators roughed things up in Chicago in 1968 at the Democratic National Convention and lost the Democrats votes in national revulsion. Now they do it at a Republican convention and still the Democrats are to lose the votes in revulsion, according to the way most people view the effects.

Well, politics is a strange world and no one ever promised it would be fair. The Democrats, who so far can't even buy a break in this campaign, should be used to this kind of thing by now.

The demonstrators were going to discredit President Nixon, block the hall so he would have to make his acceptance to empty seats, and help defeat him in November. They apparently achieved the opposite effect in all instances, as everyone told them in advance they would. It defies logic that they would have tried, but then logic has never been a long suit with this element.

There's little glory in this kind of affair for anyone, but what there is has to belong to the Miami Beach city police and the Florida state law enforcement officers. From all accounts they performed a difficult job in the best traditions of police agencies. Our hat is off to them and to Miami Beach Police Chief Rocky Pomerance for what is surely one of the most quotable lines of the summer: "I cannot understand why all these people who are for peace in Vietnam are not for peace in Miami Beach."

THE MIAMI NEWS
Miami, Fla., August 24, 1972

What someone called the biggest non-event in political history was concluded here last night, and Miamians are as relieved as the Republicans to have it safely behind them.

The Republicans must view the convention as a distinct success. They came with a rehearsed script, not to select a nominee, but to fashion an appropriately enthusiastic launching for their frontrunning ticket. They accomplished that objective despite the great probability that the proceedings would be disrupted by protesters.

The protesters failed to force the authorities to call out the troops, and thus embarrass the President. Furthermore, they managed to obscure their message by their abusive manner, which was juvenile, tiresome and trite.

If we felt any sympathy for the demonstrators, it was for the Vietnam war veterans who had something important to say, but whose point was obscured in the general confusion.

The demonstrators did score one clear success. Those who declared their intentions to get arrested were more than obliged by the police, who carted them off by the hundreds. They received quick hearings from the efficient magistrate program established by a committee of volunteer jurists and lawyers.

The law enforcement establishment in general did an excellent job. This was true of local police in particular who received special training for the conventions months in advance. The Florida Highway Patrol on the other hand was noticeably less disciplined and quicker with its clubs.

Despite the diverting sideshow, the closing session last night belonged to the Republican Party, President Nixon and Vice President Agnew.

The crisp, aggressive tone of the candidates' acceptance speeches underlined their growing confidence in the success of a campaign which has been going entirely their way.

With this sensitive convention safely behind them, who could blame them for sounding cocky?

Campaign '72:
GAO ASKS REPUBLICAN FUND PROBE; LINKS TO BREAK-IN INVESTIGATED

The Congressional auditing agency, the General Accounting Office (GAO), reported Aug. 26 that it had found "apparent and possible" violations of the Federal Election Campaign Act by the Finance Committee to Re-elect the President. The GAO's findings, involving amounts up to $350,000, were referred to the Justice Department.

The GAO cited failure to keep adequate records concerning: (a) a $25,000 contribution made to the Republicans by Minnesota businessman Dwayne O. Andreas through Kenneth H. Dahlberg, chairman of the Minnesota re-election committee for Nixon, (b) $89,000 from four checks drawn on a Mexican bank and (c) the balance of some $350,000 in cash deposited May 25 to a media affiliate of the Nixon committee. Funds from the Dahlberg check and the Mexican check had turned up in possession of Bernard L. Barker, one of five persons siezed in the attempted raid on Democratic national headquarters. [See pp. 801-804]

A delay in the scheduled release of the GAO report Aug. 23 drew complaints from McGovern's campaign chairman, Lawrence F. O'Brien, and Rep. Wright Patman (D, Tex.) whose Banking and Currency Committee was also investigating the break-in at the Democrats' offices in the Watergate buildings. After the report was released, Patman complained about reversion of the case to the Justice Department. A "strongly partisan attorney general," he said, was being asked "to prosecute wrongdoings of the political party which boosted him to such a high place in government."

The Finance Committee to Re-elect the President called the GAO report "inaccurate" Aug. 26. Maurice Stans, chairman of the committee, said Aug. 27 the report contained "serious misrepresentations" and demanded that the GAO audit Democratic fund-raising records. Democratic nominee George McGovern said Aug. 28 "we'll welcome the GAO or any other investigator who wants to look at our files." McGovern called upon the President to reveal the sources of $10 million in campaign funds collected before the new disclosure law went into effect. [See pp. 454-457]

At his news conference Aug. 29, President Nixon said technical violations of the new campaign law apparently had occurred "on both sides." He disclosed that his own staff had conducted an investigation of the Watergate affair and he could "categorically" state that the probe "indicates that no one on the White House staff, no one in this Administration, presently employed, was involved in this very bizarre incident."

(After a U.S. District Court judge had rejected a Republican request to postpone a $1 million civil suit filed by O'Brien against the re-election committee, O'Brien revealed Aug. 15 that his attorney would begin taking depositions from persons connected with the case, including Stans and John N. Mitchell, Nixon's former campaign manager.)

St. Louis Globe-Democrat
St. Louis, Mo., August 17, 1972

Sen. George McGovern, who once gave the impression that he would try to win the White House on his own merit, now appears bent on getting there by tearing down President Nixon with undocumented charges and innuendos.

This is certainly a low road but McGovern doesn't seem to mind taking it.

His latest unsubstantiated smear against Mr. Nixon is a charge that the President is "at least indirectly" responsible for the June 17 break-in at the Democratic National headquarters in Washington.

As usual, he offered no proof of the accusation.

In these circumstances most fair-minded Americans will recognize that McGovern, in desperation, has resorted to the basest kind of campaign—attacking the character and integrity of Mr. Nixon without justification.

The net result will be that McGovern, not the President, will suffer. Senator McGovern's credibility gap, which widened as he continually changed his positions on issues, will widen still further.

If McGovern keeps this up a lot of Americans will believe that he is just plain McNasty.

THE LINCOLN STAR
Lincoln, Neb., August 19, 1972

Until the matter is settled in court, and maybe not even then, people will not know how direct are the ties between the men caught snooping in Democratic National Committee headquarters and President Nixon himself.

But that will not stop the Democrats from capitalizing on the abundance of signs that point to the intruders as agents in the pay of the Committee to Re-elect the President.

The Democrats have filed suit and the issue is pending in court. In the meantime, new evidence against the President's campaign team is claimed and Nixon is being charged with at least indirect responsibility for the incident.

Former Democratic Party Chairman Lawrence O'Brien contends that new evidence shows his national committee offices were "bugged" for some time before June 17, the date the five men were caught inside the offices by Washington police. O'Brien says he plans to take depositions on the matter from a number of men prominently tied to the re-election campaign. And on the campaign trial, or the fist time, Sen. George McGovern charged that President Nixon was "at least indirectly" responsible for the break-in.

From the other side, Nixon, former campaign chief John Mitchell and other GOP officials have denied knowledge of the break-in. But the Republicans have also asked that the trial of the lawsuit be put off until after the election in November. And the evidence that has surfaced thus far is damaging. One of the men arrested was a paid employe of the Committee to Re-elect the President. A $25,000 campaign check has been traced to the bank account of another of the arrested men. Just on the surface, there are some very serious questions the President's campaign chiefs need to answer:

Is the bugging incident really serious? Is it a legitimate campaign issue? George McGovern seems to think so. He said the incident "ought to disturb every American, because if the leadership of the President's campaign will snoop and invade and wire-tap on the Democratic National Committee, what reason is there to believe it won't do that to the rest of us?" McGovern may be pressing it, but he has a point.

The Nixon campaign can't be allowed to sweep this incident under the rug. It has some explaining to do for its own good. We would hope that the President or his chief lieutenants wouldn't stoop to anything like political espionage. It would reflect badly on his high office and provide another reason to distrust public officials.

New York Post
New York, N.Y., August 28, 1972

At a time when President Nixon is being depicted as a political superman by many analysts of the 1972 campaign, the unsavory mess in Washington involving the Finance Committee to Reelect the President must be a deepening source of discomfort to the White House. Some members of the Nixon entourage must be wondering why it was necessary to get into so much trouble in a year when money is flowing so freely into the GOP treasury, and when euphoric commentators even question whether it is needed.

But what began as a seemingly minor unpleasantness is steadily assuming large dimensions, and the latest developments suggest that Mr. Nixon himself may not be able to remain aloof from the controversy, as he has tried to do so far. There is a potential storm rising that will require a good deal more effective response than the cry of "foul" recited yesterday by GOP Finance Chief — and former Commerce Secretary — Maurice Stans, who had remained mute and inaccessible for so many days when the story began to unfold.

The Administration's initial belief that the silent treatment could effectively dispose of the matter seemingly ended when the General Accounting Office, a body noted for its political independence and technical competence, flatly declared on Saturday that Mr. Stans' committee had been guilty of numerous "apparent and possible violations" of the Federal Election Campaign Act. It said the alleged violations involved up to $350,000 in gifts to Mr. Nixon's campaign.

How much of this amount was directly related to subsidizing the bugging of Democratic headquarters remains to be established; plainly part of the fiscal hanky-panky was connected to that dreary invasion. But the questions emerging cover wide ground.

More than enough has already emerged to justify Democratic demands that Mr. Nixon name a special prosecutor to press the inquiry. Certainly these proposals are "political," in the sense that this is a campaign year and that the Democrats detect pay dirt in the saga. This is how democracy operates; one of the dividends of election seasons is that people learn things normally concealed by bipartisan arrangement.

The Administration can hardly expect to evoke public confidence in an investigation conducted by the present leadership of the Justice Dept. As Rep. Wright Patman (D-Tex.) has validly observed, it is absurd to entrust Attorney General Kleindienst with the prosecution of the same political forces to whom he is indebted for his appointment. One of the figures whose role warrants full scrutiny is Kleindienst's chief sponsor, John Mitchell.

We do not profess to know where all the trails will lead if a diligent inquiry is pursued by an unfettered prosecutor. But as long as Mr. Nixon resists that course, the suspicion that a massive protective maneuver is in progress will inevitably grow. For the logical public conclusion will be that he views political risks of full disclosure as graver than the hazard of flagrant coverups by an avowed "law-and-order" Administration.

The New York Times
New York, N.Y., August 28, 1972

The findings by the General Accounting Office that the Committee to Re-elect the President has committed "apparent and possible violations" of the Federal Election Campaign Act calls for an immediate, full-scale inquiry by investigators of unassailable credibility.

The issues are far more serious than even the substantial amounts of campaign contributions and expenditures which apparently changed hands without the required public disclosure. Some of these hidden resources seem to have found their way into the pockets of those shadowy figures who were arrested in June while breaking into the Democratic National Committee headquarters at the Watergate apartments. This suggests something more sinister than illegal efforts to protect the anonymity of bashful campaign contributors.

The list of unanswered questions grows longer every day. Elusive funds have been transferred from committee safes to banks in Miami and Mexico City. Some participants in these dubious events—including at least one former member of the White House political staff—have refused to answer questions or disappeared altogether. Former Commerce Secretary Maurice Stans, who now is the chief Republican money raiser, has not to date given full and satisfactory explanations concerning the source and disposition of some of these mysterious funds. Mr. Stans moreover had also directed the crash campaign to get a maximum of anonymous cash into the campaign coffers before the new public disclosure laws went into effect last April.

The risk incurred when those who seek favorable governmental rulings are also anonymous campaign contributors was once again underscored. A charter to open a suburban bank appears to have been expedited shortly after the applicant contributed $25,000 to the Republican campaign. And according to the Federal Bureau of Investigation, all or part of that contribution, which the donor had hoped would remain anonymous, seems to have found its way into the bank account of one of the planners of the Watergate political espionage.

The White House remains silent. The Justice Department promises only that the G.A.O. findings will be handled "routinely." Does this mean that the stable doors are to be locked after the elections have gone?

Responsibility to investigate cannot be left in the hands of the Administration's own officialdom. The G.A.O., as the Congressional watchdog, lacks subpoena power. The Committee to Re-elect the President—not surprisingly—"welcomes the opportunity" to deal with the Justice Department in these matters. Indeed, a spokesman for the committee expressed confidence that the Justice Department will find the alleged violations to be "nothing more than minor and technical." This is precisely why this investigation cannot be left to a department with strong political ties to the Administration and to the Nixon re-election committee.

What is involved in these tawdry proceedings is not an obscure political caper but the integrity of the election process and of government itself. The issues range from allegations of serious financial abuses to nothing less than political espionage. The charges implicate persons close to the White House.

This is why the President himself should act at once to appoint a special prosecutor of unquestioned political independence and judicial integrity. The American people have a right to demand all the facts and the fair and impartial prosecution of any violators of the laws.

© 1972 by The New York Times Company. Reprinted by permission.

LEDGER-STAR
Norfolk, Va., August 28, 1972

The mystery that continues to surround both the attempted bugging of the Democratic national headquarters and the misdirection of Republican campaign checks ought to be cleared up for the public with as much dispatch as possible.

The questions that the events, the charges and the counter-charges have raised are serious. A large amount of money is involved, and the channeling of funds, $114,000, into the bank account of one of the five men charged in the Democratic headquarters break-in obviously has worrisome implications.

The Democrats themselves have been airing the details almost daily, but they have done so in a plainly partisan way in an effort to make election campaign progress. They have not, however, offered much enlightenment along with their rhetoric.

★ ★ ★ ★

On the other side, the Republicans, too, have been less than helpful. To a finding by the General Accounting Office of five "apparent" and four "possible" violations of election law by the Finance Committee for the Re-Election of the President in the handling of funds, the GOP has offered no clarifying response.

And the Watergate caper—as the headquarters break-in has come to be called—has long since changed in its implications from the almost ludicrous to the very ugly, with connections being made to the GOP campaign operation.

★ ★ ★ ★

There are public responsibilities here, one to bring out the facts with respect to the campaign funds —not only the apparently misdirected $114,000, but other "possible" and "apparent" violations cited by GAO—and another to establish just what connections did exist between the headquarters break-in and the Republican party.

The responsibility is a crucial one because for a long time there has seemed to be a growing public cynicism about politics and politicians. This is a trend that can only erode further the public's confidence in government.

Certainly, too, the questions that have been raised hang unhappily over the presidential campaign. So the Republicans not only owe a clear and complete explanation as a public responsibility; in a sense, they owe this to themselves as well.

THE SACRAMENTO BEE
Sacramento, Calif., August 21, 1972

Clark MacGregor, the President's campaign manager, and President Richard Nixon himself, should come down from Olympus and tell the people what they know — or do not know — about the June 17 raid on the Democratic headquarters in the Washington, DC, Watergate Apartments. The bizarre affair, known in high political circles as the Watergate Caper, is no joke.

Curiously, a $25,000 check to the Nixon campaign was traced to the bank account of Bernard L. Barker, alias Frank Carter, who was one of five men arrested at 2:30 a.m. in the headquarters of the Democratic National Committee.

And the Washington Star reported another $89,000 was channeled to Barker through the Committee to Re-elect the President.

Until the President, Republican campaign treasurer Maurice Stans and MacGregor are willing to talk about the raid on the Democratic headquarters they inevitably leave the suggestion there is Republican involvement.

At the time of the break-in, John Mitchell, then Nixon's campaign chairman, denied any GOP complicity.

When the new Republican chairman, MacGregor, was asked by reporters about the campaign contribution winding up in the bank account of one of those caught in flagrante in the headquarters of the Democrats, MacGregor invoked "legal rights" as the basis for not responding. This leaves unfulfilled the party's moral obligation to truth.

As the story of the Watergate Caper unfolds it is clear more than indignant denials and pious statements are needed. The people have a right to know, for the Watergate incident is an ugly one and is an unsettling influence upon the confidence of the people in the political processes.

Above all others, President Nixon should demand prompt and honest disclosure for the benefit of the public and so should his campaign manager.

Rocky Mountain News
Denver, Colo., August 18, 1972

ONE MORNING IN JUNE, police arrested five men inside the offices of the Democratic National Committee in Washington, D.C. The offices were in the Watergate apartment complex, which otherwise largely is populated by higher-living people, many identified with the Nixon administration.

The five accused men had in hand assorted bugging devices and a wad of crisp new money. The purpose of the trespass still is unknown, but the characters who thought up this caper hardly qualify as gents of great common sense. It was a stupid stunt, whatever the motive.

Naturally, the Democrats are trying to make this into a cosmic campaign issue and to this end Lawrence F. O'Brien, Democratic chairman at the time, has filed a million-dollar damage suit against the Committee for the Re-election of the President, which previously had employed at least one of the suspects.

Meanwhile, a Justice Department lawyer has been representing a White House consultant, whose name has been involved. A Washington judge ruled the lawyer off the case because the FBI and other parts of the Justice Department are supposed to be investigating, along with a grand jury.

But the Justice Department, which can't seem to quit while it is ahead, has gone to a higher court to keep its lawyer in the case.

All along, the White House has taken an aloof attitude toward the whole prank, while Sen. George S. McGovern is out on the hustings trying to build a big bonfire out of it.

This is not the type of issue on which the country is likely to decide a presidential election—not at least unless it can be proven that some "higher-ups" the White House or on the President's campaign committee either condoned this ridiculous affair or dreamed it up.

But until the full story is cleared up, the Republicans are running the risk of looking more and more foolish. And if they persist in trying to smoke the whole thing over until after the election, they simply will be making themselves look guilty, as well as silly.

The Evening Star
Washington, D.C., August 24, 1972

There is something disquieting about the decision of the General Accounting Office to delay issuance of its audit report on the finances of the Nixon re-election committee until Finance Director Maurice Stans and GOP bigwigs have a chance to examine and offer suggestions about the 8-page document.

The GAO, after all, works for the Congress of the United States and not for the executive branch of this or any administration. It may be true, as aides of Comptroller General Elmer Staats say, that it is standard operating procedure for the GAO to show investigative reports to the investigated agencies unless some member of Congress specifies that this not be done.

But the GAO is working with a new Federal Election Campaign Act that did not become effective until April 7 and, beyond this, the Committee for Re-election of the President is not an "agency" in the sense that the Pentagon or the Peace Corps is.

There is a strong instinct to suppose that Stans' phone calls to GAO officials an hour before scheduled release of the audit report caused Staats to delay public disclosure of a matter that is central to the Watergate bugging of the Democratic National Committee in which CRP people are suspect. If it is routine to submit audit reports to investigated agencies, why was the submission not made until after Stans had called GAO at least twice?

The GAO, like all investigative agencies, must be like Caesar's wife in irreproachability. We cannot take kindly to the spectacle of GAO officials sitting down with GOP campaign leaders in Miami Beach to edit, check, delete from or add to a report that should be based only on documents the committee is bound by law to have submitted long since.

We believe Stans has even more to explain now than he did before about how GOP campaign funds were used and now the GAO, a watchdog agency, has created the appearance of evil if not evil itself.

The Topeka Daily Capital
Topeka, Kans., August 18, 1972

When Washington police surprised those five men attempting to bug national Democratic headquarters in the Watergate Apartments, the incident was treated more like a scene from a Keystone Cops comedy than the serious campaign issue it fast is becoming.

Readers were hard-pressed to imagine just what information could be gleaned by bugs from headquarters of any political party, Democratic or Republican, that would be worth such an effort and risk.

Who, persons asked laughingly, would anyone want to have advance information on the planks the Democratic platform will include, or how much the Democratic deficit is, or does McGovern really have a chance, or what new strategy will be used to defeat President Nixon for a second term.

Lawrence O'Brien, then Democratic national chairman, took it more seriously. He immediately filed a $1 million damage action against the Committee for the Re-election of President Nixon and the five men arrested. The court since has narrowed the case to O'Brien and the five men, saying the Democratic national committee and the Nixon re-election committee are unincorporated associations and do not have the status to sue and be sued.

Since O'Brien's action, sparks have been flying in all directions. Police and Federal Bureau of Investigation agents have sorted out aliases given by the five men, and have been linking them with former Nixon aides, past employment by the Central Intelligence Agency and Free Cuba agents. A grand jury also is investigating.

The Watergate Affair took on a distinct Republican flavor when $25,000 in political contributions to the Nixon campaign were converted into a cashier's check and deposited in the account in Miami of one of the buggers. Subsequent investigation shows that similar deposits of at least $114,000 have been placed in the same account.

While influential Republican leaders, including John Mitchell and Maurice Stans, both former cabinet members, deny any knowledge of the amateurish bugging attempt, they have a deep responsibility to find the truth and tell the people of the United States exactly what they find.

If they do not, and it is possible no one in the White House is privy to what really happened, they should understand the great urgency to clear the record. While they remain silent, a believable mixture of fact and fiction snowballs and worsens.

The truth is, the Watergate Affair isn't funny anymore. It is a deadly serious campaign issue that grows faster in silence than in honest disclosure.

The Evening Bulletin
Philadelphia, Pa., August 29, 1972

President Nixon can no longer remain silent on the reported misuse of campaign funds contributed to his reelection committee.

The report of the U.S. General Accounting Office, which answers to Congress, alleges that as much as $350,000 in campaign contributions may have gone unreported or been misused in a way that suggests outright violation of the new federal laws governing election campaign expenditures.

What started out as a relatively trivial or even comic incident with the apprehension of five men with electronic espionage gear at the Democratic national headquarters last June 17 has now ballooned into a potential scandal that could have impact on the presidential election.

The response — or nonresponse — of top Republican officials so far has been silence or countercharges that the Democrats are exploiting the incident for political purposes.

And so they are. But that doesn't disprove the GAO's finding that there may have been extensive misuse of campaign funds through "apparent and possible" violations in the new federal elections expenditures law.

GOP Finance Chairman Maurice Stans' defensive request that the GAO turn its attention to Democratic spending practices may have merit but right now it is not to the point. It is the Republicans and not the Democrats who are under the spotlight.

The affair has taken on a sinister air with the revelation that some $114,000 of the allegedly misused or unreported funds was deposited to the Miami bank account of a principal suspect in the June 17 break in. The collection and disposition of these monies remain a central mystery in the entire matter.

The incident has now reached the stage where it cannot help but reflect unfavorably on some key managers in the President's campaign organization and thus, indirectly at least, on the Administration itself.

No one would suggest that Mr. Nixon had knowledge of the shadowy transactions involving some of the funds of his reelection committee. But President Nixon does offer himself as a take-charge Chief Executive and as a man well in control of all situations. Thus he is certain to be judged in part by the way in which he reacts to the Watergate affair and to the other matters involving his reelection committee's funds.

Mr. Nixon should assert his leadership now.

He should assure the American people that a full, fair and fearless inquiry will be made into all of the circumstances of the entire matter.

He should assure the American people that it will not be handled as merely another routine matter in the Department of Justice or be allowed, perhaps, to wait until after the election for attention.

It is up to Mr. Nixon to take action. If he feels the inquiry can be handled within the executive department of the Federal Government he should so state and give assurance that he will be personally responsible for seeing that it is carried out. If Mr. Nixon feels that an outside inquiry is necessary he should get this under way at once.

There is far too much involved here for the White House even to appear to be sitting this one out.

Herald-Journal
Syracuse, N.Y., August 30, 1972

Sen. George S. McGovern, the Democratic presidential candidate, and nearly every member of his staff are demanding almost hourly that President Nixon reveal sources of campaign funds and explain how $114,000 of Republican campaign money apparently landed in the office of Bernard L. Baker, one of five men arrested in the Democratic National Committee Watergate offices in June.

Atty. Gen. Richard Kleindienst has said he expects a grand jury to report soon on the Watergate affair.

A grand jury investigation is the proper way to clear the air. It probably is too much to ask of the issue-starved McGovern and his staff that they await this report.

We also suggest that a grand jury with a special outside prosecutor look into the campaign fund charges from both political parties with orders to report their findings before Nov. 1.

Such an outsider could do much to silence the chatter about the Justice Department answering to a Republican President and the General Accounting Office answering to a Democratic Congress.

The Washington Post
Washington, D.C., August 29, 1972

Well, now that the General Accounting Office's elections office has issued its report, Maurice Stans has talked again. The GAO has given us a bit more clarity about the Watergate-Nixon campaign financing affair, but Mr. Stans has contributed—against his own staff's prediction that he would have a "logical" explanation—nothing but smog. As soon as the GAO report was released, Mr. Stans rushed into print claiming that the report was wrong and that its defects were the fault of the Democrats, going on to demand a full audit of the financing of the McGovern campaign. He also claimed that there have been no "purposeful" violations of the campaign financing act and that any violations are "purely minor and technical." There is not one whiff of explanation in all this and the argument is so contorted as well as so brazen in its assault on the public's capacity to reason that it makes the head spin. The Democrats are not the point. Republican campaign financing is what is at issue.

So, since Mr. Stans would rather obfuscate than explain, let us just run lightly over the GAO report and some of the other major issues surrounding the Nixon campaign finances. First, there is the matter of several hundred thousand dollars—perhaps as much as $750,000—which was at least in part generated by a fund raising trip in which Mr. Stans participated and which was "laundered" in Mexico. That is, checks and stock certificates donated to the Nixon campaign were deposited in a Mexican bank account and then converted into dollar drafts so that the donors could retain anonymity. Then there is the confirmation of the fact that in addition to the $25,000 Nixon campaign check which ended up in the bank account of one of the men arrested at the Watergate, there was another $89,000 in Nixon funds which also landed in that account—all of it "laundered" through Mexico. Then there is the matter of at least $350,000 which was just lying around in Mr. Stans' safe. Another highlight of the report is that the GAO asserts that the Nixon campaign money managers comingled personal and campaign funds.

Much can be made of all of this, but two points at least deserve particular attention. The first is that Mr. Stans and others have been trying to give the impression that no one high in the Nixon campaign organization had anything to do with the authorization or the financing of the Watergate caper. Yet, now the GAO tells us that the $114,000 (25 + 89) in the suspect's account came out of the funds Mr. Stans kept in his safe until May 25. It stretches credulity just a little to suggest that a fund so closely held by the financial chief of the campaign committee could be tapped for a sum as substantial as $114,000 without his authority and without his having some knowledge of the use to which the money was to be put.

And then, of course, no one knows just how much was originally in Mr. Stans' safe. All we know about that money is that it was deposited in a bank on May 25, 1972, with a notation on the deposit slip indicating that it had been, "cash on hand prior to April 4, 1972, from 1968 campaign." Yet, Mr. Stans told GAO investigators that it was not money from 1968, but rather that the money had been raised this year. We have no way of knowing which is true nor is there any way of knowing now how much was in Mr. Stans' safe originally, how much was taken out of the safe and spent or for what purposes such expenditures were made.

The Mexican laundry operation also reeks. Much has been made—appropriately, we think—of the fact that the Nixon campaign managers have refused to disclose the names of the donors to the secret $10,000,000 fund raised by the campaign committee prior to April 7, the date on which the campaign financing law requiring disclosure of donors took effect. Until the GAO report, however, the lengths to which the campaign committee went in order to keep the sources of their funds secret was not clear. The disclosure of the convoluted Mexican transactions cannot help introducing questions about how the money was raised and what promises were made in order to secure those funds. The disclosure that Dwayne Andreas, the secret donor of the $25,000 that found its way to a Miami bank, received a federal bank charter in unseemly haste does nothing to relieve ever darkening suspicions.

So, there it is. The GAO has apparently done a competent job, but it admits that without subpoena power, there are "gaps" it cannot close. The rest of us can only wonder about those gaps and about what Mr. Kleindienst's Justice Department—from which we got the ITT case and the cover-up of Harry Steward's indiscretions as a U.S. attorney in San Diego—will do to restore public confidence in the electoral process in this election year. We have asked repeatedly that Mr. Stans speak out to clear this whole matter up. Apparently, he does not intend to do so. But the matter is far larger than Mr. Stans now. The questions are so numerous and so grave, that nothing less than a full disclosure by the President of all of the sources of his campaign funds and the appointment of a special investigatorial and prosecutorial team from outside the government would seem to be required to dispel the Republican-created sense that there is a great deal of dirty business in the effort to re-elect this particular President of the United States.

The Star-Ledger
Newark, N.J., August 29, 1972

The report by the General Accounting Office citing "apparent and possible" violations of the new election finance law raises serious questions that are not going to be brushed under the rug with political pettifoggery

The Republicans have been vehement in their protestations but they have revealed a remarkable lack of forthrightness in explaining the possible breaches involving the handling of about $500,000 in contributions for the Nixon campaign and the bungled bugging of the Democratic National Committee headquarters in the Watergate Hotel in Washington.

It is not enough, for example, to have the President's chief political money raiser, Maurice Stans, denounce the GAO findings in an oblique manner, an apparent attempt to divert attention from the alleged violations, which are sufficiently grave in nature to have the matter referred to the Justice Department for possible prosecution.

The matter is past the stage of partisan issue, a fact that Mr. Stans and other Nixon campaign aides would prefer to ignore, taking refuge under a plethora of counter charges. There has been a persistent lack of candor on the Republican side that has been a deeply troubling factor since the Watergate scandal, the direct links between the men arrested for breaking into the Democratic Committee offices and the Nixon campaign organization or the White House staff.

The money used to finance the aborted bugging operation has been traced; it is part of $114,000 funneled from the Nixon campaign headquarters into the Miami bank account of one of the men arrested at the Watergate.

For some curious reason, GOP campaign aides, including Mr. Stans, have not been able to fully clarify how this money passed hands, going blank on the crucial juncture when it left the committee and suddenly turned up in the possession of one of the Watergate suspects.

And it just happened that one of them was the Nixon committee's security coordinator. In another embarrassing development, the FBI identified a sixth man involved in the sleazy affair as a consultant to a Presidential assistant who handles sensitive political assignments for the White House.

The Nixon Administration has been in continual hot water over campaign financing since the disclosure early this year before the Senate Judiciary Committee of a pledge by the International Telephone & Telegraph Corp. to finance the Republican National Convention with a $400,000 contribution. The ITT backing took on unsavory implications when it was revealed that the White House and the Justice Department had been unduly solicitous in setting up an anti-trust settlement favorable to ITT.

There are too many unresolved factors in the questionable campaign financing practices of the Nixon committee for the White House to continue to remain silent on the matter. It no longer can be regarded in strictly political terms, these serious charges raised by the GAO investigation are central to the electoral process and governmental integrity.

It is certainly not a matter to be left in the hands of the Justice Department or to be treated routinely by the FBI. The allegations are neither "technical nor minor," as blithely suggested by a member of the Committee to Re-elect the President. They concern possible serious breaches of the election finance law and political spying, with troubling ties to important White House functionaries.

An independent investigation by an impartial special prosecutor would establish accountability and remove conflicting partisan factors that have obscured the fundamental issues in the whole unsavory situation. It is a responsibility that the President no longer can defer by remaining silent and unresponsive, a posture of seeming indifference that is incompatible with the gravity of the charges leveled against his campaign organization and aides in the White House.

Buffalo Evening News
Buffalo, N.Y., August 28, 1972

One night last June five men were arrested inside Democratic national headquarters at the Watergate Hotel in Washington. They were loaded down with electronic eavesdropping, or bugging, equipment. Nothing subsequently revealed about this bizarre affair has weakened the justification for the immediate Democratic reaction that this was "political espionage" by their Republican foes.

One of the arrested men, since dismissed, was employed by the GOP as a consultant on security. A bank account of another of the five apparently contained campaign funds raised by the GOP. Senior officials in the Nixon re-election campaign organization have denied any connection with the Watergate caper, but several fairly prominent figures in that organization have subsequently left rather suddenly, including one rightly dismissed by Republicans for refusing to cooperate with the break-in investigation.

We reject the brush-off notion peddled by some that this kind of insidious snooping is merely a slightly shady game politicians play. The incident itself, whatever its source, is an inexcusable invasion of privacy. And if its origin is connected with campaign purposes, the incident betrays twisted values alien to even the most crude concepts of political fair play. As Vice President Agnew said in deploring the Watergate affair, it "is not what I want to see happen in our country."

Responsibility for the break-in, then, should be fully and promptly traced to its source, whatever it may be. The legal processes involved in getting at the truth — the several investigations under way and any subsequent judicial proceedings — should move ahead without regard to autumn's political calendar. Let the legal and political chips fall where they should.

THE SPRINGFIELD UNION
Springfield, Mass., August 29, 1972

The report of "apparent and possible" violations of the Federal Election Campaign Act by the Finance Committee to Reelect the President will have to be more definitive to have much impact.

It is unfortunate that the General Accounting Office (GAO), which has a serious responsibility to the nation, would resort to speculation. Its mission is fact-finding, not politicking.

Charges that the report of the GAO, a watchdog agency which serves Congress, was made under Democratic pressure should be investigated, if "possible" wrongdoing is at issue.

Justice Department inaction on the GAO report is predicted by the McGovern forces. The latter are saying, in effect, that one political caper deserves another.

It is doubtful that the "apparent and possible" violations will become a major campaign issue — except in criticisms by issue-hungry spokesmen of the Democratic campaign.

PORTLAND EVENING EXPRESS
Portland, Me., August 29, 1972

The Republican campaign fund mystery gets curiouser and curiouser. According to a General Accounting Office report released over the weekend, the Finance Committee to Re-elect the President may have failed to disclose the source and use of up to $350,000.

The new disclosures are especially damaging in their appearance because the GAO report found that as much as $114,000 of the Republican campaign funds once passed through the hands of Bernard Barker, one of the five men caught bugging the Democratic National Headquarters.

The bugging incident coupled with the Nixon fund mystery are adding up to a powerful campaign issue for the Democrats, and they can be expected to exploit it fully and relentlessly.

Meanwhile, the GAO has turned its findings over to the Justice Department for possible prosecution. Democratic National Committee chairman Lawrence O'Brien is understandably "pessimistic" that the Justice Department will act speedily and vigorously in the case, even though it could bring the matter before a grand jury that is already meeting to look into the bugging incident.

Nevertheless, if the Justice Department decides not to prosecute on the basis of the GAO information, or if it decides to delay matters to carry out further investigation of its own, it will doubtless be more harmful than not to Mr. Nixon's re-election prospects.

George McGovern, who is anxious to get his campaign off the defensive, can be expected to seize this issue and pursue it heatedly. McGovern knows from experience how potentially potent the issue can be. Back in the New Hampshire primary campaign he exploited Sen. Ed Muskie's failure to disclose campaign fund sources with telling effect, and that was a case where no wrongdoing was even hinted.

The longer the Nixon people keep the mystery going, the worse it's going to get for them.

The Courier-Journal
Louisville, Ky., August 30, 1972

PRESIDENT NIXON'S Attorney General says that President Nixon's Justice Department should have exclusive control of the investigation into President Nixon's campaign committee's handling of President Nixon's secret campaign fund and the bugging or attempted bugging of the Democratic Party's headquarters by President Nixon's campaign workers.

And when the investigation is over, says Attorney General Richard Kleindienst, "no credible, fairminded person is going to be able to say that we whitewashed or dragged our feet on it."

Of course not.

How could any clear-headed citizen even entertain such a thought, after President Nixon has spoken out so forthrightly, has initiated such vigorous action to track down the spymaster of those five men caught skulking about the Watergate Hotel with wires and batteries and funny little microphones?

And Mr. Kleindienst—he who recently cited the thousands of illegal arrests in Washington on May Day 1971 as a laudable example of how Mr. Nixon has curbed "mob violence" around the country—who could be so cynical as to believe that anything less than a thirst for pure justice motivates his pursuit of Republican spies?

And Maurice Stans. Who could doubt that his refusal to talk about the Watergate caper is, indeed, motivated by what he says is deep concern for the civil rights of those whom a federal grand jury might indict? His fingering of Gordon Liddy as the owner of the last known hands to touch that mysterious $25,000 Nixon campaign check that came to rest in the bank account of one of the spies—who could construe that as an attempt to designate a scapegoat?

No, Mr. Stans' yearning for justice is at least as powerful as Mr. Kleindienst's. After the General Accounting Office reported "apparent and possible violations" of the Federal Election Campaign Act by Mr. Nixon's campaign committee, was it not Mr. Stans who immediately and forthrightly demanded a "full and complete audit" of Democratic Party finances, too? The public can only hope that Mr. Stans will follow up his call with a list of his specific complaints and an official request for a GAO investigation, lest his demand be mistaken for a smokescreen.

With the case of the Watergate bugging and the $10 million Republican slush fund firmly in the hands of Mr. Nixon, Mr. Kleindienst and Mr. Stans, the Democrats' demand for a "special prosecutor" is obviously, as Mr. Kleindienst put it, "political." And, of course, politics is the very last thing that should intrude into an attorney general's pursuit of his duty.

Indeed, the persons implicated in the bugging of the Democratic headquarters are, as Mr. Kleindienst said so beautifully, "entitled to all the protection of the law, like the Chicago Seven, Daniel Ellsberg and the Berrigans."

Ah, how Mr. Nixon's Justice Department protected them! If Mr. Kleindienst pursues the Republican spies half as vigorously as he hounded the critics of Mr. Nixon's war policies, his investigation will be a monument to Nixonian justice. And what will it matter if such thoroughness requires much time, and protection of the accused requires much silence, even into 1973?

O Nixon! O Kleindienst! O Stans! How cozily the Republic rests in your hands.

The Ann Arbor News
Ann Arbor, Mich., August 30, 1972

ATTY. GEN. Richard Kleindienst has promised the forthcoming investigation of the break-in at the Democratic National Committee will be the most extensive, thorough and comphrehensive "since the assassination of President Kennedy."

It is in all parties' interest that Kleindienst be held to that pledge. The Watergate caper, as this break-in has come to be known, is beginning to smell. There is a lot of explaining to do.

At this point the Democrats are foolish to let the matter drop and give up a potentially damaging issue. For their part, the Republicans are foolish if they try to cover up the mess any longer.

If Maurice Stans, as chairman of the Committee to Re-Elect the President, has nothing to hide, he will cooperate with the Justice Department probe, and in the meantime document the flow of funds which has gone through his committee.

* * *

IN addition to the bugging incident at the Watergate, Stans has to answer for a General Accounting Office (GAO) report which, after an audit of Stans' committee's books, concluded that there was an apparent or a possible violation of campaign finance laws.

Stans has dodged and ducked the issue, which unfortunately adds to the suspicion that plenty is amiss here. Stans has to explain two main questions and probably a host of sub-questions. They are:

The link between the Watergate Five and a large sum of money which passed through Stans' committee. More specifically, how did money supposedly intended for GOP campaign coffers get into the account of one of the Watergate Five?

GAO says $25,000 was contributed to Stans' committee after April 7 which makes that sum subject to the 1971 campaign finance law. Stan says that sum was in the committee's hands before April 7.

Breaking and entering and eavesdropping are not matters lightly dismissed. This clearly is a cut or two above the cheap political party espionage that goes on all the time. When the trail leads so close to the White House as it apparently does here, the country needs to know what's going on.

That is why a prompt, thorough investigation is to be encouraged. If Kleindienst delivers on his promise, there won't be any charges of "coverup" after the probe is completed.

THE DAILY OKLAHOMAN
Oklahoma City, Okla.
August 29, 1972

ODORS of politics rise unmistakably from the charges and counter-charges over the handling of some $350,000 in campaign funds by the Committee to Re-elect the President.

The General Accounting Office, the auditing and investigating agency of Congress, issued a report alleging "apparent and possible violations" of the 1971 Federal Election Campaign Act. To put the whole affair in proper perspective, it should be kept in mind that the GAO is responsible solely to Congress, which is controlled by the Democratic majorities in the Senate and House.

The GAO referred the matter to the Department of Justice for possible further investigation. This puts the monkey squarely on the back of President Nixon's administration, since the head of the department, Atty. Gen. Richard G. Kleindienst, a Nixon appointee, is considered to be strongly partisan. Obviously, it would suit the campaign strategy of the Democratic presidential nominee, Sen. George McGovern, for Kleindienst to neglect to follow up on the report so he could be accused of covering up for the administration.

For its part, the Committee to Re-elect the President, through its finance chairman, Maurice Stans, Nixon's former secretary of commerce, demanded that the GAO begin immediately an audit of the Democratic fund-raising records. He said the committee has "reason to believe" such an investigation would be "very revealing."

The McGovern campaign is also trying to make political hay with the "Watergate caper"—the June 17 arrest of five men armed with electronic gear inside the offices of the Democratic National Committee. Some of the "apparent violations" cited in the GAO report centered on a $25,000 contribution to the Nixon campaign. The money showed up in the bank account of one of the men arrested in the raid.

The GAO report did not make a connection between the "apparent violations" and the Watergate arrests. But Sargent Shriver, the Democratic vice presidential nominee, has been trying to make it singlehandedly. Recently he spoke of employees of the Committee to Re-elect the President being caught in Democratic headquarters, although the only actual link with the committee was a security coordinator who had been retained on a contract basis.

Lacking other issues with which their liberal candidate can score with the American electorate, the McGovern people hope to hurt the Nixon campaign by capitalizing on the Watergate incident. Interestingly, campaign contributions turned up by the investigation include $89,000 from four Texas Democrats and $25,000 from a Minnesota supporter of Hubert Humphrey. At this rate, McGovern may find out to his dismay just how many big Democartic contributors are shying away from his candidacy.

Campaign '72:
McGOVERN REVISES ECONOMIC PLANS IN SPEECH TO WALL ST. AUDIENCE

Democratic presidential candidate George McGovern presented revised proposals for tax and welfare reform in a speech to the New York Society of Security Analysts Aug. 29. The South Dakota senator dropped his widely-criticized proposal to provide a $1,000-per-person welfare grant and substituted a National Income Insurance plan. His new proposal would provide public service jobs for those on welfare who could work, a $4,000 floor for welfare aid for a family of four, and a shift of care for the aged, blind, and disabled from welfare to the Social Security system. McGovern estimated the cost of his revised welfare plan at $14 billion above current budgetary levels.

McGovern described his tax reform plan as "a fair share" program that would raise approximately $22 billion by 1975. The largest increase would result from his proposals to revise the taxes on capital gains, making them taxable at ordinary income rates rather than at half the regular rate or less as currently done. He also proposed tightening the rules regarding depreciation deductions for business investments, eliminating the depletion allowance for oil, gas and other mineral industries, repealing certain tax incentives for real estate development, subsidizing state and local governments to issue taxable bonds, eliminating the "gentleman farmer" tax break for losses, and eliminating tax breaks for U.S. business income earned abroad. McGovern said the principle of his proposals was that "money made by money should be taxed at the same rate as money made by men." He also called for the reduction of the maximum rate of taxation on both earned and unearned income from 70% to 48%. Tax loopholes, he charged, made the present top rate "a fiction."

McGovern also charged Aug. 29 that President Nixon had failed to spell out any specific economic plans for the next four years. "I think this may be the first national campaign in memory," he declared, "where we can know with greater certainty the results of electing the challenger than of re-electing the incumbent." McGovern said that if he were elected he would nominate Rep. Wilbur D. Mills (D, Ark.) to be his Treasury secretary.

THE WALL STREET JOURNAL.
New York, N.Y., August 30, 1972

Senator McGovern's Wall Street speech yesterday was billed as the definitive statement of his income maintenance and welfare reform plans, but it remains to be seen whether the latest versions will hold up longer than the earlier ones. For they are still tainted by a ring of implausibility.

Senator McGovern's advisers have been shuffling figures to and fro in an attempt to prove it's feasible to redistribute a lot of income without taking much of it away from anybody. It may be that they now have a series of figures that adds up, though we have doubts about even that to the extent the plan rests on the Pentagon budget cuts. But in the real world there are a lot more considerations than merely whether a plan fits neatly into a Chinese menu for income redistribution, and it seems the thinking behind the McGovern plan only spasmodically gets beyond one from column a and two from column b.

Yesterday's bombshell proposal to tax capital gains as ordinary income is an excellent example. Last May Senator McGovern took a full-page ad in this newspaper to say, among other things, that he had proposed no drastic change in the taxation of capital gains. Yet yesterday the elimination of special treatment of capital gains became the biggest item in his promised $22 billion worth of loophole closing.

Such a proposal raises a number of questions of both equity and practicality. If a capital "gain" represents merely the result of inflation, why should it be taxed at all? If capital gains are to be added to ordinary income, why cannot capital losses be deducted from it? What would be the effect on capital formation and liquidity, and therefore economic progress? These questions of course do not preclude changes in the present capital gains treatment, but they are the reasons that treatment takes the shape it does, and they ought to be thought about a bit before it is repealed.

The Senator would expand income averaging to give relief to someone who sells a business built up over the years. A summary of his proposals says capital losses would be deductible against gains, and presumably therefore not against ordinary income. Other than that, the Senator's explanation to the security analysts was "money made by money should be taxed at the same rate as money made by men." This scarcely strikes us as a rationale that has weighed all of the considerations that will come up in prolonged scrutiny.

The same lack of realism was even more pronounced in the fundamental proposition of the Senator's speech yesterday. He asks us to believe that his loophole-closing and military budget proposals would yield more than enough revenue to pay for "the total costs of additions to the national budget by a Democratic administration." Even without consulting the details, does any serious person believe that?

As for the details, Senator McGovern said his proposals would provide $54 billion in revenues for other purposes. This includes Pentagon budget cuts of over $30 billion. Pentagon experts say his severe cutbacks would actually save only $20 billion; it seems his budget neglected certain operating items, such as buying gasoline to run the trucks and tanks.

But even if the $54 billion is correct, yesterday's speech proposed or reiterated proposals to spend $39 billion for job creation, welfare and property tax reduction. Does this mean Senator McGovern is dropping his previous support for Senator Kennedy's health insurance plan, which would cost $57 billion by itself? Is Senator McGovern dropping the 100%-of-parity agricultural price supports and other expensive items in the Democratic platform? If his words do not mean that, do they mean anything at all?

Indeed, does the figure-juggling, definitive-statement game mean anything to begin with? The more we watch it, the more we doubt any plausible program of reform can be built on the intellectual exercise of juggling the figures from column to column. To propose changes that prove feasible, you have to get behind the figures and grapple with reality. Then, of course, you typically find that things are the way they are for a reason, and that the possible reforms are slow and limited, and by no means exciting enough for the purposes of an electoral campaign.

The New York Times
New York, N.Y., August 30, 1972

Much as John F. Kennedy went before the Methodist ministers in Texas to reassure them about his religious philosophy during the 1960 Presidential campaign, Senator George McGovern has gone to Wall Street to reassure the security analysts—and the nation—that he is no radical who would wreck the American economy.

The Democratic Presidential nominee has sought to quiet fears about his economic views in three ways: By dropping his original plan for a $1,000 "demogrant" for all Americans and substituting a new National Income Insurance Program with job-creation as a cornerstone; by closing out $22 billion in tax preferences while not increasing "by one penny" taxes based on wages and salaries; and by laying down an over-all fiscal program aimed at cutting defense outlays and stimulating growth without inflation. As evidence of his resolve to pursue safe-and-sane economic policies, he topped it all off by proposing to name as his Secretary of the Treasury Representative Wilbur D. Mills, the cautious chairman of the House Ways and Means Committee.

The McGovern effort to undo the apprehension caused by some of his earlier ill-considered tax proposals has not involved turning his back on liberalism. He has shown genuine daring in calling for an end to tax preferences for capital gains, declaring that "money made by money should be taxed at the same rate as money made by men." By phasing out other tax loopholes, Mr. McGovern hopes to raise more than enough revenue to make possible a steep cut in the top-bracket income-tax rate; he would cut it from its present level of 70 per cent—an unrealistic rate that an army of tax lawyers and accountants has been created to avoid—to 48 per cent. This makes excellent sense.

Mr. McGovern would raise additional revenues by repealing the unduly generous accelerated depreciation allowance of 1971 and would set realistic depreciation guidelines for business. He would, however, not drop the 7 per cent investment tax credit immediately; rather, he would gradually convert it—by 1975—into a system for encouraging increases in investment that would otherwise not be made.

* * *

Though he has made some moderate concessions to labor on measures to discourage multinational corporations from investing abroad, his program does not surrender to protectionist pressures. He is apparently thinking chiefly of measures to prevent multinational corporations from avoiding taxes by keeping earnings abroad and juggling tax liabilities from country to country.

Although it is always painful for a politician to change stands on which he has lavished much earlier rhetoric—it was this that kept President Nixon chained to his original Economic Game Plan until his bold switch of Aug. 15, 1971—Senator McGovern was wise to drop his original plan for a welfare reform plan of staggering complexity.

Mr. McGovern's new proposal seems much more realistically calculated to help people at the bottom of the income ladder—both by providing more jobs for those who can work and increased dignity for those who because of age, sickness or the need for taking care of their own small children cannot work.

The Senator's revised plan for putting a floor under family income represents a more generous, but not basically different version of the Nixon Family Assistance Plan. Whatever level of guarantee the plan eventually embraces, the Nixon-McGovern approach deserves bipartisan support.

The overriding McGovern message to the financial community was a reminder that the nation is beset by discord arising out of severe domestic and global problems which must be met by making the economic system both more expansive and fairer. What Mr. McGovern is trying to say is that he, like F.D.R., comes to rescue not to wreck, American capitalism. Win or lose, his proposals have sharpened the choice of economic directions open to America.

© 1972 by The New York Times Company. Reprinted by permission.

THE KANSAS CITY STAR
Kansas City, Mo., August 31, 1972

Sen. George McGovern now has set forth his economic Magna Carta—or at least the outlines of such a document—with the hope it will catch fire with voters who are generally content with the American position in the world and the troop disengagement from Vietnam. Generally, unless the nation is in the midst of a war or other international crisis, elections in America are determined by the bread-and-butter issues of jobs, the worth of money and taxes. Now McGovern is stating his position on these matters.

If all is not yet clear—and it can be debated whether the McGovern figures still add up—at least the senator has presented a far clearer picture of his economic principles and hopes. He will attract some votes with his emphasis on the closing of tax "loopholes" and other monetary reforms. The proposal to reduce local property taxes by an infusion of federal money will fall gladly on many ears. There are those who would like to see military spending reduced, as McGovern says he would do. In general, his theme is an old and tried political theme, the offer to do "the greatest good for the greatest number," but then that promise is implicit in almost all political blueprints.

While the senator has moved closer to realism and clarified some of his earlier statements, he now presents a much more stationary target for the Republicans who will be taking aim with heavy guns. Already Herbert Stein, chairman of the President's Council of Economic Advisers, has said that the proposed defense cut is illusory and that the open-end proposal of supplements for low-income persons holds "the threat of enormous tax increases." Of course the Republicans will not let anyone forget the original McGovern idea to give every man, woman and child $1,000—a plan that offended the sensibilities of much of the middle-class.

Tax reforms outlined by McGovern to an audience of Wall Street security analysts will cause concern but not panic among the targets of his reforms. Most of them do not believe he will become President and even if he should, there is still Congress. The pre-election appointment of Wilbur Mills as Secretary of the Treasury will not alleviate uneasiness. As for a new approach to welfare, the administration will point out the similarity of the McGovern plan to the Nixon-Moynihan plan that has not been able to get out of a Democratic Senate in three years.

What Senator McGovern is talking about is a redistribution of national wealth—the movement of money from one group to another. He is talking about jobs and how to provide for those who do not have jobs. These are all debatable issues, and the senator now has set the stage for discussions of genuine substance on economics.

THE KNICKERBOCKER NEWS
··· UNION-STAR ···
Albany, N.Y., August 31, 1972

Senator George McGovern, wearing the hat of presidential nominee, has carried his economic populism to the marketplace, where not unexpectedly he found it less than spectacularly popular.

Spelling out his revised economic policies to Wall Street security analysts, he presented a program geared to taxing income from investment on a level equal to the tax on income from sweat. Thus he would have capital gains taxed equally with earned income eliminate depletion allowances for oil and minerals, tax investment income earned but uncollected at the time of a person's death, discourage the issuance of tax exempt bonds by states and municipalities, and eliminate certain tax incentives for a number of businesses. It all adds up, he indicated, to a phasing out of $22 billion in tax preferences for corporations, the well-to-do and the rich.

Politically, the appeal of the program is akin to the early economics of Franklin D. Roosevelt although the difference is that FDR was appealing to a nation with many poor and relatively few rich. Senator McGovern may find his program may have less political clout in a nation in which the ratios have been substantially changed with millions of persons in the moderately well-to-do bracket.

(It is interesting to note that even as Senator McGovern was seeking to revive the FDR economic appeal, President Nixon was harking back to FDR with the promise that, if reelected, the first six months of his second term "could equal in excitement, in reform the 100 days of 1944." He was speaking of the first months of President Roosevelt's first term.)

Economically, Senator McGovern's program raises the question of whether such stringent measures would so discourage investors as to retard national growth and job opportunities.

That there is need of tax reform is beyond doubt. Whether there is need for as much tax reform as the senator has proposed is debatable.

What he has presented is the economics of liberalism, hoping perhaps to bring about a confrontation with President Nixon as an advocate of the economics of conservatism. This he may find difficult to accomplish, for the President is skillful in presenting an image that puts him only little to the right of center in economics and social science. Typically, the President asked only Tuesday for a "clear mandate" permitting him to create a program providing broad and progressive social programs "without raising taxes."

If it was excitement Senator McGovern sought to create in presenting his program, he failed. Wall Street took his talk in stride. If he was seeking to make the nation think, he may have succeeded better. But whether thinking will be translated into votes for George McGovern remains very doubtful indeed.

THE CHRISTIAN SCIENCE MONITOR
Boston, Mass., August 31, 1972

Even those Americans least likely to agree with George McGovern's new set of proposals for economic reform can respect his willingness to correct a clearly bad economic policy in midcampaign, and his courage in taking it to the lion's den of Wall Street for its baptism. President Nixon, after all, also changed an unworkable economic stance, though in midterm rather than midcampaign, by instituting wage-price controls.

Wall Street would appear at first blush to be the least likely forum for presenting a program designed to take $12.6 billion more in federal revenues from individuals and $9.4 billion more from corporations. That sector of the economic ladder which Wall Street symbolizes may be aghast at proposals to treat capital gains exactly the same as earned income — that is, fully taxable. Some will deplore the proposal to dissuade states and cities from issuing tax-exempt bonds, long a favorite haven of the rich.

Its corporate clientele will resent the proposals to eliminate oil, gas, and other mineral depletion allowances; to tighten up on fast-depreciation write-offs; and to revise gradually the 7 percent investment tax credit.

Doubtless it was these very proposals that led Mr. McGovern to carry the fire straight to the tinderbox as he did. The arena was bound to give his ideas fullest airing, and the best opportunity for understanding, where they would hit most directly. The dramatic element also helped focus the country's attention on the substitute proposal for his most widely known (and widely deplored) primary campaign plan to give $1,000 to every man, woman, and child.

What he has come up with is an alternative somewhat more costly but not widely different in its philosophical base from Mr. Nixon's family assistance plan. The Nixon plan, now before Congress in amended form, would provide a minimum annual income of $3,000 for a family of four (Mr. Nixon asked for $2,400). Mr. McGovern proposes a "national income insurance" program. It would increase social security benefits, create one million new public service jobs for persons now on welfare, and put a guaranteed income floor of $4,000 in cash and food stamps under a family of four. The total cost would exceed the present $7 billion of federal welfare spending by $14 billion.

The package, as put before the Wall Street security analysts, was clearly an effort to prove to the country's most economically aware audience that he is not the "radical" that his political opposition has tried to paint him. While he did not mention his original $1,000 a person proposal, he put forth an alternative that by its proximity to the Nixon program could not be easily attacked on ideological grounds. With his proposal to close out $22 billion in tax preferences for the affluent, he added a sweetener: not a cent of higher taxes on money earned in wages or salaries, for anybody, and a cutback of the maximum personal income rate from 70 percent to 48 percent.

Mr. McGovern's new package is a sophisticated political and economic effort to get out of the bind which his earlier, poorly researched and poorly articulated primary campaign programs had put him in. It differs in detail, but not in general thrust from those earlier statements of policy. It is designed to disarm his foes, or at least to blunt their arrows, while making the broadest appeal to working-class Americans who depend on earned income rather than dividends and capital gains for their living.

A large chunk of the savings in public spending would come from his proposal to cut $10 billion a year for the next three years out of the defense budget. This will doubtless prolong the debate over the question of nuclear capacity "overkill" and the incessant Pentagon demands for new weapons systems. That is not a bad thing. But the debate should also include the appalling instances of waste, duplication and cost estimate overruns revealed in congressional hearings last spring.

We would hope that in the forthcoming weeks of campaign debate, independent agencies would begin to feed the programs of both Mr. McGovern and President Nixon into their computers and give the public as fair an estimate as possible of their impact on the economy. Regardless of which candidate takes the oath of office next January, the basic questions of tax reform and redistribution of the national wealth will remain.

Mr. McGovern has, in effect, called for a change in national direction, and a change in values. It is a hard platform on which to try to win an election — an impossible one, unless he has seen something stirring in the majority mind quite different from what Mr. Nixon thinks he sees there. Senator McGovern has opened not only his arithmetic but himself to the toughest kind of scrutiny, not to mention hostile reaction. If his economic advisers, and he has some very good ones, have rightly figured their economics, it remains a question if they have rightly assessed the American people's willingness to so reorient the country's social and economic structure.

THE MILWAUKEE JOURNAL
Milwaukee, Wis., August 31, 1972

In a prudent move toward the political center, Sen. McGovern has revised and moderated his controversial proposals for a fairer sharing of American wealth. He still seeks reform in tax and welfare policies, but in ways that will be harder to brand "radical."

As before, McGovern argues not only for an enlarged economic pie, but also more equitable individual slices. The key is still tax loophole closing to reduce unfair breaks for the wealthy as well as raise urgently needed revenue. With this money, plus savings on defense, McGovern would provide local property tax relief and finance domestic revitalization programs, including welfare reform. McGovern believes his program can increase social justice while bringing prosperity for all.

But his revised proposals, still disturbing to many, are more temperate in detail. Except for an unusually bold attack on preferential treatment of capital gains, his tax reforms are mostly those that have knocked around Capitol Hill for years without success. What is remarkable is that a presidential candidate is pushing them in such itemized fashion — hitting at everything from cherished oil depletion allowances to real estate tax shelters.

Similarly, McGovern's sharply redrafted approach to welfare offers nothing novel. Above all, he pledges a decent job for every able bodied person, with the government employing those frozen out of the private economy. Anyone who refuses to work when able would not be eligible for welfare. For the aged, the halt and the blind, McGovern wants better benefits under expanded Social Security. For others who cannot work—mostly mothers with children in fatherless homes — there would be an income guarantee of $4,000 for a family of four. For the working poor whose pay falls below the poverty line, McGovern no longer has an answer, but says that various income supplement ideas are being explored.

All in all, McGovern's welfare pitch is not far different from that of President Nixon, who has called for a minimum income of $2,400 for a family of four, linked to a work requirement and provisions for supplementing the income of the working poor.

McGovern has thus come in from the fog. Sloppy research on previous, highly explicit tax and welfare proposals had left him vulnerable to charges of incoherence — a peril most presidential candidates avoid by being vague. Now McGovern has returned with toned down objectives, updated arithmetic and a pledge that his changes would not cost wage earners another cent in federal taxes. That, of course, is open to challenge.

Questions remain. Can we really expect to raise so much through tax reform? Or must we, as many economists insist and both candidates refuse to concede, look to higher taxes to meet essential national needs? How far can we go in squeezing capital gains without endangering investment and economic growth? How much can the defense budget be safely cut? Beyond many other technical questions, there is the broad matter of wealth redistribution. The poor are a minority. The dispossessed multitudes of the Great Depression are now comfortable suburbanites. Can any candidate successfully promote a share-the-wealth program when a majority of the people are well off? McGovern says only the unjustly enriched need fear, that the average man won't be nicked — yet there is much anxiety among the crucial middle class to overcome.

Whatever coming weeks may reveal, however, McGovern is in an improved posture. He can carry the battle to Nixon and fairly ask: What precisely are *your* tax and social programs for the next four years? What will they cost and how will the dollars be raised? White House responses that are nothing but attacks on McGovernism will not suffice. A real debate is needed.

OKLAHOMA CITY TIMES
Oklahoma City, Okla., August 30, 1972

SEN. GEORGE McGOVERN has now made public the latest version of his personal platform, with emphasis on a revised tax structure and on providing unearned income for all. Following established political custom, he called his proposals reforms.

But reforms should bring about a betterment of an existing situation. The McGovern attitude toward investments could only cause a worsening of the business and industrial climate, and that in turn could only produce more unemployment.

Much of America's difficulty in the international community today stems from the fact that while we have been helping other nations modernize their industrial plant and adopt the latest, most productive machine tools, we have neglected modernization of our own plants, to the point that they are no longer competitive.

WHEN foreign plants can produce American-quality goods at prices that drive American-produced counterparts off our own counters, while paying their own workers the highest wages in their history, we have lost the productivity edge that made our own high wages possible in the first place. The result is the export of jobs that were once American.

The only way American workers and industries can regain lost markets is to become truly competitive again. That means tremendous new investments in plants and tools, to make the American worker once more the most productive per hour worked in the entire world.

THAT INVESTMENT must come from two sources: individuals who buy shares and securities of American industry themselves, and through such large savings plans as their life insurance and pension funds; or from the profits of industry plowed back into the business in the traditional way. But a tax plan that discourages investments will dry up these sources in a hurry.

The Evening Star
Washington, D.C., August 31, 1972

The best that can be said for Senator McGovern's revised tax-reform and welfare proposals is that they approach the outer fringes of plausibility. No longer do they contain such unwieldy and terribly expensive ideas as the plan to give every American a $1,000 "demogrant."

And yet the new McGovern program remains flawed to a degree that surprises, considering the size and stature of the group of Democratic economists that for more than a month has labored to make the senator's original proposals more rational and saleable. About the only explanation is that his advisers tried to bite off too much. For they were trying simultaneously to: Justify enough changes in the tax system to bring in much of the enormous amount of new money McGovern obviously would need to pay for his big new social-welfare schemes; fulfill some of McGovern's earlier commitments on income distribution; assure middle-class earners that they won't pay any more taxes; and put forth an income-guarantee plan for the poor that is well-designed yet different from President Nixon's long-debated Family Assistance Plan. The effort did not quite come off.

Aside from the fact that McGovern chose Wall Street to unveil his new program, his tax-reform ideas probably will generate much more interest nationwide than his welfare plan. For they are clear and comprehensive. They no doubt will strike a responsive chord in countless Americans who feel abused by existing tax preferences that others enjoy. And if current White House stirrings are any clue, they may well lead President Nixon to come up with a program of his own for reforming the tax code.

"Money made by money should be taxed at the same rate as money made by men," said the senator. This is the essence of the McGovern tax approach, covering as it does a number of specific proposals aimed at corporations and individuals whose incomes derive largely from investments. Certainly any tax reform effort ought to redress, at least in part, the inequity that finds federal income taxes bearing much more heavily on wage-earners than on people who rely mostly on stocks, bonds, and real estate. Moreover, McGovern has hit upon some out-and-out tax dodges that cannot be justified. But on other points — notably his proposals to tax capital gains as ordinary income and to roll back recent tax breaks for business—the senator all too airily dismisses the dampening impact these changes might have on capital formation, industrial expansion and thus economic prosperity. At best it will be a tricky business for McGovern or anyone else to steer the right course between tax fairness and continued economic growth. No realistic reform plan, moreover, is likely to produce the $22 billion a year McGovern suggests.

The senator's welfare plan, at least as it appeared this week, stands little chance of commanding serious attention. It seeks to guarantee $4,000 a year to a dependent family of four, much like Senator Ribicoff's alternative to the Nixon welfare-reform plan, and it would provide one million public-service jobs. But unlike the Ribicoff or Nixon legislation, it contains as yet neither a work requirement nor work incentives. All this, it is said, might be clarified later. But then, that's the way it has been with the senator's welfare ideas all year.

TULSA DAILY WORLD
Tulsa, Okla., August 30, 1972

SEN. GEORGE McGOVERN has gone back to the drawing board to replace his halfbaked, disastrously foolish scheme of giving everyone in the U.S. $1,000 a year.

He has come up with a plan he figures will be politically foolproof. It would give to the poor, soak the rich and leave the man in the middle untouched. If McGOVERN hadn't claimed it, we would have sworn this came straight from FRED HARRIS' New Populist pap.

It has all the familiar earmarks of liberal tax and welfare reforms — except that McGOVERN is so obviously eyeing votes more than economic remedies that his plan is fatally suspect. He tried one approach and it was laughed off the street; now he comes back with another, computer-calculated to appeal to at least 50.1 per cent of the voters.

But worse than that is the *direction* of McGOVERN's program. It is aimed specifically at almost every *incentive* that has kept the American economic machine going all these years.

In the name of "closing loopholes," the Senator would remove or neutralize such provisions as capital gains tax benefits, the investment credit for business, oil and other mineral depletion allowances and the tax savings for investing in low-interest municipal bonds.

No matter what kind of tax reform the country faces, these and other tax advantages will be under attack and some changes can be justified. But McGOVERN seems to be intent on wiping out almost everything that now induces people to save money and invest it.

He appears to have no understanding of the role of this saving-investing process in our economic system—that it creates wealth, jobs and in turn more taxes for Government.

McGOVERN has his arithmetic neatly set out on paper to show that the savings from his tax program would pay for all the costs of his welfare benefits, such as guaranteeing every family of four an income of $4,000 a year, and would end up with a net increase of $22 billion in Federal revenue.

But the fact is that his figures are meaningless, *precisely* because he *does not take into account the loss of the incentive to invest.*

Who can say, for example, what wiping out the oil depletion allowance would do to the economy of the State of Oklahoma? Who would invest in the oil business, our major industry? How many jobs would be lost, how much income reduced, how great the tax loss—from this one instance of "loophole" closing alone?

The effect of the total package is incalculable, because no one has ever thrown such a total wet blanket over our free enterprise system at one time. If changes have to be made in that system, may Heaven protect us from a bungling tinkerer like GEORGE McGOVERN. His drawing board is a disaster area.

The Dallas Morning News
Dallas, Tex., August 31, 1972

CANDIDATE George McGovern has unveiled the latest model of his automatic shift, 4-speed welfare reform program—the speed at which it will increase welfare can be changed, depending on which audience he's talking to and the shift can be made with no noticeable effort.

McGovern had to recall the previous model, which would simply have granted a thousand dollars to every man, woman and child. Various high Democratic strategists apparently warned him that his blatant giveaway had so many obvious defects that it would be an unsafe campaign vehicle at any speed.

The new model also guarantees an income of $4,000 for a family of four, but there is evidence of some reworking of the grill and chrome trim by McGovern's design engineers. In a speech to Wall Streeters, he talked about jobs quite a bit in his discussion of welfare—just as Wallace has been doing for several years. And he mentioned that there is a question of income supplements for the working poor—just as Nixon has been doing for several years.

However, unlike the other two program salesmen, he didn't come right out and say that his new plan would have a tough work requirement. He said, "I will take whatever steps are necessary to guarantee a job opportunity to every man and woman in America who is able to work."

That doesn't pose much of a threat to the professional welfare clients who routinely pass up "job opportunities" in order to stay on welfare.

As for the income supplements to the working poor, he firmly asserted that the question must be resolved. He didn't say how.

However, the Democratic nominee did turn very emphatic on one point. He charged that Nixon is using scare tactics in claiming that the McGovern reforms would force Americans to pay half their income in taxes.

The fact is, declared McGovern, "No American whose income comes from wages and salaries would pay one penny more in federal taxes than he does now. Let me repeat that: No American whose income comes from wages and salaries would pay one penny more in taxes than he does now."

When McGovern repeats a promise twice like that, it is really convincing. As he has previously demonstrated, the repeating of a statement indicates that he stands behind it 1,000 per cent.

The Honolulu Advertiser
Honolulu, Hawaii, August 30, 1972

There are no doubt two statistics George McGovern never wants to hear again: One is 1,000 per cent, his degree of stated support for Senator Eagleton, his first running mate. The other is $1,000 a year, the amount he would have given each American as part of his initial tax and welfare program.

Although he now has Sargent Shriver as a vigorous vice presidential candidate, McGovern's personal image is still shadowed by the inept handling of both how Eagleton was selected and then how he was shelved.

NOW McGOVERN has unveiled a new tax-welfare program, and reactions are sure to involve an almost homogenized mixture of politics and economics.

An initial — and perhaps unfair — reaction is that the Democratic presidential candidate may be making more economic sense with his new plan but it still lacks political jazz. Others, of course, will see it just the opposite.

His accompanying idea of naming Representative Wilbur Mills as treasury secretary has some appeal. But again, it is shadowed by word McGovern never really talked it over with the surprised Mills.

There are several parts to McGovern's new program, involving the phased closing of some of the more glaring tax loopholes, a liberalized welfare program, no welfare benefits for the able bodied who refuse work, and a public-service job program to provide more opportunities.

It is economically more moderate and politically more hard-line, a shift toward the right, or at least the center.

In fact, McGovern's welfare proposals are not that much different than those of President Nixon, whose own major reform suggestions have been almost lost in the furor over those of the Democratic candidate.

MANY MIGHT FEEL that the tax-welfare debate will not be a big issue this year, that it is mostly political smoke and confusion that will only be reduced to charges that McGovern can't add right.

Still the year has produced evidence voters feel that something is wrong with the system of taxes and welfare. But they also feel different ways about what's wrong.

Some suggest the over-riding need is for a massive redistribution of income through both tax and welfare reform — that there must be more equality and minimum guarantees.

However, Irving Kristol, co-editor of The Public Interest, says the average American is not rebelling against inequities in the tax structure: "He is rebelling against taxes period."

Herbert Stein, chairman of the President's Council of Economic Advisers, says that any further redistribution depends fundamentally on "the willingness of the non-poor to give money to the poor." How willing are Americans on that question?

THE NATIONAL MOOD on these matters is most uncertain, and that is what the election debate is about.

McGovern doesn't have much of a chance at this point, and he has damaged his credentials in this area. But his ideas deserve to be studied, and a rational debate can influence Congress and set a climate for needed, progressive legislation — maybe even based on some of President Nixon's ideas on welfare.

Los Angeles Times
Los Angeles, Calif., August 31, 1972

It is human nature to want something for nothing, and politicians have been catering to this trait for as long as anyone remembers. Sen. George S. McGovern's speech to the New York Society of Security Analysts was, unfortunately, in this mold.

The trouble isn't with the Democratic presidential nominee's stated goals: to guarantee a job "for every man and woman in the country who is able to work"; to reduce the welfare rolls, and to close so-called tax loopholes which enable some affluent persons to pay less than their fair share of federal taxes.

These are objectives which enjoy broad public support, and rightly so.

The trouble comes with McGovern's insistence that he can do all this, and open the way for $15 billion in local property tax relief besides, quite painlessly; without, in fact, requiring the average, non-wealthy citizen to pay so much as one red cent in higher taxes.

As a practical matter, it isn't possible, and the South Dakotan is being disingenuous when he leads the American people to think that it is.

Although McGovern spoke in Wall Street, it is obvious that his real target was not the assembly of stockbrokers and investment counselors, but the large number of ordinary citizens who were put off by his earlier income redistribution scheme.

That plan would have involved, in effect, raising taxes on middle-income and ultra-affluent Americans in order to subsidize families with incomes under $12,000 a year.

McGovern's substitute "national income insurance" plan is several shades less ambitious, and has the political advantage of seeming to exempt middle-income Americans from having to pay for it.

Under the revised, three-part plan, the federal government would create a million public service jobs for employable welfare recipients. The aged poor would be taken off the welfare rolls by raising minimum Social Security benefits from $85 to $150 a month. And welfare recipients who are unable to work would be guaranteed a minimum income of $4,000 a year, in the case of a family of four.

The total bill, according to McGovern, would be $14 billion a year.

The Administration suggests that the McGovern package would actually cost considerably more than that. Whether or not that is so, it isn't clear that even the creation of a million public service jobs would fulfill the South Dakotan's promise of employment for everybody who is able to work.

And, whereas President Nixon's own welfare reform plan would provide benefits for the working poor—those whose job earnings leave them below the poverty line—it is not at all clear that McGovern's plan would do so. If it wouldn't, a working mother earning $3,500 a year would fare worse than a non-working mother receiving $4,000 in welfare.

These are matters which McGovern may be able to explain in the days and weeks ahead. The real trouble with his Wall Street speech is more fundamental.

When McGovern promises that "no American whose income comes from wages and salaries will pay one penny more in federal taxes than he does now," he is making two very questionable assumptions.

One is that Congress would go along with his proposal to make a massive $32 billion cut in defense spending. In fact there is no way to make a reduction of that size without endangering the nation's security—and neither Congress nor the country is ready to do that.

The other assumption is that even the most controversial elements of his tax reform plan will in fact become law—thereby providing an extra $22 billion in revenues. That is unrealistic, too.

In real life, therefore, a McGovern Administration would be faced with the necessity of either raising everybody's taxes or abandoning its national income insurance plan.

There is no question that tax reform is needed, and that several of McGovern's eleven proposals for reducing or eliminating tax preferences or "loopholes" have merit. Congress would be well advised to look before leaping into others, however.

The major case in point is the Democratic nominee's proposal to eliminate the preferential tax treatment accorded income from capital gains.

It is hard to argue with McGovern's basic point that it doesn't seem fair for Americans who work for a living to get less favorable tax treatment than people who make their money from stock market profits or land investments. The fact is, however, that the principle of lower taxation on capital gains is woven deeply into our economic system.

Businessmen are convinced that treating such profits as ordinary income would discourage savings, disrupt investment patterns and, ultimately, slow the economic growth which is essential to creation of jobs for the very people McGovern wants to help.

Maybe the businessmen are wrong. On the other hand, maybe they're right. We should try to find out before tinkering too much with a system that has been an integral part of the world's most successful economy.

That kind of searching inquiry is properly the province of the House Ways and Means Committee, where, fortunately, tax reform will be the top-priority order of business next year.

Campaign '72:

SHRIVER CITES LOST PEACE CHANCE; McGOVERN AIDE HAS TALKS IN PARIS

Democratic vice presidential nominee R. Sargent Shriver charged Aug. 10 that President Nixon had lost an opportunity for a Vietnam peace settlement when he took office in 1969. Shriver said "Nixon had peace handed to him literally in his lap. He blew it." His remarks were taken to imply that a 1969 decrease in battlefield activity had signaled North Vietnam's willingness to negotiate a settlement of the war. Two former negotiators at the Paris talks, Averell Harriman and Cyrus Vance, both Democrats, issued a joint statement Aug. 12 stating that they supported "completely Sargent Shriver's view that President Nixon lost an opportunity for a negotiated settlement in Vietnam when he took office."

Nixon Administration officials hotly denied Shriver's charges. Secretary of State William P. Rogers Aug. 11 described the allegations as "bunk" and "political fantasy." The State Department responded to the Harriman-Vance statement Aug. 12 declaring that "no record of any such so-called signal" could be found. "Mr. Harriman reportedly says it came in October or November 1968," it said. "This raises the question as to why no action was taken on the so-called signal for the next three months, before the present Administration took office."

The dispute over Shriver's statement had barely subsided when another dispute between the Nixon and McGovern camps began over a visit by Pierre Salinger, a co-chairman of the Citizens for McGovern Committee, to Paris to meet with North Vietnamese negotiators. Salinger disclosed Aug. 16 that he had met with the North Vietnamese July 18 and Aug. 9 and they had informed him "that there was no change in their position with regard to prisoners of war, that the release has to be in the context of an overall peace settlement as outlined at the negotiations." Salinger said he had told the North Vietnamese that if there was any possibility "to negotiate a peace agreement with President Nixon that they should do so without regard to the American election."

McGovern confirmed Aug. 16 that Salinger had met with the North Vietnamese at his request. The Nixon Administration objected to the Salinger mission Aug. 17. White House Press Secretary Ronald Ziegler said McGovern representatives "might say something in contact with the enemy that could jeopardize [President Nixon's] peace efforts." McGovern responded Aug. 17 charging that Nixon "has manipulated American public opinion to appear to be negotiating seriously when actually he has been stalling to prop up Gen. Thieu's government in Saigon."

The Times-Picayune
New Orleans, La., August 12, 1972

Sargent Shriver, the urbane and energetic nominee of the Democratic party for vice-president of the United States, made some very interesting statements in an interview in Maryland Thursday.

Among other things, the former ambassador to France said that President Richard M. Nixon "blew" a chance to end the war in Southeast Asia in 1969, when the vice-presidential candidate was serving the Nixon administration in Paris.

Mr. Shriver was quoted by The Associated Press as having said, "Nixon had peace handed to him literally in his lap. He blew it."

The vice-presidential candidate was quoted further as saying that better peace terms could have been obtained by President Nixon in 1969 than he can get today. The President, he said, could have offered in 1969 the same peace terms that he is offering today with a very high chance of their acceptance.

"The obvious reason," he was quoted as saying, "is in that period we had hundreds of thousands of troops there."

This suggests what we consider a most pertinent question: Does Mr. Shriver approve the course that has been followed by President Nixon in drastically reducing United States troop strength in Vietnam? If he does not approve this course, does he feel that President Nixon errs in bringing Americans home?

Mr. Shriver's position seems most inconsistent with that of his running mate, Senator George McGovern, who has repeatedly urged withdrawal. The senator has promised to bring our troops home and have our prisoners of war out of North Vietnam 90 days after he becomes President.

If having troops in the theater of war improves a President's bargaining position at peace talks, doesn't bringing them home damage his bargaining position?

Maybe Mr. Shriver has a logical explanation of his apparent disagreement with Sen. McGovern. We'd like him to give it.

DAILY NEWS
New York, N.Y., August 15, 1972

A bunch of Democrats are hastily rewriting history in an effort to get vice presidential candidate Sargent Shriver off the hook he fashioned for himself when he accused President Richard M. Nixon of muffing a peace chance early in his term.

Shriver let on that Mr. Nixon ignored a solid offer from Hanoi. But what happened, according to Averell Harriman and Cyrus Vance—U.S. negotiators in Paris at the time—was that the Reds "signalled" their pacific intentions by withdrawing some forces from South Vietnam.

The alleged signal, moreover, came in October or November of 1968—when the Democrats were still running the show. So who muffed what golden opportunity?

Sen. George McGovern has even embroidered his running mate's fable. He charges that President Nixon answered the enemy's supposed peace gesture with "accelerated" bombing.

Just to set the facts straight, there was no U.S. bombing of North Vietnam from October 1968 to April of this year. Attacks were resumed then to halt a naked invasion of South Vietnam by the North Vietnamese, using weapons hoarded during their respite of almost four years.

Just how gullible does Sen. McG. think Americans are?

The Tennessean
Nashville, Tenn., August 15, 1972

THE EXTRAORDINARY vehemence with which the Nixon administration has attacked Mr. Sargent Shriver on his statement that it had an opportunity to end the war and blew it says two things about the White House view.

★ ★ ★

The first is that he has hit on, or painfully close to the truth when he said the administration lost an opportunity for a negotiated settlement in Vietnam when Mr. Nixon first took office. The second is that the Republicans view Mr. Shriver as a formidable addition to the Democratic team and that the thing to do is to hit him hard and early.

So the Republicans have wheeled out the artillery to blast Mr. Shriver with everybody from Secretary of State William P. Rogers —who has finally been given something to do—to Sen. Robert Dole, the Republican committee chairman.

Secretary Rogers said Mr. Shriver was indulging in "political fantasy" and his comments were "bunk." Others have been even less kind to Mr. Shriver, who was ambassador to France during the period in question.

Both Mr. W. Averell Harriman and Mr. Cyrus R. Vance who were negotiators in Paris at the time have supported Mr. Shriver's statement of the lost opportunity, saying that North Vietnam at the time withdrew 22 of 25 regiments from the South back across the DMZ.

In the campaign, Mr. Nixon had said that he had a plan to end the war and he went on to say if the conflict was still going on in January "it can best be ended by a new administration that has given no hostages to the mistakes of the past; an administration neither defending old errors nor bound by the old record..."

There was then some optimism that the war could be settled. Mr. Harriman and then Mr. Vance left Paris as negotiators, but with statements that held some expectation that settlement could be had. Even Ambassador Henry Cabot Lodge, the new Nixon negotiator, seemed optimistic.

Publicly, Hanoi continued to sound tough, but reports from there by European observers suggested it had become less obdurate about peace terms, although its antipathy toward President Thieu remained strong.

At one point, President Nixon scoffed at reports from Hanoi, saying that it had given up hopes for a military victory and was now trying to win at the conference table what it could not on the battlefield.

At that point, Mr. Nixon had well over 400,000 men in Vietnam and tremendous leverage. But his comments and his peace proposals were interpreted in Hanoi to mean the U.S. commitment to President Thieu's remaining in power was firm as ever.

From that point, negotiations at the Paris peace talks were stuck on dead center and have remained there. Only the North Vietnamese know for certain how far they were willing to compromise in January of 1969, but they did signal their intent to the new administration that a serious opportunity was at hand for some new initiatives.

★ ★ ★

What kind of opportunity it was remains obscure to the American people, but judging from the administration's heated reaction to Mr. Shriver, the assertion of a missed chance is a painful reminder.

The Virginian-Pilot
Norfolk, Va., August 12, 1972

The failure of President Nixon to end the Vietnam War, as he promised in '68, is surfacing as a campaign issue in '72 in an odd way.

Sargent Shriver, who was inserted in the No. 2 spot on the Democratic ticket as a pinch-runner for Senator Thomas Eagleton, is charging that Mr. Nixon missed a "historic opportunity" to end the war in 1969—and to end it on better terms than he can get today.

While Mr. Shriver is dealing in hindsight, where politicians and lesser mortals enjoy 20-20 vision, he is in a position to know what he is saying. He served as Ambassador to France under President Johnson and was held over by Mr. Nixon, resigning in 1970 amidst rumors that he would be a candidate for office that year. (He was mentioned, as they say, for the governorship of Maryland and an Illinois Senate seat, but both came to naught.) As Ambassador Mr. Shriver was in close touch with the American negotiators at the Paris peace talks.

In an interview with reporters at his home Thursday, he said the American negotiators, W. Averell Harriman and Cyrus Vance, felt they were close to a settlement on the eve of the election in '68 and that he had thought Mr. Nixon would move quickly to end the war in early '69, as President Eisenhower had ended the Korean War soon after entering the White House in '53. "I thought he had one of the great historic opportunities of my lifetime," Mr. Shriver said "I cannot imagine why he blew it."

Whether or not Mr. Nixon "blew" a peace settlement in '69, Mr. Shriver is probably right in saying that he could have obtained better terms then than he can today. But despite the terms of Mr. Nixon's open offer to North Vietnam, there isn't any indication that the other side is interested in buying peace at any price. Hanoi knows that time is on its side, and apparently is willing to endure Mr. Nixon's punishment for a while yet.

Meanwhile, the last American combat troops are coming out of South Vietnam and the antiwar forces on Capitol Hill are mounting a major offensive to legislate our total withdrawal. The House of Representatives sided with the White House on the latest end-the-war vote when it beat down a pull-out proviso stuck to the $2.1 billion military aid bill Thursday. The amendment requiring an October 1 withdrawal in exchange for a limited cease-fire and the American prisoners' return was rejected, 228 to 178, with the Democratic leadership siding with the White House. But the antiwar forces now seem to have the necessary votes in the Senate; the issue probably will be revived soon.

Because of the disabilities that the Democrats have labored under, George McGovern hasn't had the opportunity to make much of the war. But the issue is a natural and Mr. Nixon remains vulnerable.

The Christian Science Monitor
Boston, Mass., August 16, 1972

The serious question is not whether Mr. Nixon might or might not have been able to get a quick peace in 1969, or whether he could get the prisoners back by stopping the bombing now, but whether Republican reaction to Democratic action will help the needy Democrats.

Up until the Republicans began stomping on Democrat Sargent Shriver, a redoubtable old Democrat named Averell Harriman was sulking in his tent over the way he had been ignored at the Democratic convention in Miami. And the Harriman moneybag, which happens to be well filled, was not being opened for the McGovern ticket. But Mr. Harriman has always believed, and many times has asserted among friends, that he had things lined up for a peace settlement when he handed over the negotiating job in Paris to Henry Cabot Lodge.

Whether that was wishful thinking on Mr. Harriman's part is beside the point now. He believed it. Mr. Shriver asserted it. The Republicans pounced on Mr. Shriver for asserting it. And so Mr. Harriman became involved because it was his version of 1969 that was being trampled upon. So Mr. Harriman is no longer sulking in his tent. He and his moneybag are back in the Democratic battle line.

And then there is the Lyndon Johnson angle. Secretary of State Rogers joined in the attack on Mr. Shriver by claiming that the Democrats had had three months in which to respond to any "signal" which Hanoi might have been flying at the end of 1968. This overlooks the simple fact that any signal sent out by Hanoi at that time was intended for the incoming, not for the outgoing, president. But there was the Rogers contention that Lyndon Johnson missed any boat that was missed. And Lyndon Johnson was the most conspicuous nonperson at the Miami convention. Mr. Johnson has yet to say a word of public support for the McGovern ticket. But now —it could change.

We do not know whether Sargent Shriver and former Attorney General Ramsey Clark are sharp enough politicians to do what they did to goad Republicans into words which would bring the disgruntled veteran Democrats roaring out of their tents and back into the fray. But that is what seems to be happening.

The Democrats emerged from their convention so disunited that only Republicans could put them together again. They might.

As for the merits of the Shriver-Ramsey Clark assertions about the availability of peace then and now: The fine print of the Clark thesis includes the phrase "agreement on the military and political issues." Yes, the prisoners will come home, if Hanoi is first satisfied on "political issues" which means, of course, pulling the rug out from under President Thieu of South Vietnam. Mr. Nixon could have had a quick peace in early 1969, and could get one now, by dumping President Thieu. That has always been at the heart of the issue. Nothing said by anyone in these affairs changes that central fact.

The New York Times
New York, N.Y., August 16, 1972

Secretary Rogers, former Ambassador Lodge and the State Department are being disingenuous, to put it mildly, in denying "any" knowledge of the 1969 chance for peace in Vietnam that Democratic Vice-Presidential nominee Sargent Shriver and former Ambassadors Harriman and Vance claim President Nixon "blew." Interpretations of the events of that period may differ, but there can be little dispute on the facts or the Nixon Administration's detailed knowledge of them now and then.

The new Administration's secret National Security Council study memorandum on Vietnam of February, 1969 (NSSM-1), which leaked to the press last spring and has now been published in the Congressional Record, is conclusive on these points. During his first week in office, President Nixon asked eight Government agencies for their interpretation of North Vietnam's withdrawal of large numbers of its troops from South Vietnam—the move the Johnson Administration negotiators in Paris and Defense Secretary Clifford, among others, had interpreted as a "signal" of Hanoi's desire for de-escalation of the war and a negotiated settlement.

Secretary Rogers and the State Department were among those replying that they saw a political purpose related to the Paris negotiations in North Vietnam's troop withdrawals. In response to another NSSM-1 question, they indicated a belief that Hanoi had come to Paris to seek a negotiated settlement—on terms favorable to itself, of course.

* * *

Ambassador Harriman briefed President-elect Nixon at the Hotel Pierre in New York in December, 1968, and saw him again at the White House on his return from Paris after the change of Administrations in January, 1969. Ambassador Vance, who stayed on as Paris negotiator for another month, reported to President Nixon on his return. Both negotiators gave their estimate of the situation repeatedly to Secretary Rogers and other high Nixon Administration officials. Notes on these conversations must exist in State Department and White House files.

There is no valid security reason why some of this data should not now be made public, especially after the detailed reports Henry Kissinger has given publicly about his secret 1971 negotiations with North Vietnamese Politburo member Le Duc Tho. The Harriman-Vance view is that the tenor and the context of their Paris negotiations made it clear that Hanoi's troop pullbacks were intended to initiate a reduction in the violence of the war, mutual withdrawal of American and North Vietnamese forces and substantive negotiations for a political settlement. The country has a right to the facts on which to base an independent judgment.

Mr. Shriver's personal role, which the Administration understandably has made the center of its counterattack, was essentially peripheral to the negotiations. As President Johnson's Ambassador to France, who continued for fourteen months under President Nixon, he handled some liaison with French and Soviet diplomats. But, as he has now confirmed, his job did not charge him with reporting to Washington on talks, and there is no documentary evidence that he resigned the Ambassadorship out of disagreement with Nixon policy on the peace issue.

* * *

The important issue, however, is not Mr. Shriver's role but rather whether the Nixon Administration embarked from the start on a policy that brought stalemate in Paris and the continuation of the war for another four years.

Beginning in the summer of 1968, while Lyndon Johnson was still President, and resuming in early October, the North Vietnamese removed 22 of their 25 regiments from the two northernmost provinces of South Vietnam. That signaled an intention, at the very least, of abiding by the understanding that large-scale violation of the Demilitarized Zone between North and South Vietnam at the 17th Parallel would be suspended once American bombing had halted.

The other key factor, as seen by Ambassadors Harriman and Vance, is that Hanoi agreed after arduous negotiations to seat the Saigon Government at the negotiating table in return for the admission of the Vietcong. Unfortunately, that breakthrough was largely negated first by procedural foot-dragging by President Thieu and then by his refusal to consider either legalization of the Communist party in South Vietnam or a coalition government there, conditions that made a compromise settlement impossible.

The Harriman-Vance view is that the new Administration should have set a negotiated peace as its first goal, but instead emphasized the survival of President Thieu and his Saigon Government. The same factor that made a compromise settlement impossible in 1969 remains the chief stumbling block in 1972.

© 1972 by The New York Times Company. Reprinted by permission

WORCESTER TELEGRAM
Worcester, Mass., August 17. 1972

The charge that President Nixon "blew" a historic chance to settle the Vietnam war during the early stages of his term is one of the first political salvos of what promises to be a lively presidential campaign. It sounds less than persuasive, however.

The claim has been made by former Paris peace negotiator Averell Harriman and was amplified last week by Sargent Shriver, George McGovern's running mate. They alleged that North Vietnam withdrew the bulk of its troops from the south at the end of 1968, thus giving the Americans a chance for a diplomatic settlement.

The case — if intended to discredit the administration's sincerity to bring about an honorable peace — rests on shaky grounds. For one thing, the Communist troop withdrawal occurred while President Johnson was still in office. If indeed the de-escalation was a well disguised peace offer, it was the Johnson administration that chose to disregard it.

Moreover, there is no evidence that temporary Communist troop withdrawals actually signaled Hanoi's willingness to negotiate a political settlement. Harriman and Shriver may think so — but that is only an assumption on their part, and a far-fetched one at that. For all we know, Hanoi may have switched to different strategy or decided to reorganize its forces for a future offensive. At any rate, the Communists have steadfastly refused to consider Washington's peace offers — in 1968 and ever since.

If the Democrats have proof that the Nixon administration knowingly rejected real opportunities to end the war, the American people ought to know about it. But we need more evidence than has been presented so far.

The Harriman-Shriver charge is surely not the last of its kind for the campaign. Both sides will do their best to capitalize on issues — real and imaginary. It is up to the public to separate truth from propaganda. Sometimes that isn't easy.

HERALD EXAMINER
Los Angeles., Calif., August 15, 1972

Getting nominated to the Democratic national ticket seems to bring out the worst in a man.

George McGovern revealed a basic indecision and lack of prudence in the Eagleton affair. Sargent Shriver, his new running mate, has followed by revealing a remarkable viciousness which belies his reputation for fairness and honesty.

Shriver was at his very worst recently in an interview at his Maryland estate. In an ill-considered attempt to damage the Republican cause, he said flatly that President Nixon "blew" a historic opportunity to end the Vietnam war in 1969 when he "had peace handed to him literally in his lap" at the Paris peace talks.

Shriver, who was United States ambassador to France in 1969, gave no details on who made the alleged offer, how it was made, when it was made or how the president blew it. His only elaboration was that "I can assure you we would have gotten better terms then than President Nixon can get today."

The reason why the Democratic vice presidential nominee furnished no names, dates or specifics on the alleged enemy offer is that there never was such an offer — and he certainly knows it. From the very first, and right up to yesterday, the enemy has not budged an inch from its demands that we stop supporting Saigon and get out of Southeast Asia.

Secretary of State William P Rogers, retorted to the Shriver charge by calling it "bunk" and "political fantasy" — which is certainly a kind way of expressing it.

A more accurate description would have been to label the charge as the wildly intemperate, dishonest and reckless smear it really was.

Newsday
Long Island, N.Y., August 18, 1972

One can understand Sen. McGovern's desire for North Vietnam to understand his position on immediate release of American POWS. The sentiment is honorable and indeed useful to our side in the peace talks. But to encourage or even condone Pierre Salinger's direct contact with the North Vietnamese delegation in Paris is a breach of international protocol, U.S. law and basic common sense.

There are several ways McGovern could have accomplished his praiseworthy purpose. He could have stated his policy in public; Hanoi's hearing has proven quite acute during the political campaign. Or he could have transmitted a personal message via the official U.S. delegation. Quite probably he could have won the government's agreement to have a trusted representative deliver the message in person through the front door.

It's hardly likely, though, that Pierre Salinger, a man of some experience in public relations but none whatever in diplomacy, would have drawn the assignment if McGovern gave the matter much thought.

And that's what troubles us most: the lack of thought. It's the same sort of ill-thought-out improvisation which characterized the selection and discarding of Sen. Eagleton as McGovern's running mate. McGovern's staff did not inform itself about Eagleton *before* the nomination and it certainly hadn't considered the consequences of various public statements *after* the whole business was out. Now we have the same pattern with Salinger: the initial failure to consider the consequences; the weird disclosure of the mission by Salinger himself in New York; the initial denial by McGovern in Illinois, followed by confirmation; and then the naive rebuttal to White House criticism: in effect, if Kissinger can do it, Salinger can too.

The Eagleton and Salinger episodes suggest more naivete about the conduct of government than we'd have expected on McGovern's part, or else a serious deficiency among his top advisers, or perhaps some of both. McGovern should apply the necessary cure at once. In this campaign, the issues are too serious to be decided or diverted by amateurism and improvisation.

Des Moines Tribune
Des Moines, Iowa, August 22, 1972

President Nixon's aides are persisting in their efforts to refute Sargent Shriver's contention that the Administration missed a North Vietnamese "signal" for peace early in 1969. The latest statement also takes issue with peace negotiators W. Averell Harriman and Cyrus R. Vance who backed Shriver, the Democratic vice-presidential candidate.

Herbert G. Klein, Nixon's director of communications, sent newspaper editors a 13-page "evaluation paper" on the controversy.

The dispute centers on Shriver's statement that the North Vietnamese indicated a willingness to negotiate a peaceful settlement by withdrawing part of their forces from major combat areas late in 1968 after Nixon was elected. The Klein analysis concludes that there was "no peace opportunity, real or possible," either at that time or after Nixon's inauguration.

"The contentions that the North Vietnamese had withdrawn 90 per cent of their forces, either from all of South Vietnam (Shriver allegation), or only its northernmost provinces (Harriman and Vance allegation) and that this represented a peace signal are not substantiated by the facts," Klein's explanation asserts. "As for the size of the redeployment, our best estimates indicate the NVA (North Vietnamese Army) withdrawal was only about 50 per cent from the northernmost provinces and less than 20 per cent from South Vietnam as a whole."

Those statements brought Harriman back into the argument, accusing the Administration of misrepresenting what he said. In support of Shriver both Harriman and Vance said the North Vietnamese Army had withdrawn "almost 90 per cent of its troops — 22 to 25 regiments — from the northern two provinces, which had been the area of fierce fighting."

Harriman pointed out that the Administration paper omitted his reference to *two* provinces. He surmised that the Administration reference to a 50-per-cent withdrawal from the northern provinces is based on statistics from "all five provinces of I Corps, not the two provinces Vance and I were talking about." Harriman insisted he used the same figures consistently since 1969, and public records bear him out.

In the end, the significance of the North Vietnamese "signal" was a matter of judgment, as Harriman candidly admitted. He, Vance and Shriver felt it was worth pursuing. The Nixon Administration, whether it perceived the sign or not, did not. When future historians analyze the U.S. involvement in Vietnam, the story of the "signal" probably will be no more than a footnote.

So it is puzzling to see the Administration overreacting to a difference of opinion. Not every partisan argument brings forth lengthy Administration rebuttals from Klein. Nor did his work remove the Administration's credibility problem. Instead, Klein's report only re-emphasized how sensitive the Administration must feel about its failure to end the war, the big campaign promise of 1968.

ALBUQUERQUE JOURNAL
Albuquerque, N.M., August 18, 1972

We can't help being skeptical about recent statements by W. Averell Harriman that in 1969 he handed President Nixon a chance for successful peace negotiations "on a silver platter."

Our skepticism to a large extent is based upon the timing of Harriman's claims. Had the statement been made at an earlier time prior to the election campaign, it might have carried more weight.

Harriman was President Lyndon Johnson's chief delegate at the Paris Peace Talks. He claims now that by the time President Nixon took office in January, 1969, "all the procedural questions were settled which we thought made it possible to begin really serious negotiations. Unfortunately they never took place. President Thieu, I believe, consciously scuttled the negotiations."

Henry Cabot Lodge, the U.S. negotiator in Paris starting in 1969, disagrees with Harriman's contention. He said there was no golden opportunity for peace because North Vietnam maintained its position that the United States must depose of the Saigon regime and unilaterally withdraw.

The obvious conclusion is there was no such opportunity but it is politically expedient this election year to muddy the waters of President Nixon's efforts to end the war.

New York Post
New York, N.Y., August 19, 1972

In deciding to advertise Henry Kissinger's latest exercise in diplomacy, the Administration tacitly conceded that the Vietnam war remains a central issue of the 1972 campaign. Indeed, it is now revealed that the renewal of private talks with North Vietnam was conditioned on Hanoi's willingness to permit Washington to announce that the sessions were taking place (in contrast with the deep secrecy that so long enveloped many earlier meetings). The aggressive political postures of Defense Secretary Laird and — uncharacteristically — of Secretary of State Rogers have further emphasized the degree to which Mr. Nixon recognizes the hazard involved in prolongation of the war.

In that situation it is tragic when the McGovern camp ineptly invites diversionary dispute, as it has once again in Pierre Salinger's ill-conceived Paris adventure. Whatever purpose may have been intended—and that is obscured by contradictory statements from McGovern and Salinger—the spectacle of an emissary of an opposition candidate for President meeting with Hanoi representatives was bound to provoke serious questions as well as political polemic and even legal doubts. The discrepancy in the ensuing comments palpably undermined McGovern's credibility.

At the same time the controversy has once again distracted attention from what should be the heart of the matter — the dead-end U. S. commitment to the Thieu regime.

As McGovern has contended for many months, that is the crucial obstacle to peace. That is the reason for continued internment of American prisoners. That is why our planes are engaged in a monstrous, unremitting air war. And that is why all of Kissinger's travels will be meaningless unless the Administration has told Thieu that it is time to retire.

Anything said or done by McGovern or his spokesmen that clouds those basic propositions is not only a campaign blunder; it is a setback in the battle for peace to which McGovern long ago pledged his highest allegiance.

Campaign '72:
SEVEN INDICTED IN WATERGATE RAID; TRIAL OF DEMO CIVIL SUIT DELAYED

Seven persons, including two former White House aides, were indicted by a District of Columbia federal grand jury Sept. 15 on charges of conspiring to break into the Democratic national headquarters. [See pp. 1035–1041] The two former Nixon aides were: G. Gordon Liddy, a former presidential assistant on domestic affairs and, at the time of the headquarters raid June 17, counsel to the finance committee of the Committee to Re-elect the President; and E. Howard Hunt Jr., a former White House consultant and associate of Liddy. The other five indicted were those seized by police inside the Watergate office building during the raid. After the indictments were made public, a Justice Department spokesman said "we have absolutely no evidence to indicate that any others should be charged."

Lawrence F. O'Brien, who was Democratic national chairman at the time of the break-in, said Sept. 15 "we can only assume that the investigation will continue since the indictments handed down today reflect only the most narrow construction of the crime that was committed." The same day Democratic presidential nominee George McGovern called for "an impartial investigation conducted by somebody entirely outside the Department of Justice." In a statement Sept. 16, McGovern accused Nixon of ordering a "whitewash" and deplored the "questions left unanswered" by the grand jury, such as who had ordered and paid for the espionage attempt.

The trial of the civil suit brought by the Democrats against key officials of the Committee to Re-elect the President was delayed by U.S. Judge Charles R. Richey who said Sept. 21 "it will be impossible" to begin the trial before the Nov. 7 general election. Richey said he would extend his order barring depositions in the case until the persons under criminal indictment had been tried.

(Clark MacGregor, President Nixon's campaign director, had announced Sept. 13 that the Committee to Re-elect the President had filed a counter-suit in federal court seeking $2.5 million in damages from O'Brien. The suit accused O'Brien of having used the court "as a forum in which to publicize accusations against innocent persons which would be libelous if published elsewhere.")

THE CHRISTIAN SCIENCE MONITOR
Boston, Mass., September 16, 1972

The most suspicious thing about the whole Watergate affair is the effort of the Nixon administration to keep it under wraps until after election day.

When the Democrats brought a civil suit the Republicans moved for a postponement until after election day. When this failed they moved to have the case dismissed on technicalities.

Attorney General Richard Kleindienst promised "the most extensive, thorough, and comprehensive investigation since the assassination of President Kennedy." But he didn't say anything about when or how fast.

We can think of one legitimate argument against quick pursuit of the truth in this extraordinary matter. If any trial were under way now there would be daily news stories based on allegations and implications. The daily crop of headlines would help the Democrats and hurt the Republicans during the campaign. If it were discovered in the end that there had been nothing worse than excessive partisan zeal on the part of underlings it would then be too late to undo the unfair damage already done.

This is a point. But we think it overweighed by the appearance of an attempt to sweep it all under the rug.

If the Republicans were as innocent as they say they are they should seek the earliest and most complete vindication possible. The bald effort to avoid a speedy trial of the Watergate case compounds the bad appearance already produced by secrecy about that $10 million collected just before the new disclosure law went into effect.

Republicans are loud in their claims of innocence. If they are truly innocent they should not fear complete and full disclosure. Their failure to seek it puts them in an unfavorable light.

Honolulu Star-Bulletin
Honolulu, Hawaii, September 16, 1972

The Department of Justice will render an injustice to itself and to the people it serves if it moves with less than utmost speed and energy toward a solution of the bizarre Watergate affair.

Reports of a disposition within the department to let the case lie until after the November election are, if true, a reflection not only on the department but on the President himself. The Department of Justice is the chief law enforcement arm of the nation, and for it to refrain, deliberately, from imposing the law for purely political reasons cannot be condoned as anything less than scandalous.

The issue has become so obscured by political charges and counter-charges that its real nature is hard to see. Yet the facts are that (1) five men were caught redhanded "bugging" the Democratic party's national headquarters; (2) some of these men had close connections with the Republican party's Committee to Reelect the President; and (3) one of them, admitting his complicity in an interview with the New York Times, has inferentially accused others by saying he will never testify against them.

The President himself is the titular head of his party. He also, as President, is head of all the people of both parties. If the Republican party, or any of its offshoots, such as the Committee to Reelect the President, was involved in eavesdropping on the Democratic opposition, it should be revealed.

It simply is not good enough for the White House to remain silent and pretend it never happened. On the contrary, it is the responsibility of the White House, acting through the Justice Department, to find out what happened and, if such is indicated, to prosecute those involved, be they Republican or Democrat.

The News and Courier
Charleston, S.C., September 19, 1972

As might be expected, federal grand jury indictments in the Watergate caper won't satisfy George McGovern and his supporters. Nothing will do, it seems, but that top names in the Republican Party be linked by tangible evidence to the bugging operatives caught at Democratic headquarters.

By crying whitewash over the indictments, the Democrats are telling the public they have no intention of abandoning the Watergate affair. In fact, it appears they will continue to nurture it into the significant campaign issue they so desperately need.

For voters looking for excuses not to vote for Richard Nixon, the Democrats may be scoring points with their calculated effort to paint corruption all over the Nixon administration. Even staunch supporters of the President are considering these hearty hints of wrongdoing. Tip-offs on the Russian wheat deal, funny political money from Mexico and the Watergate affair itself suggest to the hesitant that the Nixon team is at least capable of wrongdoing.

It appears, however, that hanky-panky rhetoric spawned by the Democrats is merely affirming the public's already cynical view of national politics. Manipulation of campaign money like chess board pieces (sometimes under the board, too) and operations by party spies are no surprise. Many voters may have concluded by now that the idealistic McGovern legions would be up to the same tactics were they in charge.

As Democrats couch their prime campaign thrusts around negative issues, public opinion polls show Mr. Nixon's favor with voters holding steady or growing. Democrats in Congress apparently aren't banking on a big McGovern comeback, either. As a Page One story in The News and Courier Monday noted, many Democrats are eager to educate voters on ticket splitting procedures.

The cries from the McGovern camp, where "new politics" is supposed to be in vogue, are the old sounds of "outs" trying to get in. Having grown accustomed to it all, U.S. voters seem unmoved.

The Birmingham News
Birmingham, Ala., September 19, 1972

Whoever authorized the so-called Watergate Caper made a collossally damaging blunder and in time, presumably, wil have his hide nailed to the wall.

The incident of political esplonage was illegal, morally wrong and pragmatically stupid. The proof that it was stupid is that the culprits got caught—and now have been indicted—and getting caught is the worst blunder in that sort of dirty game.

Nevertheless, the Democrats have not been able to turn the campaign around on the single issue of bugging. The damaging attempt to gather Democratic secrets may have hurt the Republicans, but how much is hard to tell when the polls continue to show a 34 per cent gap between the President and his Democratic opponent.

Some observers say that even many traditionally Democratic voters shrug off The Caper, determined to cast a rare vote in the Republican column because of the vastly more important issues of substance in the campaign.

Perhaps the Democrats have hurt themselves somewhat in capitalizing on the embarrassment of the spying incident by being too gleeful in the first place that it happened and subsequently by being too shrill in day-after-day denunciations of the Republicans.

Certainly Democratic campaign leader Lawrence O'Brien went too far in accusing Republican campaigner Maurice Stans of a criminal act when no proof has been established that the charge is true.

Democrats, who have been critical enough of some Republicans for "rhetorical overkill" should themselves take a lesson.

When the offended party becomes so wild in its charges that its own credibility is rendered suspect, the average voter is tempted to dismiss the whole thing as another exercise in partianship. This is what seems to be happening in regard to the Watergate Caper.

In the final analysis, the election will be decided by the real issues. Those made apprehensive by the McGovern candidacy are not likely to vote for him because the Democratic headquarters was bugged, as reprehensible as that was.

The Virginian-Pilot
Norfolk, Va., September 18, 1972

On Friday a Federal grand jury returned indictments against seven men in the famous Watergate caper.

That is a beginning in getting to the truth of what appears to be a major political scandal. But it is only the beginning and the business is clouded with suspicions.

Indicted in Washington were the five men arrested on June 17 within the Democratic offices in the Watergate and two former White House aides, G. Gordon Liddy and E. Howard Hunt Jr., also implicated in the bugging of the Democrats' headquarters. The seven were charged variously with burglary, conspiracy, eavesdropping, and the possession of wiretaps.

The five men who were arrested in the Watergate are Bernard L. Barker, the alleged leader of the plot; James W. McCord Jr., who was on the payroll of the Committee for the Reelection of the President as security coordinator when he was caught by the police in the Watergate; Eugenio Martinez, Frank A. Sturgis, and Virgilio R. Gonzalez. All had been involved with the CIA and Cuban exiles in the past.

Liddy was fired as counsel to the Committee for the Reelection of the President 11 days after the arrests for refusing to answer FBI questions. He had served as an aide to the Treasury and the White House prior to taking the campaign job. Hunt, who had been on the White House payroll as a consultant earlier this year, dropped out of sight for several weeks after the affair broke in June.

Both Hunt and Liddy are charged with entering the Democratic headquarters on June 17 "with the intent to steal property of another," although they were not arrested with the other suspects. They are also accused of renting rooms under false names at an adjoining motel and intercepting telephone conversations over a period of three weeks. They are believed to be the first White House aides ever indicted.

There is no question that the suspects were engaged in systematic surveillance of the Democrats, since they were caught in the act on June 17. Apparently the bugging had gone on for some time.

Who was behind the bugging in the Watergate? Who was paying the bills? Those are questions to be answered yet.

Friday's indictments do not touch upon the $114,000 in campaign funds that have been traced to Barker's bank in Miami. He is charged in Florida with fraudulently notarizing a $25,000 campaign check when he had difficulty in cashing it. (The donor was a Democrat who has since been awarded a bank charter.) Four other Republican checks, totaling $89,000, were routed through a Mexican bank to Barker's bank in Florida. The General Accounting Office has cited the Republicans for 11 "apparent violations" of the election laws in the handling of the $114,000 in campaign funds traced to Barker and the mysterious $350,000 in cash kept in the safe of Maurice Stans, the chief fund-raiser for the Republicans.

It appears that the burglary and bugging at the Watergate was financed from the Republican treasury. The links to the Committee for the Reelection of the President are suspicious.

Besides Messrs. Hunt, Liddy, and McCord, the chairman of the Committee for the Reelection of the President, former Attorney General John Mitchell, and the committee treasurer, Hugh W. Sloan Jr., both resigned after the arrests in June for "personal reasons." The current GOP line is that no one now on the payroll had anything to do with the Watergate.

While it is conceivable that the bugging was a cloak-and-dagger operation undertaken without the knowledge of GOP higher-ups, it requires the willing suspension of disbelief to stick to that view. The Nixon Administration—and especially the Justice Department under Mr. Mitchell and his successor, Attorney General Kleindienst—hasn't been scrupulous about civil liberties. It has been eager to snoop upon a variety of alleged conspirators, protesters, and simple wrongdoers.

The business at the Watergate smells to high heaven.

OREGON JOURNAL

Portland, Ore., September 22, 1972

So far, Democrats do not seem to be getting the political clout they expected from the Watergate bugging incident and the reason probably lies in the public attitude toward politics.

It has been shrugged off as just another case of political wickedness. The people have not been aroused to outrage by one group of politicians invading the offices of another group.

But breaking into private quarters and using the devious devices of electronic surveillance to desecrate another's privacy is fully worthy of outrage. Were something other than a political party involved, the public reaction might be quite different.

At least it is to be hoped that electronic snooping into private lives is not gaining the acceptance of apathetic acquiescence.

Perhaps if the Democrats would change their approach to the issue they might achieve more success. Perhaps they could paint the Nixon administration as providing the kind of climate that encourages Big Brother to break into private quarters and to bug private lives, and then to expand the incident beyond the crime in their own headquarters and picture it as a threat to the home and privacy of all citizens. Perhaps then they would get their point across.

But regardless of political mileage, the Watergate caper should help to stir public reaction against the threat of unjustified invasion of personal privacy via the sophisticated gadgets of modern technology.

Partisans of President Nixon as well as those of Sen. McGovern should sound the alarm against unwarranted electronic spying.

Watergate is not simply an evil perpetrated by one party on another. It is a case of breaking and bugging and no one knows how many cases of illegal bugging it may represent.

But the public attitude ought not be allowed to be interpreted as surrendering to or not caring about being spied upon—by government, by private agencies or by fellow citizens. With the wiretap granted certain legal standing, and applied far beyond the confines of the law, the only way to keep the bugs off will be for the people of this country to keep the heat on.

THE SUN

Baltimore, Md., September 22, 1972

With only six and a half weeks remaining until election day, it is becoming steadily more doubtful that voters will know the essential facts in the Watergate case before they enter the polling booths. This is deplorable, not because the Democrats say it is in their efforts to help Senator McGovern. It is deplorable because the standards of legal and political morality, as perceived by members of President Nixon's re-election team, have been brought into question—and left hanging. Criminal indictments have indeed been brought against five men arrested on the premises of the Democratic National Committee last June 17 and against two former White House aides accused of assisting their alleged attempt to bug and burglarize the Watergate offices of the enemy. But neither the Federal grand jury nor the General Accounting Office of Congress has dealt adequately with the broader questions: Who authorized this disgraceful episode and the free-wheeling use of GOP campaign funds so intimately connected with it?

The defendants named in the criminal indictment and the accompanying civil suit lodged by the Democratic National Committee have legal rights that, of course, must be protected. Justice cannot be dispensed to conform to political timetables. But this cannot excuse high Republican spokesmen in their blustering attempts to protect those with ultimate responsibility for the Watergate operation. Funds under the control of Maurice Stans, former Secretary of Commerce, were involved. Personnel answerable to John Mitchell, former Attorney General, figured in the case. Procedures in violation of the spirit and perhaps the letter of new campaign-financing laws apparently were condoned at high level. These are matters of serious import that should be clarified before November 7. They can hardly be considered "third rate" (to quote a White House spokesman) or political skullduggery dismissible as normal campaign background noise.

Arkansas Gazette.

Little Rock, Ark., September 20, 1972

THE NIXON GANG has the nerve of burglars, as it appears from one of the most direct evidential forms there is—arrest on the burgled premises—some of the members actually are. It would have afforded some slight degree of comic relief in a most unfunny business, indeed, if the Watergate Five (which turns out now to have been the Watergate Seven), before being flushed in the wee hours at Democratic National Headquarters, had been asked who was there and then had managed to respond weakly, "Nobody here but us chickens." As it was, there wasn't time even for that much after-the-fact subterfuge.

Yet there was Mr. Nixon himself, possibly the nerviest of the lot, saying in his first and last remarks on the case that none of the several accused men with close links to the Committee to Re-elect the President or to the White House itself was on either payroll "at the present time." This meant only that Gordon Liddy, counsel to the Committee and former White House aide, had been fired *after* he had been implicated in the Watergate scandal and had refused to answer such questions as the FBI was asking in the matter, and that the others, including, notably, the "chief of security" for the Committee, had severed for reasons of their own earlier, whether as a conscious prelude to the act of political espionage we may or may not ever be allowed to learn.

Mr. Nixon, delivering his defense and disclaimer, was as cool as he must have been on the famous occasion when he crawled through the transom at Duke to find out his test grades. He probably would have liked to lead the Watergate raid himself, and might have, had it not been for an exaggerated sense of the dignity of the office that he has come to honor only after being elected to it himself. The careful qualifier, "at the present time," apparently sailed over the heads of lot of Mr. Nixon's auditors at the August 29 news conference at San Clemente—or at least was taken at face value along with the rest of the statement, rather than being singled out for the attention it deserved—and that was supposed to put an end to the matter, which we now were supposed to believe was nothing more than a tempest in a teapot, really, much ado about nothing.

IT HAS REMAINED for Chairman Dole—who, if Nixon isn't the nerviest of the lot, surely must be—to seize upon the occasion of the formal federal indictments against the Watergate Seven to demand that the Democrats "apologize" to the Republicans for continuing to dwell on the subject. Not content with that, the chief highbinder of the GOP National Committee, demanded that the Democrats apologize to the *American people*. The Chairman stopped short of demanding that the Democrats apologize for having a national headquarters there to be broken into, pitifully financed though it may be in comparison with the operation run by Chairman Dole himself.

We suppose the Democrats could just have refrained from reporting the break-in, and thereby saved themselves from the necessity of apologizing for anything, but in that case, the Republicans might have accused them of failing to co-operate with the program by which (as is well known) the President has succeeded in sharply reducing the crime rate in the Federal District. "Might have," but we rather suspect wouldn't have, though the temptation to indulge in this final feat of nerviness no doubt would have been great. But since the Democrats *did* make the crime known —or, rather, since the non-partisan security guards they had retained for the purpose made the crime known, there was nothing to do but for the old piano player in the White House to play the thing down—"*Pianissimo*, everybody!" —for everyone else in the official Republican family to take his cue accordingly.

Thus, the Republicans have done everything they could to try to insure that the Democrats' civil suit over the Watergate goings-on is not brought to trial before the election. The federal criminal case, which we can be assured will not be brought to trial until after the election, Attorney General Kleindienst has represented as the fruit of one of the most thorough criminal investigations of modern times. We rather doubt this, but the air of finality with which Mr. Kleindienst has foreclosed on any further indictments certainly was about as an abrupt such cut-off as you are likely to see, anytime anywhere.

THE LINCOLN STAR
Lincoln, Neb.
September 23, 1972

If it were possible, the best and cleanest way to resolve the disputes surrounding the bugging of Democratic National Headquarters and the campaign financing practices of both political parties would be to fully investigate the complaints now and have the courts dispose of the cases quickly so that the people would know before the election who the culprits are.

But we are backed up against the election time-wise and so the complaints are being swept under the rug — necessarily.

Complaining that this is "a time of very intense political activity," Attorney Gen. Richard Kleindienst indicated that the Justice Department would probably delay its investigation of campaign financing violations until "it's all over in November," so as to avoid a "whitewash." And a federal judge this week halted further proceedings in the civil suits stemming from the Watergate caper until the criminal trials are concluded — meaning, in effect, that legal conclusions will not be available for the voters' edification.

The establishing of guilt might have made a blockbuster impact redounding to the Democrats' favor. But time was on the Republicans' side, if they had anything to hide. Prosecutions which are rushed, like the judge said, are fair neither to the defendants nor the public.

What remains before the election, however, will not be particularly noble or edifying. Accusations and counter-accusations will fly, mingled with only a smattering of evidence and no proof.

That dispassionate investigation and review which is needed — if it can be had — cannot possibly come before the election, the investigators, judges and prosecutors say, because of the relentless turn of the calendar.

With respect to our system of justice, we wish it no other way. There is the gnawing feeling, however, that the President's campaign organization has gotten away with something through outrageous luck.

The Philadelphia Inquirer
Philadelphia, Pa., September 22, 1972

A law professor at George Washington University has asked the federal courts to appoint a special prosecutor to investigate the attempted bugging of Democratic national headquarters at the Watergate last June and the links of the suspects with the White House and the President's re-election campaign.

John F. Banzhaf 3d charges that former Democratic National Chairman Lawrence F. O'Brien, who along with other Democrats has been calling for an outside impartial investigation of this extraordinary affair, would rather have the political issue than the special prosecutor.

We do not know how successful Mr. Banzhaf's legal manuever is likely to be. Neither do we know whether he is right about Mr. O'Brien.

We do know that the Democrats are enjoying the discomfiture of the Republicans and making the most of it. We also know that the Republican administration has refused to appoint an outside investigator, and we doubt that the Republicans are working hand-in-glove with Mr. O'Brien and other Democrats.

★ ★ ★

Instead, the White House has conducted its own investigation and assures us that it has found no one now on the staff or now in the administration who was involved.

And the Justice Department—headed, of course, by a Republican Attorney General, Richard G. Kleindienst—has conducted its own investigation, resulting in the indictment of the five men who were captured inside the Democratic headquarters, plus two former White House aides.

A Justice Department spokesman also assures us that that wraps it up: "We have absolutely no evidence to indicate that others should be charged."

Having "absolutely no evidence" does not mean that it must exist, but neither does it mean that it has been sought assiduously. There are just too many unanswered questions in this bizarre business, beginning with the question of whether any administration can be relied upon to pursue an objective, thorough investigation of itself.

★ ★ ★

Without going into all the ramifications of the Watergate affair, certain facts have been confirmed. We know that Republican fund-raisers collected some $10 million from sources they will not reveal. We know that substantial sums were sent to Mexico, but not for the sunlight, and returned to Washington. We know that some of this money passed through the hands of GOP finance chairman Maurice H. Stans and somehow landed in the bank account of one of the men indicted, and we know that Mr. Stans' stories about how this happened have been self-contradictory and contradicted by others.

We also know that Mr. Stans had a safe stuffed with campaign funds amounting to about $300,000. It is now reported that three GOP campaign officials, all former White House aides (one of them indicted), tapped that cache for purposes unknown, and that records of who had access to Mr. Stans' safe and what they did with the money were destroyed after the Watergate break-in.

Now Vice President Spiro T. Agnew has advanced his "personal theory" that "Someone set up these people to have them get caught ... to embarrass the Republican Party."

That is a bit hard to accept. What we need are not such far-fetched personal theories but facts, and the best way to try to get them all is through an impartial investigation.

The TENNESSEAN
Nashville, Tenn., September 22, 1972

THE seven men who were indicted in the Watergate break-in of Democratic headquarters have pleaded innocent to the charges, which is what the administration has been pleading all along.

★ ★ ★

The Republicans have steadfastly denied that any men of "senior status" were involved in the case of political espionage, even though two former White House aides were indicted along with the five men arrested at the scene.

The great, unanswered question is who gave the five the "go-ahead" and provided the financing for the Watergate caper. Even campaign organizations rolling in money are not noted for dispensing large amounts of cash to underlings who can use it as they see fit.

It is obvious that Mr. Maurice Stans had a personal knowledge of the checks amounting to $89,000 which ended up in the bank account of one of the men indicted in the case. He first denied, both publicly and privately, that he knew anything about the money.

The funds in question came from Texas businessmen who funneled them through an intermediary in Mexico to keep it from being known.

Subsequent and detailed testimony by Mr. William Liedtke, a leading money raiser for Mr. Nixon in Texas, disclosed that he had Mr. Stans' approval to include the Mexican funds in a batch of cash, checks and securities in the amount of $700,000 that was transmitted to Mr. Stans on April 5.

It is, of course, illegal for foreign nationals to contribute money to U.S. political campaigns, even if they are acting as a middle man in simply transferring funds on. But the illegality of the situation apparently didn't impress Mr. Stans much—and still doesn't.

However, Mr. Liedtke's testimony did refresh Mr. Stans' memory a bit and he admitted that he was aware the money came from Mexico.

The next unanswered question is how the money that Mr. Stans knew about ended up in the bank account of Mr. Bernard Barker, one of those arrested in the Watergate case.

It is evident the Republicans hope—and it has so turned out—that the seven men indicted will not be brought to trial before the elections and that, in any case, they will refuse to implicate anyone else in the Watergate case.

★ ★ ★

Maybe the whole thing can be pushed out of the limelight long enough for the public to forget it temporarily, but it is doubtful. Behind the curtain the White House has drawn between itself and the indicted men is a smell of political corruption that rises to high heaven.

THE INDIANAPOLIS NEWS
Indianapolis, Ind.
September 27, 1972

While the courts of law will determine the individual guilt or innocence of the men indicted for breaking into Democratic headquarters at Washington's Watergate complex, the larger implications of the deed are obvious enough on the face of it.

One does not have to presume the truth of campaign suggestions that higher-ups in the administration knew about or encouraged the Watergate break-in to realize the episode is symptomatic of an unhealthy climate in the nation's capital. When this many people with ties to the Committee for the Re-Election of the President and/or the official apparatus of government are involved in such an affair, full-scale investigation is obviously required.

We would add only that such scandalous goings-on are not distinctive of either party, and we recall that there were documented instances of bugging and break-in during preceding Democratic administrations as well. What we confront, all too obviously, is a growing atmosphere in which wiretaps, bugs, and intrusions upon personal privacy are becoming standard operating procedure.

That anyone would think it advisable to bug the headquarters of the Democrats in this particular election year suggests just how standard the procedure is. Why anyone would want to engage in such a bugging operation, or what anyone could possibly derive from such an enterprise, is a mystery to us. By all accounts, the Republican national ticket is home-free in this election, and the idea that its interests could possibly be served by tapping "inside" data at the disorganized McGovern headquarters is faintly ludicrous.

Despite general distaste for such activities it appears that Democratic efforts to turn the Watergate caper into a burning issue of the election have not succeeded. In the weeks that all this controversy has gone on, President Nixon's popularity ratings have continued to soar and McGovern's have continued to sink. This, too, fits past experience. We recall that in 1964 the national flap over the Jenkins case and other skeletons in the Democratic closet did little or nothing to impair the image of President Johnson.

The truth seems to be that the public makes up its mind about political candidates on deeper, visceral questions, and that issues of scandal like Jenkins or Watergate can do little to deflect such massive tides of opinion.

The Washington Post
Washington, D.C., September 25, 1972

There is something to be said for corruption. It stinks. No matter how many lids you try to put on it, the stench will out. And that is what is happening with respect to the financial manipulations and related espionage activities involved in the effort to re-elect Richard Nixon, despite the best efforts of the administration and the Nixon campaign committee to stuff more lids onto the mess.

Without being dreary about it, we know there was burglary at the Democratic Party's headquarters in the Watergate—breaking and entering for the purpose of committing a crime. We know there was bugging equipment on the premises for electronic eavesdropping. We know there was tapping of telephone lines. We know there was $700,000 stuffed into a suitcase and rushed to the Nixon campaign headquarters just before the deadline for reporting on campaign donations—and we know there was a shift in the position on milk price supports favoring dairy farmers just after receipt of some hefty contributions from associations of dairy farmers. We know there was a slush fund in Mr. Stans' safe. We know that some of the money intended for the President's campaign ended up in the bank account of one of the men arrested at the Democrats' headquarters. We know that some of the President's money was "laundered" by having checks from contributors deposited in a bank in Mexico from which nice, clean cash could then be withdrawn. We know there was a $10 million secret campaign fund and we know that one $25,000 donor got a federal bank charter a good deal faster than most people do. And we know, finally, that all this was done on behalf of the effort to re-elect the President of the United States.

But what do we hear from the President, his administration, and his high campaign advisers? First, we hear some scoffing from his campaign chief, Mr. John Mitchell . . . then a resignation . . . then, nothing. Next, from Mr. Maurice Stans, the financial chief of the Nixon campaign, we hear background promises of a perfectly "logical" explanation . . . and then silence except for vague denials when he was cornered in what Mike Wallace called the "dark reaches" of the convention hall in Miami Beach. In the civil suit brought by the Democrats, the Nixon committee and its representatives have done everything they could to make sure that the depositions being taken, which might shed some light on the whole affair, be sealed from public view and, indeed, be put off until after the election. In the criminal action, we are told that we can be told very little because of the administration's delicate sensibilities concerning the defendants civil liberties. This is the same administration which was perfectly prepared to try the brothers Berrigan in the newspapers before any grand jury was ever convened, and this is the same President who found Charles Manson guilty in advance of his trial and intervened to hold out the possibility of clemency for Lt. Calley while his case awaited review. And, now it turns out that the judge in the civil suit—a man who freely admits that he owes his position on the bench to the friendly intervention of the Vice President of the United States—has determined that the depositions cannot be taken until after the trial of the criminal action, an event which probably will not take place until after the election.

Meanwhile, the administration in whose behalf these various acts were being committed urges us to trust it and its investigations. We are assured that before his fairly precipitous departure, Mr. Mitchell conducted an investigation and that he found that everything was fine. Yet we are given no documentation. We are told that the White House counsel, Mr. John Dean, conducted an investigation in which he assured himself and the President that no one *presently employed* in the administration was involved in the burglaries and the electronic surveillance. But when asked about it on the Public Broadcasting network by Elizabeth Drew, Mr. John Ehrlichman of the White House conceded that Mr. Dean's investigation "didn't go beyond the government"—to the question of Mr. Mitchell's role, for example, or that of Mr. Stans. Mr. Ehrlichman said that the investigation was "satisfactory to us" but that it did not tell who ordered the surveillance and that even after the "satisfactory" investigation, Mr. Ehrlichman didn't know who ordered it.

And then, there is Mr. Kleindienst. He is fairly sure that the investigation into the matter by the FBI is the most thorough conducted since the investigation into the murder of President Kennedy. Yet, when queried by the same persistent Mrs. Drew about reports that important documents had been destroyed at the Nixon campaign committee just after news of the Watergate break-in, Mr. Kleindienst allowed as how he hadn't known of that. He also seemed vague about the connection of that matter with a criminal investigation until Mrs. Drew suggested that there might be an issue of obstructing justice.

And now comes Henry Peterson, head of the Justice Department's Criminal Division—in charge of the investigation—guessing that "the jail doors will close behind" the suspects before the real motivation for the Watergate break-in is ever discovered.

So, those are the investigations that are supposed to put our minds to rest.

And after that, there is the Republican rhetoric. Mr. MacGregor says that all of this will redound to the President's political credit. Mr. Mitchell, in one of his infrequent lapses into public utterance, has said that he doesn't see how this has hurt the President in the polls—as if it were merely a matter of public opinion rather than an issue that goes to the heart of the integrity of our electoral process and of our elected officials. And Mr. Agnew says in one breath that the Watergate burglary may just have been—yes—a frame-up by the Democrats to embarrass the Republicans and in the next that the Democrats are trying to make the wheat scandal into "another Watergate."

Well, if this whole thing is so good for the Republicans and if their investigations show them to be as clean as they say, why don't they tell us all? Who ordered the burglary? Who ordered the tapping? Who ordered the bugging? Who had control of Mr. Stans' safe? Who had access to it? Who were the contributors to the $10 million secret fund and what were they promised? What do the reports to Mr. Mitchell and the report to Mr. Dean really say? What is Mr. Stans' "logical explanation" of the hundreds of thousands of dollars of money laundered in a bank in Mexico? Were the secret fund books destroyed? And if so, who destroyed them?

Why don't they talk to us about these things instead of hurling around charges of "frame-up" without any supporting evidence? Until they do, the suspicion can only grow that their reason for keeping silent is that the whole thing stinks.

Portland Press Herald
Portland, Me., September 26, 1972

The importance the average American assigns to the Watergate Caper is likely to be determined more by political party affiliation than by moral standard.

Democrats are making the most of it, understandably. Republicans are playing it down, blaming the press for inflating the issue. It is not difficult to share Vice President Agnew's suspicion that the whole thing may have been an attempt to embarrass the GOP rather than a Republican plot to spy on Democratic Headquarters. After all, if the phone tapping had been completely successful there was not much to be learned by the eavesdropping. If it was an attempt to embarrass the Republicans, it succeeded.

But there is little reason now to expect it to be more than an embarrassment. It is impossible to believe that either President Nixon or Vice President Agnew could have had knowledge of such a thing. Secondly, the contemporary custom is to pay tribute to people for violation of trust, for breach of confidence. Industrial espionage is taken as a matter of course.

Daniel Ellsberg was applauded by many for the papers which never did reveal as much as they were expected to convey. It would come as no surprise to know that some who commended Ellsberg for his action are now outraged, or professing to be, over the Watergate allegations.

A United States senator from Alaska seemed to take pride in using his senatorial privilege to bypass legal restrictions and make portions of those documents public while the courts were still deliberating the matter.

The New York Times received those purloined papers and released the content. It got a Pulitzer Prize for its labor.

Using information from confidential conversations and private files, that somehow made its way into his possession, columnist Jack Anderson initiated the ITT probe. The effect of the revelation obscured any question as to how he obtained the information. Later, he revealed the nature of executive sessions on the short India-Pakistan war. The propriety of invasion of such sessions once would have been a matter of gravest concern. Anderson got a Pulitzer Prize.

The allegation of unethical conduct doesn't carry great weight any more.

Campaign '72:

SEPTEMBER OPINION POLLS SHOW NIXON FAR AHEAD OF McGOVERN

President Nixon held a 28-point lead over Sen. George McGovern in a Louis Harris poll released Sept. 25 (interviewing conducted Sept. 19–21). The 59%–31% survey findings indicated a six-point gain for McGovern over the Harris poll released Sept. 14, which reported Nixon was favored 59%–25% with 16% undecided. The same 24-point spread was reported at the time by the Gallup poll. A poll conducted for the *New York Times* by Daniel Yankelovich, Inc. and published Sept. 25 reported Nixon was leading McGovern by a 62%–23% margin in the 16 states accounting for two-thirds of the electoral vote.

After the release of the Times-Yankelovich finding, the McGovern organization released its own private sampling of public opinion that showed McGovern trailing by 22 points.

George Gallup and Louis Harris both testified before a House panel Sept. 19 on a proposed "truth-in-polling" bill. Gallup said McGovern had as good a chance of closing the Nixon lead as he did in winning the primaries. But Harris said "history is against" an upset by McGovern.

Reporting the results of a special poll, Gallup had said Sept. 10 that Nixon was favored over McGovern by a 61%–36% margin among voters under 30 years of age.

Oklahoma City Times
Oklahoma City, Okla., September 25, 1972

POLITICAL preference polls have one built-in disadvantage. They record only what the political leanings of those polled were during a recent but past period of time. They do not indicate much about what those same voters will do several weeks from now, as a number of poll-takers have learned to their chagrin in earlier election years.

The polls do have influences, however, and must be taken seriously. For one thing, as a spokesman for the Democratic National Committee said last week, they influence those who are deciding whether to donate money. Few big givers want to pour money into a losing race. On the other hand, a contributor who has been holding back may come across with a large sum if he feels that it may make the difference between victory and loss for his favorite candidate or party.

CANDIDATES, too, are influenced by these readings which purport to tell them how they are doing. The candidate who finds himself on the losing end of poll after poll may become discouraged and quit fighting for his point of view or principles. Or he may react to that same situation by becoming desperate, and lash out wildly making unfounded charges, alienating supporters of whom he has become distrustful. More than one candidate in the past has gone down in a cloud of brash promises that discredited him with the very voters he sought to win over, because of his irritation by the poll-takers.

And a series of favorable polls can be just as fatal to a leading candidate. His supporters fall away, deciding that he is so far ahead that he no longer needs money to finance travel, campaign headquarters, or advertising. On election day, many of them do not trouble to go to the election booths, because the only thing in doubt is the margin of his victory. As former Gov. Dewey Bartlett can attest, that kind of over-confidence can cost the election. Bartlett lost to the present governor, David Hall, by a margin of less than one vote per precinct.

IT is not only in elections, of course, that Americans tend to drop interest when they decide the outcome of a contest is already decided. At any football game during which one team piles up a marked lead, thousands of fans can be seen leaving the stadium during the third quarter. In football, it is merely a discourtesy to the losing team. In politics, it can change the outcome of the contest.

The situation today is almost without precedent, but only because of the wide margin separating the candidates in the polls. Those taken in areas in which McGovern expected his strongest support are not much different from those taken in "Nixon country," where the President was known to be the favorite. In most of the polls, McGovern ranks with "Undecided."

BUT all of the ingredients of a political upset are still present. Nixon backers may still repeat the patterns set by Dewey supporters in 1948, or by the Oklahomans who thought Gov. Bartlett's re-election was assured in 1970. By sitting on their hands, they could still elect the man they profess to fear and despise, Sen. McGovern.

Our history is full of examples which prove the cost of over-confidence in the political process. And Santayana quoted for us the price of ignoring the lessons of history.

Tulsa Daily World
Tulsa, Okla., September 21, 1972

WHEN opinion polls were favorable, LYNDON JOHNSON used to carry the figures around in his pocket to show everyone he met. To him, a high Gallup rating was final proof of the wisdom of his policies.

GEORGE MCGOVERN, faced with low ratings, sees the polls as worthless—or worse.

In truth, the surveys are neither omniscient nor meaningless. They are an interesting, sometimes fairly accurate means of measuring trends in public opinion.

In that light, we see no reason why they should be regulated by Federal law, as advocated by Rep. LUCIEN NEDZI, D-Mich.

It's true that polls can sometimes be used to deceive. And there is a measurable "bandwagon effect" in politics that tends to help a candidate who can convince voters he is the sure winner.

To suggest, however, that the public needs special Federal "protection" from polls is to tag the public as pretty stupid.

Where there is a bandwagon effect, it may be offset by people who tend to sympathize with the underdog. Most voters, we suspect, pick the candidate they believe to be best for a number of reasons, with little regard to his standing in the opinion polls.

But if an individual wants to vote for a candidate because he thinks that candidate is a winner or because he is an underdog, that's the voter's own business. He might make a bad choice, it's true, but that's what free elections are all about.

THE CHRISTIAN SCIENCE MONITOR
Boston, Mass., September 18, 1972

The significant fact about the presidential race is Mr. Nixon's overwhelming edge.

The latest Harris poll has the incumbent ahead of his rival by a 63 to 29 percent margin. The latest Gallup poll also showed a 34 percent lead, 64-30. This lead holds up in almost every important category of voter. By sex, where Mr. Nixon had scored less well among women voters, he now maintains his 63-29 percent lead. Among under-30 voters, he leads George McGovern by 52-42 percent. He leads among trade union members by a surprising 56-34 percent. Another traditionally Democratic category, the Roman Catholic vote, has reversed a 2 percent McGovern lead in May to a 62-27 percent Nixon margin.

But this powerful Nixon lead in the polls, greater even than the edge Lyndon Johnson held over Barry Goldwater in 1964, means both less and as much as it appears to mean.

Obviously it gives Mr. Nixon a margin that can hardly be closed in the six or seven weeks that remain in the campaign. In May Mr. McGovern had a far smaller handicap, a seven-point poll spread. But even though Mr. McGovern will surely recover at some stage in the remaining days of the campaign, it will be a matter of too little too late.

Still, a Republican win, even by a landslide, will also mean less than Republicans might hope.

If one thinks back to the Johnson landslide of 1964, and how the Democrats came apart at the seams by 1968, a landslide in 1972 does not necessarily signify a shift to Republicanism in the population. The cold fact is that the characteristic American voter is now the independent, not the party-bound voter. And this group, more easily won over by centrist policies, is also more quickly lost.

The Nixon strength also does not show the decisively conservative swing in the electorate that many have been claiming is under way. If by conservatism one means a desire for social stability, for less adventurous commitment abroad, then one can say there is a yearning to ease up and consolidate, which are "conservative" characteristics.

But what about in economics? Are not wage and price controls, and a Congress edging toward a revolutionary income maintenance program submitted by the White House, distinctly "liberal" oriented?

True, in such social issues as busing and open housing many voters are calling for a halt. But even this must be seen as a reaction to the dominantly liberal desegregation trend of the past two decades, which is still occurring.

In foreign affairs, can a United States which is on speaking and trading terms with the two Communist powers, China and the Soviet Union, be said to be on a "conservative" course?

What has happened in the past four years is that the center of the American voting public has continued its slow progressive shift. Mr. Nixon has made certain bold moves, to be sure: his Moscow and Peking openings, the wage-price freeze. But he appears to have been careful to move only when assured the majority of voters would confirm the sensibleness of what he had done.

Whether one agrees with every zig or zag or standing pat of Mr. Nixon, one cannot argue that he has not shown a sensitivity to the pace of change which the public will tolerate. In contrast, the McGovern image is that the departures for the country may be too sudden. This may be an unfair rap for the Senator from South Dakota. But it's the image he's been stuck with.

Looking ahead then, if Mr. Nixon is reelected, even a landslide margin will not necessarily indicate a downhill course through the next four years in office. The American electorate is fluid. If it is touch and go with inflation again, if there is any backsliding from such progressive legislation as environmental control and welfare reform and medical cost reduction, a sane and prudent-sounding Democrat can reverse this November's Republican advantage, come 1976.

The New York Times
New York, N.Y., September 22, 1972

Faced with the beauty of seeming numerical precision, it is once again the season to spread the reminder that political polls are not elections.

Both the large national polling organizations, Harris and Gallup, are now assigning President Nixon a stunning 34 per cent lead over Senator McGovern, and too many loyalists in both camps are acting as if the outcome of the election is no longer in doubt. It was important, therefore, to have Dr. Gallup's caveat that there is "still plenty of time" for changes of voters' attitudes. Mr. Harris, on the contrary, argued that "history is against" Senator McGovern's overcoming this kind of gap by November, but he too noted that "anything can happen—we're living in a highly volatile period."

The art of political polling has gained a strategic place in the campaigning process without sufficiently widespread understanding of its limitations. While such major organizations as Gallup and Harris have built up a deserved reputation for integrity, there is no doubt that polling is a field with more than its share of fly-by-night "experts" and downright charlatans. Hearings are now under way in a House Administration subcommittee on a bill to require full disclosure of polling methods along with any published results. Whether formal legislation is the way to do it or not, there is ample need for more effective policing, or self-policing, of the pollsters.

No intelligent judgment about any poll results can be made without knowing how big the sample was, when the questions were asked, exactly what they were and, most important, who paid for the poll — an independent organization or a partisan interest.

Reinforced with information such as this, political polls have legitimate value for reflecting, within a specified margin of error, public attitudes at the given moment. That is all. The campaign now could well be threatened by the myth that the polls should be treated as inspired prophecies. They aren't.

© 1972 by The New York Times Company. Reprinted by permission.

THE BLADE
Toledo, Ohio, September 22, 1972

However much he may have been simply trying to rationalize through scapegoatism the ineptitude of his own campaign, Democratic presidential nominee George McGovern expressed one view we long have held when he characterized public opinion polls as "a lot of rubbish." And, as a matter of fact, he has been getting no little support—albeit unintended—from some of the opinion-mongers themselves testifying at House subcommittee hearings on whether political polls affect the outcome of elections.

Two of the biggest names in the business appeared the other day, for instance, and discussed among other things whether Mr. McGovern might close the gap indicated by their surveys between him and President Nixon. George Gallup said there is "still plenty of time" and the senator has as good a chance of catching up as he did in winning key primaries last spring—which would mean a pretty good chance. Louis Harris, on the other hand, suggested it is getting late and said "history is against" Mr. McGovern's coming from behind at this point. If that contradiction is an example of the supposed scientific exactitude of the leading pollsters, it is easy to understand why the reliability of their "findings" on almost any subject should be subjected to considerable skepticism.

Perhaps the ultimate "rubbish" offered in behalf of the polls, however, came from a witness bearing the impressive title of director of social research for the Columbia Broadcasting System. Any defense he made of polling would, of course, have to be taken with a grain of salt to start with just because he represents an industry which conducts most of its operations according to surveys. But beyond that, he sought to support his contention that voters are not influenced by polls with, of all things, a poll done by an opinion research outfit. The gist of it, apparently, was that there was little or no relationship between what those surveyed knew about pre-election polls and how they actually voted. Did the so-called researchers really think the voters would have admitted it if they had been so influenced?

That is, obviously, one of the fundamental difficulties in polling. How does one determine whether the respondent is giving an utterly honest answer or one that he thinks will sound most impressive or one deliberately designed to veil true feelings he wants to keep to himself? How does the questioner tell whether his interviewee may be answering knowledgeably or covering up his lack of knowledge? And how can the pollster measure the depth or intensity of conviction to know whether an answer perhaps quite honestly given at one moment will stand up or be quickly changed the next moment because of some new information or development?

Citing a poll to gloss over these basic problems with polling is typical of the pseudo-scientific hogwash the self-styled opinion research people deal in. Not the least of dangerous influences they can have on elections or other aspects of public policy is simply that they expect to be—and in too many instances actually are—taken seriously.

CHICAGO DAILY NEWS
Chicago, Ill., September 29, 1972

If one thing was considered a lead-pipe cinch at the campaign's outset, it was that the nation's young people were behind George McGovern. They "dug" him and they liked what he stood for.

Now come Time magazine and Dr. George Gallup with surveys showing President Nixon the substantial favorite of young voters. Time's Yankelovich poll (Aug. 13-Sept. 12) gives the President a 46 to 43 per cent edge in the 18-to-24-year group. Gallup, polling in late August, showed President Nixon favored by 61 per cent of the registered voters under 30, with 36 per cent for McGovern.

While five and a half weeks remain before the election and the sentiments of young people can change fast and far, it still must come as a shock to the McGovernites who had counted on the youth vote being well in hand.

And so it had seemed a few weeks earlier to the pollsters, themselves. Yankelovich found that Nixon's position among the 18-24s had improved 8 per cent in a month. An early August Gallup poll had shown Sen. McGovern leading Mr. Nixon 48 per cent to 41 per cent in the under-30 age group.

What happened, quite obviously, was that a great many of the young idealists who had plugged for McGovern all through his spectacular campaign in the primaries changed their minds during and just after the Democratic convention.

"McGovern lost my vote and a lot of others by turning down (Sen. Thomas) Eagleton," a 21-year-old woman told Georgie Anne Geyer, sounding youth opinion in Illinois for The Daily News. And a 19-year-old Californian told surveyors for U.S. News & World Report: "I think it's a bloody shame what they did to Eagleton." It was a widely shared sentiment.

Along with the dumping of Eagleton came McGovern's retreat from previously held positions on major issues such as economics and defense funds. If McGovern backed away from his $1,000-for-everybody welfare plan and his drastic defense cuts out of fear of alienating "middle" voters, he is now discovering that these very positions helped create his "pure" image with a lot of young people. Projecting her Illinois findings nationwide, Miss Geyer estimated that "a sizable group of 18-to-24-year-olds are political purists on a scale not seen in this country since the Progressive movement early this century." Some young purists still cling to McGovern and proclaim his honesty and trustworthiness. Others have felt personally aggrieved by his position shifts, and dropped him.

The significance of the shift away from McGovern and to Mr. Nixon is considerable in view of the fact that there are almost 26 million new potential voters for this election in the 18-to-24-year age group — more than 18 per cent of the total eligible to vote. It could turn out that McGovern, in shifting to a more moderate stance, gave up more than he gained.

The Evening Star
Washington, D.C., September 26, 1972

Along with his other troubles, and no doubt contributing to them, George McGovern must bear the increasing burden of the public opinion polls.

The latest batch of these surveys spells out a tale of appalling woe for the McGovern camp. The statistics are almost beyond belief. President Nixon appears to be leading his opponent in every corner of the country, and among all social groups, income classes and ages, even the young. If the most recent New York Times-Yankelovitch poll can be believed, Mr. Nixon is even ahead among registered Democrats in the nation's 16 largest states.

McGovern and his staff, of course, would prefer not to believe the polls. Quite naturally, they are playing them down as unreliable. The fact is that, with the obvious qualification that voter sentiment can change, and may well change in the weeks before the election, these surveys are quite reliable.

The pollsters have come a long way since the time when the Literary Digest questioned a wholly unrepresentative segment of the populace and, on the basis of that, predicted Alf Landon would beat Franklin Roosevelt in the 1936 presidential race. Voter samples are now selected in a more scientific way. Margins of error are accounted for. If the sampling is small, these margins can be sizable. But they are never so large as to offset the kind of lead — 30 to 40 percentage points — that all the major polls have shown Mr. Nixon is enjoying.

It is the very reliability of polls, in fact, that is troubling many people about the whole business. For the month-by-month publication of voter opinion cannot help but have a direct influence on political campaigns and how they are run.

Probably it is true, as George Gallup and Louis Harris told a congressional subcommittee last week, that survey results do not create bandwagon effects. It is equally unlikely that, simply on the basis of polling figures, many voters would switch from the front-runner to the underdog. But any figures that show a candidate as far behind as McGovern appears to be are certain to have a depressing effect on those who might otherwise work hard for the candidate or help finance his campaign. In a presidential race, that can make a great deal of difference.

It is a problem with no solution in sight. Polls are with us to stay. They have a value, but like many another modern device, they can exact a price. This year, in morale, volunteer support, allegiance of party regulars and financing, the McGovern camp is no doubt paying a very big price every time a new set of survey figures hits the street. Perhaps the next polling go-round will show the senator has really "bottomed out" and is beginning to narrow the gap. But the turnaround would have to be dramatic to start undoing the damage.

The Hartford Courant
Hartford, Conn., September 26, 1972

In the four decades since the old Literary Digest fell flat on its face by predicting the re-election of Herbert Hoover on the strength of a straw vote it conducted among its readers, public opinion surveys have come a long way. When they are conducted by reputable professionals, experience has shown, they give a reasonably reliable cross section of the public state of mind at any given time. But as the dean of the American pollsters, Dr. George Gallup, was careful to point out in his latest report, the opinion surveys at this point in the game predict nothing about what will happen on election day.

"Polls can report sentiment only as of the time they are taken," Dr. Gallup emphasized. "They are a 'snapshot' of opinion as of the time of interviewing. By providing several readings during the course of a campaign, polls can chart the trend of sentiment — they can reflect the public's views only as of a given time."

Just how accurate are the polls even within the framework that Dr. Gallup insists on? Is a random sampling of a few hundred people an accurate reading of public opinion? Reputable professionals concede a built-in margin of error, depending on the size of the sample, beginning at about 2 per cent. Since there is always a time-lag between asking the questions and the publication of the polls — we are only now getting early September's results — it is impossible to know how a constituency would actually have voted on the day it was polled. And we do know that horrendous errors are possible. All of the British public opinion polls before the last general election two years ago showed a huge lead for Labor. Some critics blamed — or credited — the actual Conservative triumph on poll-bred complacency that caused many Labor supporters to stay home.

There are other causes of error, although most of them concern issues rather than candidates. One fine example stems from two 1966 surveys attempting to test public reaction to the Vietnam war. The first showed that 70 per cent of those questioned approved American bombing of oil storage dumps in Hanoi and Haiphong while only 11 per cent disapproved. Two months later, the same organization asked if the United States should submit the Vietnam decision to the United Nations — as recommended by doves — and "accept the decision, whatever it may be". Here 51 per cent of those sampled thought the proposal "a good idea" and 32 per cent disliked it.

Both hawks and doves used the two polls to support their contentions that public opinion heavily supported them — the hawks claiming that the first poll showed the public supporting them seven to one and the doves claiming support by three to two in the second poll. Actually the confusion arose from an over-simplification of two quite different questions.

As Dr. Gallup pointed out yesterday, the polls which will be with us until election day are subject to wide fluctuations. Only four years ago, Hubert Humphrey gained 10 points between early September and the election which he lost by a squeaker. Furthermore, the election is decided not by the national vote but by the vote by states, which could give a quite different result. Their meaningfulness will be attacked and defended according to the interests of the candidates and their supporters. They are interesting, but they are far from infallible.

RAPID CITY JOURNAL
Rapid City, S.D., September 27, 1972

Nov. 7 will be a most humbling experience for political analysts and pollsters if Sen. George McGovern defeats President Nixon. Very little being published today suggests that McGovern has a chance, and those who stake their reputations on being accurate or close to the public's pulse show little inclination to hedge.

They should remind themselves more frequently, perhaps, that McGovern is a stout contender and accustomed to swimming upstream. McGovern's 1972 fate has not already been decided, even if some political observers are already talking about 1976.

George Gallup said this week that Nixon's present wide lead over McGovern could vanish before election day. And he set forth how, historically, there has been a favorable change in the opinion polls for the losing candidate between the beginning of the campaign and the actual election returns.

Perhaps Gallup is hedging now, but we think not. He offers proof. And he also answers McGovern's complaint about "nutty" public-opinion polls that "make these things up in the backrooms somewhere." Gallup says, as he has carefully explained many times before, election surveys are not intended to "predict" what will happen on election day. Polls can report sentiment only as of the time of interviewing.

Political season polling is becoming an issue, with an indignant McGovern contributing.

Enjoying a substantial lead in the Gallup Poll, the Harris Survey, polls conducted for Time magazine and the New York Times, the President has been silent. Yet Republican leaders must be wary that Nixon's standing does not create overconfidence in GOP ranks while spurring McGovern's forces to work harder on an underdog image which could attract sympathy.

For McGovern, continual poor standings also could be dangerous, dampening financial support and worker morale.

On balance, the Omaha World-Herald believes the effects of public opinion polls to both sides seem to be so mixed that there probably is no significant influence in the long run.

They do serve several purposes. One is to give the trailing candidate something to lash out at. South Dakota's presidential candidate is not the first to do so, nor will he be the last.

THE WALL STREET JOURNAL
New York, N.Y., September 25, 1972

The recent Gallup Poll finding that a majority of younger voters support President Nixon over Senator McGovern was quite an eye-opener. It had been assumed by a great many people that the youth vote would flow automatically to liberal or even radical candidates. And the conventional wisdom even more emphatically held that youth would embrace George McGovern.

Yet the Gallup organization now finds Mr. Nixon with 61% of the under-30 vote. Even allowing for statistical error and for possibly sharper divisions among still younger voters, it seems the surprise will be not how different "the kids" are, but how much they vote the same way their parents do. In short, a youth revolution at the ballot box is unlikely.

Inevitably, then, the question is, how come? What happened to all those angry young kids who dominated the TV news, the newspapers and news weeklies?

The answer, it seems to us, is that even if all those angry young militants are still angry and militant, they never really represented amorphous "youth." They represented, at best, a youthful fringe. What many influential adults assumed were youthful attitudes, it seems, actually flowed from the adults' own preconceptions and hopes.

Some journalists and other observers also seriously misinterpreted the views of blue collar workers and the so-called ethnics. Yet the mistake here was not in glorifying the angriest of them, and hailing them as representative spokesmen for the whole group, but in ignoring them completely, in excluding blue collar and ethnic concerns and aspirations from public debate while concentrating on those of fashionable minorities.

And no minority was ever more fashionable than campus militants, whose activities were duly chronicled by the press, and whose threats and imprecations were published and treated with deference by serious reviewers. No matter that many of their thoughts were shallow and their pronouncements vague; their emoting was regarded as transcendent wisdom.

Although youth may be charting independent paths in the area of morals and manners, the great majority seems to be within the political mainstream. The irony is that so many otherwise intelligent observers tried for so long to place them outside it.

The Evening Gazette
Worcester, Mass., September 27, 1972

Polls are interesting, fairly accurate, but sometimes confusing indications of public sentiment.

If misunderstood or taken too seriously, polls can do more harm than good in informing our political process.

Take the case of four recent national polls on the presidential race. All found President Nixon leading Sen. George McGovern. But the Nixon margin ranged from 22 to 39 points. Likewise the percentage of "undecided" voters ranged from six to 15 in the various samplings.

How can this be in an age of computer science, one might ask?

Well, first, the polls were taken at different times between Aug. 25 and Sept. 22. Opinions can shift rapidly in the heat of a presidential race.

Second, the pollsters used a variety of techniques from telephoning 1,200 "likely voters" nationwide to personal interviews with 1,534 adults selected randomly. Sampling methods and size of sample can produce divergent results.

Moreover, the phrasing of particular questions can alter results in some polls. Persons who say they would "be inclined" to vote for President Nixon if the election were held today might react differently to a question stripped of room for equivocation.

So it would be wise if we took our polls with several grains of salt, remembering that presidents and other leaders are finally elected by the voters on election day, not in private polls before.

THE CINCINNATI ENQUIRER
Cincinnati, Ohio, September 29, 1972

THERE IS NO evidence that President Nixon carries the results of the latest Gallup or Harris poll around in his pocket to impress his friends (as President Johnson is said to have done at the peak of his popularity). But no one can deny that, on the face of them, the polls are providing the Chief Executive with an almost unbelievable amount of good news. It is good news, moreover, that has appeared to date to grow even better with the passage of time.

Mr. Nixon, however, would do well to ponder the observations of two of the nation's most experienced and respected pollsters.

One of them, Dr. George Gallup, contends that Sen. George McGovern has a good chance of closing the wide gap that now separates him from President Nixon.

The other, Louis Harris, says that "if I were Mr. Nixon today, I'd be worried that people would look at the latest polls and say they're for him but they don't want him to win by that much."

Dr. Gallup, in addition, touched on yet another danger when he declared that it would be "amazing if Mr. McGovern doesn't start improving his position." Indeed, as the McGovern campaign gives the Democratic presidential nominee more and more national exposure, he is all but certain to show significant gains in popularity—gains that his lieutenants will herald as a nationwide bandwagon in the Democrats' behalf.

A private poll taken by Senator McGovern's staff in mid-September has provided a measure of such encouragement —even though it showed the senator 22 percentage points behind the President.

As they have perfected their techniques, the polls have proved to be strikingly accurate gauges of national opinion. Yet the only polls that really matter will be those that open on the morning of November 7. Voters and political strategists alike would be well advised not to be swayed unduly even by the expert previews Dr. Gallup, Mr. Harris and the other pollsters offer up in the meantime.

Campaign '72:
NEWSDAY DROPS ENDORSEMENTS; MOST PAPERS BACK NIXON-AGNEW

The Long Island, N.Y., newspaper *Newsday* (circulation 440,000) announced in a full-page editorial Sept. 5 that it will no longer endorse political candidates. The paper's decision did not reflect the trend of newspaper policy. According to *Editor & Publisher* magazine, the percentage of newspapers endorsing a presidential candidate was greater in 1972 than it had been in 1968. A poll of daily newspapers conducted by the magazine showed that 76.5% of the papers responding were endorsing President Nixon and 4.3% were backing Sen. George McGovern.

Newsday
Long Island, N.Y., September 5, 1972

Nine weeks from today, America's voters will go to the polls to elect a President for the next four years. Here on Long Island, the ballot will also include candidates for Congress, the Legislature, the state judiciary and local offices.

As the campaign progresses, newspapers from coast to coast will be making their traditional candidate selections. Newsday has gone along with this tradition in the past: in 1948, Newsday endorsed Dewey; in 1952, Eisenhower; in 1956, Stevenson; in 1960, Kennedy; in 1964, Johnson, and in 1968, Nixon. In state and local races, Newsday has endorsed a broad spectrum of candidates: last year, for example, we backed 15 Democrats, six Republicans, one Liberal and one Conservative.

This fall we are going to break with tradition and endorse neither Richard Nixon nor George McGovern. Nor will we formally endorse candidates in state or local races, though we may on occasion call attention to those who appear extraordinarily qualified—or extraordinarily unfit.

The reason we say this now is because you—our readers—should know our position at the outset of the campaign, and also because we want you to understand why those of us who determine Newsday's editorial policy made this decision.

First, we believe that a newspaper's primary obligation is not to tell its readers whom to vote for but to give them the kind of information they need to make thoughtful choices. Our job is to inform—as accurately, fairly and completely as is humanly possible. In a political campaign, this also means clarifying issues, stimulating discussion, presenting differing points of view and reporting what is really going on behind the scenes as well as on center stage.

Second, we wonder if a newspaper can do its job as effectively as it should if people have reason to infer, no matter how wrongly, that it is favoring certain candidates while short-changing their opponents. Here at Newsday, we report events in the news pages and express opinions on the editorial or Viewpoints pages. Our editors and reporters understand this distinction, but we're not sure that all our readers do. That's why we want to avoid even the appearance of bias.

Third, given the steadily snowballing power of government at all levels, it seems to us that a good newspaper's role in our society—regardless of which party is in power—is to be generally skeptical, frequently critical and sometimes impertinent. Some of our news stories have made Newsday unpopular in the White House, and we have criticized the President's policies sharply in editorials. But if Senator McGovern were elected, our attitude would be no less probing and no less questioning. And on the local level, our investigative team will continue to smoke out evidence of favoritism and fraud among both Republican and Democratic office-holders. (Look for a country where the press is popular with public officials and you generally find a dictatorship.) We intend to keep sounding off when the public trust is abused; but if we endorse a candidate and he wins, it could make it harder for us to maintain our independence and do our job properly.

Fourth, we were struck by the outcry earlier this summer when the executive board of the American Newspaper Guild—which represents some editorial employes on some newspapers—declared the union's support of McGovern. Many newspapers and Guild members thought it was wrong for the union's leadership to commit its members to the support of any candidate. We agreed, and said so in an editorial. There is enough unwarranted suspicion among readers and viewers about the alleged slanting of news without nourishing that suspicion. However, if it is ill-advised for a union that represents some newsmen to endorse a Presidential candidate, isn't it equally ill-advised for a publisher to do the same and by implication identify his newspaper and his employes with a political party? That's why we hope Newsday is not alone among newspapers this year in breaking with an obsolete tradition and asserting its political independence right through election day.

Our new policy, in short, means that Newsday will not formally endorse candidates for public office. We will take stands on the issues that emerge in this and future political campaigns and on the performance of the candidates. We have already expressed our views on most of the issues facing the electorate this year—on Vietnam, civil liberties, drugs and crime, defense spending, domestic priorities, gun legislation, abortion laws, control of inflation, foreign policy, tax reforms, conservation of our resources and environment, consumer protection and a host of problems affecting the quality and promise of American life in the seventies and beyond. We'll continue to do so. In fact, we expect to be even more outspoken in our editorials in assessing how the candidates deal with these and other issues.

In the nine weeks ahead we are going to publish as much information in our news columns as we can gather that will help you make up your own minds before you step into the voter's booth on November 7. In most state and local races, we'll be meeting with the candidates and telling you what we learn about them. In the Presidential race, we'll give you complete coverage of what we still hope will be the "clear contest" that Mr. Nixon has promised; clear—and clean. May the press do its job of reporting it without fear or favor. And may the voters choose wisely.

THE WALL STREET JOURNAL.

New York, N.Y., September 13, 1972

With each presidential election comes the task of explaining our dissent from the tradition that every good newspaper formally endorses one candidate or another. The task is in many ways a thankless one, the hold of tradition being so powerful few will listen carefully to a defense of eccentricity.

Yet perhaps a redeeming virtue can be found by taking the occasion to offer a few remarks on what purpose we hope the scribblings in these columns can serve. For the reasons for our long-settled policy of non-endorsement are found in our conception of the editorialist's function. Indeed, the short reason is simplicity itself: We don't think our business is telling people how to vote.

To take the matter from the ground up, we think a newspaper's editorial columns ought to serve the same basic purpose as its other columns, which is to inform. But editorials inform in a different way, with different strengths and limitations, than factual reporting does. There is much to learn of the world that is best developed and conveyed in argumentation and speculation.

If proposal X comes before Congress, for example, ordinary news stories will quite rightly turn to a range of questions such as: Will it pass? Whose political future will it affect? Who will benefit from its provisions? Only seldom and awkwardly do news stories address a range of questions such as: Does the proposal really make sense? What would a thoughtful case for or against it look like? What is its significance in our lives and times?

Obviously these are interesting and important questions. But they are difficult to explore with the techniques of straight news reporting because no amount of digging will turn up a final answer to them. By contrast, editorials and other opinion features, precisely because the forms are manifestly those of perhaps mistaken opinion, are free to address such questions with a special rigor. The exercise, we can hope, will convey to the reader something of his times beyond what he finds even in the best news columns.

The informative value of opinion, in our experience, is best extracted by serious men working from a serious point of view. That an editorial is not merely another opinion but the opinion of a newspaper at the least means that it is the opinion of someone who is paid to take opinion seriously. At the best it means an opinion infused with insights and traditions built up over the years by successive generations of thoughtful men.

This heritage is something we believe should be taken seriously. We were flattered recently when a theologian analyzed our "theology"—even though we might not express our overview in quite the same way, and even though he didn't fully approve of the theology he found (see Notable and Quotable, alongside). We think on this newspaper or any other, it is this accumulated heritage that produces a distinctive voice, an identity that gives context and meaning to opinion. The reader understands that this is not merely a random opinion on passing events, but the insights produced by a known outlook on man and society.

The limitation, of course, is that no one outlook produces all the insights, no heritage embraces all of human wisdom. It is of course possible and highly desirable to find room for points of view arising from contrasting heritages. But in our experience men delude themselves when they believe they can weigh all the arguments and arrive at ultimate truth, or even when they believe they can really do justice to opposing points of view. What editorial columns can do is to sharpen the case for one viewpoint, stimulate the thinking of those who hold other viewpoints, and ultimately raise the level of public debate.

With this conception of our purpose, we discuss the issues of the day in presidential years as in others. We speculate where each candidate fits in the sweep of events. If the net effect adds up to a preference, so be it; if it does not, so be that too. In either event the reader will know not a mere presidential preference, but precisely what we think, and we hope he or she will have found something enlightening in the reading.

Having done that, what does it add to pin one candidate's name to your lapel? We do not see any meaningful way in which that would either add to the reader's understanding of his times or raise the level of the public debate. In fact, we suspect that such labeling is likely to detract from the level of public debate if you take it seriously. At least, we have occasionally noticed that when even the best editorial pages become involved in campaigns intended to achieve such-and-such a political result, their arguments start to remind us less of what we admire in the scholar and more of what we do not admire in the politician. Such, we take it, are the wages of courting your own "influence."

Well, that is enough introspection for another four years or so. But those are the reasons for our eccentricity about endorsements in presidential years and, for whatever it's worth, a guide to the spirit these columns aspire to in other years as well.

ARKANSAS DEMOCRAT

Little Rock, Ark., September 14, 1972

The fact that considerable attention has been given to one newspaper's self-righteous change in editorial policy prompts us to indulge in a little shop talk.

Newsday, one of the nation's largest and most protean afternoon newspapers, has decided that it will no longer endorse candidates for political office. There's nothing wrong with that; many newspapers have that policy. We don't happen to, thinking that the newspaper, like any other well-informed citizen in the community, has opinions and when it does it's part of our responsibility to offer them and tell why.

What disturbs us are Newsday's reasons for its change in policy. They are sort of insulting to the profession of journalism and the intelligence of most newspaper readers. "A newspaper's primary obligation is not to tell its readers whom to vote for . . ." was one of its reasons. Well, who ever said it was? Implicit in that statement is that newspapers have that power. That's absurd, of course. The purpose of editorial-page endorsements (the purpose of anything on the editorial page, for that matter) is simply to stimulate thinking, to offer an idea that the reader can use as sort of a backboard for testing his own opinions.

Then, even more bewilderingly, Newsday says that if it endorses a candidate on the editorial page it makes it harder for its staff to maintain its objectivity and for its readers to believe that it is even trying to do so. It caps it all with this bit of illogic: If it was wrong for a newspaper trade union to endorse a candidate (which it admits that it was), then it's also wrong for newspapers to.

This is hardly the case. The newspaper union is made up of news editors and reporters who deal with fact, not opinion — men whose touchstone should be impartiality. Not many of America's reporters belong to the union, but since it is a national organization, its endorsement of George McGovern made it appear that the nation's working press had abandoned its touchstone.

Publishers and editorial page editors, on the other hand, do not belong to unions and vary, in philosophy and style, from town to town. They do not report the news. They comment and express opinions but on the editorial page, not in the news columns. Most people with any degree of sophistication understand this and, we think, respect the integrity of newspapering about as much as they do that of most professions.

What really saddens us is the thrust of Newsday's arguments. They imply that all of us in this business are such ideologists that endorsing a candidate is more serious than marrying one, in that we will defend him even when he's wrong and stick together until death us do part. There are some newspapers that are like that but they are in the minority. Most publishers today insist on fairness in the news columns and independence on the editorial page, which means not crawling in bed with any party or politician. It also means that when you find yourself with no candidate you can conscientiously recommend to your readers, you will be man enough to admit it.

The Oregonian

Portland, Ore., September 6, 1972

The decision of Long Island's Newsday, the nation's largest suburban newspaper, to stop endorsing political candidates in order "to maintain our independence" is founded on shaky intellectual ground. Further, its stated hope that other newspapers will join it "in breaking with an obsolete tradition" demeans the intelligence of the reading public and is an undeserved insult to most other American newspapers.

Newsday's editorial basically breaks down to a few observations and inferences: That the public is unable to distinguish between news and editorial opinion; that endorsing a candidate who wins could make it harder for a paper to maintain its independence and do its job properly; and that the job of the newspaper is not to tell readers whom to vote for but to give them information on which they can base their own thoughtful choices.

The Oregonian rejects the suggestion that its readers cannot distinguish between fact and opinion.

We are also puzzled as to how Newsday arrives at the conclusion that it should continue to speak out editorially on issues but not on political candidates. If, as the paper implies, the public believes editorial opinions on candidates influence news decisions, doesn't it follow that Newsday should be silent on issues such as taxation, abortion, political ethics and other subjects for the same reason? This line of reasoning is untenable.

Does endorsing a political candidate who eventually wins make it more difficult for a newspaper to do its job properly; that is, to be generally skeptical, often critical and occasionally cynical? We don't believe so. The Oregonian and every other paper worth its paper and ink, including Newsday, has figuratively dragged candidates it has previously endorsed across hot coals on any number of issues.

Does The Oregonian presume to tell you whom to vote for? The answer is "No." Endorsements represent the judgment of the editorial board as to the candidates it deems best suited to handle the issues raised in the electoral contest. It is our opinion, presented for you to accept or reject on the strength of our reasoning or on the basis of your belief in our credibility and reliability.

Those who read editorial pages regularly establish benchmarks by which to judge opinions presented. That means endorsements will be rejected out of hand by some readers, accepted with a grain of salt by others and adopted unhesitatingly by others. In any event, The Oregonian believes strongly — and has for more than a century — that taking a stand on political candidacies is one way of fulfilling its responsibility to inform.

We also believe Newsday disregards the importance to voters of the discussion and endorsement of candidates for so-called minor office, candidates who often receive little space in the news columns.

Finally, we must ask two questions: How can issues be separated from those who propose to deal with them? And why print an editorial page if you are reluctant to express an opinion?

DAILY NEWS

New York, N.Y., September 27, 1972

This country and the world need the continued leadership of our President. I say to you delegates, to you my fellow citizens of America, we need this man.

We need this man of action, this man of accomplishment, this man of experience, this man of courage. We need this man of faith in America.

So said Gov. Nelson A. Rockefeller last Tuesday evening at the Republican National Convention in Miami Beach when he nominated President Richard M. Nixon for reelection Nov. 7.

Richard Nixon   Spiro Agnew

To us, the Rockefeller statement rings as true as the Liberty Bell before it contracted that unfortunate crack while sounding forth the glories of George Washington's Birthday in 1846.

Accordingly, THE NEWS whole-heartedly endorses Richard Milhous Nixon for reelection as President of the United States, and Spiro Theodore Agnew for reelection as Vice President.

The reasons for this support are many. We believe—

THE MOST IMPORTANT REASONS

—are these:

The Vietnam War is being wound down as fast as consists with our national honor, loyalty to our Saigon allies, the hope of getting our war prisoners released, and most Americans' detestation of Communism. We think it would be foolish, and could be suicidal, to buy Sen. G. S. McGovern's formula of cut, run and surrender.

The national defenses are potent at present. The Nixon-Agnew administration promises, if continued in power, to keep them that way. Sen. McGovern (who talks like Liberace but does not make as much sense) proposes to cut the defense budget by $32 billion—leaving us at least half-naked to our enemies, who are numerous and rapacious.

The fight against inflation is showing results. The rate of inflation has been cut in half via the temporary wage and price controls devised by the Nixon-Agnew administration. Let us allow the present White House team to carry on with this vital work. Let us on no account buy the wild-jackass economics of Sen. McGovern, keyed as they are to a promise to "give" every person in the U.S.A. $1,000 if the South Dakota whizbang becomes President. (Those "gifts" would be sweated out of all the taxpayers.)

The Nixon foreign policies are aimed at easing tensions between the free and the Communist worlds, without losing a particle of U.S. power or freedom of action. They are getting results up to now.

On the home front, the Nixon-Agnew administration for three years, seven months and one week has been dealing fairly and generously with organized and unorganized labor, religious and ethnic minorities, our young people, and the distaff part of the population.

It has stood for the rights of decent people as taking priority over the rights of criminals and crooks.

And it has refused to pit faction against faction for political or any other purposes. As the President said Wednesday night in his grand-master acceptance speech:

Let us commit ourselves to continue relentlessly to remove the last vestiges of discrimination in America. But the way to end discrimination against some is not to begin discrimination against others. . . . Americans don't want to be part of a quota. They want to be part of America—as proud, self-respecting individual citizens.

How can Americans best serve their own highest interests on Nov. 7? We think they can do so by—

VOTING REPUBLICAN

—for candidates on both White House and Congressional levels, with some exceptions as regards the latter.

Mr. Nixon has been hampered throughout his first term by the fact that Congress has been controlled by the Democrats.

Give President A Whole Team Many of these are fine and patriotic citizens, like the innumerable Democrats who plan to vote Nixon-Agnew this time around because they cannot stomach McGovern-Shriver and their platform.

But Mr. Nixon can best carry on his policies and plans if he is backed by a Republican-controlled Congress.

Why not vote to give him this backing—in hope that his second term may prove 10 times as good for us all as his first term? That would be super-good plus.

The Topeka Daily Capital

Topeka, Kans., September 10, 1972

With September well-started and only October between now and election day, support of a candidate seems to be in order.

The Capital-Journal will support President Richard M. Nixon for re-election.

The news columns of the newspapers, as usual, will be kept as free of political bias as is humanly possible.

With the many editors, reporters and copyreaders in the newsroom, each will have his or her personal preferences, but each also realizes that the pride and honor of a newspaper requires its news columns to be fair and unbiased. Each will strive meticulously and unstintingly to achieve this constant goal.

The left-hand columns of our editorial pages are reserved to express the views and opinions of each newspaper. The regular news columns, beginning with the front page, really belong to the subscribers.

Briefly, Sen. George S. McGovern of South Dakota is a conscientious candidate with good and bad points, but we believe President Nixon's achievements are of such magnitude that they weigh heavily in favor of his re-election.

The President's unflagging efforts to reach a negotiated settlement of the Vietnam war, an inherited problem, have continued unabated from the day he took office until now.

The President's program of Vietnamization of the war has allowed him to reduce the number of American troops in South Vietnam from the 550,000 there when he took office to 39,000 in late August.

At that time, the President announced 12,000 more troops would be withdrawn during the months of September, October and November, and that no additional withdrawals would be announced until after the election, but he assured concerned Americans that U.S. troops would remain in South Vietnam as long as North Vietnam holds American prisoners of war.

The President has proceeded as promised in 1968 to establish an all-volunteer Army and end the military draft. The draft will end next June 30, and draftees called between now and then will not be sent to South Vietnam unless they volunteer. American casualties—although one is still too many—have been reduced to an all-time low.

The President's efforts to obtain action on his domestic programs have been derailed time after time by a Democratic Congress which seems to find little glamor in any Republican-sponsored measure, and which actually has done little during the nearly four years of the President's first term.

President Nixon has moved boldly in the field of foreign policy to ease world tensions and erase many of the scars caused by the protracted "cold war."

His trip to Red China to talk face-to-face with Premier Chou En-lai and Chairman Mao Tse-tung can only be considered as a forward step in improving relations with mainland China. The long-range effect of this historic visit may be years in unraveling, but the start of any move can be measured in inches.

The President followed this diplomatic effort with one of equal importance — a visit with heads of state in Russia. The President's reception in Moscow was, as it was in Peking, friendly and correct, but not overcome by enthusiasm.

There are visible signs both visits will result first in improved trade relations. Russia has agreed to purchase needed grains from the United States under a three-year credit agreement. Russia also is seeking to buy fertilizer from an American company.

Although all presidents are cognizant of political pressures, and sometimes yield to them, President Nixon has not hesitated to take the rougher road in some of his decisions. He has vetoed bills which he believed provided more money for education than was needed. The clamor was deafening, but he held his ground.

He inaugurated wage and price controls a year ago last month when it became apparent he could hold off no longer in the face of mounting inflation. His acts have begun to bear fruit.

While unemployment has remained at a higher level than he would hope for, it cannot be forgotten that more jobs have become available during his term, but the entrants into the labor market have exceeded them.

All economists say business now is good and will improve. This doubtless will be reflected in lower unemployment figures in the months to come.

President Nixon's appointments to the U.S. Supreme Court have been designed to, and have, restored some balance to the liberal attitude of the so-called Warren Court. He pledges to continue appointing men or women to the court who hold similar attitudes. Slowly, but surely, the court is moving to provide as much concern for the victims as it had for criminals.

Taken all in all, President Nixon is running on a record which he can cite and all can see. It is filled with accomplishments and shows promise of more successes if he is given the opportunity to continue his efforts as chief executive.

The Capital-Journal believes his record calls loudly for his continued stewardship.

Chicago Tribune

Chicago, Ill., September 24, 1972

We have seen enough of the way Mr. Nixon has conducted the Presidency and of the way Mr. McGovern has conducted his campaign to convince us that the United States cannot afford this change at this time.

We base our decision mainly on the positions of the two sides on the major issues. First, the war. We believe that Mr. Nixon has done a sincere job of trying to find a durable end to the war and that he has been as successful as anyone could be under the difficult circumstances. The excessive use of the term "anti-war" as applied to Mr. Nixon's critics implies that Mr. Nixon is "pro-war"—and nothing could be farther from the truth. Mr. McGovern's impulsive urge to throw in the towel would not end the fighting in Southeast Asia and would encourage aggressors there and elsewhere.

With respect to foreign policy in general, Mr. Nixon has pulled off something close to a miracle. He has at once reduced the tension between the United States and the two top Communist countries while aggravating the tension between Russia and China. These steps are not without risk and can invite over-optimism. But on balance, the profound shake-up which Mr. Nixon has given to world relationships is bound to be for the better. Mr. McGovern has had little experience in world affairs and seems out of his depth in discussing them. Even the Soviet leadership, it appears, would prefer to deal with a reliable, if tough, Nixon than with an impulsive and unpredictable McGovern.

On economic policy Mr. Nixon's critics have been loud and unreasonable. The facts are clear enough. Mr. Nixon has slowed inflation down to a rate lower than now prevails in competing countries and lower than the rate at which wages are rising. The common charge that "wages are being held down while prices are soaring" is manifest nonsense. The present upturn in business has a healthier base than existed under runaway inflation and should bring unemployment down to more acceptable levels.

Mr. McGovern, by contrast, is reduced to offering [and then revising] ill-considered reforms and denouncing the wage and price controls which the Democrats themselves once demanded.

The differences are not confined to the issues. One feels that the Nixon administration knows where it is going [albeit with more Madison Avenue slickness than one would like] and that the McGovern team doesn't. At the Vice Presidential level Mr. Agnew exudes a quiet confidence while Mr. Shriver battles on with rhetorical fireworks and a good deal of demagoguery. The McGovern team is disorganized, bickering, and grasping at straws [like Watergate] which, whatever validity they may have, are of little relevance in a struggle for the most powerful job in the world at one of the most critical periods of its history. On the basis of the issues that count, and the confident direction that the government needs, it would be a frightening tragedy not to reelect the Nixon ticket.

210 — Newspaper Endorsements

St. Louis Globe-Democrat
St. Louis, Mo., September 28, 1972

President Richard M. Nixon and Vice President Spiro T. Agnew, on their record and their policies, are head and shoulders above the Democratic team of Sen. George S. McGovern and R. Sargent Shriver.

Mr. Nixon and Mr. Agnew have restored the United States to a place of world leadership in foreign affairs and brought unity and an expanding economy at home. It is essential to the nation's future that they be re-elected and be given a majority in Congress to carry out their progressive programs in the years ahead.

Senator George McGovern has been an utter disappointment from the day he was nominated. He has been a weak, vacillating, confused, opportunistic blunderer. He is the kind of man who claimed to be "1000 per cent" behind Tom Eagleton and then cynically kicked the Missouri senator off the ticket a few days later.

His running mate, Sargent Shriver, a poor substitute for Eagleton, is woefully miscast. He reminds us of Little Sir Echo, trying hard to sound like he knows what goes on in the big world, but never quite making it.

The spiteful campaign of McGovern and Shriver obviously has turned off the public. McGovern's intrusion into the Vietnam war at a time when delicate peace negotiations are going on is unforgivable. It stamps him as an unconscionable meddler, ignorant and disdainful of the consequences of his words and actions.

To appreciate what Mr. Nixon has done, with the capable support of Mr. Agnew, it is necessary to recall how conditions were when they took office in 1969, and compare them to conditions today.

The picture on the world scene was very grim. Democratic President Lyndon B. Johnson had committed more than 540,000 young American men to fight in Vietnam without any plan for either winning the war or ending it honorably.

Respect for the United States around the world had fallen to an all-time low. Our relations with the Soviet Union were extremely hostile, almost at the breaking point. We had no contact with Red China. Even our relations with our allies — England, France, Canada and Japan — were at a low ebb.

Now, nearly four years later, there has been an almost miraculous transformation. More than 500,000 troops have been withdrawn from Vietnam and our ground combat role there has been ended. Secret negotiations are progressing that could end the war almost at any time.

Our relations with the Soviet Union and Red China have been immeasurably improved by Mr. Nixon's trips to Peking and Moscow. Instead of a cold war with these countries, the United States is now embarked on a program of greatly expanded trade and cultural exchanges with these two huge Communist powers.

The prestige of the United States has been restored around the world as Mr. Nixon has shown that our nation can be both a friend of all peoples and a resolute ally, as in the case of South Vietnam.

At home President Nixon has brought about respect for law by advocating strong law enforcement and supporting legislation and other programs for reinforcing the nation's system of justice.

His appointment of Warren E. Burger as chief justice of the Supreme Court and subsequent appointments of Harry A. Blackmun, Lewis F. Powell Jr. and William H. Rehnquist had a great deal to do with the change in public attitude. They take a stricter interpretation of the law and give much more consideration to the public's right to be protected from crime than their predecessors on the Warren court.

After a long, hard fight, Mr. Nixon now appears to be winning the battle against inflation. It has been cut to about 3 per cent. As a result of wage-price controls and other economic measures, the United States now is showing one of the best productivity gains in the world and its rate of inflation has dropped below most of its world competitors.

The national economy also is enjoying a strong, steady growth that should continue for some time to come. Mr. Nixon's well balanced economic programs deserve much of the credit.

President Nixon also has been very helpful to cities. After much prodding from Mr. Nixon, Congress finally approved his revenue sharing program which could prove a boon to such cities as St. Louis in the years to come.

This newspaper believes that it is vital to the welfare of the nation that Mr. Nixon and Mr. Agnew be returned to office. They have demonstrated that they have the character and the determination to lead this nation — and lead it exceedingly well—through some of the most difficult years this nation has faced in its history.

The two opposing candidates have almost no comprehension of how foreign affairs are conducted or what is required for successful diplomacy. Senator McGovern has advocated income redistribution, gutting of our national defense and other extremist and isolationist policies.

Their name-calling, lightweight campaign has stamped them as second-raters who don't belong in the same political ring with President Nixon and Vice President Agnew.

The New York Times
New York, N.Y., September 28, 1972

In less than six weeks, we, the American people, will be choosing the President and Vice President of the United States for the next four years. But we will be doing more than that; we will be determining whether we want this country to continue along the course it has been taking during the past four years, or whether we want to restore to American political life its traditional values of democratic liberalism and social concern.

In an America striving to realize its own vision of equality and liberty under the rule of law, the Presidency requires particular qualities of character, leadership and moral force that transcend the narrow bounds of personal ambition and of party politics. It requires a perception of the things that are wrong with America—politically, socially, economically, morally—as well as the things that are right; and a sense of priorities that gives precedence to human needs and public integrity over the panoply of wealth and the arrogance of power.

The New York Times urges the election of George McGovern for President of the United States. We believe that Senator McGovern's approach to public questions, his humanitarian philosophy and humane scale of values, his courage and his forthrightness can offer a new kind of leadership in American political life. We believe he can restore a sense of purpose to the American people as a whole, a sense of participation to its component parts and a sense of integrity to their Government.

In these respects, it seems to us, the Presidency of Richard M. Nixon has largely failed.

Mr. Nixon has indeed had his spectacular triumphs; and this newspaper has never hesitated to applaud the accomplishments of the President and his Administration when we thought that he was serving the best interests of the American people, even when in doing so he was adopting policies that he had spent a lifetime in opposing. But despite his best efforts—in regard to China, the Soviet Union, economic controls and so on—Mr. Nixon has failed both in principle and in practice in other areas of public policy even more vital than those in which he has scored his successes.

Not only has Mr. Nixon failed to carry out his explicit pledge to end the Vietnam conflict, on which he won the election by a hair's breadth four years ago; he has pursued a policy that appears to move in one direction while actually moving in another. Constantly emphasizing the winding down of the war and the withdrawal of American troops, Mr. Nixon has nevertheless enlarged the scope of hostilities, undertaken the biggest bombing campaign in history and committed American prestige to an increasingly authoritarian regime in Saigon.

The Vietnam war is but one area where President Nixon has failed either to carry out his pledge or to give the nation the moral and political leadership that would indeed unite us—as he promised to do four years ago. This Administration appears to be without basic philosophy, without deeply held values, an Administration whose guiding principle is expediency and whose overriding purpose is to remain in office.

The pursuit of excellence has been subordinated to pursuit of the next election, as evidenced by some of Mr. Nixon's appointments in such ultra-sensitive areas of Government as the Department of Justice and the Supreme Court. In many of its social, economic and fiscal policies; in lax standards of probity and truthfulness in Government; in favoritism toward special interests; in its addiction to secrecy; in its disregard of civil liberties and constitutional rights, the Nixon Administration has been a failure.

President Nixon has shown himself willing to exacerbate America's racial divisions for purely political purposes; he has countenanced and encouraged an ominous erosion of individual rights and First Amendment freedoms, and has demonstrated his indifference to such dangers by deliberately selecting Spiro T. Agnew as his potential successor to the Presidency. Protected by the White House curtain, he has stood above the political battle as the odor of corruption and of sleazy campaign practices rises above the Washington battlefield.

A McGovern administration, The Times believes, would reverse the unmistakable drift in Washington away from government of, by and for the people. It is undeniable that since his nomination Senator McGovern has been on the defensive, partly because of the Eagleton episode, partly because of ill-considered comments on specific points that he has subsequently modified or corrected, and partly because of the confused management of his own campaign. But on his record, and on what he has consistently stood for in his years of public office—a consistency in striking contrast to that of his opponent—it is clear that Mr. McGovern will fight for effective and necessary reforms in American social, political and economic institutions.

What this election comes down to is a decision on the direction in which the United States is going to move for the next four years.

Are we going to continue to pursue a foreign policy that, for all its success in certain areas, is essentially based on military supremacy, on a strident nationalism and on a cynical power game that could alienate this country from substantial segments of the international community?

Are we going to continue to pursue a domestic policy that, in its fundamentals, is contemptuous of civil liberties, oblivious of deep social conflicts and racial and economic cleavages in the cities of America, and oriented toward that very "military-industrial complex" against which President Eisenhower perceptively warned us so many years ago?

On virtually every major issue from the war to taxes, from education to environment, from civil liberties to national defense, Mr. McGovern—faltering though many of his statements have been—seems to us to be moving with the right priorities, with faith in the common man, and within the democratic framework. While this newspaper does not necessarily accept his program in every detail as he has thus far outlined it or as the Democratic platform has structured it, we are convinced that the direction of American policy in the next four years would be in safer hands under a McGovern-Shriver administration than under the present regime.

There can be no doubt that Mr. McGovern is now far behind in the Presidential race. But if he succeeds in these next few weeks in getting his basic philosophy of democratic government across to the electorate, a philosophy that rejects the meretricious appeal of his opponents, Senator McGovern may yet touch a chord in the American voter that will respond to his own practical vision of an American society that cares and an American democracy that works.

© 1972 by The New York Times Company. Reprinted by permission.

Campaign '72:
McGOVERN OUTLINES VIETNAM PLANS IN NATIONWIDE TELEVISION SPEECH

Democratic presidential candidate George McGovern presented the details of his peace plan for Indochina in a television speech Oct. 10 (taped Oct. 8). Sen. McGovern said the war issue constituted the "most important" and "fundamental" difference between himself and President Nixon. McGovern said he regarded the war "as the saddest chapter in our . . . history," while President Nixon viewed it "as our finest hour." Nixon had said in his 1968 campaign he had a plan to end the war, McGovern said, and "those who have had a chance for four years and could not produce peace should not be given another chance."

If he were elected president, McGovern promised he would (1) immediately end all bombing and withdraw all U.S. military personnel from Indochina within 90 days, (2) call upon the enemy "to return all prisoners of war and to account for all missing in action," (3) send the vice president to Hanoi "to speed the arrangements for the return of our prisoners and an accounting of our missing," (4) close down U.S. bases in Thailand and remove U.S. naval units from Indochinese waters after all U.S. POWs had been returned, and (5), after all POWs were home and Vietnam veterans provided for, extend an opportunity to come home to those "who chose jail or exile because they could not in conscience fight in this war."

New York Post
New York, N.Y., October 11, 1972

In giving last night the nationwide telecast on Vietnam he had taped last Sunday, George McGovern inevitably risked the charge that he was jeopardizing "sensitive" peace negotiations. But in the absence of any clearly affirmative news from Paris, he had no honorable alternative. Moreover, nothing he said divulged any secrets to Hanoi about his long-avowed resolve to end U.S. participation in the war if elected. At the same time, his speech could help to persuade General Thieu that Congressional and popular opposition to our involvement will not fade away after a Nixon victory.

Thus, if there is substance and direction to the current dialogue, and if Thieu's refusal to step aside for a tripartite coalition is in fact now a major obstacle, McGovern's address can strengthen the pressure for a settlement. But if the talks were extended to create an illusion, it is best to have the issue drawn sharply.

For the promise of an early turn toward peace has time and again created false expectations in the country, during both this Administration and its predecessor. We have no way of knowing whether the hopes are any more valid now than before, or the product of campaign maneuvers. But clearly this is the season when the people have a right to affirm anew their weariness with a wasteful, endless war. In effect, McGovern has given them a chance to set Election Day as the deadline for fulfillment of Mr. Nixon's 1968 pledge.

This is not to say that we endorse each point in McGovern's proposed procedure for decisive withdrawal from the conflict (any more than we accept his self-description as an unwavering opponent of the war since 1963). We regret that he did not advocate active American support for creation of a coalition regime in Saigon, but suggested only we would respond favorably to such a development after our total departure. In the same context he should surely have stressed our concern about those who fear reprisal after the guns are stilled, and indicated that our economic aid in post-war rehabilitation would be conditioned by the conciliatory nature of the transition.

It is sad, too, that McGovern—like the President—seems unprepared to recognize the need for a major UN role in averting a repetition of Vietnam.

But in his indictment of the futility of the long struggle, the political and moral sterility of the Thieu cabal and the interminable squandering of life and resources, he said things that urgently needed to be said again. Equally relevant was his reminder that the portrait of Vietnam as a front line in the battle against communism had been rendered grotesque by the Administration's new relations with Peking and Moscow.

McGovern again challenged the fantasy that prolongation—rather than cessation—of the war could offer any glimpse of daylight for U. S. prisoners. He offered an earnest challenge to those for whom the war has ceased to be an issue because the color of the casualties has changed, and to whom the bombings present no problem of conscience.

On an earlier occasion McGovern said that his campaign will have been vindicated—regardless of the outcome —if it helps to convince the Administration that the worthy objective is to "save lives, not face." His speech last night was essentially consistent with that spirit. It deserves rational, considered response in Washington and the rest of the nation.

Los Angeles Times
Los Angeles, Calif., October 12, 1972

Sen. George S. McGovern's television address on the war in Vietnam was constructive and useful. He spelled out a practical program for the withdrawal of American forces, for terminating American military action. And, perhaps more important, he dealt realistically with the way America must accept this failure without losing confidence in the nation's principles.

We are uneasy about some of the details, notably the question of support of South Vietnam following an American withdrawal. McGovern has suggested (1) the immediate termination of "any shipments of military supplies that continue the war" and (2) removal from South Vietnam within 90 days of "all salvageable American military equipment."

Presumably he is not suggesting that the army of South Vietnam be disarmed. But he seems to be suggesting that South Vietnam be left defenseless. It seems to us that this question is more appropriate to negotiation. For McGovern has left nothing as an incentive for China and the Soviet Union to halt their arms flow to North Vietnam.

We think McGovern is right in refusing to make the prisoner question an obstacle to American withdrawal from South Vietnam. In practical terms, there is little the United States can do to force this issue. The potential for negotiating release of the prisoners is being explored in Paris. McGovern has proposed that only the withdrawal of American forces off shore and in Thailand would be contingent on settlement of the prisoner question.

The most useful contribution McGovern has made in the speech is the realism with which he has faced the failure of the American intervention. This is not new for him. But it is important for the nation to face the facts and not be diverted by those who insist on a peace formula contrived to justify what the United States has done. He spoke with compassion that equated the deaths of Vietnamese with those of Americans. He spoke with welcome fervor of the ideals of the nation, "the America that we learned to love in the days of our youth, a country that once again stands as a witness to the world for what is noble and just in human affairs."

But he also spoke against the backdrop of peace talks proceeding in Paris with unprecedented intensity, peace talks that could bring a cease-fire before election day. They are peace talks that have failed in the past out of boundless suspicion and distrust, not for lack of generosity in terms. But they are peace talks that have been permitted for too long to justify a perpetuation of the American intervention.

If the peace talks fail again to end the killing, Sen. McGovern has at least shown that there is another way to end the American part in the killing. So his proposals deserve a central place in the debate of this campaign.

THE DAILY OKLAHOMAN
Oklahoma City, Okla., October 13, 1972

ONCE again Sen. George McGovern's presidential campaign suffers from contradiction and indecision. Now controversy has arisen over whether he left himself a loophole in detailing the other night his plan for ending the war in Vietnam.

All along the senator has given the impression that he would rely completely on Hanoi's good faith in living up to its offer to release American prisoners of war upon total withdrawal of U. S. and other foreign forces from South Vietnam. Then, during the Democratic national convention in Miami Beach in July, he startled his ardent, anti-war followers by suggesting he would keep U.S. bases open in Thailand and U.S. ships patrolling off North Vietnam's coast until the prisoners were actually returned. Even this was too much for the bug-out people.

In the ensuing weeks McGovern and his aides sought to gloss over his backsliding error, contending his position on total withdrawal had not really changed. But in his carefully prepared televised speech Tuesday night the senator stated that after all U.S. prisoners had been returned and a satisfactory accounting received for missing men, he would order the bases closed in Thailand and the reassignment elsewhere of ships still stationed in waters adjoining Indochina. The key word is "after."

An accompanying background paper went farther, saying that if the POWs were not released, McGovern as president, would retain the option of military action to secure their return.

When this loophole was noted in a news dispatch, the McGovern people rushed out a clarifying statement. They said the background paper was misleading and that McGovern has no plan to resume military action even if the POWs weren't released.

This is precisely what worries many persons about McGovern. How can he be sure the prisoners would be returned after U.S. withdrawal? Can he really trust the Communists to keep their word and not make conditions? They have already demanded reparations. McGovern's plan included an offer of U. S. help in "repairing the wreckage left by this war." What if Hanoi held onto the prisoners as a sort of ransom until it got the amount of aid it wanted?

Significantly, even liberal, anti-war columnists believe McGovern went too far, showing willingness to accept worse terms than Hanoi has offered. He would not insist on a cease-fire, much less a withdrawal of North Vietnamese from the South.

More than that, he would hurt the Saigon government's ability to survive by taking out all salvageable American military equipment and stopping all military supplies.

By centering his war opposition on South Vietnam's President Van Thieu, McGovern ignores the millions in the South who prefer not to live under communism. Assuring them the right to make that choice is the reason we went into South Vietnam in the first place.

The Times-Picayune
New Orleans, La., October 12, 1972

Sen. George McGovern's much advertised and expensively announced plan to end the Vietnamese war has turned out to be nothing new. But also, we suspect (and no one can do more at present), it is not significantly different in substance from what President Nixon is now doing in negotiations with North Vietnam.

Sen. McGovern, suffering the outsider's lack of authoritarian grasp and also the idealist's tendency to simplify, offers unilateral American action in withdrawing from South Vietnam and dependence on appropriate Communist response.

President Nixon is doubtless trying to cast withdrawal into a full-fleshed agreement requiring specific commitments by all parties. Mr. McGovern's offer thus has the aspect of surrender; whatever Mr. Nixon comes up with will have the aspect of at least some degree of success.

Comparing the McGovern plan and the Nixon record militarily, we find that we are all but withdrawn, and that Mr. McGovern could not offer immediate total withdrawal and cessation of war activities if Mr. Nixon had not, over four careful years, gotten the troop level down to the point where final phaseout would not bring disaster to South Vietnam. Our main forces now are the Navy offshore and the Air Force based in Thailand, and Mr. McGovern, too, would keep these until our POWs are returned.

As for the political structure in South Vietnam, post-withdrawal, Mr. McGovern, again going for the simple, clean cut, would just end support of President Thieu's administration and let things fall out as they may. President Nixon, we assume from the roster of participants in the current flurry of secret discussions, is working on a formula for a new governmental structure that would be more representative and acceptable to all sides, though admittedly temporary.

One may conclude that this election is not the election for Vietnam to be a major issue, and that Sen. McGovern's attempts to make it one are not particularly helpful. At this point, there is really not much to argue about as to what must be done. The manner of its doing counts, of course, and the timeframe now apparently in effect suggests that Mr. McGovern's plan could well be overtaken by events of which President Nixon will be a major determiner.

DAILY NEWS
New York, N.Y., October 12, 1972

For all its advance build-up, Sen. George McGovern's televised presentation Tuesday night of his "detailed plan" to end the Vietnam war was just so much warmed-over hash.

There are only so many ways to say "surrender," and the Democratic presidential aspirant used them all long ago.

If anything, McGovern moved even closer to total acceptance of Communist terms. At least, that is a reasonable reading of the intent behind his promise to pull American forces out of South Vietnam, end all American air and naval action against North Vietnam, stop aid to Saigon, and —as a clincher—remove "all salvageable American equipment."

Would that mean snatching rifles out of the hands of South Vietnamese soldiers? Stripping them of artillery and tanks? Crippling their small air force?

It would be disgrace enough for the U.S. to abandon an ally. But to denude South Vietnam of every means for self-defense, delivering 17 million people into the hands of a merciless enemy, would make the U.S. an accessory to the certain butchery that would follow.

Even if Americans are prepared to stomach such a shameful and dishonorable policy, could they live with the consequences? Surely no thoughtful citizen can delude himself into believing that the—

SHOCK WAVES

—from a McGovern-style sell-out in Southeast Asia could be confined to that corner of the globe. What friend or ally—from the fringes of the far Pacific, to the Mideast, to Western Europe—would retain faith in America's pledges?

In his frenzy to turn a political profit on Vietnam, the senator blindly ignores that obvious and immediate peril. But then, McGovern's whole view of Vietnam is a blend of blindness and ignorance.

- He charges that renewed bombing of North Vietnam kills chances of a negotiated peace, forgetting that a three-and-a-half-year bombing halt brought not a single Red concession.
- He cries out against the bombing, but utters not a peep of protest against the naked aggression by Hanoi that prompted retaliation.
- He trumpets his willingness to bow to all Communist demands, undercutting at every turn President Richard M. Nixon's attempts to negotiate a fair, just end to the conflict.
- He lashes out at the "tyranny" of the Saigon regime, but callously proposes to hand South Vietnam over to infinitely harsher despots.

McGovern's Vietnam stance is so baldly disreputable on all counts that he has invited—

A SLASHING COUNTERATTACK

—which we hope Mr. Nixon will deliver promptly—and personally. The Chief Executive has fared well so far by relying on campaign stand-ins and McGovern's own talent for alienating rational voters with wild, strident oratory.

Devotion to official duties and a desire to keep the presidency above cheap politics are admirable. But Americans expect the personal touch in presidential politics, and they deserve better than the shrill solo they are getting from McGovern.

Most of all, they respect a candidate who speaks out directly for himself and his beliefs. Apathy, not Sen. McGovern, poses the greatest threat to Mr. Nixon's re-election. The best preventive medicine we can think of for that malady is some determined stumping by the President.

The New York Times

New York, N.Y., October 11, 1972

Senator George McGovern's address to the nation on the Vietnam war is a strong indictment of a politically bankrupt and morally ruinous policy. The Nixon Administration's failure to "win the peace" in Vietnam — four years after it was elected on a pledge to do so — and its continuance of the war up to this moment is one of the major issues of this campaign.

Several years ago there was at least an intellectually defensible argument for the view that it was in the American interest to prevent a Communist takeover in South Vietnam, even if that interest never corresponded in size or importance to the enormous military effort which the Johnson Administration invested in its defense. But Mr. Nixon's rapprochement with China and Russia has destroyed whatever rationale may have existed on this ground for further American military effort in Vietnam. Mr. McGovern asks the unanswerable question:

"How can we really argue that it is good to accommodate ourselves to a billion Russian and Chinese Communists but that we must somehow fight to the bitter end against a tiny band of peasant guerrillas in the jungles of little Vietnam?"

President Thieu has destroyed the second reason for American involvement — the right of political self-determination for the people of South Vietnam. Since General Thieu has suppressed virtually all of his political opposition, the U.S. in supporting him can no longer be said to be supporting freedom or self-determination.

Senator McGovern sets forth in detail his alternative to the Nixon-Kissinger policy of secret negotiations and intensified bombing. As he has in the past, he promises to withdraw American military forces completely from Vietnam within ninety days. If the North Vietnamese reciprocate during that time by releasing American prisoners of war, he would follow their action by withdrawing U.S. forces from Thailand.

* * *

The problem of making peace in Vietnam has always been political. The war has been fought to determine the political future of the southern half of the country. Since taking office in 1969, Mr. Nixon has tried to escape that inescapable fact by pursuing two contradictory policies. The pace of American military withdrawal has been tied to the success of "Vietnamization," which is a program of strengthening the Thieu Government. But the pace of the Paris peace talks has been tied by the Communists to the willingness of the U.S. to accept replacement of the Thieu Government. This contradiction has produced nearly four years of blood-stained stalemate, which President Nixon has been unable to break. The commitment to the Thieu Government has proved an insuperable obstacle to peace. Senator McGovern would overcome this obstacle by relinquishing any American responsibility for the political future of South Vietnam.

Senator McGovern was eloquent in his accounting of the terrible costs of a war which has been prolonged for far too long — the lives lost, the hopes blighted, the money squandered, the budget unbalanced and the price level inflated. The ultimate cost is moral. In a sense, the election turns upon the moral capacity of the American people to turn aside from the saving of face and away from misplaced appeals to national honor and to confront at last the true human costs of this war for all participants, Vietnamese and American. Senator McGovern's moving statement of the moral issue deserves an affirmative national response.

© 1972 by The New York Times Company. Reprinted by permission.

The Evening Star

Washington, D.C., October 11, 1972

The most comforting thing about Senator McGovern's Vietnam peace plan is that, given the good sense of the American electorate as reflected in the recent public opinion polls, his chances of ever being in a position to implement it are, to put it mildly, slight.

In last night's televised speech, the Senator from South Dakota lashed out with almost equal bitterness against both President Nixon and President Thieu. He charged Mr. Nixon with enlarging the war and being interested only in saving face and preserving the Thieu regime. The South Vietnamese government he characterized as being a bunch of thieves and drug-pushers "not worth one more American dollar, one more American prisoner, one more drop of American blood." It is doubtful if a candidate for the highest office of any nation has ever so viciously attacked a regime with which his own government is allied.

And the Democratic candidate for president had not a single word of blame or condemnation for North Vietnam, a regime which has waged war against all its neighbors, never held a free election since the Communist seizure there and steadfastly refused to abide by the Geneva protocol governing treatment of prisoners of war.

McGovern's prescription for ending the war is simply to run up the white flag in the hope that somebody in Hanoi will salute. He would unilaterally halt all bombing and other "acts of force" in Indochina, terminate the shipment of military supplies to the war zone and withdraw all American forces (and their equipment) from Vietnam, Laos and Cambodia within 90 days. The expectation is that Hanoi would return all American prisoners during that 90-day period, as well it might in return for such a sell-out.

Once the prisoners were returned and the missing accounted for, McGovern would then close the American bases in Thailand, pulling out all U.S. forces and equipment and withdrawing American naval power from "the waters adjoining Indochina." After which the U.S. would begin repairing "the wreckage left by this war" and offer amnesty to draft-dodgers.

McGovern, in short, proposes an Asian Munich, a recipe for disaster. It would leave the peoples of South Vietnam, Laos and Cambodia to the tender mercies of the Communists and endanger the security of Thailand, Malaysia and Singapore. It would undermine the faith of nations as disparate and far-flung as Iran, Israel and West Germany in the value of an American commitment. It would mock the sacrifice of the 50,000 Americans who have lost their lives in the defense of South Vietnam, the hundreds of thousands wounded there and the expenditure of billions of dollars. That McGovern made his proposals at a time when Henry Kissinger had extended his talks with the North Vietnamese in Paris to an unprecedented fourth day added a note of irony to the speech broadcast last night from the Senate wing of the Capitol.

McGovern's proposals are neither new, realistic nor imaginative. He proposes not negotiation but capitulation, not an honorable end to the war but a surrender which would lead to a further bloodbath of those who have placed their faith in the United States, not a solution but an abdication of responsibility.

The trauma of the Vietnamese war has been such that it is easy to play upon people's emotions by offering simplistic solutions. But we have no doubt that the American people will treat Senator McGovern's white-flag proposals with the contempt they deserve when the nation renders its verdict on November 7.

The Dispatch

Columbus, Ohio, October 12, 1972

AMERICANS impatient for a final end of this nation's involvement in Vietnam have every reason to doubt whether George McGovern's alternative to the current Nixon policy would be any more productive.

Reason for doubt about the effectiveness of the McGovern proposal is insertion of the element of "if" — the same "if" which has plagued President Nixon.

THE PRESIDENT has said that if the American prisoners of war now held by North Vietnam are released and the missing in action accounted for, a settlement of all other issues could be resolved and the bombing of North Vietnam ended.

Mr. McGovern's proposal does not state precisely what he would do, as president, if America met all of North Vietnam's demands and the POW-MIA condition was not met by Hanoi.

But he implies resumption of the use of force.

WHAT IS pivotal in the McGovern proposition is a 90-day stipulation for a pullout of American military forces from Indochina.

It is obvious he has faith the North Vietnamese will resolve the POW-MIA issue within that 90-day period.

IF NOT, what then? Since he has not declared U.S. military forces will be withdrawn all the way back home, it must be reasoned he would keep the bulk of them in the vicinity. That implies he believes resumption of persuasion could be needed.

Such a stance is not far from that being followed now by President Nixon.

BUT IF THIS is not Mr. McGovern's intent — and it must be acknowledged he may shift to another stance as he has all too frequently in the past — then there is only one interpretation for the latest proposal — he is telling Hanoi he wants peace — and at any price. We can't buy that either.

ARGUS-LEADER
Sioux Falls, S.D., October 12, 1972

U.S. Sen. George McGovern's plan to end the Vietnam War contained very little new material. The most notable new idea which he advanced in his speech Tuesday night was his plan if elected, to dispatch his running mate, Sargent Shriver, to Hanoi "to speed the arrangements for the return of our prisoners."

Most of the remainder of his speech was a reiteration of his ideas to hand Hanoi what it wants, with no promises in return for cessation of American hostilities and a pullout of forces from most of Indochina. McGovern would halt arms aid to South Vietnam with no agreement in return from North Vietnam, which President Richard Nixon has sought, that there be a reciprocal reduction of outside aid Hanoi receives from Peking and Moscow.

McGovern's characterization of President Nguyen Van Thieu "as not worth one more American dollar" cannot do anything but hurt the administration's present efforts to achieve some kind of settlement.

McGovern would not require a general cease-fire in South Vietnam. A statement accompanying his speech said a limited, temporary cease-fire is implied in his plan because both sides at Paris have indicated the Communist forces would not attack American troops carrying out an announced pullout. President Richard Nixon has made an internationally supervised Indochina-wide cease fire a major condition.

About the only loophole that McGovern leaves himself in an otherwise complete giveaway to Hanoi would be to keep U.S. forces in Thailand and off Vietnam's shores until America's prisoners are returned and an accounting is made of the missing U.S. servicemen.

McGovern's message to the world, and particularly our allies in Asia, is that in his view the United States is so tired of the Vietnam War that an agreement from the other side is not a necessary prelude to a settlement. In effect, McGovern proposes to hand over South Vietnam to North Vietnam, with no prior agreement of any kind or assurances about the fate of our ally and her people.

Getting the United States out of this unfortunate and terrible war is a lot more difficult than the way this country got into it. Taking the North Vietnamese on faith for their response to McGovern's unilateral offer is not the way to wind up the war. Agreements to end the conflict must be bilateral.

Surely, the American public, which has sacrificed its youth and its tax money and incurred a severe dislocation in its economy and national priorities because of the Vietnam War, will not approve of the kind of softheaded, giveaway settlement that Candidate McGovern has in mind.

The Honolulu Advertiser
Honolulu, Hawaii, October 11, 1972

Senator George McGovern's address on Indochina last night underscores an irony: The Democratic presidential candidate is most likely in a no-win situation on an issue where he has been right — that the U.S. should get out of the no-win war as quickly as possible.

For it will be Nixon who will get the credit for ending the U.S. involvement, despite the fact it has taken him almost four tragic years to do so.

The cost of those years — in American and Vietnamese deaths, POWs, bomb damage and money spent — will never be justified by the final result.

THERE IS AN "if" of sorts, that Nixon ought to produce something that can be called peace before election day. The missions of Henry Kissinger are deliberately raising expectations.

But even if the current secret talks fail again, the feeling is Nixon still has enough margin to win in November. The North Vietnamese know that, so it would be foolish, as some will do, to suggest McGovern is interfering with the chances for a settlement.

The Democratic candidate's proposals will be controversial in several ways and especially so in election season. Ideas such as sending Sargent Shriver to Hanoi lend themselves to humor or scorn.

But McGovern is still far more right than has been Nixon, who has somehow distorted the idea of American national honor into an endorsement of President Thieu, tens of thousands more deaths and bombing on a scale the world has never seen in all previous wars.

MCGOVERN'S SPEECH will mean very little in the face of his campaign mistakes and the massive indifference that marks many American attitudes on Vietnam.

We hope it doesn't happen, but the bitterest irony is that it would only mean something to most Americans after it is too late — if the war and killing by Americans continue past election day.

The Evening Bulletin
Philadelphia, Pa., October 13, 1972

Discounting the possibility that a pre-election Vietnam settlement is in the offing, and disregarding any criticism that his words might help to prevent such a settlement, Senator McGovern asserts that the choice in the 1972 election is Vietnam peace with him or more war under President Nixon.

The senator, of course, may himself have no choice but to refocus attention upon the antiwar theme. It inspired his followers in the primary and enabled him to capture the Democratic presidential nomination. It may help now to sharpen an image that has become blurred.

The Vietnam war does remain a legitimate issue, no matter how many American troops have been withdrawn by President Nixon. A peace settlement would further deflate that issue, but it is perfectly proper that the Nixon Administration is challenged for slow delivery on its promise to produce peace — on the lives lost, and the billions expended, under its policy of gradual withdrawal from Vietnam over the past four years.

If there is no peace settlement between now and November 7, Mr. Nixon by all rights should be more vulnerable to challenge on the peace terms he is offering and the military policy he is following to support them.

Yet Senator McGovern, spelling out in a major address the details of his own plan for peace in Indochina, seems not to grasp the scope of the change that has taken place since the Nixon Administration took office. Neither the content of his plan nor the tone of his approach seems calculated to win wide response.

Mr. McGovern sees the difference between himself and Mr. Nixon on the war as the most important one of the campaign. He sees America as being offered "the choice of the century." But as he presents this choice, it seems to boil down to one between good and evil. More than moral, he is evangelical. He wants the country, not just to elect a President, but to cast out devils.

But of course it isn't that simple. The country quite clearly isn't prepared to subscribe to a viewpoint which so thoroughly condemns U.S. actions, but not likewise the aggression from North Vietnam. Nor does it appear entirely humanitarian, or in keeping with an appeal to the American conscience to abandon, not corrupt rulers, but people who have fought beside Americans without assuring those allies safety or sanctuary.

The terms on which Mr. McGovern proposes finally to extract the U.S. from the war appear more sharply than ever as simply conceding the field to the North Vietnamese.

He would halt American bombing, swiftly and unconditionally remove all American forces from Vietnam, Cambodia and Laos. He would take out all American military equipment that could be salvaged, and send in no more military supplies. The Vietnamese would be left to settle their own affairs, and the U.S. would support any settlement made.

What the United States would expect would be its prisoners returned and an accounting for those missing in action. That done, American bases in Thailand would be abandoned and U.S. ships withdrawn from Indochinese waters.

This is a bit much in the way of concession to the Communists without negotiation. And the McGovern plan would not seem, at this point in time, to offer a viable alternative to the Nixon policies even if these do not seal a peace pact before November 7.

Campaign '72:

WATERGATE PROBE BARRED IN HOUSE; WIDE GOP SABOTAGE EFFORT REPORTED

The House Banking and Currency Committee Oct. 3 rejected a proposal to probe possible violations of banking laws in connection with the break-in at the Democratic headquarters in the Watergate office building and possible irregularities in Republican campaign financing. [See pp. 1132-1138] The vote was 20-15, with six of the panel's 22 Democrats voting with the majority. Chairman Wright Patman (D, Tex.), who offered the proposal, accused the White House after the vote of "engineering" the rejection of the probe, which was set under his proposal to subpoena some 40 individuals and organizations, including top Nixon campaign aides, for testimony.

Other major developments in the Watergate case:

■ L. Patrick Gray 3rd, acting director of the Federal Bureau of Investigation, Oct. 2 upheld the propriety of the Nixon Administration itself investigating the Watergate case even though it involved former Administration aides and a Republican committee. Gray said he had taken the case "under my own wing" and "there's not been one single bit of pressure put on me or any of my special agents" concerning the probe. Gray also discounted the possibility of presidential involvement in the incident. "It strains the credulity that the President of the United States—if he had a mind to—could have done a con job on the whole American people," he said.

■ Chief U.S. District Court Judge John J. Sirica issued a broad order prohibiting all law enforcement agencies, defendants, and witnesses, "including complaining witnesses and alleged victims... and all persons acting for or with them in connection with this case" from making extra-judicial public statements to anyone, "including the news media," concerning the Watergate case. Democratic presidential candidate George McGovern said Oct. 4 that he would not allow himself "to be muzzled or intimidated." Sirica eased the ban Oct. 6 by deleting the phrase referring to witnesses.

■ Alfred C. Baldwin 3rd, a former FBI agent, disclosed Oct 5 in the *Los Angeles Times* that he had monitored telephone and other conversations at the Watergate for three weeks while employed by the Committee to Re-elect the President. He said he had delivered the information he obtained to a Nixon campaign official who had not yet been indicted in the Watergate case.

■ President Nixon said at a news conference Oct. 5 that he would not comment on the Watergate case because grand jury indictments had been handed down and the case was before the courts.

■ *The Washington Post* reported Oct. 10 that the Watergate raid was but part of a larger espionage and sabotage effort against the Democrats on behalf of the Nixon re-election campaign. The paper quoted federal investigators as describing the operation as "unprecedented in scope and intensity." The story reported that a letter used in the New Hampshire primary against Sen. Edmund S. Muskie (D, Me.) was one such sabotage attempt. The letter, in which Muskie was accused of condoning the use of the epithet "Canucks" in reference to Americans with French-Canadian backgrounds, according to the story, was written by White House aide Ken W. Clawson. At the time it had been ascribed to a Paul Morrison of Deerfield Beach, Fla. Morrison had never been located.

ARKANSAS DEMOCRAT
Little Rock, Ark., October 7, 1972

Now we learn that a former FBI agent says he bugged the Democratic Headquarters at Watergate and delivered transcripts to Nixon campaign headquarters.

This adds to the already large accumulation of evidence that somebody in the Nixon campaign was employing illegal means of snooping on the Democrats. Additional evidence indicates that the snooping was ordered or at least condoned at high levels. Maurice Stans, former commerce secretary and campaign fund raiser, handled a check that went to one of the men charged with the bugging. And John Mitchell, former attorney general and later head of the Nixon campaign, reportedly controlled a secret intelligence fund, the records of which have been destroyed.

The matter has been confused considerably by political rhetoric. Some say for that reason it should wait until after the election. But the fact remains that it is a political issue. It involves very serious charges concerning one of the candidates, and the public deserves a full investigation, or at least an explanation by the Republican Party.

The charges filed against the five men who were arrested in the Watergate Offices and two other men serve more to prevent full disclosure than to bring it about. Standard prosecution procedure would have granted immunity to one of more of these alleged lower-echelon agents to acquire information about who ordered and paid for the operation. With all of them charged, none is obliged to do anything but plead his own case, which is pretty well sewed up by the fact that they were caught on the premises with bugging equipment. That is all the more reason to believe that the Nixon administration's Justice Department is not the proper agency to investigate charges against employes of the Nixon campaign for President. The FBI could be working just as well for a special prosecutor that has no connection with either party's presidential campaign.

Congress had an opening to break through the roadblocks to an investigation set up by Republicans. The House Banking Committee, under the leadership of Rep. Wright Patman, D-Tex., tried. But a committee hearing was voted down 20-15 Tuesday, when six Democrats joined the 14 Republicans on the committee in opposing it. This is a surprising and sad performance by a Congress that has been complaining about its loss of power to the executive branch. But mostly it is a blow to the chances of the public to learn more about what could be one of the most important issues in the election campaign.

The Republicans' refusal to discuss the matter and their actions to delay investigations until after the election increase the cynicism about government that permeates American society. And Congress' reluctance to do any more, in its haste to adjourn, doesn't help. We urge Patman to continue his efforts to bring about a congressional investigation. If he fails there, we wish him luck in his latest effort to get the General Accounting Office to make a study and make a preliminary report by October 26.

Los Angeles Times
Los Angeles, Calif., October 6, 1972

District Court Judge John J. Sirica has sought to prohibit further investigation of the Watergate electronic eavesdropping case with an order so sweeping that he has acknowledged it might affect discussion of the case by presidential candidates.

The order is a shocking abuse of judicial power, an obvious infringement of constitutional rights. And it is the more worrying because it has been taken on the initiative of one of those under indictment in the case with particular interest in suppressing information on the case prior to the election, because he was on the White House staff at the time of the eavesdropping. There simply is no evidence to support the premise of Judge Sirica that publicity makes impossible a fair trial. The whole history of judicial operation in an open and free society demonstrates the contrary, that the best assurance of a fair trial is freedom of information.

Neither President Nixon nor Sen. George McGovern was silenced by the judge, however.

Mr. Nixon reaffirmed at his press conference Thursday that he had known nothing of the case and that he was confident, from the thoroughness of the FBI investigation, that no one in his campaign organization was involved beyond those already among the seven indicted last month.

Senator McGovern said he would not be silenced in his discussion of the case. His fellow Democrat, Senate Majority Leader Mike Mansfield, expressed "grave doubts about the wisdom and the legality of the judge's dictum."

The campaign for silence is pervasive. A federal civil court action has been postponed on grounds it might jeopardize the criminal proceedings, and Congress gave the same reason for voting down an inquiry. If the public is to learn anything more before election day, it will be through the unlikely possibility of a speedy criminal trial, or through the press, or in the General Accounting Office study due Oct. 27.

The need for further investigation was made clearer than ever in the account of the bugging of Democratic National Committee Headquarters written for The Times by one of the participants, Alfred C. Baldwin III. His account suggested that not all of the Nixon headquarters staff involved in the eavesdropping are named in the indictment. His story makes it difficult to accept the insistence that no senior Republican campaign official was aware of this operation or in control of the large sums of money involved.

Secrecy and silence will not solve these mysteries.

The Cleveland Press
Cleveland, Ohio, October 4, 1972

There won't be any investigation of the Watergate caper or the "roaming check" story by the House Banking Committee, Chairman Wright Patman notwithstanding.

Soon after he heard that several checks headed for the Committee for the Re-election of the President had been wandering from Mexico to Florida and elsewhere, Patman saw a chance to investigate on the possibility that some banking laws had been violated.

The Watergate caper broke when five men were arrested last June and charged with breaking into Democratic National Headquarters. The s u s p e c t s since have been indicted and accused, among other things, of bugging the Democratic offices.

Later there were charges that checks contributed to the Nixon committee for campaign expenses at one point had been in the hands of one of the men accused of the Watergate bust-in.

But the banking committee has voted down Patman's plan, 20 to 15. Fifteen of the no-probe votes came from Republicans, not surprisingly, on the theory that a congressional inquiry might prejudice the trial of the defendants in the Watergate caper.

That's possible, of course, but it is fair to wonder just how sympathetic the Republicans would have been for the rights of the defendants if the defendants had been Democrats.

However, six Democratic members of the committee voted against the investigation on this same principle — or perhaps they didn't think the investigation would learn much anyway, or b e c a u s e they didn't think it was much of a campaign issue.

Until the men indicted in the bugging go to trial, we are not apt to learn much more about the reasons for this caper. But meanwhile there is no excuse for the Committee for the Re-election of the President to remain mute about those itinerant checks.

THE LINCOLN STAR
Lincoln, Neb., October 5, 1972

By a vote of 20-15 Tuesday the House Banking Committee refused to investigate the financial aspects surrounding the June break-in of Democratic National headquarters by agents linked to the Committee to Re-elect the President The vote apparently stifles the last opportunity Democrats hoped would result in public hearings on the Watergate incident before the election.

The 14 Republicans and six Democrats who formed the committee majority on the vote were in general agreement that a House investigation would mingle politics with justice and that it might prejudice the government's case against and/or violate the rights of those indicted in the break-in.

The 15 Democrats who sought the investigation predicted that public opinion would force a reversal of the committee action. And if it did, it would be for the good.

For one thing, the investigation, as proposed by Rep. Wright Patman, committee chairman, would be aimed at tracing the campaign contributions which a l l e g e d l y financed the break-in to determine whether any U.S. banking laws had been violated and to see if political favoritism had any role in awarding of bank charters. That seems to be within the purview of a congressional committee.

For another, none of the seven men indicted in the Watergate caper was on the list of those to be subpoenaed by the committee if the investigation had come off. This would have diminished the possibility of prejudice for or against any of the defendants in the civil or criminal actions.

The committee's action amounts to an abdication of the responsibility it has to set the record straight.

Rep. Henry Reuss, who fought for the investigation, best summed it up. The committee, Reuss said, has a duty to "uncover skullduggery, whether by R e p u b l i c a n s, Democrats or nonpartisans."

St. Petersburg Times
St. Petersburg, Fla., October 4, 1972

The indictment of seven men, including a recent $100-a-day White House consultant and two officials (now resigned) of the Committee for the Re-Election of the President, for burglarizing and bugging Democratic National Committee headquarters exposed the odor but not the substance of what is recognized in Washington as possibly the smelliest political scandal in our history.

Although the original arrests were made four months ago, trials of the accused men and of a related civil suit brought by the Democrats are not scheduled until after the November election.

EVEN THEN, prosecution by the Nixon Department of Justice is unlikely to provide answers to the larger questions: Who instigated the electronic surveillance of the opposition party's headquarters, who profited by it, and how and why was $114,000 in CRP campaign funds channeled by devious routes — most of it through Mexico City — into the Miami bank account of one of the self-admitted burglars.

For weeks top Democratic Party officials have brought quiet but intense pressure on Sen. Edward M. Kennedy, D-Mass., to take jurisdiction for the Senate Judiciary subcommittee which he heads, and to hold public hearings at which witnesses, including responsible officers of the CRP, could be examined under oath.

But Sen. Kennedy has "no plans" to pick up the political hot potato. Apparently, no other congressional committee is in a position to conduct an effective investigation.

THE HOUSE Banking Committee, which might have taken jurisdiction, voted 20-to-15 yesterday not to conduct an investigation, with six Democrats joining all 14 Republicans in opposition. The Justice Department had formally protested Chairman Wright Patman's plans to hold hearings and to subpoena top officials of the CRP and financial records relating to the questionable transfer of committee funds.

Meanwhile, the public is lulled into dismissing the whole affair as a "caper," the misleading headline term that the press has attached to it.

We believe, in this case, Sen. Kennedy should place the public's right to know ahead of any personal political considerations.

Wire-tapping and electronic bugging of political opponents is not a caper. It is deadly serious public business.

The Washington Post

Washington, D.C., October 8, 1972

Rancid is a word we rarely use except when dealing with environmental issues and the need to find better ways to dispose of waste in our society. But, rancid is just about the only word to apply to what we know about the Watergate crimes, the circumstances surrounding them and the allegations concerning them which have not been laid to rest. The incredible, but internally consistent and persuasive interview which Alfred Baldwin III gave to the Los Angeles Times and which was reprinted in this newspaper on Friday—even if it doesn't give all the facts about the higher-ups in this affair—gives you all you want to know and more about its character.

It tells you, in short, that the Nixon campaign committee was running, under innocuous cover and with "laundered" campaign money, a clandestine intelligence operation worthy of the Central Intelligence Agency. In the jargon of professional intelligence agents, this is what is sometimes known as a Department of Dirty Tricks. And Mr. Baldwin's account also tells us that the dirty tricks were not simply directed at Democratic Party headquarters, but that, even from underling Baldwin's limited vantage point, they were directed at a variety of Democratic political targets such as activities at Sen. McGovern's pre-convention headquarters and at the Democratic Convention itself.

Moreover, Baldwin's story—even if it doesn't exactly connect John L. Mitchell as the directing force behind the dirty tricks department—shows at best a certain lack of bureaucratic distinction between the Mitchells' personal needs, the use of government property and outright criminal activity. Mr. Baldwin tells us that he was hired by James McCord, security chief for the Nixon campaign committee, to provide security for Mrs. Mitchell after Mr. Mitchell had left the government. Before one of his trips with her, he was given eight crisp new $100 bills to pay for "food, drinks, tips and incidental expenses." And, when he got to New York, even though Mrs. Mitchell was no longer the wife of a government official, they were chauffeured around in J. Edgar Hoover's bullet-proof limousine —which presumably still belonged to the U.S. Government.

Then, Baldwin, after being personally thanked by Mr. Mitchell for the fine job he had done in taking care of Mrs. Mitchell, was shifted by McCord to the job of monitoring illegally installed wiretaps at the Democrats' headquarters. And, on the way to do that job, he was given five more crisp new $100 bills presumably to pay for the incidental expenses of his newly assigned chores for the committee to re-elect Richard Nixon President of the United States.

New hundred dollar bills weren't the only tools he was given to ply his trade. He was issued a ".38 snub-nosed police special." When he protested that he had no permit to carry a weapon, he says he was told by McCord, "You're working for the former attorney general and there's no way a policeman or any other law enforcement officer is going to question your right to carry that weapon. But, if you have any problem, have them call me." Later, he says he was told that the pistol had belonged to Fred La Rue, a former Nixon White House aide, whom McCord described as being "over from the White House" and "John Mitchell's right-hand man." That kind of White House name-dropping seems to have been fairly commonplace and to have impressed and reassured Mr. Baldwin.

The rest is like the plot of a very bad spy novel. People were using code names. A former White House official was carrying around a pistol wrapped in a towel inside an attache case. There was an abortive attempt to break into McGovern's headquarters to monitor phone calls. There was bugging equipment said to be worth $15,000. Cars rendezvoued in the night with the help of a lot of walkie-talkie conversation. Mr. Baldwin listened to about 200 illegally tapped phone calls from the Democrats' headquarters in three weeks. There was his entry into Democratic committee headquarters under an assumed name in order to find chairman O'Brien's office and to diagram it. And finally, there was Mr. Baldwin acting as lookout from a Howard Johnson's across the street on the night of the burglary, June 17.

Mr. Baldwin never questioned any of McCord's orders, because, in his words, "I felt he was acting under orders and with full authority. After all, his boss was John Mitchell, the committee director and former Attorney General of the United States."

That pretty well wraps up Mr. Baldwin's story. Of course, there are other hanging accusations, many of which we have posed in these columns. One of the latest, however, is that some of the information obtained from the illegal wiretaps was delivered to the White House itself—to Mr. William Timmons, assistant to the President for congressional relations—and also to people high in the Nixon campaign committee. Another new revelation is that a contribution of $100,000 to the Nixon campaign was clearly illegal. Because of the tortured and secret trail it took from corporate coffers to Nixon committee headquarters in a suitcase, it is hard to tell whether it was a contribution by a corporation or by a foreign national. It doesn't much matter, though. Both are illegal.

So, there you have it—guns, code names, illegal $100,000 contributions, a stash of several hundred thousand in cash said to have been controlled by the Attorney General of the United States while he was in office, and burglars caught red-handed in a venture which everybody in authority tries to paint as the bizarre caper of a few misguided individuals. Meanwhile the President tells us his investigation of all this made his Hiss investigation look like a "Sunday School exercise," and both Mr. Nixon and Mr. Mitchell tell us they don't know what was going on. If that is true, it is an admission of an enormous and irresponsible ignorance. Sen. McGovern has been roundly and thoroughly criticized (and in many instances appropriately, we think) for not having complete control over his staff. But, taking Mr. Nixon and Mr. Mitchell at their words, the McGovern staff operation looks extraordinarily controlled and competent by comparison. Sen. McGovern's people have been accused only of running around with loose tongues. The operatives in behalf of the re-election of the President were apparently running around with loose guns, committing squalid crimes, arrogantly ignoring law and minimal decency. Mr. Nixon can't have it both ways. Either he was responsible for these crimes committed in his behalf by his agents or he was not. If he was not, it amounts to a breathtaking confession of managerial incompetence and a gross abdication of responsibility.

THE DALLAS TIMES HERALD

Dallas, Tex., October 5, 1972

THE LAST effort by Democrats to make a campaign issue out of what is known as the Watergate Ca- per—the break-in last June at Washington Democratic headquarters— has failed. It is well that it did fail: It would be hard to get an objective investigation in the closing weeks of a presidential campaign.

Rep. Wright Patman's Banking Committee voted down his effort to subpoena the bigwigs of the Committee to Reelect the President—the men who Democrats have been saying for months are responsible for the raid on the plush hotel headquarters.

None of the top GOP brass acknowledges any link with Watergate and they would not have answered any subpoenas or made sport for Patman in a preelection "trial" of the incident. Patman, they say, can't even spell the word Republican. Besides, the law has taken stern notice of Watergate; the facts can be left to the courts.

SEVEN MEN, five of them caught with eavesdropping equipment inside Democratic headquarters last June 16, have been indicted. Both their trial (they have pleaded innocent) and the civil damage suits cross-filed by the political parties themselves have been safely docketed for trial after the election.

It is bad luck for the Democrats. Watergate might have been their big campaign issue if they could have convinced the public that Mr. Nixon and his lieutenants sent five scroungy adventurers to implant electronic "bugging" equipment in the opposition's headquarters.

But from first to last, Watergate has been a waterhaul. Americans are aware of the break-in and probably do believe that there is—as McGovern's campaign chief Larry O'Brien has said so many times— such a thing as "political espionage." But cynically or resignedly, Americans seem to regard it as part of the game. There is no evidence at all that they believe the President had prior knowledge of the incursion.

ALL THE same, burglary is a crime, and somebody is accountable for the break-in. One of the five intruders, James W. McCord, was security chairman for the reelection committee until a short time previous to the break-in. What's more, a large sum of GOP campaign money did end up in the Florida bank account of another of the indicted men.

The Justice Department says it has the facts and the trials might afford a fascinating look at the lower echelon aspects of professional political campaigning—the cloak-and-dagger side. The only surprise would be that higher GOP brass either ordered or condoned the goings-on.

If a congressional investigation is in order, both Democrats and Republicans on the Patman committee must have reasoned that the closing month of a presidential campaign is not the most propitious time to unearth all of the story.

THE SACRAMENTO BEE
Sacramento, Calif., October 15, 1972

The moral breakdown implicit in the Watergate bugging incident is frightening. The public as a whole seems somewhat indifferent about what should be treated far more seriously than a "caper." For Watergate can touch us all.

Evidence by FBI agents has established that the raid on Democratic National Committee headquarters and the electronic spying that went with it were part of a widespread campaign of snooping and political sabotage conducted on behalf of President Richard Nixon's re-election. The investigators pinned down, too, that these activities were directed by White House aides and the Committee for the Re-election of the President.

Nixon's press secretary, Ronald Ziegler, at one point dismissed the Watergate affair as "third-rate burglary." This soft, head-in-the-sand attitude is not shared by Chairman Wright Patman of the House Banking Committee. The feisty Texas Democrat called it "the most sordid political tactics ever employed by a major political party."

Many people are disturbed by the thought that if Watergate can be glossed over or covered up, it will invite police-state surveillance over public officials, political leaders, professional people and even the average citizen. Americans may not be aware of the extent to which governmental agencies and private companies now use computers and microfilm to collect, store and exchange sensitive information about the activities of private individuals. It is, alas, a documented fact.

If you think "it can't happen here," just go back a few months to the disclosure of Army spying on the lawful political activities of a wide range of groups, and incident reports on individual citizens. Protests and a lawsuit prompted the Army to announce it was abandoning the data bank — but turning over the data to the internal security division of the Justice Department.

Watergate should wake up Americans to the inherent threat to the precious fundamental right of privacy. Every aspect of the case demands the broadest possible airing and everyone connected with it should be brought to trial.

The New York Times
New York, N.Y., October 12, 1972

The Watergate affair has taken an astonishing and profoundly disturbing turn.

At first, it seemed that the men arrested for burglarizing and "bugging" the offices of the Democratic National Committee in the Watergate Building in Washington, D. C., were engaged in an ugly but isolated act of political espionage. But investigative reporting by The Washington Post and other newspapers has now uncovered a complex, far-reaching and sinister operation on the part of White House aides and the Nixon campaign organization. This operation involves sabotage, forgery, theft of confidential files, surveillance of Democratic candidates and their families and persistent efforts to lay the basis for possible blackmail and intimidation.

For more than a year, a secret fund existed in the Nixon headquarters which financed these "special activities" and to which only certain key officials had access. Many hundreds of thousands of dollars in cash flowed through this secret fund. Dozens of people, including numerous ex-F.B.I. and ex-C.I.A. agents, were employed in this clandestine work. High-ranking officials including some still employed at the White House and at the Committee to Re-elect the President received copies of the confidential reports prepared by these agents on the basis of their wiretapping and their surveillance of leading Democrats.

A notably dramatic episode involves a letter which surfaced in the New Hampshire primary last February. It stated that Senator Edmund S. Muskie, while campaigning in Florida, had made a derogatory reference to Americans of French-Canadian background. The letter never seemed plausible on its face but, played up by the scurrilous Manchester Union Leader, it weakened Mr. Muskie among French-Canadian voters in that city.

It is now asserted that this letter was forged by a White House staff member in a deliberate effort to weaken Mr. Muskie, then the front-running Democratic candidate. The staff man has denied the allegation, but Senator Muskie is surely right that this serious charge and the many others which have come to public knowledge in recent weeks demand a personal response by President Nixon. The veracity and integrity of the President's staff and campaign organization are at stake.

Much of the public has reportedly taken the attitude up to now that there is nothing particularly unusual in the Watergate affair. It cannot be reiterated too strongly that, on the contrary, such practices are unprecedented in American politics. No national party and no incumbent Administration has ever set out in this systematic fashion to invade the privacy, disrupt the activities, and discredit the leadership of the political opposition. These are ambitions and police-state tactics which have no place in a democracy.

© 1972 by The New York Times Company. Reprinted by permission.

THE MILWAUKEE JOURNAL
Milwaukee, Wis., October 14, 1972

Tales of skulduggery swirl ever more thickly around the Nixon administration. Yet, observers report, the public seems strangely unmoved.

Lack of exposure cannot be blamed. Many are aware of such damaging things as the ITT affair, which cast doubt on the enforcement of antitrust laws and left suspicion of influence peddling in high places; the milk case, which revealed linkage between dairy lobby donations to the Republican Party and higher milk price support; the Watergate bugging caper, with its ties to the Committee for the Re-election of the President (CREEP) and money contributed by secret Republican donors; the Russian wheat deal, with its indications of questionable ethical conduct by government officials and insider profiteering by large grain firms; and now the astonishing stories by the Washington Post, apparently based on leaked FBI information, showing widespread spying, sabotage and other sinister activity directed at the Democrats by members of the White House staff and CREEP.

If the public response is as limp as it seems, there probably are several explanations. The stories of scandal are complicated; pieces are difficult to fit together. Many of the worst charges have not been adequately proved, at least not yet — and with Congress hurrying to adjourn and wrongly willing to let the administration investigate itself, it seems that solid answers to allegations of guilt will be postponed until well after the election. It must also be noted that the president himself has not been tied to any particular misdeed, leaving people free to believe, or at least hope, that the presidency is clean even if there is some corruption in the ranks.

Perhaps the most important reason for lack of discernible public alarm is the general mood of the electorate. Apathy is the wrong word, because even the nation's rather comfortable majority seems concerned about many problems. But, as several voter surveys suggest, people are rather depressed and heavily inclined to caution and disbelief of politicians as a breed. Most voters are not thrilled by Nixon but neither are they ready to accept challenger George McGovern as, on the whole, a better alternative. They are wary of promises and of attempts by both sides in this election to claim purity for themselves while attributing only wickedness to the opposition. Many voters, in short, see things like the Watergate break-in as "politics as usual," as an example of the dishonesty that both political parties have practiced through the years.

Up to a point, of course, public skepticism is healthy. An easily bamboozled citizenry is no asset to a self-governing society. And surely both parties are capable of corruption. Yet there is danger in the mood today. One must wonder: As questions of misconduct in Washington pile up faster than answers, how long can a conscientious citizen react with a shrug instead of an outcry? At what point does sensible skepticism become useless cynicism — a mental swamp where moral indignation is smothered in the ooze?

Campaign '72:

MOST PRESS ENDORSEMENTS BACK NIXON-AGNEW FOR RE-ELECTION

U.S. daily newspapers were supporting the re-election of President Nixon and Vice President Agnew by a vast majority, according to the Nov. 4 issue of the trade magazine *Editor & Publisher*. Of the 1054 newspapers polled by the magazine, 753 (71.4%) supported the Republican ticket while only 56 (5.3%) supported the Democratic ticket of Sen. George S. McGovern (S.D.) and R. Sargent Shriver. The remaining newspapers polled had taken no formal position in the presidential race.

RAPID CITY JOURNAL—

Rapid City, S.D., October 24, 1972

Four years ago, the Rapid City Journal supported Democratic Senator George McGovern in his bid for re-election. It was a sincere endorsement, affected in part by the stature he had gained by sampling the presidential nominating waters at the Democratic National Convention in Chicago in 1968.

That same year the Journal also supported Richard Nixon for President.

South Dakota gave its vote to the Democratic senator and to the Republican presidential candidate. But now, under circumstances that may never be repeated, South Dakotans must choose between these same two men for the highest office in the land. With consternation, many find they never really knew Senator McGovern's beliefs until now. Our native son does not seem to reflect the mainstream of South Dakota's thinking. This poses a dilemma for those who see a first-time-ever South Dakota relationship with the White House.

The Nixon-McGovern question should not be decided on the basis of state pride. The question is what is good for America. We do not feel America is ready for Senator McGovern.

We see South Dakota's senator as a humanitarian and an idealist, yes. But his oratory reflects a spirit of defeatism, as if America is on its knees. We also are dismayed by his rhetoric and by his frequent changes in position, leaving Americans confused and disillusioned by his waffling.

Conversely, President Nixon has been positive and firm. Yet he has been flexible as shown by hard decisions to go to Moscow and Peking and to initiate wage-price controls. He is identified with the center of America's thinking, including the average South Dakotan. He has moved the country along at an acceptable pace and has guided us well in foreign affairs.

President Nixon has not been everything we would like in a national leader. He has, however, taken some bum raps and has been handicapped by a Congress heavy with men who coveted the presidency for themselves. Much good legislation has been passed in spite of this partisan division and because President Nixon has mustered votes when he was right. True, he has not made everybody happy.

We believe the majority agrees with his approach to disengaging us from the most unpopular war in history. Abject surrender would leave us without honor and would have worldwide repercussions.

Granted, there is disagreement, but the nation is not in the turmoil it was four years ago. There is prosperity and record employment. America's progress since 1968 is the envy of the world.

President Nixon has run the country pretty well and there is reason to believe people will be still better off under his program to decentralize government.

The times require a man who is tested and proven. President Nixon has shown that he can lead with skill and with firmness. On that basis, he should have another four years in the world's most punishing job.

Chicago today American

Chicago, Ill., October 15, 1972

AFTER SEN. GEORGE McGovern won the Democratic nomination in July, we commented that this would be a different kind of Presidential campaign; it would be not so much a contest between two parties or two candidates as between two ways of feeling. The real test was between voters who are fed up with the "old politics"—as represented by President Nixon and the entrenched leaders of both parties —and those who are offended or frightened by the new.

That seems somewhat less true now, because so many voters who might be temperamentally inclined toward McGovern have been chilled by his showing as a campaigner—the bad guesses, the disorganization, the air of frantic improvising. The question must have occurred even to the most devoted McGovern supporters: If this happened to his campaign, what would happen to his administration?

Still, personal and individual feelings undoubtedly will play a greater part than usual in the voters' choice. It is not our intention to try to change them, but to decide as objectively as possible who has the stronger case for election Nov. 7. And on the record we think President Nixon has.

The standout fact of Nixon's administration—of this decade, in fact—is the amazing change he has brought about in international relations. Ten years ago, Red China was a looming, inscrutable menace; the United States and the Soviet Union were edging close to war over the Cuban missile crisis; the prospect of total nuclear devastation was one we had to live with daily. Today, we and the Russians are busily putting together agreements on everything from arms limitation to antipollution efforts, China has become a trading partner whose interests in some respects parallel our own, and the two Communist giants are on rather better terms with the United States than they are with each other.

Nixon has shown himself adept at international dealings. McGovern has not; his view of foreign policy seems to be essentially that we should be more trusting and less assertive. We do not find it convincing.

Viet Nam remains Nixon's chief weakness. He has tried hard for peace there; the grating fact is that he hasn't got it. But here too, McGovern's peace plan is so unnecessarily sweeping that it makes the Nixon approach look better. Beyond a commitment to pull out of Indochina and leave it without American-made arms and materiel, the McGovern plan almost amounts to indemnifying the North Vietnamese for their losses in attacking the South.

On the economy, Mr. Nixon's record is one of trying hard and adopting new approaches, with respectable if incomplete success. The McGovern program of sweeping overhauls based on economic theories may have a certain adventurous appeal; we can't see that as reason enough to elect him.

There is much we like about George McGovern, much that we dislike about the Nixon administration. What we find decisive, tho, is that Mr. Nixon has shown he can handle the job ably and McGovern has not convinced us he could.

Richmond Times-Dispatch
Richmond, Va., October 8, 1972

Four years ago, fear, despair and distrust were casting long shadows across the face of America. More than half a million American men were fighting in an unpopular Asian war, the end of which was nowhere in sight. The United States and the Communist bloc were glowering at one another across a chasm of hate and suspicion, as they had been doing since World War II, and rapprochement appeared to be an Ice Age away. Here at home, inflation was mangling paychecks, volcanoes of violence were erupting on campuses and in ghettoes, and crime was transforming the nation's central cities into jungles of terror.

A New Mood

Four years ago. Today, a new mood prevails in the land. The nation is regaining hope and confidence as the seemingly insoluble problems of four years ago show signs of yielding to solutions. America's ground involvement in the Vietnam war has virtually ended, campuses and cities have become calmer, inflation is waning and the world's major powers are moving, if ever so slowly, from an age of confrontation into what promises to be an era of at least limited cooperation. No, the millenium has not arrived, but there is no question that the United States is a healthier and happier nation than it was four years ago and that the world is a more relaxed and hopeful place.

It would be naive to credit one man, and one man alone, for the conditions that have generated this new atmosphere of hope, but it would be asinine to deny that one man has played a preeminent role in the developments that have brought them about. That man is President Richard M. Nixon. It is largely because of his innovative leadership that the United States now appears to be on the high road to recovery from its domestic ailments and that the world has begun a tentative march upon what could be the high road to enduring peace.

Now, not for one moment do we ascribe omniscience, omnipotence or saintliness to this Republican President. During the past four years, he has erred more than once, and this newspaper has often been among his critics. But Mr. Nixon's mistakes have been eclipsed by his spectacular successes, and those dramatic achievements clearly justify his re-election.

The Record

Consider the highlights of his record:

He has reversed the United States's involvement in the Vietnam war, an involvement that reached its peak during the administration of his Democratic predecessor, by withdrawing most of the 540,000 American troops who were there when he took office. Moreover, he has offered extremely generous peace proposals, and only the greed and arrogance of North Vietnam—which would like to see the United States grovel, renounce its solemn pledges and abandon an ally—keep the war going.

Crashing through the frigid barriers of the Cold War, Mr. Nixon journeyed to Peking to open the United States' first dialogue with Red China and to Moscow to negotiate historic arms and trade agreements with the Soviet Union. As a result of his courageous moves, mutual fear may soon cease to be the dominant factor in relations between the U. S. and Communist bloc nations. It is no exaggeration to say that Richard Nixon has contributed more to a relaxation of world tensions than any other President since World War II. At the same time, however, Mr. Nixon has made it clear that he is no peace-at-any-price President for he is convinced that the U. S. must remain militarily strong and loyal to its friends.

Mr. Nixon's accomplishments on the domestic front have been no less dramatic than his achievements in international affairs. He has succeeded in halving the rate of inflation without plunging the nation into a recession. Business activity, in fact, is increasing. Measures that he has advanced or supported have contributed to marked successes in the nation's unending war against crime. His superb appointments to the U. S. Supreme Court—Chief Justice Warren E. Burger, Associate Justices Harry A. Blackmun, William Rehnquist and Lewis F. Powell Jr. — have increased that tribunal's devotion to the integrity of the Constitution. The President's opposition to the compulsory busing of schoolchildren for racial purposes has encouraged those who are convinced that this pernicious practice is capable of ruining public education in America. His promotion of economic opportunities for minority groups and his numerous appointments of minority group members to important governmental posts refute the charge, heard often from his political foes, that he is indifferent to the needs and aspirations of nonwhites.

This, in summary, is the record of the administration of President Richard Nixon and Vice President Spiro Agnew, and an impressive record it is. Does the opposition offer anything better or even as good? No. Democratic nominee George S. McGovern may be a thoroughly decent man, but he is one of the most unattractive presidential candidates any major party ever presented to the nation.

Senator McGovern's program features proposals that are irresponsible, dangerous and philosophically repugnant. He would expand welfarism, enlarge the federal bureaucracy, support forced busing of school children, discourage economic growth with unsound tax measures and reduce military spending to the point of imperiling the nation's defenses.

But even if McGovern's program were unassailable, he would remain unacceptable. It is a tragic fact that this man, as many members of his own party readily admit, has shown no capacity for leadership. McGovern's performance during this campaign has revealed him to be shallow, erratic and even deceptive. Operationally, his campaign has involved one blunder after another. Some of the senator's most ardent supporters during his primary campaign have deserted him because of his incredible ineptness.

America's choice, then, is between President Nixon, whose responsible and progressive record has infused the nation—and the world—with new hope, and Senator McGovern, whose irresponsible and disjointed campaign proposals have confused the nation and the world and may even contain the seeds of disaster. The choice is clear: Richard Nixon should be returned to office on November 7.

The Courier-Journal
Louisville, Ky., October 15, 1972

IT'S NO mere accident of history that before democracy died in Athens 2,400 years ago, its citizens fell into a resentful malaise with parallels observable in America in election year 1972. When people no longer trust their government but see no better alternative, their disillusionment leaves them weak, disunited and susceptible to those who don't understand or don't really want democracy.

In 23 days we elect our next President, choosing between a Republican incumbent who is running the highest-priced, most carefully orchestrated campaign in U.S. history, and a Democratic challenger whose meteoric rise in spring and summer faltered badly when he began taking his case to the country as a whole.

So what should be an epic confrontation between two men so dissimilar in character and philosophy has become a campaign characterized mostly by public apathy. Despite a war that drags on through its second decade, despite revelations of wiretapping, grain deals, official deceit and all the rest, the voters seem resigned either to a continuation of the present administration, because it is at least a known quantity, or to voting *against* whichever candidate has most stimulated their anxiety or antagonism.

We are less likely ever to go the way of Athens, however, if each citizen will at least vote; and for those who are still undecided we hope the exploration of issues and philosophies that follows may be useful.

For our part, after weighing not only the promises but the performance and character of the rival candidates, we endorse Senator McGovern and his running mate, Sargent Shriver. They represent a spirit of idealism, of reform, of compassion, of understanding of what democracy is all about and why we must preserve it, that America urgently needs if it is to overcome the cynicism, indifference and lack of clear philosophy and moral leadership that have characterized President Nixon and Vice President Agnew.

✦ ✦ ✦

One of the paramount issues of concern for the American voter is, of course, foreign policy, a field in which President Nixon not only has unusual interest and expertise, but in which he has scored notable successes. By reversing the cold-war, "commie-conspiracy" attitudes that helped keep him politically alive for a generation, Mr. Nixon has markedly improved relations between the United States and its major rivals, Russia and China, with consequent easing of tensions in such worrisome areas as Central Europe and the Middle East.

But these triumphs have been balanced by less spectacular foreign policy behavior that has troubling implications for the years ahead. We have renewed our pledges to 42 governments—among them some dictatorships that systematically use torture and secret police to maintain their rule—to protect them from internal subversion and even "political agitation"; while continuing to help them out with weapons and other aid. Our invasion of Cambodia and virtual occupation of Laos have ravaged both countries and almost certainly guarantee that they will end up as Communist states. We have lost the friendship of India, the world's largest democracy, by siding with the Pakistani dictator in his cruel pillage of breakaway Bangladesh. And, perhaps worst of all, we are becoming known as a bully-boy in global matters, cracking the whip at international conferences and in other ways alienating many of our best friends.

The nation's most critical stumbling block on the road toward peace, the war in Vietnam, has been the President's most serious foreign policy failure, despite his efforts to make us think it's over. Although our troops in South Vietnam and our weekly casualties have dropped dramatically, we have simultaneously conducted a vast escalation of our forces elsewhere in Indochina and off-shore. Since Mr. Nixon took office 45 months ago, 15,339 Americans have died in Vietnam. One hundred more Americans have been imprisoned in North Vietnamese POW camps in the past six months alone. $52.7 billion has been spent to conduct the largest bombing campaign in history and to arm the soldiers of a government that is hardly more democratic than the one it's fighting, and which—for all the proud claims of success in our Vietnamization program—is incapable of holding the country if America withdraws.

President Nixon inherited the deadlocked peace talks in Paris and they still seem deadlocked today. If we have been willing to accept a realistic negotiated peace rather than a military victory in Vietnam, that point seemingly has never been transmitted to the enemy—let alone to the American people. Yet, four years after he led us to believe he had a plan to end the war honorably if he were elected, Mr. Nixon and his surrogate campaigners are proudly proclaiming that peace on our terms is just around the corner.

McGovern's public plan

Senator McGovern, on the other hand, has opposed American involvement in the Vietnam war for nine years—during which time his role has changed from the lonely voice crying in the wilderness to the chief spokesman for millions of Americans who now feel the same grief, dismay and disgust that he has voiced for so long. In addition, Senator McGovern has offered a *public* plan for bringing our machines, our money and our men—including the prisoners—home in a matter of months. There's no reason to believe the plan wouldn't work. It's the same one used by the French to disengage themselves from their military disaster in Indochina two decades ago. It certainly stands a better chance of bringing peace than any alternative offered by the present administration.

And we must have peace. For the American people, who have lived with war or the threat of war for more than 30 years, are perilously close to a condition that Alexander Hamilton warned against during the earliest days of the Republic. War-weariness, he said, "will compel nations the most attached to liberty to resort for repose and security to institutions which have a tendency to destroy their civil and political rights. To be more safe, they at length become willing to run the risk of being less free."

One way to become less free, as President Eisenhower warned in his Farewell Address, is to join those who scoff at the suggestion that the military-industrial establishment and its political friends may not have all the answers to our national defense and how much we should spend for it. This is a major issue in the 1972 campaign, and it says a great deal for Senator McGovern that he has been willing to defy this formidable array of votes, campaign contributions and political power.

Our extravagant weapons

Senator McGovern proposes a sharp cut in defense spending without hurting our basic military capability, and this is termed a "white flag budget" by the Nixon surrogates.

Yet, some esteemed military experts agree that the Pentagon's programs (a $74.3 billion budget this year including such "bargaining chips" as the B-1 bomber and the Trident submarine) not only are inconsistent with our efforts at the SALT talks and elsewhere to slow the arms race, but may be obsolete before the weapons are built. This is the same Pentagon, after all, that pays salaries for a military establishment top-heavy with generals and admirals. We now have one of these highest-level leaders for every 1,745 men and women in lower ranks. At the end of World War II the ratio was 1 to 7,133.

Tax reform and other economic questions? Senator McGovern has forthrightly spelled out a way to close the gaping loopholes enjoyed by the rich and to readjust the tax load so that it would be less burdensome on the poor. President Nixon, for all his conversion to Keynesian economics and campaign-time oratory about the burdens of the property-owner and low-income citizen, was one of the last Americans to start talking about genuine tax reform—and still has the matter under study.

In the area of finance, both foreign and domestic, this administration has fallen far short of its promises. Our balance of payments position has continued to deteriorate, and we had a trade deficit last year for the first time since 1888. The Nixon administration has run up one-quarter of our entire National Debt, and the "full employment budget" turns out to be a euphemism for staggering deficits—more than $73 billion over the past three years. Devaluation of the dollar and proposed international monetary reforms are credits to the President, and so are the wage-price controls he finally imposed after months of prodding by a Democratic Congress. But they can hardly offset an unemployment rate that has risen from 3.5 per cent when Mr. Nixon took office to 5.5 per cent this fall, the addition of six million Americans to the welfare rolls, and the slowing of inflation but its continued erosion of the consumer or investment dollar.

We know there's plenty to be done. President Nixon's business-oriented environmental policies have permitted the continued degradation of our countryside, our waters and the air we breathe. Our cities continue to decay. Children continue to go hungry in urban and rural slums. The quality of their education is reduced to simplistic tirades about busing. Bills for better schools and medical care are repeatedly vetoed, not in sorrow but in cold lectures on congressional extravagance. Welfare reform is dropped like a hot potato when it turns out to be more vote-catching to talk of "welfare-chiselers." Public housing falters when the President refuses to tell white suburbia that it must open its neighborhoods if it ever hopes to eliminate crime, welfare and the other staggering social costs of economic and racial segregation.

The road to tyranny

The vaunted pledge of "law and order," meanwhile, turns out to be purchases of more police cars, to cope with the symptoms; not court- and prison-reform, not compassion for the impoverished and broken families in which most criminals are bred, not concern for the other ways in which we must get at the root causes of crime. So crime has increased 32 per cent since Mr. Nixon took his oath of office, and the FBI reports that America endured 5,995,200 serious offenses in 1971—410,000 more than the previous year.

(continued on next page)

(continued from preceding page)

And perhaps the most important of all, because it is so essential to our survival as a democracy, Mr. Nixon has found many ways to prove that a President who doesn't really understand or sympathize with the purpose of our Constitution can find ways to subvert the basic guarantees that have made America the goal of all who fear tyranny. While Senator McGovern has consistently defended the American citizen's sacred rights to free expression, due process of law, fair trial, fair elections, and all the other rights and liberties reserved for us through the farsighted wisdom of our founding fathers, Mr. Nixon has shown little inclination to let any of them circumvent his pursuit of his own political and governmental goals.

He is the first President in history to attempt the prior censorship of a newspaper—maintaining in the Pentagon Papers case that the First Amendment doesn't apply when matters of national security are concerned. In retaliation against his critics he has, without legal authority, jailed persons without charging them with a crime, and has searched and seized without warrant. Wiretaps without court orders have blossomed, and conspiracy trials based on such tainted evidence have been pursued relentlessly by the most politicized Justice Department since the "Red-hunts" after World War I. Mass arrests, preventive detention and no-knock searches; attempts to pack the Supreme Court with pliant men whether they're qualified or not; spying on his political opponents and now, evidently, even trying to disrupt the electoral process by espionage and sabotage—these are not the marks of a man who would have gotten the time of day from Washington, Jefferson and the others who knew how tyranny starts.

In contrast to Senator McGovern's frank disclosures of his campaign fund sources and his pledge to expose himself regularly to the view of the public and press, Mr. Nixon has run the most secretive administration in memory. His penchant for invisibility, his continual ducking of public accountability, renew all the old doubts about the integrity of his conduct of office and his stewardship of the public interest.

This, in our judgment, is where George McGovern stands head and shoulders above Richard Nixon. It has been claimed that Senator McGovern "demonstrates an economic illiteracy and global ignorance" that disqualify him for the presidency. But men and women who are talented in these fields are for hire in Washington and have been available to every Chief Executive. What is *not* for hire is integrity. A President without it may see nothing wrong in deliberate efforts to exploit racial tensions, in polarizing elements of society by playing them off against each other, in failing to provide moral leadership when it might disrupt a "Southern strategy" or alienate voters elsewhere. A President without integrity also might falter while trying to sketch in the details of some of his campaign positions, as Senator McGovern did; or mishandle the dumping of a colleague, as the Senator mishandled the tragic "Eagleton affair." But such a man also would see nothing wrong in filling sensitive government jobs with political hatchet-men, or in refusing to divulge the names of those to whom he is indebted for $10 million or more in campaign slush funds—a disturbing echo of the issue that almost caused General Eisenhower to dump Mr. Nixon from his own ticket 20 years ago. A President without integrity cannot generate the unity, the healing of wounds, the national sense of purpose, that America so desperately needs after the terrible divisiveness, expediency, cynicism and deceit of the Vietnam years.

Mr. Nixon repeatedly lectures us on the "honor" of our military commitments. But he seems totally blind to the fact that a government also can lose its honor in the bugged offices of its political rivals, on the wheat fields of swindled farmers, in the ghetto homes of hungry children.

We believe that Senator McGovern—in the respect his government associates hold for him, in the compassion for people that led him to administer the Food for Peace program and later to open America's eyes to the scourge of malnutrition among millions of our own youngsters, in his efforts to make us re-examine our priorities of spending, of human concern and of our global role—is what this nation needs now. If America in 1976 is to have anything like the greatness its founders envisioned 200 years before, it needs leadership it can truly trust.

The Miami Herald
Miami, Fla., October 8, 1972

RICHARD NIXON, candidate for re-election as the thirty-seventh President of the United States, labors under a number of liabilities.

He suffers an over-fat, somewhat arrogant campaign apparatus, guilty of such collegiate antics as the Watergate affair.

He has not ended a war which he implied he would while campaigning in 1968.

In tapping Spiro Agnew again as his running-mate he laid his hands upon a man who has pursued the dark cults of division and distrust for political gain.

He was rescued by the Senate's better judgment in the nomination of two unqualified candidates for the Supreme Court, a body which has seemed to come to reflect Mr. Nixon's seeming light regard for civil rights, and most especially the First Amendment.

In Congress the Nixon administration has struck out on five of the six "great goals" of the 1971 State of the Union address. These are revenue sharing, welfare reform, executive reorganization, health insurance and environmental clean-up.

The Nixon administration has made many boasts about reducing unemployment, exulting only last week over a figure of 5.5 per cent of the labor force. Yet it inherited a 3.5 per cent unemployment rate (which it didn't mention Friday) in 1969. Fiscally it has endured without much protest one shocking federal deficit after another. The next looks like $35 billion.

THERE are some flies, too, on George McGovern, the Democrat who hopes to become the thirty-eighth President of the United States.

Sen. McGovern's prairie populism underwent a number of sea changes as he moved East. Many of his starry-eyed followers are looking for other constellations, if any.

He stumbled over the Eagleton issue, which suggested that he, too, was a poor or ill-prepared judge of horseflesh. The men around him seem to be of exceedingly small bore.

At one time or another he has been on any given side of an issue — economics, the war, foreign policy, etc. His proclaimed tax program, before it got a scrubbing of sorts, horrified the lean cats as well as the fat ones. Either his memory or his understanding — or perhaps both — was faulty when he ascribed to President Nixon an anti-labor policy, whereas Mr. Nixon has fallen over backward in Miami Beach not to offend the labor barons. These things, to be sure, are Willkiean "campaign talk," but a harsher word from some of the thread-worn campaign accusations is demagoguery.

TO be sure, Sen. McGovern has some commendable qualities and some assets.

He was the first member of the Senate to recognize the terrible error of Vietnam and to castigate a cruel and senseless war. After flirting with isolationism on the campaign trail he has embraced a "new internationalism" which is at least specific, including the recognition of China and rational arms limitation.

His seeming zealotry is tempered by an idealism which rises from the long-slumbering American dream. Not since Adlai Stevenson (though not as well) has an American candidate spoken so eloquently to first principles.

Even so, the McGovern campaign to this point is an unmitigated disaster, supposing that Americans want a free choice and not competitiveness in the political marketplace.

For all his melodic contortions, George McGovern can't even charm a gartersnake.

With nowhere to go but up, as his supporters explained, he has yet to lift his own weight.

FOR the reasons which follow, The Herald endorses Richard Milhous Nixon for reelection.

The overriding issues, we think, are the state of the national economy and, more importantly, the state of the world in which Americans must live and to which they must contribute in the next four years.

Despite its perennial pockets of poverty which it must turn inside out, the nation is increasingly prosperous. The balance of trade has improved. The Gross National Product rose $30 billion in the second quarter. Industrial production is 1.5 per cent above the September, 1969, peak of 111.9 per cent. Wage-price controls have been administered without too much commotion and with a telling effect on the pace of inflation. In sum, the feared "Republican depression" never surfaced.

We have always said that Mr. Nixon's longest suit is foreign affairs, in which he is perhaps the most experienced President (and Vice President) in modern history.

(continued on next page)

(continued from preceding page)

The paranoid aspects of the Cold War began to diminish with his election. He proposed at the time to reach a detente with China, and he has done so. With a skill which few have yet fully realized he has balanced relations with Russia, including promising relations in trade, with the other hand. In the Middle East he has proven himself a friend of Israel and has yet managed to win some confidence from the Arab realists. Save for Indochina, the world relatively is at peace.

If the polls are any true indicator, they tell the rest of the story. The American people may not "like" Richard Nixon, a recluse among the more outgoing Presidents of our time, but apparently they trust him to govern. And he has shown that capacity, despite the historic instance of a Congress wholly owned by the political opposition.

We hope and believe the people will s p e a k overwhelmingly for Richard Nixon on the first Tuesday in November. A minority President until then, afterward he will be able to bring a needed sense of unity and purpose to the United States.

The Birmingham News
Birmingham, Ala., October 1, 1972

On Sept. 2, 1968, the lead editorial in this newspaper declared:

"*The Birmingham News* is convinced that the times demand the election of Richard M. Nixon to the presidency of the United States."

Today, four years later, this newspaper is convinced that it made a wise choice in calling for President Nixon's election.

A close scrutiny of events during the past four years provides ample proof that the nation under Nixon's leadership has made remarkable progress in many areas.

Viewing the achievements the Nixon administration has made and considering the alternatives offered by Sen. George McGovern and the Democratic Party, *The Birmingham News* is equally convinced that Richard Nixon must be re-elected to the presidency in November.

★ ★ ★

FEW PERSONS IN 1968 questioned the desperate need for a change of direction and attitude in Washington. Few among us today would argue that President Nixon has brought in Utopia or that the changes he has initiated have been fully implemented. But a great change in direction has taken place, a change sufficient to make the American people feel overwhelmingly that President Nixon should continue his policies and programs toward completion during the next four years.

The erratic, impatient and capricious alternatives offered by Sen. McGovern and his New Left followers are chilling to contemplate.

But McGovern's proposals, as unsound as they are, do give American voters an indelibly clear choice between a radical plunge into the icy waters of state socialism and President Nixon's concept of hammering out orderly change toward a better quality of life in a traditional American fashion which preserves time-tested values, free enterprises and individual initiative.

★ ★ ★

DURING THE PAST four years, the President has brought to bear two great and overriding principles:

(1) To devote administration efforts to reversing the trend toward ever bigger and bigger federal government, fostered for nearly a half century by the Democratic congressional majority, and to turn back as much decision-making power as possible to the people at state and local levels. Contained within this concept was the conviction that the federal judiciary, including the Supreme Court, should reflect strict constructionist viewpoints on all constitutional questions.

(2) To reduce or eliminate the politics of confrontation as a means of solving world problems and to establish a new era of international detente and accord with the leadership of the world's power centers.

Viewed critically and calmly, divorced from the strident, nearly hysterical attacks from opposing Democratic leadership, the achievements of the Nixon years are impressive.

The President as part of his campaign in 1968 promised to do all in his power to end the fighting in Vietnam. He said he had a plan which he deeply believed would bring an end to the war.

That plan included Vietnamization —a process of gradually turning the security of South Vietnam over to the leadership of the Vietnamese people as the South Vietnamese were trained and equipped to accept that responsibility. The second part of that plan was the orderly withdrawal of American troops as fast as Vietnamese units were capable of replacing them.

The President announced his plan only four months after taking office.

Since that time he has brought almost half a million servicemen home. In 1968, when he was handed the war by the Democratic administration, more than 500,000 U. S. servicemen were in Vietnam fighting the murderous invaders from the North at almost every level. Today fewer than 40,000 servicemen are there, serving mostly in support and advisory capacities.

And Americans can take a reasonable pride in that this tremendous transition was accomplished without abandoning the South Vietnamese to a bloodbath from the invaders from the North.

BUT LAST SPRING when it appeared that the Vietnamization program was working, the Communist die-hards of the North mounted another vicious all-out invasion of the South.

To protect our troops and to meet our commitments to the people of the South, the President, as his only alternative, ordered the blockade of all North Vietnam, the mining of its harbors and a renewal of bombing of troops and military installations.

At that time, the President again offered to withdraw all American forces from Vietnam, if Hanoi would free all American POWs and agree to elections supervised by neutral observers.

At this point Hanoi continues to go through the motions of negotiation, but no one knows whether or not in good faith.

Meanwhile the South Vietnamese grow stronger and more confident daily, and a half million servicemen can testify that the President's promise has been honored. They can take pride too in the fact that they did not abandon the little people of the South to a holocaust and that we are nearer now than we have ever been to a negotiated settlement.

IN OTHER AREAS of international affairs, even the Democratic leadership can only applaud the President's successful efforts to normalize relations with the two Communist giants, Soviet Russia and The Peoples Republic of China.

The Congress already has approved the administration's S A L T agreements with Russia which will serve to halt the arms race. Agreements have also been made with the Soviets for cooperation in space, health, science and environment. Already a number of billion-dollar agreements involving wheat and technical and engineering projects have been worked out with the Soviet Union, and similar trade agreements are expected to be forthcoming with Red China.

Political realists recognize that progress in these international areas was made in large measure because of American strategic military capability. For that reason the President insists that the United States continue to negotiate from strength. A vast number of Americans agree with the President that a strong military capability, with consonant research and development of strategic and tactical weapons are utterly necessary to give our negotiating efforts both authenticity and authority. Thus the President's call for adequate expenditures for military capability is both wise and consistent with our experience in negotiation with other world powers.

ON THE DOMESTIC FRONT, the President can properly take credit for considerable progress in the economic area.

A positive degree of stability has been achieved under the wage-price controls which the President effected in August, 1971. Nixon ordered the controls only after he had given a full exploration of voluntary efforts to slow inflation and with the urging and blessing of the vast majority of Americans.

In the area of welfare, the President has tried for three years to move the balky Democratic congressional majority toward passage of legislation that would return hundreds of thousands now on welfare rolls back into the work force where many can learn skills that will make them capable of holding higher paying jobs and becoming creative forces in American society. It appears that Congress is finally moving in this direction.

In the area of the judiciary, the President has appointed four men to the Supreme Court. In keeping with his promises of 1968, all of the men came to court with a reputation and a history of being strict constitutional constructionists. Recent decisions indicate that the court is rapidly moving away from the old Warren Court position that the court through its decisions and orders is in the business of promoting social change.

In the area of returning decision making power to the people at state and local levels, the President has successfully pushed through the legislative process the first revenue sharing bill. It is far too early to predict the results of this unprecedented move, but it is a measure which should help floundering local communities to meet growing obligations which have been thrust upon them.

REALIZING THAT MANY of our economic ills are rooted in government spending — deficit spending — the President has moved forcefully toward creating in the Congress a deeper sense of fiscal responsibility. It appears that his efforts will result in a $250 billion spending ceiling for the next fiscal year, a goal that is almost mandatory, if inflation is to be contained.

And on the international monetary scene, the President has laid down for consideration a program that will go far in stabilizing money exchange and stimulate world trade and at the same time work to bring the balance of payments between the United States and other nations back into line.

Great strides have been made in understanding the pollution problem and in creative measures to protect the environment. Progress to halt the increase in crime, to stop the influx of illicit, hard drugs into the nation and into the cities and villages has also shown marked acceleration in recent months.

THESE ARE ALL REAL, measurable achievements, but perhaps the most significant indicator of all of the administration's effectiveness is a growing willingness on the part of activist groups, on campus and off, to work within the system for solutions to social problems.

Minorities, the young, the dissenters of many stripes seem to have taken a second look at America and its institutions during the Nixon years and found what they have seen to be more good than bad.

Most seem to have decided that the goals they pursue are worth patience and negotiation through the political and social processes that are our democratic heritage.

We believe the administration's calmness, patience and the President's unflapable steadiness has helped to create this new climate.

In President Nixon we believe the nation has a highly competent and dedicated steersman, a chief executive who will lead the American people into a new era of peace and accomplishment.

We believe the record of his nearly-four years in the presidency so acclaim him. We believe the American people recognize the progress we have made under his leadership and will reelect him with an unchallengable plurality in November.

The Philadelphia Inquirer

Philadelphia, Pa., October 15, 1972

As the days dwindle down, George McGovern professes to be puzzled at the turn the 1972 Presidential campaign has taken.

It was his intention, as he said in July in the flush of his victory at the Democratic convention, to make President Nixon "the fundamental issue in this campaign." And yet here in October, as Loye Miller Jr. of our Washington bureau wrote the other day, "the issue has now become George McGovern himself."

"I've got to tell you I'm baffled at the support Nixon has in the polls," Sen. McGovern mused in an interview last week. "I have not thought he was a popular President. I don't think his record has been a good one. And that being the case I am puzzled by the polls. I just don't know what they mean."

Well, we'd like to suggest and discuss a couple of reasons why Mr. Nixon is leading — and why The Inquirer now endorses him for another term.

The first is that the majority of American voters simply do not accept Mr. McGovern's shrill assessment that the President has given the nation the "worst leadership in our history."

The second is that Mr. McGovern's vacillation on the issues and his fumbling campaign have inspired little confidence in his own capacity for national leadership.

★ ★ ★

Mr. Nixon, like any other President, has his shortcomings. And his administration, like any other, has sins of both omission and commission for which it must be held accountable.

Generally, however, we believe that this contemplative President has used the vast powers of his office well to move the country in directions that the broad sweep of history will prove sound. And it is the forest, not the trees, that should command the attention of the electorate when choosing the man who will lead the nation for four years.

By this standard, the overriding issue of our time is unquestionably the search for what Mr. Nixon himself calls a generation of peace.

That peace has eluded him in Vietnam, despite the progress he has made in reducing American involvement in a war he inherited and bringing home most of the 550,000 troops his Democratic predecessors sent there. While applauding his incessant search for a settlement that will give South Vietnam a reasonable chance to survive on its own, we deplore and oppose the bombing he pursues in the attempt to force that settlement.

We cannot, however, accept Mr. McGovern's characterization of the President of the United States as a barbaric, Hitlerian warmonger under whom, in the area of foreign policy, "we are becoming a second-rate nation in the terms that will really count."

★ ★ ★

A less passionate Democratic assessment, we believe, was one couched not in desperation campaign rhetoric but in a thoughtful commencement address earlier this year by Senate Majority Leader Mike Mansfield. Commenting on Mr. Nixon's momentous visits to Peking and Moscow, he said:

"History may well record 1972 as the year in which a corner was turned for peace. There are indications that the world is headed back toward constructive human purpose in its major international relationships... The President is responding in a new fashion to international circumstances. He is projecting not as adversary but as conciliator. In so doing, he is paying heed to the legitimate claims of a public sentiment grown impatient with the words of peace, sung to the cadence of war."

Or listen to Max Lerner, one of the most liberal of the liberal commentators, describing some of the "current wonders of America":

"The wonder of a conservative President who has carried through the most revolutionary foreign policy in the history of America as a great power.

"The wonder of the nuclear weapons control treaty, nursed for several years and completed by a President formerly regarded as a nuclear hawk."

On domestic issues, solutions to some of the economic and social problems of the country have proved as elusive as peace in Vietnam.

But "the truth is," as Eric Sevareid observed recently, "that there are no quick cures. And it may be that the man the majority will respond to is the candidate who frankly acknowledges this and promises only to keep trying, without regard to doctrines or past conceptions, until some answers are found."

As in foreign affairs, Mr. Nixon has not hesitated to break with the past in trying to change the way we approach our domestic problems.

For all of Mr. McGovern's talk about reordering priorities, the fact is that in the four Nixon years such a process has been taking place. In fiscal 1968, the last year of the last Johnson budget, 45 percent of the federal budget was spent on defense and 32 percent on human needs, or social programs. In the 1973 budget, those figures are exactly reversed. As a percentage of the gross national product, defense spending during that time has fallen from almost 9 percent to slightly more than 6 percent — the lowest level in 22 years.

★ ★ ★

If one thing has become abundantly clear, however, it is that pouring more money into old programs is no panacea. Mr. Nixon's response has been a series of such fundamental reforms as welfare reform, government reorganization and revenue sharing.

Unhappily, the same Democrats who say the people are disenchanted with the way government works and who promise them a change have used their control of Congress to scuttle many of the President's proposals. But revenue sharing seems finally on the way, and we do not doubt that a second Nixon Administration would see further innovative efforts to deal with problems that have not responded to massive infusions of cash from swollen Washington bureaucracies.

Meanwhile, runaway inflation has been brought under control, even if the federal budget has not. As a result, for the first time since the mid-1960s Americans this year are enjoying an increase — of 4.3 percent — in real, spendable weekly earnings.

★ ★ ★

Many thorny problems remain, of course. But they bring us back to Mr. Sevareid's point and to the confidence the American people have in a Presidential candidate.

It may be true, as Mr. McGovern said he supposed, that Mr. Nixon has not been a "popular" President. Certainly he does not generate the kind of affection the fatherly Dwight Eisenhower did or the kind of excitement the charismatic John Kennedy did.

But in his own way, he has quietly gone about binding the wounds that tore the nation apart during the Johnson Administration and restoring to the White House a sense of dignity and respect it seemed to have lost. His lead in the polls, a Gallup spokesman said recently, does not mean that he is invincible but that he "has managed to come across with a Presidential style. There's been a real change in the tone of what is said about him."

His administration has shown its seamier sides, as in the current Watergate affair, and though the President has not been personally implicated he must of necessity bear the responsibility for those he puts in places of trust.

That is a far cry, however, from charging — as Sen. McGovern does — that the Nixon Administration is the "most corrupt in the two centuries of American government." Such a reckless broadside says more about the bankruptcy of Mr. McGovern's own candidacy than it does about the President and will be hard to sell to American voters. According to the latest Harris poll, they indicated by a 60-29 margin that they put more trust in Mr. Nixon than in Mr. McGovern.

★ ★ ★

Which brings us to the question of why Sen. McGovern has fared so poorly in trying to sell his own brand of leadership.

He is, after all, a decent, intelligent and honorable man. But he is being measured now as a potential

(continued on next page)

(continued from preceding page)

President of all the people. And he has not measured up.

His major problem, perhaps, is one suggested by James Reston of the New York Times: "He has probably misjudged the mood of the country and emerged as the champion of militant forces that want more change than the majority of the voters desire."

That appeal to the militants won the nomination for him, even though he took only 23 percent of the votes in the contested preferential primaries. But it left his own party grievously split. In trying to repair that wreckage and broaden his support, he has damaged his credibility by waffling on so many issues that not even his original supporters know where he really stands.

In his handling of the Eagleton affair, he not only dealt his credibility a further blow but emerged as indecisive and reluctant to face up to unpleasant situations.

And in the management of his inept campaign he has raised doubts about his ability to run anything, much less the most powerful nation in the world.

Mr. McGovern talks of building "a new coalition that will bring about fundamental changes in the country." But he seems quite fuzzy himself on some of those changes, and even fellow Democrats express concern about some of the others.

Before finally abandoning his grand design to give everybody in the country $1,000 a year, for example, Mr. McGovern was asked in a television debate what it would cost and answered simply: "I don't know."

Although he insists he could cut $30 billion out of the defense budget without endangering the country, it was not Melvin Laird but Hubert Humphrey who warned that his proposals "cut the muscle in the very fiber of our national security."

And it was not Barry Goldwater but one of the more liberal Southern Democrats, Duke University President Terry Sanford, who expressed concern about the thinking behind some of Mr. McGovern's domestic proposals — "the thinking ... which sees a greater paternalistic action in supporting people, bigger and bigger government. I think that the frame of mind that one gets into in serving in the Senate causes one to look at the problems of the country in terms of massive plans. They are not going to work any more. But I think he goes a step beyond that ... Most of his programs come through as a highly centralized approach to the problems of America."

★ ★ ★

Mr. McGovern indeed offers a choice on Vietnam, where he proposes to end our involvement immediately with what such a dispassionate observer as the Times' Mr. Reston has called "virtually a formula for surrender."

But he offers other choices as well, both in his proposals — whatever they may be at a given moment — and in his casual style of leadership.

For our part, we would choose four more years of the Nixon Administration. The White House is not ready for George McGovern — or vice versa.

ST. LOUIS POST-DISPATCH
St. Louis, Mo., October 15, 1972

In January 1971 the *Post-Dispatch* welcomed George McGovern's announcement that he would run for President. We had long approved his lonely and courageous stand against the Vietnam war, and in the last 22 months we have watched him develop from a nationally unknown Senator from South Dakota to the Democratic party's able standard bearer in this crucial election. Since we have often expressed admiration for his high principles, humanity and candor our formal endorsement of Mr. McGovern for the nation's highest office may come as no surprise.

That in no way diminishes the nature of the choice, for the differences between what Mr. McGovern offers and what President Nixon promises have sharpened with the passage of time. Mr. McGovern offers a philosophy of decency and compassion directed toward healing wounds and drawing the nation together. Mr. Nixon's appeal is to less noble instincts — he would obtain a consensus of mediocrity through a process of dividing the country into selfish special-interest groupings.

There is no denying that there have been disappointments in Senator McGovern's post-convention campaign, beginning with his major blunder in dropping Senator Eagleton of Missouri as his vice-presidential running mate. We are skeptical of certain parts of his tax program; he has avoided the key issue of a guaranteed income in his welfare proposals. He has at times seemed indecisive, and he has been plagued by faulty staff work.

Yet many of the deficiencies in his campaign have been due to his own admirable qualities — a stubborn realism, flexibility, and a felt need to be straightforward. Talking sense to the American people did not serve Adlai Stevenson well, and frankness has not, at this point, been acclaimed by the people in the case of Mr. McGovern. Yet one must hope that the truth will be grasped, that in the end the voters will not be misled by the shallow misrepresentations of Administration campaigners.

On the main issues facing the American people this fall Mr. McGovern is entirely right. He would extricate the country from the calamity of the Vietnam war. He would rebuff the military-industrial-congressional complex by reducing the monstrous Pentagon budget while retaining an adequate defense establishment. He would redistribute income to change the nation's domestic priorities and give a better economic break to the poor. He would provide a leadership based on faith in the people and would restore a sense of direction to our national life.

Against this must be placed the failures of the Nixon Administration. Mr. Nixon deserves high marks for reversing himself and making friendly overtures to China; he is entitled to much credit for the nuclear arms control agreement with the Soviet Union and for seeking better relations with the Russians; he would be entitled to applause for withdrawing half a million troops from Vietnam if he had not built up United States forces elsewhere in Asia and intensified the unholy bombing of North Vietnam.

We believe Mr. McGovern would have done no less in the field of foreign policy, and that on domestic issues he would not have resorted to the policy of vote-getting expediency that has seemed to guide the Nixon Administration. Mr. Nixon is clearly vulnerable on domestic affairs. He has appealed to racial prejudice in exploiting busing and civil rights issues. With the deplorable Carswell and Haynsworth nominations he tried to discredit the Supreme Court by naming unqualified justices. He has acquiesced in wire-tapping, indiscriminate arrests and attacks on the press.

Under this Administration, favoritism to big business and special interests has dominated the Washington scene. The International Telephone & Telegraph scandal, the Watergate bugging, the wheat export deal, the raising of millions in unreported campaign funds have besmirched the Administration and have shaken the faith of the people in the integrity of their government. By absorbing power within the White House the President has been enabled to rule in secret; power is held by men who, by claiming executive privilege, can avoid questioning by Congress.

Over and above all this, there is a moral issue that must dominate the election. The American people are called to answer the question whether they believe an official government policy of mercilessly bombing a little Asian nation and its people into oblivion, for no good reason, is an honorable course for the greatest military power the earth has seen. We think it is dishonorable, immoral and self-defeating, and the antithesis of what every American ought to stand for.

That is what George McGovern believes. He would quickly end the madness in Vietnam and seek to restore America's lost honor and sense of justice. From the record there is no cause to think that the divisive and cruel war, which is of itself the source of so many domestic dislocations, will be brought to an end under Mr. Nixon's leadership. That alone is a valid reason to support Senator McGovern, but there are many more.

In view of all the considerations in this critical year, the *Post-Dispatch* welcomes the opportunity to endorse George McGovern for President of the United States.

BOSTON HERALD TRAVELER
Record American
Boston, Mass., October 12, 1972

No decision can be more important than the choice of a President, a man who will lead this country for four years. But rarely in our history has that choice been so clear, that decision so easy to make.

Without reservation, the Boston Herald Traveler and Record American endorses the re-election of Richard M. Nixon.

This is not to say that we are in complete agreement with the President's programs and views. But we do believe that his accomplishments and his record over the past four years have been good, and that they are worthy of a strong vote of confidence from the people.

More important, perhaps, is that the only alternative — the election of Sen. George McGovern — is simply unacceptable. The choice, stated briefly and bluntly, is between an able, experienced, effective incumbent who has demonstrated strong leadership at home and abroad, conducting the affairs of the nation with dignity and honor, and an indecisive, impractical and impulsive challenger whose radical views, wild accusations and ever-changing positions inspire no confidence that he would be capable of leading the nation.

The contrast between President Nixon and his opponent on most of the major issues, both foreign and domestic, is rather sharp. And in virtually every case, the President's position is much closer, we think, to the outlook shared by the overwhelming majority of the American people.

It is impossible, of course, to review and dissect all of the issues here in detail. What follows is a comparison of the candidates' stands on several of the most critical issues:

VIETNAM

As our columnist John Roche noted recently, Sen. McGovern's record of opposing the war in Vietnam is not as consistent as he pretends, and a huge credibility gap exists between his speeches on the subject and his votes in the Senate. "It was not until the Republicans took over," says Roche, "that McGovern began voting what he would probably call his 'conscience'."

Nevertheless, the Senator's position today boils down to calling for a unilateral withdrawal of American forces, a pledge to "beg" the Communists rather than bargain with them for an end to the war and the release of our prisoners, and the total abandonment of our allies in South Vietnam. McGovern's latest "plan" to end the war, unveiled Tuesday night, is nothing short of a "formula for surrender," to use the words of Columnist James Reston. It is virtually the Hanoi plan.

The main attack on the President's credibility, Roche added, "has been based on a bogus quote, a statement he never made that he had a 'secret plan' to end the war." Though the war hasn't ended, it certainly isn't for lack of trying on Mr. Nixon's part. He has gone the extra mile in offering the enemy reasonable terms for settling the conflict. He has brought home 515,000 of the 550,000 troops sent to Vietnam by two previous Democratic Presidents. He has ended America's combat role and reduced our casualties by 98 percent.

DIPLOMACY AND TRADE

In other important areas of foreign policy, Mr. Nixon has taken many bold and dramatic steps toward peace and stability in the world: opening the door to China, improving relations with the Soviet Union, initiating new agreements to curb the arms race, fostering programs designed to increase trade between nations and encourage economic competition rather than political and military confrontation.

Sen. McGovern's overall foreign policy leans sharply toward isolationism: turning America's vision inward, abandoning our alliances, curtailing our influence abroad and unilaterally scrapping much of the defense of this country and the free world in the naive hope that others might do likewise.

MILITARY SPENDING

Though he has expressed radical views on many other subjects, Sen. McGovern's attitude toward national defense is perhaps the most alarming. He has pledged to cut military spending by 40 percent, emasculating our defenses — and eliminating the jobs of millions of American workers in the process. The fact is not as well known as it should be, but Mr. Nixon has already sharply reduced the burden of military spending in the past four years, cutting our armed forces by over a million men and reordering our priorities by allotting a much larger share of federal spending for domestic needs. But the President has refused to gamble with the safety of the American people, insisting that spending less than we need is false economy which could cost us our lives and our freedom.

AT HOME

On domestic matters, Sen. McGovern's positions have changed so often or have been so fuzzy in their presentation that it is difficult to know today where he may be standing tomorrow. But in general, his views on such issues as tax reform, a guaranteed income, or combatting unemployment and inflation strike us as rather extravagant and impractical.

Some of the votes he has cast in the Senate on labor issues and civil rights, and the statements he has made recently concerning crime, drugs, busing, abortion and other controversial matters, have alienated millions of moderates and liberals who have traditionally supported the Democratic party and its nominees.

In a letter to all state and local AFL-CIO affiliates, George Meany recently complained that at the party's national convention and throughout the campaign, the McGovern people "repeatedly indicated their disregard and contempt of the trade union movement and the workers it represents." He added: "Nor does the nominee himself have a record that inspires our confidence or encourages us to commend his candidacy for the Presidency to our members. It is true that Senator McGovern has voted 'right' from a labor point of view on numerous occasions. But on the crucial issues — when the chips were down — he was to be found on the other side, aligning with forces hostile to working people."

President Nixon's accomplishments on the domestic front are not as solid as they might be, nor as impressive as his achievements abroad — though this is due in part to the difficult economic situation which he inherited and to a lack of cooperation from Congress.

CRIME, SPENDING, TAXES

Perhaps his most important domestic achievements in the past four years have been to reverse the direction of the Supreme Court and to begin a major assault on crime and drug abuse, which have been rising at an alarming rate in recent years. Mr. Nixon also deserves credit for making some progress in the war against inflation and unemployment, though his efforts were late and not as strong as they might have been.

He has not been as frugal as many Americans who are fed up with extravagant government spending and soaring public debt would like. But, again, the alternative is Sen. McGovern, whose pie-

(continued on next page)

(continued from preceding page)
in-the-sky spending schemes would send the federal budget skyrocketing toward new records. And it is to be noted that Mr. Nixon has pledged, in his next term, to "oppose any new spending program which would add to the tax burden of American wage earners."

UNITY, LEADERSHIP

Four years ago, when Mr. Nixon was elected, the nation was torn by deep and bitter divisions. Not all of our national fractures have been healed, but the President has done a remarkable job of bringing most Americans together again.

If the political polls are reasonably accurate, he now enjoys the support and confidence of virtually every identifiable segment of American society, irrespective of geography, age, religion, education, income bracket, etc. In sharp contrast, his opponent is one of the most divisive candidates who has ever appeared on the national scene. Can a man like Sen. McGovern, who cannot even unite his own party and has lost the confidence of so many people who traditionally support its candidates, realistically expect to unite the country behind his leadership?

That, perhaps, is the most important question for the voters of America to answer on Nov. 7. We have no doubt that they should and will answer it in Mr. Nixon's favor, giving him another four-year term in the White House.

BUFFALO EVENING NEWS
Buffalo, N.Y., October 7, 1972

The proper way to construct the essential question facing the voters this November is not whether to elect Richard Nixon or George McGovern as President. Rather, as with any first-term incumbent, it is whether President Nixon deserves re-election to a second term.

We believe the President's over-all four-year record clearly does entitle him to another four years in the White House. This preference is strengthened immeasurably by an opponent whose wobbly campaign performance and extreme positions on important issues betray a fumbling indecisiveness and hasty judgment that could leave seriously unfulfilled the exacting leadership requirements of this most powerful elective office in the world.

* * *

In his first four years in office, President Nixon has proved his competence in managing the vast federal bureaucracy and effectively governing this nation. He has demonstrated an extraordinary resourcefulness in devising comprehensive policies that take into account a bewildering range of complex details. Beyond that, he has shown a boldness in seizing opportunities of the moment, of acting where others merely talked, of striking out in innovative directions, particularly in foreign affairs.

Like that of any President, the Nixon record contains its flaws and ragged edges. The Justice Department has blundered at times in the sensitive terrain of civil liberties. Some of Mr. Nixon's nominees for Supreme Court vacancies would not have been our choices, and we wish his withdrawal from Vietnam could have been paced more rapidly.

But the President has unquestionably made impressive progress against three enormous problems inherited from the previous administration and bearing directly on his 1968 mandate — Vietnam and the broader issue of America's over-extended commitments around the globe, the overheated and tattered economy and the tumultuous disruptions that had convulsed many cities and college campuses.

* * *

No doubt the inner cities and college campuses are calmer today for many reasons, yet surely two concern the substantial reduction in our involvement in Vietnam and the timely reforms of an inequitable draft law. Our Vietnam involvement has not been totally ended, regrettably, but the President has essentially ended American participation in ground combat operations and has withdrawn all but about 25,000 of the nearly 550,0000 U. S. troops stationed and fighting there when he took office. After an initial period of depressing economic news, the President's dramatic New Economic Policy announced a year ago has contributed heavily to a revived economy, a cooling of the inflation that began in the mid-1960s and the promise of a more stable international monetary system. Despite some Buffalo-like pockets of severe unemployment, the New Economic Policy has also helped push the number of job-holding Americans to a record high.

Indeed, the robust economic recovery coupled with deficit federal spending could pose future risks of a resurgent inflation. But on that point alone the conservative instincts of Mr. Nixon, which tend to favor more restrained spending and a limited role for the federal government, would serve the nation more sensibly than the profligately liberal instincts of a Sen. McGovern, who supports a vastly enlarged Washington role in national life with corresponding increases in public spending.

Outside these inherited domestic problem areas of the economy and civil turmoil, President Nixon has also advanced notably inventive reforms. He was the first President to advocate revenue-sharing, the first to urge an automatic linking of higher social security benefits to cost-of-living increases in order to protect the savings of retired Americans. He was the first to ask Congress for free family-planning services on a voluntary basis for those who want but cannot afford them. In a daring and comprehensive bid to reform the nation's welfare system, he became the first President to support a national income floor for welfare families.

We hope that in a second term Mr. Nixon would press vigorously for congressional action on these and other incompleted portions of his domestic reforms, such as his sensibly balanced, public-private plan for national health insurance.

* * *

But it is in foreign affairs, where a chief executive enjoys the greatest freedom of action, that President Nixon has brilliantly broken from the frozen policies of the past to reshape America's role in the world.

His unprecedented visit to mainland China re-opened channels of communications closed for a quarter century. His firm and savvy diplomacy contributed to a ceasefire in the turbulent Middle East and probably the withdrawal of Soviet military manpower from Egypt. His administration negotiated the first limitation of strategic arms with the Soviet Union, and his Moscow visit produced other dividends in terms of concrete treaties and face-to-face diplomacy.

These among other foreign policy initiatives, thoughtfully conceived and steadily pursued, redeem the 1968 Nixon campaign pledge to try to move from an era of tense confrontation to a period of negotiation in quest of a more peaceful world. In the President's low-profile vision of the American role in foreign affairs, the U. S. would not act as some kind of international policeman. In line with this judicious pullback, military personnel have been reduced from 3.5 to 2.3 million, and defense spending which in 1968 amounted to 45 per cent of the total federal budget now is only 32 per cent.

* * *

Significantly, however, this Nixon lowering of America's profile around the world contrasts markedly with the sudden wrenching extreme of unilateral withdrawal from hard responsibilities abroad implicit in Sen. McGovern's policies and desire to slash $30 billion out of the defense budget over three years.

These, then, are the main reasons why we believe President Nixon should be re-elected Nov. 7, and thus be given an enthusiastic mandate to carry forward and complete the promise of his commendable first-term performance.

Chicago Sun-Times
Chicago, Ill., October 15, 1972

As our readers know, we have disagreed with President Nixon on many fundamental matters over the last four years, particularly his conduct of the Vietnam War and his failure to expand civil rights and to protect civil liberties. But we have supported his historic new approach to building global peace by establishing new relationships with Russia and China and we believe he has taken sound steps to strengthen the American economy, here and abroad.

In the long run, the well-being of every American will depend on stability and peace in world affairs and prosperity at home. In the next four years we believe Mr. Nixon can achieve more in these areas than his Democratic opponent, Sen. George McGovern. We are for the re-election of the President.

Because we have been so often critical of Nixon administration policies — from Supreme Court nominations to the Watergate spy episode — our endorsement was not handily arrived at. Our decision reflects, in part, a lack of confidence in the personal ability of McGovern to measure up to one of the biggest executive jobs in the world.

The Sun-Times supported Mr. Nixon for election four years ago. We said we expected him to extricate the nation militarily from Vietnam. We called for new international policies based on the pragmatic acknowledgment that the United States could not police the world. We said the President must stop the erosion of the dollar through prudent government fiscal policies and must help cities quell crimes and resolve other social problems.

Mr. Nixon's greatest accomplishment has been the creation of new American international policies that cancel long-standing attitudes toward the Communist world. It has taken courage and conviction on his part. Within his own party there linger the vain hope and the belief that Communist control of large land areas is only a temporary phase in world history and may be ignored without peril. Mr. Nixon's trips to Moscow and Peking to form "a more creative connection with our adversaries" recognized not only the realities of today's world but eased the climate of nuclear crisis that has prevailed since World War II.

Opening normal channels of trade and communication with the Communist nations may well help bring the generation of peace Mr. Nixon talks about. Russia appears willing to help cool the Middle East as part of the new relationship which is symbolized by the strategic weapons pact.

In the context of these diplomatic breakthroughs the war in Vietnam has become an anachronism, the last of the major inheritances of the old Communist containment policy. Mr. Nixon has brought home 500,000 American servicemen and has to that extent extricated the United States militarily from the war. But the policy of intensive bombing to bring pressure on Hanoi for a settlement keeps the United States deeply and immorally involved in a war Mr. Nixon in 1968 promised to end.

The intensified negotiations at Paris raise the hope that a cease-fire may be near. We do not accept the proposition that the only way to end the war is to elect McGovern. The end is inevitable. If Mr. Nixon is re-elected the pressure to end the war will continue and he must do so if he is to reach his goal of a generation of peace. It is inconsistent to do business with Moscow and Peking but not Hanoi.

Mr. Nixon has been unable to stay erosion of the dollar but he has slowed it by moving with the same daring in economics, here and abroad, as he has in international politics. The dollar is becoming stabilized in the world market and the rate of inflation has declined at home. Mr. Nixon's pledge to check spending gives hope of eventual fiscal prudence after nearly a decade of fiscal irresponsibility, typified by Lyndon Johnson's budgets.

Prices have not seemed to respond to government controls, particularly of food. The price of food remains high because of demand, reflecting the buying power of 82 million employed Americans, buying power higher than four years ago, despite inflation. We do not think controls should be ended abruptly, as McGovern advocates.

We were impressed with McGovern's forthrightness on issues and the efficiency of his staff before the Democratic convention when McGovern was challenging his own party for the presidential nomination.

When McGovern and his organization moved onto the national stage to challenge the President their weaknesses became apparent. The image of forthrightness was replaced by one of vacillation and expediency as McGovern gave the impression of overnight changes of policy in clarifying his positions. His broad promises came through as campaign oratory. His staff, reflecting his personal informal attitude, became inefficient and discordant. If we agreed with all of McGovern's views — which we do not — we would be concerned about putting him in the White House. The job requires more than a platform, it requires the ability to govern. Mr. Nixon is an acknowledged professional and disciplinarian in the art of politics and government.

Re-electing Mr. Nixon will not create the best of all possible worlds. But we have more confidence in better times ahead with Mr. Nixon in the White House than McGovern.

The Chattanooga Times
Chattanooga, Tenn., October 8, 1972

The choice of a President in this year of domestic unease and global tension calls for considered judgment of the record of the incumbent and the potential of his challenger.

Each lacks perfection but on balance we conclude the best interests of the country and its people lie with a change from the management-oriented administration of Richard Nixon to the person-centered programs of George McGovern.

By no means do we denounce in its entirety the record written by President Nixon. In most of its foreign affairs aspects, with the exception of Vietnam, it has shown a creditable boldness for which we have given Mr. Nixon unstinted support. On the domestic front, however, we believe he has turned his back on too many vital social issues. He has neglected problems of the urban areas and allowed the corrosion of individual rights. He has surrounded himself with surrogates who either permitted or failed to prevent irregularities tinged with corruption.

Nor do we endorse all the Senator from South Dakota has said or done in his remarkable march to the Democratic nomination or as his party's standardbearer. He was fuzzy in some of his pre-convention pledges. Hindsight suggests he could have handled the lamentable case of Tom Eagleton, his original running mate, with greater aplomb and kindness. His campaign organization has not run smoothly. But, as he fitted himself into the role of a presidential nominee rather than that of a lonely aspirant who no one thought could come in out of the dark, he has shown a steadily surer grasp of himself and his task.

So much for the cross currents in the decision making process which have given many thoughtful voters pause.

Compelling Reasons

The positive aspects of George McGovern's cause are much more compelling. They warrant giving him the opportunity to bring this lacerated country of ours back to a willingness not only to restate but also to live out the fundamental reasons for our being.

First, there is the man himself. He is a product of rural America with all that implies in the derivation of basic philosophies; a minister's son and briefly one himself before turning to teaching and politics as a career; a

(continued on next page)

(continued from preceding page) combat soldier, twice decorated for bravery as a bomber pilot; a legislator and administrator of experience and ability.

A dominant force in his life is a quest for peace. He is no newcomer to the search for settlement in Vietnam, having advocated disengagement of U.S. forces as early as 1963. In contrast to this Administration, George McGovern believes saving lives is more important than saving face, and that the way to end a war is to halt the fighting. This he has pledged to do.

He is no isolationist, and remains mindful of U.S. commitments to allies around the world. He is willing to retrench on over-extended efforts to act as a global policeman, especially in the expenditure of American blood and wealth in behalf of an unstable regime and a people who may not be desirous of, or ready for, our specific methods of governing. Whatever savings he is determined to make in defense outlays wil not be at the expense of the nation's strength or security.

On the domestic front, he is committed to the idea that Americans want to feel their problems are understood, their pleas for help heard. He is a willing listener and is proving an adept planner. He would encourage work as the primary source of family support, create jobs where they are needed to lessen unemployment, and provide assistance to those who have to have it to maintain a decent level of existence.

There are no confiscatory taxes in his fiscal program, but a redistribution of the burden in stricter keeping with the principle that obligations increase with the ability to pay and the accumulation of invested capital.

A Moral Force

Sen. McGovern sees in government a moral force to protect human rights and the compassion to meet human needs. There would be no "benign neglect" of obligations to minorities under his leadership.

Finally, and fortunately, there is nothing in him to suggest he would countenance corruption in government. The accumulating stench of deals with giant corporations, of favoritism to major campaign contributors, of raw political espionage, of the trade of freedom for a felon for a union's support, is offensive to the American people. We foresee no corrective action in a continued Nixon Administration.

The selection of Sargent Shriver, business man and government administrator, as a candidate for vice president adds strength to the Democratic ticket. His presence offers a welcome contrast to Vice President Spiro T. Agnew whose possible accession to the presidency raises well founded fears of further erosion of basic liberties.

On these broadly based conclusions, we support the McGovern-Shriver ticket for election in November.

Orlando Sentinel
Orlando, Fla., October 15, 1972

A MAGAZINE article not long ago spoke of the political magic of Richard M. Nixon.

In terms of achievement, often against great odds, the President might indeed be called a magician.

However, the solid attainments of his first term didn't come out of a hat. They're the result of Mr. Nixon's energy, enthusiasm, leadership, patience, an astute knowledge of government, and the desire to serve his fellow man.

✩ ✩ ✩

THINK BACK. In January 1969, when the President took office, inflation was rampant at six per cent per year, college campuses were in turmoil, cities were being burned and sacked by angry mobs, a half-million Americans were fighting a dirty jungle war — and 250 GIs a week were coming home in caskets.

The nation didn't even recognize the existence of the world's most populous country, China, and was at odds with one of the world's most powerful nations, Soviet Russia.

✩ ✩ ✩

THREE YEARS and 10 months later, as another general election nears, Mr. Nixon and the people he chose to work with him, have:

— Tamed inflation without triggering a recession.

— Restored order on the campuses and in the inner cities of America.

— Brought home all ground combat forces from Indochina and stepped up diplomatic efforts to end the war.

— Started a historic live-and-let-live relationship with the 700 million people of China's mainland.

— Initialed an arms limitation treaty with Russia that brings the first real hope of slowing, and eventually ending, the costly and perilous arms race between East and West.

✩ ✩ ✩

THE DRAMATIC visits of President and Mrs. Nixon to Peking and Moscow helped further the Nixon doctrine — that the United States can't do everything everywhere but will stand by its friends and try to live peacefully and productively with everybody, including our political antagonists.

Mr. Nixon's hopeful message, that the United States wants to live at peace with the rest of the world even though ideological differences exist, is a welcome change from the "devil theory" of international relations, a simplistic belief that "we," the Good Guys, are being swept inexorably toward an armed showdown with "them," the Bad Guys.

President Nixon insists that competition between the nations, both economic and ideological, can be peaceful. The thrust of his diplomacy is toward that goal. So far his calmly reasoned policies have been successful — so much so that the United States commands greater worldwide respect than at any time since our Marshall Plan helped a war-scarred world back to its feet.

✩ ✩ ✩

MR. NIXON IS an innovator. When it became clear the Communists were using Cambodia and Laos as protected sanctuaries from which to attack us, he gave the signal that chased them back from the frontiers.

Nor was the President too timid to order the mining of Haiphong when the closing of the enemy port was crucial to halting Hanoi's vicious 1972 offensive.

The fearful among us wrung our hands and waited for a nuclear Armageddon that never came. The Communists, we found, understood and respected the use of power, having had a great deal of practice themselves in its use.

✩ ✩ ✩

MUCH HAS BEEN accomplished these first four years of the Nixon presidency.

And many things remain to be done.

Mr. Nixon's greatest domestic programs, including family assistance and welfare reform, have been stalled by a Democratic Congress.

With time and patience they can be dislodged and enacted.

Unemployment remains a problem in part of the country, particularly among blacks, and the President has plans for putting people to work. Still, more Americans have jobs today than ever before in our history.

Sensible leadership must continue to control reckless spending if we're to stay ahead in the battle against inflation.

We're confident the voters will agree Nov. 7 that Richard M. Nixon has earned, and richly deserves, the chance to finish what he has begun, the foundation of an America stronger in sinew and greater in heart.

Oregon Journal
Portland, Ore., October 26, 1972

A big proportion of the American electorate will be going to the polls on Nov. 7 with troubled spirits.

Millions find it impossible to vote either for President Nixon or for Sen. George McGovern without mixed feelings.

That is the mood Oregon Journal editors are in as we face the duty of endorsing one of the candidates.

Yet the voter must make his mark alongside one name or the other and a newspaper must endorse one or the other. We do not consider any of the fringe candidates a real alternative.

Given these conditions, The Journal has decided to endorse George McGovern.

This choice is made in clear recognition that President Nixon is going to be re-elected by an overwhelming majority, unless the polls are far more in error than we think they are.

Part of our motivation is a belief that President Nixon doesn't deserve a landslide victory and that a victory of that scale will not be in the best interests of the country.

We are disturbed by the fact that a substantial share of President Nixon's support comes from those who voted for Alabama Gov. George Wallace in 1968 and who would be in his corner now if he were again heading a third party ticket.

We do not accuse the President of turning his back on minorities, but he has been all too willing in this political year to cater to the prejudices of those who resent the legitimate aspirations of minorities and who are indifferent to their plight.

The Journal believes the charges of scandal and corruption raised by candidate McGovern against the Nixon administration are overdrawn.

But enough questions have been raised by the Watergate affair, the ITT case and others to require more candor than has been forthcoming from the administration. The Watergate incident could and should have been cleared up long before the election. The President is prone to secrecy and mystery despite his early promises of an open administration.

While the President may not personally have ordered questionable acts by members of his administration, he at least has been careless and cynical in picking some of the personnel around him. It is not to be forgotten that he tried to appoint unqualified men to the Supreme Court until he was prevented from doing so by the U.S. Senate.

President Nixon deserves credit for what may be historic achievements in foreign policy by opening up new diplomatic and trade channels with both Communist China and the Soviet Union. These are gains which none of his critics can take away from him. The returns are not all in on his Indochina policy. Only history will tell whether the results of Vietnamization will be worth the costs paid by us and all the people of Indochina in the last four years.

And what of George McGovern?

The experience of the campaign proves that large numbers of the American people have reservations about him. It seems to say that he is not the strongest candidate the Democratic Party could have chosen.

Yet he stands for many of the right things. He is asking America to choose many of the right priorities. He is asking America to live up to its best instincts.

We believe he is a better man than his campaign has revealed, but he has been forced by the political realities into tactics and strategies which detract from his basic idealism.

It will be tragic if a crushing defeat for McGovern is interpreted to mean that America is turning its back on the best that he represents, that it is indifferent to the aspirations and needs of its disadvantaged and that it is apathetic to some of the dangerous trends in the uses of power by the Nixon administration.

The Journal has never been a carping critic of presidents for the sake of criticism. Assuming Mr. Nixon's re-election, we will continue to call the shots as we see them without partisan bias.

For now, we think the situation calls for a token of protest and an affirmation of many of the things for which Sen. McGovern stands.

The Detroit News
Detroit, Mich., October 26, 1972

The Detroit News endorses Richard Nixon for reelection as President of the United States.

For us this is the easiest decision of the 1972 election year. Mr. Nixon has proven an able and in some respects brilliant chief executive. There would be no good reason to replace him even if his opponent were a man of outstanding merit, which Senator George McGovern is not.

To say that Mr. Nixon has been faultless would be absurd. He is human and a politician and therefore subject to error and the exigencies of politics. He sometimes seems too ready, for example, to adopt rather than reform the philosophy of domestic welfarism.

On balance, however, he has moderated the plunge toward the total welfare state. Also:

He has mustered the courage to confront the previously unchallenged forces of inflation which his predecessors unleashed.

He has appointed four Supreme Court justices who give promise of a return to more literal construction of the Constitution. There is hope now for restoring balance to a process under which solicitous consideration of the rights of the accused has overshadowed the need to protect society.

He has restored a sense of order which was lacking in our society before he came into office. The streets and campuses are quieter; the sounds of rioting have faded.

He has reduced U.S. forces in Vietnam from more than half million to 36,000. While winding down a war inherited from other presidents, he has initiated with China and Russia a new diplomacy which creates hopes for an era of world tranquility.

Work so well begun should not be interrupted by an unnecessary change of presidents, by a switch from moderation to radical reaction, by a trade of good management for bad, by a retreat from responsible world citizenship into isolationism.

McGovern disturbs us because in some cases we find his ideas opaque and because in other cases we see all too well what he wants to do.

His original tax-welfare plan, a piece of demagoguery which promised everybody in the land a $1,000 annual bonus, was an impossible scheme which elicited hoots of derision from all sides. He withdrew it and offered in its place a plan which would be funded from savings he cannot guarantee and from taxes which would discourage economic growth and employment.

Vague though he may be about tax-welfare reform, he leaves no doubt about his intentions in Vietnam. He would get out of the war by simple surrender, pulling the rug from under South Vietnam, killing any chance of reasonable settlement, and jeopardizing the chances of getting back our prisoners of war.

While surrendering to Hanoi, he would drastically cut the U.S. defense budget, endangering the nation's security and sapping its ability to keep its commitments to its friends. These risks would be offset, however, by using the defense budget "savings" to buy a new American utopia.

Since the many and various McGovern programs would require much more money than the "savings" could provide, there obviously must be other sources of funds. Who will pay? Not you or you or you, of course. The money will come pouring down from heaven.

Judging from the polls, these McGovern programs and policies have left the mass of voters cold. Desperate, he now grasps at straws — the Watergate caper, the ITT episode, the wheat issue — and exaggerates flimsy evidence into ironclad proof that this administration is the "most corrupt" in U.S. history.

In the ITT case, Senate liberals sought to connect Richard Kleindienst, Mr. Nixon's appointee as attorney general, with an alleged deal between ITT and the administration. But the Senate — controlled by Democrats — confirmed Kleindienst. Obviously, the Democrats would not have confirmed a Republican appointee if they could have proven him corrupt.

In the Watergate case, no proof has been produced that any high and responsible official of the Nixon administration had anything to do with the alleged bugging of Democratic headquarters. And the Justice Department has indicted the seven accused of the breakin. It is unfair of McGovern to judge that case before it has been heard in court.

In the wheat case, neither McGovern nor anybody else has proven that insiders profited from the sale of grain to Russia. A half dozen investigations are under way. Again, why doesn't McGovern wait to see what, if anything, these investigations produce?

McGovern's petty politicking might be redeemed if one could detect in him enough of the qualities of leadership that make a man worthy of the presidency despite his blemishes. We detect few such qualities.

For example, one mark of good leadership is the ability to pick good assistants. If McGovern were elected president, what choices could we expect from him? Would he give us for secretary of state a Ramsey Clark, the McGovern dove who recently threw the whole country into an uproar by his meddling, blundering propaganda trip to Hanoi? Would McGovern take with him to the White House those "uninformed interns" whom he blames for the miscues of his campaign?

The first top-level appointment McGovern made to his prospective administration turned into a fiasco of historic proportions. He chose as his vice-president a man with a record of emotional instability and psychiatric care. After finding out about Senator Thomas Eagleton's disabilities, McGovern stood behind him "1,000 percent" and then dumped him — not because Eagleton was a bad risk for America but because it became apparent that Eagleton would lose him votes.

Indeed, the Eagleton affair seemed to set the spirit and the tone of the McGovern campaign for president. And the chaotic McGovern campaign warns of a chaotic McGovern administration. Why buy such trouble when we already have a president who is doing a good job? We cast our vote for Richard Nixon.

The Oregonian
Portland, Ore., October 22, 1972

The popular assumption, fostered by the presidential candidates of both major parties, is that the election Nov. 7 offers Americans the clearest choice in this century between men of widely differing philosophies and records.

That is probably an exaggeration, but it comes close to the truth. The nation will not perish overnight if one or the other is not elected. There is still Congress and the Supreme Court to share responsibility for keeping the republic on course. But the man in the White House can influence the future of America and the world.

In his four years in the presidency, Richard M. Nixon has begun to make history. But it is only a beginning. He needs more time and a more responsive Congress. His initiative, patience and unflagging determination to end the Cold War with the Communist powers and lead all nations toward a lasting peace already have accomplished near-miracles. But there is much more to be done. To change presidents at this stage and risk the adverse world reaction which would result would be an ill advised risk.

The shrillness of Sen. George McGovern's campaign to replace President Nixon tends to obscure, and is designed to obscure, the historic changes in national policy brought about in the past four years. Yet these, and not Watergate, or ITT, or the President's personality, will determine whether the United States continues to prosper in freedom and avoid war, or whether it will fall from world leadership into a status of weakness and servility to a monolithic rival.

The promises Sen. McGovern has been making lack substance. The accomplishments of President Nixon have lifted the spirits of all Americans and given the world new hope.

It is hardly necessary to recite in detail the steps Mr. Nixon has taken to get American forces out of Indochina, or to resist by air the massive April offensive of the North Vietnamese, thereby bringing the North and South to the verge of a cease-fire and political settlement.

Sen. McGovern started his campaign for the presidency four years ago on a single issue — withdrawal from Vietnam. But that is a Nixon program and it is being accomplished. The efforts to convince the American people that Vietnam is "Nixon's war" have been unconvincing. Now, Sen. McGovern has gone back in full cry to the unacceptable theme that President Nixon failed because he has not abandoned 19 million South Vietnamese to the Communist armies, without a cease-fire and return of American prisoners of war.

It is not in Vietnam, but on a far broader front, that the President's leadership of America has been most penetrating. He has broken through the isolationist barrier of the People's Republic of China and prepared the way for the gradual admission of its 800 million people to the community of nations.

He has negotiated with the Soviet Union the absolutely essential treaties and agreements to halt the nuclear missiles race and reduce tensions to a state of peaceful trade. He has done this by tough bargaining, step by step, without giving away American security, in the hope the Russians would reciprocate. Sen. McGovern's response is that the Communists would "trust" him if he went to the White House. But trust is a long way from the present stage of these hard negotiations, as it is in Vietnam.

The President's bold and innovative directives suspending the convertibility of the U. S. dollar into gold and forcing the major nations to work for monetary and trade reforms also changed the course of history.

His initiatives to curb congressional spending, to stimulate productivity of the economy, to reduce defense employment by 2½ million and move these workers into productive jobs, to encourage by all means possible the continuing expansion of the economy, have been no less important, if not so dramatic.

The President has done what it has been necessary to do, without flinching because he may have opposed it in the past. Thus, his Aug. 15, 1971, invocation of a freeze on wages and prices and the later wage and price controls which Sen. McGovern now attacks. These and other bold, frontal moves have reduced the rate of inflation — an inflation whose basic origins are the war in Vietnam the President inherited — from 6 per cent annually in 1969 to 2.5 per cent. Every wage earner has more buying power because of these controls.

The fight must go on. Neither the world relations nor the domestic economy has yet reached that degree of stability which must be achieved. Presidential leadership, not carping criticism and emotional appeals, must be retained. The case is clear and the choice is obvious. President Nixon must be given the four more years he needs to complete his redirection of America's future.

CHICAGO DAILY NEWS
Chicago, Ill., October 16, 1972

The Daily News urges the re-election of President Richard M. Nixon. We have no doubt — and by the look of things, the vast majority of the voters agree — that he is by a very wide margin the abler of the two major candidates to discharge the exacting duties of his office.

The blunt fact is that Sen. George S. McGovern has not made it much of a campaign. His primary fight was spectacular: He came riding out of the West like young Lochinvar leading a host of eager followers caught up in his heady promises of a spiritual upheaval.

So powerful was his spell — or so entranced were his partisans with the beauty of the image they held in their mind's eye — that his policy utterances took on the aura of holy writ. In spite of the consternation his more outlandish proposals wrought among objective authorities, the spell held right through the Democratic convention.

Then McGovern, himself, pricked the bubble and everything went to pieces.

A Lochinvar wouldn't have done what McGovern did to his comrade-in-arms, Tom Eagleton.

A real knight-errant could hardly have become — as our Charles Nicodemus put it — the greatest waffler since Aunt Jemima, hedging on his income-sharing program, on his running-mate, on his proposal to scuttle half the U.S. fleet and 10 of its 16 aircraft carriers.

It can be argued that McGovern's recent programs make more sense than those he set forth earlier in the year. That doesn't answer the basic question. The basic question is how reliable is the judgment of a man who could pitch those proposals into a serious campaign in the first place, and then retreat in such confusion that it's hard to know where he really does stand. A President of the United States had better be a man who finds out what he is talking about before he says it. The peace of the world could depend on it.

President Nixon, with the advantage of long experience in dealing with crises and wielding authority, moves boldly, but with prudence and circumspection. That is the decisive difference between the two men.

Once persuaded that strong measures were required to check inflation, Mr. Nixon made his plans and ordered the wage-price freeze. The planning was bold but sound; the plan worked.

Once persuaded that the hopes of long-range peace on Earth required a drastic new order of global diplomacy, he planned and executed his historic face-to-face negotiations with the chiefs of the Communist world. That plan is working; China has joined the family of nations, the first arms-limitation treaty has been signed with Russia, and a new and better era of international understanding has been brought into sight.

While we have shared the general sense of frustration over the prolongation of the war in Vietnam, Mr. Nixon has made his careful plan there, too, and by the look of things is doing what neither of his predecessors was able to do by bringing that war to a close. Meanwhile he has cut U.S. troop strength and casualties to a small fraction of what they were.

One need not look far for grounds to criticize Mr. Nixon.

On the domestic front he has played election-year politics with some controversial and important issues such as welfare, busing and gun control. And corruption has been unearthed in his official family. We do not minimize the seriousness of this issue. But it is fair to point out that every President within memory has had retainers less scrupulous than he, and that Mr. Nixon has not been touched personally by any hint of scandal.

The President's domestic record has also had its share of pluses: in curbing inflation, in cleaning up the environment, in control of narcotics, in bringing more women into responsible positions in government, in broadening opportunities for minorities in jobs and housing and broadening benefits for the old and ill.

Perhaps from the nature of his personality the President has tended to be viewed as more of an expert technician and consummate politician than as a humanitarian or civil libertarian.

But the task on Nov. 7 will not be to choose an image, but to elect a man qualified to lead the nation through four more years of danger, challenge and change. Richard Nixon's record establishes his credentials. He has kept his priorities straight, made headway with the big jobs, and kept the nation on an even keel and moving forward. He has earned the right to a second term.

DAYTON DAILY NEWS
Dayton, Ohio, October 19, 1972

The nation faces a melancholy choice in its presidential election next month, and most Americans seem to be responding in kind. There is little enthusiasm for either candidate, only a kind of resigned determination that somehow we must hang in.

We must, of course, for mankind is undergoing an historic sea change, the nature of which is not yet apparent, and it may well be crucial for the planet and the people that we move into this future with new ideas and ancient values, with new systems of participatory decision-making and an old, almost forgotten, humane sincerity, with a reawakening of the goodness in man combined with some sort of quantum jump in what may loosely be described as the social sciences.

Neither presidential candidate offers us even a window onto that future.

Though in serious disagreement with much of what Richard Nixon has done and is doing, The Daily News nonetheless prefers him of the available choices and endorses his candidacy for re-election.

Mr. Nixon has inflicted serious disservices on the country, most harmfully in widening the divisions of a people he promised to bring together. His cynical exploitation of the race issue in such matters as school-busing and Supreme court appointments has been not only tragic but politically unnecessary. It is a pity the incumbent President runs so scared. Had he possessed confidence in himself, he could have led in healing the racial wounds that must be cured before America can begin to become a healthier place in which to live.

It is ironic that his greatest contributions, in opening the possibilities of detente with Russia and China, have been matched by his manipulation of the fears of Middle America so as to further divide his own people. Often the President seems not really to care about people, except as political objects. He is not hostile, only indifferent, which may be the cruelest attitude of all.

Sen. McGovern seems a decent man, as Robert Kennedy said first and many have said since. Yet decency, while desirable, is hardly a qualification to lead his country through what may be its most perilous period. McGovern has some good ideas about tax reform, racial accommodation and putting to work the youthful idealism which probably is our best hope.

He does not, however, show much promise when it comes to accomplishing these ideas. He does not even demonstrate a clear understanding of precisely what it is he is proposing. His bungling of the Eagleton affair, frequent revision and recosting of his incomes policy, strange conduct with respect to Pierre Salinger in Paris and waffling on such questions as amnesty and abortion paint a disturbing portrait of what appear to be his infirmities as an executive.

Most seriously, his combined positions on defense and foreign affairs remain uninformed and dangerously, perhaps fatally, naive. They would invite Soviet adventurism and might even require it. The Kremlin moderates would be defenseless against the Soviet Union's hard-liners and predators, once the U.S. was as weak as the three annual McGovern cuts, totaling $30 billion, would render us. This weakness would create power vacuums and make it impossible to work out diplomatic agreements looking toward peace and disarmament.

The Daily News does not oppose reductions in defense spending. Some is necessary in reordering priorities for a pluralistic society in a multi-polar world. In recent months, this newspaper has proposed cuts of $3.2 billion in weapons development and procurement for this fiscal year—some 4 per cent of the total defense budget. Carried through five years, these reductions would total $16.9 billion.

Sen. McGovern's $30 billion whack is both dangerously excessive and arbitrary, however. It is not fitted even to McGovern's own foreign policy. It offers nothing but the horrors of massive retaliation to support commitments to Israel, to the new involvement the senator proposes in southern Africa or to back up Western Europe.

The senator's program of total withdrawal of assistance to South Vietnam and of partial withdrawal without prior understanding from Western Europe represent a dangerously swift U.S. recessional.

They are isolationist, whether the senator recognizes that fact or not. They move toward the Fortress America concept of Herbert Hoover at a time when no continent can be a fortress, when time and distance have shrunk so that peace and security in the world cannot be divided by any geographic barrier.

Mr. Nixon's conduct of foreign policy and security have been his strong points. For that reason, The Daily News believes he is less likely to bring disaster to America in the next four years than is his challenger.

Beyond those four years, as the postwar generation matures and its influence grows, we must find something better if we are to endure. We cannot afford, as a people, to leave our fate entirely in the hands of the politicians during the interval.

Somehow as a citizenry, during what at best will be a Presidential hiatus in the American dream, we will have to reassert our fundamental decency and struggle, even sacrifice, to come through these next four years freer, more considerate and gentler than we begin them.

The Morning Star
Rockford, Ill., October 31, 1972

The Morning Star recommends Richard M. Nixon for a second term as President of the United States.

The decision comes after a careful weighing of the performances, the public utterances, and the staff appointments made by both the President and George McGovern, the Democratic senator from South Dakota.

By opening the doors to China and Russia, Nixon probably has assured himself a place in history as an international statesman. At the same time he has turned his back on the grave social problems weighing on the nation.

The economy has not been stabilized, civil rights improvements are at a standstill, the nation's welfare system is a cesspool. An inaccessible, aloof President, Nixon has shown little concern for the common man.

Perhaps the worst thing that could be said about Nixon is that he again chose Spiro T. Agnew as the man to occupy the post just a heartbeat away from the presidency. Even with his new low profile, Agnew has never shown he has the sagacity, temperament or capacity for the nation's top job.

The McGovern promise that showed in his series of stunning primary victories has been dulled by his performance since then. He's been on the defensive, indecisively changing his position in search of an issue that would carry him into the White House.

McGovern's staff has repeatedly let him down, giving rise to serious questions about the kind of men who would surround him in the White House. His big issue — the war — has been blunted by the Nixon-Kissinger initiatives.

It's a political shame that the nation should have to make such a decision — between an indecisive idealist and a man who can't face up to his nation's own problems. But the decision must be made.

Although we cannot endorse the way President Nixon has handled the job, we do believe he has the capacity for it. We recommend his reelection in hopes that the next four years — freed from the necessity of a reelection campaign — he can use the great powers of the presidency to cure some of the nation's ills.

THE ROANOKE TIMES
Roanoke, Va., October 22, 1972

If all the indicators are true the 1972 presidential race is a total bust in stirring voter interest. Richard Nixon is campaigning less than any president since Franklin Roosevelt ran for a fourth term in 1944. George McGovern's speeches, as one writer put it, "have put more people to sleep than warm milk and crackers."

It has been a dreary campaign, devoid of the kind of debate the nation needs. The longer it runs, the less enlightening it is. Once the primaries were over and the Democratic ticket was finally settled, the country began to yawn and it has been yawning ever since.

The danger in this situation is that it will not be fully awake on election day. A president will be elected on Nov. 7 and it is imperative that he be Richard M. Nixon.

Both positive and negative considerations impel this choice. On the positive side, Mr. Nixon's most persuasive claim lies in his management of foreign policy. Particularly in his dealings with the Soviet Union, the President has sought to find a new balance of power consonant with world realities. The U.S. position in world affairs under Mr. Nixon remains that of an active leader but less of an interventionist, as it should.

The President's dramatic effort to bring China into the world community and the first-stage development of the strategic arms limitations agreements are major accomplishments of the Nixon administration.

Mr. Nixon's handling of the Vietnam War has been less adroit than his management of other foreign affairs. Still, he has enormously reduced our military involvement there. Faced with the unfortunate entanglement in which the nation found itself at his inauguration, Mr. Nixon probably has advanced our external interests as well as any president could have.

There is no question about the President's genuine desire for peace and the sooner he can complete our withdrawal from Vietnam the sooner he can press forward on the other fronts where he has made auspicious beginnings.

At home, Mr. Nixon's greatest success has been the nation's economy. Price and wage controls, as late and as hesitant as they were, have reduced the rate of inflation. Mr. Nixon demonstrated his flexibility by doing what he had said he would not do and the business climate is vastly improved over the recession of a few years ago. While the unemployment rate remains too high, more people are working for higher wages than ever before.

The negative reasons for supporting Mr. Nixon are as numerous as the positive. Senator McGovern was supposed to have the intellectual capacity to discuss the great issues in a rational, illuminating way. He has failed to do it.

Instead, he has proposed a tax revision that would destroy initiative by virtually confiscating the savings a father has put aside to pass on to his children. He has advocated a $1,000 handout welfare scheme from which he himself has been forced to retreat. And he has called for a Vietnam withdrawal that would give Hanoi even more than it has asked.

As for Senator McGovern himself, the qualities of decency and forthrightness which were attributed to him during the primaries have now faded in a wash of demagoguery and indecision. The Eagleton case and other examples of vacillation raise serious questions about his ability to administer the affairs of the nation.

There is much about the President and his style and more about some of the men who surround him and their politics—which we do not admire. Secrecy in government, poor appointments, rejection of the right-to-work guarantee, the Watergate affair and the aura of cynicism and readiness to bend to special interests that pervade high places—all of these bother us.

We believe, however, that relieved of the political pressure to run again, Mr. Nixon in the next four years can be the statesman at home he has proved himself to be abroad.

All things considered, the case for Mr. Nixon is conclusive. The Times recommends his re-election.

HOUSTON CHRONICLE
Houston, Tex., October 22, 1972

The Houston Chronicle has examined the policies and records of the two major party candidates seeking the presidency of the United States.

We asked ourselves the same questions all voters ask. Which candidate is best qualified to lead this nation? Which candidate has the strength to guide our foreign policy? Which candidate sets and pursues realistic domestic goals?

Our conclusion: We endorse Richard M. Nixon for reelection.

There is a clear choice. There are major differences between the candidates on many key issues. Let's look at those issues.

President Nixon has demonstrated strong leadership in foreign affairs. The President's bold visit to Peking ended the threatening isolation of the People's Republic of China. At the same time, he retained good relations with Japan and arranged mutually beneficial trade agreements.

The President's visit to Moscow created a detente that is easing tensions worldwide. Nixon has skillfully set the stage for more European conferences. The Strategic Arms Limitation Talks produced agreements that are a positive step in controlling the arms race, a great achievement.

In Vietnam, President Nixon has brought us to within days of a settlement under honorable terms. He has proven himself flexible in negotiation but adamant against surrender. He has shown calmness under stress and firmness in the face of pressure. Through his Vietnamization program, he brought home more than 500,000 American troops while building the capacity of South Vietnam to maintain its independence.

The President moved confidently to stabilize world monetary problems. He directed that steps be taken to correct the balance of payments deficit. New trade agreements portend greater expansion of American firms in the foreign market.

Domestically, President Nixon acted firmly to control our economy. Although he finds controls distasteful, he saw that limited ceilings were necessary to keep inflation from diluting the take-home pay. The controls Nixon placed in effect have cut the rise of inflation but have not stifled the economy. The President has wisely sought a balance between the wild spending of Congress and the need to keep business activity spirited.

And the President believes in keeping our nation's defense capabilities second to none. The expense is tremendous and there is no place for waste, but the consequences of bilateral disarmament are frightening to contemplate.

In contrast, Sen. George McGovern has failed, in our opinion, to demonstrate the necessary leadership abilities, even in the conduct of his own campaign.

McGovern engineered a Democratic Party convention that deliberately alienated many loyal party members, forcing them to put country above party affiliation nationally. He appealed to minorities with radical programs during the primary campaign, and since has shifted his position on many major issues, creating his own credibility gap.

On Vietnam, the senator took a position of surrender to Communist aggression. He deplored military actions by the United States and South Vietnam but failed to treat in the same manner the invasion of the South by the Communist armies.

The senator put forth a $1000-a-year-for-everyone plan that collapsed in fiscal ruins when his own figures were totaled. Then he retired to come up with another plan which avoids that problem by not providing specific figures.

The senator says he would slash our military budget to a point we consider would reduce the United States to a second-class power. His approach to foreign policy is naive, even passive, and he would put us on the road to isolationism, not world peace.

On Tuesday, Nov. 7, the voters will take the fate of this nation into the voting booth with them. The issues and the questions at that moment are reduced to a single point: Who do you trust?

We believe President Nixon has demonstrated his ability to perform. We also believe his philosophies are in tune with the needs and wishes of the great majority of the American people.

On such matters as the general direction the Supreme Court should take, the prudent but not emasculating reform of the tax structure, no forced busing for racial balance, a higher regard for the work ethic than the welfare ethic, no unconditional amnesty for those who deserted their country—on all these issues we think the President stands with the country, not far and unrealistically to the left of it.

We believe this country should have and wants change in many directions, but a reasoned and intelligent change without radicalism. President Nixon is the man we would trust to have sitting in the Oval Room of the White House for the next four years to preside over this change and our national security.

The Evening Star and The Washington Daily News

Washington, D.C., October 29, 1972

The candidacy of Richard Nixon was not made in heaven. There is no burning bush on the White House lawn from which emanates an unworldly voice proclaiming, "This is MY President, in whom I am well pleased."

Richard Nixon—let the fact be faced—is not a lovable person. He does not come across as a man of great principle or substantial character. He, and the men around him, show unmistakable signs of hubris, of an arrogance of power which borders on contempt for those with whom they disagree, of distrust for institutions as basic to our democracy as a free press. His White House seems more adept at marketing the Nixonian product than at bringing out the best in this good nation.

And yet seldom in a presidential year have we had less trouble in determining our preference between the candidates. We prefer Mr. Nixon.

His faults are far outweighed by his accomplishments. He does much better than he looks and sounds. Indeed, perhaps only a cool operator like the President, unburdened by a zealot's commitment, could have shrugged off the shibboleths of the past to forge the imaginative, innovative record of his first term.

It is in the field of foreign affairs that Mr. Nixon has scored his major triumphs. He has richly fulfilled his promise to bring us out of an era of confrontation into an age of negotiation. Months of painstaking bargaining with the Soviet Union have produced the first stage of the arms limitation agreement, an initial step back from the abyss of nuclear annihilation. The recent Soviet-American trade agreement is another step toward the creation of bonds of mutuality which will give each nation both a better understanding of the other and a stake in each other's survival.

Nor has this been achieved at the sacrifice of any essential American interest in Europe or the Middle East. The United States remains committed—and is known to remain committed—to the security of Western Europe. While peace has not come to the Middle East during the President's first term, neither has war. Israel is stronger today than she was in 1968 and is receiving a flow of Russian Jews pried loose by Mr. Nixon's quiet diplomacy.

Perhaps nothing staggered the President's friends and foes more than his mission to Peking, a political end-around play which only one with impeccable anti-Communist credentials such as his could have brought off. Many problems remain in our relations with Peking, but at least a start has been made. And again, this has been achieved without sacrificing the security of our friends on Taiwan.

In 1968, Mr. Nixon pledged to bring peace to Vietnam. While Henry Kissinger may have been a trifle premature in proclaiming Thursday that "peace is at hand," the Tho-Kissinger draft agreement at least provides a framework within which a peaceful settlement can take place. And it clearly meets the basic desire of the mass of Americans in that it provides for the return of the U.S. prisoners of war and the final withdrawal of American forces from the Southeast Asian conflict. In a difficult situation, Mr. Nixon has done as well as any President could.

Mr. Nixon's accomplishments on the domestic front, while less dramatic, have been substantial. We sometimes forget that he took office in the wake of the assassinations of the Reverend Martin Luther King and Senator Robert F. Kennedy, that our cities were smoking and our campuses in turmoil. Confrontation was the order of the day. If everything is not coming up roses today in America's garden, there is a quieter, more constructive mood in the land. Much of the credit is due the President.

In his approach to domestic problems, Mr. Nixon has displayed a tendency toward conservative rhetoric. But his legislative proposals have, in the main, been both pragmatic and centrist. He accepted and expanded Democratic programs which he found promising, such as subsidized housing and food stamps. He met the challenge of environmental pollution with an array of solid proposals. He proposed — and then regrettably backed away from — an imaginative scheme of welfare reform and income maintenance. On that issue, however, as on some of his other legislative failures, the Democratic Congress must share the blame.

In dealing with economic problems, Mr. Nixon has displayed both decisiveness and flexibility. His "shock" to the world trade and monetary system, demanding reciprocity for our low import barriers and realistic currency exchange rates, has improved our bargaining position with our commercial partners abroad. His restimulation of the economy, and imposition of wage and price controls in mid-1971, have made inroads both on unemployment and inflation.

Even in the field of civil rights, the area in which Mr. Nixon is perceived as most lacking, his accomplishments have been considerable. He has made an earnest effort to bring more blacks into government. He has moved against outright job discrimination, notably with the Philadelphia plan, has consistently supported minority enterprise programs, and has achieved more breakup of de jure school segregation than all of his predecessors put together. At the same time, he has made clear his opposition to such force-fed racial-integration experiments as long-range busing of schoolchildren and dispersal of city blacks to the suburbs.

Both at home and abroad, this adds up to a real record of accomplishment. So while we regard the Watergate "caper" as distinctly unfunny and feel the tone of the administration could and should be much improved, we believe Mr. Nixon has earned the right to a second term.

This is particularly so when one considers the Democratic alternative. Senator George S. McGovern is a decent, compassionate man. But that is about all one can say for him. He was a lightweight as a legislator and he has been a lightweight as a presidential candidate. Neither he nor his staff has proved — as evidenced by McGovern's abortive $1,000 give-away scheme and other harebrained ideas — able or willing to deal with complex realities. His cut-and-run foreign policy, whether applied to Vietnam or to Western Europe, would be an unmitigated disaster. His proposed $30-billion cut in defense spending would reduce this nation to the status of a second-rate power, and gravely threaten the security of the entire free world. His handling of the Eagleton affair bespeaks both a tendency to shoot from the hip and an indecisiveness which, taken together, would be a dangerous flaw in a President. His simplistic notions of the imperatives of world affairs are more suited to the pulpit than to the Oval Office.

Either through design or chance, he is the candidate of radical change who asks us to accept him on faith. Mr. Nixon, in contrast, is the candidate of continuity, of evolutionary rather than revolutionary change. He shares the values and the perceptions of the majority of the people in this country. He has a positive record of accomplishment which McGovern cannot begin to match. He has demonstrated an encouraging capacity for growth.

Which is why The Star-News endorses Richard M. Nixon for re-election.

San Jose Mercury

San Jose, Calif., October 23, 1972

The best interests of the American people, both at home and abroad, will be served by the re-election Nov. 7 of Richard M. Nixon as President of the United States.

The choice this year is clearly perceived, both as to the issues and the personal qualifications of the two major candidates for the presidency, Republican Richard M. Nixon and Democrat George McGovern. On the basis of his record, President Nixon has earned four more years in the White House. Sen. McGovern's campaign, on the other hand, has failed totally to inspire confidence in his leadership potential.

Presidential elections are inevitably and unavoidably concerned with these two aspects of choice. They are at once a referendum on the record of the incumbent administration and a judgment-in-prospect on the abilities of the challenger. Synthesized in the mind of the voter, these factors are most often expressed in the question:

"Which man will do the best job for the country — and for me — during the next four years?"

The answer to that question this year is unmistakable: Richard M. Nixon.

To see why this is so it is necessary only to look at the record of the past four years. At home and abroad the United States is stronger today than it was on Jan. 20, 1969. The prospects for peace, both long term and in the short run, are brighter; the American economy is stronger, and the opportunity to give increased emphasis to domestic priorities is greater.

Under President Nixon, in short, the United States has reached a point where history's past-due bills can be sorted and catalogued and payment can begin in orderly fashion. A second Nixon administration is certain to see impressive construction on the foundation laid down in the first administration. Consequently, a hard look at that foundation should prove useful at the present time.

When President Nixon took office Jan. 20, 1969, the United States had a field army of a half-million men bogged down in Vietnam. Today fewer than 40,000 American servicemen remain in South Vietnam, none of them in ground combat roles.

Four years ago, North Vietnam, armed and supplied by the Soviet Union and Communist China, was capable of inflicting devastating damage on South Vietnam virtually at will. Today, the South Vietnamese are able to defend themselves on the ground, and American bombing and naval blockades have reduced Hanoi's war-making potential to the extent that the North Vietnamese are edging closer to a negotiated settlement of the war.

Critics of the President to the contrary notwithstanding, Vietnamization plus air support plus naval blockade has won the war. Only the form of the inevitable peace remains uncertain. Even the timing is predictable within certain limits; it will probably come just before or not long after the re-election of President Nixon.

The end of the Vietnam war will release tremendous energies, both human and material, for concentration on America's internal problems — its decaying central cities, its urgent need for broader social and economic opportunity, the challenges of education, housing and transportation, to mention but a few.

President Nixon's policies have brought the Vietnam war close to total liquidation. His policies have, in addition, led to closer economic and diplomatic rapport with North Vietnam's principal mentors, the Soviet Union and Communist China, thus ensuring maximum long-range benefits from a peace that starts in Vietnam.

In the past four years, President Nixon has concluded a strategic arms limitation (SALT) treaty with the Soviet Union, thereby slowing down if not halting entirely the frightful, spiraling race in nuclear weapons. He has concluded preliminary trade and cultural exchange agreements with mainland China and only last week effected a major trade-agreement breakthrough with the Soviets.

China, once isolated and hostile to the Western world, is now a member of the United Nations and is busy picking up the threads of normal commerce, not only with the United States but with her former arch enemy in Asia, Japan. The momentum of these truly historic shifts in attitude has barely begun to be felt; over time they are certain to make for a more stable, peaceful world as each major power comes to realize it has more to gain from peace than from conflict.

Finally, President Nixon proved himself well aware, in 1971, that an economically weak America could not hope to discharge its duty to its own citizens much less lead in the building of a peaceful world. On Aug. 15, 1971, he invoked provisions of the Economic Stabilization Act, thus freezing wages and prices. He imposed import and monetary exchange restrictions that, in effect, devalued the dollar and placed American exports in a better competitive position.

The purpose of all this, of course, was to strengthen the dollar in relation to the other international currencies and to halt inflation at home. It was admittedly strong medicine, but it has begun to work.

The major trading nations of the world have begun serious work on developing an entirely new international monetary system. The American economy has begin to recover; the gross national product for the first nine months of 1972 is up seven per cent over a year ago, a full percentage point ahead of administration forecasts. The rate of inflation has been cut in half, and unemployment, still too high by any standard, has begun to decline.

All of which is to say the United States is far from the shambles it is pictured by the Democratic nominee for President. America is no utopia; it probably never will be, but it is one of the best social and economic structures yet devised by men.

In the past four years, Richard M. Nixon has helped guide America toward peace abroad and a better life for her people at home. He hasn't solved all the nation's problems, nor has he made that claim. He has, however, seized every opportunity to try for solutions, and he has never hesitated to abandon concepts that didn't work and to innovate when necessary.

If pragmatism is what works, then Richard M. Nixon is a pragmatist. America, indeed the world, needs four more years of that kind of pragmatism in the White House.

The Mercury urges the re-election of President Richard M. Nixon.

ARKANSAS DEMOCRAT
Little Rock, Ark., October 22, 1972

For the second time, the Arkansas Democrat recommends that its readers vote for Richard Nixon. The country, after all, is selecting a President, not a preacher. And Mr. Nixon's opponent, George McGovern, has shown to us that his chief talent is moralizing.

We don't mean to suggest that the moral tone in Washington could not be improved. It can today, could have been yesterday and doubtlessly should be tomorrow. The recent revelations of favoritism, spying and illegal fund-raising are shocking.

However, the public doesn't seem to be too upset about them, and we think the reasons are that (1) it has not been proven that President Nixon had anything to do with them and (2) McGovern is saying too much about them. No one likes a moralizer. No one really believes that the question of which man is more moral is the one the voters should be asked to decide November 7.

Yet, that is the thrust of McGovern's campaign. Like the preacher that he started out to be, McGovern has resorted to name-calling and overstatement: The Nixon administration is immoral. It is the most corrupt in the history of the country. Mr. Nixon is no better than Hitler.

Now when you are fighting the devil, this sort of thing is accepted, or at least not challenged. But political fights are different. Appealing to emotions got him the nomination, largely because he was addressing himself to the alienated and the young people to whom emotion really means more than fact. But now he is up before the entire population, and most people find all this distasteful. Self-righteousness is especially obnoxious when the record doesn't justify it.

The McGovern record

Was McGovern being honest when he kicked the old political hacks out of the Democratic convention but later went around to all of them and asked for their support? Did he show compassion for Tom Eagleton when he kept him dangling like a fish on a hook while he figured out how to throw him back without getting cut by the fins? Is he being truthful when he tells the nation that he has been against the war since 1963 but yet in 1965 was still saying things like, "We cannot run out unilaterally on our commitment to the government of Saigon." Shouldn't his integrity be questioned when he tells the American Jewish voters that he'll fight to defend Israel but serves notice to our other allies (not as politically potent) that he regards our defense agreements with them as nothing but scraps of paper? Is he more virtuous for accepting a political contribution from Playboy magazine than Mr. Nixon is in taking one from ITT?

We find McGovern to be dangerously naive when it comes to foreign affairs. He thinks that the North Vietnamese would stop fighting if we got out of Southeast Asia and would return our prisoners right away. If they didn't, he would "beg" for them. As for the Russians: "I think they would regard me as a friend and do everything they could to keep my friendship."

We find McGovern to be dangerously experimental in his economic policies. They run counter to the principle of upward mobility, which is what makes this country operate so well. For instance, he makes it appear wrong for people to work hard to accumulate wealth and would strip it from them with harsh taxes. This would eventually eliminate the incentive to make money or to save it, and soon there would be no money to redistribute, or to create the new jobs, homes and businesses.

The Nixon record

Now admittedly, Mr. Nixon does not have McGovern's sincerity or warmth, but he has made a good President. In fact, in the area of foreign affairs, he has earned himself a permanent place in the world's history books: Starting Chinese-U.S. relations, negotiating the first disarmament and trade agreements with the Soviet Union, introducing a new worldwide monetary system and bringing half a million Americans home from Vietnam are major accomplishments.

Some of his domestic achievements are very impressive. He has reduced the 6 per cent rate of inflation brought on by Lyndon Johnson's Great Society spending to 2.5 per cent, the lowest rate in any industrial nation in the free world. He has gotten the rioters and protesters out of the streets. He has prevailed upon the Congress to adopt revenue sharing, which will ease the financial pinch of states and cities and strengthen the principles of the federal system. While his record on Supreme Court appointments is spotted, he has put the Supreme Court back into the middle of the road. And he has lowered the amount of military spending from 45 cents out of every dollar in the last Democratic budget to 32 cents in the one for 1973.

Mr. Nixon will be re-elected. He deserves to be. And we predict that George McGovern, when his Senate term expires in two years, will be as soon forgotten as any Democratic presidential nominee in history. He deserves to be.

THE PLAIN DEALER
Cleveland, Ohio, October 28, 1972

Based upon President Richard M. Nixon's record of accomplishment, The Plain Dealer earlier this month urged his re-election.

World events of the four weeks since that endorsement was published have served only to strengthen our belief that Richard Nixon deserves public support for a second term as President of the United States. He has earned that honor.

When President Nixon took office, America was mired hopelessly in a futile war and was struggling to maintain outmoded cold-war ideologies. The nation was rift with dissension because of that war.

America today is closer to peace than at any time in the last nine years. Even North Vietnamese officials state that peace is within close reach.

President Nixon is responsible for this achievement. He has spared no effort to end the conflict. He has used every bargaining tool available to bring an end to the war in Vietnam.

These peace initiatives included a series of diplomatic master strokes which culminated in presidential visits to the Soviet Union and to the People's Republic of China. The visits, and agreements reached on the trips, were important to any constructive settlement of the Vietnam war. They eased post-World War II tensions and helped convince Communist leaders of the United States' sincerity in seeking an end to the war.

But, even before the diplomatic breakthrough of the past month, President Nixon had moved the United States a long way on the road to peace.

Under President Nixon's direction, more than 500,000 American combat troops have been removed from Vietnam, leaving a token force of just 36,000 men. Last month, for the first time in seven years, a week passed without an American losing his life in combat in Vietnam. Under President Nixon the exacerbating draft is being replaced with all-volunteer armed forces.

Dispatches from North Vietnam say that an end to the war could come as early as next week. Whether the war ends next week, or before the Nov. 7 election, or just after the election is speculation. But, it is apparent that peace is at hand. And for this President Nixon must receive credit. He has brought it about.

President Nixon has brought America to the point of peace not through rhetoric, not through empty campaign promises, but through hard, diligent and resourceful work.

America four years ago entrusted its destiny to Richard M. Nixon and he has handled that responsibility in a manner which commands respect.

As in 1968, The Plain Dealer again this year believes Richard M. Nixon is the best man to be president of the United States and proudly supports his re-election.

Herald Examiner
Los Angeles, Calif., October 16, 1972

John Connally — former governor of Texas, former Secretary of the Navy and former Secretary of the Treasury — was in California last week, urging the re-election of President Nixon.

A life-long Democrat, Connally feels so strongly about this year's presidential race that he heads the nationwide Democrats for Nixon movement.

"This is the time," he said, "when citizens should place their country above party."

He speaks the truth. The alternatives are very clear: On the one hand an able and effective incumbent President of well-defined views providing strong leadership in both domestic and world affairs; on the other hand an indecisive challenger with fuzzy and impractical programs that, if implemented, could bankrupt the country and imperil our ability to defend ourselves.

During his four years as President, Nixon has made many decisions and achievements which commend his re-election.

Among his accomplishments is his handling of the Vietnam war. He has wound down the American combat involvement. He has managed the military and political decisions of that conflict in a manner that makes an acceptable peace imminent. And he has done all this in a manner that has preserved American strength and American credibility in the world.

In the foreign policy field, Nixon has opened the door to mainland China. He has achieved a nuclear arms pact and other major agreements with Soviet Russia. He has reduced the military tension in the Middle East. He has lowered the American military profile abroad through the Nixon doctrine. By these steps he has removed any immediate threat of a nuclear world war.

President Nixon has taken strong action to halt inflation and increase employment. He has helped revitalize industry and has brought employment to an all-time high of 82 million at work. He has made a start toward stabilizing the dollar abroad and redressing the trade balance. Housing starts, a prime economic factor, are up 42 per cent over last year.

When Nixon took office Jan. 20, 1969, there were 543,000 American ground troops carrying the bulk of the fighting in Vietnam. That number has been reduced to 30,000, and no American is fighting on the ground. American casualties have all but ended.

The armed forces have been reduced by more than a million men. The defense budget is eight per cent below the last prewar (1964) budget. Troops have been withdrawn not just from Vietnam, but South Korea and Thailand too.

This is a responsible record of careful disengagement. We emphasize the word "responsible." Nixon has refused to let his country lose its nerve. He has not let himself or others forget the long night that would fall upon the Free World if the United States stumbled under its burden.

In 1968, there was mass rioting in cities and on campuses across America. Under Nixon, riots have become a fraction of what they were. The President has spoken out strongly for the need to respect the law and has effectively worked to solve many of the problems disturbing America.

It makes sense that on November 7, a President who has worked for peace so successfully on so many fronts should be given a mandate by his people to continue that work four more years.

In the President's own words:

"Let us reject the narrow visions of those who would tell us that we are evil because we are not yet perfect, that we are corrupt because we are not yet pure, that all the sweet and toil and sacrifice that have gone into the building of America were for naught because that building is not yet done."

The Miami News
Miami, Fla., October 31, 1972

President Nixon's continuing, sometimes bold, efforts to relax world tensions came into sharp focus with the news that the Vietnam war may be ending at last.

Whatever he might have done previously toward that end, whatever finally convinced him and the North Vietnamese that the madness must cease, the fact of the impending close of hostilities exists.

His progress in foreign relations, including the winding down of the war, will give him a determining edge as America goes to the polls next Tuesday to elect a President.

His other advantages may be defined only in the shortcomings of Sen. George McGovern who has failed to maintain public confidence in his decisiveness and in the firmness of his directions. Sen. McGovern was trapped in the Thomas Eagleton affair and made a further unfortunate mistake when he was less than candid as to whether he had asked Pierre Salinger to negotiate a peace with the North Vietnamese in Paris. The inclination would be to forgive him those early campaign gaffes if he had managed to come down strong during the ensuing weeks in those areas in which his natural sympathizers expected clearcut leadership.

People who would rather not vote for President Nixon have not found Sen. McGovern the sort of alternative they could rally round with the conviction and enthusiasm they would like to display. He has been less than positive on defense strategy following his proposed three years of $10 billion annual reductions in defense spending; although his compassion toward the poor, weak and sick is obvious, his plans are mushy and lack a central philosophical direction; he has seemed unable to grab hold of the direction of his own campaign.

In his major television appearances Sen. McGovern has been convincing insofar as his own sincerity and basic decency are concerned. Is this enough?

Other Cox Newspapers, The Atlanta Constitution and the Dayton Daily News, for example, found McGovern "not competent to be President," and lacking promise "of accomplishing his ideas." Throughout, these newspapers chose to endorse Mr. Nixon as the least dangerous choice to the nation's future.

Mr. Nixon, on the other hand, seems removed from the daily concerns of the nation.

His administration's systematic attacks on the integrity of the nation's news media have so damaged people's confidence in the information they receive that they know not what to believe. A genuine threat to democracy, which rests in the end on the wisdom of the people themselves, exists if current administration policies are pursued another four years.

Mr. Nixon put the brakes on growing racial understanding in the country by siding with those who feel the Supreme Court exceeded its authority in interpreting the Constitution. He wiped out years of slow, heartbreaking effort on the part of many Southerners who thought they were doing what their government wanted them to do when he ordered a halt to further compliance with school busing rulings and at the same time embargoed many millions of dollars appropriated to help schools, neighborhoods, central city areas and better housing projects.

He has demonstrated administrative competence and the ability to control, perhaps to too great a degree, every political and governmental aspect of his White House tenancy.

If the Democrats can't manage to reconstruct a working coalition of the many and diverse parts of the party by 1976, the voters will face again the dilemma of 1972. If Sen. McGovern can act as healer and find a way to articulate clearly and precisely what we feel to be the generous and patriotic aspirations of the American people, good for him. He hasn't done so from the stump in this campaign.

This is exactly what the polls reveal as to the country's attitudes.

It is when the choice is most difficult that a choice must be made. Therefore this newspaper endorses the candidacy of Richard M. Nixon for re-election.

Democrat Chronicle
Rochester, N.Y., October 25, 1972

President Nixon should be returned to office for another term—both because his record entitles him to four more years and because Sen. McGovern simply has not made the case for being elected President.

The odds of course are always on the incumbent, and usually heavily so. In Mr. Nixon's case, his advantages have been strongly reinforced by his sure, decisive handling of foreign affairs.

Those personal pilgrimages to Russia and particularly to China were somehow deeply reassuring to an America that no longer wants to be the world's policeman and is indeed now headed towards a defense system based in part on an all-volunteer army.

The war in Vietnam, it's true, continues to trouble many Americans and Mr. Nixon has not yet succeeded in ending it. People who want to take him at his literal word are entitled to vote against him. For Mr. Nixon is on record as having said as a candidate in 1968 that "those who have had a chance for four years and could not produce peace should not be given another chance."

But this is much too narrow an interpretation. If the war is not over, it clearly is in the last throes. Mr. Nixon has been able to wind down American involvement to a point where much of the wind has gone from Sen. McGovern's antiwar sails. The withdrawal of half-a-million troops is an achievement that no one can deny this Administration.

Despite what sometimes seems like an excessive reliance on bombing, the Nixon strategy has generally worked out. Much of the bite has gone from the protest movement in this country. There is a feeling that peace, so long delayed, is just around the corner, and the feeling does nothing for the Senator's chances of capturing the White House.

In domestic affairs, Mr. Nixon has been able to maintain the initiative most of the time. The economy is still sluggish at many points, but inflation has been checked, unemployment has been reduced, industrial production is rising. These are considerable achievements.

While the Democratic Congress occasionally rose up in rebellion, as just before adjournment, it seemed to spend most of its time on the defensive against the Administration.

The charges against the Republicans of political shenanigans and special interest deals are more serious. They make all of us uncomfortable. And it's poor consolation to Sen. McGovern, and an unhappy commentary on public values, to dismiss the charges with the comment that this is what people expect of politicians these days.

Even if it isn't true that the public is just plain cynical, it still would be carrying things to extremes to hold Mr. Nixon personally responsible. We don't believe so for a moment, and neither is there any general disposition to blame the President himself.

On the Watergate affair for example, most people, according to the latest Harris survey, don't believe that President Nixon or his top White House aides were involved "in either knowing about or giving the orders for the bugging."

Voters might be inclined to trust Mr. Nixon less if they believed in Sen. McGovern more. But the plain fact is that the Senator doesn't inspire high confidence. In this he's a victim more of his own indecision. People are not convinced that he would act boldly and decisively as President.

The indecision and mind-changing associated with the Eagleton affair and with welfare ought not on the face of it to be fatal to the cause of the Democratic challenger. After all, Mr. Nixon has changed his mind a number of times, and so have most presidents.

Wrote Vermont Royster in the Wall Street Journal a while back:

"Woodrow Wilson was elected because he kept us out of war; he got us into the same war. Franklin Roosevelt campaigned on sound money and a balanced budget; he launched a long era of deficit financing and depreciating money. Richard Nixon built a political career on hostility to Moscow and opposition to Red China; he led us to a rapprochement with both."

Most of these changes evolved over a period of time. More fundamentally, they represent the difference between the candidate and the office-holder. But Sen. McGovern has done his changing, or at least the changing that has hurt him, within the course of a single campaign as candidate. And while no one doubts his moral fervor or his deep conviction on the war issue, he still has a wobbly look about him.

With Mr. Nixon, we feel we know our man, imperfections and all. We like his capacity for leadership in a crisis.

About Sen. McGovern, we're not so sure. We can't get a clear view. And that's one reason why we think Mr. Nixon should be returned to office.

The other reason, as we said in the beginning, is that his record abundantly entitles him to be supported once again. So we cast our vote, as we did four years ago, for Richard Nixon and Spiro Agnew

THE SUN
Baltimore, Md., October 29, 1972

In making a choice between the Republican and Democratic candidates for President, voters have two principal questions to consider: Mr. Nixon's record during the past four years and Senator McGovern's qualifications to succeed him.

A president standing for re-election customarily is favored for a second term. Unless his record is very poor he goes into the political campaign with a decided edge over his opponent. He can develop his own campaign in his own way, relying more upon his actions as President than upon his political speeches to promote his candidacy. If he is skillful enough, he can make use of major events in national or international areas to demonstrate his capacity in office and hence his capacity for four more years.

Mr. Nixon fits neatly into this pattern. He has dominated events in Washington during the past year, keeping the Congress in its own shadow; he has given new and adroitly publicized directions to United States foreign policy; he has discarded in the face of realities the old Republican taboos about deficit spending, economic controls and tight budgeting and has adopted for his own use much of the liberal economic doctrine long espoused by Democrats; that is, when faced with conditions he has not himself clung to the doctrinaire. He has conducted the war in Vietnam in such a way as to earn credit for a big reduction in the United States participation and to provide a rationale for our intensified bombing attacks in North Vietnam, though a great many Americans do not accept that rationale. In these large and extraordinarily difficult matters he has acted as he believed fit, regardless of dissent and in the face of criticism that has often been heavy, within his own party and without.

Less favorably, his campaign, well-financed and well-coordinated and shrewdly directed by himself and the big White House staff, has been marred by a number of unpleasant aspects. Even the Secretary of State and the Secretary of Defense, who in the past have usually maintained a nonpartisan stance, have been active in the Nixon campaign. Indeed, there has been an excess of politicking, in our view, during recent months, an excess that has often given an unfavorable cast to executive actions. Mr. Nixon diminishes his good deeds by overt opportunism, by a play on public emotions and prejudices, by overblown showmanship. Some of his appointments to the Supreme Court, notably the two rejected by the Senate, demeaned the court as well as his own office. In civil rights he has gone with the crowd instead of showing the national leadership expected of a President; his exploitation of the busing issue exemplifies his attitude. He has tried to face down without explanation the charges of corruption and favoritism rising from the Watergate break-in, the ITT affair and the wheat sales to the Soviet Union. The list could be made longer, including, more generally, the failure to conduct the "open administration" promised four years ago.

•

Yet any administration, as it nears the end of a four-year tenure, must be viewed in the broadest terms, as a whole. One may take exception to many of President Nixon's actions and methods, as this newspaper has done, and yet conclude that his record, in particular his record of the past year and the direction in which he is now headed, makes him a better choice than Mr. McGovern. He is a better choice, that is, because he is a surer choice.

The balance sheet for the country, as we read it, shows a net gain for the Nixon administration. Inflation has been slowed. The national economy is expanding. The war in Indochina is being reduced if not yet ended. Our foreign policy is moving toward a more open and more peaceful world; and if Mr. Nixon's bold initiatives in foreign relationships come to their hoped-for fruition he may indeed be recorded, as he already claims, to have been a maker of history.

We are not persuaded that Mr. McGovern would be likely to do any better. His qualities of national leadership and of administrative management have been only dimly visible. We find it hard to discern a coherent theme in his campaign for the presidency — the kind of theme that would suggest the nature of his administration if he should be elected. To the contrary, his campaigning has seemed to shift along the political spectrum at times, moving from the left toward the center, and at other times it has seemed to drift with events, until we cannot feel sure where he really stands or what as President he would really try to do.

In these circumstances Mr. Nixon is the choice of The Sun for the presidency. On balance, the record of his first term is favorable. After months of campaigning Mr. McGovern's qualifications for the presidency are still unimpressive. If Mr. Nixon is re-elected, as we hope he will be, he will have a great opportunity to build upon the real national and international accomplishments of his first administration.

The Providence Journal

Providence, R.I., November 5, 1972

When Richard M. Nixon won his first term as President of the United States in 1968, he found a nation bloodily embroiled in a war halfway around the world, a nation dangerously divided on that war, an economy under strain, a frightening national sense of leaderless drift. For what he did in those four years, he deserves re-election Tuesday.

In foreign affairs, he undertook a realistic search for world peace, replacing the on-the-spur policy decisions that had characterized the Kennedy and Johnson years. He sought and established new and improved communications with the Soviet Union and China: the SALT agreements and pending international conferences next year are among the fruits of that policy.

These newspapers have had sharp differences of opinion with the President and his administration. In a democratic society, unanimous consensus is rare, produced usually only under the stress of major war. In urging his re-election, these newspapers propose to continue to make independent judgments of what Mr. Nixon does and does not do in the next four years.

It is and has been our judgment, for instance, that Mr. Nixon's silence in the face of serious charges of political sabotage, most particularly involving wiretapping of Democratic Committee national headquarters, has been a most serious mistake. Simply in terms of politicking, his silence licenses Democratic rhetoric.

We concur with The Ripon Society, which also supports the President's re-election, in its recent proposal that the President direct his White House and re-election campaign staffs to cooperate totally in all official investigations of what are unproven but damaging charges of irregularities. The public must have the truth.

But if there have been disappointments in his performance in some areas of domestic concern, his drastic intervention to halt the spiraling wage-price increases has turned the economy around. Every responsible American also shares his continuing concern for the steeply rising costs of government as Congress talks economy and spends lavishly.

As for Sen. George S. McGovern, Mr. Nixon's Democratic opponent, he would have walked away from a war that Mr. Nixon proposes to end after protracted and detailed negotiations. Mr. McGovern's approach to the maintenance of adequate defense could inspire revival of American-Firstism — and total reliance on nuclear weapons at times of international crisis in the absence of adequate conventional armed forces.

In his promises for domestic change, Mr. McGovern has veered with the winds of criticism in such areas as welfare reform; he promises changes that even a Democratic Congress would be loathe to approve. The South Dakotan has no experience, as Mr. Nixon has had as vice president and president, in the executive management of the nation's affairs.

Endorsement of Mr. Nixon's re-election candidacy is not an endorsement of all he has done or acceptance of what he has not done. It is an endorsement of the candidacy of a man whose national leadership must be given a major share of responsibility for the four-year emergence from the bleak, dismal prospects of 1968.

Oakland Tribune

Oakland, Calif., October 22, 1972

The time has come for all Americans to ask, what kind of government did Richard Nixon give us during the past four years? In our judgment, it has been a most able and competent government, one which has earned the continued confidence of the American people.

Think back to the election year of 1968.

The American commitment to the agonizing land war in Vietnam was approaching 600,000 fighting men. The weekly casualty counts were appalling and heartbreaking. Internationally, the war had cost us gravely in terms of respect and credibility as a world power. Domestically, our economy was staggering from the effects of the war-inspired inflation. Our streets and campuses were torn with turmoil and riots. The people of America were divided against themselves as they had not been in this century.

Richard Nixon campaigned on pledges to bring us together again, to defuse what was approaching a national hysteria, to disengage us from the Vietnam morass, to stabilize the economy and to restore us to a position of respect in world affairs.

It was a tall order. But in his now-closing first term of office, Mr. Nixon came much closer to fulfilling every one of those pledges than perhaps any of us realistically expected.

In Vietnam, Mr. Nixon brought more than a half million troops home. The American people have ample reason to believe that an end is, at long last, truly in sight. The war is no longer the country's major preoccupation. Neither are any of the potential crises which did not happen during Mr. Nixon's first term. There has been no Bay of Pigs, no Cuban missile crisis, no massive Middle East flareup threatening a worldwide holocaust.

Instead, the prospects for a peaceful future seem brighter all the time. The President has, of course, opened new lines of communication with Mainland China and the Soviet Union. Evidence of growing trust and respect between the world's superpowers abounds. There have been the Berlin accords, the SALT agreement and scores of major economic and cultural advances.

Importantly, the Nixon administration has not resorted to weakening our defenses as a means of achieving more harmonious world relations. There is no hint of a return to the isolationism of the '20s and '30s. Washington has not forgotten that in the long run world peace will depend upon the maintenance of American strength.

At home, Mr. Nixon has acted boldly and innovatively in dealing with the economic problems he inherited. His imposition of wage and price controls has for the most part been effective. Today the economy is moving ahead, inflation has been checked, the rate of price rises has been slowed, business is generally good, more people are employed than ever before, productivity is better and the nagging unemployment situation is improved.

Mr. Nixon also need make no apologies for his record in the area of social progress. Turmoil in the streets has all but disappeared. There have been no major urban riots since he took office. His Administration has instituted major new controls over the quality of the air and the water. Federally-supported mass transit programs are being made available to urban centers. Under Mr. Nixon, the federal civil rights budget has tripled, there has been a record number of appointments of blacks to top positions and record achievement in school integration.

In short, domestic tranquility has been restored and our nation enjoys new respect in the world community.

Mr. Nixon has proven to be an extremely able and reasonable leader, a man of great competence and strong character. He has done an outstanding job for his country in his first term as President. The Tribune, therefore, recommends the re-election of President Richard Nixon.

ALBUQUERQUE JOURNAL
Albuquerque, N.M., October 22, 1972

The Journal supports President Nixon's bid for re-election.

There have been a number of things in his administration to criticize and this newspaper has joined in pointing them out. But overall his term in office has been an effective one.

His economic policies have helped reduce the rate of inflation and restored confidence to the point the nation is now pulling out of the recession of a few years ago. The unemployment rate of 5.5 per cent is still a persistent problem but at the same time there are now more persons working for higher pay than ever in the nation's history.

On the other hand Sen. George McGovern's ineptness in choosing a vice presidential candidate has carried over into his campaign. His ill-conceived tax reform plan was a cynical appeal to class prejudice, and his recent switch to a campaign of vituperation doesn't befit a candidate seeking the nation's highest office.

In foreign affairs the gulf between the two candidates is even wider.

Nixon's summit meetings in Peking and Moscow were historic landmarks in dealing with the Communist powers. He can be faulted for escalating the bombing of North Vietnam, but he has reduced American troops in South Vietnam by half a million men. And the Paris negotiations appear now to have reached the hard bargaining stage.

McGovern's foreign policey — if he has any left after all his waffling about Indochina — appears to be aimed at an isolationism this nation would never accept.

Under the circumstances Nixon has to be our choice.

The Boston Globe
Boston, Mass., November 2, 1972

Nothing has divided the nation in this century like the Vietnam War. The prospect of a settlement in Vietnam which will end the killing and give America a chance for a new beginning at home is a welcome one. And because there can be a new chance for America, the choice of a President for the era of peace is the issue at hand.

We have condemned America's role in this war for the past six years. We believe the end of our involvement in Vietnam is as important as who wins the presidential election. We share Sen. McGovern's statement that "if the Administration can bring a settlement of this war, they'll have (our) full support and cooperation in any effort to bring peace."

Yet it is proper to ask why a settlement could not have been reached one, two, even three years ago. The irony of it all is that in the nine points of agreement between the United States and North Vietnam we are close to what was available to both sides after the Geneva Accords in 1954 when the United States became a party to block the Vietnam elections to keep the Diem government in power. Since President Nixon has been in the White House, 700,000 Southeast Asians have died; 20,000 Americans have been killed; more than two million refugees have been created in both parts of Vietnam; 500 more American flyers have been interned as prisoners of war; and at least $60 billion has been spent.

This is too much for mankind. Even today, the President faces the problem of whether his long-time support for the corrupt government of President Thieu in Saigon will continue to obstruct the final settlement of the war. We pray this will not be.

But neither should this obscure the work President Nixon and Henry Kissinger have done. The President inherited a bad war with 30,000 Americans already dead, and if there is a settlement it is because of his skill in bringing to bear the forces of Moscow and Peking for peace.

Others, too, have an equal place in the peace—Sen. McGovern whose candidacy has been the constant pressure in moving President Nixon toward concession and settlement, and those young people who remind us each day of the killing.

Now, if peace does come Americans must decide who can best heal the wounds of Vietnam and who can restore this nation's spirit, aspirations, and confidence in itself.

Mr. Nixon has done much to serve his country. He deserves high marks for becoming the first President since World War II to abandon cold war policies. He has opened a new era by his visits to China and his negotiations with the Soviet Union. He has pursued an end to the arms race with effective flexibility. The ABM agreement, signed in Moscow, is testament to that.

He showed a similar flexibility by imposing wage and price controls, a concept he long opposed. And many experts feel that the nation's economy, in grave trouble two years ago, has made an upward turn. The success of wage and price controls, and general acceptance of the them by both business and labor, may lead them to become a permanent fixture of our government.

But partly because of Mr. Nixon's emphasis on the war in Vietnam, relations with our friends in this hemisphere have been slighted and domestic projects sidetracked.

For three years in a row education bills have been vetoed by the President. He once said, "One area we cannot shortchange is education." He has either vetoed or failed to live up to goals in such areas as consumer protection, environmental control, and equal opportunity in jobs, schools, and housing.

He promised the nation a Supreme Court which would adhere to strict construction of the Constitution. Then he sent to the Senate two mediocre nominations which were rejected. Mr. Nixon's Justice Department has tampered with our Bill of Rights. For the first time in the history of the nation, prior restraint was imposed on newspapers in the publication of the Pentagon Papers. This, in effect, put our courts in charge of publishing three newspapers. The same department, and Mr. Nixon's new majority on the Supreme Court, gave us the Caldwell case. This landmark ruling obstructs severely investigation of corruption in government and thus blunts people's chances for decent government.

On the record, the differences between the two candidates are clear. George McGovern has carried his cause imperfectly to the people and his shifting positions on major issues have narrowed his constituency within the Democratic Party. But he has faced the issues publicly, with concern.

More than any other factor, Mr. McGovern's indecision about Sen. Thomas Eagleton hurt him. But his ultimate selection of Sargent Shriver for Vice President stands as a sounder decision than Mr. Nixon's choice of Spiro Agnew as a potential President.

The approaches to tax reform and defense spending are basic to this nation's well-being. We agree with the McGovern concept for tax and welfare reform, but not with his entire program. Further, Mr. McGovern's proposed cuts in defense spending of $30 billion over three years would lead to greater tax equity, particularly in easing the burden of local property taxes.

In all of these areas Mr. McGovern promises a response to the needs of a whole America, while the Nixon Administration has too often responded to an elitist few. Mr. McGovern has come through as a man of goodwill and decency. He reflects a level of honesty and integrity which should be implicit in this nation's leadership.

There are signs that many Americans feel they never had it so good. There has not been a major race riot in four years. The campuses are quiet. But this silence may echo the calm born of hopelessness, what Thoreau meant when he said that the mass of men lead lives of quiet desperation.

The cynicism that abounds in the electorate is directly traceable to the loss of integrity in government. Fourteen years ago, Sherman Adams was drummed out of Dwight Eisenhower's White House because he accepted a rug, a vicuna coat, and payment of a hotel bill. In Harry Truman's Administration, Gen. Harry Vaughn created an uproar by accepting a deep freeze.

These episodes now seem comparatively insignificant. Today we have testimony from an ex-FBI agent that he saw nothing wrong with carrying an unregistered revolver during the burglary of the Democratic National Committee for the Re-election of the President.

What happened at Watergate was not a caper, but a crime. The issue of Watergate is **burglary**, a secret fund to finance that **burglary**, and President Nixon's refusal to disclose the names of those who contributed to that fund.

It involved shipping Nixon campaign money through Mexico for "laundering." It involved spying, lying, and carrying guns. Men close to the President ordered the Democratic Party headquarters files ransacked and telephones tapped.

Watergate is not the only scandal of the Nixon Administration. Its handling of the ITT case, the milk-support deal, the Soviet grain deal, the mergers of drug and insurance companies—all betray a public trust and diminish faith in the government.

This is what happens when a President surrounds himself with too many men of questionable integrity, self-serving advisers whose last concern seems to be the protection of the American people.

We have had delay in ending the war in Vietnam, the brutal bombing and escalation of the fighting in Cambodia, and at home corruption in the highest places. We are given nominees to the Supreme Court who would repress the Bill of Rights. And we are given Vice President Agnew as a possible successor to President Nixon. These are not our concepts of the human values and principles that should be set for our nation.

Four years from now this nation will review its heritage of two centuries. What will we say then if we have allowed cynicism to destroy the public faith and confidence essential for the survival of a democracy?

A national election is not the implementation of a Utopia; it is a choice of alternatives. It is worth remembering that this nation sent Warren G. Harding to the White House by a landslide and elected Abraham Lincoln with the smallest percentage of any candidate in American history since John Quincy Adams.

Now, more than ever, the President should inspire the nation. He should lift the spirit, give it vision, and the courage to meet the challenges which face all of our people.

To restore these honored qualities to a troubled nation as it looks to the future, we believe the United States would be better served by the election of George McGovern and Sargent Shriver as President and Vice President.

The Standard-Times
New Bedford, Mass., October 6, 1972

It is both unfortunate and fortunate that this has been such a lackluster presidential campaign. The first, because the seeming disparity between the popularity of President Nixon and Senator McGovern has led to public apathy. The second, because the portents are that Mr. Nixon will be re-elected, as he should be.

Complacency could be dangerous, however, for the stakes are large. The voters face a choice between four years of trial and error management of U.S. (and in large part, world) affairs and four years of experienced leadership.

Senator McGovern has retreated or wavered in his views on every major issue — even to busing. This newspaper believes that this indecisiveness has not been caused by campaign pressures and political necessities, but reflects, rather, the inexperience and inconsistency of mind and outlook of the candidate himself.

President Nixon, on the other hand, has compiled a record that has been consistent, energetic and productive. In appraising that record, it is well to examine the issues that were held to be overriding when he took office in 1968, not in order of their importance:

Crime—Latest available statistics show that the increase in serious crime during the first six months of 1972 was the lowest since record-keeping began 12 years ago.

Inflation—The monster has not been obliterated; but it has been slowed down substantially through the initiative of price and wage controls.

Vietnam—The war, however torrid the current rhetoric, is fading away. Senator McGovern says he would end it on taking the oath of office. But only a negotiated peace can stop bloodshed in South Vietnam, and that may come any day.

World peace—In a larger-than-Vietnam sense, the lessening, if not the elimination of fear of a major-power conflict has been an incomparable achievement of President Nixon. He succeeded in this by arms control pacts, new relationships with the Soviet Union and Red China and by maintaining a strong defense.

(Although there is instinctive reluctance to let world opinion influence an American presidential election, the overwhelming sentiment in foreign capitals for Mr. Nixon's re-election surely is based on this Nixon achievement.)

National spirit—Mr. Nixon's four years have not brought more restlessness, racial animosity and domestic violence, as his critics predicted in 1968. These have, on the contrary, diminished greatly. For a divisive potential we nominate Senator McGovern's proposal for blanket amnesty for deserters.

A working world—Despite the antipathy for the U.S. role in Vietnam, the world has come closer together these past four years. In trade, monetary policy, inclusion of Red China in the United Nations, in curbs on drug traffic, air piracy and terrorism, and in less strident lineups on ties with the Soviet Union vis-a-vis those with the United States, the family of nations is acknowledging that progress is a collective enterprise.

These are some of the good entries in the ledger under the Nixon administration. There have been poor ones, too — the ITT antitrust case; Watergate, deals with "big labor," such as the jail release of James Hoffa; the wheat sale "leak" to large grain exporting firms, the curious, even devious handling of campaign funds.

But, as yet, there has been no evidence of personal enrichment by any administration official, and no evidence the President personally condoned any such misuse of governmental authority. In short, these have not been issues on which a presidential election should be decided, whatever the responsibility that goes with being captain of the ship.

The issues for U.S. voters in this moment of history are two-fold: World peace and the domestic economy.

In the area of peace, there must not be trial and error experiment. Senator McGovern is a novice at this infinitely painstaking, terribly crucial task. He has shown his incapacity for it by the utter naivete of his expressed belief that the United States can exert a dominant influence for peace while unilaterally cutting down, to the point of neglecting, its military strength.

However unwelcome the fact, a nation's influence in foreign affairs is linked to its accompanying military posture, in materiel and determination. If this were not so, India's masses would be setting rules for the international conduct of nations.

Senator McGovern is, therefore, advocating isolationism, because a nation dismantled of power cannot be an arbiter. His policy could only lead to the United States being forced into a predicament where the choice would be loss of freedom or fight.

On programs for the national economy, there is a striking contrast between the two candidates. President Nixon, controls notwithstanding, has followed a moderately conservative approach in encouraging investment and incentive for expanding the free enterprise system. He advocates welfare reform—and the cost of welfare is an important economy factor — based on encouraging work habits.

Senator McGovern's fiscal policies are so involved he cannot explain them the same way twice. They include the populist and discredited "soak the rich and industry" theme. He would redistribute income by taking away from those in the $12,000 and above bracket; he would virtually end inheritances. His $1,000-a-head welfare scheme ($4,000 for a family of four) would set up a permanent welfare class. It is safe to say no presidential candidate has so divided labor and alienated employers by his economic theories.

This nation would face grim prospects at home and abroad were Senator McGovern elected. There have been welcome advances in both areas under President Nixon. There will be more if he is entrusted with another four years at the helm.

THE ATLANTA CONSTITUTION
Atlanta, Ga., October 16, 1972

After all the other arguments have been completed in a Presidential campaign, voters finally must decide on the competence of the candidates.

Richard Nixon has shown the world he is competent to be the President.

Sen. George McGovern has failed to convince us that he has the competence to run the country.

The Atlanta Constitution endorses President Nixon for reelection and urges that the voters of this nation support him.

* * *

That does not sweep away all the objections which have been raised here to the Nixon administration. The current list of escapades in which the campaign is involved—the Watergate bugging case, the loans from special interests like ITT, the strange methods of handling campaign contributions—give the nation pause as it chooses a President.

Nor does the endorsement indicate agreement with many Nixon programs. When he said four years ago that one term was enough time to end the war in Vietnam, we agreed. It is one of the areas in which much of the nation finds fault.

The President probably has not moved as vigorously to disturb the bureaucracy as he should. He has not been quick enough to eliminate special interest influences.

For these and other reasons, many voters have reservations about going to the polls to vote for Nixon for another four years.

* * *

Despite the drawbacks, the President has shown himself to be a flexible man willing to adjust to the realities of the world.

His ability to deal with foreign powers, particularly China and Russia, may have been a major contribution to peace in the world. His willingness to forget old campaign slogans to treat with them persuades many that he is a man who has grown in office.

When he became President, this nation was very nearly convulsed in internal dissent. More than the college campuses were involved; the streets of major cities were choked with vast numbers of protesters. Time certainly was a healing factor, but Nixon's handling of such incidents calmed the situation.

The economy still is troublesome. There is too much unemployment, and too much nervousness about the future. Nixon had to reverse himself abruptly to impose wage and price controls. That he was willing to take his medicine, i.e. listen to those who would say "I told you so," and impose controls is a tribute to his willingness and ability to adapt.

As for those Democrats who feel that his flexibility is a major defect, it would be well for them to remember that perhaps the greatest Democratic President of this century, Franklin D. Roosevelt, was a man who changed policies until he found something that worked.

* * *

Sen. McGovern came to this Presidential race with high ideals and fervent support from idealists.

The convention and the campaign which has followed have been puzzling and disappointing.

He has said that President Nixon's policy in Vietnam is the "worst barbarism since Hitler." Surely he knows such a comparison has no validity.

McGovern has exhibited a woeful inability to deal either with his own campaign staff, his Vice Presidential candidate or the necessary fund-raising to wage a campaign. If a major portion of the President's job is management—and it is—the public has been unable to determine that McGovern has any of that kind of talent.

Nowhere is McGovern's inability to manage more evident than in dealing with the regulars in the Democratic Party. Some like Mayor Richard Daley of Chicago were thrown out of the convention. Others like 51 per cent of the Democratic candidates for Congress have refused to endorse his candidacy. A man unable to be more persuasive than that within his party is an unlikely cohesive force in holding the nation together.

* * *

Finally, then, the voting public must decide what it seeks in a President.

Party affiliation is a valid experience. In the South, it has been one of the most important factors in elections. None can say it is an overstressed element, because political parties have given shape and stability to the American political system.

In this case, however, many Democrats will wish to cross to the Republican side in voting for a Presidential candidate. Under Georgia law, it is possible to vote for President Nixon and then vote for Democrats. Such a procedure is not complicated; it can be seen clearly on the sample ballots available in polling places.

The Constitution believes that Richard Nixon is a more competent President than George McGovern would be. Nixon should get this state's votes this November.

AKRON BEACON JOURNAL

Akron, Ohio, October 23, 1972

Believing that a choice must be made on the basis of competence and the ability to govern, the Beacon Journal endorses Richard M. Nixon for reelection as President.

We like George McGovern's vision for America — a land of fair taxes, full employment, peace among ourselves and with other nations. He dares to dust off the American dream and to thrust its fierce light at us unshielded. He has had the courage and the honest caring to batter the conscience of a relatively prosperous majority with the anguish and pain of the jobless, the poor, the maimed and others among us who reckon only the day and know no tomorrow.

We like George McGovern. Like all politicians, he waffles but with more wincing than glibness. He is capable of hard calculation as evidenced by earlier short-term decisions to play down the war issue which, more than any other factor, accounts for and justifies his candidacy. But always in the end he has returned to the terrible cost in blood and honor we have paid, and still are paying, to retrieve a tragic mistake in Vietnam. He fails, however, to assess the major blame for that mistake to his own party.

The senator is a man of exceptional decency, evangelical by temperament and training, and reformist by conviction. He is the latest in a line of men who have sprung up, principally in the Midwest, preaching populism tinged with isolationism. There is in him some of William Jennings Bryan's tendency to rail against wealth, and some of Tom Watson's naive, soon-corrupted passion for fighting the prejudice of race and class with prophecy and preachment.

Such men are valuable. They have made a difference for the better in our political traditions, breaking ground in which reform later took root and, in time, flourished.

After The Sermon?

But these men have been too much possessed by what ought to be, rather than what can be. They have been more acutely sensitive to a vision, rather than to the complexities and realities of American life. And they have lacked the skill, knowledge and ability to form the majorities that transform ideas into laws.

George McGovern, we conclude, is such a man. He has offered a kind of zealous, missionary rhetoric demanding change. But he has not offered a coherent program nor demonstrated the capacity to evolve and implement one.

We think he is unprepared for the rigors and harsh demands of the office he seeks. We suspect that he has no more than a surface understanding of a broad range of problems and attitudes he would face if elected.

Moreover, he is a factional rather than a party candidate, seeking to unite the Democratic Party in opposition to Nixon rather than in support of himself. He has been from the start out of step with the majority of his own party, and out of tune with the dominant moods of America. His campaign has been deficient in organization and direction.

He has erred greatly in projecting the presidency as a pulpit. That office first and foremost is a political office requiring political skills and the toughest kind of human fiber. With all respect for the senator, we find it difficult to picture him at a bargaining table with Chou En Lai or Leonid Brezhnev.

He Loses Confidence

It was not cynicism or calculation that we saw in McGovern's wretched handling of the Eagleton affair, but lack of balance, judgment and sound political instinct. And it was not so much reckless radicalism that we saw in McGovern's tax reform proposals, withdrawn under justified criticism even of bad arithmetic, as it was an absence of knowledge and lack, or failure, of judgment.

The tax fiasco and the Eagleton tragedy had not only a common cause, but a common and costly result — a sharp loss of confidence in George McGovern. His credibility as a political leader has not gone up, but down, during the campaign, and such gains as he is now making are due principally in our judgment to distaste for the stench of political espionage and intimations of fat-cat cronyism that have mushroomed around the Nixon Administration.

We view these scandals with dismay, and the evasive, dissembling responses to them by the President's associates, with contempt. And Mr. Nixon's own failure to respond forthrightly manifests that uncured flaw which has robbed him of affection and substantial trust even as respect for him has grown.

Dissent Resented

Richard Nixon is now, as he always has been, too political, too lacking in self-esteem, to deal unblinkingly and openly with the dissent, criticism, and clash of ideas that must always characterize a republic worthy of the name. Such votes as are taken from him for this fault are lost deservedly.

But it also is true that the substantial respect and confidence he enjoys, particularly in foreign affairs, has been earned. With vision, ability, devotion, and more than a little daring, the President has achieved his major goal of reshaping the context of the Cold War.

There is now less paranoia and some promise in Big Power relationships, and a solid beginning in reducing the armaments race. Excepting Vietnam, and his unmitigated support of the Thieu regime, but including the Middle East, where he has exercised great skill in warding off a holocaust, the President's record in foreign affairs is strong, progressive and likely, we think, to be well remarked in history.

The record is less good at home. He has changed philosophically the Supreme Court, which was his right. But he also has corroded respect for the highest tribunal by making unworthy nominations and by attempting to diminish its powers rather than urging constructive alternatives to its course on busing and other volatile issues.

In the Nixon record, like that of any other President, there is a minus for every plus. Joblessness remains too high. But by imposing controls he fostered new strength in the economy. Perhaps more important for the long run, he freed labor, business and plain citizens of the myth that America possessed an engine capable of perpetually pumping out goodies. He drove home the fact that restraint, discipline and competitiveness are the price of a viable modern economy.

Bold And Prudent

Richard Nixon has been a far better President than might have been expected from his razor-thin election, his inauguration without a mandate, and his confrontation of a Congress controlled by the opposition.

He has combined boldness, prudence, flexibility and a mature sense of priorities which are prime characteristics of an able executive.

Richard Nixon without doubt is a man of vast ability, experience and knowledge capable of forming majorities in a divided country and world — capable of governing.

The people and the Congress have the power to curb his excesses, as the Senate did in rejecting court nominations and as the people can do in demanding congressional action to force disclosure and accountability for the espionage scandals.

Chance For Trust

Neither the people nor the Congress, however, can endow George McGovern with the intricate skills, experience and knowledge that the presidency requires in dealing with the harsh choices of national and world leadership.

It is on this basic proposition that we rest our recommendation that Richard M. Nixon be given a second term and a second chance to add trust to the respect he has earned.

HERALD-JOURNAL
Syracuse, N.Y., October 15, 1972

Four years ago, this newspaper backed Senators Hubert H. Humphrey and Edmund S. Muskie, the Democratic candidates, for president and vice president.

This year, this newspaper endorses President Richard M. Nixon and Vice President Spiro T. Agnew, Republicans, for re-election.

The reasons are simple.

President Nixon has proved during his four years in the White House to be strong and decisive.

Sen. McGovern, during his years in politics and eight weeks of campaigning, has proved to be weak and vacillating.

Other considerations bear on our reasoning that led to the decision made by this newspaper's publisher, its editor, the day and night editors, its chief editorial writer, and city, county and state reporters.

One is the nature of the campaign.

Sen. McGovern has descended to the low road.

As we read accounts of his impromptu remarks and speeches, we're left aghast.

He compares the President with Hitler. He questions Nixon's morality. He indicts him for low motives.

Most lately he has accused the President of conducting sham negotiations with the North Vietnamese to achieve, not peace, but political gain.

We can't risk electing such a reckless man to the presidency.

Earlier, he labeled the Nixon administration as the most corrupt in history.

He accuses Republicans of bugging, condoning windfalls and camouflaging campaign contributions.

But isn't the pot calling the kettle black?

What's been the political record of union contributions to Democrats, of Democratic wooing of ethnic and religious blocs of voters, of catering to geographic prejudices since 1932?

How did Franklin D. Roosevelt first build the Democratic coalition that has held sway, except under Eisenhower, for 40 years?

He put the coalition together by political maneuvering.

President Nixon has been trying to do the same, picturing himself this year as a candidate of "all the people" to the distress of Republican congressional and senatorial candidates throughout the country.

After digesting McGovern's irresponsible accusations, we conclude he is willing to wreck the country to win the election just as he wrecked the Democratic party to achieve nomination.

▽ ▽

Sen. McGovern, a one-issue candidate until he won the nomination, is fond of quoting President Nixon's off-hand response to a group of hecklers four years ago that those then in office hadn't ended the Vietnam war in four years. Others, he stated, should be given the chance.

Sen. McGovern isn't so fond of quoting his own record during those Democratic years preceding Nixon's election.

He voted Aug. 7, 1964, for the Gulf of Tonkin resolution to support President Johnson's ordered retaliation against attack on U.S. forces by North Vietnam. President Johnson, we recall, discussed these attacks while keeping in touch with Congress when in Syracuse two days before that vote to dedicate the Newhouse Communications Center at Syracuse University.

McGovern's statements and votes supported U.S. policy and action in Vietnam until 1969 when a Republican entered the White House. That was the year McGovern started advocating total surrender.

His statement that, "My position on the Vietnam war has not altered one iota," can be equated with his pledge of 1,000 per cent support of Sen. Eagleton.

▽ ▽

While Sen. McGovern is willing to talk about other men's pasts, he omits a whole decade from his own record.

The televised film biography of his life skips McGovern's support of Henry Wallace who ran on a platform in 1948 that dove-tailed in detail with the recommendations of our homegrown Communists of the day: dismantling of the Marshall Plan, scuttling of the Truman Doctrine, abandoning of U.S. military bases.

McGovern attended the party's convention as a delegate from Illinois.

He feels the same today as he did then, according to Robert Anson who wrote "McGovern: A Biography," published this year. McGovern is quoted by Anson as saying, "I wasn't happy with the direction the Democratic party was taking in those times. I liked what Wallace had to say about foreign policy. I still think he was essentially right."

Shortly after the 1948 campaign, Sen. Humphrey labeled Wallace's Progressive party as a "crude Communist-front enterprise."

McGovern, no wonder, wants voters to forget his record from the end of World War II to the middle 1950s.

A more positive and overriding factor in our decision to back President Nixon is his record these past four years despite the obstructionism of a Democratic-controlled Congress.

He tried and is succeeding in taking the heat out of inflation, even to imposing direct controls on prices and wages.

He wound down the war in Vietnam. Most U.S. troops are home.

Simultaneously, he has been pressing for a diplomatic breakthrough to achieve, first, a cease-fire throughout Indochina.

His historic trip to Peking opened the door to communications with China, reversing our policy of 30 years.

The journey to Moscow will produce lasting results through agreements limiting offensive and defensive arms and through the opening of channels for trade.

He achieved, finally, a compromise version of revenue sharing that is turning into the salvation of our cities and localities. Note that the City of Syracuse will post a $1.39 per thousand tax cut for 1973.

Not all of the President's "six great goals" of 1968 have been achieved: Welfare reform, national health insurance, government reorganization, a full-employment economy.

He tried.

Congress, the Senate particularly torn by a half dozen Democratic presidential hopefuls, couldn't or wouldn't work fast enough, couldn't or wouldn't work toward rewarding compromises.

There's our statement about the head of the ticket this election year.

We recommend voting for President Nixon and Vice President Agnew. They have earned the right to another term.

The Evening Bulletin
Philadelphia, Pa., October 30, 1972

Many expected the 1972 presidential election to be decided on specific issues such as inflation and prices, taxes, the war, jobs, housing or the quality of life — and government — in the United States.

But the checklist of issues has become blurred. Voters seem ready to make their choice on the known strengths—or weaknesses—of two men who seek the leadership of the most powerful and influential nation in the world for the next four years.

Senator George McGovern emerged from the Democratic Party's presidential primaries as a fresh political spirit, a moralist, a homespun populist. While some of his schemes, notably his short-lived idea of an annual federal allowance of $1,000 for all, were ill-contrived, Mr. McGovern was credited with a deep-rooted concern for people and with outspoken honesty.

But the McGovern of today is not the George McGovern of the primaries or the Democratic National Convention. He has shifted and has tried so desperately for opportunistic advantage that it is hard to tell where he really stands.

This lack of decisiveness surfaced early with Senator McGovern's inept handling of the Eagleton affair and with his obvious difficulties even with his own campaign staff.

Senator McGovern continues to speak out against federal wage and price controls which, although applied belatedly and reluctantly by the Nixon Administration, have had a degree of success in curbing runaway inflation.

In the closing days of the campaign Mr. McGovern has turned to increasingly strident attacks upon the Nixon Administration and on the President personally.

References are made to Hitler in criticizing some Administration actions. The initial purity on ideals and issues that marked Senator McGovern's candidacy has been blemished. So has his credibility.

What of Mr. Nixon?

It should be realized, first off, that there is an anti-Nixon cult dating back to the President's earliest days in politics. Nothing Mr. Nixon says, or does, will change this group.

But there are many, not frozen into an anti-Nixon stance, who worry about the way President Nixon does some things and about the ethics of some of the people around him. President Eisenhower had his U-2 and President Kennedy his Bay of Pigs. It is hard to imagine either man, though, experiencing a Watergate with all of its unsavory implications. And Mr. Nixon has yet to address himself fully and firmly to the Watergate episode and matters related to it.

There is the question, too, whether Mr. Nixon has done all he could to bring together the diverse elements of the country—acknowledging that there are some who profit from turmoil and would rebuff all healing moves.

(continued on next page)

(continued from preceding page)

There are welcome assurances now that "peace is at hand" in Indochina and that there may at long last be an end to that costly and frustrating conflict. Even if peace becomes a certainty before Election Day, enabling Mr. Nixon to keep his pledge to end our involvement during his term, there will remain many who feel he should have extricated us far sooner.

Against such sentiment must be weighed the refusal of Hanoi to respond to several past peace overtures. Mr. Nixon is to be credited, too, with having withdrawn more than a half-million American troops sent by other presidents, and for ending U. S. involvement in ground combat in Vietnam.

Placed upon the scales in the continued weighing of Vietnam as an issue must be Senator McGovern's rather naive proposal to walk away from the whole mess, with little thought to what could happen to those who over many years cast their lot with us. Nor can the fate of American prisoners of war and those missing in action be entrusted to the goodwill of the North Vietnamese or anyone else.

Foreign affairs

President Nixon displayed, in his visits to Peking and Moscow, diplomatic daring and imagination as well as a sure grasp of his country's present and future role in the world. There has been, since Mr. Nixon's historic journeys, a whole new flexibility in world relations. China and Japan are talking. Russia is out of Egypt. The Soviet Union shows a softened attitude.

Then there is Mr. Nixon's great achievement in persuading the Soviet Union to step back from the awful abyss of nuclear weapons competition.

A great distance remains to be traveled, but a start has been made. An era of direct armed confrontation with communism seems to be ending.

President Nixon appears to be ready to shift now into economic and trade competition, a rivalry that will be fully as difficult and demanding.

The people of the United States will have to hustle to compete with the workers and the goods of Japan, Germany, Russia, the European Economic Community—the entire world market. Our longtime technical and industrial superiority is being challenged and the competition will be fierce and unyielding, not just ideologic—as Americans learned in the recent Olympics.

Senator McGovern talks of a new internationalism that would be based virtually on trust alone. He displays no awareness of the importance of a strong defensive shield to honor this country's commitments and insure world stability.

Domestic needs

President Nixon has also instituted some major changes in direction at home. Through revenue sharing and in his proposals for welfare reform and government reorganization he is trying to trim back the bureaucratic jungle and turn away from the philosophy of a paternalistic Federal Government that has long dominated Washington.

Mr. Nixon has contended that the Federal Government does not always know best. He is convinced that the American competitive system remains basically sound and contains within it the power to correct its own faults.

In this belief Mr. Nixon is demonstrating the ability to determine and to reflect the national mood, the national consensus. The people want reform and progress, but not massive social and economic upheaval.

The question for November 7, then, is whether President Nixon has shown the competence and the grasp of the nation's needs and role in the world to continue in the most demanding of all jobs—or whether he should be replaced by Senator McGovern, a relatively unknown and untested contender.

It is The Bulletin's opinion that President Nixon is the better choice.

• • •

If reelected, Mr. Nixon should demand a stronger moral tone and accountability from all around him in his new administration. He should display greater concern for human needs and hopes and for civil rights and such basic rights as press freedom.

In a second term President Nixon would be unable to succeed himself and would thus be free of the political pressures that play upon a first term Chief Executive. He should then be expected to show the innovative daring in domestic affairs that he has already displayed in foreign affairs.

Mr. Nixon could assure himself an especially bright chapter in our country's history by concentrating for the next four years on helping to achieve *for all Americans* an equal share in the "American Dream."

THE NASHVILLE TENNESSEAN
Nashville, Tenn., October 29, 1972

IN THE MATTER of days, American voters will go to the polls to choose their presidential leadership for the next four years. Rarely has there been such an overcast of apathy, or a greater sense of dilemma about a presidential contest.

It is easy to understand why. President Nixon has served for four years and the nation is worse off than it was. As President, he has managed to break almost every major promise he made to the electorate in 1968, and some he made after he took office.

Mr. Nixon promised to seek an immediate end to the war in Vietnam. Four years and more than 20,000 American dead have piled up in bitter evidence that "a new administration, not tied to the mistakes of the past" has continued the mistakes, and the war.

★ ★ ★

Mr. Nixon promised to bring the nation together, but it has never been more divided, or less confident in itself.

Mr. Nixon pledged to make our lives and streets more safe from violent crime, but there has been a 32% increase in serious crimes over the past three years.

And the administration which rode a "law and order" campaign into the White House has now been involved in the Watergate burglary of Democratic headquarters, of amassing a $10 million campaign kitty in defiance of the principles and the spirit of the election law Mr. Nixon praised, of political spying and sabotage which run counter to common decency, much less a spirit of law and order.

Mr. Nixon promised an end to deficit financing. After four years, his budgetary deficits of more than $90 billion exceed the combined deficits of the Eisenhower, Kennedy and Johnson years.

Mr. Nixon promised to restore the soundness of the dollar and vowed to end what he called a "deteriorating balance of trade." Instead he devalued the dollar, which is weaker than ever, and now has the first U.S. trade deficit in 100 years.

He promised a full employment economy and an increase in jobs. But there has been an 85% increase in unemployment in his term and the jobless rate stands at 5.5%.

He promised welfare reform as his number one goal, but switched his position on it, although in four years there has been a 66% hike in the welfare rolls—from 6.2 million to 10.3 million.

Mr. Nixon vowed to reverse the increasing centralization of government and over-staffing of bureaucracy. But he has built the largest staff organization in the White House in history.

Candidate Nixon pledged his would be an open administration and that he would avoid a credibility gap by being candid with the people. No administration has been more secretive, or more opposed to a free flow of information, or has sought harder to "brainwash" the American people.

Mr. Nixon promised to give new emphasis to civil liberties and rights of Americans. The record is the opposite and ranges from attempts to undermine the Voting Rights Act to the use of criminal prosecutions and federal grand juries to stifle dissent.

Mr. Nixon promised to use the office to rally the people, "to define those moral imperatives which are the cement of a civilized society . . ." Yet evidence of corruption within his administration is piled higher than the Washington monument.

Mr. Nixon's proudest boasts are in the area of foreign policy and specifically his visits to China and the Soviet Union. But even his China trip repudiated a promise. He said in 1968, speaking of the reality of China: "This does not mean, as many would simplistically have it, rushing to grant recognition to Peking, to admit it to the U.N. and to ply it with offers of trade—all of which would confirm its rulers in their present course."

The question for the voters is whether they can continue to place their trust for four more years in a man who has said one thing and done another. Can there be confidence in an administration which bugs the Democrats while boasting of law and order, of dropping tons of bombs on Vietnam while boasting of peace, of piling up record deficits while bragging of thrift?

Mr. Nixon is inconsistent to the point that a rule of thumb is that whatever the administration says it will do, it won't and vice versa. Furthermore, he never talks of mistakes or lets the people in on what goes on. During this cam-

(continued on next page)

(continued from preceding page)

paign he has remained in a veritable cocoon of silence, seldom discussing any issues, never answering any questions, and seeking through a "canned" campaign to manipulate voters like puppets.

There is an alternative to Mr. Nixon and he is Sen. George McGovern.

Senator McGovern puts what is just ahead of expediency. He is by far the most consistent of the two candidates, but when he has been wrong, he has had the courage to admit it and discuss it. His antiwar position is of long standing and he has clung to it when some thought it was out of date. His position on the economy, on jobs, and on doing more for the "average man" were cemented in his record long ago.

Senator McGovern has a sense of honesty and integrity that his most bitter foes would have to concede. He wants what is right for this country, not what is expedient. His vision is of a better nation which can recover its sense of purpose and its sense of justice.

Senator McGovern's plea throughout this campaign has been aimed at the better instincts of people, a plea that urges them to turn away from the politics of favoritism, from the politics of "promise them anything but give them little," from the politics of manipulation and propaganda.

Four more years of Mr. Nixon can only bring a repeat of the last four with worsening symptoms: a mishandled economy, continued inflation, broken promises and a great moral emptiness in public life. But there will surely be new repressions and vengeance-taking by an administration that can't succeed itself. It is true the public opinion polls reflect a strong preference for Mr. Nixon. But this is more a commentary on the times than on the candidacy of Senator McGovern.

Senator McGovern has repeatedly said the nation can't afford four more years of political blight, corruption, intrigue, secrecy and favoritism to the few. This is not what America needs as it nears the 200th anniversary of its beginnings — beginnings which had noble purpose, greatness of vision, and a deep-seated sense of national honor.

There is a choice on Nov. 7. It is a choice between Sen. George McGovern and a President who has broken his commitments to the American people at every hand. It is a choice whether this nation will take the high road again, or continue on the low.

The Afro-American
Baltimore, Md., October 28, 1972

Senator George S. McGovern is the AFRO's choice for president in the Nov. 7 election.

In almost every essential measurement, we rate Senator McGovern, the Democratic aspirant, above Richard M. Nixon, the Republican president.

We have been forced to conclude during the Nixon regime that events have been set into motion and moods created that threaten racial togetherness and progress to such an extent so as to invite national disaster.

On a broader view we find the future of all Americans in peril unless the citizenry checks the smell of corruption, favoritism, opportunism, police state tactics, secrecy, militarism, sectionalism, ethnicism, racism and the threat to civil liberties being promoted or condoned by government officials and politicians.

George McGovern sounds and acts like a man who would rescue America from an immoral, costly war in Vietnam, assure a job for every person able to work, support the law in deeds as well as through rhetoric, give the core cities higher priorities, end political espionage, provide necessary tax reform and restore meaning to equal opportunity guarantees to all citizens.

Nixon Has Failed

Nixon has failed miserably in these areas.

Under his benign neglect policies a president of the United States is campaigning for reelection without direct public appeals to 22 million black citizens, an intended rebuff to the nation's largest minority.

Except for his black surrogates and a few well-known black success figures, Nixon has insulted black voters by purposefully ignoring them as part of his anti-welfare, anti-busing, anti-quotas, anti-desegregation, anti-poor, anti-fair housing, pro-South Africa, pro-Portugal, pro-Rhodesia and pro-Dixie political strategy.

Even when Nixon did things that normally would lead to progress, his overall policies are such failures that they negate entirely or in great measure his positive efforts.

Thus it is that when he talks of monies spent to help black people, what the results have added up to are poor people increasing in number for the first time in a decade, climbing living costs, several million more on welfare and a 10.2 rate of unemployment.

He puts money into equal opportunity areas but his policies lead him to threaten to fire cabinet members, and other federal employers, who did not understand his unconstitutional anti-busing stance, or who thought he really meant to push housing desegregation in the vote-rich suburbs.

McGovern's Stance

The AFRO does not say it has been 100 per cent in agreement with all McGovern's postures on issues we feel deeply about as a minority still struggling toward the day when we will enjoy all our constitutional rights as citizens.

But between McGovern and Nixon we think the choice clearly is obvious to more than 80 per cent of us.

McGovern is a man with the courage of his convictions. He has had some campaign bloops along the way that have not helped him. It now appears some of his trouble has been caused by the political espionage of GOP-hired party and personality assassins.

McGovern's stance on the Vietnam war, promise of a full employment economy, willingness to support a Supreme Court decision including busing as a desegregation tool, criticism of Nixon's African policies, work on behalf of poor, hungry and aged people, his challenging of the favoritism, secrecy and corruption being practiced and his public wooing of all American voters, are among the things that suggest to us he would make a far better president.

McGovern's choices for vice president, first Senator Thomas Eagleton and then R. Sargent Shriver, tells us he is more concerned about America than is a man who puts Spiro T. Agnew in line for the presidency.

Don't Give Up

Black voters cannot afford to be lulled asleep by polls and predictions that McGovern cannot win on Nov. 7. Until the votes are counted, he has a chance.

Moreover, if McGovern should lose, and by a margin even close to that now being predicted by the polls, be fairly warned that we as a group will be in deeper trouble. If the segregationists, reactionaries and conservatives snow McGovern under, the cause of moderation and racial progress will suffer another severe setback. Moderate and liberal candidates and spokesmen will become even more cautious.

Another silly election argument blacks must not swallow is the one being peddled that insists we ought not all belong to one party. That is not the issue here.

On Nov. 7, we don't vote for a party necessarily, no matter how we are registered, but for a man who will serve as president of the United States.

We must vote for a man who has shown himself to be a friend to the Constitution, to decency and to us.

We gave Nixon 25 per cent of our vote when he ran against John F. Kennedy. He got less in 1968 because of the record Kennedy and Lyndon B. Johnson made. He'll get less than 25 per cent Nov. 7 because of his own record and policies as president.

Remember this: those who insist the Democratic Party will make a comeback after McGovern is washed away, had better take a good look at the political shenanigans and big-money deals of this election year and ponder the question of what chances the Democratic Party might realistically have after four more years of it.

Future At Stake

This election is not one to be taken lightly.

Whatever the outcome, black voters must come out in numbers and stand up for justice and decency. If you don't vote you help Nixon.

We cannot survive as a people if we take our liberty and progress so lightly that we accept money or prestige payoffs to willingly shuffle along, grinning and hugging obvious enemies of our best interest.

On Nov. 7 black voters say to the watching world that we respect ourselves enough that nobody, tricky or not, can walk on us for four years and expect us to scratch our heads and turn the other cheek.

On Nov. 7 black voters should go to the polls as if their futures and those of their children were at stake, and they are, to do what they can with their ballots to help elect Senator George S. McGovern president.

The Des Moines Register
Des Moines, Iowa, October 29, 1972

THIS NEWSPAPER is politically independent. We are not committed to any political party, and we do not "support" candidates in the sense of trying to help them get elected.

It is not our function to tell readers how to vote. Our function is to report in the news columns as much pertinent political information as we can gather and to provide on this editorial page discussion and comment. At the end of a campaign we attempt to reassess the candidates and issues and to state our own conclusions.

This has been a dreary campaign with almost no illuminating debate that would clarify issues and strengthen the nation's political institutions. President Nixon, assured of reelection if the polls are correct, has felt no need to submit his record to searching debate. Senator McGovern, who had been expected to discuss the overriding issues in a thoughtful and rational manner, has resorted too often to the same appeals to class prejudice and the same kind of loose statement which some critics have associated with Nixon.

Our conclusion as the campaign ends is that, all things considered, this country would be better served by a continuation of the Nixon Administration than by transferring the presidency to Senator McGovern. We conclude this despite serious disagreement with some current Administration policies.

Any assessment of President Nixon's performance must begin by recognizing his creative statesmanship in reversing this nation's 23 years of hostility to China, in reaching an accommodation with Russia and in making a beginning toward control of nuclear armaments. Taken together, these accomplishments may well prove to be the most significant reorientation of U.S. foreign policy in recent decades.

A number of circumstances contributed to the Administration's success in these areas where three former presidents had been unsuccessful. But President Nixon's perception of America's current position in world affairs, his willingness to change a previous strongly-held position and his general leadership skills must be recognized as the major reasons.

The Nixon Administration has managed, too, to keep an uneasy peace in the Mideast through the efforts of Secretary of State Rogers and Assistant Secretary Sisco.

On the economic front, the President has done well, considering the severe inflation which he had to deal with when he entered office. He has not been doctrinaire in economic policy. He made mistakes in trying to curb the price rise by conventional monetary and fiscal means, but when this didn't work, he did not hesitate to take decisive action in applying controls and in moving toward world monetary reform.

Today, the United States has the lowest rate of inflation of any major industrial country. And the economy is moving upward encouragingly, which should soon ease the unemployment situation.

The President has failed to press hard enough for desperately needed welfare reform, but he did make innovative proposals to Congress encompassing a guaranteed basic income level, and he was the first president to do so. The Democrats in Congress must share the blame for lack of progress on this reform.

* * *

There is much to criticize in the Nixon Administration. We have been critical of the President's Vietnam policy which ostensibly has been based on guaranteeing the South Vietnamese the right to determine their own government, but which has had the effect of propping up a dictatorial regime imposed by us and prolonging the killing and destruction in a war which we should never have entered.

We have criticized certain mediocre appointments (notably some of the nominations to the Supreme Court) and the soft attitude on civil rights to woo Southern support.

We have raised questions about the moral climate in Washington. We are disturbed by the Watergate scandal and the evidence linking it with the White House, by the hidden political funds, the indication of secret deals in the ITT affair and the dairy price supports and the Russian wheat sales. We are disturbed by the Administration's lack of candor on these questions and its refusal to disclose information which would identify any who are guilty. The ugly charges of political connivance which are being made may not be true, but they will not be dispelled by silence.

We can agree with much of Senator McGovern's criticism of the Administration in these areas, but his campaign has not built confidence that an administration under his guidance could deal adequately with the crucial problems of the next four years. His failure to organize his own campaign staff, the revisions in his positions on economic policy, the vacillation exhibited in the Eagleton episode, the lack of credibility in the Salinger incident raise serious questions about his leadership abilities.

In the awesome office of the presidency good intentions are not enough. We favor a continuation of the Nixon Administration.

[At the end of a campaign we are often asked about our position in previous campaigns. In 1960 we favored Nixon; in 1964, Lyndon Johnson; in 1968, Hubert Humphrey.]

The State
Columbia, S.C., October 29, 1972

THE SOLID accomplishments of the Nixon administration, coupled with efforts to move a Democrat-controlled Congress toward further achievements, warrant the re-election of Richard M. Nixon as President of the United States for another term.

In making such a declaration, *The State* does not endorse his every action—or inaction. Indeed, we have expressed and still maintain serious reservations about certain of his policies and some of his associates. To be more specific, we question the wisdom of his advocacy of an all-volunteer army, his initiation of international realignments in the Far East which undercut Nationalist China, and—on the home front—his sponsorship of programs which promise more costs than cure for social ills.

But President Nixon has been bold and venturesome in seeking solutions to weighty problems which have plagued this country and the world in recent years. If there be risks in some of his undertakings, the prospects of success make them worth the running. He is entitled, in our judgment, to another four years in which to bring more of his policies to fruitation.

Yet despite the positive achievements we have cited, the most compelling reason for Americans to support the re-election of Richard Nixon is the utter lack of an alternative. It is unthinkable that citizens of the United States would entrust their fate to a man so manifestly unfit to lead them as Sen. George S. McGovern.

As a one-time follower of Leftist Henry Wallace, Senator McGovern has proposed radical programs ranging all the way from a massive redistribution of wealth to outright capitulation to Communism in Vietnam. In order to help finance his give-away social schemes, he would willingly gut the national defense budget. And while piously preaching of morality, this one-time "nice guy" viciously likens President Nixon to Adolf Hitler.

The Democratic party has done itself and the nation a disservice by putting forward such an incredible nominee for the Presidency. Nothing would help the party more than the complete obliteration of the McGovern influence and the reconstitution of a credible *national* Democratic party. There are hosts of Americans who consider themselves Democrats but who cannot stomach either the ticket or the platform which emerged from Miami Beach. Out of the wreckage which seems destined to ensue from the McGovern candidacy, it is to be hoped that they can rebuild a viable party and an acceptable image which will once again give real meaning to presidential elections.

The essence of American politics is the availability of a choice. This year, there is no choice but Mr. Nixon. It is a shame, for the absence of an alternative tends to neutralize the constant scrutiny and occasional criticism which should be directed at every president—Republican, Democrat, or otherwise.

New York Post

New York, N.Y., October 30, 1972

In his inaugural address on January 20, 1969, President Nixon said:

"We are torn by division, wanting unity. We see around us empty lives, wanting fulfillment... When we listen to the better angels of our nature, we find they celebrate the simple things, the basic things—such as goodness, decency, love, kindness... We cannot learn from one another until we stop shouting at each other.... I speak from my own heart, the heart of my country, the deep concern we have for those who suffer and sorrow."

Now, nearly four years later, the gap between that eloquent rhetoric and ensuing reality dramatizes some of the saddest failures of the Administration.

Now, nearly four years later, George McGovern has validly asked: "How many of you can say that your life has really improved in the last four years?"

Now, nearly four years later, the President who called for rational political discourse is abrasively promoting national division and hostility.

His contempt for the First Amendment was reaffirmed as late as October 16 when he delivered a bitter assault on media critics, university figures and "some of our top businessmen" who questioned his decision to unleash the massive air assault on North Vietnam last May.

Beyond any debate over that action, the intemperance of his attack, mingled with the flagrant invasions of the democratic process staged by the Committee to Re-Elect the President and its underground network of spies and saboteurs, raises ominous questions about the prospect of a second term.

Against that background, The New York Post declares its support for George McGovern and Sargent Shriver.

* * *

It is a common tendency to deliver editorial endorsements in the wholly one-sided language of campaign oratory. But campaign '72—including such unscheduled events as the tragic Eagleton episode—denies such luxury.

Whatever else may and must be said about Mr. Nixon, history will grant generous recognition to his missions to Peking and Moscow.

Difficult as are the problems that remain, these unconventional initiatives—like Mr. Nixon's reversal of his ancient resistance to price-wage controls—were memorable. Along with the move toward peace in Vietnam, they could have formed the central and disarming themes for his bid for re-election.

But the dismal paradox of much of Mr. Nixon's first term, as well as of his current campaign, is that the President who visualizes himself as world peace-maker has continuously played the politics of militarism and discord at home.

On the great domestic issue of new priorities, requiring major reappraisal of the Pentagon budgets for overkill, Mr. Nixon has invoked the old slogans of super-patriotism and rejected any serious debate. But what is the meaning of all the heralded steps toward detente and sanity, including the SALT talks, if any real challenge to our military is branded a menace to national security?

The nation warily rejoices at the new glimpse of peace in Vietnam. Yet even as that hope rises, the President is stridently crusading against any advocacy of amnesty—as if those who conscientiously faced jail or exile merit no different treatment from those who deserted under fire. He has cynically repudiated his own earlier positions.

Basically Mr. Nixon has moved steadily toward extension of the "Southern strategy" to the nation. His present large margin in the polls reflects his acquisition of most of the vote won by George Wallace in 1968. He has wooed that vote, both long before and during the campaign, by distortion and exaggeration of the "busing" issue, by abandonment of his Family Assistance Plan, by frontal and covert attack on the wise, humane heritage of the Earl Warren Supreme Court.

His commitment to that strategy was clearly signalled in his redesignation of Spiro Agnew.

* * *

In endorsing the McGovern-Shriver ticket, we recognize that it faces especially heavy odds, greatly magnified by the defection of so many Wallace adherents to Nixon and Agnew.

The prospect of a "landslide" achieved under those auspices should resolve any tortured debate among progressive Americans who have been disappointed—as we have—by some aspects of the McGovern campaign.

George McGovern has unquestionably committed errors on his long journey. He was wrong in initially urging termination of price-wage controls; his initial welfare reform program was ineptly improvised. He has at least had the courage to acknowledge mistakes.

It must also be said that he has been subject to frequently unjust attacks such as the charge that his opposition to U. S. involvement in Vietnam forshadowed an "isolationist" indifference to the fate of Israel. To identify Thieu's oppressive, corrupt Saigon regime with Israel's functioning democracy was a false equation. There is no true "Israel issue" in this campaign.

* * *

The essential case for McGovern rests on his consistent record of progressivism, his vision of an America reendowed with a sense of national purpose and fraternity, his demonstrated compassion and decency, his resolve to combat inequity and injustice, his dedication to the Bill of Rights.

Despite all the trials of his campaign, we believe McGovern represents "the better angels of our nature" of whom Mr. Nixon spoke in 1969. We believe he is capable of inspiring that "deep concern for those who suffer and those who sorrow" so sorely missing during the Nixon years. We cannot offer any certainty that he provides the promise of greatness. We are confident, however, that his voice will be steadfastly addressed to the best instincts of the American people.

Pittsburgh Post-Gazette
Pittsburgh, Pa., October 24, 1972

Our Choice for President

MORE THAN any presidential election campaign within our memory, this year's is focused more on what is wrong with the candidates than on what is right. Perhaps this is because both candidates are so vulnerable to criticism. That makes a choice much more difficult than if one candidate could be portrayed as Galahad and the other as Lucifer.

Both President Nixon and Senator McGovern suffer from extensive credibility gaps, a fashionable term for inconsistency. The President, for example, has failed to keep his promise to end the war inherited from the Democrats, although we give him credit for persistent efforts which have brought what appears to be a chance for an early cease-fire.

Again, the President has abandoned his role as an economic conservative in favor of Keynesian economics and enormous budget deficits.

Mr. Nixon has also made a 180-degree turn from his hard-line anti-communism toward historic advances to the Communist powers, China and the Soviet Union. But for this he is to be praised rather than criticized.

Among the President's debits must be included a couple of bad appointments to the Supreme Court, which the Senate properly rejected; allegations of illegality in campaign spending, the juvenile Watergate affair and the wheat deal, and he has shown an unfortunate propensity for exploiting public fears and biases on issues like school busing rather than trying to exert a healing influence.

The President has failed, too, to achieve certain domestic goals, like welfare reform and executive reorganization, but in fairness it should be noted that he has been dependent upon a Democratic Congress which has been inclined to collaborate only in fiscal irresponsibility.

* * *

As for Senator McGovern, unable to lure the President into a Great Debate, he has chosen to debate with himself, often with disastrous results. He has had to skin back from several untenable positions. In the primary campaigns, for example, he proposed to give $1,000 annually to every man, woman and child from the Federal treasury. Public alarm over that scheme led him to discard it for more moderate proposals hardly less costly.

The Senator's troubles began to surface after the Miami nominating convention with the miserable Eagleton affair. For the first time, a presidential candidate removed a running mate from the ticket as a result of hasty judgment and poor staff work. The dumping of Senator Eagleton was foretold even as Senator McGovern avowed that he remained behind him "1,000 per cent."

At the convention itself state delegations had been rigged to provide quotas for delegates likely to support the Senator's candidacy. That excluded many party regulars. Subsequently, Mr. McGovern has been scrambling from the left back toward the party's center in an effort to unite with the alienated. As for quotas, when questioned by the American-Jewish Committee, the Senator foreswore them as "detrimental to American society."

Again, while his relentless attack upon the Nixon war policy led to his nomination, the Senator hasn't always been a dove. He was voting for Vietnam appropriations and arguing against unilateral withdrawal as recently as 1967. In the next year, however, he was in the forefront of the effort to unseat President Johnson for his "policy of madness." But this summer he went to the Pedernales, praised the former President, and sought his benediction.

On the war issue, the Senator has also said that he would if necessary go to Hanoi and beg for the release of American prisoners. Begging, he said, is better than bombing. But the dove turns into a hawk when the issue becomes the Middle East, where he would commit American forces to the defense of Israel.

In addition to indecisiveness, Senator McGovern has shown a lamentable inability to control his staff, raising doubt as to his ability to govern anything as large and complex as the United States. He simply doesn't yet give evidence of the solid, sound thinking required of a President. The idealist is revealed as just another politician and the "new politics" fades ingloriously into the old.

* * *

While President Nixon has had his ups and downs on domestic programs, he has shown a better grasp than Senator McGovern of this nation's role in world affairs. He is phasing out a war begun by the party of his major critics and he might even have ended it except that the enemy could be holding out in hope of a McGovern victory which would mean peace on communist terms.

Contrary to the neo-isolationism implicit in the Senator's appeal to "come home, America," President Nixon has demonstrated skill as a world statesman. He has opened with China a dialogue leading to useful exchanges. Under his initiatives, our relations with the Soviet Union have gone from confrontation to negotiation and a relaxation of tensions.

As a result of the talks on limiting strategic weapons (SALT), the first important steps have been taken toward limiting the nuclear arms race. The President has also enunciated the Nixon Doctrine, which calls for the avoidance of direct American military involvement in remote corners of the earth.

At the same time, dangerous confrontations in the streets and on the campuses, which badly bruised the national soul and damaged the nation's image abroad in the 1960s, have all but disappeared.

And there is an encouraging upturn in the economy. The rate of inflation has been reduced by half. More Americans — 2.5 million more than a year ago — have jobs than ever before. Although unemployment remains unacceptably high, jobs are being created at the fastest rate in 20 years. The real income of the average worker after Federal taxes and inflation is up six per cent over the last two years. The Administration has in recent months made more strenuous efforts, as with the automobile industry, to control prices.

* * *

From Mr. Nixon's long record in public service emerges the portrait of an unlovable and not always credible professional politician who is, nonetheless, skillful and competent. Despite his streak of hucksterism, he gives us a greater sense of confidence than we can find in the amateurish and strident campaigning of Senator McGovern.

This is the first time in his three races for President that the Post-Gazette is endorsing Mr. Nixon. On balance we feel that, despite his shortcomings, he should remain in the White House for another four years. Given a clear mandate by a majority of the voters and a better hold on Congress, we believe that the President can go far to redeem his pledges.

(continued on next page)

Presidential Choice: An Editorial Dissent

Because of a division of opinion, within the editorial board of the Post-Gazette, on whom to endorse for president, the dissenting board members were asked to express their views, which follow:

* * *

THE MAN WHOM the electorate chooses to lead this nation for the next four years will have the task of restoring Americans' pride and confidence in themselves as cooperative members of the world's leading democracy.

He can turn them *away* from dwelling on their age, class and ethnic differences.

He can turn them *toward* a renewed a w a r e n e s s that, through the nearly 200-year history of this republic, they made it the most admired and admirable, the richest and most enriching, the strongest and most humane of nations.

He can make "politics" and "government" o n c e more words of respect, not opprobrium. By the personal example he sets as the symbolic archetype of The American — the collective consciousness of the people — he can replace suspicion of leadership with respect for leaders.

By speaking to his fellow Americans and to the world in words of single, rather than double and dubious, meaning, he can convince his own people and the world's that America once again is capable of producing leaders who care more for constructive change and the domestic tranquility of the populace than for power, political advancement and favoritism toward the privileged few.

We believe that nearly a decade of political opportunism and a brutal, unjust war have made Americans forget that they are one people, with the right and the capacity, given the proper leadership, to respect each other and to feel proud and confident toward their future as a nation united by the best qualities that human nature has to offer.

There is one man seeking the presidency who has the self-respect and respect for others, the quiet firmness of moral conviction and the courage to seek to unite and to lead his nation's people in giving new birth to a faith in the democratic process and the basic goodness of the American citizenry.

That man, we believe, is Sen. George McGovern. For these reasons, then, we urge the election of Sen. McGovern to the presidency of the United States.

* * *

SEN. McGOVERN has demonstrated not only the heart and courage required to sustain the loneliness of the long-distance runner, but also a strong c a p a c i t y to lead. Against nearly insurmountable odds, he won the toughest-fought Democratic presidential primary in recent history. In so doing, he skillfully amalgamated an assortment of idealistic, dedicated and cunning political managers who outwitted his opponents at the Miami Beach convention.

Sen. McGovern has the true manner of a president, rather than glamor of a President Kennedy, the wheeling and dealing of a President Johnson and the hucksterism of a President Nixon which some Americans have been conditioned to expect as characteristics necessary in their national leaders. Still more voters, we believe, have the wisdom to r e c o g n i z e in the subdued thoughtfulness, quiet firmness and intellectual anti-dogmatism of Sen. McGovern precisely that alloy of qualities which America needs and deserves from her chief executive.

Sen. McGovern is, nevertheless, deadly serious in seeking the responsibility of national leader. Thus, he did an about-face on Sen. Eagleton, but only after the nation's leading liberal newspapers virtually ordered him to drop Sen. Eagleton or lose their influential endorsements, which Sen. McGovern, as the underdog, realistically understood h e needed.

Nor should Sen. Eagleton be regarded as a hero stabbed in the back. He had neither the integrity nor the courtesy to reveal immediately his history of mental treatment.

In economic reform, Sen. McGovern's original $1,000-a-person plan differed not in basic concept but in detail from President Nixon's guaranteed-income scheme as an alternative to the bureaucratic idiocy we call "welfareism." Some form of income redistribution which preserves private-profit and incentive, we believe, is bound to come soon, no matter who is president.

In foreign policy, Sen. McG o v e r n's slogan, "Come Home, America," is a call not to isolationism but to a more responsible, less meddlesome f o r m of internationalism. Many of us, including this newspaper editorially, h a v e long a d v o c a t e d Europe's shouldering a fairer share of its security costs. So, too, have many of us urged that merely feeding the insatiable hunger of the military establishment has little to do with genuine national security but a lot to do with profiteering through disgraceful cost overruns and with cities starved for rapid mass transit and new housing.

The difference between "Come Home, America" and Mr. Nixon's Guam Doctrine is that Sen. McGovern explicitly states that to exercise unchallenged world leadership America need not defend every right-wing dictatorship in the n a m e of anticommunism, while President Nixon does not.

* * *

FOR THE vast majority of citizens who still believe that this nation can provide wise and moral leadership, we believe that President Nixon has not always used the majesty of the White House to bring out the best in America's richly diverse populace.

Rather, as in Vietnam, he has often sought to win his points with the electorate by catering to its human weaknesses and fears. Mr. Nixon did not create the race issue around which busing has spun poisonous clouds of hate and fear. But he exacerbated it.

In the triumphant arch of civil liberties, through which American democracy passes safely, there rests a keystone: the free press. From attempts at prior censorship in the Pentagon Papers case to court decisions imperiling reportorial confidentiality, President Nixon's voice rang out not once in defence of those quintessential press freedoms.

But Mr. Nixon happily used the press to trumpet his positive—but perhaps overrated—rapprochement with C h i n a and Russia. Opening diplomatic and trade channels with China was an idea whose time had long come. For military and trade reasons, it was mut u a l l y beneficial. Similarly, strategic a r m s limitations were strongly desired by the U. S. and the USSR because neither could afford the ever increasing balance-of-terror costs.

If Mr. Nixon deserves at least a modicum of praise in some areas of foreign policy, we hope that no man in the U. S. presidency ever again will allow the good name of the office and of the nation and people for which it stands to be sullied by seeming to turn his back on such a national disgrace as the "Watergate Affair." For the bugging of Democratic headquarters has gone far beyond what many cynical Americans may regard as merely rough-and-tumble politics.

Only this week, Time magazine, known for neither anti-Republicanism nor Nixon-baiting, revealed that information in Justice Department files directly links the White House to Donald H. Segretti, who allegedly was paid more than $35,000 from the Nixon campaign fund to subvert and disrupt the 1972 Democratic candidates' campaigns.

Of longer lasting importance than governmental dishonesty is the integrity and independence of the Supreme Court, on which two more vacancies may occur in the next four years. If re-elected, Mr. Nixon could appoint a majority to the Court which he has already been shaping in a way which may undo recent advances in civil liberties and rights, including those of privacy against electronic surveillance and of an unfettered press.

FOR HIS part, although the son of a preacher, Sen. McGovern is no saint. Like Mr. Nixon, he has made compromise after compromise. Both men are of this earth and wish to lead. The difference is that Mr. Nixon's long career demonstrates a propensity to compromise on fundamental issues like civil liberties and honesty in government.

Given his Senate record and h i s progressive philosophy, Sen. McGovern, once elected, will, we believe, turn this country away from overreliance on the m i l i t a r y and over-generosity to those who least need it and back to a temperate internationalism and a responsibly humane concern for the masses of people who live in his—and our—nation.

Maine Sunday Telegram
Portland, Me., October 15, 1972

Now is the customary time for political endorsements. But as a newspaper, we back off from "endorsements." In our dictionary "endorsement" means signing one's name on the back of a check — a guarantee of full approval. And we are not about to endorse any politican in that fashion. Nor, we bet, are you.

Furthemore we think political endorsements are a bit old-hat, a bit patronizing and pompous, and they often backfire. Witness the fact that our own Ed Muskie got endorsements a mile long for the presidential nomination. And a lot of good they did him.

So we are not "endorsing" anybody, or thereby suggesting that you should.

But faced with the shirt-sleeve question of "Whom would you hire as your next President, Nixon or McGovern?", we'll give a one word answer: Nixon.

And for one reason, above all others . . . We think Nixon can handle the job and that McGovern cannot.

Like you, we have watched Nixon on the job. For almost four years, his performance has been under the public microscope.

Often we did not agree with what he did, and said so.

Certainly he has not solved all the problems he promised to solve — including ending the war, stopping inflation, curbing crime on the streets.

Certainly Nixon has not developed any charisma or winning personality, in our book. When Nixon comes on our TV screen, we find him a cold fish. But then a candidate's charm, style, charisma is not what sells us. As we think about hiring a Chief Executive, we think most about ability to do the job. And in our book, Nixon makes a capable, responsible Chief Executive. McGovern does not.

Here are a few of the reasons why we think so.

Foremost job of any President today is to keep the nation secure. In our book, Nixon is fully committed and fully proven as a President who will do just that. But McGovern waffles. He promises to cut some $30 billion from defense spending, but not to weaken our defenses. We don't believe it.

Next biggest job for the next President is to end our part in the Vietnam war, if by the time we vote in November we are still in it.

McGovern says he will get all Americans out in 48 hours. And maybe he would, even if it meant total abandonment of an ally who, whatever South Vietnam's shortcomings, has suffered millions of war victims by fighting a war we have urged them to fight. Maybe McGovern would end the war in 48 hours, even if it meant accepting terms the enemy dictates, even if it meant throwing down the drain the reasons why

(continued on next page)

(continued from preceding page)

50,000 Americans died in Vietnam and 200,000 were wounded there. Maybe he would, even if it meant cutting the legs out from under America's future credibility as the one big world power on the side of law, ready to resist aggression against the weak.

But in our book the price of capitulation — or cut-and-run — which McGovern seems ready to pay is too low a deal for America to make.

In our book, we'd hesitate to hire a man with that kind of judgment to be the next President of the United States.

In our book, Nixon has done and is doing all any responsible American president can properly do to end the war, without throwing down the drain either America's honor or the basis for future peace.

For future peace hinges on more than how fast we get out of Vietnam. Most importantly it hinges on whether the United States, Soviet Russia and China can live together without war.

In our book, Nixon already has made bold but difficult progress in beginning to defuse these explosion points of world conflict. As the result of Nixon's extraordinary visit to Peking China and the United States are talking to each other, trading with each other for the first time in a generation. That makes sense.

As the result of Nixon's hard bargaining in Moscow we now have in the recently signed SALT agreements a promising start toward defusing the terrible threat of nuclear war. His next step, if re-elected, will be to bargain for limits to the massive financial burden of nuclear arms races.

Speaking of military burdens, for the first time in generations, our nation is about to end the burden of the military draft. And despite the huge costs of adequate defense today, this country is now spending a smaller percentage of our wealth on military-related programs. Today we are spending the greater part of our federal budget on human needs at home.

To achieve this significant reversal took hard bargaining with the Soviets and the Chinese. Now, to get further along the road to peace, will take a lot more hard bargaining with the Russians and the Chinese during the next four years.

Given a choice between McGovern and Nixon as to which man is the more capable and more qualified hard bargainer with the Communist nations, we'd hire Nixon to do the job.

What about jobs here at home? Who is the better man here? Along with keeping our nation secure, ending the present war, avoiding another war, the biggest job for a President is to keep America prosperous, to keep Americans at work and off welfare.

When it comes to the business of nursing the economy, of stimulating business, of making jobs, our choice is to hire Nixon over McGovern as the nation's manager.

Admittedly, Nixon certainly has wrought no miracles in curing unemployment or inflation. But most of the economy is healthy and 95 per cent of our work force is at work.

The record shows that more people hold down more jobs at higher pay today than ever before in the American economy. The record shows that inflation, once rampant at six per cent a year, is down to about three per cent today, and slipping.

Admittedly, there are also more people on welfare (which Congress refused to reform after three years of debate) and more people drawing unemployment insurance than ever before. But then there are millions more Americans than ever before, and more and more women are in the work force.

So the question is: Is Nixon or McGovern the better man to hire to remedy our economic ailments?

Looking at McGovern's record, no evidence indicates his ability to steer the world's biggest economy. When McGovern speaks about economic problems, the solutions he suggests are most often still more federal spending, still more welfare, still higher taxes. He is often vague, frequently naive.

When pressed for details as to how much it would cost to carry out his scheme of $1,000 a year for every man, woman and child, McGovern's arithmetic went into a tailspin, from which it has not yet pulled out.

So in problems affecting jobs and the pocketbooks of the nation, we'd hire Nixon over McGovern, as the more competent man.

There are of course blemishes and black spots to be found on both men's records. Nixon may be faulted for the messy Watergate affair; or in favoring fat cats in the grain sale to Russia. In deciding to hire either McGovern or Nixon, the voting public will also have to weigh the shabby treatment and the wavering mind McGovern showed in handling the Eagleton affair. They may worry over pronouncements from the McGovern camp favoring amnesty for draft evaders, for legalizing abortion and marijuana made when seeking delegate votes at the nominating convention. These are somewhat buried now that McGovern is seeking votes from the man-in-the street, where such ideas have no appeal. If elected, would these McGovern ideas be revived?

And so we back off from "endorsement", from signing our name indicating full approval on the back of either politician's check.

But given a choice whether to hire Nixon or hire McGovern as Chief Executive of these United States, the Maine Sunday Telegram would hire Nixon as the better man for the job.

THE COMMERCIAL APPEAL
Memphis, Tenn., October 15, 1972

RICHARD M. NIXON is seeking re-election as President on the basis of his record, and on that same basis The Commercial Appeal supports his bid.

Both the Republican President and his Democratic challenger, Senator George McGovern, have said that this election offers voters a clearcut choice. We agree. The choice is Nixon.

SINCE HE MAPPED the course he proposed to follow in his 1968 campaign, Mr. Nixon has moved steadily forward. In some areas, such as his reshaping of American foreign policy, he has made more progress than anticipated. In instances where formidable roadblocks have appeared, advancements have been slower. But the overall first-term batting average is impressive.

In the 1968 race, Mr. Nixon said of the Vietnam War: "We must seek a negotiated settlement. This will require patience." By now the President has withdrawn almost all of the 550,000 American troops who were in Vietnam when he took office. He has never let the frustrations of negotiating with the North Vietnamese deter him from further efforts. When the series of Paris peace talks begun by President Lyndon Johnson and continued by the Nixon administration floundered in propaganda, he turned to higher level secret talks, and has now sent aide Henry Kissinger to Paris 19 times as his spokesman.

The negotiations have indeed required patience, but the signs today are that it has not been wasted.

THERE WAS LITTLE fee'ing of trust between the United States and its two great adversaries, the Soviet Union and Red China, in 1968. Nixon was saying then that America "must risk as much to defend freedom as the Communists are willing to risk to destroy it."

But he added, "We have got to have negotiations with the Soviet."

And he guardedly expressed hope that relations with the People's Republic of China might someday reach the point where he could visit that country.

The dramatic breakthrough that made it possible for President Nixon to travel to Peking last February is a benchmark of his career. Two decades of cold war ice were broken. World tensions decreased. United States foreign policy took on a decidedly new look, and China began to reassess its position on the world stage. An important new trade avenue was opened.

Nixon's follow-up trip to Moscow in May brought agreements on matters concerning science, space and — most important — limitations on strategic arms which had been hammered out in two and a half years of negotiations. As was the case in Peking, the door was opened to forms of trade which should be mutually beneficial.

The Nixon dream of "normalized relations" with the major Communist powers was made to come true. It was a triumph not only for the President, but also for people the world over who breathed a new freedom from fear of a nuclear holocaust.

DOMESTICALLY the President has kept his promise to give the "silent majority" a voice. By showing alienated power blocs that their common interests were greater than their differences, Mr. Nixon has given America a greater sense of unity.

"The new majority," he said in 1968, "is not a grouping of power blocs, but an alliance of ideas." Nixon's ability to articulate for a diversity of people their wants, needs and feelings has brought into being that phenomenon known as the "new coalition."

His steady attack on inflation, and his efforts to keep the economy moving without overheating are producing results. His willingness to impose price and wage controls when standard methods failed to halt inflation was a measure of his determination to get the job done.

As promised, crime's annual rate of increase has been cut. An easing of

(continued on next page)

(continued from preceding page)

racial tensions has brought relief from protests and street riots. The winding down of the Vietnam War has reduced campus unrest. A head-on attack on the sources of illegal narcotics has been effective, as have broader programs of rehabilitation among drug abusers. A less experimental Supreme Court has been shaped by four Nixon appointments.

It is in ways such as these that President Nixon has brought a welcome sense of peace and well-being to much of the nation. It is a continuing quest for quality in life, and one which Nixon will give priority.

Nixon's term has not been one of total success, of course. His promise to bring order out of the chaos of federal welfare programs has not been fulfilled. He has not attained the goal of government reorganization. And he has missed by far the mark of gaining control over highly inflationary deficit spending.

GEORGE McGOVERN also has a record, but it is not one to inspire confidence.

His plan to end the Vietnam War amounts to surrender. His proposed 90-day cave-in goes even further than the demands made by Hanoi.

When he talks of curtailing government spending, it is through the sacrifice of national security.

When he proposes new taxes to mount vast social programs, it is the great middle bracket of taxpayers who would carry the load.

His vacillation is frightening — from the Eagleton affair to his stand on war prisoners to economic proposals.

His "1,000 per cent support" is something nobody covets.

FOUR YEARS AGO The Commercial Appeal liked what Richard Nixon proposed to do if elected and we backed his candidacy. He has performed as well as we expected, and sometimes better. He has proved to be a man of initiative, and he stands up well under the burdens and complexities of the presidency. He is far superior to his Democratic opponent.

We think he should be allowed to serve a second term.

The Star-Ledger
Newark, N.J., October 29, 1972

The American people will be called on soon to elect the President who will guide the destinies of the nation through another four years.

Since one of the candidates is an incumbent, his record of the past four years must of necessity become the major criterion on which to base a judgment.

The man in office, Richard Milhous Nixon, has been a controversial figure in American political life for many years. He has stirred strong support and strong opposition.

But Mr. Nixon should be judged today not on past animosities and controversies, but on his record in office. On this basis, what emerges is a President who has shown a reassuring resiliency, a sensitive awareness of the need for radical changes in foreign policy and a pragmatic acceptance of social programs historically identified with democratic liberalism.

* * *

IT SHOULD BE apparent that Mr. Nixon is not the same man he was a decade ago, when his political career was believed to be finished, or even four years ago, when he made a remarkable comeback to be elected President, an office that had previously eluded him by a razor-thin margin.

He has become a President of his times, an international leader who has acknowledged, in a responsible manner, that the world cannot survive in an unremitting atmosphere of Cold War confrontation and tension.

Mr. Nixon has moved boldly — and wisely — in the foreign field, lifting the inscrutable Bamboo Curtain that isolated Red China for too many years with a sullen distrust of the United States and its allies. He complemented this historic detente with a summit meeting in Moscow that opened the way for broad exchanges in trade, scientific and cultural areas.

The strategic arms limitation agreement negotiated by the United States with the Soviet Union, a difficult and complex accommodation that required years of painstaking negotiation, constitutes another major accomplishment for the Republican President. It represents the first significant leveling off in the reckless, unending arms competition that has critically drained the resources of both super-powers.

* * *

MR. NIXON has been the subject of persistent criticism for his failure to end the costly and unpopular war in Vietnam, but this is an issue that should be circumspectly re-examined in a fuller, overall perspective — and in contemporary terms.

It's true that the war has not ended, as Mr. Nixon pledged he would do when he ran for the Presidency in 1968. But it's also clearly apparent that it has been decisively wound down, and the American disengagement has reached a point where the U.S. role has been mostly confined to aerial operations. The fact is that Americans no longer are being sent to combat duty in Indochina.

There was criticism when the White House resumed bombing of North Vietnam several months ago, but even this must be judged in the framework of the threat created by the invasion of South Vietnam by the army of North Vietnam. The military situation to a large degree has been stabilized, and this might be considered a requisite to the peace negotiations that now appear on the verge of success.

At home, the Nixon Administration has followed a transitional approach that has generated a broad mood of consensual acceptance. There has been criticism of the President's cordial rapport with business, but this must be equated with his liberal social programs — welfare reform, which was clumsily aborted by a Democratic Congress, and revenue-sharing, the latter a fiscal formula to provide revenues for strapped states and localities.

Revenue-sharing should provide the impetus for even greater federal commitment in the future in alleviating the continuing urban crisis, a re-ordering of national priorities when the war is finally over in Southeast Asia and our resources can be channeled into urgently needed urban areas.

These are progressive initiatives that have been historically indentified with the populist philosophy of the Democratic Party. But is is apparent that Mr. Nixon is keenly aware that even a GOP administration no longer can turn the clock back on vital social issues that affect millions of Americans.

* * *

ONE PROBLEM in any evaluation of Mr. Nixon is in excising residual doubts about the younger, ambitious politician from the man who sits in the White House today. He has become a stateman tempered by his times and the exigencies and pressures of high office.

In endorsing Mr. Nixon for re-election, this newspaper is reassured by the belief that the politican, the statesman and the man has demonstrated a responsible maturity by his incumbency in the White House — a sobering experience that should serve to further broaden his outlook on fundamental human values and to firm his commitment to achieve domestic and global equability.

Campaign '72:
PROGRESS TOWARD INDOCHINA TRUCE REPORTED TWO WEEKS BEFORE VOTING

With only two weeks to go before the presidential election, White House aide Henry A. Kissinger told a news conference in Washington Oct. 26 that he believed "peace is at hand" in all of Indochina. He confirmed "the general description" of the nine-point agreement that had been broadcast earlier Oct. 26 by Hanoi radio. Democratic presidential candidate Sen. George McGovern said he hoped that a truce came soon, but expressed doubt that a full agreement was imminent. At an Iowa campaign speech Oct. 26, McGovern declared, "The question that haunts my mind is this: Why, Mr. Nixon, did you take another four years to put an end to this tragic war." President Nixon said at a West-Virginia rally Oct. 26 that there were "still difficulties to be worked out. I am confident that they can and will be worked out."

Kissinger's version of the agreement included the following principal points: (1) there would be a cease-fire in place; (2) all U.S. forces would be withdrawn within sixty days of the signing of the agreement; (3) all captured military personnel and foreign civilians would be repatriated within 60 days; (4) North Vietnam would be responsible for accounting for the U.S. prisoners and missing-in-action throughout Indochina; (5) the South Vietnamese people would decide "their political future through free and democratic elections under international supervision"; (6) the existing authorities would remain in office while the two parties negotiated about the timing of the elections and the offices for which these elections would be held; (7) a National Council of National Reconciliation and Concord would be formed to maintain the cease-fire and to supervise the elections; (8) an international conference would meet within 30 days of the signing of the agreement to form an international supervisory commission to which disputes between the parties could be referred; and (9) the parties would agree to respect the sovereignty of Cambodia and Laos and to refrain from military operations in those two countries.

Kissinger acknowledged that there was a "misunderstanding" about signature of the agreement by Oct. 31, a deadline cited earlier in the day by the North Vietnamese delegation to the Paris talks. He asserted that there had been no definite date set for the conclusion of the talks.

In its first official reaction to the accord, the South Vietnamese Foreign Ministry released a statement Oct. 27 indicating the government's willingness to accept a cease-fire but expressing strong reservations about the political settlement. The South Vietnamese also objected to North Vietnam's apparent freedom under the terms of the accord to maintain 145,000 North Vietnamese troops in areas of South Vietnam. President Nguyen Van Thieu had declared in a nationwide broadcast Oct. 24 that the reported peace terms were unacceptable.

Pittsburgh Post-Gazette
Pittsburgh, Pa., October 28, 1972

IT COMES with ill grace for Senator McGovern to carp, now that a cease-fire seems imminent, that the Nixon Administration didn't end four years ago the war that Presidents Kenedy and Johnson got us into. If it were all that easy, why didn't the Democratic Presidents end it?

It is true that the war could have been ended at any time, by either side. Peace required only that the South Vietnamese and their allies surrender or that the North Vietnamese end their aggression against the south. America's myopic doves, for some reason (political, perhaps?) haven't been able to see or to concede that there were two sides to this war.

Let us all rejoice, however, that both sides have now agreed that there isn't to be a military victory and have made concessions that should permit a negotiated settlement, as sensible people have contended all along offered the only acceptable way out.

Details of the settlement as outlined by Henry Kissinger impress us as reasonable. They also underscore the complexities of the technical and political problems involved and for which there was no simplistic answer short of surrender.

Nor should we rub our hands in smug anticipation of instant peace. Terms of the cease-fire and of the political negotiations to follow it are such that many opportunities for further conflict will remain. Close supervision by neutral powers will be required to maintain a cease-fire and to work out the intricate procedures toward self-determination for the South Vietnamese.

* * *

A world weary of the costly tragedy in Vietnam must hope that Mr. Kissinger's delicate mission will be concluded successfully and soon. President Thieu of South Vietnam should not be permitted to prevent a cease-fire, a withdrawal of American forces and an exchange of prisoners. This opportunity for peace, sought by President Nixon since the initiation of secret talks with the Communists during his first year in office, should not slip from our grasp.

Although charges of domestic politics must inevitable intrude upon the negotiations on the eve of a presidential election, they, too, should not be allowed to sway or disrupt this chance for peace.

There will be more than enough time for political reassessments and recrimination after a cease-fire takes effect and we are at long last disengaged from a war in which we should never have been involved.

Anchorage Daily Times
Anchorage, Alaska
October 27, 1972

IT IS inevitable, perhaps, that something political will be made of a peace settlement in Vietnam, when and if it comes in the next hour or the next week.

We suspect that a very great many Americans would like to accept the cease fire with grateful thanks to God that it has finally come, through whatever motive, by whatever cause.

Many, we suspect, will resent politicians of either party trying to make election-eve hay out of an event which has been so long sought, so agonizingly fought and died for.

Cheap-shot politics should be laid aside.

UNFORTUNATELY, the peace settlement, or the attempts to achieve one, seem destined to be dragged through the political gutter before election day.

Instead of rejoicing that peace is at hand and constructively trying to aid its fruition, Democratic nominees George McGovern and Sargent Shriver have been accusing the Nixon administration of dragging out the war for four years — just so it could be ended with a bid for votes on Nov. 7.

Some Republican candidates apparently are going to rise to the bait and try to answer that kind of terrible accusation with some equally bad.

AFTER WEEKS and months and years, it now appears that an end is in sight to the bloody turmoil that has ravaged Vietnam for so long.

In seeking this peace that is yet to be, the United States has been forced to make some concessions to the North Vietnam leaders who have brought so much death and destruction and tragedy to South Vietnam.

But the Saigon government, and the country it represents, still stands. Freedom still exists in Southeast Asia.

The cause, for all its cost and all its suffering, has not been in vain.

And to besmirch the efforts for peace, on the very eve of success in hopes of gaining some short-range political goals a week from Tuesday, serves no one well.

ST. LOUIS POST-DISPATCH
St. Louis, Mo., October 29, 1972

One of the few aspects of the Vietnam preliminary peace agreements about which the American public can be certain is that President Nixon has taken over the headlines less than two weeks before the close of the presidential campaign and is likely to dominate the news during the final critical pre-election period. Whether he planned it that way cannot be demonstrated, but the situation makes it difficult for his rival, Senator McGovern, to obtain an adequate hearing.

If peace comes promptly there will be rejoicing, even though it comes more than three and a half years and 20,000 American deaths after Mr. Nixon assumed office. We do not accept the explanation of Henry Kissinger, Mr. Nixon's national security adviser, that a Hanoi proposal of last Oct. 8 made possible negotiations previously impossible. We cannot believe that Mr. Nixon could not have brought about a peace three years ago if he had really wanted it.

Nevertheless, if the war is over, we will rejoice. But is it? And if it is, what are the terms? We do not fault the Administration, Hanoi or even President Thieu of South Vietnam for surrounding whatever agreements have been discussed in a verbal cloak. It is perhaps the only way to begin closing out the war in a way that will make everyone appear to be the winner. Formulas and diplomatic double-talk have had to be devised to conceal the truth; it is likely, if there is substance behind the talk, that the real facts will emerge slowly.

Mr. Nixon says he is confident recent progress will lead to "peace with honor, and not peace with surrender," which explains quite simply the reason for all the vagueness on key points. What the words from Hanoi and Washington add up to looks precious like a coalition government for Vietnam, something Washington's client, Thieu, says he will not accept. Coalition would mean the end of Thieu and general acceptance by Washington of Hanoi's conditions. If there is really to be peace, it must come on some such terms.

There is no reason to believe North Vietnam would seek peace if it were to be denied the goals for which it has fought for a generation. The U.S. bombing of North Vietnam and the mining of Haiphong harbor have not halted the North Vietnamese military machine, which has continued to nibble at bits and pieces of South Vietnam to the point at which a cease-fire in place would leave the Communists in control of vast areas of the countryside, including a dozen or so hamlets on the outskirts of Saigon. This massive infiltration is the wellspring of Viet Cong strength in the South.

It is not possible for the public to know whether the real initiative for the October effort by Mr. Kissinger came from Washington or Hanoi. Both sides have reasons to make concessions at this time, Mr. Nixon in the hope of gaining political advantage through talk of imminent peace, and North Vietnam in the hope of obtaining a better bargain before the November election than after. If the Administration moves are substantive, then it is Senator McGovern, who has fought a long and at times solitary battle for Vietnam peace and who has challenged the Administration on the issue in this campaign, and not Mr. Nixon who should be given major credit.

It is notable in this sea of words there is no *act* that would demonstrate the sincerity of either side. Could Hanoi release another batch of prisoners of war, for example? For several years we have suggested that Mr. Nixon could certify his professed desire for peace by some such positive act as accepting the retirement of 78-year-old U.S. Ambassador Bunker, Thieu's great and good friend in Saigon. If Mr. Nixon would take some such positive action before the election it would disarm the skeptics and enhance his credibility.

Lacking that, there will be ample room for doubt; but the American people, and surely all Vietnamese, will profoundly hope that this is the real thing at last.

BOSTON HERALD TRAVELER and Record American
Boston, Mass., October 27, 1972

Henry Kissinger's flat declaration that "peace is at hand" in Vietnam was, by all odds, the best news the American people have heard in many years. At terribly long last it brought the vision of real light at the end of an interminable tunnel, a promise of agony soon to end.

The vision seems real enough. For many reasons it appears all but inevitable. At the same time there is good cause to keep rejoicing at a minimum until the vision becomes reality. No treaty has yet been signed; everything could still fall apart.

Probably the best reason for optimism is that the general agreement between the United States and North Vietnam is basically fair to all concerned. In essence the fighting would stop, we would withdraw with our freed prisoners, and the Vietnamese people would solve their political differences under the jurisdiction of an international control agency.

George McGovern and other Democratic doves have been asking why President Nixon couldn't have accomplished such a sensible agreement far earlier. He couldn't have because Hanoi was not ready — and one of the main reasons was the encouragement given the Communists by the McGoverns and Fulbrights through their incessant criticism of our war effort.

Now, for various reasons, the Communists obviously have become convinced that prospects for a U. S. sell-out of its allies were a delusion. Unsuccessful in their all-out Easter invasion of the south, hammered by relentless bombing in return, they opened the door to potential peace by reversing themselves on the cease-fire issue.

Their adamant contention for years was that a cease-fire could never materialize until the U. S., in effect, abandoned Saigon to their mercies. By agreeing to a cease-fire as first step in settling the conflict, Hanoi made possible the present apparent breakthrough toward peace.

The breakthrough may or may not end the agony. South Vietnamese President Thieu is reluctant to compromise. So are powerful militarists in the north. But, finally and almost miraculously, the forces of reason appear to be transcending those of intransigence.

All wars eventually must end, one way or another. In Vietnam and Indochina decades of bloody strife are not about to be resolved in a sudden atmosphere of sweetness and light. Many bitter days and crises lie ahead.

For the present, however, the prospect that talk is about to replace killing seems a reasonable expectation. A momentous series of new possibilities — at the very least — have been set in motion. No matter what happens they will be preferable to what has gone before.

Omaha World-Herald
Omaha, Neb., October 30, 1972

Sen. George McGovern has reacted to the apparent settlement of the Vietnamese war with about as much statesmanship as could be expected under the circumstances.

He has said, as have many other critics of the President's war policies, that first and foremost he welcomes the prospect of peace, regardless of the political implications.

At the same time, McGovern has understandably tried to minimize the political benefits Nixon is expected to receive as the result of the cease-fire developments.

Mainly, McGovern has been hitting at this theme: If peace is within reach now, why could it not have been achieved four years ago, or at any other time in Nixon's tenure?

* * *

Presidential adviser Henry Kissinger seemed to dispose of the question satisfactorily in the news conference he held last week.

The main reason the breakthrough in negotiations came when it did, Kissinger said, is that North Vietnam did not until Oct. 8 relinquish the position that Vietnamese political issues should be settled before a military agreement could be concluded.

It was not until this fall, apparently, that the North Vietnamese fully felt the confluence of pressures that drove them to compromise. The pressures included U.S. military force, suggestions from Russia and Red China, the failure of the Easter offensive to make significant territorial gains in South Vietnam, and, possibly, internal conflicts in the war-ravaged North.

As we have noted, another consideration for Hanoi may have been the realization that President Nixon was heavily favored for re-election, and the hope that a pre-election war settlement would be more favorable than one concluded after Nov. 7, when Nixon would have a freer hand.

Any election-eve peace initiative is naturally suspect. We recall the widespread skepticism accompanying Lyndon Johnson's Oct. 31 bombing halt four years ago.

In the present instance, however, Kissinger's explanation seems reasonable enough. Among other things, it fits with previous predictions that Hanoi would not come to any sensible terms until the U.S. election picture seemed clear.

McGovern's claim that the end of the war could have come four years ago is acceptable if one also accepts McGovern's definition of what a settlement should have entailed.

Peace of a kind was possible four years ago, but it would not have been a peace that validated even partially the tremendous sacrifices the United States has made.

The Providence Journal
Providence, R.I., October 28, 1972

The question that haunts my mind this afternoon, is this: Why, Mr. Nixon, did you take another four more years to put an end to this tragic war?
Sen. George S. McGovern

In his first reaction to the news that "peace is at hand" in Indochina, as Dr. Henry A. Kissinger put it, the Democratic Party's candidate for the presidency suggested through the question that haunts his mind that President Richard M. Nixon could have put an end to the war four years ago. Could he have? Let's look at the record.

* * *

As long as he was President, Republican Dwight D. Eisenhower refused to involve the United States military in Indochina. When Democratic John F. Kennedy took office, he reversed that policy and opened the door to military intervention with a swarm of advisers to the South Vietnamese Army.

When Democrat Lyndon B. Johnson succeeded Mr. Kennedy, he locked this country into Indochina with a massive escalation of armed forces. What one Republican president refused to do, two Democratic presidents did — and Richard M. Nixon fell heir to a tragic, complex, and dismayingly confusing political and military mess.

To suggest that Mr. Nixon could have put an end to the war four years ago, as he proposes to do now, insults the imagination. The only way Mr. Nixon could have put an end to the war four years ago would have been to walk away from it, as Mr. McGovern proposed to do as soon as he got into the White House — if voters elected him Nov. 7.

Mr. Nixon, however, wanted more than a simplistic end of the war. He wanted to effect a situation in which there would be a cease-fire under supervision, withdrawal of all troops — American and North Vietnamese — from South Vietnam, an exchange of prisoners of war, and political resolution of Vietnamese problems by the Vietnamese.

But peace is not made unilaterally as is surrender. Peace is a bilateral or multilateral business, and Hanoi and the Viet Cong had to participate meaningfully in negotiations with this country and South Vietnam if the war was to end. Hanoi and the Viet Cong, however, fixed and pursued the goal of total takeover in South Vietnam.

Mr. McGovern has declined to credit the Nixon administration for the prospect of peace, saying that those who opposed the war deserved "much of the credit." Sargent Shriver, Mr. McGovern's running mate, went farther; he said, "The peace agreement is a triumph of George McGovern's campaign." No doubt, the McGovern-Shriver ticket brought home 500,000 American troops from Vietnam in the last four years, too.

* * *

But the question of timing remains. There are Democrats who insist that the whole peace deal was arranged to coincide with the end of the campaign. But how did Mr. Nixon persuade the intransigent North Vietnamese and Viet Cong negotiators to agree to a peace plan on the eve of the election?

The Americans have made compromises; the North Vietnamese and the Viet Cong have made compromises. There may yet be more compromises on both sides. Hanoi now wants to end the war as earnestly as Mr. Nixon and Dr. Kissinger, who did a remarkable negotiating job for the United States, perhaps one of the most difficult tasks any American diplomat ever faced.

Mr. McGovern, Mr. Shriver and other top Democrats fail to concede that Hanoi and the Viet Cong can read the returns in presidential polls as easily as Americans. Is it just possible that Hanoi and its allies realized the give-away peace plan of Mr. McGovern was a dead issue, and that Mr. Nixon was the man with whom they would have to settle eventually and why not now?

Further, the present situation may well reflect the long effort Mr. Nixon has made to firm *detente* with Moscow and open the doors at Peking. It may well reflect a war weariness in Hanoi, too, a revulsion among Hanoi's doves to the continued drain on North Vietnam's resources and manpower and the emergence of hopes for peace at long last.

* * *

Mr. Nixon did not need a peace plan to win re-election. By every pre-election indicator today, he is certain of victory Nov. 7. The refusal to recognize that while many talked peace, Mr. Nixon has it in hand is a final mark of the bankruptcy of the McGovern-Shriver campaign for power.

PORTLAND EVENING EXPRESS
Portland, Me., October 31, 1972

Both Sen. George McGovern and Sargent Shriver have hurt their candidacies, in the eyes of intelligent voters, by their fatuous and inadmissible comments on the agreement reached by Hanoi and Washington to settle the Indo-Chinese war.

McGovern has been the more restrained — welcoming the good news, saying he hopes it will prove to be correct, but demanding that the President say why it took "'another four years to put an end to his tragic war.''

Shriver, on the other hand, has directly linked the settlement to the election, and in South Carolina last week charged that the announcements from Washington were "an election maneuver.''

The vice presidential candidate even tried to garb himself in the role of prophet, saying he "predicted" the settlement would come between Oct. 10 and Oct. 22.

He was equally inaccurate in stating that the terms the President has secured from Hanoi are no better than those he "could have achieved on coming into office."

Four years ago, and consistently since then until Oct. 8th of this year, the Communists insisted on a political settlement prior to a military pact. It was the kind of settlement that this country could not honorably accept. But by early October the rulers of North Vietnam were forced to admit their summer offensive had failed, they were being subjected to a blockade, plus severe air bombardment, while Russia and Red China were warning them to take the best terms possible.

The last thing the North Vietnamese wanted was a Nixon victory and continuation of the punishment they were receiving. So they have agreed to a truce, a war-prisoner return, and other concessions. A month ago the White House probably had no idea the tide would turn. Furthermore Mr. Nixon is sophisticated enough to be aware that the coincidence of the settlement and the election will persuade some voters that he and Henry Kissinger planned it that way, which is not true.

THE DAILY HERALD
Biloxi, Miss., October 29, 1972

At long last we are on the road to what promises to be an enduring peace in Vietnam. What the public knows of the terms at this writing is incomplete. But the chief terms disclosed indicate that the war can be terminated, without the U.S. breaking faith with its commitments under the Southeastern Asia Treaty Organization.

The agreements apparently embrace a speedy cease-fire, withdrawal of American troops and equipment within 60 days, return of our prisoners, and machinery by which the Vietnamese may settle their own political differences.

Unfortunately, we are hearing the predictable charges that the entire agreement is "political" and designed to ensure the re-election of President Nixon.

Senator George S. McGovern, for example, asks why didn't the President end the war four years ago?

Senator McGovern knows perfectly well that President Nixon didn't have the power then or even now to "end the war" unless he was willing to surrender and leave the South Vietnamese people to the tender mercies of their foes in the North. This he chose not to do.

It has taken years of patient negotiations to reach the agreements now in sight. And before we entertain any charges of "politics" let us remember that Hanoi broke the lid of secrecy on the tentative agreements, not President Nixon. It has been clear that the President was willing to wait until after the elections to announce the full peace terms if it took that long to reach complete agreements.

If all goes well with the rest of the negotiations, as all Americans fervently hope it will, we can write an end to a bloody and unfortunate chapter in world history.

And the United States will emerge from the conflict with its integrity intact. We will not be in the position of a power that breaks faith with its friends and refuses to keep its solemn treaty commitments.

DAILY NEWS
New York, N.Y., October 28, 1972

"Peace" candidate George McGovern is showing little joy over the prospect of an end to the Vietnam war.

President Richard M. Nixon rates unstinting praise for negotiating with patience, diligence and skill to end America's involvement in Vietnam on honorable terms.

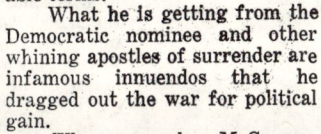

President Nixon

What he is getting from the Democratic nominee and other whining apostles of surrender are infamous innuendos that he dragged out the war for political gain.

Why, squeals McGovern, didn't the President accept a settlement four years ago? The answer is simple: Not until three weeks ago was North Vietnam willing to back down from its demand that we hand South Vietnam over to the Reds on a silver platter.

Before Oct. 8, Hanoi refused to budge from demands that the U.S. abandon its ally and skulk out of Vietnam in disgrace. A Sen. McGovern would have kowtowed to the Communists; President Nixon would not. He held out—as he should have held out, and as a majority of Americans wanted him to hold out— for an understanding that would leave the people of South Vietnam with at least a fighting chance to preserve their freedom.

The pending agreement is not much different in basics from offers President Nixon made to the enemy early in his term. But Hanoi would have none of them while there remained a glimmer of hope that it could overrun South Vietnam militarily or that the President would be forced by appeasers in the U.S. to put his name to a sell-out.

McGovern and other arch-doves have done all in their power to oblige the enemy, carping at **every move by the** President that would have proved false their defeatist gospel that surrender was the only way out of Vietnam.

Now that Mr. Nixon has come within inches of his goal in spite of all the ranting and whimpering, McGovern pelts him with lies and abuse.

It's the reaction of a small-minded, mean-souled, spiteful, malicious little man who sees his dreams of high office fading away and, in his rage, seeks to undermine public trust in the nation's leaders and institutions.

The Seattle Times
Seattle, Wash., October 31, 1972

FACED with imminent peace in Vietnam, Senator McGovern and his followers have fallen back on the suggestion that President Nixon deliberately waited until the virtual eve of the presidential election to settle on terms available three or four years ago.

We have not the slightest doubt that the American public will resist being taken in by so obvious a distortion of the known facts.

Not until last October 8 did Hanoi abandon its previously inflexible positions, agreeing that President Thieu will remain in power pending an internationally supervised election, and to a cease-fire in advance of a political settlement.

And now the Communists have backed off from their previous insistence that the peace agreement be *signed today*. Henry Kissinger remains in touch with Hanoi, and it seems likely that the last, relatively small roadblocks to a settlement will be cleared away within a matter of days.

IT is apparent that the approach of the American election created pressure for a settlement, all right, but that the pressure was on the North Vietnamese, not Mr. Nixon.

The Hanoi rulers and not Mr. Nixon made the key concessions, just as the Hanoi rulers and not Mr. Nixon initiated one last massive attempt to win the war by military means with the tank-led offensive begun last Easter.

Mr. Nixon could have responded to that offensive by reintroducing American ground troops into combat or, contrariwise, by simply closing out the American role in Indochina—McGovern style — under altogether ignominious circumstances.

Instead, he mined North Vietnam's harbors and undertook selective bombing of that country's war potential.

THE results, in two most significant ways, spelled disaster for North Vietnam.

● South Vietnamese troops, after some bad initial reverses, fought Hanoi's invading army to a standstill. Vietnamization worked.

● Second, China and Russia made no effort to challenge the American mining. Furthermore, each major Communist power made clear that its separate detente diplomacy in regard to the United States was not to be sacrificed, or even deferred in order to accommodate Hanoi's interests.

North Vietnam found itself enveloped by President Nixon's summit diplomacy and out of step with a world-wide trend of events that includes the modus vivendi movements in the two Germanys and the two Koreas.

Could all this have happened three or four years ago? The answer obviously is no.

THE BLADE
Toledo, Ohio, October 30, 1972

WITH the eruption of headlines that peace may settle on Vietnam any day now and almost assuredly will within a few weeks at most, there is an assumption abroad in the land that this dramatic — and certainly welcome — news can only redound to the political benefit of Richard M. Nixon. If any development could further enhance the President's already expected victory Nov. 7 and guarantee his re-election by the avalanche of votes he so dearly yearns for, a declaration just before Election Day that he has come to the point or the brink of delivering this nation from the curse of Vietnam would surely do it.

Perhaps it will work out that way. It can safely be taken for granted that, besides the many pundits and partisans who share this view, the President himself counts on getting landslide returns from Henry Kissinger's last-minute diplomatic coup. Yet that very fact unavoidably puts a cynical taint on the achievement Mr. Nixon hopes will serve as his crowning glory.

For the turn of events these past few days confirms a nagging suspicion of long standing that the President has all along deliberately paced his steps toward ending U.S. involvement in the Vietnam war so they would reach a triumphant climax at the precise moment to do him the most good in his bid for a second term. As far back as April, 1970 — just past the first year of his Administration — we raised the possibility that Mr. Nixon's disappointing rate of troop pullouts could be intended "to spread future withdrawals well into a presidential year when, possibly on the eve of balloting, he can dramatically reveal that . . . we are on the verge of victory . . ."

What has emerged from Dr. Kissinger's frenetic global activities in just the last couple of weeks makes it impossible to escape the conclusion that the political objective in the war-and-peace strategy extended to the cleverest details of timing. It seems evident, for instance, that public revelation of a breakthrough must have been designed to come late enough to allow no time before election for questions to arise over fine points of the settlement such as whether the Thieu regime was being deserted after all, or what concessions Mr. Nixon might have yielded in his previously "nonnegotiable" stands to bring Hanoi around to terms. Moreover, even if the final agreement could not be formally signed and sealed before voting day, there would be an advantage in giving people the feeling that settlement lay too close at hand to risk changing horses.

Yet two basic questions do inevitably press to the surface: Could not the same frenzy of travel by Dr. Kissinger, the same twists of pressure on Mr. Thieu in Saigon, the same give-and-take in enticing Hanoi to terms have produced an end to the war long before this moment on the very eve of the election? Might not many of the 20,000 American lives and thousands of wounded casualties and hundreds of prisoners and billions of dollars that the war has cost since Richard Nixon took office have been saved had the settlement been pursued with as much intensity and energy from the first of his term as it obviously has been since the first of this month?

Maybe Mr. Nixon deserves extra credit just for the shrewdness of his politico-diplomatic planning and his skill at bringing it off. But it leaves a tragic cloud over a moment of joy that the American people should not have been made to wait for so long.

DAYTON DAILY NEWS
Dayton, Ohio, October 28, 1972

It is with a mixture of grace and sour grapes that Sen. George McGovern has reacted to the tenative agreements that would end the Indochina war, or at least would end direct U.S. involvement in it.

The grace becomes Sen. McGovern, as when he expresses his hope that the accords will stick and emphasizes his support for President Nixon's efforts in that regard.

The carping, however, is both pointless and unfair. Mr. Nixon's richly authenticated reputation as a trickster permits the suspicion that he would, if he could, time peace for his own re-election purposes. But the events of the past few years do not support the suspicion.

The timing of any peace arrangement more general than U.S. surrender always has been at Hanoi's discretion, and historically North Vietnam never has composed matters for the convenience of its antagonists. Whatever else one may believe about the government in Hanoi, the conclusion is unavoidable that it performs solely according to its own self-interests.

North Vietnam obviously held on to the war like a terrier, though a wearying one. It hoped until this year that U.S. domestic politics, one way or another, would force a unilateral American withdrawal. Hanoi pinned much — too much, as things turned out — on its military offensive early this year.

Of course the United States could have quit any time during the last four years, or the last 12, and whether it should have or not remains a legitimate if moot issue. The chance for the United States to dicker its way out, however, didn't become lively until recent months, and Sen. McGovern ignores reality when he implies otherwise.

Rocky Mountain News
Denver, Colo., October 30, 1972

IT IS INSTRUCTIVE, we think, to compare the peace agreement the Nixon administration has all but signed with Hanoi to the Vietnam plan of Sen. George S. McGovern.

Any such comparison clearly shows that presidential adviser Henry A. Kissinger won far better terms from the North Vietnamese that McGovern was prepared to offer them.

The Democratic presidential candidate stated his Vietnam policy in its greatest detail in a nationwide broadcast Oct. 10.

On his inauguration day, he pledged, he would order an immediate halt to bombing and all other acts of force against the Vietnamese Communists. He also would immediately cut off all combat supplies to the South Vietnamese and would withdraw all American forces from Indochina within 90 days.

The McGovern plan did not contain a cease-fire, which is a key achievement of the Nixon-Kissinger negotiations. Thus, by his terms, the North Vietnamese, free to receive fresh supplies from Russia and China, would be able to continue attacking the South Vietnamese, who could not be resupplied with arms and ammunition.

A cease-fire, we submit, is greatly preferable to a continued bloodletting, with all the odds favoring the enemy side.

Moreover, Nixon got agreement on international machinery to supervise the peace, which McGovern did not call for. The President also gained the right to resupply his South Vietnamese ally in case the cease-fire breaks down, which is not unlikely.

On the vital issue of prisoners, Kissinger got a carefully drafted commitment from Hanoi that it would return all POWs taken in Vietnam, Laos and Cambodia and would account for Americans missing in action.

McGovern did not insist on any such precise undertaking.

In sum, the McGovern plan was such that an analyst for the New York Times (which has endorsed the Democrat for election) stated;

"The senator...invited the American people to support a plan whose military essentials amount to virtually total acceptance of the demands of the Viet Cong and their allies in North Vietnam."

By way of contrast, the arrangement worked out by the President gives the non-Communist majority in South Vietnam a chance at peace and, if the agreement is violated, a chance at survival.

Campaign '72:
NIXON RE-ELECTED IN LANDSLIDE; DEMOCRATS HOLD POWER IN CONGRESS

President Richard M. Nixon and Vice President Spiro T. Agnew won re-election Nov. 7 in a popular and electoral vote landslide with few precedents in U.S. history. The Democratic ticket of Sen. George S. McGovern (S.D.) and R. Sargent Shriver Jr. won only in Massachusetts and the District of Columbia. The Nixon ticket captured every other state, winning 521 electoral votes to the Democrats' 17. In the popular vote, Nixon won 45.9 million (61%) and McGovern won 28.4 million (38%).

Support for the President encompassed almost every sector of the electorate and every region. Nixon received 55%–60% of the urban vote, 70% of the suburban vote, 80% of the rural vote, and an exceptionally strong Southern vote, rising to 79% in Mississippi. Preliminary analysis of the results indicated Nixon picked up a majority of the Roman Catholic vote and the blue-collar vote, both unprecedented for a Republican candidate. It appeared Nixon split the vote from union families and the youth vote almost evenly with McGovern. The only groups solid for McGovern were blacks, the very poor and intellectuals. Surveys indicated that more than a third of all Democrats voted for Nixon, compared with an average defection rate of 16% for the previous five elections. Many commentators noted that state-by-state as well as nationally the Republican vote coincided with the combined vote totals of Gov. George C. Wallace and Nixon in the 1968 Presidential election.

Despite Nixon's landslide, massive ticket-splitting by the electorate enabled the Democrats to retain their majorities in both houses of Congress, gaining a net two seats in the Senate and losing only 13 seats in the House. In the 93rd Congress, Democrats will hold 57 Senate seats to the Republicans' 43. The Democrats will control the House of Representatives by a 243–191 margin.

Democrats also did well in gubernatorial races, winning 11 of 18 contests, and increasing their margin of control in statehouses by one, to 31–19.

The Charlotte Observer
Charlotte, N.C., November 11, 1972

President Nixon's overwhelming victory was not so much the evidence of a love affair with the American public as an indication that the voters wanted security against rapid change and unknown frontiers. Mr. Nixon succeeded in finding many of the anxieties of the people and in finessing concerns for which George McGovern was spokesman.

The results, we think, reflect not so much a lack of public concern about corruption, the war, inequities in the tax system and other issues which Sen. McGovern pressed as much as a lack of confidence in the Democratic candidate himself. He simply frightened a great many people. This made the campaign turn more upon personal confidence and approach than upon hard issues. But even with his success in winning that personal confidence battle against Sen. McGovern, Mr. Nixon's victory would not have been a landslide except for his deftness in co-opting much of the 1968 George Wallace support. Four years ago the President won 43 per cent of the votes and Gov. Wallace received 13 per cent, a total of 56 per cent; this time Mr. Nixon's total was 61 per cent.

Mr. Nixon spoke often of "the new majority," and his sweep of 49 states certainly included elements of something new in recent American electoral history. But there is a message also in his inability to make even the party gains in Congress which more modest presidential victories usually bring. That, too, suggests that it was public fear of Sen. McGovern himself, more than anything else, that brought about the landslide. Thus the word "mandate" hardly seems to apply to Mr. Nixon's sweep.

The campaign never clearly established what kind of leader Mr. Nixon will be in his second term. He has the opportunity to rise above the cheaper appeals which often have characterized his dealings with the public and to emerge as a great president. He could begin that emergence with removal of the tawdriness of the Mitchell-Kleindienst-Haldeman-Erlichman elements in his White House guard and by seeking people of higher caliber for his second administration.

We wish Mr. Nixon well as he approaches a second term, and we believe most of those who have opposed him should offer him their support in making the next four years — years that will end with the country's 200th anniversary — a time of renewal and strengthening for the nation.

The Evening Star and The Washington Daily News
Washington, D.C., November 8, 1972

Well, you can't, as they say, beat somebody with nobody, and that was about the size of it yesterday as President Nixon won a second term in the White House, brushing aside the unctuous opposition of Senator George S. McGovern of South Dakota, the Democratic nominee.

When the last ballots were tallied, nearly two out of every three Americans had expressed a preference for Mr. Nixon over McGovern, who ended up with only the District of Columbia and Massachusetts in his column, the weakest performance of a major party candidate since 1936 when Alf Landon stormed to victory in Maine and Vermont, leaving the rest of the country to FDR.

For a man who is hardly first in the hearts of his countrymen, a politician whose career has been marked by narrow victories and close defeats, it was a stunning, heartening performance. Yet it is obvious that the Nixon landslide was a product as much of the people's well-founded distrust of McGovern and his policies as it was of their enthusiasm for Mr. Nixon and his works. Had Governor Wallace, who won 13.5 percent of the popular vote in 1968, been in the race — or had the Democratic candidate been virtually anyone other than McGovern — the outcome would have been considerably different.

While the Solid South for the first time was going solidly for a Republican president, and traditionally Democratic strongholds such as Rhode Island, Wisconsin, West Virginia and Maryland's Montgomery County fell like duckpins, the presidential coattails proved distressingly short to GOP congressional candidates. As a wet dawn broke today, the Democrats retained secure control of both the House and the Senate.

So while Mr. Nixon will go into his second term with a substantially strengthened personal mandate, he will by no means have everything his own way when it comes to pressing his domestic program. Relieved of either the necessity or the possibility of seeking re-election, he has the opportunity to forge a record which will assure his place in history, but only if he acts in such a constructive, innovative way that a Democratic Congress will not be able to refuse its cooperation.

The Nixon landslide has one aspect to it that is wholly to the good. The size of his mandate will enable the President to negotiate from a position of great strength in dealing with other countries, both friends and foes. Mr. Nixon's accomplishments in foreign affairs during his first term were substantial, and he now has the means to build upon that record. A McGovern victory, or even a narrow victory for Mr. Nixon, would have placed in jeopardy much of the good work achieved during the past three years.

The Star-News supported Mr. Nixon's re-election this year, as it did his election in 1968. We challenge him now to improve upon the good record of his first term; to cleanse his administration of unseemly acts, to end the Vietnam War upon just terms, to heal the wounds that stem from that war and to restore to this nation and all its people a sense of mission and a faith in themselves. It is a large order. But a victory of yesterday's proportions compels high goals. Now, more than ever, the ball is in Mr. Nixon's court.

The New York Times
New York, N.Y., November 8, 1972

Richard M. Nixon and Spiro T. Agnew have now been overwhelmingly elected to a second term as President and Vice President of the United States. In accordance with the essential genius of this democracy, all Americans — including especially those who, like ourselves, vigorously opposed their re-election — recognize that the President yesterday received an unchallengeable popular mandate and that the destiny of this country for the next four years is now, for better or worse, to a large and important extent in his hands.

As we see it, the vote that has so decisively confirmed the retention of executive power by Mr. Nixon was less a vindication of specific policies of the President than an expression of mistrust of Senator McGovern's prescription for change and of his ability to carry it out. In rejecting Mr. McGovern's basic critiques of American foreign and domestic policies, the majority implicitly opted for the reality of their own affluence, garnished with a tissue of hopes: hope that Mr. Nixon really will achieve an "honorable" settlement of the war, hope that he really will succeed in curbing inflation and unemployment, hope that the second Nixon Administration really will eradicate the present ominous signs of corruption and cynicism in government and politics.

* * *

The election returns suggest that many of the issues which Senator McGovern attempted to raise did not sufficiently trouble the great majority of Americans to lead them to risk any break with the comfortable familiarity of the status quo. They involved such questions as the threat to civil liberties and to the Bill of Rights, the concentration of executive power at the expense of Congress and the people, the obvious inequities of the tax system, the power of the military-industrial complex, the widespread racial and class divisions, the massive bombing of military and civilians alike in defense of one dictatorship against another in Vietnam.

None of these issues on which the Nixon Administration has been attacked during the last four years seems to have been able to overcome the general feeling among most Americans that "we never had it so good," that the elusive peace — as Henry Kissinger so disarmingly predicted a fortnight ago — really is "at hand," that corruption in Washington is unimportant and that in any case Mr. McGovern is either too idealistic, too inept or too radical to entrust with the reins of government.

Mr. Nixon's cause was, of course, greatly and deservedly enhanced by the initial success of his policy of détente with Peking and Moscow. He himself undoubtedly considers foreign policy his forte. In the next four years he will certainly need all of his skills in achieving further progress in arms limitation and in steering this country between the Scylla of a nationalistic neo-isolationism and the Charybdis of militaristic *Realpolitik*.

But — apart from the festering sore of Vietnam — it is here at home that President Nixon is likely to face his gravest problems during his second and final term of office. It is here that he will be confronted with issues that he ducked altogether during the campaign but that cannot be ignored in the next four years.

Hidden difficulties in the economy, for example, have been concealed by enormous budget deficits and somewhat relaxed credit; but now that the election is over the time for reckoning is near. Higher taxes are all but inevitable, irrespective of campaign promises. The military budget will have to be brought under control, which is almost a contradiction in terms. Welfare reform is a must; it will be incumbent on the President to revive his former innovative leadership on this issue.

Education is far more in need of aid from the Federal Administration than any or all of the big businesses or special interests that have been receiving it through subsidies, guarantees or other forms of favoritism. The problems of the inner cities — far beyond the scope of revenue-sharing — must be genuinely tackled at the highest level of government. The President must face the busing issue, which is another form of the racial issue, with honesty and forthrightness. The same may be said of such other central social and political questions as crime and "law and order"; the sanctity of privacy and of individual rights; freedom from political prosecution and similar forms of governmental tyranny.

* * *

Mr. Nixon and Mr. Agnew could do no better during these next four years than to heed the voice of an American President who stated in his inaugural address:

"For its part, Government will listen. We will strive to listen in new ways — to the voices of quiet anguish, the voices that speak without words, the voices of the heart — to the injured voices, the voices that have despaired of being heard.

"Those who have been left out, we will try to bring in.

"Those left behind, we will help catch up.

"For all of our people, we will help set as our goal the decent order that makes progress possible and our lives secure. . . . The lesson of past agony is that without the people we can do nothing — with the people we can do everything."

Those words were spoken by Richard M. Nixon on Inauguration Day, 1969. They are even more appropriate today than they were then.

As is evident from yesterday's balloting, Mr. Nixon has the vast majority of "the people" with him; now he has the mighty responsibility and the profound obligation to "do everything": to bring this country together again in unity, in freedom and in peace. We deeply hope that he will succeed.

© 1972 by The New York Times Company. Reprinted by permission.

The Boston Globe
Boston, Mass., November 9, 1972

President Richard M. Nixon has emerged from Tuesday's election with probably more support from the people than any of his predecessors ever obtained in popular elections. And in this fact there is a great hope for the nation's future.

He knows, and he said so at the end of his last campaign that he called "the very best one of all," that he was reelected not only by Republicans but by "those millions of Democrats and independents who supported us." And he pledged himself during the next four years to "work for all Americans . . . and not for one group against another."

There seems every good reason now why he will do this. His last campaign is over, and what may have seemed to him to have been political considerations at times in the past four years can be weighed in another light during the next four.

To be sure, the nation's will as expressed at the polls may seem to some to be contradictory, since the Democrats retained control of the lower House of Congress and increased by two their majority in the Senate. In a sense the President's coattails turned out to be short sleeves.

But this may mean only that the people were voting on the issues and on the particular candidate, rather than on the basis of the party label. It all says a great deal for the independent-mindedness of a very large number of voters.

There was indeed a mandate in Tuesday's results. We see it as one to make peace in an honorable way. So, we believe, does President Nixon, who will have the support of all for his statement that world peace is "bigger than whether we are Democrats or Republicans."

What the people have said most clearly, perhaps, is that they have more faith in the President's call for a healing process than in a call for uncharted change.

This impressive demonstration, it is to be hoped, will make it easier for the country to be brought together again, and for trust to be restored. The President is now much more free to be his own man as well as the nation's, and in this endeavor, all will wish him well.

THE KANSAS CITY STAR
Kansas City, Mo., November 8, 1972

The critical question of the next four years was not answered yesterday, for on Nov. 7, 1972, the outcome was never in question.

Rather, it will be answered in the innermost thoughts of Richard M. Nixon as he interprets the landslide that was his almost for the asking.

To what purpose, now, will Mr. Nixon—in this hour of his greatest triumph—dedicate his "four more years?"

Will power renewed by this largest of public endorsements be power that can restrain itself? (Certainly it will be restrained by the make-up of the next Congress, which ideologically may be somewhat more friendly to the re-elected President but which, nevertheless, remains under Democratic control.)

Yet leadership, once and then twice bestowed, has a way sometimes of misreading the intent of those who bestow it. In this instance, there is at least the chance that Mr. Nixon might be so tempted, and if he is, the second four years may be a disappointing anticlimax to the successes of the first four years.

We trust that this will not be the case. After all, Richard Nixon, tasting now this tremendous and totally personal triumph, is freed of the pressures of presidential politics. If, as some charged and not without justification, the almost invisible Nixon of the campaign was a negative sort of leader, seeking re-election to some degree on the basis of what he opposed, there is now the opportunity for a positive kind of leadership to emerge. We believe it will, for Richard Nixon is a man with a deep sense of personal destiny, and the fulfillment of that destiny in the next four years will carve his place in the history of the presidency.

Yet in the beginning, or in the second beginning, if you will, there are doubts that need to be eased. Mr. Nixon must know—we all must know—that this campaign has left its scars on the nation. The healing of such wounds is a quality of leadership now needed so badly.

To Restore Credibility

It was, obviously, a campaign that raised questions about the credibility of both sides. In so far as the charge pertains to Senator McGovern, we need pursue it no further. For the senator, who tried so manfully in all his idealism, is now of the past. (Although we would not, as some may be tempted to do, bury his Democratic party on this morrow of its defeat.) But Mr. Nixon, very much of the future, will need to think now of his own credibility. And seek ways to restore that part of it which may have been lost in his campaign.

To do this, the re-elected President will need, in the not too distant future, to speak openly on such matters as Watergate and the distressing techniques of modern American politics that reflect no credit on party leaders.

He will need to follow through energetically on the matter of a Vietnamese cease-fire, for by no means could anyone find, in yesterday's outcome, a mandate for four more years of war—war of any sort—in Southeast Asia.

He will need, very early in his second term, to speak out to the alienated of our society, particularly to the minority groups with whom, quite frankly, he has failed to identify effectively.

He will need, it seems to us, to address himself to some of the points raised, not without purpose, by his opponent: To a fairer tax system, for example; to the control of military spending, and to the development of not only a more just but a more open society.

And he will need, not tomorrow but *today*, to substitute for the negativism of his campaign a positive program to help America come closer to realizing her dream as she moves closer to her 200th birthday anniversary.

A Record to Build On

That Mr. Nixon can, if he chooses, do these things, we have no doubt. Look back, if you will, on the accomplishments of the first four years which received the stamp of voter approval yesterday: To the evolving accommodation with Moscow and Peking, to the steady if sometimes frustrating disengagement in Southeast Asia, on the solid foundations of which the hope of a lasting peace seems now to rest.

Granted, the record at home is less brilliant. But Mr. Nixon's first administration is not without its high marks, and there can, in the second administration, be more. There can be, that is, if Mr. Nixon does not over-read yesterday's landslide, does not permit himself to drift into a negative period (or a period of retreat) as the nation deals with its pressing domestic and international problems in the next four years.

It is not our intention, on this morrow of the 1972 election, to seem negative about the future. Quite the contrary.

Soon, we will all shed the weariness of this campaign. Soon, we can at least hope, we will all begin to forget its bitterness. And soon, we trust, Richard M. Nixon, in the aftermath of his finest hour, will turn his attentions to those matters of urgent national priority that sometimes seemed to be forgotten in the months past.

Senator McGovern has conceded, graciously and in the tradition of the American political system. Richard Nixon has won, also in the tradition of the American system.

The sun, we noted, rose this morning, and it will tomorrow. There are questions to be answered; and there is work to be done. But there is in the White House a President who can answer the questions and do the work.

Mr. Nixon, in accepting his victory, has so pledged himself, speaking of a nation working together, in the next four years, toward the common goal of true peace in the world and the common, great goal of progress and prosperity at home. That, after all, is the real and awesome mandate of the Nixon landslide of 1972.

ARGUS-LEADER
Sioux Falls, S.D., November 8, 1972

Mr. and Mrs. Voter spoke decisively in the United States Tuesday—for President Richard Nixon and his policies.

The overwhelming vote for President Nixon undoubtedly stemmed from the voters' confidence that the first four years of his administration have set the nation on the road to peace. The President's handling of the Vetnam War, his initiatives with respect to Russia and the People's Republic of China and the trade breakthroughs he has made behind the Iron Curtain may be considered among the points that influenced voters.

Beyond that, the President's handling of the economic crisis from the time of the August 1971 wage-price freeze and the cooling of the country's emotions and troubles in the last four years contributed to his landslide victory. President Nixon's pragmatism in the presidency is a known quantity; what Sen. George McGovern of South Dakota offered was untried—and a change.

South Dakota voters parted company with their senator, whom they've elected four times, and stayed with President Nixon, whom they've favored as the South Dakota winner in four previous elections since 1952. The South Dakota voter, we are convinced, preferred President Nixon's approach in foreign policy and economic affairs to that of McGovern's.

The South Dakota voters also demonstrated their historical tendency to vote for the man instead of the party in choosing President Nixon on the national ticket and re-electing Gov. Richard Kneip and U.S. Rep. Frank Denholm, both Democrats. This same observation applies to the voters' choice of U.S. Rep. James Abourezk, a Democrat, to succeed U.S. Sen. Karl Mundt, and James Abdnor, a Republican, to take Abourezk's second district congressional seat.

The Democrats this year have elected more candidates to the statehouse, in both constitutional offices and the legislature, than they have for some years past.

In defeat, Senator McGovern spoke very well. Sixteen years ago he won his first term as South Dakota's first district congressman. Tuesday, he lost as his party's nominee for president. That is personal achievement of a high order, and something a South Dakotan may not do again for a long time to come.

The winners deserve their victories and the congratulations of the country. The job ahead is to translate the mandate at the polls to effective government on the state and national scene.

THE ATLANTA CONSTITUTION
Atlanta, Ga., November 8, 1972

We congratulate President Richard Nixon on an overwhelming victory at the polls in his bid for a second four-year term.

The magnitude of the landslide bore out what the major national polls had been saying for weeks. Most American voters quite simply felt that, on balance, Nixon was the better of two choices. Sen. George McGovern, a man who inspired the warmest, most dedicated devotion from a narrow band of followers, never succeeded in the campaign in projecting himself as a viable alternative in the minds of most voters.

The polls and the political indicators never showed that the Nixon-McGovern contest was even close. President Nixon, because of that, never chose really to hit the campaign trail. We understand the politics of that decision. It was a shrewd decision and probably helped boost the President's margin of victory. And it can be blamed in part on the failure of McGovern's candidacy ever to get off the ground. But this non-campaign must also be viewed as a lost opportunity, a lost chance for genuine national debate of a number of issues.

We have frequently applauded President Nixon's innovative foreign policy. That is his strong suit. His behind-the-scenes moving which culminated in his visit to mainland China must rank as one of the most creative diplomatic strokes in modern times. Even on Vietnam, that tragic war, there seems every reason to believe that a real ceasefire and peace settlement are close.

Yet, on domestic issues, there are unresolved questions. The fierce need for welfare reform, for facing up to the plight of most major cities, the need for dealing with still high unemployment, with equal opportunities for all Americans in every field. To sum it up, President Nixon has a great opportunity to try to turn his landslide mandate into momentum for dealing with significant domestic problems. We hope he seizes that oportunity.

We wish Sen. McGovern well. He had bad luck and made some early bad decisions. But he inspired a rare kind of loyalty among some of the brightest and most idealistic Americans. It is clear that he is a man who cares for his country and for the issues affecting his country, though we disagreed with many of his specific stands. His voice will still be heard on issues of national moment.

The Star-Ledger

Newark, N.J., November 8, 1972

What had been widely regarded as a foregone conclusion is now political reality. Richard Milhous Nixon, the Republican incumbent, has been given a ringing mandate by the American voter to guide the destinies of this country for the next four years, a crucial period of dynamic adjustment and change as we move from a wartime basis to a peacetime production.

The Presidential campaign was largely undistinguished in either rhetoric or sharp, incisive issues that stirred the electorate. The choice has been made; it is clear cut and decisive — and it is now part of our political history. But there are pertinent issues that reveal themselves in the vote composite, the strong endorsement given to Mr. Nixon in his bid for re-election that warrants sober reflection.

There can be little doubt that the Republican standard-bearer benefitted to a considerable degree from the negative vote cast in yesterday's Presidential election, a substantial bloc of defecting Democrats disillusioned by the faltering, indecisive campaign conducted by Sen. George McGovern, a politician with integrity and deep spiritual reserve, but one who was unable to clearly focus on troubling issues that could have united Americans behind his candidacy.

* * *

SEN. McGOVERN was severely handicapped right from the outset of his campaign — a deep-rooted alienation of old-line Democrats by his zealous, single-minded tight group of supporters and the passions aroused by the staff laxity in the Eagleton misadventure, a poignant affair with disturbing human implications that were hurtful to Sen. McGovern.

The seeds of a political debacle appear, in retrospect, to have been implanted at this critical juncture. But that could be a simplistic generalization, too, for it should have been apparent even before this denouement that the Democratic nominee never really had achieved a broad base of support, that his primary triumphs were skillfully managed, with only scent margins of popular support separating him from other major candidates.

Unfortunately for Sen. McGovern, the primary tactical adroitness that marked his successful bid for his party's nomination was shockingly absent in the contest that counted. His campaign was concentrated on the war in Vietnam, an issue sharply undermined by the imminent prospect of peace, and the shabby Republican role in the Watergate political espionage. Evidently, this was not enough.

A more fertile area — persistent, endemic unemployment and chronic inflation — was not exhaustively plumbed by Sen. McGovern, a strategic inadvertence that may have proved costly in the end. In a historical sense, the voter's pocketbook is a personal gut issue of considerable consequence in a political campaign.

NOR DID MR. McGOVERN, for some unexplained reason, follow through during the campaign on his strong advocacy of a sweeping tax reform directed at establishing a more equitable formula of tax obligation for the American people.

These were, in a full sense, critical lapses in a campaign that could ill afford forfeiting any initiative or edge that had the potential of swinging sizable segments of electoral support. Also hurtful was the cynical characterization of Sen. McGovern as a radical who espoused collectivist doctrines; that was a completely phony issue.

As for the President, it was a campaign that was mainly non-participatory in a personal sense. Mr. Nixon used the influence and prestige of his high office with political deftness, standing above the clamorous campaign charges. It was frustrating for Sen. McGovern, who not only had his own tactical problems but the added handicap of an opponent who was wraith-like, if not non-existent.

It worked for Mr. Nixon; it didn't for Mr. McGovern.

But for Mr. Nixon — and for the country — the awesome problems still remain, casting long shadows on the future. The next four years could be crucial; they mark a dynamic turning point in any national commitment directed at resolving domestic problems that had to be deferred or curtailed because of the staggering drain of the war on our resources.

THE PRESIDENT has been a perceptive and innovative molder of foreign policy, but the problems closer to home require a massive re-ordering of priorities. Considerable energy and resources must be channeled into resolving the urban crisis, the disturbing shortage of housing, the growing paralysis of transportation, a long-troubled economy, and a moral climate distressingly eroded by mounting crime that has had the chilling effect of a counter-repressive reaction on civil liberties.

If Mr. Nixon views the electoral mandate given to him by the American in any lesser dimension, than he would have taken a flawed interpretation of the popular decision to extend his incumbency in the White House for another four years.

The San Diego Union

San Diego, Calif., November 9, 1972

Two days after the stunningly contradictory election of last Tuesday people of the United States of America still are scratching their heads in an effort to define a mandate.

Most attention centers on the fact that President Nixon's coattails did not assure a Republican majority in Congress, although he personally received a historic popular mandate.

Some pundits consider the President's electoral sweep as a purely personal victory—a public accolade for his excellent four years of stewardship.

Less charitable partisans insist that the Nixon landslide is not that at all, but a no-confidence vote against Senator McGovern.

Still another expert, the statistician and economist Louis Bean, insists that Democrat-dominated Congresses are a hand-maiden of the urbanization of America. He points out that during the Republican Administrations since 1868 the Democrats' control of the House has gradually risen from 30 to 55 per cent. In the Senate the Democrat majority has climbed from 15 to 55 per cent during the same era.

Among the most popular of the contemporary theories is that the growing public distrust of Congress has led a sophisticated electorate to opt for another check and balance in government. These cynics insist that more and more people are electing a Congress of one political faith and a President of another.

They use the classic example of 1956 when Dwight D. Eisenhower received 457 of the 531 electoral votes in a landslide election. However, Republicans did not gain a single seat in the Senate and lost two in the House.

There is some truth and some fantasy in each of these ideas.

By virtue of receiving over 61 per cent of the popular vote, President Nixon did indeed receive a political mandate that Congress simply cannot ignore. Adding to the weight of his political victory is the fact that his support cut across the sociological strata of the United States. As such, the vote on Tuesday put Republicans in a strong position for the 1976 election and gave President Nixon a powerful lever in Congress.

By the same token Congress itself will be more independent and volatile because President Nixon did not have long coattails, and because many old members either retired or were defeated.

The combination of an independent Congress and a popular President may not be exactly the checks and balances that the Founding Fathers had in mind in the 1700s.

Nevertheless, they are a comforting political fail safe in this era when events at home and abroad move so rapidly.

AKRON BEACON JOURNAL
Akron Ohio, November 8, 1972

The analysts will be arguing for months over the meaning of the new Nixon mandate, but the landslide proportions of it make at least one thing unmistakably clear:

Confronted with the choices available to them, the overwhelming majority of America's voters were in no mood for change.

The outcome should take one load off Richard Nixon's mind. From the ambiguities of a "minority presidency," he now moves into that select historical group of American presidents whose voter support was not merely decisive but truly huge: Harding, Franklin Roosevelt in 1936, Lyndon Johnson.

★

And yet the "no change" mood also seemed to extend to Capitol Hill, with voters willing to leave it dominated by the Democrats. Despite the size of Nixon's majority, his coattails appear to have been cut off at the waist.

In the Senate the Democrats appear to have netted two additional seats, bringing their dominance to a 57-43 split. In the process the voters ousted such Republican long-time stalwarts as Gordon Allott of Colorado, Jack Miller of Iowa, J. Caleb Boggs of Delaware and — perhaps the most surprising for Americans who find it hard to think of the Senate without her — Margaret Chase Smith of Maine.

In the House there will be some Republican gains, but they will leave the President's party, at best, some 23 seats short of a majority. Needing a gain of 41 seats, they had added 11 as this was written, and seven other contests were still in doubt.

★

It can hardly be argued that the landslide adds up to a positive endorsement of Nixon's program; he didn't offer any. It seems, instead, to be more a negative: A whopping majority of the voters couldn't see George McGovern as "presidential," and were more moved to fear and uncertainty than to sympathy by his changing and hazily perceived programs.

This "leave it all in place" decision, then, extends also to all the continuing unsolved problems: the peace that isn't yet; the welfare mess; the inequities in taxes; the still-persisting unemployment and the still-pushing inflation; the huge Federal deficits; the still-painful difficulties of racial integration in education and housing and employment.

Let's hope, now that there is less evident need for it at the White House, that we will see a cut-down of division-building rhetoric aimed more at mustering voter support than at solving problems — and in its place some genuine leadership to help us find workable ways to lessen our troubles.

The Hartford Courant
Hartford, Conn., November 8, 1972

The pre-election polls have now proved to be entirely right. President Nixon has won an unprecedented landslide victory in the nation's voting as had been predicted, returning him to the White House for the "four more years" which had become a campaign slogan.

The Presidential campaign itself has not been a particularly distinctive one. All candidates readily agreed that yesterday's election was one of the most important ones in recent American history. With a war still to be finally ended and with all the problems of a postwar era in the offing, there could be little doubt about their assessment and the four years that lie ahead.

President Nixon himself campaigned almost entirely over the airwaves, ever keeping in mind his current Presidential duties while looking forward to another term. This is certainly as it should have been. On the other hand it did not prevent him from making puissant speeches both on the accomplishments of his Administration and his aims as continuing President. That they were telling seems plain enough from the tremendous number of votes he has drawn.

Those who supported him had good reason to do so. As The Courant had occasion to recount in backing him for another term, President Nixon has achieved notable accomplishments in foreign and domestic affairs. By negotiations with Russia and China, he has reduced world tensions. He seems on the verge of doing what two Democratic predecessors failed to do — get Americans out of Indochina and leave the South Vietnamese in control of their own destiny. Even facing a Democratic Congress, he has been able to halt the rate of increase in the inflationary spiral he inherited, made a sound gain in spendable earnings, and seen his own version of revenue-sharing enacted.

Again, in Courant words, Mr. Nixon has shown the strength and strategy in foreign affairs, the realistic, pragmatic approach in domestic matters that afford a sound plan for the progress of this nation in the next four years to which he has been elected.

And Mr. Nixon himself, in a weekend speech, has further listed what he, "or any President," might well chose as ideal targets next: A world at peace, the elimination of race and sex discrimination here at home, a country free from fear, a country that is clean, healthy and economically prosperous, one that provides quality education for all, and one in which representative government will be strengthened and renewed at state and local levels.

These are "target" plans, as Mr. Nixon said, some that cannot be completed in four years, but all of which can be pressed. On Mr. Nixon's record, it became plain yesterday that millions of anxious American voters both subscribe to these goals and believe Mr. Nixon, as President re-elect, can start them greatly on the way.

The Courant hopes, too, that Mr. Nixon will return to the policy of "an open administration" he set forth after his election in 1968 — an administration that answers questions in regularly scheduled press conferences and listens to new ideas, thereby bolstering public credibility in the legislation he believes necessary and desirable for this nation.

The country has now reaffirmed its faith in the Presidency of Richard Nixon. The job to be done, though he heads it, cannot be done by him alone. He will need the aid of an intelligently cooperative Congress. Whether his election will make it more Republican, more politically balanced, we have yet to learn. He will need the aid of every citizen who believes in this country, aid that can be shown in setting aside partisanship for the mere sake of politics now that the election has been decided. The years ahead will not be easy, but they can be made easier if we give uncommon effort to our common goals. Let us begin by wishing Mr. Nixon Godspeed as he prepares to carry on.

THE BLADE
Toledo, Ohio, November 8, 1972

BY NO stretch of the imagination can one deny that Richard Nixon rolled up an impressive landslide triumph over Sen. George McGovern. It was a total victory — one of the most impressive sweeps in history — except in Lucas County and a few other areas where the senator won.

But it was not an all-encompassing mandate, as it will no doubt be interpreted in the days ahead, in the sense that it implies a clear authorization by the electorate for Mr. Nixon to carry on in the next four years as he has in his first term. It is not that sort of broad mandate for two reasons. First, the voters clearly showed that they were not embracing the Nixon policies and promises by maintaining Democrats in control of Congress. The Nixon coattails, in other words, were extremely short or, in most cases, nonexistent. Secondly, as millions of Americans were aware, the final decision to go along with Mr. Nixon came down to a choice between two candidates, neither of whom had any real attraction for most voters. It was, in other words, a choice of the lesser of two evils.

Nevertheless, Richard Nixon will occupy the White House for four more years, and the question looms of what they will portend for the nation. Who knows, actually, considering the President's capacity to reverse positions on any given issue depending upon how the political winds are blowing?

But if it means anything, Mr. Nixon himself spelled out what could be the broad and laudable outline for his second administration in his comments during his final radio address a few days ago. He set down 10 goals which he described as "guides on election day and every day throughout the next four years, no matter who wins." They were, of course, sweeping and general in nature—a world living in peace, and a just, secure, and prosperous nation in which "every human being, regardless of race or religion, age or sex, wealth or national origin, enjoys equal rights before the law and unlimited opportunity for realizing his or her fullest potential."

That is a large order, and it would be nice to believe that this next administration could achieve all or part of that. But hopes are dimmed in view of Mr. Nixon's penchant for moving almost in directly opposite directions during his first term in office.

His goals would be more inspiring if one could overlook his performance and could put more stock in an admonition uttered four years ago by former Attorney General John Mitchell, one of Mr. Nixon's closest associates. "Judge us not by what we say but by what we do," he said, in suggesting that the Nixon administration be measured not by rhetoric but by its realizations.

We—and the nation—are still waiting.

HOUSTON CHRONICLE

Houston, Tex., November 9, 1972

We congratulate President Nixon on his massive victory and wish both him and the country a truly fruitful four more years.

The campaign was bitter in many ways and this newspaper is delighted to note that when it ended the American spirit of generosity and good sportsmanship prevailed.

Both the President in his triumph and Sen. George McGovern in his defeat were graceful and appealed to the best that is in us. Their joint aspirations for peace and equality for all, and Nixon's call for domestic tranquility and economic betterment are soothing balm for a nation unsettled by months of passionate partisanship.

Nixon's overwhelming win certainly stemmed from a combination of factors. Looming large among them, it would seem, was the President himself after his trips to China and Russia and the detente atmosphere they produced. The popularity he achieved in this respect was enormous. But perhaps the biggest factor was George McGovern. The public considered him a radical and simply would not accept him.

Nixon was not able, despite his own strength, to pull in with him a Republican House or Senate. Traditionally even a popular president has difficulty here when enmeshed in state races hinging on so many different factors than the national race. This Republican administration-Democratic Congress leads us to expect the country will travel much the same road the next four years as it has the past four.

Many mandates can—and probably will—be read into the President's landslide. The clearest we see is that the American public is tired of being wrenched at, emotionally set upon, lectured for alleged evils and told it must endure traumatic and radical change for its own good.

The public has replied, in our opinion, that it will accept change, but only in an orderly and rational manner; that it rejects the canard so clearly implied that Americans have somehow become evil at home and abroad.

The American people have shown an infinite wisdom over the years to elect presidents who were men of their times, who best fitted the way the country needed to move and act in the broad perspective of history. We think they exercised such a judgment Tuesday.

Los Angeles Times

Los Angeles, Calif., November 8, 1972

The country has given President Nixon a vote of confidence. Now it is up to him to respond to this trust.

The first order of business is the ending of the terrible war in Indochina, an ending tantalizingly close, but not yet in hand. The one theme common to the candidacies of both the President and Sen. George McGovern was the theme of End the War; McGovern's strongest claim to the voters' support was that the war is not yet ended; Mr. Nixon's, that it is about to end. Now the election is past; no serious barriers can remain to the swift conclusion of one of this country's most grievous mistakes.

The war behind us, Mr. Nixon can devote his attention in foreign affairs to the initiatives he has under way. As in his first term in the White House, the control of nuclear arms is the most important of these endeavors. Phase 2 of the strategic arms limitation talks, which deals with offensive nuclear weapons, opens Nov. 21. It is of the greatest importance to the world that the United States and the Soviet Union agree to the limitation of offensive nuclear weapons, as they have agreed to the limitation of defensive nuclear weapons.

As the President has already indicated, the new openings to the Soviet Union in trade, and to China in diplomatic contacts and trade, will be continued and expanded. It is not likely that Mr. Nixon can furnish the American people with more foreign policy surprises like the approach to China. Rather, his principal task in his next four years will be the patient adjustment of U.S. policy to the requirements of a changing world power structure. Those adjustments will heavily involve economics, which is supplanting direct political power as the principal field of competition between nations. This nation is belatedly coming to understand that the economic arrangements between, say, the United States and Japan are immensely more important to the future of the United States than are the political arrangements in Indochina.

It is especially incumbent on the President to regularize American relations with the principal American allies. Only the United States can agree with the Soviet Union to limit nuclear weapons; only the United States can deliver a blow to the international monetary system like the Nixon shock of last year; but only in concert with other nations can the United States bring about that regularization of trade and mutual defense upon which depends the "generation of peace" of which the President speaks. In the past few years the Nixon Administration has neglected its relations with the allies, Japan especially; restoring mutual consultation is high on the list of priorities.

With the election over, too, the Administration can again press toward a settlement between Israel and the Arab nations. And, with the 21st century in mind, the United States must make a new effort with the other industrialized nations to assist the poor and populous nations of the third world.

It can be said that handling of foreign policy will be easier for the President, once the war is past, than the management of domestic affairs. His general competence in foreign affairs is matched by a certain bleak insensitivity on his part to some of the pressing needs of the country.

The essential task before the nation at home is to manage the economy so that it continues to expand steadily, and to manage social programs so that they offer maximum security and opportunity. The social goals of neither party can be met if the economy falters. The new Nixon Administration should, and probably will, selectively and carefully lift wage and price controls to return as soon as possible to free market conditions.

There is a serious question about what the President's own social goals actually are. On race, he has, as we have said before, let the country down; he has carried his opposition to busing to the point that he has tended not to reconcile but to set citizen against citizen. He will have no claim to greatness as a President unless he abandons on this matter the politically expedient course he has been taking and begins to talk with the country seriously and constructively about this yet unhealed wound in the heart of American life.

Some of the social needs of the country will be met only by the application of federal funds and federal direction of social programs. The President's proposals for welfare reform were good; he now has the opportunity to return to them. He has the opportunity and the obligation also to explore some of the more innovative ideas of his Administration in housing and education, and to come to grips with a plan to provide adequate health insurance and health care for all. These programs, like the existing social efforts, require money; the President will have to take a sharp look at the defense budget, and will have to entertain the idea of a tax increase, if he is not to cut these domestic programs below acceptable levels.

Administration of domestic affairs, though, is more than programs: it is leadership, and on this score, as we said even while recommending the re-election of the President, his record is disquieting. The people cannot long tolerate his first Administration's narrow view of civil liberties, its chilling attacks on the press and on dissent. And, as we have also said, his claim to leadership will be tarnished unless he moves swiftly to clarify the facts arising from the Watergate case, and to erect impassable barriers between his Administrations and interests that would seek to influence it by gifts of money. In government there is no substitute for honesty and candor.

In foreign affairs, the prospect of four more years of Mr. Nixon is good. In domestic affairs, he is challenged to provide the kind of enlightened, progressive leadership the country must have if it is, in every way, to prosper.

Detroit Free Press

Detroit, Mich., November 9, 1972

THERE MAY never have been another presidential election like it. Richard Nixon scored a victory to rank among the all-time greatests, but the Democratic Party gained two seats in the Senate, one governorship and lost only a handful in the House to retain healthy majorities across the board.

In previous landslides, such as the defeats of Alf Landon in 1936 or Barry Goldwater in 1964, the President managed to carry Congress along on his coattails. This time there were practically no coattails. It was, as GOP Chairman Robert Dole said, "a personal triumph for Mr. Nixon, not a party triumph."

Possibly more accurately, it seems to us, is that the result was a personal disaster for George McGovern, a disaster which started in the snows of New Hampshire and was foreordained in the steam heat of Miami Beach. The campaign issues he used to win his party nomination were the same issues which defeated him before the national electorate.

This should—but probably won't—tell us something about the value of national primaries. As Sen. McGovern recognized, he was running at one edge of the political spectrum and George Wallace at the other. Between them, from early March into June, they successfully cut to ribbons the Democratic hopefuls in the middle. When Gov. Wallace was shot and his supporters turned to Mr. Nixon, it was George McGovern against the field.

If that assured his nomination, it also assured his defeat. No matter what he did after Miami Beach, he was unable to convince the voters that he was not a radical, and the American voter doesn't want a radical. As one McGovern adviser analyzed the returns, at a time of such rapid social change as now, American voters are clinging for security to traditional politics. "We're in a period of political conservatism while social change accelerates."

The lesson, he went on, is that "political change is going to have to come from centrists."

Certainly in contrast to Sen. McGovern, Nixon was a centrist, and the voters made the obvious choice. Whether they approve of any particular Nixon program, or even like the man, they feel secure with him. They want few changes and they want those small. And they showed it by giving him an overwhelming margin while keeping Congress safely in Democratic hands.

Mr. Nixon, it seems to us, was well aware of this in his gracious victory statement and in his remarks later to thousands of his supporters.

"This will be a great victory depending on what we do with it," he said. "In other words we win elections not simply for the purpose of beating the other party or the other person but to get the opportunity to do good things for our country.

"It was a great victory but the greater the victory the greater the responsibility, the greater the opportunity."

All of us can agree with the goals he has set out for the next four years: Peace in the world and "new progress and prosperity which all Americans deserve."

Mr. Nixon does not have the "new American majority" he sought, but he does have a new, if personal, mandate for four more years. He can use it to build the new American majority, which he has not really tried yet to do.

This means peace in Southeast Asia as his first order of business. It means turning to, and conquering, domestic problems, which include high on the list racism and the deterioration of our cities. They include tax and welfare reform, equalization of educational opportunities, an end to divisiveness, a rejuvenation of human rights and human dignity and a restoration of confidence in government.

We join all Americans in wishing him well.

WINSTON-SALEM JOURNAL

Winston-Salem, N.C., November 9, 1972

IT WILL take many a day for the dust to settle, but one thing is as clear as the air after a blizzard: the presidential election of 1972 was a tremendous personal triumph for Richard M. Nixon.

Only 10 years ago, after his defeat for the governorship of California, Mr. Nixon counted himself out of political contention. But on Tuesday he did the incredible, rolling up what is probably the biggest majority in presidential history.

People who do not admire Mr. Nixon may argue that he had a weak opponent, the weakest the Democrats could have fielded. True enough, but the President didn't need a weak opponent to form his majority. He correctly sensed what an overwhelming number of the American people wanted, and he organized his campaign to identify himself with their wishes.

Then why did the Democrats hold both houses of Congress and even increase their majority in the Senate?

This will take a lot of analysis and explaining. But one thing can be said now: They brought along some attractive new candidates to run alongside their solid old favorites.

So for the next two to four years we will continue to have ''divided government.''

This is no catastrophe. We had divided government under Presidents Truman and Eisenhower as well as under Mr. Nixon during his first term, and the wheels of government kept turning.

Actually, it is highly desirable that there should be some cogent checks and balances on the Nixon presidency. During his first term Mr. Nixon showed too great a disposition to extend the war-making powers of the president, too little appetite for curbing free-wheeling generals and too little moral repugnance to under-the-table and over-the-transom deals with questionable corporations and groups. It is high time for Congress to make better use of its constitutional prerogatives and to make sure that the presidential excesses or lapses of the past four years do not continue.

Given the results of the election for both the presidency and the Congress, there is good reason for the two sides to respect each other and to work constructively on the issues which, it must be said, received very little constructive discussion during the campaign.

ARKANSAS DEMOCRAT

Little Rock, Ark., November 8, 1972

George McGovern is really to blame for his own downfall. It was he who insisted on those quotas for delegates, which produced a convention that was representative of a demographic formula but little else. Certainly it was not representative of the Democratic Party because it did not include Southern conservatives, organized labor, hyphenated Americans, and local, lifetime Democratic leaders and givers.

When his unusual group got together in Miami Beach in July, it naturally nominated its godfather, George McGovern. But yesterday it could not elect him. As a matter of fact this new coalition of Democrats was able to deliver only Massachusetts and the District of Columbia — the worst defeat given any Democratic nominee since Horace Greeley carried only six states in his race against President Grant exactly 100 years ago. Incidentally, 1872 and 1972 happen to be the only years that a majority of Arkansans have ever voted for a Republican for president.

What will happen now, of course, is that the Democrats finally will realize that they went too far with their quotas, and, starting probably no later than the National Democratic Committee meeting next month, the old party leaders will move quickly to bring all Democrats back into the party, pausing only to wave goodby to Senator McGovern as he disappears into oblivion.

Let us be totally honest about it: George McGovern was not presidential timber. Neither his record nor his potential qualified him for the nomination. Not once — neither 22 months ago when he started his campaign nor in his concession statement last night — did he show the brilliance or the fire in the belly that would qualify him as a national leader. The reverse was true. His associations, his backtracking, his name-calling, his socialistic impulses and his self-righteousness made you want either to get ahead of him or to change lanes but certainly not to follow him.

On the other hand, President Nixon, while admittedly not a man you want to clasp to your bosom, at least had a good record as President. He is an efficient manager, and all Americans secretly admire that. He has proven that he knows more about foreign affairs than any President since Franklin Roosevelt. And he is smack in the mainstream of American thought on subjects like busing, patriotism, law and order and virtue. And so he was elected by the greatest margin of any American President. Not bad for a guy who just 10 years ago was defeated miserably when he ran for governor of California.

We are pleased that Arkansas joined 48 other states in voting for him. We have tried party loyalty, and, by going for George Wallace in 1968, we experimented with being a renegade. Frankly, neither stance has advanced us to a position of leadership among the states. So maybe it's time Arkansas tried switch-hitting. We'll get more respect when the Democrats start to welcome Southerners back.

Even though few if any of our Republican candidates were elected, we were proud to see that most of them got a lot of votes. Also, we were glad that some predominantly black areas gave as much as 20 per cent of their votes to Mr. Nixon. Frankly, we think it is better if neither people nor states are taken for granted.

Nixon's Landslide

Anchorage Daily Times
Anchorage, Alaska, November 8, 1972

FOUR TIMES Alaskans have voted in a presidential election.

On three of those occasions the 49th State has given its three electoral votes to Richard M. Nixon.

The first time Alaska voted in a presidential election was in 1960, a year after statehood. Mr. Nixon, campaigning against John F. Kennedy, made an 11th hour, election eve trip to Anchorage — and by the narrowest of margins he carried the state, but lost the nation.

The vote in Alaska was 30,953 for the ticket of Nixon and Henry Cabot Lodge, and 29,809 for Kennedy and Lyndon B. Johnson.

In 1964, the battle was between President Johnson and Sen. Barry Goldwater — and Alaskans helped the incumbent Democrat to a smashing landslide, casting 44,329 votes for LBJ to only 22,930 for his Republican challenger.

MR. NIXON again was the candidate in 1968, and by a slender margin he again carried Alaska as he won the presidency in a razor's-edge victory over Vice President Hubert Humphrey. The Alaska balloting produced 37,600 votes for Nixon, 35,411 for Humphrey.

And then came Nov. 7, 1972 — yesterday, and the biggest victory of all for Richard Nixon, both in the state and nationwide.

While carrying 49 states and losing only Massachusetts and the District of Columbia, the President rolled over Sen. McGovern in Alaska — with returns in the early morning hours showing a 41,809 total for Nixon to 24,362 votes for the South Dakota Democrat, a 58.5 per cent total for Nixon that was expected to hold steady through the completion of the count.

AS MR. NIXON'S triumph was no surprise nationally, it likewise was the expected thing in Alaska.

Alaska knows President Nixon, it is familiar with him. He campaigned hard throughout the territory when the statehood battle was being fought, he was President Dwight Eisenhower's vice president when statehood was won, he has been here many times as a private citizen and as President.

Not only that, of course, he stands with Alaskans on things that matter in this far northern land.

He has supported and fought for the pipeline. He has supported the military establishment and the defense requirements of the country at large.

He has traveled to and from Alaska, to Asia and the Far East; he has opened avenues for peace in a huge section of the world close to Alaska's sprawling boundaries.

FROM THE very start of the campaign, President Nixon was a winner in Alaska.

The Democratic effort, faltering from the start, was dealt its final rushing blow when Mr. McGovern came out in Seattle with a nonsensical statement that the trans-Alaska oil pipeline should be delayed while a study was made of hanging the pipe from pylons stretched across the tundra.

That wiped out all of the frantic efforts by campaign workers and Democratic leaders to wash Sen. McGovern's anti-pipeline stand and make it somehow appear to be favorable to the project.

MR. McGOVERN'S credibility was destroyed by his own words, and the presidential election was really over in Alaska from that time on — despite an off-base assessment somebody provided to the Christian Science Monitor, which then came out with a survey showing that McGovern had a chance to carry the 49th State.

As a result, the McGovern forces spent a lot of money here in a last minute television blitz, hoping to swing the state to the Democratic column.

It was money down the drain, good dollars after bad, as Alaskans gave their presidential election to Richard Nixon — a man they have known since those territorial days of so long ago.

THE MILWAUKEE JOURNAL
Milwaukee, Wis., November 8, 1972

It is Richard Nixon's moment to savor. The persevering political pro who always had trouble winning on his own will finally go into the presidential record books as one of the biggest winners ever.

Now all Americans join a devastated foe, George McGovern, in wishing Nixon well in the pursuit of peace, prosperity, justice, unity and the other lofty goals that he has set for himself and the nation. None can quarrel with the objectives.

Some speculate that such a landslide can bring out the best in Nixon. Given the constitutional limit on a third term, it is said that he can concentrate on his place in history and fret much less about partisan advantage. Others worry about a smashing victory encouraging insensitivity in office. One thing seems fairly clear: However awesome the vote totals and sweet the personal triumph, there are few signs of a massive ideological shift to Republicanism. Congress remains firmly Democratic, with Republicans losing ground in the Senate and making only a limited gain in the House.

In his own race, it appears that Nixon benefitted from an essentially negative choice. Many voters, according to pre-election polls, turned to him because they perceived his opponent as a less inspiring alternative — too "wishy-washy," a bit too "radical" or what have you.

This is not to detract from Nixon's adroit campaign. Never mentioning McGovern once by name, he was quick to scoop up leaderless Wallace legions, cultivate disenchanted Democrats, magnify administration achievements, soft pedal failures, dodge the shadow of scandal and keep his future plans cautiously vague and thus not easily assailed. In a successful effort to project McGovern as part of the nation's problem rather than part of the solution, Nixon hit at "amnesty," "bussing" and the "welfare ethic." Nixon was able to dominate the political center, stressing moderate change within the comfortable framework of continuity.

McGovern, who dreamed of building a new political coalition, helped Nixon immeasurably with a heavy evangelistic style that failed to stir, with alienation of traditional elements in the Democratic Party, with stumbling over Eagleton and economic policy. McGovern raised many of the right questions, battled tirelessly and showed courage in adversity, but he obviously misjudged the national mood — or at least was unable to articulate the need for some rather drastic changes in a convincing, nonthreatening way. In the end, McGovern himself became the major issue.

For Nixon, the urgencies of office will bore in swiftly. There is still the horrid war in Vietnam to end, and related wounds at home to heal. The Watergate affair must be cleared up, for Nixon's own sake as well as the nation's. There is the challenge of the economy with the competing demands for growth without wild inflation, high unemployment, massive federal deficits or environmental damage. Taxes and tax reform are issues that will not go away. Likewise the unfinished business of the 1960s — racial injustice, poverty, inadequate schools, faltering health care and other perplexities — must still be faced more squarely.

Campaigning in 1968, Nixon once declared: "If this country isn't good enough for all of us, then it isn't good enough for any of us." Let this now be his standard, and that of the loyal opposition, in the days ahead.

HERALD EXAMINER
Los Angeles, Calif., November 9, 1972

More than anything else, the tremendous personal victory scored by Richard M. Nixon in Tuesday's voting proves how deeply concerned the average American citizen is with preserving his democratic heritage of freedom with responsibility.

The landslide can by no means be interpreted as an outpouring of love for a beloved President. It was, essentially, an overwhelming recognition and reaffirmation of the traditional values Nixon represents.

The President has provided the nation with four years of strong, experienced and temperate leadership whose allegiance to traditional values is unquestioned.

This is what paid off at the polls. When the showdown came the American voters turned out to turn thumbs down a challenger who — no matter how personally sincere — offered little but faith in untested and extremist ideals.

The American people, they demonstrated, are overwhelmingly anxious for peace — but not at the cost of surrender to enemies who respect only strength. They want security and justice at home — but not at the cost of further compromise with those whose idea of security and justice is more handouts and unearned privileges.

George McGovern failed in his ivory tower crusade because he underestimated the basic common sense, the basic pride and the basic patriotism of his countrymen. They are proud of their country. He spoke millions of words which convinced most of his compatriots that he is not.

Tuesday's record turnout of voters belied the predictions of those who thought the average citizen was selfishly apathetic about his nation's future. The average citizen has proven once again that he cares very deeply indeed — and once again that promises to him are no match for the hard-headed and responsible kind of performance he respects.

The Greenville News
Greenville, S.C., November 9, 1972

The American people have given President Nixon an unmistakable mandate to continue his pragmatic policies of pursuing lasting, just peace in the world and a return of domestic policy-making and financial power from Washington's bureaucracy to state and local governments. Mr. Nixon has won a tremendous personal victory.

The overwhelming vote given the President also is a clear rejection of Senator George McGovern's proposals for unilateral disarmament and more drastic change at home, with emphasis upon increased Washington control of American life.

It is equally clear that the electorate has not rejected the Democratic party which has been largely in control of American affairs for four decades. Democrats retain control of both Houses of Congress, increasing their Senate strength unexpectedly with upsets in several states.

The net effect of the presidential and congressional voting is rejection of the radical change image projected by Senator McGovern and the "new politics" crowd which seized control of the Democratic convention and national party machinery. All across the nation Democratic congressional candidates won by divorcing their candidacies from the presidential race.

The President probably can count on congressional support for his foreign policy and national defense positions. Americans have made crystal clear their rejection of military weakness in a still-dangerous world.

President Nixon will have a rougher time with his domestic program. It will be touch and go on many key issues. Some of the fighting over many appealing projects will be rough.

The first order of business, now that the election is over, is to settle the Vietnam situation by ending American participation without sacrificing the country's basic commitment to the principle of self-determination in Indochina. Hopefully that can come about within a matter of weeks.

Then the country can get on with the business of pursuing worldwide peace and eventual disarmament and of coming to grips with numerous pressing domestic problems. Mr. Nixon's tremendous victory has helped to clarify the basic desires of the American people regarding those problems.

The Chattanooga Times
Chattanooga, Tenn., November 9, 1972

President Richard Nixon's second term in the White House has been assured by majorities of heroic proportions.

Mounting returns from across the nation, as of this writing, indicated his share of the popular vote in Tuesday's general election would run somewhere between 60 and 65 per cent of the total. The electoral vote sweep for Mr. Nixon was shaping up as a landslide of even greater intensity.

Sen. George McGovern, the Democratic nominee, seemed unlikely to carry more than one or two states with fewer than a score electoral votes.

The results were surprising, if at all, only in the margin of victory for the President.

Mr. Nixon has become the respository of the hopes of a vast majority of American voters, despite the fears of a great many who cast their ballots for him. Sen. McGovern simply was rejected as a candidate of presidential caliber.

The truth seemed to be that the American people were, as individual voters, sufficiently appeased by the contradictory elements in Mr. Nixon's record and wary enough of Sen. McGovern's liberal image to be cleansed of any desire to make a change.

The Vietnamese War, which many had thought would prove a burden for the President, faded as an issue as the GIs returned and a peace agreement appeared to be only a matter of days. Many of those who remembered the withdrawal of ground soldiers was accompanied—even made possible—by the heaviest bombing attacks in the history of the world would not accept the McGovern pledge of an immediate end to hostilities, come what may.

Complaints of the high cost of living were damped by the assertion that inflation was "slowing down," and the generally unpopular idea of wage and price controls made acceptable by declarations they provided "the only way out," even if they did seem to work unevenly for the profit maker and the wage earner.

Credible evidence of campaign irregularities, ranging from government favors coincidental with big donations to the most reprehensible sort of political espionage, was brushed aside as of no importance. Murder, rape and assaults rose, but because less severe crimes were less numerou, the boast of safer streets seemed justified by the gradually declining rate of climb of all reported criminal acts.

Restrictions on personal liberties became attacks on permissiveness, and neglect of urban and social problems were made to appear needed economies.

We do not regret our support of Sen. McGovern and his major objectives. Neither can we forget the record on which President Nixon has won a second term. The victory was that of a consummate politician.

He has now the mandate he sought. Our deepest hope is that he will use it to give substance to his words. In those actions he takes for the best interest of the public, we shall support him without fail, for he remains the President of all Americans.

THE DAILY HERALD
Biloxi, Miss., November 8, 1972

The 1972 campaign for the presidency of the United States lacked suspense and excitement, but even without those elements of political glamor it posed a momentous decision for the nation's electorate.

The stakes were high. The candidates gave the voters clear choices in their approaches to attaining world peace and managing the domestic economy. In overwhelming numbers, the American people endorsed the programs of President Nixon over those offered by Senator George S. McGovern.

Mr. Nixon's re-election had been widely predicted. The issues, with few exceptions, seemed to be weighted heavily in his favor.

First in importance was the war in Vietnam. The President and his aides appear to have accomplished a settlement of that tragic affair that can soon be concluded without the stain of political charges. Senator McGovern sincerely believed that the war could be ended by simply pulling out of Southeast Asia. Mr. Nixon took a longer view that envisioned arrangements for the safety of our South Vietnamese allies and commitments for an enduring peace in all of Asia. The problem of peace in Vietnam has been debated for ten years. Doubtless the debate will continue. But the hard facts seem to be that a comgination of diplomacy in Peking and Moscow, Vietnamization of the ground war, harbor blockades, and supply destruction by air has brought us finally to the point where an end is in sight.

On the domestic front, despite relatively high unemployment, the state of the economy wasn't of much help to the Democratic party's cause.

President Nixon managed to pump up the economy by imposing price and wage controls, against the advice of his political counsellors, and began a reform of the international monetary system that eventually will strengthen the dollar. And despite an increasing federal deficit, the rate of inflation has been curbed.

The issues of pocketbook and peace, in the judgment of voters around the country, were apparently on Mr. Nixon's side.

It was a bitter campaign with many charges of "political immorality" against the Administration. The divestiture of assets of ITT by the Justice Department was accepted when it first occurred as a legitimate blow against the big conglomerate. Its stock went down 12 points. But later when it was learned that ITT had offered the San Diego Convention Bureau $200,000 to help finance the GOP convention (and also advertise ITT-controlled Hilton hotels) the issue suddenly came to be viewed as a "scandal." The Russian wheat sale was also supposed to be a scandal until an audited report from Cargill, Inc., showed it lost about $6.6 million. False accusations were widely broadcast in both cases.

What remains to be explained from the welter of charges is the attempt to steal secrets from the Watergate headquarters of the Democratic party. We hope the Administration will not only cooperate in a continuing investigation, but will take a strong hand in demanding a complete exposure of all that was involved.

Such a forthright step would help unite a nation that has been torn by doubt and skepticism by a hard-fought and sometimes bitter campaign. There are political wounds that need healing. The nation's confidence in its structure of government must be restored.

Oakland Tribune
Oakland, Calif., November 8, 1972

The nation's voters yesterday made it overwhelmingly clear they prefer to continue traveling the cautious middle ground of President Richard M. Nixon rather than venture into the uncharted seas of radical change advocated by Sen. George McGovern.

It was a monumental personal victory for Mr. Nixon, who now becomes only the fifth Republican President — after Lincoln, Grant, McKinley and Eisenhower — to win two terms in the White House.

Mr. Nixon's was a low key campaign, one free of strong rhetoric and wild promises. He, essentially, chose to stand on his accomplishments of the past four years.

He had ended America's ground combat role in Vietnam, he had achieved a major breakthrough in relations with mainland China and the Soviet Union and he had stabilized an erratic domestic economy. The social upheaval which had been so common on our streets and campuses when he first took office had all but disappeared.

Yesterday's vote returns dramatically demonstrated that those achievements have won for Mr. Nixon the respect and confidence of a large majority of Americans. They were sufficiently satisfied with his performance as President to give him the "four more years" he asked for.

Senator McGovern apparently thought he detected a widespread dissatisfaction throughout the land which simply didn't exist. While respecting the South Dakota senator's sincerity and idealism, Americans were not ready for $1,000 a year welfare grants, crippling defense cutbacks and a return to isolationism in world affairs.

By the size of his victory, Mr. Nixon would seem to have received a mandate from the voters. But a mandate for what? Rather than change, the President's mandate is for a continuation and fulfillment of the pledges he first made four years ago.

A final end to hostilities in Vietnam must be the first priority. The electorate has every right to expect the President to make good on the dramatic Administration announcement in the closing days of the campaign that "peace is at hand."

Certainly the President can interpret yesterday's election results as a vote of confidence for his history-making achievements in the conduct of foreign affairs. The nation will expect him to continue improving communications and relationships with the world's major powers while still maintaining a strong national defense.

On the domestic scene, the voting majority yesterday could have voted for a radical change in the direction Mr. Nixon has taken. But it didn't. The option available was for more welfarism, for a return to permissiveness in judicial appointments, for increased federal spending and paternalism.

For the most part, those were the policies of the '60s. They resulted in an America divided against itself as it had not been in this century. They were policies which brought little but unfulfilled expectations, tension and turmoil.

Yesterday's returns make it amply clear that the only change in direction the majority of Americans want is still the one which was made when Richard Nixon was first elected four years ago.

THE SUN
Baltimore, Md., November 9, 1972

President Nixon and the Democratic leadership in Congress have a mandate from the American people, we suggest, to come to terms with each other. Mr. Nixon's sweep of the country in Tuesday's elections was a tremendous personal victory and, by the same token, a personal disaster for Senator McGovern. A strong President in office was much more than a match for a weak Democratic candidate; as generally anticipated Mr. Nixon outpowered Mr. McGovern all around. And yet, while this was a landslide victory in conventional terms, it was not the kind of landslide this country has often experienced. Mr. Nixon did not carry with him a Republican majority in the House of Representatives, as might have been expected from the record books, and his party even lost ground in the Senate, with the Democratic leadership of which he has been conducting a running battle for almost four years.

On his performance record of the past four years, it seemed to us, Mr. Nixon deserved re-election. On the congressional performance record of the past four years, the Democratic leadership deserved a setback if not a loss of power. None the less the voters have given both the President and the Democratic majority in Congress a vote of confidence, so to speak. The pattern was not uniform around the country, but an essential fact is that a great many citizens voted for the Nixon-Agnew ticket and at the same time also voted for Democratic candidates for the Senate and the House. However this fact may be analyzed and dissected, its practical meaning has to be that the people expect the President and the Congress to work together for the common good.

An immediate issue, carrying over from the old Congress to the new, is a much tighter control over the federal budget as it now stands, as well as over spending policy in general. Mr. Nixon is right in insisting that spending during the current fiscal year must be restrained. His own $250 billion limit is generously large. Both political parties have a clear duty to cut back the deficit spending which has been feeding inflation. They have a clear duty, further, to see to it that the war in Indochina is promptly ended and to work together to help heal the scars left in Southeast Asia and in this country by this costly war.

Another important matter on which the leaders of both parties in Congress, along with the President, should be able to agree and to work together is welfare. The earnest effort to improve the system, begun by Mr. Nixon and given a big push months ago by the Ways and Means committee and the House, was allowed to dwindle and die in the Senate as the session was adjourning. The need for reform is obvious, workable improvements have been drafted, and the cost of the present system continues to increase.

The voters, re-electing a Republican President and a Democratic Congress on the same day, were obviously not demanding major changes in Washington. But we do not believe they were demanding a stalemate between the White House and the Capitol, or fruitless political bickering. They seemed to be saying, in short, to the political leadership in Washington: This is it for the next two years, so get on with it.

The Washington Post
Washington, D.C., November 9, 1972

We congratulate Mr. Nixon on his political masterpiece—a singular personal triumph—which gives him more than a little license to claim unqualified vindication both for past defeats and for present performance from an extraordinarily broad spectrum, regionally and in terms of party, age, and race. His New American Majority, never mind how durable or tightly glued together it may turn out to be, did the job he asked of it and did it handsomely. That said, it should come as no secret that we would have welcomed somewhat less vindication of Mr. Nixon, or at best vindication of a less sweeping nature. Putting it another way, we would have been heartened by a little more restraint and selectivity, in the message that poured in from the vote for President Tuesday night. We would not argue that it is not Mr. Nixon's right to make of such a "mandate" what he will. But the scope of his support and its lack of focus, when taken together with the second-level returns in the contests for Congress and for governorships, and with the President's own campaign strategy, do not tell us nearly enough in any conclusive way about what it is the President now has this broad new "mandate" to do or not to do—about just what was being deplored and what was being approved.

Was it, in the case at Vietnam, the President's promise of "peace" almost any minute now—or his tough emphasis on "no surrender"? Was it the sensible welfare reform program he had proposed to Congress, or the fact that he abandoned it in favor of a crude attack on welfare "chiselers"? Was it his relentless concentration on "anti-busing"—or his regular protestations of his dedication to racial non-discrimination and equal rights and job opportunities for blacks? Did most voters know of the excesses and improprieties and even alleged illegalities in his campaign—or did they know, but not believe it, or simply not care? Without knowing what message was really getting through, it is hard to know at this point exactly what messages were being sent back.

The answers, we suspect, will only be apparent over time. So we will forego instant analyses, except as to one or two conclusions that seem to us to be inescapable. It would, for example, be a mistake to do the easy, political thing, as it were, and explain it all away in terms of the lameness of the challenge that was raised. This entered into Tuesday's landslide, no doubt; but it is not enough to account for it as a vote *against* Senator McGovern, or his particular policies; it is only fair to infer that, in a quite *positive* way, people in huge numbers, and all across the country, like things pretty much as they are, and some of the reasons for this are set forth in two articles elsewhere on this page today.

For our part, as close readers of these columns may have deduced, we do not share the popular complacency, and still less a sense that the President's record entitled him to anything like so wholesale and seemingly indiscriminate a vote of confidence. We will not elaborate today on the grounds we find for disquiet in Mr. Nixon's indifference both to civil rights and civil liberties, in his absence of elemental compassion for the disadvantaged, in what he has done to desert fundamental values and principles. But we do not concede that Tuesday's vote has closed the books on these accounts. Rather we see in the totality of Tuesday's returns persuasive evidence of something less than a readiness on the part of the voters to give the President and his party the sort of seal of approval that enabled Franklin D. Roosevelt and Lyndon B. Johnson, in comparable landslides, to sweep their party along with them.

And beyond that, we see in Mr. Nixon's "mandate" an opportunity for him to make a virtue of its ambiguity—to draw from it the support he needs to pursue his worthy quest for "a generation of peace" in the world, and to find in it reinforcement for a re-direction of his energies and the nation's resources to the urgent problems that await him at home.

ST. LOUIS POST-DISPATCH
St. Louis, Mo., November 8, 1972

What did the voters tell President Nixon in returning him to office by a historic landslide? The President declined to debate and presented no program during the campaign. In the interest of a huge popular vote for himself he refused to work for Republican Senate and House candidates lest he sacrifice some Democratic and independent ballots; so he has another Democratic Congress.

It was an extraordinary outcome for the unpopular head of a minority party, and by some criteria the mandate is disturbing. The voters were not repelled by the savage bombing of North Vietnam and, despite the lack of evidence that Mr. Nixon has finally come to grips with the basic problems of Indochina, they evidently accepted Henry Kissinger's assurance that "peace is at hand."

The people were not repelled by the Watergate scandal, which involved an attempt by Nixon partisans to sabotage the Democratic party and subvert the electoral process; the trail of guilt led right into the White House. They were not repelled by the denigration of the Supreme Court, the favoritism to big business, the assaults on civil rights and the press. In all these areas the Democratic candidate, Senator McGovern, appealed to the conscience of the American people, and it wasn't there.

Does this mean that Mr. Nixon's mandate is for four more years of the same? We are not so sure. The only hope Senator McGovern had was that the country was in one of its periodic moods for change, in a liberal direction. The mood instead appeared to be one of let well enough alone — we are not doing well but we are not doing so badly, either; let's just rock along for another four years.

Mr. Nixon's overwhelming popular vote and his unprecedented sweep of the entire South was due in part to an accident, the attempt on the life of George Wallace who polled more than 10,000,000 votes in 1968. There is no doubt that a significant portion of the votes Mr. Nixon inherited were racially-motivated, as exemplified in Administration exploitation of the phony busing issue. So it may be said that Mr. Nixon has a mandate to slow further the integration of blacks into the mainstream of society.

But there is perhaps more than race in the votes of the Southerners and hard-hats who turned to Mr. Nixon. Mr. McGovern's proposal to cut the swollen defense budget undoubtedly occasioned the fear of greater unemployment. High prices in the marketplace seems not to have turned the housewives away from the Administration in office; many voters obviously felt that even though Mr. Nixon was apparently bringing peace he would find a way to keep defense industries running.

We are not at all sure that the voters yesterday told Mr. Nixon they want four more years of the same. We doubt the country can very well stand four more such divisive years, and Mr. Nixon ought now to undertake policies that will give reality to the way he spoke of unity on election night. Indeed, he will need a good deal of unity in the nation if he is to cope with the domestic problems with which his Administration has temporized — the further decline of the cities, the necessity for higher taxes, welfare reform, the curbing of the military-industrial-congressional complex and the military budget, a greater regard for civil rights.

Since he cannot run for the White House again, and since as a practical matter he cannot transfer his appeal to Vice President Agnew or any other potential Republican presidential candidate in 1976, Mr. Nixon will be free in his next term to abandon divisive politics and bring the people together as he promised when he was inaugurated in 1969. We think many persons who voted for him, including millions of middle-of-the-road and conservative Americans genuinely worried that Mr. McGovern was simply not up to the presidency, hope that Mr. Nixon will exercise his unquestioned political skills in the interest of the general welfare.

With the vast majority of the people on record as supporting him, Mr Nixon is in an extraordinarily strong position to move the country forward. We hope he will view that as his mandate. In his China and Russian overtures, and in some domestic economic policies, Mr. Nixon has shown a commendable flexibility. He can if he will do what needs to be done, and if he does he can count on widespread support, and acclaim. The potential is unlimited.

The Birmingham News
Birmingham, Ala., November 8, 1972

The American people have spoken in unmistakable terms.

The nation went to the polls yesterday with possibly the clearest choice of direction it has had this century. Americans of many stripes opted for tested traditional values as enunciated by Richard Nixon during the past four years.

Undoubtedly some of the tremendous support President Nixon received must be put down to a repudiation of the social and political philosophies espoused by Sen. George McGovern and spokesmen for the so-called new politics.

But even historians will be hard put to find in the total popular vote any conclusion other than that Richard M. Nixon has received a full endorsement and mandate from the American people.

As the nation moves now to heal the birthing wounds that are a normal consequence of democratic renewal the tendency is to look searchingly toward the future.

Following naturally is the question: What course will President Nixon steer now that he has received the mandate, now that he has no more elections to win?

To the man who has been deeply tested and shaped by the political fires of both defeat and victory, the scope of his triumph is likely to be both sobering and a source of satisfaction. And while he works to make his country stronger and his party an effective majority he will reserve an inner eye for history and his niche in it.

His over-all commitments will not have changed: He will seek to match or exceed his considerable achievements in foreign affairs with a steady pressure for events that seem likely to bring a greater degree of world stability.

His domestic thrust will be toward creating a new sense of national equilibrium infused with a spirit of progress and refinement and revalidation of historic human values.

While seeking to lower the nation's profile abroad, he will seek to shape U. S. policy in terms of a five-sided world — the United States, Russia, China, Japan and the growing European federation — instead of in terms of American-Russian power. The evidence of the new five-sidedness of the world has grown increasingly since his visits to Moscow and Peking.

He will make determined efforts to increase American exports with a concomitant effort at home to boost productivity so that American goods can compete with cheaper and in many instances better-made foreign products. At the same time he will seek to draw clean lines between military and economic considerations, especially in the areas of U. S. foreign aid.

With a cease-fire in Vietnam and with neutral nations supervising a political settlement, he will focus attention on strengthening NATO with considerable pressure on European governments to bear a larger share of the financial and military burden.

At home President Nixon will probably move with less constraint in both economic and social areas, but he will be guided by the pragmatic considerations of what actually *can be* accomplished rather than by what he would *like to* accomplish.

Much in both these critical areas will depend on the President's already articulated goal of creating in the Congress a majority rooted in national needs rather than in narrow partisan goals. For such a majority to come into being, the administration will have to perform political acrobatics with all the attendant risks of falling from the highwire.

In seeking to solve the problems of inflation and unemployment, he will focus on measures to increase productivity — plant modernization, a better trained and a more technologically sophisticated labor force, with steady pressure to bring minorities into the mainstream.

On a selective basis he will seek for more effective restraints on government spending especially in areas which tend to push prices upward. Even defense spending will come under these selective restraints.

He will seek once again to inject into welfare philosophy pressures for moving trainable indigents into creative job situations that will gradually remove them from dependency rolls.

President Nixon is not a man given to fancy slogans and well-turned phrases. His rhetoric for the next four years is not likely to stray too far from the political pragmatism that is his seal. He will speak in terms of *real* accomplishment and of *realisticall vobtainable* goals.

Yesterday's vote is ample evidence that the President has the nation solidly behind him, and he will be the first to acknowledge as much: The big question is whether the Congress will interpret the vote as a clear command from the American people to get on with the job of helping make America the nation it is capable of being.

Only time and the tide of events can provide the answer to that question.

The Topeka Daily Capital
Topeka, Kans., November 9, 1972

President Richard M. Nixon's dream of a New American Majority became a rousing reality Tuesday and gave him a massive landslide-victory in his bid for re-election to a second four-year term.

In casting Sen. George S. McGovern aside with an almost back-of-the-hand attitude, American voters not only expressed solid satisfaction with President Nixon's administration, but also displayed deep doubts about McGovern's proposed programs and some of his more radical campaign workers.

It was, in a way, a national vote for the status quo. Not that no change is desired, but in the sense that the changes President Nixon has accomplished or has proposed are patently acceptable.

There are good grounds for considering that President Nixon won the election back in 1971 when he announced that he was going to Peking to talk face-to-face with Chairman Mao-Tse-tung and Premier Chou En-lai.

If it wasn't won that day, it was won when he added that he was going to Moscow for a head-to-head meeting with Kremlin leaders.

Both meetings were history long before election day, but their effects continue to bob up in the news. There has been an increase in trade with Red China and Russia and there will be more. Both Communist countries, supplying arms and food to North Vietnam, have urged Hanoi to agree to an end of the fighting in Indochina. And peace now is near.

Wage and price controls never are popular restrictions in this free-enterprise system, but the voters apparently did not find them overburdening.

Although President Nixon's huge vote reflected his growing popularity, it also included the product of McGovern's inept and often careless campaign. Voters preferred the low-profile tactics of the President to the constant, carping criticism by McGovern and R. Sargent Shriver, the Democratic vice presidential nominee.

Plagued from the first day by the Eagleton fiasco, McGovern never got on track. When he dumped Sen. Thomas Eagleton of Missouri from the ticket as his running-mate, McGovern sealed his doom not only nationally, but also in the Show-Me State.

By asking Eagleton's resignation because Eagleton had undergone psychiatric treatment, McGovern was, in effect, telling Missourians they had been duped into electing an unstable man as their lieutenant governor, attorney general and U.S. senator. President Nixon carried Missouri and Christopher "Kit" Bond, a Republican, became the first GOP governor to be elected in Missouri since 1940.

Some issues read correctly long ago by President Nixon were factors in the outcome of the balloting. He opposed legalization of marijuana, busing of school children to achieve racial balance, and favored allocating more money for police protection. The Gallup poll later showed these stands to be overwhelmingly popular.

California voters, often found to rush to liberal causes, voted against legalization of marijuana and busing of pupils to achieve racial balance. They also voted to reinstate the death penalty outlawed by the U.S. Supreme Court in certain instances.

President Nixon's massive vote did not carry other Republican candidates into office. There was a net loss of two in the U.S. Senate and a gain of only 12 in the House of Representatives. One House race still is in doubt. Republicans lost one governorship in the voting.

Absence of any discernible coattail effect in the election can be attributed to several factors.

The President made no particular effort to include the fortunes of other Republican candidates in his own campaign, and with party loyalties diminishing each election, it might not have made any difference if he had.

Voters are more willing than ever to split tickets and vote for candidates of their choice. Too, local issues and local circumstances usually have a greater influence on voter preferences than do presidential endorsements.

While the President will be faced for two more years by a Democratic Congress, his crushing defeat of McGovern certainly will command more attention in congressional halls, and his proposals will likely receive more and friendlier attention.

The President has said he wants to leave an imprint of responsible conservatism in his next four years in office. The voters have given him the opportunity in convincing style.

The Evening Bulletin
Philadelphia, Pa., November 8, 1972

In his stunning personal victory at the polls — more than a landslide, it was an avalanche — President Nixon has won what every occupant of the White House desires in seeking reelection and in fuller measure than most achieve.

It is a spectacular vote of confidence from his fellow citizens after four years in office. It is the affirmation of his policies at the ballot box. And it is the honor of being entrusted for four more years with the leadership of this nation. All that and more he won: the broad sweep of his triumph invests him with the political authority of a personal mandate rarely given.

None of the straws at which his opposition grasped bore the weight of their hopes. There was no hidden current of public sentiment running in the opposite direction under the vast surface movement in favor of the President. No last minute display of electoral perversity deflected the voters from the choice to which every sign had pointed.

The Nixon victory represented as well a massive rejection of the ill-starred candidacy of Sen. George McGovern, but was no less a victory for that. It disappointed Republican Party hopes in leaving Democrats in control of Congress, but there are Democrats and there are Democrats and it is the conservative-liberal tilt of the two Houses that will count in battles ahead, rather than just the party label.

• • •

No analysis of the returns, no reading of their fine print, can obscure or detract from the single fact this election writes large — that Mr. Nixon, who won his first term by narrow plurality, emerges from this contest as the choice of most Americans by an overwhelming margin.

This is the fact that needs to be fully accepted, acknowledged and appreciated by all. The obvious in these times does not always seem to register with impassioned minorities, including the free expression of the majority voice.

Yet to accept that expression, with good grace, is essential if the democratic contract we have with one another is to be fulfilled. And it is essential if we are to work together for common objectives which, as Mr. Nixon said last night, alone could give meaning to the vote.

• • •

The Bulletin profoundly hopes that Mr. Nixon, with no reward to look forward to except the gratitude of his fellow citizens and the ultimate verdict of history, will be able to use effectively his mandate for the resolution of problems old and new.

First on any agenda must be the swift conclusion of the Vietnam war. There is the building of that structure of a wider peace to which the President has pledged himself. Still dimly perceived by many Americans are the enormous changes and challenges in the world's economy, which will affect our nation's fortunes and our daily lives, and to which the United States must adapt.

Closely allied with shifting global economic relations are the measures to be taken to strengthen further and make more competitive our domestic economy. The shape of Phase III in the Administration's new economic policy has to be determined.

Mr. Nixon surely has been given a mandate to press ahead with reordering the government structure to improve efficiency, to curb its oppressive costs, and to reduce the concentration of power in Washington in favor of bringing government closer to the people.

Finally, having received such a strong expression of confidence from most Americans, President Nixon doubly owes it to them to move vigorously to help dispel those shadows cast by excesses of a bitter campaign. And even more do we hope that from his new position of strength he will move steadily ahead in his second term toward accomplishing what was proclaimed as the goal of his first — bringing *all* Americans together.

But this last is not the task of one man, even of a President with such a mandate as that now held by Mr. Nixon. It is a task for us all. That includes a loyal opposition that, working within the legitimate framework of party differences and policy dissents, nevertheless accepts and fully regards a President chosen by free expression of the majority as its President, too.

The Philadelphia Inquirer

Philadelphia, Pa., November 8, 1972

President Nixon has won re-election, by a margin which would be breathtaking were it not for the fact that it had been widely predicted by polls and by almost every intuitive observer.

So four more years is what the American people have chosen.

First off, why? Principally, we believe, because Mr. Nixon in the four previous years has demonstrated a firmness of judgment and leadership that has yielded the public confidence expressed in yesterday's votes.

He has intelligently and courageously wrought historic changes in international politics. He has brought Indochina to what appears to be the brink of peace. He has dealt firmly and very encouragingly with the economic malaise into which America was slipping dangerously. And Mr. Nixon shows every promise, in his second and last term, of furthering those advances with vigor and sureness.

★ ★ ★

But there is another important element in the re-election of the President. Although we doubt any candidate could have defeated Mr. Nixon this year, the fact is that his challenger was emphatically rejected. And we believe Sen. McGovern was turned aside because he misjudged — catastrophically, for his own ambitions — the mood of America, misjudged the nation's deepest emotional needs and its most fundamental political responses.

The campaign waged by Sen. McGovern was, by any of several standards, the longest in American political history. And, on the count of votes — which are all that count — it was among the most disastrously unsuccessful.

The central theme of the McGovern candidacy was — in an unpopular word — radicalism. It proposed that America had reached a point in history at which many of its political and administrative institutions had outlived their usefulness, had outworn their capacity to serve the will of the majority.

That idea was the real basis for all Sen. McGovern said about America's conventional fiscal institutions, its conventional foreign-policy mechanisms, its conventional educational and social-service structures and more — down through the campaign inventory.

★ ★ ★

As the campaign regressed after the Democratic National Convention, Mr. McGovern found in polls, in fund drives and in public endorsements a startling lack of response. He became frustrated, then gradually desperate. Under those pressures, the quiet organizational force which had captured the structure of the Democratic Party and its Presidential nomination began to crumble.

The crumbling exposed bad, or at best indefensibly hasty, judgments on such things as his unworkable and ultimately abandoned welfare scheme, the hyperbole of his tax-reform proposals, and the sad Eagleton affair.

But it finally exposed a more fundamental characteristic, a personal sense of alienation from the broad American middle ground.

In an interview with the Associated Press on Oct. 27, just ten days before the election, Sen. McGovern was asked whether he viewed the election as a moral question, whether he really felt that Mr. Nixon was — as he had increasingly said — an evil man. His answer:

"Well, he's conducted an evil administration. I don't like to make judgment on the man himself. The use of sabotage and espionage and wiretapping. I think those are evil practices. I think the exploiting of racial fears is an evil practice. I think the aerial bombardment of Southeast Asia by Richard Nixon is the most evil thing ever done by any American President."

Sen. McGovern then was asked if he would be able to join behind President Nixon if he were re-elected. He responded:

"I think I would try to play the role of alerting the nation to the dangers of apathy, rather than to ask them to support the Nixon Administration."

In those latter-day assessments by Sen. McGovern — in the distortions of their perspective — lie the bankruptcy of his theme and of his candidacy.

We believe there is much to be answered for by the Nixon Administration, which has not been without its failings in the areas cited by Sen. McGovern. But we also believe that by extreme overreaction to the substance and the appeal of those failings Sen. McGovern proved himself an unconvincing challenger.

★ ★ ★

As the second Nixon Administration goes forward, we shall continue to press for answers and for adjustments. But today, as tradition rightly has it, we believe America's most demanding need is for healing and for unity behind the mandate given Mr. Nixon yesterday.

It is a promising time. Free of the concerns of re-election, and — we deeply hope — free of the albatross of Indochina, Mr. Nixon can go on with the unfinished business of a historic first term.

He has brought America past the first and worst hurdles of a quarter century of rigid international polarity. He now can move on toward his promise of enduring peace in the world and stable and realistically progressive prosperity in America.

WORCESTER TELEGRAM

Worcester, Mass., November 8, 1972

President Nixon's impressive sweep yesterday did not surprise anyone who has been reading the newspapers or watching television for the past few weeks. The polls were virtually unanimous in predicting a Nixon victory of substantial dimensions.

Nevertheless, the Nixon triumph is astonishing when viewed from a slightly longer perspective. Ten years ago, Nixon was a two-time loser — for president against John F. Kennedy, and for governor of California against Edmund Brown. He looked all washed up.

But with the dogged perseverance that has marked his whole life, Nixon set about the long, long task of rebuilding his political base. In 1968, he squeaked into the White House with only 43 per cent of the vote in a three-way race against Hubert Humphrey and George Wallace. Now he has made it handsomely, with the majority he has always yearned for: It is one of the most remarkable political comebacks since Abraham Lincoln was defeated by Stephen A. Douglas for the Senate in 1858.

There were many contributing factors to Nixon's victory, including the tragic shooting of Gov. Wallace and the astonishing ineptness of George McGovern's campaign. But it may be that the negative aspects of this election have been overemphasized. Nixon went to the voters with some impressive achievements to his credit. He had wound down the American combat role in Vietnam, and come within striking distance of a truce agreement. He had made bold initiatives in foreign policy. Despite the fiery rhetoric of Vice President Agnew in 1970 and thereafter, the country was considerably quieter than it had been in 1968. Nixon may have had less to do with that than his partisans claimed, but he certainly benefited from it.

Finally, it seems beyond question that Nixon assessed the mood of the American people much more shrewdly than McGovern did. There is a deep strain of conservatism in this country and Nixon knew how to appeal to it. He saw that the nation had had its fill of sociological experiments, and he trimmed his sails to the prevailing breeze.

That looked like "playing politics" to some, which it certainly was. But politics is the key to winning elections. As he prepares for his second term, President Nixon knows that at last he has achieved a consensus of the American people. That was no small achievement, given the divisive torments of recent years. Just what sort of "mandate" that translates into is not clear, but it is clear that the President can now move more freely and with fewer constrictions than during his first term.

DESERET NEWS
Salt Lake City, Utah, November 8, 1972

If any one lesson stands out in the 1972 presidential election, it is that the middle of the road remains the safest place in American politics.

It means it is still very chancy to take extreme positions even though they have great appeal to many splinter groups and hope the total will add up to a majority.

It means that though there is no shortage of dissatisfaction about contemporary affairs, the mainstream of American political life seldom veers sharply to the left or right.

That much seems clear from the victory which President Nixon won Tuesday in a landslide of historic proportions.

Since large turnouts normally favor Democrats, Mr. Nixon's victory takes on added dimension in view of the record ballots cast in several states. But it was a personal triumph rather than a party triumph in view of the Republicans' failure to win control of either house of Congress.

The Nixon victory is partly a measure of how much Vietnam has been de-fused as a political issue by the withdrawal of U.S. troops and by the heightened prospects of a peace settlement.

It is partly a measure of how far the U.S. has come since the divisive days when Lyndon Johnson was forced to bow out from a bid for a second term and it looked like the country might be in for a series of one-term presidents.

It is partly a measure of the advantage the incumbent in the White House still enjoys in his ability to attract attention and to mobilize the vast resources of manpower and money required for a modern political campaign.

It is partly a measure of George Wallace's absence from the campaign, and of the inability of John Schmitz to match the Alabama governor in generating enthusiasm.

There's room for wondering if Mr. Nixon's failure to campaign very actively didn't contribute somewhat to the continuation of a Democrat majority in Congress.

With a Republican in the White House and Democrats controlling Congress, Americans are faced with the prospect of at least two to possibly four more years of divided government. Even so, Tuesday's vote was certainly no mandate for stalemate and stagnation. Rather, it was a mandate for cooperation between the legislative and executive branches, for steady change rather than for sharp shifts of direction.

Although Americans made it abundantly clear they preferred not to let George do it, Senator McGovern has made a deep and lasting impact on American politics.

Americans have not heard the last of the reforms with which he became identified in opening up political conventions to a broader and deeper spectrum of society. It is a healthy trend that seems bound to continue.

Nor have we heard the last of an issue he sought to raise during the campaign — the issue of morality in politics.

By their votes Tuesday, Americans made it clear that few believe direct responsibility for the Watergate affair and other episodes of political sabotage extends as high as the President himself. But no American can be unconcerned about this debasement of the democratic process, and no political leader of any real stature should tolerate it.

In fulfillment of his pledge to bring Americans together again, President Nixon should use the authority of his office so that politics becomes less a source of cynicism and more a source of idealism.

Chicago Sun-Times
Chicago, Ill., November 8, 1972

President Nixon's crushing defeat of Sen. George McGovern strengthens his hand in dealing with other nations and in pressing for his policies at home. We hope Mr. Nixon's new popular vote will inspire him to press for new domestic priorities.

As a supporter of the President's re-election, and also of Sen. Charles H. Percy, we are naturally pleased with their showing in Illinois. Many partisans for Mr. Nixon must admit, however, that the President drew many votes because of the failure of his Democratic opponent, Sen. McGovern, to catch fire with many traditional Democrats and independents.

Mr. Nixon's policies that changed this nation's posture in world affairs undoubtedly accounted for much of his support at the polls. His establishment of new relations with Russia and China were giant steps toward his goal of a generation of world peace. Voters, rejecting Sen. McGovern's pessimism about the Vietnam War, accepted Mr. Nixon's timetable for peace there, sharing his optimism that a cease fire and a return of American prisoners of war is only a matter of weeks and the delay is necessary to write terms acceptable to this nation that has invested so much in Vietnam.

In the next four years we expect Mr. Nixon to reap for America and the world many dividends from the new policies — greater world trade creating more prosperity at home and security abroad; reductions in expenditures for arms and standing armies (we believe Mr. Nixon can and should cut defense expenditures from present levels); and easing of tensions in remaining trouble spots such as the Middle East.

We also hope and expect that Mr. Nixon, freed of the burden of the Vietnam War, will devote more of his energies to the domestic scene. When he makes his second inaugural address in January, we hope that he borrows heavily from his State of the Union message of January, 1971. That is the one in which he talked of the new American Revolution and vital domestic problems. He urged Congress to put a floor under family income, to help those not able to help themselves, to clean up the environment; to ensure that no family will be denied basic medical care because of inability to pay; and to create new federal departments focused on human needs, community needs, environment and prosperity.

We would hope also for a greater regard for civil liberties, the basic underpinning of our society, than was shown in Mr. Nixon's first administration. The casual attitude that many of Mr. Nixon's associates took toward wire-tapping, invasion of privacy and the power of government over the individual culminated in the incredible episode in which men financed by Republican campaign funds broke into the Democratic Headquarters in the Watergate office building.

Because of this incident and the related use of campaign funds for other shady enterprises as well as accusations that big business contributors were given unfair favors, many of those voting for Mr. Nixon Tuesday did so with grave misgivings about the integrity of the Presidency itself. Mr. Nixon has a prime obligation to remove the cloud over the White House that Watergate and other incidents have created. He has condemned Watergate but not discussed it forth-rightly — and has thus given the impression of a moral insensitivity that has no place in the office of the President.

Without waiting for the upcoming congressional investigation of Watergate, Mr. Nixon should publicly clean house before his inauguration. Those tainted by association with the incident and mishandling of campaign funds must be publicly identified and exiled from the White House. Until these moral issues are resolved, Mr Nixon will be under a grave handicap despite Tuesday's vote. It could inhibit his program for progress and peace.

Mr. Nixon grew greatly in his first four years in the White House, particularly as a world figure. We wish him four more years of growing stature as a President concerned about the lives of his own countrymen.

PORTLAND EVENING EXPRESS
Portland, Me., November 8, 1972

Yesterday's smashing election victory for President Richard Nixon installs him in the White House for four more years, to pursue the policies he thinks are best fitted for the country's interests.

Essentially this was a victory for political conservatism, except that Mr. Nixon is not a full-fledged conservative in the accepted sense of the word. Perhaps his critics would prefer to call him an opportunist, but that is not correct either. During his first term he deviated from the right-wing norm by proposing daring welfare reforms that so far Congress has effectively thwarted, he went even farther in attacking inflation with wage and price controls, and he must have appalled many Republicans by visiting Russia and Red China, and opening up new avenues of communication with nations that basically are assumed to be our enemies.

This is not opportunism, it is what the Germans call "realpolitik" meaning that Mr. Nixon has not hesitated to abandon policies that do not work and try something else, even of an unconventional nature.

There is no reason to believe, either, that the President will not pursue the same course until he leaves office in 1977, so we can expect more surprises from the White House.

It is unfortunate that he will not have a Republican Congress to support him, but this is a cross Dwight Eisenhower had to bear, during most of his two terms, and it testifies to a political ambivalence in the electorate that we deplore. The American people are saying, at election time, that they want the U.S. system of checks and balances magnified to the extent that both the President and the Congress are put under restraint. Yet this is not responsible government, and some day it may injure us badly.

In this state, the voters turned out in great numbers to register one of the most surprising upsets in decades—the defeat of Sen. Margaret Chase Smith by Cong. William Hathaway of the Second District. The GOP loss was somewhat compensated for by the capture of the seat vacated by Mr. Hathaway. We will examine in more detail the Maine picture tomorrow.

If the election campaign was a breeze for Mr. Nixon, the next four years may not be. He must still wind up the Vietnam war, and prevent the overthrow of Pres. Thieu if possible, he must confront a hostile Congress next January after inauguration, and he must single out the most pressing domestic and foreign problems and either wheedle or otherwise extract from Congress laws best calculated to insure national security and do the things that need to be done at home.

With the votes nearly counted, it appears that the total will not surpass the 80 millions that many expected. Perhaps not as many young people went to the polls that observers predicted, and if they did they surely did not affect the final result. What did sway the outcome was the so-called "Wallace vote" that Mr. Nixon courted with his hostility to busing, his hawkish stand on the war, and other attitudes close to the hearts of the men and women who have been voting for the Alabama governor.

Even with the next election four years away, it must be plain to the Democrats that they cannot afford the luxury of idealistic liberalism. And it must be plain to the Republicans that Mr. Nixon's departure in 1977 will cost them much of the support they enjoyed in this most recent election. The choice of his successor is most important to the GOP.

Post-Tribune
Gary, Ind., November 8, 1972

American voters made it "perfectly clear" Tuesday that they want "four more years" of President Richard M. Nixon — or at least vastly prefer that to the available alternative of four years of Sen. George McGovern.

They did not in our estimation mean that they wanted a repeat of the four years they have had.

They do not, for example, want the "four more years of war" McGovern frequently charged would result from a Nixon victory. Rather they voted for Nixon in part because of his demonstrated success in winding down that war and because they believed indications that peace is near and that it hopefully will be the "peace with honor" and "lasting peace" which the President pledges.

They do not want four more years of rising prices and relatively high unemployment. They voted for Nixon in part because they believed his handling of the economy — including the question of continuing wage and price controls — seemed to offer a better chance of rectifying some of its imbalances while keeping it strong than the experimental alternatives offered by his Democratic opponent.

They do not want four more years of rising crime statistics. They voted for the President because they felt his concept of "law and order" and the beginning of a concentrated federal attack on the narcotics traffic and organized crime offered more hope than the permissiveness which many at least felt might be implicit in the McGovern approach.

They do want a continuing sense of adequate national defense. They voted for the President in part because they feared the depth of McGovern's pledged heavy defense cuts and unilateral reduction of forces. However, they do not want continuing evidence of defense waste including massive contract overrides. And they do want a relaxation of international tensions of which they see hope in Nixon's trips to China and Russia, in the continuation of SALT (strategic arms limitation talks) after partial success in the first round, and in the approaching signs of conferences aimed at reducing East-West military forces along the Iron Curtain.

They do not want — in our view — a continuation of the stalemate between the President and Congress, despite returning a Democratic majority in both houses. They hope instead that the mandate given Nixon can help direct both the executive and legislative branches toward more cooperation. And they do not want a radical shift to the right any more than they wanted the radical shift toward the left which many feared with McGovern.

They voted for Nixon in part because he kept to the middle of the road — and they do want a government on the road — not parked at the curb.

The Des Moines Register
Des Moines, Iowa, November 9, 1972

Richard M. Nixon has been reelected President of the United States by a landslide vote. He won two campaigns for the Vice-Presidency by large majorities, but those victories were the victories of Dwight Eisenhower and not Richard Nixon. He lost by a slim margin in 1960 and won by a similar edge in 1968. So Mr. Nixon must feel great satisfaction and pride in this decisive personal triumph.

It is a triumph for pragmatism and flexibility in government policy and administration.

President Nixon's reversal of American policy (and his own position of long standing) on China and his successful negotiations with Russia have been given a strong endorsement by the voters. The voters also have approved an effective anti-inflation control program and a renewal of economic growth.

President Nixon also gained voter support, we believe, by withdrawal of nearly all U.S. ground forces from the Indochina war and the indications that, finally, there will be a cease-fire. The attempts by Senator McGovern to persuade voters that the peace plan agreed to with North Vietnam is a sham and that the war will go on indefinitely were unavailing.

The voters are willing to trust Nixon once more to carry out his promise to get out of the war "with honor".

These "pluses" in the Nixon record were enough to outweigh the signs of governmental corruption, of favoritism to business interests, of cynical appeals to race prejudice, of attacks on free speech and press in the Nixon Administration.

The weakness of the appeal of Senator McGovern was a major factor. McGovern failed to convince even many of his fellow Democrats that he had the leadership quality to carry out his policies. The forthrightness which first attracted so many to his cause seemed to wane during the campaign.

In a parliamentary democracy, such as Britain's, the result of this election, nevertheless, would have been to make George McGovern President (or prime minister) — for the Democratic party, as a party, defeated the Republican party and retained control of Congress. But Nixon, the shrewd and realistic politician, is unlikely to delude himself that this election reflects a surge of new personal popularity. This was a vote of approval for the practical management of affairs as against emotional and at times extreme proposals for change.

Now Richard Nixon has no more elections to distract him. He has four more years to make his place in history. He is a proud, ambitious man. He has demonstrated that he also is a practical man, no ideologue. He could move America far toward the generation of peace he talks about. He could renew his effort to reorganize the federal government and clean out the dark alleys of conflict of interest and corruption in national affairs.

For the kind of place he wants in history, these are the things Richard Nixon must do.

Minneapolis Tribune

Minneapolis, Minn., November 9, 1972

President Nixon was right when he said Tuesday night that his landslide election "means nothing unless it is a victory for all Americans." We would put it this way: The result may have represented a resounding vote of confidence in Mr. Nixon. Or it may have been more negative than positive, a rejection of Sen. McGovern's philosophy and leadership. Either way, the President deserves full credit for winning by the decisive margin he sought, but the important question now is the use to which he will put that victory.

The campaign gave few answers. There was nothing like the great debate that ought to take place between presidential candidates every four years, because Mr. Nixon chose to address the issues raised by McGovern in only the most general way. The President has not held a press conference in two months; he limited his own role in the campaign to ceremonial appearances and one-way communications with the public. "I have tried to conduct myself in this campaign in a way that would not divide our country," he said Tuesday night. But it seems to us that divisions among the electorate are an inherent and essential part of the democratic process, and that the risk of widening those divisions is offset by the responsibility to debate the issues.

Even though this strange presidential campaign has ended, the debate has not. Mr. Nixon sees his election victory as the opportunity to "get on with the great tasks which lie before us," foremost among them being the opening of a "new era of peace." In his telegram conceding defeat, McGovern expressed similar hopes, but told his supporters that the "loyal opposition" does not "rally to the support of policies we deplore."

Whatever may have been McGovern's shortcomings as a candidate, he articulated the different policies — sometimes unwisely, sometimes unrealistically, but always forcefully — that he thought should replace those of the Nixon administration. McGovern's defeat does not remove the sources of those differences. It is not a mandate to prolong the Vietnam War, to let mounting defense budgets absorb funds for domestic needs or to ignore minorities. It is, we believe, primarily an expression of belief that Mr. Nixon has done enough things well in his first term to elect him to a second, particularly when the views of the challenger seemed well ahead of those of the Middle American majority.

But it would be a mistake to look at the presidential election as the crest of a national wave of feeling in favor of the status quo. If that were the case, the one-sided Nixon victory would be reflected in other election results. Instead, Mr. Nixon's party lost four seats in the Senate, widening the Democratic majority to 14. Sens. Gordon Allott and Margaret Chase Smith, part of the Senate Republican leadership, were among those defeated. Although Republicans gained a number of House seats, Democratic representatives retained a sizable majority.

None of this distracts from the political skill Mr. Nixon has shown in winning a popular vote of record size and nearly equalling the percentage of Lyndon Johnson's 1964 landslide. But there is another side to politics. It is one that requires the President to deal with the issues he skimmed over in the campaign, and to do so with more receptivity to new ideas than has lately been shown in the White House. As Mr. Nixon said so well four years ago:

"It's time we once again had an open administration — open to ideas *from* the people, and open in its communication *with* the people—an administration of open doors, open eyes and open minds." We agree. We would only add the words of a recently popular campaign slogan: "Now, more than ever."

THE WALL STREET JOURNAL.

New York, N.Y., November 9, 1972

Richard Nixon's sweeping presidential victory is a vindication of his record as President and a repudiation of the "new politics." Or to put the same thing another way, it is the judgment of the American people that the job of politics is to deal with reality, not to beget utopia.

For in terms of coping with the constraints of grubby reality it's difficult to fault the Nixon presidency, at least from the perspective his opponents have chosen. But in this campaign and over the last four years his critics have raised the question not of whether his policies work but of whether they are well-intentioned. The essential argument—on which the voters now side with the President—has not been over which policies meet given criteria, but over the criteria themselves. Are policies and politicians to be judged pragmatically or moralistically?

Nowhere is this more clear than in foreign affairs. Mr. Nixon's critics have condemned his policies on Vietnam; after all, war and killing are *evil*. But the same critics have saluted his policies on China and the Soviet Union; after all, friendship is *good*. Few of them seem to recognize that in an imperfect world the choices may not be so simple, and almost never do they conceive—or at least, never do they concede—that the two sets of policies may be part of a larger cloth.

Yet clearly Mr. Nixon and his administration view the policies as part of the same complex interrelationship. Enduring peace requires a mixture of toughness and flexibility. Emerging from Vietnam with some credibility will make it easier to build a lasting detente with the Communist superpowers, just as movement toward detente helps solve the problem in Vietnam. Perhaps this leaves the nation's morality tainted by association with "corrupt dictatorships" and so on, but the voters seem to think that an acceptable price for pragmatic progress toward peace. And they judge that, on the evidence so far, the Nixon approach works.

In domestic policies the same sort of division appears, except that the administration itself can be faulted for being late to recognize such realities as the budget crunch. But its critics choose to belabor it instead for not being willing enough to provide programs for the poor and downtrodden; the point is not that such programs do any demonstrable good but that they show moral concern.

On an issue like busing, the critics again see only a battle between good and evil, bigotry and tolerance. There is no recognition that the moral question itself can also be seen as one of a quota-regulated society versus an open one. And pragmatic questions, like how much trouble for what real result, are not allowed to intrude.

Finally, the critics fail to see why the Watergate episode and the like failed to move more votes. To the moralistic viewpoint they seemed the perfect embodiment of the choice at hand. But the voters did not find them connected closely enough to the President to make the choice one of good against evil. And they were perfectly capable of taking the attitude that while Watergate is deplorable and calls for a good housecleaning, its impact on the future of the Republic is not of the same order as that of foreign policy and so on.

So when the voters gave their landslide to Mr. Nixon they rejected the moralizing approach to public affairs. This does not mean morality is unimportant to them, or to Mr. Nixon. It means rather that their moral viewpoint is tempered with what some modern theologians have called "moral realism"—a recognition of the enduring imperfection of the world and, in the words of critic Lionel Trilling, "the perception of the dangers of the moral life itself."

It will be fascinating to see how the President's critics react to the rebuff he has given them. We have previously remarked on their temptation to shift fire from Mr. Nixon to the American people. We may now be told that the election proves the American people are killers, racists and moral degenerates. Indeed, there were hints of that among the television commentators Tuesday night.

Yet politicians are closer to reality, and George McGovern's remarks were not nearly as bad as he had previously threatened. Yes, there were policies "we deplore" and the suggestion that his campaign brought peace closer (is it inconceivable it encouraged Hanoi to wait before settling?). Yet some minimum restatement of his positions was almost demanded, and his congratulations to Mr. Nixon were gracious enough.

So in the wake of the President's landslide there may be reason to hope that his critics will learn enough from their defeat to reassess their posture. If they can retain their idealism but work back to a more realistic morality, they will profit and so will the nation.

THE DENVER POST

Denver, Colo., November 8, 1972

TUESDAY'S ELECTION was a tremendous personal and political victory for Richard Nixon . . . the peak of a career of a man who seemed consigned to political oblivion only a few years ago.

In a political era characterized by Kennedys and charisma, Mr. Nixon has been to many people an unlikely occupant of the White House.

In fact, as one of the most controversial and berated men who has ever taken the political trail, the President's victory Tuesday must be particularly gratifying and sweet.

But we hope the certain euphoria will be short-lived, and that it will not influence Mr. Nixon to regard the vote as a mandate for business as usual.

He certainly is a "pro," and the "pros" remember that these chaotic times carried LBJ from a landslide victory to oblivion in a few short years.

Mr. Nixon's place in history as one of our most innovative and effective presidents in the field of international politics already is secure.

We hope that in his second term he will compile a comparable record in solving domestic problems.

PUNDITS, POLLSTERS, politicians and just plain folks will be analyzing the election results for a long time, but all that needs be said now is that Mr. Nixon, after four years in the presidency, has achieved remarkable status as a leader of and spokesman for the great majority of the American people, young and old, rich and poor, blue collar and white collar, liberal and conservative.

The election indicates that the voters perceive in Mr. Nixon a man of action and attainment who, even if lacking in personal warmth and appeal, has been a dignified, forceful, flexible and highly successful White House occupant.

Maybe it's not so surprising after all that he emerged as the winner in a joust with a knight of woeful countenance such as Sen. George McGovern.

Senator McGovern was less than impressive except in his zealous commitment to the issue that caused him to seek the presidency in the first place. He rode into the fray with single-minded purpose: to slay the Vietnam dragon which has threatened the nation's safety, security and unity.

But the senator was unseated in a distasteful preliminary affair involving his erstwhile second-in-command, Sen. Thomas Eagleton, and he never got firmly back into the saddle.

In overwhelming numbers the people have voted for Mr. Nixon, whose achievements during the past four years have satisfied some of the expectations, if not the hopes, of most Americans.

MR. NIXON has not always responded to these hopes, particularly in dealing with domestic issues, but in his second term he has the opportunity to be come more attuned to the wants and needs not only of the "new American majority," but also of all the minorities who have a stake in this country.

It has been said that all people want basically the same things, including peace, security and comfort, and President Nixon has a magnificent opportunity to lead the way in helping all Americans to achieve those vital goals.

We suspect that he will seize the opportunity, for Richard Nixon has no more elections, only his place in history to think about.

THE CINCINNATI ENQUIRER

Cincinnati, Ohio, November 9, 1972

FOR A MAN WHO lost the presidency of the United States by the narrowest margin in this century and came back to win it by a margin nearly as close, the smashing triumph that has returned Richard M. Nixon to the White House must have been a deeply moving and satisfying experience.

It must also amount to a challenge whose dimensions will become clearer with the passage of time.

Buoyed though he is entitled to be by one of the most phenomenal political feats of American history, the President can scarcely avoid being simultaneously sobered by his party's failure to win control of either house in the new 93rd Congress, which meets in January.

In practical terms, that failure means that the President must look ahead to at least two more years of the tug-of-war that has left too many of his legislative initiatives simply ignored.

In longer-range terms, Mr. Nixon must realize that that he has been, to some extent, the beneficiary of the Democratic Party's unwisdom in putting forward as its presidential nominee a man who represented, at best, only a minority of the party and whose views constituted an affront to vast numbers of those who traditionally looked upon the Democratic Party as their ideological home.

Put another way, Mr. Nixon, however much he relishes his re-election, must recognize that even a victory as devastating as this one appears to have fallen short of building the "new Republican majority" of which he spoke so frequently in this year's campaign. He has won no more than an opportunity to build that majority.

One reason for the President's failure to carry more Republican congressional candidates to victory with him, very possibly, is that his most notable achievements during his first four years have been in the areas of foreign policy and national security—areas that seem remote to large segments of American society.

In part, that seeming preoccupation has stemmed from the circumstance that the President is far freer to act unilaterally in the foreign-policy field without the specific authorization of Congress. In many domestic areas, by way of contrast, he has needed—and failed to receive—congressional collaboration.

The question now is whether his overwhelming victory will persuade congressional Democrats that Mr. Nixon deserves more co-operation than they have been willing to give him during the last four years. Up to now, Mr. Nixon has been a minority President (having won the presidency in 1968 with something less than half the popular vote). Now, he will speak not only as the representative of a numerical majority, but as the beneficiary of a landslide of genuinely heroic proportions.

As the administration proceeds in the weeks ahead to unravel the problems that still stand in the way of peace in Vietnam, Mr. Nixon will undoubtedly turn his attentions more fully to domestic concerns.

The administration's revenue-sharing plan finally made its way through the 92nd Congress. But the President's initiatives in the area of welfare reform and governmental reorganization—to cite only two of the most ambitious—are still gathering dust.

The New Federalism, of which Mr. Nixon has been speaking since his inauguration, is still more of a slogan than a fact. It ought to be Mr. Nixon's purpose now to make it a reality, to reverse the 40-year tide that has deposited more and more of the nation's decision-making in Washington to the detriment of state and local governments and to the even greater detriment of the rank-and-file citizen.

Mr. Nixon, in the course of the campaign that has now come to an end, has spoken of his resolve to make the next four years—years in which the nation will be celebrating the 200th anniversary of its independence—the greatest four years in America's history.

Certainly they are years in which some basic and far-ranging changes are needed. The fact that the nation now has a President who speaks for so sizable a segment of his countrymen augurs well for converting that dream into reality.

The Honolulu Advertiser
Honolulu, Hawaii, November 8, 1972

President Nixon's landslide is more or less of the proportion expected. As such, it calls for both congratulations and an expression of caution.

The President's victory is most obviously a tribute to both his political skills and his more prominent policies. And in that there are ironies:

After a lifetime of bitter partisan combat, Nixon has scored his greatest victory by remaining personally above the battle. His was a great triumph of strategy and restraint, and it reflects both a man who has learned to change with the times and use the enormous power and prestige of an incumbent President.

THIS IS ALSO true of his policies: Whether it is at hand or slipping away, the prospect of a Vietnam settlement agreement and U.S. withdrawal was a major election-day plus.

Restoring relations with China and the widened contacts with the Soviet Union were dramatic steps that deservedly won the favor of most voters and helped add to the President's positive image.

Domestically, the nation's economy has been improving, and no doubt many saw that as a result of Nixon's praiseworthy turnabout from outright opposition to imposition of wage and price controls last year.

The fact these moves in foreign and domestic affairs involved a man of conservative image shifting to traditionally liberal positions is an irony that has struck many on the left and right.

SOME OF THE concern over Nixon's victory will be because of its very size. Landslides can raise dangerous ideas in big winners, and there are real questions over how much this year's mixture of McGovern mistakes and murky issues contributes to what some might mistakenly term the "Nixon mandate."

Even more disturbing is the possibility of dulled public sensitivity as evidenced in the reaction to implications of wrongdoing in the Watergate break-in, the ITT case, the hiding of campaign contributions and sabotage of campaigns.

Faced with some alarming evidence and disturbing charges, the Nixon organization most often evaded or gave unsatisfactory answers. Yet the public reaction was mostly "that's politics."

The danger is that that may become everyday politics for everyone, if the American people remain unconcerned and unless presidents and other high officials set and enforce higher moral standards for those around them.

WE ARE much encouraged by President Nixon's remarks from the White House last night in reply to McGovern's concession message.

They were non-partisan and statesman like. If their tone is reflected over the next four years in the President's actions, and—just as important—in the actions of those around him, the nation could well move toward a unity and a confidence that are sorely needed.

The Standard-Times
New Bedford, Mass., November 9, 1972

Americans voted themselves an unparalleled opportunity for peace and progress by giving Richard M. Nixon a crushingly decisive endorsement for another four years in the White House.

Setting aside the enigma that is Massachusetts, the breadth and depth of Mr. Nixon's margin was comforting evidence of the average voter's ability to take the long view on what is the best course for the nation.

The choice was between demonstrated performance and experience on the one hand, and experiment and untried leadership on the other. It was not a personality contest, despite efforts of Senator McGovern and his supporters to make it so. Nor was it a contest over morality in government, busing, amnesty, unemployment, Vietnam or other specifics, singly or in combination.

A majority so huge as that behind the President must have included sharply differing opinions on these issues. What united them behind one candidate only could have been a shared maturity and perception about the difficulties of progress at home and peace abroad, the record on these in the last four years and the chances for improving it in the next four.

When the voters, generally, take this high-level view, a campaign such as Senator McGovern's scatter-gunning from soak-the-rich to down-with-big-business to carping about the speed of ending a war that Mr. Nixon did not start, has no broad foundation of appeal.

On the other hand, the vote was not a personal tribute to the perfectability of Mr. Nixon, or to the Republican party. There was a lot of hope in those ballots, a trust extended, perhaps apprehensively, that the man in the White House, relieved of worry about another re-election, can work for the common good without fear or favor.

Mr. Nixon rightly appraised the feelings of the electorate when he said, in his post-election remarks, "This is a great victory depending on what we do with it. The next four years will be a time we will try to make ourselves worthy of this trust."

A sobering thought for the administration is found, too, in the marked distinction the voters made between voting for the President and for members of his party seeking election to Congress and state office. The voters sized up their candidates. Republican-held offices went to Democrats, and vice versa.

The "coattail effect" is diminishing, to be sure, but in such a sweeping presidential decision one might have assumed it would have exerted a stronger influence. The answer may be in the evidence that developed during the campaign of a growing arrogance and usurpation of power—assuming the President was not a party to the development—by administration officials in the handling of campaign funds and such transgressions as the Watergate incident.

The best answer to any elitist trend is to make sure there is some balance of authority in the halls of government.

Another message to the President and his administration came in the size of Tuesday's vote. Despite a record number of votes cast, the percentage exercising the franchise was only 56 per cent, the lowest since 1948. Some absentees may have represented the "plague on both your houses" view; others stayed home because of the predicted one-sidedness of the contest. Whatever the reason, millions did not avail themselves of the opportunity to vote for or against Richard Nixon.

Looking ahead, however, there is nothing on the horizon precluding Mr. Nixon from fulfilling his pledge to do "the very best job we can for all the people."

It is said that he may have alienated the Democratic-controlled Congress during the campaign, by vetoing some of its legislation, by such groups as the Democrats for Nixon, so forcefully led by former Governor Connally of Texas, and by interceding in some congressional races (although notably with little effect except in North Carolina).

But it is unrealistic to suppose that Congress is going to abrasively oppose a President chosen by the voters in 49 of the 50 states. Senator McGovern stood for implacable opposition to administration policies, and he ended up speaking neither for the Democratic party nor any meaningful cross-section of the voters.

Woe begone as was its standard-bearer in defeat, the Democratic party should acquire a new and stronger image from this election disaster. That was the experience of the Republican party after the 1964 defeat with Barry Goldwater. Extremists got control of the one, as they did of the other, and the reaction should be the same: Leadership more moderate in outlook, speaking for, not at, the majority.

Senator McGovern's campaign leaves one useful legacy. He was a poor loser, as he was a campaigner, signing off in an attitude of "tears and regrets," implying martyrdom for having "pushed the day of peace one day closer" although his arrogant view encouraged the enemy to stand fast, and praising himself for having "brought into the political process" young people, although, apparently, most of them voted against him.

But although he got waylaid by ethical conflicts in the campaigning, McGovern did stand for an impressive, if naive, belief that government should set standards of morality for the nation to follow. It may be a goal virtually impossible of attainment, but it is worth striving for, and the Nixon administration should give it highest priority.

All other considerations aside, the election was a stamp of maturity on the American people, their ability to understand and to make judgment. Wisely and impartially used, this maturity is the opportunity that awaits President Nixon.

Pittsburgh Post-Gazette
Pittsburgh, Pa., November 9, 1972

PRESIDENT Nixon won an overwhelming personal victory in Tuesday's election but as a result of ticket splitting of epic proportions the Democratic Party remains strongly intact as the nation's majority.

Senator McGovern's "new politics" was tested and found wanting. But that was at the national level. Back home, in the states and local political subdivisions, the old politics of the regular Democratic organizations was showing its accustomed muscle, gaining strength in the Senate and governorships and losing only 11 seats in the House of Representatives.

Mr. Nixon

Thus the President, despite his tremendous mandate, must still work with a Democratic Congress for at least another two years. The Democratic Party is not in a shambles and the new American majority which Mr. Nixon sought failed to materialize. The President is a Republican driver holding the reins of a Democratic rig.

Mr. Nixon's victory reflects a combination of circumstances: the confidence of a very large majority that he will soon end an inherited war; his demonstrated talents in foreign affairs; a general prosperity which the Jeremiahs could not distort or obscure; and perhaps of most import, a widespread revulsion to the incivilities of a permissive society in which everyone is encouraged to do his or her thing regardless of consequences, including intrusions upon the rights of others.

Senator McGovern's troubles started with his stacked delegate deck at the Miami convention and escalated from there. Aside from the ineptness of his campaign, he turned many voters of all parties off with a self-righteousness better suited to the revival tent than to the White House. In his divisive appeal to class distinctions, he demonstrated that a national candidate cannot successfully defy the law of political gravity, which centers upon Middle America.

The campaign demonstrated, too, that the people have an intuitive sense about what is right and wrong for them. They are fed up with those among us who can find nothing right with America and nothing wrong with its foes.

The dimensions of his victory must have astonished even Mr. Nixon, as shrewd and experienced a politician as he is and despite public opinion polls which proved to be remarkably accurate. He is no longer a minority President who squeaked through by a handful of votes; he now has a mandate rivaled by few leaders in American history.

How will he use it? An answer does not come easily for various reasons, not the least of them the continuing party division between the executive and legislative branches. His programs will still be at the mercy of a Congress always looking for partisan advantage in the next election.

More than that, Mr. Nixon's personal response to the challenge of his mandate will be all important. Will he, as a lame duck who has faced the electorate for the last time, be able and willing to abjure political expediency and hucksterism in favor of principle and conviction?

That is the real challenge to his leadership and we earnestly hope he will rise to it. Given the confidence expressed by a heavy majority of his fellow citizens, Mr. Nixon has the opportunity to lead them toward the admirable objectives he has set, including a generation of peace throughout the world. If he pulls it off, he could find a place among the nation's great Presidents.

OREGON JOURNAL
Portland, Ore., November 8, 1972

President Nixon's whopping re-election victory was predictable days, even weeks, before the election.

The successive findings of national poll takers revealed from week to week that Democratic challenger George McGovern simply failed to make inroads in the substantial lead in popular opinion held by the President from the time of the national conventions on.

It became obvious that suspicions of wrong-doing in the Nixon Administration were not strong enough to overcome the belief that in some areas, particularly foreign policy, the President has done a good job and that McGovern had not convinced the electorate he possessed the leadership qualities the people want in a president.

The mood the nation is in had something to do with the size of Mr. Nixon's victory. He was the beneficiary of votes that might have gone to Alabama's conservative Democratic Gov. George Wallace, if a disabled Wallace had not been prevented, by the bullets of a would-be assassin in Maryland, from again heading a third-party ticket.

Presidential campaigns frequently are bitter. This one, it seems to us, has been more bitter than usual. Both sides have departed from fair campaign practices often enough and far enough to distress millions of people and make them long for the end of the campaign.

It is time now to try to rebuild some sense of national unity, put aside extremes of partisanship and get on with the business of solving urgent problems which face this country both on the national scene and at home.

This imposes responsibilities, respectively, on the President, the Congress and the Democratic national leadership, whether it rests in Sen. McGovern or some other person.

President Nixon will be in error if he interprets the size of his victory to be a massive vote of confidence. Millions cast their ballots with troubled spirits, feeling they didn't have the best of choices either way. They will want answers to questions raised by such incidents as the Watergate affair. They want less mystery and more openness in his administration.

As for the Congress, it is time for that body to quit crying about the loss of power to the executive branch until it is willing to reform itself and conduct itself in such a way that it deserves to be the co-equal branch of government which the Constitution says it is.

The President and the Congress have been engaged in a tugging match over spending limits, and the problem has arisen largely because Congress has abdicated responsibility in fiscal matters.

This fact is conceded by some of its wiser members, including Oregon's Democratic Rep. Al Ullman, second ranking member of the House Ways and Means Committee, who wants Congress to set up some kind of mechanism for budget control.

Aside from the larger questions of war and peace, the nation's most serious challenge may lie in trying to allocate its resources in such a way as to meet its most urgent domestic problems without perpetuating dangerous budget deficits and stimulating a new round of inflation.

This cannot be done unless the President and the Congress develop a better working relationship than they have had in the last two years. The immediate problem there is not limited to partisanship but includes failures in both branches to use their powers in accordance with the extent and the limits that the Constitution intended.

Most Americans have accepted at face value President Nixon's assurances that the Indochina War is winding up. If a formal peace is not signed within the next few months, the President will be seriously handicapped in his attempt to focus the nation's attention on other priorities, both foreign and domestic.

Nobody is allowed to forget the endless and seemingly insoluble Middle East conflict. Perhaps there will be a chance to make progress on that once peace is assured in Southeast Asia.

An urgent international priority will be the building of new agreements in international trade so that the industrial powers can live with one another and avoid disastrous trade wars. A dangerous trend of protectionism is rising in the U. S. Congress and must be dealt with.

For the first time in his political life, President Nixon will now be free of the pressures of another election campaign. He has a sense of history, and one must assume that he wants to leave a record that historians will remember favorably.

The voters have given him a chance to do that. In international diplomacy, he has made impressive beginnings. If he succeeds in adding to the foundation of "a generation of peace" and if he is able to restore a sense of national unity among the diverse elements of this nation, then history will indeed remember him well.

THE RICHMOND NEWS LEADER
Richmond, Va., November 8, 1972

The final tallies are not yet in, but on the basis of the returns that we do have, Richard Nixon has rolled to a massively impressive electoral victory. It is on the order of the FDR and LBJ successes. He carried every State except Massachusetts and the District of Columbia: The only election that approaches this one is FDR's 1936 defeat of Alf Landon, when Landon won only Maine and Vermont. He is going to wind up with more than 60 per cent of the popular vote, with perhaps a 16 million to 17 million popular vote spread: The only vote spread that approaches that is LBJ's 15.9 million popular vote spread over Barry Goldwater.

So this morning we have George McGovern as the Roy Riegels of American politics. Riegels was the University of California football player who in 1929 lost the Rose Bowl to Georgia Tech by running 64 yards the wrong way. Throughout his campaign, Senator McGovern seemed always to be running towards the wrong end zone. He issued preposterous position papers. When he opened his mouth, his words were full of sanctimony, and reflected the extremist's dearth of humor. He likened the President to Hitler. He indulged in breathtaking prevarication and served up to the populace a new fangled variety of pie-in-the-skyism. In St. Louis, he stood smiling as Democratic Congressman William Clay described Mr. Nixon as "insane." He sought to tap all the nation's seemingly fashionable enthusiasms, and instead opened seismic faults between his philosophy and the philosophy of the electorate. His running-mate charged that in Vietnam, 20,000 American men have died since 1969 to serve the purposes of the Committee for the Re-election of the President. As the campaign progressed, the Senator became a fumbling, bungling, desperate last-chancer. He could not even resuscitate his eroded reputation as honest George.

"We has seen the enemy," said Pogo, "and they is us." Truly George McGovern's primary enemy in the campaign was himself and the philosophy he attempted to foist on the American public. Most successful candidates practice the politics of inclusion—attempting to bring in every possible inhabitant of the vast American middle. George McGovern practiced instead the politics of exclusion—denying that he was a centrist, and thereby leaving the public with the inevitable conclusion that he was a man of the left. If today's results tell us anything, they tell us that in American politics, the great swings on the fringes have little impact on the center. George McGovern was a candidate of the leftist fringe. Because of that, the center sent him packing.

And for his part, he repudiated the South. Not once during his campaign did he dare to venture into the deep South. He simply kissed off the 11 States of the old Confederacy and the five border States. Those States are inhabited by middle Americans —Americans with profound concerns about welfare about busing, about inflation; Americans who want to leave Vietnam honorably, who do not believe in amnesty for dodgers of the draft, who do not advocate the legalization of marijuana. It was a crippling mistake, for George McGovern thereby wrote off 175 electoral votes, or 62 per cent of the 270 electoral votes needed for victory. Mr. Nixon swept the South, and with good reason. He is the first Republican to have done that.

It probably is correct to say that Richard Nixon won a second term when George McGovern was nominated by the Democrats in Miami Beach in July; the President's re-election simply required formal ratification yesterday. The magnitude of his victory clearly should not be read lightly in Hanoi; perhaps now we shall have a quick and honorable settlement. And the size of his majority should tell us that the American electorate still is basically conservative.

In Virginia the President's success was almost absolute. On the basis of the returns at this writing, he carried every city and county in the State except Charles City County. He carried 42 of 43 precincts in Henrico, 19 of 20 in Chesterfield, and 45 of 78 in Richmond, for a total of 106 of 141 (75 per cent) of the precincts in the Richmond metropolitan area. That is persuasive in anybody's book. Virginians are moderate conservatives. They identify with the moderate conservative who resides in the White House. And that is good.

It is part of contemporary political lore to say that if a man is elected to the presidency, he is almost a shoo-in for a second term. That is a fallacy. Of the 32 men elected to the presidency, Richard Nixon is only the twelfth to be elected to a second term. He has done it in devastating style. His victory is a crushing repudiation of the philosophy put forward by Senator McGovern—a man who sought to sell the extreme as the norm. This morning the American people are heaving a sigh that Mr. Nixon has prevailed. His are good hands for the nation to be in, and the people know it. And they are justifiably exuberant on this great day after the Great Sweep.

Orlando Sentinel
Orlando, Fla., November 8, 1972

PRESIDENT NIXON, at this writing on election night, seems headed for the landslide predicted by the polls.

It surely must be considered a great victory for Richard Nixon, a man considered politically dead 10 years ago when he lost his bid to become governor of California.

It is a crushing defeat for George McGovern and his radical followers, and proves once again that the vast majority of Americans don't want their political leaders to stray too far from the middle of the road.

McGovern was viewed as irresponsible, a man who as president would trifle with the defense of the country.

Although McGovern talked of tax reform, that apparently was translated by many voters as a tax increase.

The McGovern campaign was vicious, with President Nixon being likened to Hitler. McGovern and Shriver hurled preposterous charges, and their outlandishness obviously detracted from the already suspect credibility of the Democratic standard bearer.

IRONICALLY, many moderate and conservative Democrats hoped for a Nixon landslide. Only then, they reasoned, could the Democratic party be recaptured from the radicals who seized control over the last year and nominated George McGovern in Miami Beach.

Obviously, McGovern owes his defeat as much to these disenchanted Democrats as to the Republicans.

It was these Democrats who felt betrayed at Miami Beach, and they took their revenge on McGovern and his band on election day.

WHAT DOES the landslide mean for President Nixon? The way he interprets yesterday's election could determine the course of the nation for many years.

The last presidential landslide was Lyndon Johnson's in 1964. Instead of seeing the vote as a desire for moderation, Johnson took the results as a mandate for massive and expensive social programs and a reflection of his invincibility. He moved ahead on that assumption and four years later found himself barely able to govern a country that had been split apart by his policies.

We hope that President Nixon will not repeat Lyndon Johnson's mistake.

He must recognize that much of yesterday's vote was anti-McGovern.

It was not a signal from the electorate for sweeping change. In fact, it was just the opposite. The country is tired of disruption and great governmental experiment. It would like four years of peace at home and in the world.

Americans, it would seem, voted Tuesday for a chance to catch their breath from the turmoil that has marked the last decade of our history.

Mr. Nixon, we think, will see it the same way.

The State
Columbia, S.C., November 8, 1972

PRESIDENT Nixon's first order of business, now that the election is over, should be to cleanse his Administration of the rather tarnished image it acquired during the 1972 campaigning.

This admonition is offered in the expectation that Mr. Nixon by now will have been returned to office for another four-year term. But even in the unlikely event of defeat, there still rests upon him the burden of refurbishing the reputation of the Administration and restoring public confidence in political activities which manifestly stem from the White House.

One of our continuing laments with regard to this year's presidential contest has been the lack of a credible alternative to Mr. Nixon's re-election. The mere thought of a McGovern victory had a chilling effect on any anti-Nixon comment or conduct which conceivably might have hampered his return to office.

But all such considerations are behind now. And whether President Nixon has four more years or just two more months in office, he owes it to the American people to remove the political soot which has besmirched the White House.

We suspect that removing the soot will involve removing some of the individuals who, by one means or another, have risen to positions of influence within the Nixon entourage. We can understand even though we do not approve the President's hesitancy to purge the palace guard during the heat of a re-election campaign. But now that the campaign is over, he must do whatever is necessary to re-establish the respect due the presidency.

Continued White House silence on matters such as the apparent political invasion of Democratic headquarters at the Watergate apartment complex should be replaced by White House insistence on getting at the facts and, equally important, getting the facts before the public.

Other instances of political dirty work have surfaced during the bitter campaigning of 1972, involving Democrats and Republicans alike. The raising and handling of campaign funds leave much to be desired, both ethically and legally. And the raw arrogance manifested by highly placed officials in both major parties has left a bitter taste in the mouths of countless Americans who expect something better of their political "leaders."

Perhaps it is too much to expect that partisan politics can be played by anything approaching Marquis of Queensbury rules. But Americans who still regard their governmental institutions with pride of past and hope for the future deserve better than they have gotten this year.

The man who can do most toward vindicating that pride is Richard Milhous Nixon. In the last four years, he has established his prowess as a prime mover in national and international affairs. Let him now demonstrate the same drive and dedication in giving the presidency a corresponding moral ascendancy.

BUFFALO EVENING NEWS
Buffalo, N.Y., November 8, 1972

The two most remarkable facets of President Nixon's landslide re-election victory are pretty obvious. The first is that its scope, in both popular and electoral votes, exceeded all the pollsters' expectations. The second is that it had practically no side effects.

Not only will the Republican President continue to face a Congress that is solidly Democratic in both houses, but the coattail effects of the Nixon triumph were so negligible that the Republicans actually suffered a net loss of two Senate seats and one governorship. In the House, they gained a dozen seats where they needed three times that many for a majority.

For President Nixon, the outcome is of course a most gratifying vote of confidence in his over-all leadership, especially in foreign affairs. It must give him particular satisfaction as an expression of public confidence in his conduct on the Vietnam war and the peace negotiations — the issue on which his opponent had sought so fervently and so desperately to discredit him.

Yet for all the personal gratification the President is entitled to take from such an amazing popular sweep, the far more clearcut meaning of this 1972 landslide is its total rejection of the McGovern candidacy and its total repudiation of the Democratic convention that let itself be captured by his minority movement.

The amazing thing is that the Democrats could suffer such an utter disaster at the presidential level and yet survive as the unquestioned majority party in Congress and in the statehouses. When the Republicans took this same catastrophic route in 1964 with Barry Goldwater, after all, they not only lost the presidency by a landslide but ended with their party in a shambles at all levels. This time, the Democrats emerge broke and chastened, but with as broad a base to rebuild on as they had before.

The great lesson of 1972, however, could not possibly be more emphatic for both parties — especially since it follows so closely on the same lesson of 1964. It is that neither major party, in its nominating process, can afford to turn away from the national mainstream without courting political disaster.

It is all very well to talk about a "choice not an echo" or to mount some holy crusade for a set of principles believed in fervently by a minority faction. But when it comes to nominating a national ticket at any major-party convention, that party had better take a pretty cool measure of the national mood and of the kind of opposition it is going to face, or it will invite what happened to Barry Goldwater in 1964 and to George McGovern in 1972.

What exact national mandate can be read into yesterday's returns is difficult to say—and the blandness and unruffled dignity of the President's own standoffish re-election campaign makes it all the more difficult. Except for firmly pledging himself to a course of fiscal conservatism and no tax increases, Mr. Nixon did not really seem to be asking for much more than a vote of confidence to provide substantially the same leadership for the next four years that he has for the last four years.

His landslide should certainly tend to mute his vociferously dovish Senate war critics and strengthen his leadership in the whole foreign policy area where the President's responsibilities and powers are greatest. But when it comes to initiating new domestic programs, or pushing through old ones on which he has heretofore been thwarted, the Democratic-led 93d Congress may be as hard to sell as the two opposition Congresses of his first term were.

On the Vietnam war, we can only take the Nixon landslide and the McGovern repudiation to signify a nationwide expression of confidence that the President has in fact brought us to the verge of peace, and that his generally competent and forceful diplomacy will soon succeed in tidying up the loose ends and bringing the longed-for ceasefire to reality.

THE LOUISVILLE TIMES
Louisville, Ky., November 8, 1972

The question now, it seems to us, is this: What will President Nixon do with his victory?

Or perhaps the question should be: What do the people of the United States—more precisely, what does that majority of the people who yesterday returned Mr. Nixon to office—want him to do with it? What vision do they want fulfilled? What do they want to keep and what do they want changed—and how do they want it changed?

In light of the voting, it seems clear that Mr. Nixon spoke to and for the majority of the American people. Some of us may not like that. It may offend what some of us believe the American spirit is or should be. But that does not alter what the voting indicates as a fact.

Is Mr. Nixon unenthusiastic about more generous welfare? Perhaps most of the American people also are. Is Mr. Nixon opposed to the busing of school children for the purpose of integration? It is reasonably obvious that so are most Americans. And in a democratic society it is a little difficult to say that government should not be responsive to the people, whether or not some of us deplore what the people indicate they want.

All kinds of post-mortems will be held, of course, over Sen. George McGovern's failure. We assume there will be some merit in all the explanations: that by compromise he smudged his early shiny image as the nonpolitical politician; that he made many feel he bungled the Eagleton affair; that he was too "radical" or, conversely, that he wasn't radical enough for his young early supporters.

Basically, it seems to us, McGovern failed because he misinterpreted the will of the majority of the American people, because the America he wanted them to come home to was not the America they really wanted. In McGovern's smashing triumph at the Democratic convention, a fact which now looms very large indeed was lost sight of: McGovern's support even within the Democratic Party was always paper thin. Evidence of this is provided by the fact that in eight primaries held before George Wallace was shot out of the running, Wallace outpolled McGovern by approximately 2,750,000 to 1,550,000. The primaries were in New Hampshire, Wisconsin, Pennsylvania, Massachusetts, Indiana, Michigan, Maryland, and Tennessee.

If that many Democrats (after making allowance for possible Republican crossovers where that was permitted) preferred the political philosophy of George Wallace to that of George McGovern, it seems inescapable that McGovern's dream, whatever its virtues, was not the American dream in this year of 1972.

What, then, is the American dream? More "strict constructionists" on the Supreme Court? No-work, no-eat welfare programs? An end to busing for school integration? Increasing commercial and diplomatic ties with Russia and China? Continuing the war in Indochina indefinitely? These are some of the things President Nixon has practiced or preached in the last four years. We have to assume, on the basis of the vote, that most Americans preferred these to the alternatives suggested by McGovern. This may be more a nightmare than a dream to many Americans, but there it is.

Mr. Nixon has been given his four more years. We wish we knew what he will do with them. For this is more than a time of triumph for him—it is a time of testing for him and all of us.

The Cleveland Press
Cleveland, Ohio, November 8, 1972

Although it was forecast by the polls and pre-election surveys, President Nixon's landslide re-election is a remarkable achievement.

The scope of the President's sweep was truly national. All regions and most elements of the population gave him a decisive endorsement. Few Presidents (Franklin D. Roosevelt, Dwight D. Eisenhower, Lyndon B. Johnson) have had comparable acclamation from the electorate.

The President's conduct of his office, his innovative foreign policy and his efforts to wind down the war in Vietnam obviously had the approval of the voters.

But at the same time the overwhelming majority was having no part of George McGovern. McGovern's proposals, if they ever were clearly understood, simply were not acceptable. He personally frightened voters. Nixon was unusually fortunate in his opponent.

For better or worse, the President is not personally beloved in the sense that FDR and Ike were. His triumph is based on performance, on respect for his ability more than on endearment. Which is the way it should be — the country needs a doer more than it needs an idol.

But for all this, the unusual size of Nixon's vote clearly can be laid as much to McGovern as to any other factor.

Nixon's crushing defeat of McGovern gives him an opportunity commensurate with his victory.

It immeasurably strengthens his hand in world leadership, in dealing with the Soviet Union and Maoist China, in exerting influence in the explosive Middle East, in meeting crises not yet foreseen.

The victory should be a formidable asset in concluding a settlement of the Vietnam War with the North Vietnamese Communists, for it belies their notion that the president's policies did not have the support of the country.

It also should be a strong aid to the President in dealing with the new Congress, regardless of its Democratic makeup. Especially in his efforts to close out the tragedy in Indochina in an effective manner.

And most of all, Nixon's lopsided majority should do more than any event in years to solidify the country. Already, despite his squeaky win four years ago, Nixon had presided over a significant abatement of the noisy divisiveness which preceded his election.

In short, Nixon will begin his second term in the most auspicious circumstances.

•

But the President's victory, big as it was, doesn't give him a mandate to go freewheeling through the next four years, as Nixon wisely and appropriately acknowledged.

His remarks, after hearing the election results, were filled with humility, as becomes both his character and his high position.

"The greater the victory the greater the responsibility," he said.

And so it is, or should be.

While the people gave him a resounding vote of confidence, they did not give him a rubber-stamp Congress. His coattails were narrow indeed (coattail elections have been mostly out of style since FDR). The people have faith in him, but just the same they provided a check in Congress.

Based upon what Nixon had to say on his side of the campaign, and judging by the McGovern proposals which were repudiated, the President can read into the election returns two principal directives:

TO FINISH UP the Vietnam venture in as practical and honorable a way as possible, as he has promised.

TO PUT A BRAKE on government spending, to make good on his pledge to avoid new taxation and to bring the spread of bureaucracy under control. If necessary, he now can afford to fight Congress to the teeth in this respect. He has the okay of the voters.

Just as Nixon's campaign was smirched by having too much money to waste (resulting in such things as the Watergate caper), so the government can be wasteful and enept by loose budget controls and an excess of payrollers.

Otherwise, the people can expect, as the President himself noted election night, that he will get on toward his "great goals" — a lasting peace, prosperity without war or inflation, equal opportunity for all — and that he will keep his cool, come what may, and live up to his own extraordinary abilities.

On that note, we can offer the President the most enthusiastic congratulations and earnestly wish for him historic successes in his second term. For he now is our unquestioned leader, and our national welfare and personal fortunes to a large degree will depend on his wisdom and energies.

The Christian Science Monitor
Boston, Mass., November 9, 1972

For Richard Nixon, election day was an enormous personal triumph. Above all, the voting showed approval of the way he has managed the national affairs since he became President. He has wound down the Vietnam war, put out the "cold war," and steadied the American economy. The voters liked it and, in effect, have renewed his contract for another four years. There was, clearly, no confidence that George McGovern could manage as well.

But there was lacking from this election the slightest overtone of anything revolutionary, or counterrevolutionary. This was not a mandate to the Republican Party to undo the old "New Deal." Indeed, there was no mandate to the Republican Party. It lost ground in the Senate, governorships, and local offices.

In part the result must be a continuing reaction against the previous administration. Lyndon Johnson was given an equally decisive personal triumph in 1964 — and also a Congress of his own party. And look what happened! He took the country into a massively unpopular and appallingly expensive war which undermined the national economy. The American people may be wary for a long time of again entrusting all the power in Washington to men of the same party. By giving the White House to Mr. Nixon but leaving the Congress to the opposition they have expressed a preference for as little change in the present structure of American society as may be possible.

Mr. Nixon's mandate is to manage the general public affairs of the country — which primarily means its relations with the outside world and the condition of its own economy and public services. There is no mandate to change substantially the relations of the American people to each other.

There is an important difference between those things a president does on behalf of the general community and things done which change the relations of groups of citizens toward each other. The voters seem to have been unusually sensitive this time to the distinction. Mr. Nixon has scored his geat popular triumphs in the areas which are not partisan and not ideological. He has yet to make any substantial change in the internal fabric of the American community. And there is nothing in the voting results which would encourage him to attempt any such change over the next four years.

A new system of checks and balances is being improvised by the voters to take the place of the old system which has been undermined and eroded by the growth of the presidential power at the expense of the other branches of government in Washington. It takes the form of denying to the president a majority of his own party in the Congress. Democrats are still regarded as useful.

But nothing in this precaution detracts from the broad and sweeping expression of approval of the way Mr. Nixon has handled the general public business.

He is entitled to feel confirmed in his prudent but not radical treatment of the problem of getting his country out of the Vietnam war, of his practical and rational management of relations with China and Russia and of his pragmatic management of the economy. He is entitled to take deep satisfaction at this climactic moment of his public career from the approval his fellow citizens of all parties have expressed toward him. We congratulate him and add that we are confident that he will continue to manage the general affairs of the Republic in the same practical, prudent, successful and nonideological manner over the next four years.

San Jose Mercury
San Jose, Calif., November 9, 1972

Presidential elections always reveal a great deal about the American people, the followers as much as the leaders, and Campaign '72 was no exception. Its implications will be pondered for years.

On the morning after, however, the principal conclusion to be drawn from Tuesday's voting is that the American people, in their great good sense, elected not to let George do it.

President Richard M. Nixon scored the greatest electoral victory since Franklin D. Roosevelt smothered Alfred M. Landon in 1936; Sen. George McGovern carried only Massachusetts and the District of Columbia, for a total of 17 electoral votes.

In the popular vote, President Nixon's landslide was nearly as impressive. He garnered 61 per cent of the ballots to 38 per cent for Sen. McGovern. It was a personal, not a party, victory, and it had its negative as well as its positive elements.

For example, in terms of total registered voters, the Democratic party is still very much the majority party in the United States. It would not have been possible for President Nixon to win his four more years in the White House without large numbers of Democratic votes. He got them, despite the fact that Richard Nixon has never been precisely a folk hero to the average Democrat.

Average Democrats by the millions simply could not picture Sen. McGovern in the White House; they preferred President Nixon, past politics and all. Political historians will argue for years over the degree to which Sen. McGovern's waffling on the issues and his apparent embracing of minority causes to the exclusion of all others drove his nominal partisans over to the opposition.

Nor will it be overlooked that the average Democratic voter remained loyal to his party in races other than presidential. President Nixon's coattails were not much help in the congressional contests generally. The Democrats actually gained two seats in the Senate and held their losses in the House of Representatives to fewer than 15 seats. The Democrats, in short, continue to dominate Congress handily.

The American people, as a body, trust President Nixon more than they trust the Republican party, and, conversely, they trust the Democratic party more than they trusted its 1972 nominee, Sen. McGovern.

It is interesting in this regard to note that the two-party system is alive and well in the United States. Rep. John Schmitz, the American Independent party candidate and nominal heir to the so-called "Wallace vote," polled little more than 1 million votes nationwide, or only a tenth of what Alabama Gov. George Wallace drew four years ago from supposedly the same constituency. Wherever the "Wallace vote" went, it didn't go to John Schmitz. Dr. Benjamin Spock, the Peace and Freedom party candidate, did even worse, winning not quite 100,000 votes nationwide.

In sum, the lessons of the 1972 presidential election are probably these:

Political power in America continues to rest in the center, not on the fringes, either left or right.

The two-party system is still a viable vehicle for the exercise of that power.

The American people are not disposed to surrender in Vietnam. The war there will end in compromise and negotiation, probably soon now that President Nixon's mandate is both decisive and impressive.

With a Republican President in the White House and a Democratic Congress sitting on Capitol Hill, the need for compromise and accommodation, restraint and statesmanship, will be as great in the coming four years as it has been in the past four if the best interests of the American people are to be served adequately.

Chicago Daily Defender

Chicago, Ill., November 14, 1972

A host of descriptive terms are being used to categorize the Nixon victory. Some call it a Conservative sweep, a return to the status quo; others attribute it to personal magnetism, and still others view it as an outright rejection of George McGovern on philosophical grounds. All of these to a degree approximate the character of that phenomenal triumph.

The evidence, however, is preponderantly on the side of the view that the Nixon landslide was on the whole a racist ground-swell, a white backlash by Democrats and Republicans alike who feared that blacks would dominate the political scene if a liberal like McGovern got into the White House.

The threat of a massive incursion of black Democrats in almost every essential spot in the party, from the Vice Presidency down to the office of U. S. Attorney General, brought shivering fear into the white power base. And the prominance of blacks at the Democratic National Convention in Miami where they almost took over the whole convention added much impetus to the anti-black movement which Gov. George Wallace of Alabama had spearheaded with his paranoiac stand against school busing.

With the exception of McGovern, all of the Presidential hopefuls in the primary contests declared themselves against busing and when they lost they turned on McGovern calling him a radical who backed Henry Wallace's Progressive Party in 1948. The pace of the McGovern economic reorganization was, they said, too far out of step with the mood and tempo of the American masses, and similarly was his liberal position on the race issue.

By any standard of judgment, the Nixon electoral triumph was an outgrowth of the Southern Strategy and the emphasis placed by Mr. Nixon on school busing. He camouflaged that issue under the umbrella of an inadequate educational apparatus which strains race relations rather than harmonizes them. It was an inadequacy which found accommodation in the bosom of the Southern Strategy which John Mitchell, former Attorney General had, with evil design, contrived for President Nixon in the early days of his Administration.

Mr. Nixon either foresaw the anti-black trend or gave impetus to it as a potent, fruitful means of activating the South into the Republican camp. And the strategy paid off not only on the White House's opposition to busing but also the President's insistence on putting Southerners or "strict constructionists" on the Supreme Court.

The size of the national vote cannot fail to lead to the conclusion that America is yet clinging to its pernicious dogma of white supremacy as a means of preserving the dominion of power with the implied right to treat the black citizens as semi-colonials. Only the umitigated power of the black vote can change this gloomy landscape.

Chicago Tribune

Chicago, Ill., November 10, 1972

In giving Mr. Nixon his landslide, the voters have also given him a mandate to maintain the status quo. The so-called protest vote that appeared to dominate the primary victories of Sen. McGovern and Alabama Gov. George Wallace proved to be ephemeral.

Thruout the nation, the people voted against change. Nowhere was this trend more apparent than in the plethora of special propositions put up for referenda.

Despite an apparent tidal wave of disgust with property taxes and promises by both Presidential candidates to reform this tax and to replace it with federal aid to education, four states soundly defeated efforts to eliminate or sharply limit the property tax as a source for funding education. Moreover, the proposals in California, Colorado, Michigan, and Oregon, were beaten by margins as high as 4 to 1. And in Ohio, the voters decided to retain the state income tax.

At the same time, voters gave their blessings to 75 per cent of an estimated $5.3 billion in new bond issues, many of which will result in higher property tax levies. This is in sharp contrast to the trend in recent years to reject new bond issues.

But even aside from these economic issues, the voters clearly demonstrated they oppose change. In California, for example, the death penalty was restored by Constitutional amendment and the legalization of marijuana was rejected. Abortion on demand was defeated in Michigan, and Oklahomans once again voted down liquor-by-the-drink.

Environmental issues, all but ignored by the Presidential candidates, were overwhelmingly supported in Massachusetts, Florida, North Carolina, California, and New York. In the latter state, a $1.15 billion bond issue to finance facilities for cleaner air and water was approved by a 2 to 1 margin.

There were exceptions on social issues: Maryland, Iowa, and Washington have joined the growing number of states that have turned to state lotteries as a source of new revenue. A similar measure was rejected in Colorado, where the voters also decided against using state funds to finance part of the 1976 Winter Olympic Games that had been scheduled for the Denver area.

But in general, the conservative "message" Gov. Wallace asked the voters to send to Washington last spring would seem to have been delivered. It says in unmistakable terms: Let's think carefully before we rush into any drastic changes, whether social or economic.

Herald News

Fall River, Mass., November 13, 1972

The defeat of Senator McGovern was the result of many separate factors, but one of them surely was the distaste most Americans feel for the more extreme antics of some representatives of the counter-culture.

The Democratic nominee was certainly not responsible for their excesses, yet because they supported him, he was in the public mind tarred with their brush.

How many votes did McGovern lose because of the demonstrators outside the Boston dinner where Mrs. Nixon was the guest of honor? The number is incalculable, but certainly large. It was Senator McGovern's misfortune to be associated with some persons entirely unworthy of him and the party he represented.

The President's victory will be attributed to a conservative swing in the electorate, but that notion would be more convincing if Congress had not remained more firmly than ever in the Democratic camp.

The massive vote in favor of the President does indicate, however, a real repudiation of the extremists, who, so unfortunately, clung to McGovern's coattails.

The deep moderate convictions of the American people as a whole are evident both in their election of the President and of Congress. The majority of Americans are truly middle-of-the-road, and they dislike extremism either of the left or right.

The fact that the McGovern entourage included some extremists, whether or not the senator really wanted them, played a role in the dimensions of his defeat.

THE DAILY OKLAHOMAN
Oklahoma City, Okla., November 11, 1972

VOTERS demonstrated by their choices in the general election that they exercised discrimination to a degree seldom seen.

Undoubtedly, large numbers of citizens of both major parties cast straight party ballots, but decisive votes in many cases were those of individuals who selected some candidates from both parties. Among the other candidates, only the American party received support of any consequence. President Nixon's landslide victory would have been impossible without the votes of millions of registered Democrats. The same sort of selective voting, reflecting thoughtful consideration of issues, was evident in the results for constitutional amendments and other referenda on the ballots in many states.

For those and other reasons, the Republicans should not assume a "winner-take-all" attitude. Re-election of the president should not be taken to mean that all those who voted for him approved of everything he advocated. In the past, overwhelming victories sometimes have been erroneously interpreted as blanket endorsements of all policies.

Nor should the Democratic party accept the overwhelming defeat of Sen. McGovern as an all-out repudiation of its traditional principles. The programs he advocated were different in many respects from platforms adopted in earlier Democratic conventions. In the past large numbers of Republicans have voted for Democratic candidates for president because they supported Democratic policies, but in this case, millions of Democrats abandoned the top party leaders because they didn't agree.

Democrats are reviewing their campaign, trying to figure out why they lost. They have a lot to consider. The quota system used to select delegates to the nominating convention didn't suit everybody. The switch of vice presidential nominees upset many. One state candidate declared the party must come back to midstream. Another said the platform must reflect the views of the majority of Democrats. Often during the campaign observers noted that Sen. McGovern's statements were inconsistent with his earlier declarations.

Whatever the combination of factors that spelled their defeat, the Democrats have an opportunity and responsibility to rebuild their party around the majority they retained in both branches of Congress. They may react to the indications of the desires of the electorate just as well as Republicans. Both parties must face the same problems in national and international affairs and neither can work out satisfactory answers by itself.

Problems awaiting the new administration and the new Congress are much the same as those before the session just closed. Some way needs to be found to reduce governmental spending, in spite of increasing demands for more federal handouts. High employment must be maintained while holding down inflation and prices. Peace is of primary concern, but the growing tax burdens are personal problems with nearly everybody. The list is long.

The job of analyzing the problems and hammering out solutions is not likely to be any easier in the next four years than it was in the last four.

The Virginian-Pilot
Norfolk, Va., November 11, 1972

The paradox of 1972 is how little seems to be changed by the huge landslide President Nixon scored this week.

George McGovern was swept away by the Nixon tide, to be sure. Beyond that, perhaps the most significant statistic in the election returns is that only 55 per cent of the eligible voters bothered to vote. The dissatisfaction that Mr. McGovern sought to ride into the White House was nonexistent. But Mr. Nixon's vote of confidence was curiously limited, too.

In state after state, the electorate split its tickets with a vengeance. Alabama gave Mr. Nixon 76 per cent of the vote, but returned Democrat John Sparkman to the Senate with 66 per cent of the vote. Illinois returned Chuck Percy to the Senate by more than a million votes and gave Mr. Nixon almost as big a majority, but elected Democrat Dan Walker as Governor over the incumbent Republican. Iowa gave Mr. Nixon 59 per cent of its Presidential vote, but the Democrats gained two House seats and a Senate seat there. Mr. Nixon won in Texas by a million votes, but the Democrats won 20 of the 24 House seats. In Washington Mr. Nixon was a big winner and Republican Governor Dan Evans was reelected, but the Democrats held all six of the House seats. The story was the same in West Virginia, and in almost every other state. There were no coattails, there is no clear mandate to Mr. Nixon to do this or do that.

What the country is going to get from "four more years," only the President can say—and he isn't saying yet. He made no promises in asking for a second term and he is free to do very nearly as he pleases, subject to the agreement of the 93rd Congress.

The new Senate will be the biggest obstacle to Mr. Nixon, as the old one was. Almost all the Democratic leaders—Kennedy, Humphrey, McGovern, Muskie, Mondale, and the rest—are sitting there. If Mr. Nixon succeeds in ending the Vietnam War by Inauguration Day, and if the malefactors of the "Nixon scandals" are included in the President's promised housecleaning, then a honeymoon between Congress and the White House may be prolonged. If, on the other hand, the peace talks are unsuccessful and the White House persists in disclaiming any knowledge of the Watergate, etc., then the storm warnings will be up.

The biggest changes in the House of Representative did not occur on Tuesday, when the GOP gained a dozen or so seats, but earlier when a number of veterans in both parties retired, or were redistricted, or got upset in the primaries. Almost every fourth face in the House of Representatives will be a new one.

The result of the turnover is that the House may be more Republican, but less stick-in-the-mud at the same time. If the President plans a problem-solving assault on domestic issues in his second term, as aides are hinting, the House and Senate will be compliant. The goals Mr. Nixon prescribes in his State of the Union Message will be the clue to the shape of the second term.

Finally, the elections of '72 were almost barren of bright new faces. The "comer" among the Democrats, Jay Rockefeller, was knocked off in West Virginia. The man to watch among the new Republicans is probably Christopher (Kit) Bond, elected Governor of Missouri at 33, the Nation's youngest. Among the Democrats, Dan Walker, who beat first the Daley Machine and the Nixon tide to win the governorship of Illinois, is positioned to attract attention nationally. But governors have a high mortality rate among politicians. The heirs apparent are clear in each party—Spiro Agnew and Teddy Kennedy. Isn't that where we came in?

St. Petersburg Times
St. Petersburg, Fla., November 8, 1972

In the next four years, how will President Nixon use the vast powers of leadership renewed so convincingly yesterday by American voters?

Answers to that question are as varied as the answerers. One of the most likely, perhaps, was that of author - columnist Gary Wills, who believes the new term will be "four more years of roughly the same."

BUT NO ONE can predict with any certainty. Only once before in history has a president served a term with no possibility of facing the voters for re-election. The 22nd amendment limiting presidents to two terms was not adopted until 1951. Dwight Eisenhower also was ineligible for re-election after 1956, but the differences in personalities between Ike and Mr. Nixon are so great the comparison of their second terms becomes meaningless.

What **should** be the direction and tone of leadership from the White House in the immediate future?

First, the operation to remove the cancer of the Vietnamese War ought to be completed as quickly as possible.

Then, without ignoring foreign affairs, the President should show more enthusiasm for tough domestic issues too long in need of attention. For example:

✔ At the earliest possible moment, Mr. Nixon should deal decisively with the questions of corruption and political espionage raised during the campaign. In the Justice Department, Commerce Department, Agriculture Department and the White House itself, he should clean house of those whose conduct stained the Administration. They should be replaced with new faces who can restore public confidence.

✔ The powers of the presidency should be used constructively to heal the racial divisions in our society. This means selecting themes and programs that emphasize cooperative solutions, and avoiding chest-beating about busing and private schools. There should be less evidence from the White House of a Southern strategy and more of an American strategy.

✔ In the next four years, the President should set a tone that helps to repair the nation's economic divisions. The most promising tools for that task are federal tax reforms that curb the extremes of economic inequities, health reforms that remove the dollar sign from adequate health care and welfare reforms that break the poverty cycle without pitting one group against another.

✔ **IN THEIR** desire to protect the environment, Americans are more unified in 1972 than perhaps on any other single question. Because it's a vehicle that can bring citizens together working for the common good, the environment deserves a high priority in the second term.

✔ There's also wide agreement on the need for creative leadership to control and reduce crime and drug abuse. The President should give this problem a great deal of attention. His leadership also should place the White House on the side of defending and expanding individual liberties against the onslaughts of big government.

All these things add up to a rather simple wish: We hope Mr. Nixon uses the powers given him by the people yesterday to nurture their spirit of unity. He can do that best in the next four years by appealing to the best in Americans — their optimism, their can-do attitude, their strong individualism and their sense of fair play.

The Detroit News
Detroit, Mich., November 13, 1972

Because the Democrats retained control of Congress while President Nixon was winning his unprecedented victory, some observers are calling the election a standoff and saying it didn't mean a thing except a personal triumph for the President.

In this newspaper's opinion, that version of the election is rubbish.

President Nixon was the only victorious national candidate and thus the votes cast for him reflect a national mood much better than do the votes cast for the victorious members of Congress, Democratic and Republican.

Senator George McGovern was the only defeated national candidate and the minority of votes cast for him show he not only was outside the mainstream of American political thought but outside the mainstream of his own party.

As Mr. Nixon looks ahead, he says he's going to try to follow the footsteps of a "Disraeli conservative — a strong foreign policy (and) strong adherence to the basic values that the nation believes in and people believe in." That, of course, has been his platform for four years.

The so-called intellectuals and some sheep-like college students will sneer at Mr. Nixon's comments — as they did at his speeches during the campaign — but in our view such critics, too, are outside the mainstream of American life.

It was ever thus, of course. The pseudo-intellectuals in politics often have pushed for radical change and expressed radical philosophies but they rarely took over a presidential campaign to the extent that they did this year when they mismanaged McGovern into one of the worst defeats ever suffered by a presidential hopeful.

The intellectuals are important to the country, of course. Many of their recommendations in the past have borne fruit and have become law. But at a given moment they rarely speak for the majority of the American people. They didn't again this year.

McGovern lost, it is said, because he changed his mind so often that even his followers didn't know where he was headed. That's no doubt true. But he also poor-mouthed the United States in a way that has seldom been heard except from the mouths of Communist candidates for national office. Disparagement of this country is nothing new for the pseudo-intellectuals, of course.

Nobody says everything is right with America. But the election proved the public emphatically doesn't buy George McGovern's claim nothing is right with America. The results did not prove the American people are against change. The election proved only they are against too-rapid change and against leadership that does not represent their own middle America, middle-of-the-road thinking.

In effect, the outcome emphasized support for Mr. Nixon's aims for peace but also his goal of maintaining a strong defense so that America does not become No. 2 in the world. In our view, the voters also backed his moderate views on social reforms, as well as his plans to oppose bussing, keep taxes at present levels and his other efforts to control spending and the bureaucracy.

McGovern and his friends still persist in their illusions. They saw the contest as one between good and evil and assumed they were the good. Arrogantly, they still think so. Their explanation now is that the public just couldn't understand McGovern and his social programs because he was so far ahead of everyone else.

Arrogantly, they take credit, after the election, for having brought the nation close to peace in Vietnam. In fact, they can be blamed for prolonging the war by having given aid and encouragement to the enemy — until even Hanoi realized McGovern and his doves didn't speak for the United States.

William F. Buckley contended the other day that American intellectuals are "the most misinformed people in the United States." The election proved it. So the Democratic Party could make no worse mistake than to assume that it just needs a better salesman and candidate than George McGovern to win with the same pseudo-intellectual programs in 1976.

A party that has won only a minority of the voters in five of the last six presidential elections really ought to abandon its reliance on its so-called intellectual wing and go back to building upon and serving the interests of the great middle class that first made it the majority party.

Unless it does, Richard Nixon has a good chance to make the Republicans the majority party and expand its influence in Congress and the country.

Index

ABORTION—*see CAMPAIGN Issues (Women)*
ABZUG, Rep. Bella S.
   Loses New York primary to Ryan—95, 97
AFL-CIO—*see VOTING Blocks, MEANY*
AGNEW, Vice President Spiro T.
   New Hampshire primary showing—12, 15
   Named as Nixon's running-mate—145-147
   Wins renomination as Nixon's running-mate—161-169
   Prospects of 1976 presidential candidacy—168-169, 171-173
   Comments on Watergate break-in—186, 200-201
   Re-elected by landslide vote—257-282
AMERICAN Party—*see SCHMITZ, Rep. John*
AMNESTY—*see CAMPAIGN Issues (Indochina War)*
ANDERSON, Jack
   Charges Eagleton with drunk driving; retracts charges—139
ANDERSON, Thomas J.
   Nominated for Vice President by American Party—157, 159-160
ARMED Forces—*see CAMPAIGN Issues (Military)*
ASHBROOK, Rep. John M.
   New Hampshire primary showing—12, 14-17, 19-20
   Florida primary showing—27
   California primary showing—86-87
ASKEW, Gov. Reubin
   Turns down Democratic vice-presidential offer—122
BALDWIN, Alfred C.
   Admits monitoring Dem. offices at Watergate—216, 218
BARKER, Bernard L.
   Arrested in Watergate raid—100, 184-185
   Indicted for Watergate raid—198, 200
BOEING Co.
   Contributions to Jackson's presidential campaign—49, 51
BUSING—*see CAMPAIGN Issues*
CALIFORNIA
   Primary results—84-94
   Democratic convention credentials challenged, settled in McGovern's favor—104-119

CAMPAIGN Funds—*see also CAMPAIGN Issues (Watergate)*
   Nixon & Jackson criticized for not listing contributors—48-51
   GAO asks GOP fund probe; links to break-in investigation—182-187
   GAO uncovers GOP campaign fund violations—198-199
CAMPAIGN Issues—*see also CONVENTIONS-Dem. & Rep. platforms and specific candidates*
   BUSING
     Key issue in Florida primary—21-30
     McGovern supports busing; wavers on position—22, 29, 79
     Tennessee anti-busing vote—68
     Wallace busing views—74-76
     Michigan voters oppose busing—78, 80
     Humphrey changes position—79
     Democratic party platform rejects anti-busing plank—125-128
     Nixon, Republican Party position on busing—166, 175, 178, 220, 232, 234, 245, 247
   CRIME & VIOLENCE
     Wallace shooting—71-77
     Nixon positions—163, 219-250
     McGovern positions—219-250
   ECONOMY & WELFARE REFORM
     McGovern on tax reform—91, 94, 99, 118, 188-192, 219-250
     McGovern's welfare reform proposal—96
     Nixon position on welfare; scores McGovern's $1000 proposal—161-169, 190, 192, 219-250
     McGovern revises economic plans in Wall St. speech—188-192
   FOREIGN RELATIONS
     Nixon's visits to China & Russia—161-164, 168, 209-210, 219-250
     Foreign/domestic priorities—164, 167-168, 219-250
   INDOCHINA WAR
     McGovern position—85, 93, 211-214, 219-250

     Nixon Indochina policy—163-164, 168, 193-196, 208-210, 219-250
     Nixon & McGovern positions on amnesty—166
     Shriver cites lost peace chance; McGovern aide has talks in Paris—193-196
     McGovern outlines plans to end Indochina war—211-214
     Kissinger says peace near; Saigon wary of agreement—252-256
   MILITARY & DEFENSE
     McGovern on defense spending—88, 91, 94, 118, 188-192, 219-250
     Nixon position on defense maintenance, draft—161-169 208-209, 219-250
   VOTER DISCONTENT
     Expressed in Wisconsin primary—38-47
     Expressed in California primary—86, 91
   WATERGATE & CAMPAIGN SABOTAGE
     Former CIA men caught in raid on Dem. national offices—100-103
     Nixon camp denies link—100-103
     Link to GOP special fund investigated—182-187
     Seven indicted in Watergate case; Dem. civil suit trial delayed—197-202
     Probe barred in House; court bars extra-judicial public statements; wide GOP sabotage effort reported—215-218
     Influence on Dem. campaign—219-250, 257-282
     Influence on Rep. campaign—219-250, 257-282
   WOMEN
     McGovern on abortion—91, 226
CARTER, Jimmy
   Stop McGovern campaign—92-93
CHISHOLM, Rep. Shirley
   Florida primary showing—25
CLARK, Ramsey
   Supports Shriver's charge of lost Indochina peace chance—194

COMMITTEE to Re-elect the President—*see CAMPAIGN Issues (WATERGATE), CAMPAIGN Funds*

CONVENTIONS
  DEMOCRATIC
    Demonstrators allowed to camp in Miami parks—111
    California & Illinois credentials challenged—104-112
    McGovern wins credentials fights & nomination—112-119
    Eagleton gets vice-presidential nomination—120-123
    Platform adopted with few changes—124-28
    Committee nominates Shriver to replace Eagleton on Dem. ticket—150-156
  REPUBLICAN
    Nixon, Agnew win renomination—161-169
    GOP liberals lose delegate reform battle—170-174
    Platform reflects Nixon positions; adopted with little opposition—174-178
    Demonstrations fail to disrupt GOP convention—179-181

CRIME & Violence—see CAMPAIGN Issues

DALEY, Mayor Richard J.
  Political setback in Illinois primary—31-37
  Dispute over Illinois credentials settled in Miami as Daley forces ousted—104-119
  Supports McGovern, Democratic ticket—140-141

DEMOCRATIC Party—see CONVENTIONS, & specific candidates

DOLE, Sen. Robert J.
  Denies Nixon campaign involvement in Watergate affair—101-102

EAGLETON, Sen. Thomas F.
  Selected as McGovern's vice-presidential running-mate—119-123
  Reveals mental care; forced to resign from ticket—129-139
  McGovern names Shriver as replacement on Dem. ticket—150-156

ECONOMY—see CAMPAIGN Issues

ELECTION Results
  Nixon wins by landslide; Democrats keep control of Congress—257-282

FLORIDA
  Primary results 21-30

GARDNER, John W.
  Criticizes Nixon & Jackson for not listing contributors—48-51

GENERAL Accounting Office (GAO)
  Asks GOP fund probe; links to Watergate investigation—182-187
  Uncovering of GOP campaign funds violations—198-199

HANRAHAN, Edward V.
  Illinois primary victory—31-37

HARRIMAN, Avrell
  Supports Shriver's charge of lost peace chance—194-196

HARTKE, Sen. Vance
  New Hampshire primary showing—12, 14-16, 20

HUMPHREY, Sen Hubert H.—see also CAMPAIGN Issues
  Effect of New Hampshire primary on candidacy—14, 17-18
  Florida primary showing—21-30
  Busing position—22, 29
  Wisconsin primary showing—38-47
  Wins Pennsylvania primary—52-59
  Massachusetts primary showing—52-59
  Ohio primary results—64-67
  Indiana primary results—65-67
  Nebraska primary results—69-70
  West Virginia primary results—69-70
  Michigan primary showing—78-82
  Oregon primary showing—83
  Changes busing position—79
  Maryland primary showing—78-79, 82
  Rhode Island primary showing—83
  California primary showing—84-92
  New Mexico primary showing—86, 90
  New Jersey primary showing—87, 90-92
  Declares willingness to accept Wallace as running-mate—89, 91, 105
  New York primary showing—96
  Position in California credentials dispute & withdrawal from presidential contest—104-107, 110, 114-115, 117

HUNT Jr., E. Howard
  Indicted in connection with Watergate raid—198

ILLINOIS
  Primary results—31-37
  Democratic convention credentials challenged, settled in Miami as Daley forces ousted—104-119

INDIANA
  Primary election results—65-67

INDOCHINA War—see CAMPAIGN Issues & specific candidates

JACKSON, Sen. Henry M.
  Florida primary showing—21-30
  Wisconsin primary showing—38, 40-42, 45-46
  Criticized for not listing contributors & Boeing Co. backing—48-57
  Pennsylvania & Massachusetts primary showings—52, 54, 57
  Withdraws from primaries—66-67
  Effect of presidential candidacy on Humphrey's bid—114

JACKSON, Rev. Jesse
  Dispute with Daley over Illinois credentials—114

KENNEDY, Sen. Edward M.
  Possibility of presidential candidacy—26-27, 30, 42, 46, 54-55, 57, 61, 63, 78, 81, 92, 96
  Support for McGovern—58-59, 84, 92
  Turns down Dem vice-presidential offer—120-123, 150, 155

KISSINGER, Henry
  Says peace near; denies Oct. 31 signing date—252-256

KLEINDIENST, Atty. Gen. Richard G.
  Investigation of Watergate break-in criticized—183, 187, 197, 199-201

LABOR—see MEANY, VOTING Blocks

LIDDY, G. Gordon
  Indicted in connection with Watergate raid—198-199

LINDSAY, Mayor John V.
  Florida primary showing—21-3, 26-30
  Wisconsin primary showing withdraws from race—38-47

LOEB, William
  Exchanges with Muskie—11-13, 15-17, 19-21

LOWENSTEIN, Allard K.
  Defeated in N.Y. primary—95

MacGREGOR, Clark
  Refusal to discuss Watergate break-in—184

MARYLAND
  Wallace shot while campaigning—71-77
  Primary results—78-83

MASSACHUSETTS
  Primary results—52-59
  McGovern wins primary—257-282

McCARTHY, Sen. Eugene J.
  Illinois primary showing—33, 35-37
  Wisconsin primary showing—42

McCLOSKEY Jr., Rep. Paul N.
  New Hampshire primary showing—12-16, 19-20
  Florida primary showing—27
  Massachusetts primary showing—53
  Showing at Republican convention—162, 165

McCORD, James W.
  Arrested in Watergate raid—101, 102-103
  Indicted for Watergate raid—198, 218

McGOVERN, Sen. George S.—see also CAMPAIGN Issues, CONVENTIONS
  New Hampshire primary showing—11-20
  Florida primary showing—21-23, 27-30
  Supports busing—22, 29
  Illinois primary showing—35-37
  Wins Wisconsin primary—38-47
  Wins Massachusetts primary—52-59
  Pennsylvania primary showing—52-59
  Ohio primary showing—64-67
  Nebraska primary showing—69-70
  Maryland primary showing—78-79, 81
  Michigan primary showing—78-80, 82
  Wavers on busing position—79
  Rhode Island primary showing—83
  Oregon primary showing—83
  Wins California primary—84-94
  Indochina position—85, 93, 211-214, 219-250, 257-282
  Most papers oppose Dem ticket—85, 206-210, 219-250
  New Jersey primary showing—86-87, 90-92
  South Dakota primary showing—86-87, 90-91
  New Mexico primary showing—86, 87, 90-91
  Possibility of modifying own programs—86-89, 93, 96-97, 99, 116, 119, 188-192
  Defense spending position—88, 91, 94, 188-192, 219-250
  Tax reform proposals—91, 94, 99, 118, 188-192, 219-250, 257-282
  Abortion position—91, 226
  Wins New York primary—95-99
  Welfare reform proposal—96, 188-192, 219-250, 257-282
  Involvement in credentials fights & capture of nomination—104-119
  Chooses Eagleton as running-mate—119-124
  Platform positions criticized—116, 118, 124-128, 162-169, 176, 178
  Steelworkers opposition to McGovern's candidacy—116, 121, 123, 142
  Forces Eagleton off ticket following disclosure of mental care—129-139
  Endorsed by Newspaper Guild—148-149
  Names Shriver to replace Eagleton on Democratic ticket—150-156
  Foreign/domestic priorities—164, 167-168, 219-250
  Charges Nixon complicity in Watergate raid—182, 184-197
  Revises economic plans in Wall St. speech—188-192
  Shriver cites lost Indochina peace chance; aide has talks in Paris—193-196
  Accuses Nixon of whitewashing Watergate raid; criticizes investigation—198-199, 216
  September polls show Nixon far ahead of McGovern—202-205
  Outlines plans to end Indochina war—211-214
  Effect of Eagleton episode on campaign—219-250, 260, 268-269
  Calls Nixon peace settlement 4 years late—252-256
  Loses election by wide margin; Democrats keep control of Congress—257-282

MEANY, George
  Opposition to McGovern's candidacy—113, 117
  AFL-CIO votes for neutrality—142-144, 226

MILLS, Rep. Wilbur D.
  New Hampshire primary showing—11-12, 14-15, 17, 19
  Named McGovern's choice as Treasury secretary—188-192

MINORITIES—see VOTING Blocks

MITCHELL, John N.
  Refusal to release names of Nixon contributors—51
  Denies Nixon campaign involvement in Watergate affair—100-103
  Refuses to discuss Watergate break-in—182-187
  Possible complicity in Watergate affair—199, 201, 215, 218

MUSKIE, Sen. Edmund S.
  Wins New Hampshire primary—11-20
  William Loeb encounter—11, 13, 15-17, 19-20, 21, 53
  Florida primary showing—21-30
  Busing position—21-22, 25-26, 29
  Illinois primary showing—33, 35-37
  Wisconsin primary showing—38-47
  Pennsylvania & Massachusetts primary showings—52-59
  Withdraws from active participation in primaries—59-63
  Rhode Island primary showing—83
  Oregon primary showing—83
  Refuses to endorse McGovern—89
  Position in California credentials dispute & withdrawal from presidential contest—104, 113-114, 117

McGovern offers vice presidential candidacy—150-153
Letter quoting Muskie slur attributed to White House aide—217

NEBRASKA
Primary results—69-70

NEW Hampshire
Primary results—11-20

NEW Jersey
Primary results—86-87, 90-92

NEW Mexico
Primary results—86-87, 90-91

NEWSPAPER Endorsements
San Francisco Sun Reporter endorses McGovern in Calif. primary—85
Sacramento Bee endorses McGovern in Calif. primary—85
Newsday drops endorsements—206-210
New York Daily News endorses Nixon—208
Topeka Daily Capital endorses Nixon—209
Chicago Tribune endorses Nixon—209
New York Times endorses McGovern—210
St. Louis Globe-Democrat endorses Nixon—210
Rapid City Journal endorses Nixon—219
Chicago Today endorses Nixon—219
Richmond Times-Dispatch endorses Nixon—220
Louisville Courier-Journal endorses McGovern—221
Miami Herald endorses Nixon—222
Birmingham News endorses Nixon—223
Philadelphia Inquirer endorses Nixon—224
St. Louis Post-Dispatch endorses McGovern—225
Boston Herald Traveler and Record American endorses Nixon—226
Buffalo Evening News endorses Nixon—227
Chicago Sun-Times endorses Nixon—228
Chattanooga Times endorses McGovern—228
Orlando Sentinel endorses Nixon—229
Oregon Journal endorses McGovern—230
Detroit News endorses Nixon—230
Oregonian endorses Nixon—231
Chicago Daily News endorses Nixon—231
Dayton Daily News endorses Nixon—232
Rockford Morning Star endorses Nixon—233
Roanoke Times endorses Nixon—233
Houston Chronicle endorses Nixon—233
Washington Evening Star & Daily News endorses Nixon—234
San Jose Mercury endorses Nixon—235
Arkansas Democrat endorses Nixon—236
Cleveland Plain Dealer endorses Nixon—236
Los Angeles Herald Examiner endorses Nixon—237
Miami News endorses Nixon—237
Rochester Democrat Chronicle endorses Nixon—238
Baltimore Sun endorses Nixon—238
Providence Journal endorses Nixon—239
Oakland Tribune endorses Nixon—239
Albuquerque Journal endorses Nixon—240
Boston Globe endorses McGovern—240
New Bedford Standard Times endorses Nixon—241
Atlanta Constitution endorses Nixon—241
Akron Beacon Journal endorses Nixon—242
Syracuse Herald-Journal endorses Nixon—243
Philadelphia Evening Bulletin endorses Nixon—243
Nashville Tennessean endorses McGovern—244
Baltimore Afro American endorses McGovern—245
Des Moines Register endorses Nixon—246
Columbia State endorses Nixon—246
New York Post endorses McGovern—247
Pittsburgh Post-Gazette editorial board splits on endorsements—248-249
Maine Sunday Telegram endorses Nixon—249
Memphis Commercial Appeal endorses Nixon—250
Newark Star Ledger endorses Nixon—251

NEWSPAPER Guild
Endorses McGovern—148-149

NEW York
McGovern wins primary—95-99

NIXON, President Richard M.—see also CAMPAIGN Issues, CONVENTIONS
Wins New Hampshire primary—11-20
Florida primary showing—22-23, 27, 30
Wisconsin primary showing—38-39, 41-42, 47
Criticized for not listing contributors—48-51
Massachusetts primary showing—53
Voter reaction to Wallace shooting—81
Teamsters endorse Nixon—142-144
Chooses Agnew as running-mate—145-157
Political impact of stand on parochial school aid—161, 167
Wins renomination; calls for new majority—161-69
Position on welfare; scores McGovern's $1000 proposal—161-169, 190, 192, 219-250, 257-282
Position on defense maintenance, draft—161-169, 208-209, 219-250
Visits to China and Russia—161-164, 168, 209-210, 219-250, 257-282
Cites criteria for Indochina peace; Indochina policy—163-164, 168, 193-196, 208-210, 219-250, 257-282
Position on busing—166, 175, 178, 220, 232, 234, 245, 247
Foreign/domestic priorities—164, 167-168, 219-250
GOP platform reflects President's positions—174-178
Silent on Watergate, GAO fund probes—182-187
Two former aides indicted in Watergate case—197-202
September polls show Nixon far ahead of McGovern—202-205
Most papers back Nixon-Agnew ticket—206-210, 219-250
Disavows any knowledge of Watergate raid—216
Kissinger says peace near; Nixon confident about agreement—252-256
Re-elected in landslide; victory doesn't change congressional balance—257-282

NORTH Carolina
Primary results—70

O'BRIEN, Lawrence F.
Calls for FBI Watergate investigation—100-103
Sues GOP charging complicity in Watergate raid—184-187
Accuses Stans in Watergate case—198, 200

OHIO
Primary results—64-67

OPINION Polls
Significance of polls—18
September polls show Nixon far ahead of McGovern—202-205

OREGON
Primary results—83

PATMAN, Rep. Wright
Watergate break-in investigation—183
Accuses White House of engineering probe rejection by House—215-216, 218

PENNSYLVANIA
Primary results—52-59

PEOPLE'S Party—see SPOCK
PRESS—see NEWSPAPER Endorsements
PRIMARY Elections
New Hampshire voting results—11-20
Florida primary results—21-30
Illinois voting results—31-37
Wisconsin voting results—38-47
Pennsylvania voting results—52-59
Massachusetts voting results—52-59
Indiana voting results—65-67
Ohio voting results—64-67
Tennessee voting results—68
North Carolina voting results—70
Nebraska voting results—69-70
West Virginia voting results—69-70
Maryland voting results—78-82
Michigan voting results—78-82
Rhode Island voting results—83
Oregon voting results—83
California voting results—84-94
New Jersey voting results—86-87, 90-92
South Dakota voting results—86-87, 90-92
New Mexico voting results—86-87, 90-92
New York voting results—95-99

REPUBLICAN Party—see CONVENTIONS, & specific candidates

RHODE Island
Primary results—83

ROGERS, Secy. of State William P.
Responds to Shriver's charges of lost Indochina peace chance—194-196

ROONEY, Rep. John J.
Defeats Lowenstein in New York primary—95

RYAN, Rep. William F.
Defeats Abzug in New York primary—95, 97

SALINGER, Pierre
Secret Paris negotiations with North Vietnamese stirs controversy—196

SANFORD, Terry
Loses North Carolina primary to Wallace—70

SCHMITZ, Rep. John G.
Nominated for President by American Party—157-160
Election showing—279

SHRIVER, R. Sargent
Named as McGovern's choice to replace Eagleton on Dem. ticket—150-156
Charges lost Indochina peace chance—193-196
Links peace settlement to election—253, 255
Loses vice presidential bid—257-282

SOUTH Dakota
Primary results—86-87, 90-91

SPOCK, Dr. Benjamin
Nominated for President by People's Party—158, 160
Election showing—279

STANS, Maurice H.
Alleged involvement in Watergate break-in—184-187, 198-201, 215

STEELWORKERS, United—see VOTING Blocks
TAXES—see CAMPAIGN Issues (Economy & Welfare Reform)
TEAMSTERS—see VOTING Blocks (Labor)
TENNESSEE
Primary results—68

THIEU, Nguyen Van
Declares peace terms unacceptable—252-253

VANCE, Cyrus
Supports Shriver's charge of lost peace chance—194-196

VOTING Blocks & Patterns—see also specific candidates
Nixon carries urban, suburban, southern, Catholic & blue collar vote—257-282
LABOR
Withholds support for McGovern—113, 142, 226
Steelworkers opposition to McGovern's candidacy—116, 121, 123, 142
Meany, AFL-CIO vote campaign neutrality—113, 117, 142-144, 226
Teamsters endorse Nixon—142-144
Newspaper Guild endorses McGovern—148-149
Nixon seeks support—222
Nixon, McGovern split labor vote—257-282
MINORITIES
San Francisco Sun Reporter endorses McGovern—85
Baltimore Afro American newspaper endorses McGovern—245
McGovern carries black vote—257-282
YOUTH
Illinois primary—36
Massachusetts primary—53, 56
McGovern supported—116
Nixon makes appeal to young voters—166
Polls show Nixon ahead of McGovern among young voters—203-205
Nixon, McGovern split youth vote—257-282

WALKER, Daniel
Wins Illinois gubernatorial nomination—31-37

E859 .K55 1973

WALLACE, Gov. George C.
  Florida primary win, anti-busing, racial views—21–30, 74–76
  Anti-intellectual sentiment—28
  Wisconsin primary showing—38–47
  Pennsylvania & Massachusetts primary showings—52–59
  Indiana primary results—65–67
  Ohio primary results—65, 67
  West Virginia primary results—69, 70
  Shot while campaigning in Maryland—71–83
  Tennessee primary, anti-busing win—68
  North Carolina primary results—70
  Maryland primary showing—78–83
  Michigan primary showing—78–83
  Oregon primary showing—83
  Possibility of third party bid—84, 91, 94
  New Mexico primary showing—86, 90, 92
  Democratic convention rejects conservative planks on busing—125–128
  Withdraws from presidential race; American Party nominates Schmitz, Anderson—157–160
  Wallace withdrawal contributes to Nixon landslide—257–282

WASHINGTON D.C.
  McGovern carries district—257–282

WATERGATE Affair—*see* CAMPAIGN Issues & specific individuals

WELFARE—*see* CAMPAIGN Issues

WEST Virginia
  Primary results—69–70

WISCONSIN
  Primary results—38–47

YORTY, Sam
  New Hampshire primary showing—11–12, 14–15, 17, 19–20

YOUTH—*see* VOTING Blocks & Patterns

E 859 .K55   Knappman, Edward W.
              Campaign 72

DATE DUE